Paul Ham is the author of the highly acclaimed *Kokoda* (HarperCollins, 2004) and the Australia correspondent of the London *Sunday Times*. He was born and educated in Australia and lives in Sydney, having spent several years working in Britain as a journalist and publisher.

## Praise *for* VIETNAM

'Ham's prose is fluent, trenchant, aphoristic … In the grandeur of its sweep and the precision of its detail, Ham's book is a classic of that branch of our literature which still seems to have most to tell us of ourselves.' — Peter Pierce, *Bulletin with Newsweek*

'Paul Ham has excelled with his latest book, *Vietnam: The Australian War*. It's a must-read; not as some prescriptive history lesson that must be rammed down our collective throat, but as an important part of our national profile.' — Lucy Clark, *Sunday Telegraph*

'Ham's intelligent commentary on such terrible dilemmas prompts disquieting thoughts.' — Alan Stephens, *The Age*

'A wonderfully illuminating read about a shameful episode.' — *Daily Telegraph*

'Ham speaks with remarkable clarity and rapidity … His grasp of the Vietnam War, let alone the extensive declassified documents which largely inform this book, is impressive.' — Christopher Bantick, *Courier-Mail*

'*Vietnam: The Australian War*'s harrowing pages not only enlighten, but provoke sorrow, anger, even outrage in equal measure.' — Bron Sibree, *Sun Herald*

'*Vietnam: The Australian War* should be essential reading for Australians of all ages. Only then will this nation truly understand the sacrifices our soldiers made during Australia's longest-ever military campaign.' — Peter Masters, *Australian Defence Magazine*

## Praise *for* KOKODA

'Paul Ham has written a masterpiece of military history … it grips from its first words to its last moments. It is impossible in a short review to capture the power of this amazing story.' — *Courier-Mail*

'Paul Ham has produced an exceptional book on the Kokoda campaign … Authoritatively researched, intelligently structured and beautifully written, *Kokoda* is a substantial book that will appeal to scholars, students, history buffs and readers with an interest in World War II.' — *The Age*

'… [*Kokoda*] conveys the extraordinary heroism of these men without artifice, yet manages to be deeply provocative.' — *The Daily Telegraph*

'Ham has written a comprehensively researched, moving and at times truly shocking history of an awful chapter in Australia's evolution … It is the story of ordinary people in extraordinary circumstances, of men at their best and worst.' — *The Australian*

'A fascinating and compelling read.' — *Sunday Telegraph*

'This is a book that both enriches and deconstructs the Anzac legend.' — *Courier-Mail*

# VIETNAM
## THE AUSTRALIAN WAR
### PAUL HAM

HarperCollins*Publishers*

The author gratefully acknowledges the assistance of a grant from the
Lyndon Baines Johnson Library, Austin, Texas, in researching and writing this book.

**HarperCollins*Publishers***

First published in Australia in 2007
This edition published in 2008
by HarperCollins*Publishers* Australia Pty Limited
ABN 36 009 913 517
www.harpercollins.com.au

**HarperCollins*Publishers***
25 Ryde Road, Pymble, Sydney, NSW 2073, Australia
31 View Road, Glenfield, Auckland 0627, New Zealand
1–A, Hamilton House, Connaught Place, New Delhi – 110 001, India
77–85 Fulham Palace Road, London, W6 8JB, United Kingdom
2 Bloor Street East, 20th floor, Toronto, Ontario M4W 1A8, Canada
10 East 53rd Street, New York NY 10022, USA

National Library of Australia Cataloguing-in-Publication data:

Ham, Paul.
　Vietnam: the Australian war / Paul Ham.
　ISBN: 978 0 7322 8780 1 (pbk.)
　Includes index.
　Bibliography.
　Vietnam War, 1961–1975 – Participation, Australian.
　Vietnam War, 1961–1975 – Political aspects – Australia.
　Vietnam War, 1961–1975 – Protest movements – Australia.
　Vietnam War, 1961–1975 – Campaigns.
　Vietnam War, 1961–1975.
959.7043394

Front cover image: Australian War Memorial Negative Number E00454
Back cover image: Australian War Memorial Negative Number DNE/65/1037/VN
Author photo: Susan L'Estrange
Cover design by Matt Stanton
Internal design by Mark Gowing Design
Maps on pages xv-xviii by Demap, www.demap.com.au
Battle drawings on pages 233-5 by Matt Stanton, courtesy David Sabben
Battle drawings on pages 368, 383 by Matt Stanton
Typeset in 11/14.5pt Bembo by Kirby Jones
Printed and bound in Australia by Griffin Press
79gsm Bulky Paperback used by HarperCollins*Publishers* is a natural, recyclable product made
from wood grown in a combination of sustainable plantation and regrowth forests. The
manufacturing processes conform to the environmental regulations in Tasmania, the place of
manufacture.

7  6  5  4  3　09 10 11 12

To my mother and father
and
Zuzana Lenartova


Dedicated to the Australian servicemen and women
— and their families —
who fought this politicians' war

*Better to conquer hearts than citadels*
— Nguyen Trai, Vietnamese poet, 1426


*What were we who had strayed in here?*
— Joseph Conrad, *Heart of Darkness*

# Contents

# Acknowledgements

So many people contributed to this book that my job, at times, seemed like that of a lightning rod channelling the lives and experiences of others. In particular, I wish to thank the Vietnam veterans and their families — both Australian and Vietnamese — who shared many insights and memories, sometimes in extremely fraught circumstances.

I am profoundly grateful to certain veterans whose combat experience and/or professional expertise proved essential to my understanding of the Australian war in Vietnam. (I am indebted in some cases to their wives, too, who participated in the interviews.) The list includes generals, brigadiers, colonels, majors, captains, sergeants, corporals and privates, both regular soldiers and national servicemen. They include (and the list is by no means complete): Bill Akell, Phillip Bennett, Michael Bindley, John Binnie, Murray Blake, David Booth, Kevin Bovill, Bob Breen, Bob Buick, John Bullen, Terry Burstall, John Church, Terry Cobby, Peter Cosgrove, Neville Cullen, Graham Cusack, Ray De Vere, Peter Dinham, Bill Dobell, Laurie Drinkwater, John Eaton, Ross Ellis, John Essex-Clark, Tim Fischer, Denis Gibbons, Bob Grandin, Peter Gration, Phil Greville, Ron Grey, Trevor Hagan, Philip Ham, Richard Hannigan, Nat Hardcastle, John Heslewood, Brian Honner, Geoff Jones, Michael Jeffery, Spike Jones, Tony Keech, Bill Kerr, Colin Khan, Ian Kortlang, Nick LeRay-Meyer, Greg Lockhart, Rod Lyons, Mark Moloney, Brian McFarlane, David Morgan, Paul Murphy, Graham Neil, Trevor Nye, Michael O'Brien, Bill O'Mara, Bob O'Neill, Tien Manh Nguyen, Noel Payne, Sandy Pearson, Barry Petersen, Tuan Van Phan, Garry Prendergast, John Press, Neil Rankin, Adrian Roberts, Bob Richards, Trevor Richardson, Geoff Rose, John Rowe, Hans Roser, Barry Russ, David Sabben, John Salmon, Mick Sheean, Jim Shelton, Eric Smith, Harry Smith, Morrie Stanley, Iain Stewart, Ian Stiles, Don Tate, Wally Thompson, Blair Tidey, Vo Dai Ton, Colin Townsend, Neil Weekes, Tony White, Harry Whiteside, David Wilkins, Roger Wilson and Peter Young. In addition, nurses, entertainers, former protesters and draft resisters offered their time and their memories of the war.

I am deeply indebted to a few good friends who were unusually helpful during the two years of research: John and Carol Press, who offered me a room in their home in Canberra (in exchange for a few bottles of red); Paul Murphy, founder of the Australian Vietnam Veterans Reconstruction Group in Vung Tau, who kindly arranged my interviews with former NLF commanders and journeys through Phuoc Tuy (Ba Ria–Vung Tau); Drew Blomfield, who generously organised my prolonged stay at Berghutte Ski Lodge in Thredbo during summer 2006 (where the last chapters were written); Angela Priestley and Nikki Woloszuk, for helping with research and the job of transcribing hundreds of hours of interviews. Most importantly, I'd like to thank my dear mother, Shirley Ham, who read and photocopied many documents and took excellent notes.

In Vietnam and Cambodia, many people too numerous to mention helped in all kinds of ways. A great source of information was Mr Hiep, a very engaging tour guide with an extraordinary knowledge of the Coral and Balmoral battle sites; Rose and Rod Murray, for their knowledge of Hanoi; several former commanders of the People's Army and NLF units, who offered valuable insights into the war from the other side; and my interpreter and translator, Le Minh Nguyen, who converted the D445 Battalion's official history into plain English.

I am exceedingly grateful to everyone at HarperCollins, especially Shona Martyn, Alison Urquhart, Mary Rennie and Natalie Costa Bir, and copy-editor Cathryn Game, for their friendship, care and vision. All understood from the start the scale of this undertaking, and delivered the kind of unwavering support every writer hopes for. I would also like to thank my wonderful agent, Deborah Callaghan, who once again guided the idea from a synopsis to a finished publication.

Various libraries and archives were very helpful: chiefly, the staff of the Australian War Memorial Research Centre, Canberra; the Waverley Municipal Library, Sydney; the National Archives, Canberra; and the LBJ Library, Austin, Texas, USA. The fresh American content in this book would not have been obtainable without the generous research grant from the LBJ Library. I am also indebted to Donna Coates, a researcher in Texas, who photographed hundreds of library documents and arranged them in perfect order. Thanks, also, to Roger Lee, head of the Army History Unit at the Australian Department of Defence.

A long list of friends and family members helped in all sorts of ways, but I will name just a few: Ingrid and Geoff Arnott, Camille Bentley, Drew Blomfield, Reg Carter, Christopher Coogan, Cameron Cooper, William Essex, Don Featherstone, Mark Friezer, Carina Gilster, John and Janet Ham,

Ian Ham, Shirley Ham, Emma Harcourt, Philippa Honner, Francesca Hynes, Rob Jarrett, Michelle L'Huillier, Jacqui Lang, Justin Mclean, Tony Rees, Steve Tolhurst and Helen Votrubec.

Finally, my eternal gratitude to Zuzana and Ollie, who lived with me as I wrote this book, and witnessed the monster gradually take shape and overwhelm everything in its path … Thanks for your patience, love and understanding.

## Note on Imperial and Metric Measurements

The general principle has been to present measurements, where practical, rounded in the metric scale. Exceptions were made when a measurement is in a direct quote or is an acceptably well-understood unit.

Measurements in gallons and tons have been retained as per their source because of the difficulty in determining whether a UK or US system has been used.

1 inch = 25.4 millimetres
1 foot = 305 millimetres
1 yard = 914 millimetres
1 mile = 1.6 kilometres
1 acre = 0.405 hectares
1 pound = 0.454 kilograms
1 UK gallon = 4.54 litres
1 US gallon = 3.79 litres
1 UK long ton = 1.01 tonne
1 US short ton = 0.9 tonnes

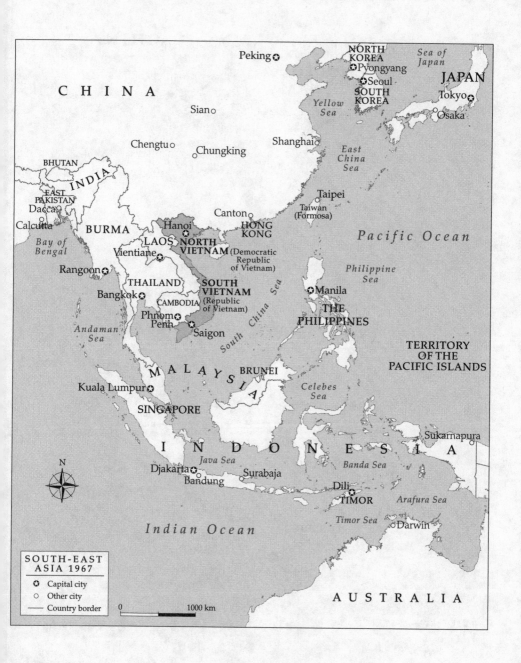

SOUTH-EAST
ASIA 1967

✪ Capital city
○ Other city
— Country border

0       1000 km

CHINA

Peking ✪

Sian ○

Chengtu ○    Chungking ○

Shanghai ○

BHUTAN

INDIA

EAST
PAKISTAN
Dacca ○

Calcutta ○

Bay of
Bengal

BURMA

Rangoon ✪

Canton ○

Hanoi ✪

LAOS  NORTH
Vientiane ✪  VIETNAM (Democratic
Republic
of Vietnam)

THAILAND

Bangkok ✪

CAMBODIA

Phnom ✪
Penh

Saigon ○

Andaman
Sea

SOUTH
VIETNAM
(Republic
of Vietnam)

South China Sea

NORTH
KOREA
Pyongyang ✪

Seoul ✪
SOUTH
KOREA

Sea of
Japan

JAPAN

Tokyo ✪

Osaka ○

Yellow
Sea

East
China
Sea

Taipei ○

Canton ○       Taiwan
(Formosa)

HONG
KONG

Pacific Ocean

Philippine
Sea

Manila ✪

THE
PHILIPPINES

TERRITORY
OF THE
PACIFIC ISLANDS

MALAYSIA    BRUNEI

Kuala Lumpur ✪

SINGAPORE

Celebes
Sea

INDONESIA

Sukarnapura ○

Djakarta ✪
Bandung ○    Surabaja ○

Java Sea

Banda Sea

Dili ○
TIMOR

Arafura Sea

Indian Ocean

Timor Sea

Darwin ○

AUSTRALIA

N

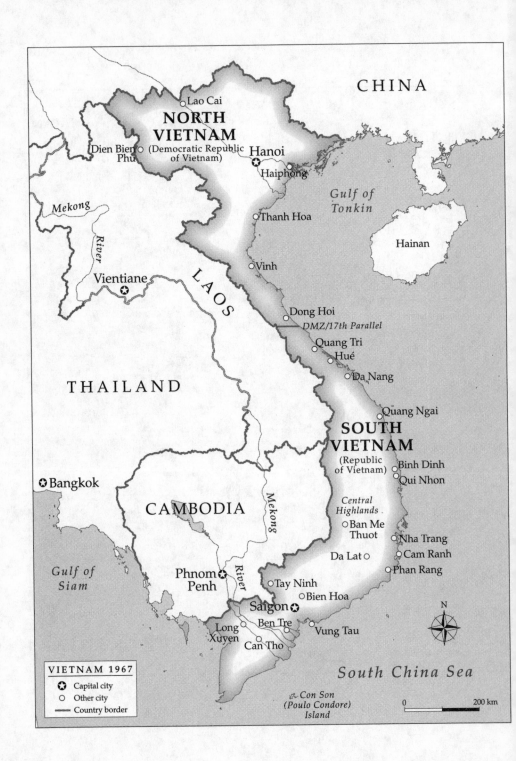

CHINA

Lao Cai

**NORTH VIETNAM**
(Democratic Republic of Vietnam)

Dien Bien Phu

Hanoi

Haiphong

*Gulf of Tonkin*

*Mekong*

*River*

Thanh Hoa

Vinh

Hainan

Vientiane

LAOS

Dong Hoi

*DMZ/17th Parallel*

Quang Tri

Hué

THAILAND

Da Nang

Quang Ngai

**SOUTH VIETNAM**
(Republic of Vietnam)

Binh Dinh

Qui Nhon

Bangkok

CAMBODIA

*Central Highlands*

Ban Me Thuot

Nha Trang

Cam Ranh

Da Lat

Phan Rang

*Mekong*

*Gulf of Siam*

Phnom Penh

*River*

Tay Ninh

Bien Hoa

Saigon

Ben Tre

Long Xuyen

Can Tho

Vung Tau

N

*South China Sea*

**VIETNAM 1967**

✪ Capital city
○ Other city
┄┄ Country border

*Con Son (Poulo Condore) Island*

0        200 km

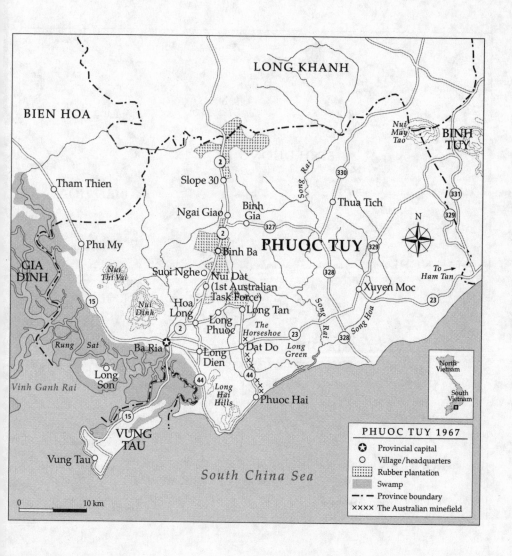

BIEN HOA

LONG KHANH

Tham Thien

Slope 30

Nui May Tao

BINH TUY

Phu My

Ngai Giao

Binh Gia

Thua Tich

GIA DINH

Nui Thi Vai

Suoi Nghe

Binh Ba

PHUOC TUY

To Ham Tan

Nui Dinh

Nui Dat (1st Australian Task Force)

Xuyen Moc

Hoa Long

Long Tan

Rung Sat

Ba Ria

Long Phuoc

The Horseshoe

Long Green

Vinh Ganh Rai

Long Dien

Dat Do

Long Son

Long Hai Hills

Phuoc Hai

VUNG TAU

Vung Tau

South China Sea

0        10 km

PHUOC TUY 1967

⊛  Provincial capital
○  Village/headquarters
▦  Rubber plantation
▨  Swamp
–·–·  Province boundary
××××  The Australian minefield

North Vietnam

South Vietnam

Ben
Cat

*Iron
Triangle*

*Battle of
Balmoral, 1968*

✖

*Battle of
Coral, 1968*

✖

N

*Operation
Iron Triangle,
1965*

**BINH DUONG**

Tan Uyen

*Ho Bo
Woods*

✖

*Operation
Crimp, 1966*

**BIEN HOA**

Cuong

*Operation
Coburg, 1968*

✖

Cu Chi
(tunnels)

Bien
Hoa

Long Binh

**HAU NGHIA**

Duc Hoa

**GIA DINH**

North
Vietnam

South
Vietnam

**SAIGON** ✪

**SAIGON & SURROUNDING
PROVINCES 1965–1968**

✪   South Vietnam capital

○   Village/headquarters

✖   Australian battles with
     enemy forces

      Built-up area

–·–   Province boundary

**LONG AN**

0          10 km

*Song Saigon*

*Song Dong Nai*

*Song Nha Be*

# Part One
# 'The place'

# Chapter 1
# Three thousand years

How dare you, barbarians, invade our soil?
Your hordes, without pity, will be annihilated!
*General Ly Thuong Kiet, in a poem rallying his Vietnamese troops*
*against the Chinese (eleventh century).*

Near Bennelong Point, Sydney, on the night of 7 April 1967, a young Australian soldier and his girlfriend were saying goodbye. They sat hand in hand under a giant fig tree at Mrs Macquarie's Chair, overlooking Garden Island wharf, where HMAS *Sydney*, lit up like a giant passenger cruiser, was docked and waiting.

It was sunset, one of those brilliant sunsets that seemed perfectly to fit the contours of Sydney, as though the city itself had been designed as the backdrop for a soldier's sad farewell: the white curves of the Opera House were then half built, yet already suggested shells, or sails, on a fantastic scale; the Harbour Bridge, dark and stern in the background, seemed to frown on the burgeoning wonder by the quay; and all was young and golden in the fading light — until the sun, as if on cue, dutifully disappeared with a last, orange blast beneath the bridge. The day expired, and the stars emerged.

Private John Binnie, 21, a grazier's son from Singleton and a member of the fifth intake of national servicemen, was due on the ship at 10 p.m. The deadline passed. 'I'm not leaving yet,' he told Victoria, his girlfriend of three weeks, and he embraced the attractive 18-year-old he already knew as 'Vic'.

'John kept saying to me, "You don't want to fall in love with a soldier",' Victoria said, forty years later. 'We sat holding hands,' she recalled, 'and feeling quite desperate. It was a beautiful night.' Would they meet again, after his tour in Vietnam? The question of marriage lingered unsaid; they were barely out of school. As 11 p.m. approached, the couple walked hand in hand back to the boat. Binnie, along with several hundred members of his battalion, then boarded the *Sydney* — the 'Vung Tau Ferry' — bound for South Vietnam. He was charged for being late — and next morning ordered to chip the rust off the deck.

The next day, Victoria and Binnie's father said a last goodbye on the wharf, then drove up to South Head, where they watched the great ship slip out of Sydney Harbour and turn north. 'His father absolutely couldn't speak,' Victoria recalled. Binnie's mother stayed at home, weeping inconsolably: 'She adored John,' Victoria said. 'She couldn't come to see him leave.' Later that day, Victoria went to visit her: 'She started drinking heavily the morning after he left for Vietnam.'[1]

David Llewelyn similarly departed for Vietnam on HMAS *Sydney*, in 1968. His memory of the ship pulling away resonates with many: 'The sailors lined the deck facing out to sea and the soldiers faced the wharf and their loved ones down below. I felt a huge ache in my stomach and as the ship started to move, I could hear this deep sobbing coming from one of the soldiers. It sounded so sad, and it was almost as if he was voicing the distress of all of us on our behalf. I had a few moments to settle down, and then the plaintive sound of a lone piper standing at the very end of the wharf came across the water … Those sounds will stay with me forever. The farewell … was particularly poignant as it was my wife of three months I was leaving behind.'[2]

Paul Murphy, the youngest of three children raised in Canberra, worshipped his father. 'A mild-mannered Labor-voting engineer' is how Murphy remembers him. After leaving school, Murphy joined an insurance company, but the lure of adventure led him to volunteer for national service. 'I was young; I wanted to go to Vietnam.'

One Saturday morning, in late August 1966, Murphy returned home on leave from infantry training. News of the Battle of Long Tan had just reached Australia: 'When Dad heard the news,' Murphy recalled, 'he kicked my bedroom door in and shouted, "Seventeen blokes have been fucking killed and you want to go to Vietnam!" It was the only time I ever saw him cry.'

Murphy's departure was awkward and 'very low key': 'You were given an hour at the airport with your family. We stood around. My brother, sister and my girlfriend all came. Dad steeled himself for it — he was a meek and mild man. I shook his hand. I should've hugged him. I kissed my mother — she later left Dad for someone else — and then I boarded the flight to Vietnam.'

Within a few months, about a quarter of Murphy's unit — Delta Company, Second Battalion, the Royal Australian Regiment — were dead or wounded: 'The blokes felt we were cursed,' Murphy later said. 'We had a wake and got pissed. But the blokes lost it ... they were sobbing for their dead mates. We were absolutely, emotionally distraught. We were 20-year-old hairy-arsed boys.'[3]

Rural Australia doted on its first 'nashos' — national servicemen — and the small Victorian town of Ensay, in the close-knit shire of Omeo, was typical. In 1964, Barry Heard, a local farm labourer, had ideas of becoming a shearer. At weekends he took his girlfriend to Young Farmers' woolshed dances. He loved the mutual support of the rural community: when a fellow local footballer died in a car accident, hundreds attended the young man's funeral. As the coffin was lowered into the earth, 'the entire community started to grieve as one,' Heard wrote, 'as our dear friend's soul was sent off with all the love this little community could muster.'[4]

One day, out of the blue, Heard — then 19 — received a 'very official letter' in a brown envelope, informing him that his name had been drawn in a ballot for national service. A number on a little wooden marble had coincided with his birth date; suddenly, he wore the badge of Ensay's first conscript: 'Apart from feeling a sense of mild panic, I had no idea what it all meant.' Nobody opposed national service in Ensay: 'It was endorsed by the Country Party, so that was that.'[5] Like hundreds of rural Australian towns, Ensay threw its first, accidental hero a farewell party: the locals bedecked the community hall in streamers and flowers, and a band called the Diamonds played. Two hundred people attended. Old diggers came over and chatted to the prized new recruit. After many handshakes, dances and hugs, Barry Heard prepared to depart for the recruit training centre at Puckapunyal.[6]

'To contain communist aggression' was the most cited reason why Australia committed 50,000 defence personnel to our longest military confrontation (1962–72). And in 1964, when Barry Heard was conscripted, the war was hugely popular, and both regulars and conscripts felt the frisson of excitement that many young men have always felt, and which politicians have always exploited, on the eve of battle. They were not only doing their duty; they were also off on a great adventure. Even reluctant conscripts felt an 'obscure sense of duty', as Heard recalled: the call of the hero, or the whisper of an ancient masculine predisposition to protect and defend. The great majority of Australian people initially accepted the political justification for sending these young men, almost half of whom were recruited at random, to a war few understood, fought thousands of kilometres from home.

The Vietnam War was the last and the most prolonged proxy battle of the Cold War, that deadening stand-off between the democratic nations of 'the West' and the command economies of the Communist Bloc. Like Korea, it was a hot frontline in the Cold War, which by 1960 had reached the brink of nuclear annihilation; an outcome narrowly averted in the Cuban missile crisis of 1962. Indeed, these terrifying forces were considered for use in the Vietnam conflict, as a bland minute to a US National Security Council meeting on 1 May 1961 noted: '... for the US to win a war in South-East Asia against the North Vietnamese and Laotians may possibly require the use of nuclear weapons.'[7]

For more than forty years, from the drawing-down of the Iron Curtain in 1946 to the collapse of the Soviet Union in 1989, two great political ideas divided the world: on one side, a democratic tradition built on universal suffrage, an open society, freedom of thought and speech, and private property; and on the other, the communist blueprint of Marxism-Leninism, essentially the state ownership of the means of production, the abolition of private property, and the control of religious belief and free speech under a one-party 'proletarian' dictatorship. The Vietnam War — otherwise known as the 'Second Indochina War' or, in Vietnam, as the 'American War' — was an undeclared war fought in an impoverished hook-shaped strip of land whose people had rarely known peace. Yet Vietnam, declared President John F. Kennedy, was 'the place' for the final clash of the superpowers.

In the early 1950s the Australian Prime Minister, Sir Robert Menzies, understood the Second Indochina War as a moral battle for the soul of man against the 'strange malignant daemon' of communism, embodied by Red China.[8] On the other side of Parliament, Arthur Calwell's Australian Labor Party (ALP) — and later, most vocally, Dr Jim Cairns — saw the Vietnam conflict as a war of 'national liberation' waged by Vietnamese peasants against Saigon despots who had the support of Western 'imperialists'. The actual picture, as we shall see, was far more intricate and layered than any of

Canberra's glib portrayals of Right versus Left, God versus Marx, and Peasant versus Empire. And in our understanding of the conflict we must first go back in time to 'the place' itself and Ho Chi Minh's expressed wish in 1946 not to eat 'Chinese shit for the rest of my life'.

Four clear themes of Vietnam's past are vital to our understanding of the Vietnam War: rice; the Chinese; Vietnam's martial history; and the fierce nationalism of the Vietnamese people. These interrelated themes permeate 3,000 years of Vietnamese history, which may be arranged into an admirably brief yet precise formulation: 1,000 years + 1,000 years + 900 years + 80 years + 30 years + 30 years. They represent, in turn, a thousand years of the Bronze Age; a thousand years of Chinese occupation; 900 years of independence; eighty years of French occupation; thirty years of the Indochina wars; and the most recent, communist-controlled period, from 1975 to the present.[9]

In the first thousand years (starting at about 1100 BC — we shall use the Roman calendar for the sake of familiarity), during the Bronze Age, a thriving rice civilisation lived in the southern provinces of China, which included the Red River basin near the ancient site of Hanoi. Setting aside their mythical roots — as the progeny of a dragon and a fairy — these ancestral tribes, chiefly the 'Viet', preserved their identity during the Chinese occupation. The Viet tribes were once believed to be the sole direct ancestors of the modern Vietnamese; yet they in fact have a very mixed ethnography, sharing Mongolian ethnic origins with the Chinese and Thais, and elements of Austro-Melano-Indonesian. The modern Vietnamese language blends elements of Mon-Khmer and Thai.

In 700 BC the Hung kings formed a federation of fifteen Viet tribes, called the Lac Viet, who wore body tattoos and bark clothing; made beautifully decorated drums, beaten to remind the rain dragon to water the rice paddies; worshipped the spirit of the sun; wove, made pots, and knew lacquering techniques; and dressed their dancers as aquatic birds on feast days. Most importantly, the Lac Viet were a relatively advanced rice culture, and used irrigation techniques and brass ploughshares.

The Au Viet, a mountain tribe with similar ethnic roots, annexed the Lac Viet in the third century BC, to form a new kingdom, Au Lac, with its capital near Hanoi. Here, the enlarged Viet people built a tremendous citadel enclosed in three walls, 3 to 4 metres high and 1,700 metres long (at the widest periphery). In 1959 thousands of bronze arrowheads were found at the site, testament to their wars of resistance against the Chinese.

A rebel Chinese general, Trieu Da, governor of the Viet, occupied the province in 179 BC and massacred any Chinese loyal to the collapsing Chi'in dynasty. This brazen grab for power failed when, in 111 BC, a Han dynasty army marched triumphantly into the devastated capital of the Au Lac. The Viet people were overrun and beaten into submission.


A thousand years of Chinese occupation ensued, which profoundly shaped the relationship between modern Vietnam and China. The steady infiltration of Han culture and the constant resistance and revolt of the Vietnamese characterised this second period of verifiable Vietnamese history (111 BC to AD 938).

The Chinese sought to impose their language and culture, modes of education, customs and Confucian belief system in a deliberate effort to overwhelm and ultimately obliterate any trace of the Viets' existence. Taoism and Buddhism, introduced from China and India in the second century BC, were absorbed into Viet customs and ceremonies and evident in the construction of pagodas. The Viet married, mourned and celebrated according to Chinese Confucian and Buddhist rites. The Chinese transformed Vietnamese agriculture: iron replaced brass ploughs; and fertiliser, new irrigation techniques, water buffaloes and horses were introduced. Rice farming massively intensified. The Chinese coupled these advances with the brutal suppression of indigenous Viet traditions.

Chinese oppression unified the Viet people in a state of permanent resistance and revolt. Unlike so many tribes that disappeared under China's awesome heel, the Viet people aggressively asserted themselves as a separate and inviolable culture. The occupying forces paradoxically accelerated the emergence of a distinctive Vietnamese identity even as they sought to crush it. Women led the most famous of these uprisings. In AD 40 Trung Trac (whose dissident husband the Chinese murdered) and her sister Trung Nhi mobilised the people, defeated the Chinese and regained the Red River Delta. During this war a third noblewoman, the pregnant Phung Thi Chinh, gave birth, strapped the baby to her back and continued fighting. Two years later, when the Chinese reconquered the Viet, these national treasures, the Trung sisters, committed suicide by throwing themselves into a river.

Other legendary female exploits followed. In AD 248 Trieu Au, Vietnam's Joan of Arc, or perhaps Queen Boadicea, clad in golden armour and riding atop an elephant, led a thousand soldiers in battle. Like the Trungs, Dame Trieu is revered in modern Vietnam; her temple is inscribed with her words: 'I want to rail against the wind and the tide, kill the whales in the sea, sweep the whole country to save the people from slavery, and I refuse to be abused.'[10]

The stories of these indomitable female warriors, no doubt embellished by the yearning for national legends, help to explain the courage, resourcefulness and relative influence of Vietnamese women. The example of the Trungs and Trieu served as lethal role models for Vietnamese female fighters in the twentieth century.

The Viet people developed a powerful sense of shared destiny, marked by the psychology of the perennial underdog, forever fighting for their right to exist: '... a thousand years of military, administrative and propagandistic efforts notwithstanding, the Chinese failed completely in their attempt to assimilate the Vietnamese ... the more [the Vietnamese] absorbed of the skills, customs and ideas of the Chinese, the smaller grew the likelihood of their ever becoming part of the Chinese people.'[11] The Viet and their related tribes stole the better ideas and influences from the Chinese. They absorbed the Confucian emphasis on family, duty and a stable social hierarchy, in which the collective will subsumed the freedom of the individual; they adopted a belief in ancestral worship and the Buddhist rites of reincarnation and the afterlife, and endowed all these with distinctive Vietnamese characteristics.

The burgeoning national identity of a people fiercely animated by their shared sense of destiny gave rise to the nation-state Viet-Nam, 'the land of the Viets'. 'When the Vietnamese, after many unsuccessful attempts, finally broke away from China, they had forever passed the stage when a people can become anything other than its own riper self.'[12]

A period of consolidation and chronic struggle, leavened by the beautiful expression of an emerging culture, a new national literature, the rise of educational and political institutions, and the establishment of a distinct Vietnamese polity under monarchist rule, characterised the next 900 years — the third period of Vietnamese history — up to the French conquest of 1883. An early succession of sound rulers, from the Ly and Tran dynasties (eleventh to the fourteenth centuries), gave Vietnam a national script (nom), religious architecture in the form of temples and pagodas, a great public works project (notably, the extension of the dykes along the Red River to the coast), a national opera (*cheo* and *tuong*), poetry, art and water puppets. This bountiful era ended, however, in degradation and despair.

The flowering of a distinctly Vietnamese culture proceeded against the background of persistent military threat, chiefly from the Chinese and the Mongols. Down Vietnam's long, porous borders a veritable sea of intruders and would-be conquerors massed. Little wonder the Vietnamese developed an indelible siege mentality and a martial culture shot through with constant suspicion and distrust of foreigners, which acquired a spiritual dimension: the more they fought off the invader, the more the Vietnamese came to believe in their divine destiny. The second Chinese Sung offensive, in the eleventh century, inspired the Vietnamese commander General Ly Thuong Kiet to write a poem to his troops; the poem can be considered the first proclamation of independence written in Vietnam:[13]

> *Over the mountains and rivers of the South reigns the Emperor of the South*
> *This has been decided forever by the Book of Heaven*
> *How dare you, barbarians, invade our soil?*
> *Your hordes, without pity, will be annihilated!*

The Vietnamese were baptised in blood. Their victory against the Sung heralded the arrival of an era of almost perpetual bloodletting. Three times they were attacked by and three times defeated the Mongol army of Kublai Khan (grandson of Genghis) during the thirteenth century, in the most savage battles of Vietnam's pre-modern era. In 1284 half a million Mongols (so the annals claim) hurled themselves at the Red River Delta; the second Mongol horde numbered 200,000 infantry and horsemen. Both were repulsed in spectacular pitched battles that prefigured General Giap's twentieth-century victories against the French.

The victorious Vietnamese general Tran Hung Dao at first used stealth and mobility, hit and run, jungle guerrilla tactics, harassment and ambush, and appeals to the hearts of the people — all the techniques of insurgency warfare later adopted by Mao Tse-tung and Vo Nguyen Giap in exhausting and defeating their modern enemies. Then, in 1287, Dao rallied his army for an open charge, in which 300,000 confused and exhausted Mongols were routed and driven out. 'The ancient land shall live forever,' Dao wrote in a victory poem. Seven centuries later, Giap, Ho Chi Minh's supreme commander, invoked Dao's triumph to steel his men for the last battle against the French at Dien Bien Phu.

Despite their victories, the Vietnamese were never at ease. They suppressed a resurgent Champa empire in 1371, deflected repeated attacks from the kingdom to the west (the future Laos), and quelled insurrections by the Thai minority then living in Vietnam. But none compared to the barbarity of the Chinese Ming empire, which successfully invaded Vietnam in 1407 and reimposed Chinese rule for twenty years. The Vietnamese were forced to adopt Chinese clothes and customs, speak the Chinese language, and worship Chinese rulers. 'All vestiges of national culture were destroyed.'[14] Those who resisted were destroyed or enslaved. 'The country was bled white. Battalions of forced labourers were sent into mines, forests and to the bottom of the sea to extract Vietnam's natural wealth for China.'[15]

Their steps towards nationhood in ruins, the Vietnamese once more built a resistance army, under the leadership of the aristocratic Le Loi, a landowner of the province of Thanh Hoa, south of the Red River Valley. The self-styled 'Prince of Pacification', Le Loi fought against the Chinese for ten years, during which he trained a guerrilla force of deadly efficiency. He deployed Dao's guerrilla tactics and taught his friends and local brigands how to live off the land and infiltrate villages. A distant tactical forerunner of the Viet Minh and Viet Cong, Le Loi's infantry took to the jungle and rural areas, recruited and terrorised the villagers, and forced the Chinese out of the countryside. The invader hunkered down in the towns and stuck to the main roads. Yet nowhere was safe. Ambush was Le Loi's speciality, and his secret weapons the hearts and minds of the population. His adviser, the poet Nguyen Trai, anticipated the doctrine of communist insurgency warfare with a line that must chill to the bone every French, American and Australian commander faced with distinguishing the enemy from the local population: 'Better to conquer hearts than citadels.'[16] That was written in 1426.

The occupying Chinese responded to this invisible enemy as the French and Americans would centuries later: they fortified the villages and built towers along the roads. At night they kept to their city fortresses, as the countryside came alive with Vietnamese peasants loyal to Le Loi.

Finally, Le Loi struck on open ground, in the field of Tot Dong, west of Hanoi, in 1426. The Chinese were gravely weakened and demoralised. In a spectacular battle, Le Loi's elephant-borne cavalry routed the Chinese horsemen and threw the invader out of Vietnam forever. Their departing ranks were granted 500 junks and thousands of horses on which to get home. In a truce accord signed two years later, Le Loi secured official Chinese recognition of the independence of Vietnam. With the exception of two attempts, in 1788 and 1979, the Chinese 'never again launched a full-scale attack against Vietnam'.[17] Le Loi is today revered as the father of the nation; the main avenue in Ho Chi Minh City (Saigon) bears his name. 'Every man on earth,' he wrote, 'ought to accomplish some great enterprise so that he leaves the sweet scent of his name to later generations. How, then, could he willingly be the slave of foreigners?'[18]

The Le dynasty endured for 300 years after Le Loi's death. It started well, with the construction of great public works and the reintroduction of Confucian learning. Its capital, Dong Kinh (modern-day Hanoi) — hence the later name for the northern province, Tonkin — presided over a realm of great estates, political order and educational excellence. The 37-year reign of King Le Thanh Tong (1460–97) can perhaps be called a Vietnamese Golden Age as it saw the establishment of a standing army of 200,000 and the revival of the great Confucian classics of the eleventh century. Le Thanh Tong imbued the nation with the jewels of Confucian learning. His fascination with maps led to the drawing of the first complete map of the country. The Vietnamese ideogram, the *nom*, was expanded and standardised.

Most importantly, Le Thanh Tong imposed a Confucian political order, an intricately layered hierarchy that survived until the French invasion 400 years later. Six ministries and their executive departments formed and implemented policies, which were handed down to thirteen provincial headquarters. These controlled hundreds of district offices, responsible in turn for thousands of communes 'each governed by the equivalent of a mayor'.[19] These endowed the village with unusual autonomy; the peasant saw the emperor's power as spiritual, rather than temporal. Hence the old Vietnamese saying 'The edicts of the emperor stop at the edge of the village'.

Overlaying the political order was a new legal system which balanced an unusually liberal code. It protected ordinary people from tyrannical mandarins, and extended property and conjugal rights to women. Those who transgressed or subverted the divine authority of the emperor were subjected to ghastly punishments in the Confucian tradition — strangulation or dismemberment (the victims generally chose strangulation, as the body remained intact in the afterlife). Disobedience to one's teacher or political chief was punished by exile, a terrifying prospect because exiled souls, sentenced to wander the world in everlasting limbo, would never be reunited with their ancestors.

The 'Golden Age' of Le Thanh Tong turned progressively leaden with the failure of later emperors to build on his achievements. Degradation and corruption marked the early sixteenth century. Of the eight rulers who governed Vietnam between 1504 and 1527, six were assassinated by relatives or usurpers. One insurrection, led by Mac Dang Dung, a former mayor of Hanoi, succeeded, and Mac mounted the throne in 1527. When the Chinese threatened his regime, Mac gave the invaders a parcel of Vietnam in exchange for a promise not to attack. The Chinese refrained, but the hated bargain set in train a series of events that would divide Vietnam between the northern and southern provinces and inflict a wound that has never properly healed, despite repeated attempts to stitch it up with accords, treaties and brute force.

The surviving Le rulers refused to recognise Mac, and threw their support behind the southern-based Nguyen Kim, head of a government in exile, who hoped to overthrow Mac with the help of the Laotian king. After five years of struggle, in 1545 Vietnam was split in two; Mac controlled the region north of Thanh Hoa, on the southern edge of the Red River Delta; Nguyen Kim controlled the great curling ribbon of country to the south. Not until 1592 did the Le dynasty (with Kim's help) overthrow Mac's last pretenders to the throne and reunite the country. But this bloody, sixty-year split seems to have penetrated the heart and soul of Vietnam. The divide cut more deeply when Trinh, a general in the Le army, assumed control of the nation and made his sons hereditary princes (while leaving a Le on the throne in nominal charge). Meanwhile, a surviving son of Kim, Nguyen Hoang, assumed command of the region south of the seventeenth parallel — the latitude along which the country would again be divided, 350 years later, in 1954.

There began a fifty-year war between north and south, during which the Trinh army, which outnumbered the south three times, launched repeated offensives. A huge land and sea invasion in 1627 was repulsed, as were seven Trinh attempts to breach two great walls erected by the Nguyen. Trinh's failure led to a stalemate, and in 1673 the two warlords signed a truce. The north and south lived in peace for a century, during which the weaker south survived primarily because it discovered and settled the Mekong Delta, a critical factor in the evolving fortunes of the 'Two Vietnams'.

The Mekong, the future rice bowl of Asia — and later the world — drew a steady stream of northern immigrants and refugees, who poured in to exploit this vast, naturally irrigated floodplain, perfectly suited for the cultivation of rice. The Chinese again cast a covetous eye on a food source even greater and more sustaining than the Red River Delta. But Asian eyes were not alone in contemplating the riches of the Mekong: by the eighteenth century Dutch, Spanish, English and French explorers had all surveyed the glittering green shoots of the Mekong paddies and drawn up their plans.

A last, great upheaval cracked the veneer of this tentative peace. In the late eighteenth century, the peasants, furious at their treatment by the feudal lords of both North and South, rose in armed rebellion. This ferocious peasant army, led by the Tay Son, a family of seemingly indomitable peasant warriors, conquered the south, butchered the Nguyens and then, in a series of brilliant manoeuvres by the youngest Tay Son brother, chased the opportunist northern invaders out of Hué and back to Hanoi. In 1788 — the year the First Fleet of convicts and white settlers established a colony in Australia — a peasant-based regime briefly united Vietnam.

The next year the Chinese Manchu dynasty again invaded Vietnam; again they were repelled. In one action, the Tay Son troops drew up near the Chinese camp outside Hanoi, and shocked the intruders with an audacious midnight attack in the middle of the Tet New Year holiday — normally a Buddhist time of peace and goodwill in both China and Vietnam. This violation of Tet utterly surprised the Manchu enemy, who were caught sleeping off the day's revelry. The event presaged a similar violation, 179 years later.

The Tay Son soon met their nemesis. In one of those passing oversights that hindsight endows with immense historic repercussions, the Tay Son failed to eliminate a young Nguyen prince, Anh, who re-entered the country from exile, swooped on Saigon with the help of Cambodian mercenaries and crowned himself 'King of Cochinchina' in 1782. Within twenty-five years Nguyen Anh had 'conquered the whole of Vietnam, exterminated all members of the Tay Son family and founded the last dynasty of his reunited country'.[20]

The French explorers who stepped ashore in the late eighteenth century encountered a strict society ruled by the Nguyen emperors from the ancient capital of Hué. Vietnam fell swiftly to the conqueror's superior technology. Yet in their reply to the French invasion may be seen the most painful and exquisite expression — both resistant and cooperative — of Vietnam's deep longing for nationhood. The coming of the French brought down the curtain on 900 years of Vietnamese independence.

# Chapter 2
# The French

When our soldiers are again threatened, as they are today, we will
be asked for more money and for more men. We will not be able
to refuse. And millions upon millions, fresh troops on top of fresh
troops will lead to our exhaustion. Gentlemen, we must block
this route.

*Georges Clemenceau, addressing the French Parliament, March 1885.*

Reminders of the French survive in the ruins of seaside villas, now the
residences of vermin; in the poinsettias on the broad avenues of
Saigon, of which a few — such as Avenue Louis Pasteur — retain their
French names; and in the broken chateaux of the old French rubber
planters. Architectural echoes of Paris resonate in Hanoi's Old Quarter,
where crippled street vendors still sell copies of the classic on the decline of
French Indochina, Bernard Fall's *Street Without Joy*.

The French occupation of Vietnam began with an invasion in 1858,
ostensibly to punish the Vietnamese for their persecution of indigenous
Catholics, who dared to convert to the Christian faith under the influence
of French missionaries. It ended with the annihilation of the French Army
at Dien Bien Phu in 1954.

The intervening ninety-four years were a bloody catalogue of French
crimes against the Vietnamese people. Let us dispense at once with the
colonial theories of 'assimilation' and 'association'. Let us draw aside the veil
of sweet-smelling nostalgia for French Indochina, look beyond the colonial

charm and failed dreams of France's *mission civilatrice* and their doughty pioneers, and consider the reality of French imperialism and how it planted the seeds of the American War. The French used brute force to create a little France in Indochina. The transient gifts of French civilisation meant little while French officials and entrepreneurs busied themselves with the rape of a nation; the theft of Vietnamese resources — chiefly rice, rubber, minerals — and the brutal subjugation of the Vietnamese people. This oppression operated on a political, military and cultural level and pervaded every aspect of Vietnamese life. The French routinely and savagely crushed all resistance. They ruled through edict and direct control — unlike the British colonial poobahs, a few thousand of whom ruled 300 million Indians by local proxies.

French apologists argue that the gifts of technology, trade and infrastructure redeemed the worst excesses of the French occupation. If so, the Vietnamese clearly did not agree. India preserved something of the British legacy — democratic institutions, the English language, an independent judiciary and cricket — but the Vietnamese retained very little that was peculiarly French: certainly no recognisable political institution, and nothing that the Vietnamese could not build themselves after decades of war. In the wake of France's humiliating departure, a despot took power in the South, and Ho Chi Minh's communist tyranny asserted its grip on the North. In the final analysis, the legacy of the French was so much ephemera, the trinkets of a souvenir culture and the baubles of a fading dream that descended rapidly into a nightmare. Indeed, as we shall see, the French were directly responsible for creating the political conditions that compelled the Vietnamese people to pursue change through violent revolution; first, under the banner of nationalism and, when that failed, communism. Those conditions ultimately led to the division of Vietnam and another long war, with America and her allies.


The French pioneers came to Vietnam ostensibly on a mission to 'civilise' the 'backward peoples of the world'.[1] This was France's pretext for joining the colonial scramble for Asia. Missionary scholars, of whom the most famous were Pigneau de Behaine in the eighteenth century and Bishop Pellerin in the nineteenth, arrived in Vietnam bearing the Bible, the cross and a political plan. French mercantile and military might loomed over the shoulders of these intrepid missionaries, probing for a chance to taste the sweet riches of Indochina.

In the mid-nineteenth century, Vietnam was a closed, heavily controlled society in the hands of a conservative, inward-looking Confucian elite who paid court to the Nguyen emperors. Indigenous Catholics were harshly suppressed. Trade with the outside world was virtually non-existent. 'A more disastrous policy for preparing to cope with change in the external environment can scarcely be imagined.'[2]

The defence of persecuted Catholics gave the invaders their excuse, and in 1858 French warships seized an opportunity to break open this closed, anachronistic society. A fleet carrying 3,000 French troops landed at Da Nang (the same landfall as the US Marines, 107 years later), with plans to march north and conquer the capital of Hué. Vietnamese resistance forced them south, where they captured the provinces of Bien Hoa, Gia Dinh and Dinh Trong, and the city of Saigon.

The beaten Nguyen emperor, Tu Duc, offered concessions in order to salvage what was left of South Vietnam. A treaty signed on 6 June 1862 ceded the three provinces, Saigon and the island of Poulo Condore to the French; allowed French warships free passage up the Mekong to the Cambodian border; gave Catholic missionaries the right to proselytise; opened three ports to French ships; granted France the right to forbid Vietnam to cede any more of its territory to a rival power; and indemnified France for the losses of the invasion, a total sum of four million piastres.

In so doing, Tu Duc lost the moral authority to rule his people. Vietnamese district chiefs and local officials were not so malleable. Their resistance was sharp and furious, and spread swiftly through the Mekong Delta. 'If you persist in bringing to us your iron and flame, the struggle will be long,' stated a village poster. 'But we are guided by the laws of Heaven, and our cause will triumph in the end.'

The French persisted, and a guerrilla war erupted in the provinces. Anxious to retain something of his ailing empire, Tu Duc offered to extend the treaty to embrace a French protectorate over all six provinces of Cochinchina, plus the payment of an annual tribute. Napoleon III accepted this generous offer, but the French colonists, chiefly the navy, were furious at the apparent sell-out. They wanted total control, not a Vietnamese-administered protectorate. They took matters into their own hands, and presented the spoils of conquest to Paris as a fait accompli. In 1867 Admiral Pierre Paul Marie Benoit de La Grandière overran the three provinces without warning or negotiation, and imposed direct French control, a prelude to possessing the entire southern region of Cochinchina. Before killing himself, one deeply shamed Vietnamese viceroy forced assurances from his sons that they would never collaborate with the French.

Emperor Tu Duc, a broken man, broadcast his country's impotence in an extraordinary appeal to the nation:

> Never has an era seen such sadness, never a year more anguish …
> Alone I am speechless. My pulse is feeble, my body pale and thin,
> my beard and hair white. Though not yet forty, I have already
> reached old age, so that I lack the strength to pay homage to my
> ancestors every morning and evening … Evil must be suppressed
> and goodness sought. The wise must offer their counsel, the
> strong their force, the rich their wealth, and all those with skills
> should devote them to the needs of the army and the kingdom.
> Let us together mend our errors and rebuild …[3]

French adventurers, possessed by a diabolical zeal for colonial riches, drove relentlessly into the Vietnamese interior, over the mountains and up the Mekong River. The sacred serpent of the Mekong, the longest river in South-East Asia, held a deadly allure. Would it offer a route to the riches of Yunnan province in China? Would it open up the Red River Delta? Would it lead to Xanadu? Alas, the Mekong — bubbling snowmelt in the Tibetan Himalayas, shooting torrent in the gorges of south-western China, swirling rapids in the upper Laotian reaches, and symbol of majesty and eternity through the paddies of the delta — proved of little commercial value as a trade route. That did not inhibit the great pioneering French explorer Lieutenant Francois Garnier from embarking on a two-year voyage in 1866, which took him up the Mekong, down the Yangtze to Shanghai and back to Saigon. His journey had bloody consequences for Vietnam. With Garnier's encouragement, an entrepreneur called Jean Dupuis began shipping arms, tin and copper between Hanoi and Yunnan.

In 1873 a group of Hanoian mandarins who controlled the local salt monopoly blocked Dupuis' fleet. In retaliation, the French raised the Tricolour over Hanoi, in direct defiance of the sovereignty of Tonkin, the northern region, and its treaty with France. Pleas for restraint from Paris had little influence in the wild east, where French opportunists tended to fire first and negotiate later. Garnier and Dupuis joined forces, suppressed the resistance, commandeered the port of Haiphong and slashed customs tariffs to suit French merchants. Garnier died in vain. Paris refused to accept his posthumous gift of Tonkin on a platter. Severely stretched in the south, the French Government put a halt to Dupuis's premature scramble for Indochina.

And so, for a time, Tonkin remained independent. The French evacuated Hanoi under the watchful eye of Paul Louis Philastre, a formidable scholar and rising star in the French colonial office. In Hué, in 1873, Philastre signed another treaty with Tu Duc that recognised the sovereignty of Tonkin and confirmed France's unconditional control of the southern region of Cochinchina.

Philastre was one of those sensitive, extremely clever young Frenchmen — he translated the Vietnamese legal code into French — who occasionally stood up to remind his colonial masters that their methods, if not their mission, were perilously misguided. He pleaded with his countrymen to respect Vietnamese culture, customs and institutions. He observed the disastrous effects of the imposition of French rule in the 'extraordinary resistance' of the Vietnamese people, 'sometimes violent, sometimes passive in nature, day by day more hateful'. Such hatred, he wrote, was shared by 'all classes of people' and 'is stronger now than at any time since the conquest. We must open our eyes.'[4]

Had they done so, French eyes may have seen the real victims of the French/Vietnamese struggle: the local people. The French imprisoned or massacred those who resisted. But the Vietnamese dealt similarly with collaborators. More than 20,000 Tonkinese Catholics were massacred and a million rendered homeless for their suspected allegiance to the French, according to Vietnamese sources.

French eyes remained firmly shut to Philastre's ideals. In 1882 a far stronger France, freed from the burden of the war with Prussia, cast a fresh gaze over Indochina in the race with their colonial arch-rivals, the English and Dutch. A booming economy at home cried out for overseas markets: 'For the first time since she went into Vietnam, France almost unanimously stood behind the imperialist aggressors in the East.'[5] Only one politician, the conservative Jules Delafosse, openly opposed the decision: 'Let us, gentlemen, call things by their name,' he told the French Parliament. 'It is not a protectorate that you want but a possession.'[6]

In pursuit of Tonkin, the French embarked on twelve years of butchery to which they gave the name 'pacification'. The full invasion began in August 1883. Prime Minister Jules Ferry authorised the dispatch of an expeditionary force up the Perfume River to Hué. On one ship was a peculiarly cruel official responsible for 'native affairs', François Harmand. Harmand gave the Vietnamese forty-eight hours to surrender. Failure to do so, he warned, would be met with the 'worst evils': 'Imagine all that is terrible and it will still be less than reality,' he warned, adding, 'The word "Vietnam" will be erased from history.'

The Vietnamese did not surrender and, true to his word, Harmand gave no quarter in the coming slaughter. Tens of thousands of Hanoians lost their lives during those twelve years of French 'pacification'. The Emperor Tu Duc died in July, 'cursing the invader ... killed by sorrow over seeing foreigners invade and devastate his empire', declared the Imperial Court. 'Keep him in your hearts and avenge his memory.'

All of Vietnam became a French colony. A final act of 'incredible brutality', in the words of civilian governor Jean-Marie Antoine de Lanessan, gave the lie to the *mission civilatrice*. In 1885, emboldened by Chinese recognition of their protectorate, the French ordered the resignation of a dissident mandarin, Ton That Thuyet, adviser to the new emperor, the 13-year-old Ham Nghe, who resided in the beautiful Imperial Palace in Hué. Thuyet refused, and recklessly ordered his Vietnamese guards to attack. In reply, a thousand French troops encircled the citadel, slaughtered the guards and stormed the interior. They burned the Imperial Library and its ancient scrolls and manuscripts, and 'stripped the palace of gold and silver ornaments, precious stones, carpets, silk curtains, statuary, and even mosquito nets, cuspidors, and toothpicks, the total valued at some twenty-four million francs'.[7] The boy emperor fled with Thuyet into exile, and the French placed a compliant stooge on the throne.

In March that year Georges Clemenceau addressed the French Parliament. The brilliance of his speech thwarted Ferry's attempt to raise another 200 million francs with which to continue pacifying the Vietnamese. As the twentieth century dawned on French Indochina, Clemenceau's words acquired the weight of dreadful prophecy. Speaking after the 'defeat' of a French unit at Langson, near the Chinese border (the drunk French commander imagined he was under attack, and retreated), Clemenceau said: 'When our soldiers are again threatened, as they are today, we will be asked for more money and for more men. We will not be able to refuse. And millions upon millions, fresh troops on top of fresh troops will lead to our exhaustion. Gentlemen, we must block this route.'[8]

They did not. The construction of roads, railways, bridges and ports, the exploitation of rubber, rice and mineral resources, and the establishment of opium, alcohol and salt monopolies, characterised French rule over Indochina in the twentieth century. Few public works benefited the local people, as Buttinger observed: the railways were the most expensive to build and operate in the world, and 'were of profit solely for the men who built them ... and for the banks that granted the loans for their construction'. These huge public works enslaved the people; the trading monopolies were the cruellest form of extortion, 'fiscal brutality' on a national scale. By fixing exorbitant prices for salt and limiting its distribution, the French instituted a public health crisis and ruined the indigenous salt producers.

A succession of governors — fifty-two between 1886 and 1926 — stamped their will on Vietnam, with little coherence or continuity. There were a few constants: resistance to French rule was mercilessly suppressed, by guillotining and imprisonment (Saigon still used the guillotine in the early 1960s); Frenchmen were paid many times more than their indigenous counterparts; and any governor who threatened to dismantle the cherished trade monopolies was swiftly relieved.[9]

Sparks of resistance kindled around the name of Ham Nghe, the exiled boy emperor. Ham Nghe led the first phase of uprisings against the French. In 1888, aged 17, Ham came down from his mountain hideout at the head of a guerrilla movement that smashed the French hold on Annam and left a trail of blood and fire. Betrayed and captured, Ham responded to his French interrogators with contemptuous silence. He was exiled to Algeria in chains and his followers executed. His brave example ignited an underground conflagration: in coming years, rebel leaders such as Nguyen Thien Thuat, Doc Ngu and De Tham, the 'tiger of Ben Tre', raised the fist of defiance to French rule.

The French responded with the ancient tactic of divide and conquer. They offered carrots to district chiefs — the right to raise taxes and local armies, for example — in return for loyalty; they persuaded mandarins and Catholic converts to collaborate; and the French generals overcame support for the local guerrillas with valuable economic grants, 'civic action' that predated by sixty-five years the similar programs of the Second Indochina War adopted by the Australian and American armies.

By the early twentieth century the French grip on Indochina seemed unbreakable. Tens of thousands of Vietnamese had died for their country;

yet it was no closer to being theirs. A new era of cooperation with the colonial power betrayed the memory of that sacrifice. French collaborators — men whom Ham Nghe had scorned as 'disguised animals' — gained the upper hand. The emperors lost their 'mandate from heaven' as the Confucian elite sank into a cushioned nomenclature of titles without substance. All over Vietnam a sense of futility and subservience to France suffocated the spirit of defiance. *Nghia*, the Confucian way of righteousness, duty and justice, had lost its hold on the Vietnamese mind. The resistance movement faded or went into exile, and an unnatural time of crushed hopes, rudderless dreams and abject servility came down on the heads of the Vietnamese people. The soldiers of *nghia* had surrendered.

Only the poets seemed capable of expressing the sadness of the soul of Vietnam. The turn of the century was a time when truths were turned upside down, when the brittle Confucian social code of Ly broke down. It was, as the poet Nguyen Khuyen (1870–1907) wrote, a time when 'water flowed upward' and his contemporaries used 'feather fans' and wore 'socks', like the French. The obsequiousness and French affectations of their colleagues disgusted patriotic Vietnamese, as Nguyen Khuyen observed in his bitter poem on the celebration of Bastille Day:

> *Firecrackers are resounding. It's Bastille Day!*
> *So many waving banners, so many lanterns hung …*
> *… Whoever organized these games has done a splendid job.*
> *Yet the more fun that these folks have, the greater the disgrace!*[10]

Where force of arms had failed, Vietnamese scholars took up the cudgels of the mind. Their sense of helplessness produced desperate satire. Listen to Nguyen Khuyen's poem about a friend who turned down the offer of a French official post, claiming he was deaf: feigning deafness was the only weapon left. Perhaps the most bitter was Tran Te Xuong, an alienated northerner who saw the futility of refuge in intellectual pursuits in a world that had changed utterly:

> *What good are Chinese characters?*
> *All those PhDs are out of work.*
> *Much better to be a clerk for the French:*
> *You get milk in the morning and champagne at night.*[11]

Tran Te Xuong's was the voice of intellectual and moral surrender. 'Both armed resistance and righteous abstention had become meaningless responses to the French colonial takeover.'[12] With Xuong's death in 1907 it seemed as though the voice of Vietnamese resistance had been extinguished forever.

Yet there *were* other ways. Younger Vietnamese adopted the Japanese model of resistance through imitation. Two men embodied this spirit of modernisation along Western lines: Phan Boi Chau and Phan Chu Trinh. Encouraged by Japan's defeat of Russia in 1905, they urged their compatriots, in speeches and underground newspapers (one of which was called *Letters Written in Blood*), to dispense with the old Confucian ways and to adopt Western ideas — the most dangerous of which seemed to be the concept of individual will. This was thoroughly at odds with the Vietnamese-Confucian idea of the collective will, and hardly appealed to the faceless Vietnamese peasant, who had never been treated as an individual.

Both men were, more importantly, strident Vietnamese nationalists, as Trinh wittily demonstrated in a speech in Hanoi in 1907, which launched the 'haircut movement'. Linking the fashion of long hair with China's Ming (read French) invasion, he urged his fellow Vietnamese to cut their hair: '… our men began to let their hair grow … and we became Chinese. But Heaven has opened our minds. We have awakened, and the entire nation is modernizing. So go out and cut your hair! Don't leave any more land for that stupid gang of parasites to colonize on top of your heads, from which they can suck your blood!'[13] The metaphor amused, and the haircut became a popular symbol of freedom. Throughout the country the 'haircut chant' accompanied the snip of scissors: 'Comb in the left hand/Scissors in the right/Clip away! Clip away!'

It would take more than a shave to resist the French. In 1908 crushing taxes, forced labour, consecutive crop failures and a collapse in the value of the piastre drove the peasants to near insanity. They revolted. Lynch mobs rampaged, demanding tax relief, seizing officials and district chiefs, some of whom received haircuts before execution. The French responded with customary overkill. They summarily executed the leaders and bundled a hundred others off to the penal colony of Poulo Condore.

Chau, then in Japan, was sentenced to death in absentia. For nearly twenty years he nurtured his nationalist dream in exile and involved himself in every act of resistance, every plan of modernisation. The nationalist leaders consulted him over the planting of bombs in the cities and the assassination of collaborators. His elusiveness infuriated the French, who gave the then Governor Albert Sarrault the special job of getting Chau's head. Eventually, Chau was captured and confined to house arrest in Hué until his death in 1940.[14]

The one nationalist voice capable of unifying Vietnam therefore slumbered in the house of Chau. The nationalist cause fragmented and lost direction. The young nationalist leaders failed to comprehend the immense social forces that were awakening, like an enraged Titan, across Vietnam: two classes, the landed and the landless, were the direct consequence of French land reform. 'Reform' meant brazen sequestration: the French colonial government, having decided that private property did not exist in Vietnam, simply redistributed the peasant holdings to wealthy collaborators — usually northern Catholics. This ran roughshod over the fact that, if they did not technically 'own' their land, the peasants held traditional title to their allotments at the pleasure of the emperors, who dared not interfere with local land rights.

Displaced peasants — forced on to French farms, or driven by war from their land — returned to find their allotments in the hands of new owners, *colons* and collaborating Vietnamese. 'Thus were created the new class of landless tenants, or *tadien* ... a class that, like the big landlords, had not existed in pre-colonial Vietnam.'[15] The construction of canals and the draining of swamps accelerated the process. The rice-land surface of Cochinchina quadrupled between 1880 and 1930, but the average peasant holding was smaller in 1930 than before the French invasion of 1858.[16]

The result was a feudal-class system of wealthy Vietnamese landlords, answerable to the French; and their serfs, the peasant tenants, worked to death on the plantations. In a few decades the French had succeeded in rupturing the sacred link between peasants and their land. In 1930, 2 per cent of Tonkinese landowners held 40 per cent of all rice lands. The remaining 98 per cent were desperately poor peasant farmers with half a hectare per family on average. A similar process applied in the southern rubber industry, where French plantation owners, anxious to outproduce the profitable British rubber plantations in Malaya, progressively corralled small family farms into great estates. The rubber and rice plantations exacted a terrible price for their success, in terms of human suffering and long-term social breakdown. One Michelin plant lost 12,000 out of 45,000 workers to malaria, dysentery and malnutrition between 1917 and 1944. The virtual enslavement of the

Vietnamese peasant was, for a time, profitable: the vast French estates produced a growing rice surplus for export (320,000 tons in 1877, 1.55 million tons in 1937). By the outbreak of World War II Vietnam had become the third-biggest rice exporter after Burma and Thailand.

French colonial pirates were no doubt responsible for these abuses, but it is worth noting that their agribusinesses differed little from the later communist collectives. The obvious distinction was that French monopolists, and not the state, owned them. But they both used indentured labour, both broke the workers, both extracted massive surpluses to enrich their owners. Other industries were equally rapacious in their demands on the Vietnamese: the coalmines of Hongay raised output from half a million tons in 1913 to two million tons in 1927 while imposing conditions of near slavery on the local miners.

Intense, widespread hatred of the French, and resurgent Vietnamese nationalism, resulted. Many Vietnamese were democratic nationalists; many were nationalist and communist; others (including several later leaders of the National Liberation Front, or Viet Cong) saw communism as a vehicle for nationalist hopes.

In the 1930s and 1940s the communist movement rapidly gained strength at the expense of the nationalists. Why? The obvious reason was that the communists were far better organised, and their slogans appealed to the peasants. The communists had repudiated the French more loudly and effectively than the nationalists, who were tainted by their links to colonial capitalism. Peasants simply rallied behind the political force most likely to evict the invader. 'The colour of the political banner under which the struggle for independence was conducted was secondary.'[17] The communists saw this. They associated their creed with every protest and every cause: the reduction of taxes, land reform, higher wages, better medical care, the right to unionise — as if only they could deliver social justice. The communists blamed colonial capitalism for mass enslavement. Stripped of French finery, this was not capitalism, of course, but the crudest form of lawless economic subjugation, more akin to rapine. It 'brought all the evils of early and none of the blessings of later capitalism ... and above all it was completely foreign, not a Vietnamese phenomenon'.[18]

The tragedy for Vietnam lay in this: the communists presented themselves as the party of freedom and 'democratic nationalism'. In fact, the end of true democratic nationalism was a depressing byproduct of the communist ascendancy. With Chau under house arrest, the nationalists had no clear leader capable of organising and guiding them. They were, in the main, headstrong, romantic intellectuals, the sons and daughters of mandarins, or the middle class. They were reckless idealists. Their party, the Vietnamese Nationalist Party (VNQDD), formed in 1927, paid little thought to mass mobilisation; instead they launched headlong into armed rebellion. In 1930 their covert plans for a series of uprisings backfired with the failed mutiny at Yen Bay military base. The French executed eighty leaders of the VNQDD, literally beheading the nationalist cause. The communists seized the opportunity, and in 1930 destroyed and replaced the local French administration in Annam with 'democratic' Soviets. Then, in 1931, a year dubbed the White Terror, the nationalists tried again to stamp their authority on the destiny of Vietnam. This time, French retribution was exceptionally thorough, and indiscriminate: 10,000 Vietnamese nationalists and communists were murdered and 50,000 deported. It was the darkest year of French rule in Indochina. The Vietnamese rebels died not in open battles but by being 'chased, hunted down, and murdered by a soldiery drunk on blood'.[19]

Their visceral hatred of the French found dark forms of expression in the best-selling poetry of the 1930s. A powerful symbol of Vietnamese nationalism was the caged tiger, as beautifully expressed in The Lu's poem, 'Remembering the Jungle — The Words of the Tiger in the Zoo'. Australia's psychological warfare units would have found it useful reading:

*Gnawing upon our resentment, we stretch out in an iron cage,*
*Watching the slow passage of days and months.*
*How we despise the insolent crowd outside,*
*Standing there foolishly, with tiny eyes bulging,*
*As they mock the stately spirit of the deep jungle …*
*Here by misfortune, shamefully caged,*
*We are no more than a novel sight to amuse them, some plaything …*
*O stately soul, heroic land,*
*Vast domain where yesteryear we freely roamed,*
*We see you no more.*
*But do you know that during our days of frustration*
*We follow a great dream, letting our souls race to be near you,*
*O formidable jungle of ours!*[20]

The stately defiance of The Lu's poem gave way to the despair of Cu Huu Can's 'Sacred Fire':

> If You only knew, Lord, how many hearts have panicked
> And shattered their wings like bats in the darkness of grief.
> If You only knew how many streams of bitter tears
> Have flowed like rivers and still not washed out life's sorrow.
> If You only knew how many souls have been decimated
> Because they picked up the flaming vessel and held it to their lips;
> Then even You, O Lord, might blush with regret
> That You had brought human life into existence.[21]

Poetry freed the mind, not the nation. These poets saw the futility of words in a world without political freedom. Only organised violence could evict the French, they believed. The proto-communists, the Viet Minh — an army of Spartan prowess forged by Hanoi's Vietnamese leaders to fight the French — understood and harnessed this belief: village by village, they drove Tonkin to bloody insurrection. 'Only force could prevail against the French, and the Communists were the most consistent exponents of force.'[22]

# Chapter 3
# Ho and Giap

The white man is finished in Asia. But if the Chinese stay now they will never go. As for me I prefer to sniff French shit for five years than eat Chinese shit for the rest of my life.
*Ho Chi Minh, to comrades after ceding control of Vietnam back to the French in 1946.*

We're blowing everything up — goodbye to our families —
*Adieu ...*
*The last French radio message from Dien Bien Phu, 1954.*

'A spectre is haunting Europe — the spectre of communism,'[1] declares the opening line, as ominous as a hearse in a plague-stricken street, of *The Communist Manifesto*. Karl Marx's aristocratic wife, Jenny (née von Westphalen), penned this line, perhaps the most chilling sentence in the library of the bourgeoisie.

The Manifesto, written by Marx with the help of Friedrich Engels — two middle-class German intellectuals — prophesied the triumph of a stateless, classless society; the consequence, Marx held, of the overthrow by the workers of the bourgeoisie. For Marx, the bourgeoisie, that 'class of modern capitalists, owners of the means of social production and employers of wage labour', were the last and most parasitic oppressors in an ancient struggle between 'freeman and slave, patrician and plebeian, lord and serf ... oppressor and oppressed'.[2] Only bloody insurrection, only 'the shock of body against body', Marx wrote in *The Poverty of Philosophy*, would achieve his revolutionary aims.³ As Karl Popper has shown, peaceful reform, union organisation and democratic pressure had no place in Marx's conception of violent revolution as the ultimate agent of social change. The workers must be organised and armed, Marx declared; the proletariat must 'deal with' its own national capitalist classes, before joining hands in a global uprising. Private property would be abolished; capital confiscated; and the bourgeoisie 'swept out of the way, and made impossible'; that is, annihilated.

The famous last paragraph of the Manifesto removes any lingering semantic doubt about Marx's intentions: 'The Communists disdain to conceal their views and aims. They openly declare that their aims can be attained only by the forcible overthrow of all the existing social conditions.'⁴ His later disciples applied this literally: millions would be denounced and condemned to exile and untimely deaths in the name of Marxism–Leninism and its Chinese offshoot. Like a plague of vermin, an entire 'class' of ill-defined, ordinary people were to be 'made impossible' because they happened to own 'capital' — which in practice often meant a farm, a shop, a small plot of earth, a machine tool. The Manifesto's last lines underlined the creed's international program: 'Let the ruling classes tremble at a communist revolution. The proletarians have nothing to lose but their chains. They have a world to win. WORKING MEN OF ALL COUNTRIES, UNITE!'⁵

And tremble they did. Marx's 'scientific' theory of communism fired the bloody insurrections of Lenin, Stalin, Mao, Fidel Castro, Ho Chi Minh and Pol Pot. If, in his lifetime, Marx did not recognise the violent seedlings as his, then we are left to wonder what he meant by the 'forcible overthrow of the bourgeoisie'. It is hard to credit the claim — repeated *ad nauseam* by Marx's legions of apologists — that the bearded intellectual would have been shocked by what was done in his name: *The Communist Manifesto* prescribed that very outcome.

Marxism spread to Vietnam via revolutionary Russia. Lenin — born Vladimir Ilyich Ulianov, in Simbirsk on 22 April 1870, the son of a college teacher — mercilessly applied Marx's theory of violent revolution to a backward agricultural economy in the grip of an absolute monarchy. The overthrow of Tsarist Russia required a period of concentrated aggression, Lenin declared: '… the liberation of the oppressed class is impossible without a violent revolution.'⁶ Having dispatched the hated monarchists,

Lenin applied similar methods to remove his moderate rivals: in 1917 Lenin 'excavated' the works of Marx and Engels in order to justify his destruction of the provisional government. His essay 'The State and Revolution', was a grim reminder to the doves in the Russian Socialist Party that their late comrades Marx and Engels had indeed intended the violent overthrow of the middle class. 'No one remembers,' Lenin scolded his timid comrades, that Marx had written 'a panegyric of a revolution by force ... by which social movements hack their way through and break up the dead and fossilized political forms.' Lenin called for 'the annihilation of the power of the State', this 'parasitic excrescence': 'Its "amputation", its "destruction" ... these are the expressions used by Marx regarding the State ...!'[7]

Such were the expressions absorbed in Paris in 1919 by a quiet, slightly built Vietnamese political activist, sometime kitchen hand and pamphleteer who went by the alias Nguyen An Hoc — one of his many pseudonyms. He was born Nguyen Sinh Cung in Nghe An province, central Vietnam, in 1890, to the son of a concubine. Cung's father shed that indignity, rose to the status of mandarin, then abandoned his family to roam the country as an itinerant healer. Cung inherited his father's restlessness on a grander scale: he would wander the world for decades, never marry or have children.

Young Cung had little formal education. His father taught him to read and write Chinese characters, and he spent a brief time at the exclusive Quoc-Hoc school in Hué (which Ngo Diem, the future President of South Vietnam, also attended). In 1911 we find him, a galley boy, aboard the French steamship *Latouche Treville* bound for Europe. In London, Cung worked as a kitchen hand with the great French chef Escoffier, who promoted his young Vietnamese favourite to the cake-baking department. After six years in London, Cung moved to Paris. There he heard that the French in Vietnam had sentenced his sister to nine years' hard labour for revolutionary activities. The young man resolved his grief into a burning hatred for the colonial power, and for a time he went by the alias Nguyen O Phap (Nguyen Who Hates the French).

At first his cause sounded democratic, if quixotic: in 1919 Cung drafted a plea to American President Woodrow Wilson (then in France for the Versailles peace talks), that 'all subject peoples are filled with hope by the prospect that an era of right and justice is opening to them ... in the struggle of civilisation against barbarism'. Wilson ignored him, but Nguyen Ai Quoc (Nguyen the Patriot, as he now called himself) found a new direction. He fell among French socialists. He wrote poems and a play, *The*

*Bamboo Dragon* — a deadly attack on colonialism, said his admirers; dull and hackneyed, thought his critics. The French authorities in Indochina banned his pamphlet 'French Colonialism on Trial', a great compliment to its wit (e.g. 'the figure of Justice has had such a rough voyage from France to Indochina that she has lost everything but her sword'). He read Lenin and Marx; in Cung's mind, Marx's theories found their sharpest and most brutal expression in the colonial enslavement of the Vietnamese people. In 1920–21 he co-founded the French Communist Party, and styled himself an expert on colonial affairs — in which capacity he went to Moscow in 1923 as a delegate to the Peasants' International Congress. He stayed for two years.

Those two years were the making of the quiet revolutionary destined to be known as Ho Chi Minh. Ho was many things: a devoted Vietnamese nationalist, a ruthless pragmatist, a sentimental idealist, a brilliant organiser, but above all, an avowed communist and disciple of Marxist-Leninist doctrine. Ho welded his Marxist ideals to a genuine longing for Vietnamese independence. 'The fate of Vietnam was Ho's obsession.'[8]

He wore khaki drill and a goatee. Graham Greene described him as gentle, simple, with no trace of fanaticism: 'Ho was a man who had patiently solved an equation.'[9] Patient to the point of stoic, Ho Chi Minh was far from gentle. Vietnam would be laid to waste before Ho surrendered and he would inflict whatever force necessary to establish an independent communist Vietnam: 'We must win back ... freedom even if we have to burn down the whole of the [Annamite] range,' he told his comrades before the August Revolution — couching his prime motives as anti-colonialist at this stage of the uprising.[10] He later said, at the height of the war with America, 'They may send here five hundred thousand, a million or even more troops, the war may drag on for five, ten, twenty years or even longer; Hanoi, Haiphong and some other towns ... may be devastated. But the Vietnamese people will never be intimidated. Nothing is more precious than independence ...'[11] Ho thus allied the concept of 'freedom' with his Marxist-Leninist vision for Vietnam.

In 1924 Ho met Stalin and other Bolshevik leaders, and later survived Stalin's purges and attempts to oust those seen as 'soft' communists. The Bolsheviks dispatched him to Canton in southern China as an interpreter to the permanent Russian delegation in China; Ho did much more than interpret. In Canton he created the Association of Annamite Revolutionary Youth to foment a Marxist revolution on the Sino–Viet border. With the support of Chou En-lai, Mao's future foreign affairs minister, the Annamites were put through Whampoa Military Academy, a training ground for revolutionary cadres. A fellow student was Pham Van Dong, future prime minister of the 'Democratic Republic of Vietnam' and one of Ho's earliest and most loyal acolytes. A high-born mandarin's son, Pham Van Dong had served six years in a French prison before fleeing to Moscow to join the Communist Party, vowing revenge.

No football match has played a more influential role in political history than that held in Hong Kong in June 1929. Amid the roar of spectators, Ho Chi Minh and his huddled comrades founded the Communist Party of Indochina. It aimed to create a revolutionary army, a 'people's army', which would free Vietnam from the French and destroy the democratic nationalists and their supporters, still led in absentia by Phan Boi Chau.

In 1931 the plan ran aground when British police arrested Ho Chi Minh; Sir Stafford Cripps, the British solicitor-general in London, saved him from extradition — and certain execution by the French. Diagnosed with tuberculosis, Ho escaped hospital and fled to China, having persuaded his doctor to report him dead. Ho's obituary appeared in the Soviet press, and the French closed his file with the words 'Died in a Hong Kong jail'.

Ho then wandered the world, a frail waif with a hacking cough, always planning the 'liberation' of his homeland. He travelled in a freezing train compartment across Siberia, or in the lower decks of freighters that plied the sea lanes between Africa, Asia and Europe. He dressed in all manner of disguises and adopted dozens of pseudonyms, his 50-year-old body racked with dysentery, recurrent malaria and tuberculosis. On one occasion he walked for five days to Mao's lair in the caves of Yenan.

In early 1941, disguised as a Chinese reporter, Ho appeared in the South China town of Chingsi. At a propitious moment Vietnamese agents spirited him across the border into Tonkin, his first footfall in his homeland for thirty years. In a cave near the village of Pac Bo, high in the northern mountains, he met two men who were to become his most trusted comrades in arms: Pham Van Dong and Vo Nguyen Giap. No three men would heap greater humiliation on French and American military pride. Giap and Dong awaited the famous exile on the bank of the Tsuy-Hu River. When he appeared — under the alias Vuong — Giap and Dong embraced the man they had revered for so long as 'Uncle' (a title that deftly absolved Ho of the blame he might have drawn as 'Father' of a failed revolution). Ho teased them; Giap was 'still beautiful, like a girl', he said.[12]

In a cave of spirit–lit limestone, the three revolutionaries drew up their plan for the emancipation of Vietnam. 'The time has come,' Ho told his comrades on 19 May 1941, to organise an army of 'patriots of all ages and all types, peasants, workers, merchants and soldiers' to fight both the Japanese and their French collaborators. They named this communist–led force the Viet Nam Doc Lap Dong Minh, later simply the Viet Minh. At the same time Nguyen Sinh Cung adopted his last and most famous *nom de plume*, Ho Chi Minh, or 'Bringer of Light'.

The young Giap was a deeply embittered young man in whose mind the desire to avenge his family's death congealed with a determined scheme to liberate his homeland. Born in 1912 to poor peasants in Quang Binh province, just north of the seventeenth parallel, Giap was a precocious student of uncommon intelligence (he took a degree in political economy from the University of Hanoi). Giap joined the resistance at 16, one of many young 'militant nationalists'. Arrested in 1933, his 'youth saved him from the guillotine', and he was later freed for good behaviour.[13]

The loss of his beloved family in events of unusual cruelty, even by French colonial standards, had a profound influence on Giap's political and emotional response to the occupying forces. In 1939 French police seized Giap's wife, Nguyen Thi Quang Thai, whom he married in 1939, and infant son; both died in prison in 1940. The same year they guillotined Giap's sister on charges of terrorism. His father was also executed. The effect of this personal tragedy on Giap — the scarring of the mind, the dull ache for revenge — cannot be understated: Giap later recalled those two brief years of family life as his happiest days. Other men might have died of grief. Instead, the experience forged a soul of iron: the 'Snow–covered Volcano', as French negotiators dubbed him, a perfect metaphor for the burning hatred that lay beneath Giap's impassive exterior.

Giap took command of the Viet Minh in 1945, and forged a communist guerrilla army of spartan resilience and astonishing will. Of boyish appearance and slight build, Giap bore little outward sign of a man destined to become one of the twentieth century's most successful and ruthless generals. He often inspected his troops in a white suit, checked tie and trilby. The French and Americans grossly underestimated him: an avid reader of military history and strategy, Giap revered Napoleon and Sun Tzu. He assumed a general's responsibility with a major's background, and compensated for his lack of military experience with a profound grasp of the political imperatives of the war. He personally ordered the assassination of village chiefs and others deemed to be French collaborators. His first victory, the massacre of two French garrisons on 22 December 1944, marked the birth of the People's Army of Vietnam.

A generation of indoctrinated boy soldiers vowed to give their lives on the orders of this cruelled spirit. Giap cared little for the individual; only for the collective result. 'Every minute, hundreds of thousands of people die all over the world,' he remarked. 'The life or death of a hundred, a thousand, or of tens of thousands of human beings, even if they are our own compatriots, represents really very little.'[14] For good reason, the French (and Americans) described battles with Giap as 'meat-grinders'. Much later, in 1969, having sent half a million young men to their deaths, Giap told the Italian reporter Oriana Fallaci that he would continue to fight 'as long as necessary — ten, fifteen, twenty, fifty years'.[15] Drawing on Mao's example, Giap, with Ho's devoted support, set forth to exhaust the invader by a thousand cuts, in a war without end. 'You can kill ten of my men for every one I kill of yours,' Ho famously said. 'But even at those odds, you will lose and I will win.'

On 17 August 1945 the Viet Minh seized the chance left by the vanquished Japanese (and their Vichy French puppets) and, in a series of daring stabs at the heart of the old colonial power, infiltrated and occupied Hanoi. Thus began the August Revolution, the 'unforgettable days', Giap wrote. Mob exuberance swept the city as Ho Chi Minh declared Vietnam free: elderly men wept; the remaining Japanese waited and watched; the French cowered in their homes; and the last emperor, Bao Dai, resplendent in his imperial robes, abdicated and prostrated himself as an 'adviser' to Ho Chi Minh. The emperor's Mandate from Heaven thus passed to a communist revolutionary in a khaki jacket and rubber sandals.

On 2 September 1945 Ho Chi Minh proclaimed the Declaration of Independence of the Democratic Republic of Vietnam.[16] His Constitution borrowed straight from America's own Proclamation of Independence of 1776: 'All men are created equal. They are endowed by their Creator with certain inalienable rights, among these are Life, Liberty and the Pursuit of Happiness ...' Ho Chi Minh pleaded with the West for recognition: 'We are convinced that the allied nations ... will not refuse to acknowledge the independence of Vietnam. A people who have courageously opposed French domination for more than eighty years, a people who have fought side by side with the Allies against the Fascists during these last years, such a people must be free and independent ...' Ho repeatedly cabled Washington; he received no reply.

Ho acted swiftly to consolidate his power. He made the right moves: he slashed taxes, dismantled the hated salt, opium and alcohol monopolies, confiscated land from the French and handed it back to the peasants. And he dallied with his most dangerous foe, the non-communist nationalists, who demanded a voice in the new People's Congress. Using all his political guile, Ho brought together sixty delegates of all political stripes to create the National Liberation Committee of Vietnam. This multilayered creation had outward peelings of democratic patriotism and a deep Red centre.

At first Ho and his comrades were careful not to besmirch their 'nationalist' credentials with Marxist dogma. From the start, the communists ran in the guise of democratic nationalists. The Viet Minh impudently presented itself as 'the unified front of all nationalists and patriots'.[17] It reassured the nationalists and the Vietnamese landlords. Ho and Giap even briefly dissolved the Communist Party in order to 'accommodate' — that is, flush out — the nationalists, thus retaining 'the ingenious political edifice' through which they dominated the nationalist movement.[18] And as Ho Chi Minh's regime closed its grip, his *faux* democrats wore the cloak of democracy with ever more cynical ostentation: in 1946 they anointed the new state a 'one and indivisible' nation of north, centre and south, ruled by a single chamber, the People's Parliament, elected by direct universal suffrage every three years. The People's Parliament was stillborn, merely another front conceived to seduce the nationalists. It did not meet until 1953. Meanwhile, the true democratic nationalists, who despised French rule as much as Ho's communists, were exposed and gradually removed — assassinated, imprisoned or exiled — and by 1954 'strangled and destroyed, never to be a serious force again'.[19] Like Lenin and Mao, Ho and Giap personally ordered the liquidation of their democratic and socialist rivals.

Yet Ho's triumph was not simply a communist plot. In the 1940s the Viet Minh forces were genuinely popular, and did represent a broad spectrum of the people. Bao Dai, Ho's new adviser, noted the 'yearning for independence that is in everyone's heart', and warned General de Gaulle: 'Should you establish a French administration here, it will not be obeyed. Every village will be a nest of resistance, each former collaborator an enemy, and your officials and colonists will seek to leave this atmosphere, which will choke them.'[20]


In Saigon the revolution met tougher resistance. French and Vietnamese clashed in vicious running street fights. The British, sent to Saigon to 'liberate' the country from the Japanese, were reliably on hand to subdue the natives. The British commander General Douglas Gracey set about re-enslaving Vietnam under French control. 'He had not come to Indo-China to preside over the liquidation of the French colonial empire, or to put a bare-faced coolie in the palace.'[21] On 23 September 1945 French troops (and even a few Japanese Marines), with Gracey's assent, put down the Vietnamese revolution in the South and reclaimed Saigon.

It was the bloody prelude to the return of the French. In 1946 Ho Chi Minh acceded to French demands that Vietnam return to French control, in order to thwart the Chinese forces of Chiang Kai-shek that had crossed the northern border after the Japanese surrender. Chiang backed the Vietnamese nationalists, the VNQDD Party, Ho's arch-enemies.

'You fools!' Ho famously defended this decision to shocked colleagues. 'Don't you realise what it means if the Chinese remain? Don't you remember your history? The last time the Chinese came they stayed a thousand years. The French are foreigners. They are weak. Colonialism is dying. The white man is finished in Asia. But if the Chinese stay now they will never go. As for me I prefer to sniff French shit for five years than eat Chinese shit for the rest of my life.'[22] On 6 March Vietnam thus became a 'free state' within the French Union (the name for France's post-war empire). The next day the ever-loyal Giap supported his leader before a hushed crowd of 100,000 outside the Hanoi Municipal Theatre, where Ho quietly assured the people, 'You know I would rather die than sell our country.'

Yet the French swiftly betrayed him. No sooner had Ho Chi Minh left for France to negotiate the details than Admiral Thierry d'Argenlieu in Saigon violated the agreement and laid outright claim to the 'possession' of Cochinchina. In Fontainebleau, after eight weeks of humiliations and concessions, Ho had no choice but to sign a fait accompli. Cochinchina and its rich Mekong Delta returned to French possession, and the North reverted to its pre-war status as a French protectorate. The 'deal', Ho Chi Minh knew, condemned Vietnam to an interminable war with France. As he inked the hated document, Ho whispered to his bodyguard, 'I have just signed my death warrant.'[23] At a press conference, he blurted out, 'It is Vietnamese soil! It is the flesh of our flesh, the blood of our blood!' Within months, Vietnam was at war with France.

The First Indochina War erupted on 21 November 1946 with the murder by Viet Minh guerrillas of twenty-three French soldiers in Hanoi, some of whom were unarmed and out shopping. In reply, France shelled the suburbs of Haiphong Harbour, killing an estimated 6,000 Vietnamese.[24] The French General Jean-Etienne Valluy stepped ashore in Haiphong on 17 December and, furious at the loss of some of his troops, warned, 'If those gooks want a fight, they'll get it.'

Valluy swiftly realised that a war against a more numerous, dedicated foe, hidden in the jungles and mountains, could not be won. Yet Paris insisted on reclaiming French Indochina by force. French socialists and conservatives clung to the chimera of empire, and thus condemned thousands of troops to the furnace of Dien Bien Phu.

In late 1953 General Henri Navarre, a reputedly brilliant French strategist who knew little of Indochina, had conceived a plan — the Navarre Plan — based on the grave misapprehension that Dien Bien Phu, a valley near the Laotian border that straddled trade routes between Laos, China and Tonkin, was strategically vital.[26] Navarre had construed early French offensives in the Red River basin as victories, but these were in fact Giap's lures — 'feinting attacks' — designed to draw a confident Gallic fish out of the cities and into the remote mountain regions to the west of Hanoi. Navarre, who had assumed responsibility for the defence of the Laotian border, responded as Giap intended. He flew in or dropped thousands of 'French' paratroopers — many were African, German or Vietnamese collaborators — into the valley of Dien Bien Phu in OPERATION CASTOR on 20 November 1953.

In March 1954 three divisions of the French Army — about 80,000 troops — were stationed in the flat, heart-shaped valley, the 'arena of the Gods', around the village of Dien Bien Phu. Navarre's defence of the cities meant he could spare only a fraction of his 500,000 troops; they were based in a string of forts on the valley floor named after French officers' wives and girlfriends: Huguette, Claudine, Eliane, Dominique, Gabrielle, Anne-Marie, Beatrice and Isabelle.

Giap's ace was his devoted army, the Viet Minh, four divisions of which he secretly positioned along the valley escarpments, supported by well-concealed Chinese 105mm guns and 37mm anti-aircraft guns. Like Mao's bandits, the Viet Minh had lived for years off the land, in jungle, swamps and mountain hides. They defended nothing; they stood to gain everything: at this stage, their political creed was reduced to one word: *doc-lap*, or 'independence'. In the months before the battle, hundreds of thousands of civilian supporters, including women and children, dragged Chinese guns, shells, food supplies and ammunition to the top of the ridges using buffalo-drawn carts and bicycles strengthened to withstand up to 370 kilograms of supplies.

At 5 p.m. on 13 March 1954 a huge Viet Minh artillery bombardment preceded the 'human sea' that poured down the mountainsides, 2,500 of whom were machine-gunned on the spot, according to French records. For fifty-seven days and nights the French withstood the Viet Minh assault. Giap's 'steel elephants' fired 200,000 rounds into the valley, about three times Navarre's estimate.[27] The waves of Vietnamese kept coming, hurling themselves into the valley, singing martial songs, such as: 'Hills and rivers are ablaze; our nation is radiant/Above the fields of Dien Bien Phu, red banners of victory brighten the sky.'[28] On a ridge high above the valley, which Giap likened to a 'rice bowl', the Snow-covered Volcano surveyed the carnage, and murmured, 'We will take the French by the throat.'

Giap's heavy artillery soon destroyed the airstrip, and parachute was Navarre's main means of resupply. The Viet Minh then overran the forts; one by one they fell: Beatrice, Gabrielle and Anne-Marie. Then, after a lull, the Viet Minh stormed the remaining strongholds, ending with the conquest of Isabelle. In the last stages, Secretary of State John Foster Dulles had urged US intervention and raised the possibility of using tactical nuclear weapons to save the French garrison. But such action was contingent on British support, and Sir Anthony Eden 'turned him down'.[29]

The world abandoned the French to their self-inflicted fate. Staring at defeat, General Christian de Castries ordered the destruction of 'whatever could not be fired'. The astonishing figure of surgeon Dr Paul Grauwin continued operating amid the cries of thousands of wounded, as the Viet Minh closed in. 'We're blowing everything up — goodbye to our families … *Adieu* …' a lone signaller radioed a passing aircraft.[30] Dien Bien Phu fell on 7 May 1954. The next day a conference to decide the fate of Indochina began in Geneva. All hostilities ended on 21 July, and the sun set on France's colonial adventure in the most tragic and humiliating of circumstances.

The French suffered 7,184 battle casualties, of whom 1,726 were killed in action. At least another 4,000 died, out of 11,721 prisoners (total French losses in Vietnam during the eight-year war were 172,000 dead or missing). Giap expended at least 23,000 of his finest soldiers, 8,000 of whom were killed in action. Thousands of French and Vietnamese lay in unmarked graves in the valley, dubbed the 'Stalingrad of the jungle'.[31]

# Chapter 4
# The Red menace

When the 'yellow peril' and the 'red peril' coalesced, the threat became total. Race, religion, ideology and recent history all combined against any rational debate on China.
*Graham Freudenberg.*

In 1946 Winston Churchill had first invoked the image of an 'Iron Curtain' falling across Europe, from the Baltic to the Adriatic. From his podium in Fulton, Missouri, Churchill had warned the Western democracies of 'the indefinite expansion of Soviet power and doctrines'. The Soviet Union fulfilled Churchill's prophecy to the letter. In the descending darkness, Stalin subjugated half the European continent, silenced dissent in the Soviet archipelago, and sponsored communist uprisings in Asia, Africa and Latin America. Marxist-inspired crises erupted in Greece, Iran, Turkey and Germany. In the 1950s communist cells fomented revolution in Malaya, Indonesia, Thailand, Vietnam, Laos, Burma and India. Some had loose links with Moscow and Peking; most were rough peasant armies living off the land. Australia and America joined the dots, however, and beheld an international communist monolith controlled by the Soviet Union and China, and intent on overrunning South-East Asia.

In the early 1950s events justified this fear. In China, in 1949, Mao Tse-tung's communist forces defeated Chiang Kai-shek's nationalists. The global shock that met the victory of Red China cannot be understated. The event horrified the West and seemed to toll the death knell of the Truman Doctrine, which had supported nationalist wars against communist-inspired uprisings, first in Greece and Turkey and later in Europe and Asia. The 'loss of China' was 'a grievous political defeat', stated a US policy document on South-East Asia in 1949. Chinese communism, if not contained, 'will be felt throughout the rest of the world, especially in the Middle East and in a … critically exposed Australia'.[1]

Mao immediately established an aggressive, expansionist policy of support for communist-backed 'liberation movements' throughout the world. Red China invaded North Korea and Tibet and threatened India and Taiwan. Indeed, a nation prepared to expend more than 400,000 young lives, as China did in the Korean War, brought a terrifying dimension to modern warfare. The coming of Mao 'altered the whole defence picture in the Far East'.[2] Left unchecked, Chinese-sponsored 'wars of liberation' would spread from nation to nation, like the flames of a bushfire leaping from tree to tree. Or perhaps South-East Asian nations would topple to Stalin or Mao, like a line of dominoes?

President Eisenhower's administration coined the domino metaphor: 'You have a row of dominoes set up,' he said on 7 April 1954, 'you knock over the first one, and … the last one … will go over very quickly. So you could have the beginning of a disintegration … the loss of Indochina, of Burma, of Thailand, of the Peninsula, and Indonesia … you are talking really about millions and millions and millions of people.'[3] Australia might even 'go', Eisenhower warned in 1961.[4]

The fall of a single domino in the chain threatened the collapse of all, American defence analysts argued. That is to say, if one Asian domino, for example Vietnam, 'went' to communism, the rest would tumble in every direction. The dominoes' contiguous borders in Asia made this inevitable, the Pentagon believed. '… the loss of any single country [in South-East Asia],' claimed the National Security Council, 'would probably lead to relatively swift submission to or an alignment with communism of the rest of South-East Asia and India, and in the longer term, the Middle East … would in all probability progressively follow. Such widespread alignment would endanger the stability and security of Europe.'[5]

The theory's focal point was the line dividing North (the 'Democratic Republic of Vietnam') and South (the 'Republic of Vietnam') under the Geneva Agreements of 1954 which marked the end of the First Indochina War with the French. The most vexing question for Australia and America was: would Hanoi break the Agreements and send its troops pouring over the border?

There were in fact two 'Agreements' negotiated at Geneva, by the USSR, France, Britain and the USA (all UN Security Council members) and the People's Republic of China. 'North' and 'South' Vietnam were effectively sidelined; Australia and other countries had observer status. The first Agreement briefly stopped men fighting; the second ensured that they would resume fighting, on a scale then inconceivable.

The first Agreement formally agreed to the ceasefire between France and the Democratic Republic of Vietnam. The second, the unsigned Final Declaration, drew a demarcation line between 'North' and 'South' Vietnam along the seventeenth parallel, with a demilitarised zone (the 'DMZ') 5 kilometres wide on either side. Within 300 days all Viet Minh forces were to regroup north of this line and all forces loyal to Saigon south of it. Civilians were free to live where they wished — without reprisals or discrimination.

Articles 17–19, the core of the Final Declaration, banned 'reinforcements' by either side (i.e. increases in arms and troops above replacement level); prohibited the establishment of military bases under the control of a foreign state; and forbade North or South Vietnam from entering into any military alliance with a foreign power. A toothless International Commission for Supervision and Control (composed of Canadians, Poles and Indians) would monitor the ceasefire and demarcation arrangements.

The demarcation line was a military boundary, not a border between two countries. In time it came to be seen as a default border between the North and South. The two Vietnams, however, had been recognised as 'states' five years before Geneva, in 1949, under a French plan known as the 'Bao Dai solution', which offered partial independence to North and South. The plan envisaged Bao Dai, the last Nguyen emperor, assuming the role of chief of state over all of Vietnam. The Viet Minh vigorously rejected this brazen French attempt to thwart communist designs, and continued fighting for a unified Vietnam under Ho Chi Minh.

The South, on the other hand, accepted partial independence, and in 1950 in fact had a stronger claim on statehood, under international law, than the North. In 1950, the USA, Britain and Australia recognised the Republic of Vietnam as a sovereign country; in 1952 the UN voted forty to five (twelve abstained) that 'South Vietnam' qualified for UN membership; by 1954, thirty-four nations had recognised the southern regime. In this sense, Saigon was hardly a 'puppet' of France.[6]

Geneva also prescribed general elections, to be held in 1956, for the 'reunification' of the country under a supposedly democratically elected president. This doomed any hope of a peaceful settlement: it condemned the South to a communist takeover by ballot, because the more populous North (15 million) would obviously deliver a block vote for Ho Chi Minh. The provision provoked 'shock, dismay and violent opposition' among the Saigon delegates to Geneva, who consistently protested, in April, May and July 1954, against elections they knew would result in communist rule.[7] On the last day of the conference Saigon's Foreign Minister, Dr Tran Van Do, tried to amend the text to record his government's disgust. Intent on getting a deal, France and Britain, for whom falling Asian dominoes held no threat, overruled him. By ignoring this plea for freedom of a people it had subjugated for almost a century, France thus heaped one last indignity on the Vietnamese people.

The South left the conference with no intention of holding elections as imposed at Geneva. The 'democratic' elections as demanded would kill off the hope of democracy in Vietnam forever. The lone figure of Tran Van Do registered his government's scorn for the proceedings with a dignity that elicited respect — and prophesied dire consequences for Vietnam. The Final Declaration at Geneva, he said, was 'catastrophic and immoral'.[8]

In short, Geneva's Final Declaration was not an agreement in any legal, diplomatic or indeed conventional sense of the word. No one signed anything; the South Vietnamese refused to accept the document; the USA, ominously, 'took note' of but refused to sign or ratify the Agreements. In an overt message of support for Saigon, America restated its longstanding anti-colonial position, 'that people are entitled to determine their own future'.

Hanoi's delegation was less combustible. After its victory at Dien Bien Phu, the Viet Minh claimed a mandate to rule all Vietnam, and refused to accept any 'agreement' that denied this. It reluctantly bowed, however, to Chinese pressure to accept temporary partition, consoled by the provision for general elections. Ho Chi Minh knew he could not pursue unification without China's help, but Mao did not want to risk the Red Army in another Korea. China actually soft-pedalled in Indochina in the mid-1950s; true, Mao gave aid to North Vietnam, but he 'discouraged Ho Chi Minh from pursuing Vietnamese unification at the time'.[9] The North Vietnamese thus discovered the limits of communist internationalism; all the old suspicions of China — albeit Red China — returned to haunt Ho Chi Minh, who bided his time.

The Australian delegation simply misinterpreted the Agreements. Perhaps it was their early departure, or plain carelessness, that produced Australia's strange response. On the face of it, Menzies' statement on 22 July 1954 echoed the US position. Australia 'noted' the Agreements, and would view any violation of the terms as a threat to international peace, etc. The Prime Minister then added: 'The United Kingdom, France, Soviet Union, Laos, Cambodia, Vietnam, Chinese People's Republic and Vietminh [sic] have undertaken, in their relations with Cambodia, Laos, and Viet Nam, to respect the sovereignty, independence, unity and territorial integrity of those States and to refrain from any interference in their internal affairs. The Australian government welcomes this undertaking.'[10] This was nonsense, as former diplomat Alan Watt showed.[11] First, the 'Vietminh' was an army, not a state (Menzies had meant the Democratic Republic of Vietnam); second, Australia's statement had in effect asserted that 'the Democratic Republic of Vietnam' had agreed not to interfere with the internal affairs of 'Viet Nam', which was meaningless. Third, neither Hanoi nor Saigon had agreed to respect the other's 'sovereignty'. Each claimed sovereignty over the whole of Vietnam.

The Menzies Government watched with mounting alarm the communist presence in Asia. For decades a deep-set fear of communism had influenced Australian politics. This fear tended outwards, to foreign countries, and yet, when an Australian brand of Marxism appeared to gain strength, Canberra's gaze turn inward, and endowed the local threat with a disproportionate influence and power. Fear of foreign Reds gave notoriety to the local version.

In truth, at its most influential, in the 1930s and 1940s, the Communist Party of Australia (CPA) was little more than a ventriloquist's doll for Stalin, with no power base outside the militant unions. By the 1950s the home-grown menace had degenerated into a self-important irritant, the political wing of hard-line unionism. Stalin's Australian mouthpiece had found a congenial home in laid-back union offices and the sun-drenched university campuses of Sydney and Melbourne.

In this light, Menzies' crackdown on the CPA seemed overplayed. The passing hysteria over 'Reds under the bed' brought to mind the infantile inquisitions of Joe McCarthy, the firebrand American anti-communist. In the late 1940s Arthur Fadden's Country Party placed the Australian communist 'in the same category as a venomous snake — to be killed before it kills'.[12] The Australian Labor Party (ALP), too, backed efforts to remove communist agitators: in 1946 Lance Sharkey, the communist leader, was prosecuted and jailed for three years (reduced to thirteen months on appeal) for sedition: 'If Soviet forces in pursuit of aggressors entered Australia,' Sharkey warned a reporter, 'Australian workers would welcome [them] …'[13] Yet the idea of the Red Army splashing ashore to an effusive welcome at Bondi Beach seemed far-fetched: in 1945, at its height, the CPA claimed 23,000 members, several unions, a few local councils and, oddly, a Queensland MP. Their hopes of the violent overthrow of the state languished in the parched indifference of the Aussie 'lumpenproletariat' — Marx's contemptuous term for conservative working men who preferred to mow their lawns, watch footy and have a beer than man the barricades.

In this light, it was nonsense to suggest that the CPA 'inflicted misery and loss upon thousands of citizens' or was organised 'so as to overthrow by force, majority rule' in Australia, as an April 1948 parliamentary censure motion claimed.[14] Nonetheless, on his return to power in 1949, Menzies set out to fulfil his election pledge to 'deal with the King's Enemies'. His attempt to ban the Communist Party failed: the High Court overturned the Communist Party Dissolution Act within twenty-three days of its becoming law. The Bill was grossly illiberal; it opened the door for any slack-jawed McCarthyite to condemn a person without the slightest evidence, as Ben Chifley argued. In reply, Menzies asked the people in a referendum whether the government should have the power to ban the Communist Party. The 'no' vote narrowly won, by a mere 52,082 votes, with three of six states returning a 'no' majority. The communists had secured — just — their democratic right to exist, however undemocratic their intentions: the referendum exemplified that beautifully naive quality of democracy in tolerating the existence of political beliefs that would seek to destroy democracy altogether.

Within a few years the CPA became 'a stumbling, groping, limping movement'.[15] Even so, the 1950s were fraught with political intrigues against the Red menace, the most influential of which were 'the Movement' and the 'Groupers': staunchly anti-communist Labor Catholics who were determined to stamp out Marxist infiltrators in the ALP and the unions. Their methods were clandestine and inquisitorial and, fired by the will and eloquence of their spiritual leader, 'Bob' Santamaria, their activities culminated in the great Split: the formation of the breakaway Democratic Labor Party (DLP) in 1956, which divided the ALP's ranks and sealed the Liberal Party's control of politics for the foreseeable future. In a sense, then,

Menzies and his successors had the Australian communists to thank for the new Liberal Party's prolonged period in the electoral sunshine.

There was another issue that conflated with the perceived — or manufactured — internal threat of communism: the belligerent to the north, China. In 1954, days before setting off for the Geneva Conference on the future of Vietnam, Minister for External Affairs (1951–60) Richard Casey, DSO, MC, delivered a sermon on the evils of communism outside Australia's borders: 'The world is very disturbed,' he noted. '… The United States of America is on our side. It is on the side of democracy, decency and right, and the forces of darkness opposed to it are very apparent and very powerful.'[16] Casey returned with a name for those forces of darkness: 'China', he told Melbourne's conservative heartland, which had assembled one wintry night in Toorak. 'With the black cloud of communist China hanging to the north, we must make sure that our children do not end up pulling rickshaws with hammer and sickle signs on their sides.'[17]

The image of Australian kiddies dragging fat Asians around Toorak was probably unrealistic. Indeed, China's actual threat to the region (and Australia) depended on the realisation of an awesome set of assumptions at the time: (1) Peking intended the conquest of South-East Asia, thus risking nuclear war with America; (2) Hanoi was the creature of Peking; (3) Hanoi–Peking sought to crush South Vietnam, as the first stage of regional conquest; (4) Saigon would fall, and trigger a pan-Asian domino effect; which (5) would lead inexorably to Chinese communist control of, or in the preferred jargon, 'hegemony over', Australia. The outcome was unlikely — China had neither the willingness nor the military capacity to overwhelm Asia and risk war with America. Yet none of the Party faithful dissented from a voice as authoritative as Casey's. International communism might be on Australia's doorstep within eighteen months, he warned.

Notwithstanding the unlikelihood of that scenario, anti-Chinese rhetoric continued well into the 1950s and early 1960s. In truth, it was designed to appease the DLP's ferocious Red-baiters, and it led the Prime Minister to deploy far more colourful language than he might otherwise have done. Australians must 'protect our lives and ideals while we have time or the day will come when we will either live to regret it, or die without having any chance to regret it at all', warned Menzies in a speech in September 1960.[18] The conservatives were willing to kowtow to the breakaway Catholic party's insistence on strong words and actions against the godless Marxists. Parroting the DLP's sinophobic squawk was a small price to pay for the opportunity to divide and conquer the ALP. In the 1961 election campaign, for example, the DLP, 'at the slightest hint by word or deed that a milder Chinese diplomatic policy might be in preparation … exploded with wrath and screamed the dishonour of sellout'.[19] No surprise, then, that fearful images of red tides, crimson seas and falling dominoes pervaded public debates, speeches and news conferences until well into the 1960s.

The hysteria would reach fever pitch during the election of 1963. A DLP TV commercial depicted a mound of human skulls, labelled 'Communism', a map showing China and an arrow leading to Australia. The Country Party even compared the Chinese threat to the Japanese in World War II: 'Domination of China by the Reds makes possible a swift military thrust down South-East Asia … similar to the Japanese pattern but backed this time … by the whole might of the Union of Soviet Socialist Republics.' The voice of rural Australia added: 'The Red glow from South-East Asia can be clearly seen on the North Australian horizon.'[20] The Country Party's constituents were well placed to see the red glow of communism: China bought 42 per cent — up from zero in 1959–60 to two million tonnes — of Australian wheat exports in 1962–63, and was Australia's eighth-biggest customer for wool. Angry opponents of the trade claimed that Australian farmers were thus feeding and clothing the enemy. The government argued that if Australia did not trade with China, others would; that it had no place interfering with wheat boards and private companies; and that Australia was not at war with China. All true to the letter, but hardly consistent with the hue and cry of government rhetoric.[21]

These awkward inconsistencies eluded most Australians. Anti-Chinese propaganda found its mark. In Australian eyes, China had replaced Japan as the yellow peril; worse, the new enemy was a red yellow peril. A people weaned on the White Australia Policy readily blended the yellow hordes of the Gold Rush years with the Red Menace of Chairman Mao. 'When the "yellow peril" and the "red peril" coalesced, the threat became total. Race, religion, ideology and recent history all combined against any rational debate on China.'[22] The fear of China, then, cemented Canberra's policy of forward defence of Australia at a distant battlefield in a foreign land.

One Australian politician did more than any other to engineer this outcome: Paul Hasluck, who became Minister for External Affairs in 1964 after Garfield Barwick, who had succeeded Casey. For Hasluck, China was not only a grave threat in the coming Asian conflagration; it was also Australia's frontline. To combat it, he persuaded a fundamental shift in Australian foreign policy: he marked Vietnam, instead of Malaysia and Indonesia, as the line of forward defence of Australia. His most consequential decision as Minister for External Affairs was to back the Americans in identifying the seventeenth parallel that divided Vietnam as the frontline in the war against communist aggression. The actual danger to Australia lurked not in Indonesia — as the Department of Defence believed — but thousands of kilometres away, at the point where the Chinese- and Soviet-sponsored Democratic Republic of Vietnam ('North Vietnam') met the American-sponsored Republic of Vietnam ('South Vietnam').

# Chapter 5
# The two Vietnams

Christ has gone South ... The Virgin Mary has departed from
the North.
*American propaganda leaflets dropped over Hanoi, 1954.*

The two Vietnams were at once very different and strikingly similar. After
the last Frenchmen packed up and left, Hanoi repossessed a region of
157,880 square kilometres that faced seemingly insuperable economic
difficulties: plundered by French, Japanese and Chinese; ravaged by famine
under the Japanese; bombed by the US Air Force in 1944–45; and 'literally
ploughed under by French tanks and Viet Minh saboteurs from 1946 until
the ceasefire'.[1] Decades of war had taught the North Vietnamese how to
blow up a railway line but little knowledge of building a water purification
plant or running the trains on time. Corruption was near endemic: the
victorious communists were no less vulnerable to temptation than the
capitalist southerners. The Red River Delta was overcrowded, desperately
poor and starving. The government could not feed its people, and in 1955
only an emergency Russian gift of 150,000 tons of rice averted famine.

One event alleviated the pressure on the North's food supply: the
exodus to South Vietnam of 860,000 people, including at least 600,000
Vietnamese Catholics (another estimate is 794,000 Catholics).[2] The
remaining 200,000 refugees who headed south were nationalists or
'collaborators'; that is, soldiers who had fought with the French, and their
dependants. The Geneva Agreements permitted the civilian populations of

both North and South to decide where they wished to live. About 80,000 communist guerrillas returned north, but several thousands of these cadres — the 'stay-behinds' — were ordered to remain in the South — 'sleeping' military cells, whose presence defied the letter and spirit of Geneva.

During this great migration, American aircraft assisted the Saigon regime in compelling people to head south, by dropping propaganda leaflets over Hanoi announcing, 'Christ has gone South' and 'The Virgin Mary has departed from the North'. Most Catholics needed no such blandishments. Their memory of persecution was a stronger spur, and 65 per cent of the total Catholic population of North Vietnam, including whole bishoprics (e.g. Bui-Chu and Phat-Diem), moved south. No doubt the first President of the Republic of Vietnam, Ngo Dinh Diem — a Catholic of medieval asceticism, installed with the full backing of Washington — reassured the faithful. If Diem's punitive regime later resembled the worst excesses of the Spanish Inquisition, most exiled Catholics did not quibble: many received good jobs, land and generally favourable treatment, factors that incensed the majority Buddhist community.

Free of these troublesome Christians, the Viet Minh leadership set itself the task of transforming the Democratic Republic of Vietnam into a grim Marxist dictatorship. The process might have been 'almost comical', in Bernard Fall's words, had it not been so terrible — chiefly for the 'third way', the fragile voice of Vietnamese democratic nationalism, which was snuffed out for good. Its origins predated Geneva, of course. From 1952 Hanoi's communist apparatchiks sabotaged and terrorised attempts at local elections. In 1954 the Population Classification Decree defined the 'class' of an individual in five stages, from 'landlord' down to 'agricultural worker', by tallying each individual's 'value', or return on investment, in quarts of rice. Every commodity or beast of burden — a piglet, for example — equalled a certain number of quarts (the peasants better understood a quart of rice than a piastre: the barter economy prevailed at village level). But the Viet Minh officials applied this method to the 'middle classes' — artisans, shopkeepers, professionals, lawyers and small landowners. In so doing, they shared with petty bureaucrats of all totalitarian regimes, including the junior Bolsheviks and the Nazi prison guards, a savage attention to detail. The *can-bo* — the lowest rung of Viet Minh cadre — ever anxious to deliver their 'quota' of class enemies, applied the decree 'with the utmost ferocity'.[3] They denounced 'rich landlords' and 'capitalists' before People's Agricultural Reform Tribunals, which imposed death sentences as though they were punishing parking offenders. Poor, envious peasants decided it was in their interest to denounce as landlords their 'wealthy' neighbours; often half a hectare distinguished landowners from the landless peasantry. Many of the victims were valiant fighters against the French, even Party members; professionals and businessmen were less squeamishly dispatched. The madness escalated until brothers denounced brothers and children denounced their parents. Reliable estimates place the total number executed in 1955–56 at 50,000; at least twice as many were sent to forced labour camps.

The classification decree ran in tandem with 'land reform' that handed property stolen by 'landlords' back to the peasants. This confiscation and redistribution of tiny plots at least retained an element of private property (unlike the mass collectivisation of the Soviet and Chinese communist regimes). But it was shockingly mismanaged, and ended up making rich farmers even richer and the poor and landless peasants left holding a worthless half hectare, one tool per family, and one buffalo for every thirteen families. The reforms were no accident or mistake: they were a planned assault on anyone deemed 'bourgeois', according to Marxist-Leninist dogma. As in Russia and China, North Vietnam's crazed class struggle used Stalin's vicious methods to apply Lenin's violent program in order to realise Marx's daft ideas. The land reforms 'formed an integral part of the demented Marxist-Leninist program for atomizing existing societies in order to create a new socialist man'.[4] To Huu, Hanoi's annointed 'poet laureate', applauded the bloodshed:

> Kill, kill more …
> For the farm, good rice, quick collection of taxes …
> Worship Chairman Mao, Worship Stalin …[5]

Like Mao and Lenin, Ho Chi Minh knew to apply the brakes when ideological excess endangered his regime. He intervened to stop the insanity in a letter addressed 'To the Compatriots in the Country': 'Errors have been committed in the implementation of unity in the countryside,' Uncle Ho conceded. In 'determining a plan for their correction', he proposed that 'those who have been wrongly classified as landlords and rich peasants will be correctly reclassified'. The victims were to be 're-established in their rights … and their honorable character will be recognized'.[6]

As communist displays of contrition went, this was unprecedented. Ho sacked those responsible — Truong Chinh, the Secretary General of the

Communist Party, was the most powerful scalp — and introduced a Campaign of the Rectification of Errors, an 'orgy of self-criticism', observed H. C. Taussig, a British scholar and observer.[7] On 31 October 1956 Giap apologised on the Party's behalf, thus: 'We attacked the landowning families indiscriminately ... We showed no indulgence towards landlords who participated in the Resistance ... We made too many deviations and executed too many honest people ... we have attacked tribal chiefs too strongly injuring local customs ...' Giap concluded: '... torture came to be regarded as a normal practice during Party reorganization.'[8] This was the regime in which the 'international community' entrusted the probable control of Vietnam via 'free elections' that very year.

Giap's prostration notwithstanding, the damage had been done: 'One cannot wake the dead,' noted Ho Chi Minh. The land reforms resulted in a serious deterioration in output per hectare, at a time of explosive population growth (3.5 per cent per annum in the late 1950s — the fruits of a policy to build the nation — and army — through breeding). The North's irrigated fields covered just 252,000 hectares, compared with 326,000 hectares in 1939, and North Vietnam had somehow to feed 600,000 new mouths a year. It could not rely on rice shipments from the South — the two Vietnams refused to trade with each other; indeed, scarcely a postcard crossed the DMZ. And between 1955 and 1961 North Vietnam failed both to increase rice yields per hectare and to expand the land under plough. Livestock production collapsed: in 1964 it reverted to the level of 1939, forcing human beings to do the work of buffalo. In the end, the communist government could not feed its own people, and surrendered to partial market forces, with incentives to encourage farmers to meet their quotas. When these piecemeal reforms failed, Hanoi pleaded for Soviet and Chinese help.

The Soviets and the Chinese came to the aid of Ho's Party, the lifeline that saved the fledgling Vietnamese Communist Party, and shored up its leader's popularity after the disastrous land reforms. In 1955 Chinese rice averted famine; 2,000 Chinese railroad workers helped rebuild the rail network; and between 1955 and 1961 the Communist Bloc gave civil loans and grants of US$1 billion to the Hanoi regime (roughly equivalent to US aid to the South at that time). North Vietnamese light, medium and heavy industry flourished on the back of this capital injection: Soviet money built eight thermal power stations, thirty-five heavy industrial plants and a huge fish cannery; and the Chinese invested in ten medium industry plants between 1957 and 1960.

Their investment was purely political: the Democratic Republic of Vietnam, as the only socialist country in South-East Asia, offered 'a communist ... jump-off point into not only South Viet-Nam, but Cambodia, Laos, and Thailand'.[9] It was the 'showcase' for communism in the region. These factors certainly lent validity to the Domino Theory and Western fears intensified in the late 1950s, when Chinese and Soviet arms started flowing into North Vietnam. This, then, was the economic and cultural state of the North by 1960: an isolated, paranoid, closed communist society dependent on Chinese and Soviet aid. Between 1954 and 1956 it presented an unthreatening face to the world. Yet two months after the deadline for the 1956 elections had passed, Hanoi activated its 'stay-behind' guerrillas in the South, who started sabotaging the local economy and terrorising villages deemed loyal to Saigon.

South Vietnam (the Republic of Vietnam) had a greater claim on statehood than the North. The Saigon regime was a full member of every UN agency; Hanoi refused even to provide agricultural statistics to the UN Economic Commission. Yet many Western observers, especially those of a left-wing persuasion, believed — or hoped — that South Vietnam would simply wither away. The Diem regime proved them wrong. It survived, and sceptics grudgingly came to accept the South's right to exist: '... slowly the idea of viability began to grow. Like water turning into ice, the illusion crystallised and became a reality ... [South Vietnam] became real in powerful men's minds. Thus, what had never truly existed and was so terribly frail became firm, hard. A real country with a real constitution.'[10] Despite these promising signs, Saigon's disastrous administration sowed the seeds of its own collapse.

Washington and Canberra strongly approved of the austere, devoutly Catholic figure of Ngo Dinh Diem, who was elected first President of the Republic of Vietnam following a rigged referendum in 1955 that dethroned Bao Dai, the increasingly errant Head of State. Diem claimed to have 'won' 98 per cent of the vote. Yet Diem's millions of southern 'supporters' barely knew this stern, unsmiling little man, who wrote of himself as deserving 'sacred respect' as the 'mediator between the People and Heaven'.[11] His motorcade drove through Saigon with scarcely a wave or a smile for the curious crowds lining the streets.

Diem, whom one US newspaper called 'the mandarin in a sharkskin suit', won his nationalist spurs as a staunch opponent of the French; to his credit he refused to collaborate. A strong, authoritarian leader, he seemed 'possessed to an exceptional degree by that common Vietnamese quality of "absolutism".'[12] Diem was proud, self-righteous, a complete stranger to compromise, and without a scintilla of affection or compassion for the ordinary people. His greatest failing was an infuriating obstinacy and refusal to change course, most disastrously when his policies wrought havoc and devastation on the countryside. He openly contemplated the annihilation of the Communist Bloc, and supported the use of nuclear weapons against North Vietnam and, if necessary, China.

'Diem is a monk living behind stone walls. He knows nothing,' observed the Australian journalist Denis Warner.[13] This had an element of literal truth: Diem had spent two years in a seminary in New York state, where he met Cardinal Spellman and then Senator John Kennedy. His austere strain of Catholicism impressed prominent Australian Catholics, such as the ailing Archbishop Daniel Mannix and the DLP's spiritual leader, Bob Santamaria.

The true colours of President Diem's weird, nepotistic regime emerged slowly, under the cover of elections that portrayed him as popular. His four southern elections were obviously rigged and 'poorly disguised exercises in totalitarian techniques'.[14] In every vote, he prearranged a 90 to 98 per cent outcome in his favour, rejecting the 60 per cent figure that US officials recommended as less incredible. In his mind he saw two kinds of people: 'wholehearted supporters and heretics to be suppressed'.[15] He expected to be obeyed not because he was popular, but because he believed himself to be morally superior, as historian Neil Jamieson observed.

Diem's 1956 Constitution did not overly alarm the American and Australian governments. One reason is that Diem's very survival — 'a political miracle of the first magnitude', stated Australian Asia specialist William Henderson — had impressed them (Henderson was among the few to see that without reform, Diem's regime threatened 'unforeseen disasters'[16]). 'Some sacrifices in individual liberty' were expected of Asian countries, remarked Richard Casey.[17] Yet Diem's constitution was nothing more than a dictator's prescription for a police state: the President had the power to 'decree a temporary suspension of the rights of freedom of circulation and residence, of speech and the press, of assembly and association ...' (Article 98). He used this *carte blanche* to great effect. In his first three years, he crushed the gangster sects — the Binh Xuyen, Hoa Hao and Cao Dai — and their private armies, and gained total control over the defence forces by playing the generals off against each other. Diem was nothing if not a master manipulator of rivals.

Diem's social and rural policies rapidly alienated the peasants, who came to loathe him. His land reforms were singularly disastrous and no less extreme than those of Hanoi, except in the reverse direction: the return of land to 'landlords' who claimed to have lost their farms during the French wars. Most had not been theirs to begin with; for example, newly arrived Catholics were given large parcels of land. Within three years, a small group of favoured farmers controlled or owned most of the land, and crushed the peasants under extortionate rents.

With absolute control, Diem, together with his noisome brother Ngo Dinh Nhu and Nhu's termagant wife, Madame Nhu, set about creating a nation in his own image: ascetic, tyrannical and medieval. His clan attempted to impose a strict Catholic moral code on free-wheeling Saigon; they closed the dance halls and 'vice clubs', and suppressed Buddhism and Taoism (whose followers vastly outnumbered the Catholics). Diem signed Madame Nhu's personal gift to the South Vietnamese people, the Family Code. It contained all one wishes to know about this beautiful, compassionless woman, aka the Dragon Lady (Madame Nhu bore a terrifying similarity to Lady Macbeth). Her decree outlawed dancing, divorce, beauty contests, fortune-telling, cockfighting, prostitution, contraception, gambling and adultery, and hundreds of other things she regarded as morally repugnant. Dancing was forbidden even in the privacy of one's home; she later threw in the singing of sentimental songs, as these were likely to undermine the war effort. The laws were strictly enforced. She imposed her regime through the state secret police, many of whom worked for her husband's Personalist Labour Party, Nhu's pet political project, created by his obsession with the obscurantist and infantile cult of 'personalism', which nobody in Vietnam understood.

In sum, the methods, if not the ideologies, of North and South Vietnam were alarmingly similar: both regimes used terror, lies, personality cults, propaganda and torture to pursue ends to which they gave different labels, but which ultimately meant the same thing: a closed, one-party dictatorship. By 1960 both men had achieved this aim. Yet while Uncle Ho remained popular in the North, Diem 'fathered' a series of catastrophic policies that made him the most hated man in South Vietnam.

The Australian and American Governments did not blink at the dark side of the mandarin in their midst. To Eisenhower, Diem was a 'miracle man'; LBJ later called him the 'Churchill of the East'. No doubt Diem had surprised everyone; in appearance, at least, his republic seemed to be working: he had ruthlessly imposed his authority on the country and spoke the rhetoric of freedom.

No country rewarded the dictator as lavishly as Australia. During his visit on 2–9 September 1957, Diem received 'more ceremony and pageantry' than the Queen's visit of 1954. 'Everywhere he was feted as a man of courage, faith and vision.'[18] A guard of honour and a 21-gun salute awaited him in Sydney, Melbourne and Canberra, where huge crowds cheered his arrival. Diem told cadets on special parade at the Royal Military College, Duntroon, that they were 'comrades of the Free World'.

The Australian press wrote glowing accounts of the South Vietnamese leader. The *Sydney Morning Herald* dubbed him 'One of the most remarkable men in the new Asia ... authoritarian in approach but liberal in principle'. The *Herald* pictured Diem eating cheese ('there's nothing like this in my country'), visiting a housing estate ('How many rooms do you have?') and, as 'the flower-loving president', driving through the Botanic Gardens. To *The Age*, Diem was not a 'morally equivocal' figure like Chiang Kai-shek or South Korean President Syngman Rhee, but 'incorruptible and intensely patriotic'. Other papers reported Diem's 'popular support'. The effusions of the Catholic press outdid the rest. Their man in Asia bowled over the *Catholic Weekly*, for whom Diem was 'his nation's saviour from Red onslaught ... an ardent patriot of great courage and moral integrity and an able intellectual'.[19] The paper fondled the details of Diem's links to Australia with creepy sycophancy: when in Rome, the *Catholic Weekly* gleefully pointed out, a brother of Diem had been a classmate of the Bishop of Sydney. In fairness, Diem had succeeded in absorbing at least 600,000 Catholics, to worldwide admiration. He was also a staunch anti-communist and the bastion of Catholic Christianity in Asia, a fact hammered home by the Democratic Labor Party and Bob Santamaria.

The Menzies Government strongly backed Diem, not least because it wished to curry favour with the DLP, thus deepening the split in the Labor Opposition. Not for nothing did Menzies personally call for three cheers for Diem at a parliamentary luncheon; bestow on the South Vietnamese President an honorary Knight Grand Cross of the Order of St Michael and St George, one of the highest imperial honours available to a non-British subject; and firmly reiterate Australia's support for the Saigon regime.

The visit of the South Vietnamese President made a powerful statement about Australia's position in the world. Our unquestioning support for the dictator entwined Australia's interests with the fate of his government. 'Australia had now associated Diem's survival with its national interests, publicly and without restraint.'[20] A natural extension of that public friendship was a future military commitment to South Vietnam — which is exactly what Diem had in mind.

# Chapter 6
# Viet Cong

It is the duty of my generation to die for our country.
*A Viet Cong soldier, in a diary captured by the Australian forces.*

I will fight the Americans to the last Vietnamese.
*Mao Tse-tung.*

In July 1956 Geneva's deadline for elections in Vietnam — to which Saigon had never agreed — came and went. This was widely anticipated, yet Hanoi affected a bitter sense of betrayal, and the communist leaders' violent rhetoric soon curdled into aggressive action: where the ballot had failed, war would prevail. Anticipating this outcome, Ho, Giap and their northern comrades had already planned the invasion of the South, which aimed to impose unity on Vietnam under the Yellow Star. The beliefs and hopes of millions of southerners who, by moving or staying in the South, had chosen not to live under communism, were simply to be trampled on.

The invasion would be slow, agonisingly slow: 'little by little',[1] by a thousand cuts, Giap and Ho intended the destruction of the southern forces and their foreign allies. 'It is part of the doctrine of People's Revolutionary War that victory is inevitable, even if it takes half a century,' concluded the counter-insurgency expert, Sir Robert Thompson.[2] It would be a revolutionary guerrilla war fought in three stages: infiltration and control of the villages by loyal insurgents; gradual envelopment of the cities; and mass uprising and open invasion, crushing all resistance south of the seventeenth parallel. Giap described his tactics, used to devastating effect against the French, in chilling detail in his book *People's War, People's Army: The Viet Cong Insurrection Manual for Underdeveloped Countries*:

> The enemy mopped up; we fought against mopping up. They organized ... local Vietnamese troops and installed puppet authorities; we firmly upheld local people's power, overthrew men of straw, eliminated traitors and carried out active propaganda to bring about [their] disintegration. We gradually formed a network of guerrilla bases ... 'red zones', which ceaselessly spread and multiplied, began to appear right in the heart of the occupied areas. The soil of the fatherland was being freed inch by inch in the enemy's rear lines. There was no clearly defined front in this war. It was there where the enemy was. The front was nowhere, it was everywhere ...[3]

Giap thus championed a highly developed form of 'indirect' warfare, the rules of which, according to the military scholar Basil Liddell Hart, were: never attack on open ground; strike at the enemy's rear; never reinforce failure; and exploit any success to the maximum. 'The ideal,' wrote General Peter Gration, 'is to cause the opponent's sword to fall from a paralysed arm, rather than to engage him directly on equal terms.'[4]

An army of astonishing versatility and ubiquity would be created to crush the Republic of Vietnam. It would comprise southern peasants, village guerrillas, provincial forces, northern insurgents and, in time, the People's Army itself, all carefully synthesised into a mutually supporting mass that permeated every level of society. All civilians would be combatants in the coming 'people's revolution'; Hanoi saw no distinction between civilians and soldiers. 'Neutrality' did not exist; villagers who refused to join the uprising would be condemned as collaborators, and mutilated or assassinated.

And so, after the widely expected failure of the elections, Hanoi moved swiftly to activate its southern comrades. In August–September 1956 Giap authorised his top-ranking colleague Le Duan to switch on the communist 'stay-behind' guerrillas in the South. In a flagrant breach of the Geneva Agreement, the guerrillas began sabotaging the southern economy and attacking government employees.[5] Hanoi thus controlled the uprising from the start. In December that year Le Duan told the eleventh Plenary Session of the Lao Dong (the Communist Party of North Vietnam) that armed revolution was the only way to 'liberate' the South.[6] From that date Hanoi planned the invasion and conquest — which they called the 'reunification' or 'liberation' — of the Republic of Vietnam.

President Diem reacted in character. His regime began persecuting thousands of suspected communists, many of them simply nationalists or democrats who disagreed with his policies. His disastrous methods converted whole provinces to Ho Chi Minh. His land reforms were shockingly mismanaged. Diem 'destroyed at a blow the dignity and livelihood of several hundred thousand peasants by cancelling the land distribution arrangements'.[7] His thugs razed poorer quarters of the southern cities to make way for commercial sites and lavish apartment blocks for the wealthy. And, as we shall see later, he brutally alienated the Montagnards, the tribal people of the Central Highlands.

The 'Denounce Communist' (To Cong) roadshow, launched in late 1956, was one of Diem's most hated measures. The typical To Cong campaign rolled into the village about once a month, and corralled the peasants into the dusty square or the *dinh*, the communal hall. Here Diemist henchmen would denounce and arrest communist suspects. Husbands were dragged away from their tearful wives and children. Those who resisted were beaten on the spot and sometimes shot. After repeated raids, many villagers grew too exhausted to care, and read their newspapers or chatted while the megaphones droned on, listing their alleged crimes.

In 1959–60 To Cong used the 'stronger methods' of murder and torture in response to more aggressive communist activity in South Vietnam. Captain Richard Ziegler, an American officer, listed them in his diary:[8] '1. Wrap in barbed wire. 2. Strip skin off back. 3. Rack by use of vehicle or water buffalo. 4. Head in mud — 1? minute. 5. Shoot thru ear. 6. Hook up to EE8 [a US-supplied field telephone through which electric shocks were applied to the testicles, vagina and breasts by cranking the handle]. 7. Sit on entrenching tool [the handle was forced into the victim's anus].' If these failed, water was forced down the captive's throat until his or her stomach swelled painfully, when it was beaten, and the 'indiv. vomits it out'.[9]

Between 1957 and 1960 Diem's regime assassinated 5,000 people and wounded or imprisoned tens of thousands. Two-thirds of the Communist Party in the South were 'lost through arrest or death up till the end of 1958 … the whiff of extermination was in the air'.[10]

The Diemist terror did little to pacify the South; indeed, it had the opposite effect. Leaders in Hanoi and Beijing decided at a meeting in May

1960 to bring forward the launch of the official armed uprising in the South (which had been unofficially active since 1956[11]): 75,000 communist-trained cadres were ordered to turn the 'political struggle' into a fully fledged war. Mao Tse-tung, via his mouthpieces Chou En-lai and Deng Xiaoping, stamped China's imprimatur on the decision, and a relieved Ho Chi Minh anticipated a huge inflow of Chinese weapons and support troops.

On 19 December 1960 sixty young revolutionaries met in the mangrove swamps of Tay Ninh province, in the Republic of Vietnam, to proclaim the birth of the National Front for the Liberation of South Vietnam (NLF), 'a broad-based, united front led by the Communists against the Diem regime'.[12] The NLF's most hardened volunteers formed an army of extraordinary resilience, cruelty and self-discipline, popularly known by its Western derogations, the 'Viet Cong' ('Vietnamese communists'), 'gooks', 'slopes' or simply 'Charlie'.

In this light, the National Liberation Front was not a spontaneous southern uprising against Diem, as so many in the Western anti-war movement later claimed. From the start, Hanoi led and controlled the NLF, which served as a cover for North Vietnam's invasion plan. 'All key [Liberation Front] positions were in the hands of [Communist] Party members.'[13] At the same time, Hanoi refused to admit 'that she is in any way involved within South Vietnam'.[14] This fooled only Western protesters and idealists; even Wilfred Burchett, the Australian reporter and communist sympathiser, conceded that the North 'arguably' provided the inspiration and leadership to the southern communists.

Disgruntled southerners were active in their own right, of course. In 1958 a loose resistance movement absorbed angry and estranged people of all political complexions. There were nationalists and communists, former Viet Minh freedom fighters, peasant representatives and members of the middle classes. The NLF subsumed most of them; indeed, some NLF leaders, such as the future justice minister Truong Nhu Tang, were nationalists at heart and tokens to the NLF's democratic veneer. The tragedy is that so many southerners naively supposed the National Liberation Front to be genuinely democratic and freedom-loving; they preferred not to believe that avowed northern Marxists controlled it. Nhu Tang later expressed shock when he learned the truth: that his NLF comrades were in fact answerable to Hanoi, which used it as a Trojan horse in which to invade and occupy the Republic of Vietnam.

Yet Hanoi's intentions were clear, for example, in the creation in South

Vietnam in 1962 of the People's Revolutionary Party, whose leaders reported directly to Hanoi through COSVN, the Central Office of (communist) South Vietnam, which directed the Viet Cong's 'parallel government' in the South, a network of political officers, tax collectors, agitators and social services. In reality, the People's Revolutionary Party was simply the southern mouthpiece of the North's Lao Dong (workers') Party. Its creation was 'only a matter of strategy', noted a memo from a Lao Dong provincial committee on 7 December 1962. Hanoi explained that strategy: '... to deceive the enemy ... the founding of the People's Revolutionary Party has the purpose of isolating ... the Ngo Dinh regime, and to counter their accusations of an invasion of the South by the North. *It is a means of supporting our sabotage of the Geneva Agreement, of advancing the plan of invasion of the South ...*'[15]

Who were the Viet Cong? wondered Western intelligence. Who led it? How did it fight? How many North Vietnamese insurgents filled its ranks? Which villages did it control? How were its fighters supplied, fed and trained? And, most critically, where did it begin and end? Were the postboys VC? The prostitutes? The lines of rice harvesters? The cyclo-drivers? The shoeshine boys? Anyone in 'black pyjamas'? (Many Australian soldiers, told that the Viet Cong wore black cotton pyjamas, found on arrival that most Vietnamese peasants wore black pyjamas.)

The structure and identity of the National Liberation Front were as elusive as the true meaning behind the organisation's title: it was a synthesis of soldiers, local guerrillas, farmers, villagers and peasants, whose connections cascaded through society, incorporating well-trained and -armed Main Force regiments — that is, units organised along proper military lines — provincial mobile battalions raised in their home provinces, local rag-tag village guerrillas (farmers by day, fighters by night) and civilian supporters.

Many Viet Cong leaders were highly politicised and attuned to the shifts in power in Hanoi and even of their ultimate Marxist benefactors. A senior Viet Cong commander, for example, wrote in his diary on 11 May 1965: 'New Situation — New Movement ... Previously the Soviet Union led the liberation movement against Imperialism. But the Soviet Union is still administering Revisionism. Today, Red China has replaced the Soviet Union in the mission of leading the liberation movement ...'[16] And they were prepared to tolerate immense sacrifice, pain and loss of life: 'It is the duty of my generation to die for our country,' a Viet Cong soldier wrote in his diary.[17]

At the other end of the scale, the ordinary village guerrillas tended to be crudely indoctrinated peasants. They 'couldn't have told dialectical materialism from a rice bowl', quipped Truong Nhu Tang.[18] They simply worshipped Ho Chi Minh; their political 'lessons' amounted to mouthing nationalist slogans: 'Nothing is More Precious than Independence and Liberty!' and 'Unity, Unity, Great Unity! Victory, Victory, Great Victory!'.[19] 'Never let the country fall under foreign domination,' wrote Huynh Chien Dau ('Huynh the Fighter'), a Viet Cong guerrilla from Phuoc Tuy province. 'Venerable Uncle [Ho] taught us: "Whenever you see any single American invader on our land, we have the noble duty to sweep him away".'[20] Their leaders refrained from administering heavy doses of Marxist ideology, which their northern comrades guzzled straight; to do so would have been considered 'the worst torture … the regime could possibly devise for them'.[21]

The Viet Cong guerrillas lived in tunnels, mountain caves or jungle hides; blended their gardens with the forests; and cooked in 'Dien Bien Phu' kitchens, underground ovens that dispersed the smoke via lateral tunnels and slits in the earth. They seeded the approaches to their camps with booby traps — mines, grenades and bamboo *punji* spikes set in camouflaged pits, their ends sharpened by elderly women and often smeared with snake venom or human excrement to speed infection. They later made use of every scrap of material stolen or salvaged from the Americans. Their Ho Chi Minh sandals, for example, ideal for the heat and jungle, were made of tyre rubber. In the early 1960s, America's Goodyear replaced France's Michelin as chief supplier of tyres. One stolen truck tyre yielded ten pairs of sandals. Their packs were often American white flour bags, whose contents had been donated to South Vietnam, and stamped, 'THIS IS A GIFT OF THE PEOPLE OF THE USA. NOT TO BE SOLD OR EXCHANGED.' Attached to their US webbing belts were, typically, a tiny spirit lamp, made of US cartridges; a hammock of US parachute nylon; a US water bottle; and a cluster of grenades made from unexploded US shells.

Peasants, fishermen, miners, cyclo-drivers, clerks, launderers and interpreters all played a part, as combatants, spies and suppliers. Women were used in combat, espionage and propaganda. Teenage girls formed their own units, known as chignon battalions (after the fashionable hairstyle). Their ruthlessness stunned foreign soldiers unaccustomed to fighting an all-female infantry. 'Combat mothers' fought by day and performed their traditional roles of mother, nurse and teacher by night. 'In the assault you command a hundred squads/Night returns, you sit mending fighters' clothes' ran a well-known poem.[22] Women manned jungle headquarters, radios, kitchens and supply centres, and entertained in jungle theatres. Crucially, with 'shovels, hoes and guns',[23] they helped to keep open the Ho Chi Minh Trail, a vast network of jungle tracks carved into the Laotian and Cambodian highlands, which broke eastwards into Vietnam via feeder trails that dissolved into tiny capillaries, the final link with the Viet Cong's secret caches and hides in the South.[24] One poet captured the sight:

> Pink brassieres hanging on trees
> Frail heels trod everywhere in the Truong Son Forest,
> Their songs resonate across the mountains,
> Determined to get the trucks to the blood-filled south.[25]

An Australian doctor examined one 30-year-old female commander, a thin, wiry woman with eyes that stared at nothing. Although four months pregnant, she had personally commanded 147 men, won 11 medals and 43 other decorations, and boasted an incredible 'scalp' count. Her husband was dead, and all she desired was to return to her mother and village on the Cambodian border.[26]

They were a teenage army, too: the Viet Cong's recruiting officers — who often used threats to rope in 'volunteers' — favoured adolescent boys and girls, preferably aged 15–20. Those older than 25 held less appeal unless they had a special qualification.[27] Extreme youth had a better chance of surviving a 'long war'; the young were impressionable, easily indoctrinated and romantic.

Until 1958 their weapons tended to be home-made shotguns, clapped-out US carbines and Garands, machetes, home-made mines, even hoes and pitchforks. Then huge quantities of Chinese and Soviet arms began flowing south.[28] By 1965, when Australia's first battalion arrived, the Viet Cong's swollen arsenal included light, medium and heavy submachine guns, rocket launchers, recoilless rifles, mortars, anti-tank rifles and, of course, thousands of Kalashnikov AK47 assault rifles, generally regarded as superior to the American M16.[29] All were Soviet or Chinese communist-made and sent south via the Ho Chi Minh Trail or by sea, to Cambodian ports and coastal estuaries, often hidden beneath the false bottoms of sampans.

Their ranks grew rapidly, too, with the arrival of northern insurgents, who packed the Ho Chi Minh Trail in the early 1960s.[30] In January 1963 the Viet Cong was a small, poorly trained force of 23,000 regulars and regional guerrillas (arranged in twenty-five battalions of varying strengths). By December 1964 it had grown into an army of 56,000 well-trained, well-equipped combat troops and 40,000 support troops. By 1964 Diem's legacy and American bombing helped to transform the Viet Cong from the 2,000-man Viet Minh remnant of 1956 into 600 fully equipped battalions.[31]

The Viet Cong's most effective weapon was terror, with which it aimed to eliminate the actual and 'potential' opposition. Its campaign of terror began in 1956.[32] Where propaganda and threats failed, VC guerrillas beheaded, disembowelled and mutilated uncooperative villagers: 1,900 cases were reported in 1957 and 1958. On 17 December 1957 'spectacular assassinations' occurred in the provinces of An-Giang and Phong-Dinh (in the Mekong Delta). In the village of Thanh-My-Tay, armed men appeared in the dead of night, read a death sentence, and 'beheaded four young men whose heads they nailed to the nearest bridge'.[33] In 1960 communist guerrillas destroyed or damaged 284 bridges, burned sixty medical aid stations and deprived 25,000 children of schooling, according to Saigon Government reports.[34]

The Viet Cong claimed it attacked only 'wicked enemy ringleaders' and Diemest 'tyrants'; in fact, most of its victims were useful members of the civilian community — village elders, teachers, doctors and farmers — who refused to join its ranks. In 1964, of the 429 village officials assassinated and 1,482 officials kidnapped, almost all were native to the area and not brought in from outside, according to one study that year; that is, they were local people, not Saigon's thuggish placemen. Their neutrality, however, damned them as 'government' supporters. There were thousands of such cases, of which a mere sample follows:[35]

- On 23 August 1960 Viet Cong guerrillas burst into a classroom and forced the schoolteachers, Nguyen Khoa Ngon and Miss Nguyen Thi Thiet, to witness, as a warning, the execution of two men tied to the school verandah.
- On 22 March 1961 the Viet Cong blew up an unarmed truck carrying twenty girls without military escort on the Saigon–Vung Tau road; the girls were returning from the Trung Sisters Day celebration. Two were killed and ten wounded.

- On 15 May 1961 twelve nuns of La Providence Order were stopped and searched on their way to Saigon. One who protested was shot dead on the spot and their bus sprayed with bullets, seriously wounding another.
- On 20 February 1962 Viet Cong guerrillas threw four hand grenades into a crowded village theatre near Can Tho, killing or wounding 108, including twenty-four women and children.

By 1963 Viet Cong terror easily outpaced the South's capacity to respond. Its methods were horrific. In 1966, an Australian doctor, R. G. Wyllie, led a civilian medical team at the Song Nai Hospital. When the Viet Cong attacked a village, his team typically received twenty to thirty casualties at once, invariably teachers, government officers, the village policemen and the hamlet chief and his family. In one case, a 20-year-old teacher received 'multiple wounds extending from behind her ears, exposing the brain, to beyond the midline in the front, cutting full thickness through the facial bones', Dr Wyllie wrote in a letter to a Sydney newspaper. A Viet Cong guerrilla had slashed her head with a sugar-cane knife as she crouched in a corner holding her hands over her face; she suffered horrific brain damage and died of blood loss. A policeman from the same village lost his jaw, nose, cheekbones and eyes, torn off by machine-gun fire: 'He died from uncontrollable haemorrhage.' The pregnant wife of the hamlet chief arrived deep in shock, with her legs 'hanging by ribbons of flesh'. She had been forced to watch her attackers strangle her husband, after which she and her three-year-old child were machine-gunned; the child died in the medevac helicopter; the woman survived, only to abort her child during the operation: '… a woman without a husband, children, or legs — because she was the wife of a hamlet chief.'

'It is enough,' Dr Wyllie concluded, 'that they were neutral and wished to remain so. Neutrality is unacceptable to the Viet Cong. It must be destroyed.'[36]

The Viet Cong 'formalised' these crimes by condemning the victims to death in absentia, in jungle courts. Guilt was presumed; there were no juries or lawyers. Death warrants were posted to the victims, or nailed to their front doors. The warrant declared that the 'criminal' had been 'tried', 'found guilty' and must be 'punished'. It was 'forbidden to execute the accused savagely', warned one Viet Cong directive; shooting and beheading were deemed 'non-savage'.[37]

The Saigon forces visited similar crimes on communist suspects, as we have seen. Wilfred Burchett claimed that Diemist thugs gouged out the eyes and drank the blood of their communist victims. Yet he singularly failed to report Viet Cong atrocities; nowhere in his many books does he report a common Viet Cong punishment: the public disembowelment of civilians in front of their families. Nor does he report the murder, for example, of children. How did the slaughter of ten orphans in a village near Vung Tau — the girls slit from their vaginas to their throats, the boys disembowelled and castrated — serve the Viet Cong's revolutionary purposes? The French nuns caring for these waifs were raped and the village chief beheaded, observed an Australian witness, who happened to be delivering medical supplies to the village at the time.[38]

'Steadily, quietly and with a systematic ruthlessness,' concluded a US study of the communists' terror campaign, 'the Viet Cong in six years [1960–66] have wiped out virtually a whole class of Vietnamese villagers. Many villages today are virtually depopulated of their natural leaders.'[39] Between 1957 and 1965 the Viet Cong assassinated or kidnapped 27,600 civilians: village leaders, teachers, business owners, government workers.[40] Most kidnappings ended in death.

In despair, Diem resorted to the classic counter-revolutionary tactic: the separation of the villagers from the communist insurgents. In 1961 he accepted the recommendation by Sir Robert Thompson, head of the newly arrived British Advisory Mission, to 'resettle' the villagers in specially fortified communities, known as Strategic Hamlets. French attempts (the 'agroville') to do so had 'failed dismally', noted the Pentagon Papers, 'because they ran into … active resistance on the part of the peasants at whose control and safety, then loyalty, they were aimed'.[41] Yet Thompson's idea drew on the success of a similar program in Malaya (where very different conditions applied), and he made explicit the importance of giving the peasants a secure alternative to communism. 'The objective of the plan was to win loyalties rather than kill insurgents,' Thompson warned; the methods, he added, must be 'clinical rather than surgical'.[42]

Such nice distinctions were lost on Diem, who, on 3 February 1962, launched the Strategic Hamlets Program in South Vietnam with the eviscerating flourish of a medieval surgeon. By August, under the charge of Diem's brother, Ngo Dinh Nhu, 2,500 fortified hamlets had been built, and work had started on a further 2,500. The Australian Government strongly backed the plan: Strategic Hamlets seemed to be the only way of saving the countryside from the Viet Cong, concluded Barwick, during his visit to Vietnam in May 1962, when he observed the 'enthusiasm and dedication' of the peasants in a showcase hamlet.[43] America largely financed this new dawn and the Australian Government allocated £250,000 of its SEATO defence aid to the cost of barbed wire, corrugated iron and other materials.[44]

The reality was rather different: the peasants were wrenched from their ancestral homes and driven cattle-like into sterile new compounds, surrounded by bamboo fences, serried spikes and Australian barbed wire. Their new homes were hovels set in vacant plots, bulldozed clear of trees and shelter. 'This is no life,' said one skinny old village elder. 'We have to be inside the gates half an hour before sunset or we'll be beaten up.'[45] They had to pay new taxes for this pleasure, and received ID cards containing their photos and thumbprints. 'The people,' remarked one US general, 'think that this is the finest thing since canned beer because it indicates to them that the government loves them, has an interest in them … They don't regard this as harassment … which, of course, it is …'[46]

Of the first 205 families to be 'resettled', only seventy volunteered; the remaining 135 were 'herded forcibly from their homes'. Their old dwellings, their possessions, their ancestral heirlooms, were torched behind them. Only 120 men of conscription age were found among these first 205 families, indicating that most had already gone over to the Viet Cong. The rest would soon follow. Undeterred, Diem 'resettled' millions of peasants into new hamlets; most were forcibly moved. By September 1962, 2.5 million people had been uprooted in the southern provinces and 1.7 million in the central provinces; a total of 4.2 million, or a third of the rural population.[47]

The mass resettlement proceeded remarkably peacefully; the Viet Cong attacked very few new hamlets. The American advisers interpreted this as success: a form of local democracy had arrived at village level 'for the first time', reported one optimistic observer. The Viet Cong had overrun 'two-tenths of one per cent' of the Strategic Hamlets, the US Joint Chiefs of Staff delightedly concluded. 'The Vietnamese people must surely be finding in them a measure of the tranquility they seek.'[48]

On the contrary, the Viet Cong infiltrated the new hamlets within weeks of their completion, as Thompson had warned. It was hardly about to destroy a string of custom-built jungle citadels, financed by its enemy, which contained 'peasants motivated as never before to support the Viet Cong'.[49] The Viet Cong easily penetrated the Strategic Hamlets; in one case, the guerrillas replaced boys on buffaloes with their own young troops, who escaped detection when they re-entered the gates. Once inside, they rounded up the hamlet leaders and shot them. Stripped of their ancestral homes, a vengeful peasantry had every reason to welcome the Viet Cong into their new precincts — especially in those where the hamlet chiefs were Diemist thugs. In many areas, of course, the Viet Cong *was* the people. Yet America's top commanders — and Australia's Brigadier Ted Serong — continued to believe the Strategic Hamlet Program a great success.

A darker truth lay behind the fiasco of the Strategic Hamlets: Nhu had put in daily control of the program one Colonel Pham Ngoc Thao, known to his mates as 'Albert', who happened to be a Viet Cong spy. Albert thus performed his job with calculated cruelty, the harsher the better. The peasants supposed their awful treatment the work of Diem, and not the Viet Cong. The odious Nhu's nodding approval played directly into Viet Cong hands.[50]

The Strategic Hamlet Program collapsed within two years. The people packed up and went home. At one hamlet in Long An province, the Viet Cong broke in and told the peasants to tear it down and go back to their native towns. They did so with relish. The hamlet looked as though a hurricane had struck it: '… the watchtowers were demolished, and only a few of its original thousand residents remained, sheltered in lean-tos.' This pattern occurred all over the South. An attempt to force the people back (OPERATION SEA SWALLOW) failed; they simply destroyed the hamlets again. The Viet Cong was the direct beneficiary: by 1964 the NLF cadres had destroyed or controlled 3,659 Strategic Hamlets (renamed 'New Life Hamlets'), according to an Australian intelligence officer attached to the CIA.[51] In sum, the Strategic Hamlets were 'the greatest gift the US gave the Viet Cong'.[52]


Diem deluded himself that he was securing the South. In March 1964 his forces reported a total of 23,500 'communist kills', mostly democrats and nationalists who opposed his tyranny.[53] His assassination squads thus silenced any hope of democracy at that time and fed the communist insurgency, whose cadres were 'playing havoc with the local administration'.[54] Diem's district chiefs simply lied about the state of security:

'How many villages are there in your district?' General Pham Van Dong asked one district official.

'Twenty-four,' he replied.

'And how many do you control?' asked Dong.

'Eight,' answered the official.

'And how many,' said Dong, smiling, 'do you tell Saigon you control?'

'Twenty-four,' said the official, sheepishly.[55]

By 1965 the National Liberation Front would virtually overrun the countryside; already, in 1963, they were beginning to encircle the bigger towns. North Vietnamese insurgents were heading south at a record rate. Ho Chi Minh had almost realised Mao Tse-tung's vision, as stated by Mao's army chief Lin Biao in a letter to Hanoi, in September 1965. The 'countryside of the world', wrote Biao, must surround 'the cities of the world' and cut down the capitalists through 'armed struggle'. Hanoi must neither surrender nor force China to intervene. This grimly laid out the Viet Cong's true role in the war: as mere cannon fodder of Chinese and North Vietnamese ambitions; expendable shock troops, charged with driving the Americans out of Vietnam. 'America,' Biao said, 'must lose stinking.'[56] In delivering up millions of southern lives to this cause, Hanoi almost granted Mao's wish: 'I will fight the Americans to the last Vietnamese.'

# Chapter 7
# Enter the Americans

Welcome to the Gallant Marines.
*South Vietnamese poster, Da Nang, 1965.*

'It was a glittering time,' Halberstam wrote of the Kennedy administration. The 'best and the brightest' of their generation spoke of a better world, of hope for the poor, the racially abused, the disenfranchised. Jack Kennedy, Bobby Kennedy, Lyndon Johnson, Bob McNamara, Dean Rusk, Walt Rostow, the brothers McGeorge and William Bundy — all shared a belief, a crusading faith, in the power of politics to engineer a better society, indeed a Great Society (as LBJ's slogan dreamed): 'They literally swept into office, ready, moving, generating their style, their confidence — they were going to get America moving again … these were brilliant men, men of force, not cruel, not harsh, but men who acted rather than waited … We seemed about to enter an Olympian age in this country, brains and intellect harnessed to great force, the better to define a common good.'[1]

The poet Robert Frost captured this spirit: '… But I have promises to keep/And miles to go before I sleep/And miles to go before I sleep …' — a poem Kennedy repeated, one icy winter in 1960, on his election tour of New Hampshire.[2]

Throughout his presidency, Kennedy was a staunch believer in the Domino Theory. Soon after his inauguration, he declared: 'The message of Cuba, of Laos, of the rising din of Communist voices in Asia and Latin America — these messages are all the same. The complacent, the self-indulgent, the soft societies are about to be swept away with the debris of history.'[3]

The young President pursued a close interest in guerrilla warfare; he saw, as few in the Pentagon did, that the jungle combat skills of a counter-revolutionary war presented a new challenge to the US forces. Kennedy tried to impose his views on a resistant Pentagon. His efforts foundered on the rocks of bureaucracy and the American generals' 'big unit' fetish, which harked back to the huge, open battles of World War II and Korea. The final confrontation between the Communist Bloc and the Free World would be a war of sweeping, pitched battles, and clear frontlines, many commanders believed — or hoped; and heck, if the enemy chose to hide in jungles and tunnels, American firepower would soon flush them out into open battle.[4]

In the late 1950s and early 1960s the American military presence in Vietnam amounted to several thousand military advisers, whose job was to train their South Vietnamese allies, the Army of the Republic of Vietnam (ARVN), in jungle combat and guerrilla warfare — skills in short supply even among the US forces. In practice, however, the Americans (and the Australian advisers, as we shall see) found themselves leading South Vietnamese units in combat. Gradually, the US advisers became part of the conflict — and the chief target of the communist insurgents.

In September 1962, General Paul Harkins, then commander of the 'Free World' forces in Vietnam (known as Military Assistance Command Vietnam, or MACV), claimed that he would defeat the Viet Cong in three years: all he needed were the Three Ms: men, money and materiel. Harkins and his successor, General William Westmoreland, who assumed command in June 1964, were strong proponents of open battle and wars of attrition — in the pursuit of which they urged Washington to send thousands of combat ground troops. To kill the enemy faster than his ability to replace the dead and wounded — such was the pitiless logic of attrition, the success of which was measured by the net body count. In time, the sole aim of US strategy in Vietnam would be simply to wear the enemy down by inflicting massive casualties, 'to persuade them that the game is not worth the candle and that he should negotiate ...'[5]

In pursuing this approach Harkins and Westmoreland were responding to a real emergency: by 1964 the South looked on the brink of defeat. And yet, 'the result of [Westmoreland's] approach,' noted the British Army's *Counter-insurgency Manual*, 'is an escalating and indiscriminate use of firepower. The wider consequences ... will often be an upward spiral of civilian alienation.'[6] In their pursuit of purely military goals, the American commanders failed adequately to understand the political dimension of the war, and the grave consequences of backing a hated despot — whose ruthless regime shortly came under worldwide scrutiny as a result of a wholly unexpected provocation.


On the morning of 11 June 1963 a Vietnamese Buddhist monk sat cross-legged on a busy street in central Saigon. Fellow monks doused his body with petrol and ignited it. The monk burned without a murmur, his palms clasped in prayer. As the flames enveloped his saffron robes and singed the stubble on his shaved head, shocked pedestrians 'prostrated themselves in reverence'.[7] Quang Duc's charred body toppled onto the asphalt as ambulances arrived. Next morning, pictures of the first Buddhist martydom, in protest against President Diem, appeared throughout the world. To international revulsion, Diem's sister-in-law, Madame Nhu, responded by welcoming further 'Buddhist barbecues'. She told a reporter: 'Let them burn, and we shall clap our hands.'[8] Dozens of ritual Buddhist suicides followed.

Superficially the Buddhist revolts, which spread to Hué and Da Nang, were a mere distraction for a regime grappling with a huge communist insurgency in the countryside. Yet the spectacular nature of the suicides showed the West a very different side to Diem's regime. The Americans and Australians had accepted Diem as the best of a bad bunch — 'Sink or swim with Ngo Dinh Diem!' US journalist Homer Bigart said of the relationship[9] — and felt acute discomfort at being seen to support a leader who persecuted a peaceful religious community.[10] Diem met the Buddhist protests with a customary leaden fist. On 21 August 1963 he declared a state of martial law. His brother Nhu's secret army arrested 1,400 monks and raided twelve Buddhist pagodas. Two days later, two disgruntled Vietnamese generals then embroiled in planning a coup against Diem contacted Lucien Conein, veteran of the French wars and the CIA's pointman in Saigon.

Vietnamese monks, hitherto seen as soft-spoken, saffron-robed, moving serenely among their people, suddenly excited a huge local following. The Buddhists' suicides became the rallying cry against the Diem family. The monks did not fit into any crudely drawn class or side. Theirs was a third way, in support of neither Diem nor the Viet Cong; they prayed for 'the creation of a government that combines the genuine will of the people for independence with their profound aspiration for peace'.[11] They embodied the spirit of the Vietnamese past, a calm, cross-legged judgement that descended on Saigon in a ball of flames.

The Buddhist suicides were protests against years of frustration with the Diem regime, culminating in the deaths, in Hué, on 8 May 1963, of nine Buddhists at a peaceful gathering to celebrate Buddha's birthday (the Viet Cong were later found to have provoked the incident). In fairness, Diem had not violently oppressed the Buddhist faith; Buddhists were free to practise their religion. That was small comfort, given Diem's preferential treatment of the new Catholic minority, which incensed the Buddhist community, to which faith 90 per cent of the South claimed to belong. The MACV was forced to confront a gnawing truth: the South could not be saved under Diem, as Henry Cabot Lodge, the new US ambassador to Saigon, stated in a cable to Dean Rusk on 29 August 1963.[12] With a nod here and a few cables there, Lodge set in motion the coup that would lead to the assassination of the Vietnamese President.

Henry Cabot Lodge arrived at Tan Son Nhut one drizzling night in August 1963. A tall, slightly stooped man with greying hair, this quintessential East Coast patrician strode through the flashing bulbs of the press with the poise of a Roman tribune. Lodge was the original Cold War Warrior: a lieutenant colonel in World War II; a leading Republican senator in the post-war era; and Nixon's running mate in the 1960 election against Kennedy. Lodge's latest posting would be his least dignified: covert executioner of the government of an American ally in war. 'We are launched on a course from which there is no respectable turning back,' he told Kennedy in a top-secret cable a week after he landed in Saigon.[13]

The coup, codenamed Bravo Two, began at 1.30 p.m. on 1 November 1963 at the prearranged CIA signal: 'Nine, nine, nine, nine, nine ...' Nhu — in a desperate effort to divide and conquer the military — staged a counter-coup at the last minute. It failed; Nhu's own troops turned on him. A mutinous battalion stormed the police headquarters and surrounded the Presidential Palace. The CIA backed the generals against Diem, yet Washington insisted the brothers receive safe conduct and the offer of US asylum. Too proud to seek American help openly, Diem telephoned Lodge at 4.30 p.m.:

'Some units have made a rebellion,' Diem said, 'and I want to know what is the attitude of the United States.'

'I do not feel well enough informed to be able to tell you ...' Lodge replied, who famously kept a small revolver in his desk drawer.

'But you must have some general ideas. After all, I am a chief of state. I have tried to do my duty ...' Diem said.

'You have certainly done your duty ... Now I am worried about your physical safety.'[14]

Later that night, trapped in the palace, Diem and Nhu appealed to General Dinh, whom they believed loyal. Dinh swiftly disabused them: 'I've saved you motherfuckers many times, but not now, you bastards. You shits are finished. It's all over.'[15] The troops captured the palace within an hour, and proceeded to loot Madame Nhu's bedroom (she was abroad) and Nhu's cellar. The brothers escaped to St Francis Xavier's, a French church in Cholon, and surrendered the next morning. Taken to a railway crossing in an armoured personnel carrier, they were shot repeatedly at point-blank range and then mutilated. South Vietnamese authorities later claimed they committed suicide.

On news of Diem's death, Kennedy left the Oval Office with a look of shock and dismay on his face. Diem's assassination stunned and embarrassed the Australian Government, which had not been informed of the coup or America's hand in it — the first of a series of intelligence-related humiliations. The Australian Government had made very public its support for a dictator and for America's role in Vietnam, yet neither Canberra nor Ambassadors Brian Hill in Saigon and Keith Waller in Washington were informed of the decision to topple Diem. In Saigon the people celebrated the hated regime's collapse. Thousands of political detainees, many disfigured by torture and years in 'tiger cages', were freed, the last Strategic Hamlets demolished and the nightclubs reopened. Saigon's overheated pressure cooker hissed with relief. Lodge cabled Kennedy: 'The prospects now are for a shorter war.' Three weeks later, President Kennedy was assassinated.

Lodge's optimism was gravely misplaced. President Lyndon Baines Johnson inherited a state under siege. The National Liberation Front ruthlessly exploited the South's political crisis. The month of Diem's death, November 1963, the Viet Cong stormed twenty-five garrisons near

My Tho and ambushed the main roads constantly, even by day. In 1964–65, the communists seemed to have infiltrated everything, and the insurgency neared its peak in early 1965, on the eve of the arrival of the first Australian battalion.

Vietnam was now at war in all but name, as the rising 'body count' showed. In 1963, 20,757 Viet Cong troops were killed in action, 3,501 wounded and 4,207 captured, according to CIA figures.[16] In the same year the ARVN (Army of the Republic of Vietnam; i.e. South Vietnamese Army) lost 5,825 troops killed, 11,950 wounded and 3,265 missing. In 1964 the ARVN suffered 32,300 casualties (killed, wounded, missing and sick), of whom 7,000 were listed as wounded.

The body count measured the rapid loss of the countryside to the communist insurgency after a run of astonishing Viet Cong combat successes against South Vietnamese troops, who were at this stage trained by US instructors. One of the earliest became the most famous: the battle of Ap Bac, on 2 January 1963, revealed the true grit of an enemy willing to stand and fight, even against US airpower. Neil Sheehan, a US reporter in Vietnam, summarised the result:

> The 350 [Viet Cong] guerrillas had stood their ground and
> humbled a modern army four times their number equipped with
> modern armour and artillery and supported by helicopters and
> fighter bombers … They suffered eighteen killed and thirty-one
> wounded, light casualties considering that the Americans and
> their Vietnamese protégés subjected them to thousands of rifle
> and machine-gun bullets, the blast and shrapnel of 600 artillery
> shells, and the napalm, bombs, and assorted other ordnance of
> thirteen warplanes and five Huey gunships. The Hueys alone
> expended 8,400 rounds of machine-gun fire and 100 rockets on
> the treelines at Bac.[17]

The 'kill ratio' was four to one in favour of the Viet Cong, which shot down five US choppers during the battle. The American commanders in Vietnam learned little from this fiasco. General Paul Harkins, then commander of MACV, absurdly claimed Ap Bac a 'victory' because 'we took the objective'.[18] The Viet Cong was not fighting for 'real estate'; it fought to inflict maximum military (and political) humiliation on the South Vietnamese and their American advisers.[19] Indeed, the battle gave a huge boost to the confidence of the communist forces: Ho Chi Minh and Giap personally instructed the National Liberation Front to unleash waves of similar offensives, under a campaign named the 'Ap Bac Emulation Drive'. Diem's death further inspired these dauntless assaults. In early 1964 Viet Cong Main Force troops attacked across the entire northern half of the Mekong Delta, while its 5th Division — soon to meet the Australian Army in Phuoc Tuy province — surged over the rubber plantations north of Saigon.

By 1964–65 Saigon's grip on the countryside resembled 'a beam that has been eaten from the inside by wood-boring beetles'.[20] All over the South, Viet Cong units besieged outposts, watchtowers and the cracked bamboo ramparts of Strategic Hamlets. Terrified Saigon troops, on pain of death, helped to arm the rampaging enemy. The surrender of 10,000 bullets was the cost of a month's survival. Between November 1963 and mid-1964 the National Liberation Front stole or extorted more than 200,000 US small arms: 'With the exception of heavy metals specialists, the US Government armed virtually every fighter — right down to the local hamlet guerrillas — on the communist side.'[21] At the same time, in the hamlets, the atrocities continued: the Viet Cong murdered 429 Vietnamese Government officials and 482 'others' (teachers and other civilians) between January and October 1964, according to US reports.[22] More ominously, terror against American personnel in Vietnam reached politically unacceptable levels: on 30 March 1965 a Viet Cong bomb exploded outside the US Embassy in Saigon, killing two and injuring forty-five Americans and inflicting 118 Vietnamese casualties.[23]


The hawk at LBJ's shoulder kept pecking away at any hint of Democrat softness on communism. The Republicans urged the President to bomb the North and send in combat troops. In 1964, as he embarked on his first presidential election campaign, Johnson was determined to appear tough on communism, and where better to display his toughness than in a little 'pissant' country miles from home, where US strength would surely swiftly defeat the communist insurgency? Yet Johnson needed a *casus belli* to justify the bombing of North Vietnam and the dispatch of American combat troops to the South. He soon found one.

On Sunday morning, 2 August 1964, the President received news of a North Vietnamese attack on a destroyer, USS *Maddox*, which had been sailing in the Tonkin Gulf, in or near enemy waters (depending on one's legal interpretation). Three North Vietnamese patrol boats had fired on the *Maddox*; it had not been hit and no Americans were injured. The *Maddox*'s captain, John Herrick, called an air strike, which sank or disabled the three boats — like trying to swat mosquitoes with a big fly swatter, remarked a *Maddox* crew member. The enemy had attacked in response to two provocations: a South Vietnamese commando raid on Hon Me Island, planned by the CIA, two days earlier, and the fact that the *Maddox* was sailing in the island's vicinity and arguably in North Vietnamese waters.

Johnson publicly responded by playing down the matter, stating he had no wish to widen the conflict (the Pentagon's press release did not even identify North Vietnam); in private, he leaned towards a firm military response. He ordered the *Maddox*, a second destroyer, USS *Turner Joy*, and protective aircraft to return to the Tonkin Gulf and 'attack any force that attacks them'. He warned Hanoi, in the first US diplomatic communication with North Vietnam, of 'grave consequences' if they took 'further unprovoked military action' against American warships 'on the high seas'. It is hard to escape the conclusion that the US warships 'were effectively being used to bait the Communists' and that the North Vietnamese were being 'treated as belligerents from first detection'.[24]

That night, 4 August, a storm blew up in the gulf. At eight o'clock, buffeted by swollen seas, Herrick claimed (and later denied) that he had intercepted messages suggesting an imminent enemy strike. Aircraft overhead saw nothing. Nor were any hostile ships visible from the *Maddox*'s decks. Yet the radar showed what seemed to be approaching torpedoes — an interpretation later shown to be false. In a panic, the US destroyers started firing wildly at the shoreline, convinced that they were under attack.

In the next few days, grave doubts intruded. Neither Herrick nor any of his officers could confirm that they had engaged the enemy. Commander James Stockdale, who flew over the scene, was certain there had been 'no incident'. 'Not one,' he told a later debrief. 'No boats, no boat wakes, no ricochets off boats … nothing but black sea and American firepower.'[25] Stockdale was later shot down over North Vietnam and spent years in the 'Hanoi Hilton'; other pilots, however, under a process called 'redebriefing', gave Washington and the US chiefs of staff what they wanted: a 'proof package' that enemy boats had in fact attacked the American fleet. That, in essence, was the basis for the Tonkin Gulf Incident: a clear act of war by Hanoi, or a chimera dressed up as fact by the President to justify US intervention? The American media, under the spell of the Pentagon, generally accepted the former, official line: US ships had been 'under continuous torpedo attack' and US jets 'diving, strafing …' and so on.

Johnson seized on this construction of the dubious events in the Tonkin Gulf as a way of pressing Congress for a war resolution. He appeared on television, speaking of 'repeated attacks' against US ships. The provocative actions of the North Vietnamese had 'given a new and grave turn' to the situation in the region, in reply to which he ordered sixty-four bombing sorties against North Vietnamese naval bases and an oil depot. The Australian Government and most ALP shadow ministers firmly backed the US air strikes, notably Gough Whitlam, who said, in Parliament's first major debate on Vietnam, '… it is difficult to think that any … head of state would have reacted differently'.[26]

On 7 August 1964 Congress overwhelmingly approved the Tonkin Gulf Resolution, which was 'the closest the United States came to a declaration of war in Vietnam'.[27] It gave the President sweeping powers to prosecute the war as commander-in-chief of the US armed forces. The resolution undoubtedly assisted LBJ's election: he won the November ballot by 16 million votes, the biggest landslide in American history, seen as a sympathy vote in memory of JFK and a vote of popular support for the war.

If the President deceived the American people over what happened in the Tonkin Gulf,[28] one fact is clear: the Tonkin Gulf Incident was the pivotal act that brought America, Russia and China into the Second Indochina War. It transformed the Soviet Union's stated policy of 'non-engagement' to one of substantial support for Hanoi.[29] The incident 'symbolised the new relationship that Hanoi required with Moscow. The nature of the war was changing … from barefooted Viet Cong with their homemade shotguns to Vietnamese Communist armies equipped with the best weapons the Communist world could produce.'[30]

China, too, rallied to Hanoi's side after Tonkin. Mao met Hanoi's leaders and agreed to extend massive military support to Hanoi. China placed troops in the Kunming and Guangzhou Military Regions in combat readiness, sent fifteen MIG jets to Hanoi, agreed to train North Vietnamese pilots, and constructed airfields near the Vietnamese border. Liu Shao-chi, Mao's number two, told Le Duan in early 1965: '… we will do our best to provide you with whatever you need and whatever we have.'[31] Between 1964 and 1965 the Chinese raised gun delivery to North Vietnam 2.8 times (from 80,500 to 220,767), bullets five times (25.2 million to 114 million) and artillery shells six times (335,000 to 1.8 million).[32] Mao secretly met

Ho Chi Minh in May 1965 and, while refusing pilots, pledged an army of support troops. 'China would be responsible for road repair in North Vietnam,' he promised. Chinese engineers and supply troops began flowing into North Vietnam: 320,000 were stationed there between 1965 and 1968. Chinese aid reached right down to daily articles, uniforms, rice, meat, sugar.[33] Most critically, China sent America its 'Rules of Engagement'. 'If the United States bombs China that would mean war, and there would be no limit to the war,' it stated. Put another way, if America limited its air attacks to North Vietnam and did not strike China, Peking and Washington would avoid a possible nuclear war.[34]

The Communist Bloc's reactions to Tonkin thus defined Vietnam as 'the place' — the superpowers' chosen killing ground — and drew the line between nuclear Armageddon and 'limited war'. Vietnam was seen as a testing ground for a new generation of weapons of limited (i.e. non-nuclear) warfare, a suitably remote battlefield that would enable the Pentagon to 'advertise our strengths as levels below brink'.[35]

On 7 February 1965 Johnson used his Resolution: American aircraft bombed North Vietnam in retaliation for the Viet Cong attack on Plei Ku airbase in which eight Americans died. Then, on 2 March, Johnson approved OPERATION ROLLING THUNDER, the concentrated bombing of industrial targets in North Vietnam. The name was taken from a hymn; the raids aimed at breaking Hanoi's will to fight. Both the Australian Government and the ALP Opposition strongly supported the bombardment. Canberra had been 'pressing for it since Christmas'.[36] Days after the first bombing runs, the ALP's Foreign Affairs Committee endorsed the US air strikes (an endorsement Calwell later withdrew).

Scheduled to last eight weeks, ROLLING THUNDER continued for three and a half years. Hundreds of US aircraft ran thousands of sorties over the Red River Delta. Between 1965 and 1968 the USA unleashed on North Vietnam triple the bomb tonnage dropped on Europe, Asia and Africa during World War II: roughly eight million tons of bombs, rockets and missiles. They destroyed factories, bridges, towns, train lines, oil refineries, ammunition dumps, farms and port facilities — personally authorised, until 1968, by Johnson, who boasted, 'They can't even destroy an outhouse without my approval.'[37] Civilians were not targeted, although more than 50,000 died in collateral damage, according to most estimates.[38] US planes spared the Red

River flood control system, the destruction of which would have killed millions. Schools and hospitals were accidentally struck: thirty children and a teacher died, for example, when four bombs hit Thuy Dan school 100 kilometres south of Hanoi.[39] A Hanoi resident who lived through the air raids told me: 'We dug tunnels to protect our families from cluster bombs. We slept in tunnels for years. After the bombing we tore branches off trees and rebuilt the roads. I got so accustomed to the bombing I wasn't afraid: I thought, maybe I'll live tomorrow, maybe I'll die. I moved school seven times.'

ROLLING THUNDER would neither confirm White House adviser Walt Rostow's mystical faith in air bombardment nor fulfil the hopes of US Air Force Chief of Staff Curtis Lemay to 'bomb 'em back to the Stone Age'. Nor would it 'stomp them to death', in the words of General William DePuy, Westmoreland's chief of operations. The air bombardment failed even to bomb 'em to the negotiating table. The opening of the air war served an incidental purpose: it partly justified LBJ's decision to send the first US combat troops to South Vietnam, whose first job was to protect the American airfield at Da Nang from an encircling force of 6,000 Viet Cong troops.

On 8 March 1965, 3,500 Marines in full combat gear — the 'nose of the camel' as the invasion force was dubbed — came ashore at Da Nang, bearing the American flag. They were greeted by smiling South Vietnamese schoolgirls bearing flowers and a poster, 'Welcome to the Gallant Marines'. In May, Australia's 1st Battalion followed.

# Part Two
# First contacts

# Chapter 8
# The quiet Australian

I was aware of [Australia's entry into the Vietnam War] before anybody in Canberra was aware of it.

*Ted Serong, the first Australian military adviser in Vietnam.*

Meanwhile, in Australia, another, more tangible threat than fear of communism drove foreign policy: colonial withdrawal. The last Europeans were preparing to leave the Far East after centuries of colonial occupation. If the age of Western imperialism dawned with Columbus's voyage to the new world in 1492, it probably closed with Japan's conquest of Singapore in 1942 and the British departure from Malaya. In the 1950s and early 1960s the signs were everywhere: in the wail of British bugles and the lowering of the Union Jack over Malaya; the abandoned French villas along the coast of Indochina; the last shipments of spices from the Dutch Antilles; and the sad faces of Eurasian orphans abandoned by French officials returning home. For Australians, the most powerful symbol of the end of colonialism was the British Government's intention to abandon Fortress Singapore and withdraw all forces east of the Suez Canal.

Signs of Britain's colonial exit deeply disturbed Australia, because Canberra had received no firm assurances from America that it would fill the gap; indeed, America had no intention of doing so. Many Australians saw Britain's intended withdrawal from Asia as treachery; Menzies spoke of a 'catastrophe'. During the 1962 Laotian crisis — when a communist takeover seemed imminent — the Prime Minister warned that if Britain 'found itself unwilling' to join Australia and America in opposing the Laotian communist insurgency, 'a painful and perhaps catastrophic problem would be presented to Australia'.[1]

In the early 1960s Australians thus contemplated a lonely future as the last Anglo–Saxon outpost in a new world of inscrutable yellow faces. Frank Hopkins, the US consul general in Melbourne, summed it up in a cable to Washington, in 1962:

> After nearly two centuries of economic and psychological dependence on Great Britain, Australians are shocked by the thought that they may now have to stand on their own feet and rely primarily on themselves … They feel that Britain is letting them down, and that the United States is failing to appreciate their plight … It remains to be seen whether Australians can find the courage, the confidence and the willpower to work out their own destiny under much less favorable conditions …[2]

In tandem with political isolation, Australians faced economic loss. Our traditional buyers in Europe, chiefly Britain, were turning inward. The European Economic Community (EEC) was busy erecting the most destructive barrier to international trade devised, in the form of the Common Agricultural Policy. Between 1955 and 1971 Australia's total exports to the founding six EEC members would halve, from 11.2 per cent. Losing markets in Europe, Australia hoped to prise open new ones in America.

An offer of military assistance to the Americans might help to achieve this goal, Canberra privately felt. Politicians will never openly admit the link between economic and military cooperation; yet it predates Clausewitz, who saw military collaboration, in part at least, as a commercial relationship. Alan Renouf, Australia's chargé d'affaires in Washington, was eager to exploit the commercial opportunity of Vietnam 'without disproportionate expenditure' by Australia. Menzies agreed. He publicly defended Australia's tenuous military alliance with America on the grounds of national security; yet the commercial opportunities of the relationship also exerted a strong claim on his mind. In 1961–62, pleading the cause of ANZUS and the South-East Asian Treaty Organisation (SEATO),[3] Menzies unleashed Barwick on the scent of a more robust US commitment to Australian security.

Menzies' hopes turned on the ANZUS Treaty, signed in 1951, as the cornerstone of Australia's military alliance with America. The treaty was grossly misrepresented and misunderstood: ANZUS merely obliged the signatories to consult each other on regional threats; it did not place an automatic obligation on America to defend us, as former Defence Minister Malcolm Fraser explained.[4] ANZUS, a very frayed safety net, was 'a vaguely worded' provision of mutual assistance and not a guarantee of military assistance from the most powerful nation in the world.[5]

'Each Party,' stated its key clause, Article IV, 'recognizes that an armed attack in the Pacific area on any of the Parties would be dangerous to its own peace and safety and declares that it would act to meet the common danger in accordance with its constitutional processes.'[6] That hardly guaranteed an American arm around our shoulder. In fact, even in 1964 Menzies was not fully aware of the extent of Washington's cavalier regard for ANZUS. This was made abundantly (and privately) clear to President Johnson on 24 June 1964, the very day Menzies sat embalmed in the goodwill of the White House. Before lunch, a presidential adviser, McGeorge Bundy, one of those dangerously cerebral political clinicians who heavily influenced the White House at the time, sent a private memo to the President: 'Once or twice,' Bundy said, 'Australians have tried to interpret our ANZUS commitment as a blank check, but Menzies has never made this mistake. He knows that we are good allies, but *the exact shape of our action under the treaty will depend on your judgment as President, at every stage.*'[7] In US eyes, then, ANZUS had a chameleon-like quality: America would decide when and how the treaty applied. In truth, Australia was not a US defence priority — as America's fence-sitting over the Indonesian and West Papuan crises demonstrated. Japan, in fact, was far more vital to US commercial interests, and received far greater military assistance, an irksome truth so soon after World War II.

Yet in one sense, ANZUS served Washington: as a diplomatic means of securing two more flags for the Vietnam War. With this in mind, Dean Rusk, the US Secretary of State, deigned to attend the first ANZUS Council to be held outside America, in Canberra, in May 1962. Rusk's purpose was to extract from the Australian Government a commitment to send military advisers to South Vietnam. Barwick opened the discussion by crudely demanding — 'come hell or high water' — a US pledge to defend South Vietnam and oppose the Chinese in the event of escalation.[8] (Barwick drew the line at nuclear weapons, although SEATO, in fact, allowed for a nuclear contingency in Asian conflicts. The fledgling post-colonial Asian governments were, at this stage, facing internal communist uprisings.)[9]

The meeting satisfied neither side. Barwick got no firm assurances from the Americans, and Rusk got a weak commitment from Australia to send a 'handful' of military advisers to South Vietnam — 'three or four', Barwick told a press conference on 9 May 1962. The newspapers were broadly favourable — a 'gesture of support to Washington' and so on — with the striking exception of the *Courier-Mail*, which warned that South Vietnam might become the battleground of a world war.

On 6 June 1962 a short, compact man with darting blue eyes stepped onto the tarmac at Tan Son Nhut airport, Saigon. He wore the rank and uniform of an Australian Army colonel, yet his reception suggested a man of greater importance: Lieutenant General Richard Weede, Chief of Staff to US General Paul Harkins, commander of the newly created US Military Assistance Command Vietnam, along with members of the Australian Embassy, met him at the airport. The Australian colonel strode with deliberation. He carried himself with a determined, oddly unstoppable demeanour — 'almost Napoleonic', observed one colleague.[10] He exuded the air of an officer who knew his own mind and his limitations, of which, observing his self-confident projection, there were very few.

Colonel Francis ('Ted') Serong was in Vietnam on an official intelligence-gathering mission. He spent a few weeks in country, visiting the headquarters of the US Military Assistance and Advisory Group, the demilitarised zone, Da Nang and the Central Highlands. 'Worse than I had been led to believe and worsening,' Serong concluded of the dismal progress of the undeclared war. He partly blamed the Saigon Government of President Ngo Dinh Diem, which had failed, in Serong's view, to draw up a strategic plan: 'Government plan? — on paper! — In fact?'[11] Saigon's US-trained soldiers had taken 'a bucket to a bushfire', Serong wrote. If Australian troops were to join this war, 'We will probably lose some, tactically. We may lose the lot, strategically.'[12] In time, Serong's tough-minded appraisals and fearless willingness to speak his mind would win him respect — and hatred — at the highest levels of the US, Australian and South Vietnamese armies and the ear of Presidents Lyndon Johnson and Diem. He would become the longest serving military adviser in South Vietnam, and one of the most influential operatives in the CIA's Saigon Station. Yet Serong is scarcely known in Australia.

★ ★ ★

An exceptionally clever boy, Ted Serong grew up in a strict Catholic family in the Melbourne suburb of Abbotsford. His father, who trained as a blacksmith, through hard work rose to become a weapons maintenance expert in the Department of Defence. The family were steeped in the ethos of survival and self-defence; Serong's father knew the mean streets of Melbourne's Irish working class, and young Ted learned how to box at an early age.

Serong attended St Kevin's College, in East Melbourne, where Irish Catholicism and Marxism were in rancorous disagreement: God and Marx were antithetical, the Christian Brothers preached, although the zeal with which they condemned communism suggested that it served a kind of symbiotic role, as a dependable demon. Catholicism was the begetter of faith, hope and charity, and Marxism the begetter of brutal atheistic regimes. If the two institutions bore interesting similarities — the control of mind and deed by an absolute, incontrovertible power (God or state); and the biblical, or historic, inevitability of a promised land (Heaven, or the dictatorship of the proletariat), young Ted Serong was not about to argue with the demagogues of St Kevin's.

Serong swam in the spiritual slipstream of a boy two years his senior, Bob Santamaria. The pair became lifelong friends. Santamaria took the lessons of St Kevin's deeply to heart and, with the help of the media, evolved into Australia's most identifiable lay Catholic; Santamaria later led the powerful lobby group the National Civic Council, whose origins lay in the staunchly anti-communist Labor 'Movement' that had prised apart the ALP and helped to establish the DLP. Santamaria had interesting friends. He befriended President Diem during the Vietnamese Catholic dictator's 1957 Australian tour, which opened a door not otherwise available to an Australian colonel. Through Santamaria, Serong would also enjoy the confidence of Archbishop Daniel Mannix, a consistent supporter of the war in Vietnam and the Diem regime. These powerful Catholic connections helped to smooth Serong's access to top officials in the Kennedy administration, the South Vietnamese Government and the CIA.

Serong's military career got off to a faltering start: Duntroon initially rejected him. It was a severe, inexplicable blow. The selectors gave no explanation. Serong was certainly fit and bright enough. So why? One explanation is the tendency for institutions to replicate themselves in their own image, after a predominant 'type'; Serong simply did not fit the identikit. He was a mite over-pleased with himself, not really 'one of us'.

Merit alone was not enough to surmount that invisible barrier. More alarmingly, Serong had shown signs of raw, naked ambition, an alarming trait in so young a man; it ran against the old school tradition of the Anglican gentleman amateur, and threatened to show up those senior to him. Others attributed Serong's rejection to his Catholicism in an Anglican heartland. Serong's biographer observed of his family: '... their Roman Catholic religion at that time constituted a major social barrier.'[13] Many Duntroon cadets had reliable Anglo-Saxon names and tended to be selected from Anglican private schools (the name Serong is derived from Portuguese; the family's ancestors were Madeiran). Serong did get into Duntroon, eventually, via the rarely used and extremely difficult route of applying for the second year. To do so, he had to complete the first-year coursework as a serving member of the defence force: so he joined the Citizen Military Force and completed Duntroon's first year in five months.

He never really forgave the Australian Army, and it showed in the eagerness with which he later leaped at American career opportunities. His thwarted ambition tended in an unusual direction. Certainly it set him apart from his peers; he was with them, but not one of them. He felt an overwhelming need to prove himself, and set his own standards higher than those of Duntroon. Hadn't he knocked over a year's work in half the time? Hadn't he graduated with top marks, and won awards for small arms handling, marksmanship and boxing? Surely he was destined for swift promotion and a shining career.

Yet as he rose through the ranks — from a staff officer in divisional headquarters in New Guinea during the Kokoda campaign in 1942 to a lieutenant colonel at Army Headquarters, Eastern Command in Sydney in 1948 — Serong developed a strident, some thought overblown, opinion of his abilities. No doubt he had intelligence and drive: he later re-established and became commandant of the Jungle Training Centre at Canungra, one of the world's toughest jungle combat courses. That success marked him out as a specialist in jungle warfare and counter-insurgency operations — precisely the skills the Americans required in Vietnam. Yet there was more to Serong than simply a self-styled jungle combat expert: his crusading, anti-communist spirit, leavened with a strong Catholic faith, forged his destiny as an ideological soldier and Cold War warrior motivated by forces that transcended his narrow military brief.

In 1957 he delivered a series of lectures to the Burmese Army, which, in classic Serong style, summoned up the demon of Marxism in an Asian theatre of war: his views anticipated many of the problems in Vietnam. He came to see himself as a regional strategic planner, on a special mission 'to prevent the spread of Communism in South-East Asia'.[14] He measured his value according to unorthodox benchmarks: he styled himself a military adviser to embattled governments, no less, and a world authority on counter-revolutionary warfare. 'Confident, innovative and highly individualistic, Serong was suited for the special combination of military, political, sociological and economic warfare being waged in Vietnam.'[15]

In February 1962 the Central Intelligence Agency approached Serong in Rangoon, where he advised the Burmese Government on counter-revolutionary warfare. The CIA's agent, a colonel who doubled as director of the US Medical Equipment Distribution Team (a CIA front), suggested that Serong's skills were needed in Vietnam. A delighted Serong — who relished this US recognition of his expertise — informed the then Chief of the General Staff, Lieutenant General Sir Reginald Pollard. Impressed, Pollard instructed the Australian Secret Intelligence Service to facilitate Serong's attachment to the CIA Station in Saigon.

The appointment of Serong carried the imprimatur of the US and Australian governments. He had been chosen on the strength of his reputation at Canungra, Dean Rusk freely admitted to the ANZUS meeting in Canberra in May 1962 that the US armed forces knew little about jungle warfare. Barwick concurred. Serong, said the Minister for External Affairs, was the only Australian officer to be considered for the job. Australia thus planted its first footprint in Vietnam as part of covert CIA operations. At that stage, still two years before the Tonkin Gulf Incident, as Serong later explained, 'the CIA were running the war'.[16]

In June 1962 Serong joined the war — then a struggle between the North and South Vietnamese, advised by the USSR–China, and America, respectively — as a senior adviser to the commander of the US Military Assistance Command, serving first under General Harkins, then General William Westmoreland; later that year, he was appointed to command the first contingent of Australian military advisers in Vietnam. His wife Kathleen and three of their six children joined him, and the family moved into a comfortable, barbed wire-lined villa in central Saigon.

Serong swiftly gained the confidence of senior figures in Diem's regime. He met Diem's 'defence minister', Nguyen Dinh Thuan (a placeman who executed Diem's orders), and Colonel Duong Ngoc Lam, the thuggish commander of the South Vietnamese Civil Guard. With their blessing, he toured the country for sixteen days and compiled exhaustive reports on the state of the insurgency: the country, he concluded, was being overrun. Through terror or propaganda the National Liberation Front had gained the support of most of the rural population — many of whom were genuine sympathisers — and were fighting the second phase of Hanoi's revolutionary struggle, using highly mobile, platoon-based attacks on southern towns and infrastructure.

Swiftly he drew up six rules of counter-insurgency operations, known as 'Field Service Regulations', which formed a ruthless prescription for bringing the war to the Viet Cong and give an insight into Serong's mind:

1. Pursuit shall follow every contact, and shall take precedence over all other considerations;
2. No mobile encounter will be broken off by any component before at least one-third of the strength of that component are battle casualties (i.e. 33 per cent of the opposing forces must be dead or wounded before retreat or disengagement were thinkable);
3. No defensive position or static post will ever be surrendered. There is only one degree of defence — to the last round and the last man;
4. Every static post will maintain one-third of its strength in continuous mobile patrols. [The Australian infantry later exceeded this, maintaining half its force in the first year, and up to two-thirds in subsequent years, on continuous patrols.]

The rules were aimed at the ARVN, whose laziness and cowardice infuriated the US and Australian army advisers (some of whom would later lose their lives as a result of ARVN desertion on patrol). In Serong's words, 'I am sickened to see these little bastards getting away with murder, and to see our boys [the American troops, at this stage] getting killed while they're graciously making up their mind whether they'll take our advice ... Poor US are doing their best, within the limitations of the pussyfooting policy which is imposed upon them.' (Not that all Vietnamese units loyal to Saigon answered to this description; many were excellent soldiers and extremely brave.)

Indeed, Serong followed through on his complaints: he demanded more power to promote the war effort. He insisted on having a right to 'goad' the South Vietnamese and 'veto' their commanders; powers that would soon bring Australian military advisers into open combat with the Viet Cong. Serong bravely aired his opinion of the disastrous state of South Vietnam to Harkins, and other senior American commanders.

As Serong's influence grew, he outshone the Australian diplomats then in Saigon. '... in the eyes of senior Americans in Saigon, Serong was Australian policy,' concluded one study of his role. 'They would often go to him rather than the Australian Ambassador for advice.'[17] In time, Serong had the ear of the President, and visited America several times for special 'sessions' with Johnson. At least two meetings with LBJ and one with Nixon were confirmed.[18]

Senior CIA sources corroborated this. Serong 'brought a quality to our operations that I thought the Americans had a very hard time absorbing', said William Colby, CIA chief in Saigon. 'The Americans were inclined to focus on military power whereas Serong ... realized the importance of the political dimension ... So the Australian contribution was very important and quite unique ...' In particular, Serong saw the importance of helping the villagers to defend themselves, Colby added. 'The Australians particularly understood that element of the effort ... Sometimes it was a little hard to get ... across to the rather hasty American ...'[19]

Serong even took on the fearsome US Marine commander, General Victor 'Brute' Krulak, a Harkins man, during a meeting of the US Special Counter-insurgency Group, in Washington, on 23 May 1963. The 'Special Group', as it was called, pooled President Kennedy's most powerful planners on the Vietnam War: Averell Harriman, the Under Secretary of State for Political Affairs; Roger Hilsman, Secretary for Eastern Affairs at the State Department; Robert Kennedy, Attorney-General; William Bundy, then a White House foreign affairs adviser; Michael Forrestal, on the senior staff of the National Security Council; and John McCone, Director of Central Intelligence. That they thought Serong's opinion worth hearing was as much a measure of his influence as of America's weakness in guerrilla warfare.

The minutes described Serong's impact on the meeting: 'May 23: Colonel Francis Serong, Australian guerrilla fighting expert, expresses doubt on the Strategic Hamlet Program saying it is over-extended, and that it has left vast areas from which the Vietcong can operate freely. Krulak immediately and violently challenges him ...'[20] Serong left the meeting convinced that few had understood him: 'My God,' he thought, 'does the fate of the world reside in the hands of those clowns?'[21] In the event, both Harkins and Krulak rejected Serong's advice on the direction of the war — as they would similar warnings from US Colonels Dan Porter and John Vann — with disastrous consequences.

Serong's belief that the Viet Cong was winning the war drew on hard facts: the northern insurgents were travelling down the Ho Chi Minh Trail at will; the South Vietnamese Army was poorly equipped, badly treated and ill-trained. Only the elite Ranger Battalions and a few Special Force units with US commando experience were willing to attack the Viet Cong. This pattern, common throughout South Vietnam, was most acute in the Central Highlands, where the ill-treated Montagnard tribes were turning their loyalties to the Viet Cong. During one exchange with Nguyen Dinh Thuan, Diem's Secretary of State, Serong glimpsed the cold heart of the regime with which he dealt. Thuan said that he had no intention of properly arming or training the troublesome mountain people. 'I suspect,' Serong wrote, 'that Thuan knows they will run out of ammunition, and that he intends them to … He means to finish this war with no Montagnard problem.'[22]

In this climate Serong grew convinced that Australia should play a much bigger role in the war. His assessment of the American war grew progressively bleaker. He scorned the US Army's approach to jungle warfare, and envisaged a group, or 'team', of specially trained, carefully selected Australian military advisers, all of whom would excel at jungle warfare and whose job would be to advise and train the Saigon forces.

Serong set about the appointment of the first Australian advisory unit with his trademark cloak-and-dagger approach. He revelled in the furtive world of the CIA, and liked to suggest to his Australian superiors that he knew a lot more than they did. Several Australian officers, who outranked Serong, simply misunderstood the latter's influence beyond his rank, chiefly within the CIA. Brigadier David Jackson seemed to think of Serong as a mere colonel who had no right to advise Harkins. 'Colonel Serong, I think, is something of an egotist,' said Jackson. 'I think that he overrated his ability to advise people like the American Ambassador in Saigon, the American commander-in-chief in Saigon. He seemed to feel that it was part of his function …'[23] In fact, that was precisely part of Serong's function.

One has only to consider Serong's unusual access to President Diem as a gauge of his influence. Serong claimed to have played a critical role, for example, in the life-and-death choice of location for the first Australian military advisers. They might have gone to Quang Ngai, near the demilitarised zone — one of the most dangerous provinces — had Serong not intervened, he later claimed. However, fresh evidence reveals that Serong initially accepted the Quang Ngai deployment plan. In a private meeting with Diem in May 1963 the President revealed to Serong, in chilling terms, why he wanted the first Australian troops in Quang Ngai province. The two men spoke in English, with extraordinary candour. Serong respected Diem, and their relationship went beyond the formalities of diplomacy; they were friends. Their shared faith eased this process: they recognised in each the unspoken 'otherness' of the lay mystic. As such, Serong felt able to say what he thought to the President.

Serong began by explaining why he felt Diem's Strategic Hamlet Program was not working — he spread his fingers out on the table to show how the fortified hamlets defended the axes radiating through the Mekong Delta, but failed to protect the gaps in between — when Diem suddenly changed the subject. 'I was disappointed,' the President said, turning a quizzical eye on Serong, 'when you did not accept my proposal to concentrate your men at Quang Ngai … Do you know why I wanted the Australians at Quang Ngai?' Serong said nothing. Diem continued: 'I reasoned that if they were all killed, your government would feel compelled to commit more troops to the defence of my country.'[24]

Serong later gave his version of this exchange:

> The President of Vietnam, God bless him, was most anxious to put support … into Quang Ngai province. Well, while I subsequently developed a great deal of affection for the President of Vietnam … it was perfectly obvious to me what [his] purpose was — namely that if there was to be such a sudden thrust by Hanoi down through that area, that we were designed to be killed so that there would thereupon be a great avenging intervention by Australia. So I wasn't having any part of that …[25]

Serong had a personal hand in choosing the first Australian military contingent in Vietnam — and, in so doing, again displayed his unfortunate, somewhat puerile trait of revelling in his earlier access to information than those more highly placed or of a grander rank: 'I was aware of [Australia's entry into the war] before anybody in Canberra was aware of it …' Serong boasted in an interview in 1971.

'Are you prepared to say how you were aware of it?' the interviewer asked, alluding to Serong's friends in the CIA.

'No … I got a message saying, "Come on up to Canberra", and when I got there I was greeted with the news that I knew I was going to be greeted with … that we were going to intervene here, that it would be a very small token intervention … on a politically visible basis.'[26]

Such arrogance contributed to his undoing. Like America's famous military rebel John Paul Vann (immortalised in Neil Sheehan's *A Bright Shining Lie*), Serong won few friends in high places by reminding them of their ignorance or shortcomings. Sometimes he went behind their backs. In December 1963 he warned Henry Cabot Lodge, then US Ambassador in Saigon, of the dire state of the South, and Harkins exploded, describing Serong's report as 'a gross and unsoldierly affront, to me, to my staff'.[27]

Serong's pessimistic insights and radical prophylactics often flew off at extreme angles. To counter the inertia and chronic instability in the South, he recommended in December 1963 — a month after President Diem's death — the appointment of an American commander-in-chief in the South and that Henry Cabot Lodge be given executive administrative powers. Serong had demanded, in effect, that America colonise the Republic of Vietnam. These were astonishing proposals from a mere Australian colonel. 'He had come to believe a Viet Cong victory was inevitable and made no bones about saying so.'[28]

A desk-bound official in Canberra set in motion the job of muzzling this rampant, rather brilliant Australian. On 29 April 1964 Arthur Tange, Secretary of the Department of External Affairs, quietly noted that Serong should not be permitted to extend his tour beyond its appointed term. Ministers would have to be involved in his removal, of course; Serong's fierce ambition had to be managed: 'In Oct '64,' Serong claimed, in a possibly vainglorious letter, 'I declined (respectfully) an invitation from PM Menzies to return to Australia to become CGS [Chief of the General Staff — the highest appointment in the armed forces].'[29]

For now — early 1963 — Serong focused on his most important task in Vietnam: as the first commander of that unique detachment, the Australian Army Training Team Vietnam (AATTV), which was destined to become the most highly decorated military unit in Australian history.

# Chapter 9
# The Team

My Darling,
... I thought that the end of the world had come last week ...
[it] was a bloody nightmare ...
*Sergeant Billy Hacking, letter to his fiancée, 27 May 1963.*

Serong chose the first thirty members of the AATTV — the 'Dirty Thirty' — from a list of a hundred officers and 200 warrant officers. 'I was invited ... to make a selection. Nearly all were ... known to me personally,' he said.[1] Selected for their combat experience and intelligence — and perhaps for their relationship with Serong — the first members were spirited away in great secrecy to a special training course at the School of Military Intelligence, Middle Harbour, Sydney. 'You have been specially selected ...' they were told on their arrival, in 1962. The thirty-six men (six were reserves) felt greatly honoured, yet for what? The nature of the Team's full role in Vietnam was confidential; they were to be instructors to the South Vietnamese, not combat troops (the first battalion of whom would not leave for Vietnam until 1965). Yet none had been told any specifics of his mission.

They got an inkling midway through the first lecture when the doors suddenly flew open. Guards appeared with batons, ordered the class to their feet and roughly manhandled each soldier to an underground prison, fitted with bamboo cages. 'The water dripped incessantly and the walls were discoloured by age and slime,' recalls Captain Barry Petersen, a veteran of the Malayan Emergency destined for an unusually daunting role in Vietnam.[2] The soldiers were stripped naked and given ill-fitting prison clothes. Then the torture training began: for the next week the men suffered food and sleep deprivation, interrogations, beatings and all kinds of humiliation. Each cell had a peculiarly offensive feature: in the Music Room a loudspeaker blared 'The Internationale' and Mao's 'The East is Red', as well as fanatical communist rants ('Comrades! We all must learn the Principles of Communism!'); the Whistlestop Room broadcast an unbroken, high-pitched shriek that drove the soldier mad from lack of sleep; in the Pit, a dungeon entered by a trapdoor, the soldier sat in pitch blackness, in ankle-deep water, in the company of a few rats. Interrogations in the Conversation Suite simulated the questions and brutality they were likely to face if captured in Vietnam: baton-jabbing, beatings, verbal abuse ('Have you no sense of decency, you dirty, filthy man?').[3]

The Australian Army's School of Torture aimed to humiliate and enrage the pupils. They prodded Warrant Officer Ossie Ostara in the testicles. 'They made rude comments about them,' he said, 'they poked you in the breast, asked if you were a girl, if you liked men. Anything to make you lose your temper. Once you lost your temper they had you.'[4] Captain Peter Rothwell spent four days in solitary confinement, living on bread and rice shoved under the door, and endured 'loud blaring music', non-stop, day and night: 'By the second day I completely lost any realization of time and space ... I started to believe I actually was captured.'[5] Warrant Officer Brian 'Snowy' Lawrence said, 'If you couldn't take the code of conduct course, you certainly weren't entitled to consider going to Vietnam.'[6] Some survivors of the School of Torture remember it with a sort of tortured affection.

The feared jungle training course at Canungra was comparatively easy. The soldiers spent five days honing their jungle combat skills, and were then told their mission — to train the Army of the Republic of Vietnam — and their true name: the Australian Army Training Team Vietnam (affectionately known as 'the Team'). After pre-embarkation leave, the men assembled at Eastern Command Personnel Depot, at Watsons Bay, in Sydney, and on 29 July 1962 a little group of family and friends farewelled the first Australian soldiers to leave for Vietnam, on a Qantas flight bound for Saigon. The troops wore civilian clothes and carried their uniforms in a bag. Their loved ones had no idea of the Team's precise destination in Vietnam. Sergeant Bill Hacking would write to his fiancée, Kathy Ginnane, from 'Nowheresville'; his precise location was strictly classified.

★   ★   ★

'Hatchet-faced professionals'[7] was how one US officer described them, as they stepped onto the tarmac at Tan Son Nhut airport. Sent to Vietnam nominally as 'advisers' to the South Vietnamese Army, Australia's finest jungle warfare exponents quickly found themselves leading combat operations. Most had overseas combat experience, and many had served in Korea and/or Malaya. Some were World War II veterans.

Serong immediately imposed his will on their deployment. Having resisted Diem's death wish to send them to Quang Ngai, he also spurned General Harkins' advice, 'to smear the Australians quite thinly over the countryside so that they would not constitute a threat to the Americans' command structure',[8] and ignored Sir Robert Thompson, the British counter-insurgency expert, who said they should be sent to the delta. No, said Serong. The Team, he insisted, were jungle warfare specialists; they would operate in jungle, not rice paddies. He decided on a 'partial spread and partial concentration' — he could not risk losing all thirty at once — in the 'strategically spectacular' northern and central provinces. Ten members joined the American advisory team at the Dong Da National Training Centre, in Phu Bai, south-east of Hué; another ten joined the Vietnam Civil Guard training centre at Hiep Khanh, north-west of Hué; two were attached to a village defence training centre at Da Nang; seven remained in the southern part of the country, four at the Ranger Training Centre at Duc My, and three in the Australian headquarters in Saigon.

Serong delegated most of his daily command duties to Colonel Joe Mann, who doubled as general supervisor of the US advisory effort. Serong's CIA intrigues and advisory role to Harkins occupied most of his time, and he neglected his daily duties to the Team.[9] No doubt the Team were a mere cog in the US-led war effort: a thousand members of the Team were eventually sent to Vietnam — 277 being in country at their peak — within a US advisory force of 16,000. Yet they punched well above their weight: many were dismayed by the direction of the US war and tried to impose Australian methods on their South Vietnamese allies. They raised, and later led, small units of Vietnamese and indigenous Montagnard soldiers, with whom they fought a series of astonishing operations.


Of the 'Dirty Thirty', Sergeant Bill Hacking was exemplary. Aged 29, fit and bright, Hacking was a weapons expert who had completed two tours in Korea. He fell in love with, and proposed to, Kathy Ginnane shortly before his departure for Vietnam. 'Darling,' he wrote, on 27 July 1962, 'when I come home, no double bed please — I don't even want you at more than an arm's distance away … All my love, Bill. PS I can still smell you (lovely) on my scarf. I am taking it with me. x'[10]

Hacking wrote to Kathy every few days; their separation was a constant torment. He asked her to put droplets of perfume on her letters; he confessed that 'just thinking of you is like a minor orgasm'; he refused to tell her the exact date of his return because 'I just want to see you again as you are, in bed …'

When the army pushed forward his return date, he became agitated and less able to tolerate the wretched conditions. Near the end, he was stationed in a remote jungle outpost, and his tone changed to one of despair. Of the American officers, he wrote: 'These stupid bastards from the land of the dollar are driving me around the twist … They are the real enemy up here, their complacency and super-man complex has got the Vietnamese hating their guts and we (at least I) are not far behind …' (7 September 1962.)

On Viet Cong terror: 'The Viet Cong have been working overtime. Christmas or not, they blew up a passenger train just down the line last night (my area) and murdered 3 civilians; I say murdered as opposed to killed because these were an old man, his daughter, and his daughter's child, a little girl …' (Christmas Day, 1962.)

On the aftermath of battle: '… we had a regular massacre about 3 weeks ago; when it was all over there were 109 good Viet Cong strewn around the area, it was a scene very reminiscent of the finish of a Grand National steeplechase. By far the biggest success … so far.' (7–12 January 1963.)

On 1 June 1963 Hacking became the first Australian soldier to die in Vietnam. The army claimed he shot himself by accident. Kathy Ginnane believes he died of 'friendly fire'. 'Billy just wanted to get home and get married,' she said.[11] In their book *The Men Who Persevered*, Davies and McKay argue that army records and the angle of the bullet suggest Hacking committed suicide.[12] Hacking's last letters provide a few clues:

My Darling,
… I thought that the end of the world had come last week …
we were moving through elephant grass that must have been
12–15 feet tall … and there isn't a single breath of air … By the
grace of God, and realisation of the fact that the Vietnamese

would never have carried me out had I given up the ghost — I
managed to make the distance. But truly darling, the last day was
a bloody nightmare … (27 May 1963.)

In his last letter, dated 31 May 1963, sent from 'a mountain top in the
middle of the very deep jungle', he asked,

Did you receive my last couple of letters, written before I left
Hiep Khanh? … I am waiting most anxiously to hear, especially
since they … probably arrived at the flat during one of your
frequent absences from Melbourne. My concern is that they will
be there when you return. I see that the fires have been lit down
on the drop zone, so the choppers must be somewhere near.
Must rush.
      As always,
      Your own,
      Bill x

Sergeant Bill Hacking died the next day, on an operation deep in
'Nowheresville', in the Central Highlands.

The Australian involvement in Vietnam was, in essence, a 'political gesture',
as Serong called it: politicians in Canberra ran the show, made all the key
decisions and routinely ignored or overrode the defence force's advice. Yet
the first soldiers had to deal with the grim reality behind that gesture: a
world of Viet Cong terror, civilian despair, and an ineffectual South
Vietnamese Army. A few remarks convey the mood that greeted the Team
on their arrival:

'The South Vietnamese soldiers were oblivious to the almost daily
news of a company or battalion being annihilated,' Captain Bob Hagarty
said. 'The [military] training centres were worse than expected.'

'The South Vietnamese were all conscripts,' Major Joe Da Costa said,
'young and inexperienced, keen to learn, but badly treated. All their equipment
was ill-fitting. They'd have size 9 boots instead of size 6 — plop plop plop all
over the place. The standards of marksmanship were pretty appalling.'

'The peasants had been bled dry by VC taxes,' recalled Captain Adrian
Clunies-Ross. There were extraordinary obstacles, not least the language

barrier, he recalled. 'You'd have to issue orders through an interpreter. You'd speak for five minutes, and they'd say two or three words.'[13]

The southern army's lack of discipline provoked most complaints. In one spectacular example, members of the Team observed several hundred South Vietnamese soldiers lined up on a ridge to demonstrate 'coordinated firepower' to a visiting Vietnamese general. As the general's helicopter landed, a soldier suddenly started wildly firing at a distant target, then another fired, and another — until hundreds opened up on a little white rabbit that hopped madly among the bullets. The soldiers then broke ranks, surged down the hill and gave chase to the bunny, which they trapped amid great hilarity. The planned air strike, artillery and mortar demonstrations were aborted. The Australian observers 'could do little but look on dismayed' at this carnival atmosphere.[14]

Clunies-Ross felt a similar sinking feeling when he joined a heliborne assault with a Ranger battalion. Before they took off, he noticed running along the tarmac a furtive Vietnamese officer trying to find a seat on a helicopter. They were all full. An American marine pilot reluctantly made room for the officer, who happened to be the battalion's commander.[15]

Their combat performance was often deeply disconcerting. Warrant Officer Allan Joyce, a veteran of World War II and Korea, described an example in his diary: 'Saw an enemy recce ptl [reconnaissance patrol] of 3 moving along the Rd ... I informed Dia Huy [his Vietnamese counterpart]. Gibbering and pointing broke out everywhere, like a pack of yokels ... ARVN raced into the clearing on the spurline to gawk, point, giggle, gesticulate in the direction of the recce ptl. Never have I witnessed such a display of childishness and lack of soldierly discipline ... Our posn was entirely compromised ...'[16]

The Team were supposed to be advisers and observers. But in these conditions they quickly found themselves leading by example, as Warrant Officer George Chinn and Captain Rex Clark experienced during a 'hot insertion' near the Laotian border. Their chopper descended into a firefight. With the South Vietnamese in disarray, Chinn and Clark took command, organised their terrified troops and secured the zone for subsequent landings. It was the start of a pattern of Australian 'observers' suddenly finding themselves leading from the front.

The enemy's fearlessness soon produced Australia's first battle casualty: Sergeant Kevin Conway, a (temporary) warrant officer with US Special Forces and an adviser to the Nam Dong base in Thua Thien province. He gave his life leading 300 Nung tribesmen against 700 Viet Cong troops, who attacked the remote outpost, at 2.45 a.m. on 6 July 1964.

The enemy opened with their customary mortar barrage; a shell demolished the US Special Forces mess. Fires broke out. The forces of the National Liberation Front poured rockets, recoilless rifle and machine-gun fire into the compound; then, at the sound of a bugle, hundreds of their finest troops raced up to the perimeter wires and scrambled through.

Conway leaped out of his camp bed, grabbed his rifle and ran to a weapon pit when a bullet struck him. He died in the pit alongside US Sergeant Gabriel Alamo. The Viet Cong eventually withdrew, leaving the fort a smouldering ruin, inflicting 115 Nung casualties (of whom fifty-eight died), and killing or wounding nine Americans. Conway, aged 35, was the first Australian soldier killed in action in Vietnam. He received the US Silver Star and the National Order of the Republic of Vietnam (South Vietnam's highest award), among several other posthumous decorations. He was also recommended for the Victoria Cross — denied because, Canberra argued, Australia was not then officially at war.

The Team enjoyed extraordinary autonomy. Captain Ian Teague, for example, pioneered an approach to 'winning the hearts and minds' that would later form the central plank of America's 'other war', the pacification effort. A veteran of Malaya and a former commando, Teague joined the Team in April 1964 and was attached to the CIA's Combined Studies Division as a case officer in Quang Ngai province, one of the most heavily infiltrated. He set himself the task of finding out who in fact formed the Viet Cong's support network; that is, the mysterious 'Viet Cong infrastructure' of political agents, tax collectors and suppliers who ran the villages sympathetic to the enemy.

Teague travelled Quang Ngai in civilian clothes to find out. He established strong links with village communities, and persuaded the CIA to back the establishment of local intelligence centres throughout the province. Bags of money and weapons started flowing, and in early 1965 Teague formed the first of his People's Action Teams (PATs). He trained them in combat, propaganda and civic action: Teague's plan was to turn the guerrilla war on the guerrillas, using their methods. He borrowed the PAT code of ethics straight from the communist textbook.[17] For example, his Four Principles were: 'respect the people, help the people, protect the people, obey orders'. His eight regulations were:

1. Always be polite
2. Pay for what you want (the right price)
3. Return borrowed things
4. Pay for breakages and damages
5. Don't be harsh or overbearing
6. Don't destroy crops
7. Don't molest or rape women
8. Treat prisoners fairly and firmly.[18]

The People's Action Teams set out to gain a village's trust, then prime it for information on Viet Cong infiltrators. For example, a PAT typically entered a hamlet, met the hamlet chief and offered various kinds of aid (all paid for by the CIA): schools, marketplaces, hospitals, roads, drainage. After a few weeks, the villagers were expected to repay the generosity by volunteering information on enemy movements and terror. The scheme initially worked, and in 1965 Captains Jim Devitt and Allan Thompson and Lieutenant David Brockett arrived to expand on Teague's success. When Teague left Vietnam in 1965 his program employed 13,500 personnel in 310 teams throughout twenty-one provinces.

Overall, the Team would perform exceptionally in Vietnam. Yet many of their actions were scarcely known to the Australian public at the time and remain obscure to this day. One reason is that the Team's members operated in small groups with US advisers, embedded in South Vietnamese units which tended to be sent into extremely remote areas. In 1965, the experiences of Warrant Officer Leslie 'Aussie' Osborn, for example, were typical of these operations. Osborn, a veteran of World War II and Korea, was awarded the Military Medal for his extraordinary heroism in Vietnam. On 29 May 1965 he served as an adviser to an ARVN battalion in Thua Thien province. When his unit came under attack, Osborn repeatedly exposed himself to heavy enemy fire to encourage his Vietnamese troops to hold their ground. When the ARVN withdrew in disorder after their battalion commander was killed, Osborn remained in position and dressed the wounds of a US officer while holding off encroaching Viet Cong troops. He took part in many dangerous operations, during which, according to his MM citation, his performance was 'consistently outstanding'. Osborn's tour was typical of many conducted by members of the Team. But perhaps the most prolonged and daunting was that of Captain Barry Petersen.

# Chapter 10
# The Montagnard chief

Maybe I was only a minor monarch, but I was as close anyone got to being the absolute ruler of his own little cabbage patch.
*Captain Barry Petersen,* Tiger Men.

You've developed far too much influence with the Montagnard
… you've developed a personality cult in the Highlands.
*Chief of the CIA's Covert Action Branch to Petersen.*

In a Montagnard longhouse in the Central Highlands of Vietnam an Australian soldier dressed in a Rhade ceremonial vest and loincloth reclined on a reed mat beside the severed head of a freshly sacrificed buffalo. A Rhade sorcerer chanted incantations as hundreds of devoted tribespeople farewelled their beloved chieftain, Captain Barry Petersen, of the Australian Army Training Team.

Earlier that year, 1965, Petersen had reached the height of his temporal powers: honorary chief of a Rhade tribe, commander of a 1,200-strong Montagnard guerrilla force, and an inspiration to the Montagnard separatist movement. He led a private army of more than a thousand mountain warriors, including forty-four Rhade eight-man sections, sixteen teams of M'nong tribesmen, several twenty-four-man training cadres and a communications section of sixteen men, all of whom worshipped their young Australian leader. Petersen's personal fiefdom incorporated the Buon Enao school and hospital, three drama and propaganda teams, and ten interpreters. He ran this vast operation with a bottomless revolving fund of five million piastres (about A$50,000), courtesy of the Central Intelligence Agency.[1] At the time Petersen was aged 29.

Petersen became one of the stranger legends of the Vietnam War: an Australian version of Colonel Kurtz, the star of our very own *Apocalypse Now* — except that Petersen was not mad. He had methods. For more than two years he survived in one of the more dangerous mountain regions, with instructions to arm the indigenous tribes, raise an army and rally the mountain tribes behind the South. Even by the Team's standards, Petersen's mission was 'enough to daunt the stoutest heart', observed Lieutenant General Tom Daly, later Chief of the General Staff, 'set down in a strange provincial town in a completely foreign environment, armed with only a vague directive and a bagful of Vietnamese piastres, with no knowledge of the language …'[2] By any measure, it was an exceptional feat of persuasion, guile and personal command. It was also deadly: Petersen raised and led a unit renowned throughout the Highlands for its merciless brutality.

As a boy growing up in northern Queensland during World War II, Petersen rarely saw his father, a staff sergeant drafted into the army to operate radio workshops. His mother raised him, although he remembers with deep affection his grandfather, a first-generation Australian of Danish ancestry, who taught him how to drag a fishing net into shark-infested waters, an experience that terrified the boy.

Petersen grew into a young man of marked aesthetic sensibility, with a keen sense of self-dramatisation. A youth of cherubic good looks, he portrayed himself in Saigon as a character out of Graham Greene: 'Seated in a rattan chair on the wide verandah of the Hotel Continental Palace on the Rue Catinat and sipping iced citron, the tart juice made from lemons and limes, I found the boulevards fascinating to behold … Whatever the sins of the French in Indo-China, their best influences contributed much to the beauty … of the cities. They saw the value of trees and encouraged their growth.'[3] That much may be said of the French occupation.

In Vietnam, in 1963, he and Captain John Healy were attached to the CIA (a fact not made public until 1990). The Australian Government agreed with Washington's suggestion that selected members of the Team be seconded to the CIA's Covert Action Branch, which had the innocuous cover name of Combined Studies Division. It undertook a wide range of tasks, chiefly the training of Vietnamese irregular troops (i.e. civilian reserves), and later became part of the US Special Forces.[4] One of its roles in 1962 was to raise an army of Montagnards (mountain tribes) from among the 63,000 tribesmen in the highlands.

Petersen was selected as the first 'Free World' soldier for the job. His experience as a platoon commander in Malaya recommended him. There he had operated among the Orang Asli, the Negrito tribes in the jungles. Using his basic Malay he had established a close relationship with two tribes, the Jahai and the Temiar. His Malayan unit's second-in-command, Major John Milner, paid close attention, and Petersen's skills reached the ear of Colonel Ted Serong, who personally informed him of his new mission: he would be set down in Ban Me Thuot, the capital of Darlac province, in the Central Highlands of South Vietnam, and given command of his own field program. The details remained vague, but 'I've managed to get the CIA to agree … you're the first one', added Serong, delighting in his vaguely sinister role.[5]

Petersen's mission began in August 1963, at the CIA's Covert Action Branch, in a pleasant villa near central Saigon, where he met his American handler, Bryan Mills, a glacially cheerful young Ivy Leaguer who wore a concealed handgun under his open shirt, as did every CIA field officer. Mills accompanied Petersen on his first flight, in September, to Ban Me Thuot, a tree-lined town of about 45,000 Vietnamese and Montagnard people set in the rusty red earth, lush jungle and coffee plantations of the Central Highlands. The CIA had commandeered a huge teak hunting lodge that had belonged to the last emperor, Bao Dai, as their headquarters ('the Bungalow', they called it).

The Covert Action Branch gave Petersen a room in the Hotel Darlac, a typewriter and 35,000 piastres (US$350, a large sum, as a Vietnamese soldier was paid 1,300 piastres a month) — but no briefing. As Mills got up to go, Petersen said: 'Hey, Bryan, you haven't told me what to do up here …' Mills replied, 'Oh, just get to know the locals. Find yourself a good interpreter and see if you can find a house to live in.' And off he went. Petersen sat alone, 'like a shag on a rock'.[6]

Petersen moved quickly: he obtained a battered old truck. He learned the basics of the Rhade dialect. He found a large house and appointed an interpreter, driver, cook, housekeeper and personal secretary. In time, the house expanded to incorporate a radio room, a classroom, an armoury and accommodation for Petersen's eight-man security detail, all CIA-funded. Within the walled garden were peacocks and a monkey, and later a honey bear, a baby leopard, deer, gibbons and a tiger cub — all gifts of the Montagnard.

Six weeks later, a light aircraft buzzed the town — the CIA's idea of knocking. Mills had returned. On his last visit, he had in fact given Petersen one specific task: to establish whether a Montagnard guerrilla force, hitherto funded by the CIA at US$2,500 a month, in fact existed.

'I don't think they exist, Bryan,' Petersen said.

'We've been paying for people who do not exist,' Mills wearily replied, with the observation that funding phantom tribal armies was a common problem for the CIA 'throughout the country'.[7]

Petersen added, however, that a 100-strong Montagnard police force existed. Perhaps they could be turned into a guerrilla unit. Mills agreed, and dispatched a letter on American Embassy paper to the baffled police chief thanking him for the smooth handover of control of his force to the Australian (in revenge for which, Petersen later claimed, the deposed police chief tried to poison him with a 'cyanide-laced chicken').[8]

To turn the police force into an army, the CIA supplied Petersen with ammunition, explosives and weapons, as well as cash, gifts, clothing, food and propaganda materials, 'in unlimited quantities on a non-recoverable basis'. Petersen was expected to mesmerise the tribes with Cinesound projectors and films; radios and stencil equipment; small printing presses; hair-cutting kits; children's shirts; rice bowls and chopsticks; toys — balloons, model boats and dolls; sewing kits and fishing rods; and toilet kits; all marked with pro-government mottos and colours.[9] 'These items, produced by the CIA, I derided as useless propaganda material,' he later said.[10]

Thus equipped, Petersen took charge of his first Montagnard force. He studied Rhade, Jarai and M'nong customs, and immersed himself in their way of life. Descended from the Malayo-Polynesian or Khmer ethnic groupings, about 650,000 Montagnards, in dozens of tribes, inhabited the Annamite Chain of mountains that straddled the strategically vital feeder lanes of the Ho Chi Minh Trail. Whoever controlled the Montagnards controlled the supply lanes of the communist insurgency. The CIA were convinced the highlands held the key to South Vietnam's security.

The Montagnards were polytheistic animists who used animal sacrifices and vested spiritual authority in the local sorcerer, usually a wealthy man. They looked 'incredibly wild', with darker skin than the Vietnamese, 'great tousled mops' of hair and 'craggy' features that 'reinforced the unreasonable, prejudiced conception of savagery'.[11] The Rhade (or 'Ede') were the most numerous. Theirs were matriarchal societies: women owned the property, and a man took his wife's name on marriage. In some Rhade villages, jural authority rested with a senior council of elderly women.[12] That did not diminish the male enthusiasm for fighting, a skill Petersen would soon use to mould the most lethal armed unit in the highlands, his 'Tiger Men'.

A long struggle for independence bound the tribes against a common enemy, the Vietnamese; the tribes yearned for a separate Montagnard nation. They trusted neither Hanoi nor Saigon, but were prepared to join the side that promised them independence. Treated as inferior *moi* (savages), they lost much of their ancestral land to President Diem's hated resettlement program, which forced Vietnamese peasants from the overpopulated pro-communist coastal provinces onto prime Montagnard tribal land. For its part, the Viet Cong proselytised, in attempts to buy Montagnard loyalty. 'The Vietnamese talk equality,' tribesmen told Gerald Hickey, an American scholar, 'but they don't mean what they say … in their hearts they want to dominate us. They are colonialists …'[13] In fact, the Montagnards had traditionally sided with the white man, who treated them relatively well: many village chiefs served as sergeants in the French Army, for example, and Australians and Americans were welcome in many Montagnard villages.

When Petersen arrived, Saigon's policies were rapidly alienating the tribes and driving many towards the Viet Cong, whose propaganda promised 'independence' if the mountain people helped to destroy the southern regime. (Hanoi delivered no such promise after the war, of course, and continues to oppress the mountain people to this day.)

In Petersen, the Montagnards found an unusual mentor: a leader, a friend and a self-styled freedom fighter. He empathised with their dream of independence. He fearlessly 'went native'; toured their villages; engaged in epic rice wine drinking sessions with tribal elders; and more than once gathered up his boots at the home of a village chief and stumbled, retching, into the night to escape a Viet Cong patrol.

His police boys' training began in earnest in April–June 1964. Petersen chose a near-empty Montagnard village called Buon Enao, a former US Special Forces camp a few kilometres east of Ban Me Thuot, as his training centre. He taught his young charges ambush skills, jungle movement, assault, and the use of radio and weapons: light machine guns, carbines and sniper rifles. Mostly obsolete American arms sent by the CIA, they were a vast improvement on the Rhade's traditional spears and booby traps, which included the terrifying 'flying mace', a clay ball covered in bamboo spikes, suspended by a vine.[14]

Impressed by Petersen's progress, Mills authorised the expansion of the force to 350, spurred by growing Viet Cong agitation in the highlands.

Northern infiltration had rapidly increased: at least a thousand insurgents — including many doctors, pharmacists, signallers and teachers — had entered Darlac province since the previous October.[15] Petersen requested help: Warrant Officer Danny Neville, a former member of Australia's SAS Regiment, joined him for two weeks, after which Serong approved the dispatch of a permanent assistant. The first was Warrant Officer Bevan Stokes.

US commanders refused to believe that the Viet Cong was overrunning the highlands. A telling insight into the American military mind at this point was their response to Petersen's secret proposal, sent to Serong and the Covert Action Branch on 1 June 1964, to train a guerrilla resistance force should the highlands fall into communist hands. 'These men are the near perfect nucleus of an anti-communist guerrilla organization,' he wrote of the tribes.[16] The CIA latched on to the assumption, not the point: Petersen 'had a defeatist attitude in thinking that any of South Vietnam might ever fall to Communist North Vietnam', the CIA replied.[17] Yet by mid-1964 Petersen, and not the CIA, had correctly gauged the direction of the highlands war. The Viet Cong was winning because neither South Vietnam nor its US sponsors gave a damn about the tribespeople. On one occasion, when the Viet Cong attacked a Montagnard village, the people pleaded for more ammunition, but the US helicopter supposed to deliver it flew off to help a GI who had cut his finger whittling. By the time the helicopter returned, the village was in flames: 'There was no sign of life below. A village had died,' wrote Petersen. 'It was one of the stupidities of that war … that the inhabitants of a village could be cruelly wiped out because an American had cut his hand, carving a bit of wood.'[18]

Daft CIA ideas seemed to come with the territory. One US officer proposed to train Montagnard deaf mutes, armed with axes and knives, 'to strike terror into the hearts of the Viet Cong'. Petersen told him he was 'creating a monster', and the idea for an army of deaf mutes was quietly shelved.[19] An ex-US Army major, Dorsey Anderson, promoted the idea of training Montagnard civilians as assassins: hairdressers and village health workers by day would become trained killers by night, using Anderson's 'assassination kits'. Dorsey 'is permitted to, and does, allow his imagination to run riot', observed Petersen. The assassins' course failed; on one visit, Petersen found 'a group of students returning from a rifle range; the rest were learning to sing'.[20]

★ ★ ★

On the night of 30 July 1964 Y-Bham Enuol, a respected tribal elder recently released after five years in Diem's prisons, invited Petersen to a buffalo sacrifice and rice wine binge at the village of Buon Ea Dung, to celebrate Y-Bham's freedom. The pair drank a great deal of whisky, wine and beer, well into the night. At one point, the inebriated Montagnard leader told Petersen the true aims of his people: first, to fight against the common enemy, the Viet Cong; and second, 'to work slowly and carefully towards self-control …' (i.e. independence from Vietnam). The evening then degenerated: at '0330 hours' Y-Bham presented his 'daughter' (in fact his niece) to Petersen; the girl was required 'to sit beside the case officer and share the one straw reed of a jar of rice wine'. At '0400 hours', Y-Bham began referring to Petersen as his 'grandfather' and his 'brother', before collapsing.[21]

Far from a serious discussion of Montagnard destiny, the meeting was a drunken parade of dreamy ideals. But it confirmed some things on Petersen's mind: the Montagnards would fight the Viet Cong if they could be shown that communism posed a threat to their survival. 'It was a way of life which would be destroyed … if the Viet Cong should be allowed to prevail.'[22] They must be politically indoctrinated along these lines, Petersen decided. 'In a freedom loving, lazy race, lacking ambition (as are the Montagnard), he must be made to realize that communism offers a threat to his freedom and … will not materially benefit him or his longhouse …'[23]

Yet Petersen also saw the dangerous logic of the plan: it encouraged Montagnard hopes of secession, to which Saigon was strongly opposed; and it cast Petersen in the pivotal role of seeming to foment such aspirations. For now, the young captain set aside these concerns in the pursuit of that elusive quality vital to any military unit: *esprit de corps*.

And he succeeded: by September 1964 Petersen led several hundred devoted warriors, officially called the Truong Son Force (the name for the Annamite Chain). But the Viet Cong dubbed the unit the 'Tiger Men', a nod at its fearsome reputation, and Petersen seized on his troops' notoriety: he ordered tiger-headed beret badges and green berets. The tiger-print uniforms — duly supplied by the CIA — gave substance to his unit's tiger-like notoriety. Drawn by its mystique and dashing fatigues, hundreds of Montagnard youths, aged barely 20, volunteered to join Petersen's unit.

★ ★ ★

Montagnard nationalist aspirations were, of course, stronger than their loyalties to Petersen. A Montagnard revolt against the South had been brewing for months: anti-Vietnamese Chams working for the Cambodian leader Prince Sihanouk's Deuxième Bureau, Cambodia's military intelligence unit, was stirring up hatred of the Saigon regime.

Tensions erupted on 19 September 1964 when Petersen awoke to news of a tribal uprising against the Saigon Government, and dispatched Bevan Stokes to alert Serong. Five Montagnard Special Forces units were threatening to attack Ban Me Thuot, in protest at bad pay, poor conditions and cruel treatment by their South Vietnamese masters. Petersen's Tiger Men were keen to get involved (in the event they did not, due to a communication error). This was not a case of disloyalty, strictly speaking: hadn't Petersen encouraged their fight for independence? Hadn't he supported their cause?

Indeed, the National Director of Police, Ong Binh, and the then province chief, Major Bui Huy Gia (a member of North Vietnam's minority Muong tribal group), held Petersen directly responsible for the rebellious mood — a backhanded compliment to Petersen's influence. '[They] both believed,' he later wrote, 'that I — a foreigner, and a mere army captain at that — had sufficient influence to prevent not only my own Truong Son force from demonstrating, but all the Montagnard.'[24] Petersen was powerless to prevent a Montagnard revolt against the South Vietnamese Government.

On 20 September 3,000 Montagnards marched on Ban Me Thuot, occupied the radio station and blocked all entrances to the city. They shot or cut the throats of nine Vietnamese Special Forces soldiers at the Buon Sarpa base; massacred the South Vietnamese Civil Guard at another post; and executed twelve more Vietnamese soldiers at Buon Mi Gia base in Darlac province. The rebels held American personnel hostage and abducted Y-Bham Enuol, the titular Montagnard leader.

The revolt had serious repercussions for the wider war. 'The central highlands,' wrote Petersen, 'which were the key to the security of South Vietnam, were … ripe for takeover by the Viet Cong.'[25] Immediately, Serong, the new CIA handler Stu Methven, and the Vietnamese II Corps commander, General Nguyen Huu Co, flew in to Ban Me Thuot to negotiate a way through the crisis.

General Co urgently asked Petersen to contact the rebel leaders, in an effort to persuade them to come to Ban Me Thuot and broker a deal. Petersen agreed. It involved a perilous journey, that night, through several rebel-held checkpoints, in pouring rain, to reach the tribal commanders dug in at his fortified village of Buon Enao. At each checkpoint, Petersen and his interpreter proceeded on foot, in the rainswept glare of the jeep's headlights (leaving Serong and an American colonel, Donald Kirsting, in the back seat). It was a deadly business: Petersen survived probably because his Truong Son soldiers recognised him through the downpour. The jeep reached Buon Enao.

In a small earthen-floored thatched hut, Petersen implored the rebel leaders to present their demands to the South Vietnamese General Co back in Ban Me Thuot; he assured them a safe passage. The discussion dragged on. At one point, Serong anxiously drew Petersen aside: 'Barry, you've got to make them agree to come back with us,' to which Petersen protested that he could only persuade, not force them. Serong interpreted this as insubordination: 'Don't you speak to me like that ... I can have you out of this country in twenty-four hours!'[26]

The five Montagnard leaders finally agreed to meet General Co, who received them with courtesy and respect, and promised to implement, or draw to government attention, their list of demands, including the right to own their land and fly their flag, elect a Montagnard representative in the National Assembly and command their own military units; the freedom to administer US aid destined for their villages; and better educational opportunities for their children.

The meeting was a triumph of reconciliation over confrontation. The rebels returned to their villages in peace. Those responsible for the massacres fled to Cambodia, where they joined the communist-backed Front Unifié de Lutte des Race Opprimées (United Struggle Front for the Oppressed Races, or FULRO) to foment further hatred of the Saigon regime.


The construction of a new base, in the Lac Thien district, 40 kilometres south of Ban Me Thuot; aggressive patrolling; re-equipping and training his Armed Propaganda and Intelligence units ... Petersen threw himself into his job in the wake of the revolt. Bevan Stokes personally handled the construction of the new base, deploying elephants to clear the airstrip. Warrant Officers Harry Pope, Larry McGarry and John 'Jock' Roy succeeded Stokes in turn, but these skilled soldiers found themselves ill at ease in a strange world increasingly dominated by Petersen's personality. The Montagnards, it seemed, bestowed their loyalty on one man.

Meanwhile, Viet Cong insurgents launched a wave of terror against Ban Me Thuot. Popular nightspots were bombed. A tiny orphan boy called

Ngoc, well known about town, carried two grenades into a packed bar and detonated himself along with many others. Enemy artillery struck Buon Enao. Many nights, the Viet Cong would haul up a flag outside Petersen's house, and in the morning he would find 'this very salutary reminder from the VC that they ... had his name in the books'.[27]

The Tiger Men responded with sudden, bone-shattering attacks. They turned Viet Cong methods on the Viet Cong. The grisly details revealed the merciless quality of Petersen's 'savages', as they were known in CIA salons. In one attack, Petersen wounded a Viet Cong; a Tiger Man finished off the victim, grinning that his Australian captain should have completed the job properly. In another instance, to Petersen's shock, a young mother dropped her child and cried out in terror when she saw the Australian; she believed Viet Cong propaganda that 'Americans' ate babies. And there were surreal moments, such as the cup of Vietnamese tea Petersen shared with an elderly couple who sat shaking with fear in their hut after an attack by Truong Son forces; outside, the village burned and the bodies of communist suspects littered the red earth.

Such experiences jolted Petersen's nerves, and a demagogic note entered his jottings. Yet, unlike Kurtz's 'Exterminate the brutes!', Petersen's handwriting did not lapse into a hate-filled scrawl; he did not consider himself omnipotent. 'Fire must be fought with fire,' he wrote. 'Communist subversive tactics have proved all too successful during the past decade. Communism could be fought with tactics similar to those used by the communists themselves. Talk and gifts will not necessarily do it ... The Viet Cong is fighting to control the population and thereby control the country. They do this by being forever in the midst of the people ...' He broadened his theme to the whole war: 'How can we Caucasian foreigners ... hope to imbue a cosmopolitan population with a sense of nationalism and a will to fight fellow Vietnamese (misguided as they might be), in a fight for survival against communism (which the majority do not even understand)? ... All we can hope to do, as an emergency measure, in stemming the tide of communism, is to exploit ... those things dear to humans — their racial traits, customs and religion if any.'[28]

He turned to civic action as the most effective form of propaganda. Petersen was among the first to see that the methods of giving aid were more important than aid in itself. 'For example: a school is built in a village ... Initially the villagers are overjoyed ... The Viet Cong or their agents then begin to "sow the seeds of doubt" in the minds of the villagers ... Why does the government provide a school and teacher? ... Is the school provided to enable the "puppet" government to "poison the minds" of the children? Will the children eventually be turned against their own parents?'[29]

His methods worked on their own terms. He shone in Montagnard affections. By June 1965 Petersen enjoyed 'undreamed-of autonomy' to recruit and train the Montagnard and lead them in battle. He commanded nearly 1,200 men, and received unlimited CIA funds, weapons and ammunition. His troops knew him 'warts and all' and were completely loyal, naming him Dam San, after a mythical warrior who challenged the Spirit of the Sun. Village chiefs bearing gifts — beautiful Rhade blankets and a black Rhade jacket and loincloth — humbled themselves before their great white protector ... this junior deity from the Great South Land.

For miles around, Montagnard villagers came with the same request: would Dam San send the Tiger Men to protect them? On condition, Petersen replied, that they send him their young men. 'No other Australian, American or any other Caucasian had quite the same free hand,' wrote Petersen, by now more than a little touched by power. 'Maybe I was only a minor monarch, but I was as close as anyone got to being the absolute ruler of his own little cabbage patch.'[30] His CIA controller, Stu Methven, dubbed him 'Lawrence of the Highlands', initially a compliment but later, given Methven's role in Petersen's demise, derisive.

The first warning of moves against him came during a trip to Melbourne in March 1965. Petersen's reputation preceded him. General Sir Walter Cawthorne, director of the Australian Secret Intelligence Service, invited him to lunch at the Melbourne Club and introduced him to Menzies. Lieutenant General Sir John Wilton, Chief of the General Staff, summoned him for a briefing. Their fascination in his Montagnard adventures satiated, Cawthorne, Wilton and Sir James Plimsoll, permanent secretary of the Department of External Affairs, all asked the young captain the same question: what would be the likely effect of Australian combat troops in Vietnam? It was the first Petersen had heard of this possibility, one that bore the stamp 'Most Secret'.

So far, so gentlemanly — the top people trusted him. Then came the grilling: Arthur Malcolm Morris, a desk officer at External Affairs, shot the first arrow. In a provocative meeting, Morris blamed Petersen for fomenting the Montagnard rebellion, and cited Saigon Government intelligence.

Caught off guard, Petersen stoutly defended himself, and a smiling Morris pronounced himself satisfied with Petersen's account. Yet the episode served as a signal warning: the South Vietnamese President, no less, had warned Canberra of his wish to see Petersen removed.

Back in the highlands, Petersen received early notice of the CIA's decision to relieve him in the form of a visit from the new American ambassador, General Maxwell Taylor. Maxwell applauded Petersen's Tiger Men as the kind of operation 'we should be conducting throughout Vietnam', then quietly wondered to an aide why an American was not capable of doing the job.

Petersen's operation fell apart in mid-1965, at the height of his powers. The CIA and Saigon decided that Petersen's star shone too brightly. The Australian officer had raised an army loyal to himself and not to Saigon. The CIA 'criticised me for not … imbuing the Montagnard with a sense of Vietnamese nationalism,' he wrote. 'I was not doing enough "flag waving" …' Petersen felt that this would only confuse the tribes, but his explanation failed to appease his paymasters.

The CIA decided he was losing touch and out of control. As Tom Donahue, Chief of the CIA's Covert Action Branch, told him later that year, 'You've developed far too much influence with the Montagnard … you've developed a personality cult in the highlands.'[31] Denis Gibbons, who photographed Petersen's last goodbye, said, 'They sacked him because he got outta hand. He became one of the tribes. He was telling the generals to get stuffed.'[32] The CIA resorted to spying on their erstwhile golden boy to support their claims: the Covert Action Branch dispatched a rival agent (whose job was to recruit another assassination — 'counter-terror' — squad); intercepted Petersen's mail and communications; tapped his telephone; and confiscated letters addressed to him by FULRO leaders. Petersen even believed the CIA planned to have him killed, had he not agreed to leave (there is a hint of paranoia in Petersen's story that an Australian chargé d'affaires in Saigon later claimed to have given clearance to a CIA plot to kill him; yet at the time anything seemed possible).

In late July the CIA's Covert Action Branch told Petersen he was being replaced. In fairness to its concerns, Petersen had spent two years in the mountains living in a constant state of extreme tension that would have destroyed a weaker man. Both Brigadier David Jackson, then commanding Australian Force Vietnam, and the Australian Ambassador to Saigon, David Anderson, thought it discreet to leave the role to an American. 'Barry was tired, he was under very great nervous strain,' said Jackson, 'and I felt ... that if he was going to live a useful life ... it was necessary that he came out from there as an individual.'[33]

The sorcerer's chant faded, and Petersen sat up. 'I felt a little foolish lying there like some Eastern potentate while hundreds of eyes were fixed solely upon me.' He laid a bare foot upon a Montagnard axe. 'Blood and rice wine were poured over my foot and a live chicken waved in circles above my head.'[34] Next a procession of his soldiers and their families bearing gifts filed solemnly past their warrior chief: they clasped more than 200 bracelets around his forearm and ten necklaces with amber-like beads around his neck.

The sound of gongs and the low boom of buffalo-hide drums reverberated through the village. 'It was time for me to drink the rice wine.' He drank his required portion through a long straw, then joined hours of drunken revelry — the culmination of two weeks of celebrations, during which 400 Tiger Men paid their last respects. It ended in a feast: three buffaloes were tethered, hamstrung, speared through the heart, butchered and roasted. The blood was drunk raw and the meat eaten amid endless speeches regaling the young Australian.

Petersen thus ended his first tour of duty. Later, as a major, he became a company commander in Phuoc Tuy. He received a Military Cross for his courage in suppressing the Montagnard revolt and the Vietnamese Cross of Gallantry for the 'outstanding success of the Truong Son Force', a unit that attained 'one of the best combat records in Vietnam'.[35] In 1972 the President of the Republic of Vietnam presented him with a lacquer cigar case containing a solid gold presidential seal. Years later, observed Serong, in 1972, Petersen '[was] still remembered by even the most distant tribesman, waiting and hoping for his return'.[36]

# Chapter 11
# 1st Battalion, Royal Australian Regiment

The takeover of South Vietnam would be a direct military threat
to Australia and all the countries of South-East Asia. It must be
seen as part of a thrust by Communist China between the Indian
and Pacific Oceans.
*Sir Robert Menzies, 29 April 1965.*

We ... were looking for a way in and not a way out.
*Menzies on taking Australia to war in Vietnam.*

At 8 p.m. on Thursday, 29 April 1965, Prime Minister Sir Robert
Menzies rose to make a statement. The Lower House of Parliament
was half-empty; the sitting members were immersed in a dreary debate on
tertiary education. Tomorrow a long weekend began. Menzies had given no
advance warning to the House; nor was he obliged to give one except on
occasions of great matters of state. The Labor Opposition leader and deputy
leader, Arthur Calwell and Gough Whitlam, were absent. Only Cabinet and
Washington had seen Menzies' speech before the great white-haired leader,
the longest serving prime minister in Australia's history, stepped up to the
dispatch box.

The Australian Government [he declared] is now in receipt of
a request from the Government of South Vietnam for further

military assistance. We have decided — and this has been in close consultation with the Government of the United States — to provide an infantry battalion for service in Vietnam … [This] decision represents the most useful additional contribution which we can make to the defence of the region at this time. The takeover of South Vietnam would be a direct military threat to Australia and all the countries of South–East Asia. It must be seen as part of a thrust by Communist China between the Indian and Pacific Oceans.[1]

Menzies thus committed Australia's first combat troops to an undeclared war — no leader had publicly spoken of war — in Vietnam. In the public mind, the phoney war was over. True, the Australian Army Training Team, supposedly 'advisers', had seen combat in Vietnam during the past three years (the Australian people were unaware of the extent of their actual involvement). Yet Menzies' decision to send a battalion of infantry soldiers, the basic combat unit, meant we were officially at war, although Canberra had not publicly used the word. War against whom: the Viet Cong? The North Vietnamese? The Chinese? Crucial questions remained unanswered; in fact, Menzies made just one passing 'declaration' of war, in a private speech to the Australia Club on 28 June 1965. Reinvoking his vision of a 'communist tide' washing into the Timor Sea, Menzies said, 'Gentlemen, we're at war, don't let's make any mistake about it.'[2]

Menzies, Paul Hasluck, Minister for External Affairs, and Shane Paltridge, Minister for Defence, had announced the decision to send combat troops at a Cabinet meeting on 17 December 1964, after a recommendation from the Australian chiefs of staff. That recommendation reflected neither the views of most senior commanders nor those of senior officials in the Defence Department, most of whom, for various reasons, disagreed with the decision. Menzies' unfortunate remark, 'a thrust by communist China' — taken out of context from a paper by Sir James Plimsoll, Secretary of the Department of External Affairs — gave the impression 'that Australia was intervening in Vietnam in order to meet a direct military threat from China'.[3] This grave hostage to fortune was a gross distortion of the Defence Department's assessment of threat. The department had argued, in several Strategic Basis papers between 1956 and 1963, that Australia's greatest threats lay closer to home — such as in Indonesia and Malaya/Malaysia. Menzies, however, with the strong approval of successive Ministers for External

Affairs, chiefly Hasluck, forced the department to rewrite its recommendations to embrace a more distant threat from China.

'Political considerations overrode thinking in the Department of Defence,' concluded an excoriating history of the department. '[Its recommendations] did not influence government thinking so much as reflect it.' Defence had been steadily 'emasculated' and failed to offer any strategic direction: 'In the continuing series of crises in the 1960s, the opinion of the department was too often ignored … Politicians made the key decisions …'[4]

Indeed, this was going to be a politicians' war, in the purest sense. Senior advisers had warned repeatedly of the folly of sending combat troops to Vietnam; their words had fallen like autumn leaves. The most senior dissenting voice was Hasluck's departmental head, Sir Arthur Tange — known as the 'last Mandarin' — who remained bitter thirty years later about Hasluck's failure to represent his cautionary warnings to Cabinet. Another, particularly acerbic critic was Gregory Clark, who had worked on the China desk. Fluent in Mandarin and Russian, with a degree from Oxford University, Clark took a close interest in Vietnam, and believed Menzies had grossly overstated the Chinese threat.[5] Clark persuasively argued against the idea, prevalent in Cabinet, that Hanoi and the National Liberation Front were the creatures of Peking. Not all of Clark's views on China were sound, but this last observation had substance. No doubt Hanoi was anxious to obtain Chinese supplies, troops and arms, but that did not mean it was an appendage of Mao's regime. Nobody listened. The austere political orthodoxy of the times shut down the oxygen of debate. Clark eventually resigned in disgust.[6]

The military's most emphatic voice in pressing for ground troops was Air Marshal Sir Frederick Scherger, chairman of the Chiefs of Staff Committee, who led the Australian delegation to the Honolulu Conference, a meeting of the US leadership in June 1964, to define a strategy for Vietnam in the wake of Diem's death. 'He exceeded his brief and virtually offered his US counterparts a battalion before any final political decision.'[7] In the end, however, Menzies, Hasluck and Paltridge decided on the troop commitment, with no debate. The trio went into Cabinet, 'to make the most important decision of their lives, with their minds made up'.[8] A fine example, indeed, of Thucidydes's remark that leaders tended to shoot first and debate later.

At the time, in the view of most Australians, there *was* a case for the troops' dispatch, as a demonstration to our US allies of Australia's willingness jointly to resist communist aggression in Asia. Menzies could hardly demand that America send forces to Vietnam without a concomitant (if not proportionate) effort from Australia. On this issue, Menzies' hawks outdid LBJ's hawks. Yet, in surely the most unconvincing performance of his illustrious parliamentary career, Menzies gravely mishandled the dispatch of the first Australian combat troops.

The events leading to the troop decision provoked claims that Menzies had deceived Parliament.[9] Saigon had neither invited nor requested Australian ground troops — ran the charge — yet Menzies presented his decision as though he were answering a desperate plea for help. Menzies 'requested the request'.[10] Or, alternatively, 'The Australian government was determined that troops should go even if the South Vietnamese did not want them and had to be coerced into taking them …'[11] Yet the story is not so simple; the truth, as always, was elusive, subtle, and as many layered as an onion.

True, the Saigon Government of Prime Minister Phan Huy Quat in 1965 was reluctant to request Australian military help, with good reason. Quat was a member of the Dai Viet (the Vietnamese Nationalist Party), and had deep misgivings about using foreign soldiers; their presence handed the communist forces a propaganda dream: '[The South Vietnamese] were highly sensitive to VC propaganda … portraying them as under US domination,' said one assessment.[12] Nor did Quat have much faith in foreign troops' ability to 'winkle out terrorists among the 14 million people in South Viet-Nam', as Rusk told Harold Holt, then Australian Treasurer, in Washington on 28 April 1965.[13]

In short, Quat had to be coerced into accepting an Australian battalion. Yet Quat was merely one of a succession of leaders of the Republic of Vietnam, all of whom Canberra had dealt with. Tran Van Huong, Prime Minister from November 1964 to January 1965, *had* requested Australian ground troops; President Nguyen Khanh wrote to thirty-four countries on 25 July 1964 pleading for military help; and earlier President Ngo Dinh Diem had appealed to ninety-three non-communist countries, including Australia, for urgent military intervention. In this light, it is misleading to claim that Saigon had no need of, or wish for, Australian troops simply because Quat hoped to limit foreign flags in Vietnam to the Stars and Stripes. Nor is it fair to accuse the Australian Government of being 'totally indifferent to the aims and expectations of the South Vietnamese'.[14] The prospect of losing the republic genuinely troubled some Australian ministers, chiefly Hasluck and Holt, who took a close personal interest in the fate of the South.


Prising a request for Australian troops out of Quat proved to be a white-knuckle ride in Canberra. As late as 12 April 1965 — little over a fortnight before Menzies' troop statement — neither Saigon, nor in fact America, had formally requested an Australian battalion. Thus, Menzies' first priority was getting an *American* request; Saigon's request was considered a formality. With this in mind, Keith Waller, Australia's ambassador to Washington, arranged a special meeting with Secretary of State Dean Rusk on 13 April. He cabled Canberra with the result:[15] 'I ASKED RUSK WHETHER I COULD INFORM THE AUSTRALIAN GOVERNMENT THAT IT WAS THE PRESIDENT'S DESIRE THAT AUSTRALIA SHOULD SUPPLY A BATTALION FOR USE IN SOUTH VIETNAM ... RUSK SAID THAT I COULD SO INFORM YOU AND THAT ... THE SOONER THE BATTALION WAS SUPPLIED THE BETTER.'[16]

That bit was easy. Now came the hard part: far from a formality, getting Saigon to accept our troops seemed as painful as extracting teeth from a tiger. Three days before Menzies' scheduled statement, the Saigon Government 'had not even agreed to the proposal of Australian troops, let alone made a formal request'.[17] Waller urged the US State Department to put pressure on Quat, who merely made positive noises.

The day before Menzies rose to speak, a sense of panic gripped elements of the government: news of the battalion's dispatch had leaked to the press, provoking a storm of protest from the ALP. On Wednesday night, UPI wires had picked up a long article by Alan Reid about the imminent dispatch of Australian ground troops.

Menzies found himself in an extremely tight fix. He had not yet received a request from Saigon for the very troops whose commitment to Vietnam had been revealed in the Australian press. As diplomats harried Quat for the vital cable, Menzies saw a way out of the deepening crisis. It lay in a letter from President Johnson, a swiftly drafted thank-you note for Australia's military support: 'Dear Mr Prime Minister,' the President had written, 'I am delighted by the decision of your Government to provide an infantry battalion for service in South Vietnam at the request of the Government of South Vietnam ...'[18] LBJ thus referred to a request that had not been received; yet for Menzies this was a diplomatic green light. If the President of the United States decided that a Vietnamese request existed, then one assuredly did, or *would*. Menzies quoted the letter in full in his statement to the House.

Quat never did, in fact, formally request an Australian battalion. He verbally accepted Australia's *offer* of a battalion. Hours before Menzies rose to address the House, Canberra received a cable from the Australian ambassador to Saigon stating that Quat had verbally accepted the 'announcement tomorrow evening by Australian Prime Minister of decision to provide battalion at Vietnamese request'. This arrived at 5.10 p.m., on the 29th, three hours before Menzies spoke. Quat's 'written request' for Australian troops arrived the next day. It was merely an acceptance of the Australian offer of troops, sent in reply to the embassy: 'Dear Mr Ambassador,' Quat wrote, 'I have the honor to refer to your letter of today's date [29 April 1965] *confirming the Australian Government's offer to send to Viet Nam an infantry battalion of 800 men … I wish to confirm my government's acceptance of this offer and to request the dispatch of this force to Viet Nam*.'[19]

In this sense, Menzies had misled Parliament: he implied that he had received a written request from Saigon when Canberra had received nothing of the sort (Quat's letter was not revealed until late 1971, when the leaked Pentagon Papers forced its release). Yet it seems that Menzies, bolstered by President Johnson's letter, genuinely believed a written request *would* be forthcoming. Thus fortified, he presented the troop decision as an urgent response to a non-existent plea for military help. He acted throughout without consulting Parliament, his advisers in the Departments of Defence or External Affairs, or the people. He offered no serious consideration of alternatives, nor an exit strategy. 'We … were looking for a way in and not a way out,' he later said.[20]

The Australian press, with one exception, strongly backed the government's commitment. Cartoonists' huge hammering fists and red tides may have mocked the threat; but the *Sydney Morning Herald*, *The Age*, *The Sun* and the Melbourne *Herald* all supported the government's line on the red scourge. This 'grave and heavy' decision, intoned the *Sydney Morning Herald*, committed Australian troops to a 'hard and bitter struggle' that was 'right and indeed inevitable'. The newspaper shared Menzies' vision of a 'downward thrust': '… what is being defended here is … the security of all South-East

Asia. It cannot be too often or too strongly emphasised that if South Vietnam is allowed to fall to Communism, then the extension of Communist influence down through the Malay Peninsula to the shores of Australia is inevitable.'[21] *The Age* conflated the troop decision with a global war against China: '... the conflict ... between Communist China and the West in South-East Asia has been joined ... There was no alternative but to respond as we have.'[22] And veteran reporter Denis Warner wrote of 'the gravest decision this country has taken since we joined Britain at war with Nazi Germany'. The *Australian Financial Review* praised this 'unambiguous expression of Australian solidarity with the United States'.[23]

*The Bulletin* applauded without reservation the policy of forward defence and warned of a direct threat to Australian lives from Chinese-sponsored communism: '... it has been plain to the whole world that South Vietnam is Australia's frontline and that the South Vietnamese have been fighting and dying for what are Australia's interests as much as their own. Since the loss of that country to the Communists would inevitably be followed by the Communisation of the rest of South-East Asia, Australia had no alternative but to contribute ... to its defence.'[24]

Only one newspaper dissented. Under the headline, 'The War That Can't Be Won', Rupert Murdoch's new national paper, *The Australian*, unequivocally condemned the decision as 'wrong' and 'reckless': 'It is wrong because it deliberately and coldly runs counter to the mounting wave of international anxiety about the shape of the Vietnam War ...' The writer, Douglas Brass, a close friend of the Murdochs, concluded: 'Australia has lined up her generations against the hatred and contempt of resurgent Asian peoples — without adding one iota of confidence or strength to the tragically embroiled American nation. It could be that our historians will recall this day with tears.' In his leader the next day, Brass accused Menzies of showing 'contempt for public opinion'.[25]

The new medium of television helped to sell the war; by June 1964 two million Australians held viewers' licences. 'The box' played to Menzies' strengths: alongside the doddery Calwell, the Prime Minister appeared statesmanlike, and he used the television to great effect. Broadcasters generally supported the troop decision; 'the telly' played up a popular story. By the time the troops sailed, Menzies' Cabinet bathed in the warm glow of public approbation and nearly all the media's unblinking support. Most Australian journalists shared the fears of the Saigon correspondent of the *New York Times*, who could write, as late as mid-1964, that if South Vietnam fell, close to 115 million people were at risk of communist takeover in South-East Asia.[26] In short, even if the Fourth Estate later 'lost' the Vietnam War, as many contend, the press certainly played a useful hand in starting it.

The ALP condemned the decision. In the finest speech of his career Calwell valiantly, if quixotically, argued against the dispatch of troops. The Labor leader's speech on 4 May 1965 accurately prophesied the 'new policy' of conscription, briefly unified the ALP and momentarily arrested Calwell's relentless, if defiant, slide into soapbox obscurity. Yet it had fatal flaws that exposed him to an eloquent savaging from Menzies, the master of parliamentary debate.

> How long will it be [Calwell declared] before we are drawing
> upon our conscript youth to service these growing and endless
> requirements? Does the government now say that conscripts will
> not be sent? ... If the Government now says that conscripts will
> not be sent, this means that the First Battalion is never to be
> reinforced, replaced or replenished. If this is not so, then the
> Government must have a new policy on the use of conscripts —
> a policy not yet announced ... There is now a commitment of
> 800. As the war drags on, who is to say that this will not go to
> 8,000, and that these will not be drawn from our vote-less,
> conscripted 20-year-olds?

He ended with a curse: 'To the members of the Government, I say only this: if, by the process of misrepresentation of our motives, in which you are so expert, you try to further divide this nation for political purposes, yours will be a dreadful responsibility, and you will have taken a course which you will live to regret ...'[27]

Calwell's prayerful denunciation set no plan of action, no sign of how and when a Labor Government might withdraw the troops. It thus confused the party and the public. Just how was the decision to be reversed? Calwell merely made a lame appeal to the United Nations to resolve the conflict. Most confusingly, he affected to support the American presence in Vietnam: America 'must not be humiliated and must not be forced to withdraw [from Vietnam]', he said.[28] This collided in the public mind with his opposition to Australia's commitment: why should America send ground troops, and not us? Why had America dispatched a mighty army across the Pacific to fight in Vietnam if no threat to Australia existed? Two days later Gough Whitlam, the Deputy Leader of the Opposition, deepened the confusion. In a broad echo of Calwell's themes, Whitlam strongly supported the American alliance: 'America's motives in South Vietnam are above dispute.'[29] Australian troops, he added, would be better deployed in Malaysia or Indonesia.

Menzies' response slashed at the ALP's most vulnerable place — its dubious support for America — like a verbal rapier. 'I would hate to be,' Menzies ended, 'the head of a government which had to say to the United States on an occasion like this: "Sorry, we can do nothing about it. We will help you with debate in the United Nations … But, as for practical action, No. That is for you" … I think that is a disastrous proposition for any Opposition to put forward.'

As the emotional power of his words faded, Calwell's argument seemed to sag and the man seemed hollow. He sought noble refuge in unpopularity. He failed to play to the circus, as he himself admitted: 'I cannot promise you that easy popularity can be bought in times like these; nor are we looking for it …' Menzies leaped on this admission, with all the 'courtly brutality'[30] for which he was renowned. Calwell had struck a 'pathetic note', Menzies said, 'when he turned to his own people and said metaphorically and literally: "We will be unpopular but we will stick to it … we are ready to suffer in an unpopular cause!"' He concluded: 'I have not the slightest doubt that … we … are on the side of the great majority. If I may end on a horrible political note, it is a good thing occasionally to be in a big majority.'

A strong majority of Australians initially supported Menzies' troop decision and the war. A fortnight later 64 per cent of Australians said they believed the claim that communism, left unchecked, would overrun South-East Asia, and an extraordinary 72 per cent reckoned China directly endangered Australia, according to a Morgan Gallup Poll.[31] 'We can't let the Americans do all our fighting' and 'It's the continuation of the ANZAC spirit' were common remarks, in a survey by *The Australian* in June 1965. 'It's better to let [the Australian troops] go than let the Chinese come here,' said a Brisbane woman. A Canberra mother, with an 18-year-old son, said: 'Let's fight this away from Australia, and try to keep the war from our shores.' Taking the war to the perceived enemy at a distant frontline — safely beyond Australian shores — had popular backing.

There were dissenting voices, however, and not only in the Australian Labor Party. One veteran of the Great War told *The Australian*: 'This is no good. Before we get into more hot water this killing in Vietnam must be stopped.'[32] The nascent anti-war movement protested that conscripts may be sent to Vietnam, and a small minority targeted the troops. Anonymous anti-war protesters sent hostile pamphlets and made abusive phone calls to the soldiers' families.[33]

The decision enraged the militant unions, who swiftly condemned Australia's new combat role in Vietnam. Such was their power at the time that the union leaders saw themselves as somehow duty bound to offer political opinions that had nothing to do with their members' working conditions. Of course, the most hardline, chiefly the Waterside Workers' Federation and the Seamen's Union, had a heavy political agenda: they were strongly influenced or controlled by communists who had been brought in from the cold.

On 3 May 1965 the Waterside Workers' Federation demanded nation-wide strikes in protest at the troop commitment. The Australian Council of Trade Unions, the peak union body, declined the unions' demands, consistent with the ALP's policy of being seen to support the troops, if not the war. Yet the proposed action portended the successive strikes to come, and continued a long and ignominious left-wing tradition in Australia of striking in wartime. During World War II waterside unions had refused to load transport ships bound for Papua, compelling the soldiers to do the job, and in 1965 the Seamen's Union shunned two US Navy ships then in Australia to commemorate the defeat of the Japanese at the Battle of the Coral Sea.

The unions were a broad church, however. The Federated Iron Workers' Union, for example, praised the American alliance and supported the fight against communist aggression. The war fractured other unions: 'Howling and screaming and jumping around' best described a meeting on Vietnam of the Victorian branch of the Australian Railways Union, during which fist fights erupted between those in favour of and those opposed to the war. Chairs were put through the windows, and no resolutions passed.

One line of attack that particularly incensed Menzies was the claim that Australia's military support for America was nothing but a 'blood for dollars' or 'diggers for dollars' deal, as many unionists and ALP members claimed (although Calwell resisted joining this attack). The callous charge reflected 'only the murky recesses of the minds of the people who made it', Menzies growled. If so, many Australian minds were decidedly murky. The people could be forgiven for thinking that Treasurer Harold Holt's trip to Washington to press the national interest on behalf of Australian exporters — at the same time as the troop decision — was hardly a coincidence. (Yet, if extracting more dollars had been his intention, Holt failed: the USA would open very few new markets to Australian exporters during the war years.)

On 26 May, in the dead of night, the first Australian combat troops to go to Vietnam were trucked from Holsworthy Barracks to Sydney Harbour. The 1st Battalion's commanding officer, Lieutenant Colonel Ivan 'Lou' Brumfeld, 38, a sharp-minded graduate of Duntroon, had been alerted three months earlier to his mission — an immense challenge, in so short a time. Political sensitivities dictated that he prepare his men in strictest secrecy. Many felt like accomplices in a clandestine, nocturnal operation. 'They snuck us out like mongrel dogs,' said Private Bill Crombie, a Scot, whose father had been killed in World War II. 'The trucks were all buttoned down; there were military police everywhere.'[34] Wives and lovers were kept away; there were no emotional farewells at the docks. The extreme secrecy expressed the slight paranoia of a government that placed the gagging of a few protesters ahead of the expression of genuine, popular support for the commitment.

At 1.39 a.m., on 27 May 1965, a company of the 1st Battalion, Royal Australian Regiment, drew away from Garden Island wharf aboard the converted British aircraft carrier HMAS *Sydney* (formerly christened HMS *Terrible*). They were accompanied by 1 Troop, A Squadron, Prince of Wales Light Horse armoured troop and a logistics unit, along with journalists Pat Burgess (*Sydney Morning Herald*), Alan Ramsey (AAP), Maurie Wilmott (*Daily Mirror*), Mayo Hunter (ATN 7) and Stuart MacGladrie (AAP); later Graham Connolly, Don Petersen, Creighton Burns and Gerald Stone joined or replaced them, in the first wave of the media stampede. (Garry Barker was one of the first Australian journalists to arrive in Vietnam, in 1962.)[35]

The troopship slid out of the harbour using only its navigation lights. A soldier's wife, who tearfully watched it leave the Heads, told a reporter, 'There they go; now we begin the letter writing.'[36] Another wife lay in hospital, expecting their baby 'any minute' as her 21-year-old husband sailed to war. John Eaton, on sentry duty on the deck, witnessed the craggy brow of North Head slip away in the shimmering moonlight: 'We were all so excited, so impressionable … the mood was like the Australian Rugby Team heading overseas for a test match.'[37]

★ ★ ★

'You Go to an Unjust War!' screamed a thirty-foot banner draped over the sandstone cliffs, near the mouth of Sydney Harbour.[38] Intended for the eyes of the soldiers on deck, the banner was the handiwork of the Women's International League for Peace and Freedom (WILPF), a communist-influenced organisation founded in 1915 (then named the Sisterhood of International Peace).

WILPF's members were among the early foot soldiers of the anti-war 'movement'. The word tends to misrepresent its coherence. The early anti-war protesters formed, in fact, a motley collection of small groups, of broadly left-wing sympathies, from all social groups and ages. Consider WILPF: in 1965–66, a group of well-heeled matrons from Sydney's most elegant suburbs ran its New South Wales branch. They included Miss Gladys Armstrong, of Mosman; Mrs Muriel Briot, of Mosman; Mrs Erskine Levick of Vaucluse; and Mrs Marjorie Mason, of Castlecrag. The president was Mrs Betty Gale, of Cremorne.[39] The ladies angrily rejected newspaper reports claiming that communists controlled their organisation. They were not alone: the Campaign for Nuclear Disarmament, the Association for International Co-operation and Disarmament, the Australian Peace Council, Women for Peace, Another Mother For Peace, the Union of Australian Women, Save Our Sons, and Christian Women Concerned were all, at one time or another, cast as communist fronts.

Yet undeniably a Marxist imp sat on the shoulders of many of these organisations. A mildly comic irony was that nice middle-class women had unwittingly given the Communist Party of Australia a new lease of life. On the other hand, many protesters were unfairly tainted throughout the war: for example, members of Save Our Sons, founded by Joyce Golgerth in May 1965, in general protested out of moral conviction and concern for the young men. They wore blue-and-white sashes to identify their mission.

In early June, as the *Sydney* sailed north, a small reconnaissance party led by Major John Essex-Clark flew to Saigon. They disembarked at Singapore in civilian clothes, which fooled nobody, then changed into their army uniforms on the plane. In Saigon, they prepared for the battalion's arrival, by sea and air.

The 1st Battalion were regular, professional soldiers, most of whom had served in Malaya, and who 'did not think much about the politics of their deployment'; it was simply 'another job against the Asian Communist'.[40] On the *Sydney*, they participated in strenuous training exercises, daily target practice (shooting at balloons or empty beer cans), and played volleyball and deck hockey. There were movies and a 'Cross the Line' party. Padre Gerry Cudmore delivered fifty hours of lectures on the primacy of religion and the evil of communism. He put 'the fear of God and the fear of Communism' into them, according to one recollection.[41]

A US Navy patrol boat met the ship in Vung Tau Harbour, in the Republic of Vietnam, at 6 a.m., on 10 June. Among ten American soldiers on board was Private Don Dali, of the 173rd Airborne Brigade. 'We arrived alongside at the break of dawn,' Dali recalled. 'We were greeted with cheers. The Aussies gathered all around us asking lots of questions. We showed them how our weapons worked … they offered all of us their rations of beer. Not wanting to offend anyone … we obliged.'[42] Landing craft were lowered over the ship's side and cargo nets dropped. As the troops approached the shore, the stench of rotting vegetation and excrement assailed their nostrils. Within minutes they were 'in country', standing on the beach. And as they gazed about the 'funny country', the first intimations of revulsion — towards a society crippled by poverty and disease, in the grip of a war on the verge of being lost — played upon their thoughts.

Major Essex-Clark (later Brigadier, DSM), a great, leonine officer with a rugby forward's physique and a ready opinion on his mustachioed lips, had been busy preparing for the first operations. He drew largely on his experiences in Malaya: 'I used my imagination, current readings, old books and my experience in UW [unconventional warfare].' Essex-Clark was a battle-hardened veteran of thirteen years' experience; he'd served with the Rhodesian Light Infantry, fighting guerrillas in Rhodesia and the Belgian Congo, and with the 17th Gurkha Division in Malaya. 'I spent many a long night,' he said, 'studying, inter alia, Tanham's *Communist Revolutionary Warfare*, Praeger's *The Guerrilla and How to Fight Him*, Fall's *Street Without Joy*, the British *ATOM* [*Anti-Terrorist Operations — Malaya*] …'[43] But written doctrine meant little after the first shots were fired, he wrote. The point, he noted, was to know the enemy's tactics, to get inside his head.[44]

# Chapter 12
# The Iron Triangle

We should have stayed there and fought the VC to a standstill,
but using our Australian tactics. God I feel down …
*Corporal Lex McAulay, after OPERATION IRON TRIANGLE.*

'Welcome Australians' and 'Long Live Australian-Vietnamese Anti-Communist Spirit' read the Vietnamese signs at the gates of the Bien Hoa airbase, in May 1965. Uncomfortably, these signs were erected before the Australian 1st Battalion had officially been told its destination, lending an eerie sensation that it was being watched.

The diggers entered a strange and terrible world. The great clanking monster of the American war machine, sandbagged, wired and fortified, rose amid the old rice paddy and rubber plantations 25 kilometres north of Saigon near the nondescript provincial capital of Bien Hoa (literally 'Land of Peaceful Frontiers'). Bien Hoa's northern frontier was anything but peaceful: it encroached on the jungles of War Zone D and the dreaded Iron Triangle, an area bristling with Viet Cong troops.

The Australians were attached to the US 173rd Airborne Brigade and operated under American command. As such, they were a very small cog in the vast US military machine. In May 1965, 50,000 American combat troops were in country; by December a further 150,000 would arrive. And that was just the beginning. By comparison, Australia then fielded one infantry battalion, of whom 600 were combat troops; 80 advisers (the Team); a 73-man air force unit equipped with six Caribou planes; an 8-man surgical team; a group of civil engineers; and a few dairy and signals experts.

The 173rd Brigade was an elite parachute regiment of about 3,500 troops, flown in from Japan in May; they claimed the title of 'toughest fighting men in Okinawa, if not the entire US Armed Forces'.[1] The 173rd, nicknamed the 'Sky Soldiers', chose the music from the TV series *Rawhide* as its theme song. When saluting, the paratroopers bellowed, 'ALL THE WAY, SIR!' to which their officers yelled back, 'AIRBORNE!' They were a 'get in quick, do the job, then get out' unit, the perfect answer to Westmoreland's 'find, fix and finish' strategy of defeating the enemy in quick time. When Major John Essex-Clark arrived, in July 1965, Brigadier General Ellis 'Butch' Williamson, the 173rd's commander, told him, 'Once the Cong feel the mobility, cold steel and fire-power of airborne soldiers, the war will be over. We'll be back in Okinawa by Christmas.' The Americans were passing through, on 'Temporary Duty', and the signs were everywhere, right down to the US soldier's habit of 'indiscriminate defecation', observed Essex-Clark.[2]

Yet here, under a roasting sun, the Americans were building a huge airfield that would eventually sustain a small city. It was 'a high-tech hornets' nest dropped into a quiet, green landscape'.[3] The Australians' job was to help secure the airfield and the surrounding area, in readiness for the arrival of 11,000 troops of the US 1st Infantry Division, the 'Big Red One'. Williamson warned his men that 'any successful attack on Bien Hoa airbase … will result in extreme embarrassment to US and Australian Forces'.[4]

Essex-Clark and Williamson disagreed at once about where to deploy the Australian troops. Their disagreement set the tone for a deeper conflict of military cultures. The American commander, 'a lean, silver-haired, devoutly religious, fiercely anti-communist officer',[5] favoured a small patch of young rubber, which Essex-Clark dismissed as indefensible and virtually uninhabitable. Instead, he recommended a wide 'prairie' on the eastern flank, with a four-mile defensive arc.

The allies worked to an exhausting schedule: 'In a few days,' records a 173rd Brigade history, 'thousands of sandbags were filled, miles of wire laid, forests cleared, and acres of stump blown.'[6] The monsoon started. Every afternoon the rains pelted down and reduced everything to a soup of red mud. The troops lived in sandbagged tents; rubble, empty ammunition boxes, jerry cans and a melange of other stuff littered the hastily dug lines. The encroaching vegetation was 'charred and twisted into grotesque shapes' from continual attempts to burn and defoliate it.[7] Latrines were mere holes in the ground. Over this putrid Gomorrah the Phantoms roared and the Hueys bore down, amid the background chatter of machine guns and semi-automatic weapons, all resolved by night in the pop and crump of mortar and artillery. Attempts were made to 'beautify' the place with banana trees, aluminium huts and recreation halls, and in the violet evenings some troops watched John Wayne movies under the stars.

'Boy, what a hole of a place this is,' Corporal Ron Kelly wrote to his wife, Dinane, on 10 June 1965. 'Boy it is stinking hot … I love you and miss you so very very much and want you so very much … all my love and kisses Ron xxxxxxxxxxxxxxxxx.' On 16 July he wrote: '… we sit up every night and listen to Hanoi Hanna as we call her. She is like old Tokyo Rose … She refers to us as Australian mercenaries and would like the addresses of our wives … so they can write to get you all to explain to us we are no good … She said last night that 150 Yanks were killed and 1,000-odd wounded … in one small attack from the Vietnam Freedom Fighters. Oh!! Hell she is a real laugh!'[8]


The 173rd Brigade swiftly carved out a foothold in a country under siege. By mid-1965 the Viet Cong was on the verge of overrunning the South. Every week Saigon received news of the annihilation of a South Vietnamese company or battalion (about 350 men). On 11 May the communist forces captured the capital of Phuoc Long province and mauled a Ranger battalion, killing five out of forty US advisers. On 11 June the enemy destroyed a South Vietnamese airborne regiment and killed or wounded its twenty American advisers. Acts of Viet Cong terrorism against civilians peaked in 1965: 1,895 were assassinated and 12,778 kidnapped.[9]

The National Liberation Front exploited lax security to build a lethal intelligence network. Its spies steadily infiltrated the South Vietnamese Army; indeed, many Vietnamese soldiers were 'two-timing' in both armies, chiefly in the area of Ben Cat. A young platoon commander, Second Lieutenant Clive Williams, an Englishman who joined the Australian Army eighteen months earlier, wrote to his parents that 'Viet Cong or sympathisers' comprised 10 per cent of all uniformed Vietnamese.[10] And that was inside the American airbase.

The civilian population harboured unknown numbers of enemy sympathisers: their bicycle-borne scouts were faster transmitters of intelligence than foot soldiers or trucks, observed Lieutenant Colonel Lou Brumfield at the time. US forces employed Vietnamese cooks, cleaners and clerks within their lines — many of whom had NLF links. One cavalry unit even retained the services of a brothel within their base, and 'enemy women cadre' were reported to be acting as waitresses in American snack bars armed with 'Red China-made poison', according to one US intelligence assessment: 'This applies to all bars in Bien Hoa ...'[11] Bien Hoa was, unwittingly, 'one of the few army camp towns in the world that successfully caters for two opposing armies at the same time'.[12] For their part, the more cautious Australians refused to admit any Vietnamese labour within their small base at Bien Hoa.

All Vietnamese civilians — including children — were treated as suspects: '... be on the look out for strange or unusual behaviour of Vietnamese citizens — e.g. children going into their homes as you come by,' stressed a US Intelligence Bulletin.[13] Bar girls leaving early signalled an imminent attack, according to the South Vietnamese National Police.[14] Taxi drivers would not approach the base four hours before a Viet Cong attack.

Nor were US and Australian radio signals secure. On several occasions the enemy intercepted signals of brigade operations.[15] The security breaches went far deeper: Essex-Clark and Captain Alan Thompson discovered in October, to their shock, that a unit of South Vietnamese troops actually appeared to be coordinating Viet Cong actions: by day, the 7th ARVN regiment were loyal to Saigon; by night they were loyal to the Viet Cong.[16]

In this tense atmosphere, the slightest provocation drew an instant and deadly reaction. Overkill became the norm. When the US forces received, on 29 June, unconfirmed reports of Viet Cong boats on the Song Be River, they responded with 'napalm, rockets and 750-pound bombs'.[17] In a designated killing zone (later called Free Fire Zones), anything that moved tended to be 'taken out', including farm animals. The Viet Cong exploited the Americans' trigger-happy tendency by deliberately attacking from the cover of civilian hamlets. The logic was simple: excessive US retaliation destroyed the people's villages; the civilian survivors, if they were neutral or pro-American before the attack, were certainly Viet Cong after it.

At dugout level, the Aussies and Yanks struck up lasting friendships. The two armies laughed at each other's oddities: 'The Yanks here wear really gaudy uniforms with great big badges — they have no idea of soldiering, they look like Christmas trees ...,' wrote one officer.[18] The Americans, in their starched fatigues and caps, mocked the grimy diggers in their baggy jungle greens and floppy bush hats. They look dressed for a safari, not a war, Butch Williamson reckoned. The diggers were poorly paid, too: two and a half days' leave for every month served in the theatre; tax concessions of up to £270 per year; and a tiered 'Vietnam Allowance', starting at seven shillings and sixpence per day for privates. Australian troops then stationed in Malaysia received twice the allowance, and the Americans four different allowances. Australian conditions soon improved but never matched US levels.[19]

The Australian lines were ragged, almost primitive beside the slick Americans'. Corporal Trevor Hagan's platoon slept in a graveyard on the first night. The diggers' tents were wretched World War II contraptions with flammable coatings; the troops used Raven Oil to soften and waterproof their old boots. The Australian kit, dating from the 1940s, was falling apart at the seams: on 10 July Brumfield made the point by ripping apart a tattered shirt in front of Dr Jim Forbes, Minister for the Army. The story reached reporter Alan Ramsey, whose dispatch — headlined 'Diggers' uniform "rotten"' — deeply embarrassed the government. Nor did a diplomats' questionnaire, sent to the diggers in error, ease Canberra's discomfort: it requested details of the frontline troops' expenditure … on wine and dinner jackets.

If the diggers and the GIs hit it off, the higher ranks were less compatible. Many senior Australian commanders — Brumfield and, when illness sent him home, his successor Lieutenant Colonel Alex Preece — felt deep unease about the US strategy of attrition, which was so alien to the Australian experience of counter-revolutionary war in Malaya. They also shunned US or South Vietnamese interrogators as 'we found their methods to be too brutal', remarked Essex-Clark.[20]

Many Australian officers took particular exception to the 'body count' by which US commanders measured the progress of attrition. The tally of 'kills' scarcely reflected the level of village security or rural support for Saigon, the Australians felt. Even on its own terms, body count was failing. The Americans routinely exaggerated the kill total; for example, after a heavy battle near the Dong Nai River, on 6–9 July, Williamson enthused: 'The toll we extracted … was fantastic. We killed 56 Viet Cong by body count and at least 150 more by estimation … Probably over 200 more were wounded. We destroyed well over 300 buildings, 100 tons of rice, numerous domestic animals … In short we literally tore up one of the Viet Cong's best battalion size organizations … I am proud of all of us. Keep up the good work.'[21]

Lieutenant Williams, whose platoon participated in this action, witnessed a different outcome: '… in this op,' he wrote in July, 'most of the VC escaped … The US "estimates" are usually greatly overestimated …' The Americans would never admit failure, he added, citing the example of Alpha Company of the Airborne 1/503rd Battalion, who walked into an ambush. Thirteen Americans died, and thirty-three were wounded: 'They got no VC bodies and claimed 35 kills, it really annoys me.' Williams questioned the US arithmetic, not the strategic (or moral) case for the body count. Like many Australian officers, he had no choice but to join the 'body count' race: 'We only claim when we get bodies, the Yanks claim when they can produce nothing,' he told his parents. '[The Americans] are obsessed about keeping the kill ratio at 3 to 1 in their favour. Ours is at present 4 to 1 …'[22]

Notwithstanding the exaggerations, the American and Australian units published a daily 'Viet Cong Body Count Scoreboard', which tallied enemy 'Killed in Action', 'Prisoners Captured', 'Weapons Captured' and so on. Platoons competed for the highest score. The Australian soldiers were instructed not to exaggerate: every 'kill' had to be verified. One patrol took this literally: a soldier removed a finger from a dead guerrilla, wrapped it in toilet paper, and presented it to his commanding officer. Radio Hanoi later denounced the Australians as 'cannibals'. Australian officers privately regretted this 'indiscretion' in the heat of 'combat success'.[23]

General William Westmoreland, who succeeded Harkins as the supreme commander of Free World forces in Vietnam, received new powers on 26 June 1965 to commit US (and hence Australian) troops in combat — without requiring Saigon's approval. This freed him to impose attrition to the full. In fairness, he had little choice: only massive firepower could break the advance of the communist insurgency. In this sense, Westmoreland defended attrition as an emergency strategy; yet its continuation later marked the absence of any clear American strategy in Vietnam. 'Westmoreland's tactic,' remarked Colonel John Nagl, a US strategist who explained the disastrous consequences of Westmoreland's war in his classic *Learning to Eat Soup with a Knife*, 'was to "pile on" as many troops as were available, supported by close air support, artillery, and even B52 strikes, to kill as many of the Viet Cong and North Vietnamese Army soldiers as possible.'[24] It succeeded in temporarily forcing back the enemy; yet, in virtually every large US action, chiefly OPERATIONS MASHER, CEDAR FALLS and JUNCTION CITY, the devastated killing fields were, within weeks of the US 'victory', 'literally crawling with what appeared to be Viet Cong'.[25] Perceptive Australian officers noted the futility of killing people without winning local support. 'This operation,' stated a blunt Australian after-action report in August, 'will have no lasting effect on the VC ... unless the pressure is maintained by continued patrolling' to stop the enemy returning.

For Westmoreland, failure was unthinkable, victory a formality: the rising pile of Viet Cong bodies would force Hanoi to see sense and give up the fight. This thinking completely misread the enemy's resolve and history. At a darker political level, several US commanders misunderstood the point of the Viet Cong, who was, in Hanoi's eyes, an expendable source of southern manpower. Far better to bleed the southern communists — many of whom were tainted with democratic or nationalist ideals — than waste the North's prized People's Army. Hanoi thus fed its southern comrades into America's mincing machine, which was all too ready to receive them.

A horrific accident produced the Australian battalion's first casualties. On 26 June, returning from his first operation on a cattle truck, 21-year-old Private Billy Carroll leaped off in the rush to get a cold drink and a shower. As he jumped, his grenade pin caught and released; the striker lever sprang loose; and the explosion blew out his stomach. Privates Mick Bourke and Arie Van Valen sustained awful wounds, of which they soon died. A further ten soldiers, including two American troops, lay wounded, some severely. Captain Michael Le Bars rushed over to find bodies 'groaning and twitching on the ground' and a severed leg 'from the groin to the foot on the driver's side of the vehicle'.[26] Second Lieutenant Bill Kaine fought back a flood of nausea as he dressed the wounds of an American, who mumbled: 'Leave me, I'm dead. Help someone else.'[27] Kaine stayed, and saved the American's life.

The Menzies Government refused to pay for soldiers' remains to be flown home, under the policy that interred them in the nearest Commonwealth cemetery (which was at Terendak Barracks, in Malaysia). This deeply upset the families: Carroll's 20-year-old wife, Mindy, received news of his death while cradling their infant son. A Sydney businessman, Ron Wiggins, stepped in and paid to return the bodies of Carroll and later Private Billy Nalder, shot through the chest by a sniper.

★ ★ ★

Meanwhile, the Team's initial successes were foundering because it lacked the numbers to impose its ideas on the American brass. The People's Action Teams set up by Ian Teague and his jungle warfare specialists, for example, lost focus and fell apart under American leadership, which sacrificed quality in the rush for quantity, recalled Lieutenant David Brockett. As the PATs rapidly expanded nationally, desertions, Viet Cong infiltration and theft became commonplace, and patrols and ambushes were farcical, reported Brockett.[28] In the end, the US commanders replaced the PATs with new 'hearts and minds' teams, called 'Revolutionary Development Cadres', which failed to attract popular support.

The failure illustrated the striking contrast between Australian and American methods. The Team (and later Australian combat units) concentrated on grassroots infiltration in a gradual war. They championed individual skill, marksmanship ('one shot, one kill'), map reading, stealth, avoiding known tracks, ambush and counter-ambush, tracking and, 'above all, patience', as McNeill explained. It was a lesson born at Kokoda and honed in Malaya. 'The Aussies used squads to make a contact,' observed David Hackworth, America's most decorated soldier, 'and brought in reinforcements to do the killing; they planned in the belief that a platoon on the battlefield could do anything …'[29] The American Army, on the other hand, was trained to fight short, big unit wars, involving battalion- or division-strength battles, and applied massive indirect fire on wide areas. The American longing for a decisive, open confrontation, along the lines of the vast pitched battles of World War II, 'seemed almost to become an obsession'.[30] The gradual infiltration and conversion of hostile villages — over years, if necessary — simply did not fit the US war plan. A drawn-out guerrilla struggle in the jungle seemed somehow unworthy of American firepower and training.

Instead, the Americans sought to flush out the enemy through brazen scrub-bashing and massive firepower. The careless courage of the American ground troops amazed the Australians. The elite US paratroopers would stride down the jungle paths, smoking and chatting, radios blaring, their shoulders emblazoned with red-white-and-blue patches. An Australian company involved in a joint ambush was 'astounded at the [in]discipline of US soldiers and their use in ambush of transistor radios, cigars, loud noises and mass sleep'.[31] They used little camouflage. 'The Yanks made themselves targets,' said Private Terry Burstall. '"Bring 'em on," they said. But it was foolhardy courage, crashing through the bush.'[32]

Yet the Americans had a lot to teach the Australians: about heliborne assaults, air and artillery support and much more. In this sense, Vietnam was a testing ground for new manoeuves using weapons of incredible destructive power. The fact that they were utterly unsuited to a guerrilla war did not inhibit their deployment: 'We used 'em because we had 'em' was a common American refrain.

The Team had grown to about 100 by now. The new members differed from the 'Dirty Thirty' in one critical respect: they were permitted to join and lead their South Vietnamese soldiers on combat operations. 'Serong was all for the Team going out on combat operations,' said one Team member, 'but the government didn't want anybody to get killed, and all this garbage ... Serong changed all that. We would train for six weeks, then go out for a week.'[33]

Indeed, one harrowing example, in the remote outpost of Tra Bong in late 1965, demonstrated just how far the Team would be expected to lead the South Vietnamese in battle. The redoubtable Captain Geoff Skardon established the Tra Bong post, 30 kilometres west of Quang Ngai, in August that year, on the orders of Lieutenant Colonel Alex Preece, who had succeeded Serong as commander of the Team (Serong stayed in Saigon as a CIA operative and adviser to the US Army). Tra Bong was one of nineteen Vietnamese Special Forces forts in which members of the Team served. Their purpose was to destroy Viet Cong supply and communication lines and protect friendly villages from enemy attack. Yet, in many cases, the National Liberation Front 'owned' the villages, often through terror or bribes, and lived and fought behind these civilian shields. It made the job of civilian protection extremely difficult, if not impossible.

Preece, eager to utilise Australia's jungle skills, seized on an American request for help in establishing the base, and Skardon flew in to survey the designated site: a narrow valley carpeted in rice paddies beneath jungle-clad mountains, 900 metres high, through which an unsealed road ran parallel with a little river. The proposed location, Skardon saw, was highly vulnerable to a Viet Cong attack.[34] So he selected instead a hill 500 metres from the airfield with better protection. The base would include a Special Forces 'A' team of twelve advisers (eight Australians and four Americans); a South Vietnamese Special Forces unit; a few hundred Vietnamese 'irregulars' (none of whom was properly trained); and a company of Montagnard Nung tribesmen (the last to be led by Australian Warrant Officers Bill Abigail and Alf Seal). After his recce, Skardon returned to his helicopter to find a group of Vietnamese peasants surrounding the aircraft and begging to board ... to escape Viet Cong terror attacks, they pleaded.

Skardon's first operation — to clear a hamlet of enemy forces — got off to a farcical start. It was the local soldiers' first ride in a chopper, and they laughed and waved to their friends and families, hundreds of whom came to see them off: '... the excitement of a helicopter ride clearly outweighed any thoughts that they were about to land in a hostile environment,' Skardon observed.[35] No sooner had they landed than confused reports were received of Viet Cong troops inside the hamlet. Before Skardon could confirm the reports, his Vietnamese irregulars started shooting. Excitably, they shot an enormous number of rounds at an unseen target. The Australians raced down the lines, tearing the weapons from the soldiers to stop the inferno, at which point nine shaking enemy soldiers stood up in the targeted area and surrendered. 'The volume of fire, though not directed at [the Viet Cong], obviously had the desired effect!' Skardon concluded.[36]

The hamlet chief told the Australians that his 150 villagers were fed up with Viet Cong terror strikes, and demanded to be moved to Tra Bong. Skardon agreed, and airlifted the villagers' pigs, chickens and ducks; cattle were dropped by parachute — in one instance six cows floated earthward, to the delight of the Vietnamese soldiers. 'Rounding up the rather cranky beasts ... was a gala event and provided much light relief,' recalled Skardon.[37] (Dropping livestock by parachute was common practice: even the occasional elephant floated into outlying posts during the war.) Bulldozers and heavy equipment were also airlifted to remote regions; in one case, in Quang Nam, a bulldozer strung to four parachutes crash-landed through dense jungle, and a race ensued between the Viet Cong and Australian-led troops to reach the valuable machine. Australian Warrant Officer Reg Collinson got there first and, with bullets cracking about him, jumped into the cage, pumped the engine and crashed through virgin jungle to safety.

In September Captain Felix Fazekas succeeded Skardon as Australian commander at Tra Bong. The tall, Hungarian-born Fazekas had a picturesque Prussian demeanour: as a student in Budapest during World War II, he had helped resist the advancing Russian tanks. He later emigrated to Australia.

Fazekas strengthened Tra Bong's defences. As well as extra rolls of wire and the appointment of a Nung 'praetorian guard' at the gates, he introduced the novelty of filling 44-gallon drums with petrol. These were to be ignited and rolled flaming down the hill in the event of human wave attacks. Fazekas also sent out daily patrols, one of which, on 13 November, included Warrant Officer Kevin 'Dasher' Wheatley, who had been posted to Tra Bong in October 1965. Dasher was 'a good bloke' in the best Australian tradition, said one of his mates: down-to-earth, fair, sports-loving and always ready for a beer. He carried his pack low and loose because the knocking against the thighs kept him going, he explained.

Wheatley's reputation for bravery had already been established. Earlier that year, he had been pinned down in a ditch by the overshots of South Vietnamese troops then locked in a firefight with the Viet Cong. At the sound of the machine gun, a little Vietnamese girl had broken from her mother's grip and run screaming onto the road near a US command post. When Wheatley saw the little girl, he jumped up, sprinted down the road, grabbed her in his arms and scrambled back to cover, shielding her with his body. Such spontaneous heroics, of a strictly unmilitary nature, were in Wheatley's character. The event helps to explain Wheatley's performance several months later in the action for which he received the Victoria Cross.

As well as Wheatley, Fazekas's patrol at Tra Bong included six other Team members and Vietnamese Special Forces led by Second Lieutenant Quang, who immediately compromised the mission by insisting on a new route, which risked fatally exposing Wheatley and his men to the enemy.

Wheatley and fellow warrant officer Ron Swanton were crossing a rice paddy at the head of about sixty Vietnamese irregular troops when Viet Cong soldiers, dug in nearby, opened fire. Most of the Vietnamese irregulars broke for the jungle in terror. One was shot, and Swanton tried to carry him to safety while Wheatley covered Swanton and radioed Fazekas for support. Suddenly, Swanton fell too — wounded, with a bullet through the chest. Wheatley raced across the paddy and dived down beside his friend.

Fazekas and Sergeant Theodore Sershen, of the US Special Forces, rushed to Wheatley's aid. As they left, to Fazekas's fury, Quang refused to offer any help. Yet, of their own volition, a few brave Vietnamese soldiers got up and followed the Australian and the American, who had gone off alone through Viet Cong territory to rescue their stricken friends.

Within 150 metres of Wheatley, Fazekas heard him shout, 'God, somebody help us, somebody do something!' Wheatley then 'began to drag his wounded comrade across the fire-swept paddy field to cover'.[38] His Vietnamese comrades had all bolted, with the exception of a medic who dashed across the field with a bandage for Swanton. The medic pleaded with Wheatley to leave Swanton and run. Wheatley refused, and continued to drag Swanton towards the jungle, miraculously surviving heavy machine-gun fire. His ammunition ran out as he neared the jungle fringe. At that point, a South Vietnamese private, Dinh Do, ran out to help Wheatley drag Swanton the last few metres to cover. Later, Dinh Do described the two Australians' last moments alive, in his statement supporting Wheatley's recommendation for the Victoria Cross:

> My platoon … started to run away when I saw Warrant
> Officer Wheatley half-dragging, half-carrying WO Swanton
> from the rice paddy to some heavy undergrowth. I helped him
> [Wheatley] in the last stages and asked him to run with us. He
> refused to leave his friend and he pulled the safety pins from the
> two grenades he had. I started to run when the VC were about
> 10 metres away. Then I heard two grenades explode and several
> bursts of fire.[39]

Meanwhile Fazekas had blazed a path across the open paddy to the hamlet, destroyed the enemy positions, and returned to help his two warrant officers; both were already dead. For his actions and rescue attempt, Fazekas was awarded the Military Cross. The bodies of Wheatley and Swanton were found the next morning, lying together, shot repeatedly at close range through the head and chest. Wheatley had been due home in two months. His personal effects included several cables to his favourite pub, the Civic, in Sydney, counting down his return home: 'TEN DAYS TO DASHER DAY', 'NINE DAYS TO DASHER DAY' — and 'ROLL OUT THE BARREL, THE KING IS HERE'.

Dasher performed one last service — posthumously — for the Australian Army. The Department of Defence had hitherto refused to pay for the return of soldiers' remains to Australia. The department insisted that they be interred in the nearest Commonwealth military cemetery. Families who wanted to cremate or bury their sons in Australia had to pay for their sons' return. The public outcry over the government's refusal to bring Wheatley's body home — sparked by a letter to the press from his sister-in-law — helped to change the policy. Soldiers' corpses were henceforth returned to Australia for burial, at government expense.

In Bien Hoa, the Australian troops were engaged in weeks of uneventful patrolling, interspersed with sudden, blinding moments of absolute terror.

Australia's first contact had an element of saloon-bar bathos: a fist fight between Captain Bob Hill and two Viet Cong soldiers, on whom Hill had stumbled near a forward sentry post. The same night he received a grenade wound, yet stayed fighting with his men — one of several acts of extraordinary resilience under fire for which he received the Military Cross.

A patrol led by Second Lieutenant Peter Sibree conveyed the horror of close-contact guerrilla warfare: pinned by enemy fire, with two men severely wounded, Sibree's huge corporal Terry Loftus flung a headless Viet Cong corpse across the field of fire to protect the wounded; Lance Corporal Dave Munday continued to fight with hideous wounds (he later lost a leg), for which he received a Military Medal. There were dozens of similar moments: fleeting, furious clashes on jungle patrols, the chief purpose of which was to keep the enemy off balance.

The soldiers could never relax. The enemy was constantly probing their perimeter — spectacularly on 26 August, when a Viet Cong mortar attack on the Bien Hoa airbase destroyed or damaged forty-nine aircraft — and delayed plans for the first huge US–Australian operation.

OPERATION IRON TRIANGLE (September to October 1965) set out to destroy the 'Iron Triangle', a dagger-shaped wedge of defoliated country pointing at the heart of Saigon and bounded by the Saigon and Thi Tinh rivers, and a line between Ben Suc and Ben Cat to the north. On the south-western edge were the notorious Ho Bo Woods, and further south the enemy-held district of Cu Chi. The whole area seethed with enemy troops, who remained elusive despite a huge defoliation effort to strip the area of jungle.

In late 1964 Westmoreland had ordered the chemical saturation of the Iron Triangle in the first massive application of herbicides, including Agent Orange. Two months after the spraying, leaflets and loudspeakers had warned civilians to evacuate the area, now a 'tinder-dry fire trap' of leafless trunks and sticks.[40] The people obligingly fled. Aircraft then doused the triangle in thousands of gallons of petrol, set alight by napalm and white phosphorus incendiary bombs, in a process nicknamed 'making matchsticks'. The defoliation of one heavily wooded area, during OPERATION SHERWOOD FOREST on 18 January 1965, involved 101 crop-dusting sorties, which sprayed 83,000 gallons of herbicide, fired 85,000 rounds of ammunition and dropped 760 tons of bombs (chiefly napalm, diesel fuel and white phosphorus). The 6,000 inhabitants of the area were forced to abandon their homes, which were destroyed. By mid-1965 the Iron Triangle had been sprayed, burned, bulldozed and bombed so completely that it resembled 'a waffle iron'.[41]

And so, when the Sky Soldiers of the 173rd Brigade and the Australian 1st Battalion ventured into the Iron Triangle, in September 1965, they beheld a region of struggling regrowth, devastated farms and flimsy villages, many rebuilt in soil that literally oozed defoliant. Their mission, to October 1965, was to secure the area and the roads for the arrival of the US 1st Infantry Division. They were to sweep through and 'find, fix and finish' the enemy.

The usual overture of B52 strikes, helicopter gunships and artillery warned every man, animal and leech of the start of something big: a massed American air-mobile assault, 'a roller-coaster helicopter ride accompanied by screeching Wagner and a thundering Guy Fawkes', mocked Essex-Clark. 'It is madness, and the surrealism makes me laugh with incredulity … it is utter fantasyland.'[42] After the softening up, the infantry went in, to find desolation; the enemy had simply taken the hint and fled. Yet if the operation failed to find or fix the communists, it finished the civilians' way of life: both Americans and Australians emptied the villages, captured enemy suspects and — after handing out cold drinks and sweets for Vietnamese children — moved on. It was left to Saigon's troops to decide whether to burn the cleared hamlets, so IRON TRIANGLE ended with the burning of many 'VC camps' and a lot of angry villagers. Days later, the Viet Cong crept back into the smoking hamlets and resumed taxing and threatening the survivors at will.

The whole experience was acutely frustrating and futile. Deep dismay festered in the Australian ranks. Corporal Lex McAulay, a Vietnamese speaker, expressed the mood in a letter to his wife:

> Our life is reduced to the bare essentials — Will it rain? …
> When is the next resupply? What time am I on picket? The
> outside world just ceases to exist … Viets fall into two categories
> — those carrying weapons and those not. The first type we shoot
> on sight — the second type … there's not much we can do
> about … The country is so beautiful, but there are always signs of
> war — destroyed houses and villages, bullet holes in everything,
> and there is hardly a building that has not been damaged or
> destroyed. The poor bloody Viets are trying to build a decent
> country but the VC are destroying any progress as fast as they
> can. Bloody politics.[43]

Mines and booby traps scarred the body and brain. During OPERATION IRON TRIANGLE, they had been everywhere: on gates, in rubbish, on boards, near *punji* and along tracks; in rafters, thatched roofs, rice bags, haystacks and dung piles.[44]

The sight of one's mates blown to pieces deadened morale; many survivors went into deep shock. When a huge mine blew the engine out of an armoured personnel carrier on Highway 13, several soldiers were thrown 20 metres into a muddy rice paddy. The driver died, the rest suffered shrapnel wounds and shock. One turned psychotic, and had to be evacuated to Australia. The victims were all from Charlie Company, which had also borne the brunt of Carroll's grenade accident, and were dubbed the 'Hard Luck Charlies'.

'It was soul destroying,' said Private John Eaton. 'You would hear the explosion up front and then the cry "Medic forward" … the wounded digger would be treated and then we … stepped off again and waited for the next blast. Boom!!! and we would just repeat the process.'[45]

'We hit a mine,' said Hagan. 'I went 10 feet above the jungle and landed on an ants' nest. One bloke was blown in half. I picked up his shoulders, someone picked up his feet. We went different ways. I had three bits of shrapnel in my chest; had 'em in me for thirty years.'[46] The experience sent him slightly off the rails: 'Animal Hagan' lost his corporal's rank after several drunken episodes. 'I don't know how many charges I got … I once drove a horse and cart into a bar.'[47]

The 1st Battalion at one point swept an area known to be heavily mined, east of Highway 13. Majors John Healy and Ian McFarlane lost several troops: Ross Mangano and Terry Loftus (respectively 50 kilograms and 100 kilograms, and great mates) were blown into the air. Mangano landed with a mangled leg, which was amputated; despite his own terrible injuries, Loftus crawled to help him. Mines also killed two New Zealand gunners of 161 Battery, Royal New Zealand Artillery, which arrived in July. Perhaps the most disturbing case was Lieutenant John MacNamara's 8 Platoon — again, Charlie Company. Mines and booby traps wounded him and eleven of his men. 'My war was over,' he wrote in October. '8 Platoon, strength nine, almost ceased to exist.' In revenge, one officer proposed setting grenades under Viet Cong bodies, as 'the VC always attempt to remove their own dead'.[48]

In this climate of terror, mistakes were made and soldiers' remarks — made in the heat of battle — shocked Australians who heard their report at home. The press leaped on the first 'atrocity' stories.[49] Alan Ramsey, the AAP correspondent, reported the shooting of an 'unarmed' Vietnamese couple. In truth, Private Jeff Porter presumed the couple were Viet Cong soldiers. 'When they were 20 yards away they saw us and turned and ran, and I let them have it,' Porter said. 'I gave them a fifty-round burst — if they weren't dead they were pretty sick.'[50] While the report enraged anti-war protesters at home, in Vietnam Ramsey briefly lost his press accreditation.[51]

By the end of OPERATION IRON TRIANGLE, the 1st Battalion had suffered two dead and thirty-six wounded, most of them mine victims. When he returned to base, Lex McAulay wrote to his wife: 'We should have stayed there and fought the VC to a standstill, but *using our Australian tactics*. God I feel down …'[52]

Australian officers blamed America's brazen tactics and indiscriminate firepower for the operation's failure. Major Brian Harper, of the 1st Battalion, described it as 'rushed and careless' and the 'random B52 bombing' as being of questionable value.[53] Major McFarlane was scathing: 'To push troops through heavily booby trapped areas is to guarantee casualties,' he wrote. 'The use of air strikes on en[emy] camps is ineffective … Pilots … have NO conception of what a village/camp looks like … Arty [artillery] fire from US guns is too haphazard and inaccurate for even reasonable safety.'[54]

Butch Williamson, commander of the 173rd Brigade, declared the action a triumph: 'The Iron Triangle is no more … One more enemy bulwark (psychological and physical) has been completely marked off the situation map. My pride in the Brigade continues to be well founded. AIRBORNE, ALL-THE-WAY.'[55] The 173rd Brigade awarded itself a body count of 116 Viet Cong killed, four wounded and 115 captured. Yet only five rifles and four grenades were recovered, so either the enemy were unarmed or most of the victims were civilians. The brigade lost nineteen dead and 110 wounded — 90 per cent of them in mines or booby traps.

OPERATION IRON TRIANGLE failed to find, fix or finish the enemy in the area. In January 1967 the Viet Cong returned. In response, the Americans launched the largest search and destroy mission of the war: the forest was obliterated, the town of Ben Suc levelled, its 6,000 inhabitants 'resettled', hectares of jungle flattened and kilometres of tunnels demolished. Scarcely a cockroach survived. In 1968 the Viet Cong again reoccupied the Iron Triangle, from which they launched the Tet Offensive against Saigon.

In time, the US–Australian relationship at Bien Hoa became unworkable. Westmoreland had assured Australia's Chief of the General Staff, Lieutenant General Sir John Wilton, of Australian tactical autonomy, yet on large joint operations, this did not work. More than once Brumfield openly cursed American tactics; for example, on patrols that required stealth and silence the US troops often fired parachute flares and star shells that turned night into day or, when the Australians had requested a single ranging round, US batteries would fire all their guns on the target, in a 'mad minute'.[56]

In American eyes, however, the Australian tactics seemed timid, over-cautious, slow and ineffective. America's immense firepower, they felt, overruled the need for careful, gradual patrolling, grid square by grid square. A sense of transience permeated the US ranks: flush out the enemy, destroy him and go home.

# Chapter 13
# Cu Chi

The velvet darkness is all-engulfing; the adrenaline rush subsides as it becomes harder to catch your breath. You become light-headed, then dizzy and confused as the air runs out. Reason and sense evaporate as the darkness claims you. That's how it felt to be a Tunnel Rat.

*Captain Sandy MacGregor, MC.*

In October 1965 morale plunged. Four big actions had demanded forty-five days in the jungle, without a break. The usually buoyant Second Lieutenant Williams wrote: 'The battalion is going rapidly downhill … The ops are always hard with much fighting, all with no tangible results. The Yanks are losing a lot of troops here. The official rate of kills is 5:1 in favour of us, but in fact it is about 1:1 … All the officers in one [US] company and a whole platoon [were] killed … There is no doubt we are winning, but is it worth the cost?'[1] Lex McAulay observed severe tension and some demoralisation in the rifle companies; one soldier 'went to pieces two days ago — the mortars firing was the last straw'.[2]

Then came the 'bloody Hump', OPERATION HUMP, so named because once they were over it, ran American thinking, their tour would end. Napalm and B52 carpet bombing heralded the US–Australian offensive against a Viet Cong supply tributary running off the Ho Chi Minh Trail. For the first time, the enemy met his opponents in open battle. The two armies clashed in a damp, leech-ridden forest near the junction of the Be and Dong Nai rivers,

20 kilometres north-east of Bien Hoa. An American major, James Hutchens, walked into an early ambush: 'The whole earth seemed to erupt furiously before our eyes. Staggered claymore mines exploded all around us … we could hear the piercing screams of young men whose bodies lay punctured and shattered …'[3] The Viet Cong pumped rounds into the dead or wounded Americans, which 'rolled' their bodies in the soil. Their infuriated buddies charged with bayonets and fired round after round into enemy bunkers.

Further south, on 8 November 1965, the 1st Battalion's Alpha Company, led by Major John Healy, moved across the northern fringe of the Gang Toi plateau. Lance Corporal Richard 'Tiny' Parker's section led the company through thick jungle up 'Hill 82'; they advanced in single file, strung out over 300 metres. As Parker's men reached the top, the Viet Cong opened fire at close range, using machine guns, small arms and grenades. Parker, 24, and Private Peter Gillson, 20, were among those hit. The enemy kept firing bullets into Gillson's body, eliciting tears of fury in his platoon sergeant, Col Fawcett, who three times tried to drag in his friend's corpse (Fawcett was later awarded the Military Medal for this attempt). Yet to their intense frustration, the Australians were forced to abandon the bodies of Parker and Gillson to the enemy.[4]

'… I have a son,' Mrs Gillson wrote to her husband's platoon commander, when informed of his death, 'which Peter never saw. He is only 4 months old … I only hope that his son will grow up to be as fine a man as Peter … PS excuse my wording in this letter but I just don't feel up to writing just yet.'[5]

The dust-off (named after the radio call sign for medevac choppers) helicopters flew in to retrieve the wounded and take out the recoverable corpses. Frantic medics slid about the bloody chopper floors tending the severely wounded. The dead were zipped up in tidy green body bags with any severed body parts. Somewhere, on the ground, the Viet Cong dragged away their casualties, leaving crimson trails through the mud and vegetation.

Captain Peter Rothwell later captured in a poem the moment the dust-offs arrived at Landing Zone Princess:

*A sound*
*then a roar*
*a second green bird*
*comes to rest*
*on the sodden princess*

> ...
> *A bundle of bags drop*
> *The undertakers alight*
> *a joke*
> *a grin*
> *here we are*
> *let the play begin*
> ...
> *This is the age of the package deal*
> *we have zip-ups*
> *custom made*
> *seven by four*
> *man oh man*
> *It's a clean clean war*[6]

Butch Williamson claimed a great victory in OPERATION HUMP: the 403 (later raised to 700) Viet Cong dead represented 'the largest kill, by the smallest unit, in the shortest time in the Vietnam War to date'.[7] One US battalion received a Presidential Unit Citation. Yet the brigade had suffered heavy casualties, and failed to secure the area. The Viet Cong continued to use the Bien Hoa area as a major supply route for the rest of the war.

Two hamlets, two armies, two very different methods of attack ... In November 1965 OPERATION NEW LIFE aimed at capturing a reportedly huge rice harvest in the La Nga Valley (the rice, it later transpired, did not exist), and destroying the Viet Cong in the area. Duc Hanh had been a 'strategic hamlet' and, like most, now lay firmly in Viet Cong hands. A sharpened bamboo palisade, a deep moat and rolls of barbed wire surrounded it. The 1st Battalion, temporarily led by Major Mal Lander in the absence of Brumfield, and with combat planned by Essex-Clark, surveyed the hamlet by air and gathered local intelligence. The Australians decided to ignore the obvious approach, the main road (an ideal VC ambush point, as it later proved). The troops advanced instead through the jungle from the south-east. Meanwhile, armoured personnel carriers (the Prince of Wales Light Horse) launched a dummy frontal assault along the main road from the east.

Rothwell, who commanded Delta Company, drew on his Malayan experience in leading the south-easterly assault, launched at a vulnerable point where the jungle met the hamlet's moat. At dawn his men waded the moat while two companies (Bravo and Charlie), led by Majors Ian McFarlane and Jim Tattam, swung north to block the escape routes. No preliminary air strikes or artillery bombardment — in fact, no warning — preceded the attack.

Rothwell's men broke from the moat and raced across the village square firing from the hip; they instantly silenced the Viet Cong snipers, hidden in the first huts. Sergeant Jim Carnes, a Korean veteran, routed a machine-gun pit, leaving eleven Viet Cong dead (for which he received a Military Medal). Machine-gunners fired through the thatch roofs of the huts, forcing the occupants out; about ninety Viet Cong troops were captured, wrote Rothwell.[8] His men searched the tunnels with smoke and tear gas; the people emerged, crying and wailing. 'I can still see the old grandma striding through the gas, tears streaming, abusing the Australians,' wrote Lex McAulay. 'Behind her was a waiting crowd of old men, women and kids ...' By 3 p.m. the Australians had captured the hamlet: sixteen Viet Cong troops lay dead, the rest surrendered, for two Australian casualties.

A single Vietnamese civilian died during the battle, in the 'greatest act of love and devotion I have ever witnessed', wrote Lieutenant Bill Giles. A Vietnamese boy had aimed a pistol at Giles from a funk hole covered in planks. Giles's men decided they could not enter without being killed, so they dropped in an M26 grenade. The sound of children crying followed the blast. 'When we lifted the lid we found a woman and three youngsters ... none of them were injured though they were all in a state of shock. Lying on the floor was a man's body — the father. He had caught the grenade and laid down on top of it. He was unarmed. This was the most tragic event that occurred to me during my tour of Vietnam ...'[9]

After a huge show of US air strength left the area, dozens of 'ralliers' (defectors) surrendered under the 'Hoi Chan' — open arms — program. Vietnamese women shouted to their husbands and sons, who were hiding in the jungle, that it was safe to return.[10] In time, a terrified new village chief and his deputy were flown in to Duc Hanh, which was handed over to Saigon's control.

Compare this with the American attack on nearby Thanh Duc, another Viet Cong-fortified hamlet, on 1 December 1965. Air strikes and a rolling artillery barrage saturated the thousand-square-metre area, after which twenty-two US armoured personnel carriers crashed through the main village gates and disgorged the GIs, who fanned out to complete the hamlet's destruction: forty suspected Viet Cong and an unknown number of civilians lay dead; their surviving families homeless and in shock.[11]

OPERATION NEW LIFE had a tragic, all-too-familiar footnote. A few months later, the Viet Cong launched bloody reprisals: they attacked Duc Hanh, destroyed the South Vietnamese troops, razed the village and killed many of the 3,500 civilians. 'The South Vietnamese Government was incapable of taking control after US and Australian units had cleared [the enemy] … This was the refrain for the remainder of the Vietnam War.'[12]


The diggers' first Christmas in Vietnam brought gifts of beer and cigarettes sent by anonymous donors 'to an Australian soldier'. Following an old tradition, the Australian officers and sergeants served lunch to the troops. That afternoon Bob Hope entertained the Bien Hoa base, and Lucky Starr, Don Lane and the 18-year-old Lynne Fletcher performed on a converted semitrailer. The soldiers, who had heard of the anti-war protests via the press, constantly asked Lane to remind the Australian people back home 'not to forget about us because we get the feeling that many do not care that we are here …'[13]

The patrols and operations swiftly resumed. For some they never stopped. Ron Kelly's platoon was sent out on Christmas Eve and Christmas Day: 'Well, darling,' he told his wife, 'it would have to have been one of the worst xmas's I have ever spent … By hell everyone was so very wild about it.'[14]

In January 1966 came OPERATION CRIMP, a huge airborne thrust into the notorious Cu Chi district: 'a massive attack … to strike at the heart of the Viet Cong machine', stated one US Army report.[15] It would be Westmoreland's first divisional offensive, deploying 8,000 troops of the US 1st Division, the 173rd Brigade (incorporating Australia's 1st Battalion), helicopters, tanks and armoured carriers. Their mission: to eliminate the Viet Cong headquarters in Military Region IV, which enclosed Cu Chi district. Its destruction was part of Westmoreland's plan — a direct echo of French thinking — to ring Saigon in a series of giant forts, creating a permanent citadel against Viet Cong attack.

The huge airborne armada took off from Phu Loi on 7 January 1966, bound for Cu Chi district. Not a soldier on board had an inkling of the kind of battlefield they were about to enter.

Buried in tunnels beneath the loamy soil at Phu My Hung village, the Viet Cong's 7th Cu Chi Battalion awaited the onslaught. Lieutenant Nguyen

Thanh Linh had known of the attack for days: Viet Cong spies riddled the South Vietnamese Army; and the B52s, reconnaissance spy planes and artillery shells confirmed this information. The Viet Cong was accustomed to American 'softening up', yet the barrage they were about to endure was on a different scale.

Linh, who would later command the Cu Chi Battalion, somehow had to inspire his fearful teenage troops, a thousand of whom had volunteered to defend the Phu My Hung tunnels, the biggest subterranean network in the Cu Chi tunnel complex. The young soldiers peppered him with anxious questions: would an old carbine bullet kill a big American? Would a bullet kill a big black American? 'I reassured them their bullets would kill if they struck the right spot ... Four days later, the Americans came. We watched with heavy hearts the helicopters endlessly landing men ...'[16]

At 2.45 p.m. on 11 January, a soldier called Tran Bang recorded the invasion in his diary: 'Have spent four days in a tunnel. About eight to nine thousand American soldiers were in for a sweep operation. The attack was fierce ... a number of underground tunnels collapsed. Some of our men were caught in them ... It is not known what has become of sisters BA, BAY, HONG HAN and TAN HO ... Fifteen minutes ago, enemy jets dropped bombs; houses collapsed and trees fell.'[17] The diary was among nearly 8,000 items captured by the Americans and Australians the next day.

In 1965 the Cu Chi tunnels formed part of an underground labyrinth that stretched from the 'gates of Saigon to the Cambodian border': more than 200 kilometres of subterranean passages, fighting tunnels, meeting rooms, hospitals and food caches.[18] Their strategic value lay in their proximity to Saigon; they honeycombed the main land and river routes into the city, and formed 'a spring board for attacking Saigon, the enemy's brain centre', said Mai Chi Tho, who fought in the tunnels (and became Party Chairman of Ho Chi Minh City after the war). 'It was like a thorn stabbing in the eye ...'[19]

American aircraft had shelled, napalmed and defoliated Cu Chi to a blackened cinder. This typhoon of fire rarely ceased. Cu Chi was a 'Free Fire Zone': anyone or thing that moved inside was an automatic target. US pilots routinely offloaded unused ordnance and napalm over the area on their flights back to base. The Viet Cong had lived beneath this barrage since 1960, when they reactivated and strengthened the tunnel network, dormant since their fathers, the Viet Minh, used it to fight the French. They lived, ate, slept, made love and defecated underground; women gave birth in those dark recesses. They lived on small balls of rice and tapioca, and emerged only to fight, patrol and collect food.

The tunnels were intended for a combative, not defensive, role, designed with interlocking arcs of fire and connecting fire tunnels: 'Their sheltering purpose is only significant when they serve our soldiers in combat,' noted an extraordinary enemy document captured in September 1967.[20] They were fighting tunnels.

American boots touched Cu Chi's soil in January 1966 and swept forward along a 1,500-metre front; soldiers soon started to fall, victims of invisible snipers. The losses mystified the US commander, Lieutenant Colonel Robert Haldane: where was the fire coming from? A US platoon sergeant, Stewart Green, solved the mystery. He sat down on what he thought was an insects' sting; a search revealed a nail, part of a wooden trapdoor 'perforated with air holes ... with bevelled sides that kept it from falling through into the tunnel below'. The shout of the discovery 'brought Colonel Haldane on the run'.[21]

Green volunteered to enter the hole. He emerged with hospital supplies — from an underground dispensary. The Americans pumped smoke in using a Mity Mite agricultural blower; moments later, to their astonishment, wisps of smoke issued from hundreds of holes in the jungle floor.

'Before I go,' said American Lieutenant Colonel George Eyster, who lay mortally wounded by an enemy tunnel sniper, 'I'd like to talk to the guy who controls those incredible men in their tunnels.'[22] Those were his last words. Neither tear gas nor smoke would force the occupants out, because the tunnels' zigzag design, many layers and sealed trapdoors restricted the fumes. (The Australians later requisitioned diesoline vapour, to little effect.[23]) The allies had somehow to engage in underground battle, fought against an army of troglodytes. Thus were born the Tunnel Rats: phenomenally brave military engineers whose job was to enter the tunnels, salvage any documents and weapons, and destroy the network.

None would forget the sphincter-clenching fear of crawling through a booby-trapped underground pipeline. Only a rare kind of man could bear it, and to this day the Rats are set apart as 'oddball heroes', in the words of US Lieutenant General Fred Weyand. 'The velvet darkness is all-engulfing,' wrote Australia's Captain Alex 'Sandy' MacGregor, who led the first Australian tunnelling unit. 'The adrenaline rush subsides as it becomes harder to catch your breath. You become light-headed, then dizzy and confused as the air runs out. Reason and sense evaporate as the darkness claims you. That's how it felt to be a Tunnel Rat.'[24]

Two kilometres east of the Saigon River, in the Ho Bo Woods near the Cu Chi district, Australia's 1st Battalion alighted on a tunnel network that belittled anything yet seen. The earth's 'unfathomable entrails' interred, MacGregor later stated, the headquarters of the southern command of the National Liberation Front.[25]

Major Ian McFarlane's Bravo Company secured the new landing zone — the location of which had provoked another stoush between the Americans and Essex-Clark, who insisted, after a quick aerial reconnaissance, that the LZ selected by the US Brigade staff from a map alone was in fact a heavily fortified Viet Cong area. He selected a less exposed assault landing zone, but nobody, it seemed, had alerted US gunships to the change. Shortly, they started strafing the Australians, who leaped into the surrounding scrub. Nor did smoke signals and frantic radio calls stop a US artillery bombardment. The Australians, caught in the open, ran about like headless chooks, one of whom happened to be the visiting commander of the 5th Battalion, Lieutenant Colonel John Warr, seen diving into a pit in his officer's peaked cap, lightweight summer dress shirt and shiny black walking shoes. A furious Essex-Clark got on the radio to the American commander, and the 'friendly fire' ceased.

The Australians crept over the living earth; soon the sniping started. Lieutenant Jim Bourke's platoon dived into a sunken section of a road, unaware that they had entered a Viet Cong killing ground. The enemy immediately started firing from inside a hollowed-out mound that resembled a giant termite's nest with firing slits. Bourke was shot through the cheek at near point-blank range, spat out teeth and bits of jawbone, and continued leading his men until he fainted from blood loss. Corporal Ron Smith received hideous wounds from two bullets through the eye that shattered his skull (he miraculously survived, after a prolonged dalliance with death in an American hospital).

Two medics died: Private Merv Wilson was racing forward to treat Bourke's smashed jaw when a sniper shot him in the neck; Chris Clark, a bandsman who doubled as a medic, ran up to staunch Wilson's spurting jugular and received a bullet in the back. Side by side, Wilson and Clark bled to death. The jawless Bourke directed Lance Corporal Jim Pratten to attack and destroy the mound. Under cover of relentless machine-gun fire, Pratten's section charged, fired into the slits and tossed in grenades.

All over the field, the soldiers witnessed similar attacks on tunnel entrances. Ian McFarlane's company entered a forest bristling with snipers, seeded with booby traps and *punji* stakes, and laced with trip wires connected to shells and grenades dangling from branches, one of which blew McFarlane and several men off their feet. McFarlane, himself painfully injured, kept commanding. Eight Australians were killed and thirty wounded in the Ho Bo Woods, including Captain Ken Bade of the 105th Battery, who suffered shocking chest wounds and became the first Australian officer killed in Vietnam.

The 1st Battalion was fighting above a human anthill. An 'eerie feeling of hearing men scuttling around underground' was how Essex-Clark described the sensation.[26] Below ground, they could hear the subterranean army; above, the whimpering of women and children, 'probably lamenting the fate of their husbands, fathers and sons who were trapped in the tunnels below …'[27] The civilians were seen to loiter, terrified, in bunkers. The Viet Cong withdrew behind this civilian shield, and Australians found themselves staring down their sights at women and children. No kind of training could prepare a soldier for such conditions: a nightmarish combination of the primitive (bamboo booby traps), the high-tech (AK47s and rockets) and the pathetic (a Vietnamese child). All were weapons of war.


The Royal Australian Engineers (3rd Field Troop, 1 Field Squadron) formed the first unit of Australian Tunnel Rats led by MacGregor, a rugby prop toughened by two years' military service in Papua New Guinea. His men included Corporal Bob Bowtell, Denis Ayoub, Les Colmer and Barry Harford. Colmer and Harford hailed from Broken Hill, and their mining background proved useful in the coming ordeal.

MacGregor developed a new approach to tunnel warfare: blasts of fresh air were pumped in after smoke and tear gas, to improve the conditions for the Tunnel Rats (who would enter in gas masks). His sappers were also equipped with tunnel search kits, which included miners' lights strapped to their hats. 'After we'd blown smoke, then tear gas, then fresh air down the tunnel, I sent a couple of men down to investigate.' The men would enter in pairs; one checked for booby traps, the other paid out telephone line. The tunnels tended to drop straight down, then double back up, like the U-bend under a sink. Typically, wrote MacGregor, 'there wasn't room enough to turn around. It was terrifying down there, armed only with a bayonet to probe for booby traps and a pistol to defend yourself.'[28]

The Rats lowered themselves in, and a chill rippled over their legs, thighs, groin and genitals. Getting out was like snatching their limbs from a shark-infested pool. The further they went, the more intricate the system became, with drops, twists, turns, alcoves, rooms ... a vast military complex unfolded in the depths of the earth.

One tunnel in the Cu Chi complex emerged under the original landing zone, in another firing mound, vindicating Essex-Clark's decision to change its location. If the battalion had landed there as planned by the Americans, 'we'd have been meat in a hot metal sandwich', MacGregor later wrote.[29]

Australia's first tunnel casualty, Corporal Bob Bowtell, tried to wriggle from one level to another through a trapdoor that measured 40 by 30 centimetres. He got stuck and in the process lost his respirator. He shouted for help, but inhaled smoke and fell unconscious. Jim Daly frantically tried to drag Bowtell's inert body from the trapdoor frame until he, too, almost suffocated in the process. The Australians eventually dragged out Bowtell's body.

Within days, four teams of six Tunnel Rats were working underground, from dawn to dusk. They salvaged thousands of documents, equipment and photos. 'Every day dawned to startling revelations,' wrote MacGregor, who later received a Military Cross for his leadership.[30] 'We had stumbled upon hospitals and classrooms containing so much equipment that the Americans assumed we had found the Viet Cong headquarters.' They found booby-trapped bags and even Parker pens wired to small explosive devices. Ayoub came upon an underground weapons workshop: the grenade casings were made of tomato juice tins or beer cans, and the fragmentation material of blue metal road gravel. In future, Australian patrols were ordered to 'burn, bash and bury' all their used ration cans.

With telephone line and a compass, the Australians penetrated 56 square kilometres and mapped 17 kilometres of Cu Chi tunnel, according to captured NLF documents, exposing a large part of the network, which yielded ninety weapons (including Chinese-made anti-aircraft guns), 7,488 documents, 760 medical items, ammunition, grenades, rice, radios and a vast array of general stores. The intelligence revealed the structure and operations of vital enemy command posts, as well as a list of enemy agents operating in Saigon: most seemed genuine, although, as a Viet Cong leader later said, the Americans liked documents 'so we made sure they got many'. After the search, MacGregor's men destroyed or lined the tunnels with tear gas crystals: 'Our intention was to … leave those parts that we couldn't destroy as uninhabitable as possible.'[31]

OPERATION CRIMP ended with 128 enemy killed, 91 captured and 509 suspects taken for interrogation; 1,031 refugees fled the area — many of whom would later rejoin their tunnel regiments. The 173rd Brigade lost 22 killed and 106 wounded, of which Australians accounted for 8 dead and 29 wounded. The operation destroyed a fraction of a huge tunnel network, according to a training officer in Cu Chi, Captain Nguyen Huot. The Viet Cong soon redug and reoccupied the tunnels. They never ceased digging: Cu Chi remained an enemy stronghold for the duration of the war. Yet CRIMP did succeed in establishing the extent of the tunnel network: hundreds of kilometres of additional war zone, all underground.

The months rolled by, and the Australian troops had little relief or rest. Discipline occasionally lapsed, most sensationally in the case of Gunner Peter O'Neill, a renegade soldier of insolent reputation who on his own account had left the lines without permission to visit the brothels of Bien Hoa. In February 1966 O'Neill received three charges for serious, separate offences and failed to appear at two field punishment parades. In response, his battery commander Major Peter Tedder, a precise 30-year-old Duntroon graduate, ordered O'Neill to be 'restrained' — handcuffed to a steel picket by day, for seven days. O'Neill was later discharged, amid inflamed press coverage that accused the army of brutality. Tedder himself was court-martialled, but the charges were dropped. The 'confused, anomalous and anachronistic' state of Australian military law led Tedder mistakenly to believe that he had the authority to chain a repeat offender to a fixed object. The law was later amended.[32]

In the last few months of their tour, the Australian troops played a small, if effective, role in a series of immense US operations, including ROLLING STONE, SILVER CITY, DENVER and ABILENE. (During the latter, Australia's cautious tactics failed to impress America's Havana cigar-smoking Brigadier General Jim Hollingsworth, who challenged Preece to a US$100 bet that the Australians could not protect his base from mortar attack in coming operations. Preece won the bet.) At dawn, like a sinister dirge, the sound of the helicopter rotors would herald the next airlift to a grid reference somewhere in this alien land.

ROLLING STONE was supposedly a road security mission. It turned into an enormous firefight for the very survival of the US 1st Infantry Brigade headquarters, a lightly defended American fire support base and brigade base, which, Australian patrols had observed, was extremely vulnerable to VC attack, with no barbed wire or fortifications and few sentries. On 22 February 1966 Preece assumed the worst and directed Essex-Clark to warn the Americans of a major attack. Heeding it, the Americans helicoptered in reinforcements late that afternoon.

Preece's intelligence had been correct: at eight o'clock that evening, 2,000 enemy troops drew up within sight of the noisy, well-lit US base. Out of the darkness, a scatter of twinkling lights lit up the forest; the lights advanced, accompanied by the awful popping sound of mortars firing — a prelude to a 'waterfall' of rifle fire as 'thousands and thousands of rounds' whizzed over the American and Australian dugouts, as McAulay recalled.[33] The Viet Cong charged — straight into 'Bourbon Baby' and 'Bad Fox', two widely separated M48 tanks, used as almost sacrificial 'standing patrols', deep in the surrounding rubber plantation, which the rapidly advancing Viet Cong very quickly overwhelmed and destroyed.

Out in the rubber, a small Australian patrol of Privates Walter Brunalli, John Eaton, Rod Gearhardt, Jim Daly, Rick Forno and Barry McLeod witnessed the fireworks. Eaton vividly remembers 'red and green tracer rounds streaming through the night sky; the eerie moving shadows created by flares swinging beneath parachutes; the thunderous explosions of mortars, claymore and artillery along with canister rounds from the tanks …' At one point, a Viet Cong soldier mistakenly attached himself to the tail of the patrol; Gearhardt and Daly shot him point-blank when he started talking in Vietnamese.

The attack on the US base failed, and the Viet Cong withdrew, leaving 150 bodies. Most were buried in a bulldozed hole; others were hauled away with meathooks and ox carts, the sound of which put Essex-Clark in mind of 'the tumbrels carting the condemned to the guillotines of the French Revolution'.[34] The Americans lost eleven killed and seventy-two wounded in a battle that their very carelessness had provoked. Prisoners later told their interrogators that they had marched 25 kilometres and arrived exhausted to attack a 'soft' American target. The Viet Cong had forced women and children to carry their ammunition and supplies right into the battle, 'so a large number … were also mown down. The fools who parade around protesting and praising the VC ought to see this,' McAulay wrote.[35]

Their last big operation, SILVER CITY, saw the Australians ambushing and patrolling around BUGS BUNNY, a landing zone. The cartoon rabbit's name would later haunt 162 American wounded, medevaced out of one of their most frenzied battles: 345 Viet Cong were confirmed dead, many of them young women, who fought in hand-to-hand clashes with knives and bayonets. If these huge firefights met the American body count quota, they failed to fulfil Westmoreland's broader strategic goals. Attrition was supposed to force an early Viet Cong surrender. It had not, and the 173rd Airborne, the *Rawhide*-singin' paratroopers from Okinawa who reckoned they would be home by Christmas, would stay in Vietnam for another six years and suffer 1,533 dead and 6,000 wounded.

In April, Major Ian Fisher's company (Delta) drew the short straw for the 1st Battalion's final action: to protect the establishment of the First Australian Task Force, soon to arrive in Phuoc Tuy province, to the south-east. The rest of the battalion packed up and flew or sailed home. Despite their criticism of the US Army's strategy and tactics, they never forgot the American friendship and the constant and mostly reliable combat support of the US Air Force and Artillery. 'None of us in 1RAR would forget the many more times that we were glad to have US support nearby,' said Essex-Clark.[36]


In June 1966 Australia's 1st Battalion marched through Sydney in an exuberant ticker-tape welcome home parade. Anti-war activists were scarce; one elderly man struck a hairy protester with his crutch; a woman hit two more with her umbrella. A more spectacular action, however, would sear the memory of that day in the soldiers' minds. As the troops passed the Town Hall, a young woman suddenly broke from the crowd. Nadine Jensen, a 21-year-old secretary from Campbelltown, rushed up and threw red paint over Lieutenant Colonel Preece and another officer, both of whom marched on. Fined $6 and put on a good behaviour bond, Miss Jensen told the court she did not belong to a peace organisation; she said she was personally opposed to the war; and no, she did not need psychiatric care. Her lone act, however, showed the burgeoning peace movement the power of media stunts as a way of embarrassing the government and humiliating the returning troops.

The battalion lost twenty-three killed in action and 130 wounded. Mothers were left silently grieving their dead sons. Nelly Clark, mother of the bandsman Christopher Clark, who gave his life trying to save another's, summoned the strength to reply to her son's platoon commander:

Thank you very much for your kindness in sending me Christopher's photo, and thank you for the nice things you said about him. I still find it hard to believe, he was such a lively kid and he was so good to his young brothers and sisters, the little ones still speak of him, they don't realize — which is just as well. I hoped and prayed that the army had made a mistake, but I guess I knew really they don't make mistakes like that, but I find it very hard to make myself realize that he will not come back ...[37]

Part Three
# The Australian province

# Chapter 14
# Nashos

At the top of the pile is the General, then there's the Brigadier,
the Full Colonel, Lieutenant Colonel, Major, Captain, Full
Lieutenant, Second Lieutenant, Warrant Officers 1 and 2, Staff
Sergeant, Sergeant, Corporal, Lance Corporal and Private ...
Then there are rats and mice, blowflies and cockroaches. Then
there are YOU FUCKING RECRUITS.
*An army instructor to a group of national servicemen.*

'You are hereby called-up for national service ... You are required to
present yourself to Colonel Dunstan at Army Training Depot,
Docker Street, Wagga ... You will catch the train leaving Albury at 8.47
a.m. ...'[1] Thus Rick Bensley received his call-up notice, on 15 June 1965, as
part of the first intake of national servicemen. In time the army expanded
on this masterpiece of brevity: John Binnie's 'dreaded brown envelope'
arrived on 29 June 1966. It said: '... you have been selected for National
Service Training ... you have been allocated for a period of 10 weeks Basic
Recruit Training.' Binnie was to 'bring a minimum of civilian clothing ... a
pair of rubber thong-type footwear for wearing under showers ...' As well,
he would need: '1 Tin Black Boot Polish; 1 Tin Brasso; 2 Polishing Cloths;
1 Marking Pencil; 1 Old Toothbrush (for cleaning rifle) ...' A 'neat and trim'
haircut was desirable before 'you march in to the battalion ...'.[2]

The call-up was the last in the five-stage process of becoming a national
serviceman. First, all 19-year-olds were required to register for national service;

second, conscripts were selected at random by a national ballot, dubbed the 'lottery of death', in which young men whose birth dates matched a series of numbered wooden balls were conscripted; third, conscripted students, apprentices, married men and members of the Citizen Military Forces, theologians, the medically unfit or those who could demonstrate conscientious objection or family hardship were eligible for exemption or deferral of their service; fourth, those remaining who passed their army interview and medical examination were recruited for the army, then 'called up'; that is, ordered by law to attend their nearest recruit training centre. The recruit's civilian job, if any, was technically protected until he finished his two years' service.[3]

Parents, wives and girlfriends submitted, with sadness or pride, to the political expedient that snatched away their sons, husbands or lovers. At the sight of the sullen brown envelope on the kitchen table mothers sat down and softly wept; fathers proudly clapped their sons on the shoulders … and shuddered at what lay ahead. Richard Hornery's mother 'was devastated' when her son's number came up. 'Having lost a daughter and a son when they were infants … I think it terrified her she may lose another son.'[4] John Binnie later realised 'how much your parents suffer, and how brave they are until you return'.[5]

Compulsory military service for home duties has always been popular in Australia, in war and peace. The issue that divided the nation was whether a man should be conscripted to fight overseas. That would prove to be the government's most serious Achilles heel.

Australians had previously resisted government attempts to draft young men for overseas service. To a dismayed Billy Hughes, who damned the result as unpatriotic, the nation rejected by slim majorities, in two referenda in 1916 and 1917, conscription for overseas service in Europe. By 1916, 28,000 volunteer Australian soldiers had been killed or wounded on the fields of France or the beaches of Gallipoli; the people drew their own conclusions. During World War II, in the face of bitter Labor opposition, Prime Minister John Curtin forced through legislation that empowered the government to conscript youth to fight in the islands on Australia's northern perimeter. In the 1950s Menzies introduced a popular national service scheme for military training of 18-year-olds, with no obligation for overseas service, although Menzies 'would probably have included this provision if it had been politically possible'.[6] During the Vietnam years, those opposed to conscription for overseas service consistently outnumbered those in favour, according to six Morgan Gallup polls between 1965 and 1967 (the polling company tended to bury these explosive findings at the end of its reports).[7]

Yet there were powerful forces in favour of conscription for overseas combat. The initial factor influencing the plan to introduce conscription was the Indonesian Confrontation (the stand-off between Indonesia and the newly formed Federation of Malaysia), together with the prospect of the UK's withdrawal east of Suez. The Returned and Services League and Bob Santamaria's National Civic Council were ardent supporters. The RSL's 1963 annual report pressed for compulsory overseas military service: Australia and Britain were 'the only [member countries of SEATO] not employing a compulsory service scheme', the RSL noted.[8] In 1967 the RSL's New South Wales president, Sir William Yeo, expelled a member for opposing the league's support for conscripts to serve overseas. In this light, the RSL's widespread failure to support the same soldiers on their return seems less forgivable. Intriguingly, a little-known and powerful advocate was the US Government. The Johnson administration actively lobbied the Menzies Government to conscript Australian men for Vietnam to boost Australia's available pool of infantrymen. '[Conscription] is a policy which the United States has been pressing on the Australians for some time,' noted a memo to McGeorge Bundy, a senior White House aide, the week after the government tabled the National Service Bill.[9]

A powerful dissenting voice came from the Australian Army. In 1964 the army needed at least 10,000 more men to meet their desired target of 33,000. The top brass hoped that better pay and conditions would lure more volunteers. They objected to the concept of random selection for national service because they did not believe it possible to train for combat a reluctant civilian lad whose name had popped out of a hat. How did you mesh him into a regular army fighting unit? As late as 25 October 1964 the Australian Army and the Joint Chiefs of Staff strongly resisted conscription unless 'it provided for full-time service for at least two years, including an obligation for overseas service'.[10]

In the teeth of army resistance, the politicians decided on 4 November 1964 to introduce a compulsory national service scheme. Events including the Tonkin Gulf Incident, unrest in Papua New Guinea and the insurgency in Vietnam combined with the Indonesian Confrontation and the situation in Suez to outweigh the army's objections. Conscription was seen as necessary. The *Sydney Morning Herald* welcomed the decision as 'Preparing Against War with Indonesia'.[11] Menzies announced the new policy in his Budget Speech on 10 November 1964, along with a 58 per cent increase in defence spending in the three financial years (ending June 1968) of US$2.75 billion. Again, there was no debate, no discussion. The army required rapid expansion to meet the Asian threat, Menzies warned, and could not rely on volunteers alone.

The President sent his perfunctory approval. On the eve of Hasluck's visit to Washington, on 24 November 1964, Dean Rusk was advised that Australia had just introduced conscription with overseas service for the first time in its history. (The advice overlooked conscription for overseas service under the Curtin Government.) 'I am sure Hasluck,' advised William Bundy, 'would greatly appreciate an indication from you that we regard this politically courageous decision as an important step forward for Australia and for us.' Rusk replied, with a sharp note in the margin: 'Compliment him!'[12]

The National Service Act was a political and legal abomination — vague, obtuse and ill-presented. When the then Minister for Labour and National Service, William McMahon, tabled it on Remembrance Day 1964, a gale of questions struck him: on what medical grounds were young men exempt? How were university students to be affected? Would the conscript be forced to serve overseas? Where? Why conscript men in peacetime? (War had not been declared.) Where is the justice in conscripting 'minors', who are not permitted to vote?

McMahon's responses were as confusing as the Act. In time, a little clarity shone through: the physically and mentally disabled, students of theology, the clergy, 'conscientious objectors' (a term open to legal interpretation) and full-blood Aborigines were all exempt from national service, McMahon said. His desolate performance fuelled public resentment. The president of the University of Queensland asked about the terms of deferment for medical and married students; months later, McMahon replied, with vacuous arrogance, that students who 'failed to be diligent in their studies' would be forced to join the army.

The draft captured first-generation Australians of British, German, Polish, Austrian, Dutch, Yugoslav, Italian, Greek, French, Danish, Finnish and South Sea Island extraction, and, of course, New Zealanders and Britons resident in Australia. The exemption of Aborigines was divisive: the ALP claimed it patronised indigenous people; conservatives argued that blacks should serve if they wanted the benefits of citizenship. So Aborigines were added to the draft. But the decision never received legislative assent, and Aboriginal troops in Vietnam tended to be volunteers, such as Kenny Laughton, Geoff Shaw, Richard Tilmouth and Ray Orchard. Orchard, of Bundaberg, took a year to persuade his father to sign the form. One day, his father 'took it in his old cane-black hand … and he said, "If you want to go, well go".'[13] There were a few Aboriginal conscripts: Charles Tilmouth, for example, was called up and served eighty days in Vietnam in 1970, before being medevaced home: 'I was pretty badly wounded.'[14]

Luck would decide who went to war. Since only a fraction of the 761,854 men who turned 20 between 1965 and 1972 were needed, the government decided a national ballot, or raffle, was the fairest way to draft them. Every few months, a prominent Australian — a politician or sporting hero — drew a series of numbered wooden balls from a ballot box. If your birth date corresponded with the number on a ball — about one chance in twelve — you were conscripted. You had won the raffle! 'There was a joviality about its conduct I found insulting,' recalled Michael Leunig, the cartoonist, whose number came up in the first ballot. 'It was a media circus … the whole process typified the stupidity and callousness of Australian attitudes.'[15] The first annual call-up in mid-1965 drafted 4,200 men. Next year, two draws generated 6,900 recruits, raising the army's strength to 37,500 by December 1966. At its peak, the lottery drafted four intakes of 2,150 20-year-olds per year, producing an annual total of 8,600. From 1967 to 1971 there were, at any one point, about 16,000 national servicemen in the army (i.e. 36–38 per cent of the total strength). These conscripts represented 66 per cent of the total number 'balloted in' as recruits; the rest had failed to pass the physical or psychological standards of the army.[16] Conscripts were most heavily concentrated in the frontline rifle companies, of which 40 per cent were conscripts.[17] In total, 15,381 national servicemen served overseas, a third of the Australian Army force sent to Vietnam.

The ballot provoked ALP fury. Calwell denounced the lottery as 'rank injustice piled upon utter folly'. 'The Labor Party,' he told the House on 12 November 1964, 'opposes utterly and absolutely conscription for the youth of this country for service overseas … These boys, with not only their careers, but possibly their lives at stake, are to be selected by some form of lottery, or Russian roulette.' Condemning the 'unlucky dip', Calwell asked: 'Is this equal treatment before the law? Such a system will open the door for the exercise of every kind of privilege and pressure.' In the end, he claimed, those selected 'will be young fellows whose families lack influence and friends'.[18]

Calwell tended to foul the moral high ground when he claimed it: to suggest a class conspiracy badly smudged his case. The ballot did not exempt the rich (although it did allow university students to defer their service). It was eminently 'fair' insofar as a random selection could be. It was a lottery, not an American local draft committee, which did tend to draft the poor, blacks and uneducated. 'It was probably the fairest way to organise it,' said Don Chipp, then Chairman of the Liberal Back-bench Committee on Labour and National Conscription, and an advocate of military intervention in Vietnam.[19] The sons of the great and the good, wealthy businessmen, professional people, sporting stars and celebrities — Keith Gent, the Essendon footballer, and Normie Rowe, the pop star — all were conscripted.

If the ballot was 'fair', the principle of random selection seemed grossly unjust, if not immoral. The lottery repelled many Australians, and with good reason. Why should one man in twelve be randomly selected to fight, and possibly die, for his country? The celebrity-drawn marbles demeaned the Anzac tradition; courage and self-sacrifice hardly resounded to the roll of a dice.

Another source of deep unease was that, in 1965, under 21-year-olds could neither vote nor drink. In the eyes of the law they were mere boys; to the government, they were old enough to fight and kill, throw grenades and fire a machine gun. The vote was later extended to 20-year-olds, but in 1966, the year of Long Tan, a conscript did not have the right to vote for or against the government whose policies decided his fate: to fight, to kill or be killed. Protest groups seized on the issue, and their first effective campaign — 'Conscripting Australia's voteless youth!' — widely resonated with the public, much to the government's discomfort.

The great myth about conscription was that national servicemen were forced to serve in Vietnam. In fact, most battalion commanders offered to re-post those who did not want to go. 'The national serviceman,' Brigadier Colin Khan DSO recalls, 'had to specifically volunteer for overseas service by signing a declaration during Corps training ... all national servicemen who served in Vietnam volunteered to do so.'[20] Many conscripts do not recall being asked to sign a form, but in practice most were offered a verbal exit. Very few withdrew; the great majority went to Vietnam enthusiastically, for the sake of their mates, out of a sense of duty, or simply for the excitement and adventure.

Or fear. Some battalions' methods of weeding out 'cowards' probably ensured that many recruits stayed quivering in the ranks. Company sergeant majors were known to shout, 'Any little cunt who doesn't want to go to Vietnam, step forward now!'[21] 'We were asked: all those who wanted to go to Vietnam form up on the right, those who don't … form up on the left,' recalls Corporal Barry Middleton.[22] The courage required to step out possibly matched the courage of going to Nui Dat. The few who did were sometimes paraded in disgrace, then bundled out of the barracks like rubbish bins, their self-esteem in shreds, according to several accounts. One young man, a schoolteacher, who decided to withdraw from serving in Vietnam, was told by his commanding officer, in front of his battalion, 'You disgust me.' In fairness, the army generally dealt carefully and discreetly with such cases; officers simply wanted the best soldiers. Captain David Wilkins told members of the 5th Battalion that those who did not want to go 'may leave the room now and there won't be any recriminations … Our aim is to get the best team.'[23]

Despite this, the press and anti-war activists peddled the myth that conscripts were being forced to go to Vietnam. Later in the war, Lieutenant Colonel Keith O'Neill, commander of the 8th Battalion, challenged journalists to find a single reluctant soldier aboard HMAS *Sydney*. The press raced about, interviewing all and sundry, and found not a single reluctant soldier.[24] In short, the national servicemen who went to Vietnam were far from 'reluctant soldiers', as Lieutenant General Wilton observed.[25] When the Liberals were re-elected in 1966, Gregg Lindsay's battalion celebrated because 'an ALP victory would have seen an end to the Australian commitment. A wave of relief and jubilation swept the whole battalion.'[26]

The nashos were brighter, on average, than the voluntary recruits, and lent colour, irreverence and, in some cases, a touch of glamour to the Australian Army. They knew the latest music and fashions and how to chat up girls. Many had useful skills: rural sons like Binnie and Heard were familiar with rifles, and mining communities delivered engineers (and Tunnel Rats). The conscripts had 'experience, maturity and frequently education, rarely experienced in recruits [who tended to be 19 when sent to Vietnam]', observed Brigadier Colin Khan.[27] The nashos dared to ask questions, too.

'[They] demanded to know the reasons why,' said Khan. Officers and NCOs had to explain why things were done. 'It made better infantry leaders of all we Regulars,' Khan wrote.[28]

The lottery also captured the odd misfit, layabout, delicate boy and the utterly inept. Most of these were screened out. One poor dairy farmer, 'thick as a brick', believed a story that the condom issued with his pay packet was a balloon, to be inflated and presented on leave to his mother with 'I Love Mum' written on it. (He did so, and she complained to the army, as Barry Heard hilariously relates.)[29]

Of course, there were many superb regular soldiers of dynamic character, courage and leadership. And the sergeants had one way of offsetting their slight unease amid these hip young men from civvy street: training. The fresh-faced conscripts were in the army now. And they were going to feel it.


Amid tearful mothers and braying protesters, the new conscript walked the gauntlet of the Save Our Sons ladies' vigils that huddled outside local military induction centres. After further medical checks he set off for one of three 'holiday resorts', as the nashos called the army training centres. Victorians, Tasmanians, South Australians and Western Australians went to freezing Puckapunyal, or 'Pucka', a hundred kilometres north of Melbourne; Queenslanders and northern New South Wales recruits went to freezing Singleton, in the Hunter Valley; and the rest of New South Wales went to freezing Kapooka, near Wagga Wagga.

At the railway station they met their 'CSM'. Nobody knew who or what this stood for: 'City stationmaster? Coffee, scones and a muffin?'[30] wondered Barry Heard. The recruits shortly divined the letters stood for Company Sergeant Major, invariably a stiff, lantern-jawed bloke in a crew cut and perfectly creased khaki uniform. The sight provoked laughter among Heard's mates. 'Looks like a green emu ... Looks like he's just cacked his daks,' they muttered.

The mood of a school excursion animated the bus trip: laughter, singing, whistling at girls. 'Getyagearoff!' the new recruits yelled at passing sheilas. The CSM and his army colleagues sat up front, stiff and tight-lipped throughout, and were always sure to address the riotous assembly with 'please' and 'would you mind' and 'thank you'; that is, until the bus reached Puckapunyal, Kapooka or Singleton.

The moment he arrived at his designated holiday resort, the nasho experienced the odd feeling of being verbally clobbered. A huge bullet-headed instructor, the dominant caricature, boarded the bus and bellowed down at him: 'RIGHT. GET OFF THIS FUCKING BUS OR YOU'LL DO PUSH-UPS UNTIL THIS PLACE IS BELOW SEA LEVEL', followed by: 'FORM UP IN THREE RANKS, GIRLS!' After a pathetic attempt to form up, Heard's gang abandoned the effort and milled about, or 'just sauntered off'. Shortly a 'square-jawed, mean-looking, six-foot six-inch part animal' addressed the apparent ringleader: 'Hey, you — yes, you — you ugly six foot of sewer sludge. Get your arse over here ... now!'

And so it began. A ceaseless bark. Dawn parades in underwear. The issue of linen, armoury, uniforms. Hair reduced to stubble. Ten weeks of marching, jogging, ceaseless drill, spitting, polishing, climbing ropes, stripping and cleaning rifles. Up at 5 a.m., lights out at 10 p.m. Nights in freezing huts (four groups of sixteen to a dorm, at Pucka) set in treeless, desolate training camps. No contact with home for the first three weeks.

The conscripts and regs were treated exactly the same. They were invariably 'Girls', as in 'Let's fuckin' try it again, shall we, girls?' and so on. The instructors had a fine line in scatological humour; for example, 'When I say shit, you say where!', or:

'What are ya, 11 Platoon?'
'SHIT, SERGEANT!'
'How old?'
'THREE WEEKS, SERGEANT!'

Robin Harris found his place in the pecking order, courtesy of a sneering corporal, 'At the top of the pile is the General, then there's the Brigadier, the Full Colonel, Lieutenant Colonel, Major, Captain, Full Lieutenant, Second Lieutenant, Warrant Officers 1 and 2, Staff Sergeant, Sergeant, Corporal, Lance Corporal and Private ... Then there are rats and mice, blowflies and cockroaches. Then there are YOU FUCKING RECRUITS.'[31]

Regs endured the same regime, as Brian Hennessy found when he volunteered for the army: 'You are a despicable little grub, recruit. Wattarya?' To which Hennessy snapped to attention and shouted, 'I am a despicable little grub ...'

The furious corporal shouted back, 'You are a despicable little grub ... WHO??'

'I am a despicable little grub … CORPORAL!'[32]

The nashos quickly learned the game. To admit to being a grub or 6 feet of sewage was a minor price to pay for avoiding a unit punishment. One man's error disgraced the rest, all of whom were punished (extra miles, more press-ups). Better to muck in and perform than risk the wrath of your mates. The system was eminently practical.

The army's fastidiousness amazed the conscript. Everything had to be spruce; every step at a march; their fart sacks immaculate. When some slept in sleeping bags, to avoid making their beds, a furious sergeant paraded the recruits with their sheets over their heads. Pets were banned: when an instructor caught an ant walking across a dormitory floor, he charged the nearest recruit with 'harbouring a pet'.

The men were lectured on politics, history and personal hygiene. The army padres tended to cover the evils of masturbation and sexual sin. In one case, a padre warned the recruits not to fondle a girl's breasts as 'they may get excited and tempted to sin', to which a nasho muttered, 'Why the frigging hell does the silly old fart think we go for their tits?'[33] Instructors often stooped to pranks designed to humiliate; for example, recruits were forced repeatedly to salute a tree that had an officer's badge on it; wash clean dishes; or impersonate a dying fly, often in mud, and so on.

Many conscripts complained of petty-minded, ill-educated regs who held rank in recognition of long service rather than any manifest ability and who treated them like children. Financial penalties were particularly despised. 'I have never in my life,' said one, 'been so belittled and [unable] to retaliate … without fear of losing money.'[34]


There was method in the meanness: slowly, the recruits were being moulded into a mutually supportive combat unit. They strove to survive, then to endure, and finally to conquer the challenge, as a team. They helped the genuinely weak and threatened the lazy. And soon, beyond the fear and loathing, a kind of respect for their instructions — and even their instructors — began to emerge.

A sense of pride in their achievements kindled during the next stage of training: infantry corps. This involved three months in an infantry battalion, with lessons in how to fire new weapons — the machine gun and rocket launcher — and how to throw grenades: 'Pull the pin, let go the clasp, count to two, call "grenade", throw the grenade at target, duck, three, four, boom.'

They practised assault tactics, contact drill, ambush formations, hand signals. 'I had a wonderful time … one of the fondest times in my life,' Barry Heard later wrote.[35] Close friendships formed; nicknames (Booster, Chunder, Snoggons, Grunter, Turd) stuck. The men had greater freedom; they were allowed to 'hit the boozer'.

At the end of infantry training the recruits were promoted to 'Private' and posted to their permanent units. Most went to rifle companies in infantry battalions. Of the first batch, for example, John Binnie went to the 7th Battalion (7RAR) and Gordon Knight to the 6th Battalion (6RAR). Nine battalions would eventually go to Vietnam on a rotating basis; most served two tours. Others were posted to transport, engineers, signals or medical corps. In each case, national servicemen made up 30 to 40 per cent of the ranks.

A few gifted national servicemen — the 'Kings of the Call-up', as one paper reported — were selected for an officer training course.[36] The Scheyville Officer Training Unit near Windsor, west of Sydney, aimed to make a platoon commander of a national serviceman within six months. As such, it was certainly as tough an officer training course as the elite Portsea Cadet School in Victoria and Royal Military College, Duntroon, Canberra. About 120 cadets from each intake of 2,500 national servicemen were selected for Scheyville, according to their intelligence and personality. In total, Scheyville produced 1,871 second lieutenants between 1965 and 1973, compared with Portsea's 1,287 and Duntroon's 465.

Named after the prominent freemason William Schey, the school demanded 'the best of the best — and then some', recalled David Sabben, a cadet.[37] It was a case of being 'broken, remoulded, trained, challenged and tested', wrote Gary McKay.[38] A near-unbearable, continuous assessment process yielded a 30 to 40 per cent failure rate. Some cadets were failed the day before their graduation. 'The cost in shattered 20-year-old egos was high and often psychologically traumatic,' remembered Gregg Lindsay.[39]

It is impossible to comprehend the challenge facing the Scheyville cadet without grasping the extreme demands on a platoon commander: the platoon is the core combat unit and Vietnam the ultimate platoon-level war. The platoon commander must lead thirty men into a combat zone; excel at navigation, tactics, advanced weapons and a multitude of other things; understand the strengths and weaknesses of his men; earn their respect and loyalty; and conquer his fear. 'I had to be better than all my soldiers,' Sabben said, 'in order to instil in them the confidence that I deserved to lead them.'[40] Sabben's platoon sergeant, in his thirties, was a veteran of three wars; Sabben was just 21.

The process of creating such a man began the moment he arrived, when the usual cropped head of the regimental sergeant major leaped on the bus (cadets cannot forget RSM Larry Moon) and started yelling. The yelling never stopped. 'As they tumbled out we had them running, and they didn't stop running till the end of the course,' said Moon. 'We did terrible things to them,' he smiled.[41]

'The clear message was "You are going to war, and diggers will die if you don't get it right",' Lindsay recalled. Memories of civilian life, of rugby and the beach, faded and 'you found yourself with real issues, of real consequence. And at 20 you take yourself very seriously. We were putty in the hands of the military.'[42]

Members of the Team returning from Vietnam adapted the course for the conditions of that war. Chief instructor Stan Maizey made the field exercises 'as real as possible'. They rehearsed heliborne assaults and hot insertions. Mock Vietnamese villages, 'complete with hides, false walls, dogs and chooks',[43] were erected, to train the cadet in the tactics of the 'other enemy', the Vietnamese civilians, 'who would throw a grenade at the drop of a hat'.[44] Members of the Women's Royal Australian Army Corps Officer Cadet School dressed as Vietnamese civilians, in black pyjamas and conical straw hats. Lessons in dining etiquette rounded off this military Pygmalion, and a second lieutenant was born: a platoon commander, jungle warfare expert, officer and a gentleman hewn out of the ganglionic blob of untested youth.

Rugged, razor-back country blanketed in dense rainforest surrounds the Jungle Training Centre in Canungra, a few drab administration buildings in the foothills of the Beechmont plateau, south-east Queensland. Passing this final, three-week course was mandatory for all soldiers bound for Vietnam. Founded in World War II, the dreaded Canungra had lain dormant for ten years until, in the mid-1950s, Colonel Serong reshaped the centre to meet the physical demands of modern jungle warfare.

Serong made the course tougher than previous years, a lot tougher. A gauntlet of instructors prodded and shouted as the troops pelted along the obstacle race, against the clock, over a cargo net strung above bog holes, up a suspended pole, down a flying fox, through barbed wire, over fences, down into muddy puddles and up a wooden tower suspended 10 metres above Canungra Creek, into which they plunged. One ferocious instructor tended to kick the fingers of soldiers immobilised on the ladder, as several veterans later recalled. The 'battle inoculation range' involved launching mock assaults as Vickers machine guns chattered overhead and simulated artillery and mortar fire threw up clods of earth, 'adding to the smoke and confusion of battle'.[45] The night assaults saw hundreds of men charging through flares and tracer and exploding shells. Yet, however well contrived, such rehearsals scarcely touched on the chaos and terror of actual night operations in Vietnam.

Their year's training culminated in a huge, battalion-strength mock battle, using artillery and armour, at Shoalwater Bay Training Area near Rockhampton. The men who passed were deemed ready for war. They were the fittest and best trained troops ever to leave Australia, as several battalion commanders remarked. The national serviceman in particular, observed Colin Khan, 'despite the fact that he came from a generation considered by some to be "long-haired dissenters", was the equal of any soldier to leave our shores'.[46]

# Chapter 15
# To Nui Dat

Q: I take it you went to Canberra at some stage before you went
to Nui Dat?
Brigadier Jackson: No.
Q: You didn't. Oh … you were [not] given any specific briefings?
Brigadier Jackson: No. I was not told anything in fact … I went
up there pretty much without any previous knowledge … I spent
one day at Intelligence Centre in Sydney and then [was] told
something about the Vietnamese people and their habits …
*Brigadier David Jackson, 1st Australian Task Force commander, 1966.*

'Just put a ring around Phuoc Tuy province,' smiled Major General Ken
Mackay one day in August 1965. Mackay, soon to command Australian
Force Vietnam, the military administration unit based in Saigon, was chatting
to General Bill DePuy, Chief of Staff to Westmoreland, about where to
deploy the 1st Australian Task Force, which had been formed to defend a
chosen Vietnamese province, with tactical independence from the Americans.
By now it was clear the US experiment with the 1st Battalion, then in Bien
Hoa, simply had not worked at a tactical level — despite the generally good
relations between the troops — and the Australians were to get their own area
of operations. Ultimately they would remain under US operational control
but would be free to exert far more tactical autonomy.

The Australian commander had rejected the Mekong Delta, Bien Hoa and
Phan Rang: 'If we're going to come in with a force,' Mackay told DePuy, 'this is

the place … it would suit us. Now flog off this other area, flog off this and that, do what you like, but don't let this one go … until we've checked it out.'

'OK, we'll put a thumb mark on it for you,' said DePuy, with a laugh.

It was a relaxed meeting of close friends in the sumptuous, air-conditioned offices of the American Military Assistance Command — Vietnam (MACV). 'This was the happy situation I was in with Westmoreland's staff,' Mackay recalled. 'This is the way you do this sort of liaison.'[1]

A little more thought went into the decision than DePuy's arbitrary thumbprint: Westmoreland had reinforced the idea of the 'Australian province', in talks with Lieutenant General John Wilton, Chief of the General Staff, and Brigadier David Jackson, designated commander of the Task Force.

Wilton approved. Phuoc Tuy met his strict criteria: it was strategically useful; thick with enemy (i.e. there was a job to do); did not border Australian no-go areas, such as Cambodia, Laos or the Demilitarised Zone; and offered ship and air access for easy insertion and, if necessary, evacuation. Most importantly, Australian troops could fight their own tactical war here, undisturbed. American tactics, Wilton privately mused, were likely to hasten the destruction of the far smaller Australian forces. 'Although for military tactical reasons we really had to be under [US] operational control, I preferred not to be included in an American position,'[2] he said later.


Phuoc Tuy was a rough rectangle 30 kilometres from north to south, 60 kilometres from east to west, bounded by the South China Sea to the south, the Rung Sat marshes and Saigon River to the west, Binh Thuan province to the east, and Long Khanh province to the north. In 1966 about 103,000 people lived here, sprinkled over thirty villages and more than a hundred hamlets. Two-thirds were Buddhist and a third — three times the provincial average — Catholic.

Mountains, jungle, grasslands and swamps claimed most of the province. The May Taos rise 2,500 to 3,000 feet over the north-east corner; the Nui Thi Vai and Nui Toc Tien Hills to the west of Nui Dat; and the impenetrable Long Hai range buffets the South China Sea to the south-east. On the latter summit a shambles of enormous boulders still block the entrances to a labyrinth of caves, known as the Minh Dam Secret Zone, headquarters of the Viet Cong provincial forces.

The chief sustainers of life in Phuoc Tuy were rubber and rice-growing, fishing, salt, wood-cutting and charcoal-burning. The province's rice crop grew mainly around Dat Do and Xuyen Moc. The busy fishing ports — including Long Phuoc Hai, one of the most productive in Cochinchina — had great strategic value as marine supply depots. Tiny craft also secreted ammunition and food to the Viet Cong through the Rung Sat (or 'Jungle of Death'), a vile, brackish waterway of malarial channels teeming with insects.

Phuoc Tuy offered the perfect terrain for guerrilla warfare. 'It has a long coastline,' observed one Australian officer, 'a complex delta area of mangrove swamps, isolated ranges of very rugged mountains, and a large area of virtually uninhabited jungle containing all the most loathsome combinations of thorny bamboos, poisonous snakes, insects, malaria, dense underbrush, swamps and rugged ground conditions that the most dedicated guerrilla warfare expert could ask for ...'[3]

It was also of strategic value. Whoever controlled Phuoc Tuy controlled a deepwater harbour — Vung Tau — at the mouth of the Saigon River, connected by road to the heart of Saigon. With Saigon's riverside port heavily congested, Vung Tau was a supply lifeline. 'We saw the province as very important strategically,' Nguyen Gia Ho, the National Liberation Front's former propaganda chief in Phuoc Tuy, told me in 2005. 'It was one of four fronts to Ho Chi Minh City.'[4]

In the early twentieth century wealthy French colonial officials and plantation owners took their holidays in Phuoc Tuy — at the coastal port of Vung Tau, then named Cap St Jacques, the 'New Riviera'. The French haute-monde would drive down to their seaside villas from Saigon, sometimes stopping en route to hunt. A 1930s travel guide warned of wild animals: tigers, panthers, stag and wild bullocks, most of which had disappeared by 1966.[5]

The French thoroughly suppressed local resistance in the province, deporting Vietnamese nationalists and nascent communists to the island of Poulo Condore: 'The red seed of Phuoc Hai' — the province's first communist cell, established in 1934 — took a breath and died, and the people lapsed into 'postures of non-violent resignation'.[6] The Japanese occupation briefly interrupted the French colony's pleasures, but resistance flared up again after the Japanese departed, when Phuoc Tuy produced its own answer to the heroic Trung sisters: Thi Sau, a 15-year-old schoolgirl, tried to assassinate the province chief on Bastille Day, 1948. A French firing squad executed her four years later, the day after she joined the local Communist Party.

When the French left, the Viet Minh overran the province, which soon became one of 'the major Viet Minh bases of the South'.[7] Their Viet Cong sons succeeded them. In 1962 most of the locals — '70 per cent', according to one communist history — were corralled into 132 Strategic Hamlets, virtually all of which were destroyed or 'liberated' by the Viet Cong in the next two years. In February 1964 the National Liberation Front 'maintained the initiative and called the tune' in the province, according to the military attaché at the Australian Embassy in Saigon. Only Ba Ria, the provincial capital, had any link with Saigon: 'In the remainder of the area, the VC operate almost unopposed.'[8]

Many Vietnamese Catholics fleeing the North settled in Phuoc Tuy, in newly built, heavily fortified villages such as Binh Gia, where a little church replaced the usual Buddhist pagoda. By 1964 the village's 6,000 inhabitants were part of an 'iron guard' of militant anti-communist villages surrounding Saigon — prime targets for Viet Cong rural guerrillas. In the last week of 1964, about 1,600 Viet Cong attacked and occupied Binh Gia, on a scale hitherto unseen by Free World advisers. It took seven battalions — about 4,500 of South Vietnam's best troops — to reclaim Binh Gia, not without severe casualties: 201 killed and 192 wounded, and 68 missing.[9] In fact, the ferocity of the attack helped to persuade Westmoreland to call in US ground forces. The battle was a 'watershed'.[10] At Binh Gia, as at Ap Bac, the enemy showed that he could stand and win. The Australians would soon confront some of these troops at Long Tan; yet when they arrived, few Australian commanders had even heard of the battle of Binh Gia.[11]

The National Liberation Front had proliferated with astonishing speed. At the start of 1966, the communists fielded 174,000 more soldiers than their opponents in the South.[12] By July 1966 the People's Army had deployed 460,000 troops in North Vietnam and 230,000 in the South. That month 200,000 North Vietnamese youths joined up, and infiltration from North to South was running at 4,500 a month that year, compared with a monthly rate of a thousand a year earlier.[13] The success of the American counter-offensive had provoked this massive enemy concentration: Westmoreland's war of attrition, as an emergency strategy, had succeeded in thwarting Hanoi's invasion plan, halted the communist attempt to cut South Vietnam in half, and driven the Viet Cong back to the guerrilla stage of revolutionary war.

Still, in 1966, the Viet Cong virtually controlled Phuoc Tuy. By night, their cadres infiltrated the villages with ease. 'Before your forces arrived,' Nguyen Gia Ho said, 'the National Liberation Front controlled the province: that was why the Americans thought it was so peaceful.'[14] On the eve of Australia's arrival, enemy forces virtually saturated Phuoc Tuy. On 23 November 1965 the 5th Division of the National Liberation Front established its headquarters in Ba Ria. It comprised the 274th and 275th Regiments, provincial mobile units, notably the formidable D445 Battalion, raised on 19 May 1965 at Long Tan village, as well as thousands of local guerrillas. 'There were by this time seven battalions of Viet Cong with heavy fire support units active within the province,' noted Bob O'Neill, who became the intelligence officer of Australia's 5th Battalion, which arrived in May 1966.[15] Their base areas covered the Hat Dich area to the west and the Minh Dam Secret Zone, encompassing the Long Hais, Long Dien and Dat Do. Meanwhile, several regiments of North Vietnamese had been sent to contiguous or nearby provinces, in Bien Hoa, Long Khanh and Long Binh, including Special Forces battalions, logistics and rear echelons, and artillery detachments.

To visualise the depth of communist infiltration, picture the province at night. In every village — with the exception of Binh Gia, and a few isolated Catholic hamlets — the Viet Cong came alive, fed off the peasants, taxed the farmers and threatened or murdered collaborators. Some communities, notably the 'fighting villages' of Long Tan, Hoa Long and Long Phuoc, were thoroughly communist; many were neutral (in spirit) or terrorised into submission. In March 1966 an American intelligence estimate reckoned that 32 per cent of the province's villages were pro-South, 12 per cent pro-Viet Cong and 56 per cent neutral.[16]

Surveys failed to detect the underlying reality. In early 1966 most people in Phuoc Tuy obeyed the Viet Cong, whether forcibly or willingly. By day the province chief, Lieutenant Colonel Le Duc Dat, exerted nominal control over Ba Ria and Vung Tau and a brief slice of Highway 15, and a semblance of authority in Xuyen Moc and Phu My. 'All districts except Ba Ria itself were heavily infiltrated,' Bob O'Neill observed. Even the capital was unsafe: the Viet Cong mortared Colonel Dat's house in retaliation for his support for the US assault on Long Phuoc. 'By the time the Task Force arrived in May 1966, the National Liberation Front had effectively won the war in Phuoc Tuy.'[17]

In early 1966, Brigadier Jackson personally reconnoitred the province.

Phuoc Tuy, he grimly concluded, 'was an area which had gone bad … The VC were pretty much in control of it.'[18] The war, he said, 'was lost from a military point of view'.[19]

Into this explosive climate the Australian Government dropped two battalions of well-trained troops, almost half of whom were (on completion of training) 21-year-olds chosen by raffle.

It was early 1966, and a turbulent time in Canberra. In January Treasurer Harold Holt — energetic, buoyant, eager to engage 'the Asians' — succeeded Menzies as prime minister when the latter resigned after eighteen years in office; Malcolm Fraser, a tall, patrician grazier with an acute political mind softened by a damp strain of *noblesse oblige*, replaced Dr Jim Forbes as Minister for the Army; and Allen Fairhall succeeded Senator Shane Paltridge as Minister for Defence. Hasluck remained at External Affairs. The fit, urbane Holt, of Wesley College and Melbourne University law school pedigree, was well liked; he had managed not to derail the economic boom. His first statements as prime minister linked him indelibly with Vietnam: he promised to treble the size of the Task Force and to issue a medal for service in South Vietnam (in reply, in a little corner of Hyde Park, Sydney, a dozen defiant youths burned their draft cards). Holt's new guard inherited a decidedly bleak military situation in Vietnam, and a political powder keg at home, as the burgeoning protest movement rallied around the first few draft resisters.

In sending a fully supported task force, the army had won the argument over the government's cheaper preference for a second battalion. Fearful of the political fallout of losing a battalion, the Holt Government bowed to the army's advice of the bigger, costlier deployment. In 1966 the 1st Australian Task Force (1ATF) incorporated two infantry battalions, armoured and artillery units, a Special Air Service squadron, engineers and helicopter squadrons, a reconnaissance flight, an intelligence unit and signals, logistic, medical and provost support units. All would be rotated each year. Technically the Task Force was under the operational control of the US II Field Force Vietnam, yet tactically it was largely autonomous, a self-contained combat unit under Australian tactical command with responsibility (with the ARVN) for securing the countryside in Phuoc Tuy. As such, the Australians offered a control experiment for a very different kind of war.

The Task Force's first commander, Brigadier Oliver David Jackson — erstwhile commander of the Team and Australian Force Vietnam (the

Saigon office that liaised with Canberra) — received no briefing before he took up his new role, as revealed in a later interview:

> Q: I take it you went to Canberra at some stage before you went to Vietnam?
> Jackson: No.
> Q: You didn't. Oh ... you were [not] given any specific briefings?
> Jackson: No. I was not told anything in fact ... I went up there pretty much without any previous knowledge ... I spent one day at Intelligence Centre in Sydney and then [was] told something about the Vietnamese people and their habits ...
> Q: And no other briefings?
> Jackson: And no other briefings. I was given no directions or briefings ...[20]

In fact, Jackson's only clear instructions came from Westmoreland, who said simply: 'Take over Phuoc Tuy.'[21] At the same time, the Australian Government approved a series of 'tasks' for the Australian Task Force. They were:

1. to secure and dominate the assigned Tactical Area of Responsibility (TAOR) in Phuoc Tuy province;
2. to conduct operations related to the security of Highway 15 (linking Vung Tau and Saigon) as required;
3. to conduct other operations in Phuoc Tuy as required;
4. to conduct operations anywhere in the ARVN III Corps Tactical Zone (CTZ) and subsequently in the area of the adjacent province of Binh Thuan in the ARVN II CTZ as agreed by COMAFV and COMUSMACV (Commander Australian Force Vietnam and Commander US Military Assistance Command — Vietnam, respectively).[22]

The tasks were vague and open-ended, subject to constant reinterpretation and offered no strategic objective; that was America's job. As such, Jackson was not the first Task Force commander to interpret the tasks in his own way. He thought his job also involved 'the far more important' task 'of getting in among the people. Stay with them, giving them security and helping them to a better way of life.' He pressed on his staff the importance of civil affairs and improvements to village security, water supply and shelters.[23]

Were the troops, then, to double as plumbers and carpenters? Asked what he thought the Australians were supposed 'to do, to achieve' in Phuoc Tuy, Jackson later replied, 'Well, I don't think anybody could solve that question …' General Mackay seemed similarly in the dark. Had he heard of the Joint Strategic Initiative supposedly drawn up with the Americans? 'Never heard of it. Probably useless when it was developed anyway …'[24] An exasperated Brigadier Sandy Pearson, a later Task Force commander, witheringly remarked that 'we weren't given a task' in Vietnam. He added, 'It's the first war we've gone into without a strategic or political aim …'[25] And Major General A. L. MacDonald later thumped his oar in, asserting: 'The Australian Army's role in Vietnam was to ensure the security of the people in Phuoc Tuy … I never regarded that as being the real role … the real role was to demonstrate to anybody who wished to know … that we were as opposed to communist aggression as they were …'[26]

Taken at face value, it seemed the Australian commanders had no idea what they were supposed to be doing in Vietnam. Yet that misses the political subtext of these remarks: an implicit finger pointing at Canberra. The government had not given them a mission other than to 'conduct operations' as the army saw fit, and so on. The commanders were politely — and understandably — shifting the blame. No one said so openly, but the army's top brass were under no illusions about their true role in Vietnam: as a token political force, a mere gesture, to satisfy the Americans. The Australian Task Force was nominally under the operational control of America's II Field Force Vietnam, and the Australian Force Vietnam merely had a veto role in regard to their employment. The commitment had no strategic military purpose whatsoever. The journalist Peter Samuel got it right, writing in 1969: 'The Australian Government would appear never to have thought in depth about the role of the Australian forces or formulated a strategy for the Task Force in particular.'[27]

Unburdened by these political considerations, David Sabben, a platoon commander, stated with crystalline clarity what he believed to be his mission in Vietnam: 'The Australian aim in Phuoc Tuy was to isolate the Viet Cong and North Vietnamese Main Forces from the population.'[28] In short, to protect the people. Yet many of 'the people' were either afraid of Australian protection — or were Viet Cong.

★ ★ ★

After last beers at a local Liverpool pub, a chilly parade at Holsworthy Barracks, and an emotional hour with their families, the advance party of the 5th Battalion, Royal Australian Regiment, the first combat unit of regs and nashos, boarded a Qantas Boeing 707 bound for South Vietnam (the rest went on HMAS *Sydney*). It was the night of 12 May 1966. 'The crowd became excited and then cheered' as the troops boarded. As the plane taxied to the runway, recalled O'Neill, 'we saw the small distant faces and waving arms recede quickly into the distance …'[29]

A week later, the 6th Battalion based at Brisbane's Enoggera Barracks prepared for their departure. Returning from leave, Major Brian McFarlane, a company commander, spotted one of his troops, Private Gordon Knight, of Newtown, at Sydney airport, saying goodbye to family and friends. McFarlane paused and watched; he meant to go over and introduce himself to his soldier's family but, 'when I next looked they had gone … the moment was lost. Lost forever.'[30]

At 40,000 feet the azure coastline gave no sign of the racked nation below. A ribbon of yellow sand divided the sea from the mottled green jungle. And then, like hundreds of flickering mirrors, the rice paddies of the delta flashed by; urban smudges and skids of smoke soon mingled with the fields, and rooftops, animals, shops and vehicles crashed into the great metropolitan shambles of Saigon. The pilot suddenly plunged earthward, to avoid the Viet Cong's anti-aircraft guns, and pulled up on the tarmac of Tan Son Nhut airport.

A scene of mayhem greeted the soldiers as they stepped out into the sweltering heat and dripping humidity: the scream of supersonic Phantom jets; the whiff of diesel oil; the thumpa-tumpa-thumpa of helicopter blades; the hundreds of species of airborne vehicle; the interminable bustle of American soldiers, jogging here, marching there, landing, taking off; the loudly welcoming, and strangely sullen, 'Negroes', so alien to the Aussies; the exaggerated nonchalance and cowboy swagger of the white Americans, indomitable, in charge, winning. Everywhere were signs of an indeterminate threat: the steel mesh on the bus windows to block grenades thrown by passing cyclists; the hatred in the eyes of the hungry Vietnamese who huddled near the airport lounge; the distant crump of artillery and air strikes.

On the tarmac McFarlane's company passed about a hundred 1st Battalion troops, awaiting their flight home. Many were quiet, absorbed in thought; and their welcoming banter could not disguise the grey pallor and thousand-yard stare of these young men; men whom the war had changed utterly.

Baby Herc transport planes flew the fresh battalions to Vung Tau, where they soon met their complement, arriving by ship. The troops converged on a little slice of coastline on the dunes high above Back Beach, commandeered by the 1st Australian Logistic Support Group. The liquid air and close heat had an asphyxiating effect and clung to everything. Daily monsoons flattened the sand dunes and turned the roads to mud or pools, and the stench — none forgot the stench that overhung the place, of faeces, rotting food, old fish and something else, something putrefying, human or animal …

Westmoreland, in green fatigues with 'creases that would slice bread', flew out to greet the rest of the troops arriving on HMAS *Sydney*. 'Gentlemen of the 5th Battalion, I salute you,' he announced to the amazed ranks that lined the ship's deck. The supreme commander threw a salute, at which one digger awkwardly farted, provoking a stir in the ranks.[31] Shortly, the landing barges were lowered, and the troops headed for the beach. At the break the ramps went down, and they splashed ashore with rifles ready to find on the sand Americans on leave, sunbathing and drinking beer. The beach was a US transit area, and 'waterfalls of glinting beer cans and food containers' seemed to cascade down the dunes, observed Lieutenant Colonel David Rouse, who commanded 1st Australian Logistic Support Group.[32]

It was a dreadful place from which to supply an army, with soaring temperatures, sandstorms, flooding and daily subsidence. To stabilise the sand against the wind and rain required 60,000 to 80,000 tonnes of rockfill: 'You'd have a dunny on top of a sand hill one day,' explained Rouse, 'and the following day you'd have the dunny standing up and the sand hill 6 feet below it.' Tippers and dozers operated around the clock: not until August 1967 would the Australian base at Vung Tau possess a tarmac heliport and all-weather roads. The standards of hygiene — this was the future site of the main Australian field hospital — were shocking: 'The blow-flies, the flies, the filth, the grime and the lack of everything was indescribable,' said Rouse.[33] Yet even these filthy dunes were hard won: Jackson actually threatened to order HMAS *Sydney* to turn back unless the Americans made room for the Australian support base.

The troops acclimatised in temperatures of 35 degrees Celsius amid the daily afternoon deluge. Patrols of the surrounding hills soon found the ruins of a French villa, embraced in creepers: Vietnamese graffiti covered the whitewashed walls; snakes, rats and scorpions had the run of the rainswept rooms. Whenever he encountered these desolate reminders of the French,

Bob O'Neill heard the same imploring whisper from the past, 'What do you newcomers think you can achieve?'[34]

In May the Australian battalions departed for Nui Dat — the Task Force base — aboard a convoy of trucks with seats facing outwards in case of ambush, and floors heavily sandbagged against mines. As they passed Hoa Long, 'we didn't get many waves, only hostile looks', Corporal Spike Jones recalled.[35]

Their destination, Nui Dat — 'hill of earth' — would be the home of the Australian Task Force for the next six years. Wilton had chosen it earlier that year on a fly-over: 'One day there'll be an empire down there, won't there?' he remarked to Jackson.[36] The hill and surrounding area met Wilton's conditions: big enough to accommodate 3,000 men and an airstrip big enough to receive Hercules transports; able to withstand enemy attacks of divisional size; sited on elevated, open ground so that artillery could fire in any direction without endangering civilians; beyond the artillery range of the Nui Dinh Hills and Long Hai Mountains; and close to a water supply and a road link to Vung Tau. To the arriving troops, however, it was a desolate little plateau of coarse scrub topped by a little knoll, and surrounded by old, disused rubber plantations and a few Viet Cong-controlled villages.

'We built the camp up from nothing in the most atrocious weather conditions,' recalled Lieutenant Colonel Colin Townsend, the 6th Battalion commander. 'There was bloody mud everywhere. Boots just wore out, everything perished.'[37] Mildew discoloured everything. The erection of every tent, tin shed and boozer, the construction of the Task Force headquarters, the laying down of gun emplacements and sandbags, the clearance of an airfield and helicopter pad, the establishment of the Special Air Service (first in the rubber, then on the little summit), the defoliation of the surrounding vegetation, the rolling out of perimeter wire, the endless digging, digging, digging of weapon pits, toilets, drainage, shower blocks, and the constant patrols into the tactical area of operations (which every soldier had to perform, including the service corps); all these actions shouted defiance to the brooding, silent countryside. The Viet Cong watched and waited ... and took the measure of this novel enemy, who oddly eschewed steel helmets for floppy hats and chose to camp in the boondocks ... yet whom they quietly dismissed as merely another American mercenary.

The people were curious: 'The young willowy girls in their black and white *ao dai* dresses moved in knots of giggles to and from school,' wrote Michael O'Brien. 'The street urchins grinned and begged. The placid, patient farmers worked their paddy under their conical straw hats.'[38] But the people's faces expressed fear: for years many had endured Viet Cong infiltration, extortion and terror; now they had a choice. But would the Australians stay or make their lives more dangerous? Would these *uc dai loi* ('army from the south land') stay to protect us? wondered fearful locals not yet loyal to the enemy.

Brigadier Jackson tried to answer that question. During the tense first month, he and the province chief drove down to the Viet Cong-controlled village of Hoa Long, stood in the marketplace and announced: 'The Australians have come here to help you, and they have come to stay. And whatever the VC may feel about this, It's too bad for them. Because they are not going to exist in this province in the way they have in the past.'[39]

The Task Force's location certainly unsettled the Viet Cong, conceded General Hoang Phuong, chief military historian of the Socialist Republic of Vietnam.[40] Nui Dat straddled the Viet Cong supply line, from the urban centres in the west to their mountain hides in the east. The destruction of these impudent *uc dai loi*, this minor US ally, also had great political value to the Viet Cong's armed propaganda units. In fact, the communist forces were already planning the annihilation of the Australians. Nui Dat's 'frontlines' were north, south, east and west. Everywhere you looked on the map from that earthen mound, Viet Cong villages, hamlets and mountain hideouts stared back.

The supply disaster kicked in immediately. For several weeks no defence stores, barbed wire, tents, sandbags or star pickets arrived, due partly to the primitive state of Vung Tau and, more distressingly, the result of the Australian wharf labourers' refusal to load HMAS *Jeparit*, a transport ship. And so, for weeks, the soldiers slept under hutchies (waterproof sheets thrown over a branch or stick for temporary shelter) in the steaming heat and pouring rain, with an inadequate water supply, no drainage or sewerage, no garbage removal and certainly no laundry service. The men later sent their jungle greens to Ba Ria.[41]

The toilet blocks were roofless shacks situated above a huge hole topped with four seats. There were no partitions. The stench was indescribable. 'I'd never, never experienced this before,' recalled David Morgan, a later arrival, 'sharing the same toilet with three blokes straining and grunting at the same time as me.' Flares were dropped into the holes to kill the swarms of insects, 'with spectacular visual effects'.[42] The shower block contained four canvas bags with shower nozzles, raised by a pulley system connected to the corrugated iron roof.

Skin conditions, chiefly 'crutch rot', were immediate health concerns, recalled Corporal Geoff Jones, a 6th Battalion medic: 'Your genital area, the scrotum particularly, and all of the inner part of the thighs became great red welts that would ooze and seep, and it was difficult to walk, but you had to walk.'[43]

By day they dug and dug — weapon pits, perimeter pits, gun pits — laid sandbags, built pathways and fortified the perimeter with rolls of wire and mines. Some units did a little landscaping. Harry Smith's Delta Company, 6th Battalion, tried to beautify their lines with banana trees along the pathways, to which a senior officer snorted, 'What are you trying to do? We're here to fight a war!' Smith refused to live in mud and squalor: 'My attitude was that we should fight hard and come back to comfort.'[44] And all the while, the Viet Cong observed this bizarre sight, of a foreign army daring to build a fortress bang in the centre of 'their' province.

The defoliation of Nui Dat, or 'base area vegetation control', began immediately. The ground spraying teams defoliated 5 square kilometres of countryside around the 13-kilometre perimeter wire and out to the Horseshoe (a hill thus shaped north of Dat Do). The verdant shambles of jungle, forest and old rubber encroached on the Task Force perimeter, and posed 'a considerable hazard', advised scientist George Lugg and Major E.S. Holt, who developed a ground spraying plan for defoliating the area around the Task Force Base. As thick vegetation offered cover to Viet Cong patrols, and the farms provided a source of food, further defoliating the immediate area was a sound military decision: it cleared the field of fire, removed the enemy's cover and helped to preserve the soldiers' lives.[45]

Spraying herbicides was then considered a minor task, one of hundreds in the daily routine. At the time, few gave much thought to the associated health risks.[46] The defoliation of Nui Dat was merely part of the defoliation of Phuoc Tuy, one province of forty-six, in the wholesale defoliation of the jungles of South Vietnam.

The Kennedy administration had authorised this environmental destruction (OPERATION RANCH HAND, which ran between 1964 and 1970).[47] In Phuoc Tuy, for example, thickly afforested parts of the province — chiefly 'Slope 30' north of Nui Dat, the Thua Tich region in the remote north-east, the Rung Sat swamps, farms deemed to be under Viet Cong control, and the isolated forests east of Xuyen Moc — were regularly doused in three different herbicides (including Agent Orange, one of the most lethal) by US aircraft. These 'Traildust' operations flew low over the designated targets spewing long streams of defoliant. Elsewhere, this chemical deluge targeted the Viet Cong supply lines, chiefly the Central Highlands, the delta and river estuaries, and the Ho Chi Minh Trail.

In 1965 defoliants destroyed enough food to feed 245,000 Vietnamese people for a year — a propaganda gift to the Viet Cong. Indeed, defoliation alienated innumerable villages and rural communities, and generally failed to uncover the enemy, who fought on from his tunnels, mountain caves and areas of uncleared jungle. The Free World forces persisted, however, and sometimes timed the destruction of 'enemy' crops for the end of the harvest: the effect on the villagers' spirits can be imagined. 'The idea,' explained an RAAF officer who participated in these spraying operations in 1968, 'was not to destroy [the food] but to make it unpalatable ... because [we] reckoned it was better to keep them busy tending the crops to harvesting stage ... that meant they would have less time for fighting.'[48]

# Chapter 16
# The village

I thought the psychology of destroying Long Phuoc ridiculous. If
they weren't VC sympathisers, they sure were after they were
moved and their homes destroyed.

*Denis Gibbons, veteran Australian war photographer.*

Private Errol Noack — a handsome young man, six foot five, and a
terrific athlete — died on the first day of the first operation, ten days
after he arrived in Vietnam. Noack was the first national serviceman to be
killed in action and the only son of Walter Noack, a divorced factory worker
of Port Lincoln, South Australia.

One day, in mid–1966, a policeman, a padre and an army captain
knocked on Walter's door. The captain said: 'I've got some bad news,' and
handed Walter the telegram.

At first, Noack's father would not believe it: 'Errol was such a terrific
kid,' he said later. I raised him … his mother cleared out when he was just a
baby. He was great the whole time. When he left school, we worked
together tuna fishing and in factories.'[1]

'He will be buried with full military honours in Vietnam,' the army
captain gently informed the distraught father.

'You won't do that. You'll bring him back,' Walter replied.

The captain insisted on the usual army protocol, to which Walter said:
'This is different. Errol was conscripted. He was taken from his home and sent
to Vietnam whether he wanted to go or not.' The captain argued that there

may not be time, to which the boy's father demanded: 'They found it possible to get him across there, and they can find it possible to bring him back!'

Canberra went into an overnight huddle. The next day, it was announced that Errol Noack's body would come home. The Task Force borrowed a lead coffin from the Americans; it arrived at Adelaide airport, draped in the Australian flag. Walter insisted on viewing his son's corpse, into which the Americans had thoughtfully injected embalming fluid. 'He looked … like he was asleep — it was all natural colours.'[2] Before the funeral, anti-war protesters daubed the slogan 'Errol Wayne Noack, aged 21: his was not to reason why' over the Cross of Remembrance in Adelaide.[3]

Noack died of friendly fire on 24 May 1966; the cause of death was not revealed until much later. That afternoon his unit — a company of the 5th Battalion — patrolled in roasting heat, in long grass. The sweat turned their jungle greens black, the colour of the Viet Cong's 'pyjamas'. As darkness fell, Noack joined a forward post during his company's relief; he stood up, and a burst of machine-gun fire riddled his back. Corporal Ron Nichols, the company medic, dashed forward and dressed his wounds, but Noack died on board the American dust-off helicopter.

Noack's death was a political event, and Canberra sought to contain the damage. Malcolm Fraser, Minister for the Army, demanded immediate details from the generals. 'I was sensitive on the political side,' Major General Mackay, commander of Australian Force Vietnam, in Saigon, later recalled. Mackay used deception to buy time: 'I made sure the communications [with Canberra] didn't work … I don't know whether it was legal or illegal, it didn't matter, but my main concern was to be quite certain what killed this man.' Mackay ordered an autopsy; the army doctors claimed that an AK47 (enemy) bullet had killed Noack. '… never once has there been any suggestion that this first national serviceman was killed by anything other than Communist fire, and that's what I was guaranteeing,' Mackay concluded.[4]

Mackay's guarantee, in this instance, was worthless; or he simply withheld the truth. No soldier had any doubt what killed Errol Noack: '… nothing shook the conviction of the men … that Private Errol Noack had died as a result of a tragic error,' concluded the official historian.[5] When the truth emerged, the government and army were accused of a deliberate cover-up. It was, of course, a sad accident, the first of many 'friendly fire' incidents common to all wars.[6]

★  ★  ★

The battle for the soul of the Vietnamese village occupies a special place in the annals of human suffering. The Vietnam War began in the village. If the Viet Cong controlled the villages, it controlled the countryside and could then gradually encircle the towns and cities.[7] Each village comprised several hamlets. The hamlet was the country's hearth, rice bowl, shrine and home to that most resilient character, the Vietnamese peasant. The peasant's peculiar tragedy was to live in the eye of the storm of a superpower-sponsored proxy war. It is difficult to conceive of a more terrifying place than to exist between the sights, on the one hand, of Sino-Soviet-backed communist guerrillas and of American, Australian and South Vietnamese troops on the other. The villagers were forced to choose.

The rival demands on their loyalties tore apart thousands of South Vietnamese communities. The US reporter Stanley Karnow, who visited dozens of hamlets in the early 1960s, found the people 'muddled, frightened, weary'. 'One thread seemed to run through their conversation,' he wrote. 'They were not participants in the conflict, but its victims. They sympathized with neither Diem nor the Viet Cong, only leaning to the side that harassed them less.' One old man explained their situation with the parable: 'If a son is mistreated by his father, he may adopt another.'[8]

The Vietnamese peasants were bound to the plot that their ancestors had farmed. '[The peasants'] love for their plot of land is stronger than all other preoccupations,' wrote one Phuoc Tuy province chief, in a local history.[9] They were fiercely loyal to this little world, the gates of which, metaphorically at least, were closed to imperial intervention — and, by extension, government meddlers and foreign intruders. 'Royal decrees yield to village customs,' ran a popular saying. This powerful sense of place, of one's ancestral roots, showed in the great migration home during Tet, the lunar holiday, and in the peasants' reluctance to travel beyond the village precinct.

In this light, the April 'resettlement' by US and South Vietnamese troops of the villages of Long Phuoc and Long Tan understandably inflamed local hatred of the foreign forces on the eve of the arrival of the Australian troops, who completed what the Americans had begun.

A pagoda, well-constructed homes, ornamental trees, deep shaded wells, fishponds and a little patchwork of market gardens where pineapples, bananas and root crops grew; such was the pretty village of Long Phuoc, a kilometre south-east of Nui Dat, in early June 1966. Orderly hedgerows and fences marked the village perimeter, and there was a stand of clean young rubber to the south. Elsewhere the bright green paddy fields were strangely denuded of women in conical hats. Indeed, the one thing missing from this village were people: Long Phuoc was a ghost town.

Scars of war blotted the picturesque scene. Six weeks earlier the American 173rd Airborne Brigade had bombed and napalmed Long Phuoc and killed or captured the embedded Viet Cong enemy forces. Their orders had been to 'secure the area' for the Australian Task Force. A B52's 1,000-pound bomb had levelled the village's granary, leaving a hole 6 metres deep and 45 metres wide. It had been a fierce battle. The Americans had lost nineteen dead and ninety wounded. They counted eighteen enemy bodies, and extensive blood trails suggested a further forty-five enemy dead.

The civilian occupants of Long Phuoc — mostly the families of Viet Cong troops — were then forcibly resettled at nearby Hoa Long, Dat Do and Long Dien; the occupants of Long Tan were similarly evicted. 'The people were streaming along the road, carrying their possessions,' observed Second Lieutenant Adrian Roberts, commander of an Australian armoured troop, then on a familiarisation operation with the Americans. 'I remember an old lady was carrying her sewing machine. These were the first refugees I had ever seen. It was sad.'[10]

Long Phuoc was hardly a neutral community: it had been a fortified Viet Cong-controlled base, harbouring riflemen by night and wood-carvers by day, and served as the headquarters of the National Liberation Front's provincial committee. Like a mini Cu Chi, it stood on a little maze of tunnels, one of which ran 3 kilometres to Long Tan. While it existed, it offered an enemy fortress within a few kilometres from Nui Dat. Under every home, beneath every bed or kitchen table, or behind false walls, trapdoors fell away to reveal bunkers and tunnels. The approaches to Long Phuoc had bristled with *punji* stakes and booby traps.

In late June, three Australian companies — about 300 soldiers — of the 6th Battalion, plus flame-throwing and demolition units, stood on the threshold of this deserted rural idyll. Their orders were to destroy the place. 'We were to search the village, kill any enemy, take any caches of food or equipment, and destroy the tunnels and the village,' recalled Corporal Spike Jones.[11] All buildings except churches and pagodas were to be levelled. The destruction of Long Phuoc — OPERATION ENOGGERA — began on 21 June 1966.

The Australians moved in from the north, and warned by loud hailer of their intentions. A few residual snipers replied. It was a wealthy village, prosperous, clean; many homes had traditional carved furniture with mother-of-pearl inlay and Buddhist icons — bought, remarked one officer, with the proceeds of Viet Cong plunder, or 'taxes', on the surrounding countryside. 'Every time I moved my headquarters from house to house,' said one company commander, 'I felt like moving in permanently.'[12]

The Australians blew up or torched the lot. It took a week. 'Once we cleared each house, we burned them as level as we could,' said David Sabben.[13] 'House by house, tunnel by tunnel,' reported the journalist Pat Burgess. The engineers of the 1st Field Squadron, under Major Warren Lennon, spent days underground, with pistols and torches, luring any hidden survivors to the surface. Then they demolished the tunnels, using TNT, diesoline and plastic explosive. Above ground, the infantry burned the homes with flame-throwers. Everything went onto the pyre: 'hand-carved candlesticks, the old exercise book, the flimsy parasol, the tiny rubber thong …'[14]

'6RAR … completed the destruction of an enemy battalion-sized base,' remarked a satisfied Brigadier Jackson in his Commander's Diary.[15] The Task Force had successfully 'denied the village to the VC for later use,' Jackson wrote, and salvaged 43 tonnes of rice, several tonnes of salt, ten rifles, booby traps, more than 4,000 *punji* stakes, and several unexploded 105mm shells (in the process of being turned into mines).

Few troops shared Jackson's enthusiasm. Nothing in their training had prepared them for this: 'We knew we had to do it … but we did not like it,'[16] said Townsend, the 6th Battalion commander.[17] Sabben took a more hard-headed line: 'When you start a house burning and all the ammunition in the roof starts exploding, you understand that there is a good reason for doing it and you don't question it.'[18]

Later that year, the Task Force let the exiled villagers return twice a week to till their fields. Policing this proved difficult, and sometimes deadly: at least fourteen times in September 1966, for example, Australian artillery fired on cattle and people on the road linking Hoa Long and Long Phuoc. Four were warning shots — standard procedure for any civilians entering a Free Fire Zone, but that failed to explain the remaining cases.[19] The civilians were probably bombed in error, one is left to conclude, or, in the official historian's dry observation, 'Direct engagement of civilians in these circumstances could have occurred.'[20]

A Free Fire Zone with a two-day 'safe' period proved impossible to regulate. On one occasion, Australian gunners, at the province chief's request, bombed Long Phuoc after 200 alleged Viet Cong re-entered the ruins of the town. The guns ceased firing after ten minutes, but air reconnaissance revealed the damage done: some farmers killed or injured, and others trying to rebuild their makeshift shelters, with no sign of the 200 enemy. Indeed, in 1967, the Australians abandoned the curfew and let former residents return at any time, somewhat defeating the original case for the forcible removal of the people of Long Phuoc.[21]

The demolition of Long Phuoc and resettlement of Long Tan (which was allowed to remain standing) were not typical acts of the Australian war. In fact, most enemy-controlled villages in the proximity — even the hotbed of Hoa Long — would in future be cordoned and searched, and not destroyed. American units, on the other hand, razed hundreds of villages suspected of harbouring Viet Cong insurgents; usually they warned the civilians, by loud hailer, to get out (many, reluctant to abandon their homes, stayed and died). The most spectacular example was the American destruction of the village of Ben Suc, a Viet Cong stronghold east of the Iron Triangle, during OPERATION CEDAR FALLS, on 8 January 1967. The people and animals were removed and their homes torched. The bulldozers flattened anything that would not burn — buildings, fences, ancestral graveyards. Then the US 1st Division engineers 'stacked ten thousand pounds of explosives and a thousand gallons of napalm in a crater in the centre of the ruined village, covered them with earth, and tamped it all down with bulldozers'. The five-ton explosion annihilated the tunnel system beneath Ben Suc. Nothing survived, certainly not the ancestral graves, some of which led into the tunnel system: '... we were bent on annihilating every possible indication that the village of Ben Suc had ever existed,' wrote Jonathan Schell of the *New Yorker*.[22] Then the whole area was defoliated, napalmed and torched, leaving a smouldering ashen mess, and more than 700 Vietnamese dead.[23] Most were Viet Cong troops; yet the fact that the enemy often forced themselves into civilian areas was lost on the American war machine, which tended to attack 'Viet Cong' villages with little discrimination. Thus, in 1965 reporter Neil Sheehan witnessed the destruction by air and sea bombardment of a prosperous fishing village in Quang Ngai, home of 15,000 people; 180 civilians died. Sheehan saw fifteen other hamlets similarly levelled and twenty-five severely damaged that year, with high civilian casualties. He was told to ignore these 'stories' and 'go cover' a firefight in Plei Ku.[24]

The destruction of Long Phuoc and resettlement of Long Tan sowed dragon's teeth in the countryside. Where some civilians had been sullen or neutral, they were now vengeful and embittered. 'I thought the psychology of destroying Long Phuoc ridiculous,' the photographer Denis Gibbons said later. 'If they weren't VC sympathizers they sure were after they were moved and their homes destroyed.'[25]

Hoa Long boiled with displaced Viet Cong families. Yet the complexity of the war confounded settled conclusions. Certain friendly hamlets in Hoa Long later welcomed the Australian presence, according to a 1967 survey by a Vietnamese 'Census Grievance Team'.[26] And, for a time, the people lived without fear of Viet Cong threats and taxes. 'We can enter into every hamlet ... now there is not any destruction [by] VC,' said one. 'Residents believe perfectly in the defence of the Australian Army.' A 52-year-old Hoa Long mother, whose sons were in the South Vietnamese Army, had been repeatedly kidnapped and threatened. 'Then the Australians arrived,' she said. 'Now ... my sons came home to celebrate "Tet" with the family and left the next morning.'[27] Others were neutral farmers who simply pleaded to be left alone. 'He who is VC, capture him, but we are honest people. Let us go on earning our living,' said one. And some were lepers, living in huts on the outskirts of the village, as an Australian reconnaissance unit found to its horror: 'Sweet Jesus, they're lepers,' whispered Robert 'Dogs' Kearney, peering into a hut full of people wrapped in rags, 'outcasts in a war zone.'[28]

The destruction of their homes understandably put the local families of the National Liberation Front in a murderous mood. 'At Long Phuoc this late afternoon,' wrote Huynh Chien Dau, after the US bombed the village, 'sadness covers the countryside ... trees stand lonely in deserted pathways; corpses of buffaloes and bulls lie all over the fields. Houses are reduced to rubble and ashes. We all feel profoundly sad.'

Huynh, a heavily indoctrinated northerner, had joined the National Liberation Front in Ba Ria in 1962. He was not a local; rather, a communist insurgent whose job was to inflame provincial hatred. The US bombardment of Long Phuoc played into Huynh's hands. His captured diary is filled with apocalyptic visions and cries for vengeance: 'I look up and see through the dark clouds the shadow of a demon, a hideous monster ... Four fighter planes over Long Phuoc strafed and bombed it ... Chains of bombs were raining down ... with blood and broken bones splashed everywhere. Screams of husbands who lost their wives, of children whose mothers were killed ...'

'Avenge yourselves,' Huynh wrote. 'Oh! People of Long Phuoc! Unite! Rally yourselves, stand firm for the national cause! ... Imperialist Americans and their lackeys! Our people of the South will deal a fatal blow ... We will crush you, kick your head into a hole ... the surviving people of Long Phuoc are determined to suck your blood and taste your liver for revenge!'[29]

By mid-1966 Nui Dat remained extremely vulnerable: only a few rolls of barbed wire and claymore mines defended the 13-kilometre perimeter. The Australians simply did not have the time or resources to complete the job: half the Task Force were out on offensive patrols by day; by night, others had to patrol and ambush around the base. And when they were not on patrol, the troops were busy with construction and menial jobs. Security provisions banned the entry of any Vietnamese into the base — including builders, launderers, cleaners and, with a few rare exceptions, interpreters. (One interpreter, Khien Dinh Nguyen, was attached to an intelligence unit in Nui Dat from June 1966 and became a much-trusted ally; he now lives in Sydney: 'We interrogated suspects,' he said. 'I can say the Australian troops were no. 1. I never saw any torture.'[30])

Then the first big combat operations began (as distinct from the small patrols around the Tactical Area of Responsibility — TAOR — which involved everyone, including cooks and clerks). The operations were given homely titles, such as SYDNEY, BRISBANE, HOBART, WOLLONGONG, ENOGGERA and BATHURST. Their purposes varied: some were 'search and destroy' missions, aimed at clearing the enemy from the province; others were 'cordon and search' (of villages) and 'ambush and reconnaissance' patrols.

The operations were exhausting, uncomfortable in the extreme, unnerving and often terrifying. Yet they broke the tedium: the diggers were at last doing what they had been trained to do. Operations tended to last several weeks, usually involving companies and sometimes the whole battalion, on a slow slog through the scrub, clearing thousand-metre grid squares marked on their waterproofed maps. Stepping out of the wire was an arresting experience. 'You shook off your fears, and stepped into Indian country. You had your finger on the trigger, and your sights up,' said one digger. They moved off the tracks, through the jungle and scrub, a few hundred metres at a time, and stopped and listened. None experienced a sharper assault on his senses than the forward scout, the eyes and ears of the patrol, up front, alone, and 'switched on as you have never been switched on in your life'. Moving, pausing, listening 'for the slightest unusual sound … or lack of it. You haven't lived until you've walked that lonely road,' wrote Brian Hennessy, a 6th Battalion reinforcement and forward scout.[31]

The American commanders disapproved of these Aussie stealth tactics, which added little to the overall body count. The Australians were 'very inactive', with poor results, Westmoreland wrote. Successive Task Force commanders ignored these criticisms, and the Australians continued fighting the war their way.

The enemy were 'everywhere' in those early months, recalled Major Brian McFarlane. 'It was incredibly unnerving for the troops, especially those out in the boondocks at night in twos and threes on standing and listening patrols.'[32] 'Most early encounters were short, sharp vicious brawls,' remembered Lieutenant Peter Dinham, of Alpha Company, 6th Battalion.

The units communicated via a command network that linked battalion to company and company to platoon. There was also an administrative net, allowing the battalion commander to listen in on intra-company communications. All commanders kept their radios on 24 hours a day. Every function had a radio appointment title: so, for example, the battalion commander was Sunray; battalion second-in-command, Sunray Minor; the operations officer, Seagull; the medevac helicopters, Dust-off; the army liaison helicopters, Possum. These simple codes never changed, so sophisticated enemy listeners soon understood them. However, the short range of the VHF radios and the great number on the air made it extremely unlikely that the enemy gleaned any useful day-to-day information.

On operations, you left no trace of yourself. On ambush or patrols, the rules were: no fires or hexamine (a pellet-fired stove), no cooking, no movement, no shaving, no use of soap, no urinating or 'crapping in ambush sites'.[33] The soldiers defecated in the rubbish holes, to control the odour. (The Viet Cong, who did not observe the same discipline, were often detected by the smell of their unburied excrement; their chilli-flavoured sweat was also distinct.) By night, the platoons camped in defensive, diamond-shaped 'harbours', with 24-hour sentries, behind a claymore mine shield.

Nature tormented the toughest constitutions: vipers, kraits, wasps, chomping ants, scorpions and, in the wet season, regiments of waving leeches and clouds of malarial mosquitoes. Veterans share endless stories of ghastly encounters with these pests — often exaggerated over time. The chomping ants were not man-eaters; the snakes were shorter than 40 feet long; and there were no credible encounters with tigers. Nevertheless, harrowing stories prevailed, of green wasps and hornets, which had an excruciatingly painful sting — an attack by swarms required medical evacuation. Snakebite almost killed a few soldiers. Leeches were the most loathed: they would lock on to a man's eyelids while he slept, or slither up his thigh and attach themselves to his scrotum or, on occasion, actually crawl inside the penis and swell up, causing intense pain. The soldiers took pleasure in devising ways to kill the pests: a favourite method was to impale the leech on a bamboo thorn and roll it inside out.

The roasting sun and pouring rain were more debilitating torments, barely tolerated by heavily burdened, fair-skinned men unused to the tropical climate: several diggers died of heat exhaustion, and hundreds were medevaced. In the monsoon season, red mud got into everything: the webbing, rifles, boots, sleeping bags. The rain reduced the infantryman's world to a sodden, mildewed, stinking mess, and dreadful skin diseases — fungi, rashes, chafing, blisters and all kinds of suppurating encrustations and furunculous infections — disfigured their bodies.

Diggers wore one set of clothes on operations — army greens, bush hat (often with coloured tape around their hatbands, to avoid friendly fire), sweat scarf, socks and boots — usually no underwear, to reduce chafing; and certainly no flak jacket or steel helmet, which were standard in the US Army. Helmets, it was felt, were too hot, offered little protection, and impaired the soldier's ability to detect enemy sounds.

Each infantryman carried 25 to 30 kilograms — more than the soldier's load on the Kokoda Track. On long operations his metal-framed pack normally held four days of rations (resupplied by helicopter drop); a 'hutchie'; a ground sheet; a 'silk' (the inner layer of the army-issue sleeping bag); a mosquito net; insect repellent; a small hexamine stove; a cup and eating utensils; as well as a book, radio, writing gear and cigarettes. In his pockets or pack he carried extra rifle magazines with twenty rounds in each. Attached to his webbing were: two hand grenades, one coloured smoke grenade (to direct helicopter landings); up to six water bottles; an entrenching tool or fold-up shovel; and a machete. He carried a rifle (either the self-loading or an M16) or, in the gunner's case, the M60 machine gun. In addition, each section (i.e. ten men) shared the weight of: 700 extra machine-gun rounds — in belts, often worn Mexican bandit-style; several claymore mines; one rocket launcher; one M79 grenade launcher; extra batteries for the platoon radio; C4 plastic explosive; mine detonators (*not* carried by the person with the claymore, for safety); and extra smoke grenades. In June, most of these soldiers' provisions were available; large supplies, such as tents, hospital equipment and infrastructure, were still delayed.

The basic Rules of Engagement — that is, the conditions in which soldiers were permitted to fire on the enemy — were open to wide interpretation: 'It is often difficult to distinguish between the VC and civilians,' the rules noted. 'As a general rule a person will NOT be engaged unless one of the following conditions applies: a) They open fire first; b) They are seen to be carrying arms; c) They are breaking curfew; d) They fail to stop when challenged and are not obviously friendly; e) They are obviously hostile.'[34]

The battalion commanders tended to adapt these rules. For example, Lieutenant Colonel Warr, of the 5th Battalion, advised his unit to '(a) Fire only, (i) When fired at; (ii) When a suspect is about to commit a hostile act; (iii) If a suspect attempts to run through a cordon and fails to halt after challenge'. If fired on from a house, the soldiers were advised to take cover and call the interpreter forward to 'advise occupants to surrender'. If this failed, the village chief should speak to the householder: 'If the occupants still refuse to surrender, burn the house. These are the only circumstances under which houses are to be burned.'[35]

Two rules were later added: 'Don't harass women and children' and 'Soldiers will not be used to search women'.[36] Some soldiers objected that Vietnamese women and teenagers were active combatants: in an early case a soldier swept forward to discover 'a KIA, and It's a sheila!'. He gazed down on a beautiful young Vietnamese woman who moments ago had been trying to kill him.[37]

The Rules of Engagement played to the politicians' sensitivities, and did not consider the safety of the soldier. Warr later conceded that his instruction 'If in doubt, don't shoot' endangered the troops. It also ensured that not a single 5th Battalion soldier knowingly fired on a Vietnamese civilian. Viet Cong troops were actually amused by their new enemy's apparent care and respect for civilian life.


The case of an 11-year-old girl, of Hoa Long, who had 'accidentally' cut herself with a knife while husking corn — so ran the complaint — alerted the Australians to the shocking complexity of the war and the near impossibility of separating friend from foe; of trying to aid the people while defeating the Viet Cong, who were, in many cases, inseparably linked through family and kinship ties. It also demonstrated the extraordinary courage of the Australian medical teams.

On 21 June, while medics were preparing to depart to treat the girl, a Land Rover hurtled into Nui Dat carrying a severely agitated driver, Provost Corporal Bill Collins, and his passenger, Corporal Ian Brown, who lolled about with a bullet through the head. They had just come from Hoa Long village, where a crowd of sixty people, mostly women, had surrounded the car. At a shout the crowd had dropped to the ground, to reveal four armed men, who riddled the Land Rover, hitting Brown.

The medical team treated Brown and departed for Hoa Long. They found the little girl dead. She had not been husking corn: the Viet Cong had disembowelled her. A deep cut split her stomach from the breastbone to the lower abdomen; a second cut slashed across her stomach in a cross-shaped mutilation. It transpired that the girl's mother lived in the southern, pro-Saigon part of Hoa Long, and her husband was a soldier loyal to Saigon. The sobbing mother bravely told the Australians that the Viet Cong had slaughtered her daughter to draw them into an ambush, in reprisal for their attempts to win the villagers' confidence. The Task Force organised a proper Buddhist funeral for the little girl. The Australian civic action teams were unfazed: at huge risk, they never ceased trying to help the locals, and 'continued their work uninterrupted in Hoa Long as in other villages'.[38]

Throughout July, firefights and the 'fearful joy' of bullets flying — as digger (and bush tucker man) Les Hiddens later described them — were daily occurrences.[39] Time seemed to go super-fast or super-slow during these adrenaline-charged contacts, interspersed by strange silences and a sense of being underwater, of 'scuba-diving', wrote Haran and Kearney, and 'a pulsating of blood rushing around behind the eyes, inside the ear, and the sphincter … clenched to prevent something embarrassing happening. Eyes focused on the branches and leaves of the interesting bush in front of you … No green leaves. All is black and white. There is a grating sound, like sandpaper … It's coming close by. It's coming out of your mouth. It's you, breathing.'[40]

And suddenly, your greatest mate — the bloke you'd trained with, lived with, drank with — was dead. On 9 July Gordon Knight — the nasho whose farewell party his commander Brian McFarlane had regretted not meeting at the airport — was shot through the head. An enemy patrol had forced an old man driving an ox cart into the suspected Australian ambush, a common tactic as oxen apparently reacted to the odour of Europeans. Knight died in the ensuing firefight. A popular soldier, his loss profoundly demoralised his mates.

Then came the first night 'cordon and search' operation, of the village of Duc My, near Binh Ba, the home of lowland Montagnard tribes who had been forcibly removed from their mountain homes by the Diem Government. Many were thus vulnerable to Viet Cong entreaties or, if these failed, threats: a year earlier, the enemy assassinated a Montagnard leader on the Duc My playing field. The tribes 'looked incredibly wild alongside the men from Binh Ba', observed Bob O'Neill. 'They were smaller and much darker … instead of smooth, neatly parted hair they had great tousled mops … Straggly wispy beards sprouted from their chins …'[41]

On 14 July O'Neill led a night patrol to Duc My, to check for sentries and watchdogs. They waded a swamp, and crept down the aisles of rubber — 'the white ribbed Gothic arches' of the canopy high overhead — to the edge of the village.[42] They found it unguarded. So, around midnight on the 19th, in a torrential downpour, three Australian companies (led by Majors Bruce McQualter, Noel Granter and Paul Greenhalgh) closed on three sides (armoured carriers guarded the fourth) and paid out cordon rope around the village. The only mishap occurred when one Private Clarke took a wrong step in the darkness and plunged into a 16-metre well. His platoon hauled him out with cordon rope.

Before dawn an Australian aircraft flew low over the village, and the pilot warned the villagers through a loud hailer that they were surrounded. Shocked, the enemy Montagnard dashed out of their homes and 'tried to break through the cordon by means of sheer speed'.[43] There were sudden face-to-face encounters, decided by the quickest draw; others tried to escape, Ulysses-style, by hiding amid cattle being driven from the village or in the back of ox carts.

The villagers were screened and interrogated; the identifiable Viet Cong were sent off to prison camps. The care and restraint taken in surprising, then securing, the village circulated among the terrified civilian inhabitants: 'By the end of the day our soldiers were getting along very amicably with … this former Viet Cong village,' concluded O'Neill.[44] Far better to tame a village than to destroy it, he decided. A 'Viet Cong village' did not mean all the inhabitants were enemy, of course: at Duc My, as elsewhere, the locals often had little choice but to obey the Viet Cong intruders — until the Australian soldiers offered them one.

# Chapter 17
# Long Tan — warnings

> I had this tremendous feeling of responsibility that all these
> people around me were in great peril and I could do nothing
> about it … I just disintegrated totally.
> *Captain Bob Keep, Australian intelligence officer.*

A cyclo's nod … a shirt hung on a village fence … a candle burned on an ancestor's altar … a stack of rice husks: no intelligence system could detect the secret signals between civilians and guerrillas in a revolutionary war.[1] Somehow, the Australians had to read the local mind; Nui Dat was exceptionally vulnerable. Here they were, a great pile of men and materiel, dropped into enemy territory, in a lightly fortified camp with little local knowledge. How, they wondered, would they distinguish 'the people', whom they were there supposedly to protect, from the communist enemy? So often the two were indistinguishable.

In early 1966 the signs of enemy movement were as elusive as the wind, borne on a whisper, secreted in a parcel, a message or a rumour, feeding 'this uncomfortable feeling that something funny was happening in Phuoc Tuy and nobody could put their finger on it', noted the Task Force commander, Brigadier Jackson. 'In the first few weeks there were considerable rumours … of something new developing in the Province … even the Province Chief was unhappy …'[2]

A sense of being surrounded, of never knowing who to trust, pervaded the little base, unrelieved by South Vietnamese field agents who deliberately exaggerated to justify their jobs or said what they thought their paymasters wanted to hear. A week before the Task Force deployed to Nui Dat, Brigadier Jackson learned to his horror that eleven Viet Cong battalions were apparently operating within a 5-kilometre radius of Nui Dat, a claim later discredited. The sheer abundance of enemy sightings diminished the credibility of the few reliable reports. An attitude of measured scepticism greeted every new report. Jackson and the Task Force intelligence officer, Major John Rowe, settled on a worst-case scenario of 3,000 new enemy troops in the province.[3]

Some reports were more credible: on 27–28 July news of a thousand-strong Viet Cong force moving from Long Son Island towards Ba Ria reached operations adviser Captain Mike Wells, who ran a team of warrant officers in the field. A further agent's report, on 27 July, witnessed an enemy battalion encamped in the Long Tan rubber plantation; oddly, this was omitted from the enemy build-up figures lodged two days later. Airborne 'Red Haze' technology, an infra-red system that detected heat emissions from human bodies, fed the impression that a large number of fresh enemy troops had entered the province.

In mid-1966 Australian SAS patrols detected a more lethal foe than the locally raised Viet Cong. For the first time, North Vietnamese units had infiltrated Phuoc Tuy in the form of a regular battalion of the People's Army.[4] These pith-helmeted, Kalashnikov-armed units had so far been detected only on the extreme western border with Cambodia.[5] Unknown to the Task Force, the new foe arrived with clear instructions. In February, Hanoi's Central Military Committee, headed by Giap, had handed down a clear strategic vision to the northern insurgents and their southern comrades. They decided to intensify massively the offensive against the Americans and their allies, by ordering their southern comrades to: (1) conduct a 'war of concentration', with as many campaigns in as many locations as possible; (2) raise the standard of guerrilla warfare by coordinating the combat operation of guerrillas, local troops and Main Force units; and (3) harmonise the military and political struggle. All civilians — women, children, farmers and the elderly — were to be inducted into this war of 'national liberation' against Saigon's 'imperialist lackeys'.

The Australian SAS, as the 'eyes and ears of Nui Dat', were well placed to divine the enemy's intentions. In Vietnam, the SAS earned a reputation for being 'the most offensive men alive'.[6] A five-man patrol was capable of laying down immense firepower. Yet these 'thinking thugs'[7] were primarily intelligence gatherers, not assassins; they 'prowled like a cat, quietly studying the movements … of the Viet Cong', whom they detected by the enemy's uniforms, weapons and base camps.[8] While reconnaissance was their chief role, they were also 'hunter/killers' where necessary or opportune. They built a fearsome reputation both with the Australian soldiers, who called them 'super grunts', and with the Viet Cong. The SAS were extremely difficult to detect and very aggressive, said one Vietnamese prisoner of these *biet kich uc dai loi* ('Australian commandos'). The Viet Cong — so the rumours went — placed a price of 6,000 piastres (A$60) on an SAS head. Later in the war, some villagers claimed that the capture of an Australian *ma rung* (or 'phantoms of the jungle') paid a reward of US$5,000, dead or alive. As such, the SAS were in great demand, and had an exceedingly stressful job. One patrol commander, returning from a contact, wrote to his fiancée, 'My hands are still shaking from this morning's efforts.' It took him four hours to steady his hands, he wrote.[9]

On these reconnaissance missions, the SAS were barely discernible. Typically, they wore US camouflage uniforms of Woodland green pattern, made of rip-stop cotton. Many replaced their bush hats with mottled sweat scarves or berets. Some had green mesh gloves. Anything shiny — such as watches — was covered with a piece of cut sock. Their full load weighed at least 30 kilograms, and possibly 35 to 45, depending on their choice of weapons and length of patrol. Inside their shirts they carried bladders, containing two quarts of water. Black, green and ochre face paint completed the picture of Australia's deadliest jungle fighter.

They excelled at bushcraft and used a wide variety of techniques to locate the enemy. They studied the enemy's cooking and eating habits — the Vietnamese loved a pungent fish sauce, *nuoc nam* — the age and combinations of footprints, broken foliage and slashed bamboo. They used the water tables, too: the enemy guerrillas dug wells no deeper than necessary. Sometimes the SAS relied on the US 'sniffer' planes that used heat sensors to detect human concentrations beneath the jungle canopy. On at least one occasion, an SAS patrol closed on a family of monkeys leaping amid the foliage. In mid-1966 the SAS were relied upon as never before to discern the intentions of the National Liberation Front. Yet their warnings were curiously downplayed. On one occasion, an SAS sketch of a North Vietnamese soldier raised no particular concerns at Task Force headquarters.

\* \* \*

Brigadier Jackson underrated the threat for one appreciable reason: pride. Australian overreactions had already humiliated the Task Force, Jackson felt, and he did not wish to cry wolf twice and double the embarrassment. Earlier, in June, a worried Jackson had warned Australian Force Vietnam in Saigon of the enemy build-up. Lieutenant General John Wilton, Chief of the General Staff, dismissed Jackson's concerns. Obviously the Viet Cong would react to the Australian presence in an area they 'had completely controlled for many years', Wilton told Allen Fairhall, Minister for Defence (his predecessor, Paltridge, died in 1966). In any case, a major surprise attack 'had no place' in the Viet Cong's tactical doctrine, Wilton added — in this, he was mistaken — and was most unlikely because the Viet Cong would 'expose himself to very heavy casualties'.[10] Jackson accepted Wilton's assurances. Jackson 'simply refused to believe the Viet Cong would attack the base', said Second Lieutenant David Harris, the Task Force liaison officer (and later Jackson's aide).[11] This thinking grossly underestimated the Viet Cong's fury over the destruction of villages within 'Line Alpha', the radius that determined the limit of enemy mortar range — chiefly Long Phuoc — and the eviction of the people from Long Tan, which severely disrupted the NLF political structure in the province.

As a precaution, however, in late July, without consulting senior members of his staff, Jackson sent a favourite officer, Captain Bob Keep, of the Task Force Intelligence Section, to the American headquarters II Field Force Vietnam in Bien Hoa to seek American support in case of an attack. Keep returned humiliated. The Americans 'almost laughed us out of court', recalled the Australian assistant planning officer, Major Alex Piper, who passed on Keep's message. The Americans were spending vast resources trying to provoke a Viet Cong attack; Australian concerns of a pre-emptive strike seemed absurd. 'Dammit, if only the enemy would fight!' summed up the dismayed US attitude.

Keep's gut feeling persisted, however, and a little later he paid a visit to Major Peter Young, the Australian assistant military attaché, who passed on his worries to American intelligence for assessment. 'They drew blanks,' Young said later.[12] American planes checked the province and found nothing. As for Keep's field reports and other alerts, the US rated them 'F3' — 'of dubious reliability'.[13]

The crisis mysteriously passed. On 31 July new agents' reports discredited the earlier ones, and Australian patrols found no signs of the phantom battalions. Yet doubts lingered during those black nights of pouring rain when distant sounds so strange to the Australian ear — of the jungle, the lowing oxen and the wood choppers, amid the specks of flickering light — preyed on the mind and sharpened the senses.

In this air of deceptive calm the infantry lightened up a little: some 5th Battalion troops indulged in a little light R&R at Long Hai: they swam and played touch football on the beach; the battalion's band entertained the locals ... at the very base of the mountain range that sheltered the Viet Cong's headquarters. The Long Hais served as the sanctuary — the Minh Dam Secret Zone — of the D445 Battalion, a well-trained, well-armed guerrilla unit descended from Binh Xuyen river pirates who had fled the Rung Sat swamps in the late 1950s when Diem's troops swept through the vile waterway.[14] Not all were Party faithful: disgust at Diem's policies, or a desire simply to avoid the South Vietnamese Army, which tended to send soldiers away from their homes, drove many into the Viet Cong fold. Seen as 'Phuoc Tuy's own', the D445 Battalion had a special connection with many villages, through family or friends. They were a vital link in the chain between the peasant guerrillas and two Main Force Viet Cong regiments (274th and 275th) of the 5th Division. A formidable synthesis thus connected the smallest hamlet guerrillas with their provincial (D445) commanders under the overarching political apparatus of the National Liberation Front, itself ultimately answerable to Hanoi.

These Main Force guerrillas planned to attack Nui Dat as early as June 1966, according to the captured diary of Colonel Nguyen Nam Hung, deputy commander of the 274th Main Force Regiment.[15] At a political level, the defeat of this impudent, minor and untested foe — who happened to be America's closest ally — would show the local people who owned the province and prove immensely embarrassing in Canberra and Washington. Far easier to strike a newly arrived American ally than America itself: the *uc dai loi* were a prize there for the taking.

In early August, Captains Bob O'Neill and Bryan Wickens, intelligence officers of the 5th and 6th Battalions respectively, flew over the province and entered a few villages with interpreters. 'There was obviously an increasing amount of enemy movement,' said Wickens. 'I got the impression ... that they could be building up to something. Colin Townsend ... was just as concerned as I was!'[16]

O'Neill, a Rhodes scholar and later a distinguished academic, gained an insight into the Viet Cong network during OPERATION HOLSWORTHY, a cordon and search of the town of Binh Ba, on 7–8 August 1966. Binh Ba, due north of Nui Dat, then a Viet Cong stronghold, blocked Route 2, thus preventing 6,000 Catholics of the village of Binh Gia from reaching the Ba Ria markets. Indeed, 'the Binh Ba 10,000' became a catchphrase for any rumoured attack on the Task Force. Yet, as O'Neill later discovered, the residents of Binh Ba collaborated with the Viet Cong out of fear, not sympathy. Rowe concurred: 'We had the sense that the population was deeply penetrated and afraid.'[17] Indeed, after they 'liberated' Binh Ba, the Viet Cong executed the village chief, publicly humiliated lesser officials and quietly 'disappeared' those who resisted taxation and conscription.[18]

The Australian 5th Battalion closed the cordon on Binh Ba in the grey hours of a monsoonal night. With visibility at 20 metres, a tragic error occurred. Australian troops mistook as an ambush two black–clad figures in the pouring rain. They fired, and later found a 10-year-old Vietnamese boy, dead, and his mother, mortally wounded — both had been outside the curfew. A third figure ran away. The Australians signalled for a medevac but the woman died. The mother and child were buried in marked graves.

Inside the town, the Australians beheld scenes of despair. The Viet Cong had bled Binh Ba of food and supplies, and only the shrivelled, spent host of an enormous parasite remained. When offered food, the locals surged forward, knocking down Lieutenant Colonel Dat, the province chief; one villager bashed an old lady in the face with a can of milk, so desperate was he to get food.

Bob O'Neill sat in a small hessian enclosure in the town square, into which the villagers were brought one at a time. Of the 169 men interrogated, seventeen were confirmed as Viet Cong and seventy-seven detained as suspects. They volunteered a surprising amount. 'The only way which I knew to get information from people was to be pleasant to them,' O'Neill later wrote.[19] A distinct hostility to the Viet Cong permeated the community. Many hoped the South Vietnamese Government would return and the Australians stay to protect them. Their loyalties were contingent upon the promise of long-term security. For three days, Major Bruce McQualter's company returned to assist the township: they treated the sick, attended church and played soccer with the children. Over the next nine days, Captain Tony White, the 5th Battalion's medical officer, and his medcap (Medical Civic Action Program) team, treated 1,200 patients: for tuberculosis (a tenth were afflicted), bronchitis, skin diseases, worm infestations and malaria. The people were severely malnourished; most lived on meagre rice supplies, grown locally, a direct result of the Viet Cong blockade of Route 2 to Ba Ria.

Within two days of the Australians reopening Route 2, '500 people travelling on Lambrettas, ox carts, bicycles, tractors and army transport moved south to Ba Ria', reported Lieutenant Colonel Warr, and the Catholics of Binh Gia drove down to Nui Dat to thank the Australians with gifts of limes, bananas and several live chickens.[20] Similarly, the Montagnards at Duc My broke into wild applause when told the Australians were staying in Phuoc Tuy, and invited the foreign soldiers to their homes. 'It seemed incredible that a few weeks beforehand I had been creeping around these houses in the depths of night,' recalled O'Neill.[21] The cordon of Binh Ba showed one facet of the people's feelings, of course; it did not reveal the extent of the enemy's support elsewhere in the province.

Meanwhile, another, vastly more sophisticated form of intelligence crackled away in the background: electronic warfare, or signals intelligence (SIGINT, as it was later known). Signals was a new field of intelligence of which 'key commanders had no knowledge … some struggled to come to terms with it', noted Warrant Officer Blair Tidey, a later student of electronic warfare.[22] No published army doctrine explained electronic warfare in 1966; few senior officers — and not one battalion commander — had access to it. Yet Australian signalmen were at the forefront of electronic warfare, thanks to the pioneering work of Lieutenant Colonel Col Cattanach, who elevated SIGINT from a mere US 'postbox' to a highly valued intelligence source.[23]

Throughout Australia's war in Vietnam, a top-secret signals unit — 547 Signal Troop — supplied a constant stream of electronic intelligence. In 1966, only four people in the Task Force (outside 547 Signal Troop) officially knew the source — such was the importance of preserving its integrity: Brigadier Jackson, intelligence officers Rowe and Keep, and operations officer Major Dick Hannigan.[24]

The first sixteen men of 547 Signal Troop, led by Captain Trevor Richards, were rushed up to Vietnam in June 1966, grabbed some equipment from the Americans and 'started cooking with gas' in a nondescript, fan-cooled corrugated iron shack at Nui Dat. It had two long benches with ten operator positions, each equipped with two Collins R391 high-frequency receivers and a tape recorder. Richards's men worked on a

24-hour basis, in three shifts.[25] By picking up high-frequency Morse code that 'bounced back off the ionosphere', they could locate an enemy Morse code signal 'to within 400–500 metres'. In fact, the radio fixes were much more precise, but Richards built in a margin of error of 500 metres to ensure that the Task Force treated the reference as intelligence and not as a 'target acquisition'.[26]

The detection of a regimental radio did not signify the location of the regiment, explained Richards: 'I could say, "This is where the enemy's regimental radio is"; but where his headquarters was, we couldn't say; where his men were, we didn't know.'[27] Answers to those questions relied on human interpretation. 'Signals intelligence was more an art than a science,' Richards recalled. After intercepting, coding and decoding, 'there was a lot of room for interpretation'.[28]

On 29 July 1966, Richards's signallers locked on to the crackling sounds emitted by two enemy radio sets, shortly found to belong to the Viet Cong 5th Division's 274th Regiment in the far north-west of Phuoc Tuy and the 275th Regiment near Xuyen Moc (22 kilometres east of Nui Dat). The 275th's radio, for so long dormant, broadcast long messages and frequent traffic: the Australian decoders conjectured that North Vietnamese reinforcements had joined or were joining the regiment and preparing to move (this chimed with later revelations in captured diaries).

In coming days, the 275th's radio did just that: it moved westwards, in small bounds, towards Nui Dat. The Australian signallers tracked the early fixes and extrapolated these in a direct line for the Task Force base. It was an astonishing discovery, with grave implications. Yet Richards, a relatively junior officer, had to persuade the Task Force of the seriousness of the findings; Jackson would take a great deal of persuading.

Richards cut a slightly odd figure around Nui Dat. Nobody knew precisely what the signalman did, although the antennas that protruded from his shack and Land Rover were heavy hints. 'I doubt if anyone observing them thought they were listening to "Good Morning, Vietnam" all day,' said Dick Hannigan later.[29] The SAS drew its own conclusions: whenever the signalman, clutching his mysterious papers, appeared at SAS Hill headquarters, the SAS soon found itself out on a very active patrol.

Richards carried a great weight on his mind, and naturally sought to offload it on the Task Force's two intelligence officers, Major John Rowe and Captain Bob Keep. Rowe and Keep had sharply divergent views on the relative importance of signals intelligence. Rowe saw SIGINT as one source of many, such as SAS reports, infantry patrols, airborne radar, field agents, prisoner interrogations, enemy documents, civilian sources, and a reasoned analysis of all the facts; Keep, along with some senior Task Force officers, had 'an almost blind faith in the correctness of the [SIGINT] reporting to the point where it eclipsed all other sources'.[30] There were cultural issues, too: career intelligence officers tended to regard signalmen in the same light as today's computer geeks: nerdy technicians reliant on machines, with little style or panache.

The two worlds collided in June 1966, under a rubber tree at Nui Dat, where Rowe stood shaving one morning. Richards snapped to attention, saluted and said, 'Just to let you know I've arrived — Sir!' to which Rowe, according to Richards's version, responded dismissively. The signaller felt immediately sidelined, and in future resolved not to communicate through Rowe. (Rowe has no recollection of this meeting; he said later that if it happened, he certainly did not intend to cold-shoulder Richards or signals intelligence, with which he had worked closely during the past five years.)

John Rowe's character leaps from the pages of a John Buchan novel: tall, handsome, privately educated, he carried himself with an air of effortless brilliance and old-world charm. A strain of ruthless pragmatism held together the outward impression of a beguiling military spook faintly redolent of 007. Many considered Rowe one of Australia's finest intelligence officers. He moved in important circles: his father-in-law, Brian Hill, was the Australian Ambassador to South Vietnam, from 1961 to 1964. Little surprise, then, that when Rowe arrived at muddy, half-formed Nui Dat in 1966, he seemed to stride about the Australian base with a sense of imposing arrogance, earned partly from his stint with American intelligence in the 173rd Airborne Brigade at Bien Hoa in 1965, where he had warned against a parachute drop of hundreds of American troops into a valley that supposedly contained seventeen Viet Cong regiments and a huge rice harvest. Well before the drop, Bien Hoa tailors were 'doing a roaring trade in combat jump badges', Rowe discovered. The air drop, he told the Americans, was suicide. They used helicopter and road convoy instead, but found little resistance: American signals had detected regimental radios but no regiments. Nor was there any rice, as the local agricultural adviser told Rowe: 'No one has planted rice here for years ... We're starving.'[31]

The experience was salutary: in time, Rowe despaired not only of the state of American intelligence but also of the whole direction of the US-led war, which he felt was 'unwinnable' (his 1968 novel, *Count Your Dead*, distilled these feelings). And it deeply qualified his faith in radio fixes in isolation of other intelligence: 'In the 173rd Airborne Brigade, we had many experiences of regimental radio sets ... and rarely did attacks eventuate. The SIGINT made it seem as if we were going into Dien Bien Phu ...' Only infantry patrolling could confirm the importance of Richards's radio fixes. 'We all knew what was out there,' Rowe said later. 'We all knew there was a risk of regimental attack.'[32] Rowe, however, also knew that only SIGINT could pick up a regimental radio moving like a torpedo in slow motion towards Nui Dat, but at this stage he was unaware of the briefings between Jackson and Keep.

In the first two weeks of August 1966 Richards's men tracked the Viet Cong 275th's radio in daily increments of about a kilometre, heading towards the Task Force. 'This was pretty important stuff ... it was the one grain of gold amongst all the crap,' Richards said.[33] He was determined to sound the alarm — and found a willing ear in Rowe's second-in-command, Bob Keep. This precociously clever, recklessly ambitious young officer leaped at the opportunity to pass on the secret findings direct to Jackson, who felt a paternal affection for Keep: indeed, in higher circles, the pair were nicknamed 'Batman and Robin'.

Keep's motives were human, all too human: he coveted Rowe's job. The radio fixes offered a chance to ingratiate himself with Jackson and further his career. 'You knew it wasn't a ten-man foot patrol,' he later said. '... the least it could be was regimental if it was North Vietnamese. If it was Viet Cong ... it was something equivalent ...'[34]

Each night Keep and Richards pored over the signals intelligence, which Keep took straight to Jackson at Task Force headquarters. He thus bypassed Rowe, his superior officer, and operations officer, Dick Hannigan — an act of clear insubordination if not actual betrayal. And so, on the eve of Australia's gravest clash of arms in the Vietnam War, both Rowe and Hannigan were comprehensively out of the loop. For his part, Jackson either presumed Keep had kept Rowe informed or simply chose not to intervene in his favourite's methods. Either way, Jackson's conduct amounted to grave neglect and possibly a dereliction of duty, some believed.

On about 6 August, Brigadier Jackson summoned Rowe, Keep and Richards to Task Force headquarters to discuss the remarkable radio fixes, about which Rowe and Hannigan, at that point, knew nothing. Caught on the hop, Rowe advised Jackson that the radio 'could mean 275th Regiment was advancing. It could also mean a recce element of the 275th's regimental headquarters with the commander weighing up the situation — and there was an additional range of possibilities. The best way to clarify the situation was with infantry patrols. All else was conjecture.'[35]

After the meeting Rowe exploded. 'I gave Keep a rocket,' he later said. 'It was an act of serious insubordination.'[36] He reprimanded Keep 'in the strongest terms for not having kept Hannigan and myself informed of these SIGINT developments, which were of the utmost importance ...'.[37] Keep apologised profusely, praised Rowe's 'masterful' interpretation of the threat at short notice, and promised to brief Rowe and Hannigan fully in the future — a promise he failed to fulfil.

There was a darker dimension to the crisis, manifest in Keep's increasingly odd behaviour. It had a tragic outcome. Keep claimed to be unwell. Malaria and encephalitis were suggested. The illness seemed to flare up in late July: he appeared to 'be losing his sense of reality and was succumbing to personal neglect ... All the while he was painting a picture of impending catastrophe,' concluded the official history.[38] His teeth were turning green; he failed to wash; he looked unkempt. He took to wearing sandals, a Hawaiian shirt and a sarong.

Keep then appeared to suffer a kind of breakdown. Intimations of death and destruction obsessed him. He saw the approaching enemy radio as a portent of annihilation, and persuaded himself that only he discerned a truth that eluded lesser mortals. His exaggerated sense of self-importance reached 'drama queen, soap opera' levels, as Rowe acidly observed.[39] Keep later admitted, 'I had this tremendous feeling of responsibility that all these people around me were in great peril and I could do nothing about it.'[40] On 9 August he was sent to the field ambulance at Vung Tau.

The dramatic implosion of the mind of a brilliant young intelligence officer thwarted by his superiors in a valiant attempt to rescue the Task Force is one, apocryphal version of Keep's demise. The true account, a secret for forty years, tells a less edifying story, of a distressed young man facing a court martial for homosexual behaviour. That morning, 9 August, Jackson sent for Rowe to discuss the crisis. When Rowe arrived, 'Jackson looked deeply troubled and sad'.[41] He quietly informed Rowe that Group Captain Peter Raw, the senior air force officer at the Task Force, 'intended to press court martial proceedings against Keep because Keep had made homosexual advances to the Air Force officer who was sharing a tent with Keep'.[42]

Rowe advised Jackson to suppress the scandal, 'as an act of kindness'.[43] Keep would be sent home on medical grounds, 'if the doctor agreed to cooperate'.[44] On the 15th, two days before the Viet Cong mortared the Task Force base, Keep was flown in disgrace to the RAAF Field Hospital at Butterworth, Malaysia.

The officers at platoon, company and battalion level were completely ignorant of this fierce little drama played out at Task Force headquarters. Captain Charles Mollison cannot have known (as he implies in his book, *Long Tan and Beyond*) of the SIGINT reports at the time — a case of being wise after the event.[45] Lieutenant Colonel Colin Townsend, the 6th Battalion commander, knew nothing of a possible regimental build-up in the rubber plantation near the village of Long Tan. 'The days immediately before LONG TAN,' he later wrote, 'gave us little or no warning of the impending events.'[46] Townsend later unreasonably admonished himself for not taking full advantage of 'the evidence' of enemy activity, which amounted to a few dubious agent reports; minor enemy contacts; the sighting of a few enemy carrying a 'large circular shaped object' (which later proved to be the mortar base plate); the movement of 150 civilians south of Long Tan; and the intercept of a Viet Cong radio by a passing Sioux helicopter on 13 August.[47] The area usually bristled with such reports and activities. They differed little 'from previous indications of enemy activity'.[48]

Jackson did of course have the information and in mid-August sent out a series of company patrols in the area. They found nothing. Yet his junior officers, Captains Rusty Steele and Brian Goodwin and Lieutenant David Harris, continued to believe the brigadier had downplayed Keep's information (the source of which they were officially unaware). In mid-August, several officers in Task Force headquarters agreed with Keep's belief that 'we were going to be attacked', said Harris. On the eve of the battle of Long Tan, 'Jackson did not believe that the enemy was strong enough or so stupid as to place themselves at risk from our substantial artillery and attack the base ... nearly all intelligence received was treated with suspicion and usually downgraded,' Harris said.[49] Harris was not alone. Similarly thwarted on this front were his senior officers, Steele and Goodwin, who repeatedly tried to alert Jackson to the poor base protection. 'We had very little wire out,' Harris plaintively recalled. Nor were there any mines, bunkers, concrete reinforcements, or overhead protection for the weapon pits.

★ ★ ★

In the early hours of 17 August a few soldiers were playing a game of Crown and Anchor in a mate's tent. 'People drifted down to the game leaving one fellow in the weapon pit,' recalled Private Peter Ainslie.[50] The game finished, and the soldiers retired. Moments later, at precisely 2.43 a.m., a series of great explosions ripped through the Task Force base. They leaped up, grabbed their rifles and scrambled to their weapon pits.

More than a hundred mortar rounds and recoilless rifle rounds struck the base. Within seven minutes, the guns of the Australian 1st Field Regiment (103 and 105 Batteries) and New Zealand's 161 Battery blasted back into the night. In the darkness and confusion, Major Harry Honnor, commander of the New Zealand guns, took compass bearings on the sound and flash of the enemy mortar fire, in order to aim the counter-fire. The enemy barrage continued for twenty-two minutes, wounding twenty-four Australian soldiers (two seriously), and destroying or damaging seven vehicles and twenty-one tents. Silence resumed. All units prepared for a possible enemy charge: none came.

When the news reached Keep's hospital bed in Malaysia, he felt as though he'd woken from a nightmare and found it real. He went to pieces: 'I just disintegrated totally … So in some ways it was, you know, a personal tragedy that I wasn't able to get the message through. But then it was too late for me.'[51] This was almost delusional. After Keep's departure, Richards himself had directly informed Jackson of the proximity of the Viet Cong radio. Yet until the last, Keep believed that he and only he knew the awful truth, until he was bundled back to Australia for 'medical reasons'.

At 4.50 a.m. Jackson sent Bravo Company, 6th Battalion, to find the mortar position, thought to be near the deserted village of Long Tan. Led by Major Noel Ford, the eighty-man patrol, which included forty-eight men rostered for leave the next day, crossed the swollen Suoi Da Bang creek, passed over vacant rice fields and ascended a gentle slope of low bush and banana trees. At 8.10 a.m. they found the mortar base plates, site of five mortars and weapons pits; apprehended and released three female fruit-pickers; and found three cows, which they requested permission to shoot. A scorpion stung a soldier, who required medical attention.[52] At 10.30 a.m. Noel Ford lost the main track; he lost and regained it several times, as it disappeared into paddies, broke up or double-backed on itself. Later that morning, Townsend ordered Alpha Company and a platoon from Charlie Company — both already out on patrol — to join the search. Charles Mollison, the officer commanding Alpha Company, later reported heavy enemy radio 'jamming his transmissions'.[53] The two companies searched all day and stayed in the field that night. They found no further signs of the enemy, but they felt the enemy: 'It was a very eerie feeling,' recalled Lieutenant Peter Dinham, a platoon commander with Alpha Company. 'The whole forest was deathly quiet. Normally there were cicadas and birds, but there were no animal noises. It was almost as though the people were there, watching us through the rubber.'[54]

Meanwhile, sixty-seven mortar craters were counted in Nui Dat. Jackson and his senior officers set out to inspect the damage. They drove down 'Canberra Avenue', where Captain Jim Townley jumped out and found a mortar fin in a crater. 'Look, sir,' he said, 'an 82mm Chicom or Soviet mortar round!' Jackson disagreed: it was merely a 60mm, he said. Townley chose not to argue; yet he later made plain that the fin had the distinctive lug of the Chicom 82mm mortar, a weapon only the Main Force Viet Cong or North Vietnamese possessed. 'By insisting that the tail fin was from a 60mm mortar,' Harris later explained, 'Jackson wanted to believe that we had only been attacked by local or provincial enemy troops.'[55] This denial chimed with the Task Force commander's general downplaying of the intelligence. In fairness, hindsight is a harsh judge; yet many of those on the spot were amazed at the brigadier's poor preparation and cavalier attitude, manifest in the shoddy base fortifications and the decision to proceed with a rock concert the day after the mortar attack.

At noon, 18 August, Corporal Spike Jones's men located the enemy's recoilless rifle firing position: 'The rubber was quiet, eerie and still … as we moved ahead there were blood stains, blood trails and medical dressings … there were also remains of body parts …'[56] The night shelling of the 17th had been accurate.

That morning 108 soldiers of Delta Company, 6th Battalion, commanded by Major Harry Smith, were ordered to relieve Ford. Meanwhile, Little Pattie and Col Joye and the Joy Boys had flown into Nui Dat and were setting up for the afternoon's rock concert. As Col Joye tested the mikes, American artillery fired harassing rounds in a flight path directly overhead. 'If they're going to do that during the show,' Joye announced, 'they'll have to come in on the beat!' At about 11 a.m., in bright sunshine, Smith's company moved through the gap in the wire; they knew nothing of what the signalmen, Jackson and his staff knew. Second Lieutenant David Sabben's platoon led the company out, as Harry Smith shouted, 'OK, Sabben, we want to get there quickly. Go for it!'[57]

# Chapter 18
# Long Tan — action

11 Platoon has taken heavy casualties, almost out of ammo, and
the platoon commander is dead.
*Major Harry Smith, 4.30 p.m., 18 August 1966.*

The troops moved out in single file through the stifling noonday heat.
They would miss Little Pattie. The sound of the concert faded until
only the dull bass could be heard over the scrub, like the beat of a distant
war drum.

'What do you reckon's out there?' Lieutenant Colonel Townsend had
asked Major Harry Smith.

'Probably a mortar platoon of thirty or forty men,' Smith replied.
Something was out there, Smith thought, as he joined his company, on the
three-day patrol called OPERATION VENDETTA.

They were 108 men — 105 Australians and three New Zealanders —
of Delta Company, 6th Battalion, Royal Australian Regiment, about forty of
whom were national servicemen. If thoughts of home, perhaps, or their
families or their girlfriends flashed through the minds of these young
soldiers, their faces betrayed not a sign. Intimations of heaven in hell were
unwelcome: here, their immediate task mattered most, then they looked
forward to ephemeral pleasures: a shower, a beer, a rest.

Harry Smith, 33, had trained them as if he were training a commando
unit. Himself an ex-commando, Smith aimed to distill the best from his
men. 'Anyone who fails to live up to my expectations will be moved on,'

Smith had said.[1] He could be insufferably demanding, and pushed his men to their limits and beyond. If the battalion did a 20-kilometre route march, Smith drove his company 5 kilometres further, and fittingly adopted the hit song 'These Boots Are Made for Walking' as the company theme and two battered old boots as its logo. In time, his soldiers respected him: his driving personality had invested them with something above the ordinary.

Never a 'yes man', Smith stood out in the deeply conservative culture of the Australian Army. The son of a World War II tank sergeant, Harry had the army in his bones. A short, fair-haired man, supremely fit and a natural rebel, young Smith had his own ideas about self-discipline: as a cadet he was dishonourably 'stood down' for 'borrowing' twenty .303 rounds with which to shoot rabbits.[2] Raised in Hobart, where his father worked at Cadbury's chocolate factory, Smith was conscripted in Menzies's earlier 1951 national service scheme (for service within Australia) and joined the regular army in 1952, as a corporal, aged 19. His rabbit-hunting days improved his marksmanship, and he completed the tough Portsea officers' training course with relative ease: Smith topped the Field prize and came second in the Staff prize. At Infantry School in Puckapunyal, 'I got top marks in all phases of weapons and field work,' he said; diffidence did not come easily to him. Posted to Penang during the Emergency, Smith earned his nickname 'the Ratcatcher' (which his detractors changed to 'the Rat') when he broke up a well-oiled midnight poker game in the Kuala Kangsar barracks with: 'At last — got you, you rats!' In Malaya he fired 'my first angry shot' at a wounded Chinese terrorist, who appeared to be holding a grenade: 'I recall firing far too many rounds into him — it was an overreaction, but I just wanted him well dead and unable to throw the grenade at the patrol or me. We did not find the grenade.'[3]

A ruthless, self-driven man, then, Smith demanded absolute loyalty from his troops. 'He made a point of knowing all his soldiers, who was married, those that may have had personal problems. He never asked us to do what he wouldn't do himself,' Geoff Kendall said later.[4] The Ratcatcher did not suffer in silence the authority of superior officers with whom he disagreed. Smith 'rarely saw eye to eye' with the 6th Battalion commander, Lieutenant Colonel Colin Townsend. Townsend once intimated that Smith had been disloyal during a training operation at Shoalwater Bay, in which Delta Company had excelled. On the contrary, Smith had deployed Special Forces jungle techniques, which Smith claimed were superior to basic infantry methods and better suited to the kind of war they would fight in Vietnam.

Dave Sabben led the file across the scrub to Suoi Da Bang creek. The forward troops slashed through grass 2 metres tall with machetes. His diggers would rather be drinking 'a coldie' and 'watching Little Pattie doing the Twist' than 'under a 40 kg pack and an unforgiving sun', Sabben thought.[5] Sabben — Second Lieutenant David Sabben — was a highly intelligent, remarkably self-assured 21-year-old Scheyville graduate who famously volunteered for national service because he felt it his national duty. Sabben was that rarity: a young man prepared to fight for 'freedom' and 'democracy' in a complacent generation which tended to take such ideals for granted.

The son of a customs officer, Sabben spent his childhood in British Honduras (Belize), where his father's duties included 'Receiver of Wrecks' and 'Inspector of Lighthouses'. It was a child's paradise. Young Sabben hoped to become a marine biologist or ornithologist, but his family could not afford to send him to university so he joined the workforce. Then, in 1965, along came the Indonesian Confrontation, and Sabben hankered for his number to come up: 'I packed my bags and presented myself at Victoria Barracks,' where 'I argued with them until they put me on a train to Kapooka.'[6] The press hailed Australia's first voluntary conscript. Sabben soon met his match in Harry Smith, who gave the young officer a tongue-lashing when Sabben appeared on parade wearing Italian-crafted shoes instead of regulation army shoes. An astonished Sabben had met a man even more exacting than himself, and their friendship has endured. At Scheyville, Sabben excelled at map reading, and topped the subject with 100 per cent in one test. No wonder his platoon (12) led the company out of Nui Dat.

Second Lieutenant Geoff Kendall, who commanded 10 Platoon, reached the Suoi Da Bang creek not far behind Sabben. A first-grade Rugby League player from Tara, Queensland, Kendall had answered 'yes' to an advertisement in 1963: 'Would you like to be an officer in the Australian Army?'[7] Images of a dashing young lieutenant flooded his mind. After graduating from Portsea, Kendall served under the exceptional Major Peter Phillips. Kendall, a reg, at first looked dimly on the conscripts: 'I remember regarding the prospect with horror.'[8] They lacked deference. When one nasho strolled past him with his 'thumb in bum, mind in neutral … I let him get about 5 metres past and then roared, "Don't you salute officers?"' The nasho turned, and with a quite genuinely contrite look, said, 'Oh, Jesus — sorry, mate!' After Long Tan, Kendall afforded the conscripts the deepest respect.

Second Lieutenant Gordon Sharp's 11 Platoon followed. Sharp was a reluctant conscript. He never warmed to the army, but decided that if he must go to Vietnam, he would go with the best. He swore he would survive Scheyville if it killed him. Oddly, Sharp strove to excel in a pursuit that left him feeling cold. A senior cameraman by training, he mixed with the media circus more comfortably than with his fellow officers. Yet here he was, leading thirty diggers towards a rubber plantation in a war zone. The tragic irony of Sharp's brief military career was that Scheyville named a graduation prize after him.

The troops beat through the tall grass, crossed the creek and headed for the rubber. Prominent characters among them were the platoon sergeants, whose temperaments ranged from fatherly calm to bull-headed intolerance: the gruff giant Jack Kirby, veteran of Korea, was a prodigiously brave and universally liked company sergeant major; the bruising Bob 'the Skull' Buick (sergeant, 11 Platoon), another huge reg, joined the army after a troubled working life — his aggressiveness earned him enemies and grudging respect (Buick used to say of his men, 'If those bastards don't like me it doesn't matter, because the only time they'll have the opportunity to shoot me, they'll be shooting at somebody else'); the avuncular James 'Paddy' Todd (sergeant, 12 Platoon), the oldest in the company, who had served in Korea and Malaya; and the soft-spoken Sergeant Neil Rankin (10 Platoon), whose decency and temperance (he did not drink) some mistook for weakness.

In the rear, with Smith's headquarters, was Captain Morrie Stanley, the only graduate of Duntroon under Smith's command. A gentleman officer, Stanley, 35, won the respect of those who might otherwise have branded him a 'Duntroon wanker', as the diggers tended to label the products of the elite military college. Stanley was a rugby-playing New Zealander and a superb marksman; his father had been, for a time, a weapons instructor. Exceptionally brave, Stanley chose to sing 'Maori Battalion' over 'Waltzing Matilda' at the Duntroon initiation ceremony. As Delta's forward observation officer, Stanley (attached to 161 Field Battery, Royal New Zealand Artillery) had the nerve-shredding job of guiding the artillery to their targets. This involved radioing grid references for the enemy's location on the maps back to his artillery commander, Major Harry Honnor, and the gunners at Nui Dat — who adjusted their sights accordingly. Stanley thus calculated where to aim, or 'walk', the shells.[10] It was an inexact, deadly science, in which he relied crucially on his radio operator, fellow New Zealander Lance Bombardier Willie Walker. Stanley and Walker were, literally, the forward 'eyes' of the big guns.

In the hands of these officers lay the fate of about a hundred young Australian men — average age 21 — who now approached the western edge of the Long Tan rubber plantation, 2.5 kilometres east of Nui Dat. They arrived a little after 1 p.m. Major Noel Ford, of Bravo Company, whose thirty-two men they were relieving, showed Smith the blood trails, Ho Chi Minh sandals and detritus of yesterday's shelling. The soldiers formed a circular, defensive perimeter, ate their combat rations and waited. The sound of Col Joye and Little Pattie performing to hundreds of cheering soldiers drifted across the scrub. 'Back at the bloody Task Force,' Harry Smith said, 'the main preoccupation was with the bloody concert; we could hear the music all the way to Long Tan.'[11]

Meanwhile, stationed to the east of the rubber plantation, was the Viet Cong's 5th Division: 1,400 troops of the 275th Regiment, joined by a crack North Vietnamese battalion and supported by 350 local guerrillas of the D445 Provincial Battalion. Another 5th Division regiment — the 274th — lurked to the north-west, 15 to 20 kilometres away. And a third was in the process of being formed. In total, at least 3,250 enemy troops were in the area.

'You ask, what were our intentions at the Long Tan battle?' Nguyen Nam Hung, commander of the 274th Regiment, told me later. 'Our intentions were to decimate you; to knock you out. Those were always our intentions: to liberate Ba Ria province, all of south Viet Nam and to realise the call of Uncle Ho, beloved leader of Viet Nam.' The communist forces sought nothing less than the 'annihilation' of the Australian Task Force, as corroborated by the official history of the D445 Battalion: 'In the rainy season 1966, the command of the 5th Division coordinated with the headquarter of Ba Ria — Long Khanh Province to annihilate the Australians in the Ba Ria battlefield.'[12] They were supremely confident of victory: the Australian mercenaries' 'minds were weak'. 'You fought for no ideals, only on American orders,' the 274th's commander said.[13]

In early August all officers of the National Liberation Front and People's Army, 'from platoon level upwards', were ordered to meet at a river junction to the east of Long Tan village to finalise the battle plan, according to the official communist history.[14] Their units were well armed, with AK47 assault rifles, grenade launchers, light machine guns, and recoilless rifles; every man carried two or three grenades. Some 'grenadiers' carried bags of grenades. They planned a two-stage offensive, according to Nguyen Nam Hung and Nguyen Minh Ninh, deputy commander of the D445 Battalion: (1) to lure the Australian forces into the open and destroy them; then (2) to attack the weakened Task Force base.[15] The recapture of Nui Dat was in itself unimportant. The paramount aims, they said, were to prove their supremacy to 'the people' and to destroy the Australian Government's will to fight. Their ultimate goal was 'armed propaganda': to win the all-important political war in the province. To this end, the National Liberation Front and People's Army planned 'an ambush battle against the Australians in the rubber plantation at Long Tan', as a prelude to the destruction of the Task Force, claimed the official communist history.[16]

At about 3.00 p.m. Delta Company entered the Long Tan rubber. Smith ordered a one-up arrowhead formation: Kendall's platoon led, with Sabben's on the left, Sharp's on the right and Smith's headquarters in the middle, shielded on each side. The three groups of thirty men moved quietly through the rubber trees. The plantation ran up a gentle slope; the high canopy of old rubber trees obscured the clouded sun and revealed the patchy undergrowth in shreds of light. The afternoon rains had not yet come. On the forward slope were younger trees: trails of white, sticky sap spiralled down their trunks to the bowls. From one perspective, the long lines of rubber suggested a perfectly aligned regiment of trees; from another, the lines seemed to merge, and play tricks on the mind: where were the columned aisles? Had they merged into a rough forest?[17]

'All's quiet, sir,' Smith radioed Townsend. Of several tracks, Smith chose an easterly one 'on a toss of a coin'. 'My plan's to advance to the east and get to the jungle tonight,' he told Nui Dat, and ordered a two-up advance: Sharp's platoon moved up level with Kendall's, in the lead; Sabben's fell back to guard the company headquarters.[18]

The Australians advanced across a wide, 600-metre front, and the platoon commanders kept in constant radio contact with Smith. At about 3.40 p.m. Sharp's forward scouts crossed a road through the rubber; moments later they surprised six to eight enemy troops, who were chatting as they walked down the road, utterly unaware of the Australians. Buick opened fire, hitting one; the rest fled.[19] Smith had been expecting black-clad local guerrillas, with bolt-action rifles or carbines; these men wore jungle greens and camouflage, and carried Kalashnikovs. At the time, neither he nor Townsend realised they were members of the People's Army of North Vietnam.

'Contact with 6–8 VC dressed in greens,' Smith radioed the Task Force.[20] The news pricked the ears of Second Lieutenant David Harris,

Jackson's aide, who warned the Task Force commander of its likely import. Indeed, the encounter seriously damaged the communist case for a Vietnamese 'ambush' of the Australians, and suggested the 'ambush' was blown, or the start of an encounter battle that surprised both sides (see chapter 18, note 16).

On full alert, Smith's men continued into the rubber; up front, Gordon Sharp's platoon quickened the pace to catch the fleeing 'Viet Cong'; soon, about 300 metres separated Sharp's platoon from the rest of Delta Company. At 3.55 p.m. his men cautiously examined a small rubber tapper's hut, and found nothing. They resumed the pursuit; unknown to Sharp, he was heading directly for the 275th Regimental headquarters.

The Australian troops gave the impression of a much larger force, which confused the Viet Cong.[21] Unlike the Americans and French, the Australians were spread wide and deep all over the field, and not in a bunched line, on high alert, in assault formation. The enemy attack, when it came, fell on Sharp's single, peripheral platoon, a small, rogue element of twenty-eight diggers separated from the main body of Delta Company.[22] The enemy's disorder and precipitate action made the coming clash every bit as shocking and confusing to him as it was to the Australians.

At around 4 p.m., Lance Corporal Barry Magnussen, in Sharp's lead section, raised his head, 'so I could see what was in front'. He beheld 'Enemy! Lots of them!'[23] At 4.08 p.m., a 'million little lights' flashed out of the rubber: streaming tracer, and every one of them a bullet.[24] They flew overhead 'like supersonic fireflies', Smith recalled.

Suddenly rocket-propelled grenades and machine-gun fire tore into Sharp's platoon: four Australians fell instantly. Tracer poured through the darkening plantation. The volume of fire from the front and flanks pinned Sharp's men to the ground: bullets slammed into the rubber, splintering the trees and splattering the soldiers with sap. 'You could not put your hand up without getting your fingers shot off,' Private Peter Ainslie recalled.[25] The opening barrage lasted fifteen minutes. Buick's reaction was to 'get into them, and hope they don't bug out';[26] yet the volume of fire stunned his men. 'We were taken completely by surprise,' Buick later said. 'When I saw them I thought, "Fuck me, that's not in the book."'[27]

Sharp radioed for artillery: 'It's bigger than I thought … They're going to attack us!'[28]

Morrie Stanley, by Smith's side, relayed Sharp's target grid references to the guns. The artillery responded with devastating effect: the Viet Cong's forward troops were cut down, and a massed charge momentarily thwarted. Stanley and Walker kept the radio operating in the most testing conditions; if the shells came in too close, Stanley 'actually shouted a number of times over the radio net the word "Stop".'[29]

At 4.25 p.m. Harry Smith radioed Nui Dat to send urgent reinforcements and the return of Bravo Company; he warned Townsend of a company-sized attack on Sharp's platoon: 'I want Noel [Ford] to come back to Long Tan …' Ford's men mysteriously stayed put, somewhere in the scrub, under Townsend's orders, and seemed to be 'forgotten for an hour!', Smith later recalled.[30] In fact, Ford had not received, or failed to hear, the radio instruction to move.

'I need helicopter reinforcements to come in at the rubber edge!' Smith shouted above the din. Townsend refused this demand: the 'landing zone' was insecure (what landing zone?); Australian choppers were not then available; and no one asked for US Army support. In truth, no stand-by reaction forces were then available (the 5th Battalion was operating elsewhere in the province). Townsend proposed instead a relief force of Alpha Company, to be conveyed on armoured carriers later that afternoon. Meanwhile, Delta Company would have to fight on alone.

Sharp knelt briefly to check the artillery's accuracy. A bullet hit him in the throat; he died almost instantly. Sergeant Buick took charge of the platoon, now besieged on three fronts; somehow, he kept in radio contact with Smith, about 400 metres to his rear. Sheets of AK47 fire swept the rubber; in reply rushing shells split the enemy lines. Private Ron Eglinton hammered away with his M60 like a man possessed. When mud clogged the ammunition belt he spat on the rounds and loading mechanism. Although wounded, he kept firing. He kept firing as though his body were welded to the gun. On the ground, an unknown number of Australians lay dead or wounded.

'11 Platoon has taken heavy casualties, almost out of ammo, and the platoon commander is dead,' Harry Smith shouted to Townsend at 4.30 p.m.

The diggers' gung-ho self-confidence skipped a beat: this enemy had had far more combat experience. To boost morale, the Australians began to shout out each other's names above the din. When a bullet passed through Private Barry Meller's open mouth and out his right cheek, 'I don't remember him flinching,' Buick recalled. 'In fact I think he kept on talking.'[31]

At 4.50 p.m. Smith demanded every gun at Nui Dat: 'The VC at probably battalion strength are attacking 11 Platoon on three sides!' he shouted. 'I want all the artillery fire we can get!' Stanley sent the order. It was declined: two idle gun batteries were still attached to the 5th Battalion, then to the north. Incredulous, Smith got on the radio to Townsend: 'I want ALL the guns in support — the whole regiment. Give me all the guns they've got!'[32] Townsend again blocked Smith's demand, with an officious 'Let the artillery look after the guns'.[33] Smith had reached the threshold of his patience and demanded the guns. A moment later Stanley told him, 'We've got the guns of the whole regiment!'[34]

Eighteen Italian L5 Pack howitzers and six US 155mm self-propelled guns turned their cannons on the Long Tan rubber field. Not since the Korean War had so many guns acted in support of Australian infantry: twenty-four guns, each firing five, sometimes ten, rounds a minute; each shell with a 'lethal zone' — a shrapnel radius — of 30 to 50 metres. Yet Stanley's targets were indistinct; the New Zealander had no clear grid fixes on the enemy's position. He could scarcely hear the platoon commanders' radios. A miscalculation ran the risk of raining death down on his own men, spread out 200 to 400 metres ahead.

Nature intervened. 'Rain such as I have never experienced before or since … a veil between the heavens and the earth,' Townsend later wrote, of the gathering storm.[35] It was as though the battle had shattered a dam in the sky: huge droplets merged into sheets and poured through the canopy. The red earth absorbed the water, sponge-like, and sank into a sea of mud. The rain fell so heavily that 'you actually ingested water by breathing!' said Kendall.[36] 'The heaviest squalls raised a mist of muddy spray,' said Sabben. 'It was almost like walking into a thin, wet, red mist.'[37] And it was a godsend: the mist, like a low fog, enshrouded the prostrate Australians. They saw lightning, but heard no thunder; only a puny rumble beneath the sound of battle.

Time passed in flashpoints, like a time-lapse photo, or slowly, like some terrible accident experienced in slow motion. Dozens of enemy troops swung behind Buick in an attempt to encircle his remnant, half of whom were now killed or lying wounded in the mud. This Viet Cong detachment failed to detect Kendall's men, flat in the deepening puddles across their path. Kendall watched and waited. 'Christ … We'll be able to shake hands with them soon!' thought Private Kevin Branch.[38] At the last moment, Kendall shouted, 'Fire!' Harry Esler 'blasted away from the hip' as did every man: at least twenty Viet

Cong fell, like puppets whose strings were slashed. A bullet struck Kendall's signaller, Brian Hornung, in the shoulder, and destroyed his radio set, silencing communication with Stanley and the vital artillery.

Further forward, Buick's few survivors clung to the mud, almost surrounded. Eighteen were dead or wounded. The vital artillery, which held off the advancing lines — now 100 metres away — seemed to come hurtling in ever closer. Radio operator Vic Grice managed to replace Buick's radio antenna, which had been shot off; yet the Viet Cong jammed the frequency, and the pouring rain and deafening noise made transmission exceedingly difficult. Their near-exhausted ammunition deadened hope.

Back at company headquarters, Smith and his few men crouched in the rain; Stanley scratched away with a Chinagraph pencil on his mud-smeared, laminated map. Lacking radio contact with Kendall, he had no target references for the artillery — leaving Kendall's platoon exposed. Suddenly a young signaller, Private Bill 'Yank' Akell, the carrier of the spare radio, saw, with awful clarity, what had to be done. Without a care for himself Akell grabbed the radio, jumped up and ran 200 to 300 metres down the ranks of rubber trees — he shot two Viet Cong soldiers on the way — and shouted, 'Mr Kendall! Mr Kendall!'

'I took off,' said Akell later. 'I had no idea where I was going except to find 10 Platoon. The enemy rounds were cracking overhead, and the more they cracked, the more I sort of was very keen to find Geoff Kendall.'[39] He found Mr Kendall. With the comms restored, Kendall called in fresh artillery and withdrew his wounded to company headquarters.

Smith's company faced the very real threat of annihilation. In the next twenty minutes, Smith radioed a string of urgent requests to the Task Force base, all of which were delayed or declined:

1700: I need helicopter ammunition resupply — all types — to be dropped through the trees at our position, on coloured smoke indicators.
1702: I want an air strike across the front of 11 Platoon, napalm and rockets between [grid references].
1715: 11 Platoon appears surrounded and 12 Platoon, which has gone out to the right (south), is pinned down.
1720: Send reinforcements by helicopter![40]

'Totally impossible,' Townsend replied to the last demand. The weather and the enemy prohibited it. There was no landing zone. And the rain made an air strike unlikely. Instead, Townsend repeated his decision to send a relief force aboard a troop of armoured carriers.

At about this time, Sabben's platoon moved forward in an attempt to reach Buick. They advanced through pouring rain into hellish fire: for an hour AK47s and machine guns pinned Sabben's men down. A medium machine gun swept the plantation to draw Sabben's fire, but 'we waited silently as the rounds burst through the rubber trees above our heads', showering the Australians in leaves and twigs and splattering their faces with rubber sap. And when the Viet Cong again attempted to encircle Buick's survivors, Sabben intercepted them — firing at an 80-metre range. 'They withdrew, dragging their casualties,' Sabben recalled.[41]


Twelve of Buick's twenty-nine men were now fit to fight. The enemy were 50 to 80 metres away, dark shapes lining up in the rubber, 'belt hugging' the Australian line to escape the shells, which hurtled harmlessly over their heads. 'Holding the belt with one hand and punching with the other,' the Viet Cong described this tactic.

Thinking his men had moments to live, Buick radioed a jaw-dropping instruction to Stanley: Buick called in artillery on himself. Stanley asked Buick to confirm the grid reference. Buick repeated the instruction; Stanley refused to execute it: 'I was not prepared to adjust the fire onto his position. Certainly he insisted, strongly.'[42] Instead, Stanley 'walked' in the bombardment from 100 metres to about 50 metres. At that very moment, the Viet Cong troops were lining up for another assault. A sort of loud babble, or war cry, preceded the attack. Then came the dreaded bugle blasts, three short notes signifying 'Wait!', 'Ready!' and 'Go!'

'All we've gotta do is hit the fucking bugler!' one Australian muttered.[43] And then, as if on cue, the artillery struck: a few shells slammed into the main concentration of the 275th Regiment: 'A whole echelon was wiped out.'[44] Forty Viet Cong troops disappeared, 'shredded within seconds', Buick recalled. Moments later, another thirty-six shells — 15 kilos of steel and high explosive — burst along the enemy lines, sending hundreds of steel splinters in every direction. The projectiles' forward momentum and the slope saved the surviving Australians from the back-blasted shrapnel.

A great gap opened up in the Viet Cong lines, and then, to Buick's horror, fresh Viet Cong troops rushed up to fill the gap. They clambered over the bodies of the dead and wounded, elbowed to the front, actually eager to die. The whistles and bugles blew, and the dreadful advance resumed. 'We could hear a whistle … seemed they were coming again … they were!' Lance Corporal Barry Magnussen said.[45]

Fear made an eternity of seconds; calls for artillery were redundant in an instant; pleas for relief were useless in minutes. A skinful of adrenaline drove the senses, attuned to the slightest movement, sound, sight, smell. As in a dream, the soldiers beheld the lightning, the coloured tracer, the smoking remains of rubber trees, blown apart then drenched; they heard the moans of the wounded, the roar of battle and, in meek reply, the thunderclaps; they smelled the cordite and the dead and the red mud. The officers were trained to perceive these conditions of war as somehow normal. 'You're always asking yourself, "What is not normal here?"' said Sabben, '"Is it normal to be taking fire from there? Can I bring the arty in closer?"'[46] Not until much later would some remember that afternoon as the freakish denouement of a lonely little Armageddon.

The shelling gave Buick a moment's reprieve. Relief had not come; their ammunition spent, they were doomed either way. A handful of Buick's men remained alive: Eglinton's teeth were broken and his tongue bled from trying to unjam his gun; he had no rounds left to lick. Lance Corporal Robbins pulled the pin on his last grenade and lay on it: 'I decided I would lay there and play dead.' He murmured the Lord's Prayer to himself and waited for the end.[47] Buick fashioned a club out of his rifle butt, ready for the onslaught.

Their only hope was to make a dash for it, Buick decided. The word went around. On Buick's shout, 'GO! GO! GO!', the survivors jumped up and ran.[48] Buick's signaller Vic Grice died of a gunshot the moment he raised his head; two more soldiers were wounded (one for the second time). Private John Heslewood and several others waited a few moments, 'as the incoming fire was so heavy'. 'As we rose,' said Heslewood, 'the fire built up like a drum roll with tracers going over the top.'[49] Magnussen prayed — 'I said to God, "If you're ever going to help, do it now"'[50] — then leaped up and raced after the rest. On the way, he stumbled on the wounded Barry Meller and tried to drag him out, but Meller pleaded, 'Leave me, leave me, come back later.' They sprinted 80 to 120 metres through the rain, rubber and crack of bullets, stopped and regrouped; ahead Buick saw a cloud of yellow smoke billowing through the gloom. Sabben had had the prescience to throw a smoke grenade. 'My job was to keep the corridor open,' he said.[51]

As they ran towards the smoke, Buick's men yelled out their names. The 12 Platoon medic, 'Doc' Davis, rushed out to help bring them in. Several of the wounded crawled in unaided. At one point, a heap of mud seemed to move towards them. They took aim: 'I could see our kids lining me up,' recalled Paddy Todd later. 'I was yelling, "You silly bastards … Don't shoot! Don't shoot!"'[52] Private Buddy Lea helped drag Todd back the last few metres; the medics removed his boots to find his ankles and legs peppered with shrapnel splinters. The survivors fell back to Smith's headquarters, where Corporal Phil Dobson, the headquarters medic, raced from body to body, tearing open shirts to treat gaping wounds. Meanwhile 12 Platoon fought off another major assault, before falling back to Smith's headquarters where Delta Company regrouped in a classic 'clock' formation, in readiness for renewed assaults.

Back at Nui Dat, time passed according to the clock. The five o'clock briefings conference started at the designated hour, in a tent adjacent to the Operations Centre. Those present included Townsend, Major Dick Hannigan, Lieutenant Colonel Dick Cubis, Group Captain Peter Raw, Captain Trevor Richards and about thirty others. (Major Rowe had returned to Australia with hepatitis.) Hannigan almost immediately cancelled the meeting as news of the seriousness of the battle came in. The officers went to the Ops Centre, where the Task Force commander Jackson sat brooding over the incoming news.

Jackson visibly ailed as the pressure mounted, and Cubis and Hannigan assumed his most pressing tasks. The brigadier withheld the order to dispatch the carrier-mounted relief force, as he feared that would severely endanger Nui Dat. Only a handful remained to defend the base, and the survival of the Task Force, Jackson insisted, was more important than Delta Company's relief. He readily believed signals intelligence that another enemy unit — the 274th Main Force Viet Cong Regiment — was camped somewhere to the north.

So the armoured carriers were put on stand-by — for reasons unknown to Lieutenant Adrian Roberts, a brave and sturdy officer who commanded the carrier troop designated to transport the relief forces. Roberts awaited the green light with intensifying impatience. The delays continued; the arguments persisted. Townsend eventually persuaded Jackson that Delta Company's annihilation overrode the risk of an attack on the base. At 5.30 p.m. the brigadier gave the nod for the carriers to move. An exasperated Roberts, who had been waiting an hour, presumed that the cause was Alpha Company's disorder. Exhausted after returning from an operation, they were consuming a barbecue and beer at great speed. Now they were being scrambled, in some disarray, to return to the battlefield aboard Roberts's carriers.

Meanwhile the gunners blasted away at Stanley's targets in the distant rubber. The gunners overcame drenched aiming points, fogged sights, shells without fuses. Cooks, clerks, anyone available, helped to unpack the shells and screw in the fuses. The concert had long ago dispersed, and Little Pattie was flown, in near shock, back to Vung Tau. Col Joye, however, had been 'captured and held' by some soldiers as a joke, and would spend the night at Nui Dat. The Task Force base had become — in the mind of Jackson and many of his officers — a fortress under siege.

At 5.45 p.m. the ten carriers roared to life. Lieutenant Roberts's orders were to lead the machines, which contained a hundred infantrymen, to the battle and 'break up the attack'. (Townsend would fly out later, by helicopter, Roberts was told.[53]) A Portsea graduate and experienced cavalryman, Roberts observed the rawness and confusion around him with mounting concern; everything seemed deliriously ad hoc. His squadron commander, Major Bob Hagarty, shared his alarm: Hagarty had spent two years in Malaya and done a tour with the Team. They were 'old army' men, who long ago learned to contain the panic that visibly gripped some of their less-tested colleagues.

The carriers were squat tub-shaped vehicles mounted with .50 calibre machine guns manned by the crew commanders, who sat up top. Thinly armoured, of no use against anti-tank weapons, the vehicles had a top speed of 30 kilometres per hour. Inside, the soldiers bumped about in the cramped, boiling cabin; the sky and the trees were visible only through the hatch above. 'It was like being inside a washing machine,' recalled Private Terry Burstall.[54] The carriers' radios were virtually useless due to the horrendous background noise; three were fitted with new radios, which emitted a screeching sound; in any case, the infantry was totally unfamiliar with the system, said Roberts, who had no choice but to communicate with his passengers by yelling through the hatch above the roar of the engine.

Immediate delays dogged the expedition: the carriers could not find the exit from Nui Dat. Roberts had not been told of the relocation of the exit, concealed in the complex barbed-wire fencing erected by 1 Field Squadron engineers, who had to be fetched to guide the convoy through.

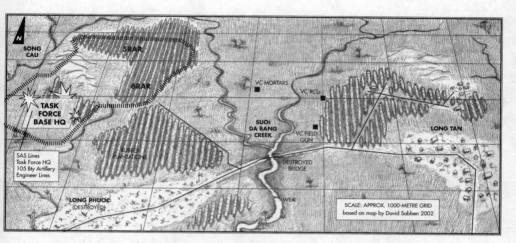

1. THE 17 AUGUST BOMBARDMENT OF THE TASK FORCE BASE,
SHOWING VC MORTAR SITES

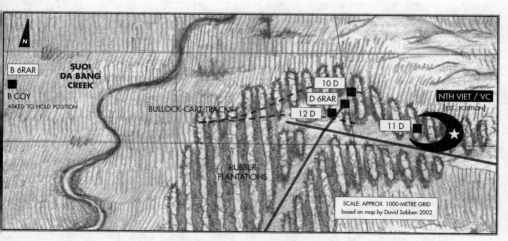

2. 11 PLATOON D COY LOCATION AND FIRST ENEMY ENVELOPING MOVES
1600–1630 hours, 18 AUGUST 1966

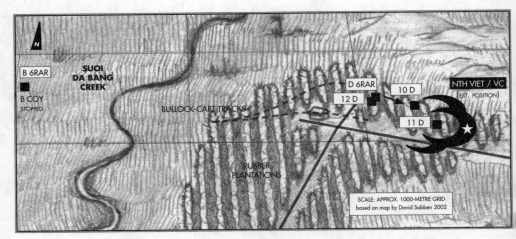

**3. 10 PLATOON D COY MOVES NORTH-WEST OF 11 PLATOON TO HELP**
1630–1700 hours, 18 AUGUST 1966

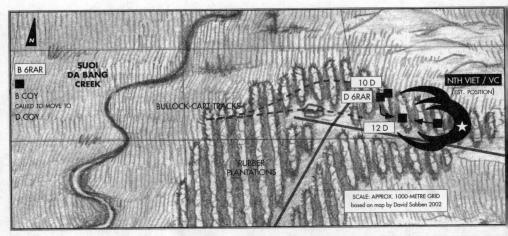

**4. 10 PLATOON D COY RETURNS; 12 PLATOON MOVES SOUTH THEN EAST**
1700–1800 hours, 18 AUGUST 1966

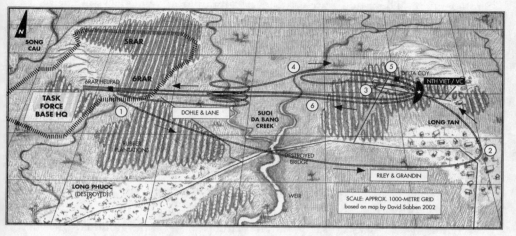

## 5. ROUTES TAKEN BY RAAF AMMUNITION RESUPPLY HELICOPTERS,
## FROM 1800 hours, 18 AUGUST 1966

**1.** Riley and Grandin (R&G) move forward to locate Delta Coy while Dohle & Lane (D&L) take a holding pattern over the river. **2.** R&G overfly Long Tan village, turn north-west towards the battlefield. **3.** R&G call for smoke and see 'orange', which was thrown by the enemy. They circle anti-clockwise and see 'red'; this was 'correct'. **4.** R&G rejoin with D&L and guide them to Delta Coy position. **5.** Ammo drop made '...right into CSM's lap...' **6.** Both helicopters return to Task Force helipad.

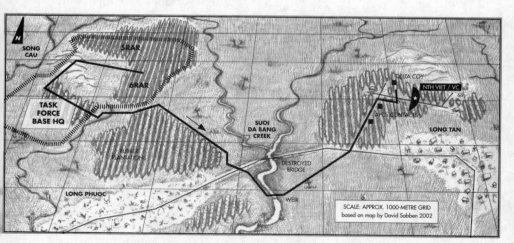

## 6. ARMOURED PERSONNEL CARRIERS, RELIEF FORCE ROUTE

Meanwhile, a grave dispute between the army and the RAAF imperilled Smith's men. They desperately needed ammunition, and Jackson had approved the ammunition resupply, to be dropped by helicopter.[55] But the RAAF's Group Captain Peter Raw opposed the plan; he refused to permit his pilots to hover at treetop height, in a monsoon, exposed to heavy ground fire. Raw invoked the Department of Air doctrine that required forward landing zones to be 'relatively secure'.[56] Permission may even be needed from Canberra, Raw suggested.

The word 'Canberra' surged through Jackson like an electric shock. Relations between the RAAF and the army, already strained, now fell apart. 'Well, I'm about to lose a company!' Jackson fumed. 'What the hell's a few more choppers and a few more pilots!'[57] Raw demurred and insisted on sticking to correct procedure.

A disgusted Jackson sent for the Americans. None doubted the exceptional courage of the US rotary wing pilots. Air Marshal Sir Alister Murdoch, Chief of Air Staff, RAAF, had just visited Nui Dat; his liaison officer casually promised a few Hueys within twenty minutes. Raw had little choice: either send the Australian pilots or leave the RAAF open to charges of failure. In any event, Raw's own pilots scorned 'correct procedure'. Flight Lieutenant Frank Riley insisted on flying to Delta Company's relief and 'would go on his own, if necessary'.[58] Flight Lieutenant Bruce Lane felt the same way. 'At last a little RAAF guts!' thought Jackson, greatly heartened.

Riley and his co-pilot Flight Lieutenant Bob Grandin boarded one helicopter; Flight Lieutenant Cliff Dohle and Lane flew the second; there were two machine-gunners per helicopter. Major Owen O'Brien and Warrant Officer George Chinn volunteered to hurl the ammunition boxes down to the men. Chinn, the 6th Battalion's formidable RSM, 'forcefully and almost insubordinately' demanded to go, 'come what may'. Grandin was less keen; he felt it a suicide mission: 'It was insanity. I felt petrified. I tried to talk Riley out of it. Frank said shut up, stop giving me the shits.'[59]

In the drenching rain, Graham Cusack, the helipad duty officer, wrapped ten to fifteen tins of ammo in blankets and loaded them into each aircraft. The Hueys' rotors dissolved in a blur, and the machines flew into the storm with only their flashing anti-collision lights on. They had five minutes to jettison their vital cargo before the enemy exploited the cessation of the guns. It was 6 p.m., and near dark. Green and red tracer slashed the sky.

As they approached, the air crews scoured the flickering rubber for the smoke grenade that would reveal Smith's headquarters. But Riley flew too far.

Delta Company signaller: 'Smoke thrown. Over.'

Grandin: 'Roger that. I see orange smoke.'

Delta Company signaller: 'No! No! Wrong! Wrong!'

The Viet Cong had tossed orange smoke to confuse them, a common ruse. Delta's signaller threw the red smoke again, and this time the helicopters saw 'red'. Riley guided Dohle through the pouring rain towards the smoke, with the Huey's flashing red strobe light visible.

A moment later, in the shelter of the storm, Riley and Dohle were flying low over Harry Smith's headquarters. O'Brien and Chinn heaved the ammo boxes out as the helicopters did a tail-rotor turn through 180 degrees at treetop level. 'They fell right into Jack Kirby's lap,' Smith recalled.[60] 'You bloody beauty! Right on target!' shouted a witness, Corporal Graham Smith. Jack Kirby grabbed the boxes, slung the bandoliers of bullets over his shoulders and rampaged about the rubber 'like a man possessed', sharing ammunition with every man. The soldiers snapped the rounds into the magazines, slammed the magazines into the breech and resumed firing.

In the artillery lull, three American F4 Phantom jets swept down on the rubber, yet the pilots could scarcely see the targets in the downpour. They dropped their ordnance, including napalm canisters, behind the Viet Cong lines, and flew away. Stanley urgently recalled the artillery.

The ammunition arrived at the last moment. The Viet Cong had tested the limits of the *uc dai loi* and lined up to resume the attack, in full regimental strength. Smith's company, which had formed a circular perimeter in readiness for the coming onslaught, saw black human shapes racing between the trees, then a line, a much longer line, arose hideous and unending between the rubber trees. Then came the bugles. 'That was shocking, that was horrendous,' said Akell. 'You saw them lining up, you heard the awful sound. They were spread out in an extended line in the pouring rain. You could see these black figures coming your way. Your mind is going a hundred miles an hour. I thought, this is my last moment on earth.'[61] Some soldiers silently prayed.

At a quick jog, enemy troops in their hundreds advanced on the Australian remnant. Re-armed, Smith's riflemen opened up, and Stanley guided the artillery to the target: the shells burst amid the enemy lines. The second lines dived for cover behind the bodies, then leaped over the dead to resume the rush: 'They were coming forward all the time over their piles of dead.'[62] Jack Kirby ran around 'screaming encouragement to the blokes', Private Bill Doonan recalled. At one point, Kirby raced forward and scooped up a wounded young reinforcement 'like a bag of spuds', and took him back.[63]

At times the enemy came within touching distance: Akell shot a Viet Cong soldier crawling 3 metres away. Others were shot as they raced up to drag out their comrades' bodies; nothing — not twenty-four howitzers — deterred the Viet Cong's brave attempts to retrieve casualties.

The attacks became bigger before they died. At about 6.15 p.m. Smith reported enemy heavy machine-gun fire from the south-east and the start of 'continuous assault waves of probably battalion strength'. At 6.20 p.m. Smith ordered Stanley to 'drop fifty metres' — drop the shells 50 metres ahead of the company position — but Artillery headquarters warned of friendly casualties at such close range.

'Annoyed,' Smith recalled, 'I grabbed the radio handset from my signaller and told 6RAR to tell the gunners to fire the bloody guns where I want them or they will lose the lot of us.' The gunners obeyed and dropped to 50 metres.[64]

The enemy came through the trees in waves of twenty ... straight into the artillery barrage. Those who fell were instantly replaced, with fresh waves, 'so you got this kind of rolling effect, which you couldn't stop'.[65] Brian Halls saw a line of humanity disappear in a shell burst, again to be instantly replaced with fresh troops.[66] 'It looked as if the dead were coming to life,' Sabben remembered.[67] The close shelling devastated the Viet Cong lines. 'We could not advance even a step to eliminate the remainder of the Australian force, as a result of the "artillery rain",' states the D445 history.[68]

Meanwhile, the armoured carriers, moments out of Nui Dat, were suddenly ordered to stop; two were ordered to return to fetch Townsend, who had been refused a chopper. The delay severely taxed Smith's patience: 'If they don't hurry up and get here then they might as well not come at all!'[69] One platoon was almost lost, and the other two were '75 per cent effective', he said.

The other eight carriers made for the western bank of the Suoi Da Bang Creek. Their delays put Alpha Company commander Captain Charles Mollison in a black mood, which now approached boiling point; Roberts, too, was frustrated in the extreme. He had chosen the quickest route, but the appalling conditions held him up. He sat on a plank across the open hatch to see over the gun shield: the rain sheeted down on the darkening field. The carriers wallowed through the thick red mud of a bullock track and down a steep slope to the creek crossing. 'All the while a torrential monsoon downpour served to mask the sound of our approach,' Roberts recalled. One by one the amphibious machines splashed into the current and floated across, buffeted along the side of a small dam in 2 metres of swirling water. One carrier stayed back to guard the crossing; the remainder (now reduced to seven) pressed on towards the roar of battle.

Then, at the track that led into the rubber, Roberts received another order to halt, to await Townsend. He ignored it and pressed on. The carriers moved forward, in a line seven abreast, 40 metres apart, covering a 200-metre front and moving astride a sunken road, which formed a convenient axis towards Delta Company. The crews strained their eyes through the incessant downpour for signs of Smith's men.

Suddenly, the crew commander of the most easterly vehicle saw them: not Delta Company but black figures moving through the night, in an orderly formation, apparently oblivious to the squat machines looming through the rain. The Viet Cong had neither heard nor seen the convoy's approach; the carriers had their headlights off, and the noise drowned their engines. Lieutenant Peter Dinham shouted to open fire. Sergeant Frank Alcorta instantly rolled off the top of his carrier, and Private Ron Brett followed, leaping to the ground. Dinham urged the crew commander to lower the rear ramp, and his ten men streamed out and attacked. The Viet Cong scattered — more in fear of the line of armoured vehicles than the brief contact. The brave, spontaneous action of Dinham's men nonetheless stunned the enemy. Later, eight Viet Cong bodies and blood trails suggesting forty wounded were found; several had been dragged away with vines looped around their ankles.[70] The contact lasted just six minutes and helped to break the enemy's obvious attempt to attack Delta Company's rear (they were later found to be members of the D445 Battalion).

Roberts shouted to Mollison to get his men back inside. The carriers were moving deeper into the rubber when a huge explosion destroyed a tree in front, and the carriers halted again. An enemy anti-tank team, armed with recoilless rifles, blocked progress. Roberts's machine-gunners swiftly cut them down. Roberts paused: he was concerned that further anti-tank units may be up ahead. Tensions erupted between the two men: Roberts told Mollison 'where to go in fairly plain terms'; in response, Mollison threatened Roberts (with a pistol, some allege, a claim Roberts later dismissed as laughable).[71]

A little later, an enemy machine-gunner raked Corporal Peter Clements's carrier, hitting him in the stomach. He fell back inside; the carrier crushed the enemy machine-gunner under its tracks. Impulsively, Roberts ordered the carrier to take Clements back to Nui Dat, a mistake he later defended as an act of compassion. Yet at the time it infuriated Mollison. (Clements would die of his wounds nine days later.)

At last the carriers reached the battleground. The six remaining machines charged into the enemy lines like a herd of wild buffalo, machine-gunning or crushing anything that moved. The Viet Cong replied with heavy machine-gun fire and a kind of explosive bullet that burst against the rubber trees in puffs of white latex. 'The bullets were going over our heads,' said Corporal Cameron Jamieson. 'You see this slow-moving tracer and you feel you can almost dodge it.'[72] They pressed 500 metres into the rubber plantation, leaving behind a wide trail of devastation. The carriers proved the last straw for the Viet Cong that terrible night: their crews busted through the enemy lines with machine guns blazing — a decisive moment in the battle often lost in the infantry's louder versions of events. The D445 officer, Nguyen Duc Thu, later recalled his despair at the sight of the armoured vehicles: 'We saw the tanks [carriers] coming and we knew that we did not have the weapons to fight them.'[73] Firing ceased at about 7 p.m. when the rain, too, seemed to switch itself off. The darkness closed over the battlefield; little fires died in the steaming night.

At 7.10 p.m., the carriers converged on Delta Company. Some of Smith's men stood and cheered. Mollison emerged waving his pistol, 'like Roy Rogers without his horse', joked one observer.[74] Around this time, Townsend arrived, and the nine carriers formed a defensive square around Delta Company, to the rear, and lit a landing zone for the dust-offs with their interior lights.

All over the field the Viet Cong gave up the fight and withdrew. Kirby organised the wounded and helped bring in the dead. The wounded were pumped with morphine and laid together, awaiting medevac to Vung Tau; an American chopper with flashing strobe lights was the first to arrive, followed by all of No. 9 Squadron's fleet, which landed without lights. Roberts, with the help of Trooper Jock McCormick on the radio, controlled the flights in and out using hand torches. 'None of us had ever done this sort of thing,' Roberts said later. 'But it worked. Thank God.'

Townsend radioed Jackson: so far, he confirmed, one platoon destroyed, sixteen wounded and sixteen missing in action. Not for the first time,

Jackson hung his head in his hands in despair; some said he trembled for his career. 'It looked like a disaster,' wrote McNeill.[75] The Task Force felt it was staring at a terrible defeat. Smith and Townsend spent the night on the battlefield, in the back of a carrier, arguing and debriefing; Smith's company stayed, too. Now and then, throughout that terrible night, an Australian patrol crawled out into the darkness towards the sounds of moaning.

# Chapter 19
# Long Tan — aftermath

The Australian mercenaries, who are no less husky and beefy
than their allies, the US aggressors, have proved good fresh targets
for the South Vietnam Liberation fighters … In two days ending
18th August the Liberation Armed Forces wiped out over 500
Australian mercenaries in Ba Ria Province.
*Radio Hanoi, 5.49 p.m., 27 August 1966.*

The birds were singing in the morning light as the sun rose upon another scene of human devastation. At Smith's headquarters, the soldiers stirred, stood to, brewed up and were ordered back to the battlefield. 'Oh Christ!' murmured Corporal Laurie Drinkwater. Many were similarly aghast. Kendall argued that a fresh company should go. Yet Harry Smith insisted that Delta would lead the assault back in, for the sake of morale and 'to see what we'd lost or won'.[1] He had refused an order to return to Nui Dat: his men lay dead somewhere in the rubber plantation. Perhaps some were alive. Ghastly rumours of the mutilation of corpses did the rounds.

Delta Company walked back down the aisles of trees, ahead of the armoured carriers. The mood was funereal, the atmosphere cave-like, upon re-entering the canopy of rubber. 'Shoot anybody you don't know,' Jack Kirby warned. Nobody spoke; the flies broke the silence as they approached.

They crept upon a landscape denuded of life: the trees were leafless stumps and the earth a tangle of red mud, body parts, splinters, rubber sap and slime. 'I thought I was on another planet,' said Drinkwater, as he surveyed the aftermath of the howitzers: 3,500 shells had burst in an area no larger than two football fields. The packs of 10 and 12 Platoon lay untouched where they had left them, a little camp site within a massacre.

White blood ran from bullet holes in the rubber trees and smeared the shattered trunks. On the ground they saw tens, then scores, then hundreds, of corpses, in grotesque positions, half-buried, dismembered, frozen in acts of blind self-sacrifice.[2] Wild pigs snuffled about the field, feasting on the remains. Bodies were obliterated; fragments that were once part of a human being were found in the limbless trees. Here and there whole corpses lent a semblance of dignity to the flesh, legs, heads and arms that scattered the battlefield, examples of what the bits and pieces might have been. 'I more or less turned off, I didn't have any feeling at all,' Drinkwater said, years later.[3]

The Australian dead lay where they fell, unmolested by the enemy, undisturbed by artillery. Most had their rifles by them, or in their hands. 'They died firing,' said Bryan Wickens. 'It was the bravest thing I'd ever seen and I'd been in seven theatres of war.'[4] A professional, ex-British Army soldier, Wickens had earlier dismissed the conscripts as 'not ready for it'. After Long Tan, 'I found them to be the bravest soldiers'. The experience, he said, later compelled him to 'change my nationality to Australian'.[5]

The unbroken hiss of radio static could be heard. Vic Grice, an Australian radio operator, had died sitting up, with the 'squelch' of his radio off, like a cardiograph flat-lining. He appeared to be smiling. Here was Lieutenant Sharp, the reluctant soldier, lying on his side, with one hand outstretched, reaching for an AK47; his shattered Armalite lay 6 metres away. And shortly they found two miracles: Barry Meller, wounded in the mouth and leg, propped against a rubber tree, was waving. 'What took you so long?' he said; and there lay Jim Richmond, face down in the mud, shot twice in the chest, yet alive. Richmond later described 'hoping that the artillery wouldn't get me … I was worried about my mother, and I kept thinking, if I died she would be up shit creek, so I prayed a lot and made a lot of promises, but I'm afraid I never really kept any of them … It was the longest night I've ever known.'[6]

The Australians were unmoved by the growing pile of enemy corpses. The Viet Cong bodies represented a job; the dead had no names. Their remains were to be counted and buried. Yet privately, many Australian soldiers came to respect this enemy, to admire the blind courage, or faith, or belief, that compelled so many young men to hurl themselves at artillery. They searched, as they counted, the Vietnamese bodies and found photos of mothers, wives, girlfriends and children; an unremarkable thing, yet it rendered human what were yesterday 'gooks' and 'nogs'. Many of the dead were mere teenagers. Most were well-dressed North Vietnamese, giving the lie to Hanoi's claim that none of its troops operated in the South. The pile of captured weapons included a heavy machine gun, a 60mm mortar, two recoilless rifles and four rocket launchers, of Chinese or Russian make. Harry Smith personally relieved a dead North Vietnamese of a prized Tokarev pistol.

Three wounded enemy troops had a chance of survival: one boy was shot in the groin. An Australian medic poured iodine into the wound, picked the dead maggots out and dressed it. He and another wounded were medevaced and the third, lightly wounded, put under guard and interrogated. He confirmed that the plan was to attack the Task Force base. The three spoke with North Vietnamese accents, the province chief told Hannigan. Two hopelessly wounded Viet Cong were put out of their misery. One had half his head missing; Buick shot him. 'I killed [him] out of pity for the poor bastard,' he wrote later.[7] 'I hope someone would have done the same for me if the roles were reversed.' David Harwood dispatched a second wounded Viet Cong, found writhing in agony. There was no routine killing of the wounded, as the journalist Ian Mackay alleged.[8] But a few Australian soldiers went off their brains and mutilated the dead. One corporal completely snapped, picked up a Viet Cong corpse by the feet, swung it around and smashed its head open against a tree, claimed Allen May.[9]

Base wallahs, 'experts', curious commanders and the media swiftly descended on the battlefield. Bob Buick actually punched a major who flew in for a 'look around' and made insensitive remarks. When a journalist started asking 'all these dumb questions' Buick stuck his rifle in the reporter's stomach and said, 'If you don't fuck off and leave me alone I'll fucking kill you.'[10] Jack Kirby hung the reporter by the collar of his shirt on a rubber tree.

It took three days to bury the Vietnamese, amid the constant hum of flies. The Australians called for bulldozers, but none came; so all the enemy corpses were buried by hand. Many of these young men had never seen a corpse. 'You lift them, and you've got the brains pouring out the back of the head … I mean it was grim stuff, it really was,' said Bill Akell.[11] Several vomited. It was Drinkwater's birthday on the day he joined the burial party. 'Happy birthday, Drinkie,' someone said, as they dug. On the second day, pigs exhumed the bodies from shallow graves; the swine continued to do so for weeks. In places, rigor mortis raised limbs from the earth. In one case, a digger hung a sign, 'The Claw', around a desiccated arm sticking out of the ground. The bodies were reburied.[12]

The Australian wounded were flown to the 36th US Evacuation Hospital in Vung Tau, in the care of Australian and US doctors and a very pretty young Red Cross worker called Jean Debelle — later nicknamed 'Jean Jean the Sex Machine' — one of the few Australian female aid workers in Vietnam at the time; her presence clearly assisted the troops' recovery. The Australian dead were flown home and interred with full military honours. Graham Cusack had the dispiriting task of receiving the Australian casualties' kit. 'Their guns, webbing, packs — bloody with bullet holes in them — all came to me,' he said, years later, with tears in his eyes. 'At the time, I didn't know if the men were dead or alive.'[13]

The total Australian casualties were seventeen killed in action, one subsequently died of wounds and twenty-one wounded. The Vietnamese casualties were carefully tallied: 'Final score: 245,' states Townsend's log.[14] He estimated that 350 wounded were dragged away. In fact, the body count ceased before the bodies were counted, according to Sabben, as Canberra demanded a figure for Friday afternoon's newspapers, so 245 became the official 'score'. Yet the enemy casualties were in fact a lot higher. During OPERATION MARSDEN in late 1969, the Australians captured a Viet Cong dispensary that had a list of dead and wounded attributed to Long Tan: '878 KIA/Missing/Died of wounds and approximately 1,500 WIA'.[15]

The press and the politicians leaped on the casualty figures as evidence of a great victory snatched from the jaws of defeat, and so on. 'REDS SURROUNDING DIGGERS WITH "ELASTIC RING"'; 'CHARGING OVER PILES OF DEAD'; '11 CONSCRIPTS IN LIST OF KILLED'; 'REDS "LOST 500 TO 600": FRASER'; 'DIDN'T WANT TO FIGHT, BUT DIED A HERO' (on the death of Sharp); 'LUCKIEST BLOKE ALIVE' (on Meller's discovery).[16] So ran the Australian headlines, on 21 August 1966. The enemy were 'drugged like zombies', remarked at least one reporter; others hailed the 'little battle' as 'one of the great stands of military history'.[17]

The politicians basked in the reflected glory. 'Our forces in their latest engagement,' cabled Prime Minister Harold Holt, 'have aquited [*sic*] themselves with skill, effectiveness and high courage in the best Australian tradition. Please tell them that Australia is proud of them ...'[18]

The Task Force renamed the Delta Company patrol 'OPERATION SMITHFIELD'.[19] The Battle of Long Tan was thus bundled up after the event to look like a pre-planned Task Force triumph that had started on the 17th, when the Viet Cong mortared the base. OPERATION VENDETTA ceased to exist.

The loss of eighteen Australians for at least 500 Vietnamese was an astonishing military feat, and gladdened Westmoreland's eye for the body count. 'Your troops have won a spectacular [victory] over the enemy near Ba Ria,' he wrote. 'Aggressiveness, quick reaction, good use of firepower and old fashioned Australian courage have produced outstanding results.'[20]

In hailing Australia's 'biggest battle', America's NBC network reported the novel discovery that these odd 'diggers' fought with cans of beer in their packs. 'Beer is part of the rations they carry in battle,' stated Dean Brelis, presenter of *The Today Show*, who added: 'In battle, the Aussies don't wear steel helmets because they make too much noise ... They are a brave, loyal people. The United States is lucky to have them on our side. We don't have many friends in Vietnam.'[21] Regrettably, he failed to mention whether the Australians won the Battle of Long Tan with Vic Bitter or XXXX.

The communist press reliably lied. The Australians had sustained terrible losses, claimed Radio Hanoi. 'The Australian mercenaries,' stated a broadcast at 5.49 p.m. on 27 August 1966, 'who are no less husky and beefy than their allies, the US aggressors, have proved good fresh targets for the South Vietnam Liberation fighters ... In two days ending 18 August the Liberation Armed Forces wiped out over 500 Australian mercenaries in Bar Ria Province.' Peking's international wire service repeated the claim.[22] The Viet Cong 5th Division conceded '60 wounded and 30 deaths'.[23]

Viet Cong propagandists presented Long Tan as a victory, of course, and paraded the message through the villages, in order to demonstrate their supremacy over the *uc dai loi*. Ba Lian, the political officer from D445, moved around the province telling people all about the big battle in the rubber plantation. 'He realised that the war could not be won without the support of the people,' wrote Burstall.[24]

Many years later, in Vung Tau, I had lunch with Nguyen Minh Ninh, a commander of D445 Battalion (which played a subordinate role in the battle). He corrected this misrepresentation, and conceded the loss: 'Your artillery stopped us from launching the next stage of our plan, to attack your Task Force. We lost many troops. We were forced to end the engagement. We had great respect for the Australian troops: you fought as we did. Some of you fought better than we did.'[25]

The Australian artillery 'caused many casualties', confirmed the D445 history. The Australian guns 'used a dangerous trick … to divide our formations', it states. 'After combat, the temporary command ordered the soldiers to withdraw. Mrs Chin Phuong's militia and others bravely carried the wounded soldiers to a safe area.'[26]

In the postmortem, the Viet Cong and North Vietnamese realised they were up against a far tougher adversary than hitherto thought; never — not against the French or the Americans — had they encountered an enemy willing to call artillery down on their own heads. Their belt-hugging tactics had no purchase against such a force. In fact, so heavy were Vietnamese casualties from close-ranging Australian and New Zealand artillery that the Viet Cong were ordered never again to attempt a direct attack on Nui Dat; indeed, on no subsequent occasion during the war would the Task Force face a regimental or larger offensive. Even the communist forces admitted that the Australians had severely thwarted their movements: 'The D445 Battalion could not carry out any major combat/attack operations at battalion level after July 1966 because of the enemy's frequently unexpected raids,' said the D445 history.[27]

Yet, in other respects, the D445 and 5th Division were never defeated in Phuoc Tuy, and proved a constant thorn in the side of Australian attempts to control the province. After Long Tan, the Viet Cong seemed to recede, only later to flare up unexpectedly. '[The Australians] could not succeed in destroying the D445 … who existed right under the noses of their heavy weapons, where even a mouse might be killed,' one communist history states.[28] In time, North Vietnamese regiments flowed into Phuoc Tuy and steeled the local forces with new weapons and slogans: 'All for the South!' and 'All for Victory against the American Invasion!' The propaganda offensive never died; villages were continually subdued or terrorised. Those who welcomed Australian protection and aid were branded 'collaborators'. Vengeance was merciless.

★　★　★

On 21 August 1966 — the same day the exhausted Delta Company survivors returned to base — Townsend ordered Smith urgently to submit his recommendations for bravery. Canberra needed heroes to placate the public outcry over the loss of eleven nashos. Smith recommended, among other awards, Military Crosses for Sabben and Kendall, a mention in dispatches for Sharp and Military Medals for Buick, Bill Moore and Akell. (The medal fiasco dragged on for forty years.) In sum, Smith's recommendations were almost all downgraded, without notice, weeks later. Not for thirty years would Smith learn the truth of what happened.

The Australian Government rubbed salt in by refusing South Vietnamese decorations to the diggers. The Queen had not formally approved the foreign awards, as was customary, Canberra argued. Expecting a reversal of the decision, representatives of President Thieu personally went to Nui Dat to pin the medals on the soldiers. Thieu, then the second most important man in the country — after Ky — was denied the chance: Vietnamese awards were unacceptable. Embarrassed, Thieu ordered his staff to fetch Vietnamese gifts — national dolls and cigar boxes — from Ba Ria, and handed these out. 'Minutes before we marched on to the parade,' said Akell, 'we were told there'd be some delay. We waited until noon. Then we were given a doll each.' For the next thirty-eight years the Australian Government would repeatedly deny the soldiers' right to their South Vietnamese medals.

The Americans later bestowed the US Presidential Unit Citation on Delta Company — the equivalent of the President awarding the second-highest medal for gallantry to each member of Delta Company. It was most appreciated, in the absence of any comparable recognition by the Australian Government. Years passed. In 2005 I visited Harry Smith, whom I found at home in Hervey Bay, fit and gung-ho, wearing a sweater emblazoned with three huge letters, 'USA'. 'It is embarrassing,' he said, 'to think that the Americans rewarded us but the Australian Government put us down.'[29]


The soldiers were given several days' R&R. They drained prodigious quantities of beer, played sport, went surfing; some waterskied behind a patrol boat. A bevy of bar girls met the troops' bus in Vung Tau.

Yet Delta Company, especially 11 Platoon, was never the same. Some soldiers, especially the new recruits not trained to Smith's exacting standards, broke down. There were spectacular binges, many offences and much erratic behaviour. Even Kendall, who went on to a fine career in military intelligence, lost the plot: in the months after Long Tan, he stole a jeep and collided with a local. Smith threw him out of the company.[30] Neville Cullen, who aided the Long Tan burial and later excelled as a dust-off pilot, was demoted after the battle: 'I was caught walking along a road drunk with a pistol in my hand.'[31]

Bruce Fletcher, the official war artist, immortalised the battle in his vast canvas of soldiers lying in mud as the carriers arrived. Fletcher tells his own, intriguing story. He volunteered for Vietnam because 'no one else would'.[32] When Fletcher arrived at Canungra, an instructor bellowed, 'Who the fuck are you?'

'I'm the fucking war artist, sir,' Fletcher replied.

He was instantly popular with the soldiers, not least when, the moment he got to Nui Dat, a captured weapon accidentally discharged and shot him in the ankle.

At the field hospital, Fletcher turned an artist's eye on a common medical condition, a 'pastie penis', so badly infected with venereal disease that it discharged only pus. This got Fletcher thinking, 'Would the War Memorial want a painting of a pastie?' Later, 'a terrible mine victim' arrived. Fletcher saw 'something roll off the stretcher — a dog's bone?' It was the victim's leg: 'A Goyaesque scene imprinted itself on my mind,' he later wrote.

In remission, Fletcher positioned himself outside a local brothel, where the girls 'caressed his plastered leg, which itched like mad'. Meanwhile, he watched US Army trucks distribute mess slops to starving little ginger-haired kids, the Eurasian outcasts. 'In putrid pools, pink lotus flowers swayed in the gentle breeze,' Fletcher wrote.

Within the wider war, Long Tan was a minor afternoon's clash, a sideshow. Yet it captured American attention: 105 Australians and three New Zealanders, with expert control of their artillery and the timely — and lucky — arrival of carrier support, had routed a North Vietnamese-led regiment and a Viet Cong battalion. In that sense, it astonished. This ought to be put in perspective, however. The Americans and South Vietnamese sustained far greater casualty rates than Long Tan every week. For example, just two months after Long Tan President Johnson received his usual situation report. The total US casualty figures for '24 hours' ending 11 a.m. on 18 October 1966 were: 154 Viet Cong/North Vietnamese army killed, 231 (estimate) wounded; 27 South Vietnamese troops killed, 51 wounded; and 10 Americans killed, 58 wounded. The casualties over the previous week (9–15 October) were 993 Viet Cong/NVA killed, 1,490 (estimate) wounded; 189 South Vietnamese killed, 504 wounded; 74 Americans killed, 447 wounded (no Australians were killed, 12 wounded). Since January 1961 the body count was: 149,846 Viet Cong/NVA dead and an estimated 224,659 wounded; 40,232 South Vietnamese killed and 80,527 wounded; and 5,584 Americans dead and 31,337 wounded.[33]

The victory of a single Australian rifle company, with artillery and armour, over an enemy force fifteen times its size, is what defined Long Tan. The soldiers later erected a simple white cross in the rubber plantation. No one was debriefed; they simply continued the tour. On 21 August the troops returned to Nui Dat, to a few rows of empty tents.

# Part Four
# All the way ...

# Chapter 20
# ... with LBJ

... And so, sir, in the lonelier and perhaps even more
disheartening moments which come to any leader, I hope there
will be a corner of your mind and heart which takes cheer from
the fact that you have an admiring friend, a staunch friend that
will be all the way with LBJ.
*Prime Minister Harold Holt to President Johnson, 29 June 1966.*

'Saving South Vietnam' was now the main goal of the war, declared the
fresh rhetoric of Prime Minister Harold Holt in 1966. A majority of
Australians still strongly supported the war in Vietnam; yet the stated reasons
for our involvement were reshuffled and arranged in new priorities. People
were growing sceptical of the Domino Theory and the threat of China.
Hence the victory at Long Tan was particularly welcome at a time of
growing unease about the war. The government played down the regional
threat, which had faded due to more stable governments in South-East Asia,
and focused on our moral obligation to the Vietnamese people and our
allegiance to America. When the ALP's Kim Beazley (senior) asked, in
March 1966, why Australia was at war in Vietnam, Holt replied:

Our first objective is to help the Government of the Republic of
Vietnam, at its request ... to resist the armed aggression of
Communist North Vietnam ... Our second objective is to free
15 million [*sic*] people of South Vietnam from the threat of

oppression and terror ... The third objective is ... to honour our treaty commitments ... Fourthly, by denying victory to Hanoi and Peking in South Vietnam we will ensure that the spread of Communism in South East Asia is checked ... Fifthly, we do not seek to overthrow the regime in North Vietnam ... We simply want the North to stop its aggression ...[1]

At a stroke, the Australian troops were cast as freedom fighters, linking arms with the Free World in saving South Vietnam from Marxism. In reshuffling the priorities of the war, the Prime Minister had tacitly acknowledged the fading relevance of forward defence against tumbling dominoes, the original *raison d'être* for Australia's commitment. China, steeped in domestic crises, was no longer considered a regional threat, and the Soviet Union preferred not to upset its delicate coexistence with the USA.

That is not to dismiss the moral case for protecting South Vietnam; even Whitlam, in the 1950s, had supported a UN-backed war in the hope of preserving a filament of democratic freedom south of the seventeenth parallel. It is simply to pose the question: what, precisely, were Australia's national interests, in a war in which the regional threat had dissipated?

Nobody seriously pursued the question. The media simply criticised Holt's lack of 'hard facts' about Vietnam or contested his claim that we were 'winning'. The peace movement brayed in its usual, ill-informed fashion. Few challenged the government on its own terms: that is, to explain Australia's continuing national interest in the struggle for South Vietnam as the regional threat faded. The short answer, of course, is that we had treaty obligations, to Washington and Saigon, and trade opportunities with America.

Holt's sunny optimism, athletic figure and perennial suntan lent his public statements a kind of persuasive buoyancy. The Prime Minister seemed always to be 'leaving on a jet plane', and the novelty of air travel and television gave his feather-duster leadership a certain glamour in the eyes of ordinary Australians, few of whom could afford to fly. Holt took a large press contingent on his lavish trips, and exploited the media limelight to the rafters. The press loved the free jaunts to exotic lands aboard his airborne bandwagon. From 21 April to 1 May 1966 the Prime Minister visited Vietnam, Thailand, Malaysia and Singapore; at Bien Hoa, he mucked in with the troops in an open-necked shirt and a bush hat. It was great television.

In June that year Holt shuttled home for a SEATO conference in Canberra, where he triumphantly informed delegates that the Free World was applying the 'Domino Theory in reverse': the market economy would spread through Asia and conquer the Communist Bloc through sheer economic advantage. He then flew off on a grand tour of Washington and London, a trip that would define his prime ministership. On meeting Holt, Dean Rusk cabled the President from Canberra: 'I FOUND HOLT ONE THOUSAND PER CENT IN SUPPORT OF WHAT WE ARE TRYING TO ACCOMPLISH IN SOUTH EAST ASIA.'[2]

Harold Holt's relationship with the President started well, and the two became firm friends. On 1 February 1966, in his first letter to LBJ, Holt strongly backed the American bombing of North Vietnam. His support was 'very much more than a public posture', Holt wrote. 'It reflects, Mr President, the strong belief of myself and my colleagues ...'[3]

Warm words flowed and glued the friendship in advance of Holt's spectacular reception in Washington on 27 June 1966. His arrival coincided with the resumption of the US bombardment of oil refineries in Hanoi and Haiphong, a politically awkward event for many Western leaders who opposed the bombing, chiefly because it was not sanctioned by the United Nations. Yet such concerns had no traction here, in a meeting between the staunchest foreign allies in the war. The Australian Prime Minister received a full state reception with a nineteen-gun salute, military bands and sumptuous dinner engagements. On 29 June, on the south lawn of the White House, in the bosom of American power, under the lights of the world's media, Holt uttered his immortal pledge that bound Australia irrevocably to the American-led war in Vietnam:

> I am here, sir, not asking for anything [he told the President]. You
> have in us not merely an understanding friend, but one staunch
> in the belief of the need for our presence with you in Vietnam
> ... And so, sir, in the lonelier and perhaps even more
> disheartening moments which come to any leader, I hope there
> will be a corner of your mind and heart which takes cheer from
> the fact that you have an admiring friend, a staunch friend that
> will be all the way with LBJ.[4]

The line 'all the way with LBJ' had been the President's 1964 election slogan. Quoting it, Holt gave the impression that Australia uncritically supported American policy. A storm of protest greeted the speech at home; the media and the ALP portrayed Holt as the presidential poodle — or joey, in the pouch of an American 'roo, as cartoonists portrayed him. Australia had offered a 'blank cheque' to the White House, the ALP claimed. Even supportive newspapers reminded Holt that Australia was a US ally — not a satellite.

In truth, Holt had no intention of going 'all the way', in the sense portrayed by the press and his ALP critics. Behind the scenes his Cabinet carefully calculated just how far it would go.[5] (In time, Australia showed that it had no intention of going even a fraction of the way, despite Whitlam's claim that the Coalition Government went 'further than LBJ' in its anti-communist rhetoric.[6] The nation had fielded 300,000 soldiers in overseas theatres during World War II; to Vietnam, it sent scarcely a brigade.) 'All the way' was a slogan, not a policy. If it seemed embarrassingly servile to the press, at the diplomatic level it helped to cement a genuine friendship between the President and the Prime Minister. It worked — so much so that Treasurer Billy McMahon later felt emboldened to cast America as our 'huckleberry friend', in a quote from the 1961 hit 'Moon River': 'Wherever you're going, I'm going your way/Chasing the rainbow's end …' and so on[7].

In this sense Holt's speech went down very well, especially with his colleagues. 'We are proud of you,' cabled 'Black' Jack McEwen.[8] Most Australians shared the deputy leader's sentiment: 62 per cent approved of Holt's speech.[9] Never before had the Australian people seen the world's greatest power so lavishly entertain one of their prime ministers. The media's hostility — Holt was portrayed as LBJ's puppet — barely dented ordinary Australian pride in their beaming new leader who bestrode the steps of the White House like the little mate of a colossus.

The visit achieved little else. The President offered nothing in the way of economic substance. On Walt Rostow's advice, Johnson rejected Australia's key trade requests. America's huge metal stockpiles had cut demand for Australian zinc and lead, regardless of whether 'you prevented the reimpositon of import quotas', Rostow advised LBJ on 17 June. To the vital question of Australian access to US wool markets, Rostow urged the President to 'refuse any liberalisation of wool tariffs' unless Australia relaxed its barriers to US tobacco. And the Australian sugar industry could forget about US access under a mooted international sugar agreement. 'None of our specialists think it has a chance,' said Rostow. Exempting Australia from the hated interest equalisation tax should also be resisted, Rostow told the President (notwithstanding the fact that America had agreed to exempt

Japan). On meat and dairy products, the President merely agreed to 'try' to prevent new protectionist legislation.[10] Holt had come 'asking for nothing from America', which was just as well, because he did not get anything.

Yet there was something about this laid-back Australian optimist that played well in the Texan's mind. LBJ saw Holt's growing difficulties at home: the looming Australian election, and the ALP's hostility to the war. Johnson also liked Australians: he warmly recalled his time as a young navy officer in Townsville. Now, as then, Australians proved staunch allies at a time when the world seemed to be abandoning Uncle Sam. In this light, the President had little hesitation in agreeing to tour Australia and New Zealand that October, en route to the Manila conference on regional security. Holt, a deft hand with a spear gun, justly hailed the visit on 22 October 1966 — the first by a US president — as the 'biggest fish I've ever speared'. The timing was a calculated triumph: just before general elections in Australia and New Zealand. Cables flew between Washington, Canberra and Wellington to plan the most powerful motorcade ever to glide through the Antipodes.

Media hysteria and a huge spike in support for the war marked the build-up to the presidential trip. Even without the LBJ factor, the war was immensely popular. In August 1966, the month of Long Tan, 64 per cent of Australians strongly approved of Holt's support for American policy in Vietnam; only 23 per cent were opposed. Two in three Australians backed the call-up for military training of 19-year-olds; 63 per cent being in favour and 26 per cent against.[11] Only a slight majority opposed conscription for overseas service. News of the 'dawn of a new era in the Pacific', as the papers hailed the presidential visit, further excited popular backing for the war.

LBJ's first stop was New Zealand, whose conservative government strongly supported the war, in spirit at least; in substance, it fell well short of delivering the arms and men LBJ wanted. In 1966 Prime Minister Keith Holyoake had authorised the dispatch of a battery of gunners and a few support troops (later, two companies of infantry soldiers were incorporated into Australian battalions).

In Wellington the catafalque party broke the American flag, and Johnson stepped on to the tarmac into the blameless company of the New Zealand Governor-General, Sir Bernard Fergusson, 55, a British-born Old Etonian formerly of the Black Watch Regiment. Sir Bernard was the third Fergusson GG, after his father and grandfather. His maternal grandfather, the

Earl of Glasgow, had held the post in 1892–97, as had his wife's cousin, Lord Cobham. Perhaps the President — a master of the hustings — felt slight unease in a country that so blithely elevated its Fergusson family. Indeed, the US Embassy in Wellington felt inclined to explain the idiosyncrasies of this fiercely British little nation, whose people the President's Briefing Book described in tones reminiscent of Gulliver's discovery of a strange new species. 'SUGGESTIONS ON APPROACHING THE NEW ZEALANDERS', it stated. 'New Zealanders tend to be a bit more reserved and standoffish … They are … somewhat fearful that their prized conservative, insular, rural, protected society may be wrenched irreparably by industrial development and [their] greater participation in world affairs …'[12]

Of Sir Bernard, the briefing warned: 'He dresses immaculately, wears a flower in his lapel and a monocle. He is a Presbyterian.' Accompanying this description is a picture of the knight with a sword and ostrich-plumed hat. His wife, Lady Fergusson, the former Laura Grenfell, had a 'slight speech impediment, somewhat in the nature of a cleft palate. To an admirable degree she has overcome shyness … She usually drinks wine punch in preference to stronger drinks …'[13]

Having done with the Fergussons, the President endured a visit to a New Zealand sheep farm, owned by a farmer opposed to the war. New Zealand intelligence had failed to unearth the man's dubious past, and the local press had a field day. 'This was a big goof by the Government of New Zealand,' Tom Johnson of the US Embassy told the White House. 'I went to the farm and met the man. He seems like a solid citizen … will not raise Vietnam … will show the President his grazing land and a sheep shearing operation.'[14]

At the time, Walter Cronkite deigned to interview Keith Holyoake. The legendary CBS anchorman growled that even 'little New Zealand' was divided over the Vietnam War, to which Holyoake replied, with a rhetorical flourish: 'What other way is there? What other way is there to convince the communists of China and of North Viet-Nam who have announced to the world they're going to conquer South Viet-Nam by these horrible communist guerrilla tactics? What other way is there to prove to them they can't do it?'[15] The idea of New Zealand standing up to communist China played well on US networks.

The Central Intelligence Agency closely monitored the antipodean peace movement. In Australia, fanatical fringe elements, chiefly Maoist and Leninist groups, had drawn up 'elaborate plans' for protests, the CIA observed.[16] Local ASIO operatives warned their CIA counterparts to expect 5,000 demonstrators on the streets of Sydney. They singled out a mob of 'Extremist Greeks', the Democritus League, who were embedded in the Communist Party of Australia. Apparently, these Red Greeks were 'particularly dangerous'.[17] Risks of 'rough demonstrations' in Brisbane, a notorious hotbed of 'strong Communist Party activity', were taken less seriously because the Queensland police 'will probably take fairly aggressive action'.[18]

Meanwhile, 'the word was out that they were going to kill the President' in Townsville, warned Charles 'Chuck' Lipsen, a presidential bodyguard. Lipsen, who had 'never heard of the damned place', was aghast at the groundless rumours. He decided to approach local union bosses to help him lock down the town. '… man, I don't want to get him bumped off here, for God's sake, you have got to help me,' Lipsen pleaded with the trade union burghers. He even organised signs that proclaimed 'LBJ is fair dinkum'. 'It's Australia's highest compliment,' he later explained.[19]

A more serious death threat came four days before LBJ arrived in Sydney. An anonymous male caller to a newspaper threatened to 'get' Johnson when the presidential motorcade passed through the city. The caller held Johnson responsible for the loss of his son in Vietnam; in response, New South Wales police scoured the files of Australian servicemen killed recently in Vietnam in an unsuccessful effort to identify the caller.[20]

For the President, the threat was personally wounding. He shouldered a heavy responsibility for the consequences of his actions in Vietnam, as shown in his reply to a letter from the brother of a dead American soldier:

> I have read your letter [Johnson wrote] not once but twice, and I am still unable to find the words to express how strongly I respect your grief. I did not know your brother, and I cannot, therefore, know what you feel so deep in your heart. But every morning, when I read the daily report of the men who yesterday died in Vietnam, I feel inside what I cannot express, even to my wife — an aching emptiness, a sadness — all the more painful for I must go on to that day's work without showing it … The struggle in Vietnam is a thousand contradictions, so the death of one man seems a thousand times more senseless. But I do not believe, I genuinely do not believe, Gordon Lippman died for an empty cause.[21]

The presidential tour was judged a great success. Hundreds of thousands thronged the streets of Sydney and Melbourne. The visit was symbolic of a new warmth in relations. 'The excitement and enthusiasm generated by your visit ... was absolutely unprecedented,' US Ambassador Ed Clark later cabled the White House.[22]

The media were universally upbeat. 'LBJ is with Australia all the way' was a typical headline. 'If this is the dawn of the Pacific Era,' wondered Melbourne's *Herald*, generously, 'where better to start it than Sydney on a Spring morning in 1966?' The *Sydney Morning Herald* speculated, 'It is not exaggerating Australia's influence to see ... the first faint outline of a special relationship between Australia and USA in the Pacific.'[23] The US media portrayed Australia as a threatened ally in need of American protection. In this observation lay the visit's historic relevance. 'Today,' reported Jack Perkins, of NBC TV, echoing John Curtin twenty-four years earlier, 'Australia looks more to the US than Britain as its closest friend, ally and chosen protector. It was as such that it welcomed President Johnson.'[24]

Johnson laid the hand of a fatherly protector on Australia's shoulder. He warned that if the USA pulled out of Vietnam, Asian countries would swiftly fall, and 'the aggressor would get to Australia long before he got to San Francisco'.[25] Yet he had no fear of that happening. 'North Viet Nam could achieve no military victory,' declared the Joint Statement issued in Canberra.

The President enjoyed a lavish — if at times frenzied — reception. In Melbourne, spectators surged over the barricades and surrounded his vehicle, delightedly shaking hands. In Brisbane, he waded into the crowds, to meet and greet; women swooned and young men fought to shake the presidential palm. Lady Bird was a great hit. The President's speeches were exceedingly well received, both in Parliament and in the press. He praised Australia's 'rock-like dependability' over the war in Vietnam.[26] He turned Holt's speech to the Prime Minister's advantage, pledging, at a luncheon in Canberra, 'There is not a boy wearing uniform yonder today who does not know that when freedom is at stake, when brave men stand shoulder to shoulder in battle, Australia will go all the way — and America will go all the way — not part of the way, not a third of the way, not three parts of the way but all the way, when liberty and freedom are won.'[27]

He declared his love for Australia's pioneering spirit. To rapturous applause, he spoke of sights in Australia to gladden the heart: the rich herds, the handsome and spirited women, and the sun-bronzed and rangy men, tall in the saddle. Australia, he declared, was the 'Texas of the South Pacific', and he conferred on 'the nation of Australia honorary citizenship of the Lone Star State of Texas'.[28]

The sensitive issue of Australia's trade relationship with America was carefully excised from the script. Yet privately Holt and McEwen did reach favourable agreements on the price of wheat and lamb. And Johnson's team also discussed the nuclear energy plant at Lucas Heights and America's 'rent-free' space stations in Canberra, Carnarvon and Woomera, which would play a key role in NASA's Apollo Space program.[29]

The protesters made a lot of noise during LBJ's visit, but failed to excite much support or interest. They were a 'fiddling minority', noted Clark, 'completely overwhelmed by the multitude'.[30] They made headlines out of all proportion to their size — at most, 5,000 in a crowd of 500,000 in Sydney, where Premier Robert Askin infamously instructed his driver to 'run over the bastards'. A few militants hurled paint and rotten eggs at the President's bubble-top, bullet-proof limousine and prostrated themselves before it. In Canberra, about 2,000 demonstrators, 'many of them bearded youths and girls wearing T-shirts', blockaded the main entrance to the President's hotel and 'screamed hatred'. Johnson and his wife were forced to use a rear entrance.[31]

There was one serious incident, in Melbourne, where two old boys of Melbourne Grammar, John and David Langley, threw red and green paint on the President's windscreen. It obscured his chauffeur's vision and forced the cavalcade to stop. The paint also drenched three secret servicemen, who were later treated for possible eye damage. The crowd turned on the Langleys. 'One old lady hit me with an umbrella,' recalled David, who claimed that security guards beat up his brother in a laneway before bundling them off in a paddy wagon.[32] Frustrated by their failure to impede the presidential progress, anti-war activists turned their ire on the mounted police. In Sydney, 'fights and scuffles' broke out when Johnson's motorcade reached Hyde Park. Police almost fell from their horses as protesters pelted the poor animals with fruit.

The tour exposed a deep rift in the ALP. The great public support for Johnson forced Calwell to express support for the American-led war. Yet the ALP's federal president, Senator J. B. Keeffe, dismissed the trip as a cheap political gimmick and called on 'all Australians' to show America that 'this country is not in favour of selling the lives and souls of young Australians ...

in Vietnam'. Calwell disowned O'Keeffe's remarks, which were roundly condemned by the ALP's leaders and the press.[33]

Indeed, as the tour ended, support for the war soared: 70 per cent of Australians said they approved of US policy in Vietnam, and 66 per cent backed ROLLING THUNDER, the bombing of the Hanoi–Haiphong industrial complex. The President and Lady Bird left Australia with warm memories, a bronze sheep, a boomerang, a bark painting and other gifts (on a separate occasion, incidentally, they received two albino kangaroos).[34]

The Manila Conference on South-East Asian security on 24–25 October 1966 — whence Holt and Johnson repaired — amounted to a photo opportunity for the 'Free World forces' and a lot of platitudinous nonsense. As a 'display of unity', Manila merely underlined global disunity over the Vietnam War. No doubt the Manila Seven — America, South Vietnam, Korea, Australia, New Zealand, the Philippines and Thailand — stood as one: one superpower and a gaggle of little flags. But where were the nominal SEATO members: Britain, France and Pakistan, or indeed any European power? Where were the so-called opponents of communism in Asia: Indonesia, Malaysia, Taiwan and Singapore? Manila merely highlighted the world's dismal support for the 'Free World' in South Vietnam.

The delegates dusted down LBJ's 'Fourteen Points for Peace'. These set the conditions for 'unconditional discussions' with Hanoi about 'mutual de-escalation'.[35] The fourteen points also called for genuine 'free elections' in South Vietnam and pledged US$1 billion for national reconstruction, in which the North was invited to participate. In reply, the communist side offered 'Four Points', demanding the total withdrawal of US military personnel and weapons in Vietnam and the ending of acts of war against the North; the 'peaceful reunification' of Vietnam in accordance with the Geneva Agreement; the settlement of the internal affairs of South Vietnam in negotiations with the National Liberation Front; and the removal of all foreign interference. Australian 'anti-war' groups, such as the Vietnam Action Campaign and others, aligned their policies with Hanoi's agenda.[36]

The Joint Communiqué, signed on 25 October, presented 'saving South Vietnam' as the chief goal of the war: 'We are united in our determination that the South Vietnamese people shall not be conquered ...'[37] The signatories pledged four 'Goals of Freedom' in Vietnam (and Asia):

1. to be free from aggression;
2. to conquer hunger, illiteracy, and disease;
3. to build a region of security, order, and progress;
4. to seek reconciliation and peace throughout Asia and the Pacific.[38]

Manila, Holt claimed, 'would have a heartening effect on the world as a whole'. On the contrary, the Manila conference prescribed a fool's paradise, the impossibility of which simply drew attention to the delegates' impotence.

Back home, in November, Holt's Liberal–Country Party Coalition won the federal election in the biggest landslide since Federation. The result was seen as a complete vindication of his policies in support of conscription, America and the war in Vietnam. The Liberals won 50 per cent over the ALP's 40 per cent of votes, a margin greater than any won by Menzies and hitherto the largest governing majority in Australian history. The President's visit, the great split in Labor, the public clash between Calwell and deputy ALP leader Gough Whitlam over conscription and troop withdrawal (the ALP had no policy on 'when') all contributed to the result. The Democratic Labor Party, whose madder leaders supported an Australian nuclear capability, helped to scupper the ALP's hopes by absorbing the working-class Catholic vote. Holt emerged with a clear mandate to prosecute the war as he saw fit. Yet the victory cast a dangerous hostage to fortune: it boxed Australia — and the Prime Minister — into a long, ugly war with no exit strategy. 'All the way' handed an open-ended commitment.

The ALP, a house divided, looked on with bitter disappointment. The Opposition Leader, Arthur Calwell, had campaigned on the divisive issue of conscription. His style — impassioned, working class, fiery — had repelled the voters. 'You are beyond military age,' he had shouted at an elderly draft supporter. 'I will not allow you or Holt or [Frank] McManus [Deputy Leader of the DLP] ... to plunge your arthritic hands wrist-deep in the blood of Australian youth.'[39] And Whitlam and Calwell were bitterly divided during the campaign. Conscripts should be withdrawn 'as soon as possible', Whitlam said, leaving space for negotiation. Calwell unconditionally demanded the immediate withdrawal of all nashos (a move that would have endangered the regs). Whitlam accused Calwell of 'debauching' the debate on Vietnam, and felt entirely vindicated by the thrashing the ALP received at the 1966 election.[40]

The election result eclipsed Calwell, in mind and spirit. The sad demise of the Labor leader played itself out to a largely indifferent public. In the ensuing months, the poor man lost his bearings and lashed out at imagined betrayers. He made fantastic claims. In a series of wild statements, he described Australia as no more than a 'state' of America and compared the Prime Minister to a US state governor. On 15 January 1967 a bitterly depressed Calwell, unable to bear his electoral rejection, accused America of planning to drop a hydrogen bomb 'possibly on Peking' in an effort to win the war in Vietnam and the next US election.

The American Embassy in Canberra sent the White House a cruel prognosis on the Labor leader's sad decline:

[CALWELL] BELIEVED PRESIDENT WOULD BE WILLING TO DROP
BOMB AND DESTROY HUNDREDS OF THOUSANDS OF PEOPLE
SINCE 'HE HAS ALREADY DESTROYED HUNDREDS OF
THOUSANDS OF PEOPLE BY DROPPING NAPALM AND
PHOSPHORUS BOMBS IN VIET-NAM'. THOUGHT USG WOULD
DROP BOMB 'IF THERE WERE NO ALTERNATIVE' … CALWELL IS
SUFFERING HARDENING OF ARTERIES WHICH CUTS DOWN ON
BLOOD FLOW TO BRAIN AND THUS AFFECTS FULL LUCIDITY.
SITUATION COMPLICATED BY OVERINDULGENCE IN ALCOHOL.
PROGNOSIS IS FOR FAIRLY RAPID DESCENT TO SENILITY.[41]

In early 1967 an event accelerated the creeping divisions over Vietnam: the visit to Australia of Air Vice Marshal Nguyen Cao Ky, Prime Minister of South Vietnam. Ky had insisted on the trip, to the consternation of Cabinet, which found itself in the awkward position of reluctantly welcoming a South Vietnamese ally whose moral and political character had dismayed even American hawks. Ky, just 36, had a reputation as a brash, reckless young playboy, who styled himself a fighter ace. He had won his spurs in the Vietnamese Air Force. A left–wing chorus damned him as a fascist dictator and a mass murderer, citing his policies in the South. Calwell threw a sally of vituperative barbs at the South Vietnamese leader: Ky was 'a butcher', a 'moral and social leper', a 'little quisling gangster', whose visit would 'shock every Australian except those who condoned and tolerated murder, brutality and injustice'. It sickened Calwell to think that 'magnificent young Australians were being killed defending the political and social rottenness which Marshal Ky personified'.[42] If there were some truth in Calwell's statements — Ky was hardly a wholesome character — the Labor leader's splenetic hatred drowned the justice of his case. Ky had notoriously expressed his admiration for Hitler, although it seems his admiration was boorish and naive, akin to Italian satisfaction at Mussolini making the trains run on time.

The visit became a public relations contest between Ky and Calwell. Ky easily won: his charm, apparent modesty and plea of thanks to the Australian people belied Calwell's portrayal of him as a sadistic brute. Ky's beautiful young wife worked her silken charm. The couple seduced their chaperone, Richard Woolcott, then information officer at the Department of External Affairs. 'I believe,' Woolcott said at the time, 'that Ky is uncorrupt at present and he seems determined to act against corruption in Viet-Nam.'[43] Ky, he added, had 'something of the almost infectious sincerity, drive and energy of Lee Kuan Yew'. Before he met the press, Woolcott media-coached the South Vietnamese Prime Minister in how best to deflect insinuations that Ky was a 'dictator'. Woolcott advised him to 'defer to other members of his delegation, particularly to the foreign Minister Dr Do … He did this very deftly at the National Press Club Luncheon.'[44] Indeed, Ky's intelligence and patriotism impressed the media. Peter Howson, Minister for Air, who accompanied Ky, similarly thought him 'incorruptible, a patriot, tough and a quick learner'.[45]

The enthusiasm for Ky and signs that Holt would meet American demands for more troops enraged the anti-war agitators. Their every action seemed to fall like snowflakes on the sunburned land, sizzle and melt away, and their awareness of this impotence inspired a violent militancy in their ranks marked by the determination to destroy or deface what they could not change.

An American victory pledge marked the opening of 1967. In Saigon, General William Westmoreland earmarked the year for the completion of his three-phase victory plan: to defeat the communist insurgency; destroy the North's ability to wage war; and commence 'nation building' in South Vietnam.[46] Australian Brigadier David Jackson celebrated the New Year in Phuoc Tuy with a message to the Task Force: 'We need have no fears for the future. It is now clear that Communist aggression against the people of South Vietnam will fail.' Meanwhile, in the field, an Australian reconnaissance platoon celebrated Christmas around a lemon tree decorated in toilet paper and barbed wire.[47]

# Chapter 21
# Draft dodgers

Dear Arsehole,
You are a shameful low swine … And don't think I'm afraid to
sign this — but my wife disapproves.
From a true Australian
*Letter to Simon Townsend, draft resister.*

Blessed by a strong economy, the youth of the 1960s spilled upon an era
gilded with opportunity. Unprecedented Western prosperity — the
last decade of a thirty-year economic boom — set the sixties swinging.
Economic historians of the period concluded that the average Australian
became richer more quickly between 1939 and 1968 than at any other time
in our history.[1] The age lent the slightly ironic title to Donald Horne's 1964
book *The Lucky Country*. In material terms, Australians were indeed lucky:
the job market was in rude good health, the nation enjoyed great natural
wealth, and a real sense of economic security prevailed, freeing the young to
contemplate and act on issues beyond their own immediate survival. Jobs
were plentiful, and the young did not feel any need to worry about their
future security.

The baby boomers enjoyed educational opportunities undreamed of by
their parents' generation, assured through the injection of new Commonwealth
funds into the tertiary education system: 83,320 were enrolled in Australia's
eleven universities in 1965, compared with the post-war peak of 32,453 in
1948. Many were 'teenagers' (the word was coined in the 1960s): by 1965 just

under 40 per cent of the population — 4.3 million people — were younger than 20.

No dominant 'student voice' had yet emerged: the students represented all extremes, all positions. In the early days, a strong conservative student body checked the advance of the apparently ubiquitous left-wing 'hippie'. For example, the statement 'That we are right in Vietnam' won 312 votes for and 200 against during a Melbourne University debate in 1965. Future ALP foreign minister Gareth Evans, then president of the university's Students' Representative Council, defended the result: Australia had to support the USA, he said, to ensure that 'the whole of Asia is not going to topple ... into the Communist camp'.[2]

Soon, however, one issue bound a majority of students — whether as a matter of conscience, politics or plain fear: their opposition to conscription for overseas service, as decreed by the *National Service Act 1951–64*. ALP leaders Dr Jim Cairns and Tom Uren addressed one of the early protests against conscription in November 1964, and peace activists were quick to see draft resistance as the most powerful weapon in their arsenal.

Sit-ins, teach-ins, student pranks, debates, academics' letters and small protests marked the first demonstrations. In one 'teach-in' — all-night debates — on 23 July 1965 the Catholic author Morris West tore into Menzies' 'terrible blandness', and pleaded for 'mercy teams', not troops in Vietnam. The barrister Tom Hughes QC responded powerfully in defence of the government, and even received the support of the ANU student newspaper. In another teach-in, Liberals conceded that Cairns's rhetorical brilliance and agile mind had rumbled the dour, intellectual Hasluck, whose lame performance probably lost him the succession.[3] Indeed, the government's spokesmen began to look stale, sarcastic and crudely simplistic alongside the eloquence and passion of men like West, Cairns, Francis James, lay editor of the influential *Anglican* weekly newspaper, and the Reverend Alan Walker, of the Central Methodist Mission in Sydney, prompting *The Bulletin* to wail that the government had done little to 'popularise the tremendous issue involved ... the issue of our survival as a free people'.[4]

A solid majority supported the war, but a passionately self-righteous minority was in the ascendant. They were not yet a 'vast, latent sea of disquiet and disenchantment' in the anti-war Reverend David Pope's dream, yet they whipped up the 'tepid mediocrity' of public debate. That did not mean it curdled into a constructive argument; on the contrary, the arguments of the peace movement so often degenerated into 'the grossest sort of emotionalism'.[5] The students failed to follow through the logic of their beliefs: those who supported Hanoi promoted aggression; they supported war, not peace — a war they dearly hoped Hanoi and Peking would win.

In late 1966 Australia's peace, or pro-Viet Cong, groups contemplated a bleak future as an ineffectual minority in a nation that overwhelmingly supported the war. The electorate had spoken. Yet the one issue that troubled a slim majority was national service for overseas duty: was it right randomly to conscript a 19-year-old minor — at least at call-up — too young to vote or drink, train him and send him to a foreign battlefield? Quietly at first, then with rising indignation, most Australians replied 'no'. In this, the anti-war agitators heard the tick of a political time bomb. They embraced as one of their own a new kind of rebel, the 'draft dodger', the popular nickname for conscientious objectors.

Female activists pioneered the anti-conscription drive and offered their homes as the hearth of draft resistance. When the second Australian conscript died, in mid-1966, the dogged SOS mothers publicly mourned. The Women's International League for Peace and Freedom protested in black veils. Then they decided to act. On 6 July 1966 a meeting took place at the Cremorne home of Mrs Betty Gale, the league's president. On this cool winter's day the league urged its members to join parents and teachers in forming a Bill White Defence Committee.[6]

Bill White. The peace movement flew to his name like fans to a pop star. White's birth date had popped up in the first ballot, in March 1965. A clean-cut young schoolteacher from Gladesville, Sydney, he refused to serve on humanitarian grounds. He had no political agenda and belonged to no anti-war group. Although naive, he quickly became well informed. His father-in-law had been a conscientious objector during World War II. White's pretty wife Claire quietly supported her husband throughout. For the role allotted them, the couple could have been cast by Hollywood. 'Bill White is a handsome, strong, tanned, athletic boy, manifestly intelligent, sincere, determined but possibly a little overwhelmed by it all.'[7]

On 20 December 1965 the Sydney Court of Petty Sessions rejected White's application for full exemption from national service. It ordered him to perform non-combatant duties. He refused. He refused even to perform basic medical tasks. He denied the right of any government to order him to participate in the war effort. His views were personal, derived, he said, from a childhood abhorrence of violence, chiefly schoolyard bullies and the trauma of killing a bird with his slingshot. On 21 March 1966 White appealed to the District Court for exemption from national service. The judge grilled him on his knowledge of military history: the Napoleonic Wars and Hitler's invasion of Czechoslovakia. White knew little of these events; nor did he know the amount Australia spent on the Colombo Plan in proportion to defence in 1958. Clearly, his 'conscientious objection' to Vietnam was based on pure emotion and not 'reason', Judge Cameron-Smith concluded.

On 18 July 1966, the day of his call-up, the New South Wales Public Service sacked Bill White. He was removed from his classroom. He pleaded guilty to refusing to comply with the National Service Act. 'I am opposed to a state's right to conscript a person,' White explained, to his growing media posse in September. 'The National Service Act is the embodiment of what I consider to be morally wrong and, no matter what the consequences, I will never fulfil the terms of the act.'

His political detractors called him a coward and a communist. The older women who worked with Claire, also a teacher, mocked her husband, eliciting tears in his young wife. On 22 November 1966, days before the general election, four beefy policemen dragged Bill White from his home. The press filmed the scene for the evening news, and the image was a defining moment of the war. White spent a month in military custody. Parents of children at Denistone East Primary School, where White taught, signed petitions to free him; his headmaster praised him as an 'outstanding young teacher'.[8] 'Release Bill White!' chanted protesters. On 30 December Bill White was 'discharged' from the army, and a court upheld his plea to be recognised as a conscientious objector.

Anti-war protesters appropriated White's stand to their cause, under the Bill White Conscientious Objectors' Defence Committee. Yet White's defiance did not reflect their demands. White opposed conscription according to his own principles, not a political agenda. Unintentionally, however, he served the interests of the militant left and thus became a lightning rod for the nation's ire: 72 per cent reckoned he should have served, according to a February 1967 poll. He also inspired a few dire ballads and poems, such as Willow Macky's appropriation of 'The Wild Colonial Boy':

> *There was a young Australian boy,*
> *His name was William White,*
> *A conscript of the Vietnam war,*
> *He did refuse to fight.*
> *'They've raised no hand against our land,*
> *This war is cruel and wrong!'*
> *Declared this brave Australian boy.*[9]

This was not merely a dreadful lyric; it also misrepresented White's position.[10]

The anti-conscription campaign rose on the tide of the anti-war movement in Australia and in America. As 1967 drew on, many Americans turned away from a war that had claimed the lives of 16,000 young men — 9,000 of whom were killed that year — along with hundreds of thousands of Vietnamese. By the end of February 1967, 106 Australian soldiers had died in Vietnam: thirty-one were conscripts, yet conscripts comprised only 25 per cent of personnel in Vietnam. The fact that most served with the infantry — there was no time to specialise in non-infantry roles — did little to douse the popular myth that nashos were being used as cannon fodder, which fuelled the campaign against conscription.

A healthy young man could avoid national service, legally, in two ways: by volunteering for the Citizen Military Force, or by registering as a conscientious objector (students could defer military duty). Appellants for conscientious objector status had to show a conscientious belief that did not permit their participation in military service of any kind at any time. It was 'not sufficient' to object to a particular conflict, such as Vietnam. A true objector opposed all wars, on grounds of faith or reason, and not emotion. Nor did the Word of God guarantee a ticket to exemption. In 1966, Edgar Collett twice appealed against a court's rejection of his case. Collett had cited his allegiance to the Exclusive Brethren, a secretive religious sect, yet his biblical studies had not impressed a Nambour magistrate. In Perth, a judge similarly remarked that the Sixth Commandment on which Danilo Covich based his case 'is directed at killing in the nature of murder and does not apply to the killing which takes place in the course of military operations …'.[11]

The severity of the law varied state by state, yet most applicants were granted full exemption: of 1,242 conscientious objector cases that went to

Vo Nguyen Giap (left) and a frail Ho Chi Minh, in Hanoi in the 1940s. Giap, dubbed the 'Snow-covered Volcano', masterminded the defeat of French forces at Dien Bien Phu; Ho Chi Minh ('Bringer of Light') vowed to fight for decades to unify Vietnam under his communist vision.

Colonel Ted Serong, the first commander of the Australian Army Training Team Vietnam, in 1963. A brilliant maverick and counter-insurgency expert, Serong later worked exclusively for the CIA and advised the Saigon Government during the collapse of South Vietnam.

AWM

LEFT: Australian Captain Barry Petersen (far left) with Americans Colonel Lou Conein (CIA), Stu Methven (CIA) and a Special Forces officer, in Darlac province, 1964. In an echo of Colonel Kurtz in *Apocalypse Now*, Petersen was sent by the CIA to raise a battalion of tribesmen. The tribes worshipped him as their Dam San, or 'warrior leader'.

AWM

RIGHT: Warrant officers Kevin 'Dasher' Wheatley (left) and Leslie Dowsett, of the Australian Army Training Team, with Montagnard tribesmen in Quang Tri, Vietnam, 1965. The Team was sent to Vietnam to train South Vietnamese and tribal troops, but members swiftly found themselves leading combat operations.

AWM

LEFT: Young women were frontline combatants in the National Liberation Front (Viet Cong). Hanoi and the NLF preferred to recruit teenagers as young as 15, who proved more susceptible to communist propaganda.

ONASIA

'The takeover of South Vietnam would be a direct military threat to Australia ... part of a thrust by Communist China between the Indian and Pacific Oceans' — thus Prime Minister Sir Robert Menzies committed Australia's first combat troops to the undeclared war in Vietnam.

FAIRFAX

GETTY

ABOVE: In 1965 the first American and Australian ground forces were sent to Vietnam. The US strategy of attrition inflicted devastating firepower on the NLF, and measured success according to the net 'body count'.

AWM

Soldiers of the 1st Battalion, Royal Australian Regiment, on patrol heading towards a rubber plantation. In 1965 they were deployed as part of the US 173rd Airborne Brigade, but Australian jungle combat differed sharply from US tactics.

Major John Essex-Clark (left), who became operations officer of 1RAR, discusses troop deployment with Captain Bob Hill. Essex-Clark, who argued strenuously with the Americans over the best tactics, would receive the Distinguished Service Medal, and Hill, the Military Cross, for leadership and bravery in Vietnam.

'A hard day at the office' is how Lieutenant Colonel Jim Bourke captions this photo of him lying wounded on a stretcher, about to be evacuated by a US 'dust-off' helicopter, on 8 January 1966. Forty years later Bourke led a team to recover the remains of two Australian soldiers whose bodies had been lost in Vietnam.

An unperturbed Colonel Alex Preece (far right) continued to lead the 1st Battalion on its return–home parade through the streets of Sydney after a young anti-war protester smeared red paint over his shirt, 8 June 1966. The young woman, covered in paint herself, attempted to smear more soldiers before she was arrested.

The first intake of national service recruits for the Vietnam War leave Central Station, Sydney, for twelve weeks' training at Puckapunyal army base in Victoria. Between 1965 and 1972, a total of 63,790 were called up in a random 'birthday ballot' — dubbed the 'lottery of death' — for two years' military service with an obligation to serve in Vietnam.

No machine was more loved by the troops in Vietnam than the Iroquois 'Huey', their ambulance, godsend and supporting gunship. Early in the war, US choppers were more supportive of the Australian ground troops; but the RAAF's 9 Squadron demonstrated great courage as their experience grew.

LEFT: Australian troops spray herbicides in Phuoc Tuy province in order to deny the enemy the cover of jungle. At the time, the Australian Government knew that herbicides such as Agent Orange were extremely toxic but denied for decades any link between chemical defoliants and soldiers' illnesses.

RIGHT: Lance Corporal Geordie Richardson (left) and Sergeant Bob Buick treat Private Jim Richmond who was found alive the morning after the battle of Long Tan, 18 August 1966, in which Delta Company, 6th Battalion — with artillery and armour support — defeated more than 1,500 enemy troops.

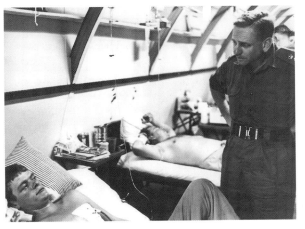

Lieutenant Colonel Colin Townsend, the 6th Battalion commander, visits Private Richmond at an evacuation hospital in Vung Tau, August 1966. Eighteen Australians and an estimated 500 enemy were killed in the battle of Long Tan.

AWM

ABOVE: Private David Collins guards a captured Viet Cong soldier found on the Long Tan battlefield by Australian troops on 19 August 1966. After Long Tan the enemy attempted no further regimental attacks on the Australian base.

BELOW: 'The biggest fish I've ever speared,' said Prime Minister Harold Holt, a keen spearfisherman, of his success in securing LBJ's agreement to visit Australia in 1966. Holt had earlier committed Australia to serve with the American-led forces in Vietnam with the memorable phrase, 'all the way with LBJ'. Holt later drowned off Cheviot Beach on 17 December 1967.

FAIRFAX

AWM

LEFT: Major Harry Smith (right), officer commanding Delta Company during the Battle of Long Tan, receives the ribbon to the Military Cross for gallantry from Brigadier David Jackson. At the time, Smith was furious at the decision to downgrade the awards he had recommended for his officers and soldiers who fought at Long Tan.

In 1966 Delta Company, 6RAR, received Vietnamese dolls and cigar cases in recognition of their bravery at Long Tan. The Australian Government denied, at the last minute, their promised South Vietnamese medals because, Canberra argued, the Queen had not given her consent. Almost four decades later the South Vietnamese awards were approved.

Huge crowds converge on President Lyndon B. Johnson's motorcade in Swanston Street, Melbourne, during his visit to Australia in 1966. After LBJ's trip, 70 per cent of Australians said they approved of US and Australian policy in Vietnam, and 66 per cent backed ROLLING THUNDER, the bombing of the Hanoi industrial complex.

court during the war, 72 per cent were granted total exemption, 14 per cent non-combatant duties and 14 per cent refused exemption. Many more registered as conscientious objectors, but their birthdays were not drawn in the ballot. In the same period, 3,082 men were investigated for breaches of the National Service Act. (Between 1965 and 1972, 63,735 conscripts served in the army, 19,450 of whom were sent to Vietnam.)[12]

By late 1967 a handful of draft resisters were becoming household names and were loathed or loved depending on one's political complexion, such as Denis O'Donnell, Desmond Phillipson, Michael Matteson, Chris Campbell, Errol Heldzinger, John Paull, Mike Jones, David Graham and Robert Mowbray. Many relished the publicity and attendant fame. They had a lot of fun, too, hiding from the police in basements and scurrying from house to house. Some hoped to make a political statement. A few, such as White and, later, John Zarb, had no other agenda than the dictates of their conscience.

Many went to extraordinary lengths to avoid national service: David Pepperell pretended to be mad. 'I researched it with my aunt, a nurse, and we came up with manic depression.'[13] He turned up at his army medical unwashed and unshaven; he twitched and rolled his head throughout the interview and behaved paranoically. Others fled. Andrew Blunden, one of the first to burn publicly his registration papers, left Australia ahead of the police, and stayed away for nineteen years. Karl Armstrong sought, and received, 'political asylum' in China, then moved to another hotbed of freedom lovers, Albania. Mike Matteson hid 'underground' and eluded the police for years. Denis O'Donnell, a recruit, turned against the war after seeing photos in *Rampart* magazine of mutilated Vietnamese children, most of whom were in fact victims of Viet Cong atrocities, an inconvenience the magazine failed to acknowledge. O'Donnell applied for exemption; incidentally, on reading his case, his senior officer, who had spent a year in Vietnam, said, 'Private O'Donnell ... if I was being posted to Vietnam [again] I would take my service pistol out and blow my brains out.' Others, like John Wollin, pleaded their religious convictions — 'Love thy neighbour' and 'Turn the other cheek' — in refusing the draft.[14] The most popular illegal way to avoid national service was simply to fail to register: almost 12,000 youths took this course between 1965 and 1972, and only about 200, on average, were prosecuted per year. The rest slipped through the net. Another option was, of course, jail.

★  ★  ★

An exceptional case overshadowed the politically motivated self-martyrdom of many draft resisters: that of Simon Townsend, a journalist and skilled self-promoter, who failed two appeals to be exempted on grounds of conscientious objection and was jailed. Like White, Townsend seemed a genuine conscientious objector: he had no political motives; his upbringing was conservative. He found national service and war morally repugnant. The judge was not convinced and decided, in early 1967, that Townsend's pleas were based on 'self-preservation of his person and his career as a journalist'. Townsend refused to appear for his army medical, which would have failed him, thus removing his 'nuisance value'. For this reason, the judge interpreted Townsend's actions as deliberately provocative, and sentenced him on 22 May to a month in Long Bay Jail.

Townsend persisted in defying the law. When, in early 1968, he again refused the call-up, the army deemed him a recruit and jailed him in Holsworthy military prison for twenty-eight days. He disobeyed prison rules, refused to salute and found himself in solitary confinement for several days, on bread and water. Every half hour a guard rapped on his cell door, at which Townsend had to shout out his name. The *Sydney Morning Herald* condemned this punishment as 'a well-established Communist technique for breaking down prisoners'.[15] Although Holsworthy was hardly comparable to the Soviet Gulag, National Service Minister Philip Lynch's ill-judged description of the treatment as 'normal' hardly reassured the public. The Military Board ordered the punishment to cease.[16]

Townsend is an interesting, faintly tragic figure, with a quirky, self-effacing sense of humour befitting the one-time Woy Woy correspondent of the *Central Coast Express*. 'I was a law-abiding young man, a conservative young man,' he said, years later. 'But I objected because I was a total pacifist. I think conscription is evil. If a war is worth fighting there would be volunteers.'[17] At his trial, the government's barrister asked, 'What would you do if your mother was being attacked and raped?' Townsend replied, 'I'd do what I could to inflict damage on her assailant … That wasn't the right answer.'

Townsend had little time for the anti-war 'movement', and distanced himself from them: 'A lot were cowards or religious zealots. I detested the term "conscientious objector". I loathed the idea that my conscience was any more pure than anyone else's. I wish people had called me a "conscription objector".' He reserved special contempt for protesters who attacked the soldiers: 'I've always remained angry at the way the soldiers were treated. It was appalling. The people who did chose the wrong targets. They were idiots. I never once went to a demo; I hated the way the protesters provoked the police.'

Townsend received bundles of hate mail. Many letters contained white feathers, and one contained a bullet. 'Most said they wished I was dead, and told me what a cowardly cunt I am. I went through a period of five years of being hated, a person to be spurned,' he said. Women sent several letters; none came from soldiers. Townsend cannot forget one correspondent who wrote:

> Dear Arsehole,
> You are a shameful low swine … And don't think I'm afraid to sign this — but my wife disapproves.
> From a true Australian.[18]

A brief American comparison is worth a look: there, a local Draft Committee, not a court or legislative tribunal, heard appeals for exemption from military service. The committees were notoriously corrupt and vulnerable to bribes, local favouritism and so on. In August 1965 a law passed that punished those who burned their draft cards with a five-year jail term. Of the 25,000 young Americans who burned their cards — most in public — only forty-six were indicted and thirty-three jailed. Of these, most were draft resistance leaders.

More than 500,000 American men committed draft violations, of which 35 per cent were accused and 12 per cent indicted (less than a fifth of these led to jail terms). 'Draft board screw-ups' — that is, errors, bribes, failures to find the conscript, local influence — led to the dismissal of the rest. Many fled to Canada, others went underground. Some feigned madness: one bloke smeared peanut butter on his scrotum and thighs, and showed up stinking of excrement. Asked by the horrified doctor if he usually slept in his faeces, the conscript tasted the peanut butter with his finger and said, 'Yup.' The army decided it could do without him.[19] So, too, it dispensed with the services of a young man who showed up wearing a tattoo, 'FUCK THE ARMY', across his right hand.

Chevy Chase and Jimi Hendrix pretended to be gay, as did a heterosexual ballet dancer who, asked whether he could kill a man, replied enthusiastically, 'Yes, I think so, but it could take weeks!' When Cassius Clay (later Muhammad Ali) refused the draft, he was stripped of his World

Heavyweight title and sentenced to five years in prison (and freed on bond). Only demonstrable religious faith confirmed conscientious objection. Appellants had to show a letter from a priest that demonstrated lifelong faith. Pacifist Mormons, Quakers, Mennonites and Jehovah's Witnesses had a better chance than other faiths. The secular faced a much tougher task proving the dictates of their consciences, as the actor Richard Dreyfus found. Intriguingly, near the end of the war Dreyfus debated the ethics of Vietnam with Donald Rumsfeld, then a young Nixon Cabinet member, who walked off the TV show.[20]

Doctors were more vulnerable to bribes than priests, and many American parents paid their local doctor to 'fail' their son's medical examination. 'Doctors ... would write you a letter for a certain amount of money. It depends how rich your family was ... the affluent draft resister had a far better chance of winning because of all the advantages he had,' noted one US draft counsellor. An average Latino or black kid 'had real difficulty expressing himself in English' — vital in filing a successful claim as a conscientious objector.[21]


The Coalition's charmed electoral position and frequent, insufferable arrogance inflamed the youthful rejection not only of the war but also of the entire conservative legacy of the 1950s.

The slightly deadening conservative consensus of the Menzies years was starting to fragment. The old Lib/Lab duality, the Manichean delineation of Good and Evil, Right and Left, seemed to be crumbling. A more complex patchwork ruffled the landscape of the mind. The first conscientious objectors were ciphers for the feelings of an emerging 'moral minority', who tended not to be students or communists. They were ordinary Australians — young and old, rich and poor — defined by their consciences, not their politics. Many were religious leaders, professionals, business people and academics, middle-class folks with no political axe to grind. They simply believed the war was morally wrong. They included faith-based opponents of the war, such as Catholics for Peace, Pax and assorted Anglican priests championed by Archbishop Strong. Satirists, poets, artists and intellectuals joined the hue and cry for peace. The Ex-Services Human Rights Association of Australia exerted a strong influence; its leader, Allan Ashbolt, an ABC presenter, presented the intellectual face of the socialist left.

Bourgeois bohemians tended to subsume the old communist cadres. Indeed, even the Communist Party of Australia adopted a gentler, fluffier pose, discarding its loyalties to Moscow and Peking to pursue socialism in 'peaceful coexistence' with the mainstream. Where political power had failed, the older Reds sought change through social power. They took to proselytising a new message of peace and love, suggesting the faintly insidious idea that the left had a monopoly on peace and love.

Militant voices were softer in society and in Parliament in the first half of 1967. In February, Calwell stood down and took his red-faced Irish rage to the backbenches. Whitlam comfortably defeated Dr Jim Cairns and Frank Crean for the ALP leadership, thus ending his debilitating rivalry with Calwell over Vietnam and conscription. Whitlam immediately moderated the tone of dissent. Conflict resolution took priority over troop withdrawal and the issue of conscription. Addressing 'current realities', not party ideology, marked Whitlam's reign in Opposition. A powerful parliamentarian and brilliant orator, he set the party on a course of victory at the cost of tainting the ALP's precious 'purity'. As leader, he reinvoked the spirit that underlay his withering attack on the ALP's Victorian controllers of mid-1966. 'We construct,' he told a jeering audience, 'a philosophy of failure, which finds in defeat a form of justification and a proof of the purity of our principles. Certainly the impotent are pure. This party was not conceived in failure, brought forth by failure or consecrated by failure. Let us have none of this nonsense that defeat is in some way more moral than victory.'[22]

In the ALP's new Cabinet the pure were sidelined with their dreams and the pragmatists held centre stage. Unions exerted little influence on ALP policy towards Vietnam. The militant dockside unions were ignored, and the ALP stood aside as the Holt Government dealt a pre-emptive strike against the most disruptive union leaders; for example, the government forewarned Albert Monk, the ACTU president, of the shipment of bombs, artillery and other weapons to Vietnam; the civilian crews were paid off, and the navy commandeered the transport ships, or transferred ordnance to military vessels. Many Seamen's Union members opposed their leaders, and were angry at this loss of work. Even so, throughout the war, HMAS *Jeparit*, HMAS *Boonaroo* and other transport vessels faced the threat of constant delays caused by union action. The soldiers were furious: strikes delayed their most critical morale boosters, Australian beer and letters from home.

★   ★   ★

With the soggy old communists in retreat, a new strain of militancy took root on tertiary campuses. The ALP's crushing election defeat in 1966 and Whitlam's moderation angered students of the left. Their lack of a voice spurred them to act. These student radicals were especially virulent at Monash, La Trobe, Melbourne and Sydney universities. They were always a minority — but a very vocal one. They preferred violence to peaceful methods, and actively supported and raised money for the Viet Cong. They longed for a communist victory as the best way of ending the war.[23] In this sense, they were not 'anti-war'. They despised democracy as the façade of bourgeois tyranny; indeed, their articles and pamphlets shared the dream, if not the eloquence, of *The Communist Manifesto*.

The student leader Michael Hyde, for example, turned to Mao for inspiration: 'I joined the Maoists of the Monash Labor Club, which had nothing to do with the Labor Party. We stood four-square against parliamentary politics. We stood for revolutionary violence, and we worked for a revolution in Australia. In 1967, we started to send money to the Viet Cong. We supported the NLF [National Liberation Front] …'[24]

The student Labor clubs and political societies jockeyed for supremacy. In Sydney, Trotskyists were dominant; in Melbourne, the Maoists had the upper hand; in Brisbane, anarchists prevailed. Among their idols were some of the most brutal dictators of the twentieth century: Mao Tse-tung, Joe Stalin, Fidel Castro and of course Lenin. Their Australian acolytes were, in Brisbane, Brian Laver; in Sydney, Mike Jones and Bob Gould; and in Melbourne, Michael Hyde and Albert Langer. The press idealised these angry young men as 'fiery', 'gifted' and 'brilliant'; their media popularity heralded a shift in the press, too. Whitlam dismissed them as 'a handful of exhibitionists'. The Liberals and the DLP viewed them as traitors, and passed the Defence Force Protection Act, with ALP backing, in August 1967, to stop the militant left sending financial aid to Hanoi and the Viet Cong.


A generational solipsism marked the young adults of the 1960s. Economic prosperity freed them to dream, yet many loathed the very system that delivered this freedom. Never had youthful exuberance enjoyed so much luxury, so much time and money, buoyed by the prosperity of the market economy they affected to despise. They knew better. They knew better than their parents, the World War II generation. They drank heavily of that most potent elixir of youth: wilful ignorance; and, in the end, a great many

Western youths performed a free public relations exercise on behalf of a string of communist dictators, in Moscow, Peking and Hanoi. Their slogans of equality, peace and love lent a spurious substance to this nihilistic dream, this Age of Aquarius. The forces of revolution and reaction were on a collision course. And bit by bit, like a great ship turning at sea, Australia's support for the war gradually shifted direction. Like hundreds of little tugboats, the political misjudgements, draft resisters, death notices and protesters nudged Australian and American minds on a new bearing. To sustain the metaphor, this great movement wrenched Western society from its settled anchorage.

Perhaps the world was on a better course; perhaps not. But sadly, the soldiers in Vietnam were not on board: they were passengers in a different time and place. They saw events in a completely different light. Not only were their horrific experiences — the loss of friends, the terrible months of fighting — ignored and demeaned but also their very story would soon be erased from the political and social script of the times. As we shall see, a unique aspect of the Vietnam War is the collective cruelty of a nation that ordered, with the threat of a two-year jail term, a 20-year-old lad to go to war — then damned him for going.

# Chapter 22
# R&R

*Uc dai loi*, cheap Charlie,
He no buy me Saigon tea,
Saigon tea cost many many P,
*Uc dai loi* he cheap Charlie ...
*Uc dai loi*, cheap Charlie,
He no go to bed with me
For it cost him many many P
*Uc dai loi* he cheap Charlie ...
*Uc dai loi*, cheap Charlie,
Make me give him one for free
Mama-san go crook at me
*Uc dai loi* he cheap Charlie ...
*Uc dai loi*, cheap Charlie
He go home across the sea
He leave baby-san with me
*Uc dai loi* he cheap Charlie ...

*Sung by bar girls in Vung Tau, to the tune of 'This Old Man'.*[1]

*Uc dai loi*, always broke
He is just a hopeless soak
He try to give bar girl a poke
*Uc dai loi* he one big joke.

*A later variant of the song.*

Saigon had deliciously degenerated since Madame Nhu's 'no dancing' regime of 1963. By the mid-1960s the party had returned. Bars, nightclubs and dance halls proliferated. Saigon was 'a vast brothel', observed the Australian journalist Murray Sayle.[2] Graham Greene's 'House of the Five Hundred Girls' rather understated the situation:[3] that year there were 56,000 *registered* prostitutes in South Vietnam. Deviance flourished within the 'folded petals of Saigon's poisonous flower';[4] anything went, and no one cared. Embassyland was a gay glissade; the Australian Embassy harboured a posse of Lotharios and queers who were free to orient their sexuality without the bother of Australian legal or social restraints.

The denizens of Saigon thrilled to the war from the rooftop bars of the Caravelle and Rex hotels: the bombing runs were entertainments, a firework display. Along the grand, poinsettia-lined boulevards the Vietnamese rich held parties of obscene ostentation: lobster, French wine, *foie gras* and caviar were flown in, while people in the backstreets huddled in shanties fashioned out of flattened Coke cans and nibbled on handfuls of rice. The riverside Majestic and the Hotel Continental — dubbed the 'Continental Shelf', and redolent of *faux*-French decadence — were scenes of nightly revelry; at the Majestic a few US cents bought a tango partner. Sex, drugs, gambling, dancing and rock 'n' roll were consumed in Caligulan quantities. 'It was party, party, party!' shrieked one Australian nurse.[5] All of Saigon seemed to inhale the star-spangled twilight of this incontinent city, as though living on the cusp of a thrilling apocalypse.

The American war machine financed the whole raucous indulgence. South Vietnamese influential enough to enjoy American patronage had a grand old time on the black market: graft and palm-greasing were popular sports. Corruption was the cholesterol in the veins of the South Vietnamese economy, which survived entirely on American life support (and would promptly collapse in 1973 when Congress turned off the aid pipeline).

Many Australian soldiers yearned to join in the Saigon party, and felt cut off in 'the Dat'. True, each battalion had a boozer, canteen, cinema, Salvation Army tent and chapel; some tents had stereo equipment and televisions bought at the US Army's Post Exchange, or PX. These did little to alleviate the sense of fighting a war in a dusty old camp on the margins of the excitement. A typical day for the troops in Nui Dat began at 0630 with reveille and flag raising, a Paludrine (malaria medication) parade, breakfast, inspection of lines and weapons, then duties. If not on operations, they did base duties. Lunch was cold meat and salad, then a second Paludrine parade at 3.15 p.m., followed by sport: football or cricket. At 1645 the wet canteen opened, with a beer ration, honoured in the breach, of two cans per day. After a barbecue dinner, the flag and sleeves were lowered, the perimeter patrolled, claymore mines armed and sentries posted. Later, they might watch a film.[6] 'Saw *Dr Zhivago* one night,' wrote Private Philip Ham (a distant relative). 'All the cold and snow seemed so out of place in our hot and sticky climate.'[7]

Leave was variously called Rest and Convalescence, Rest In-Country (the preferred American term), Rest and Recuperation or Rest and Relaxation (the latter usually applied to overseas leave). The process of self-demolition usually began with the first beer in the company boozer: the Australians typically drank Victoria Bitter, Tooheys or XXXX (and smoked Viscounts, Marlboro and Benson & Hedges). The amber nectar had a special place in the Australian war: it raised morale, counselled the grief-stricken and mediated disputes. It was the binding fluid of the bereaved and broken; the soothing spirit of the demoralised and demented. 'We were an alcoholic army,' smiled John Rowe.[8] Not in his deepest depression would the digger resort to narcotics or, to any extent, marijuana. From February 1969 until the end of the war — the 'psychedelic period' — only twenty-eight Australian cases of drug use or possession, all involving marijuana, were reported.[9]

An Australian beer shortage was thus unthinkable. In the worst-case scenario, the troops resorted to American or Vietnamese beer. On 1 November 1967, for example, a stern memo warned that the troops faced a 'cut in beer rations' as supplies from Australia were delayed. The diggers 'may have to accept an increased ration of US beer'.[10] In time, their fury at the unions' refusal to load HMAS *Jeparit* acquired a darker dimension.

The soldiers' happiest distractions were the entertainers: the singers Lorrae Desmond, Little Pattie, Sylvia Raye, Dinah Lee, Johnny O'Keefe, Lucky Starr, Beth McDonald, Jill Kennedy, Cathy Wayne (aka Cathy Warnes), Maureen Elkner, Lynne Fletcher, Ingrid Hart; the bands Col Joye and the Joy Boys, the ABC Show Band, the Chiffons and Xanadu; go-go dancers like Elizabeth Burton; and comedians David Burke and Ray Gilson. There were many more. They performed on the backs of trucks, on helipads and river pontoons, and in football stadiums.[11] Soldiers were 'encouraged to participate' in the concerts, but there was to be 'no unruly behaviour.'[12]

Bare-chested diggers gyrating with mini-skirted go-go dancers was considered ruly; drunken gropes were not. The singer Normie Rowe, a national serviceman, sometimes performed with the entertainers on stage.

Mid-decade the war swung to Dusty Springfield, Aretha Franklin, Diana Ross, Otis Redding, the Beatles, the Rolling Stones, the Mammas and the Pappas, the Bee Gees and the Animals. Particular songs resonate deeply in veterans' minds, such as 'These Boots Were Made for Walking', 'Sugar and Spice', 'I Can't Get No (Satisfaction)' and 'Son of a Preacher Man'. The soldiers' anthem was the Animals' 'We Gotta Get Out of This Place'.

At Nui Dat the performers played in the rough open-air amphitheatre, Luscombe Bowl. A makeshift dressing room and toilet block were built for the female singers. Before that, Lorrae Desmond had to perch herself on a 'throne' behind a canvas partition over which her head was visible; on one occasion, forty soldiers marched by and saluted her.

The soldiers adored Lorrae, a curvaceous, sharp-witted blonde with a fine cabaret voice. 'And I loved the troops,' she said.[13] Her silver-sequinned fishtail dress dazzled amid the dull greens and greys of Nui Dat. 'Their mouths fell open …'[14] She'd wander among the men, and chat away: 'What's your name, soldier? Where are you from, soldier?' On Lorrae's lips, 'Leaving on a Jet Plane' evoked intense homesickness. She felt a maternal affection for the troops, and they reciprocated with a 'wave of love'. 'I knew I had to return,' she said later. 'The boys were starved for entertainment. And they needed to know Australians supported them.' Lorrae returned four times to Vietnam. As Lucky Starr said, 'We didn't do it because we wanted to earn a quid … I did it because no other bastard was there.'[15]

The 'round eyed' girls from home drove the troops wild. When Lynne Fletcher, aged 18, performed at Bien Hoa, 'all these boys popping out of their huts like rabbits, seeing … a girl from home, an Australian girl'.[16] Soldiers warmly remember Sylvia Raye's pure voice, cropped hair and lithe figure. 'Hundreds wanted to dance with us. They seemed so young … They wanted us to ring their mums or girlfriends when we got home. They were very respectful and polite,' she said. 'I kissed everyone!'[17] When Claire, Xanadu's singer, blew a soldier a kiss in the middle of Sonny and Cher's 'I Got You Babe' half a dozen diggers ran up to the stage and lifted her gently to the floor. 'It was corny stuff but everyone had a ball,' recalled the band's drummer, Don Morrisson.[18] On one occasion in 1965 the New Zealand gunners got in on the act, firing a shell at the pelvic climax to a go-go dance by Pat Wordsworth (aka the Big Pretzel).

The girls wore mini-skirts, knee-high boots, tassels, bikinis, sequins, flares, satin shirts and fur-lined waistcoats. Jill Kennedy draped her bikini'd body in feather boas and padded French bras.[19] Ingrid Hart arrived with four suitcases: one for shoes, one for underwear and one for her drip-dry showgowns, from which she wrung the sweat. (A skilled entrepreneur, Hart later established one of the largest private entertainment agencies in Vietnam.)

The American concerts were much larger, and often uncontrollable. Brawls were common, tears invariable, especially when they sang 'The Star Spangled Banner' or the Marines' Hymn: '… all these big tough guys, tears running down their eyes,' Jill Kennedy recalled, 'and they'd be absolutely belting it out, and it really used to touch me … I'd be crying, trying not to let my mascara run.'[20]

In time, strippers, drugs and carelessness dealt chaos to the American concerts. Australian dancer Elizabeth Burton flew in by helicopter to 'a bald hill, a steel girder, a generator and a tent'. She put on her fringe bikini, and emerged to thousands of blokes, 'on tanks and trucks … the bald hill was a mass of people. They said that we stopped the war — and the Viet Cong were watching at the bottom of the hill.'[21] The grunts went berserk when 'three lovely Negro girls' stripped before the American Beach Club at Vung Tau; fights started, and the US military police arrived with sticks swinging, according to witness Corporal Spike Jones.[22] On rare moments, the performers came under fire. During the Chiffons' 'My Boomerang Won't Come Back', a deranged GI tossed a grenade into the crowd, killing his officer and wounding sixty-two troops. On another occasion, sniper fire pinned down Jill Kennedy on stage. The Australian singer Cathy Wayne was shot dead in error when a drugged GI tried to kill his commanding officer during a show called 'Sweethearts on Parade'.[23] Ingrid Hart witnessed the scene: 'He used a silencer on his weapon, missed his target and shot Cathy straight through the heart.'[24]

In time, the Australian officers and padres agreed to relax the 'no strippers' rule, and in 1968 the first 'exotic dancer', a tiny Vietnamese stripper, strutted her stuff at Luscombe Bowl. Suddenly, she ripped off her bra, straddled the shoulders of a burly military policeman, threw back her head and simulated sex with his neck, recalled Terry O'Farrell. The crowd boiled over and surged towards the stage, to be stopped by military police and 'outraged vicars'.[25]

Australian strippers were unwelcome to army pooh-bahs, who refused to invite Sandra Nelson, an 'erotic dancer' from the Paradise Club in Kings Cross, to Nui Dat. 'When's Sandra Nelson coming up?' Captain John Bullen, with mock innocence, asked an Amenities Fund meeting on 22 May 1968. After the uproar subsided, Major Brian 'Bronx' Honner, representing the 1st Battalion, 'jumped to his feet & said, "And why not? I believe she wants to come, and the troops want her here, so why isn't she coming?"'

'Argument subsided,' wrote Bullen, '1st Battalion's casualties having been heavy in the last week.' So he proposed that she be invited. Major Stewart Kendall, who chaired the meeting, added: 'However, gentlemen, I doubt that the Brigadier would approve.'[26] 'Thinking seriously about it,' Bullen later wrote, 'such a visit would raise morale a lot ... She needn't take her clothes off — just being here would be a boost to morale ...'[27]

When he heard of the invitation, Major General A. L. MacDonald, then commanding Australian Force Vietnam, 'exploded, and booted bums' all down the ranks to find 'the prime culprit'. The prime culprit escaped lightly; indeed, Bullen's Topographical Survey Troop was later asked to host the next concert party, 'the first minor unit ever to receive this highly pleasurable task'.[28]

It would be unfair to portray the Australian Army as one of almost ceaseless priapism. Some troops were celibate throughout the tour. A minority of troops were sexually incontinent; many partook a few times — once or twice, claimed Captain Gavin Hart, head of the 'Special Treatment [i.e. VD] Clinic' at the Australian Field Hospital in Vung Tau.[29] Some soldiers remember widespread infection; others recall a very low rate. It seemed to depend on the unit, the mood of the men and the extremity of the operations; the infection rate fell during the course of the war. Yet the prostitutes' almost universal infection rate ensured that even one-timers caught the disease.

Vung Tau, the seedy old French resort, served as Australia's off-duty playground. Restraining the troops was a dirty job, but someone had to do it. In September 1966, alarmed at the decline in moral standards, Australian Force Vietnam cabled Nui Dat: 'CHAPLAINS' were to be used as 'REGULAR INSTRUCTORS ON SELF-DISCIPLINE, DANGERS OF SOCIAL DISEASE ... AND THE NEED FOR STRONG MORAL VALUES ...' Just 10 per cent of soldiers attended religious services, the cable sternly noted.[30]

The Roman Catholic padres conceded the need for reinforcements. They summoned the bishop of Phuoc Tuy, no less, to flail the soldiers' consciences. Few attended the bishop's sermons.[31] As a last resort, some padres appealed to the soldiers' health as a means of restraint, and embraced the condom. 'I still remember on our way into Vung Tau,' said Bob Gully, 'the padre running up to the trucks and shoving a handful of condoms at us. Most were blown up as balloons.'[32]

Fresh back from combat operations, the troops literally swan-dived into the bars of Vung Tau — the Blue Angel, Rose Bar, Lily Bar, Minh Bar, or those named after US states, the Texan, Californian and so on — mostly along Tran Hung Dau and Phan Than Gian streets, where 'a bevy of bored harlots flocked around us squeezing various bits of anatomy while they chorused, "You buy me Saigon Tea … I give number one suck fuck!"'[33] Or, 'You Number One Boom Boom! I love you bookoo' and so on. During the first twelve hours, 'the blokes drank and shagged themselves stupid', a 6th Battalion medic observed. 'There was very much a sense of imminent death.' The Australian and American officers preferred the less spectacular charms of the Pacific Club, the US Open Officers' mess in Vung Tau, where demure Vietnamese girls in *ao dai* danced up close, whispering discreet invitations.[34]

Some preferred the subtle charms of a 'haircut'. One local hairdresser, for example, charged $1 for a haircut, $4 for a haircut and hand relief, and $5 for a haircut, hand relief and oral sex. 'After a $1 haircut,' insisted Spike Jones, 'we went to the steam bath, to sweat out the red mud and clean the pores … and then to the Blue Angel …'[35]

Local escort agencies met the soldiers' 'special needs': 'Brian's Dating Service', for example, advertised 'a girl for a week or the rest of your tour'. Brian catered for all tastes, including 'sadists and masochists'; he boasted 200 girls on his books. He ran 'an excellent all-nighter service', including a private bus that took 'the scenic tour into Vung Tau': 'There you choose your girl. In the morning Brian will take you to the airbase for your chopper ride in. No more worries about getting through the wire without being caught … All Brian's girls are guaranteed to be clean, but if you are unfortunate enough to get the dreaded drip, Brian supplies free treatment.'[36] Brian went broke.

Sometimes the prostitutes pursued the soldiers in the field. On OPERATION DUCK, a road security exercise, 'enterprising Vietnamese ladies' on Lambrettas plied their trade along the roadside. At the end of the operation, several soldiers had the clap, the roads were secure and 'the girls' had 'a vast collection of soap, money, cigarettes'.[37]

Thousands of girls were recruited and primped to sell their bodies, for cash or goods, under the whip-tongue of their 'mama sans' — odious old madams who preyed on pretty young Vietnamese women. Many were farm girls who remitted their earnings to their families: some earned US$400 a month, double what their fathers earned in a year on the land. A few educated bar girls identified with the heroine of the famous Vietnamese poem *The Tale of Kieu*, who sold her body to save her family from ruin.

Unconfirmed rumours claimed that 'enemy' prostitutes concealed razorblades inside their vaginas: the journalist Hugh Lunn was not the only Australian to flee a brothel, on the point of intercourse, because he feared connecting with a blade or catching venereal disease (or being bumped off).[38] Most prostitutes, however, were not Viet Cong agents: they were simply trying to survive. Some undoubtedly worked for the enemy, and Australian intelligence sometimes 'passed on' misinformation to suspect prostitutes (and often received, in return, a dose of the clap).[39]

The bar girls, regardless of their loyalties, if any, certainly wielded a damaging biological weapon. No illness afflicted the Australian (and American) armies with the pervasiveness of venereal disease. In 1966 and 1967 more than 80 per cent of soldiers in some infantry units caught VD, according to monthly medical reports. In October 1966 the Australian forces recorded a VD rate of 943 cases per 1,000 men, the highest of the war, reported Brendan O'Keefe, the official medical historian.[40] Manpower wastage was negligible, however, thanks to immediate and effective treatment.

'Venereal disease' covered a range of sexually transmitted conditions, including gonorrhoea, penile sores, ulcerations and lesions. The worst cases suffered rapidly advancing lesions on the foreskin. 'Exquisitely painful,' noted one doctor.[41] 'Shaft ulcers' in the uncircumcised were treated by retracting or removing the foreskin, and at least one army surgeon earned the nickname 'Rabbi'.

Some cases of VD had tragic consequences. A married sergeant with two children contracted an especially severe strain; the infection turned gangrenous and 'took one side of his dick off', said a witness. 'So he stuck a gun in his mouth and blew his head off. The army said he was KIA in an ambush. His wife and kids still think he was KIA.'[42] A few young men chose never to indulge. An especially tragic case was a young national serviceman — the son of a pastor — who 'wouldn't swear, wouldn't drink, wouldn't do nothing', recalled Barry Kelly. 'He'd just sit on his bed and read his Bible.' One day, just before Christmas, the lad pulled out a pistol and shot himself in the chest.[43]

Efforts at controlling the VD epidemic were 'conspicuously unsuccessful'.[44]

Yet Canberra demanded that something be done, as the infection rate was politically damaging. Since nothing could be done to restrain combat-worn soldiers from visiting bar girls or to police the use of condoms, efforts were made, from 1967 to 1970, to control the unfortunate 'carriers' — the bar girls — and 'reduce the pool of infection'.[45] The Australians thus introduced identity cards for approved — that is, 'healthy' — prostitutes; later, bars had to be licensed. In 1969 an American program attempted to subject all prostitutes in Vung Tau to a monthly vaginal examination and fortnightly injections of penicillin. It also attempted to license bars; prostitutes with VD were denied identity cards. These schemes failed. Local Vietnamese officials with a hand in the vice trade refused to cooperate. In 1970, the mayor of Vung Tau, who boasted, to general mirth, of the lack of prostitutes in his town, cancelled the US program. VD rates 'promptly doubled'.[46]

Sport — beach volleyball, rugby, cricket, sailing and surfing — offered a healthier alternative to sex. In August 1967 the Australian Amenities Fund placed an order for six small surfboards, six long boards and several fibre-glass repair kits; several small yachts; three power boats; twenty water ski ropes and five water skis; and a hundred hogshair dartboards.[47] The soldiers surfed as the bombs fell. The 'Phuoc Tuy Surf Club' at Vung Tau introduced surf flags and volunteer 'life savers'.[48] 'I learned to surf in Nam,' said Brian Sewell.[49] The Australians played volleyball and rugby against South Vietnamese and American teams.

And the men were allowed one trip ('R&R') during their tour. Some chose Thailand, Taiwan or Hong Kong. Thousands of American troops took leave in Australia, a US-designated R&R site from 1 September 1967, after the State Department assured a Joint Chiefs of Staff inquiry that 'American Negro Personnel would not encounter formal discrimination' (black American soldiers had been refused entry to Australia during World War II). By March 1968 about 6,800 American servicemen per month were spending R&R in Australia, mostly in Sydney and the Gold Coast.[50]

The few hundred Australian women who served in Vietnam — other than visiting entertainers — were nurses, secretaries and aid workers, and they had an extraordinary war. They were hugely popular: 'round eyes' received constant attention from the troops. Anne Barber, a PX secretary, had 'a romance every night'. Helen Keayes (now Nolan), an Australian staff reporter in the US Army, had 'six dates in one night'. Men, Keayes recalls, 'used to beg us to talk to them or sit at their table — they'd lie on the ground in front of us and say, "Me Me Me".'[51] Keayes learned how to pilot a chopper, flew with Phantoms, and scorned generals who butted in to dance with her. She persuaded the PX to stock tampons, and possibly helped to improve the Viet Cong's standard of female hygiene (many PX items found their way into enemy hands), as author Siobhan McHugh records.[52]

The plentiful supply of prostitutes reduced the likelihood of rape and sexual abuse. Yet there were several attacks on white women. A 16-year-old virgin, the singer Maureen Elkner, accused an Australian soldier of raping her.[53] There were several savage sexual attacks: one occurred on a beach near Da Nang, where six GIs pack-raped the dancer Elizabeth Burton at gunpoint. The men dragged her into a hut, put machine guns to her head and a 'German luger in my mouth', then took turns, she recalled, 'just like dogs lusting after something'. She did not report the attack; after the war Burton found some solace in Buddhism in America.[54]

A few Australian women had affairs with African-American soldiers. Such dalliances were generally frowned on as they disturbed the precarious racial fault lines of the unofficial 'apartheid' that applied in the US Army, in which blacks tended to stay together and frequent their own bars, such as the Soul Brothers Club on the edge of Vung Tau. Elizabeth Burton's love affair with a 'Negro' prompted the American Military Entertainment Board to deport her as 'a race-riot risk'.[55] Others married their usually white American lovers and found happiness; in a few cases, their boyfriends died in combat, of heroin addiction or committed suicide. This was the state in which Jan Graham, an Australian journalist, found her horribly mutilated American fiancé: the Viet Cong had cut off his penis, stuck it in his mouth, and sewn his testicles into his ears.[56]

For all these horrors, the Australian women relished their war experience as the most exhilarating time of their lives. Three participated in 'combat actions': Keayes accompanied a bombing mission; Hart served as a rear gunner on a night convoy; and Graham held a machine gun during an ambush.

If the soldier survived booze and the clap, he probably did not escape a bar brawl. The Australian Army's charge sheets contain many accounts of fights with the 'Yanks' and the 'nogs'. The slightest provocation triggered bar brawls; a few spilled out on to the streets like a Wild Western pie fight and drew huge crowds.

The perpetrators were lightly disciplined. Indeed, military punishments were finely calibrated. Drunken brawls were at the low end of the scale of offence. Far more serious was falling asleep on sentry duty, which usually incurred twenty-eight days' field punishment and seven days' forfeiture of pay.[57] In one extreme case, a sentry was found 'reading a book and listening to a portable radio'.[58] A soldier who 'unlawfully discharged his weapon' usually got prison with hard labour. Those with self-inflicted wounds, a rare occurrence, were dishonourably discharged from the army; and fragging — throwing grenades into officers' tents — of which there were three reported Australian cases, were treated as murder or manslaughter.

The vast majority of charges were for minor infringements and bad language. Perhaps the most thorough use of 'INSUBORDINATE LANGUAGE' graced the Horseshoe in late 1969, when Private 'RG' told his platoon commander, 'I don't give a fuck. You can get fucked. This whole fucking platoon can get fucked.'[59] The charge sheets were admirably precise. Private 'GS', for example, was charged with 'USING INSUBORDINATE LANGUAGE TO HIS SUPERIOR OFFICER' in that 'he, at Nui Dat, Republic of South Vietnam, on 25 Sep 68 at approximately 1850 hrs, said to Cpl PF, "You are just a cunt, piss off out of my tent, you are not a Corporal, arsehole".'[60]

The soldiers often had a point: the petty wielding of power infuriated the national servicemen. An order to pick up cigarette butts was ignored, on the grounds that 'this is children's work'.[61] Another nasho complained to his over-fastidious corporal, 'You are always sounding off at me … I take no notice as it goes in one ear and out the other as 90% of it is just hot air.'[62]

Most soldiers knew where to draw the line, and in general the Australian Army was remarkably well behaved in Vietnam. There were on average just forty-five charges a year, of which only about twenty led to court martials, most for drunkenness, according to the Army Manning Reviews, 1967–71.[63] The rate increased towards the end of the war. The Australian military police had to deal with the messy aftermath, and often felt the sharp end of the infantryman's abuse, as John Arnold relates in *Cop in a Baggy Green Skin*, his wonderfully droll account of life as an MP. The MPs nonetheless performed an excellent job in general: they calmly subdued drunken, traumatised soldiers, broke up street brawls and scraped off the wreckage of the night, often at great personal risk.[64]

# Chapter 23
# February 1967

Surely God weeps.
*Private Brian Hennessy, after the Battle of Bribie.*

February was the cruellest month. A series of horrific accidents, mine explosions and one near-disastrous operation battered the soldiers' spirits. February 1967 produced more Australian casualties than any other month of the war.

The year 1966 ended well enough, claimed Lieutenant Colonel Colin Townsend, commander of the 6th Battalion, with 'unit *esprit de corps* at a peak'.[1] Many troops, sensing the futility of recent operations, disagreed — and this sense permeated the highest levels. Since Long Tan, 'we have done nothing particularly noteworthy', Major General Mackay told General William Westmoreland, except 'a lot of hard, slow, patient, infantry foot-slogging'.[2] At one point, a dispirited Lieutenant Colonel John Warr, commanding the 5th Battalion, wondered what the hell they were doing in Vietnam, and asked his intelligence officer, Bob O'Neill, to propose an answer: was it to kill Viet Cong, bring the enemy to battle, separate the people from the enemy, offer civic aid, restore Saigon's control or cut the Viet Cong supply lines?

The 5th and 6th Battalions were already doing these things, in a succession of operations: the cordon and searches of Ngai Giao[3] and Hoa Long;[4] civic action in Binh Ba; tedious 'road runner' patrols along Highway 15;[5] the clearance of the Nui Thi Vai and Nui Ong Trinh Hills;[6] the assault on Long Son Island;[7] and December's interminable search for the survivors of D445 Battalion.[8] There were useful operations, such as OPERATION VAUCLUSE (8–24 September), up the Nui Dinh Hills, to destroy an enemy headquarters, during which B52 bombers flew in support of an Australian assault for the first time. The bombs decapitated the hilltop, and up went the 6th Battalion, which encountered a 'flattened forest ... covered with a patina of minced, blood-stained clothing and webbing equipment', observed Major Brian McFarlane.[9]

The Australians encountered their most hated enemies — booby traps and mines — on two assaults up the Nui Thi Vais, in October, when pineapple grenades dangling from vines seriously wounded thirteen troops. When one blew, Private Doug Bishop, the youngest on the patrol, thought someone had kicked him in the backside. He spent a month in an American field hospital with multiple shrapnel wounds in his buttocks and legs, after which he resumed fighting. The troops spent days near the summits, destroying caves and bunkers with flame-throwers. Lieutenant Dennis Rainer's platoon attacked and killed several Viet Cong soldiers in a heavily camouflaged camp, and salvaged stores, a radio transmitter and the diary of the deputy commander of 274th Regiment, Lieutenant Colonel Nguyen Nam Hung. Hung had just escaped.[10] Eight soldiers were decorated after this exhausting operation; Lieutenants Mick Deak, Dennis Rainer and John McAloney received Military Crosses, the latter for extraordinary courage in personally assaulting a cave network. (Deak, interestingly, inherited a German title after the war and became known as Baron Michael von Berg.)

During these mountain offensives, Bob O'Neill interviewed a 19-year-old Viet Cong prisoner who shed a little light on communist recruitment methods. Two years earlier, the boy had attended a secret political rally in the jungle.[11] He went with friends, who idolised these Vietnamese 'Robin Hoods'. The Viet Cong detained and forced him into uniform. He fell into depression. 'All he wanted to do was to withdraw from the conflict,' observed O'Neill. 'He thought we were French.' O'Neill gave the young man a can of Fosters, after which 'this strange sad product of the war flew out of our presence but not out of our minds for he was the essence of our problem'.[12]

In October 1966 and January 1967 the Task Force cordoned the Viet Cong stronghold Hoa Long village. Most of the village's 3,000 residents were strong Viet Cong sympathisers; six teams of nine interrogators screened every resident able to carry a gun, after which Australian civic aid teams went in: they renovated Hoa Long's two schools, built a new marketplace and threw a big party for the children, with free helicopter rides. Indeed, the cordons had the flavour of a 'county fair': movies were screened, musicians performed and the people were fed and treated for dental and medical problems. The Australian Army even sent letters of apology for the inconvenience.

It had little effect. The people of Hoa Long accepted Australian welfare and resumed supporting the Viet Cong. Major General 'Tim' Vincent, Mackay's successor as Commander, Australian Force Vietnam, scornfully observed, 'I don't believe that the medcaps or the dentcaps had a direct military return ... I don't think the marketplaces mattered a tinker's cuss.'[13] 'The Hearts and Minds campaign,' concluded Lieutenant Colonel John Warr, 'does not seem to be working in this village. The villagers appear sullen and uncooperative.'[14] The erection of a barbed-wire fence 2 metres high around Hoa Long merely inflamed an already hostile people.


Then February arrived. The first week found Harry Smith's company out on a patrol south-east of Long Tan, in a field of rice paddies and light jungle.[15] With Smith sick in hospital, second-in-command Captain Murray Weaver was in charge. On the 6th Weaver's forward artillery observer, Lieutenant Barry Winsor, called an artillery strike on a distant Viet Cong position. Something went wrong. 'I heard the rounds coming in and knew they were going in the wrong place,' Winsor recalled. 'I yelled "Down" and went to ground ...'

Four of twelve rounds fell directly on Delta Company's headquarters. Sergeant Major Jack Kirby, rifleman Douglas Powter, signalman Barry Kelly and gunner Richard Cliff were killed instantly or died of wounds. Thirteen were wounded, some severely. A large piece of shrapnel slammed into Kirby's right shoulder, perforated both lungs and major blood vessels, and flew out of his left armpit. Captain John Taske, the regimental medical officer, found Kirby conscious: 'He ... rapidly slipped away and died in my arms.'[16] Kirby's death came as a mortal blow: a hero of Long Tan, 'an idol, mascot and good luck charm',[17] he had seemed invincible. The wounded joined the deeply anguished Harry Smith in hospital.[18]

Nor was the 5th Battalion spared that grim February. Days later, during the search of the village of An Nhut, near Dat Do,[19] Australian soldiers triggered a 'friendly' booby trap intended by the South Vietnamese for the

Viet Cong. The explosion cut down the company commander Major Donald Bourne, second-in-command Captain Robert Milligan and New Zealand artillery observer Captain Peter Williams. Within days a second Australian company had lost its headquarters: three dead, five wounded. Bourne died on his birthday — he had turned 35 — on his first operation as company commander. Milligan, dux of Portsea, had two weeks to serve before returning home to marry. 'I just sat down and cried my bloody eyes out,' noted a fellow officer in his diary.[20]

February's mine attacks were retribution for Long Tan and the mountain bombardments. The most devastating struck on the 21st, during the first assault (OPERATION RENMARK) on the Long Hai Mountains, the dragon-shaped range that abuts the South China Sea, south-east of the Task Force. The range had exerted a mystical hold on the people: Buddhist monks had carved pagodas and monasteries out of the rocks; their pilgrimages to the summit ended in 1954. The Long Hais henceforth acquired a reputation as an impenetrable communist redoubt and as headquarters of the provincial Viet Cong.[21] Intelligence warned, 'Booby traps are likely to be encountered anywhere in the area of operation.'[22]

Major Bruce McQualter's company led the advance on the foothills of the Long Hais aboard a convoy of armoured carriers that rumbled towards the foothills. The approach roads were heavily mined and blocked and the bridges destroyed, so the carriers travelled over the scrub and paddy. The mood was convivial and relaxed, with the hope of a swim later that day. One popular platoon commander, Lieutenant Jack Carruthers, 'looked cheerily defiant' and his huge red moustache 'none the worst for the dust that covered him' as he rode atop the leading APC.[23]

At 2.07 p.m. a dull blast flipped that carrier on its side, tore off the turret and rear doors, and sent one track hurtling through the air like an elastic band. The driver and crew commander died instantly; the soldiers on top were thrown off. One was crushed under the somersaulting vehicle. The men inside were blown out the back door. The mine's enormous destructive power — the equivalent of a 500-pound bomb — cut a one-metre hole in the carrier's steel floor.

McQualter and medics dashed down the column to the lead carrier. As they neared, one of them detonated a second mine — an M16 'jumping jack' — that leaped into the air and would cleave in two, castrate or rip the arms off anyone nearby; its shrapnel could kill within 20 to 30 metres. McQualter was struck in the head.

Captain Tony White, the battalion's medical officer, flew in to the carnage aboard an army Bell bubble helicopter. At this stage, the RAAF was still reluctant to help collect army casualties, for procedural and cultural reasons (this changed later in 1967, when it flew anywhere it was required) so American pilots and the little army Bells performed the evacuations.[24] White displayed prodigious courage in the moments ahead. 'The chatter of the rotors faded … replaced by a soundtrack of suffering, groans, cries and mutterings,' he recalled.[25] His friend McQualter, just conscious, urged him to treat the platoon casualties first — then passed out. Carruthers lay unconscious nearby, his moustache soaked in blood (both he and McQualter later died in hospital); Sergeant 'Tassie' Wass sat propped up against his backpack, with 'both elbows smashed' and his 'forearms dangling from the clumsily butchered joints'. Further on White beheld what appeared to be a great pile of discarded uniforms: a closer look revealed the remains of dead and wounded. Here lay the mutilated corpse of Mick Poole, just 20, who had played tenor horn in the unit band and 'was a favourite with village kids'.

'The situation was out of control,' recalled White. 'Horror was piled on horror.' Near the flipped carrier lay the torso of its driver, missing the lower half of his body. 'Blood was already drying on the exposed ribs.' From beneath the wreckage protruded 'a detached arm, its hand still grasping an M16 rifle'.[26]

It dawned on White that he and other medics were working in the middle of a minefield — into which one officer, Lieutenant Michael Langley, had actually walked, to assist. The medics moved from body to body. Snap decisions focused every mind: who needed life-saving aid? Who was not in immediate need? Who was beyond hope? The sappers entered the chaos with mine detectors and marked the safe routes with tape. Even the downwash of the helicopters risked detonating a mine, yet Captain Campbell repeatedly flew in to retrieve the wounded. The dust-off took an hour and a half. The blast killed nine, wounded twenty-six and severely damaged morale.[27] A grim footnote measured the calibre of this enemy: parts of unexploded B52 and US Navy shells had comprised the mine that destroyed the carrier. These were the raw materials of the Viet Cong's booby trap factories, in which thousands of such shells were cut open at great risk and the contents recycled.

★ ★ ★

The quiet courage of retrieving wounded from a minefield is often forgotten alongside the more spectacular kind that won the Victoria Cross. In February 1967 the Team earned its second cross. At the time, several members had the thankless task of leading ('training') the Ruff Puffs, the South Vietnamese Regional (RF) and Popular (PF) Territorial Forces, recruited at province and district levels, and were sub-units within the ARVN. The Ruff Puffs tended to be poor shots, badly equipped, underfed and better at pillaging than protecting the villages — 'six to eight pigs plus a hundred-odd fowls or ducks in a normal day's operation,' reported two Australian advisers. 'From a Psycho War point of view ... we have only left behind in the villages more VC sympathizers than before [our] arrival,' their report added.[28]

One Australian who led them to better things was Major Peter Badcoe, a short bloke in thick black-rimmed spectacles who, in three separate actions, earned every metallic ounce of his Victoria Cross. Badcoe was an unknown quantity — 'an enigma', observed McNeill — even among his closest friends: 'He did not smoke or drink, nor did he mix readily ... Badcoe seemed most at ease when the conversation drifted to exploits of past military heroes ... his energy and aggressiveness knew no limits.'[29] He insisted on placing himself in the line of fire at every opportunity — an enthusiasm his colleagues found a little perplexing. He was, after all, an artillery officer. Yet during his first week in country he single-handedly destroyed an enemy bunker: eschewing air support, he dashed from tree to tree with jerry cans of petrol, poured it in the blind side of the bunker and ignited the fuel with a white phosphorus grenade. 'The effect was like napalm. The bunker destroyed, the company moved forward.'[30]

On 23 February 1967 Badcoe led an RF company south-east of Hué, to root out Viet Cong guerrillas. As they crossed a rice paddy, a friendly platoon came under heavy fire, and two American advisers were shot. Badcoe dashed towards the enemy, firing and weaving as he ran, yelling encouragement to the South Vietnamese, who poured after him and inflicted heavy enemy casualties. Badcoe destroyed an enemy machine-gun post.

Badcoe's next big performance was his last. On 7 April, hearing radio reports that several South Vietnamese units (including the feared Hac Bao — Black Panther Company — of the 1st ARVN Division) were in deep trouble north of Hué, Badcoe leaped into his jeep with Sergeant Alberto Alvorado of the US Army and sped towards the battle. The South Vietnamese were not authorised to call in air strikes without an Australian or US adviser present, so their presence changed the odds. They found the South Vietnamese soldiers caught inside a cemetery. Badcoe ran between the tombstones and rallied the men to attack; when they hesitated, he kept racing forward and attempted to attack, single-handedly, a Viet Cong machine gun. Twice he raised himself to throw a grenade; on the second attempt the gunner riddled him with bullets. Alvorado dragged Badcoe's body back and called an air strike, which destroyed the enemy forces.

Badcoe's memorial service in Hué attracted one of the biggest crowds of Americans, South Vietnamese and Australians at any commemoration of a dead soldier. 'He was courageous to an infinite degree — almost fearless,' Colonel Arch Hamblen Jr, US Army, told the service.

There is a moving photograph of nine fit young Australian soldiers, eight of whom were in their early twenties, all close friends: Privates William Trevenen, Malcolm Mustchin, David Webster, Brian Waters, Wayne Riley, Donald Rumble; Lance Corporals Victor Otway (aged thirty-three) and Garry Chad; and Corporal Robin 'Spike' Jones. They were 1 Section, 5 Platoon, B Company, 6th Battalion. After OPERATION BRIBIE only Jones was left standing.

Some believe OPERATION BRIBIE to be the closest Australia came to a military defeat in Vietnam. Sheer persistence, luck and firepower avoided that fate. Afterwards the soldiers gainsaid the sensational press reports of an Aussie 'triumph'. 'We had been soundly thrashed,' said Trooper David Clifton, an APC crew commander. 'It was us who copped a hiding,' reckoned Private Robin Harris of 5 Platoon, B Company.[31] These were exaggerations: the Australian forces had stood their ground and inflicted between fifty and eighty Viet Cong casualties; yet they almost lost a company. '... we, that is the Vietcong — North Vietnamese and 6RAR, thoroughly "belted" each other that afternoon of February 17, 1967 — that, I believe, is the "awful truth" of Operation BRIBIE,' Bravo Company commander Major Ian Mackay wrote later.[32]

The battle of Bribie was a defining event in that terrible month, during which 4,600 Australian men participated in or supported actions that changed their lives irrevocably. Victory vindicated the losses of Long Tan; yet February left the men in a different mood: quieter, sadder ... and a hell of a lot older.[33]

On 17 February Lieutenant Colonel Colin Townsend's 6th Battalion was ordered to intercept substantial Viet Cong forces that had persistently attacked several towns and villages in great strength and fired on US aircraft;

it was thought the enemy forces were withdrawing to the east through the thick scrub known as the 'Light Green'. The aim of OPERATION BRIBIE was to intercept and destroy them.

Brigadier Stuart Graham, who had succeeded Jackson as Task Force commander, imposed an impossible deadline on the operation: nightfall. The risk of another attempt to attack the Nui Dat base preoccupied him. The Task Force, he believed, lacked the resources to defend itself. In consequence, 'it was like fighting a war with one hand behind your back', Townsend later said. BRIBIE 'smacked of ad-hocery and haste', Major Brian McFarlane observed.[34]

Alpha Company, led by Major Owen O'Brien, flew off at 1.30 p.m. aboard fifteen American helicopters — earlier than planned, as the American pilots had other jobs. 'Use them or lose them!' went the thinking.[35] Fifteen minutes later the choppers touched down, and the soldiers leaped into the eddying red dust and disappeared into the scrub.

The landing zone had not been secured. An hour earlier, a squadron of armoured carriers bearing McFarlane's company had left Nui Dat for this purpose. Initially a lack of field artillery coverage slowed progress; later, as the paddies were dry, the column kept off the roads to avoid mines and the risk of enemy ambush. This meant that every 30 to 100 metres the carriers had to cross a paddy bund. 'I simply had not allowed for the hundreds of bunds, which slowed us down,' the squadron commander explained later.[36]

The animals were silent as the Australians entered the Long Green. Birds and buffaloes seemed endowed with a sixth sense denied humans, who presumed to enter a place no beast dared. They seemed to know what eluded humans; and suddenly, rifle fire crackled out of the jungle. Six soldiers of Second Lieutenant Graham Ackland's platoon fell. In reply, Ackland's recklessly brave Sergeant Frank Alcorta attacked, hurling grenades. The company withdrew 250 metres. Alcorta crawled out, still firing, and dragging Private Ron Brett, whose leg had been shredded (it was later amputated). The Australians had landed on top of tough dug-in forces, who were eager to fight.

Soon Major Ian Mackay's Bravo Company flew in, under heavy fire. A hundred soldiers leaped from the skids, in Australia's first 'hot' helicopter insertion. Soon, Mackay held a quick orders group. 'We're going in ... We're going to attack straight up the centre,' he told his platoon commanders.[37] 4 and 5 Platoons pressed into the scrub, 6 being held back in reserve. Visibility closed to a few metres. Shortly, the Australians entered the enemy's 'killing field': a wide U-shaped arc of Viet Cong troops, who watched and waited. The further the diggers went, the more they exposed themselves to withering enfilade.

Suddenly machine-gun, rifle, grenade and mortar fire dropped the forward Australians. Lieutenant John O'Halloran's 5 Platoon were 40 metres in front on the right flank and took the brunt. Mackay ordered 6 Platoon to move through 4 on the left, to help O'Halloran. 'Fix bayonets!' shouted the platoon commander, Sergeant 'Butch' Brady. He gave the unusual order 'because we were in such close proximity', Mackay said later.[38] His men were going to assault 'up the guts' of the enemy force.[39] The weapon immortalised at the Nek in 1915 failed against the Viet Cong's .50 calibre heavy machine guns: Brady's attack was cut to pieces, and O'Halloran and his twenty-eight men remained stranded and unreachable. They retained radio contact — just — and Mackay desperately ordered O'Halloran to 'advance and silence the machine gun — if possible'. Mackay was under huge pressure to meet Graham's night deadline, and did what any commander probably would have done in the circumstances: attack, and keep on attacking in order to retrieve the situation.

A deeply apprehensive O'Halloran — like Ackland, a graduate of Scheyville — relayed the order to Corporals Spike Jones and Kerry Rooney, in front. Rooney immediately saw the consequences — his men were probably going to die — and he asked them whether they realised what they were about to do; he added, to a mate, as they got into position, 'See you round.'[40] Also told to fix bayonets (most lacked bayonets, or did not hear the order), they prepared to assault across 60 metres of fireswept open scrub. On O'Halloran's shout, the two Australian sections 'as one arose' from the grass 'and ran forward yelling and screaming'.[41]

Rooney's eight men, with their rifles blazing, ran directly at a machine gun. Most fell at 35 metres. Although wounded, Rooney leaped up and charged the gun a second time, alone — to divert the fire from his wounded comrades. He fell dead virtually in front of the barrel, under the astonished eyes of the Viet Cong. 'He actually made it into the enemy bunker system,' witnessed Private Robin Harris.[42]

On the right flank, Spike Jones's section attacked at extremely close range; three machine guns opened up at 20 metres, killing three Australians and wounding five. 'We were virtually surrounded to our front and left and right … the area was criss-crossed with enemy fire lanes,' Jones recalled.[43]

Jones tried to save Private Brian Waters, to no avail, and lay hard against the ground, raked by fire amid his own casualties, within earshot of the Viet Cong. Moments later Harris tried in vain to rescue the badly wounded Dave Webster (whose brother had died in a motorcycle accident shortly before he left for Vietnam). Webster died.

The attack stalled. The men had gained perhaps 40 metres of bush. A dozen lay wounded, moaning. The platoon's stretcher-bearer, Dick Odendahl, crawled about the battlefield under devastating fire, trying to administer first aid and drag in the wounded. With rising desperation, the stranded O'Halloran sent two machine-gunners, Privates 'Mick' Burchell and 'Shorty' Arnold, up to help his beleaguered sections: both were killed dragging their guns across open ground.

O'Halloran then shouted down the radio for carriers, artillery, reinforcements, anything … where the hell were they?! The armoured carriers had by now arrived, yet they lay idle on the fringes of the scrub. The infantry later claimed the carriers were unable to traverse the boggy, close terrain, a claim found to be false.

An attempt by Alpha Company to assist Bravo Company failed. 'Why are you stopping?' a corporal shouted to a soldier during the move.

'Because we were told to advance until we came under fire,' the soldier replied.

'*Heavy* fire!' shouted the corporal.

'Well, they are only little bullets but there's a fucking lot of them!' the soldier said.[44]

It seems improbable that so many things could go wrong during BRIBIE, yet they did. Mackay's forward artillery observer, Captain Jim Ryan, had the precise job of walking in the shells. The enemy had once more 'snuggled up to us'.[45] As at Long Tan, rounds falling short or hitting the tops of trees risked wiping out the Australians. Ryan radioed O'Halloran's compass references to the gun battery located forward near Dat Do, which somehow managed to plot the position. Soon, a few shells tore in about 50 to 100 metres forward of O'Halloran's sections — and found their targets. Screams were heard in the scrub beyond. The Australian wounded took the chance to crawl back to safety.

Then two rounds fell short. One struck a tree; another fell about 15 metres to the right of O'Halloran, killing two Australians and wounding eight (some were wounded a second time). O'Halloran pleaded for the artillery to stop, as the Viet Cong slammed a rocket-propelled grenade into the area, wounding Sergeant Merv McCollough. Of O'Halloran's twenty-eight men, eighteen lay dead or wounded. Then a third round crashed into the treetops where Private Chris Gannon was helping the wounded. When a mate of Gannon's received a cricket ball–sized shrapnel wound in his bum, Gannon 'grabbed him by the balls' to reassure him that they were intact. Moments later the same bloke copped a bullet in the ribs. Enraged, Gannon, armed with an M60 machine gun, surprised three Viet Cong at a range of 10 metres.

'I pulled the trigger,' Gannon recalled. 'I pulled until the gun stopped, out of ammo. I had fired a hundred rounds into them.'[46]

At 6 p.m. Mackay shouted down the line for the armoured carriers, the only hope of saving his forward platoons. At last the carriers rumbled forward — moments earlier they had been preparing to return to Nui Dat! — and crashed into the scrub in search of white smoke that supposedly marked Mackay's company position. Yet white smoke was everywhere: small bushfires had started, detonating stray ammunition and grenades clipped to the dead, hurling shrapnel and body parts into the air. Two carriers veered off towards a small bushfire. Mackay then threw coloured smoke, and the drivers found him.

The Viet Cong were determined to wipe out the armoured vehicles — and they had the weapons to do it. A powerful recoilless rifle round struck the hatch of Geoff Strachan's carrier, which Trooper Vic Pomroy was driving. Pomroy, a well-known Victorian football player, died instantly. A second round struck the carrier, rewounding several men inside. Private Barry Bartsch received shrapnel in his head as he tried to drag wounded men aboard. Incredibly, the badly wounded Private Robin Harris managed to crawl off Pomroy's disabled carrier, across the bloody field and onto another carrier, to safety.

If man were capable of creating hell on earth, he did so at BRIBIE. The battle raged for five hours. Both sides fell back, carrying or dragging their wounded. Major General Tim Vincent, in Saigon, urged Graham to pursue the enemy. There would be no repeats of the failure to follow up the retreating enemy as at Long Tan, Vincent intimated.

Graham enlisted the help of the American forces in the area, who obliged in force: the 2nd Battalion, 47th Mechanized Infantry Regiment,

1st Brigade, 9th Infantry Division, US Army, supported by the self-propelled Battery C, 1st Battalion, 11th Artillery Regiment, US Army — with tanks — appeared on the darkening horizon like a great dust cloud from which star shells flew and burst in a luminous patch of light above the immense procession. Silhouetted in the sky were hornet-like shapes that shortly revealed themselves as Iroquois gunships and reconnaissance aircraft. Soon, 112 armoured vehicles including tanks thundered into vision like a herd of armour-plated reptiles, a display of might that 'kept us open-mouthed until the dust threatened to choke us', McFarlane wrote.[47] On the battalion command net the voice of the American commander, reportedly the son of General George S. Patton, announced: 'This is 2/47th Mechanized Infantry Battalion. One hundred and twelve armoured vehicles will pass by your location in one to five minutes. Please identify to my helicopters by smoke your locations on the ground. Then please keep your heads down. Indicate Charlie's escape routes and we'll go zap him.'[48] And off they went. That night American Phantoms unleashed fireballs of napalm over the pulverised feature.

'Where was the sense of it all?' McFarlane wrote later. 'Why had we been sent on this ill-conceived mission in haste, when [the Americans] could have done the job with ease? … Who was co-ordinating all this? Our Brigadier must have known of the capacity of the American forces nearby to back us up with armour … Why had he not asked for heavy support in the first place? National pride? National arseholes!'[49] In this McFarlane reflected the fury of many in the battalion. Indeed, after BRIBIE, Major Mackay and other officers urged senior commanders to request tanks to support future Australian operations. Major General Tim Vincent, the commanding Australian Force Vietnam, had pressed for tanks prior to BRIBIE. Canberra delivered the tanks — a year later.

Next morning, the diggers encountered an Australian boot with a foot still in it, lying on the edge of the smouldering shambles. The words *Du Me Uc Dai Loi*, which some later interpreted as 'Get fucked Australian', were scrawled in blood on the side of a disabled carrier. Private Brian Hennessy approached a burned-out tree: 'It's not a tree, It's a burned pig. My God … It's a bloke. He's one of ours … Where are his arms and legs? He's just a roasted lump of meat.' American napalm had cooked the Australian dead. 'How can I describe that place?' pleaded Hennessy. A 'terrible empty hollow dread' came over him. 'Surely God weeps,' he wrote hopefully.[50]

They found one survivor, Private Vic Otway, miraculously alive in a shell crater, shot through both legs. He had played dead to prevent the Australians rushing forward to rescue him. He was the only sign of life, human, animal or vegetable. Of the thirty-seven Australian casualties, nine were killed in action and twenty-eight wounded. Six of the dead and twelve of the wounded were from O'Halloran's platoon, whose survivors would remember Bribie as though it happened yesterday.

Sergeant Neil Rankin later attempted to identify the bodies: 'They'd all been burned with napalm,' he recalled, 'and their ammunition had exploded. So you can imagine what they were like. A piece of jelly in a body bag.' Photographs were useless; a few dog tags were still attached to the remains.[51]

Corporal Spike Jones personally packed up his dead soldiers' possessions: three Western Australians. A grim consolation was that one had not seen the 'Dear John' letter waiting for him at Nui Dat before he died. 'All he'd talked about,' said Jones, 'was getting out and going back West, increasing his acreage, planting wheat and getting married to his girlfriend. She wrote that she had someone else. I burned the letter.'[52]

# Chapter 24
# The minefield

I'm not one to boast, but my dick is now longer than my left leg.
My left hand was a mess of fingers hanging all over the place ...
Abdominally I took a penetrating wound at the base of the flak
jacket, which opened me up exposing my intestines.
*John 'Jethro' Thompson, Australian sapper.*

Brigadier Stuart Graham's first misfortune was to succeed Jackson on the
brink of February's disasters. The deadening experience blighted
Graham's first few months as Task Force commander. Yet a far greater
tragedy — in terms of its long-term consequences — marked his tour of
Vietnam: his decision to build an 11-kilometre minefield from the
Horseshoe to the sea, as a barrier to the Viet Cong. If this immense project
was 'the greatest Australian military bungle since World War II',[1] then at the
very least we should consider the motives of the man who made it.

Graham does not deserve to be remembered solely as the architect of
that fatal monument. He had a superb, if unorthodox, military record before
Vietnam. He won the King's Medal at Duntroon in 1942, served in North
Africa, Italy and Bougainville during World War II, and was awarded the
Military Cross as a young company commander of exceptional intellect.
Reputed to possess the sharpest brain in the Australian Army,[2] Graham
became director of Military Intelligence (1960–64) and commandant of the
Canungra Jungle Training Centre (1964). He received an OBE in 1963,
aged 43. He had a firm grounding in military history and a sound grasp of

tactical theory. During a visit to Vietnam in 1961 he had concluded that the war was all but lost, 'a situation ... akin to that which had existed before the French defeat at Dien Bien Phu'.[3] He was thoughtful, clever, imaginative and markedly stubborn.

Brigadier Graham 'had the ability to read the situation much better than anybody else', said Major Stan Maizey, Graham's devoted operations officer, years later.[4] 'Stu Graham,' concurred Colonel Nat Hardcastle, 'was completely loyal, not only to his soldiers but also to his superiors — unlike those who suck up to those above them and kick those beneath them. But if he got something into his head, he'd go with it ...'[5]

Others are more critical. In his ingenious book on the minefield, Dr Greg Lockhart, a Vietnam veteran, portrays Graham as a politicians' soldier with a strategic perspective utterly unsuited to the war being fought.[6] He argues that Graham shared with many high-ranking officers — notably Wilton — an ideological approach to the war that tended to eclipse their military judgement. Graham was heard to shout at a junior officer during an interview, 'Communism is evil! Communism is bad! You are a serving officer and you have no right to think anything else.'[7] The anecdote illustrates a cast of mind that understood the enemy as a disease, a plague that must be contained and eradicated.

Graham shared with other Cold War warriors a determination to seal off the human carriers of the disease. Like his American colleagues, he tended to view the world in terms of barriers that would contain the communist threat. Graham was certainly not alone in believing that the Berlin Wall, the seventeenth parallel, the Korean DMZ, the McNamara Line (a proposed electronic barrier across Vietnam that would supposedly curb infiltration) and even the little double wire fence erected around the village Hoa Long would contain the Marxist enemy.

The idea that a minefield, or a booby-trapped fence, might impede the Viet Cong simply misunderstood the nature of the enemy: the National Liberation Front permeated South Vietnam like a circuit of veins ending in local capillaries that disappeared into the rural areas. A basic understanding of these military and political links joining the People's Army of North Vietnam, the Main Force Viet Cong, the provincial battalions and the village guerrillas, should have corrected the thinking behind the minefield. Yet Graham persisted in seeing the enemy as somehow separate from, or separable from, the local population.

★ ★ ★

Graham left Sydney for Vietnam on New Year's Day, 1967. He arrived in Saigon as Westmoreland prepared to launch OPERATION CEDAR FALLS, for which the American mission statement read simply, 'TO KILL VC'.[8]

Graham did not see 'killing VC' as his core mission. He instinctively felt his task was to protect the South Vietnamese people from Viet Cong insurgents. This presupposed the existence of 'people' who wanted Graham's protection; in fact, Graham did not seem to realise 'the people' of Dat Do and Long Dien were his enemies. 'The local people largely *were* the VC,' Lockhart argues.[9] To an alarming degree, Graham was unable to distinguish friend from foe.

Many villagers, of course, despised the Viet Cong, yet were *afraid* to resist them or to accept Australian protection. Their thinking ran: 'One day, the Australians will go home. The Viet Cong will probably take over. So we'd better get used to them.' So they chose to live with the communists out of fear and pragmatism. Graham saw that the only way to break that nexus was to offer loyal or potentially friendly villages real, long-term security. He drew up an eleven-point plan that recast the Australian mission in Vietnam: '... to help ensure the security of the main areas of the population ... and so enable the government to restore law and order and get on with the job of developing the social, economic and political life of the Province. Inevitably that would involve killing VC but it would be only one of the ways, and sometimes even not necessarily the most important way, of achieving our mission.'[10]

This slice of Graham's mind reveals an intelligent and humane man who was forced to take a position that he sensed was deeply flawed but, once committed to it, he became irrationally dedicated to it. Graham's mission, as it trickled down to the officers and NCOs, seemed confused. Are we here to rebuild or defend this benighted society, the men wondered? Must we perform both simultaneously? How?

The Americans were unimpressed. They wanted clear, decisive action and 'massive formations', not careful patrolling and quiet efforts to win hearts and minds. Lieutenant General Jonathan Seaman, commander of II Field Force Vietnam to whom Graham reported, dismissed the Australian with the withering remark, 'Not aggressive'. Westmoreland, who visited Graham at the end of January 1967, found the Task Force 'very inactive': the 4,600 Australians had generated 'very little combat power', he concluded. The rotation of battalions would leave a month of inactivity during the changeover, Westmoreland added.[11] (The Americans simply replaced individuals, not units, a system that maintained continuity but deeply damaged morale.)

To his credit, Graham persisted with his mission, to try to isolate the Viet Cong and win the support of the population. It amused and sometimes impressed the Viet Cong, this Australian attempt to capture the loyalties of people the Viet Cong regarded as 'theirs'.


In drawing up his plans, Graham had somehow to work within Canberra's political expedients and constraints, in a situation the politicians manifestly failed to understand. The vulnerability of Nui Dat deeply preoccupied him. With only two battalions in hostile territory he felt daily the encroaching threat to the little Australian outpost — rather like a wagon train in Indian country. Graham eschewed 'chasing main forces around the jungle under the guise of "offensive action"'.[12] He meant to flush out the enemy by blocking his supply lines. His predecessor, Brigadier Jackson, had warned him of the 'meagre' control of the Long Green, a heavily forested supply route between the Viet Cong mountain bases and the Dat Do rice hub.[13]

Graham proposed to cut this vital enemy artery and thus block the Viet Cong from entering the province's population centres. Stranded in their mountain redoubts without supply, they would soon be flushed out and forced 'to move against the Task Force',[14] in reply to which Australian forces would assuredly destroy them. That was the idea, and it won strong plaudits with Graham's intelligence staff. Yet the Australians already lacked the combat troops necessary to fulfil the many existing demands of constant patrolling, searching for the enemy, cordoning villages, and maintaining and protecting Nui Dat. They were grossly overworked, and had scarcely a break between operations. By March, the Task Force 'was seemingly powerless to prevent [Viet Cong] movement through the Long Green and into the centre of population and money', wrote Stan Maizey.[15] Canberra, however, ever-sensitive to the political fallout, refused to send reinforcements. 'We asked Army Headquarters for another battalion,' said Maizey. 'We asked them for some tanks. The Army Headquarters said no ...'[16] (Not until 1968 were a third battalion and tanks sent.)

So Graham had to fulfil with two battalions a job that required at least three and ideally four or five. That left one option, he argued: the minefield. The politicians, he later claimed with some justification, had forced the decision on him.

The minefield would be 11 kilometres long and 100 metres wide, stretching from the Horseshoe (a hill near Dat Do, 8 kilometres south-east of Nui Dat) down to the sea. It would contain more than 20,000 American-made M16 'jumping jack' mines. Saigon Government units were expected to guard this ribbon of death: military doctrine insisted that barrier minefields be patrolled night and day.

A chorus of highly placed voices — the departing Brigadier Jackson; the province chief, Lieutenant Colonel Dat; and the new Task Force intelligence officer, Jim Furner — supported the barrier. Generals Wilton and Daly in Canberra and Vincent in Saigon were all to a varying degree aware of, and concurred with, the idea: it seemed tactically sound, in principle. Both Daly and Vincent later claimed to have disagreed with the minefield — 'I laughed and said, "There's no such thing as an unliftable mine",' Vincent later recalled. Yet at the time, neither he nor Daly openly opposed or vetoed it.[17]

The battalion commanders, Lieutenant Colonels John Warr and Colin Townsend, were vehemently opposed. So too was Major Brian Florence, officer commanding 1st Field Squadron, a bomb disposal expert with the unenviable job of laying the barrier. Florence warned Graham that a determined enemy could breach the barrier and steal the mines at any time. In which case surely the minefield simply handed the Viet Cong thousands of jumping jacks on a plate? Warr's opposition packed an emotional punch: his men had suffered dreadfully in February's mine attacks; Warr himself had been wounded by a mine in Korea, where the Chinese lifted and relaid allied mines. Later Lieutenant Colonel Eric Smith, commander of the newly arrived 7th Battalion, condemned the idea and directly warned Graham, 'I didn't think we could trust the ARVN to guard the minefield.'[18] Even at the highest level, the minefield concept met resistance. President Thieu had earlier warned Westmoreland that the Viet Cong would take 'great delight' in breaching barriers of the kind Graham proposed. Not even the most can-do American took seriously the McNamara Line, a proposed barrier across the country.

The diggers privately ridiculed the idea: the notion that a minefield would block the enemy failed to account for the ubiquity, courage and resourcefulness of the Viet Cong. The troops had seen children collecting live cluster bombs and the consequences of the Viet Cong's fearless dissection of unexploded shells. Yet the top brass did not consult the diggers, of course.

Graham stubbornly deployed a series of lame arguments in defence of his plan. Since the enemy already had an ample mine supply, he argued, why would they risk life and limb attempting to steal more from a protected minefield in which every second mine had an 'anti-lift' grenade attached?[19] This argument absurdly suggested that the enemy preferred old, clapped-out mines to a free supply of new ones; in any case, the dangers of mine-lifting meant little to an enemy hardened by the experience of turning live bombs into booby traps and mines.

The mine-laying project began in March 1967.[20] Every day, in the blazing sun, hundreds of soldiers of the Australian 5th Battalion drove thousands of metal pickets into the earth and strung up tons of barbed wire. They, and their successors, the 7th Battalion, built two wire fences, 2 metres high, 100 metres apart and 11 kilometres long. It was 'a shit of a job', said Private Warwick Binney.[21] At one stage, Eric Smith's battalion was erecting 2,000 metres of wire fences a day. In the lane between them the Australian engineers laid the first of 23,000 M16 jumping jack mines, of which 11,058 would be attached to grenades, or 'anti-lift devices', designed to explode once the pressure of the mine was removed.

The jam jar-sized jumping jack M16 mine measured 10 centimetres in diameter and 7 to 10 centimetres high, weighed over 3 kilograms and contained 2.5 kilograms of TNT entombed in a cast-iron core inside an inner steel casing. It leaped in the air and exploded at knee to waist height seconds after the application of slight downward pressure to three small prongs protruding from the earth (trip wires could also trigger it). The pressure freed the firing pin, which struck a cap, igniting a two-second fuse. This lit a small charge that threw the mine up, and in turn ignited a two-millisecond delay fuse that detonated the TNT. The huge compressed energy fragmented the cast-iron core, sending thousands of pieces of shrapnel in all directions. The mine was lethal within a 25-metre radius, could kill at 75 metres and wound at 200 metres.[22] The height of the blast ensured that if a nearby victim was not cut in half, he probably would not walk or make love again. This American invention was not only a killer and disabler but also a cheap and effective method of devastating morale. The sight of their mates lying mutilated on the earth would haunt the witnesses for the rest of their lives.

'If you're near the blast,' said Corporal Walter Pearson, 'it can tear your buttocks off, it can tear your calf or thigh off, and if it doesn't completely dismember you it does such tremendous damage that you die of blood loss.'[23]

Two soldiers were required to insert this diabolical double-whammy into the earth: first the grenade, then the mine. The slightest disturbance might trigger the grenade's switch and initiate the firing chain. The most nerve-racking part was removing the safety pins, as about 10 per cent of mines were found to be defective. The job demanded the sharpest concentration; Graham's insistence that an anti-lift grenade be attached to every second mine intensified the pressure on the sappers.

'You dig a hole roughly 10 inches deep and 10 inches in diameter,' explained Bob Coleman, a mine-layer of 1st Field Squadron. 'You place a hand grenade in the hole, and place the mine on top. Your mate half fills in the hole, then takes out two safety pins of the anti-lift grenade. Then you lower the mine, and fill in the rest of the hole, leaving three little pins sticking out of the earth. Then you remove the safety pins from the mine ...'[24] Any movement of the mine, just a few millimetres, triggered a massive explosion that would kill or maim two engineers.[25]

The sappers were ordered to lay a thousand mines a day. They began with a few hundred, then rapidly increased. Local children, animals and the Viet Cong hampered progress. The children tended to play or fly their kites near the site. At night, the Viet Cong heaved animals into the minefield, which set off dozens of freshly laid mines. Flying pigs, hens and dogs were a common occurrence. Bits of animals were found all over the minefield the next morning, and the mines had to be relaid — a deeply dispiriting job. On one occasion a dog sprinted through the trip wires, detonating the grenades attached to the fence as it ran.


Determined to complete the job before the June rice harvest, Graham demanded faster results. Dreadful accidents were the consequence. On 6 April Private Teddy Lloyd triggered a mine: it killed him instantly and wounded two others. The next day another mine blew, mutilating a platoon commander. 'I couldn't stop him bleeding,' said the distraught medic, Ross Woods. 'I didn't have any more towels and shell dressings.' The officer took two hours to die. A 5th Battalion patrol found his boot two days later: '... on close inspection it contained his foot.'[26] Word spread of the severed foot in the lone boot, and years later the image made a macabre cameo appearance in Corporal Barry Heard's nightmares.[27]

The toll rose. Neil Innes retrieved the body of an American who had entered the minefield to collect wood, an act for which he received a Military Medal.[28] And there was the awful case of John 'Jethro' Thompson, of 1 Troop, 1st Field Squadron. On 9 May 1967, when he should have been rotated, Jethro was ordered to resume arming the mines. Suddenly 'I was flying through the air. All the dust and crap seemed to float down covering me in very slow motion. My hands were spewing blood and I could not feel my left leg.'[29] Later he realised he'd been 'hit from left to right':

My left leg was only attached by shreds high up in my thigh. I'm not one to boast, but my dick is now longer than my left leg. My left hand was a mess of fingers hanging all over the place … My buttock and right leg were badly lacerated. My left eardrum was perforated, and a piece of shrapnel lodged behind my left ear … It's still there. Abdominally I took a penetrating wound at the base of the flak jacket, which opened me up exposing my intestines. I thought … what a bloody mess.[30]

He lost his right hand, his left leg, his gall bladder and his small intestine. His mates put his severed leg in the basket beside him as the chopper winched him up. He lived. He still lives, in Queensland, and, although ill, 'is extremely mobile, absolutely positive about life and enjoys a glass of good red over a long lunch'.[31]

In May five sappers died of mine accidents: Ray Deed, Dennis Brooks, Greg Brady, John O'Hara and Terry Renshaw.

The government responded with a press release. In an egregious example of political hand-washing, Canberra eschewed any responsibility for the accidents and blamed the men. The troops had died through 'a momentary lack of concentration and attention to detail', said the statement, released on 16 June 1967 by the Minister for the Army, Malcolm Fraser. 'Who loses concentration with a pound of TNT in their hands?' Lockhart later remarked.[32] The media release claimed that 'every man involved in the mine-laying operations had received his basic training in this subject' in Australia, and that the sappers had conducted 'intensive rehearsals' before laying the mines.[33]

This was simply untrue. The sappers had received no training in mine-laying in Australia, according to Major Florence,[34] nor had they the time to conduct 'intensive rehearsals'. The rehearsals were virtually all 'on the job'. 'None of the sappers, none of our senior NCOs, none of our officers … nobody had prior experience laying a minefield. It was all on-the-job training,' said Jethro Thompson.[35] Most Australian sappers had never seen an M16, notes Lockhart, nor had any laid a mine attached to an M26 anti-lifting grenade, an unusually stressful job even for experienced mine-layers. 'I would get splitting headaches from the concentration required,' said one sapper.[36] To address this ignorance, two engineers — Captain Graham Moon and Sergeant Bryan Nolen — took a crash course that amounted to 'a stroll through an unmarked minefield', after which Nolen opened an M16 with a can opener to inspect the new weapon.[37] Nor did Canberra attempt to address the fundamental issue: that the minefield was a direct consequence of the government's refusal to reinforce the Task Force.

By the end of May, with five Australians dead and ten wounded, Graham prematurely ordered mine-laying to cease. The minefield had reached the unstable dunes near the sea.

'We saw the fence as an obstacle … so we resolved to destroy it,' said Duong Son Minh, a Viet Cong soldier.[38] On the night of 28–29 May 1967 enemy troops breached the minefield's fence with wire-cutters. Hung Manh, the first to enter, would become the most celebrated of Phuoc Tuy's mine-lifters. An orphan who grew into a combat engineer of great skill, Hung volunteered, after several ceremonial drinks, to lift the first mine. He cut his way through the booby-trapped concertina fence and felt his way forward with his fingers: soon, they brushed three prongs. He dug down on each side, raised the mine, then heard a 'click': the damp grenade underneath had failed to explode. He lifted the mine and grenade, and returned to his waiting 'suicide squad'.[39]

The example of 'Hero Manh' spread, and mine-lifting teams strove to emulate his example. 'You'd leave tiny bits of white paper,' said Mac Linh Xuan, a courier and one of the first to breach the minefield. 'You'd sprinkle them so you could return on the right path. It was very frightening but my feelings of hatred helped me.'[40]

Mine-lifters competed for the highest number of mines lifted in a night.[41] A three-man team held the record of 160, claimed a local Vietnamese history. Their courage inspired rich folklore; young men were drawn to the job like kamikaze pilots. 'We lifted a whole section,' boasted

Mac Linh Xuan. 'On some nights I led groups of fifty or sixty porters carrying mines back.'[42] In time little teams of mine-lifters actually lived in the minefield, in carefully dug bunkers.

Between June and August 1967 the Viet Cong stole about 2,000 mines, according to a defector's account. By September they claimed to be lifting 200 mines a night. Women and children participated: their delicate fingers were suited to digging gently down the sides of a mine to check whether it had a grenade underneath. Not without losses: at least thirty-six Vietnamese lifters died, and scores were wounded; but they extracted an arsenal of new weapons. Indeed, the diggers nicknamed the minefield 'Charlie's ordnance depot', said Graham Edwards, who lost his legs in 1970 in a mine blast.[43]

The South Vietnamese troops were not, in fact, ordered to defend or protect the minefield, according to Lockhart. The local forces were simply not properly positioned to defend it from local guerrillas from the west, who did most of the mine-lifting. The failure to guard the barrier was therefore not the fault of the South Vietnamese soldiers but a miscalculation by higher command. In any case, the Saigon forces lacked the numbers. The job demanded several battalions installed in observation posts, with interlocking arcs of fire, night and day, along the 11-kilometre length. 'You needed search lights and flares; every inch must be covered,' said Major Brian McFarlane.[44] Asked how many patrols the South Vietnamese troops were doing to protect the minefield in late 1967, a senior Australian officer replied, 'None.'[45]

Graham left Vietnam in October, having persuaded himself of the minefield's success. It had imposed a 'logistic stranglehold on the Viet Cong', he wrote. 'Charlie is virtually finished in Phuoc Tuy Province. He has lost the people and the resources and without these he cannot live.'[46] Most disagreed, not least a report by the US agency Civil Operations and Revolutionary (later Rural) Development Support (CORDS) on Phuoc Tuy at the time, which bluntly stated, 'Little permanent damage has been inflicted upon the [Viet Cong] infrastructure [in Phuoc Tuy] and its capacity to carry out its mission.'[47]

The minefield did — briefly — realise Graham's intentions. Local communist histories do record the disruption to food supplies, movement and communications in the Long Green area.[48] However, it was short-lived — and probably exaggerated, in the tradition of communist propaganda. The minefield did not force local cadres 'to eat bamboo shoots, dig for roots and eat jungle vegetables in place of rice' to any great extent, as the local communist history claims.

The National Liberation Front saw the point of the minefield well before its completion. 'To cut our liaison corridor and isolate Minh Dam, in order to enable the puppet army and authorities to carry out pacification,' noted a crystal-clear remark in the local history.[49] The Viet Cong thus prepared well: they stored food supplies in different locations; employed or coerced civilians as extra carriers and smugglers; and called in provincial favours and so on. They used the Rung Sat waterway, for example, as a means of supplying the Viet Cong cadres to the south-east of Saigon because 'the land route had been cut off by the Australians', said one former Viet Cong soldier. Hanoi later honoured these Rung Sat 'Marines' as 'the bravest of the brave', said Lieutenant General Mai Thuan, a retired North Vietnamese infantry commander.[50]

Australian mines started killing or wounding Australian soldiers as early as May 1967. Men of the 2nd Battalion were badly hit within weeks of their arrival. In OPERATIONS CAIRNS and ATHERTON (July–August 1967) Delta Company lost most of a platoon to mines, killed and wounded. 'The blokes felt we were cursed,' said Private Paul Murphy. 'None of us were killed by rifle fire. Mostly by mines. They were anti-personnel mines — ours, lifted by the Viet Cong. Morale fell off a cliff. There was no consulting, no briefing. We just carried on. Our commanders said nothing, did nothing. We had a wake and got pissed.'[51] Later Alpha Company endured similar mine casualties and, from 1968, Australian M16 mines were responsible for the majority of Australian dead and wounded. The Task Force began dismantling the barrier in 1968, in a race between Australian mine-clearing teams and the Viet Cong to reach the mines. The process would take almost three years.

In this light, the minefield cannot, in honesty, be seen as anything other than a gross error of judgement at the highest levels of the Australian Army. This is *not* wisdom in hindsight; at the time, as shown, many had warned against the idea. 'Graham listened but he didn't hear,' said Brigadier Sandy Pearson, a later Task Force commander. 'He was pig-headed, obstinate ...'[52] In his defence, Graham attempted in Vietnam to direct a campaign markedly different from Westmoreland's ultimately disastrous war of attrition. Graham's ideas — if not their execution — of denying the enemy's supply, of separating the Viet Cong from the people, seemed a sounder and more humane basis for winning the 'other war', the battle for hearts and minds. In this sense, the minefield was a singularly disastrous expression of a way of thinking that, in its otherwise useful applications, helped Australia to win a tactical victory in Phuoc Tuy.

This disaster did not harm Graham's career: he received a DSO for service in Vietnam, and was promoted to the rank of major general. He rarely spoke of the minefield; yet the episode left him a bitter man, said close colleagues. The government never acknowledged its shared responsibility for the decision by a commander who lacked the troops required to do his job.[53] In time, the Viet Cong swept around the minefield like a ripple around a breakwater.

# Chapter 25
# The hamlet without a soul

Twice the hamlet chiefs and their deputies have been killed by
the VC. This fact makes the people … panic-stricken. Now
nobody dares to be a hamlet chief … Nobody would dare to do
it even if he had three heads and six hands.
*A local woodcutter at Ap Suoi Nghe.*

The 5th and 6th Battalions returned home in May and June 1967, to
tumultuous receptions: an estimated 400,000 people with streamers and
confetti cheered the soldiers marching through Sydney, with scarcely a
protester in sight. The 2nd and 7th Battalions, which replaced them, had
strong military personalities — especially so in the case of the 7th, the 'Pig'
Battalion. Lieutenant Colonel Eric Smith, the 7th's first tour commander,
unwittingly coined the name during basic training. Disgusted at his troops'
drunken destruction of the canteen, Smith put the whole battalion on a
charge. 'You're a mob of pigs,' Smith angrily shouted as he read out their
punishment, 'and if this happens again I'll turn you into a temperance
battalion and the laughing stock of the army.'[1] Smith's speech left an
indelible mark on his men, the mark of the swine. Henceforth, 7th Battalion
diggers tended to greet each other with 'Oink!' instead of the customary
'G'day'. The occasional grunt even lingered after a salute. Mysterious pig
images appeared around the barracks; a horse painted pink was found
tethered outside Smith's office. Higher authorities tried to stamp out 'this
pig nonsense': 'But you can't stop a tide like that,' Smith said. Thus began the

7th Battalion's lifelong relationship with pork, which continues to this day. 'I wanted a battalion spirit, not a company spirit,' Smith said.[2] He certainly got one — and the unit's camaraderie helped the men in Vietnam.

In the second half of 1967 the Viet Cong seemed mysteriously to melt away. They abandoned many of their bunkers and hideouts, and avoided the main towns and usual routes. They seemed to have left the province. Yet had they fled to the borders, as Brigadier Graham claimed? Had the Australians 'removed the claws'? Was the enemy on the run?[3]

Undeniably, the battles of Long Tan and Bribie had severely weakened the communist forces. Numerous missions had dealt heavy blows to enemy movement and logistics, most spectacularly OPERATION PORTSEA in March–April, the first joint US–Australian–South Vietnamese action under Task Force command, which captured 218 tonnes of rice and tens of thousands of rounds of ammunition and reopened the highway to the eastern village of Xuyen Moc. Yet to claim that these actions 'removed the enemy's claws' denied the fact that the Viet Cong thus far scratched when and where it chose. The 275th Viet Cong Regiment, supposedly routed at Long Tan, continued to elude destruction despite Graham's claims that it was a spent force.[4]

In fact, the National Liberation Front cadres had simply decided not to fight. No doubt their recent drubbing had diminished their appetite for combat; a foe who applied guerrilla jungle tactics as patiently as they, who hunted down and ambushed *them*, and who called artillery down on himself, posed a disturbing new development. Indeed, communist sources argue that the Viet Cong was, after Long Tan, *ordered* to avoid the Australians, to preserve its strength. Another, powerful reason for its disengagement, at this point, was the preparation for the Tet Offensive of 1968, the secret planning for which began in mid-1967. The Viet Cong, in short, was not driven out or defeated; it was reinforcing, consolidating and awaiting the signal.

Consider the disappointing results of the two biggest operations yet undertaken in Phuoc Tuy: BROKEN HILL (7–13 June 1967) and PADDINGTON (9–15 July). Both had the same ambitious purpose: 'to destroy 274 Viet Cong Main Force Regiment', states the 7th Battalion history, or, in the US manner, to 'find, fix and finish' the enemy.

In BROKEN HILL the Australians were to act as the 'anvil' to the American 'hammer'. The US and South Vietnamese forces[5] blasted through the area with the aim of driving the enemy into the Australian trap. Very little actual fighting occurred; a few Viet Cong troops were trapped. Conducted near Binh Ba — again[6] — the operation succeeded in detaining 112 civilians, including twenty-six children, on the first day. The next day the Australians released all but two: the president of the Chau Duc District Women's Committee and a Viet Cong female food supplier.[7] In short, the only suspects hammered against the anvil that day were two women. Where were all the men? In hiding, of course, with their regiments.

'Look, I don't think your Task Force commander is aggressive enough,' Westmoreland complained to Major General Tim Vincent at MACV headquarters in Saigon one June morning.

'Well, you're so wrong,' said Vincent. 'We've freed Xuyen Moc ... and this is as far as we can go.' Vincent drew a line along the provincial border, and added, 'If you're expecting me to go bounding off into the far mounds with only two battalions, well, I'm not going to do it.'

'Well, Vince,' replied Westmoreland, 'why don't you generate an operation and I'll give you the troops?'

'All right,' said 'Vince'.[8] Graham agreed. Thus began the biggest joint operation mounted in Phuoc Tuy during the war, OPERATION PADDINGTON.

PADDINGTON, a search-and-destroy mission in the May Tao Mountains, had everything: thousands of troops, hundreds of Hueys, convoys of machines. The operation deployed nine battalions of American, Australian and South Vietnamese troops, plus SAS and most Australian support units. The US units included the 1st Brigade of the 9th Division, a US Mechanized Battalion, two artillery batteries and the US 1/11th Armoured Cavalry Regiment — the latter alone fielded an 'Army within an Army', 1,300 armoured vehicles, thousands of men and supporting aircraft. The American commanders hovered overhead, and occasionally swooped down to bellow orders at an unfortunate 'lootenant'. In total, 15,000 Free World troops set out to find, fix and finish a Viet Cong regiment. The overture to this vast manoeuvre was an American cavalry charge, of tanks and armoured carriers, up Route 329; there followed an airmobile assault involving a battalion of Australians aboard a swarm of helicopters; then huge blocking forces were dropped into the combat zone, north-east of Xuyen Moc. The only things missing were the great, lumbering strains of *The Ride of the Valkyries* and the immortal line 'I love the smell of napalm in the morning'.

The operation ended — 'called off', said Vincent later — with a series of blanks. The Free World forces had flung a giant net over a giant zero: a massive effort chasing a phantom.[9] The US hammer fell on ninety-two Viet Cong soldiers (KIA), of whom the Task Force accounted for thirty-one, a pathetically low body count in Westmoreland's opinion. They 'found, fixed and finished' hundreds of empty tunnels and bunkers; otherwise this American show of strength served merely as a training exercise for a very different war.

'We missed 274th Regiment by a hair's breadth,' Graham said angrily. He had supposed the Viet Cong were 'shivering in their bunkers' and as 'good as dead'. Most had simply withdrawn: 1,500 men slipped through the Free World forces meat grinder. How? The Viet Cong had simply noted the impossible odds and disappeared into the jungle or across the border to Binh Tuy. A horizon black with hornet-like Hueys and the earth a-jitter with the vibrations of scores of tanks and carriers were powerful hints to all but a comatose sentry. Some hid unnoticed in their bunkers as the American cavalry crashed past, as Lieutenant 'Nobby' Clark recalled: 'we ... scrambled into our pits expecting battle. But it was only the over-developed American sense of drama, akin to the cowboy shooting up Western towns. It was their way of saying ... "You Aussies can leave it to us now". They always cleared ahead by fire — .50 cals [machine guns] certainly cut up the jungle. They also scattered every VC in the district.'[10] On one occasion, the relieving commander of a US artillery battery mistook a circle on his map — which in fact represented the Australian forces — for an enemy target and opened fire. No one was hit, but 'the next day my men wanted to go and punch the Yanks up', recalled Sergeant Roy 'Doc' Savage. 'I think I aged ten years that night.'[11]

Undaunted, Graham 'strongly recommended' that the large joint operations continue; only with US help, he argued, could they successfully assault the enemy mountain bases, which, he believed, were now isolated from 'the people'.[12]


By late 1967 the province seemed secure. One barometer was the extraordinary success of South Vietnam's presidential elections, held in September: 83 per cent of eligible voters turned out to vote; in Phuoc Tuy,

91 per cent took part, the largest proportion of any province. There were numerous claims of fraud and cheating, of course; the Thieu–Ky presidential ticket had allegedly demanded a 70 to 90 per cent result from their village placemen. In the event, Thieu received just 34 per cent, the rest being divided among the other ten candidates. 'The elections were fair and free — indeed remarkably so,' concluded a team of Australian electoral observers led by Sir Allen Brown CBE.[13] In Phuoc Tuy Australian protection emboldened many to go to the hustings despite weeks of Viet Cong posters threatening severe retribution. Indeed, the sapling of democracy appeared to be struggling to life in South Vietnam, despite Western cynicism and communist intimidation.

The National Liberation Front responded with more terror. In Phuoc Tuy, women and children were the victims of shocking attacks. Five children died of horrific wounds sustained during a Viet Cong M16 mine attack, in retribution for their parents accepting Australian medical and dental aid; two civilians were found face down, dead on a road in Hoa Long, their hands bound with wire — punishment for welcoming Australian aid. They were two of thousands of examples of the methods of an enemy bound by no Rules of Engagement and no military law, for whom civilians were expendable. For Hanoi, a Marxist victory over South Vietnam justified any act of terror. This was the regime to which Western peace groups donated money, medical aid and 'moral support'.

Yet American methods also made a mockery of the very idea of 'rules' of war. One little-known example involved the use of war dogs, trained to hunt down the enemy. Most of the 2,000 American war dogs were trackers, but a substantial number were 'gook killers', trained to inflict savage deaths. The US war dogs proved so effective that the enemy put a bounty on the lives of the dog-handlers, a hundred of whom were dead by 1967.

The 7th Battalion was the first Australian unit to use tracker dogs, in May 1967. They were mostly black Labradors donated by the RSPCA and trained in Australia — purely as trackers, to pursue the smell of human waste, food and blood trails. On their first outing, Cassius and Justin led a platoon to ten Viet Cong soldiers; the dogs 'were directly responsible for two kills [by riflemen]', said a report.[14] In early missions, the animals failed to 'point' at the hint of danger and almost led their handlers into danger.[15] Later, the dogs did learn. Caesar, for example, would stand still, ears up, and stare straight down the track, and freeze within sight of the Viet Cong. 'Caesar ... stared at them,' recalled his handler. 'Not a muscle moved in the war dog's body. Did he know what we were going to do to them? Did he perceive them as enemy?'[16]

During one action, Cassius collapsed and died of heat exhaustion, and was medevaced to Vung Tau. The postmortem noted a friable spleen and a 'cooked appearance' of the heart, kidneys and thyroid.[17] Cassius's death provoked much press comment; the Minister for the Army even promised to launch an inquiry — such was the national concern for the first canine casualty. By October the dogs had proved their worth: 'Each unit has had "kills" resulting directly from the employment of dogs,' said Vincent's office, which strongly recommended their continued use.'[18]

On 6 August, a ferocious three-hour firefight on the banks of the Suoi Chau Pha River, north-west of Nui Dat, interrupted Graham's 'hearts and minds' campaign. The 7th Battalion that day received its first 'blooding'.

Eric Smith sent Alpha Company, under Major Ewart 'Jake' O'Donnell, into dense jungle thought to be thick with enemy forces. Surprise was imperative in OPERATION BALLARAT, a twelve-day battalion-strength search-and-destroy mission. On the first day they ran into a company of the Viet Cong 274th Regiment.

Lieutenant Neville 'Nobby' Clark felt the first 'electrifying thumbs down' and the cry 'CONTACT! WAIT OUT!' A silent pause ensued after an Australian machine-gunner shot two Viet Cong soldiers coming down the track, then a roar of fire and smoke enveloped the jungle. Viet Cong rockets whooshed into Australian positions, which replied with machine guns, rifles and grenades. 'They opened fire with all their machine guns at once,' said Sergeant Brian Adshead later. 'They were only about 10 metres to my front.'[19] The battle disturbed a wasp nest, and several Australians were stung so badly that they needed medical evacuation.

Barry Heard, the nasho from Ensay and company signaller, ran forward, fell and lost contact; his radio went down. Heard's handset whistled and jammed. 'I attacked the handset … with my can opener, scraping out the mud.' As he lay there he experienced the strange sensation of being 'outside my own self'. Suddenly a vision 'blasted into my head' of a grave, atop Connors Hill, in East Gippsland: the grave was his. 'It probably lasted a split second, but its presence went to the core of my being.'[20] Heard crept forward and tried to staunch the bleeding of a dying friend, whose last words were, 'I'm going, mate.'[21] Forty years later, Barry Heard dreads the arrival of 6 August.

At the height of the battle, seven Viet Cong machine guns faced six Australian ones, at a range of about 30 metres. 'Every twig, every blade of grass half an inch above my body was shot off,' wrote one soldier, caught in the open. A white mist of spent gases and burning oil from hot barrels covered the field and slowly drifted away.[22]

There were acts of phenomenal courage on both sides; we know only the details of the Australian examples: of O'Donnell who, directing his men behind an anthill just metres from the enemy lines, dashed into incoming fire to drag a wounded medic to safety; of Second Lieutenant Graham Ross who repeatedly led his platoon into attack, and twice lifted the wounded to safety (although hit in the leg, he shunned help until others were treated); of Private Dennis 'Bottles' Battersby who, although shot in the right arm, hurled grenades with his left, dragged out a wounded man and withdrew only after his wounded arm 'went numb'; and of Sergeant Brian Adshead who shouldered Private 'Hoppy' Hoppner to safety under heavy fire. Private Keith Downward's action defies belief: he edged forward to within 10 metres of a Viet Cong machine gun, leaped up, charged, killed its operator, captured the weapon and, although wounded, managed nonetheless to haul a wounded mate out, too. Eight Australians received bravery awards, including three Military Crosses, to O'Donnell, Ross and Clark, and a brace of medals to the pilots of No. 9 Squadron who flew in, under intense fire, to retrieve the wounded.

The end came with the boom and crump of Australian artillery, the sweetest sound to the infantry's ear. Lieutenant Clark walked in the rounds from Fire Support Base Giraffe. As at Long Tan, the artillery proved decisive; the Viet Cong withdrew.

The chaplain was sent for, to administer last rites to the dying and reassure the living; the Catholic padre landed via winch from a hovering chopper. Five Australians were dead or dying and twenty wounded: Sergeant 'Jock' Sutherland, a Scot, was one of the worst cases of the war. When an enemy rocket exploded a metre from his position, he lost an eye and a leg, and suffered deep, multiple shrapnel wounds. He had no pulse on arrival at hospital. Doctors frantically pumped litres of donated blood into his system, and somehow he revived. Sutherland's recovery profoundly moved the battalion: even Westmoreland visited this miracle man, and recommended him for the Congressional Medal of Honour. He received a Distinguished Conduct Medal.

After the battle, several young soldiers were propped against trees, shocked by the rockets and shells that had exploded around them. 'After giving them reassurance and cradling them in our arms until the crying and shivering subsided, they recovered sufficiently to return to their duties,' Captain Don Gillies, a company second in command, wrote later.[23] An exception was Private Tony Carr, who sat against a tree smoking a cigar. Of his ten-man section, only Carr remained; the rest were dead or wounded. He greeted his sergeant with, 'Well, we fucking well showed 'em today, eh, Sarge!' The remark stuck in Sergeant Adshead's mind, because he was not sure who had showed whom, and Carr had hitherto been the quietest member of his platoon. Heavy rain fell during the night, and although cold and wet nobody bothered putting up their hutchies. They huddled together to keep warm. Next morning they resumed their twelve-day patrol.

> Dear Dad,
> … Our next Op starts on Monday 5th and is expected to last
> about 15 days … We are going to resettle about 3 villages. This is
> the last area in the province that is under VC control. The aim is
> to erase the area completely. This means all houses are to be
> destroyed, crops burned etc. The people will go to a new village
> closer to Nui Dat. It is expected Charlie will react violently to
> the move, as the area is his main source of supplies. Should be
> interesting! Glad that the money and the doll have arrived OK.
> Take a few dollars out of the change and get yourself a Father's
> Day present …[24]

Thus Sergeant Bill Fogarty wrote home on 31 August 1967 about the 'resettlement' of Slope 30: three hostile villages that were to be destroyed and their residents moved to a new, Australian-built hamlet called Ap Suoi Nghe ('hamlet of sweet water').

At Slope 30, three roads converged on a bustling marketplace that, on the face of it, looked just like any other. Rice and supplies came down from the northerly Long Khanh province; medical supplies, cloth, wire and telephone cables flowed in from the west. Contraband, weapons and ammunition made the perilous journey via the Rung Sat. All exchanged hands under the guise of a civilian marketplace.[25]

Slope 30 was Viet Cong heartland. It was an important procurement and supply depot for the 5th Division of the National Liberation Front. The local Viet Cong's families lived here; these were their ancestral homes. Their claim on the soil long predated their political sympathies; they farmed rubber, banana, coffee and cashew plantations.

In July, a South Vietnamese unit wedged itself into this hostile territory, at Xa Bang.[26] The intrusion provoked hostilities. Graham agreed with Lieutenant Colonel Eric Smith that the area posed a threat, and ordered its destruction: 'I decided to clear Slope 30 lock, stock and barrel ...'[27]

On paper, OPERATION AINSLIE seemed straightforward: to build and protect the new hamlet of Ap Suoi Nghe; to clear 200 metres either side of Route 2, move all villagers from Slope 30 to the new hamlet; and to destroy their former homes.[28] The new hamlet was 4 kilometres from Nui Dat, easier to control and well within artillery range, ran the military rationale. The reality proved rather messier.

The Australian civic aid teams flew over and alerted the people by megaphone to gather in the village square and prepare for 'evacuation' (most had been warned and were already packed). The infantry landed a kilometre away, and used the local people to guide them safely to Slope 30, through a minefield. 'I got criticised for this in the media,' said Smith, 'but the people knew where the mines were.'[29]

The Australian forces entered the villages, searched the homes and interviewed hundreds of civilians. The overwhelming majority were women (many of whom were pregnant), children and the elderly. No adult males were found in the village of Cam My, for example; they had all joined the Viet Cong forces in the scrub.

On 11 September the first families were loaded aboard a convoy of army trucks. Shortly 250 families, along with their goods and chattels, children and squealing pigs 'churned along the newly bulldozed roads', reported the journalist John Bennetts. Ap Suoi Nghe offered a 'new start' in the 'best homes in the province', claimed the Task Force press release.

On the contrary, the families arrived to a treeless grid of half-built shacks set in mud. The homes were arranged in neighbourhood blocks, like a peculiarly bleak caravan park. No attempt had been made to replicate the circular spirit of the traditional Vietnamese village. Many of the huts lacked roofs or were otherwise incomplete; the Task Force offered a prize of A$10 to the best home completed within three months.

The Australian engineers were still laying sewerage and building wells when the people arrived. They looked 'sullen, resentful and confused', yet were not openly hostile. 'The people,' said Major Des Mealey (commanding B Company) 'seemed to have accepted the fact of their removal and co-operated well. Everything possible was done to protect the rights and property of the individual.'[30] Indeed, the troops assisted the people with every task, however small: loading and unloading their belongings, reassuring the older folk, helping pregnant mothers, amusing the children, delivering food supplies. Major Don Paterson (commanding D Company) praised his men for their 'extraordinary understanding'.[31]

Smith personally intervened to ensure that every last pumpkin found its way to Ap Suoi Nghe. The pumpkin harvest had been forgotten, so Smith sent the helicopters back to Slope 30 and had them loaded. Unfortunately, the pumpkins differed in size and quality, and belonged to different hamlets. The next day Smith got a call from the Task Force commander: 'Smith, about those pumpkins ...'

'Yes, we got those out.'

'You've mixed 'em up ... You see, Smith, there are pumpkins and there are pumpkins!'[32]

The Task Force band meanwhile sounded a cheerful 'oompah', yet the notes fell flat in the mud of that desolate day. Nothing could disguise a deep and growing resentment in the minds of these forcibly relocated people.

'They hated us,' remembered Private Paul Murphy, whose company (Delta, 2nd Battalion) helped build Ap Suoi Nghe. 'This was no Grace Bros service — just what the trucks could carry. What they couldn't carry we destroyed. Old ladies were crying and wailing; they'd just been thrown out of their ancestral homes. There were very few men. In the new village they got a three-sided corrugated iron shed, with a flat roof. "Welcome to your new home," we said. They'd been at Slope 30 for hundreds of years with their rubber, ducks and chooks. And we stuck them into this slab of land and expected them to thank us. But we didn't just walk away — we connected the water and supplied rice. Militarily there was a justification for it.'[33]

On military grounds it was judged a success. Slope 30 yielded valuable intelligence and evidence of hostile intent that seemed to vindicate OPERATION AINSLIE. Documents revealed the location of nearby Viet Cong base camps and, alarmingly, a detailed sketch of Nui Dat and the plan of another attack on the base. When questioned, local rubber-tappers confirmed the heavy Viet Cong infiltration of the area. 'The VC move towards SLOPE 30 every day, normally in squad groups,' they told the Australian intelligence officers.[34]

The demolition of Slope 30 took about two weeks. 'We burned all houses, buried shelters, and generally rendered the place useless to the enemy. Scorched earth It's called,' wrote Lieutenant Nobby Clark.[35] The vegetable and fruit farms 2 kilometres to the west were sprayed with defoliant and the crops destroyed. By October 1967 nothing remained of Slope 30. 'We picked up all these people, moved them on, and burned their villages down. There was no resistance,' concluded Smith.[36]

Brigadier Graham hailed the operation as a triumph. A major enemy supply depot had been destroyed — an excellent example of economic warfare, he contended. Denied food and weapons, the Viet Cong would assuredly wither on the vine in their jungle hideouts, he insisted. The resettled families would find their new circumstances a marked improvement on their previous desperate existence in 'the Communist Utopia'.[37] No longer would they endure the Viet Cong stealing their produce; no more would they suffer malnutrition and poverty in a richly fertile area, he wrote. Thus spoke Graham the ideologue. In this, Graham misapprehended the will of the people at Slope 30: the civilians had sacrificed their own wellbeing to supply their husbands and sons in the jungle. Graham seemed not to consider the possibility that, in this case, their dire conditions were self-inflicted.

During its first year, the new hamlet was classified as a 'refugee centre', a cruel euphemism. From what were the people seeking refuge? They had been forced at gunpoint to flee their homes into the arms of those who held the gun. The Americans subjected hundreds of thousands of peasants to the same pattern all over South Vietnam. As the war drew on, the 'refugee centres' filled to bursting point.

Eight months later Captain John Bullen, of the topographical survey unit, visited Ap Suoi Nghe to subdivide blocks of land for agricultural use. He noted 'small boys everywhere ranging from … the cigarette-smoking 9-year-old leader … down to Stalky, a 2-year-old who never wears any clothes'. Many of the children lent a hand, carrying equipment or driving the Land Rover. A five-year-old acted as 'chainman' on the forward end of the survey chain. Those older than five were taught to drive the Land Rover, 'and one 8-year-old can drive the bull-dozer'.[38]

In May 1968, the villagers were allocated little 1-hectare plots in a land ballot. These failed to prosper. An accidental defoliation mission destroyed 90 per cent of the first harvest. Bogus land titles — which on inspection reverted to French title-holders then living in Paris[39] — Saigon's interference, bad roads and growing insecurity condemned the project. A curse seemed to hang over the little Australian-made hamlet.

The villagers' true sympathies soon became clear. The umbilical link with their Viet Cong comrades did not end because the people were relocated. Enemy troops quickly reconnected with their friends and families in the new hamlet, threatened those who refused to cooperate and soon controlled Ap Suoi Nghe by night — a fact lost on the then Minister for the Army Phillip Lynch, who visited South Vietnam in April 1968. Of this trip, Major Peter Murray, commander of 547 Signal Troop, wrote despairingly to his wife: '... if [Lynch] is going to meet the Headman and Councillors which we put in, he should also meet the VCs. They run the joint every night and exert as much control and authority as our blokes ...' After Lynch leaves, 'the village will quieten down and back will come Charlie! Somehow It's funny.'[40]

Then the Viet Cong struck. In August 1968 a band entered the hamlet, dragged out the Saigon-appointed hamlet chief and his deputy, and decapitated them. Later, they assassinated their replacements. Henceforth no one wanted the job, an instant death sentence, as a local woodcutter told an American Field Survey: 'Twice the hamlet chiefs and their deputies have been killed by the VC. This fact makes the people ... panic-stricken. Now nobody dares to be a hamlet chief ... Nobody would dare to do it even if he had three heads and six hands.'[41]

Yet the Australians were forgiven, for good reasons. Throughout 1968 the villagers welcomed the *uc dai loi*, who came bearing gifts: a school, farm supplies, a market, a water supply and a medical dispensary — part of Australia's ramped-up civic aid effort. The Viet Cong looked on with amusement.

In time, the hamlet fell into disarray. Construction of the promised church and pagoda was abandoned. In 1970 an Australian psychological warfare unit spent five days in Ap Suoi Nghe and wrote it off as a 'hamlet of the poor'.[42] A year later Captain Peter Hudson, officer commanding 1st Psychological Operations Unit, made the same visit: 'The attempt to move people to a "western" type hamlet structure is depressing.' Hudson contemplated something worse: a 'hamlet without a soul'.[43]

The Americans seemed to learn little from the failure of PADDINGTON. On 27 October the Task Force embarked on another massive joint operation.

The 2nd and 7th Battalions, with armoured personnel carriers, SAS, reconnaissance and engineers, joined 13,500 American and South Vietnamese troops on OPERATION SANTA FE, a 'search and destroy' mission that ran for three weeks. Once more, tanks, carriers, helicopters and long lines of troops converged on the country, this time the hilly forested area 23 kilometres north-east of the Task Force base.

It was a pestilential place, crawling with vermin, lice, leeches and other insects. For weeks, in pouring rain, the troops pushed back and forth through dense scrub, long grass, greasy banks and swollen rivers. They crossed and recrossed the Song Rai River about a dozen times. Skin diseases were endemic, malaria hospitalised eighty-seven soldiers and an unknown fever struck down a further fifty-nine. In December 111 more cases of malaria were reported (the mosquitoes were able to bite through the soldiers' uniforms, claimed one after-action report).[44]

They did more searching than destroying. Lieutenant Colonel Noel 'Chic' Charlesworth, commander of the 2nd Battalion, dismissed the operation as 'a bit of a run around'. Smith concluded: 'The Americans made so much noise. The 274th Regiment ran away. We hardly succeeded in trapping and killing any of them.' Brigadier Ron Hughes, Graham's successor as Task Force commander, clutched at straws in declaring SANTA FE 'fairly successful' because it reduced the Viet Cong's 'waning influence in the province'.[45]

A miserable event during the operation epitomised the awful fate of Vietnamese civilians caught in the middle. Second Lieutenant David Webster's platoon accidentally shot an elderly couple and two children, aged about 10. A little girl fled screaming into a cave, with a bullet in her shoulder. Bob Richards, the company medic, went forward immediately. The old woman 'had been hit in the leg; her foot was hanging off about 4 inches from the top of the ankle'. He patched her up as best he could, and found her husband 'half in the creek and badly wounded; he was hit in the groin'. Then, under covering fire, Richards removed his webbing and entered the cave: 'It was very dark and fairly confined. I found the girl and half dragged, half carried her out … she was in shock … the bullet had gone in through the shoulder … there was no exit wound — she died a little later.' The little boy 'died as I reached him. He was definitely in extreme shock. I did feel useless, as there was nothing I could do for them.'[46]

In despair, the Australian platoon carefully buried the two children on the riverbank. The elderly couple and the woman's foot were airlifted to hospital. The man later died. The accident formed a cold reminder of the use to which the Viet Cong put civilians: as lures, trap-layers and shields. Civilian families were treated as 'family production cells' whose 'duty' — often forced on them — was to set booby traps (one of which failed to explode near the landing zone). The Australians had not even seen these unarmed civilians in their sights. It was a profoundly depressing experience.

SANTA FE rumbled along, achieving little except 126 enemy killed, by official 'body count', of which the small Australian contingent were responsible for thirty-eight. The 7th Battalion tracker dogs were credited with leading the troops to inflict two 'kills'. Australian casualties numbered eleven: three dead and eight wounded, most by mines and booby traps. Again, the statistics disappointed Westmoreland.[47]

By the end of 1967 it seemed the Australian war in Phuoc Tuy had degenerated into a gloomy roam through a desolate land, without even the prospect of a battle to sustain the interest of the men.

# Chapter 26
# To January 1968

The picture of the world's greatest superpower killing or
seriously injuring 1,000 non-combatants a week, while trying to
pound a tiny backward nation into submission on an issue whose
merits are hotly disputed, is not a pretty one.
*Robert McNamara, US Defense Secretary, to President Johnson.*

Prime Minister Holt's electoral triumph in November 1966 contained
the seeds of his government's demise. Holt had bound his party's
political destiny to an open-ended war that grew ever more unpopular.
Something happened in 1967 that turned many Australians in dismay from
the creature they had elected — rather like Dr Frankenstein, who shunned
the monster he had so passionately conceived. The hatred of conscription,
the body bags, the television footage, the emergence of an aggressive protest
movement: all added to the creeping sensation that Vietnam might have
been a terrible mistake.

As nightly images of death and despair appeared on TV screens,
middle-class opposition to the war curdled into revulsion. A reliably fickle
press spun with the weathervane of popular opinion: where a year earlier it
had strongly supported the war, the *Sydney Morning Herald* now chastised the
corrupt regime in the South: '... we are fighting for a nation that does not
really exist', an editorial noted.

A deep sense of unease settled over mainstream Australia. 'All the way' ...
towards what? people asked. Australians, like Americans, were experiencing a

deep shift in their political orientation, and the Vietnam War exerted a sort of lunar power on the tide of thought. And gradually the people turned: the Corio by-election in mid-1967 saw an 11 per cent swing to Labor. Yet the tide moved not in the direction of the traditional left. A new way of thinking about the world, and Australia's place in it, seemed to be struggling for a voice. That is not to suggest that a majority had simply changed its mind about Vietnam. The great Australian midriff was not so impressionable, and most supported the war. Australians had seen far greater casualties in World War II; they sensed the value of freedom at a time when more than half the world lived under the jackboots of Moscow and Peking. The erosion of mainstream support for the war happened gradually, like the action of a subterranean stream on the undertow of a glacier.

One event paradoxically served both to heighten and to diminish the perception of the communist threat to Australia — depending on how you viewed the world. On 1 June 1967 the White House received a top-secret cable from a 'classified source' in London confirming Britain's plan to withdraw its military bases from South-East Asia. 'White faces', the British suggested, were no longer welcome in the Far East. The British had already withdrawn in spirit, as Holt discovered during his tour of Asia in May. 'Dear Lyndon,' he wrote to the President on 3 May 1967, 'It saddened me … to find no reference in any country to Great Britain or the part it could play. It was as though England was, in substance, turning its back on three-fifths of mankind.'[1]

Holt reacted to the confirmation of his fears by denouncing the precipitate British withdrawal as 'a gross breach of faith'.[2] He made the same point, more diplomatically, to Prime Minister Harold Wilson on a trip to Britain on 13 June. Canute-like, the Australian leader seemed to think he could hold back the historic forces that swirled around him. Unfortunately, the British abandonment of Fortress Singapore was not a negotiable item. On 18 July 1967 Downing Street set in motion the phased pullout. Coming twenty-five years after the Japanese bombed Darwin, the news deeply disturbed older Australians who looked to the British for Anglo-Saxon spine in Malaysia and Singapore. And yet, rather than interpret British sanguinity as a sign that the communist threat to the region had diminished, Canberra presented it as a worsening regional threat and urged a greater war effort. 'We don't live in some sort of lotus land,' Holt told the Canberra press gallery on 19 July.[3]

★ ★ ★

Meanwhile, conservative doubts about the war deepened, driven in part by the huge cost of the war to the Australian economy. Defence expenditure had grown on average by 22 per cent per year in the four years to 1967. That growth rate would soon seriously damage the domestic economy, warned Treasurer Billy McMahon. Most new defence spending went on American military equipment, severely burdening Australia's balance of payments with the USA, and raising the prospect of domestic tax rises to pay for the war. Yet Malcom Fraser, the new Defence Minister, argued against any scaling back of the war effort: Australians had overwhelmingly voted for 'forward defence' and national service, he noted. How could the government simply change course?

These domestic disputes dared not publicly admit the darker economic reality, which lay in America's refusal to make any economic concessions to Australia. On 4 June Holt wrote to LBJ about the high US tariffs on Australian wool. Wool, the Prime Minister wrote, helped to generate the foreign exchange Australia needed to pay for the 'imports essential for our development and defence'. New Zealand, he added, exported 67.4 per cent of its wool to the US duty free; Australia's duty-free percentage was 0.1 per cent.[4] The President promised to look at the problem, and did nothing. Much as he liked his little Aussie buddy, LBJ did not wish to upset American farmers at a time of deep uncertainty.

Once again, with cap in hand, Holt made his mid-year pilgrimage to Washington, and once again the President ever so nicely rebuffed him. Australia had got a 'raw deal' on raw wool in the Kennedy Round of Trade Talks, Holt told the American Australian Association on 13 June. Nor had America made any concessions on sugar, dairy products, meat, lead or zinc, he argued. 'Australians import $68 per head from the United States, and the United States imports less than $2 per head from Australia.'[5] Australia bought a quarter of its imports from the USA, totalling US$800 million in 1967, an increase of US$700 million since 1948–49; Australian exports to the USA were about US$375 million, an increase of US$300 million since 1948–49, half the growth rate. Holt simply sought a balance in trade opportunities.

Yet Holt unhesitatingly supported America in Vietnam, 'particularly the continuation of the bombing [of North Vietnam]'. As to why Australia was involved, he now said: '... because we saw this communist inspired aggression as a threat to free people and small nations — small nations in particular — everywhere.'[6] In a speech to the Far East American Council, he pledged again to 'go all the way with LBJ'. Perhaps his effusive welcome and lavish White House dinner — breast of Cornish hen, green beans amandine, *bel paese* cheese and 'Glace Zara' washed down with Wente Pinot and Beaulieu Cabernet Sauvignon in the company of Hubert Humphrey, Clark Clifford, Dean Rusk, Bob McNamara and their wives[7] — had softened the Prime Minister's mind? He seemed to offer everything; he got nothing.

The US Ambassador to Australia, Ed Clark, far better conveyed the extremity of Australia's economic situation, in an extraordinary memo to the White House on 13 December 1967. Stressing the severe economic pressure on Australia following harsher European trade restrictions, Clark wrote:

> ... our continued unwillingness to grant [Australia] even a
> fraction of the relief which has been granted to Japan ... is a
> constant source of irritation and embitterment to our Australian
> friends who have consistently supported us right down the line.
> They are our strongest supporters in Viet Nam and they are
> paying their own way there at considerable cost to their own
> balance of payments. The cost of the new weapons which they
> are purchasing from us is almost staggering for a country with
> fewer than 12 million people. Australia has consistently supported
> us in the United Nations on the China question ... It has been
> extremely disappointing to me personally not to have been able
> to secure some assistance for a good friend in need of it ...[8]

Clark's letter had no effect. The only war-related economic benefits of 1967 were a contract worth US$6.5 million a year to supply sugar to US troops in Vietnam, and tourism, or R&R (in October alone, 2,085 US servicemen visited Sydney and the Gold Coast, and spent US$628,500).

Meanwhile, the Americans were in the market for more troops, and in mid-1967 Johnson's chief procurers — presidential advisers Clark Clifford and Maxwell Taylor — flew to Australia in a hungry mood. Johnson's war was perilously expensive; the Pentagon spent US$25 billion a year on South-East Asian operations, forcing the President to press Congress for hefty tax rises to pay for it. A bigger war effort from America's allies would help Johnson sell the war to Congress, as Clifford later explained to the New Zealand Government: 'One additional New Zealand soldier might produce 50 Americans.'

Taylor and Clifford swooped on Canberra on 30 July with one goal uppermost in their minds: the extraction of at least another, and ideally two or three more, Australian battalions for Vietnam. In the dulcet tones of Washington's most consummate powerbrokers, the duo set out their demands during a marathon session with the Australian Cabinet. The threat to South Vietnam, Taylor stressed, was far greater than the danger to Malaysia or Indonesia (with or without the British); Australia should concentrate all its overseas military resources in South Vietnam, he insisted.

At first, Holt obfuscated; Cabinet demurred. Only Black Jack McEwen, the deputy leader, stood strongly in favour. Two months of private deliberations followed during which Brigadier Graham's frustrations, the Task Force's request for tanks and a timely article by Denis Warner urging more troops for Nui Dat tipped the scales America's way. On 6 September, the Foreign Affairs and Defence Committee confirmed the dispatch of a tank squadron, four helicopters and eight pilots, another ten Skyhawk pilots, 64 naval maintenance personnel and 125 additional support personnel to South Vietnam. More importantly, they agreed *in principle* to offer a third infantry battalion: 1,200 troops, about 40 per cent of whom would be national servicemen. Washington was fully informed; the Australian Parliament and people were kept ignorant.

There would be no dollars for these diggers: McMahon and Hasluck, in Washington to negotiate the fine print, failed to win any economic and defence concessions in exchange for the troops. America refused to reduce tariffs on Australian beef, mutton and other commodities, or to offer any help in filling the security gap in Malaysia vacated by the British. McMahon succeeded only in delaying the payments on the F111 fighter aircraft. In fact, US Defense Secretary McNamara turned the tables and belittled the Australian offer. He warned of the 'intolerable pressures' Congress had placed on the President and that 'none of America's allies were bearing their fair share of the load'.[9]

On 6 October — without informing Parliament — Holt wrote to the White House and confirmed the offer of a third battalion and a squadron of Centurion tanks. The tank supporters, chiefly Major General Tim Vincent in Saigon, were delighted. They had lobbied hard for armour. Intriguingly, Graham, an old armour man, did not support the dispatch of the Centurions. The tanks were too old, he said, and required helicopter support to deliver spare parts. Canberra overruled him.[10]

The fresh combat and support troops doubled Australia's commitment, to more than 8,000. 'This puts us at the full stretch of our present and planned military capacity,' Holt reminded the President. Any additional commitment 'I would regard as publicly unacceptable'.[11]

The fact is that the third battalion did not satisfy the Americans. The Australian offer 'was not enough', the President flatly told Hasluck in a meeting in the White House on 10 October. America was three times as far from Vietnam as Australia: 'If our effort in Viet-Nam was proportional to the present Australian commitment we would have no more than 100,000 men there.' Hasluck replied that 'great people bore great responsibilities' and that Australia's commitment was the 'maximum possible' without new legislation.[12]

Holt told Parliament of the decision on 17 October, ten weeks after receiving the US request. The third battalion, he said, would help turn the 'tide' of communism, which had not abated in light of the British withdrawal.[13] There was no debate. Labor and peace groups reacted with predictable ire; media outlets were generally sceptical or hostile. The story even made *Pravda*, the Soviet news daily, which scorned Australia's troop increase as 'cannon meat for Vietnam in exchange for mutton for the USA'.[14]

Two months later, the President sacked his Defense Secretary. The removal of Bob McNamara raised hitherto unthinkable questions: was the Australian Government throwing fresh troops at a doomed enterprise?

McNamara's public about-turn can be traced to 18 March 1967, when he rejected Westmoreland's appeals to dispatch 200,000 fresh US troops (which would have brought the total Americans in country to 670,000); extend the war to Laos and Cambodia; increase the bombing and mining of North Vietnam; and send infantry across the Demilitarized Zone. The whole package would have cost another US$10 billion a year.[15]

Behind McNamara's refusal lay the apostasy of a man who seemed to embody the Western crisis of confidence over Vietnam. Bitterly disillusioned, McNamara ranted 'with rage and grief and almost disorientation' — the outward signs of a deep psychological crisis that culminated in his complete recantation of his personal support for the war.[16] In a long, dark memo to the President on 19 May 1967, the Defense Secretary painted a terrifying picture of a war that had acquired a momentum all its own and was hurtling out of control. It 'must be stopped', said the man who shared a heavy responsibility for starting it:

There may be a limit beyond which Americans and much of the world will not permit the United States to go. The picture of the world's greatest superpower killing or seriously injuring 1,000 non-combatants a week, while trying to pound a tiny backward nation into submission on an issue whose merits are hotly disputed, is not a pretty one. It could conceivably produce a costly distortion in the American national consciousness and in the world image of the United States — especially if the damage to North Vietnam is complete enough to be 'successful'.[17]

Two principles now governed the American war in Vietnam, he said: (1) to see that the people of South Vietnam are permitted to determine their own future; and (2) this commitment ceases if the country ceases to help itself.[18]

McNamara prescribed a bitter pill: the gradual withdrawal of US troops; the transfer of responsibility to the South Vietnamese (a policy dubbed 'Vietnamisation'); the opening of negotiations with Hanoi; and an end to the bombing of North Vietnam. The threat of China, the spread of communism and the Domino Theory, as stated by Eisenhower, Kennedy, Johnson, Rusk, Casey, Menzies, Holt, Hasluck and — most vehemently — by McNamara himself were either exaggerated or simply no longer existed, the Defense Secretary believed. The war had degenerated to a fight in a little country of no strategic value.

Yet McNamara the rationalist failed to list a third — and most powerful — case for the American role in Vietnam: to maintain American prestige in the world. Having engaged, America could not simply 'lose'; US pride was at stake. Rogue states would get the wrong message — a view that sparked a bushfire of rebuttals to McNamara from the Pentagon. America's Joint Chiefs of Staff were rumoured to be ready to resign en masse if Johnson blinked. Instead, McNamara was forced to resign, in December 1967.

The Defense Secretary's metamorphosis little changed the Australian Government's thinking. The reinforcements would proceed to South Vietnam, as planned, in early 1968. Ironically, the deployment of the third battalion highlighted the actual poverty of Australia's commitment, in the eyes of the new Defense Secretary, Clark Clifford, who noted that 300,000 Australians had fought overseas during World War II. If Australians really were 'all the way with LBJ', why were they so reluctant to send more troops to Vietnam, he wondered. Later, Australia's piecemeal war effort helped to change Clifford, too, from hawk to dove.[19]

To raise the added troops, conscription was strongly enforced. In late 1967 a stream of 'draft dodgers' brought forward a government decision to impose a tougher National Service Act. The Bill, debated in late 1967 (and enacted on 1 May 1968), proposed spot fines of up to $200 on those who destroyed or falsified call-up notices; the appointment of single magistrates, without juries, with powers to impose two-year prison sentences on anyone who refused to serve; and the incarceration of draft resisters as common criminals in ordinary jails, a measure the RSL and the army greeted with relief.

The most sinister measure doubled to $400 the fine on anyone who failed to report young men they knew to be dodging the draft. In effect, the government was proposing that the Australian people dob in their families and friends. Informing went against the very grain of a society apparently built on mateship and a fair go. The so-called pimping provisions provoked uproar, and the ALP drew its first real blood; Gough Whitlam likened the government to a police state that imposed one vast 'apparatus of tittle-tattle under the law'. The policy sat well in the worst totalitarian regimes, he said, 'where pimping is erected into patriotism, where informing is a virtue'.[20]

The Australian people responded with contempt for this encroachment on their liberty: they burned more draft cards, held 'fill-in-a-falsie' parties and inundated the national service office with thousands of fake forms. 'Resist the draft!' became a national rallying cry. Dogs and cats, the artist Clifton Pugh's wombat, and several Liberal politicians were 'called up'. The system started to buckle under this deluge of ridicule. Even a few sober-minded conservatives came out in protest at the illiberality of the Liberals.

The storm gathered around the name of one man, John Francis Zarb, a Melbourne postman. On 2 November 1967 a court rejected Zarb's conscientious objector plea on the grounds that the Act did not recognise objection to a particular war. Zarb had said he would fight to defend Australia against an invasion, but refused to 'aid and abet' the 'unjust and immoral war' in Vietnam.[21] In October 1968 he was jailed for the mandatory two years in Pentridge Prison.

An extraordinary multi-partisan chorus demanded Zarb's release: peace activists, unions, Labor and Liberal voters. 'RELEASE POSTMAN ZARB' became a middle-class slogan. Activists draped 'FREE ZARB' posters over the balcony of the visitors' gallery in the House of Representatives. Thousands protested outside Pentridge, and Amnesty International adopted Zarb as a political prisoner. 'We have pursued John Francis Zarb,' said Labor MP Gordon Bryant, in a speech that resonated across the political divide, 'in a way in which no Australian Government ought to pursue its subjects. Where is our humanity? Where is our common sense? Where is our decency? Where is our sense of perspective?'[22]

Postman Zarb was released in August 1969 on the same day as Warrant Officer Ray Simpson received the Victoria Cross. Unthinkable a year earlier, a daring editorial in the *Sydney Morning Herald* spoke of 'two very different kinds of courage'. Zarb 'deserves respect', the paper wrote, for being prepared to risk prison for his beliefs. The sentiment enraged many, who saw no equivalence between the actions of a 'draft dodger' and a recipient of the Victoria Cross.[23]

Harold Holt died on Sunday morning, 17 December, while spearfishing off Cheviot Beach, near Portsea, Victoria, in storm-tossed seas. Wild rumours surrounded his death: had the CIA, a Chinese submarine or an alien abducted the Prime Minister? No, 'wild surf' had taken Holt's life.[24] He deserves to be remembered for more than the unusual nature of his death. Ahead of his party and most of his country, Holt believed Australia's economic and political destiny lay in Asia. He abhorred racism, and stood out as a pragmatist in a government of ideological hawks. 'He saw that we had to begin … to build a new community in Asia,' President Johnson told caretaker Prime Minister Jack McEwen, on landing at Fairbairn RAAF base in Canberra, in December 1967, to attend his close friend's funeral.[25] The President, who sat in the front pew with Harold Wilson and a youthful Prince Charles, had earlier cabled Lord Casey: 'I WAS PROUD TO COUNT HIM AMONG MY MOST TRUSTED FRIENDS …'[26] Zara Holt, the late Prime Minister's wife, a 'jolly, prattling, bouncy kind of woman' who had enchanted Washington, was inconsolable.[27] 'The world is a lonelier place today,' Lady Bird wrote to her.[28]

The state funeral offered neutral ground to engage in a 'quiet and tactful discussion', Rusk proposed. And so, on 21 December 1967, the President attended a sombre meeting of the Australian Cabinet.[29] The meeting elicited extraordinary candour in sympathy, perhaps, with the spirit of honesty occasioned by the death of a friend. McEwen began by stressing Australia's determination to 'stand with the US right to the very end'. Australia, he said, set out with America 'to frustrate an effort to enslave a nation'.[30]

The President responded as though the ghost of McNamara were speaking through him: the war was about salvaging a country, not a region, he said. Australians had shown courage 'in taking sacrifices to prevent a little, independent country from being gobbled up'. Falling Asian dominoes, Johnson now acknowledged, had never threatened America, protected by the underrated fact of the Pacific Ocean; nor did LBJ believe China or the Soviets were any longer militarily able to launch a Pan-Asian domino effect. Sweeping away years of political and military dogma, the President declared, in his arresting Texan drawl, 'The US could probably survive even if South-East Asia were lost to the Communists.' American pride now underwrote the American rationale for war. Australia, he added, in a passing nod at ANZUS, was 'one of the principal reasons that we have committed our power so fully to this part of the world'.[31] This remark was nonsense, of course, but decent nonsense, at a sad time.

On a graver note, the North Vietnamese were 'building [their] forces in the south', the President warned. 'Two divisions from the North were coming into South Vietnam.' Yet 10,000 fresh American troops were due in South Vietnam within eighteen days, he added, hoping to steel Australian resolve and nudge the local commitment higher. At the same time, Saigon's Assembly was debating the call-up of 65,000 young men.[32]

Washington hoped that the funeral might offer the President a chance to discuss communist incursions into Cambodia with Prince Sihanouk.[33] It was deeply concerned about North Vietnam's use of Cambodia as a supply route, which 'was developing to a serious point very rapidly'.[34] Yet the Prince had cut Cambodia's diplomatic relations with the USA, so he sent his toothless Foreign Minister to Holt's funeral in his place, and Cambodia's awful fate continued on its grim trajectory. Undaunted, the US State Department suggested the dispatch of a high-level Australian official — possibly even Hasluck — to relay American concerns to Phnom Penh. Rusk's telegram, to the US Embassy in Canberra, proposed 'a series of strikes' across the Cambodian border. The proposal was, of course, preposterous. Using the nation's Foreign Minister as a messenger for the US plan to bomb Cambodia 'raised major issues', replied Waller, Australia's Ambassador to Washington; Hasluck did not go.

The Australian war effort entered 1968 equipped with a new Task Force commander, Brigadier Ron Hughes, who chose to abandon Graham's 'hearts and minds' campaign in favour of a return to 'hunt and kill' tactics. An emphasis on 'body count' would be the hallmark of Hughes's tour; for example, when an SAS patrol failed to shoot three Viet Cong seen washing in a creek, Hughes demanded to know why.

In tandem, Hughes launched a prolonged and bloody effort to deny the Viet Cong the rice harvest, in a series of operations from November to January dubbed FORREST.[35] Viet Cong villages were cordoned and searched, to ensure that they stocked only 'reasonable quantities of rice'.[36] There were sporadic firefights. In one battle, Lance Corporal Bob Richards, a 7th Battalion medic, received multiple shrapnel wounds, in the arm, knee, calf and neck. 'There was a continual call of "medic" in my ears,' he said. He half-crawled, half-staggered to treat others worse than himself; two soldiers died in his arms (a chapel in Wahroonga, Sydney, is dedicated to one, Bryan Cullen). Hit again, Richards continued trying to respond to shouts of 'Medic!'[37] His mention in dispatches noted: 'The display of courage by this young stretcher bearer inspired his comrades, who eventually beat off the enemy counter-attack and held the camp.'[38]

The two-month operation left four Australians dead and thirty-five wounded (for forty-seven enemy killed in action). Jumping jack mines almost certainly lifted from the Australian minefield caused many of the casualties: On 27 November Private Jeff Rivett died and Private Noel Pettitt lost both legs and later died. (Pettitt, a conscientious objector, was sent to Vietnam after he lost his appeal against doing national service.) On 30 November a huge explosion killed Private Ron Bell and wounded Private Frankie Hyland (who later died). It wounded a further eight, one of whom, Private David Haynes, radioed for help before passing out from blood loss. He received a Military Medal. Mick Logan, a strong athlete, had both legs amputated, and another soldier lost the tip of his penis. When the latter recovered, he wrote to his mates back home, 'It works!'

'I was sorry to hear of the casualties,' wrote Lieutenant General Tom Daly, Chief of the General Staff, in Canberra, to Tim Vincent in Saigon, 'but you can't make an omelette without breaking eggs.' Daly, perhaps Australia's most respected soldier, added: 'If only we could cut down on the booby trap casualties I would feel much happier.'[39]

The first of three Australian 'fraggings' was said to have occurred at this time, an extreme example of the strain on some young men. At 8 p.m. on

10 December, at a remote fire support base near the Nui Thi Vai Mountains, Gunner Leonard Newman allegedly tossed a grenade into the sleeping pit of Lieutenant Robert Birse, of 106 Battery. As he lay dying, Birse groaned that a grenade from Newman's bunker had caused his mortal wounds.

Earlier, Newman, a national serviceman, had shown signs of severe mental instability, which excessive quantities of beer failed to ameliorate. The day before, Birse had reprimanded him for buying beer outside the base and drinking it inside. Newman also felt bitter at being denied leave to visit his wife and new baby. 'I am going to give Birse a scare and throw a grenade in his tent,' he told fellow soldiers on the night of the attack. 'It will blow his tent and gear to the shit-house but it won't hurt him.'[40] Newman's conviction and five-year sentence for manslaughter were later quashed on appeal due to lack of evidence. The military authorities construed a symptom of Newman's behaviour — excessive drinking — as the cause of the tragedy, and cracked down on off-duty drinking, a measure that further reduced morale.


Christmas came. In Vung Tau, the chaplains held 'Carols by Candlelight', and the 2nd Battalion band played.[41] Australian television screened a few cheerful soldiers' Christmas messages. At Nui Dat the diggers got stuck into a turkey feast served, as tradition decreed, by their officers and NCOs. A cigarette company gave the troops a hundred cigarettes each.

Two days later the 3rd Battalion, 'Old Faithful' of Korean War fame commanded by Lieutenant Colonel Jim Shelton, disembarked at Vung Tau and flew to Nui Dat. Shelton had been rushed up to Vietnam, and his men were not yet combat-ready, with only six months' training. During final exercises at Shoalwater Bay, the King's Shropshire Light Infantry soundly defeated them in a mock battle, and several company commanders were sacked on the spot. The tank squadron, which learned of its deployment via the ABC news, soon followed.[42] None, of course, had any idea of the bloody maelstrom they were about to enter.


In the wider world, portents of doom and pleas for peace crowded the closing days of 1967. Religious leaders appealed to Johnson's conscience to stop the war. The Pope re-sent his Christmas message of hope: 'We cry to them in God's name to stop.'[43] The evangelist Billy Graham, in his New Year sermon, warned that mankind faced 'the final conflict between good and evil that would end the world'.[44] The world survived January. Yet in that month, a new shock reached Australia: the British had decided to pull out all troops in Asia far earlier than planned; by 31 March 1971 not a single British soldier would remain in the 'Far East'.

In this atmosphere of spiralling uncertainty, Johnson's Fifth State of the Union Address, on the 17th, was sombre in tone, almost contrite. Gone were the grand pledges to end poverty and build a 'Great Society'. Behind the measured statement lay a man deeply depressed by a year of 'continuous nightmare', Johnson later said.[45] The President, observed a Republican senator, carried 'the most burdensome problems the mind of man is capable of conceiving'.[46] In February 1968 the Viet Cong troops added the straw that broke the President's back: they rose against the southern cities on a scale hitherto inconceivable.

Part Five
# The Year of the Monkey

# Chapter 27
# The Tet Offensive

... to bury alive whole families including the children on no
stronger pretext than they refused to take up arms defies the
imagination ...
*Warrant Officer Campbell, in a letter to his wife.*

It became necessary to destroy the town to save it.
*A US major to journalist Peter Arnett.*

In July 1967, seven months before Tet, Major Peter Young, Australia's
assistant military attaché, proposed for discussion at a dinner party in
Saigon the topic 'that we are losing the war'.[1] A chat about the unthinkable,
then, in the company of some of the finer minds in the intelligence
community: Ted Serong, now indisputably one of the most powerful CIA
operatives in Vietnam; Major Jack Fitzgerald, a gifted analyst with US
military intelligence; Denis Warner, the Australian journalist and probable
ASIS retainee; the CIA's deputy station chief; and the British MI6 agent in
Saigon, who, with a tuck of his silk hanky under his cuff, promptly stated
that he did not wish to participate in 'defeatist talk'.

Young was unusually well informed, even among this intimidating
company. He had served with the CIA in Da Nang in 1962, and had
clearance for the US Current Intelligence and Indications Branch (CIIB) and
Westmoreland's Black Book, the Weekly Intelligence Estimate of the
American forces. Young, a self-confident English émigré — whose detractors

claimed that the brashness of his personality was surpassed only by the quality of his sources — was privy to the higher levels of US Army intelligence, to which only Serong and one or two other Australians were admitted.

As dinner proceeded, Young and Fitzgerald outlined 'one of the most brilliant pieces of intelligence assessment in the war', argued Denis Warner later. Not only did they tip the Tet Offensive; they also 'tipped the time'.[2] They contended that North Vietnam could neither defeat the US in open battle nor continue pouring young lives into the American meat grinder. Hanoi had one choice: a single massive uprising — 'a short, sharp nationwide attack aimed at the cities', with the political aim of triggering a revolution in the South — a strike of such scale and precision as to surprise the American forces and shock the West. Young and Fitzgerald timed the conflagration for the Buddhist lunar holiday of Tet 1968, in the first week of February.

The dinner paused and ruminated. Then Serong replied in his slow, calm voice, like the tolling of a funeral bell. He accepted the major offensive theory, but insisted, with great prescience, that the South Vietnamese would fight back and fight well and that the southern people would reject any call for an uprising from Hanoi.[3] Warner agreed, as the party repaired for cigars and port.

In September, Fitzgerald delivered the thesis to Westmoreland's weekly intelligence briefing. He decked the office out as a North Vietnamese war room complete with red flag; 'Fitz' even strode in dressed as a People's Army colonel. His presentation provoked gales of dissent.[4] 'So violent was the response,' said Young (who was not present), 'that the briefing team was withdrawn.'[5] Westmoreland's men claimed that Fitzgerald's scenario grossly overrated the Viet Cong's strength.

Young sent his own predictions coded FREEFALL to the usual Australian authorities in Saigon. He had to disguise his US SIGINT sources; a secret service operative even inspected Young's typewriter ribbon. The Australian generals — chiefly Wilton and Daly — ignored or downgraded it; the Australian Ambassador in Saigon suppressed it; Canberra never saw it. Only Vincent, a signaller, took a close interest. In the gung-ho climate of the American war, Young and Fitzgerald had committed a kind of thought crime: they had failed to 'report positively', Warner observed.[6]


Tet is a time of peace and reflection in the Buddhist year, which falls in the first week of February in the Julian calendar. Hitherto, the Vietnamese had broken the New Year peace only once, in 1789, against the Chinese. 'To us Vietnamese,' said one southern soldier, 'Tet means ... a period of renewal for everything: Time, Nature, Human Beings and even Inanimate things ...'[7] Lieutenant General Vinh Loc described Tet as 'a combination of many festivals. It honors the family and brings them together, it commemorates the ancestors ...'[8]

In January 1968, as every year, the villages and cities bristled in anticipation of the coming holiday. Enlivened by the prospect of the Year of the Monkey (*Tet Mau Than*), the frantic pre-Tet ritual gathered pace: soldiers went home on leave; women scrubbed their houses and bled their poultry; men stockpiled food and rice wine for the family feast; flags, posters and streamers adorned the streets. The war seemed strangely to recede. All over Vietnam, cyclists bore enormous loads home. Cumquat trees adorned rural hovels and seaside villas. Children's faces brightened at the prospect of firecrackers in the streets. It was as if the war had been put on pause; yet it still crackled to life in peaceful places: near the end of 1967 Buddhist monks renewed their protests. Vietnam, they declared, was the 'grass that gets trampled when the elephants fight'.


In the weeks before Tet, the American commanders talked confidently of winning the war. 'North Vietnam ... has lost the initiative in the south,' stated a military assessment of 18 December 1967.[9] On a trip to Washington, Westmoreland told Congress that the enemy was 'almost on the ropes ... we are grinding the enemy down'.[10] The war had stopped the spread of Chinese-backed communism in South-East Asia, he claimed.[11] The Viet Cong, declared Robert Komer, the ebullient head of CORDS, 'can't put more than a company-sized unit into the field anywhere in South Vietnam'.[12] Phrases like 'lights at the end of the tunnel', 'corners turned' and 'an enemy on the run' littered the end-of-year briefings. Hanoi's breaking point had surely arrived, believed Westmoreland, convinced that his troops were killing the Viet Cong faster than Hanoi could replace them. In the six years to January 1968, 246,529 Viet Cong and North Vietnamese troops had died, compared with 15,696 Americans and 52,742 South Vietnamese.[13] In 1967 alone communist dead totalled 85,036; the US and South Vietnam had lost 9,050 and 10,404 troops respectively.

Serong disagreed. 'There is some misguided talk around here,' he observed in his diary that month, 'that this war of attrition is to our advantage. [The Americans] do not seem to realise that the initiative … is with the enemy. Two thirds of the casualties he incurs are in operations that he initiates. Therefore, if he is being worn away, it is at his own wish — and therefore a deliberately chosen strategy, which he can break off any time it appears to him uneconomic.'[14]

In short, the communist casualties were *planned*. Yet the US Military Command refused to accept that a people could tolerate such bloodshed; in this sense, the West projected its body-bag tolerance level on to the enemy. That is not to say that the North Vietnamese and Viet Cong chose to die on the Japanese or Chinese scale. Their higher casualties simply reflected the tactical reality: they lacked air power. Even so, their 'kill rate' more than matched a Chinese calculation that it required one Vietnamese division to destroy one US battalion.[15]

In Hanoi, the ailing Ho Chi Minh had become a figurehead, Giap remained in control of the military, and political power devolved onto Prime Minister Dong and Le Duan, the ruthless, smiling secretary general of the Lao-Dong (Communist) Party, which ultimately controlled its southern comrades through the Central Office of South Vietnam (COSVN — the southern communists' political headquarters).

For Le Duan, the 'liberation of the fatherland' relied on the Vietnamese capacity to suffer horrific casualties and endure appalling hardship. Le Duan grimly satisfied himself that the National Liberation Front — his frontline fighters — held both qualities in abundance. 'Short of being physically destroyed,' wrote Konrad Kellen, a Rand Corporation analyst, 'collapse, surrender, or disintegration was … simply not within their capabilities.' Indeed, American Republicans contemplated nuclear annihilation as the only way to defeat what an anonymous US general called 'the best enemy we have faced in our history'.[16]

Hanoi now proposed to put into effect their southern comrades' readiness to die. The Tet Offensive was not conceived as a suicidal last resort, 'a one shot, go for broke attempt', as Westmoreland claimed. On the contrary, Hanoi believed the time had come to strike for all-out victory.[17] The offensive would deal the Americans and their allies 'thundering blows so as to change the face of the war', Le Duan reckoned in a letter on 18 January 1968.[18] Yet Hanoi mistakenly assumed that southern soldiers loyal to Saigon were willing to desert and rally to the Red standard, and it vastly overrated its support among the South Vietnamese people. One had only to look at the huge turnout to the 1967 general elections in the South to gauge the burgeoning support for the Saigon Government, which the South Vietnamese increasingly saw as the lesser of two evils. Also, the ARVN were heartened by the immense firepower of the US arsenal and a better relationship with the foreign forces, after jointly fighting in a series of huge operations. Moreover, the South Vietnamese people — especially those living in the cities, where the Viet Cong couldn't easily reach them — entertained the idea that the South could win. Gone was the siege mentality of 1965. And, of course, many city dwellers had come to rely on and enjoy America's wealth and huge investment in the South Vietnamese economy.

COSVN drew up the plans for the 'General Offensive — General Uprising' (*Tong Cong Kich — Tong Khoi Ngia*) in May 1967. The chief architect, General Nguyen Chi Thanh, commander-in-chief of the South Vietnamese communist forces, presented them to Hanoi in July. He then overdrank, collapsed and died of heart failure at his farewell party; so Giap assumed direct responsibility for the offensive. A massive arms and troop build-up proceeded in South Vietnam throughout late 1967: 'Every region or zone had to build up a force of two to four infantry battalions. Their objective was to infiltrate Saigon …'[19]

The Soviet Bloc gave US$750 million and China US$250 million to North Vietnam in 1967 — Mao's Cultural Revolution had severely weakened his ability to aid the offensive. Yet Chinese political influence never wavered: 'Mao suggested … a strategy of annihilation', a suggestion that Ho Chi Minh reckoned 'logical and reasonable'.[20] At a meeting in October the Politburo in Hanoi made the grave decision to launch the mass offensive during the Tet holiday, 1968; the aim was to create shock and hysteria in the cities and to reclaim the rural areas. But Hanoi needed a diversion, a massive feint, that would distract the American giant: Giap chose the northern provinces around the Route 9–Tri Thien front and Khe Sanh. Although these areas were seen as 'second in importance', Giap would attack them in strength, 'for the purpose of drawing out American troops for destruction, thus giving support to other battlefields, foremost of which was Saigon–Hué–Da Nang, and most directly that of Hué'.[21]

Thus began the bloodiest of diversions. Westmoreland looked 'with satisfaction' at the escalating combat along the DMZ. 'We'll just go on bleeding them,' he said, in late 1967, 'until Hanoi wakes up to the fact that they have bled their country to the point of national disaster for generations.'[22]

He dispatched the First Army Division to the northern hill provinces, as Hanoi hoped. Indeed, he even told the visiting Gough Whitlam on 20 January 1968 that he expected a huge battle — the 'daddy of them all' — just south of the demilitarised zone at Khe Sanh, a remote American mountain outpost, near the Laos–Vietnam border.[23]

Westmoreland felt vindicated when, on 21 January 1968, North Vietnamese forces started shelling Khe Sanh. The final confrontation, for which he had longed, had arrived at Khe Sanh. On 15 January he had cabled to a US admiral:

> THE INTELLIGENCE ON ENEMY MOVEMENTS IN QUANG TRI AND
> THUA THIEN AND THE ADJACENT AREAS OF LAOS AND THE DMZ
> HAVE PROMPTED ME TO MODIFY CURRENT AND PROJECTED
> OPERATIONS … THE ODDS ARE 60–40 THAT THE ENEMY WILL
> LAUNCH HIS PLANNED CAMPAIGN PRIOR TO TET. MY OBJECTIVE
> IS TO PRE-EMPT THIS ATTACK.[24]

On 21 January, after the enemy bombed Khe Sanh, Westmoreland diverted all B52 missions to the area:

> I CONSIDER IT IMPERATIVE THAT WE USE MAXIMUM AIR
> FIREPOWER … TO MEET THE ENEMY THREAT IN I CORPS …
> I WISH TO STRESS THE ABSOLUTE NECESSITY FOR
> COORDINATION OF ALL ELEMENTS OF THE COMMAND TO
> BRING FIREPOWER AGAINST THE ENEMY … THE SERIOUS
> THREAT WE FACE IN I CORPS AND KHE SANH IN PARTICULAR,
> DEMANDS THIS. I HAVE DIRECTED MY AIR DEPUTY TO ENSURE
> IN MY NAME THAT THESE AIR RESOURCES ARE APPLIED TO
> THIS END …[25]

Four days later, on 25 January 1968, Westmoreland and South Vietnamese President Thieu agreed to break the usual Tet ceasefire — as observed in I Corps Tactical Zone — with a pre-emptive strike against an expected massed invasion across the DMZ.

Others quietly disagreed: a fortnight earlier Lieutenant General Fred Weyand had warned Westmoreland of an uprising in the southern cities. Something 'pretty goddamn bad was coming', Weyand said, citing his intelligence, 'right in our backyard'.[26] Lieutenant General Sir John Wilton, then chairman of Australia's Chiefs of Staff Committee, agreed. Weyand even requested Australian help to defend the northern approaches to Saigon and the giant Long Binh logistics base near Bien Hoa. 'Say, Ron,' he asked the new Task Force commander, Brigadier Ron Hughes, 'would you mind bringing your Task Force up to this area here?' Weyand waved at a map.[27] In an overt example of political interference at tactical level, Canberra insisted that the Task Force be confined to Phuoc Tuy. Vincent and Hughes compromised on a division of labour: in January 1968 two Australian battalions went to Long Binh, and 'Old Faithful', the fresh 3rd Battalion, stayed at Nui Dat.

The 'superb diversion' of Khe Sanh, as Thompson called it, lasted seventy-seven days and cost 325 American lives and 1,643 wounded for an estimated 10,000 Viet Cong and North Vietnamese dead (most in B52 saturation strikes). That was the human cost of a bluff: the blood Giap expended in order to persuade Westmoreland that Hanoi actually valued this relatively unimportant mountain redoubt.

For Westmoreland Khe Sanh became a point of honour, a 'false love object' in a personal battle, he felt, with Giap.[28] He thus ordered the Marines to defend the indefensible: a valley surrounded by communist-controlled hills and riddled with enemy artillery. He meant to draw Giap into believing that he (Giap) could launch another Dien Bien Phu. The key difference, this time, was America's immense air power. 'Do you believe,' Vincent asked Westmoreland at the time, 'that you will destroy him by air … to teach Giap a lesson he will never forget — that there will be no more Dien Bien Phus?' Westmoreland replied, 'Yeah, that's it.'[29] Johnson firmly backed Westmoreland in Khe Sanh: the President did not want 'any damn Dinbinfoo!'[30]

'Courageous' does not adequately describe what these two armies did at Khe Sanh. Both sides were shelled out of their minds. They fought with a dogged, almost bestial spirit. The Marines clung like limpets in a rock pool within range of Vietnamese guns, which were entombed in caves on the mountainside to avoid B52 Arc Light and napalm strikes. Several divisions of the People's Army lined the hilltops, and for three months they rocketed and shelled the marine bait locked inside 5 square kilometres of slightly raised valley floor.

The vastly outnumbered Marines lived on airlifted supplies in stinking, sandbagged hovels and daily fired at anything that moved on the slope beyond the barbed-wire rolls that suspended, every morning, communist assailants whose corpses rotted where they hung or were shredded in daily target practice. Marines *defending* were 'like antichrists at vespers';[31] at Khe

Sanh they lived up to their reputation as 'the finest instrument ever devised for killing young Americans'.[32] Their buddies' bodies daily lay piled amid heaps of blood-soaked jungle fatigues outside the makeshift triage room.

When the siege lifted, Khe Sanh was the most bombed scrap of earth in human history. For the Americans, it was all a pointless nightmare. Just as they would abandon Hill 937 (Hamburger Hill), a useless mound for which 630 Vietnamese and seventy Americans died in 1969, so the Marines were ordered to abandon Khe Sanh soon after they claimed it (somewhat negating Westmoreland's later claim that the valley was an 'excellent jumping-off point for cross-border incursions into Laos'.)[33] By then Hanoi's decoy had worked, and the Tet Offensive fell on the southern cities.

The mysterious disappearance of Viet Cong radio signals preceded the New Year holiday. In Phuoc Tuy, on 10 January 1968, the airwaves were silent. Not a whisper, not a crackle, reported 547 Troop's signals intelligence. It was as though the enemy had ceased to exist.

After midnight on 30–31 January 1968 Australia's Major General A. L. MacDonald succeeded Vincent as commander of Australian Force Vietnam, Saigon. MacDonald was a trying blend of puritanism and vindictiveness, a man who commanded by fear and who seemed to revel in the heartless sport of tormenting the subjects of his rather spectacular, if pointless, grudges (it took him twenty-five years to forgive an officer who laughed at him when he dived into a muddy trench in Korea).

General MacDonald arrived in Saigon more than usually grumpy. He moved literally into the line of fire, in a villa right next to the presidential palace. Two hours and fifty minutes into his command, on the morning of 31 January, a series of tremendous explosions ripped through the city. MacDonald looked out his window to see 'a Vietcong gang of bandits trying to gate crash the Palace'.[34] They were a small snatch of the huge forces then concentrated in and around Saigon. 'Nobody, and I repeat nobody … foresaw the magnitude and geographic extent of the Tet Offensive of 1968,' he said later.[35]

At 3 a.m. a truck and a taxi pulled up outside the American Embassy in Saigon. A Viet Cong squad of nineteen commandos tumbled out, blasted a hole in the wall and dashed in firing their AK47s from the hip. Within moments they killed four American soldiers; five Vietnamese policemen fled. A night duty officer locked himself in the fortified code room.

Simultaneously, a great burst of 82mm mortars and 122mm rockets struck Bien Hoa airbase.

South Vietnam awoke to scenes of blood and chaos. The bleary-eyed civilians were confused: had Tet come early? They looked out on running street battles, shells, rockets and mortars as thousands of Viet Cong — 70,000 troops — descended on the urban centres in a series of flashpoints that lit up every city like the lights on a 'pinball machine'.[36] The coordinated violence rippled through Hué, Hoi An, Da Nang, Qui Nhon … The People's Army even rocketed the huge US airbase at Cam Ranh Bay. The highland towns of Ban Me Thuot, Plei Ku and Kon Tum were aflame, and the delta rice hubs of My Tho, Can Tho and Ben Tre were overrun. 'Compatriots and fighters!' shouted the appeal of the National Liberation Front. 'The hour has struck! Let the 14 million South Vietnamese rise up and deal mortal blows at the American aggressors … !'[37]

On poor, wretched Saigon fifteen crack Viet Cong battalions fell in the bloodiest reveille in Tet history: welcome to the Year of the Monkey. One commando unit rammed a car packed with dynamite through the gate of the Saigon radio station, slaughtered a platoon of sleeping guards and grabbed the microphones. But their message declaring Saigon 'liberated' never went to air. South Vietnamese technicians had cut the station's link to the transmitter, 14 kilometres away. At a loss for what to broadcast, the technicians subjected the awakening city to a medley of Viennese waltzes, Beatles songs and military marching music. Surrounded inside the station, the commandos later blew themselves up.

Sent to Long Binh in January, Australia's 2nd and 7th Battalions straddled the enemy's main assault routes to Saigon, in the eye of the storm, with orders to block any attack on the huge logistic base (as part of OPERATION COBURG).

On the first night of Tet, Viet Cong sappers detonated an ammunition dump: fire showered the sky as the Australians raced for their weapon pits. On 31 January waves of communist youth overran the village of Trang Bom, 1,500 metres from the Australian position near Long Binh. The 2nd Battalion reclaimed it that afternoon; the Viet Cong attacked again the next day; again, the Australians reclaimed it, in savage house-to-house fighting.

A company of the 7th Battalion (Delta) went forward to search the area. Lieutenant Dave Webster's platoon advanced to the threshold of an enemy camp, later found to be of battalion strength, and was almost overwhelmed. In the ensuing melée, Webster's men were caught under heavy fire. He radioed back, 'Things look desperate, half my blokes are casualties, we are pinned down, we have almost exhausted our ammunition and they are ranging mortars and M79 on to us and I can see more en[emy] than I have in my callsign.'[38] Webster refused to withdraw, as ordered, as that meant leaving his wounded behind. Back at Delta's headquarters, Lieutenant Ross Ellis, commanding the company's 3rd Platoon, 'literally begged' his company commander, Major Don Paterson, for permission to go forward and help Webster. Eventually, Paterson agreed to send a 'stretcher-bearer party': Ellis led ten men, draped in belts of machine-gun rounds, through 800 metres of jungle towards Webster's platoon. They found Webster's men 'in shock', the wounded lying in agony and their machine guns out of order. 'It was amazing that the complete platoon had not been wiped out,' Ellis said.[39] His medics set to work on the worst cases, and Ellis, alert to a battalion-sized enemy, aligned his machine-gunners with Webster's and radioed for artillery and air support. For one awful moment Ellis accidentally threw white smoke — the colour used for enemy — to mark his own position, and swiftly radioed the error to the guns. In time, the enemy withdrew under the barrage.

Meanwhile the 7th Battalion's Major Graeme Chapman, commanding Charlie Company, moved east as part of a Task Force detachment. On 5 February he sent his three platoons forward to clear a bunker field in which his recce patrols had heard 'many VC talking'. The next day, the Australian lines witnessed a napalm strike a mere hundred metres ahead, which billowed through the jungle but failed to penetrate the enemy tunnels; the Viet Cong reappeared and taunted the Australians with shouts. Then, on 7 February, Lieutenant Mark 'Pinkie' Moloney's platoon advanced through thick forest to clear the high ground. They emerged in enemy territory. 'We were met by silence,' recalled Private Clive Swaysland. 'We were alone among the bunkers.'

The bunkers suddenly came alive. Several of Chapman's men fell. Corporal Graham Griffith twice exposed himself to enemy fire so that the wounded could be saved; Gunner Michael Williams, although wounded in the head, remained at his post and passed vital fire orders to the artillery. 'He protected the radio with his body,' said one witness. Both men received Military Medals.

In the melée some dark impulse seized 'Pinkie' Moloney. According to witnesses, Moloney collected six M72 rockets and charged forward in a single-handed attack on the bunkers. He destroyed several until he staggered and collapsed, with shrapnel wounds from the base of his skull to his buttocks. He lived. 'This was one of the greatest acts of individual bravery I witnessed,' said Swaysland.[40] Indeed, Lieutenant Colonel Eric Smith later recommended Moloney for a Victoria Cross (which was denied).

'I tried to get involved as often as I could, to keep the diggers with me,' Moloney later recalled.[41] Everyone who took part excelled, notably Sergeant Tony Keech, who expertly coordinated the mortars and rolled to the rescue of Private Mike Williams, wounded 10 metres to his left: 'I rolled over, pulled out a shell dressing and I tied it under his chin.'

The battle raged for seven hours, and the Australians routed the enemy bunkers; Eric Smith described that day as 'one of the most brilliant actions fought by an Australian rifle company'.[42] One loss provoked an act of despicable malice: when news of Private Mick Ayres's death, of terrible wounds, reached Australia, anti-Vietnam protesters phoned his parents and said, 'He got what he deserved.' They then daubed the family home in red paint.[43]

Some Australian troops flew into Saigon during Tet. Terry O'Brien and Peter McMillan, of 110 Signal Squadron, were among ten signallers dropped into the furnace of the city, a brown dystopian landscape of 'smoke, bomb craters, cluttered housing but no movement', wrote McMillan. 'Out the window I could see burned out US planes along the airstrip …' Six hundred Viet Cong had been killed in attacks on Saigon airport over the previous days. 'As we taxied in the pilot warned us … to expect sniper fire.'[44]

The Australian signallers were trucked to Phu Thu, where they witnessed surreal scenes: at the wreckage of the racecourse, 300 Viet Cong corpses lay on the grass; at the radio transmitter base, an Australian unit was holding a roll-call in the open: 'a show of strength, typical Army rubbish', McMillan wrote. Here, the ten signallers were issued one pistol, one rifle and a magazine between them, for protection during the 8-kilometre drive in an open truck to the Free World Building.

Thus began their journey, hurtling through this unreal city, 'crashing through barriers and south Vietnamese road blocks, sending drums flying … The streets were a mess, rubble, burned out cars, deserted apart from ARVN soldiers in positions everywhere, behind trees, in ditches, on roofs.'[45] They sped over the wreckage of levelled blocks, ducking to avoid sniper fire, and reached the Free World Building, where they received their rifles. 'Thus ended my first twenty-four hours in Vietnam,' said O'Brien, shaken by the memory forty years later.[46]

Tet came to Phuoc Tuy in a sudden resurgence of violence that mocked the idea of an enemy 'on the run'.

'We have the chance of a thousand years ... to fight for the country's freedom,' declared Le Dinh Nhon, party secretary of the Viet Cong's Provincial Committee, in a pep talk to D445 Battalion on the eve of the onslaught. The troops 'shouted slogans ... almost all soldiers of D445 believed that this was the last battle ... Everyone thought of seeing their homes and families in several days after the victory.' One soldier cried, 'Goodbye to the forest!'[47]

Six hundred Viet Cong troops moved by night along the powerlines towards Ba Ria, the province capital. They entered the town at 5 a.m. on 1 February, and swiftly overran it. The South Vietnamese forces, nominally responsible for urban defence, put up little resistance. The Viet Cong charged into government buildings, police headquarters and an American housing complex, and occupied the hospital, city theatre and cathedral. At dawn the Viet Cong flag flew over Ba Ria.

The fall of Ba Ria in a single night utterly contradicted the impression of provincial security that the army generals had fed to Canberra. In Saigon, in late February, MacDonald repeated Vincent's view that the enemy was virtually defeated in Phuoc Tuy and that Tet had inflicted only slight damage on the province. Yet not only had Ba Ria fallen but also every village had felt the force of the offensive. The Viet Cong cut the road between Vung Tau and Nui Dat for three days, forcing RAAF Caribous to deliver 220,000 kilograms of supplies to the Australian Task Force base at Nui Dat, briefly marooned in the province.[48]

The 3rd Battalion reacted swiftly: at 8.15 a.m., three hours after the Viet Cong entered, a convoy of armoured personnel carriers bearing a hundred Australians under the command of Major Horrie Howard rumbled towards Ba Ria.

A barrage of rocket-propelled grenades and light machine-gun fire welcomed them to the capital. The Australians swiftly dispersed and began prising the enemy from his suburban redoubts. Trained for jungle war, the Australians had no set procedure for 'street fighting in the main town', remarked their commander, the distinguished Korean War veteran Lieutenant Colonel Jim Shelton.[49] Yet house by house, street by street, the Australians and South Vietnamese troops slowly freed Ba Ria, thanks largely to the firepower of the armoured carriers led with exceptional courage by Second Lieutenant Roger Tingley, who laid down massive suppressive fire as the troops bolted across street junctions.[50]

Three Phantom jets strafed and napalmed the residual Viet Cong positions, after which the enemy 'ceased to be effective', noted a glib after-action report. Helicopter strikes set free a hundred trapped civilians and released two personnel carriers disabled during the rescue of an American civilian. At night 500 illumination rounds lit up the city like a theme park, and the air bombardment continued unabated.

Eventually the communist-led forces conceded defeat: on 4 February the D445 was 'ordered to withdraw', stated the official unit history.[51] It acknowledged thirty-five killed and 108 wounded — about accurate — yet claimed a great victory over an 'American' cavalry unit: 'Battalion 445 destroyed twelve tanks.' The armoured carriers, none of which were destroyed, were all Australian.[52] Later, the people of Ba Ria helped to identify Viet Cong captives and warmly thanked the Australians for freeing the city, according to soldiers.


The communist forces fell upon the once-beautiful, ancient capital of Hué with the ferocity of a Mongol horde. The city of 145,000, on the shores of the Perfume River (Song Huong), was the murmuring, once pounding, heart of the democratic nationalist movement, the Dai Viet Party, whose members held a candle for a unified Vietnam free of foreigners and Marx. They would suffer for daring to propose a 'third way': long before Tet, the People's Army had been determined to exact a terrible punishment on the city's recalcitrant population.

On the riverbank rose the seat of the Imperial Palace, the Emperor's Citadel, a 2.5-square-kilometre fortress within whose walls was a mini-city, a maze of roads and zig-zagging moats. The walls were 5 metres high and a metre thick, and enclosed the ancient heart of traditional Vietnam.

On the night of Tet, nine members of the Australian Army Training Team were stationed with South Vietnamese units in and around Hué. It was a night of low fog and faint moonlight, observed Warrant Officer Terry Egan, as he moved south of the city along the snaking Perfume River with his ARVN Reconnaissance Platoon. Egan had earlier received a radio message from Warrant Officer Ernest 'Ossie' Ostara, at Nam Hoa, warning of an impending North Vietnamese offensive.

Egan's platoon dug in and looked back on the lights of the city, a few klicks north. At 3.40 a.m., on 31 January, the 'whole horizon … erupted in a cacophony of gunfire'.[53] Those distant flames contained the last gasp of the Vietnamese Nationalists. Several regiments of People's Liberation Armed Forces (PLAF) rampaged through the city, violated sacred sites and slaughtered civilians. Then they launched a daring night assault on the citadel itself: hundreds of PLAF fighters penetrated the walls and dug in; some were chained to their weapons to prevent them running away. The battle resembled a tropical Stalingrad, with gun emplacements and snipers embedded in the city's ruins. Elements of both North and South Vietnamese units were later accused of mutilating corpses; some of the bodies were found strung up like bleeding harlequins on the city walls. Yet by dawn, to the city's horror, the blue-and-red flag of the Viet Cong flew over the citadel. Hué had fallen in a single night. It would take twenty-five days to reclaim, in one of the bloodiest confrontations of the war: the battle for Hué was a fight for the very soul of Vietnam.

US and Australian advisers guided and often led the South Vietnamese battalions in this most bitter kind of siege warfare. It was a dispiriting business for Warrant Officer Don MacDonald, an adviser to the 4th ARVN Battalion. Under intense mortar fire, the battalion's South Vietnamese commander broke and ran, and the rest of his men 'fled in chaos'. The Americans and Australians were left behind holding 'their weapons and one radio'.[54] This shambles preceded the 'disgusting experience' of the night of 1 February, when the same battalion sat, immobilised with fear, in a buffalo pen. Utterly demoralised, the ARVN troops retreated to divisional headquarters by mingling with long streams of refugees.

Yet other Saigon units fought with great courage. American and South Vietnamese Marines reached the city on 7 February and surged through the streets to the citadel walls. Egan's platoon guided them in. Like predatory beasts, they fought every inch into the maw of the fortress, with heavy losses. US tanks and 'the Thing', or Ontos, a tracked vehicle armed with six recoilless rifles, poured fire onto the North Vietnamese gun emplacements in the walls. At one stage, Egan came upon the isolated ruins of an ARVN Engineer compound in which four Americans lay wounded. Under heavy fire he and an American mate dashed into the compound, lifted the wounded into a disused truck (the only shelter near the chosen landing zone) and called in a dust-off. Meanwhile, several Australian warrant officers joined elite South Vietnamese Ranger units in attacking the citadel walls. They caught the retreating North Vietnamese in the open. Many enemy troops died tied to their weapons. 'It was the first time I had seen a dead enemy soldier tied to a crew-served weapon supposedly to prevent [him] from running ... I let one of them escape back into a tunnel. I was going to kill him for no reason, just for the sheer pleasure of it ... This was after advising the Commanding Officer to burn the sugar cane, as that would get the bastards on the run!'[55]

The battle for Hué raged for weeks. During the assault, a marine died for every metre gained, their bodies slung across the tanks that plied 'Rocket Alley'. On 24 February, under constant pounding, the communist forces' astonishing stand collapsed, and the South Vietnamese flag reappeared over the citadel: communist casualties were 2,642. Tens of thousands of civilians lost their homes; artillery destroyed whole neighbourhoods. Diseases stirred in the putrefying aftermath and, within weeks, the American and Vietnamese medical teams inoculated 35,000 residents against cholera and typhoid. Nevertheless, the battle for Hue was a defining moment for the South Vietnamese forces, many of whom fought with great courage and persistence in routing the People's Army. The victory impressed their Western allies, who now saw the ARVN — at its best — as capable of defeating the North Vietnamese.


The Vietnamese communists visited an atrocity on the people of Hué that went largely unreported in the West and disturbed no television meals in Australia or the USA. To this day many of Australia's former anti-war protesters remain unaware of the Hué massacre.

Mangled in a mass grave in the lime pits near a swamp on the outskirts of the city were found 3,000 civilian corpses, shot, clubbed or bayoneted, their hands tied behind their backs. The North Vietnamese had spent February hard at the grisly task of rounding up and killing anyone whose names appeared on lists of Dai Viet; that is, the middle classes, government officers, teachers, doctors ... anyone who failed to rise against the Saigon regime. Another 2,800 were unaccounted for, suggesting total deaths of almost 6,000. The innocent were summarily shot or, to save ammunition, clubbed and stabbed to death. About 800 were buried alive. Tuan Phan, a

16-year-old boy, was forced at bayonet point to bury his fellow citizens; he later escaped Vietnam and now lives in Cabramatta.[56]

The massacre fulfilled to the letter the Liberation Front Directive of 2 December 1965, sent to regional and district commissars, party and political training schools: 'In areas temporarily under enemy control: We are to exterminate … key and dangerous elements of such parties as the Vietnamese Nationalist Party.'[57]

'The atrocities … by the VC are incredible, and every day reveals mass graves,' wrote Warrant Officer Campbell to his wife. '… the story of what happened is self-evident by the condition of the bodies including many many children. One can understand the hate that lets them strangle military types with wire and decorate the walls with the bodies but to bury alive whole families including the children on no stronger pretext than they refused to take up arms defies the imagination …'[58] After Hué, Campbell lost any shred of respect he had felt for the enemy.

In late February, the Tet Offensive collapsed. The 'liberation of the South' failed. Most southerners had refused to rise; most southern soldiers stayed with their units. The vast majority chose the Saigon Government and the American forces and their allies over the communists.

In March the Americans retaliated, using massive, often indiscriminate force: slicks of gunships, convoys of armour, batteries of artillery and tens of thousands of troops fanned out over the country and laid waste to the resistance. A wisp of smoke was all that remained of Ben Tre; the collateral damage included hundreds of civilian dead. 'It became necessary to destroy the town to save it,' a US major told the journalist Peter Arnett.[59]

The American response to Tet tore the heart out of the National Liberation Front. The Viet Cong lost 45,000 of its finest troops in the conflagration. Hanoi thus expended tens of thousands of its Viet Cong comrades in a deadly litmus test of the political will of South Vietnam. It miserably failed. Yet the sacrifice served Hanoi's political interests: the Politburo would henceforth impose its command on the South, virtually unchallenged by the political opportunism or residual nationalism of its NLF comrades. In this slow loss of power lay the tragedy of the Viet Cong, defeated 'both by their military and political enemies in Saigon, and by their fellows in Hanoi'.[60]

Tet shocked Western television viewers and drew waves of sympathy for Hanoi and the Viet Cong. The cruel irony was that just as the South Vietnamese people most emphatically expressed their support for Saigon and their foreign allies, they lost support where it mattered most: with American taxpayers. Westmoreland looked foolish standing amid the ruins of the city after his victory pledge of 31 January, when he had claimed that Tet was a diversion from the real attack at Khe Sanh. 'The man who thought he was baiting was unable to understand that he had been baited.'[61] 'The Communist leaders,' stated a top-secret cable from Washington to the Australian Government, on 17 February 1968, 'could plausibly claim a great victory ... in that all major towns and cities were penetrated at will.' As a political weapon against the West — Hanoi found to its surprise — Tet mightily succeeded. 'Overseas, the reputation of the Viet Cong has probably never been higher,' Washington concluded.[62]

# Chapter 28
# Coral

'After that lot, why do they keep fighting?' an amazed soldier
asked Captain Phil Davies about the North Vietnamese troops.
'I didn't have an answer,' Davies said.
*Phil Davies, after the battle of Coral.*

If Captain John Bullen did not exist, *M.A.S.H.* would probably have
invented him. In many ways an Australian Hawkeye, Bullen contemplated
the war with a sense of detached dismay; he saw the darkest comedy in
the most inauspicious circumstances. As the officer commanding 1
Topographical Survey Troop, Bullen in fact had a hawk's eye view of things:
his men adapted the field maps to the immediate situation on the ground.

Bullen kept a diary, in which, one night in early May 1968, while
serving as duty officer in the Nui Dat Command Post, he reported a radio
conversation with a helicopter pilot. The pilot had requested permission to
shoot 'six cattle north of Nui Thi Vai'.

'Did you say CATTLE, i.e. cows?' wondered Bullen.

'That is affirmative.'

'Why do you want to shoot them?' Bullen inquired.

'Because they're Viet Cong cattle, that's why.'

'How can you divine the political beliefs of a cow when you're in an
aircraft and the cow's on the ground?'

'If we don't kill the cattle, the Viet Cong will eat them, so let's get in
first.'

'What, and kill the poor beasts in case someone else does? Fair go, mate.'

'May I engage them with machine-gun fire?'

'No. Leave them alone.'

'What! Are you Viet Cong or bloody RSPCA?'

At that moment a more senior officer, Major Ian 'Morelli' Maclean, the operations officer, entered the command post. 'What's the fuss about?' he asked Bullen.

'RAAF want to shoot up some cattle, alleged to be of Viet Cong sympathies,' Bullen explained.

Maclean half-heartedly approved the attack, and Bullen got on the line: 'Hullo RAAF! Permission granted to engage cattle with machine-gun fire.'

'... Am engaging the enemy now.'

The next day the RAAF reported the 'successful slaying' of two cattle, killed in action. The other four escaped, noted Bullen with satisfaction.[1]

In the following days, Bullen observed the build-up to a battle:

Saturday 4th May:
Went to pictures tonight — Peter Ustinov in 'Romanoff &
Juliet'. First 20 minutes were excellent, but then I was called out.
Emergency: Task Force going further north, & not coming back
as expected. Big VC attack expected. Maps needed in a hurry for
the new area of interest ...

Monday 6th May:
Quiet day — perhaps the lull before the storm. Evidence of big
build-up of Viet Cong strength ...

Monday 13th May:
Forward elements of Task Force moved yesterday & today ... to
about 30 km north of Saigon ... a North Vietnamese Army
battalion mounted an assault in the early hours of this morning.
[Our] gun position was partly overrun ... Plenty of excitement
for 12 Field Regiment, this being their 1st month in Viet Nam.

Bullen later inserted: '13/5/68 was the day that Australia nearly suffered its greatest catastrophe of the whole war. Although realized by very few at the time, the Task Force HQ ... came within an ace of being wiped out by

North Vietnamese Army. The political consequences of this would have been disastrous …'[2]

Bullen referred to the battle of Coral, fought 40 kilometres north of Saigon against the finest troops of the People's Army of Vietnam (PAVN). Coral — and Balmoral, which immediately followed — were part of OPERATION TOAN THANG ('Complete Victory'), which ran from April to June 1968 and involved seventy-nine combat battalions and 70,000 American, South Vietnamese, Thai, Korean, Australian and New Zealand troops, many of whom were already out on prolonged operations in the area. TOAN THANG aimed to crush 'Mini Tet', a renewed offensive the destruction of which would be Westmoreland's parting shot: in March the allied supreme commander learned that he was to be returned to America and 'kicked upstairs'.

Tet claimed a greater scalp that month: on 31 March a deeply unnerved President Johnson told the American people: 'I shall not seek, and I will not accept, the nomination of my party for another term as your President.' LBJ also announced a halt in the bombing of North Vietnam and a pledge to open negotiations with Hanoi. The Australian Government was not alerted to the President's decision, which acutely embarrassed the new Prime Minister John Gorton. In fact, the local press read the speech before the Prime Minister, who understandably felt that America, in whose support Australians had expended life and limb fighting, owed its staunch friend some notice of such momentous events.[3] 'This is no way to treat an ally!' Gorton shouted, and severely reprimanded Australia's Washington Ambassador, Sir Keith Waller, for failing to alert Canberra. Gorton expressed Australia's disappointment and great embarrassment that one of America's closest allies should have been given so little opportunity to [study] the President's proposals'.[4]

Westmoreland's announced departure and LBJ's resignation — the President would leave office later that year — emboldened Hanoi. From March to June 1968 the People's Army poured south, at the rate of 12,000 troops a month, to replenish their southern comrades lost during Tet. In tandem, Hanoi launched a new assault on the political front: on 13 May the communist leaders agreed to start 'peace negotiations' in Paris. In the perverse dialectic that now bound Hanoi and Washington, 'peace' meant ratcheting up the war to new levels of slaughter. Like chips in a poker game, tens of thousands of young lives were to be dealt in a series of marathon hands in which the side most willing to prolong the carnage held the aces. Bluff was not enough: the few old men in Hanoi had to show they meant what they said. They were quite prepared to toss a generation of Vietnamese boys and girls — like so many expendable rag dolls — at southern cities in order to entrench their psychological advantage in Paris. During Mini Tet, they ordered 119 attacks on military targets throughout South Vietnam. No fewer than thirteen battalions penetrated Saigon, shelled the city and threatened to rain down a hundred rockets per day for a hundred days, a gesture of indiscriminate slaughter the UN Secretary General U Thant denounced as 'barbarism'. The chief victims were, as always, young Vietnamese soldiers and civilians.

America was caught between the proverbial rock and a hard place: to invade North Vietnam invited domestic outrage and risked provoking China; to withdraw meant humiliation. Hanoi ruthlessly exploited America's political limbo, and the body count rose. In one week during TOAN THANG, the US Army sustained 652 killed and 2,225 wounded — the worst seven days of the American war.

Major General A. L. MacDonald in Saigon determined that Australian troops should participate in these huge 'out of province' actions. In consultation with US Lieutenant General Fred Weyand, he agreed to send two Australian battalions (the 1st and 3rd) to support the defence of Saigon against Mini Tet. The battalion commanders — Lieutenant Colonels Phillip Bennett and Jim Shelton — only received verbal orders before this complex operation, which was placed under the operational command of US II Field Force Vietnam, commanded by Weyand (whose immediate superior was General Westmoreland). This meant that the Australian battalion commanders, who answered directly to the Task Force and not the Americans, had very little influence on the events that followed.

The region proposed for the operation lay on the border of Bien Hoa and Binh Duong provinces, known to the Americans as the 'Catcher's Mitt'. Situated just north of the town of Tan Uyen, it was a transit point for enemy soldiers infiltrating from War Zone D to Saigon. Here, the Australians were supposed to block enemy withdrawals from, and reinforcements to, the capital. The Americans approved the scheme, and instructed two US brigades to operate in a similar role on either side of the Australians. The allies were to be dropped into country thick with communist forces, and used as bait — as 'tethered goats' — to lure the enemy into the open.

The Australians codenamed the area 'Surfers' and subdivided it into Bondi, Newport and Manly areas of operations; at the centre of each a 'fire support patrol base' (e.g. Coral) would be positioned, if necessary. The Vietnamese knew the area not as a homely reminder of Australian beaches or an American baseball glove but as Uyen Hung, a district of Bien Hoa north of the Dong Nai River. It measured about 10 kilometres north to south and 15 kilometres east to west, flat, nondescript land, with low scrub, interspersed with rubber and patches of saplings.

A fire support patrol base is a separately defended location set up temporarily to protect weapons systems, such as artillery and mortars, firing in support of infantry and armoured operations in the allocated area of operations (AO). A well-defended base may take a day to develop; guns, other weapons systems and defence stores would be airlifted in by Chinook and protection provided, usually by an infantry company, wire, sandbags, claymore mines, anti-personnel mines and bulldozed bunds or earthworks to protect weapons and crews. FSPB Coral (named after an Australian officer's girlfriend) was the biggest to be occupied in South Vietnam by 1ATF, and the location allocated was a circle designated originally at around 500 metres in diameter. Units to be sent there included Advanced HQ 1ATF, Tactical HQ 12th Field Regiment commanded by Lieutenant Colonel John Kelly, 102 Field Battery and 161 NZ Field Battery, 1RAR Mortar Platoon (of four mortars) and various detachments, such as Engineers and Signals and a Directional Locating Radar detachment. Each field battery contained six 105mm M2A2 howitzers, which had a range of 11 kilometres.

In early May, Lieutenant Colonels Phillip Bennett and Jim Shelton, commanding the 1st and 3rd Battalions respectively, flew over Surfers on a reconnaissance mission. Both were highly experienced commanders battle-hardened in Korea, yet they would have a particularly tough war in Vietnam.[5] The pilot, fearing ground fire, refused to fly below 1,500 metres. The Australian commanders thus gained a very poor impression of the battlefield. 'It was very hard even to get a feel for the ground,' they agreed. 'We could see very little — and no sign of the enemy.'[6]


A steady flow of intelligence claimed that the Australians faced a multi-regimental threat at Coral. Three reinforced North Vietnamese and Viet Cong divisions were readying for a fresh assault on Saigon, according to intsums (intelligence summaries) in early May. Major Geoff Cameron, Task Force intelligence officer, issued a special warning on 9 May that the 7th NVA Division was active in the area, and again, on 11 May, that North

Vietnamese 'of divisional size' were 'very fit and well equipped', unlike the Viet Cong, who were 'sick, half-starved'.

Bennett and Shelton were at no time issued with written intelligence summaries or assessments and were given only a general verbal briefing at the Task Force Command orders group. The two battalion commanders were sceptical of what they did receive; much previous intelligence had proved groundless. Yet, like Lieutenant Colonel Townsend before Long Tan, they were not privy to top-drawer intelligence: they saw neither US signals intercepts nor the extraordinary report of an American Long Range Reconnaissance Patrol (LRRP), on 10 May, two days before the battle: 'At least eight NVA [North Vietnamese Army] regiments and as many NVA "Infiltration Groups" (each a battalion-plus sized unit) were now known to be operating within or moving into the area west, north and northeast of Saigon,' the 'Lurp' reported.[7] Several of these units, chiefly the 141st and 165th Regiments of the 7th Division, and the independent Dong Nai Regiment, were moving on a collision course with the site designated 'Coral'. 'The total enemy strength was potentially more than a two infantry battalion task force could handle, but the Australian commanders were not unduly worried,' stated a US history.[8]

Shelton's men were responsible for securing the helicopter landing zone. They did so with the army's peculiar skill at creating a mess of things and turning the mess to advantage. In fairness, nobody had actually seen the terrain. Shelton had assumed it was a stretch of low scrub, ideal for a landing zone. On 11 May he sent his second in command, Major Geoff Cohen, to liaise with the headquarters of the 'Big Red One' — the American 1st Infantry Division — a company of which was meant to support the Australian airlift. 'Liaise' does not quite describe the ensuing farce. When Cohen flew in to the US base, the Americans had neither heard of him nor the imminent Australian deployment at 'Bondi'. In fact, the Americans placed Cohen, who arrived straight from operations — dirty and without rank badges — under close house arrest for two hours.[9]

The Americans had other reasons for eyeing Cohen with deep distrust: earlier, they had arrested an Australian found belting east on a motorbike, manifestly AWOL and passing himself off as a colonel. Elsewhere 'Australian' radio messages — Viet Cong fakes — almost duped the Yanks into sending rescue squads.

Eventually cleared, Cohen, the 'guy with the funny hat', set off at the head of a company of US grunts to find Coral. They arrived at dawn the next day, severely delayed, and re-established radio contact with Shelton. Yet the problems continued: a thicket of saplings up to 3 metres tall covered the chosen landing zone. None had foreseen this. 'The whole operation had changed before we got there,' recalled Shelton, on whose shoulders the multi-battalion airlift weighed.[10] In such a huge airlift, involving so many units, there was no time to change the site. So Shelton ordered the first slick of Hueys — Major Bert Irwin's Bravo Company — to land a few hundred metres south-east of Cohen's position, patrol back to the original landing zone, chop down the trees and clear it for the rest of the force. This convolution added greater delays. 'We just got later and later,' recalled Shelton.[11] He unfairly blamed himself; yet if one must seek blame, it began further up the food chain, and in the confluence of accidents and errors that created a state, familiar to every soldier, of SNAFU: 'Situation Normal, All Fucked Up'.


The airlift began: the gunner reconnaissance parties flew in to Coral on the morning of 12 May. Lieutenants Ian 'Scrubber' Ahearn (of 102 Battery) and Rod Baldwin (New Zealand 161 Battery) expected to find the landing zone secured and Shelton's men *in situ*. Instead, they met American infantry dressed to kill, in flak jackets and helmets, with eyes ablaze. Air strikes pounded the area. Asked about the strength of the enemy, one Yank drawled, 'This whole place is Indian country.' The airlift had 'stirred up a hornet's nest', Major Cameron later recalled.[12] That, of course, was the intention.

Shortly the air filled with the sound of Chinooks, each with a howitzer dangling underneath: the first guns of the 161 Battery. Baldwin marked out the New Zealand position nearby, but Ahearn had difficulty establishing his battery's location. He radioed the regimental reconnaissance party under the gunner major, Brian Murtagh, to find the precise location. Ahearn asked Murtagh to throw a smoke grenade, took a compass bearing on the distant smoke, and led his small party out through the American infantry and finally located Murtagh 1.5 kilometres away — an unplanned delay that put Ahearn's men at great risk.

On the smudge of earth dubbed 'Coral', Major Murtagh, designated commander of the base, tried to stamp some order on the encircling chaos. Murtagh, second in command of 12th Field Regiment, probably lacked the experience to coordinate a fire support base of such scale: he had chosen to place the two artillery batteries wide apart; the New Zealanders were 1,500 metres to the west, at the original designated grid reference. Murtagh defended the 'enormous gap' between the two batteries as necessary to cover the hundreds of troops in between. Dubious, to say the least, Ahearn 'had no prerogative to advise', and off he went to recce his area. In the rubber trees, incidentally, Ahearn fell upon 'a hundred freshly dug weapon pits', an AK47 bullet and Ho Chi Minh lollies.[13] The discovery bothered no one; Murtagh carried on unperturbed.

Soon the Chinooks bearing Ahearn's guns of 102 Battery landed, followed by the first troops of 1st Battalion (the exact reverse of the usual sequence in the Operational Order). All afternoon, the Chinooks and Iroquois landed more troops, as plumes of napalm rose across the horizon to the south-west, amid the dull boom of US artillery. An air of utter confusion breathed through these preparations. Some units were sent to the original landing pad, others to the hastily located 'new' one. Murtagh ordered 3rd Battalion's Delta Company, commanded by Major Peter Phillips, 300 metres north-west, to block a route into Coral; yet this left the fire support base with no infantry protection. Tony Hammett's company (Delta, 1st Battalion) was sent about 1,500 metres north. During this peregrination, Hammett's men passed two North Vietnamese skeletons sitting up, as though at rest, still wearing their grey uniforms. 'This is the guy you are fighting,' Corporal Paul 'Richo' Richardson told his men. 'That's his dress and gear … get a good idea of it.'[14]

Meanwhile, Captain Michael Bindley did his best to coordinate the landing zone. Yet nerves frayed. Soldiers noticed a 'funny' — as in strange — atmosphere so unlike the usually boisterous mood. Tempers flared in the intense heat. One private threatened to shoot another, after a dispute, and a New Zealander collapsed from heat exhaustion. When a US observer asked why the man's buddies had not called a dust-off, Bindley replied, 'I can't explain New Zealanders to you, but I'm sure he'll be all right.'[15]

Later that afternoon, an American brigadier general landed unannounced in a sparkling new helicopter with horns painted on the nose. Bindley, caked in red soil, scruffy and tense, snapped to attention. The US general warned the Australians of the heavy enemy presence in the area; his unit had suffered hundreds of casualties. His last words were: 'Tell your commanding officer that you won't need to go looking for them. They'll come looking for you.' (Bennett has no recollection of this exchange being reported to him.) The GIs accompanying the general kept their heads down. 'You don't wanna go

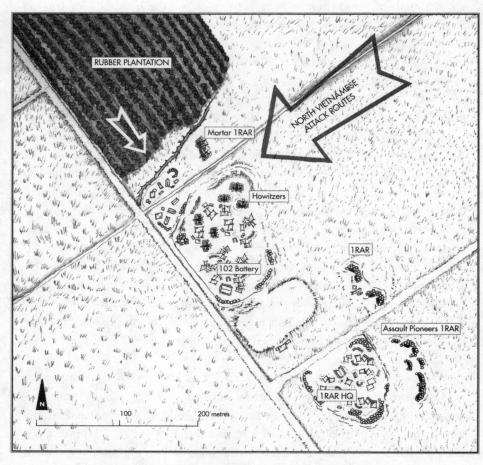

RUBBER PLANTATION

NORTH VIETNAMESE ATTACK ROUTES

Mortar 1RAR

Howitzers

1RAR

102 Battery

Assault Pioneers 1RAR

1RAR HQ

N

100    200 metres

BATTLE OF CORAL: FIRST NIGHT ATTACK ON EASTERN AREA OF
FIRE SUPPORT BASE CORAL, 12–13 MAY 1968

out there, man,' shouted a huge Negro, waving at the scrub as he flew away. 'It's tiger country.'

The Australians did go out there. Near twilight, three infantry companies of 1st Battalion were fairly scattered all over 'tiger country': Major Colin Adamson's Alpha Company went about a thousand metres north-east of Coral, to a bamboo thicket; Hammett's men were a kilometre to the north; and Captain Bob Hennessy's Bravo Company headed a thousand metres south — closer than previously instructed — as Bennett issued new orders to his riflemen to move their ambush positions nearer Coral to stiffen the inadequate base defence (company commanders on the ground don't recall receiving these orders). Charlie Company went 2 kilometres south to protect the road into the Coral area. Inside Coral, Bennett's headquarters was being quickly laid out, with limited underground space. Yet great care was taken to confirm grid references for all subunits.

Meanwhile, Lieutenant Tony Jensen cast a troubled eye over his mortar platoon. His men were perilously exposed. Corporal Bob Hickey's mortars, for example, were about 50 metres from the edge of a three-metre-high rubber plantation on the edge of the perimeter, easy pickings for a stealthy assailant. (Hickey, incidentally, had been transferred from a rifle platoon to mortars on account of his wife's nightmares. Apparently she had complained to an army chaplain of recurring, extremely vivid dreams of her husband's death; she appealed to have him moved to a safer unit. Her nightmares may have returned had she known Hickey's position that night.)

Worse, the mortars and guns lacked the usual infantry protection. Jensen's platoon commander, Captain Hugh McInally, expressed extreme disquiet at the absence of protective troops. 'Eventually people will learn that mortars can't protect themselves!' McInally said, and strode off to do something about it.[16] Jensen, too, went to find the infantry; he received dubious assurances the Australian soldiers were somewhere 'in front'.

At the going down of the sun FSB Coral was half-completed and badly exposed. No barbed wire or claymores were laid; little overhead protection had been erected; and the radio net and telephone system were incomplete. Jensen and Ahearn, who had tied in their machine guns' arcs of fire, were unable to locate any of the 3rd Battalion infantry who were supposed to be protecting Coral (they were stationed to the west). Despite this, all defensive activity ceased at the evening stand-to, leaving the artillery 'very underprepared', recalled Second Lieutenant Matt Clelland.[17] The gunners at least had time to dig weapon and sleeping pits to about 1.5 metres deep, and the mortar men fell exhausted into their shellscrapes — a bare 60 centimetres deep — in fitful sleep; the sentries stood guard, without the faintest idea of what moved out there in the twinkling darkness.

The North Vietnamese units had been watching the Australians all day. The confused airlift proceeded under the very eyes of two North Vietnamese regiments camped nearby.[18] And now, as darkness closed, with a downpour covering the sound of their footfalls, hundreds of People's Army troops crept softly past the scattered Australian infantry out in the scrub and dug in within a few hundred metres of the Coral perimeter.

As midnight approached, the rain stopped. A sliver of moonlight penetrated the light cloud cover. Silhouettes were discernible in the distant scrub. The cackle of chickens and a woman's far cry interrupted the dreadful silence. Around midnight, Jensen's mortars had a brief contact with a North Vietnamese recce patrol ... then the silence returned.

Out in the darkness the Australian infantry had a few contacts, but nothing to suggest the size of the North Vietnamese forces then flowing through them. The biggest contact occurred at 2 a.m., 2 kilometres north of Coral, when an enemy patrol walked into an ambush sprung by Delta Company. The enemy retaliated with RPGs, hitting the trees above Second Lieutenant Dick Utting's platoon. 'It was the worst night of the war for us,' said Gordon Alexander, Delta Company's FO.[19] 'Half of Dick's Platoon was hit — two killed instantly and ten wounded. Private Larry Shepard, with a terrible head wound, was choppered out with the wounded but died later that night.' A badly wounded Australian's horrific screams in the darkness 'put the fear of Christ up my blokes', one soldier recalled. Another received shrapnel in both legs, the right arm, stomach and base of his penis. 'That bastard's made me into a hermaphrodite!' he shouted, as he surveyed his torn body.

Back at Coral the loudspeaker on the gun position boomed out: 'Fire Mission Battery Contact!' The gunners ran to their guns to answer the call for fire; round after round landed on the grid reference ahead of Delta Company's men. Then the dust-off Hueys flew in to pull out the wounded; as the stretcher-bearers loaded the groaning men aboard, helicopter gunships circled above, pumping fire into the surrounding bush. A short lull followed, during which 102 Battery pointed three guns north to give instant support to the infantry, should the North Vietnamese return. Meanwhile, Bennett alerted his fire control centre for artillery and helicopter gunship support, battlefield illumination aircraft and fixed-wing air strikes against the attackers. In short, the contact better prepared the Australians for the possibility of a massed attack.

At about 2.30 a.m. the North Vietnamese struck: Chicom rockets, rocket-propelled grenades and mortar rounds pounded the Coral perimeter; every Australian dived into his shallow pit, squinting into the blackness. Somewhere out there, hundreds of North Vietnamese were creeping up to the edge of the base. Some nestled, undetected, metres from Lance Bombardier Andy Forsdike's machine gun.

The bugles sounded. Flashes of green tracer — fired to mark their assault lanes — preceded the charge. And then the North Vietnamese arose: a line of shadows materialised 50 metres in front of the Australian base, and rows of 150 to 200 enemy soldiers, in groups of ten, ran at the mortar and artillery positions and surged towards the bunds that protected the Australian guns. They fired their AK47s wildly into the air as they approached. In the first five minutes both Australian battery and forward machine-gun posts were 'overrun'. One gun was already in North Vietnamese hands, and the mortar line was 'a chaotic jumble of men and stabs of light from the muzzles of small arms'.[20]

In the moment's grace between recognition and death, the Australians reacted with astonishing speed. 'Our training kicked in' was the soldiers' refrain. Forsdike's machine-gunners swung their weapons on the attackers. Jensen's mortar crew leaped into their shellscrapes and opened fire. Enemy swirled around Forsdike's men: the young bombardier's M60 jammed. He wrestled with it. Two men fell to his rear: one dead, one wounded. Forsdike's survival strains belief.

The North Vietnamese tore into the camp, hurled grenades over the bunds, jumped into the gun placements and sprayed rifle fire at the gun crews. At number 6 gun, Matt Clelland 'emptied his pistol' into the enemy.[21] Gunner Christopher Sawtell was shot at point-blank range. Private Greg Ayson found himself weaponless, 'crawling around the pit armed with a machete'. He later grabbed Private Mick Grimes's rifle, as Grimes withdrew, wounded (a North Vietnamese corpse was later found wearing Grimes's spare jungle greens).

The crew of number 6 gun, led by Max Franklin, were forced to abandon their position, as the North Vietnamese raced over the bund and ransacked the gun area — a sandbagged hole in the ground — stealing food, ration-packed chocolate and clothes.

The enemy ran straight towards the muzzles of the three guns that had been — luckily — turned to shell the earlier contact. The Australian gunners responded by firing over open sights — straight at the oncoming Vietnamese troops: Sergeant John Stephens's howitzer crew shot splintex, or 'beehive' rounds, each packed with 7,200 arrow-shaped darts, directly into the enemy mass, for which Stephens received a Military Medal. One North Vietnamese soldier jumped in front of the cannon muzzle, and was obliterated. The gun crews further back tumbled out of their pits to join the fight. Off on the right flank, near battalion headquarters, Lieutenant Les Tranter's anti-tank platoon sent a firestorm of shrapnel at the enemy, while the guns of the 161 Field Battery and the 3rd Battalion mortars, from their position 1,500 metres west, began to pound the enemy in response to calls from the mortar platoon.

Overhead was a scene of blazing congestion: US gunships hovered and dived, sending a rain of bullets into the darkness. Then out of the night loomed a kind of spaceship, nicknamed Spooky, or Puff the Magic Dragon, a C47 Dakota, ablaze with flares and dazzling lights. This diabolical aircraft circled the battlefield and spewed a waterfall of fire to the earth. Each of its three miniguns could strike a circle 10 metres in diameter with 400 bullets at a range of 1.5 kilometres in a single four-second burst. The guns made a 'terrible, tearing sound', recalled the signaller Alan 'Jack' Parr, who guided Spooky down on the mortar command net. Above everything illumination flares attached to little parachutes swung earthward, casting monstrous shadows on a world that seemed to rock back and forth in the dangling light.

By now the North Vietnamese had captured Jensen's mortars. They swung them around and tried to fire back on the Australians, at a near-vertical cannon trajectory (they even attempted to dismantle and carry one mortar away). The mortar rounds popped harmlessly beyond the base. In the chaos, Jensen saw one option: to call splintex across his own position. Jensen first had to convince Battalion HQ then arrange with Ahearn in 102 Battery for the lethal fire. 'Stay down!' he shouted to his men, then flattened in weapon pits. 'Splintex coming in.' He radioed the signal, and a shower of little daggers swept across his position, puncturing wood, flesh and metal, and pinning one Vietnamese soldier to an Australian mortar.

From their distant harbours, out in the scrub, the infantry looked back on Coral. 'I think the Fire Support Base is being attacked,' Lieutenant John Salter told Corporal Richardson.

'Oh, jolly good,' replied Richardson. 'Who is up there protecting them?'

'No one,' Salter answered.[22]

The truth blackened the joke. From their distant redoubts the troops beheld 'a firework display', recalled Lieutenant Geoff Bowcock, which seemed to draw down from the sky the 'beautiful scarlet rain of encircling miniguns' amid the 'hard white glow' of the flares. Flickering in and out were the anti-collision lights of helicopter gunships, which hovered above Coral like great black bats.[23]

Both sides 'fought like threshing machines', wrote Adamson later. The enemy withdrew under devastating firepower and was 'severely mauled', said Bennett the next morning: the gunships and fighters, the bravery of the Australian mortar and artillerymen, and the efficient operation of the 1st Battalion command post (notably the fire support control centre) had saved the base from being completely overrun. The ashen-faced Australian survivors rested amid the shambles, many in a state of shock. The wounded were airlifted to Vung Tau, and Staff Sergeant Terry Loftus packed the personal effects of the dead for dispatch to Australia. Somewhere in the jungle hundreds of North Vietnamese soldiers dragged their comrades to makeshift field hospitals, and the 'strange, mournful mutter of the battlefield' subsided into a birdless silence.[24] On the earth before Coral lay hundreds of pairs of Ho Chi Minh sandals. Fifty-two NVA bodies were recovered and buried in a mass grave.


North of the Coral it had been a desperate night for Delta Company. As Tony Hammett's men secured the landing zone for the removal of the two dead, Geoff Bowcock's platoon had another enemy contact. Hammett decided to respond immediately by attacking in company strength with artillery cover and a gun-ship strike (the latter went awry). Hammett ordered 'Fix bayonets!' to an incredulous assault group and the company advanced.

'It was the most remarkable sight,' said Gordon Alexander, 'with John Salter's Platoon in front in extended line; Company HQ Group next and the remnants of Dick Utting's platoon behind; moving forward across open ground; firing from the hip; with artillery being 'walked' around 200 metres to the front as we went forward. We had advanced about 75 metres across the open field. Suddenly, on our left flank, a figure popped out of an old weapon pit and fired at the company line. Corporal "Greasy" Jones turned and made an incredibly brave personal attack on three NVA in the weapon pit.'

Jones continued firing until he took out the enemy position. Delta Company suffered not a single casualty in the attack, and the depression from the terrible night lifted. 'As we surveyed the battle scene,' recalled Alexander, 'we all felt confident and on top of the situation.'[25] Salter's courage in leading the forward platoon during the attacked earned him a Military Cross.

There followed two days of patrolling, punctuated by sudden, platoon-strength clashes. On the 14th the Australians had nine contacts — the highest number during the operation.

Two men received Distinguished Conduct Medals during this 'lull': Lance Corporal David Griffiths who, although shot in both arms, attacked three enemy soldiers and captured two, before being medevaced; and Private Dick Norden. Norden's action prompted Sir Roden Cutler VC to remark quietly, when decorating him, 'I do not know what one has to do these days to win a Victoria Cross.' Caught in an ambush, Norden had rushed forward under covering fire to retrieve two Australian wounded — his section commander and forward scout — shot 20 metres ahead.[26] As he ran, Norden, himself wounded, shot a Vietnamese soldier, then, out of ammunition, grabbed the dead man's rifle and continued firing until he reached his section commander, whom he dragged to safety. Norden then raced forward, again under fire, and reached the now dead Australian scout, whose corpse a Viet Cong rifleman was using as a shield. Norden killed this soldier, returned to his section, ran forward a third time with grenades and cleared the area so that the scout's body could be retrieved. Norden single-handedly saved his section commander's life and reversed the enemy's advantage 'with complete disregard for his own safety'.[27]


By nightfall on 15 May Coral was better fortified. Two days earlier, Bennett had recalled all his companies to the base, around which they formed a battalion defensive position. Dannert wire, sandbags, overhead cover and claymore mines were flown in, but the Task Force elements, located behind Bennett's headquarters, had prior use of these. The infantry was left to scrounge for wire and defences from Task Force and US units. As a result, some units remained exposed: Lieutenant Neil Weekes recalls having 'one strand of concertina wire' in front of his platoon[28] and a big gap in the perimeter between his men and the next platoon to the left.

The night was beautiful, moonlit, 'a bloody perfect night' for an attack, thought Corporal Richardson, as he dozed off in his hole. The People's Army agreed. At 2.30 a.m. on the 16th the North Vietnamese returned to Coral. Adamson's Alpha Company bore the brunt of it: 400 craters were later found inside his perimeter. The men hugged the earth in their weapon pits as shrapnel hurtled about overhead. 'All I could see was a purple haze,' recalled

Corporal James Archbold, a national serviceman decorated for heroism, who witnessed the terrifying march of enemy mortar rounds falling up and down the Australian lines. A direct hit on one pit ripped off the sandbag cover and bent the barrel of the soldier's rifle, which was hanging on a peg to protect it from the mud. The occupant suffered ruptured eardrums, no more.

The familiar pattern of green tracer — 'like a king-sized spider web', remembered Sergeant Gus Ballentine — signalled another enemy charge. Everyone dived into their weapon pits, as though 'a dingo had appeared next to a rabbit warren', said Captain Phil Davies. Ahearn, woken from a blissful sleep, and Lieutenant Bob Lowry ran to their battery command post 10 metres away, where they found the staff, 'with eyes like organ stops … frozen in time'. A mortar round almost followed them in the door, blowing away the sandbags at the entrance. Ahearn shouted: 'Fire mission battery', and they got into position.[29]

Once more the chill bleat of Vietnamese bugles touched the marrow of every man. This time, the Australians were ready. Bennett's headquarters and his fire support control centre were poised to send a firestorm at the enemy. When the forward artillery observers called in 'unlimited' fire support, no less than sixty cannons, pre-planned air strikes and even naval gunners opened up on the enemy charge. The result was carnage: hundreds of North Vietnamese troops ran at the combined firepower of almost nine gun batteries, eight mortars and three helicopter gunships.

Overhead, like a tiny sparrow buffeted inside a thundercloud, Flying Officer Roger Wilson flitted about in his little Cessna 'Bird Dog'. An RAAF pilot attached to the US Air Force, Wilson had perhaps the most dangerous job in the skies. As a forward air controller (FAC), his job was to fly in low, spot ground targets and fire smoke rockets to identify them. The Phantom jets then bombed the smoking target: the FAC served as the eyes of the fighters. Wilson described Coral that morning as 'the worst I'd seen. There was so much artillery coming in, we couldn't plot it so we just flew around hoping it would miss us — the Big Sky Theory, that's called.'[30] By the light of the flares, Wilson guided in repeated napalm strikes.[31] The soldiers lit hexamine tablets in their firing pits, seen from the air but out of enemy view, giving the fighter pilots a clear line of lights from which to coordinate their attack.[32] Within moments three silver-bellied Phantom fighters armed with 113-kilo bombs and napalm bore down on the battlefield with 'a banshee scream', their tailpipes aglow.[33]

'After that lot, why do they keep fighting?' an amazed soldier asked Captain Davies. 'I didn't have an answer,' Davies said.[34] Bennett himself later praised the courage of the North Vietnamese: they were 'exceptionally good' soldiers, he said, 'the highest standard we met … in Vietnam'.[35]

Indeed, only by penetrating the Australian lines could the enemy escape the terror in the sky. 'They came with satchel charges and bangalore torpedoes blowing my wire,' said Adamson.[36] Weekes's platoon desperately defended the widening 150-metre gap in the Coral perimeter, at which the Vietnamese ran like men possessed. Weekes walked in artillery to within 50 metres — 2,500 rounds were fired around his position that night. His machine-gunners spat belt after belt into the gap (one private cooled his machine gun by urinating on it). Anticipating hand-to-hand combat, Weekes ordered, 'Fix bayonets!' Nobody moved. 'Hell,' someone cried back. Weekes repeated the order. They fixed bayonets — but were soon forced to abandon part of their position, in which the Vietnamese quickly planted a machine gun and started spraying Coral.

Bennett, who carefully monitored the company radio net, called Weekes and proposed the use of mortars at close range. The decision, however, rested with Weekes. In an echo of Buick at Long Tan, Weekes agreed and called mortar fire down on himself — the third time in Vietnam an Australian soldier had called fire on his own position. Bennett warned that it may cause Australian casualties. 'I have no alternative,' Weekes replied. His men dived underground as the 'friendly' mortars, perfectly positioned, burst just metres away. The shrapnel lightly wounded one Australian, yet destroyed the Vietnamese machine-gunner. Twenty enemy dead were later found around Weekes's platoon, which lost almost a third of its men. Weekes later received the Military Cross for extraordinary heroism. If the Vietnamese had broken through Weekes's platoon, 'they would just spread out inside the base and you've lost control', explained Wally Thompson, the much-admired company sergeant major, years later. 'The platoon and company held, so the battalion held.'[37] By 5.30 a.m. the surviving Vietnamese troops fell back in disarray.


As dawn approached, terror and loss forged moments of Australian brutality. When a lone North Vietnamese soldier burst into flames (the rockets in his pack had ignited), he staggered about trying to beat out the fire. 'Everybody concentrated on him,' recalled one Australian corporal, 'and he was being hit all over the place. He … went up in a big flash. We all cheered.'[38]

A blood-red sun rose on the stillness of the battlefield; clouds of flies blew about and the parachute flares were still smoking. 'The air stank of explosives, kerosene and dirt, and not a bird was seen or heard,' wrote Adamson.[39]

Brigadier Hughes, the Task Force commander, emerged in the sunlight and dusted himself down. Hughes had spent part of the night between the rear wheels of his American caravan; he now looked forward to a period of rest and convalescence, in Singapore.

The burial parties again set to work. 'We had to roll bodies over with toggle ropes to make sure they weren't booby trapped,' Bombardier John Dellaca recalled.[40] The Australians buried a further thirty-four corpses in a mass grave. Sixteen Australians died in the two attacks on Coral (eleven in the first attack on 13 May), and forty-seven were wounded, including Second Lieutenant Tim Fischer, who nursed a deep shrapnel wound; Private John Eaton sat by and patched up the future Deputy Prime Minister of Australia. A few men suffered mental collapse: one private was found standing in a weapon pit amid North Vietnamese bodies, brandishing his rifle at anyone who approached and shouting, 'Stay away ... they're mine.' Another lad grew so jittery that he threw grenades at the slightest provocation. Both were sent home.[41]

The Australian wounded were first medevaced to the US Field Hospital at Bien Hoa and later transferred to the Australian Field Hospital at Vung Tau where Colonel (Dr) Don Beard dreaded the sound of a chopper landing, 'because I didn't know what dreadful injuries it would be bringing me,' he wrote on 16 May.[42] One badly wounded private 'looked up at the stars and his thoughts went straight ... to the girl he was going to marry when he completed national service'. Dr Beard operated on 'nine boys' on the 17th, with serious shrapnel wounds to the legs, chest, face, arms or abdomen. The wounds of one patient, Sergeant Austin Credlin, had nothing to do with the battle; they were the result of being gored and tossed in the air by a thundering herd of water buffalo. On the 20th 'I had a huge operating list'; thirteen men awaited surgery. 'This was going to be a battle!' Seven more cases arrived that night. Utterly exhausted, Dr Beard's mind started playing tricks. 'There were still a lot of planes flying about & I wondered if one were measured for me,' he wrote. Underlining that sentence, he added: 'I really don't know what it means. It is a terrible feeling to have written something in cold blood and not to understand the meaning behind it ...'[43]

# Chapter 29
# Balmoral

It's a measure, I guess, of [Hanoi's] skill, that they were able to
indoctrinate these young kids. I never saw the grey eminences
who were directing them; we only saw the young kids …
*Major Peter Phillips, of the enemy at Balmoral.*

With Brigadier Hughes in Singapore on R&R, Colonel Don Dunstan took temporary charge of the Task Force at Coral. A leader of uncommon gifts, Dunstan commanded with few words and a winning smile. A shrewd delegator, he 'knew how to be lazy when it was sensible to be lazy', remarked one colleague. He quickly endeared himself to the troops, not least by abandoning the 'dry' policy at Coral and ordering crates of beer; in error, the US helicopters delivered sarsaparilla, then Reschs Diet Lager.

Dunstan decided (with MacDonald's approval) to move an Australian battalion 4.5 kilometres north of Coral, 'bang under the noses' of another North Vietnamese regiment. He meant to immerse Australian troops deep inside enemy territory and provoke another battle. The Australians designated the site Fire Support Base Balmoral, in the Newport area of operations set in undulating 'golf course' terrain bounded by rubber plantations just east of the village of Binh My. There the Australians would deploy another 'tethered goat' tactic — in which the troops were sent to a remote fire support base as 'bait' to lure enemy attacks — as part of Operation TOAN THANG, the broad defence of Saigon that involved tens of thousands of Free World troops.

Dunstan chose Lieutenant Colonel Jim Shelton's 3rd Battalion for the job. At first, Shelton resisted the order. 'I was very concerned about it,' he later said.[1] Shelton plainly did not want to go. He stressed his usefulness in the battalion's present location, west of Coral. Dunstan listened, 'smiled in the lovely way he did', Shelton recalled, and said, 'You had your chance at [Fire Support Base] Coogee. Now move.'[2]

On 24 May Shelton moved. Before he left, he made two critical decisions. He welcomed the support of Australian tanks — the first time in Vietnam that Australian tanks and infantry were to attack the enemy in bunkers — and he decided on a 'cold' insertion. Instead of flying his battalion in American-style, thus alerting the enemy to its arrival, Shelton sent his advance troops to Balmoral on foot ... quietly. Shelton 'was determined not to repeat the mistakes at Coral', said Major Geoff Cohen.[3] That morning two companies — about 200 men — plus armoured carriers, set off for the new base. After a few skirmishes on the way, they arrived that afternoon, and immediately started digging in and laying wire.

The ten Centurion tanks (plus a Centurion bridgelayer and two armoured recovery vehicles) of the 1st Armoured Regiment had roared into Coral a day earlier, after a long journey from Nui Dat. They had crossed many brittle wooden bridges that swayed and nearly buckled under their immense weight. Dunstan shared Shelton's faith in tanks, chiefly their bunker-destroying capacity, which Dunstan had witnessed at Bougainville during World War II. In time, the Australian troops would feel similar affection for these 52-ton monsters, each armed with quick-firing 20-pounder ordnance and three machine guns (one .50 and two .30 calibre). The tanks carried sixty-two cannon rounds and thousands of machine-gun rounds.

Their arrival raised many unanswered questions: would they withstand mines and recoilless rifles, which shattered armoured carriers? How would they manouevre in muddy jungle terrain? Would the 'tankies' and the infantry — two very different cultures — get on? Nobody knew.

On 25 May four tanks, under the command of Second Lieutenant Mick Butler, clanked and strained towards Balmoral, under the protection of 1st Battalion troops, across country bristling with North Vietnamese units. They had a few sharp contacts en route, which were easily beaten off. Their 'intimate' fire support impressed Captain Bob Hennessy's escorting company (then reduced to two platoons to facilitate their return to Coral by helicopter); the infantry, warming to the tank crews, known as 'turret heads' and 'gasoline cowboys'. The tanks reached Balmoral in the late afternoon, and were swiftly concealed inside wire and mines. As night came, they rolled forward in pairs and the infantry companies occupied the ground between them.

With the tanks' arrival, Fire Support Base Balmoral was complete. As at Coral, the Australians were the worm at the end of the line, bobbing about in enemy-held territory: picture a lightly elevated circle of scrub about 300 metres in diameter, enclosed in rolls of catwire and mines, and guarded by 400 infantrymen deeply entrenched in sandbagged holes. In the centre were the 3rd Battalion's Regimental Aid Post, ammunition store, a fuel dump and Shelton, in his little underground headquarters, keeping constant vigil by radio contact with each of his subunits.

As darkness fell, Shelton prepared psychologically for the likely clash ahead. Beneath the commander's cheerful demeanour lay an innovative officer of resilience and mental toughness. Among his innovations that day were Shelton's Mortar Marauders, the M125A1 mortar carriers, which ran short, fast scoots around the Balmoral perimeter intended to fool the enemy into thinking these were the only armoured vehicles at the base.

Fired up to emulate the 'great victory' of the North Vietnamese 141st Regiment against the Australians at Coral — so communist sources claimed — the 165th Regiment attacked, as expected, in the early hours of 26 May. By then, the Australians were almost impatient for action. At 3.45 a.m. Shelton was on the phone in his bunker when Major Ian McLean, the Task Force operations officer, interrupted, 'Sir, we don't have to wait any longer ... they are here now.'[4]

The usual mortar and rocket barrage heralded the assault, along with a diversionary attack from the south — a classic example of Mao's dictum, 'Make a noise in the east; attack in the west'. Vietnamese troops tried to blow the southern defences with bangalore torpedoes, but were cut down by a claymore mine.

The real attack swept down from the north-east, as hundreds of Vietnamese shadows crept across the 'fairway', a brazen attack over open country that amazed the Australians. It seemed the enemy thought the northern defences were more vulnerable. Butler had privately disagreed with Shelton's decision, in consultation with Captain Bruce Richards, the APC troop leader, to position the tanks at the northern edge of the perimeter: surely the enemy would not attack over a field as smooth as 'a billiard table'? Yet here they were, in the open, utterly fearless, and running straight for the Australian base.

Visibility was good: illumination rounds lit up the battlefield like a football oval during a night match. The tanks' canister rounds, as well as mortar and artillery, cut down the first wave of Vietnamese 'shock troops'; Shelton then radioed for 'Spooky' and the US gunships, whose immense firepower broke up the rest of the attack. By 5 a.m. the North Vietnamese melted back into the forests, dragging away their killed and wounded. At dawn the Australians cleared the battlefield and buried the dead.

That day a unit of 1st Battalion troops launched the first combined Australian tank–infantry assault since World War II. Major Tony Hammett's Delta Company — deeply nervous at the prospect of an unrehearsed tank attack — and a tank troop led by Captain Gerry McCormack (part of Major Peter Badman's C Squadron) set off to destroy the enemy bunker system encountered the day before on the way to Balmoral. This first real test worried the soldiers, who thought these great, noisy machines would simply warn the enemy. 'We might as well be banging drums,' said one digger.[5]

The four tanks and two support vehicles rumbled away at the centre of three platoons, which moved forward in staggered zigzag file. At 10.30 a.m. the formation stopped, the men brewed up, and Hammett called in an air strike — delivered by Australia's Canberra bombers — on the nearby enemy bunkers. After noon, John Salter's platoon, to the right front of the company, made the first contact, on a large enemy bunker position. Gerry McCormack's tank, travelling immediately behind Company HQ Group, moved forward towards Salter's platoon. As it reached Company HQ Group, an RPG round hit just under the turret: 'It was a miracle Tony Hammett and I weren't hit,' said Gordon Alexander. 'Gerry had fixed a black umbrella above his Commander's hatch (placed there against regulations but for comfort under the blazing sun) and it was completely shredded. Gerry himself, lucky to escape unscathed, made the fastest close hatch you could imagine.'[6]

The tanks opened fire. Like hundreds of machetes working at once, the pellets hacked a field of fire through the jungle. For three hours the tanks sent round after round into the heavily concealed bunker field, or rolled forward and crushed the bunkers under their tracks.[7] In one case, three rocket-propelled grenades struck a tank. 'You'd be lying there and hear a clang!' recalled Sergeant Ray Curtis. 'It would be an RPG deflected off the tank, and the bloody rocket would whiz off into the scrub.'[8] Then the infantry, went in, backed up by a flame-thrower that shot tongues of flame into the bunkers, roasting any residual life. An unknown number of North Vietnamese were shot, burned or crushed under the tank tracks. There were no Australian casualties.

The Australian units destroyed at least fourteen bunkers before Lieutenant Colonel Phillip Bennett ordered them back to Coral. The success of the first tank operation prompted elation. 'A tremendous feeling' welled up in the company, reported Hammett. The tanks had proved 'brutally effective', the official historians stated; many soldiers would have perished had they attacked the bunkers on their own. The tanks' performance at Balmoral laid to rest any arguments against their use in jungle warfare.


To Australian amazement, on the morning of 28 May, the North Vietnamese returned to Balmoral. For fifteen minutes, they mortared the base with frightful accuracy, thanks to the courage of their nocturnal scouts who crept up and measured the distance with lengths of string! Then, in an exact replica of the earlier attack, only bigger, at least 800 North Vietnamese threw themselves on the tethered goat. As foolish as they were courageous, the attacks were suicidal, reminiscent of Japanese determined-to-die units. Perhaps the Vietnamese were drugged, some wondered. Those who reached the wire met a hail of canister and rifle fire, and fell, chiefly at the feet of Major Peter Phillips's company, which withstood the brunt of both attacks (for which Phillips's leadership earned him the Military Cross).[9] Some corpses hung on the wire until dawn.

The US gunships and Spooky again poured fire all over the field, as flares swung earthward casting a dazzling light on this pointless carnage. A few North Vietnamese huddled in old B52 bomb craters tried to shoot them down with heavy machine guns. In a sudden crazy attempt to destroy them, Corporal David Mancer raced out to the edge of the perimeter with a bag full of hand grenades and started hurling them into the craters (an action that contributed to his Military Medal); yet only the combined firepower of gunships, tanks, carriers, machine guns and rifles, in a deafening 'mad minute', ended the fire issuing from the craters.

An examination of the North Vietnamese bodies revealed that most were boys aged 15 to 17. The Australians were fighting an army of teenagers,

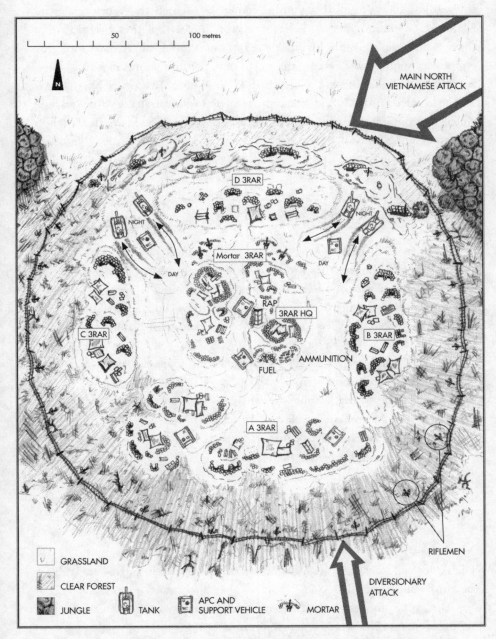

**50** | **100 metres**

**N**

MAIN NORTH
VIETNAMESE ATTACK

D 3RAR

NIGHT

NIGHT

DAY

Mortar 3RAR

DAY

RAP

3RAR HQ

AMMUNITION

C 3RAR

B 3RAR

FUEL

A 3RAR

RIFLEMEN

DIVERSIONARY
ATTACK

GRASSLAND

CLEAR FOREST

JUNGLE — TANK — APC AND
SUPPORT VEHICLE — MORTAR

BATTLE OF BALMORAL: AUSTRALIA'S 3RD BATTALION POSITIONS DURING
FIRST NIGHT ATTACK, 3.45 AM, 26 MAY 1968

and the destruction of so many young lives disturbed many Australian soldiers. '… to waste all that young manpower seemed to be criminal,' said Major Peter Phillips afterwards. 'It's a measure, I guess, of [Hanoi's] skill, that they were able to indoctrinate these young kids. I never saw the grey eminences who were directing them; we only saw the young kids …'[10]

The Australian Task Force returned to Phuoc Tuy on 5 June. TOAN THANG ended, and the 2nd Battalion returned to Australia, to a ticker-tape welcome home, in Brisbane. Lieutenant Colonel Lee Greville's 4th Battalion arrived at Vung Tau on 1 June to replace it.


Meanwhile, when not hard at work on his maps, Captain John Bullen was busy chronicling the events back at Nui Dat:

> Monday 27th May:
> Apparently the film 'Tammy' was shown last night to the complete disgust of all. All that need be done now to bring everyone to the brink of revolution is to show 'Pollyanna'. Surely more suitable films for soldiers can be selected than 'Tammy'.

> Friday 14th June [on Bullen's landing at Nui Dat with an American lieutenant]:
> He said to me, 'Where are we?'
> 'First Australian Task Force, Nui Dat.'
> 'Is this an Australian camp?'
> 'Yes, can't you see the kangaroos?'
> 'What! Say, where are they?'
> 'Over there, under the rubber trees. They're everywhere.'
> 'You guys bring 'em with you?'
> 'Yes. Never travel anywhere without them.'

The American flew away with his nose against the glass, scouring the rubber for 'roos, Bullen recalled.

Bullen fastidiously logged the infection rate of venereal disease. In July he uncovered 112 new cases, across all units:

> Casualties: 1 Officer, 111 other ranks; Diseases: 58 gonorrhea, 54 NSU.

Origin: Vung Tau 80, Singapore 11, Bangkok 9, Hong Kong 4, Ba
Ria 2, Xuan Loc 2, Long Binh 1, Saigon 1, Taipei 1, Tokyo 1.
Some surprises amongst this, especially Xuan Loc. No one from
the Task Force has been there in July except for one tank from the
Armoured regiment which broke down ... with a damaged
suspension for a few hours — plenty long enough for the
transmission of social diseases. Ba Ria is also a surprise, since no
one goes there except on duty, but I have heard of soldiers on
laundry visits to Ba Ria trading 2 apples for a quick session around
the back of the barn, and one soldier was charged for stealing army
property after trading a crate of apples for a longer session. He won
much unpopularity for raising the price & ruining the market ...

Thursday 18th July:
... Was seized at lunch to make conversation with a visiting
writer, a former French general in Indo-China ... He remarked
that the Australian & US forces in this Province are now located
in exactly the same places & strengths as the French about 15
years ago. His implication was quite clear that we are also fighting
a losing battle in Viet Nam.

Thursday 1st August:
... A most spectacular case of homosexuality occurred in the
canteen of RAEME Workshop of the Armoured Squadron last
Sunday afternoon in front of a large audience, & as a result 3 men
are facing General Court Martial. Quite the most sensational floor
show I've ever known of. Seems unnecessary to make all this fuss
though. All concerned were drunk & had accepted a dare.[11]

On his return from Singapore, Brigadier Hughes hailed the Australian stand
at Coral and Balmoral as military triumphs. Westmoreland similarly praised
the battles as rupturing a vital attack path to Saigon. Major General
MacDonald, too, felt that the results vindicated his decision to pursue more
aggressive actions outside Phuoc Tuy. 'They were very savagely attacked ...
and had a darned good fight,' he said later.[12] Even President Johnson heard of
the 'magnificent Australian victory' at Balmoral in a letter from the chairman
of the US Joint Chiefs of Staff, on 29 May 1968, in which the Australians

repulsed '1,000 North Vietnamese' of the 165th Regiment, 7th NVA Division.[13] The letter failed to mention that the Australians were equipped with tanks and gunships against a regiment of teenagers.

Indeed, some troops were unpersuaded by the merits of Coral and Balmoral. Lieutenant Ahearn thought then, and now, that the battles served little purpose: '… we only waited to see what the enemy would do to us.' The operations 'certainly weren't offensive … I don't think we had any aim apart from maintaining the integrity of the fire support bases.' Others drew cold comfort from the battles' opportunity cost. 'If they were attacking us, they were not attacking someone else, so we had occupied their minds for a while,' said a sceptical Lieutenant Salter.[14] These criticisms seem unduly harsh: they overlook the fact that Coral and Balmoral blocked vital sections of the North Vietnamese advance on Saigon and repelled several heavy regimental attacks, for relatively few casualties. Both operations were part of a 24-day onslaught, ending on 5 June, which included, in the second half of May, thirty-six 1st Battalion platoon fighting patrols and ambushes and sixteen company fighting patrols. 'The scale and tempo of operations was the highest mounted by the Task Force during the Australian involvement in South Vietnam,' concluded Lieutenant Colonel Bennett.[15]

At about the time of Mini Tet, in mid-1968, an essay appeared in Canberra that deeply disturbed the politicians and sent a tremor through the Australian military establishment. Lieutenant Colonel Peter Gration, head of the 1st Australian Civil Affairs Unit in Vietnam (and future Chief of the Defence Force, 1987–93, as a full general), submitted the essay anonymously for the Oswald-Watt Memorial Prize. The essay won. Extraordinarily prescient, its contents would surely have wrecked Gration's career had he revealed his name at the time; instead, he kept his authorship secret until 2005, when he kindly offered the essay for use in this book.

Gration's unsigned essay shocked those in Canberra who felt the war must be won, or was being won:

We are losing the war in Vietnam [Gration began]. At the time of writing the enemy has both the tactical and strategic initiative. During the Tet offensive in February 1968 he demonstrated his ability to attack cities and installations throughout South Vietnam, whilst pinning down large American installations in the North …

The enemy achieving this numbers barely a quarter of a million, including some 120,000 North Vietnam regulars. They are opposed by massive American, South Vietnamese and other 'Free World' forces outnumbering them by six to one. The allies enjoy total air superiority, and have used it to drop a tonnage of bombs which long since exceeded the World War II total. We also enjoy total armoured superiority and a technological superiority giving such facilities as infra-red photography, defoliant agents and radar-controlled bombing. The cost to the United States is some seventy million dollars per day. Clearly something is drastically wrong.

... Our doctrine ascribes the communist control of the people to the unrelenting and pitiless use of terror. Giap gives the more plausible explanation that ... winning the people lay in the twin political aims of throwing out the French (and now the Americans) and overthrowing the landlord feudal class ... Great stress is placed on education of the people with the will to win. Our thought tends to underestimate the overriding importance of this factor ...[16]

Westmoreland's war of attrition had utterly failed, Gration wrote. The American commander had hoped to destroy the insurgents completely and 'by civic action rebuild a free and democratic society'. Of this, Gration wrote: 'Unfortunately the military situation has now deteriorated so far that effective civic action on a nationwide basis is no longer possible.'

In short, 'the price of the objective is proving much higher than expected and probably more than the objective is worth ... The worst effect, however, is likely to be that the United States and not the Communists will be forced to step down because the effort required is so much greater than the prize to be won.'

'The outlook is therefore bad,' Gration concluded. He recommended the 'grand strategy' of containing communist Vietnam by focusing on building democracy in the neighbouring nations, starting with Thailand: 'Here, at a fraction of the cost, the people can be won.' In Vietnam, he recommended the cessation of bombing, de-escalation of operations and peace talks leading to a coalition government that 'would almost certainly be communist-controlled within three years'.[17]

Gration's analysis echoed the feelings of many officers on the ground, as Bennett observed in 2007: 'This essay did reflect the general view held by many Australian commanders serving in Vietnam in 1968 and 1969. They were, however, heavily involved in commanding combat operations and [stating such views] would have undermined the morale of the soldiers under their command.'[18] At the time, Gration's recommendations were ignored, of course. A vast military complex, driven by powerful men in Washington and Canberra, was committed to the war's prosecution. Senior Pentagon military strategists believed the Vietnam War served a critical role, as a demonstration of US resolve and as a training ground and weapons-testing environment, in readiness for a possible third world war with the Communist Bloc. In a small sense, at ground level, Balmoral had served this purpose: as a testing ground for the Centurion tank in densely jungled terrain; and learned essays in military academic journals tend to present this as Balmoral's ultimate military legacy. On a much bigger scale, the Pentagon prosecuted the war as a 'live exercise' on which to experiment with a new range of 'limited' (i.e. non-nuclear) weapons and technology. Nowhere did this 'experimental war' reach a more lethal level than in the air.

# Chapter 30
# The air war

The bombing of the North was tactically unsound. All it did was
to make the North Vietnamese more determined. It outraged the
[US] air force that they had to attack targets decided in
Washington. McNamara's approach was absolutely appalling.
*Air Vice Marshal Hans Roser, Australian F-4 Phantom pilot.*

I met Air Vice Marshal Hans Roser (retd) at the Commonwealth Club in
June 2005. A straight-talking, rugged-looking bloke, Roser seemed the
epitome of the retired fighter ace. In Vietnam, he served as an F-4 Phantom
fighter pilot, attached to the US Air Force, a world far removed from the
leathery silence of a Canberra gentlemen's club.

The F-4 Phantom was the most feared and, to the American and
Australian ground troops, beautiful weapon of the war. Airmen mocked it as
'double ugly' with twin cockpits and a rather abrupt, sloping nose, sometimes
daubed with shark's teeth or the breasts of a blonde triumph, joined to a
neckless, tubular body. In the air, however, it was a different story: infantrymen
in combat were tearful with gratitude as the Phantoms swept down from the
blue heights and unloaded salvation in the form of 500-pound bombs,
Sidewinder missiles and napalm canisters. To US and Australian soldiers the
Phantoms were angels of hope and life; to the Viet Cong and North
Vietnamese, they were instruments of a uniquely awful death.

'Yes, of course we flew bombing missions over Laos and Cambodia,' said
Roser.[1] To have admitted this at the time would have provoked political

uproar. The Australian Government officially prohibited Australian participation in cross-border attacks. Yet it happened regularly. Australia's six Phantom pilots — Squadron Leaders Lyall Klaffer (who served in 1965–66), Allan Reed (1967–68), Roser (1969–70) and Ian Whisker (1970–71), and Flight Lieutenants John Ellis (1969–70) and Lindsay Naylor (1970–71) — all flew missions over southern Laos, Cambodia and, occasionally, North Vietnam. Roser flew 165 sorties over South Vietnam, 200 hours by day, thirty by night; only twice was he pulled off cross-border missions. Sometimes the pilots were unaware that they had breached the border. 'Laotian jungle looked pretty much like South Vietnamese jungle,' explained Lindsay Naylor.[2] Others claimed to be unaware of the policy: Klaffer, of Korean War vintage and a legendary, slightly notorious, figure, apparently knew of no limits to his deployment and flew ten out-of-country missions. Not that the Phantoms had much success along the Ho Chi Minh Trail, Roser acknowledged: 'It was ridiculous trying to interdict guys on bikes in a Phantom.'[3]

The Australian Phantom pilots chiefly flew in support of US and South Vietnamese troops, and to bomb Viet Cong movements, 'from the DMZ to the delta', said Roser. 'We did take a lot of ground fire … you could see all this tracer flying up at you.' They escorted defoliation and reconnaissance missions, the latter often over North Vietnam; Klaffer in fact trained Phantom reconnaissance squadrons in the USA. On rare occasions — in the Long Hais, for example — the Australian Phantoms supported Australian infantry. 'We couldn't have helped those guys at Long Tan,' Roser added. 'It was pissing down.'[4]

The Phantom typically carried twelve 500-pound hidrag bombs, four Sparrow radar missiles, four Sidewinder missiles, napalm canisters and two external cannons. They often dropped white phosphorus incendiary bombs; anti-personnel cluster bombs (CBUs) that spewed thousands of bomblets over a wide area; and 'area denial' chemicals (i.e. defoliants). Occasionally they carried 2,000-pound bombs.

The Phantoms were at times inaccurate and often missed their targets, recalled Roser. At one point he gave his squadron 'a bashing about their poor bombing. You could see the bombs were miles away from the targets.' The standards of accuracy were even less exacting on the flight home to the US airbase in Phu Cat, when the Phantoms jettisoned all unused ordnance over 'Viet Cong' territory — such as the Cu Chi tunnels and other 'Free Fire' zones. 'You had to expend them — you couldn't land with them. You'd drop your bombs on a bridge, or just nothing, jungle,' said Roser.[5]

A peculiarly fearless species of pilot, the forward air controller, or FAC, guided the Phantoms to their targets. The FACs — such as Flight Lieutenant Roger Wilson at Coral — flew low over battle in little Cessna Bird Dogs, looking for ground targets, which they marked with white smoke rockets, then radioed the location to the Phantom pilot (hence 'Hit my smoke!'). The mental pressure was extreme: the FACs were in radio contact with two and often three sources — on the ground and in the air — in the midst of heavy ground fire. Between 1966 and 1971 the RAAF sent thirty-six FAC pilots into Vietnam, on detachment to US units, who knew them by their radio call signs, such as Sidewinder, Jade, Slugger and Drama.

Among the pioneering Australian FACs were Squadron Leaders Vance Drummond, the first in South Vietnam, and Rex Ramsey, and Wing Commander Tony Powell. Younger pilots followed, including Squadron Leader Graham Neil, Flight Lieutenants Brian Fooks, Garry Cooper, Roger Wilson and Doug Riding, and Flying Officers Mac Cottrell and Dick Kelloway. (Several, including Riding, Neil and Wilson, went on to achieve high rank in the RAAF.)[6] Most were highly decorated: twenty-three received British Commonwealth decorations, of whom two were awarded the Distinguished Service Order and fifteen the Distinguished Flying Cross. The FACs also received twenty-six US awards, including six Silver Stars. Adorning Flight Lieutenant Garry Cooper's chest by the end of the war were US Silver and Bronze Stars; the British and US Distinguished Flying Crosses (the latter with two oak leaf clusters); the US Air Medal, with eleven oak leaf clusters; the US Army Commendation Medal; and the Republic of Vietnam's Cross of Gallantry with Silver Star. These men were inordinately brave, and made the difference between life and death for thousands of ground troops; they were also the forward sights of an unusually devastating weapon, which has since been banned under the Geneva Conventions.

Men have been dropping burning oil on each other for centuries. Yet of all the ordnance used in Vietnam, napalm posed a unique horror. 'We dropped a lot of napalm,' Roser acknowledged. 'It was very effective for breaking up an attack. It would suck up all the oxygen, so if you didn't die from burns you suffocated. It was a terrible weapon, which they banned in the 1970s.'

'Napalm' has become a generic term for jellied petroleum. In World War I, Germany and the Allies used liquid petroleum in flame-throwers. But it burned *itself* too quickly. In 1942 Harvard University scientists and US Army laboratories found a way to 'jelly' gasoline that slowed its burn rate. Mixing an aluminum soap powder of naphthene and palmitate with gasoline produced a brownish sticky syrup that burned more slowly than liquid petroleum.

These 'primitive' napalm bombs incinerated 40 per cent of targeted Japanese cities during the Pacific War; 165-gallon versions were dropped on Chinese troops in the Korean War. Later, US scientists devised a variant, dubbed 'Napalm-B', or Super-Napalm, which used polystyrene and benzene, producing a more stable, less flammable compound. Yet once Napalm-B caught fire — using a special igniter — it proved extremely, *gradually*, combustible, literally sticking to and 'melting' the victim's flesh from the bone.[7] 'This napalm does melt the flesh,' a shocked witness of its effects on Vietnamese children told mortified readers of the American *Ladies Home Journal*. 'And the flesh runs right down their faces ...'[8] The US Air Force routinely used Super-Napalm in the aerial bombardment of Vietnam.

A napalm strike produced spectacular roiling bubbles of flame that sucked the oxygen out of the targeted area and sent globules of roasting jelly in every direction. From a distance, the sight inspired one photojournalist to remark, 'Oh my God, [It's] so beautiful', and wish for colour film. Napalm was also used to incinerate defoliated jungle and roast the enemy's mountain hides; for example, Chinooks would drop large bladders of jellied petroleum into the mouths of caves in the Long Hais, which the Phantoms ignited with a missile.[9]

The world saw first-hand the work of napalm on human flesh in 1972, when the South Vietnamese Air Force napalmed in error the friendly village of Trang Bang. A little nine-year-old girl called Kim Phuc ran screaming from the ruins, her arms dangling like a harlequin, her back covered in burning jelly: 'Her body radiated heat, and chunks of pink and black flesh were peeling off.'[10] The press photo of this burning waif running naked at the camera did more than any other image to turn the world in revulsion from the war: the photo 'doesn't rest', observed the German combat photographer Horst Faas.[11]

The bombers had a broader function, as the agents of mass destruction. The most devastating of these was the B52. 'The B52s were so terrible, you cannot imagine in your mind what it was like,' Pham Truong Thanh, a captain in the People's Army, told me in 2005, with a visible shudder as he recalled a B52 strike forty years earlier. Codenamed 'Arc Light', a multiple B52 strike approached the potency 'of a tactical nuclear weapon'.[12] A single B52 bomber carried up to eighty-four 750-pound bombs. They struck from altitudes far beyond the range of most ground fire and inflicted devastating physical and psychological effects on enemy units.[13] In theory they were restricted to bombing communist bases in relatively uninhabited areas; ground radar and lasers directed these bombing runs, which were in fact highly accurate. At their peak, in 1968, B52 pilots few 1,800 sorties per month; no Australian pilots were involved, but the ground troops heard the dull boom and felt the earth shake at a distance of 30 kilometres.

The USA lost fifteen B52s over North Vietnam, in an ultimately futile effort to destroy the infrastructure of a people accustomed to rebuilding their battered cities at startling speed. 'It's a peasant economy; they're used to using rough ground,' said James Cameron, a British journalist who visited North Vietnam. 'When a road is cut, they go around it … When a bridge is destroyed they replace it with a … bamboo mat bridge.' Nothing moved by day; the bamboo bridges were disguised. 'Only at dusk does everything come out and move.'[14] And Hanoi had the help of some 320,000 Chinese support troops.

The Australian air war[15] began in 1964 with the dispatch of new, Canadian-built Caribou transport planes to Vung Tau, as part of the RAAF Transport Flight Vietnam. The Caribous operated what was basically a 'milk run' between Vung Tau, Saigon and other cities. Dubbed 'Wallaby Airlines', the Caribous worked extremely hard, delivering troops, mail, food, ammunition and livestock — live ducks, pigs and cows — into combat zones. In one month, for example (March 1965) six hauled 1,010 tons of materiel.[16] By comparison, the US Air Force shifted 5,095 tons, with seven times the number of planes. Large livestock was sometimes parachuted in. On one occasion a cow fell through its airborne crate: '… the crate came down beautifully by parachute, the floor kept going with the cow still on it,' said the loadmaster, 'hurtling through the air with its nostrils flared.'[17] The Caribous flew 850 sorties per month and, although often fired on, none was lost. The only casualty was a leading aircraftman, who received a bullet in the buttocks.

On 14 December 1966 the Australian Cabinet agreed to send a squadron of bombers to Vietnam, a decision received warmly in Washington and Saigon. On 19 April, the first of twelve Canberra bombers, of No. 2 Squadron, flew to their new base, at Phan Rang Bay, in Ninh Thuan province, 250 kilometres north-east of Saigon. The RAAF's No. 5 Airfield Construction Unit had spent months working in intolerable heat to complete the base on time.

The Canberra touched down to American fascination in this lumbering, slightly eccentric-looking bird: slow, ungainly, usually equipped with six 750-pound bombs, it cut a slightly unfortunate sight alongside the gleaming bodies of the US F100 Super Sabres. Yet in action the Canberra would prove to be a remarkable success.

Within four days, the Canberras flew their first missions under the operational command of the US 35th Tactical Fighter Wing. These were 'Skyspot' radar-guided bombing missions flown at night at a safe 6,000 metres. In the next ten weeks the Canberras dropped almost 1,200 tonnes of bombs on 900 targets and supported several huge US ground operations, including JUNCTION CITY, DIAMOND HEAD and PERSHING. In February 1968, they helped to obliterate the Tet Offensive with missions over Khe Sanh, Hué and Quang Tri and occasional sorties near the Cambodian and Laotian borders. (If any Canberras strayed across, it went unreported in Canberra.)

The Canberras were more vulnerable to ground fire, on account of their slowness, low-altitude bombing runs and old, nose-mounted bombsites: 'Their loss rate was expected to be heavy.'[18] Yet such fears proved groundless, chiefly because ground fire, timed to strike faster-moving planes, flew harmlessly across the Canberra's nose. In fact, the up-blast of the Canberra's own shrapnel proved more dangerous, until the Department of Air raised the aircraft's minimum altitude, from 350 to 366 metres.

A statistical deluge measured the progress of the air war. By 1969 the Canberra squadron had inflicted 16 per cent of assessed bomb damage, despite the fact that the Australian pilots accounted for only 6 per cent of bombing missions. That year, the Canberras received the 'best record based on [bomb damage] of any operational unit in South East Asia'. Their airmanship proved 'outstanding', remarked the American colonel in command of the Fighter Wing.[19] The Canberras, answering to the radio call sign 'Magpie', became the pride of successive Australian wing commanders:[20] in its four years in Vietnam, No. 2 Squadron completed 11,696 combat missions, dropped 76,389 bombs, killed an estimated 3,390 enemy troops (786 confirmed), and destroyed 15,568 bunkers, 8,637 dwellings, 1,267 sampans and 74 bridges.

Most pilots were sceptical of these success ratings. They judged themselves by their survival rate and accuracy rather than by the gross tally of targets destroyed (one pilot mounted a 16mm movie camera in the bomb bay to film the effectiveness of the falling bombs). By this measure the Canberras proved outstanding: only one Canberra was actually lost to ground fire. And they were remarkably accurate, typically depositing half their payload within a 38-metre circle of the enemy target, thus minimising civilian casualties. In fact, the Canberras' most perilous early encounters seemed to be with the US Air Force. For example a low-altitude Canberra found itself flying amid hurtling trees blown into the sky by an Arc Light strike mistakenly cleared for the same target and initiated thousands of metres above the Australian pilot. A less spectacular encounter involved an incoming American bulldozer, whose driver insisted on breaking up a stricken Canberra whose nose wheels had failed to unfold on landing.

Not until 3 November 1970 did Australia lose a Canberra. That night Flying Officer Michael Herbert and Pilot Officer Robert Carver were returning from a mission at a safe altitude in clear skies. At 8.22 p.m. they disappeared from the radar screens. Sixty-seven search missions found not a trace. A court of inquiry failed to solve the mystery, thought to be the result of a catastrophic mid-air collision or possibly a surface-to-air (SAM) missile.

The squadron lost a second Canberra on the afternoon of March 1971, in a story touched by the miraculous: two SAM missiles slammed into the aircraft as it began a bombing run west of Hué. The second SAM, 'like a flying telegraph pole', shattered the cockpit's perspex canopy. Wing Commander John Downing and Flight Lieutenant Al Pinches were forced to eject:

> The sudden inrush of air through the pilot's canopy had created
> instant chaos in the small, dimly lit compartment … The force of
> the second explosion had also blown the sun visor of his helmet
> down over [Pinches's] eyes … Reacting to the pilot's instruction,
> he fired the detonators which blew away the aluminium cover
> above his seat and left him sitting exposed to the sky. The
> ejection seat was activated on Pinches' second attempt, propelling
> him out of the Canberra just moments ahead of the pilot. Later

he would recall being above the aircraft when he saw Downing
blasted up through the remains of the canopy.[21]

Downing and Pinches parachuted earthwards as the Canberra pitched, ablaze,
into the mountains near the Laotian border. Slapping through branches onto
a steep ridge, Downing sustained a broken kneecap and deep lacerations on
landing; 400 metres away, Pinches hung suspended by his parachute a metre
above ground with four broken vertebrae in his back. The two men spent the
night alone, in pouring rain, in great pain. The next day they made radio
contact with an American rescue aircraft. 'Then I heard it ...' recalled
Downing, 'the chopper ... What a beautiful sound.'[22]

The Canberras flew their last missions in Vietnam on 31 May 1971.
The squadron received two unit distinctions: the US Air Force Outstanding
Unit Award and Saigon's Cross of Gallantry with Palm.

Surely no machine has been more loved than the Bell UH-1B Iroquois
'Huey'. It was the troops' ambulance, godsend, gunship and all-round taxi
service. 'The joy of seeing the aircraft coming ... really has to be
experienced to be fully appreciated,' said one SAS soldier.[23] The helicopter's
sound — the thumpa-tumpa of the rotary wings — would live in the
soldiers' minds for the rest of their lives.

In March 1966 Holt announced that an RAAF helicopter squadron
would proceed to Vietnam. This was No. 9 Squadron, based for the duration
at Vung Tau, and flying daily to Nui Dat's Kangaroo pad or Luscombe Field,
the embarkation points for combat operations. Its main task was to insert
and extract the soldiers into and out of combat zones. 'Hot insertions' and
'hot extractions' demanded rare courage: medevacs flew at a top speed of
196 kilometres per hour, an exhilarating experience above the treetops, and
landed with the support of a ring of helicopter gunships to extract the
wounded. They resupplied soldiers with food and ammo (often with hot
meals and even ice creams); dropped propaganda leaflets; airlifted captured
rice to friendly villages; and sprayed the province with insecticide. Later they
were deployed on 'olfactory reconnaissance missions', fitted with 'people
sniffers' (infra-red detection equipment for pinpointing ground activity).

Just before Tet 1968 a new kind of helicopter appeared in Vung Tau,
dubbed the 'Ned Kelly', a prototype of the Bush Ranger gunship, adapted
from the Iroquois. In the great Australian tradition of improvisation, the

RAAF cobbled together the final model from whatever bits and pieces it could winkle out of the US Air Force. The Bush Rangers made their debut in June: an extraordinary armour-plated hybrid equipped with two seven-tube rockets and two 'miniguns' — six-barrelled machine guns capable of firing 4,800 rounds of 7.62mm ammunition per minute, with an accurate range of a kilometre. These deadly freaks became operational on 21 April 1969.

For the American helicopter crews, no task seemed too onerous; their Australian counterparts, however, were less appreciated. Accustomed to US pilots swinging in to help on call, the Australian infantry at first maligned the RAAF pilots as cowards. In fairness, No. 9 Squadron pilots were comparatively inexperienced, and — at first — their aircraft lacked the armoured seats and door-gun mounts installed on US rotary wings. Nor did the pilots have flak jackets, to start. Yet the diggers 'expected them to operate at a standard of personal daring at least as high as that of the Americans; so any example of caution was remembered and recounted'.[24] The RAAF failed to shake the charge notwithstanding many acts of great courage, of which this is one example:

On 3 October 1967 Corporal John 'Snow' Coughlan, an Iroquois crewman, was winched to the ground to rescue the American survivors of a downed helicopter gunship, burning in Viet Cong territory north-west of Nui Dat. A US gunner, with shattered knees, had crawled from the wreckage in shock; the three remaining crew were severely injured inside the burning machine. Coughlan got them out and onto the winch amid the constant hazard of the aircraft's exploding machine-gun rounds, set off by the intense heat: '… there'd be a lull of fifteen or twenty seconds in which we could move closer to the burning aircraft … Then one or two more [rounds] would go off and we'd hit the deck …'[25] Coughlan received the Conspicuous Gallantry Medal, second to the Victoria Cross among decorations then available to non-commissioned RAAF officers.

In the peak year — 1968 — forty-six Australian helicopters flew in Vietnam. Their crews included sixteen Royal New Zealand Air Force officers, five of whom received the Distinguished Flying Cross out of sixty DFCs awarded in total to the RAAF — about half of which went to Australia's No. 9 Squadron. That performance rather qualified the charge of cowardice. Yet the RAAF's alleged timidity 'became an instant part of army lore'. 'We never redeemed ourselves in the army's eyes,' said Bob Grandin, a co-pilot at Long Tan. 'We had air force guys who resigned rather than fly in Nam.'[26]

Several RAAF units, of course, served in the Australian war, the details of which are beyond our scope. For example, Nos 36 and 37 Squadrons, equipped with C130 Hercules aircraft, provided a constant lifeline, transporting troops, supplies and equipment between Australia and Vietnam, and ran medevac flights to bring the sick and wounded back to Australia. The Qantas troop-carrier — the 'Skippy Squadron' — flew 300 flights to and from Saigon during the war.[27] In addition there was the 161 Reconnaissance Flight, a highly decorated army helicopter unit; the Army Light Aircraft Squadron; Base Support Flight (later called Operational Support Unit); and the RAAF's airfield defence guards and construction units, both of which did a magnificent job, which has been little noticed. The ADGs performed a multiplicity of tasks, earning high decoration: they conducted many ground patrols, and flew as air crew/gunners, FAC observers and observers on Canberra bombers.

The Royal Australian Navy also lent backbone to the Australian air war: in reply to US demands for more helicopter pilots the RAN sent a small Helicopter Flight Vietnam, which joined the US Army's 135th Assault Helicopter Company and flew in some of the worst battles of the US war, suffering a far higher casualty rate than RAAF units. The heroic story of the RAN Helicopter Flight, virtually unknown in Australia (and told in Eather's *Get the Bloody Job Done*) formed a piquant sideline to the army/RAAF dispute. Incidentally, an obstacle to the smooth working relationship with the Americans was the RAN's penchant for facial hair, which was 'complete anathema to the United States army, who associate beards … with hippies and such like people', warned Major General MacDonald.[28] The sailors' beards had to come off, but a smooth shave did not stop the old salt Lieutenant Commander R. A. Waddell-Wood from winning a DFC for his courage over land.

As the air war expanded, the Australian Government faced a highly damaging interservice command crisis. It began in 1966, when Prime Minister Holt endorsed lines of command that effectively placed the RAAF 'under army control', noted a peeved Peter Howson, the Minister for Air.[29] In the eyes of the Chief of the General Staff, Lieutenant General John Wilton, the army commanded all before it in Vietnam: the combat forces were overwhelmingly army, and army officers held the two most powerful jobs, commanding the Task Force in Nui Dat and Australian Force Vietnam in Saigon.

The army may have regarded Vietnam as 'its war', yet initially it approached the RAAF delicately: Wilton tactfully proposed, in 1965, that Australian helicopters should accompany the 1st Battalion in Vietnam. Air Marshal Alister Murdoch, seeing little value in US-style jungle operations, refused. Murdoch's attitude angered Wilton. After all, sixteen of the RAAF's twenty-four Iroquois were bought essentially to support the army.[30] Surely only a fool would deny Australian troops the support of their own choppers?

From that moment, the army acted in a less transparent manner; indeed, it seems the RAAF heard of the army's commandeering its choppers in a leaked press article published ten days before its announced departure. Outmanoeuvred, the RAAF did not go gently into their disquieting new role. Their petulance often confounded the chain of command, at the heart of which lay the question: who controlled whom? Neither the government nor High Command gave a clear answer, which had grave repercussions in the field: the army felt very undersupported in Vietnam, and came to regard the RAAF's reluctance to face ground fire with contempt.[31]

'The RAAF were very obstructive at my level,' recalled Lieutenant Colonel Eric Smith, commander of 7th Battalion. 'They were under orders not to get casualties.'[32] Many RAAF pilots sympathised with the army. 'The RAAF policy on helicopters was a bit absurd,' said Air Commodore Roger Wilson later. 'They told them, "Don't lose any aircraft, be safe". Hell, there was a war going on.'[33]

At command level, the two services patched together a fragile truce by appointing the RAAF commander in Vietnam as deputy to the commander of Australian Force Vietnam. A succession of air commodores held the former, unenviable role.[34] It rarely worked to the RAAF's satisfaction. When Air Commodore Jack Dowling, for example, gently suggested 'some joint planning', his then superior (army) officer, Major General Mackay, snapped that 'the army had done all the planning that was necessary'.[35] The dispute is still being thrashed out in defence circles, and if the operational demands of the Vietnam War did not 'terminally poison'[36] the relationship between the army and the RAAF, they surely marred it for decades.[37]

The US-led air war, in which the RAAF played a small, if visible, part, failed to deliver the swift victory the Americans expected. 'We can reach any target in this world with our air force,' General Curtis LeMay, Chief of Staff of the US Air Force, had boasted in 1965. 'The North Vietnamese should touch his nape, otherwise it will be entirely destroyed by our bombardment, thus driving the North Vietnamese back to the Stone Age.' LeMay meant it: in 1966 and 1967 US aircraft flew 8,000 to 10,000 bombing missions monthly over North Vietnam, destroying on average US$60 million worth of roads, railways, bridges, ports, petrol stores, missile bases and so on, near Hanoi and Haiphong, according to CIA reports.[38]

Such massive US air power was critical in destroying the Tet Offensive. Yet the air war drew immense criticism, on strategic, economic and ethical grounds. The bombardment of a guerrilla army embedded in civilian areas was a tactical disaster and a human tragedy. America rapidly lost the support of the people, because fighters and bombers could not discriminate between friend and foe in a guerrilla war, as the British guerrilla warfare expert Robert Thompson bitterly explained: 'I do not oppose the use of napalm ... [but] to use napalm ... or any conventional weapon of mass destruction ... in this type of war in inhabited areas is utterly to be condemned. This is a war for the people, which means that damage and civilian casualties must be limited.'[39]

High civilian 'collateral damage' was the inevitable result. US aircraft often strafed running civilians, because US Rules of Engagement deemed any 'running person' to be Viet Cong. Even when civilians stayed still, they were often bombed in error. When young peasant women and their children made a point of not running, in an open field, in 1965, US aircraft napalmed them anyway. A pregnant woman survived: her arms required amputation; her eyelids were scorched away; and her nipples burned off, making it impossible to feed her child.[40]

Nor was she an exception: between 1965 and 1974 South Vietnam suffered 1,160,600 civilian war casualties, of whom an estimated 301,000 died. A large proportion were victims of air strikes: US aircraft dropped 13 million tons of bombs and 400,000 tons of napalm on South Vietnam. The US General Harold Johnson, US Army Chief of Staff, concluded: '[We] were indiscriminate in our use of firepower ... I think we sort of devastated the countryside.'[41] The experience of German-born Hans Roser qualifies this impression; he rejects any suggestion that civilians were targeted in Vietnam: 'I was a boy in Germany during World War II. Allied aircraft deliberately killed 30,000 civilians in Hamburg in one night. It was worse in Dresden. In Vietnam, civilians died. But we did not target them.'[42]

By 1968 the air war was costing the American taxpayer more than US$250 million a month but with little effect on North Vietnam's capacity to wage war in the South. Hanoi's ability to mount the Tet Offensive was 'final proof that attacking the North by air was not worth the cost'.[43] By then, General William DePuy's 'solution', of dropping 'more bombs, more shells, more napalm ... till the other side cracks and gives up',[44] had manifestly failed: 'The bombing of the North was tactically unsound. All it did was to make the North Vietnamese more determined. It outraged the air force that they had to attack targets decided in Washington. McNamara's approach was absolutely appalling.'[45] In 1966–67 the US Defense Secretary personally selected the North Vietnamese targets; after his resignation, in 1967, McNamara 'recanted', arguing that the logic of attrition by air would lead to 'the virtual annihilation of the Vietnamese people'.[46] As one US general said, 'I can go on killing Viet Cong forever, but where's that going to get us?'[47]

# Chapter 31
# The press offensive

[The Vietnam War was] wondrous … like a big Luna Park every
day of the week. Let's try a new ride. Let's jump out of a chopper
… Let's watch people getting blown up by mines. Let's shoot a
few gooks.
*Jan Graham, Australian journalist.*

The Vietnam War threw up more imposters and charlatans in the
name of war correspondent than I can remember.
*Denis Warner, Australian journalist.*

During the Year of the Monkey, the press, which had hitherto generally
supported the war or stuck to feel-good stories of heroism and
mateship, vigorously changed its tune. The media *reacted* to growing middle-
class disenchantment with the war: they did not initiate or promote anti-war
feeling; they reflected and fed off it. The 1968 Tet Offensive was the catalyst
for this shift in the media's line on the war, the moment most of the press
joined the anti-war bandwagon. Editors, sensing dismay and revulsion in
their readers, viewers and listeners, sought to reflect the public mood (they
ran a business, after all), and soon both press and public tended to share and
mutually reinforce their response to the war. In time, editors published
reports and photos safe in the knowledge that their readers were now
receptive to anti-war coverage. A sensational example was the 1968 picture
by Eddie Adams, of Associated Press, of the summary execution of a Viet

Cong guerrilla. On the second day of Tet, Brigadier General Nguyen Ngoc Loan, the feared commander of the 'white mice' (the National Police), roamed the streets of Saigon in a ferocious mood. Many of his men were dead, including a friend who lost his wife and children in a Viet Cong attack. When a bound Viet Cong soldier was brought before him, Loan raised his revolver and shot the captive, point-blank; Adams's photo of the execution captured the moment the bullet entered the victim's head and made front pages throughout the world.

Intimations of defeat leavened the journalists' copy: not only was the war a crime, it was also a losing battle. The media generally reported Tet as a sign that the allies were losing the war. The US cause had suffered an incredible setback, it concluded: 'Where are we winning?' (*The Australian*, 1 February 1968); the 'pain of war' must end (*The Age*, 2 February 1968); allied commanders were 'outgeneralled' and had 'surrendered the initiative' (*Sydney Morning Herald*, 2 February 1968); gun-toting calls on America to 'get tough' (*Daily Telegraph*, 2 February 1968). The lesson of Tet, the *Telegraph* concluded, 'is that more bombs are needed on North Vietnam'.[1] The weeks passed with little follow-up or analysis. Walter Cronkite, CBS anchorman, growled, '… we are mired in stalemate …' When he saw the film of the attack on the US Embassy, Cronkite wondered, 'What the hell is going on? I thought we were winning the war?' The event 'was the first time in history a war has been declared over by an anchorman'.[2]

In this light, the media utterly miscast the Tet Offensive. Few reported it for what it was: a comprehensive Viet Cong defeat, both in military terms and, more importantly, as a test of southern loyalties. The fact that the South Vietnamese had refused overwhelmingly to rally to the communist standard received little airplay. The media even failed to report the communist atrocities at Hué. One reason is that most of the press corps rarely left Saigon or paid much attention to communist atrocities. When blood and gore and piles of corpses lay on the journalists' doorstep, they presumed America had lost the initiative, and filed panic-stricken reports. In March 1968, 60 per cent of Americans regarded Tet as an American defeat in Vietnam, according to a Harris poll.

After Tet, the relationship between the military and the media — hitherto fraught but workable — rapidly deteriorated and never recovered. On 9 June 1968, during Gorton's visit to Nui Dat, Major Peter Murray wrote of the 'smouldering dislike' and 'mistrust for the press' that had spread 'throughout the force now, as a result of the rubbish they persist in printing'.[3] Yet the power of the Western media had a marked influence on Hanoi, which redirected its offensive at US homes, at US 'hearts and minds'. The Western body bag became a propaganda tool. Even the conservative press sought only 'bad news'. 'I spoke to a journalist from a right-wing paper,' said Brigadier Colin Khan DSO, 'and he showed me a cable from his editor asking simply for reports on what was going wrong.'[4]


The Saigon press pack was, in general, a cheerful, louche young tribe of star-struck hacks, heroes of their own personal drama, who hung around the Caravelle and Continental hotels waxing drunkenly about their latest 'assignment' in juvenile imitation of the Graham Greene or Ernest Hemingway of their imaginations while drawing their sustaining verbiage from that great round-up of half-news, the Five O'Clock Follies, at which Westmoreland's PR men told sweltering fibs about the body count and 'light at the end of the tunnel' that one cannot dignify as lies because they were stated (and often reported) as revealed truth, regardless of the fact that nobody believed them.

Of the 600 to 700 accredited foreign correspondents (of whom about eighty were women) in South Vietnam in 1968, 'only 50 gave journalism a better name than it deserved', wrote Michael Herr, correspondent for *Esquire* magazine, author of *Dispatches*, and demonstrably one of the fifty.[5] And certainly the Australian journalists such as Denis Warner, Denis Gibbons, Alan Ramsey, Creighton Burns, Pat Burgess and several others were among that number. Yet the majority of the Saigon press pack were 'not first-rate', as Jack Valenti, the influential president of the Motion Picture Association of America, told LBJ. 'Most of them [were] strictly third-class. Most … cover the war from the bars in Saigon.' Yet the US Army's press officers, for whom the media had lost any scrap of respect as early as 1965, encouraged this inertia. 'The press briefing officers try so hard to point up the favorable aspects of the war, they lose all credibility,' Valenti wrote. 'The [US] Army has no friends among the press.'[6]

Inexperience was part of the problem. It was easy to get a press card, and hundreds of cub reporters did. Vietnam was the 'longest running front page story in history!' gasped a reporter from UPI. You simply presented yourself at the US Army Press Centre in Saigon, with a South Vietnamese visa and a letter from your employer. No combat training was required. Freelance journalists needed only a letter from their news agency.

The new reporters were told the ground rules on security and no-go zones, and off they went — no doubt topped and tailed in their safari suits, 'CBS jackets' or 'Abercrombie & Fitch combat gear', with their names stitched on the breast pocket: hence John Shaw, *Time*; Michael Herr, *Esquire*; or, to general hilarity, 'Alan Williams, *Queen*'. Thus Sean Flynn, the son of film star Errol and the French actress Lili Damita, went to war, a 6-foot thrill-seeker whose flashing eyes, perfect teeth and sculpted face marked him down as a matinée idol. (Flynn and his buddy, Dana Stone, later disappeared in Cambodia whence they rode on motorcycles, the 'easy riders' of the Mekong.)

Saigon's black market equipped the correspondents for all their needs in the field: mosquito net, canteen, knife, canned foods, rubber air mattress, camouflage, first aid pack, water purification tablets, aspirin, maps, cleft sticks, condoms (used as waterproof containers for carrying film, identification papers and matches) and an 'optional' pocket pistol. '... you will be the target of enemy fire, exactly as if you were a combatant,' Associated Press's Malcolm Browne warned Peter Arnett. 'If you are wounded in a convoy ... you probably will be shot to death. The Vietcong generally does not take wounded prisoners ... because of the difficulty of keeping them alive in the jungle.' Arnett chose a Mauser machine pistol, Sean Flynn a pearl-handled revolver and Denis Gibbons a Colt .45.[7]

The Vietnam War rarely impinged on the average reporter's mind above the level of 'a great story'. The reporter's 'eye' for news tended to be that of the atrocity junkie, hero-hugger, weapons fetishist or war pornographer. Reporters, in general, were not interested in the causes or complexities of the conflict; as a result, they produced 'an entirely superficial view of the situation', observed Major General Colin Fraser.[8]

Hardened reporters grew addicted to the adrenalin rush. 'Vot I like eez boom boom. Oh yes,' said Horst Faas; he meant the sound of artillery. Jan Graham, an Australian wire reporter, remembered her ten years in Vietnam as 'wondrous ... like a big Luna Park every day of the week. Let's try a new ride. Let's jump out of a chopper ... Let's watch people getting blown up by mines. Let's shoot a few gooks.' She was being only half cynical, admitting that 'I could watch [the gooks] being slaughtered and feel no pain'.[9] Nora Ephron of *New York* magazine summarised the consensus: 'War is not hell. It is fun.'[10]

The Vietnam War was great fun for most journalists, most of the time. The fearless, or mad, British photographer Tim Page said he found war —

all war — glamorous: 'There is a lot of sex appeal and a lot of fun in weapons. Where else but in Vietnam would a man get a chance to play with a supersonic jet, drive a tank, or shoot off a rocket, and even get highly paid for it? … You can't take the glamour out of a tank burning or a helicopter blowing up. It's like trying to take the glamour out of sex. War is *good* for you.' Clare Hollingworth of the London *Daily Telegraph* entertained a love of weapons, and boasted that she could dismantle a machine gun faster than any man.[11]

Few journalists bothered with Vietnamese history or the complex background to the war. They were on an adventure. A minority went out on combat operations; most were 'day-trippers' who flew in and out of battle zones, usually after battle. Still, a few were recklessly brave — or plain mad. Forty-five journalists were killed and eighteen listed as missing during the war. US Marines laughed in amazement at the idea of Herr *volunteering* to cover Khe Sanh. Four Australian journalists — Bruce Piggott, John Cantwell, Michael Birch and Ronald Laramy — were shot dead on 5 May 1968 when they drove, against army advice, into Saigon's Cholon district at the height of Mini Tet. On approaching the Viet Cong, they shouted '*Bao Chi*' ('Press') to a machine-gunner, who riddled them regardless. 'We wouldn't have gone there with a thousand blokes,' said the signaller Terry O'Brien.[12] Yet these reporters died bravely trying to do their job. As non-combatants, the better journalists reckoned they could, or should, go where the infantry could not or dared not go.

One was Denis Gibbons. An extraordinarily brave combat photographer, Gibbons was among the few Australian reporters to join the diggers on operations. Wounded six times, he earned the nickname 'Mad Bastard'. Himself a former soldier, Gibbons won the soldiers' respect, and was the only journalist to patrol with Harry Smith's company. 'Harry refused to have any press or PR along,' said Gibbons. 'When I went into his tent, he said, "I suppose you're gonna knock the shit out of us."'[13]

It is hard, at first sight, to see why the first casualty of the Vietnam War should be the 'truth': after all, the press had unfettered freedom to report the war as it saw fit. Vietnam was the first — and probably the last — uncensored war.

Westmoreland granted the media unprecedented freedom. He believed that censorship was unenforceable in a war covered by so many journalists, of so many nationalities, in so porous an environment. 'Greater benefits might be derived from a policy of maximum candor,' he wrote.[14] Dean Rusk agreed (and later changed his mind), fearing that any attempt to muzzle the press would provoke 'national hysteria'.

The US Army detailed this extraordinary freedom in a little public information booklet — surely never to be repeated — that promised reporters 'whatever transportation is reasonably available to assist them in performance of their mission'. They should be 'afforded the highest priority possible next to requirements for tactical emergency troop movement ... Every possible courtesy will be extended.'[15]

This historic document — signed by Major General Nguyen Bao Tri, Minister for Information and Open Arms, Government of Vietnam; Barry Zorthian, Minister Counselor for Information, US Mission, Vietnam; Roger Bankson, Colonel, US Army, Chief of Information, MACV — was admirably clear:

RELEASABLE AND NON-RELEASABLE INFORMATION:
... The policy is to provide maximum information to
correspondents, consistent with security ...

RULES FOR DISCUSSIONS WITH CORRESPONDENTS:
... Media interviews and/or photographs of casualties are
authorized if ... the casualty/patient does not object.

ASSISTANCE TO CORRESPONDENTS:
AREA ACCESS: There will be no restriction on the movement of
accredited correspondents ...

SUPPORT: ... Local commanders will ensure that visiting
correspondents are properly received, briefed, escorted and
afforded whatever conveniences and services are reasonably
available ... correspondents will be treated as commissioned
officers with the simulated rank of major ... in such matters as
messing and living accommodations.[16]

The basic principle was simply to divulge anything, within security constraints. The only 'non-releasable' information was troop movements, Free World casualty figures, future operations, Rules of Engagement, and intelligence activities. Thus reporters, like impatient partygoers hailing a taxi, had the run of the helicopters, and flew hither and thither chasing scoops, dropping into operations, joining battalions. US officers were even expected to treat accredited journalists — in the mess at least — with the rank of 'major'. A pimply youth with a press card suddenly found himself enjoying the perks of a US commissioned officer.

However, a kind of unofficial censorship operated in the US Army: lies. Most 'facts' about the war were based on 'misinformation or misunderstandings' in a landscape 'rife with duplicity and misrepresentation', wrote AP bureau chief Malcolm Browne in his *Short Guide to News Coverage in Vietnam*. Certain US commanders could be counted on to tell 'bald-faced 180-degree whoppers', Browne wrote. In the field, too, deception was the norm: only the results of successful operations were shown to the press.[17]

The 'body counts' were the most shameless example of US hyperbole. The 160 Viet Cong dead after the Plei Ku campaign had mysteriously reached 869 by the time of the press conference.[18] Denis Warner, who supported the American-led war, noted the 'huge discrepancy' between Westmoreland's body count and the number of enemy weapons actually captured. Either the Americans were lying or the bodies were civilian. 'What no one will accept indefinitely,' Warner wrote, 'is the persistent attempt to win by pretense what has not been won on the ground.'[19]

From 1968, the Australian Government took a sterner approach to press censorship. Disturbed by the fallout over the water torture case (see below), and an increasingly hostile media, Canberra imposed its own censorship regime in Vietnam. In September 1968 Australian Force Vietnam gained new powers to restrict reporting in Australian combat zones. Under the rules, reporters were not to meet or quote any Australian soldier 'without having first been cleared by a PR officer'. The army threatened to withdraw 'all privileges and facilities' from reporters unless they complied.[20] The new rules met with great hostility: '… the most blatant attempt to impose censorship at source that I have ever encountered in any army in any war at any time,' Warner complained.[21] The restrictions were later partly relaxed.

At the same time, the Australian diggers' contempt for the Saigon press corps deepened. In 1968 the soldiers were especially scathing about the quality of media coverage of the war. Journalists would return from operations and dispatch stories that bore no resemblance to the soldiers' recollection of events. 'Even when Sean Flynn came out to Nui Dat, he wrote a story glorifying himself as saving an Aussie,' said one company commander. 'Flynn was there on the spot but got the war totally wrong.' Visiting reporters were treated with scorn, such as when the journalist Don Wise arrived at Bien Hoa dressed in a tiger-patterned marine's suit. The diggers laughed: 'Geez, mate, we're saved! Bloody Tarzan's joined us!'[22] Wise received every comfort. The CSM 'did everything apart from tucking me into bed and kissing me good night', Wise said. Later, he heard an officer ask the CSM: 'Did you make Mr Wise comfortable and welcome?'

The CSM replied, 'Yes, sir. We put him right out with the point platoon, nearest the enemy, like we do with all those bloody journalists.'[23] They might have accorded Wise greater respect had they known that he was a former World War II soldier, who had been imprisoned on the Burma Railway and was awarded the Military Cross.

Yet the media were, to an extent, complicit in the process of censorship. The sheer brain-numbing horror of the war turned reporters, unwittingly, into their own worst censors. Veteran reporters were so inured to the carnage that they became part of the war machine and not 'detached' observers of it. Old media hands eschewed the terms 'war crime' and 'atrocity' as quaint, morally earnest phrases that lost meaning in one vast war crime, as they understood the war. In time, they drowned in military euphemisms, and failed or refused to give the proper names for what they were seeing. Who were we to decide what constituted an 'atrocity'? argued Peter Arnett.[24] Indeed, the better correspondents liked to think that they dealt only in 'facts', not 'atrocities', a term that implied a judgement, Arnett claimed. Yet whose facts? Westmoreland's PR men called an atrocity an atrocity when committed by the Viet Cong, and a civilian a civilian when identified as one of 'our' civilians.

In this atmosphere, words ceased to connect with any recognisable reality. A jarring discord between language and meaning clashed in the reporters' minds: what they saw in the field bore no resemblance to what they were being told. In Vietnam, the US Army created a parallel realm, a fantasyland with its own language and moral code, where 'daisy cutters', 'pineapple bombs', 'jumping jacks' and 'Arc Light' sought to crush the insurgency so that 'accelerated pacification' could win 'hearts and minds' before 'Vietnamisation' took over. This was war by public relations, a world utterly decoupled from what was really happening. In 1968 the army 'spokesmen spoke in words that had no currency left as words, sentences with no hope of meaning in the sane world', wrote Herr.[25] The sane world of Mum's apple pie, meat and two veg, baseball and cricket simply had no point of contact with the surreal nightmare of Vietnam. Language itself became a casualty of war.

Indeed, many journalists 'went noggy', in the sense that their reality, their norm, was Vietnam and not the world of the readers for whom they wrote. The Australian journalist Phillip Knightley observed this disturbing tendency in his book *The First Casualty*. When Philip Jones Griffiths, a British photojournalist, witnessed the shelling of Vietnamese civilians, he did not bother selling the story: 'If I had gone back to Saigon and into one of the agencies and had said, "I've got a story about Americans killing Vietnamese civilians", they would have said, "So what's new?" It was horrible, but certainly not exceptional, and it just wasn't news.'[26] On one military operation, Peter Arnett 'watched hooches burning down, I saw the civilian dead. I did not write about war crimes either ... we were told of the civilian dead and how they died, but we didn't make judgments because we were witnesses, and, like witnesses to robbery, accident, or murder, surely it was not for us to be judge and jury.'[27] Like Graham Greene's English correspondent in *The Quiet American*, Arnett and other hardened reporters cast themselves as aloof, detached, *uninvolved*. Yet their very detachment failed their readers: their unwillingness to report civilians as targets meant that genuine atrocities committed on both sides went unreported.[28]

The My Lai massacre was the most egregious example of this tendency. Saigon correspondents ignored the story; it became 'news' only when a freelance journalist in the USA, stunned by what he heard, wrote about it. 'The My Lai massacre was revealed ... not by a war correspondent on the spot, but by a reporter back in the United States who was capable of being shocked by it,' Knightley wrote.[29] Reporters in Saigon were thus jolted, by a report from the USA, into hunting down American excesses that they had hitherto ignored as unexceptional.

Most of the Saigon press corps (and their editors) tired of communist attacks on civilians, and simply ignored this side of the war. 'We were watching civilians butchered by Viet Cong, children butchered by Viet Cong,' said Major Brian McFarlane. 'Not one of these reporters mentioned the thousands of civilians the VC knocked off.'[30] In the first six months of 1967, 3,798 civilians were killed in assassinations or other terrorist acts, and 'our Press has scarcely reported it'.[31] The Hué massacre was largely ignored. One reason is that the Viet Cong's attacks on civilians were considered a routine part of the war. In this sense, US and Australian editors imposed a double standard: white 'war crimes' were newsworthy; 'Asian on Asian' ones were not, and the distinction intensified after Tet.

This helps to explain the Australian media's delayed reaction, in 1968, to news of an alleged Australian 'atrocity': the so-called water torture incident, which first appeared in October 1966. That year, it was virtually ignored; in 1968, the story of the 'war crime' took more column inches of newsprint than the Tet Offensive and Long Tan. The water torture incident horrified a credulous nation and branded the Australian war as cruel and barbaric.

The facts lead to different conclusions. This is what happened: a platoon led by Second Lieutenant John O'Halloran traced a radio wire, found in the Nui Dinh Hills, to a cave. Inside they found a US radio and, wedged into a crevice above, 'like a spider suspended from the roof', a young Vietnamese woman.[32] The Australians detained her; she spent the night tied to O'Halloran, who told her she would be shot if his men were attacked. Cold and silent, unmoved by the sight of a snake that made the Australians jump, this 23-year-old 'hard-core Viet Cong' trembled and vomited when a helicopter arrived the next day; she seemed to believe stories that Australians flung captives out of aircraft.[33] She was delivered safely to Nui Dat on 25 October 1966. Under questioning, she gave her name as To Thi Nau and her position as head of the communist Military Proselytising Committee in Hoa Long. As a trainee radio operator, she relayed signs of Australian and South Vietnamese movement along Route 15 to the Central Office of South Vietnam (COSVN), in Tay Ninh province, part of the enemy's central nervous system.[34] She was critical in any plan to ambush an enemy road convoy.

Dragged to the interrogation tent, she started to scream when her gag and blindfold were removed. Her interrogator, an Australian warrant officer, Ken Borland, shouted and banged his fists when she refused to speak, then threatened the 'water treatment'. She was held down, her nose blocked and a small quantity of water from a jerry can was forced into her mouth. Major Alex Piper, the staff officer responsible for organising the interrogation, was 'a bit stunned' when he entered the tent to find Borland administering the punishment, which Piper soon ordered to cease.[35] She had swallowed less than a cup. Her interrogation lasted half an hour, after which she was photographed and handed over to the South Vietnamese.

At the time, Brigadier Jackson ordered an investigation; the woman's treatment was clearly against the Geneva Convention. Borland, it later emerged, had no authority to interrogate prisoners, and was removed from further 'duties'. 'The matter should have finished there,' states the official historian. 'The act amounted only to harassment ... Any suggestion that an atrocity had been committed was without foundation.'[36] Jackson, satisfied that he had dealt with the case, decided not to alert Canberra.

Three journalists witnessed the prisoner's arrival and part of her interrogation: John Sorrell of the Melbourne *Herald*, Geoffrey Murray of AAP and Gabriel Carpay, a freelance photographer. None reported the 'water torture' in 1966; only Murray filed a story, on the woman's capture, which failed to mention her harsh treatment. Murray later said: 'I had no intention of writing a story along "torture" lines', acknowledging that he lacked the information. Sorrell later claimed that military censorship had prevented him writing the story in 1966, a claim the army denied;[37] yet in 1968 all three reporters would report that the woman had been tortured (in fact, none had been allowed into the interrogation tent). Carpay, who waited outside the tent, later recalled: 'The warrant officer ... returned carrying a jerry can. The can was obviously full ... I heard the prisoner moan ... Shortly afterward, I heard the WO say words to this effect: "I wish they had left the bitch to me. I could have taken her into the scrub and ... made her talk".'[38]

Eighteen months later, in March 1968, an American journalist, Martin Russ, 'revealed' in his book *Happy Hunting Ground* that Australian soldiers had 'water tortured' a Vietnamese civilian; his only source was a conversation with two Australian journalists, one of whom was Sorrell. Attuned to the growing anti-war feelings of their liberal readers, the Australian media leaped on the story as evidence of a home-grown atrocity: here was the face of Australian evil in Vietnam.

The hysteria drove Phillip Lynch, the new Minister for the Army, to declare on national television that he could find 'not one scintilla of evidence for the charge'. Lynch looked a dill the next day when Sorrell wrote a sensational account of the 'torture', which the inexperienced Lynch, ignoring the army's protests, accepted as essentially true. Prime Minister Gorton then added oil to the fire: the woman had been well enough to pose for photos after her 'torture', he told Parliament.

'A bit wet perhaps?' interjected a Labor MP.

'Yes, a little wet, I agree,' said Gorton.

The remark inflamed the anti-war movement: campuses were aghast, and academics threatened to shop the Prime Minister to philosopher Bertrand Russell's tendentious 'International War Crimes Tribunal' in Paris — a mock court modelled on the Nuremburg War Crimes Trials at which solemn Marxist intellectuals, acting as 'judges', held Western politicians personally responsible for war crimes in Vietnam.[39] The government's boorishness and flippancy merely added to the outrage, and seemed tacitly to confirm that Australian soldiers had tortured a Vietnamese woman. The 'water torture' case became part of the popular mythology that Australian troops were routinely committing atrocities: '… that the case is the only one cited in evidence,' wrote historian Peter Edwards, 'suggests that the opposite was true: a distinct absence of war crimes in the Australian war in Vietnam. That did not register at the time.'[40]

Amid the uproar, Martin Russ scored an embarrassing own goal. In an article in *Life* magazine, on 1 April 1968, he virtually refuted his own claim. 'I didn't see … the Aussies use torture. The incident with the girl I wrote about was hearsay. I wasn't there … You hear a lot about torture,' he wrote.[41] This admission did little to silence the hysteria. Once uncorked, the atrocity genie spread. Other journalists dusted down their dim memories of civilian deaths and reprinted them; 'war crime' hunters came out of the woodwork; and the word 'massacre' was used as loosely then as 'genocide' is today. Editors and media proprietors jostled to satiate the public demand for 'news' that seemed to confirm their ballooning idea of Australian soldiers as savages. The episode supplied an 'atrocity' when the media were particularly receptive to one, and equipped anti-war groups with a new weapon.


It was the novelty of *seeing* war for the first time that led many Australians to oppose it. By 1968 more than 95 per cent of Australian homes had access to television, and four million Australians — a quarter of the country — tuned into the news between 7 p.m. and 8 p.m.[42] In this sense, the *technology*, the TV — and not the messengers, the reporters — lost support for the war. Had TV cameras filmed the bombing of Dresden or Tokyo, viewers may similarly have turned away in horror. Western viewers weaned on the notion of war as heroic, rule-bound and 'just' were suddenly seeing thousands dead, millions of refugees, unspeakable suffering … in short, the things common to all wars.

Commercial television tended to play down this grim reality, and cast the Vietnamese people as bit parts in a largely American–Australian story of great blokes avenging the Western dream of good triumphing over evil. US and Australian television made little attempt to explain the background or rationale for fighting the war. 'In each night's TV news and each morning's paper,' wrote President Richard Nixon, 'the war was reported battle by battle, but little or no sense of the underlying purpose was conveyed. Eventually this contributed to the impression that we were fighting in military and moral quicksand ...'[43]

In Australia, the ABC attempted to give a fuller picture. Yet the public broadcaster displayed several toe-curling examples of editorial cowardice: it caved in to a government demand to rewrite the script of a film on Cambodia (and agreed to excise, for example, the words 'built by Communist China' from a description of a Cambodian factory). And it self-censored reporter Tony Ferguson's tape of an exclusive interview with Wilfred Burchett by destroying it because the ABC's Controller of News viewed Burchett as a traitor. Surely that view made Burchett more newsworthy, not less? This idiotic act of editorial vandalism served neither the 'public interest' nor the historical record.

After all, Burchett, the son of an Australian farmer, was the best-known Western reporter to cover the war from the communist side. He unapologetically backed the regime in Hanoi, had met and interviewed Ho Chi Minh, and enjoyed access unrivalled among his Western colleagues to the highest levels of the Vietnamese communist hierarchy.

On his journeys through Vietnam, Burchett cut an ungainly figure in his broad hat, wide girth, black pyjamas and Ho Chi Minh sandals. Yet his undoubted reporting skills were wasted in the service of tyrants: a lifelong supporter of Stalin and Mao, Burchett was a paid 'consultant' to six communist governments. He reported the Korean War from the communist side, and fabricated stories about US germ warfare. Unforgivably, Burchett described the North Korean prison camps as 'one long holiday', and played down communist brutality, for which Australia's Korean veterans justly accused him of high treason. Brigadier Phil Greville, for example, spent ninety days in solitary under severe interrogation during his internment in a Korean prison camp.

Later, Burchett spoke openly of his admiration for Pol Pot, scripted 'Hanoi Jane' Fonda's North Vietnamese broadcasts and arranged for his old mate, the *New York Times* writer Harrison Salisbury, to visit North Vietnam, the first US reporter to do so. Burchett met Nixon in Peking, and Washington considered (and rejected) the idea of using him as an intermediary in negotiations with Hanoi over the return of US prisoners. Accused by Jack Kane, a DLP leader, of being a paid member of the KGB, Burchett sued Kane for defamation — a case Burchett failed to prove and for which he had costs awards against him. Burchett died in Bulgaria in 1983, too soon to witness the implosion of the political experiment to which he had devoted his life.[44] It is regrettable, nonetheless, that part of his extraordinary life ended on the ABC's cutting room floor.

Did the media lose the war? The short answer is, no. This tiresome refrain of soldiers and politicians ignored the fact that until 1968 the Australian media were almost unanimous in their support for the war and troops. Editors gave little oxygen to the anti-war protesters and draft resisters, whom they dismissed, until 1968, as cowards and communists. Only then did the media's support wane — long after public feeling, stirred by students, unions, politicians and clerics, had turned against the war. The media thus largely followed public sentiment. The generals, chiefly Westmoreland, grossly overstated the media's influence.

The more severe charge against the press concerns the quality of coverage and the failure to report the biggest stories. Many media outlets simply misreported the Vietnam War. They miscast Tet as a loss, failed to follow up 'running stories', and later relished accounts of allied 'war crimes' when editors felt the public was ready to receive them. They maligned the troops after so wholeheartedly supporting them. Editors ignored stories on the Vietnamese civilian tragedy (e.g. US newspapers refused to publish Martha Gellhorn's articles about the effect of the war on civilians). 'Ours was a babble of voices that lost all credibility,' said Keyes Beech, a US correspondent.[45] 'The Vietnam War threw up more imposters and charlatans in the name of war correspondent than I can remember,' concurred Denis Warner.[46] Some fine investigative articles and documentaries occasionally obtruded on this bleak picture; in fairness, most reporters in the field simply did what they were told. Back home their editors sold a complex 'story' as though it were a John Wayne shoot-out or an American (and Australian) crime against humanity. The public bought both versions of Vietnam.

# Chapter 32
# Body count

Do you have to notify Australia? Mum will only worry.
*An Australian soldier, who lost his leg in a mine blast.*

CONFIDENTIAL
DEPARTMENT OF THE [US] ARMY, HEADQUARTERS,
II FIELD FORCE VIETNAM
FOR THE COMMANDER
RELATIVE STATISTICS, March 1968:
1. Free World Forces KIA/WIA/MIA (TOT): 1,397/5,666/84
2. VC Casualties KIA/PW (TOT): 12,929/991 [...]
5. Civilians KIA/WIA by F[REE WORLD] Ops
(TOT): 118/183
6. Civilians KIA/WIA by VC Ops: 380/892
*Monthly Statistical Report.*

The report quoted above is an example of the monthly 'profit and loss' account in the 'American Measurement of Progress' bulletins sent to Free World commanders. The figures, crunched by huge early computers, referred to the statistical 'blip' of Tet, February 1968, in III Corps, one of four combat zones. Of the 7,147 Free World casualties listed, the overwhelming majority were South Vietnamese and American. Ninety-six were Australian, of whom fourteen were killed in action and 82 wounded.

June was more typical: that month III Corps lost 784 soldiers killed, 3,134 wounded and 41 missing in action; for these, 4,767 Viet Cong gave their lives. In the process, the allies were responsible for killing 117 civilians and wounding 73, while the Viet Cong killed 133 and wounded 312 civilians (how many civilian casualties were accidental is unknown).[1]

The monthly figures were consolidated into six-monthly reports: thus, in the first half of 1968, 5,806 Free World soldiers and 42,030 communist troops were killed in action, a 'kill ratio' of seven to one in favour of the allies. In the same period, the Australian forces lost 55 men for 691 Viet Cong dead, a 12.5:1 kill ratio; the Task Force, by this measure, was a far more deadly 'killing machine' than the American commanders believed.[2]

The statistics offer a glimpse of the 'body count', the fundamental measure of American military progress for most of the war — not-withstanding the later effort of General Creighton Abrams, Westmoreland's successor, to capture 'hearts and minds' in his 'accelerated pacification' program. In America's 'nonlinear war', with no frontline or clear political or territorial goals, the number of enemy killed apparently revealed who was 'winning'.[3] 'The military *kill*' became 'the primary target, simply because the essential political target is too elusive for us, or worse, because we do not understand its importance'.[4]

By body count alone, America and its allies were winning: 'The communists were … being defeated in almost every battle they were engaged in.'[5] In late 1968 and 1969 the enemy body count soared: in the bloody first quarter of 1969, 48,590 enemy died, a kill ratio of '6.37:1'.[6]

Westmoreland's 'kill ratios' were, of course, meaningless in isolation. The objective of attrition was to strike the 'cross-over point' — when the number killed exceeded the enemy's ability to replace them and exhausted Hanoi's will to fight. The magic figure was the 'Enemy Net Loss' (ENL), which supposedly determined the extent to which the North Vietnamese were failing to replace their dead. The Americans measured this by subtracting the total Enemy Replacement Rate (ERR) from the Enemy Gross Adjusted Loss (EGAL). The Enemy Net Loss in the second quarter of 1969, for example, was 1,693 soldiers, or 27,163 (EGAL) minus 25,470 (ERR); that is, the Vietnamese communist forces fell short of replacing their dead and wounded by 1,693 troops in the period; by this measure, the Free World forces won the war in the second quarter of 1969.[7]

Yet they did not 'do the math': according to a US Department of Defense review, American commanders overstated the body count by at least 30 per cent.[8] Sixty-one per cent of US generals in Vietnam described the corpse tally as 'often inflated', in a survey in late 1967.[9] US soldiers routinely exaggerated the kill rate to meet their 'quotas' of enemy dead. An impressive number of kills reflected well on subunit commanders. Rival units held body count races, with scoreboards for the largest number of 'kills'. They had a strong incentive to exaggerate: 'If [a commander's] predecessor had accounted for 3,449 Vietcong [dead] during his year, then he must account for 3,450 if he wanted another star.'[10] At troop level it degenerated into farce: 'What's the body count? What's the body count?' officers implored their troops after a battle. The men rarely gave round figures: 311 KIA sounded more convincing than 300.[11] The wounded were guesses, based on blood trails. When a US colonel implicitly criticised a young major's performance by claiming a far greater kill rate, the major answered, 'That is your war, Colonel. It's not mine.'[12]

Civilian deaths were often included in the count. US forces captured a sixth more people than weapons, suggesting a huge civilian death rate, according to one analysis. Not so, argued Westmoreland: unarmed casualties were usually supply handlers, porters and part of the communist 'infrastructure'.[13] Even if the figures were accurate, the US commanders simply 'measured the measurable'.[14] By 1968 Giap, on the other hand, was measuring progress not by the absolute tally of American dead but by 'the traffic in homebound American coffins' and their impact on US public opinion.[15]

By this time, too, body count had lost all credibility both as a measure of success and as a 'war management tool', as Westmoreland himself acknowledged. US generals variously condemned body count as 'the bane of my existence', 'a blot on the honour of the Army', 'a fake — totally worthless', 'a great crime and cancer in the Army', 'often blatant lies' and 'gruesome — a ticket-punching item'. Most disturbingly, said one, body counts 'were grossly exaggerated by many units primarily because of the incredible interest shown by people like McNamara and Westmoreland. I shudder to think how many of our soldiers were killed on a body-counting mission — what a waste.'[16]

A succession of Australian Task Force and battalion commanders similarly held the US emphasis on body count in contempt.[17] The Australian major generals in Saigon, however — notably Mackay, Vincent and MacDonald — were closer to the Americans and tended to be strong believers. Vincent, a strident advocate, argued, for example: 'If you took Long Tan out of it, our average kill ratio was about 2½–3 to 1; only about ½ to 1 man better than the South Vietnamese Army and 1 to 1¼ men less than the Americans. It was not a very creditable performance … Some people would disagree and say killing is not a measure of success. I think it is …'[18]

The body count psychology impinged at every level, from the largest operations to the smallest skirmishes. The American commander at II Field Force Vietnam demanded kill rates from all subunits, including the Australian Task Force. In 1968 the SAS was ordered to stay in the jungle after a successful contact 'to try for a few more kills'.[19] In fact, many SAS veterans reckoned they were used, at times, simply to improve the Task Force's kill ratio. If an infantry battalion took casualties but did not kill any Viet Cong, SAS troops were sent out to even up the 'ledger'.[20] According to this benchmark, the SAS was perhaps the most lethal unit in Vietnam; many units lost one soldier for 300 to 400 enemy killed.[21] One SAS squadron celebrated its first '100 kills' with a barbecue. The SAS kill rate far exceeded that of the infantry: '… infantry on their own … kill at about 3 to 1,' Vincent wrote: 'On the other hand, our SAS now have 81 kills to their credit with one Aust DOW [died of wounds] and one Aust WIA.'[22] Between 1966 and 1968 the SAS took part in 24 per cent of Australian contacts, yet inflicted 173 of the total 410 enemy KIA in the period and sustained just 19 wounded compared with 73 for the infantry, according to a report by the Australian Army Operational Research Group.[23] They achieved this largely through a combination of stealth, ambush and sudden, devastating firepower.

The blur of statistics in the US Blue Book on war casualties and in Australian after-action reports tends to resemble a corporate balance sheet; yet behind these figures were thousands of dead young men, implied widows, fatherless children and inconsolable parents. The wider story of the bodies, on both sides, killed or wounded in action, the civilian losses, the sick, the families — the whole human impact of war — lost definition and dignity in this statistical deluge.

> … the nearing throb of pulsing drums
> grows louder in the sky
> The press of wind — the metal sting …
> My friend — don't let me die … !

*Now the pulsing drums are overhead,*
*The metal basket lowered*
*But I feel no wind ... I hear no drums ...*[24]

This poem, 'Dustoff', by Tony Pahl, a helicopter gunner with No. 9 Squadron, RAAF, evoked the hopes and fears of the wounded as the medevac approached. Just getting the dead and wounded out of a combat zone was a harrowing ordeal. By 1968 the RAAF's dust-off service had improved on earlier years, yet some pilots still shunned the most dangerous missions, which US pilots accepted.[25]

At Vung Tau, medical teams met the choppers and rushed the badly wounded into surgery. 'Nothing you had done previously could have prepared you for what we witnessed,' said Pam Barlow, a sister at the 1st Australian Field Hospital in 1968.[26] 'You used to see a knee joint just ripped open, feet blown off, legs stripped of flesh,' recalled Dr Michael Naughton, an Australian surgeon.[27]

The 1968 offensives exhausted the little Australian field hospital in Vung Tau; the 8th Field Ambulance was stretched to the limit. To meet the new demands, on 1 April 1968 the new 106-bed 1st Australian Field Hospital opened in the sand dunes of Vung Tau, equipped with an intensive care unit, a separate VD ward, and rooms for triage, surgery, pathology, X-ray, dentistry, physiotherapy and psychiatry.

On 3 March 1968 Colonel (Dr) Don Beard arrived, in the 'lull' between the first and second Tet offensives, to lead the surgical team. Beard, a medical officer during the Korean War, 'restored humanity to a hospital which was close to losing its way', observed Dr Marshall Barr, his assistant, who admitted his own 'slide towards brutishness' in a ward blinded by the 'dehumanizing effect' of the war.[28]

An unusually compassionate man, Beard quickly 're-established the principle that all patients — friendly and enemy — were equal and all would be treated with courtesy and kindness'.[29] On occasions, Beard and other surgeons were forced to put Australian and Viet Cong patients in the same wards — especially during the maelstrom of Mini Tet, as he recorded in his first four days on the job:

Day 2/5th March 68: ... a helicopter came in with a wounded
Vietcong prisoner who had been shot through the thigh ... with
a huge gaping hole where the bullet had come out. The entrance

wound is a small puncture wound but as the bullet tears through the tissues, its energy is dissipated sideways & this is what tears the muscles and other softer tissues. If it hits the bone, then all the fragments do their damage too …

Day 3/6th March 68: … [operated on] an NZ boy who stood on a mine, one leg blown off, one amputated; another boy had extensive shrapnel wounds to abdomen, of which 2 feet of shredded bowel had been removed. It was a miracle that either survived.

Day 4/7th March 68 … very badly wounded NZer flown in at 1700 hrs. [The soldier had trodden on a mine in the Long Binh Hills.] I thought he was dead, both legs being blown to pieces. He had stopped bleeding because he had virtually no blood left. He had no pulse or blood pressure, but was still breathing faintly, with an occasional gasp. He was a Maori called Private Haenga … The blood was pumped in rapidly so that he got about 5 pints within 20 minutes. I then felt a flicker of pulse for the first time …

Removal of the dressings revealed shocking wounds — quite the worst I had ever seen. The mine had gone up behind him & virtually blown off the backs of both legs from the feet to the buttocks.

The soldier was 'virtually exsanguinated'. Both legs were broken, and 3 inches of sciatic nerve had been shot away in one leg. Beard decided to amputate:

This is a terribly difficult decision to be made on the table with a 21 year old boy. I amputated through the site of the fracture in the lower femur & managed to close the stump with a flap of skin from the undamaged shin. Next I had to … cut away all the dead muscle. It bled furiously & we had to pump blood in as fast as we could go. By now we were up to about 18 pints of blood transfusion … several times we thought we'd lost him. We had to wait 30 minutes before we could start on the other leg …

Almost six hours and a 30-pint blood transfusion later, the young Maori was still alive. Beard and his team were utterly exhausted and the theatre a mess of blood, plaster, dead tissue, transfusion packs and linen. The doctor got a few hours' sleep; then, just before 3 a.m., a medical orderly shone a torch in his face:

> 'Private Haenga is bleeding & it won't stop & his pulse is fading fast.'
>
> My heart sank … & off we set again … I cut off all the plasters and one by one clipped & tied off hundreds of small bleeding points — vessels that would normally stop bleeding themselves, but … he had none of his own blood to clot. The blood we were pouring in was pouring out again … eventually I did get on top … and stopped all but minor oozing.

At 8 a.m. Haenga awoke, smiling, after thirteen hours of surgery, nine and a half of them under anaesthetic. After further operations and a major skin graft, he was sent home to New Zealand, to his waiting fiancée. 'Between us we had won a fight with death …', concluded Beard, just four days into his new job.[30]

In March 1968 Beard's surgical team confronted the medical consequences of multiple mine victims. On the 19th, still in 'my swimming trunks and thongs', he rushed to operate on five cases, all of whom were victims of M16 mines, almost certainly lifted from the Australian minefield. Two lads lay alongside each other, chatting away in a morphine-induced high. One had lost a leg, blown off at the calf; the foot was still in its boot, on the stretcher.

'How are ya now, mate?' said the other soldier. 'How's the leg? Did you feel the mine click when you put your foot on it?'

'No,' he replied, 'but I felt a bang when it went off. This is a great way to get a homer. Now we'll be back in time to see the start of the football …'

Neither soldier complained, Beard recalled. They showed 'only gratitude' and a determination to overcome their disabilities. At one point, the soldier who had lost a leg asked, 'Do you have to notify Australia? Mum will only worry.'

Beard treated two Viet Cong patients that March, a boy and a girl. Their stories were ineffably sad. The teenage male soldier, an only child, had recently heard that 'both his parents were dead'. The girl soldier, whom a comrade shot through the arm as she surrendered, had married in January. Her husband died the next month, during Tet, while fighting in Ba Ria. 'She has now discovered that she is pregnant,' wrote Beard. 'She is only 16.'[31] Beard clung to the hope that the couple, who seemed friendly, might fall in love. They left the hospital, bewildered and frightened, 'not knowing what the future holds for them'.[32]

In May 1968 a note of despair entered Beard's diary. 'It is not day 87 but day 90,' he wrote on 1 June, with a shaking hand. 'For the first time since I arrived here I have not been able to keep up. The last three days have been a nightmare & at times I've almost wanted to go away and hide …' However, the 'constant flow of wonderful young men' replenished Beard's spirits, and his formidable composure returned.[33]

The Viet Cong sick and wounded had no such facilities. Lacking helicopters, they were dragged off the battlefield with ropes or vines, or bundled away in wheelbarrows to dismal field hospitals in caves, tunnels or jungle clearings. A typical jungle hospital, codenamed K76A, had no intensive care facilities and used the crudest anaesthetics and an ordinary wooden bench for operations. They had little or no supplies of blood, steroids or barbiturates.[34] Viet Cong troops routinely stole their medical supplies from civilian hospitals, often with the cooperation of the hospital staff. In Phuoc Tuy, they regularly entered Ba Ria Hospital. 'They had guns and you'd watch them filing past,' said one Australian nurse, 'and they'd get their penicillin, morphine, and take it back up into the hills … half the staff could have been VC.'[35] In the end, Ba Ria hospitals became too dangerous, and Australian nurses were withdrawn.

Several Australian aid workers found themselves helping sick and wounded South Vietnamese as well as casualties of the National Liberation Front. Barbara Ferguson, an Australian teacher who worked with World Vision and other agencies, survived the communist forces' bombardment of an American camp just before Tet: 'When the first attacks were over,' she said, '… we visited the province hospital where we saw a locked ward full of VC and/or NVA wounded. We offered them water but they refused our help when one of the older prisoners said it was poisoned.' Later, Ferguson worked with the Vietnamese Red Cross in Saigon; she noticed places she and her drivers visited often came under fire within days or hours of their visit. The drivers assured her she was safe: 'But it wasn't until after they were arrested that I found out that they were accused of being VC,' she said. Ferguson spent eight years caring for the victims of war. On a later occasion she shared a bunker with a family of Vietnamese Christians during a 'rain of VC rockets' and witnessed seven people die on the street. Elsewhere, she witnessed a baby being born on the side of the road.[36]

★  ★  ★

As in all wars, the civilians got the worst of it. Surgical teams from Australia's leading public hospitals (including Sydney's Prince Henry, Royal Prince Alfred and St Vincent's hospitals, and the Royal Melbourne Hospital) did their best to assist, as part of Australia's SEATO obligation. South Vietnamese doctors were extremely scarce: of 859 doctors in the South in 1967, all but 158 were in the armed forces, the rest being spread thinly over a nation of 12 million people.[37] There was a 'continuous transfusion' of foreign medical help, observed the medical reporter Dr Alister Brass, a special correspondent for the *Medical Journal of Australia*.[38]

During Tet, the number of civilian war casualties soared.[39] Between October 1967 and March 1968 the Australian Surgical Team at Bien Hoa — with five doctors, including Graham Wilson and Sam Mellick, and seven nurses — completed about 500 civilian operations. (At the time, an Australian medical team comprised two surgeons — one general, one orthopaedic — an anaesthetist, a physician, a general practitioner, and seven nurses.)[40] Wilson's team recommended the appointment of a full-time plastic surgeon. A year later, in August 1969, Sir Edward 'Weary' Dunlop, the legendary survivor of the Burma Railway, led a surgical team at Bien Hoa, which performed 637 operations. The plastic surgeon, however, had not yet arrived.[41]

They desperately needed one: Super-Napalm, B52 bombs and white phosphorus presented the surgeons with a new and dreadful challenge. Hideous burns so disfigured the victims as to render them monstrous. The worst victims arrived like mummies, cocooned in bandages, which were slowly unwound to reveal faceless creatures, their noses and mouths seared into a 'pale creamy colour' and their hands and feet charred into 'large, wrinkled, loosely fitting gloves'.[42] American and Australian doctors attempted long skin-grafting procedures, but many Vietnamese victims, unable to bear the shocked reaction to their appearance, would live out their days in caves.

Meanwhile, medieval diseases returned to torment the Vietnamese people. A World Health Organization report concluded that plague and leprosy reached epidemic levels between 1962 and 1968.[43] In 1967, 4,532 cases of bubonic plague were reported throughout twenty-seven of South Vietnam's forty-one provinces; 1959 had not seen a single case. Flea-riddled rats spread the disease, and serious eruptions in humans occurred in Nha Trang, Cam Ranh and Vung Tau. Doctors blamed 'tunnel living', which generated waste and encouraged vermin. Leprosy claimed 25,000 people in

1967, the total number of Vietnamese lepers being estimated at 75,000 that year, and higher in 1968. Cholera and tuberculosis were endemic in 1967–68. In 1968 half the outpatients at the Australian-run hospital in Long Xuyen were tubercular.[44] The foreign medical teams did an astonishing job in intolerable circumstances. The quiet, stoic involvement of the Australian civilian nurses, 'these ordinary and extraordinary girls', reduced hardened surgeons to near tears of appreciation.[45]

Yet things broke down; spirits collapsed; some staff were unable to bear such concentrated suffering. During Tet, one Australian nurse beheld 'the lawns of the hospital chockers with dead people from all the outlying districts. It became a morgue for the whole area. At the time I pulled down a curtain and I didn't talk about it. I didn't talk about it for years. I drank a lot then, I drank vast amounts.'[46] The corpses drew rats that scuttled about the hospital at night, running over the feet of the sick and the dead.

On arriving at the Long Xuyen hospital, Brass wrote this incomparable portrait of a moment in the hospital's life:

A young Vietnamese nurse was lounging in a deck-chair at one end of the room reading an elementary English text about Peter Rabbit and his furry friends. Some days before, in an absent-minded moment, she had lifted up a bottle into which pus was draining from an amoebic abscess of the liver and allowed it to run back into the patient. A mother and father were dabbing alcohol on the forehead of their feverish child, a thin, sick five-year-old who had had a laparotomy … A teenage youth in black pyjamas with a .45 bullet wound through his left thigh nodded cheerfully. How did they know he was not a member of the Viet Cong? I enquired. 'All of them may be as far as I know,' I was told. 'We never ask.' Lying on a stretcher was a middle-aged woman with high cheek bones and matted black hair. She was shocked, soaking wet and shivering, and she was moaning softly, rolling her head from one side to the other. Muddy, blood-stained bandages were loosely tied over her right shoulder, and a wet X-ray film propped up against the wall showed a mosaic of bone fragments where the head of the humerus and the outer part of the scapula should have been. An old man with thinning grey hair and black baggy pants was squatting beside her, looking dazed and helpless.[47]

The moaning woman, it emerged, was the wife of a hamlet chief in Kien Phong province, in the Plain of Reeds. At five o'clock that morning, Viet Cong soldiers had burst into their house, shot her husband and wounded her. 'The old man was vague about what had happened to her children ...'[48]

The children. The children — and the elderly — were the most vulnerable. Easily the most overworked were the pediatric and geriatric wards. 'Nearly all children admitted are seriously ill requiring very intensive care,' an Australian surgical team leader at Long Xuyen reported.[49] The blood bank relied on fifteen donors daily.

The orphanages overflowed. Tens of thousands of children were herded into these embattled institutions, which were heroically staffed by nuns and international aid workers who performed the most thankless jobs. Prominent Australian examples were Rosemary Taylor, who spent eight years caring for Vietnamese orphans, and Barbara Ferguson (mentioned previously), who joined the Vietnamese Red Cross. Many orphans were napalm victims, and lacked legs and arms; many were abandoned 'Amerasians'. The orphanage at Vung Tau received regular visits from Australian soldiers, who gave toys and medicines to the children. They were the lucky ones: most orphanages were charnel houses, from which up to 80 per cent of children never emerged. Hunger added to the misery amid scenes of starving waifs lying three to a cot, 'opening and shutting their mouths like little birds'.[50] Some orphanages and indeed hospitals gave up, and relegated their worst cases to 'dying rooms', where children beyond hope were abandoned behind closed doors.

The dreadful suffering of Vietnamese children went on and on, and scarcely impinged on the actions of the men of violence, who continued their war, tested their weapons, and mouthed their banalities and ideologies that no sensible people believed in any more. At Bien Hoa Hospital dreadfully wounded children lay in cots plugged into drips, rocking from side to side, in intolerable pain, their very existence a reproach to heaven and earth. Of what value were 'freedom' and 'liberation' in a world prepared to inflict this on a 10-year-old boy, riddled with dozens of steel fragments from a claymore mine and already a veteran of three open chest operations? The boy lay in the care of Professor Hugh Dudley, of Monash University, Melbourne, along with rows of other little bundles jutting out in their beds like exhibits in a metaphysical charge against humanity. Would it have vexed the consciences of the men in Hanoi, Washington and Saigon, who had inflicted this abomination on the world, and who had the power to stop it, to hear of the three-year-old girl blown up, her dad dead, her mum a weeping wreck beside the bed where her daughter twitched with hunger, unable to feed without a tube directly into her stomach, 'in the hope that some nourishment could be forced into her' before she died? No, the war got worse, 'peace talks' decreed as much; and not even the 'un-human' cases served the only use left them, as silent, dreadful protests — *un-human*, because a child victim of napalm or white phosphorus really went beyond pity or sorrow into the realm of appalled curiosity, that we should gaze on this charred thing, 'crisp, brown, crackling', of unknown sex, vaguely identifiable as humanoid, yet hideously transformed from the beautiful little person it had been.[51]

Civilian hospitals were both desperately sad and strangely happy places. Nomadic tribes of orphans tended to camp near the hospitals, drawn by some primal instinct that perhaps this place would care for them or house their parents. Inside, the visitor encountered the poor hygiene (the lavatory was usually a hole in the ground) and the chronic shortage of drugs, syringes and morphine. The hospitals all relied on foreign aid and often resorted to traditional medicines, such as cumquat peel and ginseng for tuberculosis; dwarf palm for dysentery; liquorice and ginger for malaria; and white mulberry for infected wounds.[52]

Then a more heartening prospect gladdened the eye: Vietnamese families, washing and feeding the patients, changing intravenous drips and drainage bags. Mothers rarely left the sides of their children's cots, which usually contained several little patients; indeed, every scrap of space was given over to the patients and their entourages. Families sat for days and weeks beside the beds, and nightly lit joss sticks, prayed and slept in hammocks strung up in the wards … swinging shadows of sleeping loved ones. 'I am sure,' wrote Susan Terry, a sister at Royal Melbourne Hospital who spent a year as a nurse in Long Xuyen, 'there can be no more devoted nursing, no more tender loving care, given anywhere in the world than the Vietnamese lavish on their sick …'[53] There were other sources of hope: in the limb workshops, in the utter dedication of the few Vietnamese doctors, and in the pockets of aid workers all over the country. Examples include Dr Pat Smith's renowned hospital in the Central Highlands (where Ruth

O'Halloran, a nurse from Wagga Wagga, worked) and the thriving hospital in Qui Nhon, founded by a civilian New Zealand team, which was the first foreign medical team into Vietnam.[54]

The foreign medical teams worked wonders in Vietnam. They inoculated thousands and repaired harelips, cleft palates and other deformities. 'Look at my baby — Australian doctors!' local mothers would cry. Clearly, the foreign surgeons did not 'abominably disfigure' the children, as Viet Cong propagandists warned the parents. The Australians dealt sensitively with their Vietnamese counterparts and respected local customs. 'The reason we feel so close to the Australians,' said Dr Nhi, a gynaecologist at Long Xuyen Hospital, 'is that you try to understand us, you try to see how we think … You don't just watch and pass judgement.'[55]

Yet the medical teams' efforts went largely unrecognised at home. In fact, on their return, Australian civilian doctors and nurses were generally ignored, maligned by anti-war activists, or criticised for 'treating the enemy', because their duty of care extended to all civilians, including, unavoidably, the families of Viet Cong. The obscene implication is that they should have let wounded soldiers or civilians suffer or die.


The fifty-five Australian Army padres and chaplains who served in Vietnam performed the roles of counsellors and confidants. They eased anxieties on operations and comforted grief-stricken or traumatised young men. And, of course, they delivered last rites, often on the battlefield, a role in which some felt helpless. 'My God, why didn't you make me a doctor instead of a stupid priest?' Father Stan Hessey of the 8th Battalion thought, as he knelt 'feeling totally useless' beside a mortally wounded soldier.

'Padre, where is God in all of this?' a dying soldier beseeched Hessey.

'God isn't in our battle,' he replied, and said later, '… but God was within that dying boy.'[56]

To some troops, the chaplains' very presence in Vietnam seemed morally incongruous: 'Had a lecture from a chaplain. It really confuses one when you find a man of God amongst a group of trained killers …'[57] Some soldiers lost all faith in the 'chaplains' bullshit', as one US grunt said: 'Whatever we were doing … murder … atrocities … God was *always* on our side.' One enraged GI almost assaulted a US chaplain who talked of a 'noble sacrifice for the sake of their country' after a battle in which many of his buddies died.[58] Yet many American and Australian soldiers, even those without faith, found the chaplains' presence a kind of hope in hell. They would pray in combat. 'I could hear a whimpering moan from a Viet Cong body,' said Private Terry Cobby, 'and I cried to myself, "Oh, I can't take this!" and my mate and I opened up and ended his suffering ... I said two rosaries and promised God the world if only we could live through this night.'[59]

The Australian boys' remains were sent to a mortuary at the American field hospital at Long Binh. Phil Johnstone, an assistant mortician, flew the 'body runs', hosed down the corpses and disposed of personal effects. He dreaded finding letters in the pockets; a letter from one soldier's wife wrote that 'their kids needed shoes and stuff like that ... things my wife said to me. I should never have read that letter.'[60]

The chaplain had the traumatic job of informing the families of the death of a son. A uniformed notification officer usually accompanied him. As Captain Michael Bindley, a notification officer, said, 'It was an attempt to improve on a cold telegram' — or, if casualties' names leaked out, the press.[61]

Bindley recounted the details of his disturbing visits in note form. Here are two:[62]

- Notification on member of 2RAR ... suffering from serious shrapnel wounds and loss of leg. NOK [next of kin], father ... at party with family and friends. Proceed to location. 9 p.m. news on car radio announces details of incident including KIAs and serious wounds. Arrive at address as given, sounds of party inside. Knock on door answered by woman; inform her I am from Army and wish to talk to soldier's father. Woman informs everybody in shocked voice who is at door. Cries that soldier has been killed from inside, as they have heard 9 o'clock news. Statement by me, in loud voice, 'It's all right, he is not dead; has only lost a leg.' Reaction to my dreadful statement one of apparent relief. Pause as I give details to NOK, asked to stay for quiet drink, declined as I felt like hiding somewhere.
- Call at approximately 3 p.m. with details of KIA and NOK location ... small shop in Newtown ... door answered by female, sister? Immediate recognition of situation by family. Padre immediately takes control and comforts family. Remain as long as necessary until friends and relatives arrive to comfort family. Return journey require pitstop at local Newtown pub, go directly

to toilet. On return to bar (in uniform) one of the drinkers shouts, 'Up the Viet Cong'. Immediate reaction to shirtfront individual, push against wall and inform him of what I have just done. Comments create absolute silence in bar (may have known KIA and family?). Silence enough time to realise that immediate withdrawal the best course of action. Another notification completed. No follow up or debriefing provided by the system.

Second Lieutenant Malcolm Brown, a notification officer, received an order to inform a Singleton woman of the death of her husband. Brown drove to the Hunter Valley with the duty chaplain in an olive-green Kombi van. Here is Brown's account of what happened:

> The woman, pathetically small, her stomach bulging with an unborn baby, came to the door. As soon as she set eyes on us she knew. She joked about the state of the house and the chaplain smiled.
>
> 'Have you got some news?' she asked as she ushered us into the living room.
>
> 'Yes,' the chaplain replied.
>
> 'Bad news?'
>
> 'Yes, bad news. Yes, killed. By a mine.'
>
> The screaming started immediately. She screamed and screamed. People seemed to come from everywhere. The woman's mother, her own tears streaming down her face, shouted at the tiny trembling woman to control herself ... The woman retreated to the kitchen. The chaplain whipped away a knife he saw on the table. 'They're likely to do anything in those first few minutes when you break the news to them,' he said later.
>
> 'I'll kill Gorton, kill him, kill him, kill him,' the woman howled.
>
> The chaplain sat quietly beside her, comforting her as best he could. She sobbed and said she did not want the baby. Then we left. We'd spent over an hour there. We had shattered a woman's life and cast a shadow over the future of an unborn child.[63]

Later the woman gave birth to a healthy baby.

Malcolm Fraser, then Minister for the Army, arrives at Saigon Airport in 1967 for a tour of the Australian bases. Later, as Defence Minister, Fraser would resign in disgust at Prime Minister Gorton's leadership, declaring, 'I do not believe he is fit to hold the great office of Prime Minister' in a speech that effectively ended Gorton's career.

1 Section, 5 Platoon, B Company, 6th Battalion, photographed before the battle of Bribie, February 1967. (L–R back row) Privates William Trevenen, Garry Chad, Vic Otway, Malcolm Mustchin and David Webster; (L–R front row) Corporal Robin 'Spike' Jones, and Privates Brian Waters, Wayne Riley and Donald Rumble. After Bribie only Jones was left standing; the rest were wounded or killed in action.

Go-go dancer Pat Wordsworth, known as the 'Big Pretzel', performs for Australian troops at Bien Hoa. The Australian concerts were tame by comparison with the Americans', where strippers, drugs and brawls were common.

Entertainer Lorrae Desmond shares a joke with a soldier at Luscombe Bowl in Nui Dat. The Australian soldiers loved her, and she returned their affection by performing five times in Vietnam, provoking the anger of protesters at home.

Brigadier Stuart Graham (right), the Australian Task Force commander in 1967, meets General William Westmoreland, commander of the US Forces, at Nui Dat. Westmoreland criticised Graham for failing to achieve the required 'body count'. Graham aimed, instead, to separate the Viet Cong from the people. To this end, he insisted on the construction of an 11-kilometre minefield, with tragic consequences.

Australian troops watch a spectacular air strike on a suspected enemy position in the Long Hai Hills in Phuoc Tuy. The Long Hais, notorious for mines and booby traps, served as the Viet Cong's provincial headquarters. Attempts to capture them led to many Australian casualties.

Khóc thương kẻ chết, người đi.
Gia đình tan nát cũng vì Cộng nô.
Đắng cay, mỏn mỏi đợi chờ,
Mẹ già, con dại bao giờ gặp anh ?

SP-2141

A 'Chieu Hoi' leaflet encourages Viet Cong troops to surrender and join their fellow countrymen who were loyal to Saigon. The leaflets were distributed by plane over communist-occupied areas.

The poem reads:
*Crying and mourning for the deceased and the departed,*
*Families fell apart because of the communists,*
*Desperately waiting in bitterness,*
*When would your mother and young children see you again?*

Binh Ba, South Vietnam, April 1969: Army dentist Captain Richard Brewer extracts a young Vietnamese woman's tooth, closely watched by villagers. An army dentist regularly toured villages in Phuoc Tuy province with a medical civil aid team attending to illness and injury among the people.

Brigadier General Nguyen Ngoc Loan, the feared Saigon police chief, shoots a Viet Cong prisoner in the head during the Tet Offensive. Eddie Adams's photo appeared on newspaper front pages around the world and turned many Westerners against the war. Loan claimed he acted in revenge for the deaths of several of his men during Tet.

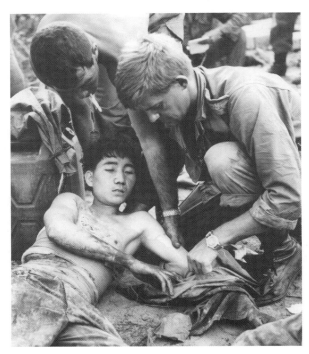

During the war, many Viet Cong casualties were sent to the Australian Field Hospital in Vung Tau, and often shared wards with wounded Australian troops.

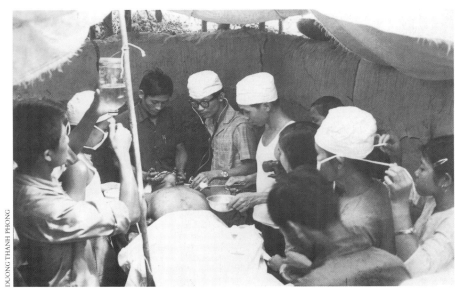

Viet Cong field hospitals tended to be underground or in depressions covered by tarpaulins and camouflaged by the jungle. The enemy forces always attempted to recover the bodies of their dead and wounded, and stole supplies of morphine and medication from hospitals in the main towns.

A defining image of resistance to the war: on 22 November 1966, primary-school teacher Bill White was arrested for refusing the draft and dragged from his home by burly policemen. Anti-war groups rallied to his cause and launched a 'Free Bill White' campaign.

Draft resister Simon Townsend is arrested on 1 February 1968. Like White, Townsend argued that he acted in accordance with his personal beliefs, and not as part of an anti-war group. He received hate mail and white feathers. After the war he hosted *Simon Townsend's Wonder World* on television.

MAKE LOVE NOT WAR

Andy Blunden, 21, a civil engineering student, burns his national service registration card at an anti-conscription rally outside Prime Minister Harold Holt's residence in 1966. Despite the high profile of 'draft dodgers', they were in fact few in number.

LEFT: Soldiers of the 7th Battalion, Royal Australian Regiment, march through Sydney on their return from Vietnam, 26 April 1968. Many returning troops received a cold reception, and soldiers remember with bitterness the hostility of a nation which had earlier voted overwhelmingly to send them to war.

BELOW: Corporal Trent Grall (left) and Lance Corporal Barry O'Brien of the 7th Battalion prime M16 'jumping jack' mines, some of the more than 20,000 mines used in the minefield laid by the 1st Australian Task Force from Dat Do to the coast. Later, the Viet Cong would lift 6,000 or so jumping jacks and use them against the Australian troops.

ABOVE: Captain Trevor Anderson treats minor ailments of members of the New Zealand W Company during a resupply in the field. On 21 July 1969 Anderson was called out to assist a wounded platoon which had walked into a minefield. After treating the eighteen wounded men, he was hit by an exploding mine and blinded.

Families expressed sorrow in heart-rending ways. One mother wrote to the army requesting that her son's birthday gift, which she had sent before his death, be shared among his platoon. In its inimitable way, the army cabled Saigon with her request:

1. NOK HAS REQUESTED THAT ARTICLE DESCRIBED BELOW, POSTED TO DECEASED FOR BIRTHDAY, BE DISTRIBUTED AMONGST MEMBERS OF DECEASED SOLDIER'S PLATOON.
2. DESCRIPTION OF ARTICLE: SQUARE PACKAGE COVERED WITH UNBLEACHED CALICO, ADDRESSED TO DECEASED SOLDIER. PACKAGE CONTAINS BOOK/CAKES ETC.[64]

The dead soldier's platoon, company and sometimes battalion commanders often wrote separately to the families:

It is not a duty obligation which occasions me to write to you
but a knowledge of the great sense of loss you must feel …
To say that [your son] was a good soldier would be far from
sufficient … The degree of esteem in which your son was held
by his friends has been movingly demonstrated … His loss to
them had a dramatic effect. I realise words alone cannot ease the
pain of this tragedy for you. However, I would ask you to
accept the heartfelt sympathy of the members of the Fourth
Battalion …[65]

In reply to one such letter, a mother asked whether anyone had found her son's wallet 'as it has all his private papers in it'. She explained: 'I want to get everything fixed up as soon as possible, because … I have just found out that I have cancer and I may join my dear son at any moment.' The boy's battalion commander replied that his wallet was 'destroyed during contact with the enemy. The only contents salvaged was in fact the money which was credited to [your son's] account.'[66]

The father of a national serviceman 'accidentally killed in action' wrote to the battalion commander: 'As he was our only child his passing has left a void in our life which can never be filled. Our sorrow is more for him as he graduated as a BSc this year in order to become a worthy citizen … As parents of a soldier "accidentally killed in action" is it possible for us to have details of just how his death occurred?'[67] The young man had been accidentally shot by 'friendly fire'.

Phil Johnstone placed the bodies in the coffins and sealed them. Sometimes only a head survived a direct hit, so he added sandbags to make up the weight.[68] Other Australian morticians did the same. The boxes went home aboard a Hercules transport plane. The soldier's personal effects followed. Nothing would heal the parents' agony of rereading letters they had sent to their sons, returned along with his clothing, wallet and souvenirs. The funeral proceeded. The army provided wreaths, dignity and a rifle salute. Meanings were made of the loss.

The North Vietnamese families received no word of what became of their sons and daughters. For propaganda reasons, Hanoi publicly refused to accept the huge casualty rate and so, in reliable totalitarian tradition, simply told the families nothing. The mothers' fury sparked a long struggle between 'Mrs Thap's Soldiers' and 'General Giap's soldiers', a little-known story of Hanoi's cruelty, as told by a North Vietnamese defector who rallied to the Australians in March 1971.

In 1968 the influential Mrs Nguyen Thi Thap, Women's Commissioner of the Central Headquarters of the Lao Dong (Workers) Party of North Vietnam, led a delegation to see Prime Minister Pham Van Dong. Mrs Thap demanded that thousands of wives and families be told the fate of their menfolk. The women naturally wished to mourn and hold funeral services in the Buddhist tradition; otherwise, the souls of the dead would wander the earth and never rest. Some women hoped to remarry — legally. Fearing an outcry over any official confirmation of the catastrophic death rate, the North Vietnamese Government refused. A war of words ensued between 'Mrs Thap's soldiers' and 'General Giap's soldiers': 'Giap versus Thap' was a source of constant rumour and anger in North Vietnamese ranks.[69] Giap won: Hanoi refused to publish casualty lists.

As for the South Vietnamese, their grief and funeral marches were tragically commonplace. Major Peter Murray drew this beautifully sad portrait of a passing bier in a letter to his wife:

Yesterday I watched a Vietnamese funeral … First came an old Peugeot sadly in need of paint and panel beating. It carried 12–14 people all curiously studying us and without any apparent reverence for the recently departed. Then the hearse drawn by a horse as old as the Peugeot. The golden-painted, wooden-framed dray was draped with white and red ribbons, golden bells, prayer paper and tinkling milk bottle tops. The cheap coffin lay bedecked in white silk. Walking in haphazard order behind the cart came a charade of professional and genuine mourners all dressed in black. Men and women in no particular order; the men looking about them casually and the women wailing. The small column wound its way along the crowded and busy street overtaking stationary cars and carts double-parked at the roadside and pedestrians darted through the mourners without regard to conscience. Basket weavers and roadside carpenters ignored the procession and children merely glanced up from their kerbside game. Traffic gave no sympathy [to] the pathetic little group … One or two soldiers displayed some interest, but only as much as they would to a passing girl …[70]

# Chapter 33
# A politicians' war

The coat of arms of my own country, sir, is borne on one side
by a kangaroo and on the other by an emu. Neither one of these
creatures, so the botanists tell me, is physically able to move
backwards; they can only move forward. We will and we have …
*Prime Minister John Gorton, in a speech to President Johnson.*

As 1968 fell towards 1969, humanity contended with the assassinations of
Martin Luther King and Robert Kennedy, American race riots and the
violent student uprisings in Paris and other European cities. Meanwhile,
America, like a wounded predator seeking refuge in a cave, began its long
psychological withdrawal from the world. Febrile social commentators and
religious zealots warned of the End, of Judgement Day, of a sickness
spreading over humanity. 'I heard this cacophony over and over,' wrote Lady
Bird Johnson, the First Lady, in her diary. 'What is our country coming to?
What is happening to us? Are we a sick society?'

The Soviet Union invaded Czechoslovakia and crushed Dubcek's
'socialism with a human face'. Most Western socialists offered little protest,
setting an odious double standard alongside their vilification of US forces in
Vietnam. It is a gross anomaly that so few raised a placard against the real
'imperialist' of the 1950s and '60s, the Soviet Union, which simply annexed
Eastern Europe at will and packed thousands of 'dissidents' off to the
Siberian Gulag. An intriguing exception was Australia's new 'Independent
Communist Party', led by the unionist Jack Mundey, the Aarons brothers

(Laurie and Eric) and Ann Curthoys, which claimed the dubious distinction of being the 'first' Communist Party in the world to oppose the Soviet invasion of Czechoslovakia. They presented their break with Moscow as a proud political virtue at a time when most Australians believed they should have hung their heads in shame for taking so long.

In Australia, 1968 had been a 'dull' year, said one newspaper. Protesters rocked the Prime Minister's car; 66 per cent of young people 'believed in God', said a survey, and a narrow majority of Sydney University students claimed to have lost their virginity. Don Lane was king of TV, and a new prime minister set forth to 'do it his way'.[1]

Recasting the political narrative: Black Jack McEwen's impressive caretaker role after Holt's death ended in early 1968 with a leadership struggle that degenerated into an unseemly scrap between Gorton, Hasluck and Billy McMahon. The Liberal Coalition needed a leader who could command a popular following and match the ALP's Gough Whitlam at the dispatch box. Hasluck's dour manner scratched him early in the race, and McEwen's intervention scuppered Billy McMahon, whom many said was a fine Treasurer (a refrain that seemed rather to disqualify than enhance McMahon's accession).

The leadership of the nation thus landed, by accident, in the lap of John Grey Gorton, a party-loving, patriotic, whisky-drinking, whimsically lecherous and rather likeable gentleman farmer and former Hurricane fighter pilot, who had a clear advantage over the rest: he was telegenic. His battered face and raffish smile announced, 'I'm everyone's best mate'. In the distorting little frame of the new medium, Gorton seemed to be a man of the people, one of us, a good bloke after our own hearts and minds.

Gorton initially charmed the Australian people. He was 'a freewheeling extrovert who, at the drop of a hat, would climb into swimming trunks, don a surf lifesaver's cap and pull an oar in a surfboat, swill beer or play darts at a workers' club, dance cheek-to-cheek all night with the prettiest girl in the room. Gorton liked to project himself as the prototype of the typical Australian, egalitarian … blunt to the point of rudeness, but good naturedly so.'[2] Shot down over Singapore during World War II, Gorton's crash-landing left him with a crumpled nose that 'makes him look like an ex-prize fighter', noted a White House profile.[3] Gorton seemed the genuine Aussie article, except that he tended to pronounce Australia 'Orstralia' in the English aristocratic manner; had attended Shore, Geelong Grammar and Oxford University; and married an attractive American, Bettina, from Maine.

As Prime Minister, Gorton ran the country in the style of the boisterous publican of a rowdy hotel. He affected a general welcome, yet in practice admitted mostly malleable yes-men, pretty young women and 'advisers' who were prepared to stay up all night to hear his baffling bar tales. True, Australians rather liked a party, but as time passed the people looked askance at the sight. The image of their leader gallivanting about the world stage, an embarrassing quip on his unruly lips, in the thrall of his 21-year-old private secretary, Ainsley Gotto, possibly added to the gaiety of the nation but did little to dignify the office of Prime Minister.

Gorton's relations with Washington started awkwardly — 'Gorton is very different from Harold Holt', the White House diplomatically observed — and quickly lapsed into an acute trans-Pacific embarrassment. Gorton naively distanced his government from Washington, partly to silence Labor's bleat that Australia was the fifty-first state of the Union. Yet his intentions went much further. With some prescience, Gorton sensed that the failing adventure in Vietnam would provoke an American return to pre-World War II isolationism. This bothered him as it would damage the ANZUS alliance and shut down US military aid as Britain withdrew from Malaysia and Singapore, forcing Australia to adopt an independent defence policy; indeed, he saw this outcome as probable, if not inevitable.

Gorton alarmed Washington. Contradictions and inconsistencies assailed his policy pronouncements. In one breath he refused further military support to America; in the next he warned of a heightened military threat from China. Washington bridled at the Australian leader's defence posture, which Gorton impulsively characterised as a 'Fortress Australia' mentality before withdrawing the allusion.[4] Yet the Prime Minister's ardent nationalism did little to dispel the metaphor. Indeed, his first act on winning office was to freeze the numbers of troops in Vietnam. He imposed the troop ceiling before Tet — and reinforced it afterwards. 'Australia won't increase its troop commitment,' he told the Canberra press gallery. He thus closed the door on the future military demands of 'forward defence', effectively terminating the policy that had taken us to war in Vietnam. The rationale for Australian involvement had ended, Gorton believed. Yet the soldiers would fight on, under a prime minister who no longer believed in the reasons for which they were fighting.

On 27–28 May 1968 Gorton did his bit for the US alliance: he made the obligatory pilgrimage to the White House, as guest of honour at the troubled court of LBJ. White House scribes drew an unflattering pre-visit sketch of the Australian leader. Gorton, they warned LBJ, was a shallow thinker and a conclusion-jumper who lacked experience in foreign affairs. 'He tends to say what first comes into his mind.'[5] Gorton's rash statements were attributable to his cocksureness, insularity and inexperience.[6] 'Nevertheless,' one brief magnanimously added, 'the anxiety which he expresses is unquestionably felt to some degree by a great many Australians. Having had the traumatic experience, in 1942, of being let down by their first great protector, they are hypersensitive to anything that could be construed as a sign of wavering on our part ...'[7]

If so, Washington was not about to ease Australia's 'hypersensitivity'. Days before Gorton arrived, Secretary of State Dean Rusk, in a private memo to the President, firmly ruled out any further US military commitment to Australian security. America would not step into the boots of the last British soldiers to leave Malaysia and Singapore in 1971. Nor would America give Australia 'a blanket guarantee of protection under ANZUS', Rusk reminded Johnson. 'Suggest you tell Gorton, as we have said before, there is no question of our "filling the gap".'[8]

At the exchange of toasts in the State Dining Room of the White House, the President leavened his speech with the usual statesmanlike hyperbole: 'Right now [our] partnership is being tested — tested in the hardest way that the ties between nations can be tested ... In Paris we shall remain patient but firm in the quest for an honourable peace ...'[9]

Gorton's reply to this august company exceeded the standards of buffoonery he had led his country to expect of him. The American administration, however, was unfamiliar with Gorton's laid-back Aussie style and found the speech risible. 'I must first of all thank you, sir,' Gorton drooled, groggily, 'for extending such a warm welcome to myself and my Maine lady — that is spelled with an "e"... I speak as a convinced Confederate; at least I would have been then. Things don't change that much ...' Well, they do, and they had, at least in America. The President had been advised that Australia's White Australia Policy was 'still substantially in effect' and that Gorton himself 'firmly advocated the continued exclusion of coloured immigrants' and 'sympathized with the racial policies of Rhodesia and South Africa'.[10] It was awkward for the president, who had genuinely tried to improve the lot of Black Americans, to host a lunch in honour of a defiantly white Aussie who identified with the rulers of apartheid.

Gorton concluded with a vision of Australia and America going forth in the manner of a large rodent and a flightless bird: 'The coat of arms of my own country, sir, is borne on one side by a kangaroo and on the other by an emu. Neither one of these creatures, so the botanists tell me, is physically able to move backwards; they can only move forward. We will and we have ...'[11]

The joint communiqué at the end of the visit was an exercise in staggering futility. Along with the usual blather about the 'continuing search for peace' and so on, it 'reaffirmed specifically the importance of the ANZUS Treaty as an expression of the United States' continuing strategic interest in the region'.[12] Rusk, of course, had eviscerated the very substance of that intent in his private memo to the President two days before (a direct echo of his neutering of ANZUS before Menzies' visit, in 1965).

If Gorton's few 'advisers' — the Prime Minister travelled with hand-picked mates distinguished by their very ignorance of foreign affairs — hoped that their leader's inanities had ended, they were soon disabused. Asked at a press conference on 28 May whether ANZUS covered Malaysia and Singapore, Gorton displayed a worrying ignorance of the hallowed treaty. 'ANZUS is a treaty,' he began. 'I think it applies in certain defined areas. But I would want to check this with the External Affairs people before I was sure that was correct. But by and large, I think it has been, what shall I say — I cannot think of the exact words — a matter never spelled out whether it applied in the Malaysia and Singapore area or not.'[13] Gorton was, unwittingly, correct: ANZUS was merely an agreement to discuss when and where it applied (and Rusk had made very clear in private that it would *not* apply to Malaysia or Singapore when the British left).

The next day, in a speech to the National Press Club in Washington, the Prime Minister alluded for the second time to Australia's need for an 'Israeli-type defence' policy, were America to withdraw precipitately from South-East Asia. The allusion drew on a siege mentality that said more, perhaps, about Gorton's dogfight with a Japanese Zero than the shared history of Israel and Australia.

The media tried, unsuccessfully, to interpret Gorton's strange performance. The *Daily Telegraph* swooned over 'the most eloquent and stirring' oratory that an Australian prime minister had ever made on such an occasion; the editor was in earnest and not, apparently, making a wry dig at previous standards of public discourse.[14] Only the *Australian Financial Review* got a handle on the scale of the debacle:

It is difficult to decide [it said] whether Gorton is a very raw tourist casually tossing thoughts this way and that from the top of his head, or whether he is the Prime Minister of a troubled nation delineating policies for the future. Either way, he comes perilously close to making an ass of himself. If he is to be taken seriously ... he is setting in train drastic alterations to the fundamental policies that guide the Australian nation. He has chosen to inform his nation and its friends of these changes from the capital of a friendly but nonetheless foreign power ...

... if the PM's action in waiting until he is abroad to issue casual pronouncements on vital policy matters is disturbing, his blinkered view of Australia's interests as being confined by Australia's borders is much more so ...

The ANZUS Treaty is hardly relevant to the security of South-East Asia as a region ... There are stirrings in the power structure of Asia which will eventually be of transcendental importance to Australia ... Yet our PM wants to opt out ...[15]

The *Financial Review* knew the half of it. During the trip Gorton rarely went to bed before 3 a.m., and insisted that Miss Ainsley Gotto and Len Hewitt, head of the Prime Minister's office, stay up to chat about world affairs over nips of whisky. 'After several days he was so groggy that his public speaking performances were affected,' Gotto told John Dorrance, political officer at the American Embassy in Canberra, in June. Her 'most difficult task', she said, was getting Gorton to read his briefing papers, which he dismissed as 'so much bumpf'. He prepared his speeches at the last minute, with Gotto's help.[16]

Extraordinary as it may seem, Gorton sought the counsel of this 21-year-old woman over his own departmental advisers. He refused to invite 'those External Affairs people', whom he loathed, on his global peregrinations. Partly intended as a puerile snub to Hasluck's department, Gorton's elevation of Gotto led some to describe her as the government's 'foreign affairs adviser'. The joke was oddly self-fulfilling; this intelligent, wilful young woman did in fact have Gorton's ear. In time, Gotto actually exerted 'a tremendous degree of influence over Gorton'.[17] Gotto even presumed to screen official briefs sent to the Prime Minister and controlled 'to a dangerous extent' which government ministers had access to him. She was 'the most influential little so-and-so in

Canberra', concluded A. T. Griffith, Assistant Secretary for Defence and External Affairs in the Prime Minister's Department.[18]

During his Asian tour in mid-1968, Gorton flew to Vietnam to visit the troops. They looked in dismay at this grotty, unkempt bloke who arrived with his shirt unbuttoned and his boots dirty, and who was largely unaware of the details of Coral and Balmoral. Nevertheless, their leader made an effort to rise to the occasion: 90 per cent of the Australian people were behind you, Gorton told the ranks. 'Hundreds of citizens [are supporting you] for every one who is not.' He dismissed the latter as 'any nut who carries a placard or sits in the middle of the road'.[19] When the reporter Pat Burgess asked about recent Tet setbacks, Gorton mistook him for Wilfred Burchett, defended the diggers and stormed off.

At the Five-Power summit in Kuala Lumpur on the future of Malaysia and Singapore in June 1968, Gorton returned to his theme of Australian independence. He opposed Australia's long commitment to the policy of forward defence, and favoured a self-reliant national defence policy and the phased withdrawal of our overseas forces. Yet he vacillated under pressure. In the end, Hasluck and Defence Minister Fairhall persuaded Gorton to agree to keep Australian forces in Singapore and Malaysia until 1971. Their semblance of unity failed to dislodge an impression of 'defence dither', reported the *Sydney Morning Herald*.[20]

Personally, Gorton believed a policy of self-reliance best served Australia's interests, and he favoured an early troop withdrawal from Vietnam. Yet his Liberal and Country Party colleagues were opposed to pulling out the troops — not necessarily on principle but rather because a quarter of their seats were decided on Democratic Labor Party preferences, and the DLP fiercely rejected any withdrawal from Vietnam. 'To question this doctrine was to strike at the heart of the DLP's obsession — the ever-present threat from the North.'[21]

Later in the year Gorton's performance descended to the level of farce, in the eyes of Washington, Cabinet and Parliament. In their Prime Minister, the Australian people rather hoped for someone who dignified human endeavour and tended not to remind them of their own failings. By this criterion, Gorton disappointed. At times, a kind of perilously ill-scripted vaudeville act seemed to be posing as the nation's leader. In June 1968 Peter Lawler, Deputy Secretary of the Cabinet Office, alerted Dorrance, at the American Embassy in Canberra, to a crisis of confidence at the top: Gorton had 'personalised' and 'politicised' the public service, Lawler said. Gorton had rejected any advice from External Affairs, a punishment for a feud with Hasluck, whose staff 'cordially hated' the Prime Minister. Gorton, Lawler concluded, appeared to be 'playing' at being Prime Minister: it was 'virtually impossible to find a government parliamentarian who had anything good to say about Gorton's performance'.[22] In such terms, a White House memo entitled 'The Performance of Prime Minister Gorton' apprised President Johnson of the state of Australia's leadership.[23]

Johnson and Gorton never hit it off; relations further deteriorated on 31 October when LBJ announced, for the second time that year, a pause in the bombing of North Vietnam without bothering to alert — far less consult — the Australian Government, which was informed the next day via an unannounced visit to the Lodge by William Crook, the American Ambassador. Crook's warm invitation to an embassy party that evening took the edge off Gorton's indignation.[24]

Gorton headed for the embassy party in the company of the 19-year-old journalist Geraldine Willesee, the only female member of the Canberra press gallery, whom he escorted from an earlier press bash. The couple lurched headlong into the night, the whiff of whisky on Gorton's breath, and promptly strayed off course towards a Black and White Ball at the Rex Hotel. Gorton's press secretary Tony Eggleton, in the back seat for the ride, reoriented the entourage towards the relative dignity of the American Embassy where, to general amazement, Gorton sat and chatted privately with Miss Willesee about great affairs of state. Herein lies our historic interest in the episode: during their exchange, Gorton treated Willesee to an exclusive insight into his thoughts on the Vietnam War. The Prime Minister told the teenage scribe that he sincerely wished to withdraw Australian forces from South Vietnam, but government policy prevented him from doing so.[25] His big night out thus became a matter of grave national interest. How many soldiers' futures rested on his failure to act on that drunken admission? It is mere conjecture, of course. The following day Willesee wrote up her sensational scoop. Her editor, Ken Braddick, refused to publish it, and within weeks, 'having decided she had become a liability, sacked her'.[26]

The story of Gorton's erratic performance ran on and on. His foolish, if harmless, antics — he never 'propositioned' Willesee — upset his more restrained colleagues, including the self-important puritan Edward St John QC, son of a Boggabri clergyman, who attacked the Prime Minister's embassy dalliance 'with a young woman who was *not* his wife' as prejudicial to Australian relations with America. Not only that; Gorton also had a 'frivolous approach to leadership', St John dared to suggest.[27]

Notwithstanding his persecution by St John, Gorton remained popular, and most ordinary people forgave his misdemeanours as the wayward eccentricities of a sound Australian. They liked him. He amused them. Gorton worshipped at the altar of a good public opinion.[28] His shameless populism at the expense of clear policy worked in 1968, thanks to a generous press honeymoon: reporters delighted in his regrettable tendency to make serious policy announcements to them before informing Cabinet and the House. Gorton indeed behaved as if the government were 'a one man band'.[29]

Amid all the merriment in Gorton's court, questions about the future of Australian soldiers in Vietnam — serious questions that involved the lives of several thousand young men — were set aside, postponed, subsumed. True, Gorton privately wanted the soldiers home. For now, however, his conversation with a 19-year-old girl was the extent of his public accountability. He would not address the issue publicly until December 1969. Until then, the soldiers, unaware of their leader's musings about their fate to a teenager, fought on.

Gorton's party could not last. Front bench disunity, backbench defiance, the media's nose for a looming shambles and the rise of a credible Opposition lit the slow burn towards electoral defeat: amendments to the national service legislation were rejected in the Senate; Gorton's colleagues 'made boner after boner' in and out of the House; and Whitlam's Labor Party repeatedly held the government up to look 'like an incompetent collection of uninformed fools'. Gorton had made a serious strategic blunder in not calling an election in late 1968, at the height of his popularity, when Labor reeled from Whitlam's imperious decision to resign as Opposition Leader and seek re-election to consolidate his control of the Labor Party. Yet by 1969 Whitlam had a new mandate, and Gorton's honeymoon was emphatically over.

Gough Whitlam combined political cunning, parliamentary principle and intellectual depth to a degree rarely seen in Australian political life. He deployed a barrister's ego, a profound knowledge of history and a mastery of the English language that outgunned most of his adversaries — Liberal and Labor — who seemed strangely diminished in his presence. Political journalist Alan Reid thought him cat-like, easy to distrust and possessed of the fleeting, cruel wit of one of Noel Coward's female characters in *Private Lives*: he 'clawed rather than punched'.[30] In Opposition, Whitlam embarked on wide-ranging reform of the Labor Party, jettisoning traditional nostrums, such as the White Australia Policy, and embracing modernisation; in the process Labor became more 'middle class', and more electable.

Yet if Whitlam seemed as unreachable as a cucumber sandwich to most Labor stalwarts, he certainly understood the political perils of the Vietnam conflict. His involvement went way back. In 1954 he had ruled out Australian participation — the first public voice to do so — except as part of a United Nations force. Alert to the essential conservatism of the Australian electorate, Whitlam trod a cautious path through Vietnam's political minefield. He refrained, once Australia had committed troops, from condemning the war. He wisely resisted setting deadlines for the return of the troops. Initially, he backed America's involvement — and the bombing of the North — but later rejected both. The one policy he consistently opposed was conscription for overseas service: a Whitlam Government would end immediately the policy that obliged 21-year-olds to fight outside Australia. Whitlam's essential problem, like the ALP's, was this: how to oppose the war without seeming to attack the troops and damaging the American alliance.

His anti-war views progressively hardened. In January 1968 Whitlam toured Vietnam and visited the Mekong Delta and Hué, in the company of the Australian Ambassador and a few American dignitaries. With a statistical precision bordering on madness, his American chaperones attempted to sell the war to this towering sceptic. Apparently, 21,173 fish had been put in rural ponds in South Vietnam under 'resettlement programs', Whitlam heard. Could it be true, Whitlam asked: might it not be 20,000, or 30,000?[31] On his return to Australia, he roundly condemned the war, and set his nose to the grindstone of winning office.


While this political tragicomedy played itself out at home, in Vietnam 8,500 Australian defence personnel were trying to do their duty, as instructed by a government and nation that seemed to have lost interest in them.

The politicians cared little for the operational war, except insofar as they sought to limit casualties: body bags were a nuisance at election time. Their indifference to the forces' operational activities was sadly evident during Major General MacDonald's twelve-month tenure as commander of Australian Force Vietnam. Nobody in Canberra took any interest in MacDonald, despite his unceasing dispatches: '... from about May through to August [1968] I think I went for over three months without getting any communication whatever from the Department of Defence in Canberra, which I suppose suited me fine but I must say on reflection it strikes me as being rather peculiar.' Not even the Australian Embassy in Saigon sought his counsel. 'I don't know what reporting the Embassy did in my time. I've no idea,' MacDonald said.[32] Brigadier Sandy Pearson, who succeeded Ron Hughes as Task Force commander, similarly remembers receiving not a single communication from Canberra. Other commanders experienced the same sense of being marooned, neglected. Major General Vincent asked Andrew Peacock, the new Minister for the Army, whether the government had considered the need to review the Task Force's structure. Peacock, then visiting Saigon, said, 'No. No, this has not been considered in the last twelve months that I am aware of.'[33]

The sense of abandonment percolated down to the troops. Many diggers recall an encroaching isolation, a distant indifference to their lot. Set adrift from their national anchorage, they were left to fight ... for whom? For what? An awful loneliness descended on many soldiers' hearts and minds, and deepened as opposition to the war approached a crescendo.

Australia's more thoughtful officers already felt the war a doomed campaign. The better commanders at Australian Force Vietnam and the Task Force 'understood the war was a lost cause': 'They saw Australia's involvement for what it was: a diplomatic gesture rather than a military necessity.'[34] In essence, the troops were being asked to risk their lives to fulfil a diplomatic courtesy to America.

At home the politicians' silence on Vietnam did not suggest a lack of interest in defence matters — far from it. Canberra was the seedbed of the politicians' war, in which successive Liberal governments had 'emasculated' the Defence Department and overrode or ignored senior public servants and defence experts.[35] Morale plummeted as 'politicians made the clear decisions' and ignored the advice of senior defence experts. The Foreign

Affairs and Defence Committee virtually usurped the role of the Joint Chiefs of Staff (echoing McNamara's political hijacking of the Pentagon). The chief culprits were considered to be Menzies, Holt, Hasluck, Paltridge (Minister for Defence, 1964–66), Malcolm Fraser (Army Minister 1966–68, and Defence Minister 1969–71) and Gorton.[36]

At a time when Australian defence policy needed an urgent overhaul, 'defence dither' took hold. Talk of an 'independent defence policy' was mere rhetoric. Yet the words were there, the future had been written: the 1968 Strategic Assessment Paper outlined the end of forward defence and the first steps towards self-reliance. Australia contemplated the post-colonial world alone, and not only because the British were leaving. The Americans, too, were pulling in their horns. In July 1969 newly elected President Richard Nixon unveiled the Guam Doctrine, which prescribed self-defence for Asian nations that had hitherto relied on American help. America would come to our aid only if openly attacked. That prospect no longer vexed the departmental boffins who drew up Australian defence policy: from 1968 they proceeded on the assumption that 'no direct threat to Australia was seen as evolving within the next decade'.[37] China, mired in domestic crises, had not only ceased to be the bogeyman of two years earlier; it had also simply dropped off the list of threats. And ultimately, as Canberra realised, the abandonment of South Vietnam was the logical result of the redundancy of forward defence. Whatever the moral case for saving South Vietnam, many in Canberra now decided that it was simply not in Australia's national interest to defend the southern majority, whose possible defeat no longer posed a regional threat. But the problem remained: how to extricate ourselves from the quagmire?

Meanwhile, the Vietnam War ground on, with the self-generating momentum of mutual hatred that the human hand in its creation seemed helpless — or politically unwilling — to stop.

# Part Six
# WHAM

# Chapter 34
# Australian Viet Cong

The Vietnam Action Committee was not truly anti-war; it supported the war in the sense that it wanted Hanoi and the National Liberation Front to win.
*Peter Edwards, Australian historian.*

Dr Jim Cairns, Bob Gould, Albert Langer, Michael Hyde, Jean McLean, Brian Laver, Jack Mundey, Mike Jones, Germaine Greer, Allan Ashbolt, Ann Curthoys, Hall Greenland, Bernie Taft, Meredith Burgmann, Norman Rothfield, Tony Dalton, Harry Van Moorst, Anne Summers, Garrie Hutchinson, Michael Hamel-Green, Michael Matteson, Father Val Noone, Francis James, Michael Leunig, Bruce Petty, Richard Neville, the 'New Left', Students for a Democratic Society, the Monash Labor Club, La Trobe, the Vietnam Action Campaign, SOS, the Communist Party of Australia, the Independent Communist Party of Australia, the Communist Party (Marxist-Leninist), *Oz, Lot's Wife, Nation Review, New Statesman, Tribune, Resist, Black Dwarf, Ramparts, Old Mole, Red Moat, L'Enrage, Black Barb, Red Ned*, the *Spanner and Sickle*, the Campaign for Nuclear Disarmament, Maoists, Trotskyists, libertarians, anarchists, Leninists, Democratic Socialists, Social Democrats, Mao Tse-tung, Che Guevara, Fidel Castro, Uncle Ho, Jean-Paul Sartre, Bertrand Russell, Herbert Marcuse, Norman Mailer, Tariq Ali, Roland Barthes, Noam Chomsky, Dr Benjamin Spock, Allen Ginsberg, Tom Wolfe, Jack Kerouac, Ken Kesey, Truman Capote, Timothy Leary, Henry Miller, Simone de Beauvoir, Peter Brook, le Corbusier, Stanley Kubrick,

Andy Warhol, Jean Arp, Jacques Derrida, Malcom X, Federico Fellini, Warren Beatty, Louis Malle, Jerzy Grotowski, Sigmund Freud, Francis Bacon, Roy Lichtenstein, Lucian Freud, Joseph Beuys, Marilyn Monroe, Mary Quant, Yogi, Twiggy, Marianne Faithful, Ursula Andress, Jane Fonda, Yves Saint Laurent, Cassius Clay (Muhammad Ali), *Breakfast at Tiffany's, Dr Zhivago, Bonnie and Clyde, Dr Strangelove, Hair, Marat/Sade, The Graduate, Deep Throat, Easy Rider, M.A.S.H., Guess Who's Coming to Dinner, Barbarella, 2001: A Space Odyssey, Midnight Cowboy, Don's Party, The Kandy-Kolored Tangerine-Flake Streamline Baby, Catcher in the Rye, Portnoy's Complaint, The Electric Kool-Aid Acid Test, On The Road, The Little Red Book, The Little Red School Book, Kama Sutra*, feminism, structuralism, existentialism, Marxism, Dadaism, conceptualism, the Beautiful People, proletariat, bourgeoisie, hippies, civil rights, women's lib, gay rights, Flower Power, Black Power, the Beat Generation, Paris, Haight-Ashbury, Rive Gauche, Berkeley, St Germaine, King's Road, Altamont, Kent State, Carnaby Street, Greenwich Village, Woodstock, the Berlin Wall, 'the Year of Protest', 'the Summer of Love', 'the Age of Aquarius', 'Make Love Not War', 'Free the Female Body', 'Burn the Bra', 'Give Peace a Chance', 'Bury Lynch/Lynch Bury', 'Draft Beer, Not Boys', 'Hell No, We Won't Go!', 'One side right, one side wrong/Victory to the Viet Cong!', 'Hey, Hey, LBJ/How many kids did you kill today?', 'Ho, Ho, Ho Chi Minh/There to struggle/There to win!', 'One, Two, Three, Four/We don't want your fucking war/Five, Six, Seven, Eight/Stop the bombs, Negotiate!', love-ins, sit-ins, teach-ins, street theatre, the Factory, the moon-walk, dialectical materialism, tune-ins, fellatio, drop-outs, communes, happenings, free sex, the Pill, abortion, free love, cunnilingus, contraception, baby boomers, beads, flares, the bikini, the mini-skirt, nudity, hair, pop, rock 'n' roll, Elvis, Aretha Franklin, Dusty Springfield, the Grateful Dead, The Mamas and the Papas, Country Joe McDonald, Bob Dylan, The Doors, the Small Faces, Joe Cocker, the Animals, Creedence Clearwater Revival, The Beatles, the Rolling Stones, Brian Jones, Janis Joplin, Jimi Hendrix, the Kinks, Led Zeppelin, Velvet Underground, The Who, *Sergeant Pepper's Lonely Hearts' Club Band*, grass, pot, hashish, speed, Mary Jane, bongs, Buddha, LSD, barrels, strawberry fields, Californian sunshine, coke, magic mushrooms, scag, No. 9, purple hearts, hearts and minds, hallucinogenics, heroin, helter-skelter, WHAM …[1]

This tumble of people, pop and paraphernalia provided the stuffing of the social revolution in Australia during the 1960s; these were some of the voices, sounds and influences that heralded the overthrow of the established order. 'We felt we were on the threshold of a new world, when we could change things,' recalled Michael Hamel-Green, a prominent activist jailed for resisting the draft.[2] In retrospect, the decade seems rather to have left a faint indent on time's shifting sands, blown in the wind like other youthful fads and ideals, the pale-faced prelude to a long, adult hangover of dazed disillusionment. 'It was a time of collective self-importance,' wrote Australian art critic Robert Hughes, 'which masked — not very effectively — a striking indifference to the way the world actually did and might work. The depths of tedium that can be plumbed by sitting around half stoned, listening to people chatter moonily about reuniting humankind and erasing its aggressive instincts through Love and Dope, are scarcely imaginable to those who have not suffered them,' concluded Hughes, who did suffer them.[3]

And yet if not quite the decade of peace and love, it certainly was a period of profound social upheaval. The Pill freed people to copulate without the risk of impregnation; women's lib did much to change the position of women in the workplace; and the bikini and mini-skirt were novel distractions from braless overalls. The silent majority, however, block-like in their suburban redoubts, remained pretty much impervious to the 'political earthquake'. If a blast of the Swinging Sixties occasionally disturbed their quietus, the 'burbs sighed at distant calamities, bemoaned 'the youth of today' and carried on — lighting the barbie, playing pokies, watching footie and hoisting their Hills Hoists sublimely uninterested in the revolution being waged in their name. Still, even their stalwart conservative members could not avoid hearing the angry young people for whom the pivotal event of the decade was the Vietnam War. In the late 1960s the war touched everyone. The most settled legatees of the Menzies era were not immune to its power to shock, divide and transform. Vietnam opened the sluices of querulous reflection even in rural and conservative Australia, whose grazing pillars contemplated the shock of the 1960s with a mixture of fear, loathing and incomprehension.

Vietnam was the litmus test of your political character. Where you stood on the war pigeon-holed your position on politics, racism, society, art, the environment and so on. The Vietnam War broke up dinners, parties, families and friendships. To be heard mildly defending the cause, if not the war, in fashionable intellectual circles was the social equivalent of announcing one's Nazi memorabilia collection over the canapés. 'Thinking Australians' were almost universally opposed to the war, reflecting the local triumph of Ho Chi Minh's bid to win the hearts and minds of the Western cognoscenti.

'The war was heartfelt,' said Garry MacDougall, a Newcastle University student in 1969–73. 'Its horrors, injustices and obscenities arrived every day. Youthful energy drove us into a furious determination. My first action was occupying the Defence Minister's office in Newcastle. We had entered that twilight zone of illegality ... anything could happen. We had a freedom that allowed us to fully exercise our minds. I look back in some horror at my earnestness ... The art of gentle conversation was unknown to me! Everything was a battle, an argument to win over people to an anti-war position ...'[4]

'I opposed the war because I was sickened by what I was reading and seeing,' said Joan Coxsedge, a member of the Victorian Moratorium Committee and a leading anti-war organiser. 'That we had lined up behind the most powerful military force in the history of the world using the most sophisticated and diabolical weaponry to destroy an impoverished nation ... A war against the earth itself, killing and maiming all living things. In that sense I saw it as a fundamental assault on life that was obscene and revolting.'[5]

'I judged everyone on how they viewed Vietnam,' said Dr Meredith Burgmann, a tireless anti-war activist (and later prominent academic, Labor politician and, for eight years, the president of the New South Wales Legislative Council). 'I was mad as a cut snake. My first arrest was in Martin Place, for obstructing access to a men's toilet. I thought I was lying down in front of Gorton's car. They whacked me into Silverwater. I was a good Anglican North Shore girl. My grandfather was a bishop; my mum changed from thinking that Menzies was a great man ... everyone assumed I was rebelling against my parents; yet my parents supported me! I believed in "One side right, One side wrong/Victory to the Viet Cong". I think I was a combination of pacifist and desperately wanting the VC to win ... I wanted them to win because they were right. We certainly didn't target the soldiers; that would've been unbelievably unpopular ... Up until 1968 most of the protest movement was organised by the Communist Party. They were crucial. I was never a member; I was a fellow traveller. I remember we had a day of rage in 1969. We believed in guerrilla activity, whatever gave the establishment grief. We attacked the Stock Exchange. I spray-painted "US Blood Money" across the Exchange [others sprayed "Smash Capitalism" and "Murderers"]. We burned the American flag in the middle of the trading floor, then all hid in the toilet ...'[6]

Antipodean resistance spread to Britain, whence some draft resisters fled to avoid conscription. In 1968 a little émigré group called 'Australians and New Zealanders Against the Vietnam War' used to protest outside Australia House.[7] One member, Garrie Hutchinson, left Australia not simply to avoid national service: 'I remember Tet as a defeat [for the Viet Cong], one of the most depressing events of 1968. I didn't think the NLF [National Liberation Front] could win, and this was an important factor in my leaving Australia.'[8] He spent weeks showing 'NLF propaganda films around England'. At Oxford University, it seems that a youthful Bill Clinton, himself in Britain to avoid the draft, probably attended the presentation.

In the late 1960s Australian support for the Viet Cong was not seen as an aberrant or militant position; a broad cross-section of the anti-war movement chanted the slogans and distributed the propaganda of Hanoi and the National Liberation Front. Several peace organisations were used, wittingly or not, as communist fronts. The Communist Party of Australia, for example, commandeered the Australian Peace Council as an instrument of Soviet foreign policy.[9] The radical Vietnam Action Committee, according to one study, 'was apparently chosen [to perform] the role of coordinating agent for the Communist Party in the protest movement'.[10] There were many less obvious manifestations of the disquieting contradiction that allied 'peace' and 'Marxism'. The goals, for example, of the National Liberation Front were indistinguishable from those of the Association for International Cooperation and Disarmament (the latter claimed to have only 'two or three Communists' on its socialist committee).

Australia's student Labor clubs and left-wing political societies all, to a greater or lesser extent, supported Hanoi and the National Liberation Front. In this sense, they and their leaders — Mike Jones and Bob Gould in Sydney, Michael Hyde and Albert Langer in Melbourne, and Brian Laver in Brisbane — were pro-war, insofar as they desired a communist victory. The peace movement hailed them as heroes; the Liberals and DLP condemned them as traitors and passed the Defence Force Protection Act, with Labor backing, in August 1967, to stop the militant left sending financial aid to Hanoi and the Viet Cong.

Many pro-Viet Cong Australians raised cash for the Viet Cong, in defiance of Section 3 of the Act: tens of thousands of dollars were dispatched to North Vietnam and the National Liberation Front. Bob Gould's Vietnam Action Committee strongly supported the Viet Cong, and raised funds and medical supplies on behalf of the NLF, as did many Australian campus groups. The committee was 'not truly anti-war', noted historian Peter Edwards; it too supported the war in the sense that its members 'wanted Hanoi and the NLF to win'.[11] Francis James, a lay Anglican and pro-Viet Cong activist, claimed to have personally raised $14,000 and sent it to the communist supporters and civil aid groups in North and South Vietnam. In a similar spirit, the Sydney University Labor Party Club, in March 1966, created a fund to provide medical supplies to the Viet Cong, called 'Medi Cong'.[12] On one occasion an 'Aid for the NLF' delegation from the Monash Labor Club visited the Cambodian Ambassador in Canberra, to inquire whether they could mail money to Liberation Front representatives in Phnom Penh. They wrote to Prince Sihanouk requesting a contact address for the front and enclosed a cheque. The Prince readily assisted and expressed his 'keen sympathy' for the students' cause.[13] In 1968, soon after Tet, the Monash veteran Michael Hyde delivered cash in person to the National Liberation Front's representative in Phnom Penh.[14] He and his colleagues were hauled before a university board and 'found guilty' of financing the enemy. The press flogged them as traitors. On 12 July 1969 a Mrs E. Mclean, 34-year-old secretary of Save Our Sons, delivered medical supplies to North Vietnam. She even got a receipt.[15] The same month the Monash Labor Club received a telegram from the National Liberation Front, stating, 'Thank you for the precious support given to our bureau …'[16] One Monash student remarked, 'If the funds so collected resulted in bullets being fired at Australian soldiers, there was nothing that could be done about that.'[17]

The financial donations were obviously treasonable at a time when Australian soldiers, for better or worse, were being sent to fight the recipients. '… the whole idea of collecting aid for an enemy against whom Australian troops were engaged was regarded by the overwhelming majority of the Australian people as treasonable, and utterly repugnant,' wrote the critic P. T. Findlay. 'In fact, so intense was public reaction that it developed into a profound distaste for students generally, who … came to be seen as the spoiled darlings of an affluent society, in need of nothing so much as a good spanking.'[18] Interestingly, not a single pro-Viet Cong Australian volunteered to fight with the National Liberation Front in the spirit of those brave foreign intellectuals who joined the Republican army in the Spanish Civil War. Yet they were not afraid of engaging in violence at home.

Fierce demonstrations erupted in 1968–69, in response to the strengthening of the National Service Act. A militant minority whipped up protests billed as 'non-violent' into bloody clashes with police. The provocateurs were standard-bearers of 'Student Power', an international movement of students giddy with passionate self-righteousness who found their most violent expression on Parisian campuses. A standard student guerrilla tactic was to hide behind peaceful demonstrators, then suddenly rush out and throw firecrackers and marbles at the hooves of police horses, to incite 'police violence'.

The Monash Maoists, the university's intellectual thugs, were skilled at inciting violence. On 4 July 1968 they pelted police with rocks, bottles and fists, smashed the windows of the American Consulate and brought down a police horse. They repeated the performance in July 1969: Karl Armstrong excitedly described 'attacking' the American Consulate in Melbourne, with a group of Monash students 'in solidarity with the NLF', and hurling 'a stack of marbles' under police horses' hooves. Petrol bombs were thrown and windows smashed. 'It was a heavy demonstration but a good one,' Armstrong said, in that 'it achieved headlines around the world'. The Monash and La Trobe Marxists believed 'it was right to use revolutionary violence', he added. Their members had even joined the campus 'Marxist-Leninist rifle clubs' to practise shooting.[19] These inane acts might have satiated their pent-up rage, but they also tarnished the legitimate, non-violent demonstration and reinforced the impression that a mob of crazed malcontents led the protest movement.[20]

In reply, the Australian Security Intelligence Organisation (ASIO) stepped up its secret monitoring. The militants, ASIO argued, used violence as a political weapon, to incite gormless youth to 'rise' against 'oppression'. ASIO infiltrated campuses and protest groups, and compiled huge, often wildly exaggerated, dossiers that reached entertaining levels of scrutiny. Their agents closely monitored the ABC, for example, an organisation clearly saturated with dangerous Reds:

AUSTRALIAN SECURITY INTELLIGENCE ORGANISATION
29 APRIL 1968
Communist Party of Australia Interest in Australian Broadcasting
Commission and Other Broadcasting Stations. In the last month,
in perusing reports coming to this office, the Deputy Director
General NSW Operations [ASIO] noted that the ABC appeared
to be targeted by the Communist Party of Australia ...:

1. Assistant General Manager, Clement SEMMLER (of German descent, born in South Australia) was a close friend of Frank HARDY, the Communist journalist in Northern Territory. SEMMLER is a strange, highly strung temperamental type …

2. Visit of General Manager and Chairman, Sir Robert MADGWICK, to Russia. The Russians, through the embassy at Canberra … want an exchange agreement with the ABC on radio and television …

6. Rupert Ernest LOCKWOOD — *This Day Tonight*. LOCKWOOD, until March of this year the Moscow 'Tribune' correspondent, a member of the CPA [Communist Party of Australia] from 1952 to 1968, the author of the infamous Document 'J' which was exposed in the course of the Royal Commission on Espionage, was to appear on the ABC programme *This Day Tonight* on 25 March 1968 … in connection with Czechoslovakia.

7. Glen Craig HAMILTON — Roger William MILLISS. Roger William MILLISS, a member of the CPA from 1966–68, and a full-time employee of Quality Films, a CPA trading venture, has continued to be in contact with Glen Craig HAMILTON, a journalist of the ABC. [Hamilton sent regular articles to *Tribune* under the pseudonym VIDOR — sparking an investigation in 1969 of a communist conspiracy in the ABC] … It is quite possible that the material which appears in *Tribune* as a critique of television, and is written by 'Vidor' may well be written by HAMILTON. [In the margin of his dossier, Milliss has written, 'Duh!']²¹

Alongside the extremists in the protest movement were many well-meaning middle-class people who sincerely opposed the war on moral grounds. Their protests were mostly peaceful, law-abiding assemblies of decent citizens — chiefly teachers, the clergy, academics and lawyers — who took to the streets in an orderly manner, bearing inoffensive placards. They did not overtly support the Viet Cong, but they sympathised with the communist forces, whom they tended to portray as a barefoot peasant army wielding shotguns and machetes against 'American imperialism'. They persisted in thinking of the Viet Cong as a spontaneous nationalist uprising in a defensive war against Saigon despots (and not, as proved the case, cannon fodder for Hanoi's invasion of the South).

The clerical community provided a rich vein of dissent, the Church of England being in the vanguard. Bishop John Moyes of Armidale was among the most prominent to land a velvet fist on Menzies' chin; Francis James helped to rally the rural Anglicans. Never had such high-ranking churchmen publicly opposed a government (provoking a long letter of rebuttal from Menzies).

The Methodists were probably the most consistent opponents of the war, chiefly in the figure of the Reverend Alan Walker. In a speech on 30 August 1965 Walker condemned the Western presence in Vietnam as being 'without justification', and claimed the struggle was a civil war, 'fought by Vietnamese people against Vietnamese people'. Australia has on moral grounds 'surely no right to hold the bodies of Vietnamese men, women and children as a shield for Australian bodies'.[22]

On the other hand, Roman Catholic Church leaders tended to support the war, with the strong backing of the breakaway Democratic Labor Party. Notwithstanding the vocal exceptions of a few younger, radical priests, such as Father Val Noone and his Melbourne comrades,[23] most Catholics viewed South Vietnam and the Philippines as the last bastions of Christian teaching in South-East Asia. Sydney's Catholic Information Bureau had declared that Menzies' decision to send troops was 'not only morally justifiable but right and commendable'; the innocent people of South Vietnam were 'facing a threat [from] a godless regime which they certainly don't desire'.[24]

Nevertheless, the most powerful reproach to Vietnam came from those opposed to conscription for overseas service, who included the parents of national servicemen and, in time, members of Australia's conservative heartland. When Robert Wilton, son of Lieutenant General Sir John Wilton, chairman of the Chiefs of Staff Committee, burned his national service deferment notice in 1969, crowds turned up to applaud. In heart-rending letters to the editor, fathers attacked the random ballot that condemned their sons to a faraway battlefield. A broad spectrum of people ridiculed Gorton's wayward leadership and despaired of the ever-worsening violence in Vietnam. Conservative matrons and their golfing husbands started to wonder: what will bombing this peasant society really achieve? Why are we sending our boys to this obscure and dreadful place? How exactly has the destruction of thirty-five sampans made Australia more secure?[25]

A broad alliance — academics, business leaders, clergymen, unions, students — took action. They chose to incite young men to resist the draft.

In 1969 a powerful 'Don't Register' campaign openly defied the absurd new law that criminalised anyone who urged others to refuse national service. Dr Jim Cairns stated that if he were of conscription age he would refuse to register; Cairns, along with a hundred others, was briefly arrested for his beliefs, in this ludicrous political game.

Dr Terry Smith and university professors Charles Birch and Charles Martin threw down the cudgels on behalf of the older generation and openly invited 19-year-olds to dodge the draft. Birch's appeal to parents and the elderly was brilliantly effective. 'We have drifted into the position,' Birch told them, 'where young people are being forced against their will to fight in an unjust war because the average Australian is a gutless rabbit as far as the erosion of his rights are concerned. The time has come for all us oldies to support and aid all those young people who ... refuse to be conscripted.'[26] Five hundred fellow academics signed similar 'incitement statements'.[27] The law itself was brought into contempt. By late November 1969 more than 8,000 people had signed 'incitement statements' that urged young men to refuse national service.[28]

An array of voices opposed to national service — right and left, secular and religious, young and old — rallied around Professor Birch's Committee in Defiance of the National Service Act (CDNSA), which bought a huge advertisement in *The Australian* on 3 July 1969 publicising the names of hundreds of supporters. They included Liberal reformers (Gordon Barton); Labor politicians (Tom Uren); academics (Alex Carey); clergymen (Reverends Alf Dickie, Frank Hartley and Malcolm Black, who was sacked from his Wollongong parish for his anti-war activities); unionists (Jack Mundey, secretary of the Australian Builders' Labourers' Federation); and a full-throated body of student radicals (Barry York and Michael Hamel-Green). The committee's executive officers numbered the freed and suddenly popular Simon Townsend; a Sydney barrister (Murray Sime); the secretary of the Ex-Services Human Rights Association (Les Waddington); and the co-founder of the Liberal Reform Group (Ken Thomas).

Self-prosecution was their shrewdest weapon. Modelled on an American tactic, the committee charged its own members with inciting the young to refuse the draft. Hundreds of respectable citizens, including the novelist Patrick White, thus incriminated themselves and 'surrendered' to the police. Even the government, helpless before the 'criminal' masses of its own creation, saw the absurdity of trying to punish these middle-class miscreants.

Resisting the draft now enjoyed the imprimatur of the Great and the Good. It became a respectable rebellion, in a society that increasingly looked on the war — and, ominously, the soldiers — as something shameful, something to hide. Two years earlier, 'draft dodgers' were condemned as cowards and unAustralian; in 1969 they were seen as local heroes.

Middle-class values seemed to turn upside down. 'The year 1969,' wrote Ann Curthoys, 'seems to have been a turning point in public opinion about the war ... The government began to lose the moral and political authority it had so comfortably enjoyed to date.'[29] For the first time since 1946 more people aged between 12 and 35 supported Labor. According to an August Gallup poll, 55 per cent of Australians supported the troops' return from Vietnam. The media and the ALP sensed the shift in popular opinion, and drew a far tougher line on troop withdrawal. The hitherto impervious bedrock of the Australian right started to give, and even a few nervous Liberals took part in their first anti-war protest. Mindful of being tarnished by association, they declared, 'We do not condone violent revolutions. We are not communists. We abhor the terrorist activities of the Viet Cong. But ...'[30]

With an election looming, Gorton decided on a statesmanlike trip abroad. On 1 May 1969, having happily installed Hasluck as Australia's new Governor-General, the Prime Minister flew to Washington. There he cemented an excellent relationship with the new Republican President Richard Nixon, who had defeated Hubert Humphrey in the 1968 presidential election. Gorton chatted with Nixon privately for an hour before meeting senior White House and Defense officials, including National Security Adviser Henry Kissinger. The President seemed receptive to the Australian leader's concerns: Gorton wanted firm assurances of continued American involvement in post-Vietnam regional security in Asia, particularly in relation to the Soviet naval presence in the Indian Ocean. 'By any reckoning, Gorton's two days of talks on these subjects were a success.'[31]

The Australian public heard little of Gorton's actual achievements. The press again seized on a single phrase. 'Sir,' Gorton said, addressing Nixon at the end of a long, windy speech at the White House dinner, 'we will go Waltzing Matilda with you.' Echoes of 'all the way with LBJ' resonated with editors, who piled on the mockery. Cartoonists drew a drunken Gorton waltzing on the toes of Dick Nixon. Gorton had again saved his 'most embarrassing verbal clangers' for the White House, reproved the *Courier-Mail*. It was one thing to enjoy 'Waltzing Matilda' — as Gorton did — but quite 'another, graver matter' to turn the song into a foreign policy, tut-tutted *The Age*. Gorton, of course, was simply speaking in the spirit of friendship at a banquet held in his honour. It was perfectly natural for him to allude to a symbol redolent of the Australia he loved in defining a relationship so important to Australia's national interest (and in fact 'Waltzing Matilda' was his preferred choice as national anthem).[32]

Gorton returned to fight the federal election, set for 25 October 1969, against a Labor Opposition flush for the first time in years with the prospect of victory. In a pre-election speech on 1 October, Whitlam promised, along with a smorgasbord of delicacies (including a universal health scheme and emergency grants to schools), to bring all Australian troops home from Vietnam by June 1970. Gorton's pre-election campaign generally stuck to domestic issues and the economy (which was booming). In deference to the Liberal heartland, and his new mate President Nixon, however, he promised to stay the distance in Vietnam for as long as the USA remained: '… we will not unilaterally withdraw. To do so would … betray our allies, and, I believe, to imperil our future security.' He refused to end conscription.

A slim majority returned Gorton to office; the voters slashed the huge Liberal mandate from thirty-nine seats to seven. The 7.1 per cent swing to Labor dealt a near-terminal blow, and had it not been for Democratic Labor Party preferences, Gorton would not have survived. Once more the Catholic working-class vote saved the Liberal Party's neck.

The election result enraged the protest groups. A big rally in December, briefly attended by Bob Hawke, president-elect of the Australian Council of Trade Unions, openly supported a North Vietnamese military victory. Whitlam wisely shunned these fleeting spectaculars and drew sustenance from the election result: the public mood had massively swung. He consolidated his earnings and appealed for party unity — most emphatically in a thoughtful letter to the West Australian branch of the ALP. Parliament, not protest marches, was the proper forum 'to explain and expound the Party's policies', he wrote. Only a Labor victory, Whitlam declared, could end Australia's involvement in this 'physically, politically, socially and morally debilitating and divisive war'.[33] With that, the Labor leader marked off 1969 as a dress rehearsal for the real thing in 1972.

Little then did he realise it, but the soldier in the sodden jungles of Vietnam bore the great weight of these arguments on his shoulders, along with his pack and rifle and water bottle. Political and religious interests had appropriated his job to their own agendas. He fought for, or against, arguments at home of which he had no knowledge or involvement. Civilian Australia, watching the war unfold on their televisions, regarded the soldier as a symbol — of freedom or barbarity, Christ or cruelty, democracy or destruction. And in time the troops painfully beheld an awful truth in Graham Greene's remark: '... to the soldier the civilian is the man who employs him to kill, who includes the guilt of murder in the pay envelope and escapes responsibility.'[34]

# Chapter 35
# Accelerated pacification

To win hearts and minds — take the people by the nuts and their
hearts and minds will follow.
*Major David Millie, AATTV.*

A tough, barnstorming commander, General Creighton Abrams 'could
inspire aggression in a begonia', observed one reporter.[1] Not for
nothing was a tank named after him. Yet in Vietnam, Westmoreland's
successor was the unlikely champion of an apparently gentler, kinder war —
the 'other war'. Body count, Abrams made loudly clear, had not worked;
attrition had rested on three false premises: that massive US firepower would
break the communist spirit (it had not); that American troops would take
the initiative in the field (they had not); and that progress could be measured
by counting corpses (it could not).[2]

In a population that had never known security, Abrams thus set himself a
challenging task: to speed up the 'pacification' of the Vietnamese people. He
demanded faster village protection and more widespread civic aid, public works
and gifts of food, dental and medical assistance, coupled with stronger local
government authorities and a more pervasive propaganda or psychological
warfare operation (psywar). Abrams was a great believer in this 'other war' — or
'better war', in the historian Lewis Sorley's optimistic phrase,[3] otherwise known
as 'accelerated pacification'.

The idea of 'pacification', of 'winning the hearts and minds' (or
WHAM), was nothing new. President Kennedy had championed the concept,

which the US Army studied then largely ignored. The Marines were an exception. They were old hands at WHAM. 'We are fighting two wars,' wrote General Victor 'Brute' Krulak, commanding the Marine Corps in Vietnam. One aimed to 'defeat a military aggressor'; the other hoped to seal 'the lasting friendship and willing cooperation of the Vietnamese people'.[4]

Brute Krulak unwittingly demonstrated why pacification had so far failed: protecting the people was always the 'other' war, a *separate* job. The two were never properly integrated. Westmoreland prosecuted a huge conventional war in tandem with a piecemeal 'hearts and minds' offensive, which threw crumbs to the survivors of a maelstrom: 'Bomb 'em and feed 'em, bomb 'em and feed 'em, bomb 'em and feed 'em,' in one US pilot's devastating summary.[5] 'Pacification was hardly anything more than a swollen, computerized tit ... a costly, valueless programme that worked only in press conferences,' wrote Michael Herr.[6] Perhaps, but that denied the sincere efforts of WHAM's many adherents in the American and Australian armies.

The Vietnamese communist forces perfectly understood the idea. For them, 'winning hearts and minds' was *a weapon of war*; pacification meant *armed* propaganda, *armed* proselytising. It required two things to succeed: (1) the integration of the military and political offensives; and (2) a willingness to use or threaten civilians with violence if gifts and promises failed. For the communists, WHAM was a weapon, not a confidence trick: *if bribes failed, use bullets.* The North Vietnamese/Viet Cong made the brutal nexus daily; in time, so would the Americans, under the Phoenix Program.

Abrams stood on the threshold of a devastated land, offering loaves and fishes to the homeless, the childless and the fatherless. It was as though the Four Horsemen of the Apocalypse had been told to tether their mounts and witness the milk of human kindness ripple over the aftermath of their gallop through the countryside.[7] It was a credit to his determination that Abrams actually believed he could succeed in winning back these displaced and brutalised people, herded out of Ben Suc and hundreds of other villages: 'A civil population may be controlled by placing it in enclosures, but that does not mean that it has been pacified.'[8] Unperturbed, Abrams untethered Robert 'Blowtorch' Komer, chief of CORDS, to drive forward America's milk and honey offensive.[9]

An exceedingly gung-ho American adviser, Komer claimed this 'other war' offered the Vietnamese people 'the crucial assurance that their future will be better than their past'.[10] It could hardly get worse. To this end,

Komer rehabilitated Colonel John Paul Vann, whom he installed as his deputy. Vann understood the failings of the US strategy better than most. Among the first to see the importance of the 'other war', Vann wrote, way back in 1963, that South Vietnam needed a vibrant middle class built through 'democratic, non-violent socio-economic change'.[11] Then, he was ignored and removed from his position. Now, as a civilian adviser, he had the power to stamp his ideas on the war.

Yet Abrams's subordinate commanders privately scorned the idea. They paid lip service to pacification and carried on fighting a war of attrition. The GIs were psychologically ill-equipped to respond to the new regime: suddenly they were being asked to convert, not to kill; to proselytise, not to pulverise.[12]

Exceptionally resistant to the new imperative was Lieutenant General Julian Ewell, dubbed the 'Delta butcher' for his obsession with kill ratios.[13] Ewell had encouraged a 'competition between battalions and companies for the highest monthly body count'[14] and threatened to relieve subordinates if they failed to reach their quotas.[15] 'The goal,' said Ewell, 'is to make the pressure of losses felt all the way to Hanoi in order to create a favourable climate for the peace talks in Paris. Our immediate goal is to attrit the enemy at a rate of 6,000 per month by the end of April [1969]. This figure is the break even point … In order to achieve a reasonable kill rate, a brigade needs two to ten contacts [per night] … Keep a close eye on your kill ratio.' In May, Ewell sent another memo: 'If you aren't getting one kill per company day, you're not in the ball game.'[16] The American OPERATION SPEEDY EXPRESS, nominally a pacification program in the Mekong Delta in early 1969, reflected Ewell's approach. It resulted in an estimated 11,000 Vietnamese deaths, of whom 5,000 were 'non-combatants'. The US 9th Infantry Division, under Ewell, was responsible for this carnage; indeed, the 9th prided itself on 'killing a hundred Viet Cong a day every day'.[17]

Notwithstanding Abrams's new broom, Ewell was promoted — at the time, the army's machinery still rewarded a high body count — to the command of II Field Force Vietnam, which incorporated the Australian Task Force. In his new job, Ewell demanded a kill ratio of at least twenty or thirty to one. The Australians deeply disappointed him. In March, April and May 1969 the Task Force managed only 11:1, 15.3:1 and 9.3:1 respectively.[18] As such, Ewell placed Phuoc Tuy in the 'disaster category', sparking dissent among Australian commanders — notably Lieutenant Colonel Ron Grey, the tough commander of the 7th Battalion — who judged performance by other benchmarks. (Ewell's successor later visited the Task Force and apologised for his predecessor.)[19]

The Australian commanders paid lip service to US orders, but in practice ignored the US approach and carried on their own tactical war, which since 1965 had involved a form of pacification under Australian Civil Affairs units. This 'hearts and minds' campaign imposed an exhausting burden on the troops, who were expected to behave as 'Ambassadors of Australia', to show 'respect for human life' and to 'protect, defend and preserve life by giving security'. Their job was the 'alleviation of pain and suffering' through civil aid and charity — 'winning hearts and minds by actions'.[20] Civil Affairs teams were to improve living conditions, build the economy and 'emphasize the concept of freedom and worth of the individual'.[21] They were also expected to continue killing the enemy: violence interspersed with altruism.

Before 1967 the Task Force had installed a few schools, windmills, dispensaries and water storage facilities. The results were disappointing: the twelve Australian windmills were slowly shutting down (only five would be operating by 1971) and the people showed 'no interest' in maintaining them.[22] By early 1967 civic action had 'almost ceased', or amounted to a land grab, the 'worst form of handout mentality'.[23] Only the medcaps and dentcaps were operating.

This changed in June 1967 when the recently formed 1st Australian Civil Affairs Unit made a determined effort to win the trust and, hopefully, active support of the local population.[24] The unit's ten officers and thirty-nine other ranks received $100,000 in seed funding (soon to increase to $2 million). The first commander, the energetic Lieutenant Colonel John McDonagh, stamped the unit's mission statement on the wall of his office in Nui Dat: 'To win the support of the local population for the Government of South Vietnam and … goodwill towards our forces and Australia generally.' The failings of Civil Affairs may be traced to this absurd statement: true, many Vietnamese villagers felt goodwill towards the Australians, yet it was not automatically converted into loyalty towards a remote, bullying, unpopular government. The idea was 'fanciful', concluded Lieutenant Colonel Peter Gration, who commanded the 1st Australian Civil Affairs Unit in 1968.[25]

That year, spurred by Abrams's 'accelerated pacification', the Australians stepped up the local aid program. Every company would field a 'civil affairs' detachment. 'What do you want from us?' a series of Task Force questionnaires asked the Vietnamese people. In 1968 Gration introduced a new approach: village 'self-help', which became a catchphrase in the new policy of 'Vietnamisation' initiated by Brigadier Pearson in Phuoc Tuy in 1969. Villagers were compelled to invest their own time and money in the projects, to encourage them to take pride in their new classrooms, wells, latrines and so on. When John Vann visited Phuoc Tuy that year, he was impressed to find his 'hearts and minds' ideas had already been activated, if on a very small scale.

In April 1969 Brigadier Sandy Pearson, the Task Force commander, launched the troops down the path of tactical 'pacification': a series of integrated hearts and minds offensives, which set out to separate the people from the Viet Cong, win village loyalties and instil a self-defence mentality in the hamlets.[26] The effort severely disrupted Viet Cong supply lines and village infiltration, despite heavy Australian mine casualties and constant American displeasure. In tandem, Pearson pursued concentrated civic action — the 'political arm' of pacification — delivering aid, medical care and infrastructure. In fact, for a few brief months, the Australian political and military offensives seemed to fly in the same orbit.

Then the experiment abruptly ended. Ewell's scorn and the arrival of Pearson's successor, Brigadier 'Black Jack' Weir, forced a return to 'search and destroy'. Civic action, however, continued — albeit as a separate job — in the hope of capturing that most elusive prize: the hearts and minds of the Vietnamese peasants.

And so, with the assistance of South Vietnamese Revolutionary Development cadres, and the 'Ruff Puffs' — supposedly in charge of security — Australian Civil Affairs teams threw themselves at the job of improving provincial living standards. Throughout 1969 farmers were shown how to use fertiliser, obtain credit and improve farming techniques; fishing facilities were upgraded and better nets and techniques adopted; an animal husbandry program aimed to put more swine and poultry in the Vietnamese diet, to raise protein intake; and Phuoc Tuy's forty-seven secondary schools received new equipment, teacher-training facilities and library books. A USAID-funded supply of 'counter-insurgency commodities' flooded the province with building supplies and foodstuffs. Water, sewerage, electricity and other public works were upgraded. In tandem, local administration was strengthened — indeed, in March and April 1970, all seventeen villages and sixty-one hamlets in Phuoc Tuy held local elections, and the elected chiefs were trained and supported.[27] Xuyen Moc in east Phuoc Tuy received a fishpond, a well for each hamlet, ten beds for the dispensary and fire-fighting equipment; the main school received a new water pipe, latrine, 124 desks and playground equipment.[28] USAID paid most of the bills.

Children were special targets of civic action, because children were the path to their parents' hearts. 'Toys, mooncakes and sweets' were among the shower of goodies liberally sprinkled across the province.[29] Children were priorities for medcaps and dentcaps. 'You have to laugh when you see the kids getting needles,' said one 7th Battalion soldier. 'They cry and run everywhere. They are very sad to look at. They are under-fed, have sores and big fat bellies through malnutrition.'[30]

A happy example of Gration's self-help in action was the construction of a little school at Ong Trinh in late 1969. The villagers invested VN$150,000 and the Australian Task Force VN$270,000. Within two weeks Australian soldiers (of the 5th Battalion, second tour) and local Vietnamese were cheerfully mixing concrete, laying bricks and painting walls as the Ruff Puffs stood guard. In time, the Australians developed close relationships with their fellow workers; a little too close, in fact, where a few local women were concerned.

If the project management erred on the anarchic — tools went 'missing', workers arrived late, interpreters misinterpreted instructions, and the British linear measurement system provoked 'chaos, misunderstandings and interminable arguments' — it all ended happily, with much back-slapping and handshaking, and a volleyball competition between the Australians, the villagers and the Ruff Puffs. The people of Ong Trinh genuinely regretted the Australians' departure, as shown by their gifts and gratitude, and their apparent fear of the consequences of accepting Australian aid. 'This project,' Gration later wrote, 'embodies all the features of good civic action and is thoroughly endorsed as a guide to units in planning future projects.'[31]

More schools were built at Hoa Long and Dat Do, and opened with similar fanfare in late 1969. The soccer field at Hoa Long and the new Boy Scout troops were particularly welcome, and villagers gave Christmas presents to the *uc dai loi* in appreciation. A poor blind widow, for whom the Australians built a new home, wrote, 'For your efforts ... we do not know if the two words *tri an* [gratitude] are sufficient to repay the sacrifices and assistance of the Australian Force ... I now have a wonderful new home with a value of 86,000 piastres.' Although she could not see her new home,

'I was able to visualise pictures from the words which the Australian captain translated with such graciousness ...'[32]

In fact, some villagers — even Viet Cong sympathisers — went out of their way to protect the Australians from Viet Cong attacks. In one extraordinary instance, while a Civil Affairs team built a road, the local people walked ahead of the grader to protect it from mines. (The driver happened to be a good-looking, blond-haired Aussie who had received several proposals of marriage.)

The Viet Cong tolerated these outbreaks of mateship between locals and the *uc dai loi*, so long as the people stayed 'loyal'. At one point, Lieutenant Colonel Nguyen Van Kiem, a former commander of the D445 Battalion, even urged villagers to accept Australian aid 'because the revolutionary government was not in a position to help them at that time'. He made sure they knew via infiltrators, however, whose side they were on, 'so it was impossible for the Australians to win the people's hearts'.[33]

Indeed, as the war ground on, Gration recognised this, at least insofar as it applied in rural communities: 'The idea of turning people around to support [Saigon] was almost impossible. They were under Viet Cong control. We never knew of any case of the villagers giving us militarily useful information. We were a long way from doing any converting.'[34] One elderly Vietnamese man told me that Viet Cong villagers routinely accepted presents from the Australian Army and then 'gave them to the VC'.[35]

The RAAF rallied to the cause. Every air unit had a Civil Aid team — often led by a chaplain. Their efforts stepped up in 1968–69, and took many forms: English-language courses, school construction, cottage industries, youth clubs, medical care and — the airmen's specialty — orphanages. At Vung Tau the RAAF built a new orphanage for 200 children, while at Phan Rang they lavished special attention on the Tan Tai orphanage, giving toys, bicycles, swings, slides and seesaws.[36]

Three RAAF chaplains were awarded MBEs for their aid work in Vietnam. At great personal risk, for example, Chaplain Pat McCormick, padre to Canberra Bomber No. 2 Squadron in 1967, became closely involved with the Tan Tai orphanage run by two sisters of the Immaculate Heart of Mary. The North Vietnamese placed 'a substantial reward for his head', wrote Peter Taylor, an RAAF officer and airfield defence guard who escorted McCormick to the orphanage. 'That is how much the North feared his input. I, and all those who served him, would have willingly laid down our lives for him.'[37]

McCormick risked his life to ensure that the aid was properly allocated. When a corrupt Highlands province chief refused to distribute the aid, McCormick held his revolver to the official's head and forced him to honour the agreement. Air Marshal David Evans AC DSO AFC, McCormick's commanding officer at the time, remembered McCormick as 'the most saintly man I have met in my lifetime'.[38]

Gration's successor, Lieutenant Colonel Paddy Outridge, took a harder line on civic action: Outridge made aid conditional on village loyalty to the allies and Saigon. Aid had to be earned: behind the carrot was a very big stick. Uncooperative villages or those sympathetic to the Viet Cong were simply denied aid unless they demonstrated loyalty to Saigon.

The WHAM production line continued unabated, however: new projects kept coming on stream. In one month, May 1970, Australian Civil Affairs teams performed 433 dental extractions; medically examined 699 people; launched a pilot sanitation scheme in Hai Van hamlet; refurnished schools in Long Huong and Long Hai; sponsored children's picnics and sports days (and took 120 children from Phuoc Le elementary school to the Buddhist shrine in Vung Tau to celebrate Buddha's birthday).[39] To top this off, a few troops organised a children's athletics carnival on the beach. In total, the Task Force medically examined a record 5,435 Vietnamese people in May alone, and a similar number received dental care. It is worth noting, in passing, that this effort coincided with the Australian Moratorium and the height of hostility towards returning troops. The disconnect between perception and reality cannot have been more marked: in Vietnam, the soldiers were building schools, entertaining Vietnamese children and inoculating babies; at home, they were being called 'baby-killers'.

The Viet Cong retaliated to the Australian hearts and minds offensive with its own forms of 'civic action' — or armed propaganda — at which it was a past master. The D445 Battalion's 'conversion' of a Catholic mass, as told in the unit's official history, offers a fascinating, if one-sided, account of communist proselytising:

D445 organized an armed propaganda, opinion-raising campaign in the Dat Do Area. At Noel Night (24th December 1969), some good looking, healthy men in each company of the battalion were selected … (led by Tam, deputy commander of D445) to participate in propaganda in Dat Do Church. A machine gun was placed at the police station gate 300m from the Church, to prevent the enemy entering. Twenty other men (and Tam) entered the church.

At first, the civilians were frightened of the 'Vietnamese Communists' (VC). Tam asked the vicar if he could address the civilians. The vicar agreed. Tam took the microphone and talked in a friendly way to the Christians and then announced: 'Any Saigon soldier present who brought his weapons into the church, please hand them over to us, and you will be forgiven.'

After a few quiet minutes, a Vietnamese Puppet lieutenant handed over a pistol. Then, two soldiers handed over their grenades. The civilians all clapped their hands loudly. After an hour of propaganda, Tam said: 'You are free to pray, you will not be harmed.' At the end of the prayers, everyone gathered around to talk. Someone said he did not believe in the Vietnamese Puppet propaganda any more. It was a great victory in the political field …[40]

Psyops, or psychological warfare operations, were a key part of the allied pacification effort. At one extreme, psyops dealt in emotional appeals and friendly chats with villagers. The Australian psyops units would 'sit down and talk to the locals', recalled Derrill de Heer, who served in psyops. 'We'd organise sports carnivals — soccer matches, volleyball — the kids loved it. We'd get films from USIS, some by Walt Disney. Catholic villages asked for religious films, such as *The Robe* with Richard Burton.'[41]

At the other extreme, psyops dealt in crude mass propaganda. Australian psyops teams and South Vietnamese Revolutionary Development cadres put up thousands of posters throughout Phuoc Tuy, such as: 'ALLIED FORCES IN PHUOC TUY PROVINCE ARE HELPING THE GVN TO BUILD A BETTER PLACE FOR YOU TO LIVE IN …'[42]

Psyops aircraft dropped millions of leaflets that aimed to demoralise the enemy, for example 'WHY BE A STATISTIC?' on a flyer covered in numbered tombstones. Or they struck at Buddhist fears: 'If you're killed, no one will know. Your spirit will wander forever. So fill in your name for a decent burial and keep this leaflet on you.' The American psywar introduced a more direct approach: '... Only DEATH is near. Do you hear the planes? Do you hear the bombs? These are the sounds of DEATH: YOUR DEATH. Rally now to survive.' On the reverse side was a grisly photo of a bomb victim.[43] The Viet Cong replied with its own pamphlets, poorly translated, which made little impression. One exhorted the 'AUSTRALIAN SERVICEMEN' to 'OPPOSE THE US AGGRESSIVE WAR IN SVN! DEMAND IMMEDIATE REPATRIATION!'

Psyops planes flew hours of voice missions, using loudhailers strapped to their wings: 'ATTENTION VC UNITS IN THIS AREA!' one aircraft yelled at the Viet Cong forces huddled in the forest at Bau Ham. 'Why do you continue to stay in the jungles, away from your loved ones, starved and suffering hardships for a cause which has given you no victories ... Return to your home and loved ones ...' Or this, to the 'illegal farmers' (i.e. those who fed the enemy) of Xuyen Moc: 'You are wrong to aid the enemies of the people of Vietnam. Your actions give the Armed Forces no choice but to destroy your crops and hunt you down. Return to your village and your families before this happens. You will be able to live a happy and prosperous life.'[44]

The American psyops planes sometimes broadcast macabre messages, designed to terrify, such as the grotesque sound of a baby wailing and the ghastly shriek, 'Friendly baby, GVN baby. Don't let this happen to *your* baby! Resist the Viet Cong today!'[45] Or the bored pilots simply played whatever took their mood: rock 'n' roll, 'Happy Birthday', 'Those Magnificent Men in their Flying Machines' or nostalgic Vietnamese tunes; all of which added to a sense of the war as a kind of surreal holiday interspersed with violence, the darkest cosmic jest.


Civic Action certainly achieved lasting incidental success of a purely humanitarian kind. Phuoc Tuy enjoyed great improvements in medical conditions and living standards. Australian medcaps virtually wiped out malaria and plague in the province. By 1970 almost all schoolchildren had been inoculated against plague, as part of the Plague Control Program.[46] The economy had advanced, too: Phuoc Le market was a bustling hive; the highways were 'a flurry of activity' — farmers could get to market and children to school; even private investors were investing in the province. Thatched roofs were sprouting 'an ever increasing number of [TV] antennas', one report noted.[47] Major General Robert Hay observed far more cattle in Phuoc Tuy at the end of his tour than when he arrived. And they were free to graze.

No one seriously contended that these advances won Viet Cong villages over to Saigon. Pacification failed as a military weapon because it was not integrated into the tactical war; it offered no clear long-term sense of security; and it suffered from a 'stop-start' mentality; that is, Task Force commanders had different tactical imperatives. Yet views on the efficacy of pacification profoundly differed. Pacification was 'the most productive period ... in the Task Force's operational history'.[48] 'Territorial security has been greatly improved,' said one hopeful Australian report in 1970, leading to an 'economic revival'. The hamlets and villages boasted a new generation of willing young leaders, who had helped to establish a 'system of government' at grassroots level 'despite the numerous risks'.[49]

The great difficulty was converting these civil gains into military and political benefits: field intelligence barely improved; Saigon never really controlled the countryside. The province and district chiefs were notoriously corrupt (in fact, on this count, one US report judged Phuoc Tuy the 'worst run province'[50]). Nor did the Australian counter–insurgency concept develop the indigenous forces: the Task Force pacified away to its heart's content without involving the South Vietnamese troops — a grave error.[51] And while the American program achieved comparatively less in other provinces, whatever the success of Australian methods they were applied in isolation. A little oasis of Australian civic action was not going to win the war.

In fact, the Free World forces failed to solve the great riddle of the peasant mind: in whom did the people invest their loyalty? 'Much of the country is controlled by neither side,' Komer observed in 1966, a situation that applied, to a greater or lesser extent, in 1969.[52] He was half-right; indeed, at times, the military's grasp of ordinary human psychology seemed extraordinarily deficient. Clearly, the people were loyal to their families and fellow villagers, a fairly universal human trait. Outsiders — foreigners, Saigon's thugs *and* Viet Cong — were seen as threats or transient benefactors, or both. The villagers acted accordingly. Sticks seemed to work better than carrots. 'They understand force,' complained one USAID representative, 'and iron leadership and threats. If someone says, "We'll kill your family if you don't do what we say", and they mean it, they are respected.'[53] AATTV member Major David Millie, an acute observer of the war, who made great efforts to help the people, noted with despair in his diary, 'To win hearts and minds — take the people by the nuts and their hearts and minds will follow.'[54] He found that the people responded movingly to whoever offered them stability, peace and protection. Yet so often the people's terror of Viet Cong reprisals inhibited their gratitude, let alone collaboration: only a furtive smile, or a child's innocent cry, '*Uc dai loi* number 1!' expressed their appreciation. Therein lay the true sadness of South Vietnam.

At the grassroots level, the war often destroyed the best civic intentions. Tanks and armoured carriers, pesticides and bombs wreaked havoc with agriculture. 'War damages' hardly appeased farmers who had lost their farms. One old farmer whose rice harvest had been destroyed started yelling at a truck of passing Australians; they tossed him a few packets of cigarettes to 'pacify' him. He kept yelling, so a sergeant pulled a pistol and said, '*Didi mau* [bugger off].'[55] Many soldiers simply could not switch off the psychology of the trained killer and switch on the milk of human kindness.

Families who lost their children were beyond reach. Civilian deaths warranted the payment of solatium to the grieving relatives, in line with a Vietnamese custom indicating shared grief. 'It is *not* compensation,' wrote Lieutenant B. L. Smith, a Vietnamese speaker and an acute observer of the war. Smith served with the 1st Australian Civil Affairs Unit from June 1969 to June 1970, and despaired of the military failure of civic action in many villages:

> ... we (Australians and Americans) are being taken for a financial
> ride. I really think that all officials, from the top ... right down
> the ladder, are not concerned with the country of South
> Vietnam and its free future, but with their own *personal* financial
> future ... They are after their own ends, and profit, and almost
> seem to make a game of, not IF they can take us, but by HOW
> MUCH they can take us, and they invariably do ... Some people
> obviously don't care whether the Communists or the present
> GVN govern them. AND THEY ARE NOT PREPARED TO HELP
> THEMSELVES OR US NOW, INCLUDING A LARGE PORTION OF
> SOUTH VIETNAMESE SOLDIERS ... Right now I feel we should
> leave the war to the South Vietnamese and see if they really
> would fight to maintain their freedom. Personally I would say
> within 12 months their whole system would fail and SVN
> would become Communist.[56]

His bitterness is appreciable. War, terror and bribes had obviously made the people deeply distrustful and bred a ruthless survival instinct, of which Brigadier Serong perceptively observed: 'The Vietnamese doesn't like the cheerful giver. To him the man who gives cheerfully isn't to be trusted. Either he gives because he wants something from you later, or he gives cheerfully because the gift is worthless. If neither of these is true then the man is a fool, and he still isn't to be trusted.'[57] True enough, as a behavioural observation; yet not a characteristic peculiar to the Vietnamese.

# Chapter 36
# Binh Ba

We had received radio messages saying 'the civilians have been
evacuated' and 'do what you have to do' — I did not interpret
this as meaning shoot who you like and issued radio orders to my
troop to ... have regard for any civilians who may still be in the
village.
*Captain Ray De Vere, after the battle of Binh Ba.*

So once again into this strange and twisted world headed fresh troops of
the Royal Australian Regiment: all nine battalions would serve in South
Vietnam at various stages between 1968 and 1971. All except the 8th and
9th would do two tours. The 2nd and 6th Battalions, on their second tours,
included two companies — Victor and Whisky — of New Zealand troops
(hence the 2nd Battalion ANZAC), about 40 per cent of whom were
Maoris, who swiftly earned a reputation for ferocious courage (the 4th
Battalion in 1971 had only one New Zealand company).

In November 1968 the newly formed 9th Battalion, the 'baby battalion',
arrived in Vietnam; the 5th and 6th followed in 1969. Their training had
changed little since 1965 and seemed less suited to the evolving combat
conditions, in which bunker attacks and platoon, rather than company, patrols,
were more prevalent. 'In my opinion,' Brigadier Colin Khan said years later, 'my
battalion had been prepared for entirely the wrong form of war.'[1] At times the
training failed to reach the standards of previous years, a sign of institutional
boredom. 'This battalion,' stated a Shoalwater Bay report just days before one

unit's departure, 'showed a marked lack of interest and enthusiasm in its participation in the exercise ...' Poor standards of communication, poor air coordination and inexperience with artillery were the chief failings, concluded the report.[2] Three battalions were similarly criticised after their Shoalwater trials, and several platoon and company commanders were sacked as being unfit to lead their men in combat. In action, however, most officers and troops would rise to the challenge with their usual tenacity, belying the few poor pre-departure reports on their combat-readiness.

Again, as it had done on sixteen previous occasions, HMAS *Sydney*, over three trips, ferried the fresh battalions to South Vietnam. As the troopship approached Vung Tau, the men, like thousands before them, returned their beer cards and meal discs, packed up their hammocks, pillows, lashings, clews and mattresses in the bedding cages, and slept on the deck in blow-ups.

They anchored off Vung Tau at dawn. 'The risk of enemy attack on HMAS *Sydney* whilst at anchor ... is very real,' stated the ship's routine warning. Artillery bombardment, 'floating charges' and 'swimmers carrying charges' were possible.[3] The Navy Diving Team, the aquatic equivalent of Tunnel Rats, plunged into the sea and swept the ship's hull for mines. The job demanded phenomenal mental and physical courage: on one occasion, an Australian Navy diver got into an underwater knife fight with a Viet Cong mine-layer.[4]

Then in stages during 1968–69, like all those before them, the 4th, 5th, 6th, 8th and 9th Battalions, in full battle order dress, roared ashore on landing craft and splashed up the beach under the indifferent gaze of a nation stupefied by war. On several occasions, a few boozy Americans laughed from their deckchairs at this melodrama. Once more, the stench of rotting vegetation and human excrement assailed the troops' nostrils; once more, these fresh 21-year-olds recoiled in revulsion from scenes of a society crippled by poverty and disease. And again, the departing units greeted these fresh arrivals with jeers, jokes and eyes like saucers ...

At the sprawling bush fortress of Nui Dat, the fresh troops occupied the vacated tents and dugouts; some added a few personal touches: 'Finished my pit today,' wrote one digger in his diary on Sunday, 16 March 1969. 'She's a beauty, got a few artillery boxes & put all my writing gear & toilet gear in ... also had a box to put my food in, a shit hot set up.'[5]

Then they set off on their first exhausting foot patrols, in roasting heat or pouring rain, bearing loads of up to 50 kilograms (including water and ammunition). The battalion histories amply cover the details of these interminable patrols through the boondocks.

One vast operation conveyed the sense of futility in the final years. In January and February 1969, the 4th, 5th and 9th Battalions joined US, Vietnamese and Thai troops on a massive sweep across Phuoc Tuy, Bien Hoa and Long Khanh provinces. The Australian part of the operation, dubbed OPERATION GOODWOOD and fought in north-west Phuoc Tuy, was conceived by Brigadier Sandy Pearson as a search and destroy operation. Pearson made a point of flying out regularly with his units, a preference shared by his predecessor Brigadier Ron Hughes. The troops would often look up to see the brigadiers hovering overhead in a little Bell bubble helicopter, an aircraft the men likened to a 'flying sperm'.

GOODWOOD, fought in dusty, dry conditions using Spooky flare ships, starlight scopes and tracker dogs (Trajan, Milo and Marcus), involved dozens of short, sharp platoon-level firefights, succeeded in finding and destroying 2,000 enemy bunkers, and inflicted 235 enemy dead, for which the Baby Battalion lost thirteen men.[6] Avoiding civilians was a constant hazard: 'Despite Psyops briefing to village chiefs, voice aircraft etc, civilians still entered forbidden areas,' noted an exasperated Lieutenant Colonel Lee Greville, commanding the 4th Battalion. 'But due to constant and correct application of the Rules of Engagement they were not fired upon.'[7]

The sweep through the hamlets yielded a sad portrait of desperate, war-exhausted innocence, observed Philip Ham, a nasho in the 5th Battalion. 'What did our platoon find?' he wondered, after searching the village of Xom My Xuan, whose 1,244 occupants were mostly woodcutters, charcoal burners and 'VC suspects'. Ham listed:

1. A sick boy covered with blankets in a hammock.
2. A straw ceiling, probed with a bayonet, revealed a male civilian
   in hiding. His wife and young baby were in the house
   shedding many tears. He was taken away and … found to be
   an ARVN deserter.
3. A freshly dug piece of ground in the backyard … The elderly
   female occupant claimed that it was the grave of her recently
   departed husband. Doubts about this. The engineers were
   called and [dug up the grave]. Sure enough the woman was
   telling the truth.

4. Spreadeagled dried rats were hanging in kitchen awaiting the cook.
5. Beneath practically all beds was a hole dug for use as an air raid shelter. These had to be searched.
6. All houses ... had the occupants' religious beliefs amply displayed, in the form of Buddhas, JC and whatever ...[8]

GOODWOOD was among Australia's final multi-battalion operation to be fought across the borders with third-country forces. From 1969 most operations tended to be platoon and company size, and restricted to Phuoc Tuy. That year, the operations came and went in a blur of codenames of little interest to the ordinary soldier: OPERATIONS BOUNDARY RIDER, KING HIT, KINGSTON, FEDERAL, CAMDEN, TIGER BALM, OVERLANDER, SURFSIDE, SABRE TOOTH, TONG, TWICKENHAM, LAVARACK, MUNDINGBURRA, TEKAPO, ROSS and MARSDEN. They were fought in a bewildering array of areas of operations and fire support bases, often named after the officers' wives or girlfriends: Maree, Kerry, Sally, Nick, Janice, Dyke, Tiki, Bruiser, Susan, Thrush, Elaine and Polly.

Fleeting contacts relieved the tedium, and some officers and soldiers began to wonder whether their commanders were deliberately avoiding the enemy, to limit casualties. Dreary officers' logs and laconic soldiers' diaries articulated this mood of boredom and routine horror.

Found sandal tracks one day old. Found footprint — 3 hrs old ...
Loc[ated] 10 bunkers, fishing gear, ammo ... Detonated a mine
— one Aust WIA ... Loc several spider holes during recce ...
Loc 2 graves 3 weeks old ... Found blood and bandages 2 days
old in an old camp ... Found 5 fish ponds, the fish were not big
enough to eat ... Contacted 2 en[emy] — result en cas unknown
... Detained 3 old women ... Found 6 old graves ...[9]

David Keating's diary recounts a bleak month, May 1969, relieved only by a Normie Rowe concert:

Sat 3 May 69 ... had a concert with Normie Rowe & Kiwis —
they were shit hot. All the fellows from 4RAR gave Normie a
hard time when he came on but they were soon singing with
him. When he left they wanted more ...

Sun 11 May 69 … We saddle up & climbed the eastern side of the Nui Thi Vai mountain … Lt Lee was killed yesterday.

Mon 12 May 69 … got Lt Lee's body out this morning and also another fellow who was shot in the legs … We reached the caves at 4.30 and gave them a rough search …

Wed 14 May 69: Was awoken by a claymore mine going off and a short burst of Armalite fire. Apparently a noggy was sneaking out before curfew which is at 6. He tried to get out at 5.30. They missed him.

Mon 19 May 69 … One of our mortars dropped short & hit one of our fellows in Charlie Company … 3 Aust WIA — own mortars.[10]

Time and again fresh battalions learned the same lessons, patrolled the same country, and 'discovered' caves and bunkers that previous units had 'discovered'. It was a khaki carousel, 'Hunting the Snark': '… us looking for him looking for us looking for him …'[11]

Suddenly a battle, a clash of unusual ferocity, the longest of the Australian war, broke the boredom. It was sustained over two days at the rubber-tappers' village of Binh Ba, a few kilometres up the road from Nui Dat. At 8.10 a.m. on 6 June 1969 a rocket-propelled grenade flew out of a house in Binh Ba and struck the turret of a passing Australian Centurion tank heading up Route 2 to support the 6th (ANZAC) Battalion; it seriously wounded the operator. The tank commander, Lance Corporal Harvey, fired a burst of his machine gun on the house, and returned to Nui Dat.

A stray, stupid provocation, by a teenage guerrilla, thought some. After all, Binh Ba was presumed to be thoroughly 'pacified' and hardly a hotbed of Viet Cong (or People's Army) insurgents. About a thousand farmers and rubber-tappers lived in this tranquil village of linear French design, whose neat houses had concrete walls, tiled roofs and wooden shutters. According to South Vietnamese warnings, however, the enemy had infiltrated the village, and the tank attack hardened suspicions that Binh Ba had fallen into North Vietnamese hands. An Australian Ready Reaction Force led by Major (later Major General) Murray Blake received thirty minutes' notice.

'My instructions,' recalled Blake, 'were to … mount a clearing operation of the village.' In short, to destroy the enemy in Binh Ba. 'There does not look to be much in this,' a quietly confident Blake told his company sergeant major as they prepared to depart.[12] His force comprised the 5th Battalion's Delta Company, four tanks (B Squadron, 1st Armoured Regiment), an armoured carrier troop commanded by Captain Ray De Vere, and a supporting gun battery. Corporals and sergeants led the platoons in an action dubbed HAMMER, to be fought, appropriately, in the Anvil area of operations.[13]

Later that day Lieutenant Colonel Colin 'Genghis' Khan, of the 5th Battalion, assumed overall command, relieving his shrewd 6th Battalion counterpart, Lieutenant Colonel David Butler, who had initiated HAMMER. A popular, dashing soldier, Khan was an inspirational speaker who liked to address his men with his slouch hat hanging off the revolver at his hip. Khan was a great believer in tanks, and relished this chance to see them perform in 'urban terrain'.

The Binh Ba civilians were to be moved before the attack. 'We told the village chief to move the civilians,' said Brigadier Pearson, who kept in close touch with Khan from Nui Dat.[14] Later, the district chief informed Blake directly that the people were 'out of the village and it was now clear for the Australian force to "do what you have to do".' A few hundred civilians had been herded into a schoolhouse, the district chief said, adding that only two enemy platoons had entered the village. In fact, elements of a North Vietnamese regiment had commandeered virtually every house.[15]

The reaction force, with tanks in the vanguard and the troops aboard carriers in the rear, pulled up about 250 to 300 metres short of Binh Ba, just beyond 'useful' rocket range. From here they observed the scene on the fringes of town. Sergeant Brian London, commanding 10 Platoon, 'saw a lot of people — 30 or 40 — running, as if to take up defensive positions'. The next moment, he saw smoke trails of rocket-propelled grenades 'heading in our direction'.[16]

The tanks responded by destroying, one by one, the first six houses from which the rockets issued. The armour then rumbled into the town from the east. They pulled up at each house. If the occupants refused to surrender, the Centurions fired high explosive rounds through the doors or shutters, destroying everything inside; then the infantry mopped up.

To the amazement of the Australians, the enemy units stood their ground … and actually chose to fight the Centurions. Fire poured from the houses, forcing the tanks to accelerate to new positions, while Blake's riflemen fought a fierce little war in the rear.

Not long into the attack the Australians met a group of civilians — who, contrary to the district chief's assurances, had not been evacuated — trying to escape north to Duc Trung. Blake gave permission to 11 Platoon to dismount and assist them. This was very risky: some 'civilians' were, in fact, North Vietnamese troops who had discarded their uniforms and mixed with the fleeing residents (one, when told to put his hands in the air, revealed his webbing under his shirt, Blake recalled). Escorting the civilians was 'My first bad decision', he said later, as it coincided with the worst of the fighting.

Within moments, a massive enfilade of rockets and machine guns stalled the Australian advance in the centre of town. 'I looked out at a scene of enemy running everywhere,' Blake recalled. The ensuing firefight was 'ferocious, intense, savage and chaotic', as Blake tried to respond to about eight radio nets babbling away: 'I spent a lot of time switching frequencies and telling people to "wait out".'[17]

Within an hour the armour-busting power of the enemy's new (RPG7) rocket-propelled grenades struck two Centurions, disabling one and wounding several crew members. One rocket actually grazed the back of Second Lieutenant Brian Sullivan, who sustained tail fin cuts to his left shoulderblade and head (and later received the Military Cross for his courage at Binh Ba). The Australian tanks and riflemen fought back with the ferocity of men who sensed that they were surrounded.

Many enemy troops fled and sought refuge in houses to the south, which the Bushranger helicopter gunships attacked at close range. 'Checks had to be conducted' in case civilians were inside, said Captain David Wilkins.[18] The restraints, however, were difficult to apply in the fog of war, and gave the advantage to the enemy. Australian efforts to escort civilians to safety seriously held up the advance. 'It took longer than anyone would have wished, but I could not leave them there,' Blake recalls.[19]

Several civilians ran screaming from their homes: a woman emerged 'in a terrible state, crying and gesturing to a partly collapsed bunker'. A search yielded a 15-year-old boy in 'shock but [with] no signs of physical injury'. Still the screaming woman kept pointing at the bunker. Another search yielded the body of a little girl, blown in half. 'We could do little to help the mother apart from wrapping up the body … and assisting her and her son to reach a safe area to the rear,' London recalled.[20]

By midday the Australians were caught in heavy fire with one tank disabled (the other three stayed operational with fresh crews). Blake decided to break out to the south; they succeeded on the second attempt, with remarkably few casualties (thanks largely to the firepower of the armoured vehicles). Undoubtedly, however, the North Vietnamese insurgents had successfully repelled the first assault on Binh Ba.

That afternoon, four fresh tanks swung to the west of the village, rejoined the infantry and launched a second assault. This time, the soldiers advanced on foot, in a mutually supporting formation. Each platoon formed five 'house-clearing teams' of two to three men. 'If you get into trouble,' London told his men, 'remember we have a tank and two carriers at our rear. Get word to me by runner if you need them. Any questions?'

Meanwhile, the 5th Battalion's Bravo Company sealed off the village's entrances and exits. 'Our task was to ensure that no enemy forces left or entered the village,' said Private Bill O'Mara. 'Most, if not all, the women and kids were in relative safety in the local school house.'[21]

Hidden snipers met the Australians as they returned. One struck Private Wayne Teeling in the neck; he died before his platoon commander could reach his body. The Australian tanks replied with a high explosive round that smashed into the house; six enemy dead were found in the ruins. Captured documents revealed their identity as 1st Battalion, 33rd North Vietnamese Regiment. For the first time, a battalion of the People's Army had moved to within 3 kilometres of Nui Dat.

Utter chaos gripped the village that afternoon. Sergeant London briefly lost control of his men during a savage firefight; hand-to-hand fighting broke out, of an intensity no Australian soldier had yet experienced in Vietnam. The anarchy heightened the risk of friendly fire: at one point an Australian carrier fired on an Australian platoon in error. 'To say that the battle … was fierce and confusing is an understatement,' London recalled.

Second Lieutenant John Russell's experience typified the mayhem. Sighting enemy soldiers in a house, Russell alone 'burst through the doorway, to be fired on by a VC at close range', records Wilkins. The enemy missed; Russell leaped behind a screen, which three enemy soldiers punctured with rifle fire and hurled a grenade over the top, badly wounding Russell in the legs and chest. Thinking the Australian dead, a North Vietnamese peered over the screen, at which Russell 'greeted him with one between the eyes'. In the chaos, Russell hurled himself out the door. 'What are you doing back here, skip? You're dead!' said one of his men.[22] The house, it later emerged, was the North Vietnamese battalion's headquarters.

At dawn on 7 June the struggle for Binh Ba resumed — animated by a moment of farce. Outside the village the Australian troops, thinking the hundred soldiers who approached through the Binh Ba rubber to be friendly South Vietnamese, waved; the 'South Vietnamese' waved back. In fact, they were North Vietnamese soldiers, and the sudden, mutual recognition triggered a great volley of fire, as the enemy fell back through the rubber.

At about 10 a.m. the Australian forces returned to the town: of the twenty-one Australian clearing teams that morning, private soldiers led twelve. 'The raw leadership of the private soldiers was outstanding,' Khan said later. The western half was thoroughly cleared by noon; the eastern half fell that afternoon — and the South Vietnamese Regional Forces completed the destruction of the escaping communist forces.

O'Mara joined the final mop-up through the rubble, at dawn on the 8th: '… it was chaos and carnage.' At this point an Australian TV journalist arrived and asked the troops to re-enact the battle. 'Do it again, fellas,' the reporter said (recalled O'Mara), 'do it for the camera … throw some grenades.' Some soldiers accommodated the reporter; O'Mara refused: 'I thought, that's sick. I told the reporter to piss off. Where was he an hour ago?'[23] Shortly, the Task Force Civil Affairs Unit arrived to help resettle the homeless.

The enemy dead were laid out in the village square on the district chief's orders, 'as a salutary warning to villagers not to harbour the enemy'.[24] This lesson failed to acknowledge that many residents had had little choice: the enemy simply commandeered their homes.

Barry Roe, a 19-year-old regular, dug a mass grave with an excavator and helped gather the remains. 'It was just a matter of running around … and picking up bodies … hunks of flesh, arms, legs, and chucking them in the bucket.'[25] On one burial party, O'Mara had an especially macabre experience: 'One bloke dug a grave with me. The bodies wouldn't fit; so the bloke took out a machete and was going to fix that. I almost shot him.'[26]

'The battle for Binh Ba ranks as one of the major military victories by the Australian Task Force,' concluded Sergeant London, who received a Distinguished Conduct Medal for his role. The soldiers claimed between ninety and 107 enemy killed, depending on your source. 'We killed a hundred people and buried them in this schoolyard,' said a veteran who visited Binh Ba in 2005.[27] Yet the 5th Battalion after-action report tallied forty-three North Vietnamese KIA 'by Body Count' and six wounded 'by Blood Trail' (for one Australian KIA and ten WIA, including eight tank crewmen).[28] There was a simple explanation for this discrepancy: the after-action report excluded about sixty casualties inflicted by South Vietnamese forces, explained Wilkins.

The dead included an unknown number of civilians: women, children and the elderly died at Binh Ba. 'Some civilians were … unable to escape,' stated Lieutenant Colonel Khan's report.[29] That did not tell the full story: the North Vietnamese used the villagers as shields. In such a war, the Australians lost if they fired and lost if they did not. In a separate operation, for example, Viet Cong soldiers broke out of a cordon by sending 'women and children in front', Blake recalls. 'Our soldiers did not open fire and let all the people pass.'[30] In fact, at several points during the chaos of Binh Ba Australian troops risked life and limb trying to protect civilians.

The truth did little to diminish claims that the Australians had committed a massacre at Binh Ba. In 1985 a Vietnamese official told the ABC's Richard Palfreyman that Australian soldiers had fired on civilians at Binh Ba even after the People's Army had withdrawn; she described the Australians as 'barbarous'. Such official hostility is understandable (if not credible); less explicable are the testimonies of some soldiers, who remember Binh Ba as a civilian 'bloodbath'. Such claims suggest the play of guilt or trauma on the mind. A serious effort *was* made to protect the people, as Blake and other officers recalled. 'We had received radio messages saying "the civilians have been evacuated" and "do what you have to do" — I did not interpret this as meaning shoot who you like and issued radio orders to my troop to … have regard for any civilians who may still be in the village,' said Captain Ray De Vere, who received a Military Cross after the battle.[31] Indeed, soldiers later found the schoolhouse 'chockers with civilians … The older men, women and kids were let out unharmed at the end of the battle.'[32]

Some civilians refused to leave their homes or were members of the People's Army in disguise. The Australians could not always tell the difference, said Nguyen Van Tan, a former Viet Cong naval sapper and guide. 'There were many civilian casualties,' he told me. 'They were all buried in one grave behind the school.'[33] He failed to mention that, after the battle, civilian survivors warmly thanked the Australians for ridding their village of the North Vietnamese, whom they loathed. 'If there'd been heavy civilian causalties,' reckoned Lieutenant Colonel Peter Gration, who headed the Civil Affairs effort in the aftermath, 'the people wouldn't have received us so enthusiastically.'[34]

Yet the memory of the civilian dead and their screaming families has never left many of the soldiers. It nearly broke several young Australian men, who sat whey-faced in the aftermath as others laughed and joked. Private G. Johnson wrote of the carnage, 'I have seen a sight under heaven that only God understands.'[35]

The soldiers later prayed. On 12 June the 5th Battalion held a dawn service in memory of recent losses, including civilians at Binh Ba. A chaplain read from Psalm 130, and the congregation of soldiers standing in the field repeated, 'Out of the depths I cry to you, O Lord … Let your ears be attentive to the voice of my supplications; If you, O Lord, should work iniquities, Lord, who could stand?'[36]

# Chapter 37
# Vietnamisation

Simpson ... covered the withdrawal of the wounded by
personally placing himself between the wounded and the enemy.
*Warrant Officer Ray Simpson's citation for the Victoria Cross.*

He organized [Montagnards] who were not wounded to crawl
out on their stomachs with wounded on their backs.
*Warrant Officer Keith Payne's citation for the Victoria Cross.*

In 1968–69 the South Vietnamese Territorial Forces were joined by a third, rather more bedraggled group, the People's Self Defence Force (PSDF), a Dad's Army of old men, women and children. Boys and girls aged 15 were given their first rifles with which to defend their hamlets. Saigon had long refused to arm the People's Forces 'for fear of weapons falling too readily into the hands of the Viet Cong'. That changed after Tet with the 'Vietnamisation' of the South, the US-led policy that aimed to make South Vietnam militarily self-reliant.

Most Australian soldiers had little contact with their South Vietnamese allies: the occasional joint action, a beer or a brawl in Vung Tau, an encounter in the villages. With the exception of a few trusted interpreters, South Vietnamese troops were not allowed into Nui Dat. The Australian Task Force fought its own isolated campaign; and perhaps its greatest failure, some believe, was this inability to establish a working relationship with the Army of the Republic of Vietnam. Still, many troops in the Task Force did conduct operations with their South Vietnamese allies. Bravo Company 6RAR/NZ Battalion patrolled with ARVN units in September 1969. Peter Simpson vividly recalls participating in a six-man Australian detachment from 5 Platoon, sent with South Vietnamese troops to trace enemy blood trails. And several Australians struck excellent personal relationships with their ARVN allies.

One example was John Press, a mustachioed, quick-witted captain of the 7th Battalion who pursued his brief with empathy and latitude. In 1970 Press was liaison officer between the Task Force and the Dat Do district headquarters: 'My major responsibility was to ensure that our patrols and the ARVN operations did not clash.' He made daily solo visits to Ruff Puff posts, often at considerable personal risk. He seemed oddly bullet-proof. He would drive into town and muck in with the local troops. The Viet Cong was surely well aware of Captain Press. 'Beer and soup in the marketplace plus church on Sundays kept me from harm,' he said. He attended Mass with Catholic Vietnamese on many occasions. His visits would also entail games of Vietnamese poker and Chinese chess, with the odd shot of rice wine. 'It was no wonder that I put on over a stone.'[1]

Another soldier who became deeply involved with the South Vietnamese was Warrant Officer Wally Thompson, later to become the first regimental sergeant major of the army and a national treasure. He served three tours, including a period with the Team near the Laotian border with a battle-toughened ARVN battalion. He ate Vietnamese food and lived as they did. 'I was very fond of them. I found them very brave. The Vietnamese soldier had a job to do and he did it. If he complained he got a rifle butt over the head. A lot of our soldiers didn't have time for Vietnamese — their only experience was bar girls, pimps and rip-off merchants. They never saw the families ...' Notwithstanding his mateship with the South Vietnamese, Thompson resisted going native. 'You mustn't "go noggy",' he said. 'Your objective is to train them to your standard, not join them and do things their way ...'[2]

Not that he ignored local sensitivities. To do so could have lethal consequences, as Private Roy Hornsby observed during a joint operation with the ARVN in 1969. Resting in a bamboo patch, Hornsby witnessed a huge American master sergeant produce a tin of biscuits and offer them to a South Vietnamese officer called Hau, who squatted in the clearing. Hau misunderstood, so the American casually threw the tin over. It landed in the dirt, 'the equivalent of throwing an old bone to a dog' — in full view of Hau's Vietnamese peers. Hau started cursing the American, who made light of it, at which Hau advanced in a rage, 'frothing at the mouth', drew his Colt .45 and 'aimed it directly between the eyes of the American'. The terrified GI was evacuated, never to be seen again. 'He was a big-talking smart arse but a changed man after this incident,' Hornsby recalled.[3]

No less confronting were South Vietnamese reactions to an Australian belief that they (the South Vietnamese) were less well endowed. It got about that the *uc dai loi* reckoned they had bigger penises than Asians in general and the Vietnamese in particular. One day, Private Hornsby awoke to the sound of yelling outside his tent: '... several ARVN soldiers ... all had their pants half down and were waving their penises in our direction. I have to say that they had picked their display team well ... it caused some anger among the Australians, as it was very challenging ...'[4]


Australian Army Training Team members were, of course, embedded with the South Vietnamese as advisers, trainers and leaders, and played a direct role in preparing the Vietnamese for the leadership of the war. In the late 1960s the Team led a series of exhausting projects which more or less pursued this goal. Major David Millie, for example, with his men led the resettlement of 6,000 refugees in Quang Tri province; Major Harry Bell pioneered the development of the Mobile Advisory Teams; Captain John Leggett helped raise Revolutionary Development cadres; Captain Bob Guest established a Regional Force Training Centre near Hoa Long; Major Graham Templeton led the first Australian detachment into the Mekong Delta; and several warrant officers created the first Village Defence Advisory and Night Operations teams (as part of John Vann's pacification effort).

In 1969 many of these projects were focused primarily on one overriding aim: 'Vietnamisation' of the war. Crudely implicit in that unfortunate term was the eventual departure of the Free World forces, leaving South Vietnam to fend for itself.

Team members spread themselves widely over the country and achieved the best results when personally training the South Vietnamese troops, chiefly in combat and patrol tactics. Mostly, however, they instructed the Vietnamese instructors, such as at the training centres in Dong Da, Duc My and Hiep Kanh. These were less happy experiences. The South Vietnamese instructors had lower — or more realistic — expectations of the average Vietnamese trooper, and the Australians' more demanding lessons were (often conveniently) lost in translation.

The Team took its skills on the road. It pioneered the use of Mobile Advisory Teams (MATS) and Mobile Training Teams (MTTS), which advised and trained Revolutionary Development cadres and the Ruff Puffs in the most remote and dangerous parts of the country. Major Templeton and several warrant officers formed two-man mobile teams. Instructing fearful city-bred South Vietnamese troops in rural security was an exhausting, perilous and often thankless job. The Australians were unable to prevent them plundering the villages in their care. In one instance (of many), hungry South Vietnamese soldiers stole hundreds of ducks and chickens from villages in the delta — villages they were supposedly 'pacifying'. As punishment, the province chief chicken-whipped each thief about the head with his stolen fowl, after which the miscreants thrust their rather bruised birds back into their packs, and put their helmets on.[5]

Team members were nothing if not adaptable. They often tolerated poor results in silence, in accordance with the culture of compromise ('harmony') that prevailed in the South Vietnamese Army. They tried to instil a sense of discipline in their Vietnamese troops, who in fairness were abysmally paid and badly fed, and lived in cramped, crowded quarters. Many South Vietnamese soldiers were press-ganged into uniform and deprived of contact with their families; their casualty rate almost matched that of the Viet Cong. No wonder many preferred a joke and a drink (and later narcotics) to the Team's rigorous standards. Not all South Vietnamese soldiers answered to this description, of course. The elite Ranger battalions and Special Forces were superbly trained — often in America and Australia — and most performed with great courage; so, too, would many ordinary infantrymen as the communist invasion loomed.

Cynicism dogged the Team's work. Yet occasionally instructors broke through the lethargy and resistance, as Captain David Savage showed in his long, hard struggle for control of his Vietnamese trainees at the Australian LRRP school in Van Kiep.[6] Savage's persistence briefly conquered the indolence of the ARVN and redrew the school's responsibilities and disciplinary procedures. It was a short-lived victory, however: on 23 May 1970 Van Kiep closed because the Australian school taught different tactics from the American. The case for uniformity, if not efficacy, prevailed, and the Van Kiep cadets moved to the American LRRP Wing near Duc My.

During these last years, a brace of military decorations reflected the courage, perseverance and local leadership of the Team, qualities most emphatically demonstrated in the extraordinary actions of Warrant Officers Ray Simpson and Keith Payne.

In May 1969 Simpson and Payne were advising Montagnard Mobile Strike Forces ('Mike Forces') on the Laotian border, deep in the province of Kon Tum. Their mission was to resist North Vietnamese infiltration along the Ho Chi Minh Trail, from Laos and Cambodia. Kon Tum is a land of jungle-clad mountains, bamboo thickets, low mist and steady drizzle. B52 Arc Light bombing had cratered the surface, replacing the dense jungle with a wasteland of mud-caked hills, and the scene of hundreds of 'Yard' (Montagnard) warriors scrambling up the defoliated, pocked slopes lent a sense of primeval authenticity to this atmosphere of antediluvian gloom.

Simpson ('Simmo') had fought on Morotai, Tarakan and Rabaul in World War II, in Malaya during the Emergency and with Vietnamese Special Forces at Khe Sanh and Ta Ko, where he had been badly wounded and earned a Distinguished Conduct Medal; this was his third tour of Vietnam. 'He was a man's man,' observed Ian McNeill, author of The Team, the unit's official history. Simpson's toughness belied 'an intellect nurtured by his avid reading of military history'.[7] His historic role model was the German commando Otto Skorzeny.

We do not know the words of comfort Simpson used to sustain his fellow warrant officer Michael Gill, on the night of 6 May 1969, as Gill lay dying of horrific gunshot wounds. We do know that Gill passed away in the company of the man who ran over fire-swept ground to save him. Units of the People's Army had attacked at 2.30 p.m. as Simpson's men neared a clearing where Gill, at the head of a Montagnard platoon, had been fatally wounded. Simpson dragged him to safety and, in a hoarse mixture of Montagnard dialect and Australian expletives, yelled to his 'Yards' to resume the attack. In the meantime, Simpson crawled to within metres of the North Vietnamese bunkers and tossed in hand grenades. He then covered his unit's withdrawal.

Simpson's next action demands that we suspend disbelief in the resolve of one human being to stare down death, alone and under terrific fire, in the interests of his fellow soldiers. On another clearing, at the top of a small hill, a US Captain Green lay dead after rushing forward to aid a wounded Australian, Warrant Officer Kelly. When Kelly radioed his position, he was hit again. The terrified Yards sat down and refused to fight; many disappeared into the jungle. A fragment of advisers — Simpson, Captain Peter Rothwell, Warrant Officer Brian Walsh and US Sergeant Holmberg — were left to extract Kelly under the noses of enemy bunkers. Simpson again crawled into no-man's land and held the enemy with grenades and rifle fire, as Walsh and

Holmberg dragged the wounded Kelly out and Rothwell hacked away with his machete to create a helicopter landing zone — even as enemy troops encroached. 'The whole area was sprayed [with enemy fire],' Holmberg said. Simpson, still in the open, took the brunt of it: his only shelter, a tree, was 'ripped apart'. 'Simpson ... covered the withdrawal of the wounded by personally placing himself between the wounded and the enemy,' concluded his citation for the Victoria Cross.[8]

Later that cold, wet night the shattered Yards, for whom Simpson had little sympathy, sat milling about, utterly demoralised: 'I observed a leaderless rabble ... sitting around doing nothing. The Yards refused to obey their leaders and the advisers.'[9]

To his disbelief, just over a fortnight later, Lieutenant Colonel Russell Lloyd, then commanding the Team, 'found himself writing a second Victoria Cross citation'. Warrant Officer Keith Payne, a quietly spoken father of five, seemed to undergo a metamorphosis in Vietnam. A veteran of Korea and Malaysia, Payne commanded a Montagnard company of the 1st Mobile Strike Force Battalion to the south of Simpson.

On the morning of 24 May US fighters scrambled to make the best of a clear blue sky and pounded the ridge line ahead of Payne's battalion. That afternoon Payne and a second Mike Force Company moved over country littered with corpses towards a bare, flat hilltop encrusted with bombed North Vietnamese bunkers. The clearing was 300 metres by 120 metres, a scrap of open ground fringed by jungle in which the North Vietnamese lay concealed. As the two companies spilled onto this clearing, withering North Vietnamese fire struck from three sides. Many of the Yards fell; some fled. Payne ran up and down their prostrate lines, firing his rifle, grabbing and hurling grenades, and temporarily deterring the enemy. Wounded in the head, with shrapnel splinters in his hands and arms, Payne forestalled his company's chaotic retreat and, in the covering fire of two helicopter gunships, led their withdrawal from the hill in relative order. At the base, he organised his surviving Yards into a perimeter for the night. Above, the People's Army surged onto the plateau.

Although wounded, Payne did not rest: he went back up the hill, through enemy lines, that night — alone. On four separate occasions he reached the plateau, and managed to drag, lead or carry forty Montagnard soldiers to safety: 'At 9 p.m. he crawled over to one displaced group, having tracked them by the fluorescence of their footsteps in rotting vegetable matter ... He organized others who were not wounded to crawl out on their stomachs with wounded on their backs.'[10] He also rescued three wounded US Special Forces sergeants.

At 3 a.m. on the 25th, at the head of a battered line that included 'his interpreter, his radio man and forty Montagnards', Payne staggered into his lines. '... he had found us,' recalled an elated Sergeant Gerard Dellwo, of the US Special Forces.[11] 'His sustained and heroic personal efforts,' said Payne's citation, '... undoubtedly saved the lives of his indigenous soldiers and several of his fellow advisers.'[12] Of Payne's original eighty-nine soldiers, thirty-one had survived; he helped rescue many more. Was he afraid? 'My God yes, yes, I was,' Payne later said.[13]

The Team joined US and South Vietnamese Special Forces in dozens of actions that led to high decoration: Felix Fazekas, Geoff Skardon, Vin Murphy, Stan Krasnoff, David Savage, Peter Rothwell, David Paul and many others advised and led Montagnard or South Vietnamese troops in the most desolate places ... for a fort, a hill, a bunker field. The exhausting relief, for example, of the Special Forces base at Duc Lap in August 1968, recounted in Savage's book *Through the Wire*; the siege of the small jungle fort of Ngok Tavak, where Captain John White and US Marines faced an encircling enemy in a battle they knew they could not win; and the eighteen-day siege for the fort at Dak Seang in April 1970, where ten Australian advisers effectively commanded the battalion-strength relief effort (one died and two were wounded). Of the hundred Montagnards killed or wounded, twenty-one suffered awful burns when a US napalm canister mistakenly fell on their platoon, and the Montagnard death chant rose above the pitiful moan of the victims through that terrible night.

In 1967 North Vietnamese and National Liberation Front forces assassinated 285 government officials, 603 civil servants (teachers, medical workers and so on) and 2,818 other civilians, for unspecified 'crimes', according to US records. The next year they abducted 10,332 civilians, double the number of the previous year.[14] The upsurge in local terror was often indiscriminate, as Douglas Pike, an authority on the Viet Cong, wrote: 'The Viet Cong strategy precluded the disinterested onlooker. Not even children were excluded — particularly not children, one might say. All people became weapons of war.'[15]

In response the CIA recommended the 'neutralisation' of the 'Viet Cong Infrastructure', jargon for the NLF's parallel administration, or Provisional Revolutionary Government, and its support system that entwined the countryside. President Thieu accepted the CIA's advice: to meet local terror with terror. This was the genesis of the Phoenix Program, or Phung Hoang, which set out to train and deploy snatch squads: hit men whose jobs were to arrest and interrogate — and if necessary kill — non-combatants who supported the Viet Cong. The Vietnam War thus descended into a darker circle.

The Phoenix squads were known as 'Provincial Reconnaissance Units' (PRUs). Secretly raised in 1966, they were not recognised until 1969 when a Saigon Government Decree identified their role as 'conducting paramilitary operations ... in order to destroy the Viet Cong Infrastructure'. Or, as McNeill writes, 'to destroy [the Viet Cong Infrastructure] by encouraging defections, killing and capturing, or neutralizing its effect through counter-propaganda'. In short, they were trained assassins.

Technically, their targets were members of 'revolutionary committees' or 'liberation committees' elected by villages, according to William Colby, the former CIA chief in Vietnam. In practice, they were anyone who supported the communists: village chiefs, propaganda teams, couriers, tax collectors, saboteurs and farmers who fed the Viet Cong. Of course, these collaborators were exceedingly difficult to identify, so Phoenix relied on 'census grievance' lists: ostensibly an avenue for villagers to air their grievances; in reality a covert means of identifying Viet Cong sympathisers. Terrible mistakes were made.

The US commanders dubbed the role of Phoenix 'Infrastructure Neutralisation' — a fine example of the syzygy between the ugliness of the euphemism and the savagery of the act. Between 1967 and 1973 CIA-sponsored 'counter-terror' and 'hunter-killer' teams 'neutralised' an estimated 40,000 Vietnamese, and 'hundreds of thousands' were sent to secret interrogation centres. William Colby's own records show 20,587 dead between 1968 and 1971: '... he likes to believe that most were killed in military combat.'[16] In fact, as Colby himself recognised, Phoenix became an instrument of savage reprisal: 'A lot of very bad things were done on both sides.'[17]

Attacks on non-combatants were as old as Thucydides and the Peloponnesian War. Yet the very premeditative nature of Phoenix as a political weapon distinguished it from the indiscriminate slaughter of civilians by an army on the march. Phoenix became the centrepiece of the 'other war', which aimed to meet Robert Komer's target of 3,000 'VCI' neutralised every month, under Abrams's Accelerated Pacification Campaign.[18] Komer thus imposed a 'body count' on non-combatants whose hearts and minds had resisted other forms of persuasion.

In strictly military terms, Phoenix implied that the South could win only by wiping out the communist support network, the parallel government; thus America, too, had taken the possibility of a neutral 'civilian' out of the equation. Understandably, Phoenix proceeded in conditions of strictest secrecy (the details did not emerge until 10 August 1987, in *Time*'s cover story, 'Under orders from the CIA', the key source of which was Ted Serong).

The Australian Task Force was well aware of the operation of the Phoenix program, but most soldiers knew very little of its extent, such was the secrecy surrounding it. Some units participated indirectly; for example the 2nd and 8th Battalions' involvement in OPERATION PHUNG HOANG in Long Le, a South Vietnamese attempt to 'hunt down any VC cadre', especially 'propaganda', 'economic' and 'civil affairs' elements.[19]

One Australian, however, was steeped in Phoenix: Ted Serong. Having quit the army in 1968, Serong continued to work for the CIA in South Vietnam, with the title of Brigadier and later Brigadier General (or just 'the General'). That year he founded South Vietnam's National Police Field Force, a CIA-funded paramilitary organisation, and recruited two old mates, the legendary ex-commandos George Warfe DSO MC and Fred Lomas MC, to run the unit's training school in Da Lat. The school turned out thousands of snatch teams for the Phoenix Program. Serong's authorised biographer, Anne Blair, skirts over Phoenix with only brief mentions of it.[20] Yet at several levels Serong *was* the Phoenix program.

A few Australian advisers and CIA-attached commandos were also closely involved. Team members trained Provincial Reconnaissance Units (PRUs), or Viet Cong 'neutralisation' teams, in Phuoc Tuy. Some advisers refused, or complied reluctantly: training death squads (as they were seen) impugned many soldiers' sense of dignity, or confounded their duty of civilian care. Some clung to a notion of what the war should be, not what it had become. Others were impatient with notions of 'rules of war' in a war in which both sides honoured them in the breach, and willingly trained

South Vietnamese Phoenix cadres to become as deadly as the enemy they pursued.

Michael Currie, seconded to the CIA as a propaganda officer in 1968–69, trained a PRU in the Rung Sat Special Zone; his troops were 'mercenaries', he said, 'and very brave': they 'racked up ... more kills per week than the whole Australian Task Force put together'. While some turned into 'petty hoodlums and stand-over men', Currie defended Phoenix on the grounds that 'we were fighting a war and the Viet Cong were bad bastards'. Currie's views were deeply coloured by his own shocking experiences: he had witnessed the disembowelment of a pregnant woman at the village of Duc Tho, an atrocity her husband, the village chief, was forced to watch before the Viet Cong beat him to death. He lost count of the number of assassinations at Suoi Nghe, 'the artificial village we Australians built, God help us'.[21] His most miserable memory was the death of a young woman whom the Vietnamese Information Service — a CIA propaganda unit — had trained in leaflet production. The Viet Cong captured her at Xuyen Moc, 'shot her, chopped out her tongue and stuffed it up her vagina'. For Currie, this was a 'graphic visual symbol that our propaganda was non-productive'.[22]


Phoenix was, for a time, devastatingly effective: the combined impact of PRUs and Serong's paramilitary police drove the enemy 'crazy', noted a satisfied Abrams, who applauded Serong's methods. In the first quarter of 1969, Phoenix matched the Viet Cong kill rate, according to US 'Infrastructure Neutralisation' figures: 4,005 'VCI' — mostly non-combatants — were 'neutralised'. Over the same period the enemy assassinated 4,947 civilians, winning the 'other war', just, that quarter by a net gain of 942 dead.[23] The number of Phoenix-related deaths rapidly rose: between 1968 and 1970, the US Defense Intelligence Agency reported a near four-fold rise, from 2,559 to 8,191.

By 1970 Phoenix had demoralised and broken the Viet Cong support system. The communist support cadres were virtually wiped out in several provinces. After the war, North Vietnamese leaders convinced the historian Stanley Karnow that Phoenix was 'the single most effective program ... used against them in the Vietnam War'.[24] Phoenix had been 'extremely destructive', said General Tran Do, the deputy communist commander in the South.[25]

Colby later defended Phoenix as 'a decent program': only top Viet Cong cadres — committee chairmen, local chiefs — were targeted, he claimed. In 1971 28,000 'VCI cadres' were captured and 20,000 killed. Most died in combat, not as a result of assassination, Colby claimed.[26] Yet many were 'non-combatants' or simply mistakes, avowed Frank Snepp, a senior CIA agent. Serong was more direct: 'Yes, we did kill teachers and postmen. But it was the way to conduct the war. They were part of the Viet Cong Infrastructure. I wanted to make sure we won the battle.' He compared the 'excesses' to traffic rules: '... everyone goes over the speed limit from time to time.'[27] In reality, by 1970 squads of wild-eyed, often drugged, Vietnamese killers roamed the countryside and indiscriminately rounded up and tortured suspects or civilian sympathisers — on both sides. 'Ordinary villagers were arrested ... and tortured or arbitrarily executed,' wrote Truong Nhu Tang, briefly the National Liberation Front's Minister of Justice, who later fled Vietnam.[28]

Yet despite its 'success', Phoenix also inflicted terrible suffering on civilian communities and steeled Hanoi's resolve. The Australian Task Force chose a different response to the Viet Cong's local terror: 'acorn operations', set up under the Counter Intelligence section of the Task Force's 1st Divisional Intelligence Unit. Acorns acted on more precise information than Phoenix; they cross-referenced censuses, field agents' reports and local intelligence. Blacklists were drawn up and suspects quietly weeded out during village cordon and search operations. 'Our efforts predated Phoenix and were based on our Malayan experience,' explained Ernie Chamberlain, an intelligence officer.[29] In fact, acorn operations were more effective and better resourced than the Phoenix system, argued Blair Tidey, an Australian intelligence expert, 'a point not lost on US intelligence officials in Phuoc Tuy'.[30] Indeed, as Phoenix degenerated into an arbitrary manhunt (eventually abandoned in 1971) General Abrams himself ordered the adoption of the more discriminating, if painstaking, acorn tactics.[31]

Meanwhile, notwithstanding the victorious conclusions of their computers, the Americans were losing the official war: for example, in the first three months of 1969, the US command had coded most roads in South Vietnam GREEN (i.e. relatively secure); B52 Arc Light strikes had destroyed 12,877 bunkers and 24,100 metres of trench line; and 'crop dusters' had defoliated 410,000 acres of 'enemy cover', or jungle.[32] Yet these figures were a poor reflection of the reality.

Perhaps the clearest sign of US failure was in the air war. In the three months to 1 April 1969, US fighters and bombers flew 52,396 sorties, of which 6,676 were in support of allied ground troops in combat: an increase of 2,600 over the previous corresponding quarter, in 1968; that is, during the Tet Offensive. This, reflected a US analyst, showed 'the general increase in ground activity'.[33]

To say the least, in the three months to 1 April 1969, the North Vietnamese/Viet Cong renewed their offensive across *all* fighting categories: they mounted 352 assaults or ambushes (169 in the same period in 1968); 631 attacks by fire (358); and 3,417 anti-aircraft attacks (2,722). Tet in 1969, if not as sudden or shocking as Tet in 1968, was, by this count, far more deadly.

In fact, the Free World forces were gazing at the profile of an enemy who would never surrender and who was somehow able to replenish his massive losses at will (one reason was that 320,000 Chinese support troops served as the North's supply backstop, freeing all young Vietnamese for combat duties). Neither the devastation of Tet nor the huge operations of 1968 and 1969, nor Phoenix, broke the North Vietnamese will to fight. Indeed, a whole generation of young northerners accepted death as their fate. Their motto, found tattooed on many bodies, was 'Born in the North to die in the South'.[34]

Part Seven

# Homecoming

# Chapter 38
# Morale

We were … waiting for these bloody things to go off … we just looked at each other. We couldn't believe they were sending [us] in.
*Private Alan Handley, 8th Battalion, on fighting in a mined area.*

In wonder the world watched the moon landing on 21 July 1969. Beamed back to earth, the images of Neil Armstrong's first lunar footprints appeared on a small black-and-white television in Cam Ranh Bay, South Vietnam, and transfixed Beverly Milner, of the RAAF Nursing Service Vietnam. Milner flew with an all-male crew of the US Air Force Medical Air Evacuation System as far north as Quang Tri province, near the seventeenth parallel. Her Australian nurse's uniform made her a 'natural curiosity' among her patients — most of whom were American soldiers. 'I was often asked by the patients to speak "Australian",' she recalled.[1]

Nurses were crucial to restoring the wounded soldiers' morale. Yet few inquired about the nurses' morale, which came close to buckling as the war ground on. 'I think I was a pretty cool-headed person,' said Fay Lewis, an Australian Army nurse. 'But I think that it eventually got to us … you were sending home week after week planes full of young, mutilated people. Most people see amputated limbs as nice rounded finished-off stumps. We didn't get that. We had the ragged ends.'[2]

Indeed, mines were the curse of Australia's last years in Vietnam. The wounds horrified the medical teams: M16 jumping jacks — most of them lifted from the Australian minefield — caused more than 50 per cent of Australian casualties between September 1968 and May 1970, the height of the 'mine war'.

The first multiple mine injuries came during OPERATION PINAROO, an attack on the dreaded Long Hais Hills in March 1968. For the first time, the Australians successfully occupied the Minh Dam Secret Zone, the Viet Cong provincial headquarters — but not without heavy losses: forty-six casualties (ten killed and thirty-six wounded), mostly as a result of M16 mines. Private David McKenzie lost both legs and his right arm in the assault. On 15 April another huge mine explosion delivered six casualties to Dr Don Beard's surgery. Two arrived dead; the rest were 'boys to whom I had been talking on Monday', Beard said, consoling himself that the survivors were missing 'only a few odd fingers and toes'.[3]

The government kept very quiet about the minefield: few knew of Canberra's shared responsibility for the decision to build it. Even the suggestion that mines were killing or maiming the diggers sparked domestic fury. When Michael Leunig drew a cartoon depicting a soldier's leg blown off, he received 'a lot of flak' and was considered unpatriotic. Later, 'a very nervous and distraught woman' — the mother of a soldier who had lost his leg to a mine — rang to thank Leunig for drawing attention to the issue. In fact, mine casualties were so politically sensitive — and a gift to the anti-war movement — that before the 1969 election Canberra actively intervened in the tactical war to limit them.

The Task Force tried to remove the source. Attempts to destroy the barrier minefield began in 1968 and dragged into 1970. Centurion tanks hauled great steel mats across the field. This failed, as repeated mine blasts disabled the tanks' tracks. Next, giant steel 'skirts' were hitched to the backs and fronts of a trial tank, but it simply rolled most mines in the sand, detonating some. Then Major E. S. 'Tim' Holt suggested that Viet Cong ralliers (defectors) be paid to lift the mines: if the Viet Cong could lift 2,000 by night, surely the ralliers could exceed that by day? Holt's idea was not pursued. 'The barrier minefield was becoming a nightmare,' wrote the historians McNeill and Ekins, in a momentary departure from their customary reserve.[4]

Not until late 1969 did the Task Force find a way of destroying the minefield. Major Rex Rowe, then commanding 1st Field Squadron, Royal Australian Engineers, and Captain John Power, officer commanding 1st Field

Squadron Workshop, devised a solution: to attach an offset axle 15 metres behind an armoured carrier and fit a series of grader tyres to the axle, which would trigger the mines at a safe distance from the carrier. The carriers were fitted with an extra steel plate at the rear, and the drivers wore heavy body armour: flak jackets and helmets. They drove the machine at top speed alongside the minefield — a 'thunder run' — then suddenly veered sharply into it, triggering the mines as they went. The grader tyres would jump up and down like piano keys, as the mines popped up behind. 'You can just imagine how dangerous and frightening it was for these poor buggers,' said Rowe, who drove several thunder runs himself.[5] On one occasion a mine almost blew his carrier over.

Yet the method worked: within six months, this contraption had destroyed most of the M16s. Many unexploded mines — damaged by the weather — remained, and were bulldozed into great holes: 'Dear Mum, Dad & family,' wrote Frank Delaney, a sapper who participated, in December 1969, '... We are now at a place called DAT DO. This is a minefield the Australians laid a few years ago & now we're pulling it up ... They use armoured tractors, dig big holes ... then push the mines from either side into the hole, then cover up the hole ... every now and again we hear a few mines going off ... All my love, Frank xxxx.'[6]


Mines instilled a raw, livid fear in the soldiers' hearts and minds that could be debilitating. Mines were invisible, hidden, loathsome killers; they disabled, disembowelled and emasculated; both sides used them throughout the war. The thought that the Viet Cong had lifted thousands of Australian M16s — Brigadier Weir reckoned they lifted 6,000 of more than 20,000 laid — weighed on every soldier's mind. 'The whole time your mind was on overload, overload with fear of mines,' said Bill Akell.[7] So prevalent was the fear of mines that Rex Rowe advised the Task Force that operations must not be allowed to grind to a halt as a result of 'mine neurosis' or political sensitivities.[8]

The specific fear of mines nourished the general fear. Some soldiers cracked up, for reasons other than mines. Reinforcements had a particularly hard time. Most filled the shoes of dead soldiers and were thus instantly stigmatised. In 1968 one reinforcement in Major Brian Honner's company 'came tearing back from a patrol with eyes like saucers. He was so young. He was shaking all over. He said, "They're shooting at me."' Honner read him the Riot Act. 'You've left a bloke out there on his own,' he fumed. Honner then picked up his rifle and cocked it; the soldier returned. 'That night,' Honner said, 'I found him. He was crying. I said, "It's OK, mate. We're all frightened."

'He cried, "Were you really going to shoot me?"'

'I said with a half smile, "It was lucky you got out fast."' Honner added: 'For many of us, Vietnam was absolute terror a lot of the time.'[9]

Surprisingly few soldiers suffered total mental collapse. Those most vulnerable were regular soldiers with existing personality disorders, such as 'Private C', who demanded to see a psychiatrist 'so I can get out of this rifle company'. An examination revealed a psychopathic personality. Private C had not made any friends, performed at an inferior standard and was a known liar and 'mouth'. There were eight similar cases. Oddly, support troops in Vung Tau experienced a higher rate of psychiatric disorders than combat troops, ascribed to several reasons; for example, spending long periods in a combat zone doing menial tasks when others were out fighting.[10] Fear could immobilise the toughest infantry platoons, as Captain David Wilkins learned: when his men responded with 'collective paralysis' to his signal to assault a cave, he 'couldn't believe it. Not a soul moved! ... I said to the nearest soldiers ... "Well, I'm going. Who's coming with me?" With hearts in their mouths, they began the assault.'[11]


In the field, three fingers signalled a land mine.[12] But neither hand nor verbal warnings saved ten members of the 5th Battalion from a mine blast on the night of 9 March 1969. Second Lieutenant Brian Walker misunderstood his orders, cut through layers of wire fence and led his men into a minefield near Hoa Long, from which they fired on friendly South Vietnamese forces, thinking them Viet Cong. In the darkness, trip wires detonated at least two mines. Walker probably died of South Vietnamese gunshot wounds, although it seems that the blast blew his body onto the concertina wire.

Rescue teams went in, with torches and bayonets. For four hours, in the darkness, sapper Raymond Ryan prodded towards the victims. Corporal Peter Jones assisted, tending each wounded man in turn, then Ryan too, who lost a foot to a mine.[13] Afterwards, the nerves of the survivors were 'ratshit', said one soldier. 'I was howling in the morning.'[14]

Far more mine casualties followed. Fifty-eight Australians were wounded and nine killed, mostly as a result of jumping jack mines during OPERATION ESSO, a 5th Battalion attack on the Long Hais in August 1969. For the first time, the enemy used mines as an offensive weapon, planted not in permanent defensive positions but moved about, near road blocks and ambush sites, around friendly villages, on farms and within 20 metres of occupied homes. They even surrounded the body of an assassinated village chief with mines. The Long Hais were literally heaving with jumping jacks: some jumped 'in excess of 12 feet' inflicting casualties within a '45-yard radius', noted the ESSO after-action report.[15]

The 'Lessons Learned' from this operation (listed in the after-action report) offered little consolation. The troops were reminded not to 'bunch' together on patrol; to clear any roads or previous patrol areas before reuse; and to assume that all South Vietnamese posts were mined or booby-trapped. Every soldier should be on the constant watch for natural objects — sticks, leaves and snails' shells — that might hide the M16's three telltale prongs. When a mine blew, troops should not 'do the human but wrong action of moving to the assistance of the wounded'. They should painstakingly clear lanes between the wounded and the helicopter landing point. A *hoi chanh* (Viet Cong defector) added a depressing footnote: most of the mines in ESSO, he said, were jumping jacks lifted from the Australian minefield.[16]

Between 1969 and 1971, the 4th, 5th, 6th, 7th, 8th and 9th Battalions struck land mines in such profusion as to render largely superfluous LIFESAVER, the Task Force training exercise in mine safety. On OPERATION MUNDINGBURRA, in July 1969, the troops encountered 169 M16s and 176 M26 grenade booby traps. Of the sixty-four Australian and New Zealand casualties (three of whom died), most were mine casualties. The 6th Battalion commander, Lieutenant Colonel David Butler, was himself slightly wounded. Soldiers of the 7th experienced sixty-four mine incidents, of which forty-six were Australian-laid mines.[17] After one mine incident, a distraught soldier returned to Nui Dat and tore up the 'Body Count' scoreboard in his unit lines. The 8th and 9th Battalions would endure the worst of the mine war.

Even mine attacks had lighter moments. After one blast, Private Roy Hornsby and Corporal Brian 'Doc' Mills probed towards the wounded, one of whom had 'crawled off ... in a state of total shock and would not respond to our urgings not to move'. Hornsby finally reached a wounded Maori soldier: 'I undid his boot ... His leg was shattered and looked like coagulated jelly. I told him that it looked OK and did the boot back up.' While waiting for the chopper, Hornsby took the Maori's hand and squeezed it every time he groaned: 'Finally he made me realise that it was the hand-squeezing that was the problem.' Hornsby hadn't noticed that the

New Zealander had lost some fingers 'and I was squeezing the bloodied stumps ... I told him how sorry I was ... we actually laughed about it ... it seemed bizarrely funny. I don't know who that NZ soldier was, but if he ever reads this I apologise once again.'[18]

The stream of mine casualties dismayed the Australian Government and the defence forces. The new Task Force commander, Brigadier Stuart Black Jack Weir, came under great pressure to avoid them. In Weir's pre-embarkation briefing, Major General Tom Daly, Chief of the General Staff, stressed the vital importance of keeping the casualties down. The CGS, Weir later recalled, 'was alarmed about ... the casualties we were receiving from mines ...'.[19]

Neither the Australian nor New Zealand governments openly instructed Weir to avoid casualties, but the message got through. 'I believed that I had a responsibility not to over-commit the Australian troops just prior to the Australian election and during the election period,' said Weir later. Daly acknowledged Canberra's 'indirect pressure' on him to minimise casualties.[20] A tacit understanding, then: both nations faced elections in late 1969, and mine casualties — particularly from Australian-laid mines — were an electoral liability. Weir told *nobody* (his emphasis) about this political interference: 'I just deliberately directed the forces at my disposal into areas where I knew we were not going to have significant contact.'[21] Domestic political concerns thus directly influenced Australia's tactical war — a disastrous situation for any military commander, because avoiding the enemy to satisfy Canberra in the short term gave the People's Army and the Viet Cong breathing space to regroup and inflict more casualties later.

A bald, hirsute, swarthy man of seismic mood swings, Brigadier Weir had physically — and mentally — changed from the dynamic young platoon commander in Papua, 1942, and courageous company commander in Korea, 1951. Indeed, in Vietnam Weir seemed to lose his bearings: he was very ill and very cranky. 'You could never take for granted that he'd be civil,' recalled one officer. 'You were never sure if you'd get raved at, shouted at. He'd suddenly change from being placid to a raving lunatic.' In fact, a military psychiatrist was sent up to Nui Dat 'to observe the behaviour of the Brigadier' at close quarters 'and make a report favourable to his removal from the post of Task Force Commander'.[22]

'With some misgivings I entered the presence,' wrote Dr Griff Spragg, the army psychiatrist appointed to 'study' Weir. The trouble was, Spragg knew Weir; they had served together in the 2/3rd Battalion in Papua, twenty-eight years earlier.

'Do you remember me, Sir? Spragg, Sir.'

'Yair. What are you doing up here?' Weir gruffly replied.

'Psychiatrist, Sir.'

'Hmm. Psychiatrist, eh?' snarled Weir, with perhaps a hint of trepidation. Spragg decoded Weir's next remark as 'You can stuff off'. Over the ensuing fortnight, with sometimes hilarious coincidence, Spragg popped up in Weir's life like an importunate ghost, to which the increasingly rattled Brigadier would shout, 'YOU! What are you doing back here?!' or, when Spragg bumped into Weir's table in the Grand Hotel, 'Watch what you're bloody well doing — YOU!' At one point Weir fled Pernier's, a French restaurant in Vung Tau, to escape the ubiquitous Spragg, who lurked minder-like in the shadows. Spragg did not complete his diagnosis of Weir, but entertainingly described their tag-team encounters in his book *When Good Men Do Nothing*.[23]

In fairness, Weir's frustration was understandable. He found himself caught in a vice between Australian politicians and American generals — chiefly that unreconstructed body-count enthusiast General Julian Ewell. 'I had no intention,' Weir said later, 'of producing body count in vast numbers at the time of the elections in both Australia and New Zealand.'[24]

In 1970 the Long Hai Mountains loomed again … the scourge of the Task Force. Weir knew the Long Hais and their role in the French war, and at first he shunned the ominous shadows to the east; he did not want to lose Australian lives in a futile assault. And so OPERATION HAMMERSLEY (10 February to 3 March 1970) began harmlessly enough, as a mission to secure a quarry near the base of the mountains; it ended as a tragedy-strewn, battalion-strength effort to destroy the D445 Battalion once and for all.

The salient points were these: after many small mine incidents and ambushes, the 8th Battalion encircled and came within hours of wiping out the Viet Cong's provincial battalion. At that point, on 18 February, Colonel Peter Falkland, deputy Task Force commander (Weir was on leave) ordered their withdrawal. Unknown to the soldiers, Weir had arranged a B52 strike on the mountains — to hit the very area where the 8th had now successfully cut off the enemy. Within an ace of a final showdown with the provincial battalion, the Australians were pulled back to a safe 3,000-metre radius, during which time the Viet Cong escaped — and not only because the B52s struck twenty-four hours late. The enemy knew about the air strike well before the Australian troops, who first heard of it that day: '… the enemy knew in advance that the strike was coming,' wrote Robert Hall, historian of the 8th Battalion. 'Because the target was only 7 kilometres from Dat Do village, the strike required province and district level approval. The VC had penetrated both levels …'[25] The Australian officers were furious at the pullout. 'Mike Jeffery [the future Governor-General, who commanded Bravo Company] was absolutely ropeable … I think he threw his map down,' recalled Lieutenant Colonel Keith O'Neill, the 8th's commander.[26] A political expedient had cut short the operation: the troops' training and very job — to engage the enemy in combat — were thus utterly undermined.

A day later, the Australians returned to the Long Hais, to find little damage: the bombs had failed to penetrate the narrow entrances of the caves. The large underground rooms were mostly untouched. The D445 had fled — temporarily. The soldiers destroyed the contents of the caves; but the Long Hais could not be held 'unless continued allied presence dominates area', warned O'Neill.[27] (Sure enough, within weeks the South Vietnamese forces appointed to guard the summit collapsed, and the Viet Cong reoccupied its mountain headquarters.) A deeply disillusioned O'Neill would later return to the relatively safe pursuits of pacification: village security and ambushing. Yet the sudden Australian withdrawal did not prevent the realisation of Canberra's worst nightmare: in the last days of HAMMERSLEY, mines inflicted the heaviest one-day toll of the Australian war …

MOST DISTRESSED AND CONCERNED AT CASUALTIES SUFFERED
BY 8RAR IN THE LONG HAI AREA. IN VIEW OF OUR EXPERIENCE
I AM AT A LOSS TO UNDERSTAND 1ATF UNDERTAKING
OPERATIONS IN AN AREA IN WHICH THEY HAVE ALWAYS BEEN
COSTLY AND OF DOUBTFUL VALUE …[28]

Daly sent this cable to 'Uncle Hay', as the diggers nicknamed General Robert Hay, then commander of Australian Force Vietnam, after a Saigon press release had alerted the media to 'light casualties' sustained in two mine explosions in the Long Hais.[29]

In fact, that day, 28 February 1970, was the single worst day for mine casualties in the Australian war. Two mines almost destroyed a platoon of the 8th Battalion, leaving nine dead and fifteen wounded.[30] In total OPERATION HAMMERSLEY killed eleven Australians and wounded fifty-nine, most in mine accidents; ten resulted from friendly fire. None had experienced such carnage so suddenly. The survivors prodded lanes to the groaning survivors and called in the dust-offs. They felt fury, fear and — understandably, if irrationally — hatred for the Viet Cong. Weir flew in to console the survivors. It had been much worse in World War II, he said, a tactless remark that enraged Corporal Peter Salkowski, who, covered in gore from helping the wounded, abused the brigadier: 'We were still covered in blood and shit, no rations, no nothing ... We were like ... a little pack of animals ... So I had a go at him. I had to apologise, which I didn't ... wouldn't.'[31]

'CONG MINE KILLS 9 DIGGERS' ran a typical headline. Dr Jim Cairns made a serious point in Parliament about the futility of repeated attacks on the Long Hais against 'mines taken up from minefields laid by our own troops'.

Yet the political fallout and rage against the war should not detract from the soldiers' courage. It is impossible to overstate the guts required to extricate a wounded man from a minefield. Very few troops succumbed to mine neurosis, despite their near-daily encounters with mines. Almost all 'controlled their fear and went where they were ordered to go'[32] — even when, as Private Alan Handley recalled, they were sent into known mined areas: 'We were ... waiting for these bloody things to go off ... we just looked at each other. We couldn't believe they were sending [us] in.'[33]

Several troops were highly decorated for their actions during HAMMERSLEY, not least Mike Jeffery, who earned the Military Cross. Jeffery's company excelled at ambushing the enemy largely due to 'outstanding morale and efficiency', said the citation. 'It was my company's effort; they did it,' said Jeffery, who commanded the SAS after the war. 'This medal belongs to them.'[34] Many other subunits also maintained their esprit de corps. One was Major Graham Dugdale's hard-driving company of the 9th Battalion, which included Lieutenant Peter Cosgrove's platoon. Twice in one week in October 1969 Dugdale's troops stormed Viet Cong bunker systems over the Long Khanh border; at one point, Cosgrove himself charged an enemy group, remembering halfway that he had left his webbing and ammunition belt behind. A fellow officer tossed it to him.[35] (Cosgrove would receive the Military Cross for this action, and later pursue a highly successful military career: he led the liberation of East Timor as commander of INTERFET, the International Forces in East Timor, and, in 2002, was made Chief of the Defence Force.)

Yet signs of a faltering in morale accumulated. Mines, friendly fire, postal delays, Viet Cong atrocities and the enemy's increasing number of young and female troops, all fed a terminal sense of futility and disgust, in many units. Second Lieutenant Neil Smith's letters home reflected many soldiers' feelings. They vividly chart the thoughts of one young officer, circa 1969–70, whose mood veered from keen optimism to despair:

9 Dec 69
Dear Mum and Dad ... this will be my last letter from Nui Dat for a while. We leave tomorrow, by US helicopter, for our first operation. We'll be out for at least four weeks straight ... I am very keen, as we all are at the moment ... The Task Force Commander was over today giving us pep talks, and the CO actually called a Battalion parade to raise morale ...

13 Dec 69
... I'm filthy and beginning to smell. It has rained the last two days ... so there is mud everywhere. I'm reddy brown all over, even my skin is changing colour ... I'm afraid we're off to a bad start in SVN. We have had several probes and sightings but have hardly fired a shot in anger ... all 8RAR have got so far is a few weapons ...

22 Dec 69
[Smith hears news that Australian trade unions had urged the soldiers to desert.] ... What's this about the Unions telling the soldiers to mutiny? Which soldiers? We are pretty well out of touch with the outside world ...

Xmas Eve 69 [a postal strike delays the mail again]
Dear Mum and Dad,
    A few hours ago I was in a very bad mood ... the fact that It's Xmas eve in this forsaken place and I haven't received any

mail from Kathryn for about four days didn't help … Gee I was angry when I didn't get any mail today …

… As you probably know It's a ceasefire tomorrow, which is a load of crap, doesn't make any difference to us. Only gives the Nogs a free hand to reorganize themselves. The poor sods in this area … are nearly starving, though full of fight … mainly North Vietnamese regulars …

… I feel rather lonely and sad at the moment. This is a bitch of a way to fight a war. Nothing happens for days, and you know no one is really safe. Yesterday 6RAR captured some VC — men, women and children — one woman actually smothered her baby because she had been told the Australians would eat it! They also found a group of wounded VC by the stench of their gangrene; one poor sod had half of his face shot away and was being eaten … by maggots. Merry Xmas. A light plane has been flying around with loudspeakers playing carols — it left after being fired at by a machine gun …[36]

Smith survived the war to pursue a successful military career; in 1969 he commanded a platoon in the 8th Battalion.

Flagging morale led to more offences. Charge sheets listed a rising rate of 'absent without leave', drunkenness, disobeying orders, neglecting to shave, disregarding malaria rules and using insubordinate language. If they drank their daylights out, very few Australians took drugs. 'Drugs were there, we could have had anything … you'd go down to the Vietnamese villages and you could buy it. But we loved our beer,' said Bill Dobell.[37] Self-inflicted wounds (SIWs) were rare, and the few cases tended to occur after a demotion or other humiliation. In one sad case, a former military policeman, ashamed of being demoted and terrified of his new posting to a rifle company, shot himself in the foot.[38]

Brawls were more common. The origins of one of the bigger bar fights of the Australian war, in 1971, were unclear. Did the Vietnamese pickpocket start it? Or the Green Beret, in a tussle with the New Zealander? Or the Australian warrant officer, drinking at the bar? It seems the latter, who joked that South Vietnamese troops were poor soldiers. The comment ignited a brawl that spilled onto the streets outside the Hong Kong Bar in Vung Tau.

Military police sent for reinforcements: fifty-five were soon on the scene and promptly joined in. Then a truckload of South Vietnamese Marines — many drunk or drugged — also leaped into the melée. 'One had an M16; he fired a shot into the air,' said a witness. 'I saw an NZ soldier try to cross the road … four ARVN chased and caught and punched him to the ground; civilians joined in …'[39] An Australian sergeant received a bullet wound in the chest. The street fight led to the closure of Vung Tau for three days. That rather damaged the bar girls' trade: 178 bars employed 3,000 prostitutes in Vung Tau at this time.

Saying goodbye was such sweet sorrow. One digger, robbed by 'his' prostitute, smashed a kerosene lamp and torched her house. 'She stole my wallet,' he explained. He did a runner through Vung Tau 'with more dogs and nogs than you could throw a stick at'. Sergeant John Arnold relates many similar incidents in *Cop in a Baggy Green Skin*. A portrait emerges of this brave man roaming Vung Tau, up-ending drunks, arresting the violent and showing dishevelled diggers the way home. He intervenes in strip shows and confronts wild gangs of local 'cowboys'. Often abused and physically threatened, Arnold stayed remarkably calm, greeting miscreants rather like a British bobby on a lonely beat around an Asian Gommorrah.

There were more serious manifestations of tension. In one of three reported cases of 'fragging', in 1968–69, a private placed an unfused claymore mine near the bed of his sergeant as a warning; in another, a soldier blew up the unoccupied living quarters of a staff sergeant. Then, on 22 November 1969, an officer died: Private Peter Allen allegedly placed a grenade near the bed of Second Lieutenant Robert Convery, a well-regarded Portsea graduate.

That night, Allen had consumed at least seven cans of beer with his 9th Battalion mates. He nursed a long-standing grudge against Convery, and described at his court martial how he killed the officer: 'I went to my webbing and took out one grenade and then sneaked up to Mr Convery's tent … I then went around to Mr Convery's side of the tent and put the grenade on the bed … as soon as it exploded I ran down to my tent and got into bed where I slept for a short time until Cpl Hargreaves woke me …' He added: 'The thought to kill Mr Convery has been with me for some time and last night … I carried it out.'[40]

Lieutenant Cosgrove was one of several witnesses in the case. Months earlier, he and other officers had encountered the accused completing field punishment — 'digging a hole … and when the hole was finished, filling it in again' — for a separate offence. 'I have never seen such a hate-filled look as that which he was bestowing on us,' Cosgrove recalled.[41]

Australia's wavering morale never plumbed the same depths as it did in the American forces. In 1970 cases of threats of fragging and gross insubordination were commonplace in US units: 788 confirmed fraggings occurred between 1969 and 1972 (not all led to deaths); 500 chargeable acts of insubordination occurred in 1969 (double the previous year); and the rate of desertion was twice the peak in Korea.[42] Some grunts began to see their officers as the real enemy. In August 1969 an entire US company refused an order to move out, the first of several 'mass mutinies'. One GI expressed a common sentiment: 'I just work hard at surviving so I can go home and protest all the killing.'[43]

Racial violence proliferated: the inexperienced, usually white officers could not control mixed-race units sick with mutual loathing and racial violence, and suffused with drugs, chiefly marijuana, heroin and opium: 30 per cent of US troops were estimated to have used drugs, chiefly narcotics, in 1971.[44] General Abrams's own VIP pilot allegedly trafficked heroin between Bangkok and Saigon. Many US and South Vietnamese troops smoked the black resin of opiates in home-made bamboo pipes; some took LSD before going into battle. Perhaps hallucinogenics made the war bearable.

Several Australians witnessed the decline of US morale at close range. 'The US Army was actually breaking up before my eyes,' said Warrant Officer Wally Thompson, who spent a lot of time with the American units in 1970. 'I could feel it. Blokes were wandering around in beads, without their uniforms. When two soldiers got Bronze Stars, only the commanding general and the adjutant attended. They just read a bit of paper. Nobody came to see these blokes decorated. It was just a routine.'[45]

'The Yanks once showed me around,' recalled Colonel (now Brigadier) John Salmon. 'I was appalled. The officers were scared of the soldiers. I could smell marihuana. The officers' mess was a funk hole to escape the soldiers. I was disgusted at the lack of authority. On operations they'd just fire up everything — "prophylactic fire" they called it — every bush and boulder.'[46]

Brigadier Sandy Pearson had a more enlightening experience. Asked to train a freshly arrived American battalion — 'they've got green, webbed feet', a US colonel warned him — Pearson sent six hand-picked warrant officers from the Team down to the delta. 'We'd never seen such a bloody shambles,' Pearson said. 'They were 80 per cent black; one was wandering around in his undies, one wore a tin hat.' There were terrible racial tensions and a distinct lack of morale. Six weeks later, the battalion went into battle and captured a Viet Cong arms depot, and the US colonel rang Pearson to thank him. 'He was so pleased, you'd think he'd won the battle of Cassino,' said Pearson later.[47]

Communist morale also fell drastically in 1969–70. Hanoi's breathless propaganda utterly misrepresented the gloom in the ranks. National Liberation Front combatants 'balked at sacrifice and hardship and had abandoned their posts', stated captured documents in 1970. Some troops 'displayed a lack of solidarity'. In response, COSVN, in Tay Ninh province, prescribed more rigorous 'political indoctrination courses and ideological guidance … to heighten their fighting spirit'. Only correct 'political attitudes' would cure the defective troops. The party credited 'brilliant combat achievements … only where Party leadership was effective'. In other words, only total obedience to the Communist Party would lead to 'the final victory of the Revolution'.[48]

The Pied Pipers of Hanoi thus led hundreds of thousands of young people to premature graves. Down the Ho Chi Minh Trail they came, hungry, sick, scared, under constant risk of aerial bombardment. 'Because of grave hunger,' wrote one North Vietnamese youth, 'traded sandals for two chickens … had a good meal. I had to shoot throughout the night to drive the tigers away.' Later, he added, 'Many soldiers and cadre died of cold and starvation here …' On one night, B52s struck for five hours: 'I was deafened by the explosions … Trees were felled everywhere and the dust rose in columns. I had the feeling I was in a storm.' On 18 August 1969 he wrote, 'Life has become more miserable and difficult.' Then Uncle Ho died: 'Alas! I feel deep sorrow over the death of our Uncle.'[49]

After months of such torment, these bedraggled youths staggered into the ranks of the Viet Cong, who were themselves recruiting boy- and girl-power. In 1969–70 Australian troops would hold fire, in disbelief, as the face of an armed child stared down their sights. 'Because of the age of one of the enemy (he looked to be about 14 years old),' ran one after-action report, 'Private G held fire for fear that they could have been village children.'[50] This was a common occurrence, as many Viet Cong documents attest. The backpack of 'Tu', a dead child soldier, contained a letter to his mum in which he asked her for money to buy a radio, reminded her that he was in Ba Ria and told her not to worry. An abandoned sampan yielded a letter to the Ba Ria Politicial Section, appealing for 'VC secret agent Kim My', a 16-year-old girl, to be admitted to the party's spy network; and a destroyed bunker revealed a carefully typed page that explained 'the method of employing 10- to 15-year-old children as agents'.[51]

The deepest blow to communist morale was the death of Ho Chi Minh, on 3 September 1969. Hanoi distributed Uncle Ho's last will and testament to the soldiers as a propaganda boost. All communist cadres must study 'Uncle's Testament',which should be 'used as a guideline for all activities'.[52] The diary of Nguyen Vu, second in command of the D445 Battalion, shows the reach of Ho's power and offers a glimpse of the effect of his death on one distant, southern guerrilla. The Australian 7th Battalion found the diary on Vu's body, at Dat Do, on 17 September 1970.[53]

Nguyen Vu dutifully wrote out Ho's political lessons, under the headings 'MARXIST IDEOLOGIES' and 'THE WORKING CLASS' (his capitals). Ho's 'PRINCIPLES OF WARFARE' reminded Nguyen Vu to 'attack the enemy's morale' and 'combine the military with the political', adding: 'FIGHT FOREVER TO DEFEAT THIS AMERICAN PLAN AND REUNITE OUR COUNTRY AS ONE ...'

'Uncle Ho died on 3 Sep at 0947 hrs — 1969. Participated in mourning ceremony for Uncle Ho at La Nga. Studied the Testament of Uncle Ho at [COSVN — the Central Office of South Vietnam], cried twice. Stayed in Cambodia 1 Oct 69 — 1 May 70.' His mood darkened: 'Since I joined the revolution, 1969 was the worst year of my life. I spent more time away from home ... The love of my country is gone. Spring is unhappy.'

The lunar New Year in Cambodia in 1970 brought no joy: 'I welcome the spring coldly ... I have no cigarettes ... This is probably the saddest New Year of my life.' He dreamed of going home to Phuoc Tuy: 'Oh God! I wish that I could be back in my home province ... Maybe God punishes me?' And then he fell in love with a young girl: 'I have only known you a short time,' he wrote to her, 'yet my heart is full of love for you. I hope to meet you again on the day that [our] country is rejoined.'[54]

# Chapter 39
# Moratorium

Our spirit is opposed to violence, opposed to hate, opposed to every motive that has produced this terrible war. And in developing our own spirit, we shall change the spirit of other people. We *can* overcome, ladies and gentlemen ... and we shall overcome.

*Dr Jim Cairns, addressing the First Moratorium.*

'MINUTES OF MEETING CALLED BY REV JOHN LLOYD, CAPRICE RESTAURANT, TUESDAY, DECEMBER 9, 1969, 6 P.M.

'Rev Lloyd moved Resolution 1 on the Agenda that: "This meeting endorses the decision ... that 500,000 citizens be encouraged to participate in a national Vietnam Moratorium Campaign to be held [in Melbourne, on 8, 9 and 10 May, 1970]."'

Someone moved that 'all' replace '500,000'. The motion was carried. The Reverend Lloyd then moved that 'We support the Vietnam Moratorium Campaign', the aims of which were: (a) the withdrawal of Australian and all other foreign troops from Vietnam; and (b) the repeal of the National Service Act.

The first Moratorium Committee comprised, according to the minutes: Dr J. Cairns, J. Newell, D. Hudson, Mrs J. McLean, L. Carmichael, P. Butcher, J. P. Ryan, T. Poulton, Revd S. Moore, T. Dalton, Sam Goldbloom, L. Hedley, R. Wilson, M. Maher, Revd A. Dickie, H. Van Moorst and the Revd J. Lloyd. The committee's next meeting, chaired by

Dr Cairns on 16 December 1969, agreed to add the adjective 'immediate' to the noun 'withdrawal' in point (a) above.[1]

These intense deliberations in one of Melbourne's smarter restaurants started the machinery of the first Australian Moratorium. It would be a mass demonstration of anti-war feeling, as agreed in November that year at a 'national consultation' of all peace and protest groups — a veritable pageant of acronyms, AICD, CICD, CDNSA, VAC, SOS and so on.[2]


The Vietnam Moratorium remains the largest and most sustained public protest movement in Australian history. The word 'moratorium' technically means the temporary suspension of an activity. The word avoided the negative connotations of 'strike', although it had the same intent: the maximum disruption of the normal flow of business over three days. 'Our intention is to bring commercial and industrial life to a halt,' said Cairns.[3] It would be a non-violent protest in the Gandhian tradition.

The US Moratorium had demonstrated its power as a visual expression of collective dissent. In October 1969 more than 500,000 Americans protested in 1,200 US towns against the war; in November, 250,000 people converged on Washington in a 'march against death', the largest demonstration hitherto seen in the capital. President Nixon's attorney-general compared it to the Russian Revolution. Dozens of nations followed the US example, with huge marches in West European cities.

The Moratorium attracted massive campus support. By 1970 the baby boomers, a demographic bubble of unprecented size, were nearly all young adults. Australia's student population doubled between 1960 and 1970, from 53,391 to 115,630. In 1972 it reached 128,076.[4] A majority in 1970 strongly opposed the Vietnam War. Revulsion at the television images and the government's widening 'credibility gap' swelled the ranks of students opposed to the war.

Meanwhile, many conservative-minded taxpayers no longer believed the war served Australia's national interest. Saving South Vietnam, in the absence of any wider regional threat, was not worth the cost in blood and treasure. The case for forward defence had collapsed: in China, Mao, like Francis Bacon's 'Screaming Pope', oscillated on his throne in a state of besieged impotence; Indonesia had entrenched a peculiarly intolerant right-wing dictatorship; and most Asian countries had asserted their independence. In fact, the creation of the Association of South-East Asian Nations (ASEAN) in

1967 — binding Malaysia, Indonesia, Singapore and the Philippines — raised the prospect of a reverse domino effect, the ripple north of capitalist one-party states. And in 1968 Brezhnev's Soviet Union had supplanted China as the chief communist exporter of human suffering — to Europe, with the crushing of the Czechoslovakian uprising.

Yet understandably the defence forces recommended caution. The Australian chiefs of staff echoed their Pentagon colleagues in advising against any precipitate pullout from South Vietnam; they rightly feared that US faith in 'Vietnamisation' was grossly optimistic. They feared a 'bloodbath', and recommended a gradual withdrawal, in stages, to allow South Vietnam a chance to save itself. In 1969 President Nixon made the first cuts in the Pentagon's huge combat presence.

In January 1970, US Vice-President Spiro Agnew refused publicly to support the preservation of South Vietnam. During his Australian visit, Agnew emphasised Nixon's commitment to the Guam Doctrine, which precipitated the US military withdrawal from South-East Asia.

The Australian Government had little choice but to follow. On 16 December Gorton announced broad, if vaguely timed, plans to withdraw Australian troops, in tandem with (and dependent on) the US exit. There was none of the fanfare that greeted the beginning of the end of past wars: the media simply welcomed what was seen as inevitable. Nor did Gorton's decision temper, as he hoped it would, the fury of the resurgent peace movement, incited to violence by its revulsion at the latest news coming out of South Vietnam.

The revelation in November 1969 of the My Lai massacre had the single most powerful influence on the Moratorium and Australian attitudes towards the war. That this should be so demonstrated Australia's immersion in the American experience of Vietnam, and underscored our ignorance of, or indifference to, the Australian soldiers' predicament.

On the morning of 16 March 1968 C Company, 1st Battalion, 11th Brigade, 23rd Infantry Division of the US Army entered the hamlet of My Lai, part of the village of Song My, in Quang Ngai province. Acting on the orders, the men said, of Lieutenant William Calley Jnr, they rounded up the villagers and shot or grenaded them: 347 unarmed people died, according to the criminal investigation; another ninety died in a neighbouring hamlet at the hands of a separate US company. The Vietnamese monument at

Song My lists 504 civilians dead. Most were old men, women, boys, girls and babies: 182 women (of whom seventeen were pregnant); 173 children (of whom fifty-six were younger than five months old), and sixty men older than 60. One GI aimed his pistol three times at a baby and succeeded in shooting it on the third attempt, to the laughter of his fellow troops. They 'beat women with rifle butts and raped some and sodomized others before shooting them'.[5] They broke for lunch, then resumed the massacre. Any survivors were picked off: a little boy wearing only a T-shirt ran over to clutch the hand of one of the dead. A US soldier, said a witness, 'dropped into a kneeling position 30 metres from this kid and killed him with a single shot'.[6] The water buffaloes, pigs and chickens were shot and hurled into the wells, and all the families' homes burned. Calley dumped his victims in an irrigation ditch.

A year later, Ronald Ridenour, a helicopter door gunner, sent details of the massacre to Washington. An inquiry was launched, and in September 1969 Calley was charged with the murder of 109 'Oriental human beings' (later reduced to 102). The papers ignored the story — the *New York Times* buried it on page 38. Then a US freelance reporter, Seymour Hersh, tracked down and interviewed Calley. After several major news agencies rejected his story, Hersh sold it for US$100 to an obscure news service. The details shocked a world unused to the normative civilian casualties of America's war: some believed My Lai an aberration; others 'an inevitable by-product of the very nature of the war'.[7] Most US soldiers did not deliberately exterminate civilians; yet My Lai surprised few people in Vietnam. No foreign correspondent in Saigon reported it; a few dead gooks were not newsworthy.

The horror of My Lai lay in the soldiers' almost lazy, amused dispatch of a Vietnamese community. That condemned My Lai more, in Western eyes, than the Viet Cong's routine and politically 'necessary' massacres of unsupportive civilian hamlets, such as when, on 5 December 1967, the Viet Cong overran the Montagnard hamlet of Dak Son near the Cambodian border. They used grenades and flame-throwers to murder 252 villagers, almost all unarmed women and children. They then torched the village, killing any survivors hiding in the matting huts.[8] The survivors returned to the village, 'to look for wives, children and friends. They held handkerchiefs and cabbage leaves to their faces to ward off the smell of burned flesh that hung over everything ... Charred children were locked in ghastly embrace, infants welded to their mothers' breasts.'[9]

Few people outside Vietnam remember the Dak Son massacre; although fully reported at the time, it received nowhere near the condemnation that attended My Lai.

My Lai imbued Australian protesters with the spirit of insurrection. The unions were among the first to act: they called for a mass mutiny in the army. Two hundred trade union officials representing thirty-two unions met in Melbourne on 15 December and urged conscripts to disobey orders and troops in Vietnam to 'mutiny against the heinous barbarism perpetrated in our name against innocent aged men, women and children'.[10] The call prompted Attorney-General Tom Hughes to consider bringing proceedings against the unions under the Crimes Act. On the same day thousands of protesters marched through Sydney bearing posters saying 'Ho Chi Minh to win'. A photo of the march appears in the Army Museum in Hanoi, with the caption 'Despite the police oppression, the Australian people raised flags and slogans on the main street of Sydney'.[11] Bob Gould, who appeared in one of the photos, said: 'We tried to provoke the troops. They were not very receptive. But we hid three American deserters. A very wealthy North Shore matron found a way of getting them passports for Sweden.'[12]

Union bosses ordered their members to strike in protest at My Lai. In November 1969 the Sydney branch of the Waterside Workers' Federation refused to reload the *Jeparit*, the military supply ship that shuttled between Sydney and Vung Tau. This time the ACTU did nothing to restrain them, and the Royal Australian Navy had to load the ship. Vital supplies were delayed. The postal unions also urged their members to take industrial action.[13] (The army got its revenge against mail and waterside strikes: in 1968 John Bullen's tireless topographical unit printed the first 'Punch a Postie' leaflets. Thus, 'Soldiers of Australia!/Unite Against Postal strikes!/Punch a Postie on RTA [return to Australia]/Sock it to 'em diggers!' 'Wallop a Wharfie' soon followed. 'Contemptible', 'despicable', 'in the worst possible taste', retorted the Postal Workers' Union. The press leaped on the story, and the Task Force, from the commanders down, were elated at 'a huge and most successful joke'. Bullen became something of a local hero around Nui Dat.[14])

Anti-war activists seized on My Lai; they ignored the fact that Australian soldiers were not involved, never operated in the area and had not committed a single verifiable 'war crime' in Vietnam. Images of the massacre blanketed pre-Moratorium publicity: thousands of posters displayed grisly images of dead Vietnamese children; leaflets declared that My Lai 'shocked every Australian'. An American war crime became the lightning rod of Australian feelings against the war. My Lai subsumed all debate, all argument — indeed, in a way, all thought — in a national spree of self-righteous indignation. Australia had 'joined the wrong side of an immoral war', argued these grossly simplistic screeds.[15] The Committee in Defiance of the National Service Act urged young men to 'Think' — in posters depicting a dead Vietnamese boy — 'Think of the My Lai massacre. Whose side are you on? The Vietnamese kid with his guts blown out? Or the soldier who pulled the trigger? If the Government conscripts you to kill Vietnamese, don't say later: "I was obeying orders." The German and Japanese war criminals said that and the world condemned them.'[16]

Such propaganda suggested the Australian soldiers were jointly responsible for an American atrocity. A deeply misleading perception took hold. The Australian people knew little about their own troops in Vietnam but a great deal about the worst excesses of the American war.[17]

In response, militant student groups espoused open violence. In late 1969, at the recently opened La Trobe University in Melbourne, a group of 'Maoist communists' [sic] declared themselves committed to 'destroying the university' as part of their revolutionary struggle against capitalism.[18] 'You'll see very few peace symbols around La Trobe,' they warned. 'The solution to the problems of US imperialism ... is the clenched fist.'[19] (In their midst was a fascinating campus character called Dale Cooper, an ASIO mole, who infiltrated the 'Engineering Socialists', a Maoist cell in the engineering faculty. Dale used to join their readings of communist literature and helped publish their newsletter *Spanner and Sickle*. He then reported it all to ASIO.[20])

Not to be outdone, the Monash Labor Club laid out its violent agenda. Upset at being excluded from the Moratorium organising committee, they demanded the removal of a clause prescribing a non-violent march. Even the 3,000 diehard members of the Communist Party of Australia disagreed with that course. More sober minds of the Old Left and middle-aged 'peaceaucrats' — men such as Dr Cairns and Reverend Lloyd — outvoted and reined in these uppity extremists.

Dr Jim Cairns stood at the heart of the Moratorium. The Labor member for Lalor was a kind of socialist matinee idol, the political apotheosis of the anti-war movement. Cairns had achieved that rare thing: he combined high political office, a radical agenda and a reputation for sincerity. Some of his apostles thought him 'Christ-like'.[21]

Cairns inspired or infuriated Australians. A hero to many, he plainly misunderstood the Vietnam War, chiefly in the extent to which he refused to accept the central role of Hanoi and the profound involvement of the Soviet Union and China. He believed the National Liberation Front primarily a spontaneous uprising against the Saigon regime, and not an organisation whose leaders were directly answerable to Hanoi. Arthur Calwell and Cairns's comrades on the left shared this view. 'The National Liberation Front,' Calwell said, as late as August 1968, 'was created not by Peking or Hanoi, but as a reaction against continuing US support — both political and military — for barbaric, reactionary and repressive Saigon governments …'[22]

If Calwell failed to enthuse, Cairns's charm, intellect and oratory persuaded millions of Australians of the rightness of his beliefs. Cairns succeeded because he brilliantly articulated the *emotional* case against the war. He was correct that America's often indiscriminate use of massive firepower had inflicted terrible suffering on the Vietnamese people. Yet he failed to appreciate the sources and designs of North Vietnamese aggression. He cared not to examine the distinctive Australian war in any detail (and made several grossly ignorant claims about Task Force operations). Still, he was consistent, courageous and conscientious. And now, at great personal risk, Cairns chose to stamp his forceful personality on the largest mass movement in Australian history.


The hum of working bees rose; donations poured in; and a great assortment of interest groups rallied to the ideal of 'peace': the clergy, teachers, university professors, the unions, politicians … The businessman Gordon Barton printed one and a half million posters; full-page advertisements appeared in major newspapers; sponsors and citizens sent money. A full-time administrator, Susan Fialkin, a veteran of the US Moratorium, flew in to help.

It was more a middle-class uprising than a student or workers' revolt. Jean McLean, who sat on the Melbourne committee, was a married working mother of two; the marcher Harry Ward, aged 45, a Monash University medical lecturer. 'I wanted Australia to have no part in what I saw as an immoral, deceitful, cruel, inhumane war to control another country,' he said. 'Reports of atrocities committed by American forces only reinforced my view.'[23]

The hum became a rumble and the rumble a roar. The sheer exuberance of the event overwhelmed its stated demands. The Moratorium became much more than a single-issue pressure campaign: it outgrew Vietnam. It became a stand against all war; a display of 'people power'; an anti-establishment fusillade; a socialist revolution ...

In the bowels of Melbourne's Congress for International Cooperation and Disarmament an assembly line of revolutionary foot soldiers painted the Moratorium's giant slogans. One was the technician Gerry Harant. 'There was never any danger of the Langers [Albert Langer, the militant activist] and others who dominated the debates [doing] the real work,' he said. Harant and his fellow proletarians had a novel approach to signwriting: 'After a meeting which had laboriously — and furiously — debated the "main slogan", we would meet in the basement and paint whatever slogans we felt were appropriate. It was a situation of workers' control.'[24]

The First Moratorium fragmented Australian opinion.[25] Seventy-five Labor MPs supported it, although a handful were aghast at Cairns' support for what they saw as an anarchic display of public defiance. Whitlam loftily dismissed the event as hopeless. The RSL attacked the Moratorium as a betrayal of Australia's national interest and 'our young men on the battlefield'. (The RSL, Vietnam veterans said later, constituted the greater betrayal by refusing or discouraging their applications for membership.) The churches offered no coherent or uniform opinion: when Melbourne's Catholic Archbishop declared the Moratorium a threat to public order, renegade priests Val Noone and Garry McLoughlin accused him of 'making an unholy alliance with the Herods and Pilates of our day'. A few hours off work and even a broken US Consulate window were 'nothing compared with the blood bath of Vietnam'.[26]

The secret services went into overdrive. In April their intelligence summaries predicted mob violence. The Central Crime Intelligence Bureau named Bob Gould, founder of Resistance (formerly SCREW — the Society for the Cultivation of Rebellion Everywhere), as a dangerous figurehead. The bureau had traced '25 young people including eight girls' to Gould's sinister Blue Mountains training camp where they had received 'lessons in guerrilla warfare'.[27] Meanwhile, ASIO informed the Prime Minister and the Department of Immigration of Gould's proposal on 6 April to invite Viet Cong and North Vietnamese delegates to the

Moratorium.[28] No doubt there *were* aggressive elements within the Moratorium movement. John Tully, for example, an executive member of the Tasmanian Moratorium Committee, was charged in April 1970 for firing rifle rounds into the offices of the Department of Labour and National Service in Hobart, and Edward Blume-Poulton, a self-described soldier of the 'People's Liberation Army', had inflicted malicious damage valued at $11,000 to Commonwealth property.[29]

Two events raised the political temperature to boiling point: President Nixon's decision, announced on 29 April 1970, to invade the supposedly neutral kingdom of Cambodia in response to the communist uprising that followed Prince Norodom Sihanouk's deposition; and the gunning down of four students by US police during a demonstration at Kent State University on 4 May. The attack on Cambodia enraged world opinion — and deeply embarrassed the Australian Government, which was not warned of the decision. Indeed, days before Nixon's announcement, Foreign Minister Billy McMahon had agreed to Australian participation in a regional conference on the preservation of Cambodian independence!

In conservative minds, the nation's moral compass seemed to be spinning out of control. Gorton called on Whitlam to stop Cairns's 'excursion into storm trooper tactics'.[30] The Attorney-General, Tom Hughes, delivered a long parliamentary speech on 14 April 1970 in which he accused the organisers of being a communist front and of sending 'a dangerous invitation to lawlessness and violence'. That the nation's most senior lawyer should decry 'the naked physical power of the mob' who sought 'to force or embarrass a government into taking steps in conflict with the policies upon which that government secured a mandate to govern' seemed rather to draw attention to the government's vulnerability.[31] The newspapers, once strong backers of Hughes, attacked the speech as peddling outdated clichés from the 1950s.[32]

In the eyes of the silent majority, the Moratorium seemed to affront the principles of duty and self-sacrifice, law and order; a rush of sentimental ideas about peace and love and the possibility of a perfect world had captured the hopes and dreams of a generation. The conservatives damaged their argument by wielding the hysterical language of overkill. The Moratorium heralded anarchy and the end of civilisation, blared Liberal and DLP politicians. On the eve of the march, ten Liberal politicians warned, in a letter to the papers, that the Moratorium represented a 'fifth column more monstrous than anything Hitler could have devised'. Billy Snedden foamed about 'political bikies who pack-rape democracy'. Even the respected Bob Santamaria feared anarchy, and hoped for a 'miracle' to prevent an almighty 'blue'.[33]

In the end, it was simply a peaceful demonstration: millions watched 200,000 banner-waving Australians walk by, sit and speak, over three days. Dr Cairns led the largest group of 70,000 down Bourke Street, Melbourne, in a peaceful demonstration of free speech and assembly, the defence of which was apparently one of the points of the war. However idealistic their vision or flawed their understanding, the First Moratorium's participants embodied the genius of democracy to accommodate peaceful dissent.

Cairns addressed his 400 slightly nervous Moratorium marshals before they marched: 'Our spirit is opposed to violence, opposed to hate, opposed to every motive that has produced this terrible war. And in developing our own spirit, we shall change the spirit of other people. We *can* overcome, ladies and gentlemen … and we shall overcome.' It was pure Cairns: straight from the heart. 'He was such a hero to everyone,' said cartoonist Michael Leunig. 'Everyone trusted him, and he inspired people without whipping them up.'[34]

So off they set, sixty abreast, at the head of thousands: 'Bliss was it in that dawn to be alive/But to be young was very heaven!' Wordsworth's lines of youthful hope tinged with melancholy, written after the French Revolution, captured a sense of the spirit of that day.[35] Line after line, men and women, boys and girls, in long hair and crew cuts, suits and beads, chanting anti-war songs, waving placards and banners — 'Give Peace a Chance', 'End the War Now', 'Bring the Troops Home', 'Resist the Draft' — interspersed by a few angry young Maoists with Ho Chi Minh posters, who had to be restrained … and a fringe element of roadside hoons and skinheads who sneered.

'It was like a great, big, slow-moving river,' said Leunig.[36] Towering over all was a huge banner that jointly condemned the Soviet Union, China and America for killing innocent people, in Vietnam and elsewhere. This blanket statement suggested a moral equivalence between Stalin and Mao on one hand and America on the other, a preposterous notion that nobody troubled to contest on this day of peace and love, rich in ephemeral hope. The white-helmeted police were restrained and good-humoured, and the crowds cheered them three times. Cairns spoke with purpose and dignity, and only once exploited the mood for crude political gain. 'We must try to get rid of the Gortons … and Sneddens and the hatred and violence they breed,' he said. A ripple of approval surged over this human ocean and subsided into smiles.

The same spirit breathed through marches in Sydney, Brisbane, Adelaide, Perth and Hobart, and in dozens of rural towns. In Sydney, 20,000 marched down George Street to the Town Hall, watched by 1,700 police. Overall, the police, politicians, ASIO and even a glum DLP conceded that the First Moratorium had succeeded as a peaceful demonstration. The only violence occurred in Adelaide, where twenty-one soldiers of the 3rd Battalion, recently back from Vietnam, had a 'running battle' with a thousand 'peaceful Moratorium marchers', claimed the papers. Five soldiers were arrested, and the twenty-one faced disciplinary charges at their Woodside barracks. Other soldiers stood and watched the Moratorium: Bill Dobell recalls several marchers calling him a 'murderer and rapist'. His father happened to be the police sergeant in charge of the march, 'but I didn't know he was there at the time'.[37]

The war at home began in the soldier's head, in the unbearable psychological juxtaposition of his bizarre experiences in Vietnam with an acute awareness of the hatred his uniform provoked in many young Australians. Gary McMahon, a veteran of two tours with the 6th Battalion, felt this painfully when he mingled with demonstrators. He wanted to 'see what it was they had to say because I wanted the war stopped too'. He found the demonstrators 'ignorant of anything to do with the war'. They were 'there for a day out. It was fun for them. Some of them were listening to the speakers, but as I listened for their reaction I realized that they had no idea ... They knew nothing about Vietnam ...'[38] They, too, accused the soldiers of rape and murder.

Jim Cairns did not overcome. The Moratorium failed to achieve its goals. Gorton could not be seen to make policy at the beck and call of a street march (he had in any case already initiated one key demand of the protest, the withdrawal of the troops). The Prime Minister rather lamely repudiated the Moratorium as an attack on democracy and his right to govern according to the will of the ballot box. That rather dignified the protesters' influence; yet these massed parades *were* 'new approaches to politics', as Gorton acknowledged. Nor did the march impinge much on the spectators: not one respondent in a straw poll said the Moratorium changed their mind on Vietnam. Seventy-four per cent of Brisbane residents said the Moratorium had not altered their views; 52 per cent still supported national service; and 48 per cent did not want Australia to pull out of Vietnam.[39]

Wilfred Burchett, the Australian journalist and communist sympathiser who supported Hanoi, meets National Liberation Front cadres in the Cu Chi 'liberated zone'. Left-wing protesters admired him; the government and most Australians considered him a traitor.

Prime Minister John Gorton cuts a dishevelled figure during a visit to Nui Dat, eliciting little respect from the soldiers. Gorton told sceptical troops that the Australian people were behind them '90 per cent' and dismissed the other 10 percent as 'any nut who carries a placard or sits in the middle of the road'.

LEFT: Gough Whitlam (right) saw the danger of opposing the war until popular sentiment made it politically acceptable. His first priorities as prime minister in 1972 were to end national service and return Burchett's passport; yet many Australians, not least Malcolm Fraser, were repelled by his swift engagement with Hanoi and his refusal to admit more South Vietnamese refugees into Australia after the war.

The Victoria Cross was awarded four times in Vietnam to: (left) Warrant officer Kevin 'Dasher' Wheatley, posthumously; (below left) Major Peter Badcoe, posthumously; and (below) Warrant officers Ray Simpson and Keith Payne. All served with the Australian Army Training Team Vietnam, regarded as the most decorated unit in Australian military history.

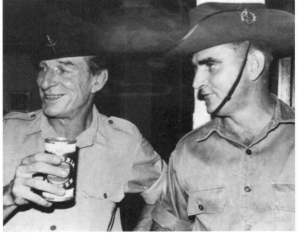

ABOVE: The battle of Binh Ba, South Vietnam, June 1969: Bodies of North Vietnamese Army (NVA) troops who attempted to hold the village are laid out in the square to be checked for documents before burial. In the foreground are two Australian soldiers who participated in the battle. Contrary to claims that Binh Ba was a massacre of innocents, the Australians took the extraordinary precaution of warning civilian residents of the attack and led most to safety before the battle began.

BELOW: A gung-ho Lieutenant Colonel (later Major General) Ron Grey, commander of the 7th Battalion (second tour), steps from his helicopter during operations in 1971. Grey steadfastly refused to submit to American demands for a higher 'body count', and stuck to Australian jungle warfare tactics, which helped to secure Phuoc Tuy province.

ABOVE: Private Ron Jones instructs South Vietnamese soldiers in how to load an M79 grenade launcher in late 1969. Training of the Vietnamese stepped up in 1970 as part of 'Vietnamisation' — a process the French had earlier called 'yellowing'.

The war at home intensified in the late 1960s: here, anti-war activists entered the Australian Stock Exchange and daubed 'murderers' across the share board. An exchange employee can be seen headlocking a young anti-war protester, Meredith Burgmann, later president of the New South Wales Legislative Council. Below, protesters burn the American flag on the Stock Exchange floor.

**FOUR OUT OF FIVE OF THESE MEN CHOSE THEIR CAREERS**

**ABOLISH CONSCRIPTION NOW**
**VIETNAM MORATORIUM SEPTEMBER 18**

The Moratorium marches of the 1970s began as a protest against conscription; they grew into something far bigger — a mass rebellion against the established order. Pre-march publicity also depicted images of children massacred at My Lai, wrongly implying that Australian soldiers were somehow involved, which fed the grotesque impression of the Australians as 'baby-killers'.

Dr Jim Cairns (centre, in scarf), Tom Uren, Jean McLean and Victorian state Opposition Leader Clyde Holding lead an estimated 70,000 people in the largest political protest ever witnessed in Australia, the first Moratorium in Melbourne, May 1970. Later moratoria failed to capture the same peaceful anti-war spirit and the last mass march in 1971 turned violent.

The novelist Patrick White, on 19 December 1969, was among thousands of Australians who signed a statement in defiance of the National Service Act despite the threat of a fine or jail. The government was powerless to act in the face of widespread self-incrimination by middle-class professionals, artists and celebrities.

ASSOCIATED PRESS

The image that never rests: a little girl, Kim Phuc, her body burning with napalm, runs from a village bombed in error by the South Vietnamese in 1972. The photo did more than any other to turn the world in revulsion from the war in Vietnam.

FAIRFAX

Dr Jim Cairns (left), as Minister for Overseas Trade, shares a podium at Sydney's Town Hall with Nguyen Van Tien, a leader of the communist 'Provisional Revolutionary Government' of South Vietnam, in front of a portrait of Ho Chi Minh (26 April 1973). The meeting, so soon after Australia's withdrawal from Vietnam, disgusted the troops. Cairns gravely underestimated China's and Hanoi's involvement in the war. Two years later, Hanoi's forces occupied the South and started dismantling Tien's provisional regime.

Dr Tien Nguyen, a medic with a South Vietnamese Ranger Battalion, spent three years in a re-education camp before escaping Vietnam as a 'boat person'; he is now a doctor in Sydney and a leader of the Vietnamese community in Australia.

Abandoned army boots litter the outskirts of Saigon after the southern troops fled the approach of Hanoi's People's Army in 1975. The city's fall heralded the beginning of ten years of leaden Marxist rule that culminated in famine. In 1986 Hanoi was forced to introduce gradual free-market reforms.

ABOVE: The last flights from the roofs of CIA safe houses (pictured) and the US Embassy in Saigon, April 1975, were among the most humiliating and haunting images of the American war in Vietnam. The ambassador of the world's most powerful nation was forced to flee the encircling communist forces to a ship anchored offshore. Loyal Vietnamese employees of both the US and Australian embassies, though promised a safe exit, were left behind.

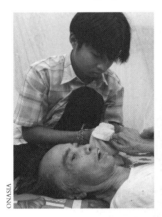

ABOVE: Agent Orange and other defoliants poisoned an estimated 3.5 million Vietnamese people. Nguyen Van Diem, a 64-year-old former soldier, has high levels of dioxin poisoning. Paralysed, mute and deaf, he has no money to pay for his only son, who cares for him, to have an Agent Orange-related health check.

ABOVE: The Welcome Home Parade, Sydney, October 1987. They came in their tens of thousands: war veterans (many just 40 years old) and their families, representing every unit that served in Vietnam across the three services. Each Australian soldier who did not return was represented with a flag carried by a family member or friend. Whatever one thought of the war, the soldiers had given not only what was asked of them, but far, far more.

Canberra's indifference was, in protesters' eyes, like a proverbial red rag, in reply to which the activists stamped and snorted and committed acts of daily public defiance: conscientious objectors went 'underground' and would pop up in public to embarrass the authorities; five women chained themselves to the public gallery in the House of Representatives, in protest at the jailing of draft resister Louis Christofides, himself famous for sitting down on a railway line to stop a train carrying nashos; 3RD, a pirate radio station, voted on whether to resist a police siege peacefully or by throwing marbles down the stairs. Conscripts deliberately failed their psych tests with neurotic answers: one well-known footballer, later a famous AFL coach, circled 'yes' when asked if he sometimes felt like jumping from high places.[40] Others pretended to 'be gay' according to a booklet on how to avoid the draft: '... wear white slacks, have your hair cut camp', but 'don't overact; homosexuality is a crime in Australia'. The same booklet urged conscripts to 'arrive [at the army] rotten drunk' and 'serve and sabotage ... ignore all orders ... use veiled insolence ... Let them lose their tempers.'[41] Counter-productive tactics included daubing anti-war graffiti on shrines to the fallen in the world wars, sending soldiers' names and addresses to the Viet Cong, and even attending soldiers' funerals waving pro-Viet Cong banners.[42] One group made a half-hearted attempt to firebomb the Australian offices of Honeywell, makers of napalm. Students also attacked their university regiments: the Sydney University Regiment had to defend itself from violence on two public occasions. In one case, protesters pelted Sir Roden Cutler VC with tomatoes.

Few of the draft resisters were prepared to go to jail for their beliefs. And they were always a tiny minority. The outcry against conscription bore no relation to the actual scale of draft resistance: of 482,000 men who had registered for national service by 1970, 38,000 had joined the army, and only 88 refused the call-up: 99.8 per cent of young men had complied with conscription. Only a handful were jailed (Brian Ross was among the last to be released, on 21 September 1970, after scores of protests). Those who escaped jail enjoyed the notoriety and their lives on the run, and provided a circus for the press. When four draft resisters emerged from hiding to speak at the Third Moratorium, crowds escorted them back to the 'sanctuary' of Melbourne University, openly provoking the police to arrest them. In September 1970 the same four — Michael Matteson, Tony Dalton, Michael Hamel-Green and John Scott — popped up again at Melbourne University to hold a press conference, and escaped while the police broke through the student barricades ('a cannon to bring down a sparrow', said the Hobart *Mercury*).[43] In November, when Matteson made a surprise appearance on *This Day Tonight*, the ABC current affairs show, the police stormed the studios to arrest him; he fled out the back door. Matteson repeatedly eluded capture, and the media hailed him as a folk hero, 'the Scarlet Pimpernel of the Underground'.[44] In April 1971 five women — Jo Maclaine-Cross, Jean McLean, Irene Miller, Chris Cathie and Joan Coxsedge — were jailed for a fortnight at Fairlea Women's Prison, charged with 'wilful trespass' for handing out 'don't register' leaflets to young men arriving to register for national service at the Department of Labour and National Service in Melbourne. Their incarceration provoked widespread strikes and demonstrations in support of the 'Fairlea Five'. The media went for the emotional jugular: how could the government jail five Aussie mums over Easter?

These student stunts paled beside the defiant stand of a deep-dyed establishment figure. On 16 June 1970 the Reverend Douglas Trethen, headmaster of Newington College — one of Sydney's Great Public Schools — wrote a letter to the *Sydney Morning Herald* in which he publicly encouraged '20-year-olds, in good conscience, and in loyalty to God rather than Caesar, to defy the National Service Act'. Trethen presented his letter as a moral meditation on the 'evil' of conscripting young men for war by selective ballot. 'Mr Gorton … for Christ's sake, stop,' he wrote, echoing Pope Paul: 'We cry to them [both armies] in God's name to stop,' the Pope had pleaded, or the war will end 'in the train of bitter slaughter'.[45]

Trethen had technically broken the law. He resigned, was charged under the Crimes Act and placed on a good behaviour bond. In crushing this obviously decent man, the government looked more ridiculous than oppressive. Dissenting Church leaders, chiefly Bishop John Moyes, Reverend Alan Walker and Reverend Gloster Stuart Udy, rallied to Trethen's side. The case further infuriated liberal opinion. 'All the churches in Australia,' Whitlam reminded Parliament on 29 September 1970, 'have advocated exemption from the provisions of the National Service Act on the grounds of conscientious objection to a particular war.'[46]


The descent of the peace movement into a cantankerous and irrelevant farce proceeded in tandem with the degeneration of the political debate. Menace and intolerance marked the build-up to the Second and Third Moratoria, on 18 September 1970 and 30 June 1971. Left-wing extremists heavily influenced both events. Numbers were down, and they had little of the spirit of May 1970. The Moratorium committees invited representatives of North Vietnam and the National Liberation Front; the government, however, refused visas to the Vietnamese communist delegates.

The second parade turned violent. Street 'sit-downs' and amplification were banned and a time limit imposed. Confusion over the rules led to provocation. The police were especially aggressive and, in Melbourne, baton-charged in a phalanx; it is unclear to what extent they were provoked or acted on orders. Each side blamed the other. In Sydney they arrested 173 people in running battles: several were hit very hard and a girl broke her wrist. Police violence played into the hands of the Maoists, the so-called 'super-leftists' of Monash and La Trobe, who, when not *in cognito*, got about in little Red Guard caps and Chinese quilted jackets. No doubt a small group did provoke the police, or at least the horses. These blameless animals were easy targets: extremists would rush out of the crowd with sharpened sticks or flagpoles and prod the horses' bellies. 'I actually saw a police horse stabbed in the stomach,' Federal policeman Peter O'Brien recalled. Or they would throw welded three-inch nails under the horses' hooves and rush back 'behind good people'. Michael Hyde, the Maoist-turned-children's author, blamed the horses, which he claimed were 'intentionally used to provoke us'.[47]

Yet the Moratorium did leave a lasting imprint on the social landscape in one respect. It helped to launch Women's Liberation, whose proto-feminists fired the first salvoes at their male chauvinist comrades in the anti-war organisations. In February 1971 women's libbers succeeded in steering the Third Moratorium in their interests, to help curb 'sexist, chauvinist and discriminatory practices and attitudes to women'. Women would be equal partners in the crusade and not 'mere assistants or decorative accompaniments for male achievers'.[48] Women wanted equal *opportunities* as well as pay, declared the pioneering voice of Germaine Greer. Anti-war slogans, such as 'Girls Say Yes To Boys Who Say No', which adorned several female marchers, were not quite what Dr Greer had in mind. Nonetheless, opposition to the Vietnam War catalysed the emergence of the Australian feminist movement, whose members recognised, with troubling clarity, that male chauvinism did not end where 'peace' and 'love' began.

# Chapter 40
# Platoon

[When Andrew Peacock visited] we were told not to say anything about the war, to give no personal opinions. Peacock wandered around. When he left, everything went back to normal, and away went the cricket equipment … We thought, 'This is bullshit.'
*Bob Gully, 3rd Battalion.*

Phuoc Tuy felt safe: in 1970, the roads were open, the villages functioned, and the Viet Cong and People's Army had withdrawn to the province borders or into the mountains. Even US Generals Weyand and Michael Davison (who succeeded Ewell) were persuaded that Phuoc Tuy, that year, was well on the way to 'full pacification'.[1]

SAS patrols continued their deadly carousel around the province. 'We had hunted out our province and there were no VC left,' said SAS legend Sergeant Frank Cashmore.[2] The later SAS actions were thus frustrating, often futile and occasionally prone to overkill. In late 1971 Cashmore led a ten-man patrol of 2 Squadron, in an ambush of the forward elements of 274th Regiment enemy group. The firefight took thirty minutes — long by SAS standards. Claymores, rifle fire, two M60 machine guns, 40mm grenades and 500-pound bombs by air strikes rained down on the shrubbery. After this devastation, just four bodies were found; two were officers, one a forward scout and one a female soldier, who was heard dying under dead fall where she had crawled leaving her webbing belt, with a hole in the location of her spine.[3]

That did not mean Phuoc Tuy *was* safe. Throughout 1970 fresh communist forces — mostly North Vietnamese units — had massed along the northern border with Long Khanh province and linked up with the Viet Cong mountain redoubts. Viet Cong morale had struck a low; supplies were scarce, and troops had little stomach for combat. The huge offensives of 1968 had decimated their ranks. They specifically feared the Australians and avoided contact. 'The enemy,' said Lieutenant Colonel John Church, commanding the 2nd Battalion, 'had faded away and were really only trying to live.'[4] Indeed, the provincial guerrillas were 'forced to live off jungle plants', according to one prisoner captured in September 1970.[5] Other prisoners verified his account.

Despite their ravaged lines, the Viet Cong had no intention of quitting; theirs was an open-ended battle. Their masters in the People's Army were not especially concerned about the Australian 'mercenaries', of whose mooted departure they were obviously aware. Their priority was the sabotage of 'Vietnamisation' — the 'yellowing of the army', as the French had called it; their chief targets were not the foreigners but the Vietnamese troops loyal to Saigon. For this reason, and in the interests of self-preservation, the communist forces kept clear of the Australians and fought only if confronted. The enemy 'avoided any major contact', observed Major General Colin Fraser, then commander of Australian Force Vietnam in 1970.[6]

'It was a platoon war now,' said Lieutenant Philip McNamara, who led a platoon in the 2nd ANZAC Battalion (and later, as a brigadier, commanded the SAS), 'and every time the enemy tried to do something they got a bloody nose.'[7] Lieutenant Peter Cosgrove similarly recalls operating, with rare exceptions, at platoon level throughout his tour.[8] The Task Force had not confronted a multi-regimental enemy attack since Long Tan in 1966. 'The Australians controlled the province from 1966,' conceded Major Chinh, a decorated former Viet Cong fighter who now lives near Nui Dat. Former D445 commander General Minh agreed: 'Your tactics matched ours,' he told me during a tour of the province in 2005.[9] A controversial example of this tactical success was the 2nd Defence and Employment Platoon, a ready-reaction force created in May 1969 with the aim of inflicting lethal incursions into enemy-held territory. The platoon performed with exceptional results under its British-born commander, Corporal Jim Riddle, before being unceremoniously disbanded after only weeks in the field, leaving no trace of its existence (not until July 2008, under constant pressure from Private Don

Tate, a former platoon member, would the Australian government formally recognise that the platoon had existed).

Yet to some extent Australia's tactical success was illusory. The enemy had chosen to withdraw and was consolidating, resting, waiting. 'The Task Force never owned Phuoc Tuy Province,' concluded a review by the Chiefs of the General Staff in 1971.[10] In fact, in June that year four unarmed Viet Cong (including three women) were captured in a well-hidden tunnel '*inside the perimeter of C Company, Fifth Battalion, where they had spent the night …*', concluded an after-action report.[11]

And Suoi Nghe would rarely enjoy peace. From the end of 1968 an Australian Mobile Advisory Team (MAT) was stationed in the Australian-built hamlet with a South Vietnamese Regional Force Company. The MAT, part of the 1st Australian Reinforcement Unit, comprised seven soldiers led by Lieutenant Bill Kerr, whose job was to train and advise the Ruff Puffs. Kerr's unit diary records an atmosphere of terror within the isolated village. One hamlet chief, who repeatedly offered to resign, is described as 'too frightened to think straight'; a joint patrol was 'a shambles', with the South Vietnamese arguing, confused or falling asleep. One passed out from drunkenness.

Overall, however, Australia's war of stealth and concentrated clearing patrols had undoubtedly transformed Phuoc Tuy from the Viet Cong-controlled province of 1966. Most provinces were relatively secure. A few American officers took an interest in the limited success of the Australian war. Colonel David Hackworth urged his superior officers to adopt Australia's infantry tactics. The Australians were patient, surprising and lethal, observed Hackworth, who had led US troops in Korea, Germany and Vietnam. Their methods cost far fewer military and civilian casualties (proportionally) than the American approach. Hackworth's men even 'began practising what the Australians preached'.[12]

On 31 May 1970 a seriously ill Brigadier Weir went home. His successor as Task Force commander was Brigadier Bill Henderson, a genial and caring man and veteran of World War II, Korea and Malaya. Henderson was similarly, softly, told to limit casualties; the soldiers were not to go on dangerous missions and risk a politically embarrassing catastrophe, so close to the withdrawal.

These constraints would test the morale of the three fresh units in Nui Dat that year, the 2nd, 7th and 8th Battalions, led respectively by Lieutenant

Colonels John Church, Ron Grey and Keith O'Neill, battle-hardened commanders who prepared their men well for the 'platoon war' Vietnam had become. They were determined to be involved: Church sometimes flew over operations in his command helicopter, and on one occasion he was shot down in dense jungle and survived.[13]

Grey stood out as the platoon commanders' commander. Nuggety, hard-driving, he dealt ruthlessly with those not up to the mark. Twice wounded in Korea, Grey was one of the key authors of the basic guidelines for patrol and ambush used in Vietnam. He struck fear in many soldiers, who cannot forget their bruising encounters with Grey at the Canungra Jungle Training School, where he served as Chief Instructor, Battle Wing. '*Generally* speaking,' Grey told his instructors at the time, 'none of you have anything to fear … Let me tell you this,' he continued, gesturing to the door, 'out there are heaps of people who will give you hundreds of reasons why something can't be done. I don't want them. I want the few, the very few, who get the job done — against all odds. You have to ask yourself: which group do I belong to? The one that gives excuses or the one that *gets the job done*?' Grey added, with an icy smile, that those in the first group should 'save yourself some angst and get out — right now'. He then told them the story of General Giap: 'one man who got the job done against all odds'.[14]

In Vietnam, Grey distilled his tactical knowledge into a concise checklist:

- You cannot go into action with an open book in your hand … you must know a hell of a lot …
- You must continually resist suggestions calling for exaggerated caution …
- More trouble is caused by a failure to give clear concise orders than any other single reason …
- Surprise is the salt that flavours battle. Aim to deceive the enemy …[15]

Incidentally, a captured Viet Cong booklet called *Tactical Ambush Principles for Infantry Companies* made several similar points, and showed just how far the Australians and the Viet Cong were fighting the same war.[16]

Political constraints, mine casualties, anti-war feeling at home and the pathos of 'Vietnamisation' circumscribed the Australian war, and might have more seriously dented unit morale had it not been for stubbornly high spirits in the ranks of the fresh battalions.

Yet 'It was frustrating that we couldn't impose our will on the war,' Church said later.[17] His soldiers shared his frustration. 'The politicians couldn't tolerate another Long Tan,' said one. 'More than once we came across enemy and were told to withdraw,' said another, from a different battalion, adding: 'We were all champing at the bit to have a go — that's what we were there for. We were very pissed off. We thought, what in the fuck are we doing here? Why spend millions on training us all …?' The Task Force was instructed to keep casualties as low as possible 'while aiming to achieve limited military goals'.[18]

At the same time, nobody wanted to be the last to die in a war that was supposedly ending. Some diggers welcomed the 'go-slow' tactics; others could not bear the long, eventless patrols. Nerves frayed; a few cracked up. Asked at his court martial why he refused to go on sentry duty, one soldier replied, 'I am too nervous … I am neurotic and fear I might shoot someone … as nearly happened on two occasions … I am in a continuous state of nervous tension.' Bob Gully of the 3rd Battalion remembered an especially nerve-racking firefight in March: 'Their bugles were blowing, we were shitting ourselves. Half a dozen guys were gibbering idiots, nervous wrecks …'[19]

Meanwhile, mines dropped the worm of fear in the soldiers' heads. Mines swiftly claimed the first 7th Battalion victims: the much-liked Lieutenant Rob Pothof, dead, and four soldiers wounded when a huge mine struck their armoured carrier. The platoon's 'morale slumped dramatically' after the loss, two months into their tour.[20] Mines struck again on 12 May, badly wounding Privates Graham Edwards, the future Western Australian Labor politician, who lost both legs, Rod Gillis and Corporal Barry DeBomford. And again on 6 June, in the sand dunes between Phuoc Hai and the Long Hais, three died — including the myopic Private Stanley Larsson, whose case prompted political interference of 'staggering stupidity', wrote Major Kevin Cole, the operations officer.[21] Although a good shot, Larsson had poor eyesight and wore strong glasses. Andrew Peacock, Minister for the Army, had rejected his parents' application to have him withdrawn from active service in Vietnam. After the boy's death, Canberra reversed that ruling: anyone with poor eyesight should be transferred from 'at risk' postings, such as rifle companies. Yet Larsson's eyesight had had nothing to do with his death, nor had it hampered his ability as a rifleman. The government reacted in a knee-jerk manner to assuage public sensitivities, Major Cole bitterly concluded.

In later mine tragedies, a blast shattered the legs of Sergeant Tom Bourke and removed the spleen of Private Leigh Christie. Bourke, a double amputee, survived the war with great fortitude, but his case added to a devastating family tragedy: his brother Michael had died in Vietnam in 1965, and Michael's wife had earlier lost her first husband in Vietnam. The war thus visited a triple blow on this poor woman: two husbands dead and a brother-in-law disabled.

In 1970 the Task Force launched one of the biggest multiforce operations, OPERATION CUNG CHUNG. It was certainly the longest, lasting from June 1970 to February 1971 — 122 days of deadly tedious, small-unit movements. CUNG CHUNG's ultimate aim was to separate 'the people' from the Viet Cong, which descended weekly to collect taxes and supplies. The idea persisted that the people and the Viet Cong were separable and not, in many villages at least, umbilically linked.

Both Grey's and Church's battalions participated. There were exceptional moments: at one point, during an attack in broad daylight, the enemy advanced bearing small trees to avoid air detection, rather like a Vietnamese version of *Macbeth*'s Birnam Wood or the shrubbery scene in *Monty Python and the Holy Grail*. During another contact in a bunker system, a journalist flew in to observe the Australian troops in action. The reporter plied a corporal with Scotch and tried to lever 'atrocity' stories from him, recalls Lieutenant (now Major General, retired) Michael O'Brien.[22]

On its own terms, OPERATION CUNG CHUNG was a great success: it shielded the villages and destroyed many of the communist forces. The operation severely mauled the D445 Battalion, a quarter of whom were killed or wounded (fifty out of a battalion strength of 201, according to captured documents). One Viet Cong company was reduced to three soldiers, and the D445's entire mortar unit surrendered. The Australian offensive drove the survivors back into the May Tao base area, where they remained for months.

On 12 August 1970 members of the Australian 8th Battalion inflicted the deadliest and most controversial ambush of the Australian war, in the rice paddies 5 kilometres east of Nui Dat. At 3.15 a.m., on a clear, moonlit night, a platoon of Charlie Company, led by Sergeant Chad Sherrin, caught a line of fifty Viet Cong guerrillas leaving Hoa Long laden with food supplies. Nineteen people, including six women, died in the claymore shrapnel storm.

Political sensitivities had banned the claymore in Australia, so the troops were taught how to use the weapon on the job in Vietnam (leading to several accidental deaths). The curved vertical mine sat above the ground on small plastic legs. Packed inside were thousands of steel balls and a kilogram of plastic explosive. The soldier triggered the mine by pressing a hand-held actuator, or 'clacker', connected by wire to the detonator; usually, six claymores were fired into the 'killing ground' at once: '... very few of those caught in the initial blast of six claymores survived,' wrote Major Iain Stewart, who identified the claymore's use as an offensive weapon during OPERATION LAVARACK in 1969. 'Those not killed outright were so shocked or otherwise immobilised that the machine-gun fire which followed quickly finished the task.'[23]

Task Force headquarters deemed Sherrin's ambush a great success. 'We have waited for this for a long time,' Henderson said.[24] Congratulations flowed from American and South Vietnamese commanders, a sign of the rarity of an ambush on this scale at this stage of the war. 'Dear Brigadier Henderson,' wrote the US Lieutenant General Michael Davison, '[the] dedication and true professionalism demonstrated by your forces have significantly enhanced the eventuality of forcing the enemy out of Phuoc Tuy Province ...'[25]

A photograph of the aftermath shows Sherrin's men searching the bodies with forensic thoroughness; the corpses were then bulldozed into a hole. Having lost so many of their own to Viet Cong mines, the Australians felt few regrets. In the equation of war, 'this was a legitimate ambush of a VC resupply party' and not, as Dr Jim Cairns claimed in 1976, a 'cold hearted attack on peasants straggling back into Hoa Long a few minutes after curfew'.[26] For this and other actions, Sherrin received the Military Medal, revealing the breadth of disagreement between the army's and Cairns's impressions of the war.

The atrocity hunters were determined to apply their laws of human behaviour to a lawless world. They failed to see that, amid all the slaughter and madness, the Australian troops did try to adhere to the rules of war. In the eyes of the Viet Cong, this effort seemed almost naive; certainly the enemy scorned or laughed at the foreigners' odd respect for civilian life and failure to see that civilians were not to be avoided or protected but harnessed to one side of the war effort. Consider this no doubt well-meant reinforcement of the Australians' duty of care, sent as 'Lessons Learned' after OPERATION CUNG CHUNG:

> CIVILIAN MOVEMENT: It is particularly frustrating ... when following up an enemy withdrawal route to meet a number of civilians often including children. Use of the helicopter is essential ... to give warning to the troops following up, thus preventing the chance of civilians being fired upon ...
> BURYING OF ENEMY DEAD: If at all possible enemy dead should be brought back and handed over to district officials [for] proper burial of the body in accordance with Vietnamese custom. If it is not possible to return the body ... the face should be covered before burial and district officials informed of the location of the grave [after large actions, this did not happen, and the bodies were buried in mass graves].
> FREE FIRE ZONES: Civilians openly violate the promulgated Free Fire Zones ... Care and patience is required, especially ... before granting a ground clearance. If in doubt don't shoot ...
> BODY COUNT STATISTICS/SUCCESS INDICATION: Statistics are not the only indication of progress ... security of civilian population, degree of civilian access, state and attitude of local forces, amount of road traffic ... are all signs of success or otherwise ... [Helping local forces to defend their villages] will win more than weeks of talking and drinking tea at comd levels.[27]

In May 1971 the American Rules of Engagement were adapted to suit the changing conditions of the war. That month the US Army issued new rules designed to 'insure against the indiscriminate use of firepower'. Sadly, these said more about what the US had failed to do in a decade of war: '... every effort must be made to avoid civilian casualties, minimize the destruction of private property,' the new US rules stated. No US commander could initiate direct fire against enemy targets without 'securing approval of the province or district chief', and civilians were to be warned via leaflets or loudspeakers of 'indirect fire missions' and given ample time to escape them. Pilots, too, were told to 'minimize civilian casualties and civilian property damage ...'[28] The new rules were mercifully free of euphemism and spared the reader the mental torment of 'accelerated pacification', 'circular error probability' and 'infrastructure neutralisation'. Yet, while some clauses were tragically overdue, others were, in effect, unworkable.

All wars produce them: confidence men who insinuated themselves into lucrative roles as dealers, black marketeers and gambling pooh-bahs. Joseph Heller's Milo Minderbinder in *Catch 22* was the most entertaining fictional model. That is not to suggest anything illegal or untoward about the TAB set up by Captain Ian Kortlang in 1970. 'I had never been to the races in my entire life,' said Kortlang; yet something about the silver-tongued 2nd Battalion's quartermaster (who later pursued a successful career as a political spin doctor) appealed to Church, who appointed Kortlang to run the TAB in the unit canteen.[29]

'The TAB became quite a big thing,' said Kortlang. 'We even had a detachment TAB that we'd send out to the field to take bets. We were making quite a profit.' Kortlang's bookies backed the 1970 Melbourne Cup winner, Baghdad Note, and were well up — until they lost a small fortune and went out of business. At a betting meeting in February 1971, a tipster whom the soldiers trusted picked eight winners. 'We were totally cleaned out,' Kortlang recalls. Soldiers' bad debts exacerbated the problem — at one stage the TAB's losses ran to $2,000, of which Church paid the shortfall out of his own funds.[30]

Kortlang's abstinence in other areas gave him added energy to run the TAB: 'I made a pact with a mate that we'd go through Vietnam without sleeping with any prostitutes. I think we were the only ones who didn't!' Still, he enjoyed chatting with bar girls — 'though I never went any further' — and, if asked, gave his name as 'John Church': 'We all did.' It seemed Vung Tau's prostitutes had clients named after several other battalion commanders. In all, Kortlang had a rather pleasant tour: 'I tasted my first croissant in Vietnam.'[31]

In December 1970 the 8th Battalion went home and was not replaced, marking the first time since 1962 that the Australian forces in Vietnam had been reduced in size; two months later the 7th Battalion ended its tour, and in May the 2nd returned to Australia. Henceforth, a two-battalion Task Force would maintain the commitment, comprising the 3rd and 4th Battalions, commanded by Lieutenant Colonels Peter Scott and Jim Hughes, who relieved the departing units at Nui Dat in February and May 1971. Scott and Hughes both drew on deep experience as Korean War veterans. Jim Hughes's combat background also involved the Malayan Emergency and the Indonesian Confrontation, making him the only battalion commander with such wide experience. Scott was renowned for issuing orders to his ground troops from a helicopter — and once was forced to land after taking ground fire. The 4th contained one company of New Zealand troops, and was thus designated an ANZAC battalion; it was the last Australian battalion to fight in Vietnam.

One of the 4th's platoon commanders was Second Lieutenant Gary McKay, a thickset former rugby player, national serviceman and Scheyville graduate. McKay vividly recalls flying to Vietnam. 'Everywhere I looked I could see bomb and shell craters,' he wrote in his bestselling memoir *In Good Company*. The villages were 'quite pretty where there weren't bomb holes and burned out areas'.[32]

Disrepair and neglect met his eyes on arrival at Nui Dat: the Australian fort resembled a forlorn, rundown outpost in a small guerrilla war. Although still a sprawling military base, the vacated (3rd) battalion lines were abandoned to scavengers and nature. The rest appeared to be sinking in a sea of red mud. McKay's tent had large holes in the roof, and the sandbag walls were 'in hopeless condition'. Under the rotting floorboards were found old magazines, grenades and the detritus of nearly seven years of soldiers' rotation. The trucks were rusting and badly maintained; and a few Vietnamese locals were now allowed inside Nui Dat, as labourers and 'vegetation controllers'. The rolls of barbed wire were a tangle of overgrown vegetation. 'The wire no longer constitutes a substantial obstacle,' warned Major Jerry Taylor, a 4th Battalion company commander, 'but rather presents an ideal avenue for penetration by enemy sappers.' Taylor recommended instant defoliation to clear the barrier: 'The wire abounds with old ammunition, grenades and claymore, many of which have been there for months/years.'[33]

They swiftly got down to work: digging, sandbagging, the usual patrols, then the prospect of a large engagement. The Australians anticipated OPERATION OVERLORD — the last brigade-sized operation (including one US battalion) — as a rare chance to participate in a multi-unit airlift. US air power made it a 'safe' operation, concluded Canberra. OVERLORD's unfortunate name hankered after the great conventional battles of World War II, a residue of the wishful thinking that obsessed US commanders right to the end. Their mission was to break the enemy strength — mostly the North Vietnamese 33rd Regiment — on the Long Khanh–Phuoc Tuy border.

Once again, the People's Army commanders received ample prior warning of the approaching conflagration: cavalries of Centurions and armoured carriers clanked and rattled over the red earth, while the sky darkened with squadrons of Hueys ferrying the platoons north. The American pilots and door gunners were fresh, gung-ho 20- to 23-year-olds; many had inscribed peace symbols, iridescent stars and stripes, and 'obscene graffiti' on their helmets, McKay observed. They were careless, too careless for McKay's liking. The helicopters skimmed the trees, to avoid ground fire, and dropped to the landing zone as six Cobra gunships sprayed the jungle fringes. As the skids neared the ground, the American pilots screamed, 'Get your mother-fucking asses outta there!' McKay and his men fell to earth, expecting immediate contact. In the scrub, all was silent. Not a hot insertion after all, McKay thought: the Americans were merely shooting up the trees.

Then, from somewhere deep in the forest, spectral figures appeared: bewildered youths decorated in bits of high technology, in no identifiable uniform; their helmets bristling with cigarette packets, Zippos, chewing gum and other junk stuck into rubber bands; their rifles and machine guns slung over their backs. 'We couldn't believe our eyes,' McKay wrote, on seeing his American comrades. 'Not one man was capable of firing in the direction his eyes were looking.'[34] Most seemed to care little about the war or the danger to themselves. Many were certainly drugged. In fact, as McKay later discovered, the US gunners who fired in support of Australian troops were often stoned on the job. The Age of Aquarius had come to Nui Dat.

OVERLORD lurched, at times, into farce. When McKay's men tried to set an ambush, the GIs chattered away in the rear. 'They had no noise discipline to speak of. They spoke out loud.' McKay invited a US platoon commander forward to hear the racket, at which the latter yelled at his men to 'put a sock in it, you guys!'. The US troops laid claymores as though they were laying a picnic. McKay observed one GI stroll to the extremity of the firing lead — without his rifle — and shout back to his commander if the site was OK.[35] This was, of course, one platoon's experience. In general the Americans did offer constant and reliable support to the Australian operation, according to Major Brian McFarlane, who was forward throughout the operation. It was during OVERLORD, incidentally, that the Defence and Employment Platoon suffered heavy casualties while patrolling the Task Force headquarters perimeter.

The operation, later dubbed the Battle of Long Khanh, achieved little; most of the enemy shunned open combat. The tanks rolled over and with difficulty crushed the bunker systems and some of their occupants. For McKay, it ended with his partial temporary blindness when the sap of a local vine got in his eyes: 'I started to get the most excruciating pain in my eyes.' He was led to the dust-off in a blur and spent four days in hospital.

The climate and exhaustion and sense of futility seemed to conspire against them; yet the Australian platoons doggedly performed the task for which they were trained. There was something defiantly professional about this unwavering sense of purpose. We can only marvel at McKay's concern that the smell of shaving cream might alert the enemy to his presence, and his care for his men (medics must watch for skin diseases; 'Happy Birthday' must be sung at a whisper!) — measures that demonstrated the existence of military order and professionalism in a world gone mad.

Even during its closing stages, the Australian war drew unlikely enthusiasts. What strange impulse possessed Carlo Mikkelsen, a Dane, to fly across the world in 1970 and fulfil his ambition to serve as a Tunnel Rat in the Australian Army? 'From the start it was always my intention ...' he said. He applied to the New Zealand and Australian embassies in Copenhagen. His request baffled the New Zealanders, but the Australian Army accepted and trained him: the Dane's ambition — to crawl along booby-trapped Vietnamese tunnels on behalf of the Antipodean war effort — seemed eminently sensible, to him at least. Mikkelsen arrived in Nui Dat in 1970, and beheld 'a pleasant sprawling tent city adequately shaded by mature rubber trees'. Clearly he felt quite at home. During his tour, this remarkable Viking helped clear five tunnel systems, fulfilling a military ambition that must rank as the oddest in Danish history. His abiding memory is of New Year's Eve, 1970–71: '... we were lying in ambush [when] a voice came over the radio saying "Australia — we kill you, Australia — we kill you".'[36]

Some soldiers, during this last eventless slog about the province, experienced feelings of intense isolation and abandonment. Many felt that they were mere pawns in a political game. 'We seemed to be dispensable,' said Barry Middleton, a nasho. 'I had the sensation of being treated like a mushroom — kept in the dark and fed bullshit.'[37] Several officers recall being ordered to 'back off' from an assault because heavy casualties were politically unacceptable.

The political show went on, however. When Andrew Peacock, Minister for the Army, visited Fire Support Base Beth near Xuyen Moc in June 1971, the diggers were ordered to appear happily occupied. 'We were told to clean our rifles, write letters home or relax; they brought in cricket equipment,' said Bob Gully. 'We were told not to say anything about the war, to give no personal opinions. Peacock wandered around. When he left, everything went back to normal, and away went the cricket equipment … We thought, "This is bullshit." '[38]

The spiral of violence threw up tales of criminal insanity scripted to delight Hollywood producers and satiate anti-war activists' thirst for evidence in their case against America and Australia. Some stories made Colonel Kurtz's war in *Apocalyse Now* seem positively quaint. Thus Michael Herr encountered the smiling maniac who handed him a plastic bag full of Viet Cong ears; the grunt who, dragging a corpse behind him, 'was gunna skin this dead gook'; and the demented colonel who hoped to end the war by dropping piranhas into the rice paddies: 'He was talking fish, but his dreamy eyes were full of mega-death.'[39] 'Everyone' had heard of the man in the Highlands who was 'building his own gook': obtaining body parts was 'the least of his trouble', Herr noted.[40] Some GIs thought of themselves as big game hunters, and were photographed standing on Vietnamese corpses. A few psychopaths arranged their victims' heads in rows, or strung their ears like beads.

Such depravity was not restricted to the grunts. 'I do like to see the arms and legs fly,' said Colonel George Patton III, son of the World War II legend, who brought a Viet Cong skull along to his leaving party. Another US colonel allegedly ordered the heart cut out of a Vietnamese corpse and fed to his dog. General James F. Hollingworth, of the US 1st Division, used to fly over in his chopper, 'zapping' Vietnamese, as Nicholas Tomalin of the *Sunday Times* reported.[41] The general's remarks were entered into the US Congressional Record. There were better-organised atrocities, of course, such as the few stray units — 'the badaas [*sic*] of the badaas' — that made up the US 'Tiger Force', originally the reconnaissance platoon of 1st Battalion, 327th Infantry. Formed to 'out-guerrilla the guerrillas', the Tigers got high on killing and mutilating. Little except their uniforms distinguished them from mass murderers. The Tiger Sam Ybarra silenced a crying Vietnamese baby by decapitating it, according to the Pulitzer Prize-winning book *Tiger Force*.[42]

The Australians and New Zealanders recorded a few isolated instances of more conventional depravity. Some Australian units imitated their American counterparts by putting up body count scoreboards — 'at least one ... was topped, for a time, with a human skull'.[43] Intense feelings of revenge, after mine blasts, provoked the odd extreme reaction: some soldiers pumped round after round into enemy corpses, 'to make sure they were dead'.[44] A few men mutilated or jumped on bodies to make them fit narrow graves. And a few lost all semblance of humanity. Stuart Rintoul records anecdotes of Maoris 'converting ... WIAs into KIAs' and of a few Australians murdering or raping civilians. One of Rintoul's sources, who gave his name merely as 'Jack', claimed that his men dragged two boys out of a house and shot one to make the other talk; the Vietnamese interpreter then pushed the survivor's face into the victim's brains. Elsewhere, a witness called 'Michael' alleged a case of necrophilia: a bloke 'screwed' a woman 'who was already dead', 'Michael' said.[45] One wonders at the credibility of 'Michael', who also happened to string Viet Cong ears around his neck, 'with my dog tags and crucifix', and sold the necklace as a souvenir when it started to smell.[46] The trouble with these stories is that they seem familiar, especially the one about the Maori wearing an ear necklace: the same rumours did the rounds.

There were, however, several confirmed cases of Australians killing enemy troops when they might have captured them; for example, the armoured carrier commander who ran over fleeing North Vietnamese during OVERLORD. 'We just went crazy,' said a carrier driver. 'We screwed them into the ground ... while they were trying to crawl and run away.'[47] This particular soldier had earlier befriended a South Vietnamese widower and his two daughters, an act of 'collaboration' for which the Viet Cong punished the father by cutting his daughters' throats. The premeditated savagery of Viet Cong attacks on civilians often cast the Australian troops in the role of avengers by proxy: one platoon, for example, shot dead a woman who had allegedly murdered children in Binh Ba to 'encourage' the people to pay their Viet Cong taxes.

The horror stories — some rumour and anecdote, others true — made easy headlines and fuelled political objections to the war; they did not show the public the true picture. The vast majority of soldiers — Australian and American — did not commit war crimes (unless, of course, one views the war as a crime). One cannot judge an army on the basis of a few anonymous accounts or the cruelty of an unhinged 'reconnaissance' platoon lost in the jungle. Rintoul's most ghoulish stories are unsourced. In any case, claims sourced to interviews do not constitute evidence. The majority of Americans and Australians were not reduced to such acts. Yet Phillip

Knightley and other reporters tend to blame the 'Americans' or whole US divisions; for instance, 'The Americans mutilated corpses', or 'The Twenty-Fifth Infantry Division left a "visiting card" ...'[48] A US division has about 20,000 combat soldiers.

Western hair-shirt historians have similarly failed to condemn communist attacks against southern civilians. This is a form of racism by omission. It implies that 'we' — the West — should behave according to certain prescribed moral or Christian standards whereas 'they' — the 'Asians' — may be excused because brutality and contempt for individual life was supposedly 'part of their culture'. This is nonsense. To have any meaning at all, shared human values must have universal — not racially or culturally confined — application. If the most heinous acts of cruelty may be justified by reference to one's race, culture or political beliefs, then the whole idea of a shared humanity becomes impossible.

It is worth remembering that Viet Cong attacks on civilians were not the consequences of sick, diseased brains bent on revenge; they were planned by intelligent, cogent beings in the name of a political ideology. Thus the Viet Cong assassin Nguyen Van Thich could calmly describe how he stabbed to death a pregnant young woman — 'for the Party and the Revolution' — then regret that the baby also died. 'I should have waited for her delivery,' he said.[49]

# Chapter 41
# Last days

... the people [had] asked us what they would do when we left.
In fact they knew and we knew what the fate of many would be.
All we could do was turn away in shame.
*Major Brian McFarlane, the last Task Force operations officer.*

Scenes of wantonness and laxity in the Australian Embassy in Saigon marked the opening of 1971. Several embassy staff, not noted for their probity, had sunk further into the folds of the city's poisonous flower. Even the usually impeccably turned-out creased command of Australian Force Vietnam seemed in want of a little starch: saluting and dress standards, for example, were distinctly lacking (largely as a result of the American style of billeting that separated officers from NCOs and the latter from the soldiers). The diggers' quarters were particularly poor, and requests to improve them were declined. An ongoing investigation into black marketeering had led to charges against ten Australians, during which the investigating officer allegedly received a death threat. Despite these setbacks, which were ultimately of a fleeting and petty nature, the soldiers performed well over long hours and basic discipline was sound. The commanders' minds tended to focus on the great issue of the day: when and how would the troops be withdrawn, which Gorton had vaguely announced in December 1970. The question prompted responses in Saigon that reverberated at the highest levels of the Australian Government — with destructive consequences.

Few Australian soldiers felt the sharp end of the politicians' war more keenly than Lieutenant General Sir Thomas Daly, Chief of the General Staff, 1966–71. Daly was a soldier's soldier, utterly devoted to the army and with a healthy suspicion of the political mind. So it was acutely galling to find himself, along with the army he so loved, the target of a ferocious press campaign orchestrated by 'someone in the Defence Department'.[1]

The extraordinary sequence of events that led to Daly's media mauling culminated in the resignation of Defence Minister Malcolm Fraser and the bringing down of Prime Minister John Gorton.[2] It began innocuously, on 3 February 1971, when Headquarters Australian Force sent field commanders a set of budgetary 'guidelines' that flagged a need to complete thirty-two existing civic action projects before starting any new ones. The guidelines, for budgetary planning purposes only, were taken from the end-of-tour report by Lieutenant Colonel Paddy Outridge, then commanding 1st Australian Civil Affairs Unit, which recommended that no new military civic action projects should start in 1971. Australian forces were to vacate the medical and educational fields, since the Vietnamese 'were now able to develop these functions', the report concluded.[3]

Understandably, the Australian Army was reluctant to commit troops to new schools or hospitals. 'We didn't want to leave half-finished monuments to our inefficiency all over the province,' the Chief of Staff, Colonel John Salmon, explained. The South Vietnamese, working on unprotected Australian projects, would have 'had their throats cut in a week'.[4]

The guidelines, in any case, were simply that: they had to be cleared with the embassy and approved in Canberra's estimates before implementation. Major General Colin Fraser directed that they be signed by Colonel Salmon, the Chief of Staff. Chiefs of staff in Saigon had a stressful if rewarding job: they acted as a lightning rod for crises. Part of their role was to coordinate messages rippling between the commander of Australian Force Vietnam in Saigon (Major Generals Fraser and Don Dunstan being the last two) and a number of civil and military authorities, such as the Australian Embassy in Saigon, the South Vietnamese Government, the Chief of the General Staff and the defence forces in Canberra, and US Army headquarters. Unless the headquarters was properly structured 'in this sort of system', said Salmon, 'you spare the Commander, but you damn near kill the chief of staff'.[5]

In Saigon, Salmon duly signed the Civil Affairs document and marked it 'CONFIDENTIAL'. This did little to prevent a disgruntled army insider from leaking the document to ABC journalist Andrew Swanton, who duly reported — without contacting Salmon — that the Australian forces were planning to 'abandon' civic action. 'The ABC report,' Salmon later said, 'had been misconstrued and misinterpreted.' In fact Swanton partly repudiated his story in a follow-up; this was ignored; the fuse had been lit.

When the so-called 'crisis' broke, Major General Colin Fraser was away from the headquarters, visiting the American operation LAM SON 719 in Laos, and Salmon had the job of replying to a flurry of 'FLASH' signals from Admiral V. A. T. (Victor) Smith, Chairman of the Chiefs of Staff, concerning the civic action leak. On Fraser's return on the evening of the next day, he dismissed Salmon's prepared signal response as unnecessary, describing the event as 'a 48-hour wonder' and left for the Mekong Delta the following morning, when the flurry of signals resumed. Needless to say, Salmon and the staff found this extremely stressful and again prepared a signal for Fraser, who said the matter was 'a storm in a teacup' and declined to become involved. Fraser claimed that Salmon was 'over-reacting'.

The ABC's story had serious repercussions in Canberra, since news of a decision to 'abandon' civic action gravely undermined the authority of Malcolm Fraser. The Defence Minister was unaware of any plans to drop civic action, which went directly against government policy, and he turned to Lieutenant General Tom Daly for answers. In fact, if anything, Fraser hoped to increase aid as the troops withdrew. (In taking this view, the Defence Department failed to see that civic action relied crucially on the army; the two were an integral part of counter-revolutionary warfare that went back to the Malayan Emergency and earlier. The army, in fact, had initiated civic action in Vietnam as early as 1965 when John Rowe oversaw the operations.)

The fuss over Swanton's 'scoop' might have faded had not further sensational coverage followed later that month in the *Canberra Times* and *The Australian*. The latter story, by Alan Ramsey — whose source was Malcolm Fraser's office — particularly infuriated Daly. Ramsey's story accused the army of disloyalty to the government and feeding false information to the Defence Department (i.e. Fraser).

Daly initially dismissed Ramsey's article as an 'imaginative rehash' of 'distortions, half-truths and untruths'.[6] Yet, when added to the media's 'intermittent sniping at the performance of the army in Vietnam', Ramsey's claims were 'just too much for the army to stomach'.[7] In reply, Daly took the highly unusual step of counter-briefing trusted journalists Max Hawkins of the Melbourne *Herald* and Ian Fitchett of the *Sydney Morning Herald*. In so doing, the general set himself up for a battle by proxy with the Defence Minister, through their preferred hacks.

On Monday, 1 March, before he met 'his' journalists, Daly got a call from a disconsolate Gorton, who said that 'someone in the Defence Department' had been secretly feeding the press information 'highly critical of the army and its leadership'. Gorton and Daly met at once, not 'in secret' as the media claimed, to discuss who might be behind the leaks. Daly suggested that recent reports of civic action might have 'upset' Fraser. Gorton dismissed this, but asked about Daly's relations with the Defence Minister. They were 'pleasant', Daly replied, although not without the occasional disagreement (Daly had strongly objected, for example, to a proposal to base a Task Force in Western Australia). The meeting ended.

In the next day or so, Daly briefed Hawkins and Fitchett. The army, he said, firmly rejected any claims that it was going behind the Defence Minister's back, and scorned as 'the sheerest fantasy' suggestions that military civic action and Civil Affairs were being precipitately abandoned: civic action had been 'the army's brainchild', he said.[8] All that was proposed was a phased and orderly handover to the South Vietnamese.

Yet a series of devastating press rockets, chiefly from Peter Samuel in *The Bulletin* and Bob Baudino in the *Daily Telegraph*, drowned Daly's counter-attack. Fraser was the ultimate source of both articles. *The Bulletin* alleged a lack of trust between the Defence Minister and the armed forces and suggested a 'revolt' over civic action; the *Daily Telegraph* claimed that Fraser had ordered the Joint Intelligence Organisation (part of the Defence Department) to report ('spy', it implied) on the army's activities in Vietnam — a claim Fraser denied.

A furious Daly met immediately with Fraser and said he was fed up with the press attacks and 'would stand no more of it'. 'Malcolm,' Daly recalled, 'gave me one of his well-known down the nose looks and asked, in a somewhat aggressive tone, what I meant …' Daly replied that he happened to possess a substantial media arsenal of his own: 'numerous communications … highly critical of the Defence Department' from officers through to service wives.[9] Fraser's political antennae pricked, and he agreed to issue a press statement, on 3 March, in which he firmly denied all the press allegations against the army: there was no disagreement; the army had not failed to consult him; civic action was not being abandoned, and so on.

In sum, the source of the allegations now roundly denied the allegations. This may seem, to inelastic minds, inconsistent. Yet it is a well-trodden political tactic to make a damaging, non-attributable claim, then deny it. Fraser, explained his official biographer, 'found himself between Scylla and Charybdis, between the need to show loyalty to an army that had not kept him properly informed, and the responsibility for the consequences of briefings he had himself initiated. Torn between the two, he chose to back his army and deny a story like Samuel's ... The alternative was politically unthinkable.'[10] In truth, Fraser 'found himself' in a dilemma of his own making.

Fraser, a proud, sensitive man with a leviathan ambition, had a tendency to obscure honourable intentions in the dark arts of subterfuge and intrigue. No doubt he had grounds for feeling the army had let him down; yet a poorly briefed politician ought perhaps ask himself the reason before blaming others. He distrusted Andrew Peacock, the Minister for the Army, and deceit came readily to the lips in an atmosphere in which relations between Defence and the army were exceptionally tense. The claims and counter-claims fed a climate of distrust that culminated on 4 March 1971 in another explosive Ramsey article. It claimed that Daly, in his meeting with Gorton, had accused Fraser of 'extreme disloyalty' to the army.[11]

This was a political powderkeg. A shocked Daly arranged an immediate meeting with the Prime Minister, whom he found 'in the throes of having his portrait painted by June Mendoza'.[12] As Gorton posed, Australia's top soldier got cracking on a press statement with the help of the Prime Minister's chief amanuensis, Miss Ainsley Gotto, who typed. After several drafts Daly and Gorton (and presumably Gotto) agreed on a media release that soundly refuted Daly's 'disloyalty' comment. 'At no time did Sir Thomas Daly "denounce" the Minister for Defence or accuse him of disloyalty,' it said, which did little to appease Fraser.

Murkier forces swam beneath these whipped currents in the form of everyone's mate, the grinning Prime Minister. It was Gorton who had given Ramsey's damaging article the green light. Offered the chance to confirm or deny Ramsey's story, the Prime Minister kept mum. Ramsey interpreted this as the nod for front-page treatment. By his inaction, Gorton had let a story run that severely damaged his Defence Minister — a lapse of judgement that Gorton later regretted. Ramsey then poured oil on the fire by publicising the fact that he *had* given the Prime Minister the opportunity to kill the story.

That was the last straw for Fraser, who promptly resigned and took the phone off the hook. In a devastating resignation speech to Parliament on 9 March, he accused Gorton of 'disloyalty to a senior Minister' and 'a dangerous reluctance to consult Cabinet'. Of Ramsey's story, he said, 'one sentence [from Gorton] would have killed the report'. He concluded: 'I do not believe he is fit to hold the great office of Prime Minister.' In reply, Gorton gave a rambling, highly embellished version of events, to which Ramsey famously interjected from the press gallery: 'You liar!'

This sordid political drama riveted the Australian public, for whom the climax did not disappoint. The mock-Shakespearian plot ended with a satisfying lurch into self-destruction, a scatter of body parts and the exit of a minister, no doubt pursued by a bear. The next day, the Liberal Party voted thirty-three for and thirty-three against Gorton's leadership — one of Gorton's 'mates', who held a deciding vote, was apparently off sick. Gorton was forced to cast the deciding vote against himself because at least four Liberals threatened to cross the floor and undermine the government in the house. To avoid that very public humiliation, Gorton fell on his sword. His mates later claimed that he had nobly stood down. Billy McMahon then easily defeated Billy Snedden in a ballot for the leadership, and promptly reshuffled Cabinet. As Fraser languished on the backbench, Gorton was made ... defence minister. And so, in March 1971, it was Gorton who went to Vietnam to discuss the gradual withdrawal of the Australian troops.

In a postcript, Daly wrote a stout defence of the army in whose interests he had acted. 'I was consumed,' the general explained, 'by a deep sense of outrage at the treatment being meted out to those splendid men and women who had given so much for their country in incredibly difficult circumstances. They deserved far better than to be unjustly pilloried by little men scratching away in their coward's castles.' Uppermost in his mind were the gentlemen of the press, none of whom had bothered to call him before rushing into print, he later claimed, in an unpublished article on which this account is partly based.[13]

★ ★ ★

Before Gorton's arrival in Vietnam in March 1971, Major General Dunstan and his staff had gainfully committed themselves to OPERATION TIMOTHY, a 'mini-withdrawal' between March and July of 650 soldiers, none of whom worked in Civil Affairs. Signals flashed between Canberra and Saigon, revealing the extreme tension and fraught complexity of the withdrawal. 'We were made to feel quite keenly the political nature of this war,' Salmon recalled.[14] TIMOTHY was ultimately subsumed by OPERATION INTERFUSE, the withdrawal proper.

During Gorton's visit to Vietnam, the former prime minister chiefly involved himself with finding out how the Civil Affairs crisis started and the welfare of the troops in Nui Dat and Vung Tau. In Saigon he met the people of importance, and assured President Thieu that no Australian combat units would leave that year.

At the end of July, a Cabinet leak alerted the Australian Task Force to the probability of an imminent withdrawal. Although secrecy forbade any detailed planning outside the inner loop, Major General Dunstan had already held 'IN CONFIDENCE' discussions with Salmon and various commanders about a phased withdrawal of all troops by May 1972. This was the genesis of OPERATION INTERFUSE, the details of which were not revealed to the Task Force in Nui Dat until weeks later.

In early August Dunstan returned to Australia for Chief of the General Staff Daly's annual exercise. While he was away Prime Minister Billy McMahon declared that the Australian troops would be out of Vietnam by Christmas; at the same time McMahon cut national service from two years to eighteen months. This effectively enabled half the national servicemen in Vietnam to go home almost immediately, if they so chose. 'It was the stupidest bloody political decision,' Salmon recalled, not least because it threatened to deprive the withdrawal plan of many soldiers with specialist skills.[15] McMahon's haste was pure politics, playing on the public mood; the decision simply ignored the danger of a rushed exit from a province that faced an external threat. Political rather than operational factors dictated the pace of the pullout and thus endangered the soldiers. McMahon, now a figure of fun with the media, who mercilessly lampooned his big ears and short stature, was forced to adopt a more phased alternative to avoid the 'simultaneous discharge' of 6,000 nashos (in Australia and Vietnam).[16]

In Vietnam, concerned staff from Saigon, Nui Dat and Vung Tau met and got on with the withdrawal planning. Canberra sent several teams to assist, and agreed on the allocation of aircraft and shipping. One team under

Lieutenant Colonel Ben O'Dowd (of the battle of Kapyong fame) was sent to help restructure the force necessitated by the possible withdrawal of the nashos (about 200 of whom availed themselves of an early discharge; a large majority loyally elected to stay with their units until the end of their tour); a team from Treasury under Mr (formerly Colonel) 'Bing' Crosby authorised the disposal of stores other than weapons, which greatly facilitated accounting; a team from Quarantine approved the cleaning of equipment before loading and thus avoided delays on arrival in Australia. Vietnam accounts were closed promptly, unlike those of the Korean War, which had dragged on for years. Army Headquarters in Canberra greatly assisted in what swiftly took the form of a very efficient and effective withdrawal; even the government, despite its dilatory actions, proved responsive to the army's needs.

The Australian troops heard the news on Radio Vietnam on 19 August 1971: they would be 'home by Christmas'. It was no great surprise, as rumours had flown for months. Major General Don Dunstan, now commanding Australian Force Vietnam, dispatched the withdrawal orders the next day. The pullout would begin in October, after which Task Force operations would be handed over to the South Vietnamese. A few elements of the Team would remain until late 1972 and embassy guards until 1973.

President Thieu expressed no 'surprise or concern' at the new timing, despite Gorton's earlier assurances. Yet Australia's departure could hardly have come at a worse time for the South Vietnamese: it coincided with the October presidential elections, when the Viet Cong usually stepped up its aggression. General Minh could spare only a single regiment to replace the Australian Task Force, he said.[17]

The Australians — and the few New Zealanders — did not go gently. The last few months were no less exhausting or dangerous than earlier years. The elections ratcheted up the tension, as communist forces pressed down on the borders. Australian intelligence repeatedly warned of 'a major build-up of VC forces in Northern Phuoc Tuy province'.[18] The Viet Cong launched a spree of abductions and assassinations in Long Khanh province.

Nor were communist cross-border incursions any less frequent; throughout 1971 they clashed with the Australians in the Long Hais, Dat Do and Xuyen Moc, to name but a few. On 21 September, in IVANHOE, the last big Australian operation of the war, North Vietnamese units of the 33rd Regiment attacked the 4th (ANZAC) Battalion at Nui Le, near the

Courtenay rubber plantation to the north of the province. The enemy deployed more advanced weapons, including, ominously, rockets and anti-aircraft guns. US Phantoms replied with napalm, missiles, flechette and 500-pound bombs. Second Lieutenant Gary McKay's men witnessed an American napalm strike at 150 metres. 'It was incredibly frightening,' he wrote. Australians died in the battle, to the dismay of people back home who naively presumed the war was over. Bravo Company suffered sixteen wounded; Delta Company suffered five dead and eight wounded.[19] Badly wounded in the chest, Private Ralph Niblett told McKay and Private 'Jethro' Hannah that he did not think he would make it to the VFL Grand Final. They assured him he would be OK. Then, McKay recalled, 'Ralph just looked straight into our eyes and said, "No, I'm not. I'm stuffed."'[20] Those were his last words; Niblett expired on the helicopter just two weeks before going home and thus became the last national serviceman killed in action. Later, McKay himself was badly wounded in the shoulder by two AK47 rounds; the dust-off could not get to him, and McKay spent an agonising night without morphine in the patient care of Corporal Michael O'Sullivan, who kept pressure on the wounds to stanch the bleeding while the wounded officer 'bit soundlessly down on his identity discs, his only antidote to pain'.[21] McKay survived, and received a Military Cross in recognition of his command during these last actions.

The Viet Cong had come full circle, back to the first 'guerrilla' phase of revolutionary warfare with which it had launched the insurgency in 1960. They tried to tax and murder uncooperative villagers. Their special targets were the People's Self-Defence Forces — 'dad's armies' and 'children's brigades' — hundreds of thousands of southern peasants armed with old guns, picks and machetes, whose existence showed the scale of local resistance to the resurgent communists, and gave the lie to Western notions that 'the people' all supported the National Liberation Front.

Friendly and Catholic villagers were terrified of the enemy's advance, and implored the Australians to stay and protect them. In Xuyen Moc 'there was much wailing, gnashing of teeth and carrying on', recalled Lieutenant Dennis Bird, of the Mobile Advisory and Training Team, 'not just because we were leaving, but because they seemed to believe it was the end of their life. Once we were gone, that was it. Most of them were Catholics and had nothing to gain under a Communist takeover and they knew it ...'[22]

Hundreds of field reports suggested an encircling threat, provoked by the impending presidential elections: 'VC boasted about the ambushing and killing of the Long Le District chief'; 'VC are forcing people ... to give them clothes and to pay $VN4,000–5,000 tax' — such were typical reports. Viet Cong fighters burst into homes and demanded food; terrorised fishermen and rubber workers; and assassinated village chiefs (including the Binh Ba chief). Death notices proliferated. 'To avoid a useless death,' warned one, 'the people whose names are listed below must ... turn your arms against the oppressors and return to the revolution.' The thirteen listed were all part of the ragtag People's Self-Defence Force.[23] Age was no protection: thus Le Van Luc, a 60-year-old fisherman, died 'BY MACHETE STROKES TO NECK & HEAD', according to the note pinned to his chest.[24] The brave new chief and deputy chief of Suoi Nghe, the Australian-built hamlet, received six warnings that they faced death for 'their part in the Vietnamisation of the war'.[25] Under interrogation, a Viet Cong prisoner called Sergeant Nguyen Van Phuong revealed a 'general directive' to 'strike fear into the hearts of the people' during the elections. 'Everything possible will be done to discredit ... Vietnamisation,' he said.

Meanwhile, the enemy sought any scrap about the Australian departure. On the night of 12 September eight Viet Cong infiltrated Hoa Long and demanded to know what the villagers knew. At the same time, the 274th Regiment was preparing to 'take command of Route 2 after the Australian forces withdraw'.[26]

Indeed, road security was downgraded from CODE GREEN to AMBER or RED. A Task Force circular on 18 September warned of an 'INCREASING NUMBER OF MINE AND AMBUSH INCIDENTS OCCURRING ON ROADS EVEN IN DAYLIGHT ...'.[27] In response, Saigon erected more road signs, such as: 'WARNING: YOU ARE ABOUT TO ENTER ONE OF THE MOST DANGEROUS COMBAT AREAS IN VIET-NAM: A PUBLIC HIGHWAY. PLEASE DRIVE CAREFULLY.'[28] But the Australians were just as likely to encounter the enemy off the roads: on 12 June 1971 a rocket detonated claymore mines on an Australian personnel carrier, killing seven Australian troops and wounding three.[29]

There were deeper reasons for the upsurge in guerrilla violence in Phuoc Tuy: COSVN had, in fact, earmarked the province for a more important strategic role in the communist takeover of the South. It proposed Ba Ria as the headquarters of communist operations over three provinces: Phuoc Tuy, Bien Hoa and Long Khanh.[30] The provincial capital would play a central part in the eastern advance on Saigon, as would Vung Tau's deep-water harbour, 'part of the breathing apparatus of Saigon', the South Vietnamese General Vien told Major General Fraser in early 1971. The Vietnamese attached great importance to having access to it, Fraser concluded.[31] And yet the fresh Viet Cong incursions were the last resort of an exhausted army, most of whom clung to the border areas awaiting a chance to pounce once the *uc dai loi* left.

On 5 October Brigadier Bruce McDonald MC, the Task Force commander, departed Nui Dat, taking the 'wizard box' — the intelligence link — with him. A veteran of Sarawak, McDonald's caring manner earned him the nickname 'Mother McDonald', an image that belied his aggressive pursuit of the enemy on the northern borders.[32] McDonald's valedictory speech praised the troops for proudly upholding 'the Anzac tradition forged by our forefathers over half a century ago'.[33] Colonel Phil Greville, one of Australia's finest military engineers, succeeded him as the last Task Force commander, with responsibility for the 1st Australian Logistic Support Group and the oversight of the immense withdrawal plans at Vung Tau.[34]

Next day the 3rd Battalion, its tour cut short by four months, flew out to HMAS *Sydney*, to return to Australia. Only one battalion, the 4th, remained in Nui Dat, in tense conditions: since August, the diminished Australian contingent had feared an attack on Nui Dat. The battalion had just two dust-off helicopters on stand-by at all times (although another sixteen helicopters of 9 Squadron, RAAF, were available if needed).[35] Despite the severe tension, the lone 4th Battalion maintained constant pressure on the enemy, and deployed as many platoons outside the wire as were available in the remaining weeks; the Australians sought to create the illusion of strength by sending out mock SAS insertions and calling air strikes. Fictitious radio signals gave the appearance of normal traffic. It seemed to work: there were only three minor contacts that last month.

On 7 October the east gate of Nui Dat was shut for good. In the next four weeks the remaining units were trucked or flown to Vung Tau. On 5 November the full 4th Battalion held a memorial service at Nui Dat. On 7 November the infantry companies began departing. Delta Company, a mortar unit and one armoured carrier troop were the last Australian units to leave. Major Jerry Taylor, commanding Delta Company, said later that he had never been so afraid as during those final weeks at Nui Dat (Taylor had earlier, on 21 September, earned a Military Cross in recognition of his courage during an attack when his company was surrounded by an estimated 1,000 North Vietnamese troops).

On 6 November — a day before D–Day, 'departure day' — the advance party of South Vietnam's 946 Regional Force Company trudged nervously into Nui Dat. 'We watched them toiling slowly up the hill towards us,' recalled one Australian witness. 'They wore an assortment of uniform, civilian clothes and webbing, all in varying degrees of shabbiness and disrepair. One of them had the torso of a monkey wired to the foresight of his M16: his evening meal presumably. They might have been figures of humour or ridicule, but I felt overwhelmingly sorry for them. I think we all did, because nobody said anything and nobody laughed.'[36] They were doomed to an uncertain fate. The people were 'dead scared', remembered Greville. 'They weren't looking forward to it. But they were very brave.'[37] Many shared the fears of Major Ko, a South Vietnamese officer who told Graham Walker: 'When the Australians leave, Phuoc Tuy Province will collapse like a card house in the wind.'[38]

At 1910 hours on 6 November the last Australians in Nui Dat blew up any unusable ammunition. Patrolling and ambushing continued until dawn of 7 November. Major Hogarth's Bravo Company were the last riflemen out; and at 1341 on D-Day 1971 the armoured carriers of 1 Troop, A Squadron, 3rd Cavalry Regiment, became the last of the Task Force to leave Nui Dat. The radio Command Net shut down at 1500; the 4th Battalion's duty officer made his final log entry: '1800. Op SOUTHWARD concluded. End of operations.'[39] Brian McFarlane, the last Task Force operations officer, recalled the melancholy journey from Nui Dat to the sea:

> As the long line of armoured vehicles carrying my headquarters
> elements made the journey down through the towns and villages
> with which I had become so familiar, I looked at the people
> going about their business and wondered what was to become of
> them … the people [had] asked us what they would do when we
> left? In fact they knew and we knew what the fate of many
> would be. All we could do was turn away in shame.[40]

Inventory lists, write–offs, the closure of accounts, decisions on what to take and what to leave — all the manifold tasks of an army on the move — occupied the last months in Vung Tau. HMAS *Sydney* and *Jeparit* and AV

*John Monash* were moored at various times in the harbour, along with a heavy-lift Japanese ship, SS *Harima Maru*; Qantas charter flights and RAAF Hercules were on hand to help.

The scale of the job astonished the few who remained to do it. On 12 November, for example, the diminished Task Force disposed of 18,000 platoon rations valued at $26,814 and 5.8 tonnes of canned meat, valued at $7,265.[41] Most were given to the locals, as a last 'civic action'. Meanwhile, in Saigon the Australian Force headquarters wrote off its projectors, TV sets, boats, billiard tables, ice-making machines, electronic organs, refrigerators and sewing machines. 'Swimming pools' that 'cannot be cleaned and packed' were to be left to decay *in situ*.[42]

All vehicles — Land Rovers, trucks, tanks, armoured carriers, concrete mixers, rock crushers, containers — and stores were steam-cleaned after washing to fumigate them, in line with strict Australian quarantine rules. The twenty Centurion tanks each required 57,000 litres of water and 156 hours of work to clear the red mud.[43]

As the troops flowed down to Vung Tau, the meagre facilities were stretched to breaking point. To accommodate 3,400 soldiers, Greville utilised First Australian Logistics and Supply Group, the R&C Centre, the beach annexe and part of an old US Army school, on loan from the South Vietnamese and stripped of wiring, switches, taps and so on … a portent of the mass scavenge to come. 'The sewerage lines were all blocked and the water supply of doubtful potability,' Greville observed.[44]

Greville and his men superbly overcame these immense obstacles, without loss of life or luggage. Shipload by shipload slid away. On 3 December 1971, 170 remaining troops held a barbecue and concert in the Wheatley Stadium in Vung Tau.[45] There was much pomp and circumstance, as President Thieu flew onto the deck of HMAS *Sydney* to bid them farewell. The last Australian infantrymen left Vung Tau at the end of February 1972.

The circumstances of the Australian Army Training Team's departure were distinctly unedifying, and reflected badly on the Australian Government. The Team was ordered suddenly to cease activities, to abandon its South Vietnamese trainees and close down courses with a day's notice.

On 8 December Lieutenant Colonel Pat Gowans handed over 'Australia House' — the kangaroo-emblazoned home of the Team in Da

Nang, witness to nine Anzac Days and the beery interludes of 700 Australian advisers — to American officers. There were emotional scenes: tearful South Vietnamese generals thanked the Team's last man in Da Nang for a contribution that had lasted nine years; in Phu Thu, 20 kilometres south-east of Hué, Vietnamese, Americans and the last two Australians said goodbye over a barbecue in the sand dunes, and Warrant Officer Bert Addington enthralled the audience with a reading of *The Sentimental Bloke*, 'in that desolate strip so far from home'.[46]

At midnight on 5 March 1972 Australian Force Vietnam ceased to exist. In its place a core unit of 128 men formed the Australian Army Assistance Group Vietnam. It included a Saigon headquarters and, in Phuoc Tuy, a few advisers, engineers and jungle warfare instructors whose job was to train the Cambodian Armed Forces of the Khmer Republic.[47] Most were former members of the Team.

On 2 December 1972 Gough Whitlam's Labor Party persuaded a narrow majority that 'It's Time' for a change of government and just defeated the Liberal–Country Party Coalition, ending twenty-three years of conservative rule. Whitlam's first three decisions were to abolish conscription (and free seven jailed draft resisters); issue Wilfred Burchett with a passport; and order the last few troops out of South Vietnam. The Team was given ten days to pack up and quit the country.

The pace and priority of the announcements delighted the peace activists, disgusted the army and created deeper divisions in Australian opinion. 'It was done in a screaming hurry,' said Brigadier Ian Geddes, commander of the Army Assistance Group in Vietnam. 'The Vietnamese reaction,' recorded McNeill, 'was one of disbelief that after more than six years in Phuoc Tuy the [last few] Australians would leave in less than six days.' The soldiers were embarrassed and ashamed. A grubby political expedient had soiled their genuine sense of duty to this benighted country. The older hands had hoped to stay in Vietnam at least until the expected 1973 ceasefire; Whitlam's haste 'was a violation of both honour and form'.[48]

On 17 December Australia lowered its flag over the Free World forces building in Saigon for the last time. Next day, the Army Assistance Group flew home. Geddes toured the country once more, to thank the Vietnamese with whom the Australians had trained and fought for a decade. A platoon remained — thirty-five men — to guard the Australian Embassy in Saigon.

On 11 January 1973 the Governor-General, Sir Paul Hasluck, proclaimed the cessation of Australian hostilities in Vietnam. Australia's longest military campaign had ended, and the withdrawal had been completed without casualties, loss or mishap — a triumph due primarily to the quality of the commanders on the spot and the exceptional planning in Saigon, Vung Tau and Canberra.

Meanwhile, the South Vietnamese had picked Nui Dat to the bone: wood pallets, fixtures, lavatories, nails … all were stripped and carted away. In 1972 only the concrete slabs in the washing areas remained. The Vietnamese names returned, and Luscombe Bowl, the Eagle Pad, the Long Green, the Horseshoe and the Warburtons disappeared with the foreigners. The undergrowth reclaimed the earthen outlines of Australian tentage and serried dugouts, and the old rubber trees stood alone once more in the battlelines, their white sap bleeding unseen by any 'round eye'. Only the painted boulders of the Australian gun emplacements, like the broken fists of a lesser Ozymandias, reminded the cowherds of the *uc dai loi*. The wind blew around that dismal place, in silence now; the boom of artillery shells and the beat of rock 'n' roll resonated only in the local memory. The rain pelted the defoliated valley, once our Tactical Area of Operational Responsibility, into a muddy wasteland. Too frightened to stay, the few Vietnamese soldiers packed up and moved their families to Ba Ria as the forest, thick with Viet Cong, closed in.

# Chapter 42
# 'Baby-killers'

Yours wasn't a war, mate! You didn't fight in the trenches. You
were on a twelve-month holiday!
*An RSL member to a national serviceman just returned from Vietnam.*

Did you fall over chasing after a Vietnamese woman whilst trying
to rape her?
*A young woman protester to a crippled Vietnam veteran.*

Most troops sailed home aboard HMAS *Sydney*.[1] US Chinooks flew the
joyful soldiers to this 212.7-metre floating city on the decks of
which, like thousands before them, the men stood and watched Radar Hill
and the Long Hai Mountains diminish on the broadening horizon. Through
the evening downpour the departing Australians watched an electrical storm
flash about the great, jutting brow of the Long Hais, a Zeus-like thunderbolt
of defiance. Soon Vung Tau was but a twinkle in the twilight, and the
soldiers settled in for two weeks of winding down. On the first night they
took long showers and devoured a hot dinner with a few beers. 'We drank
the ship dry,' recollected one private. Captain Ian Kortlang recalls enjoying
roast lamb and mint sauce with his fellow officers, then 'we just laid around
on the deck and got suntans'.[2] The mood was happy and relaxed; the men
could not wait to get home. The *Sydney*'s sailors had seen the same ritual
repeated twenty-two times since 1965. In 1971 the ship's flamboyant
Captain Scrivenor joined the troops on the quarterdeck each night, to

watch movies or entertainment. Neptune's Party on the Equator was more boisterous than usual … then, within days, the troops beheld the shores of Australia.

At Townsville, a band played as the battalions came ashore.[3] A great banner, 'WELCOME HOME!', fluttered over the town, and an enthusiastic street parade greeted the men. The ship then proceeded to Brisbane and Sydney where, in 1971, striking dock workers had refused to put gangplanks in place and the soldiers were forced to disembark via a steep rear stairway.[4]

Others flew home: one day they were in the jungle, the next they were on a plane to Australia. Most, given the option, preferred the glamour of jet flight. An exception was Captain John Bullen, one of very few officers who *chose* to take the ship home. As it turned out, he chose wisely.

'Finally we were going home,' Private Terry Spriggs recalled, as he walked across the tarmac at Tan Son Nhut airport in Saigon, to the waiting Qantas 707. 'I wept for my mates who didn't make it.' On board, euphoria took over: 'We were clapping, cheering, crying and with that sense of comradeship I'll take to my grave. It was magic: guys talking about their families, wives, girlfriends waiting to meet them … The moment came, the lights of Sydney. Jesus, I can't describe the scene aboard that 707. We touched down and taxied to the terminal, doors opened — we were home. Guys were kissing the gangway; it was wild. Going through customs I still couldn't believe I was back in Aussie, not until I was through the customs door … and there was my brother. I burst into tears and nearly hugged him to death …'

Then, into this scene of private happiness, marched a crowd of 'shitwitted protesters', Spriggs recalled: '… these motherfuckers come bursting in carrying placards. One I'll never forget as long as I live, this poxy-ridden excuse for a female, screeching and carrying a placard saying, "CHILD KILLERS".'[5]

Spriggs escaped lightly. On another flight a soldier wept as the plane banked above the lights of Sydney; moments later, outside Mascot airport, hundreds of demonstrators pelted him and his fellow troops with rotten fruit.[6] Gary Blinco flew into rain and bitter cold: 'I looked dismally around the terminal. A protester with a pimply face and long greasy hair pressed close to me: "How many women did you rape? How many children did you murder?" I shoved him roughly … "Get fucked, dickhead, or I'll break your neck"', Blinco said. The protester shrank back to his friends, 'visibly shaken by the menace he saw in my eyes'.[7]

'I got on a Pan Am flight,' recalled Harry Whiteside, who served his last year of three tours of Vietnam with a US unit. 'I'd been in the field for nine days. I stank everyone else out. Customs went over me like a rat up a drainpipe. Outside were all these civilians, mostly young women. They started to spit on me and call me a baby-killer. I realised I'd spent years overseas shooting the wrong people ... the enemy were at home.'[8]

Among the more disturbing stories was that of David Morgan, a diligent young signaller, who landed in Sydney at 1 a.m. amid the usual emotional scenes. His connecting flight left the next day, so he and a mate, Scotty, spent a night in Kings Cross. Next morning they returned to the airport, in their uniforms, where a large group of demonstrators waited:

> They see Scotty and I getting out of the taxi and they make a rush for us. They yell at us with obscene language, calling us killers of little Vietnamese children, murderers, and that we should be in jail. They jostle and heckle, as we try to make our way to the entrance. As I am about to enter ... I notice a woman lunging towards me, with her head in a forward motion. The next thing I know a large gob of spit hits my left cheek ... As soon as I got through the terminal doors ... I drop my baggage and wipe my face with my left fist ...
>
> I turn to Scotty: 'Do you believe this, that bitch spat on me ... They are fucking traitors to our country' ... I go to the men's toilets to wash my face and left fist ... luckily I am able to wash with hot water ...

Later, at home, Morgan received a registered parcel. Inside were his medals, the Vietnam Medal and the South Vietnam Campaign Medal. 'I am in shock, as I thought the medals are presented to you on the parade ground ... I find it ... very disrespectful of the Government to send my medals by mail.'[9]

Twelve months in the jungle had attuned the soldiers' senses to two colours: the black and green of the war zone. Australia's sharp primaries dazzled their eyes. Home was an olfactory delight, too: the fresh smells of eucalyptus, salty sea breezes, clear, unpolluted air. The 'round-eyed' children, healthy, happy.

And the brazen opulence and complacency of this huge country, their home. After months of strict orders, tense whispers and endless oaths, the laid-back Aussie vernacular sounded so strange, like a foreign dialect.

As he came through customs, Barry Roe saw a huge sign, 'Welcome Home, Barry'. His father said, 'Jump in the car and we'll go home now …' Jump in the car? wondered Roe. A day before he had been in a war zone: now here he was at a party of aunties and uncles and old friends. 'I just got bombed out of my brain and stayed that way for three or four weeks.'[10] Thousands of others experienced the same dreamlike sensation. 'Our bodies were here but our brains were in Vietnam,' remembered Claude Zavattaro.[11] 'People would say "How did the football go on the weekend?" or "How did Essendon go?"' said Ian Kortlang, 'and you think, "Why is it that in this world I feel like I am in the wrong place?"'[12]

Every city held ticker-tape parades. In the latter years they tended to be sombre affairs, with none of the jubilation that greeted soldiers home from the world wars. 'I felt ten feet tall, I really felt good,' said John Skinner, 'but what I didn't realise was that most people were only curious. They weren't cheering us home. They were just lined up to see something.'[13] In Adelaide, Bob Saillard marched past a crowd of silent lunchtime shoppers, 'not doing any cheering or anything. There was no welcome home at all.'[14] The men felt like curiosities, slightly freakish, emblems of a grave mistake. Their photos show ranks of unsmiling eyes that seem to bore into the back of the man in front, as if afraid to make eye contact with the crowd. No young women ran up to kiss them.[15]

On 17 November 1971, 500 soldiers, 450 airmen and 250 sailors marched in one of the last parades through Sydney. Emotions were mixed: relief and joy amid a deep sense of unease. From the stairs of the Town Hall, the perennially suntanned Minister for the Army, Andrew Peacock, beamed down on this scene of social dislocation like a Cheshire cat at a funeral.

Within days of their return the national servicemen were discharged. The process was swift and terminal (and had applied many times since 1967, of course): the men nominated their preferred place of discharge, 'provided it doesn't cost the Army any more money than if they sent you to your town of call-up'.[16] There, an administration officer announced: 'You will be discharged on [date] for the reason that the period of your engagement in national service has expired.' There was no debriefing, and certainly no 'counselling'. At Watsons Bay, for example, the discharge cell for Eastern Command asked the departing nashos a few perfunctory questions about their future. 'At Southern Command Discharge Centre,' recalled Phillip White, of 8 Field Ambulance, 'you were written off the records, and told very politely that if you weren't off the base in one hour, you would be charged with trespassing.'[17] The army cast them aside, like redundant draught-horses. On the morning of their last day of national service the nashos were paraded before their commanding officers, who thanked and bade them farewell. They were then 'marched out'.

He marched out in a mind of his own, a stranger in his own town, a 21-year-old recluse gazing in at a party to which he had not been invited: girls in miniskirts, new dance styles, new music, long hair ... And as he wandered in a daze through this peculiar world of peace and prosperity, sudden movements, familiar sounds — the beat of a helicopter, a car backfiring — snapped him back to Vietnam. It was the beginning of a lifetime of not being able to forget.

Few dared wear their uniform after discharge, but the nasho's short hair and estranged expression often betrayed him. His very conservative appearance evoked the Menzies years; he was untouchable, a figure of revulsion, in the eyes of militant protesters. Having obeyed the law of his country, he now experienced the bizarre sensation of being treated as little more than a common criminal, the target of actual social hatred for doing what his government and the people had asked of him.

No doubt the regular soldier ran the gauntlet, too; but he was relatively insulated inside the bosom of the army. The nashos simply walked away; many would not see their fellow soldiers for decades. None had expected a hero's welcome; they simply hoped for understanding, to be heard. It did not happen: Australians preferred to forget the war. The soldier could not. More painful than the protesters' crude abuse were the endless little moments of indifference and carelessness of friends and families, who simply had no point of entry into their son's or mate's world. At first, a young man would attempt to respond, to tell his side. He turned his shoulder to the nation's fury, or indifference, and tried to *explain*. Yet what followed was an act of collective national cruelty towards thousands of young men whose 'offence' had been to fight a war their government and the vast majority of Australians had supported.

With his rising anxiety and inner terror of this strange society, the young nasho cast about for an escape, or at least a willing ear. He alighted on the supposed diggers' refuge, the Returned and Services League. Surely the RSL would support him. Surely the RSL would understand. After all, RSL members were old soldiers. Alas, most — although not all — RSL branches either refused or discouraged admission and membership to Vietnam veterans. 'Yours wasn't a war, mate! You didn't fight in the trenches. You were on a twelve-month holiday!' brayed one RSL member at Ross Jack, of the 7th Battalion — a typical remark.[18] 'The RSL offered little support; the RSL didn't believe it was a real war,' stated General Peter Gration (retired), former Chief of the Defence Force, years later.[19] 'The RSL didn't want to know the nashos,' added Wally Thompson, the three-tour veteran who became the army's first RSM.[20]

In response, thousands of returning soldiers set up their own veterans' associations and shunned the RSL — many still do. 'I'll never join it,' said Bill O'Mara of the 5th Battalion in 2006.[21] Others were forgiving. 'I didn't join the RSL until 1997,' said dust-off pilot Neville Cullen. He is now deputy president of the Redcliffe RSL, in Queensland. And it must be stressed that not every RSL branch rejected the soldiers: many rural RSLs were very supportive, as Tim Fischer and other farmers' sons recall.[22]

Every soldier, in every kind of social situation, remembers the war at home as though it were yesterday. Some acts of callousness beggar belief. 'I had to go to Victoria Barracks,' recalls Neil Birnie, a signaller, 'and my wife pushed me in my wheelchair. When we were in St Kilda Road I got spat on twice.'[23]

Terry Burstall, of Delta Company, 6th Battalion, came home to Ballarat and walked into his old pub. 'A bloke said, "Weren't you going to Vietnam?" My step-dad said, "What the hell are we doing there?"' (Burstall's father, also a soldier, died in 1943 in New Guinea.) Of this kind of reception, said Burstall wearily, 'You just gave up.'[24]

'These ardent left-wingers would poke you in the chest and abuse you,' recalled Peter Dinham, a regular officer and Long Tan veteran. The regs were reluctant to wear their uniform outside barracks, 'but [Major General] Don Dunstan changed that, and said you're in the Australian Army and you should be proud to wear your uniforms'.[25]

'You never mentioned [Vietnam] on a job application,' said Laurie Bunworth, of 1APC Squadron, '... if you wanted the job.'[26] Indeed, many employers routinely refused jobs to Vietnam veterans, whom they saw as socially tainted, irascible and uneasy with civilian authority.

Nothing changed for Aboriginal veterans. Ray Orchard's local pub continued to refuse to serve him and his brothers a beer, because, said the publican, 'when you mob get together you create a problem'. Orchard, one of Australia's few Aboriginal soldiers, said, 'Hold on, I've just come back from Vietnam.'

'I couldn't care less,' replied the publican.[27]

Normie Rowe, the cavalryman and conscripted pop idol, tried to perform again but 'it was all wrong — I looked around, felt uncomfortable, like I was on a different planet … it was another four or five years before I really felt confident.' He took his dog and a few bottles of Bacardi and 'beach-bummed' for eight months.[28]

The army chaplains were generally disapproved of in civilian church circles. Their fellow clergymen would mutter, 'Fancy being part of a war machine, fancy associating yourself with a war like that; fancy claiming to represent Christ in a place like that', recalled one army chaplain. 'Some weren't game enough to say it to my face. I found that very hard to accept, and not easy to forgive.'[29]

Nor were nurses or entertainers spared. Army as well as civilian nurses were routinely criticised, said Dorothy Angell, head of Civilian Nurses, Australian Surgical Teams, Vietnam. 'They were getting set upon. Most of us have lived with it for … years.'[30]

Even the entertainers were abused for singing to the soldiers. On one occasion in Adelaide, Lorrae Desmond was heckled during her show: 'I told the heckler he didn't know what he was talking about … I told him to blame the government if he wanted to blame anyone …'[31]

Senior commanders also felt the nation's wrath. At one dinner party among wealthy bleeding hearts, an angry female lawyer abused a battalion commander. The soldier sat quietly through her tirade, then stood and said, 'Madam, you disgust me', and walked out.

Some soldiers' children were bullied or humiliated at school; even a few teachers participated in the abuse. Ray De Vere MC, now chairman of RSL Care in Queensland, recalled one egregious incident. 'My son, aged 12, and my daughter, 13, were at a school camp,' he said, 'and it had just been announced that I'd been awarded a Military Cross.' De Vere's son proudly told the class, at which the teacher said: 'How many women and children did he kill to get that?'

'My son and daughter got up and left,' De Vere remembers, with deep sadness, adding proudly, 'My son wanted to punch the teacher on the nose.' De Vere went to see the school's headmaster that day. 'I want the teacher concerned,' he said, 'to make a public apology to the entire school, and write a letter of apology in local newspaper: I will settle for nothing less.' The headmaster agreed to 'look into it', and promised to support De Vere if the allegations were true. During the school holidays, which had just begun, the headmaster rang De Vere to say that the teacher responsible had vanished. The Victorian Department of Education, De Vere believes, had arranged an immediate transfer.[32]

The collision of war and peace had a terrible social cost: families were torn apart; marriages broke down; lovers fell out; old friends got into fights: the clash on the home front literally split the nation. It affected all ranks: a colonel, for example, returned to find himself 'a stranger in my own home. My wife and children were all anti-war marchers.'

When Harry Whiteside, an SAS veteran, arrived home, in uniform, at the railway station in Griffith he found that 'My old man had gone to Labor, all because of the Vietnam War. I took my uniform off real quick.' In the town pub, a few locals unwisely insulted Whiteside. 'I put one bloke in hospital for five weeks,' he said without pride.[33] Neville Cullen fell out with his sister: 'She was one of the protesters, into Joan Baez and all that,' Cullen recalls. 'She was really hostile to the war.'[34]

'I went to a pub in Bankstown with some school mates,' said Laurie Drinkwater, a Long Tan veteran. 'I was standing in the same corner of a pub in which I used to drink. Someone said, "You joined the army or something, didn't you?" I started to go downhill.'[35]

Peter Molloy, who lost his right leg, found his childhood companions 'just cold. They sort of said hello.' Brian Sewell's 'best mate — I was best man at his wedding — didn't want to know me when I got back'.[36] One of Brian 'Chick' Hennessy's oldest friends approached him at their local pub at Point Lookout and said, 'You're a baby-killer, Chick!' Hennessy said he came within seconds of monstering the bloke.[37]

To the soldiers, old beyond their years, their civilian friends seemed naive and immature, barely men. Most, of course, were just ordinary young Australians. 'I honestly didn't notice at first,' said Gary McMahon, 'but after a few weeks I couldn't stand being around any of my old civilian friends.

They were like children.'[38] That probably said more about the influence of two tours of Vietnam on McMahon than the immaturity of his friends. 'None of us thought we'd changed, we thought everybody else had,' said David Morris. The opposite was surely the case.[39]

Some 'old mates' were monumentally insensitive or just plain stupid: 'Within a few weeks I was back at work,' said Terry O'Brien.[40] 'I was in the toilet one day, and one of my mates rolled a cracker under the door … I nearly died of a heart attack but he thought it was a great joke.'

The returned troops always ran the risk of ambush by the Australian supporters of Hanoi and the Viet Cong. Barry Heard, who lost close friends at Suoi Chau Pha, enrolled in a university course in Melbourne. He kept to himself. On one occasion, in the café, 'Fifty students burst in … They were recruiting fellow brothers and sisters for a student rally to show solidarity with Hanoi … I left immediately.'[41] Richard Hornery, a trainee engine driver when called up, worked with a guy with whom he had been the best of mates. 'On my return I met him for a drink … when out of the blue, and I quote, he said: "You murdering bastard, you killed my brothers and sisters when you were in Vietnam." Shocked, I asked him what he was on about … I thought he may have been joking. His reply was that he had joined the Communist Party while I was away and as I was fighting against Communism I was now his enemy. We have not spoken since.'[42]

Parents tried to understand the stranger in their midst who used to be their son. They were shocked by their sons' language, long periods of silence and bursts of rage. Mothers and fathers struggled merely to comprehend their sons' experiences; empathy was impossible. Some soldiers wondered whether they could love their families any more. Bernard Szapiel used to adore his family. When he got back from Vietnam, 'I just stood there … I had no tears, I had no feeling.'

Gary McMahon's experiences were typical. His family and friends told him that he had changed dramatically. 'After a couple of weeks … some of them were scared of me. My mother was devastated by the change. She said that I had gone away young and carefree, always laughing, and had come home … emotionless and cold, a nervous and jumpy wreck.'[43] Laurie Drinkwater had the same sad falling-out with the parents he once loved: 'I went home to my parents. We argued like hell. I used to get on real well with them.'[44]

Some families strove to 'normalise' these strange, introspective young men, cynical before their years and prone to long, brooding silences … They expected their boys simply to fit back in. When Barry Heard came home to Ensay, he found his family huddled around the TV, which had been installed in his absence. 'Any attempt at conversation was greeted with "Shhh!" … Whereas before there were yarns, dinnertime stories, socialising, and popping in for a cuppa … I couldn't hack it.'[45]

Others were absorbed in their own lives and seemed indifferent. If they were not watching TV, many parents preferred not to hear their sons' stories. They were tired of the war. It bored them. 'I remember saying around the dinner table, "I think I may have killed someone over there,"' said Philip Ham. 'I was very upset. My mother just said, "Dear, I don't think you'll be decorated for that." She said nothing more on the subject. I didn't talk about it … I went back to my job as a draftsman at Comalco.'[46]

New Zealand troops received a similar reception. Nick Quigley, a New Zealander who fought with the Australians, promptly left his family in Auckland and returned to Australia: 'At least there I knew other veterans and we could relate.'[47]


Sexual relations were a battlefield. Wives and girlfriends found themselves in bed with strange, wild-eyed men. 'We went to bed and made love,' said one soldier, 'but it was disappointing … She said I was too rough.' His wife said: '… it was like going to bed with a stranger. I so much wanted it to be soft, gentle and romantic. He was rough, even aggressive.' Some men were afraid to have sex; others hated their wives' talk of 'love'. The word suggested the impossible in this unreal dream. Some relationships broke down within days of the soldier's return: 'I got engaged before I left,' said Drinkwater. When he got home, 'My fiancée came to the wharf. I stayed with her for three days. Then I went down to Sydney. I never went back. I couldn't handle it.'[48]

Yet many wives heroically stayed with their men on this 'hundred-mile journey', little realising what lay beneath the man by their side. They, too, had endured much in their husbands' absence, including continual harassment, poison-pen letters and abuse over the phone.[49] 'My wife was president of the Royal Australian Regiment Wives Club,' said Lieutenant Colonel Colin Townsend. 'She helped other soldiers' wives. She received continual, abusive phone calls. She was a servicewoman in World War II. What those wives did was astonishing …'[50]

Cruel and insensitive treatment of servicemen's families recurred throughout the war, said Maxine Sheldrick, a regular soldier's wife. Wives of nashos were on the frontline, she said. One appalling example was a young teacher whose colleagues made her life a misery because her husband was a conscript; the poor woman was 'forced to tell her children to deny their father as they were being victimised', wrote Sheldrick, who greatly appreciated the army's support for service wives. 'Vietnam,' she said, 'would have been much harder, probably unbearable, for my family in a civilian community' where 'isolation … lack of support systems, and lack of understanding from an uninterested or even hostile public put many of these women under extreme pressure …'.[51] Indeed, Ian Ferguson's wife, he said, 'never, ever voluntarily admitted to anybody that I was in Vietnam because the wives were the ones receiving the flak and not us'.[52]

But it was not all a tale of woe. Many families and couples reunited and survived the trauma of war. When John Binnie returned, he and Victoria married, and they remain happily married — one example of many couples who have lived with, and conquered, the demons of the past.

Psychologists have technical terms for it; but one secular word better describes the soldiers' emotional response to their treatment: hate. It was pure, unalloyed hatred, incandescent, a kind of boxed-up loathing. True, a few veterans joined the anti-war movement, and set up groups such as Veterans Against Vietnam. Yet most soldiers shared the feelings of Bob Gibson. 'More than I could ever express I hated those anti-war protesters,' he said.[53]

In fairness, most protesters did not target the troops personally; many were simply expressing their peaceful objection to the war. Yet this often enraged the soldiers, some of whom responded violently to peaceful protests. Any act or word against the war seemed to deny the sacrifice of their mates, killed or wounded. Had the soldiers given life or limb for no reason? That was the terrible question implicit in any rejection of the war. Such feelings partly explained Laurie Drinkwater's outburst on a construction site one day. 'A bunch of hippies came in wanting us to sign a petition against the war. I went right off. I shouted, "What would you know, you bunch of long-haired cunts? Get a haircut and get over there [i.e. to Vietnam]!"'[54] Drinkwater had helped to bury the dead after Long Tan.

Occasionally, ex-soldiers and pro-Viet Cong activists came face to face, with dire consequences. Three months after national serviceman Rick

Bensley came home from Vietnam he returned to his job as a bank teller in Wagga Wagga. One morning, 'a bloke came in and wanted to send some money to an organisation that was highly supportive of the Viet Cong', Bensley recalled. In reply, Bensley drew his bank-issue Smith & Wesson .38 and gave the customer ten seconds to get out of the bank. The customer fled; Bensley was given the day off.[55]

As the months passed, many Vietnam veterans simply gave up and shut down. They drew a curtain on the past. Some packed up and left Australia, or went bush. A debilitating state of denial ensued: either the nation did not want to know or the soldier could not explain. Thus began a long, painful — and ultimately explosive — period of silence. 'The men were mentally adrift for years,' said Colin Townsend, months before he died.[56]

Many went through life never mentioning their Vietnam service. Neville Cullen later became director of nursing at Mount Druitt Hospital: 'None of my colleagues knew I was a Vietnam vet.'[57] Bill O'Mara worked for ten years with the stockbroker Bain & Co. and told none of his colleagues that he had been in Vietnam. Years later, when an acquaintance found out, she casually said, 'So you were one of the baby-killers?'[58] Nobody outside Ross Jack's immediate family even knew where he had been: 'Civilian friends thought I'd been away interstate and I let them continue to think that. I didn't say a word for twenty years.'[59]

Was the public's hostility in the soldiers' minds? Not a single anti-war protester has admitted that he or she attacked the soldiers. 'We were very conscious of not abusing the soldiers,' said Bob Gould, founder of the Vietnam Action Committee, a view shared by anti-war leaders.[60] 'I saw the soldiers as the meat in the sandwich and always placed the blame for the catastrophe squarely on the government which sent them there,' said Joan Coxsedge.[61]

Are we to conclude, then, that an anonymous Fifth Column leaped out of the crowds, abused the soldiers and melted away, never to be seen or heard from again? Perhaps silence is the only refuge open to them. If so, their silence condemns them: none has publicly recanted; none has apologised.

Nor did the government act to stop this abuse. To their undying disgrace the politicians of the day — both Liberal and Labor — did or said little to defend the soldiers, 40 per cent of whom were sent to Vietnam under the Liberal Coalition's national service legislation. Rallying to defend the troops in what had become a very unpopular war was hardly a vote-winner; so the politicians said little, and their silence scapegoated the troops. 'There was a fair bit of standing aside and letting the troops take the flak,' observed General Gration.[62] They 'switched the war off like a TV soap', said Lieutenant General Daly, later.[63] Indeed, not one politician said as then Prime Minister John Howard has said over Iraq, if you oppose the war, blame him; don't blame the soldiers.

Some soldiers did engage with the more callous or ignorant of their detractors, did break through even the most insensitive acts, as related in John Coe's book *Desperate Praise*. A wounded soldier, who had just left a repatriation hospital on crutches, encountered an aggressive female student in the street.

> '... did you fall over chasing after a Vietnamese woman whilst trying to rape her?' she said.
>
> The soldier stopped and thought, 'I have heard of this attitude, I've seen it from a distance, but here I am confronted with it.'
>
> She continued: 'You people and the Americans have plundered the innocent Vietnamese for many years now. Eventually the Vietnamese will gain victory over you despite your barbaric acts ...'
>
> The soldier interjected: 'You have first-hand experience of this situation?'
>
> 'No, I don't, and neither do you because you wouldn't have a bloody clue ...'
>
> The soldier paused, and thoughtfully replied that, despite 'your recently acquired knowledge ... you can't come to terms with any reality beyond your own'.
>
> 'Oh I see,' she shot back, 'the philosophical digger. Well, I suppose you should be a digger, a digger of graves, and I suppose you should be philosophical because you've obviously got a guilty conscience, which you should have.'
>
> 'Look, darling,' said the soldier, 'I think I am not philosophical, I'm just bitter. I'm very bitter about the fact that I'm not you.'

'What the hell are you talking about?' she asked.

'Well, I estimate your age to be roughly … mine, and I'm blue collar, I suppose. I suggest that you're highly motivated … you're going to become a white-collar or professional person and things are laid open to you as far as the future is concerned … You'll be making all the money shortly, upon graduation you'll have a job, a comfortable job …'

He concluded: '… some people are getting their arses shot off … if you're that concerned for humanity why don't you do something for them?' And he hobbled away on his crutches.[64]

# Part Eight
# **Endings**

# Chapter 43
# The North invades

Plei Ku *fini*, Kon Tum *fini*, Ban Me Thuot *fini*, Hué *fini*.
Everything *fini*.
*South Vietnamese Government official, March 1975.*

Gough Whitlam's visit, as Leader of the Opposition, to China — as yet unrecognised by Australia — in July 1971 was seen as especially insensitive at a time when two Australian battalions were fighting Chinese-supplied troops. Yet his Labor colleagues hailed the visit as a diplomatic 'coup'. No doubt the visit played well in Peking, where Prime Minister Chou En-lai, Mao's senior genuflector, basked in the public relations triumph of being seen merrily chatting with a political leader of America's closest ally in Vietnam. Whitlam told Chou that he believed all 'foreign troops' should be withdrawn from Vietnam, Korea and Czechoslovakia; he did not specify whether these should include Soviet and Chinese troops. He refused to be drawn into denouncing ANZUS; but his servile admission that the American people 'will destroy' Nixon if the President refused to pull out of Vietnam drew heavy censure at home. 'If Mr Whitlam thinks that this wholesale selling out of friends to gain a despot's smile is diplomacy, then Heaven protect this country if he ever directs its foreign policy,' thundered the *Sydney Morning Herald*.[1] Indeed, many Australians found Whitlam's actions repellent. Fraser branded Whitlam 'China's candidate'. The then Prime Minister McMahon accused the Labor leader, on 12 July, of being 'a spokesman for those against whom we are fighting'.

McMahon's remarks — if in sympathy with many feelings — were lazily imprecise. We were not, and never had been, at war with China. Days later, McMahon was also made to look embarrassingly out of touch when President Richard Nixon announced a spectacular diplomatic rapprochement with China. Neither McMahon nor Whitlam (as he pressed the Chinese flesh) was aware of Nixon's plan to visit Peking to seek 'peace in our time', which the President announced on 15 July 1971 — three days after McMahon had referred to China as 'our enemy'. America's favourite ally once again found itself well out of the loop. In public McMahon looked ridiculous; yet in private his government had, in fact, been making similar attempts to open a dialogue with Peking. Nixon's announcement inflicted the added, if unintended, wound of making the coincidence of Whitlam's China trip seem politically prescient — when in reality Washington had treated Australia as though it were just any non-aligned country.

Once in power, the Whitlam Cabinet salted, in small, symbolic ways, the death throes of Saigon. Within months of gaining office, on 2 December 1972, the Labor Prime Minister scrapped aid to South Vietnam and Cambodia, recognised the People's Republic of China and established diplomatic relations with Hanoi (on 26 February 1973). Labor enacted these measures with unseemly relish: it was as though the Republic of Vietnam had never existed — or had no right to exist, which is exactly what many on the left had always believed, or wished. Of what value, too, were the soldiers' sacrifices? wondered Second Lieutenant Gary McKay MC, as he lay in a military hospital bed in mid-1972, reading a newspaper that contained press photos of Dr Jim Cairns shaking hands with a North Vietnamese trade union leader on the steps of Sydney Town Hall. It had the effect of a kick in the guts. 'The soldier … really is just a pawn for the politicians,' he thought.[2]

The last few members of the Team in Vietnam witnessed the coming of the end. In April 1971 Captain Adrian Roberts (the cavalry commander at Long Tan during his first tour) and Warrant Officers Bill Noble and Graham Millington were instructing a South Vietnamese Armoured Brigade in Quang Tri province, which buffeted the demilitarised zone. The brigade included a tank squadron newly equipped with the monstrous M48 American tanks.

The Australians were under the command of US Lieutenant Colonel Abraham Muscari, one of those exhausting American polymaths who not only knew every inch of the M48 but also cooked Italian food and played the banjo, often during rocket attacks. Muscari and the US and Australian advisers soon confronted the first of many seemingly insuperable problems. The language barrier, bad enough on routine duties, seriously impeded the war effort during tank instruction. For one thing, the names of key tank parts, such as 'rangefinder', were untranslatable. Nor were the tanks familiar to the Australians. Muscari dealt with this by instructing the instructors. He showed Roberts and his men how to operate the tanks; the Australians then demonstrated this to the Vietnamese, who learned by imitation.

Other infuriating difficulties remained. The tanks were huge, and their tracks were much heavier than those of their predecessor, the M41. Changing the tracks proved exhausting for the slightly built Vietnamese. More ominously, the tanks arrived without vital spare parts, helmets, headsets, radios and tools. To make up the deficiency, Roberts and other instructors were reduced to scavenging in US Army rubbish dumps: huge mounds of American scrap and discarded machines destined for disposal. Somehow, they equipped the new Vietnamese tank squadron, but the Australian advisers did not complete the operators' training. In November 1971, to the 'barely concealed scorn of the Vietnamese', the Team was ordered to concentrate in Phuoc Tuy province, in readiness for departure to Australia.[3] Team members left the border zone, well aware that their former charges were now naked to the storm.

The question that deeply preoccupied the remaining Americans and Australians was: could South Vietnam save itself? Many South Vietnamese officers were well trained; the Ranger battalions were tough and decisive. And the southern army substantially outnumbered the North. Yet the Australian advisers feared for the ordinary troops, the Army of the Republic of Vietnam. 'My own opinion,' Captain Bernard McGurgan reported in 1970, 'is that if the [Vietnamese forces] are left to themselves, training will go by the wayside and they will return to their original ways ...'[4]

Dread signs of weakness showed in February 1971, when the South Vietnamese mounted their own massive attack on communist supply lines in southern Laos. Despite huge US air support, the offensive, called LAM SON 719, failed; the North Vietnamese surrounded and destroyed the southern incursion. The loss raised serious doubts about the republic's chances of survival. Yet the North also suffered grave losses: sixteen of its thirty-three battalions and at least seventy-five of 110 tanks were destroyed — mostly as a result of US air power.

The episode reflected the wider malaise in the South Vietnamese Army, whose morale fell drastically as foreign support ebbed away. This was sadly evident in the frantically cobbled together 3rd ARVN Division, raised to fill the void left by the departing Americans in Quang Tri. These wretched soldiers, scarcely trained, eyeballed three divisions of North Vietnamese then poised to cross the border. At the time, they were the first line of defence of South Vietnam.

Less reassuring were the Ruff Puffs — the Regional and Provincial (or Popular) Forces. Sloth and cowardice were endemic in many of their units. One RF Battalion, the 302 in Ba Ria, was fairly typical. The commander took long siestas after lunch, the intelligence officer was a layabout and philanderer, and other officers had little training or initiative, observed Warrant Officer Len Opie. In Dat Do, the PFs spent most of their time 'ambushing cafés', recalled Major Robert Musgrove.[5] Lieutenant Colonel John Sullivan, chief instructor at the short-lived Jungle Warfare Training Centre, witheringly dismissed his Vietnamese trainers as 'lazy, indisciplined to the degree of being insolent and arrogant'. The students displayed an 'abysmal lack of even the rudiments of military knowledge'.[6]

The South Vietnamese troops were, however, capable of extraordinary bursts of courage that amazed their dismissive advisers. On Long Son Island, for example, a Vietnamese patrol was caught in a three-way Viet Cong ambush. Their captain, Truong Hoang Dung, yelled 'Charge!' — an Australian-taught last resort — at which his men ran straight at the enemy, who fled in disorder. These were isolated cases; the Team saw few glimmers of hope.[7]

A less tangible sign of doom lay in the eyes of the ordinary people in the cities and the rice paddies. Civilian morale had started to buckle as the South Vietnamese economy shrank in tandem with the US pullout; Da Nang, Hué and other northern cities were battle-scarred and emptying, their shops looted and dilapidated. Runaway inflation hobbled the domestic economy, and theft at gunpoint became commonplace. Darkened warehouses on the banks of the Mekong ran a roaring black market in the detritus of war; swathes of South Vietnam resembled a US military rubbish dump.


Amid the portents of disaster for the South came a flicker of hope. On Good Friday, 31 March 1972, the North Vietnamese struck. Through the clouds of a huge rocket and artillery barrage 15,000 communist troops swept across the border. At first they prevailed. The hapless 3rd ARVN

Division fled in panic: officers and soldiers tore off their uniforms, threw away their weapons and commandeered civilian vehicles to escape with the lines of refugees.[8] The communist Easter Offensive overran the border provinces and penetrated deep into Kon Tum, Plei Ku and Tay Ninh. Viet Cong guerrillas in the delta simultaneously attacked more than a hundred outposts.

In a pattern echoed in many other provinces, the Easter Offensive swept through Phuoc Tuy; it was as if the Australians had never been there. They attacked with a 'strength and ferocity' that 'overcame all before it'. April 1972 'saw the highest level of enemy activity in Phuoc Tuy since the worst days of the Task Force' (in 1966).[9] At least 1,600 fresh troops entered the province and reinforced the 33rd NVA Regiment, the 274th and 275th Viet Cong Regiments and the D445 Battalion. 'They could have marched through the province with a band in front' and 'would not have been seen unless they went through one of the towns'. Within a month, the Saigon government seemed to have lost control of the countryside. '… it was for all the world to me,' Major Roberts said, 'as it had been in 1966 at the very beginning … as if we had never really been there.'[10] South Vietnamese troops made a brief, bloody stand at Binh Ba, then fell back to the larger towns.

In May, the Viet Cong engulfed the towns; cut off Xuyen Moc and Duc Thanh; occupied Dat Do and Hoa Long; blocked all major roads, including the vital Route 15 that linked Saigon to Vung Tau; menaced the provincial capital of Ba Ria, which was then packed with refugees; and mortared the Van Kiep training centre, where two Australians, one American and one New Zealander (Majors Geoff Carter and Bob Blair and Warrant Officers Graham Wease and Dave Morrison) were sitting down to large bowls of thick soup. When a mortar bomb exploded nearby, these veterans instinctively ducked, then resumed their lunch and chatted about their experiences of mortar attack. It transpired that Wease had been mortared in Korea ('I shed some blood there') and Morrison in Anzio.[11]

Then an extraordinary thing happened: the ARVN soldiers turned and retaliated. In one of the most confounding and exhilarating outcomes of the war, they stoically fought back and soundly repelled the first communist invasion. In Phuoc Tuy they held Ba Ria, and within weeks Ranger units recaptured the smaller towns. At Hué Muscari's tank squadron turned their M48s on the North Vietnamese waves, and helped to stop the invader's southern thrust. Better news came in from I Corps, near Da Nang, where the senior Australian adviser reported that South Vietnamese units were defeating the communists in every engagement. The ARVN showed themselves willing to fight with astonishing fortitude, backed by millions of People's Self-Defence Forces, the village paramilitaries loyal to Saigon.

The communist Easter Offensive collapsed. 'So severely were the invading forces punished that it was three years before they could mount another major offensive.'[12] Phuoc Tuy was typical of the rest of the country: '... the South Vietnamese Army was able to hold on to every one of the forty-four provincial capitals except Quang Tri, which it regained a few months later,' wrote a recent American history.[13] 'In terms of fighting spirit,' said Dr Tien Nguyen, now an Australian citizen who fought with a Ranger battalion, 'we had an edge over the enemy, we had a stronger spirit and that showed during the 1972 taking back of Phuoc Tuy.'[14] The South Vietnamese successes were, however, critically reliant on US air support, a rapidly disappearing resource. Without it, the South was extremely vulnerable and the promises of 'Vietnamisation' illusory.

In Saigon, fearing for the lives of Australia's civilian embassy staff, the then Ambassador, Arthur Morris, had considered activating OPERATION TANAGRA, code for the evacuation of all Australian personnel from South Vietnam. In the calm that followed the victory it proved unnecessary. A mood of limbo characterised the remainder of 1972; few discerned the face of the coming storm through the euphoric blur of the Paris peace talks.

After crushing the Easter Offensive, many southerners prayed for a settlement. In November 1972 murmurs of a breakthrough in Paris animated Saigon and put a brief stay on hostilities. Yet the proposed treaty — which Kissinger had secretly negotiated with Hanoi, at the exclusion of Saigon — amounted to a death sentence for South Vietnam.[15] Kissinger had accepted Hanoi's key demand that all foreign troops be removed from South Vietnam *without* a concomitant obligation on North Vietnamese forces to withdraw, too. Under the deal — hitherto kept secret from South Vietnam — the present troop dispositions, North and South, would remain ... leaving a dagger at the throat of Saigon. In exchange, Hanoi would agree to return all US prisoners and vow not to renew hostilities. When he learned of the proposed settlement, an enraged President Thieu rejected the deal, and only Nixon's promise to intervene if Hanoi broke the terms persuaded the South Vietnamese leader to reconsider.

'You have my absolute assurance,' Nixon wrote to Thieu, 'that if Hanoi fails to abide by the terms of the agreement, it is my intention to take swift and retaliatory action.' Yet the White House failed to inform Congress of the promise; Nixon had vowed unilaterally to rescue South Vietnam without proper recourse to the American taxpayer. Thieu added the letter to thirty others he had received from Washington in the past four years, pledging to defend the South if Hanoi attacked.[16]

In mid-December 1972 the peace talks seized up, on 'technical issues'. The breakdown enraged Kissinger. Le Duc Tho, the chief North Vietnamese negotiator — a man of gimlet-eyed inscrutability — had absented himself from the talks, prompting American suspicions that Hanoi was buying time in order to strike further into South Vietnam, entrenching its military advantage at the ceasefire. It was also a political ploy to ratchet up Western opposition to the war. 'The longer they can hold things up, the more and more dissent will there be in the United States,' Sir Robert Menzies had said in November 1969. 'The whole will to win will be weakened in the United States, and subsequently in Australia. And therefore Hanoi knows that this is a tactical victory. It makes me ill!'[17]

In response, Nixon deployed his 'Madman Theory', in which the President 'wanted the North Vietnamese to believe ... I might do anything to stop the war'.[18] The 'madman' was not merely theoretical. When Hanoi failed to respond to a 72-hour deadline for the resumption of talks, Nixon ordered the 'Christmas bombing' of North Vietnam, and a wave of B52s struck military installations in Hanoi and Haiphong. Hanoi hailed the ensuing 'Dien Bien Phu of the air' as a victory, which 'shattered the US illusion of negotiating from a position of strength, and pushed them into a position of total failure'.[19] On the contrary, after eleven days of incessant American pounding (18–29 December, with a day off for Christmas) — during which US aircraft dropped about 28,000 tons of bombs on North Vietnam, more than in the past three years of war — communist resolve melted, and Le Duc Tho, under pressure from China, agreed to resume negotiations. A faint tic of anxiety disturbed his hitherto implacable features on his return to the negotiating table.

World opinion, and Whitlam's Cabinet, accused Nixon of mass murder, mindless brutality and the indiscriminate slaughter of innocents (the Swedes compared the President with Hitler). All the evidence suggests that civilian casualties were, in fact, limited: the strikes were concentrated on military bases and oil depots, and bore no comparison with the planned slaughter of tens of thousands of innocents at Dresden and Tokyo, and in British cities during the Blitz. Hanoi put the civilian casualties at 1,600, suggesting that the true figure was far fewer and nowhere near the West's apocalyptic upper estimates.

Outrage at the bombing prompted Whitlam's first cable to Nixon, in which the Prime Minister mildly reproved the President and warned that Australia intended to rally Asian governments to press the US to resume negotiations with Hanoi. The President did not bother to reply: such were the bitter fruits of a decade of going to war with the White House. Meanwhile, Australian waterside unions refused to unload US ships; American unions retaliated in kind against Australian ships. In the face of US economic reprisals, Whitlam was forced to rein in his diplomatic offensive. He urged his colleagues henceforth to use 'discreet and restrained' language towards America, not words like 'atrocious' and 'barbarous'.[20]

Nixon and Kissinger overturned the South's reluctance to sign the peace treaty with a threat: unless Saigon signed, America would pursue separate peace talks with Hanoi, at the exclusion of the South (which in any case had already been happening). Thieu gave in. The President of the Republic of Vietnam placed his Buddhist–Confucian trust in the Judaeo–Christian honour of the Americans. It was his only hope. 'The Paris agreement is only a piece of paper,' Kissinger assured him. 'What counts is the power of the American President to back it up. If you sign the agreement, you have the power of the American President behind you.' On 27 January 1973 the two Vietnams, the USA and the Provisional Revolutionary Government of the South (the parallel government of the National Liberation Front) signed the ceasefire.

The next day the wail of air raid sirens over Saigon signalled the end of hostilities. 'I stood on the roof of the Duc Hotel and toasted the new era with a Bloody Mary,' said Frank Snepp, a CIA analyst in Saigon.[21]

Australia was among the first Western nations to befriend Hanoi. In January Australian passports were validated for travel in North Vietnam; on 26 February, after preliminary soundings by Alan Renouf, ambassador to France, Canberra recognised the Hanoi regime and agreed to diplomatic relations. Whitlam insisted that the new relationship did not alter Australia's relations with Saigon; still, Labor hardliners demanded that Australia also recognise the revolutionary government of the National Liberation Front.

Sensing the political fallout of too hastily befriending those who, a little over a year earlier, had been attacking Australian soldiers, Whitlam decided instead to offer the Viet Cong an 'information office' in Australia.

Nixon hailed the ceasefire as 'peace with honour'. Yet there was no peace and less honour (as Le Duc Tho acknowledged, by refusing to share the Nobel Peace Prize with Kissinger). Indeed, neither Hanoi nor Saigon had any intention of abiding by the terms of Kissinger's worthless scrap of paper; the President merely hoped it might buy time — a 'decent interval' — to distance his administration from the coming debacle. Within weeks, Hanoi resumed the suffocation of the South, and Saigon, urged on by Kissinger, made a desperate land grab for the countryside.

Meanwhile, with Soviet and Chinese help, Hanoi set about rebuilding the North's military installations. It worked at an astonishing rate, spurred on by a restless spirit of questing vengeance. It would stop at nothing to reclaim the South, and planned to do so on a scale hitherto unimaginable to foreign observers. Of course, this last, open phase of the revolutionary war had been in the minds of the communist leaders since 1954. Having defeated the Americans and their foreign mercenaries, according to the communist script, Hanoi would now fulfil the final act of this bloody symphony: the overthrow of Saigon and its 'ruling class' in open invasion. Kissinger's Paris deal thus handed Hanoi the card it needed: the right of thirteen North Vietnamese divisions — 160,000 troops — to stay in their posts in South Vietnam, without fear of US air power. As a precaution, on the eve of the ceasefire, the communists hid their weapons: tank regiments buried their tanks near city centres. One northern tank commander told me, 'We were fighting to the last minute before 1 February 1973; then we hid our tanks under the sand, and put trees over the tanks.'[22]

Hanoi used the next two years constructively. It rebuilt its forces, roads and supply lines — most importantly, an oil pipeline down the Ho Chi Minh Trail (first laid in 1972). It did so with the full assistance of the Chinese and Soviet dictatorships, to which the inconveniences of Western democracy did not apply. Mao and Brezhnev were not accountable to taxpayers, Parliament or Congress or the court of public opinion; they scorned such institutional expressions of civilisation as marks of Western weakness. Their desire to humiliate America and plant a Red foothold in South-East Asia — and not any real friendship with Hanoi — drove their continued support, and they competed fiercely for influence over the North Vietnamese Politburo.

By 14 March tens of thousands of North Vietnamese reinforcements and Soviet and Chinese communist weapons were flowing south, in broad daylight, in utter breach of the Paris Peace Treaty, 'so brazenly' that there were 'traffic jams along the Ho Chi Minh Trail'.[23] Between January and September 1973, 140,000 tons of supplies travelled south — four times more than 1972 — including 80,000 tons of military supplies. Between January 1974 and April 1975 Hanoi sent US$2.6 billion worth of military supplies down the Ho Chi Minh Trail, more than the previous eleven years combined (1963–74). Free of US air strikes, the communists could invade with impunity. 'We cease and they fire,' said Nixon aptly of the 'ceasefire'.[24]

As this enormous war machine manoeuvred into place, Washington destroyed Thieu's trust. The Democrat-controlled Congress severed South Vietnam's lifeline. First it repealed the Tonkin Gulf Resolution, which had taken the USA to war in Vietnam in 1964, then it cut the cash flow to Saigon: '… on or after August 15, 1973,' read the key part of the legislation, 'no funds herein … appropriated may be obligated or expended to finance directly or indirectly combat activities by United States military forces in or over/of/from/off the shores of North Vietnam, South Vietnam, Laos or Cambodia.'[25] Nixon was helpless to fulfil his personal promise to Thieu. The South Vietnamese President hung his head and wept; and within a year Nixon, embroiled in Watergate, had been impeached and ejected from office.

In Australia and America, Vietnam faded from the public mind, the press lost interest, and the protesters dispersed and pursued careers. Few showed much concern for the plight of the South Vietnamese, 80,000 of whom — soldiers and civilians — were killed in 1973. In fact, the first year of the ceasefire was the bloodiest of the war, 'the most murderous truce this century'.

The year 1974 ushered in twelve months of grey consolidation … the twilight before the coming conflagration. The OPEC oil crisis drained Western petrol supplies to South Vietnam while soaring inflation cut Saigon's purchasing power by 80 per cent. North Vietnam was relatively unaffected, as it drew on the Soviet Union's huge protected oil reserves. Nor would the South receive any further charity from America: wealthy Vietnamese diverted the remaining USAID into overseas bank accounts and foreign university places for their children.[26] Four-year law degrees at US universities were popular ways of avoiding conscription and getting troublesome students out of the country. 'The government hopes by this device,' said the last Australian adviser in Saigon, Brigadier Ted Serong, 'to keep the potentially explosive students quiescent … [It] cannot last much longer.'[27]

Hanoi calculated how long the South's dwindling military supplies would last, and let the slow bleed of time do the rest. By the end of 1974 the South Vietnamese armed forces received an arms 'ration' of 1.6 rifle rounds per day per man (compared with 13 for the US Forces when in Vietnam); machine guns 10.6 rounds (versus 165); mortars 1.3 rounds (16.9); and 105mm howitzer shells per gun 6.4 (36.5).[28] Stories of the Ruff Puffs buying grenades with their pocket money were true, remarked Colonel Hoang Ngoc Lung, a senior ARVN intelligence officer, who had fled the North in 1954.[29]

By the end of 1974, the tables had turned. Like an overripe banyan tree, North Vietnam groaned under the weight of its riches in men, materiel and food supplies. The main roads south were open, the waterways negotiable and the arsenals stacked with new weapons. In 1973–74, 150,000 North Vietnamese youths — their mothers' contribution to the war effort — joined the military, and 63,000 insurgents had entered South Vietnam in the six months to March 1975, double the number in the corresponding period in 1973–74. Many were enthusiastic teenagers, easy prey to the propaganda and promises of their elderly comrades who contemplated with equanimity the sacrifice of a generation of children to fulfil the sacred testament of Uncle Ho.

Hanoi launched the conventional invasion of South Vietnam — conceived by Ho and Giap almost twenty years earlier — in the first week of March 1975. The 'Third Indochina War', as some call it,[30] involved twenty North Vietnamese divisions. They spread over the countryside like an oil slick: three converged on Ban Me Thuot, the strategically vital Montagnard capital where Barry Petersen had raised a battalion in 1963; others went straight down the centre towards Kon Tum.

Brigadier Ted Serong reappeared at this stage of the war, in a ghostly cameo as adviser to the Saigon Government. In contemplating the evacuation of the Southern Highlands, Thieu consulted 'his astrologer and a mysterious Australian named Ted Serong'.[31] Serong urged Thieu to evacuate the northern provinces, where two-thirds of the southern troops were stationed. Thieu initially rejected the Australian's advice, as he could not tolerate the loss of Hué. Events soon compelled the President to do as Serong urged. First came the loss of Ban Me Thuot, which laid bare the eastward corridor to the city. The battle 'was over by 10.30 on 11 March', noted General Van Tien Dung, Hanoi's commander in the vanguard. Its collapse forced Thieu to order the evacuation of the highlands. Then came the far heavier blow to southern morale: the swift abandonment of the provinces of Plei Ku and Kon Tum as Hanoi's forces concentrated on the centre. Thieu's withdrawal slogan, 'Light at the top, heavy at the bottom', was thus forced upon him — and not, as he liked to think, a plan. In his unrivalled account of the invasion, Frank Snepp described the atmosphere in Thieu's Cabinet at the time of his decision to surrender the northern provinces:

> Thieu sat for a moment, fingers templed, chin resting on them …
> He looked around the table, searching the faces for an answer.
> There was none. They were all the perfect courtesans, all
> deferring to him. He fumbled in his pockets, cleared his throat,
> then gave the decision, almost in a whisper, a turning point in the
> history of the war. Kon Tum and Plei Ku would have to be
> abandoned, he said. The strategic withdrawals, 'Light at the top,
> heavy at the bottom', would begin there. The room went dead
> silent … Thieu ordered them to keep their silence. Tell no one of
> the plan, he said, not even the Americans. They had had their
> chance to help, and had failed him.[32]

The reality on the ground of 'light at the top' was the chaotic southerly exodus of hundreds of thousands of soldiers and civilians, 'rivers of struggling, panic-stricken humanity', strung out along the national highways. Highway 14 from Kon Tum buckled under the long columns of heavy armour which nosed through the civilian jam of jeeps and jalopies, leaving them bogged in a ribbon of mud.

The North Vietnamese Army moved swiftly to close the escape routes, forcing this human tide to the coast. Nearly 150,000 citizens of Quang Tri City staggered and limped towards Hué, which was soon cut off and shelled. On 25 March the ancient capital fell to the communists, for the second and last time, and the flag of the Provisional Revolutionary Government flew once more over the doomed citadel. By the end of March, the People's

Army had overrun most of the northern provinces and pressed as far south as Tay Ninh, within artillery range of the Iron Triangle, the figurative gates of Saigon. 'Plei Ku *fini*, Kon Tum *fini*, Ban Me Thuot *fini*, Hué *fini*. Everything *fini*,' said a South Vietnamese official.[33]

The death of Da Nang was especially sad: 35,000 North Vietnamese troops converged on the coastal city swollen with half a million civilian stragglers fraught with premonitions of a massacre. The invaders stayed their hand, letting 'the worm of fear and anticipation do its worst'.[34] The ARVN commander in Da Nang abandoned his men; other officers shed their uniforms and fled. On 30 March, thirty-two hours after Hanoi's troops had encircled the city, about a hundred thousand leaderless South Vietnamese soldiers surrendered.

The terrified civilians scrambled for a seaward escape route. On the waterfront, thousands crowded aboard barges, tugs … any vessel they could find. One CIA agent witnessed the horror on the decks of an American cargo vessel, *Pioneer Contender*, where 1,500 South Vietnamese troops 'sprawled, lounging, fighting among themselves … and practicing their aim at the hapless Vietnamese civilians in their midst'. To one side an 'ARVN trooper was in the process of raping a Vietnamese woman', while thirty-five American evacuees stood 'cringing by the gangway'.[35] Later 7,000 people crammed on to this death ship, and at least a thousand fell or were pushed overboard as the soldiers fought up the gangplank. Hundreds drowned or were crushed between the *Contender* and the barges buffeting its hull. Meanwhile, at the Marble Mountain airstrip, South Vietnamese troops menaced the remaining Americans and climbed at gunpoint onto the last flights out; hundreds chased the last plane down the runway, 'grabbing at its wings and fuselage'. Civilians and their pathetic bundles were left standing on the tarmac.

After midnight on the 28th the shelling of Da Nang began. The first three rounds hit the city; the fourth landed on a barge, killing everyone on board. The ships drew away as the North Vietnamese destroyed the airfield and sealed the city's fate. Later, a CIA man aboard the *Oseola* looked down from the ship's watchtower on the decks of distant barges, where the 'standing dead' were wedged upright among thousands of living passengers. On abandoned vessels the sticks 'poking up from the mounds of clothing, suitcases and steaming waste were … human limbs'.[36]

Millions converged on Saigon. Thousands of survivors of the evacuation of Da Nang and other northern cities sat in and around Tan Son Nhut airport in Saigon, 'motionless and silent on the hard cement floor, elbows propped on suitcases, their eyes staring wide and unblinking in amazed shock'.[37] Day and night, the great lines of walking evacuees flowed into the besieged city. Meanwhile, Ted Serong waited and watched; his family had gone home. The last Australian military adviser in Vietnam was determined to witness, alone, the destruction of the project to which he had devoted his career.

# Chapter 44
# The fall of Saigon

We were told to stop all South Vietnamese people previously
employed by the Australian Embassy from getting on the aircraft.
*Mick Sheean, Australian airfield defence guard, April 1975.*

South Vietnam simply ran out of bullets, Ted Serong said later. 'The
General,' as Serong was known in the court of Thieu, struck some as a
charlatan; yet they overlooked another Serong hidden beneath the folds of
his many guises: a steadfast friend and a man who genuinely grieved the loss
of his adopted country.[1] At a seminar to the Rand Corporation in 1970,
Serong offered a glimpse of this quality. 'You're the higher of two alpine
climbers,' he said, 'attached to the same rope; the lower climber depends on
you.' Suddenly the rock face crumbles under your combined weight, 'and
you realise you can only survive if you cut the rope'. The question, Serong
asked, is when do you cut the rope? 'You don't,' he told his audience, 'you
both fall together.' The Rand lesson said a lot about why, in 1975, Serong
agreed to serve Thieu's new Defence Minister on condition that 'your first
order is to ban ... helicopters as command posts. Put the damn generals on
the ground to die with the troops.'[2]

If Serong lent a faintly Mephisphelean voice in Thieu's ear, he
performed a Virgilian role on the ground, guiding people to safety, helping
the evacuation ... descending into the last circle of the past fifteen years. He
stayed on, a soldier 'defeated in all his initiatives', working not to win battles
any more but to give the South Vietnamese a fighting chance to save their

lives.[3] He witnessed the collapse, 'on foot, gathering information, arranging documentation for escapes in the last days; on foot, checking a road for ambushes; demonstrating the proper use of a weapon in a dumb show; inspecting the site of a battle'.[4]

Serong saw what was happening: the implosion of morale, the collapse of supply lines … a nation in despair. 'The whole month of April 1975 was horrible, horrible,' said Dr Tien Nguyen, who served with a Ranger battalion. 'Morale went right down. Everything was cut off, everything was down. We didn't have enough ammunition; we had no artillery or air support … As a doctor it was terrible because there wasn't much you could do. You had no evacuation, no helicopters, and the communists had blocked all the roads. Our friends at the air force said, "Sorry, mate, no petrol, no fuel, can't help you."'[5]

On 29 March 1975 Flying Officer Geoff Rose, a Hercules co-pilot with No. 37 Squadron, was settling into routine operations after the exhausting relief of Darwin, devastated by Cyclone Tracy the previous Christmas. He and his wife were expecting visitors over the Easter long weekend 'when there was a knock'. It was the squadron navigator, Peter Gerstle. 'Can't tell you where, Geoff,' he said, 'but pack your bags … and come to the squadron — ASAP!'[6]

Rose had been chosen for 'Detachment S', an RAAF humanitarian mission sent at the request of the Saigon government to assist the American evacuation of thousands of refugees. The detachment, consisting of seven Hercules, departed Richmond that day, led by then Wing Commander (now Air Commodore) John Mitchell.

On the 31st, Mitchell briefed his airmen at Butterworth airbase in Malaysia. Da Nang had fallen to the communists, he said; Nha Trang and Cam Rhan Bay were probably next. The detachment's final destination awaited Canberra's decision, but the Prime Minister happened to be on the Gold Coast and unreachable. A day passed; Nha Trang and Cam Ranh Bay fell to communist control. On 2 April the RAAF got the nod to fly to Phan Rang. They descended into a state of chaos: thousands were trying to flee the North Vietnamese steamroller. 'The RAAF personnel couldn't control or identify the people desperately trying to clamber aboard,' Rose recalled. On one occasion, a 'refugee' left his AK47 rifle behind on one of the aircraft. The next day Phan Rang fell, and all Australian aircraft were recalled to Saigon.

The first evacuees were hundreds of orphans, the unwanted products of foreign soldiers and Vietnamese mothers, who would sell their babies for as little as US$10 on the black market, 'much as cattle', reported the ABC's Neil Davis.[7] The young Adelaide social worker Rosemary Taylor spent eight years in Vietnam caring for these unwanted infants. At great personal risk she rescued hundreds of babies from the streets and countryside, and picked some infants out of rubbish dumps where their terrified mothers had abandoned them. In April 1975 Taylor's orphanage in Saigon contained 600 children — some of whom had been evicted from orphanages overrun by the North Vietnamese. 'If we feel the obligation,' Taylor, a former nun, said in February that year, 'to send our men to fight and die, to protect some barely understood cause in a foreign country, surely it is natural to feel the same obligation to help clear up the debris caused by the fighting — in this case to care for the child victims of the war.'[8] Alas, the Australian Government, by its actions, disagreed.

The American-led OPERATION BABY-LIFT, an international effort to help these 'children of the dust' — the 'non-people' of Vietnam — began with a tragedy. On 4 April the American crew of a C5A Galaxy, at the time the world's largest transport plane, loaded 200 Eurasian and Amerasian orphans aboard the first baby-lift flight. Moments after take-off hatch trouble forced the plane back to Saigon. On its approach to the airstrip an explosion blew off the bottom ramp. The sudden decompression sucked dozens of children out of the hole, and the plane crashed in a rice paddy. Two hundred died, including 143 children, as well as the volunteer aid workers Margaret Moses and Lee Mack, who became the last Australians killed in the Vietnam War. 'We could see a huge pall of smoke rising in the northern distance,' said Geoff Rose. 'Nobody knew the cause of this disaster, but all speculated that the Galaxy must have been either shot down or sabotaged.'[9]

Rose co-piloted the next flight of war orphans with Flight Lieutenant John Stone. They were mostly abandoned babies: '... a pathetic sight to see so many tiny, helpless babies and young children crammed into the back of our aircraft. The smallest babies were simply placed in cardboard boxes, their only form of security.' As the plane ascended through the darkening sky 'there was none of the usual banter between crew members'. At 10,000 feet the crew exhaled 'a collective sigh of relief'. Only two Australian planeloads of children left Saigon that day; two further RAAF BABY-LIFT flights flew out on 17 April, evacuating another seventy-seven children.[10]

Yet Canberra cancelled further flights to avoid incurring the wrath of Hanoi. A cable from Australia's new consulate in the city warned: 'AFTER SPEAKING OF THEIR HIGH REGARD FOR MR WHITLAM, HUY [THE NORTH VIETNAMESE FOREIGN MINISTER] SAID THAT THEY TOO WISHED FOR GOOD RELATIONS WITH AUSTRALIA, BUT OUR RECENT SELFISHNESS HAD NOT HELPED: "OBVIOUSLY ... TAKING ORPHANS AWAY FROM VIETNAM WAS NOT HUMANITARIAN BUT PART OF AN AMERICAN PLOT."'[11]

The RAAF's Detachment S stayed in Saigon until the last week of April. Its main jobs were to fly aid to the huge refugee centre on Phu Quoc Island and to help pack up the Australian Embassy. The airmen witnessed the final blow descend on the stricken city.

In April, Saigon fell into pure panic. There were daily explosions, endless rumours of enemy atrocities: '... much talk of the imminent, final onslaught — and the final bloodbath,' said Rose. Every day, the queues outside the airport terminal grew longer and more desperate: '... as we struggled to make our way through, frantic people would grab at us with desperate pleas and offers.'[12]

Rose was awoken at dawn on 8 April by the sound of a jet fighter screaming out of the mist towards downtown Saigon. Seconds later, he heard an explosion: a South Vietnamese defector had bombed the Presidential Palace. The shells smashed through the ceiling but did not harm President Thieu.[13]

The 9.00 p.m. curfew was more strictly imposed and emptied the streets of Saigon. After their nightly debriefings members of Detachment S repaired to the rooftop of the Embassy Hotel to watch the artillery flashes on the horizon and the prowling C119 Black Shadows that droned around the outskirts, dropping parachute flares and strafing new ground targets. 'Tracers flashed from air to ground — and ground to air,' Rose recalled.[14]

On the night of 14 April a huge explosion shook Rose's hotel. He dressed and ran up to the rooftop, 'to see a giant fireball rising, and flames lighting up the north-eastern sky'. North Vietnamese artillery had struck Bien Hoa's ammunition storage depot, 30 kilometres north of Saigon, rendering the vital airfield virtually inoperable.

The mood so deteriorated that Group Captain Lyall Klaffer, attached to the embassy to oversee RAAF activities, relocated the entire detachment to the safety of Bangkok. The shuttle flights to Phu Quoc Island continued.

The end was nearer than anyone knew. In early April a CIA field agent had sent an update on communist plans: Hanoi had issued a new 'resolution', he said. It demanded the 'liberation' of all territory north of

Saigon and warned of an attack on the capital on an unspecified date 'with no allowance whatsoever for a negotiated settlement'.[15] On 15 April in Washington, Lieutenant General Weyand warned the Senate Appropriations Committee that Saigon faced collapse within a month without further financial support; 200,000 Vietnamese might die if Saigon fell, argued Secretary of Defense James Schlesinger. Congress was unmoved; no further US aid would be forthcoming.

In Saigon, the machinery of diplomacy ticked over in a world of its own. US Ambassador Graham Martin was an old soldier of the Cold War generation. He admired Serong, whom he had described as 'a brilliant retired army officer of another country'. Serong thought rather less of Martin, but stayed closely in touch and witnessed the ambassador's last days in the city.

By April, a severe bout of procrastination had seized Martin, whose actions manifested a state of 'deliberate unpreparedness'. Even at this stage, Martin persuaded himself that a negotiated settlement was possible. The man was 'a culmination of the megalomania that has marked all US ambassadors in Saigon', remarked one colleague; 'a kind of conjuror and Madison Avenue pitchman' and 'a perfect extension of the Nixon White House'. As Saigon fell around him, Martin cast himself as the last hope for civilisation in a barbarian world, the fading light of the American dream in a delusional, self-directed melodrama that bore no relation to the reality — thus Snepp bitterly portrays him. Martin's devoted subordinates saw him differently, as a steadfast and devoted public servant. His minions 'were mere extensions of himself', Snepp acidly observed.[16] As such, they affected the patrician ease of their boss and failed to rise to the calamitous events around them. Whatever happened, nobody dared panic.

On the fringes of the city, the North Vietnamese forces massed for the final assault. Le Duan instructed his frontline commanders to 'execute the general offensive in the shortest time ... ending in April 1975 ... [act like] lightning, reckless and unexpected'.[17] Hanoi's political elders hoped to celebrate Ho Chi Minh's birthday (19 May) in Saigon.

On 20 April, after twelve days of ferocious fighting, the last brave stand of the crack 18th ARVN Division ended with the communist capture of Xuan Loc, in Long Khanh province, which abutted Phuoc Tuy,

50 kilometres north-east of Saigon. The gatehouse to the city had fallen. On 20–21 April the People's Army pressed down from the north-west, where it relieved the exhausted moles in the labyrinth at Cu Chi; from the south-east they overran Ham Tan district and joined local units in Phuoc Tuy.

On the night of the 21st, in a tearful two-hour television address, President Thieu resigned. 'If the Americans do not want to support us any more, let them go, get out! Let them forget their humanitarian promises!' he said.[18] He handed power to the arthritic, near-blind 71-year-old Tran Van Huong, who pledged to hold on until 'the troops are dead or the country is lost'. Huong's caretaker role lasted a few days, during which he tried to open 'peace' negotiations with the North Vietnamese. His own generals would have none of it; in reply to the loss of Xuan Loc they dropped their last CBU55 cluster bomb directly on the 341th NVA Division's headquarters: 250 died instantly in the suffocating firestorm. Elsewhere, on Nixon's nod, American aircraft secretly rejoined the war, dropping 15,000-pound daisy cutters on enemy units near Xuan Loc. If such pointless carnage eased the humiliation of defeat, it certainly fortified communist resolve: the shelling of Bien Hoa soon obliterated the vestiges of the airbase. Meanwhile, tank commander Quang Tan studied his maps of downtown Saigon; Tan's 203rd Armoured Brigade had been anointed the honour of 'liberating' the city, with the special task of capturing the Presidential Palace.

In the last week of April, about eighteen divisions of the People's Army stood on the threshold of Saigon. The vanguard jostled for the order to strike.


The evacuation of Saigon started with a stampede and ended in tragedy. The Vietnamese feared a bloodbath; ghastly rumours had circulated for weeks. Stories of communist torture left some hysterical with fear. Teenage girls imagined the enemy would tear off their fingernails, punishment for using nail polish, a very bourgeois activity; mothers of children by foreign soldiers dreaded the slaughter of their caramel offspring; Catholics who had fled the North in 1954 were particularly afraid of 'special treatment'. The bloodbath stories were part-US propaganda and part sincerely believed; people naturally dwelt on the precedents of Hué and Da Nang.

On 18 April the first CIA 'black flights' secretly lifted Vietnamese women and children to Phu Quoc Island. The regular airlift began two days later. 'Non-essential' US Embassy staff were flown out. One by one the foreign offices closed. The British and Canadians packed up and flew out. The safari-suited British Ambassador glided to the airport in a silver Jaguar and promptly abandoned his Vietnamese staff to the idea of communist mercy. Most embassies similarly left their native employees, although aid agencies and several US multinationals made creditable efforts to evacuate Vietnamese staff.

Conscious of this being 'their' war, the American, French and Australian embassies stayed longer: Ambassadors Martin, Merillon and Price insisted on playing the end game. To the last week, Martin believed in the possibility of a political solution, thus sealing the fate of thousands who might otherwise have been rescued, had the ambassador 'panicked'.

At 9.30 p.m., 25 April 1975, a convoy of CIA limousines with their headlights off screeched to a halt on the tarmac at Tan Son Nhut, 'like paddy wagons in a *Keystone Cops* chase scene'.[19] Ex-President Thieu stepped out, thanked his driver and boarded a US aircraft. Martin farewelled him at the stairs with a simple 'Goodbye'. Thieu flew to Taiwan, then to America, to live on his offshore millions; he would never return. The next day the caretaker President Huong agreed under pressure to hand over the presidency to General Duong Van Minh — dubbed 'Big Minh' — with whom the Provisional Revolutionary Government, the Viet Cong's 'government in waiting', had said it might negotiate. Martin believed the ruse, designed to lull the South into a false sense of security. In fact, Minh's accession had no effect whatsoever on what had always been a fait accompli: the days of bluff were long gone; the People's Army was now exerting 'military pressure for *military* reasons', as Snepp bleakly concluded.[20]


Four RAAF airfield defence guards — Mick Sheean, Trevor Nye, John Hansen and Ian Dainer — had flown to Saigon as part of Detachment S with strict orders to protect the embassy and staff; protect Australian vehicles travelling to and from the airport; search all personnel before boarding; prevent 'unauthorised people' boarding any RAAF aircraft; and act as Ambassador Geoffrey Price's bodyguards. They were each armed with a pistol.

In mid-April, at the Australian Embassy, which was on the third floor of the Caravelle, the airmen assisted the staff in frantically packing. 'There was a lot of confusion and panic,' recalled Sheean. 'They were worried about being stuck in Vietnam.' In their midst stood the ambassador, a bearded, worried diplomat who acted directly on instructions from Prime Minister

Whitlam in Canberra. 'Any telexes we received were quickly read by the ambassador and immediately destroyed,' Sheean recalled.[21]

Each day, the RAAF guards escorted embassy vehicles between the Caravelle and Tan Son Nhut airport, through thousands of South Vietnamese people desperate to escape; many promised money, gifts or sex in return for freedom. A Vietnamese businessman offered Sheean US$20,000 to marry his daughter, an offer Ambassador Price encouraged. The marriage could be annulled in Australia within a week, Price suggested. Sheean declined.[22]

As they loaded up the Hercs, heavily armed South Vietnamese soldiers often threatened the airmen unless they received a safe passage. One night, two soldiers broke into Sheean's hotel room, forced him against a wall and held a gun to his head. One shouted, 'We not go, you not go', and pulled the trigger on an empty chamber. They burst out laughing and left.[23]

The embassy staff were scheduled to leave Saigon on Anzac Day, 25 April 1975. Sheean, Nye and others were tasked with shredding the last sensitive documents, which included cables from Australia's new consular office in Hanoi. 'We shredded and shredded and shredded,' Nye recalls.

Some cables proved extremely sensitive. In March and early April, Whitlam cabled his ambassadors in Hanoi and Saigon with instructions to press the leaders of the two Vietnams to seek an armistice. A distinctly warmer message went to Hanoi, to whom Whitlam promised friendship and long-term aid for post-war reconstruction, and stated that he 'understood' (but 'could not condone') the Politburo's recourse to military action to defeat 'Saigon's intransigence'. Whitlam's missive to Saigon, which never arrived, merely urged Thieu to negotiate and begin the process of reunification.

The substance of the cables, marked 'Confidential', was leaked to the press the day before Saigon fell. In this context, Whitlam's appeal to Hanoi seemed 'unforgivably callous'.[24] In fact, the *Sydney Morning Herald*, in a full-length editorial on 30 April, virtually accused the Whitlam Government of treason in 'the gravest political scandal since Federation': 'A Government which cannot be trusted, which abuses its power and command of secrecy, forfeits its right to govern. It should be brought down.'[25] One restless backbencher certainly agreed: Malcolm Fraser believed Labor had forfeited its moral right to govern and this intensified his desire to bring down the Whitlam Government.

At 6 p.m. on 25 April, Australian Ambassador Price and his entourage drove to Tan Son Nhut for the last time. Price had tried and failed to obtain visas for his fifty-five Vietnamese staff; Whitlam, the supposed champion of multiculturalism, had blocked his visa requests until it was too late. Indeed, Whitlam had no intention of helping Australia's former allies in South Vietnam; in a handwritten note he branded their leaders 'war criminals'. Ever obeisant to the will of Hanoi, Whitlam's office cabled Australia's embassy in Saigon shortly before the fall: 'Locally engaged Embassy staff are not to be regarded as endangered by their Australian Embassy associations and therefore should not, repeat not, be granted entry to Australia.'[26] Price's last signal to Canberra ended with the fittingly banal: '... all I need say now is thank you for all your support and close up the shop. Goodbye from Saigon.'[27]

Meanwhile, North Vietnamese tanks were on the outskirts of the city and the standard of the People's Army 6 kilometres away. 'It was just chaos,' said Trevor Nye. 'There were masses of people running everywhere, like you'd see in one of these terror movies.'[28] South Vietnamese officers threw off their uniforms and fled; thousands of pairs of army boots littered the roads and airport grounds.

The RAAF airfield guards spent the day loading Ambassador Price's Hercules. They were ordered to check each item — by hand — for bombs. The embassy's luggage included Vietnamese *objets d'art* — paintings, sculptures, silk fabrics; Persian carpets; a Mercedes-Benz and the beginnings of an Asian menagerie: individually crated exotic birds, cats and 'at least two dogs', the pets of embassy and UN officials. Nye today alleges that Price 'stole' some of the goods; Bob Gordon, the military attaché in Saigon at the time, and Price's son Christopher reject this allegation. They also claim that in the final days Price argued bitterly with Whitlam in favour of evacuating his Vietnamese staff — to no avail.[29]

With the Hercules about to take off, Ambassador Price issued 'an order that made us feel sick', Sheean recalled. '*We were to stop all South Vietnamese people previously employed by the Australian Embassy from getting on the aircraft.*' The order decreed that no Vietnamese should be evacuated without official approval.

The patient Vietnamese staff waiting on the tarmac broke down and wept. 'We gave them our money, cigarettes, or anything else we thought might help them,' said Sheean. Price handed his drivers the keys to the embassy's vehicles (a Kombi, a Volvo and others) and emptied his wallet of spare cash, 'to try to help them exist until the new order was installed'.[30] The drivers 'cried and shook with disbelief'. Price tried to explain that 'he could not cut through the red tape to get them out. They were to go over to the

American Embassy to see if they could get out that way.'[31] Price ordered the four airmen to use force to prevent any Vietnamese staff from boarding the aircraft: 'We were to use whatever means necessary to carry out this order,' said Sheean.

'Price abandoned his driver,' said Nye, visibly sickened forty years later. 'I still have nightmares about those drivers … we were just about crying because as soon as they left the airport they'd be dead. How far were they going to go in Australian Embassy cars?'[32] The embassy's Vietnamese accountant, also left behind, reportedly said: 'It is shameful, and Australia's name will never be forgotten because of it.'[33]

Price had acted on direct instructions from the Prime Minister, who 'controlled the whole exercise', Air Commodore Mitchell, commander of Detachment S, wrote later. '… the Prime Minister and his staff … were never fully aware of the gravity of the situation. And when that realisation finally dawned, they blissfully went quiet, but not before they refused the evacuation of thirty Vietnamese support staff, some of whom had served Australia for more than twenty years.'[34] These clerks, drivers and interpreters were unable to afford exit visas, for which wealthy Vietnamese were prepared to pay up to US$100,000 in the last days.

Hundreds of Vietnamese with official refugee status were also left behind. In the last weeks, the embassy had received asylum applications from 3,667 adult Vietnamese, of whom 342 were approved and just seventy-six actually reached Australia.[35] Whitlam attempted to justify the abandonment of so many people to certain 're-education' and probable death on the tendentious grounds that he needed to build a constructive relationship with the new communist rulers. In short, the Prime Minister deferred to the will of Hanoi, a decision Labor's hard-nosed 'realists' defended as sensible — and the sacrifice of a few, admittedly loyal, South Vietnamese, as regrettable. Others condemned Labor's refugee policy as a monumental act of inhumanity, political expediency and bureaucratic indifference. Several Liberal politicians believed that no upper limit should apply to Vietnamese refugees. That was easy to say when in Opposition, of course; yet three Liberal politicians in fact flew to Saigon to study the crisis, and Malcolm Fraser was especially outspoken about Labor's mishandling of this human catastrophe. Later, as Prime Minister, Fraser honourably opened the gates to Vietnamese refugees and Australia's former allies.

A final shock awaited the four RAAF airfield guards: the embassy's Hercules had no room for them. The luggage they had taken a day to load

occupied all the available space, and they were told to remain in Saigon —
on the tarmac.

The flight's captain, John Stone, objected, Nye recalled: 'He said it was
unAustralian to leave people behind.' The ambassador overrode the captain.
'I'm leading this operation,' Price is reported as saying, 'and these men will
not be coming on this aircraft.'[36] A few journalists offered their seats to the
airmen, but a civilian exchange 'would've been unheard of in the RAAF',
said Nye.

Ambassador Price, his Australian staff, thirty-four Vietnamese nuns, two
children, some journalists and the embassy's treasure and pets flew out of
Saigon at 7.00 p.m. on Anzac Day, 1975. On the tarmac they left scores of
approved Vietnamese refugees, thirty embassy employees and four RAAF
servicemen. That they chose to flee on the day Australians traditionally
honour the courage of fallen soldiers added to the ignominy.

'We sat on our bags,' Nye recalled, 'with four pistols and four rounds
each … no food, no water, no communications … We had a couple of
smokes. We tried to look like tourists. We figured out, if the enemy came,
we'd head for the scrub. But we were all thinking, "Hey, we might be here
for the rest of our lives, and end up bloody dead or in prison in this
country."'[37] Several hours later, an Australian Hercules diverted from
Thailand landed — at great risk — to collect them.

The last Australian officer to leave South Vietnam was, fittingly, the first to
be sent there: Ted Serong, who spent his last days rallying his South
Vietnamese soldiers. A surviving ARVN unit, whose officers had died or
deserted, asked him to command them, and Serong agreed, in a futile effort
to buy a little time.

On 28 April Radio America played 'White Christmas', the secret signal
for remaining CIA agents to assemble at nominated pick-up points. Serong
walked through the broken city with a Vietnamese woman who had been
abandoned by her husband and children. As they approached the crowds at
the gates of the US Embassy, Serong said, 'Stick to me.' The woman, called
Xuyen, said later, 'I knew that wherever I went, I would follow him, eyes
closed.' Two Marines whisked them inside, beyond the reach of the bawling,
grasping crowd. Later that night Serong and Xuyen flew to the ships and
were evacuated with 4,000 others in the hold of the cargo vessel *Green Port*,
of New Orleans.[38]

In Xuyen's eyes, Serong embodied the hopes and failures of her country: '... this hero,' she wrote, 'after thirteen years of fighting ... found himself with his back to the wall. The defeat of Vietnam was as humiliating for him as it was for us. He seemed to want to linger in Saigon until it was too late. Without me, I am sure he would have looked after people asking for his help until the last moment ...' She added, 'Here is not just the defeat of Vietnam but the end of the American adventure ...'[39]

From his command post in a thatched hut near Ben Cat the North Vietnamese commander General Van Tien Dung ordered the final push of the Ho Chi Minh Campaign, 'the most beautiful product of the age', he later called it. At dawn on 29 April — the day before South Vietnam ceased to exist — North Vietnamese batteries rocketed Tan Son Nhut airport. Hundreds of civilians died in the attack. It was 'an important signal', conceded the CIA station chief at its morning briefing in the US Embassy, to which someone whispered, 'Like a bullet through the brain.'[40]

At 10.51 a.m. (Saigon time) President Gerald Ford ordered the initiation of 'OPTION IV' FREQUENT WIND, the emergency heli-evacuation of all Americans and as many Vietnamese as possible. All US Embassy officials were to leave Saigon by nightfall, insisted Kissinger. In the embassy compound, Marines felled a beautiful tamarind tree to accommodate the Chinooks; even here, vegetation had to make way for the war. A little after noon thirty-six heavy-duty helicopters left the deck of USS *Hancock*, anchored offshore, and flew to Saigon — the start of the largest heli-evacuation in history. As they landed, the backdraught scattered bags of rubbish that contained CIA code words, top-secret cables and the names of South Vietnamese agents, thus fatally compromising them.

Ambassador Martin wandered the embassy grounds with the stoop and sickly pallor of a 'walking dead man'. At times his little black poodle, Ninh, trotted along on a leash behind him. For all purposes redundant, Martin successfully evacuated the dog.

Outside, hundreds of thousands of Vietnamese thronged the streets along the embassy walls, their faces pressed against the gates pleading for a lifeline. Inside, 2,000 approved Vietnamese queued for the ride of their lives. The famous last airlifts from the embassy roof were 'a vision out of a nightmare', Snepp remembered. '[The helicopter] was already waiting for us, its engines setting up a roar like a primeval scream. The crew ... wore what looked like oversized football helmets, and in the blinking under-light of the landing signals they reminded me of grotesque insects rearing on their hind quarters.'[41] Over Phuoc Tuy, a fleeing US helicopter took ground fire from Ba Ria, once the capital of 'Australia's province', now in the hands of the People's Army.

Throughout that day US pilots flew 630 rescue missions and evacuated 5,595 Vietnamese and 1,373 Americans from various points in Saigon. In total, 65,000 Vietnamese were rescued aboard US aircraft during April.[42]


Orange, red and black were the colours of the night before the start of Year Zero. The sounds were the boom of artillery, the cries of drunken soldiers, the screams of women, and the rat-a-tat of machine guns. The embassy's electricity failed. Spotlights beamed from the eyes of American helicopters that hovered over the darkened city.

The CIA station ceased classified communication at 3.20 a.m. on 30 April. In his last cable Tom Polgar, station chief, dissolved into the clichés of a man miscast for the moment. 'It has been a long hard fight and we have lost,' he told Washington. '... Those who fail to learn from history are forced to repeat it. Let us hope that ... we have learned our lesson. Saigon signing off.'

Near dawn Ambassador Martin boarded the penultimate heli-lift looking 'frail, so terribly frail'; photographers immortalised the last flights out from the embassy roof. In the compound below, hundreds of Vietnamese faces looked up at the burnished sky, flush with hope. They did not know that they had just been left behind.


Around noon, a communist tank — No. 843 of the 203rd Armoured Brigade — broke through the gates of the Presidential Palace. The Australian cameraman Neil Davis was there to film it: the tank 'didn't quite make it the first time, and one gate fell off its hinges,' said Davis. 'It backed off and smashed through again ...' A soldier waving a huge flag of the National Liberation Front leaped off the tank and ran towards the palace. Davis kept filming as a North Vietnamese ran over screaming, 'Stop, stop!' To which the Australian photographer replied, 'Welcome to Saigon, comrade. I've been waiting for you.' Hours earlier, the cameraman had sat quietly with the President, Big Minh, inside the palace. 'I asked him if he was going to stay,' Davis recalled, 'and he said, "Yes. The other side will be here shortly."'[43]

The weeks of celebrations culminated in a victory march through 'Ho Chi Minh City': '... the people were crying with happiness, smiling but crying,' observed Pham Truong Thanh, a North Vietnamese captain. He did not see the others, the millions of South Vietnamese who silently dreaded what was to come. Nor did he mention the fate of his southern comrades, the National Liberation Front, whose fighters were hastily 'merged' with the People's Army in time for the victory march, at which not a single Viet Cong regiment marched under its own standard. It was as if the NLF had never existed.

The conquest of South Vietnam delighted Western peace groups. 'I cheered when the guerrillas marched into Saigon,' said the activist Bob Gould.[44] His comrades in Australia, America and Europe similarly applauded the unconditional surrender of Saigon to the communist forces. Two of Whitlam's trusted advisers, John Menadue and Gregory Clark, heard the news at a barbecue on the south coast of New South Wales, over the Easter holiday, as Clark later wrote: 'We celebrated, quietly but deeply.'[45]

# Chapter 45
# Cabramatta

... when I looked into her eyes they were expressionless. They
were dead. They were the eyes of Vietnam — the eyes of
someone who had borne the unbearable.
*Jon Swain, on meeting a young Vietnamese 'boat person'.*

In May 1975 Hanoi ordered the release of its prisoners of war. 'Go back to
your home,' they were told, 'and be good citizens. Your country is united.
We've got to hold hands and rebuild.' And it seemed Hanoi meant it. 'It was
beautiful,' Dr Tien Nguyen, a medical officer captured in the last days of
Saigon, bitterly recalled. 'I was so stunned, how noble. And they gave us all a
small amount of money for the bus fare home. The communists were very
clever, I have to admit.' Tien Nguyen's family had presumed he was dead: 'I
walked into my house like a ghost. My mother and father just burst into
tears; they thought I was a ghost.'[1]

For a few weeks, a sense of peace and reconciliation seemed to prevail.
And in this atmosphere of feigned goodwill, an edict went out 'inviting' all
South Vietnamese soldiers and government officials to attend a short political
're-education course'. They were to bring only enough luggage for a month.
This seemed a sincere gesture of 'concord and reconciliation', and the soldiers
felt inclined to cooperate: after all, hadn't the victor behaved with
commendable restraint in the days after the conquest? Truong Nhu Tang, the
National Liberation Front's Minister for Justice, even drove his own brothers,
who had fought for Saigon, to the re-education pick-up point.

'I tell you this was very clever,' repeated Dr Nguyen, in his surgery in Sydney's Cabramatta. 'I became living proof of the generosity and the kindness of the new revolutionary government. They released me and the like ... to hook all the others.'[2] In the next few months thousands of former soldiers and government officials turned themselves over to the new regime.

Their families expected to see them home in weeks. Weeks passed, then months, then years. In fact, tens of thousands would never come home. Communist 'people's tribunals' condemned them as 'lackeys of imperialism' who owed 'blood debts to the people'.[3] They were packed off to 're-education camps', the Vietnamese equivalent of the Soviet Gulag. Officers and senior government officials were imprisoned for ten to fifteen years, ordinary troops for lesser terms, with hard labour and little food and in appalling conditions. By the end of 1976, 300,000 South Vietnamese were held in concentration camps and faced years of hard labour. They cleared land, ploughed fields, deactivated minefields and endured endless humiliating chores, such as polishing the shoes and cleaning the toilets of party bosses.[4] Resistance met with severe punishment: beatings, solitary confinement, occasional torture and often death. 'Ralliers' — defectors to the southern army — were summarily shot. The combination of paltry food rations (200 grams of rice a day), slave labour conditions and disease ensured that thousands suffered a slow, agonising death. In one camp, in Nha Trang, fifty people were consigned sardine-like to each cell. In total, the liberators of South Vietnam executed a conservatively estimated 65,000 people; a further 250,000 perished in re-education camps.[5]

In 1980 the dissident poet Nguyen Chi Thien, who spent years in re-education camps, smuggled out a sheaf of handwritten poems entitled 'Flowers from Hell'. In one, he wrote:

> If Uncle and the Party, let's suppose,
> Allowed free movements in and out,
> Grandfather Marx's paradise
> Would soon become the wilds where monkeys roam.[6]

On their release, usually sick and frail, the 're-educated' former soldiers and officials joined their fellow southern citizens in the larger prison, soon to be called the 'Socialist Republic of Vietnam'. The proletarian paradise treated them and their families as untouchables: they had little hope of a decent job. Many drove cyclos or swept roads; the lucky ones returned to their villages.

I met several ex-ARVN officers — skilled, highly intelligent men — living in hovels beside the highways, broken in body and spirit. But not in mind: they were happy to discuss their experiences, as their remarkably cheerful wives served beer or tea. And some returned to their jobs; for example, a crooner in Vung Tau was imprisoned; his crime had been to entertain the Australian soldiers, although his father had been highly placed in the Saigon Government. After several months in a re-education camp, he was released and allowed to resume singing. He was still performing, in 2005, at a nightclub on the beach-side promenade, where he told me his story over a beer between sets.

The National Liberation Front and its 'Provisional Revolutionary Government' was disbanded and its leaders marginalised. The dream of sharing power with Hanoi evaporated. It was an especially painful awakening for the Viet Cong leaders. 'The true outlines of power revealed themselves with painful clarity ... Suddenly all the creeping fears were realised,' Truong Nhu Tang wrote. Hanoi permitted a few token National Liberation Front leaders in the new National Assembly 'elected' in March 1976. Yet virtually all the assembly's members were carefully screened northerners and COSVN officials who could be relied on to rubber-stamp communist policies at bitterly derided 'Yes conferences'.

The National Liberation Front had thus sacrificed hundreds of thousands of lives for an ideology in which they had no input, and a new nation over which they had no power. Within a year the NLF ceased to exist. On 2 July 1976 Hanoi declared the country 'unified' under this suffocating Marxist regime, and a stream of Soviet 'advisers' were welcomed to Vietnam to pick over the southern corpse. The Russians were 'stuffed down our throats', wrote a disgusted Truong Nhu Tang, who soon quit as the NLF's 'Minister of Justice' and later fled the country to Paris.

> ... a miasma of disgust hung over most ... who stayed [he wrote later]. It was a time of unalloyed cynicism on the part of [Hanoi] and stunned revulsion for those of us who had been their brothers-in-arms for so long. Now, with total power in their hands, they began to show their cards in the most brutal fashion ... the Vietnam of the future would be a single monolithic bloc, collectivist and totalitarian, in which all the traditions and culture

of the South would be ground and moulded by the political machine of the conquerors.[7]

If Truong Nhu Tang's surprise at this outcome strains credulity, his comrades were similarly shocked at the speed with which the North subsumed them. In 1976 a few diehard Viet Cong leaders administered last rites to their movement in the dance hall of the Rex Hotel, soon to become an official Communist Party brothel. This bitter little party of thirty ex-guerrilla leaders cranked up a few maudlin revolutionary songs … 'but we knew finally that we had been well and truly sold'.[8]

As for the Montagnard, they were denied even a semblance of autonomy, and driven from the mountains like wild animals. Of the 250,000 'resettled' to the coast, about a third made it. 'We annihilated them as they fled,' wrote the North Vietnamese General Trin Dung in his book *Great Spring*.[9]

Hanoi stamped its authority on South Vietnam with withering speed. The Politburo and its three most senior members, Prime Minister Pham Van Dong, General Secretary Le Duan and the Paris negotiator Le Duc Tho, were now the ultimate repositories of power throughout a 'unified' Vietnam.

Leaden Marxist rule, hopeless economic management and forced rural collectivisation marked the post-war decade, and exacerbated the pain and anguish of war. Just as Stalin and Mao had yoked the peasants, their human cattle, to the plough on a vast scale, so too would Ho Chi Minh's heirs use the same techniques, not once but twice. Hanoi showed that it had learned nothing from the famine of 1956, and repeated the folly on a grander scale between 1975 and 1986. The communist 'reforms' — chiefly the nationalisation of agriculture — failed miserably: the landless peasants had little incentive to work on state-owned cooperatives, a fact that always eluded socialist idealists such as Dr Jim Cairns. Yields plunged; costs soared. 'By the late 1970s,' concluded Dr Nguyen Van Khanh, associate professor of social sciences at the Vietnam National University in Hanoi, 'agriculture in Vietnam fell into serious crisis.' Average food production per capita collapsed, 'while the farmers had to give more and more back to the cooperatives and the government'. The peasants' 'minuscule income continued to shrink'.[10] Far from being the creative force that Marx had championed, the peasants and workers had become 'no more than a raw commodity' to be broken on the anvil of progress, as historian Orlando Figes observed of their Russian counterparts.[11]

The Four Horsemen came galloping back, with Famine leading the charge. Average per capita food production in the northern provinces fell from 15.4 kilos in 1976 to 10.04 kilos in 1980, barely enough to sustain human life. The most disastrous indicator of Vietnam's post-war economic collapse was rice production. In 1979, after four years of Marxist rule, Vietnam could not feed itself and was forced to import 2 million tons of rice. This, in a country Nature had endowed with perfect conditions for rice cultivation.

The best that can be said of this catastrophe is that Hanoi honoured the Last Testament of Ho Chi Minh to the letter: 'I hope,' he wrote, 'that our Party will do its best to contribute effectively to the restoration of unity ... on the basis of Marxism–Leninism and proletarian internationalism ...'[12] Leaving a message of 'boundless love' for his people, Uncle Ho looked forward 'in anticipation of the day when I shall go and join Karl Marx, V. I. Lenin and other revolutionary elders' in the communist afterlife.[13]

Famine forced the abandonment of this economic insanity. At the 6th Party Congress in 1986, Hanoi relinquished the ownership of the means of production, and adopted sweeping market reforms under the slogan 'Vietnam is on the path of renewal [doi moi]'. The farmers' land was returned; free market incentives were introduced. The transformation was phenomenal. Within three years, in 1989 Vietnam could feed itself *and* export a rice surplus; in 2002 it produced approximately 34 million tons of rice, double the yield of 1986.[14] Today it is again the world's second-largest exporter of rice, after Thailand.

In the intervening decades, millions have thought of escape from this post-war tyranny; more than a million have tried. Many of those who survived the flight went on to build new lives in America, Canada, Australia and Europe. Theirs is one of the most heart-rending stories of the war: unable to bear the new dictatorship, they put to sea in any vessel they could find, risking years in prison if caught and an uncertain fate if they escaped. Perhaps 10 to 20 per cent died at sea of starvation, pirate attack or drowning.

The *Sunday Times* journalist Jon Swain described the refugees' experiences in *River of Time*, his exquisitely told memoir of the tragedy of Indochina: 'The suffering of the Vietnamese boat people was almost beyond imagination,' he wrote, 'it consumed anyone who came into contact with it ...' The 'boat people' represented a spectrum of Vietnamese society:

farmers, professionals, government officials, teachers, writers, lawyers, students, former soldiers, young men of draft age, prostitutes, fishermen, labourers, cyclo-drivers and disillusioned Viet Cong. There were single mothers of Amerasian children fleeing official discrimination; ethnic Chinese persecuted by Vietnam's anti-Chinese government; and ordinary soldiers, ostracised for joining the 'puppet army'.[15]

Two stories convey the extremity of their suffering. The fifty-two survivors of a vessel that had carried 110 people experienced an ordeal 'as harrowing as any I have encountered', wrote Swain. The boat had drifted for thirty-seven days with engine failure. As the food ran out, a former air force corporal and his teenage followers armed themselves with knives and robbed the weaker passengers of food and water. Driven mad by thirst, the people drank sea water and their own urine. An American ship, USS *Dubuque*, circled, gave them some supplies and a map, and sailed away, ignoring their pleas that the engine was dead. When the food ran out, their suffering 'became unendurable', and the gang started killing passengers and eating them. The last to die was an 11-year-old boy, whom they drowned, 'cut off his head, dismembered the body, cooked the flesh and distributed it'. When the survivors finished relating their story to Swain, 'a terrible sadness filled the air': they hung their heads in shame, as all had participated in cannibalism. The air force corporal was jailed.

Swain found 16-year-old La Kieu Ly, the sole survivor of a pirate attack on her boat, lighting candles for her sister in a makeshift Catholic church in a refugee camp near the Thai–Cambodian border. Hers was a story of unimaginable agony. Ly, her 10-year-old sister Kim and their aunt had put to sea in a 7 metre fishing boat with nineteen others. A few hours offshore, Vietnamese fishermen stole their money. Then, nearly two days later, Thai pirates rammed and sank them. Everyone was left to drown — the pirates beat off the men with knives — except six females, including the two sisters. They became the pirates' playthings, 'repeatedly raped and terrorised with fists, hammers and knives'. Ly remembered Kim's cries as three fishermen raped her little sister in succession. 'Her last memory of Kim was of a sobbing, pain-racked little bundle of humanity, begging for life. No trace of Kim was ever found,' Swain wrote.[16] After tiring of the older girls, the pirates tossed them overboard, including Ly. She managed to stay afloat for nine hours, when another Thai fishing boat found her, nursed her back to life and left her with police at the port of Nakhon Si Thammarat. When Swain heard her story, 'I remember thinking with humility how she reflected the special dignity of Vietnamese women and their instinct of survival. But when I looked into her eyes they were expressionless. They were dead. They were the eyes of Vietnam — the eyes of someone who had borne the unbearable.'[17]

The world reacted to the plight of South Vietnam's refugees with general indifference: they were the wretched of the earth, the losers of the war. In Western cities, most student protesters had outgrown their youthful exuberance and were pursuing careers and having families. Their salad days at the barricades were but a thrilling memory; the significance of this huge exodus seemed little to trouble the West's settled conscience. Few marched against Hanoi's cruelty. Yet here were more than a million Vietnamese people prepared to risk an awful death at sea to escape the regime so many Western protesters had supported.

There were exceptions, of course. One was the irrepressible Bob Gould, furious at the Whitlam Government's refusal to take more Vietnamese refugees: 'I wouldn't have set conditions on boat people — let them all come here, I thought. Whitlam set up a wall. I felt like punching him. We stuck our noses in; we had a moral obligation to take them.'[18]

Humiliation awaited the surviving 'boat people', who arrived at their destinations disease-ridden, impoverished and unwelcome. Many had been farmers and soldiers, business-people, politicians and professionals. Now they found themselves in squalid Thai and Indonesian refugee camps, held for months while they applied for asylum clearance. America and Canada generously accepted them, as would Australia in the late 1970s.

The first Vietnamese boat people landed on the north coast of Australia in 1977. Some sailed straight into Darwin and presented themselves to the police; others dragged their boats ashore on the empty coastline, and set out on foot to find signs of human habitation. Two years after the war ended, 1,636 boat people had reached Australian shores.[19]

On arrival, they were medically checked aboard their boats, floating pits of disease that were quarantined, sprayed and decontaminated. Most of the survivors had severe head and body lice and scabies. The obviously sick were transferred to hospital, and the rest were given a thorough medical examination; they were X-rayed and their blood and urine tested. Dr Ella Stack CBE, mayor of Darwin in 1979, listed their most common medical conditions as epilepsy, severe anaemia, asthma, chronic abdominal pain, hepatitis, abdominal malignancy, trachoma, shrapnel wounds, syphilis, gonorrhoea, malaria, congenital malformations, mental retardation and wrist injury with ankylosis. The incidence of tuberculosis was 2 per cent, compared with an Australian rate at the time of 0.01 per cent. Yet, she added, most were treatable and their general health was 'surprisingly good'.[20]

The first refugees were taken to the Darwin Quarantine Station and given food and shelter. 'The children seem to have a fantastic ability to eat vast amounts of ice cream!' Dr Stack observed. After a few weeks' orientation, they were dispersed around the country, with government support.

Many went to Sydney and settled in Sydney's western suburbs, chiefly Cabramatta, a suburb close to the migrant relocation centre and better known in the late 1990s for drugs and crime. That is to see one side of the story; another exists, rarely portrayed in the press, of a relatively prosperous, self-sufficient community of Vietnamese émigrés whose older citizens continue to observe the rituals of their ancestors. Dr Tien Nguyen spent three years in a communist re-education camp, survived a terrifying escape by boat and arrived in Australia in 1979, where he has lived ever since. As federal president of the Vietnamese Community in Australia, he speaks today for a vibrant, active society of almost 200,000 Vietnamese (of whom 154,807 were born in Vietnam, according to the 2001 census; many arrived later, to join their families; and others are second- and third-generation Vietnamese Australians). They are members of the worldwide Vietnamese diaspora of more than two million people, living mostly in America, Canada and Europe. As such, 'Cabramatta' is both a symbol and a place.

Among the émigrés were soldiers who fought alongside the Australians and Americans, whose story is virtually unknown outside small reunions or the occasional protest against the media's insensitive portrayal of their homeland. A small group of them marches on Anzac Day, such as Vo Hoa Son, nicknamed 'Sonny' by the diggers, one of eight trusted interpreters in Nui Dat in 1968. He escaped in 1975: he and a friend, Moon Lee, commandeered a small German vessel on the Saigon River. At Vung Tau they took on many others, including Sonny's future wife, Linh, then 16 years old. They survived a near mutiny and sailed an abandoned fishing vessel to southern Thailand and Singapore, where they were processed for Australia. The couple were among the first refugees held in Queensland's Wacol Migrant Centre, in 1975. Since then, they have prospered and raised four children, two of whom have completed university degrees.

Less fortunate was Khien Dinh Nguyen, another interpreter in the Australian intelligence section during the war, who spent two years in a re-education camp. His father, a province chief, received a ten-year sentence, and his brother, a lieutenant colonel, thirteen years. 'We did hard labour, we carried big logs, they kicked you in the back, they swore at you,' he said. 'They'd say, "You are defeated, you must work"; they'd say, "Communism is the best doctrine in the world." If you were weak, you'd die or commit suicide.' The regime released Khien's father in 1985; he died in 1986, aged 62. In 1981 Khien lived in Vietnam, unable to escape. His first wife had fled to Australia, 'but she married someone else', he said. After seven years her new husband committed suicide. 'Before he died he told her to sponsor me. Which she did. She filled out two forms in Thailand. I then wrote to the Australian Embassy for six years, asking for asylum. In 1994 a man from the Australian Embassy came to see me: I was allowed to emigrate in 1995. I remarried; I have three children.'[21]

One of the most extraordinary stories of survival is that of Colonel Vo Dai Ton, a Special Forces commander who led secret reconnaissance missions behind enemy lines in Cambodia and Laos, for which his unit received a US Presidential Citation for 'extraordinary heroism'.[22] On three occasions Ton parachuted into North Vietnam. In 1976 he escaped by boat to Australia, where he settled with his wife, Tuyet Mai, and their son.

The pain of exile and news of his suffering compatriots compelled Ton to return to Vietnam. In 1980, of his own volition, he accepted an invitation from his old unit to help raise a guerrilla army and overthrow the communist regime. This courageous folly ended in their ambush and capture in 1982, on the Laos–Vietnam border. Vo Dai Ton was dragged away in shackles, hung from the ceiling of a prison cell and beaten for hours. 'They made me admit to working for the CIA … There was no trial and there were no charges,' he told me in 2005.[23]

In 1982 Hanoi paraded the colonel as a 'very important spy' for the CIA and forced him to confess before the world's press. Ton, by now a frail, wizened figure, stepped up to the microphones and started to read a prepared 'confession'. Suddenly he stopped and declared, in a firm voice: 'I will not betray the people who have helped or assisted me. I continue to maintain my political support for freedom and liberty. I am prepared to receive any verdict declared on me!' He was bundled away, admonished and led back in. This time, he tried to stab himself with a sharpened chopstick, hidden in his shoe, 'to die for my country', but the police grabbed him before he could retrieve the weapon and hauled him away again. The press conference was shut down, but not before Neil Davis filmed the ensuing pandemonium and smuggled the film out to Australia where the world — and Ton's wife — caught a glimpse of him alive.

There followed forty-five days of torture. The beatings resumed when Ton regained consciousness … the prelude to years in prison. For the next ten years, one month and seventeen days Vo Dai Ton inhabited a cell 2.5 by 3 metres in a common criminals' jail outside Hanoi. Twice a day he received a teacup-sized bowl of rice and once a month, a slice of pork.

'I had no contact with the outside world … I never saw another prisoner. I made up stories to survive, I memorised poems in my head,' he said.[24] His captors tortured him ninety-six times — he kept count; the torture damaged his eyesight and hearing. Far worse, he said, was the chronic isolation, where time and silence did the torturer's work. He stayed sane by writing and reciting poems, memorising hundreds.

International pressure led to his unexpected release, on 9 December 1991. He weighed 47 kilos and 'felt 80'. At 6 a.m., dressed in an old suit, he flew to Bangkok with two Australian Embassy officials. His wife scarcely recognised him when he got home, but they resumed their marriage and he regained his strength. In 2005 he lived with his wife in a bungalow in Greenacre, Sydney, where he wrote poetry. Widely recognised as a leader of the Vietnamese in exile, Vo Dai Ton became president of the Alliance for the Restoration of Vietnam.


In 2005 I met a Vietnamese man described by his doctor as 'the worst case of post-traumatic stress disorder I have seen'. His name is Tuan Van Phan. He served in the Army of the Republic of Vietnam from 1971 to 1975, during which he was exposed to loud explosions, sustained multiple injuries and 'was trapped in a collapsed trench for some hours', states his doctor's report. After the war he spent two and a half years in a re-education camp, and escaped to Thailand in 1978. In 1988 he received asylum in Australia. This thumbnail sketch barely scratches the surface of Tuan Van Phan's real story.

I met him in Cabramatta: a gentle, dignified man, with a loving wife and two pretty daughters. Tuan Van Phan has a good job, wears a suit and seems a prosperous, middle-aged businessman. The first sign of what lies beneath is his marked sensitivity to the possibility of beauty. Nature upsets him; his scarred universe seems to have no place for wonder or lyricism. 'When I see the sunlight, I cry … when I look at the birds, and their wings, I cry … when I hear the old music of my country, I cry …' he said.

In 1968 Tuan Van Phan was a 16-year-old schoolboy living in Hué. During the Tet Offensive he witnessed thousands of his fellow citizens being rounded up and led away. Many worked for the South Vietnamese Government and were staunch southern nationalists or Catholics. He, too, was captured.

'The communists took us to a farm in the mountains. During the daytime they hid us in civilian houses; at night time it was unforgettable. We had to dig ditches at night. I saw the people in chains in these holes with their hands tied together … And a man would say, "This is for what you did to the people, so you deserve to die." They shot them in the chest. Women and children and nuns and priests …

'We buried them, but some people were still alive. They fell down like that into the ditch, still alive. We were ordered to bury them alive. "Fill or die" is what I was told. I buried people alive. I had to do that over and over for many nights.' He was forced at gunpoint to throw dirt in the faces of people screaming for mercy.

As he spoke, Tuan Van Phan wept: 'I am 53 now and it is still horrible. I did not want to bury alive my own people. "Do it or die, I'll shoot you, I'll shoot you," I was told.' He witnessed the executions of his uncle and friends. When the Americans and South Vietnamese forces recaptured Hué, he joined the army, became an artillery officer and fought at the battle of Da Nang. At the fall of Saigon he was captured and tortured.

'My second wife understands me, because she was also tortured by them,' he said. He has severe nightmares, of 'bullets, so many bullets … I cover my head with my hand … My wife shakes me, she says, "Darling, darling, we are home."'

He wept, then gathered the strength to speak: 'After I emigrated, I saw people laughing, people playing. But I cry. I cry. I need to speak for the dead. I wish someone would take these memories away, so I can be a normal person. They have broken my mind … I sometimes feel suffocated, so suffocated … Why was I in that situation as a boy? Why was I forced to do those things?'

He turned from Buddhism to Catholicism, and was baptised in 1982 after the birth of his first child: 'I go to church each week. The priests teach love and forgiveness.' But he cannot forgive; his doctor prescribes rest and exercise, and medication.

Reminders of Hué induce a sharp longing for his birthplace. He especially loved the beautiful old bridge over the Perfume River. 'Did they fix the bridge?' he asked Vietnamese exchange students on a visit to Sydney in 2005, and he reminded them of the thousands killed in Hué in 1968. One said, 'What are you talking about?' The students had never heard of the massacre; Hanoi had erased the fact from the historical record. Tuan Van Phan broke down 'in front of all those strange, young people'.

We stood in the mall in Cabramatta, like strangers from another age. Tuan Van Phan smiled at the Vietnamese schoolchildren in Little Saigon. 'These people don't see my two faces,' he said.[25]

# Chapter 46
# Agents Orange, Purple, White, Green, Pink, Blue ...

Reglone, Grammoxone, Tordone and Hyva ... as far as I
personally am concerned ... they could be four horses running at
Rosehill on Saturday.
*Jim Killen, Australian Defence Minister, 1980.*

The war on the environment did not cease at the ceasefire. The poison's silent ministry swam in the plasmic slipstream, permeated the food chain and watertable, entered the molecular realm and insinuated itself into the very chromosomes of life. There, it rearranged the knit and form of the human being. The diabolical consequences may be seen in the grandchildren of Vietnamese soldiers, a parade of little grotesques, the last gasp of this unspeakable war. 'What else can possibly explain the systematic convergence?' wondered the British journalist Christopher Hitchens.[1]

This is the aftermath of ecocide, the planned destruction of an ecological system. Between 1962 and 1970, as part of OPERATION RANCH HAND, the US Air Force sprayed 72 million litres of herbicide — 66 per cent of which was Agent Orange — on South Vietnam. Fifteen kinds of chemical defoliant — a veritable rainbow of toxicity — were used: Agents Purple, Green, Pink, White, Blue and Orange (I and II), as well as dinoxol, trinoxol, bromacil, diquat, tandex, monuron, diuron and dalapon. In addition, six different kinds of insecticides drenched southern towns and forts, in an attempt to kill malaria-carrying mosquitoes.

'Never in human history have people witnessed one country's making a war to [sic] the living environment of another,' Senator Gaylord Nelson told a US Senate Hearing in August 1970. RANCH HAND largely achieved its goal of wiping out the cover of the Vietnamese jungle: more than 20 per cent of South Vietnam's forests were destroyed and thirty-two of the forty-six provinces sprayed in an ecological catastrophe that has had 'no parallel in commercial agriculture or in warfare'.[2] During 1967, the peak year, the American program destroyed 600,000 hectares of forest, and the US Government requisitioned all domestic stocks of the active chemical agents 245-T and 24-D, to maximise the supply to the spraying teams.[3] In the delta and the Plain of Reeds, for example, 'we ... made a desert', wrote Daniel Ellsberg, the former marine and Pentagon insider (who later leaked the Pentagon Papers to the *New York Times*), as he flew over a river in the spring of 1966: 'On one side of the river, green, extremely lush countryside — in fact, as beautiful as I had ever seen — and on the other [Viet Cong] side, a desert. Dry, nothing living, no vegetation.'[4]

Defoliation largely failed to achieve its military purpose — to deny the enemy the cover of the jungle — because the guerrillas concealed themselves in other ways: underground, or in the villages and hamlets. In any case, it was impossible to kill off all the forests, which tended to grow back in the hot, wet climate. Worse, the widespread spraying simply alienated great numbers of farmers and rural inhabitants. Later in the war, the Australian Task Force conceded that the results did not justify the cost or effort and that claims for damages from local peasants were 'tying the administration into knots'.[5]

The US and Australian governments were aware of the possible harmful side effects of defoliants as early as 1968, when a US study found that small doses of Agent Orange were teratogenic in mice. This coincided with newspaper reports of birth defects in children born in parts of South Vietnam that had been heavily sprayed with Agent Orange. Yet only in recent years has a scientific consensus accepted a link between herbicides and medical conditions in Vietnam veterans and their children. That acceptance has taken almost forty years of rage and confusion, claim and counter-claim, personal tragedy, political denial and the adulteration and distortion of evidence. In the meantime, the poisoning of a nation's ecology has revisited those most exposed — the soldiers and the Vietnamese people — and many veterans have died of chemical-related medical conditions.

★ ★ ★

When the Australian press first reported the effects of herbicides on soldiers, in 1978, the Australian Government simply denied that veterans had been exposed to chemical defoliants. The case of Bernard Szapiel, in December 1979, fuelled the controversy. His commanding officer, Brigadier Jim Shelton, confirmed that Szapiel's platoon had patrolled through Agent Orange-infected areas. Hundreds, soon thousands, of cases emerged. The government responded with further denials, prevarication and promises to 'inquire' into a potential risk that its own published papers had flagged as early as 1968.

The politicians were either lying or ignorant or both, the soldiers thought. 'We could smell the stuff, taste it,' said the infantryman Gary McMahon. 'It was in the air, in the water we drank, the food we ate, the bush we patrolled. In some cases it was sprayed directly on top of us, but even if it wasn't, the spray drift spread it all over South Vietnam.'[6]

Indeed, by the end of 1968, US defoliation aircraft had dropped more than a million litres of Agent Orange on Phuoc Tuy: 90,960 litres in 1965 and 204,660 litres in 1966, which doubled to 534,390 litres in 1967, the most concentrated year of herbicidal control. (Agents Blue and White were also applied, in far smaller quantities.) The drenching fell back to 242,560 litres in 1968, when spraying in Phuoc Tuy officially ceased. By the end of the war, almost two million litres of defoliant had fallen on Phuoc Tuy.[7]

Australian and New Zealand troops routinely participated: by late 1967 the Task Force had liberally applied a range of herbicides to the countryside. In the biggest spraying mission (from December 1967 to January 1968), 'a total of approximately 40 hectares was sprayed with a knock-down, or quick-acting, herbicide, while some two hectares were sprayed with a sterilant or growth-retarding chemical', stated the government's own report, in 1982.[8] RAAF helicopters, fitted with 3-metre spraying booms on either side of the aircraft, were heavily involved in spraying insecticides from 1966 to 1971 and a range of herbicides from 1968 to 1971.

In light of this evidence, the government was plainly lying when it suggested the Australian troops had not been exposed to dioxin-containing defoliants. On long operations, they could not avoid bathing in and drinking herbicide-polluted water, wrote Lieutenant Colonel Brian Avery: 'The use of chemicals was so widespread that any soldier who went into the field was exposed.'[9] Many ingested chemicals by eating local food, chiefly seafood.

Some troops consumed shellfish from the Rung Sat marshes, one of the most heavily sprayed areas of South Vietnam. Navy personnel drank supposedly purified estuarine water, which is thought to have contributed to the high cancer rate among naval veterans of Vietnam.

'We were ... covered in whatever it was they sprayed,' one soldier recalled. 'It was like a shower of rain. We didn't know what it was ... Three days later we walked through with flame-throwers and burned everything.'[10] Numerous others testify to similar experiences. Captain David Wilkins witnessed defoliation in the Warburtons (the Nui Dinh–Nui Thi Vai Mountains), 'done by aerial spraying, using chemicals such as ... Agent Orange'.[11] The SAS regularly passed through sprayed areas. And support personnel remember mixing it. 'We sprayed the bloody place with Agent Orange,' said Fred Beal, a radio mechanic with the 1st Australian Logistic Support Company. Beal participated in at least three crop-dusting missions: 'I was mixing the bloody stuff, 44 gallon drums. It wasn't just the bloody jungles; it was used on the bloody paddy fields. It killed everything, not only the vegetation; it killed animals ...'[12] Defoliation was simply a routine part of the war.

The soldiers were also directly exposed to insecticides, such as DDT, malathion and dieldren, applied in vast quantities in and around Nui Dat to kill mosquitoes, cockroaches, scorpions and snakes. (Dieldren is now banned in Australia as a carcinogenic.) Insecticides were sprayed beneath the floorboards, inside tents, living quarters and messes, between sandbags, around grease pits and rubbish bins, and in kitchen waste areas. Denis Rayner, who served in the RAAF at Phan Rang in 1967–68, recalled US aircraft 'flying low over kitchen areas and living quarters', spreading a film of malathion over everything. The spray often 'saturated those in the open and fell freely into the swimming pool' in Vung Tau, said one witness.[13]

Agent Orange was the media's favourite herbicide, and the most lethal. Fifty per cent of Agent Orange is made up of the toxin 245-T, whose active agent is the chemical TCCD, better known as dioxin. Of seventy-five different dioxins, the strain in 245-T is the most poisonous synthetic chemical in existence; a tiny amount produces malignant tumours in laboratory animals. 245-T was also a key component in Agents Orange II, Purple, Green and Pink. Six US chemical companies supplied the herbicide: Dow Chemical, Hercules, Monsanto Corporation, Uniroyal, Diamond Shamrock Corporation and Thompson-Hayward Company.

'The sick part,' wrote Gary McMahon, 'is that dioxin does NOT kill plants. It could have been removed from 245-T without affecting its purpose ... but TCDD was not removed from 245-T because that would have increased production costs.'[14]

At first, the press and Parliament applied the term 'Agent Orange' as a catch-all generic, implying that it alone had caused the problem. This was simplistic. 'You had a dozen toxic agents in Vietnam,' wrote Dr Samuel Epstein, author of *The Politics of Cancer*, 'some ... are unequivocally carcinogenic ... What you had in Vietnam was a toxicological cocktail.'[15] Restricting the debate to 'Agent Orange' allowed Defence Minister Jim Killen to avoid a broader discussion of the range of herbicides in use, during Question Time in Parliament:

> Mr J KERIN asked Killen, upon notice, on 23rd November
> 1978: How many servicemen and servicewomen were affected by
> the defoliant Agent Orange while serving in Vietnam?
> Mr KILLEN: The Australian Defence Health Services (ADHS)
> have no documented cases of personnel who have been in
> contact with Agent Orange.
> Q. What is the long-term effect of Agent Orange on an
> individual at various levels of contact?
> Mr KILLEN: The long-term effects of Agent Orange are not
> fully known to the ADHS ...
> Q. What are the range of illnesses caused by Agent Orange?
> MR KILLEN: Ingestion of large undiluted quantities of Agent
> Orange could cause gastrointestinal upset, mild central nervous
> depression and difficulty in swallowing. Occasionally skin contact
> can produce harmful effects on the peripheral nervous system
> causing pain, tingling, or paralysis of long duration ...[16]

On 27 March 1980 Killen was again asked to describe the chemical agents used in Vietnam. He replied: 'I asked my department what toxic herbicides were used ... this was the answer I was given: Reglone, Grammoxone, Tordone and Hyva. I do not wish to be disrespectful to the honourable gentleman, or indeed to this House; but as far as I personally am concerned ... they could be four horses running at Rosehill on Saturday.'[17] The joke damaged Killen and the government, which seemed grossly ignorant of a matter that, as MPs' questions showed, reflected profound public anxiety.

$$\star \quad \star \quad \star$$

A rising number of veterans complained of severe medical conditions and the anxiety deepened. Rex Voltz blamed chemical poisoning in Nui Dat for his medical problems and violent personality. Regardless of whether his claims were valid, nobody at official level took much notice. In despair, in 1980, his wife Paula wrote to the government appealing for help. Three months later, she received an official letter alerting her to the welfare services available. On Boxing Day in 1981, Rex Voltz hanged himself from a tree in a public park in Melbourne. With withering efficiency, the Department of Veterans' Affairs then promptly informed Paula that she was entitled to a $300 burial grant.

Brian Day was exposed three times to defoliants, the last while decanting the chemical from 55-gallon drums in Nui Dat. That night he started vomiting and sweating, and lost consciousness; days later he contracted a severe skin rash. In 1979 army doctors dismissed his persistent medical complaints as hypochondria. He was admitted to a military psychiatric ward, and treated for two years for a personality disorder, after which he received a pension for skin rash.

Thousands of veterans recorded similar complaints in the early 1980s (in 1983 4,000 of them joined a class action in New York against the manufacturers of herbicides) but Veterans' Affairs made 'no attempt ... to view these ailments as part of an underlying syndrome'.[18]

No case was allowed to set a precedent. Colin Simpson's experience made the point: in 1980 Simpson argued that his exposure to toxic chemicals in Vietnam had caused his lymphatic cancer. After his death, his wife pursued his claim, and in 1982 the Repatriation Review Tribunal awarded her a widow's pension. The case seemed to acknowledge a link between cancer and exposure to defoliants, and veterans saw this as setting a precedent. It did not: every case would be treated on individual merit, the government insisted. Joseph Gavin's case was a near replica of Simpson's, but his widow's appeals were twice rejected — and finally accepted after the Repatriation Commission intervened.

In 1980 the government embarked on a long process of denial, delay and obfuscation. It began with a concession: the announcement of a $2 million royal commission presided over by Justice Phillip Evatt into the possible side effects of chemicals used in the Vietnam War. The government also admitted, for the first time, in an August report, that Australian soldiers had sprayed and been exposed to chemical defoliants and insecticides in and around Nui Dat. It denied that Agent Orange was involved. Unknown to Parliament at the time were US military records of defoliation that listed Phuoc Tuy province as one of the most heavily sprayed of the war.[19]

On 1 April that year Senator Colin Mason added a more sinister dimension to the debate: a possible link between chemicals and birth defects in veterans' children:

> ... 350–400 children of Vietnamese veterans have been claimed
> to have birth defects. Missing fingers and other limbs, club feet
> and cleft palates are amongst the worst deficiencies ... TCCD or
> dioxin, the contaminant, is the teratogenic. That means that it can
> have the effect in the first few weeks of pregnancy of deforming
> the foetus. However ... it may be mutagenic, that is, that the
> genes themselves can be carried on by the father and that this can
> lead to deformity in children. That is what has to be established
> about Agent Orange ...[20]

The royal commission proposed to do just that. Submissions flowed in from all over the world. In its submission, the Vietnam Veterans' Association of Australia listed members' symptoms as severe headaches, rages, depression, anxiety, convulsions, blood pressure changes, liver and kidney dysfunction, rare cancers, bronchial problems, muscular twitching and numbness, nausea, abdominal and urinary problems, heart conditions, loss of libido, neurological problems, sweating and increased salivation and bowel problems. Their wives, they said, were prone to stillbirth and miscarriages, and their children suffered an abnormally high rate of congenital defects, including talipes, harelip, cleft palate, absence of limbs and digits, absence of bones, asthma, enlarged heads, enlarged livers, spina bifida, internal haemorrhaging, learning difficulties, heart problems and skin rash. Such conditions were 'predictable given the exposure to chemicals', the VVAA said.[21] The veterans did not seek *ex gratia* compensation; they sought treatment. Nor did they claim to have evidence of a link between herbicides and their children's health problems. They agreed that more research was needed to establish whether child deformities were passed through chromosomal alterations in the veteran's sperm.

As Evatt ploughed through this vast body of material, the Department of Defence published the desk-crushing *Pesticides and the Health of Australian Vietnam Veterans*, which argued that most Australian soldiers were unlikely to have been exposed to herbicides (yet conceded that their direct exposure to *insecticides* was 'highly probable').[22] This flew in the face of the soldiers' actual experiences and the government's own information. The report also contradicted itself; for example, it accepted that exposure to chemical defoliants carried health risks, yet argued that in Vietnam these were slight because the troops used protective clothing, gloves and respirators; it then scored an own goal by adding that the soldiers rarely used protection due to the heat and the 'routine' nature of the job. With a similar lack of logic, the government report accepted the evidence of 'spray drift' across South Vietnam, but failed to explain why the Australian troops escaped it: perhaps they were upwind for the duration of the war? This is not meant lightly: the Department of Veterans' Affairs later tried to disprove spray-drift contamination by matching wind direction and velocity in Phuoc Tuy to RANCH HAND spraying missions over several years. On this evidence, the Australians could not have been exposed to Agent Orange, Veterans' Affairs solemnly told a Senate hearing in September 1982. The US National Academy of Sciences' Herbicide Tapes — the 'Herb Tapes' — rubbished such claims by finding no relationship between the flight path of US spraying planes and herbicide damage; defoliation occurred well outside flight paths; and spray drift could not be quantified or 'even merely approximated', it concluded.[23]

*Pesticides and the Health of Australian Vietnam Veterans* also tried to claim that chemical defoliants were 'not toxic' to humans unless directly sprayed on the skin. Direct exposure, it agreed, could cause fatigue, muscular aches, dizziness, nausea, blurred vision, sweating, insomnia, blackouts, convulsions and anorexia. But these were brief side effects that lasted 'for a relatively short time after exposure ceases'. While 'chronic' exposure — that is, a regular herbicidal drenching — 'can cause abnormal sperm to be produced' (a condition known as teratospermia), healthy sperm production would resume after the exposure to herbicides ceased. If it did not, 'the genetic constitution of the man' was the cause, said the government experts.[24] In short, the soldiers' (or their wives') genes were to blame for birth defects in their children. Either that, or the mother had exposed herself to dangerous chemicals while pregnant, the government said. One rarely encounters women who crop-dust or work with herbicides while pregnant.

Nevertheless, the government conceded that veterans 'may have been exposed to mutagenic chemicals in Vietnam'. If so, these 'would be expected to produce a small number of diverse abnormalities or metabolic defects *without any consistent pattern emerging*'.[25] Hardly a consoling thought, and one that cried out for more research.[26]

The government was also quick to reject any link between chemical exposure and national servicemen's death rates in its vast *Mortality Report* (1984), the first of several. A comparison of 19,205 war veterans and 25,677 veterans who did not go to war found that the former tended to die earlier than the latter; however, both groups' death rates were actually lower than expected for Australian males, due to the 'high standard of health required of enlistees' (later known as the 'healthy worker effect').[27] The exceptions were the Royal Australian Engineers, who did appear to be dying at a faster rate than the general public. The sappers' harrowing experiences of laying and lifting mines and creeping about Viet Cong tunnels surely contributed to this statistical blip. Of course, in 1984, Vietnam veterans were still relatively young men.

On 6 July 1985 Justice Evatt tabled his findings. The royal commissioner had gathered 2,000 exhibits; transcribed 7,000 pages of interviews; travelled to Vietnam, Europe and the United States; and drawn on international medical expertise. In conclusion, Evatt rejected any link between chemical exposure and the development of cancers and other diseases in Vietnam veterans. He did so with the triumphant statement, 'Agent Orange: Not Guilty' and proclaimed that this 'good news should be shouted from the rooftops'. The suggestion that chemical defoliants had caused birth defects in veterans' children was 'fanciful'. The government had no case to answer, Evatt concluded.[28]

At first, there was stunned silence, then outright fury. The Vietnam Veterans Association condemned the report as 'unacceptable'. 'There are so many errors ... that it may justify a mention in the *Guinness Book of Records*,' it stated.[29] Scientists in Australia and abroad were astonished at the conclusions.

As the dust settled, deep flaws in Evatt's methodology emerged. Most seriously, the commission had simply lifted large chunks of its conclusions from the submission by Monsanto, a leading US manufacturer of defoliants. In one volume, entitled *Cancer*, Evatt adopted 75 per cent of his material directly from Monsanto's submission, noticed Tim McCombe of the Vietnam Veterans Association. Even such phrases as 'Monsanto submits' were replaced by 'The Commission submits'. In the ensuing uproar, Evatt was accused of colluding with a leading US manufacturer of Agent Orange.

Other perversions emerged.[30] Evatt simply ignored the testimony of two Swedish doctors whose research strongly suggested that certain herbicides used in Vietnam were carcinogenic. In response, Professor Olav Axelson accused the commission of 'flaming lies' and 'suppressing and distorting information'.[31] Similarly, the commission ignored or downplayed the evidence of several key medical witnesses, who variously listed the potential effects of exposure to 245-T (with its dioxin contaminant) as cancers, birth defects, low sperm count, loss of libido, skin diseases, loss of neuromuscular control and sensation, and other conditions.[32] Their testimonies had little bearing on Evatt's conclusions.


In time, mounting evidence, in Australia and abroad, demonstrated a clear link between cancer and herbicides, and utterly discredited the Evatt Royal Commission. A watershed case was that of Michael Schar. On 23 December 1991 the Federal Court, drawing on scientific evidence, upheld the judgement that Schar's brain tumour was the result of exposure to chemical defoliants sprayed near Nui Dat in 1968–69 — a precedent that cleared the way for many successful claims.

More persuasively, in 1991 the US Institute of Medicine conducted a comprehensive review of the health effects of exposure to herbicides in Vietnam.[33] It established, for the first time, epidemiological evidence of a clear link between human exposure to herbicides and soft tissue sarcoma; non-Hodgkin's lymphoma; Hodgkin's disease; chloracne; respiratory cancers; prostate cancer; multiple myeloma; porphyria; Type 2 diabetes; and, in the children of veterans, spina bifida and acute myelogenous leukemia. The Australian Government later accepted the US findings.[34]

It was not until 1998 that the full extent of Australian soldiers' exposure to herbicides was revealed, when the mother of all tomes came crashing down: *Morbidity of Vietnam Veterans: A Study of the Health of Australia's Vietnam Veteran Community*, published by the Australian Department of Veterans' Affairs. This huge document drew on 40,030 veterans' responses — an astonishing 80 per cent response rate — to a detailed questionnaire. The findings were profoundly disturbing: 25 per cent of Vietnam veterans reported that they 'had been diagnosed with cancer of some description since their first day of service in Vietnam'; at least 30 per cent reported mental problems: panic attacks, anxiety disorders, depression and post-traumatic stress disorder; and 27 per cent said their children had suffered a major illness. Compared with the national average, Vietnam veterans' cancer rates — based on these responses — were between three and ten times higher (depending on the condition); depressive disorders at least twenty times the normal rate; congenital abnormalities in veterans' children three to eleven times; spina bifida in children at ten times the average; missing body parts in children substantially higher; and deaths from suicide in veterans' children three times the expected rate. Female veterans — aid workers and army and civilian nurses — also recorded significantly higher rates of cancer, heart disease and birth complications.[35]

'The results, if confirmed,' concluded Veterans' Affairs, 'have significant policy implications for veterans' welfare and that of their families [and] raise major concerns about the health of veterans' children.' Veterans' Affairs recommended that the results 'be validated as a matter of urgency'.

Most of the results were confirmed: in 2005 fresh slabs of evidence tumbled off the government's presses.[36] Two huge cancer studies confirmed that rates of Hodgkin's disease in veterans was double the national average, chronic lymphoid leukaemia 50 per cent higher, eye cancer 70 to 75 per cent higher and cancers of the lung, colon, head, neck, prostate and throat significantly higher.[37] National servicemen who served in Vietnam were 23 per cent more likely to die earlier than those who did not serve in Vietnam, three times more likely to die from pancreatic cancer, and twice more likely to suffer head and neck cancers and alcoholic liver disease. However, the results carry an important rider: nashos *in general* were likely to live longer than the public at large. Why? Because most soldiers — nashos and regs — being 'healthy workers', in the government's view — had stronger constitutions than average people. The nashos in particular 'exhibit a strong healthy worker effect'.[38]

In 2007 I asked Australia's recently formed Repatriation Medical Authority (RMA) for a clear statement of current policy. Dr Justine Ward, the RMA's principal medical officer, confirmed the presence of 'a herbicide/dioxin factor' in three types of leukaemia (non-Hodgkin's lymphoma; myeloma; Hodgkin's lymphoma); four types of cancer (malignant neoplasm of the lung, prostate and larynx and soft tissue sarcoma); and five types of disease, including diabetes mellitus, peripheral neuropathy, chloracne and porphyria.[39]

After forty years, one might think a politician would feel, at the very least, a responsibility to acknowledge past mistakes in relation to the chemical poisoning of soldiers. None has done so in Australia. In New Zealand, the government agreed in 2005 to offer a formal apology to veterans who had been exposed to a toxic environment in Vietnam. In fairness, the Department of Veterans' Affairs today recognises that it failed Vietnam veterans in the past;[40] the department is now one of the more responsive and effective of federal government bodies and receives a consistently high approval rating from many of its 'clients' — although a considerable number of veterans continue to give the Department of Veterans' Affairs a very poor approval rating. And in 2007 the Federal Government announced — after a five-year campaign by veteran Geoff Parker and his wife, Sue — a $13.5 million study of medical conditions in veterans' children.

Vietnamese mothers have no doubt about what caused their children's shocking deformities. Dr Ton That Tung first recorded, in 1980, the proliferation of mutations in South Vietnamese children whose fathers had been heavily exposed to herbicides. His Western critics discredited his findings on the grounds that he had served in the Hanoi Government; yet they were consistent with those published in *The Lancet*, the British medical journal, a year earlier. Neither the Vietnamese findings nor the *Lancet* study had any influence on the Australian Government's thinking at the time.

Christopher Hitchens went to Vietnam in 2006 to report on the effects of herbicides. What he saw almost broke his faith in the power of words to describe the things before his eyes: tiny legs and arms bent at impossible angles; children's faces that seemed too big or small for their skulls; twitching children lying tethered to their cots on the floor. Dark thoughts of euthanasia flew away, Hitchens wrote, when he observed the heroic work of Dr Nguyen Thi Phuonh Tan and the clinic's happier treasures: a laughing little armless 10-year-old who skipped in and signed her name with her left foot. Her father, a soldier, had died of leukaemia at the age of 42.[41]

As the politicians' self-justifying memoirs are sloughed off and forgotten, ignorant future generations may wander in dismay through these clinics of deformed infants and think: how did these children get that way? 'Some of the victims of Agent Orange haven't even been born yet,' Hitchens observed, 'and if that reflection doesn't shake you, then my words have been feeble and not even the photographs will do.'[42]

# Chapter 47
# 'Totally and permanently incapacitated'

In thy faint slumbers I by thee have watched,
And heard thee murmur tales of iron wars ...
Cry 'Courage! To the field!' And thou hast talked
Of sallies and retires, of trenches, tents ...
Of prisoners ransomed, and of soldiers slain,
And all the currents of a heady fight.
*Lady Percy to Hotspur, Shakespeare,* Henry IV.[1]

Have you ever looked in their eyes? It frightens me.
*Diane Poulton, wife of a Vietnam veteran.*

'I ran the house like the Gestapo' is a common veteran's remark. Terrifying mood swings, blinding aggression, drunken binges, paranoid inertia and explosive silences composed the little hell they made of their homes. Such were the components of the sandbagged mind. 'I can't hold a job'; 'I've got no future'; 'I'm stuffed, rooted, finished ...' etc. Their wives and children walked on eggshells around these seething, self-pitying old brutes who would contemplate the world from inside their living room perimeter with the ineffable loathing of the chronic alcoholic. Shakespeare's Lady Percy knew the half of it: many Australian wives lived in terror of their husbands' tantrums and violence. 'I was the enemy,' said one. 'He's walking around like a time bomb,' said another. Or: 'The only emotion he ever showed was rage.' Talk of 'love' fell like a plumb in a disused well; conventional love found no place in the minds of young men who had seen the worst of human hatred. Sex had a machine-like quality, or ceased. Terrible nightmares, sweat-drenched sheets, shouts and sudden jolting actions punctuated these epic nights, in which the entire platoon seemed to share the marital bed. In their husband's delirious sleep-fighting, wives were taken on midnight operations. 'Watch that bush!' one soldier told his wife, or: 'Contact! Wait out!' Another wife found herself sitting up in bed preparing to 'move out'. 'Get your rifle ready!' her husband cried. By day, the nocturnal troops awoke to inflict new miseries on their families; their children ran away, or hid, or fought back — to face verbal or physical abuse. One soldier forced his five-year-old daughter watch him gut a bunny; another, in a fit of rage, smashed his son's cricket bat.

Divorce delivered years of loneliness. 'Where is my son today? Where is my daughter?' these broken men would plead, to the wind, to the sky … to the past. 'My friends have been the trees, the sun, the stars,' wrote one deeply alienated soldier. 'My relatives are the grass, the fish, the birds, the ants …'[2]

Others survived the slide and built relatively content, if not sober, lives. But the demons were never far away. The soldiers had seen the beast beneath the veneer of civilisation. 'All our lives are about meeting standards and values,' said Harry Whiteside, an SAS veteran. 'In war there are no standards or values. War takes a blender to standards and values, and turns it up full bore. Men come back from that and spend the rest of their lives trying to find out who they are.'[3]

The lucky ones found out, with their families' patience and care. Thousands owe their survival to the unsung heroines of this story, their wives, whose devotion and tolerance in the most difficult and often violent circumstances slowly won back these wrecks of men. With such help, many soldiers dragged themselves out of the darkness. Many did not. 'It seems like they can't get rid of their anger, their hate,' said Diane Poulton, whose husband tried to commit suicide. 'Have you ever looked in their eyes? It frightens me.'[4]

Yet one cannot write of a soldier's trauma without sensing the scorn of those who tend to rubbish the soldiers' complaints and argue that these young men were *predisposed* to being self-destructive drunks, paranoiac maniacs, wife-beaters and malingerers. According to this line of thinking, the soldiers' characters were always prone to psychological problems and alcoholism regardless of Vietnam: don't blame the war; blame the man.

Indeed, like everything else about the Vietnam War, the story of the aftermath is one long, ugly conflict. Let us briefly hear the soldiers' stories, then consider their detractors' claims.

David Booth, an ex-SAS soldier, worked as an ambulance paramedic after the war. The job exacerbated the symptoms of post-traumatic stress disorder common to thousands of veterans: he has recurring incandescent dreams of death by gunshot, bombs or falling from great heights. Unlike most of us, who tend to wake before we die, Booth dreams on *after* the bullet has entered his head or his body strikes the rocks. '... then follows an indeterminate time of being dead ... The "blackness" of this is difficult to describe,' he explains, in personal notes given to his doctor, entitled 'Fucked in the Head'.[5]

'Fucked in the Head', written in 1996, while in his late forties, is a captivating self-diagnosis by a man with the literary skill to articulate precisely what is going on in his head. It was indeed fucked; yet this description of his struggle with the psychological scars of war is also a triumph of self-willed recovery. Booth cannot recall, in his scattered notes, the moment 'I went bananas; of my old life before a cake mixer reached into my skull and turned everything into spaghetti. All I have is a notebook full of the bad poems which I wrote through the nights ...'

Veterans will identify with his sudden bursts of near-uncontrollable rage. One day he made a low offer on a house to an estate agent when 'there popped out of an adjoining cubicle a man who ... immediately started going off his face about my insultingly low offer etc etc':

At first I was bemused, then puzzled and finally I became angry ... he snuck through my defences before I could get the clamps on the lid ... Had I not turned my back on him and walked straight out of the office, that man would have been dead. I would have hurled him bodily through his plate glass window, then sawn his head off on the jagged edge. Followed by his arms and legs. This took place about twelve years ago and the ignorant little prick is still alive and unslaughtered ... I was truly a hair's breadth from going berserk. My reaction, being so extreme, really did shake me up, and that may explain why I have this fear of my own anger.

Booth found solace in the company of Keith Meredith, of the Perth Vietnam Veterans Counselling Service. 'Keith listened … Then he started to tell me about myself … Quite simply, he told me I was a classic case of a thing called post-traumatic stress disorder … there are thousands more like me around.' Keith's diagnosis 'fitted me exactly. I had no problem accepting it, it was like a raft drifting by and I grabbed it. That conversation was like talking to God.' He applied for a pension at the Department of Veterans' Affairs in Perth. Thus began a seemingly endless round of letters, forms and delays. One day, in desperation, he rang the department and said that if they did not make a decision, 'I would come down to Perth with a can of petrol and incinerate myself on their doorstep, with the press watching. I meant every word, although I was actually going to do it at the Vietnam War Memorial.'[6]

For others, personal tragedy often triggered what lay beneath. When Bernie Cox's father suffered a heart attack during a Balmain versus Norths rugby match, Bernie shouted to the bewildered medics: 'Can we get a dust-off in here?' Seeing his father die brought on a series of nightmares, so Bernie went to see a psychiatrist, 'the first I'd ever seen. I told him a few things and said, "Look, I think this post-traumatic stress thing is all bullshit." He said, "No, mate, It's not bullshit. Eighty per cent of rape victims have it, 40 per cent of people in combat have it and you definitely have it." '[7]

On 6 June 1970 Mick O'Halloran lost his three closest friends in a land mine in Vietnam. He got over it and lived a tolerable life. Then, years later, his youngest son died: 'The only complication is that my son, who I loved dearly, died suddenly … at age 24 and he has drifted into my nightmare and is tangled in with my mates who were killed.'[8]

Others felt paranoid or sociopathic. David Hall's experiences are typical:

I have a 32-year-old daughter who appears to hate me. I met my second wife [in 1976] and I have one 13-year-old daughter by her. They both appear to dislike me intensely too, though I have never missed a support payment … I have a total intolerance for bullshit, which translates to the fact that I don't socialise and no one wants to socialise with me either. This is peaceful, but it is also gut-wrenchingly lonely … So I drink a lot, mainly wine … It's the only friend I have. I am unable to sit at a dinner party and talk inanities like house prices and which school is best and 'Tell me how your diet is going' … I have never walked into an RSL club or been on a march. I have never worn my two medals from Vietnam. I have never watched a movie about Vietnam, except for *Rambo*, which dealt, I thought, with a Vietnam veteran suffering from PTSD.[9]

In a rundown Randwick bungalow lives Dr Denis Gibbons, alone, surrounded by boxes containing thousands of photographs of war; the photos are his. A man of exceptional physical courage and high intelligence, Gibbons was awarded an Order of Australia for his multi-award-winning photojournalism in Vietnam. He has several university degrees. Wounded six times in Vietnam, he received a gunshot wound to the head, and multiple shrapnel wounds on two occasions, and almost broke his back after being blown 10 metres in a mine blast ('If it goes again, I may be a paraplegic'). He suffers from acute post-traumatic stress disorder: 'My brain is imprinted with war. I get the shakes. I wake bolt upright in bed, screaming … I refuse the pills. What's the point of deadening your brain?' For twenty years Gibbons did not see his children — three boys and three girls. 'They're all bright and successful. One day my youngest, Sean, put his hand up … So I see Sean.'[10]

These days Gibbons spends a lot of time watching classic Hollywood movies. 'I love movies of 1930 to 1953, the golden years of Hollywood. I've got hundreds of 'em … I hate modern movies — "Fuck this and fuck that", the massacre movies …' Every few years he visits Broadway: 'I stay at a little pub off Broadway, and I see all the musicals and shows for three weeks. One day Sean and I will go over.'

Something happened to these men in Vietnam, the depths of which society has yet to fathom. Many have tried to lead 'normal' lives: they married, had children and found jobs; they attempted, unaided, to self-diagnose, to make sense of what they had become. The worst cases lapsed into a misanthropic limbo, neither dead nor alive, 'doomed for a certain term to walk the night'.[11] And like the ghost of Hamlet's father, they did indeed carry a terrible message for their sons.

The Trojans and the Greeks suffered from it, as Homer records in *The Iliad*. Shakespeare described it in *Henry IV*. During World War I they called it 'shell shock'; in World War II and Korea combat neurosis and combat fatigue and, after the Gulf War, Gulf War syndrome. Victims of rape and violent crime share the symptoms. Today, psychiatrists prefer the term post-traumatic stress disorder. The condition afflicts about 13,000 Australian Vietnam veterans. To call it a 'disorder' suggests that an unblemished, orderly mental state should be the healthy response to war. On the contrary, doctors see PTSD as the reaction of otherwise healthy minds to an extremely disorderly situation. Or, as Dr Victor Frankel put it: 'An abnormal response to an abnormal situation is normal behaviour.'

This is a very recent view. Until 1980 Western health authorities did not recognise PTSD as a genuine medical condition. Soldiers were told to stop moaning and get on with their lives. A parade of experts suggested bizarre explanations for the troops' complaints; for example, a professor of chemistry at the University of Tasmania attributed veterans' complaints to their widespread use of marijuana, and a psychiatrist at Sydney University suggested that soldiers' intense guilt over 'atrocities' had caused their psychological problems. Such diagnoses simply revealed the experts' profound ignorance of the war.

Then, in 1980, the American Psychiatric Association's *Diagnostic and Statistics Manual of Mental Disorders* affirmed PTSD's legitimacy as a mental illness. Veterans' psychological problems were professionally accepted as 'normal reaction[s]' to stressful situations.[12] This was an important turning point, as Dr Kristy Muir shows in her excellent study of the psychological effects of World War II and the Indonesian Confrontation on Australian veterans: exposure to the acute stress of war, rather than a predisposed personality disorder, was the major cause of mental illness in veterans.[13]

Since then, doctors and military experts have refined our understanding of PTSD. 'Once the condition has become chronic — usually if it has persisted for two years or more — there is no cure for it,' observed Philip Morris, professor of psychiatry at Queensland University. PTSD has also been linked to physical diseases, such as heart conditions and cancers, according to a study published in *New Scientist* in 2005.[14]

Vietnam veterans registered a higher rate of PTSD than veterans of earlier wars, for several reasons, the most obvious being that, given a medical explanation for their condition, they were more likely to seek treatment. They were also from a generation who were more likely to speak their minds; veterans of previous wars with 'combat stress' tended to keep quiet about it. The particular combat conditions in Vietnam exacerbated the trauma. Brigadier William Rodgers, a former director of Australian Army Medical Services, claimed that the stress levels in the Vietnam campaign were up to

200 times greater than stress levels in World War II.[15] In Vietnam, the infantry soldier experienced months in combat zones, far longer than in previous wars; the intense psychological strain of fighting an invisible enemy in mined areas and bunker systems; a high incidence of accidental civilian deaths; and a greater willingness to shoot to kill, as a result of more advanced training methods — as Lieutenant Colonel David Grossman shows in his classic *On Killing*. In World War II, on average, just 15 to 20 per cent of riflemen actually fired at an exposed enemy soldier, Grossman argues (drawing on earlier findings by the historian Brigadier General S. L. A. Marshall). This figure rose to 55 per cent in the Korean War and 90 per cent in Vietnam, he states, as advanced training overcame the soldier's natural reluctance to kill another human. 'Man is not, by nature, a close-range interpersonal killer,' Grossman concludes[16] — one reason bomber and fighter pilots, who inflicted far more casualties than infantrymen, suffer lower rates of PTSD.

Despite the acceptance of PTSD as an illness, many people continue to dismiss Vietnam veterans' complaints as bogus and their compensation claims as fraudulent. 'They're lazy, rorting malingerers,' a senior Defence Department official told me in 2005. 'Some want pensions for being turned into drunks; others say they were in actions they never were in. Then they hit retirement and claim a pension.'[17]

Several high-ranking soldiers agree. 'I find that many of the PTSD disability claims — a new and disgraceful industry motivated by greed at the taxpayer's expense — to be abhorrent and that many of these patently false claims diminish my self-respect as a soldier,' said one retired brigadier, who examines claims for the Department of Veterans' Affairs.[18]

Indeed, in the 1990s a 'rising chorus of complaint from outside psychiatry' insisted that PTSD had turned a generation of veterans into 'hopeless, dependent, welfare junkies', according to historian Ben Shephard, who argued that many soldiers were either predisposed to such problems or fabricated their symptoms for financial or social gain.[19] Dr Dale Atrens, a former reader in psychology at Sydney University, in his essay 'Madness and Neuromythology' claimed that PTSD was 'fictitious' and a prop for financial dependence. However, he also denounced the entire psychiatric profession. Psychiatry had 'hitched its wagon to the ascendant medical star on false premises', he wrote, because the 'idea that madness is a disease does not have reasonable basis in science'. Most war veterans' mental health diagnoses were simply a 'gateway to litigation', and a soldier's trauma was 'cause for sympathy, little else'.[20]

Clearly some veterans have cheated the system, lied about their military service or simply joined an available bandwagon. A strong incentive was the value of the package, which is rather misleadingly called a Totally and Permanently Incapacitated (TPI) pension and worth around $900 a fortnight, tax-free, with free travel and other perks. The pension is available to veterans who can show that they were in a combat zone, suffered combat-related stress, or saw or handled corpses, among other criteria. This annuity — lavish by international standards — has certainly encouraged a welfare mentality in Vietnam veterans. 'The nature of the compensation system encourages people to be ill,' said one medical authority tactfully. The sheer volume of recipients — 25,000 (about half of whom have been diagnosed with PTSD)[21] — and veterans' insistence that the payment is rightful compensation, *not* welfare, has to some extent removed the stigma. Perversely, some veterans wear the label 'Totally and Permanently Incapacitated' as a badge of honour, a kind of additional medal. That rather inverts the traditional idea of honour.

At the heart of the case against the 'TPI industry' is the idea of predisposition. Government and professional critics have long argued that Vietnam veterans were *predisposed* to psychological problems and alcoholism, regardless of Vietnam. Probably some recruits had borderline personality disorders, and certain soldiers would have gone to jail had they not volunteered for the army. And every generation, of course, produces some young men destined for Alcoholics Anonymous.

Yet as a general explanation the predisposition theory falls down in several ways. First, it is unprovable — because we cannot know how these men *might* have turned out had they *not* gone to Vietnam (it is true, however, that certain personality conditions — childhood trauma, mental disorders, lack of social support — do appear to influence the onset of PTSD, according to Dr Justine Ward).[22]

Second, on its own terms, the idea that a soldier was predisposed to mental illness overlooks the fact that the opposite outcome was far more likely: all the signs suggest that the soldiers, had they not gone to Vietnam, were predisposed to lead healthy, normal lives. The troops sent to Vietnam were carefully screened and selected; the nashos in particular were hailed as the 'cream of Australia's youth', the 'finest young men of their generation' and 'some of the best soldiers Australia has produced' (to pool a sample of their commanders' comments). The government's own mortality studies refer to them as 'healthy workers' who enjoyed the 'healthy worker effect'. How does this square with a 'predisposition' to long-drawn-out personal breakdown? The troops cannot have been both exemplary young men *and* latent psychopaths.

Indeed, if they *were* predisposed to chronic psychiatric problems at the time they enlisted or were drafted, why did the army's screening fail to detect these maniacs before it sent them off to war? To claim years later that a soldier was always likely to become a drunken misfit and sociopath — *regardless* of his war experience — is an implicit admission of an extraordinary failure of judgement by the military and the government. No doubt the military 'psych tests' at the time were fairly rudimentary; yet army instructors had a year to observe their recruits performing in the harshest circumstances. Another way of looking at it is this: how could it be that the government's *random* national service scheme captured such a disproportionately high number of latent sociopaths, drunkards and wife-beaters?

Of course it did not, and the soldiers were not. The simple truth is that PTSD is, in most cases, a genuine medical complaint, as most doctors now agree. Understandably — in the absence of any medical help on their return from Vietnam — many veterans sought relief in drink and drugs, which contributed to their higher rates of cancer, liver and lung disease. Cause and effect were thus confused. 'To the extent that veterans were not encouraged to seek help for symptoms precipitated by their war experience,' explained Dr Ward, 'a large number of them would not have been diagnosed until they had serious problems. Furthermore, the use of alcohol and cigarettes to lessen anxiety … has contributed to higher than expected rates of physical illness.'[23]

Vietnam veterans should stop moaning and get on with their lives, say their critics. 'World War veterans didn't moan and seek compensation' is a typical remark. This misses the point. Vietnam veterans are unique, in one important respect: unlike returning soldiers in previous wars, they came home to a deeply hostile reception. Veterans of the world wars received a heroes' welcome, which greatly assisted their recovery, say psychiatrists. The psychological trauma of returning to indifference or hatred is a unique phenomenon, believes Dr Karl Koller, a leading psychiatrist to Vietnam veterans.[24] Indeed, it gravely magnified their subsequent breakdown, agreed Dr Ward. 'We know that social support buffers the effect of stressful events,' she said. 'The lack of social support experienced by Vietnam veterans on their repatriation is likely to have contributed to higher than expected levels of psychological illness.'[25]

Far from rorting the system, many veterans down the years have in fact failed to apply for the benefits available. Former servicemen, such as John Casey, Terry Loftus, Noel Payne and others, have spent years trying to find and help these lost soldiers. Payne's organisation, the Armed Services Assistance Centre (of which he is president), conducts up to a thousand interviews a year with veterans; 60 to 70 per cent are eligible for compensation. 'One moment they're the town drunks; the next, heroes with a chest full of medals,' Payne said. He found one ex-infantryman living in a corrugated iron shack. 'He was a deadset fruitcake. He couldn't stop crying when he heard what we could do for him. He went for tests. Doctors said he suffered from massive psychological damage.' Veterans' Affairs gave the man a pension, and in time he was rehabilitated. He now lives with his wife and children in a $60,000 Queenslander, sits on an RSL board and wears four medals. (Payne has caught up with a few fakes, too. In one extreme case, a bloke took the identity of his brother, a veteran who died in a car crash. 'He already had a disability pension and a service pension. He came to us for a top-up!')[26]

Hundreds of Vietnam veterans have committed suicide since the war; the rate is slightly higher than that of the general population. To suggest that these men were predisposed to suicide is a gross insult. Often their deaths were intimately connected with the war: one veteran drove from Perth to Adelaide, parked outside his battalion's headquarters and gassed himself to death. Some simply disappeared, such as Major Noel Ford, who vanished off Bondi Beach. He commanded Bravo Company during the battle of Long Tan, an experience from which, his colleagues say, he never recovered. Or consider Ron Witty, whose brother and father also served in Vietnam. His brother committed suicide; his father died of cancer; and his mother, unable to cope, took to drink and died of alcoholic poisoning. 'In my family,' said Witty, 'the war's killed three ... and only left half of the fourth.'[27]


Perhaps the most extraordinary story of survival is that of Graham Edwards, the Western Australian politician. Edwards lost both legs in a mine blast. On his return to Australia he spent three years in military rehab. Having left school at 15, he welcomed this opportunity to improve his education. The army sent him to a civilian institution in Toorak, which offered 'basic primary school' English, maths and woodwork. In the first month, his class was taught to make a breadboard, during which a fellow disabled soldier, Tom Bourke, 'did his block in spectacular fashion and told the powers that be to stick this program up their fundamental orifice and stormed out'.

Edwards decided to persevere. After completing the breadboard, he found himself learning how to make a pair of moccasins. 'It did not seem to faze them that a man with no legs should be making moccasins.' He requested a transfer back to Western Australia. After a year of arguments about his future, Edwards was discharged. 'The army got its way. No thanks. No goodonya, mate. No best wishes for the future. Just sign here and piss off.' He took a commercial secretarial course in typing and shorthand: it made sense to train his hands. Yet it had drawbacks. His artificial legs, which were held on by suction, often fell off halfway up the steep flight of stairs to classes: 'I had to sit on my bum and drag myself up or down the stairs and attempt to put them back on.' Most of his classmates were adolescent girls, and encounters were awkward: 'I would be sitting in the quiet of the classroom, surrounded by these young girls, when the suction on the sockets of my legs would break. The loud fart-like sound ... was a moment of indescribable embarrassment.' He completed the course, and searched for a job to support his wife and child.

The army offered him a job in a sheltered workshop, working alongside disabled youths, sorting paperclips and separating lids from glass jars. Edwards recalls almost punching the officer who showed him over the premises: 'I stumbled down the stairs with ... tears welling in my eyes. Three years of mind-numbing rehabilitation and education. Three of the worst years in my life and all they could offer me was a job in a sheltered workshop. I can't remember what I told my wife that night. I think I told her nothing. But I know this: I determined I would never put myself under the control of the system again.' Today, Edwards is the federal Labor MP for Cowan.[28]

Many diggers and officers survived the war relatively unscathed; indeed, for some the experience was possibly character building. Many pursued fulfilling careers and had relatively happy family lives. To survive Scheyville was to survive life, and former cadets have been conspicuously successful:

in politics, Tim Fischer (former Deputy Prime Minister and Minister for Trade) and Terry Gygar (a Queensland Liberal MP for fifteen years); in business, Marcus Blackmore (health care), Darrel Jarvis (corporate finance — he helped reshape the Holmes à Court empire), Gordon Alexander (advertising), and Wayne Banks and Tony Sonneveld (pest control). Dick Adam became Assistant Police Commissioner in New South Wales and Gary McKay a military author. Twelve Scheyville graduates stayed on in the army and reached the rank of brigadier: Gary Byles, Wayne Jackson, Peter Kilpatrick, Peter Pursey, Angus McNeilage, John Mears, Neil Turner, Brian Vale, Duncan Warren, David Webster, Neil Weekes and Jeff Wilkinson. Others devoted their lives to charity and community work, returned to Vietnam to help rebuild, or adopted Vietnamese children.

And Australian veterans have proved remarkably adept at helping themselves. They formed veterans' associations, counselling services, wives' clubs and retreats; together they fought bureaucratic indifference, social marginalisation and the hostility of the RSL.[29] Many have made a strong recovery. David Booth, for example, slowly began to see the 'Alps, rather than Himalayas' on the horizon and pulled himself out of the Slough of Despond. To his fellow veterans, he advises: 'I'm not speaking for you. As I said, I don't know shit. But … I can say this. Hang in, take charge of your life when you can, and learn the delight of showing all the appropriate emotions even if you don't really feel them: It's a start.'[30]

Thousands simply resumed their lives. It did not occur to them to press for compensation; they felt they had done their duty and did not feel entitled to 'entitlements'. Some were too proud to admit to problems. In this light, the Vietnamese experience is interesting. 'I didn't volunteer for the army. I didn't demand a salary,' said Nguyen Van Mac, a North Vietnamese captain whose experience is common. 'Today, I get terrible head pains at loud noises. After the B52 strikes, I was bleeding from the ears and nose.'

Do you receive a pension or compensation? I asked.

'I do not expect payment. I was doing my duty. I sympathise with our government.'[31]

# Chapter 48
# Welcome home

I believe I downgraded a few [awards] myself, and scrubbed
others at the time.
*Lieutenant Colonel Colin Townsend, Commander, 6th Battalion.*

At an officers' dinner in Canberra in 1987 someone raised the subject of
the Welcome Home Parade, to be held on 3 October. What did the
officers think? Would they be marching? A lieutenant colonel and several
lower ranks — majors, captains and lieutenants — spoke in turn: yes, it was
a good idea, but no, 'I probably won't be marching'. The march was for the
diggers, not commissioned officers. The last to speak was a corporal, the
only non-commissioned officer present, who firmly told the table: 'This
march is being organised by the soldiers and they expect the officers to
attend.'

'To a man,' said Captain John Press later, 'everyone at that table
marched.'[1]

And so, under that spirited inversion of authority, this great gesture of
national reconciliation proceeded. 'All the committee were privates and
NCOs, and we were going to be dealing with generals,' said Peter Poulton,
chief organiser of the National Reunion and Welcome Home Parade, as it
was officially called.[2]

The idea originated in America in 1986, when hundreds of thousands
of Vietnam veterans marched, limped or rolled through every major city, to
a huge reception. Political gestures and civilian amends were the themes of

the day; for example, the slogans 'Honor the warrior, not the war' and 'It's not too late to say we're sorry'.[3] Poulton and five other veterans who saw the Chicago march wondered whether it could work in Australia. They adapted the idea as a simple welcome home parade, the traditional kind that so many troops were denied when they returned from Vietnam.

Sir Colin Hines, the president of the New South Wales RSL, admired and supported the idea, as would many RSL branches.[4] The media rallied, too: the ABC promised a full live broadcast to 288 local TV stations, and *The Ray Martin Show* offered live commentary. Major General Sandy Pearson AO DSO OBE MC (retd) gladly accepted the role of patron, to the dismay of some of his crusty colleagues. Politicians instinctively wanted a place in the sunshine of reconciliation. Yet Prime Minister Bob Hawke's Labor Government was in an uneasy position: Hawke had led the ACTU during part of the waterfront strikes that had so damaged the soldiers' morale. He now cast that role as a mere difference of opinion. 'There is, of course, no denying the fact,' he wrote in the parade program, 'that the Vietnam War was one of the most divisive and disturbing issues in Australia's history. But equally, whatever our individual views on the merits of Australian involvement, all of us acknowledge the courage, dedication and sacrifices of our forces in Vietnam.'[5] That did little to dispel the soldiers' feeling that Hawke's union leadership had directly undermined their 'dedication and sacrifices'.

The soldiers came in their tens of thousands: veterans and their families, representing every unit that served in Vietnam, across the three services, from all over Australia: the cities, rural towns, outback stations, Cabramatta, bedsits, motorcycle clubs … The domestic airlines and hotels offered cheap packages; the defence forces made beds available in their Sydney barracks.

This immense crowd converged on the city in the 'greatest emotional outpouring Sydney has witnessed in decades', reported the *Sun Herald*. Rowdy Friday night reunion parties flowed into the dawn service at the Cenotaph in Martin Place where, at 4.30 a.m., the largest gathering ever to assemble there joined in remembrance.

Brigadier Colin Khan DSO broke the silence after 'The Recessional' — 'Judge of the Nations, spare us yet/Lest we forget — lest we forget' — with simple words in memory of the dead, so few in number, yet somehow more knowable than the great honour rolls of the world wars: '… on this, the dawning of a great day of reunion, we pay homage to our particular 500 colleagues who will not be marching with us today ...'[6] His Excellency Air Marshal Sir James Rowland AC KBE DFC AFC, Governor of New South Wales, read the dedication — 'Let us therefore ... dedicate ourselves to the ideals for which they died. As the dawn is even now about to pierce the night, so let their memory inspire us to work for the coming new light into the dark places of the world ...' — and laid the wreath.

A bugler played. The chill wail of 'The Last Post' pierced the heart of the sternest general and summoned up Australian battlefields past, of beaches and plains, deserts and jungles ... and of the almost forgotten few, the Vietnam dead. The president of the New South Wales RSL read Laurence Binyon's 'Ode', whose spirit resonated with deeper poignancy in the minds of war veterans of just forty years:

> They shall not grow old
> As we who are left grow old,
> Age shall not weary them
> Nor the years condemn;
> At the going down of the sun
> And in the morning ...
> We will remember them.

Whatever one's view of the war, the soldiers had done what was asked of them: thus were they ushered into the pantheon of the Anzac.

At 7 a.m. the great crowd moved on to the Domain. Little reunions flared within this larger reunion, like bubbles popping on the surface of a simmering sea. Old friends rediscovered each other, and relived in seconds the shared experience of a lifetime. Then they formed up, each under their unit's banner. 'I was staggered by the crowd. The ground was packed and so were the trees and balconies,' said one veteran.[7] 'There were bagpipes tuning up, kettle drums rattling, men yelling and cooeeing mates they hadn't seen for years, marshals yelling orders,' recalled James Ibbetson, of the Royal Australian Army Service Corps (RAASC). 'We were lined up twelve abreast in each section, 200–odd to each under their respective banners. The tension rose to almost tangible proportions as we waited for our turn to march off.'[8]

Twenty-five thousand Vietnam veterans marched, witnessed by a crowd estimated at more than 400,000. A flag, borne by his mother, father, wife, son, daughter or friend, represented most of the Australian dead, as twenty flags that should have been issued were not. The forest of standards led the parade, and the long line unwound behind them: the parade leaders; the disabled veterans; the sole living Victoria Cross recipient, Keith Payne; the Team; the Army and Air Force Nursing Corps; the Royal Australian Navy; RAN Helicopter Flight Vietnam; the crews of HMAS *Sydney*, *Brisbane*, *Perth*, *Hobart*, *Vendetta*, *Jeparit*, *Boonaroo*; Headquarters Australian Force Vietnam; Headquarters First Australian Logistics and Supply Group; Headquarters First Australian Task Force; the Royal Australian Armoured, Artillery, Engineers, Survey and Signal Corps; the infantry — the 1st, 2nd, 3rd, 4th, 5th, 6th, 7th, 8th and 9th Battalions, Royal Australian Regiment; SAS; chaplains; Australian Army Aviation; the Intelligence Corps; Royal Australian Army Service Corps, and Royal Australian Army Medical Corps; Royal Australian Electrical and Mechanical Engineers; Royal Australian Army Aviation Corps; Royal Australian Army Provost Corps; Civilian Military Force Observers; RAAF Contingent Vung Tau, Caribou Flight, No. 35 Squadron, Base Support Flight, No. 9 Squadron, No. 2 Squadron, No. 5 Airfield Reconstruction Squadron, No. 1 Operational Support Unit; the Red Cross; Salvation Army; war correspondents; war artists, photographers and historians; civilian medical teams; entertainers; Everyman's Welfare Service; representatives of the New Zealand Army, US Marines, Army, Navy and Air Force, and armed forces of South Vietnam, South Korea, Thailand and the Philippines. Peter Poulton and the march organisers took up the rear.

Men in wheelchairs, men with walking sticks and men with the slightly stiff gait of those on prostheses set the pace. The flag-bearers led the march down Hunter Street and slowly up George Street, through hundreds of thousands of cheering spectators. 'During the march,' recalled one woman, 'I went up to a soldier who had stopped in the heat and taken off his hat. I simply said, "Thank you". He broke into tears.'

'… [at] every step, tree, fence, scaffold, people were yelling, "Good on you … It's about time",' recalled Roy Gunning of the Royal Australian Navy. Old soldiers bearing the medals of the Great War 'were patting us on the back, and World War II nurses … even grandmothers throwing rose petals over us, throwing kisses as we marched'.

In George Street the applause swelled beneath huge signs, 'At last welcome home' and 'Sydney honours the VV', amid spectators ten deep in places. At the Town Hall, many soldiers pointedly refused to salute Prime Minister Hawke, who stood at attention on the official dais. 'What's he doing there?' 'Who invited him?' some mumbled. 'I heard this murmur go back through the ranks … what a hypocritical bastard,' recalled John Priestland, of 161 Independent Recce Flight.[9] 'When I saw the Prime Minister there,' said one veteran's wife, 'a feeling of real bitterness came over me.'[10]

The crowds were struck by the number of decorations: Vietnam was a war without heroes, wasn't it, some wondered. Stories of the soldiers' courage had not impinged on the public mind. Yet here were rows of medals flashing in the Sydney sun. Here, for example, was Sergeant Ron Allan DCM, who twenty years ago had rushed forward under fire to drag the wounded to safety. Here, too, Corporal James Archbold MM: ambushed in a convoy, he had leaped out, shielded the wounded driver on the road and returned fire. Corporal Phillip Baxter MM, although wounded in a mine blast, had quickly marked lanes towards the more severely hurt and calmly reassured them; Private Keith Downward MM crawled to within 10 metres of an enemy machine-gunner, captured the gun and later, although wounded by a hand grenade, continued to fight until ordered to withdraw; Lance Corporal David Griffiths DCM kept firing despite being shot in both arms; Private Tom Hardwick MM, a stretcher-bearer, retrieved a wounded soldier at night, under fire, stopping now and then to apply mouth-to-mouth resuscitation; Sapper Neil Innes MM saved the lives of two American gunners, one unconscious, the other convulsing within 20 centimetres of a second mine; Warrant Officers John Malone QCBC (Queen's Commendation for Brave Conduct) and John McEwan-Ferguson (QCBC) carried Vietnamese civilians to safety across flooded waters during a 48-hour rescue mission; Major John Murphy MC, of SAS, reconnoitred the Nui Thi Vai Mountains, hanging 45 metres from a helicopter wire; Captain Amy Pittendreigh and her small nursing contingent provided constant service to the sick and wounded; and Private Peter Wilson MID, in shock from a mine explosion, saved the life of a severely wounded soldier by using his bootlaces as a tourniquet …

This is a sample of hundreds of awards.[11] In total, Australians in Vietnam received four Victoria Crosses; thirty-seven Distinguished Service Orders; nine Distinguished Service Crosses; fifty-four Military Crosses (one with bar); seventy-eight Distinguished Flying Crosses; forty-two Distinguished Conduct Medals; eighty-five Military Medals; twenty British Empire Medals; and 604 mentions in despatches (MID). Six veterans received the Companion of the Order of the Bath (CB); twelve the

Commander of the Order of the British Empire (CBE); eighteen the Office of the Order of the British Empire (OBE); and forty-eight the Member of the Order of the British Empire (MBE).[12] National servicemen received 107 awards, including nine Military Crosses, twenty-two Military Medals and forty-six MIDs — which is low, given the praise heaped on their performance and the fact that they made up 40 per cent of rifle companies. As a result, allegations of army bias were never far from the nashos' minds.

The performance of the three Australian helicopter units belied the disparaging claims against some pilots: No. 9 Squadron earned thirty of sixty-six of the RAAF's DFCs; the navy's Helicopter Flight Vietnam received three of four navy MBEs, eight of nine DSCs and all six DFCs as well as several high US awards, including a Silver Star to Sub-lieutenant A.C. Perry; and members of the 161 Independent Reconnaissance Flight, an army unit, were awarded twelve DFCs, the first time the army had won this award.[13]

'The most highly decorated unit in Australian military history' is the oft-repeated accolade attached to the Australian Army Training Team Vietnam. Some infantry criticise this unlikely medal cluster as politically driven; yet it seemed richly deserved, as any fair-minded study of the citations shows. As well as four Victoria Crosses, members of the Team were awarded two DSOs, three OBEs, six MBEs, six MCs, twenty DCMs, sixteen MMs, four BEMs, four Queen's Commendations and forty-nine MIDs. Added to this were numerous US awards including one Distinguished Service Cross, eighteen Silver Stars, sixty-four Bronze Stars as well as 376 Republic of South Vietnam awards. This, across a unit that totalled merely a thousand men. The USA bestowed the unique honour on Keith Payne VC of upgrading his Silver Star to a Distinguished Service Cross and entering his citation in the Hall of Heroes at the John F. Kennedy Center for Military Assistance at Fort Bragg, North Carolina.

For 'extraordinary heroism' at the battle of Long Tan, Harry Smith's Delta Company, 6th Battalion was awarded the highest US unit decoration for valour in battle, the Presidential Unit Citation. Only one other Australian Army unit — the 3rd Battalion for Kapyong, Korea — has earned this distinction. The 6th Battalion's individual awards were: Lieutenant Colonel Colin Townsend, DSO; Captain Morrie Stanley, MBE; Major Harry Smith, MC; Sergeant Major Jack Kirby and Corporal John Carter, DCMs; Sergeant Bob Buick and Private Ron Eglinton, MMs; and Lieutenants Adrian

Roberts, Geoff Kendall and David Sabben, Warrant Officer Jack Roughley, Corporals Phil Dobson and Bill Moore, Bombardier William Walker and Private Bill Akell, MIDs. In addition, the chopper pilot Flight Lieutenant Frank Riley received a DFC and Flight Lieutenant Cliff Dohle an MID.

We tread warily in the controversial realm of military decorations. Conspiracy theories and 'anomalies' abound in an awards system that is deeply imbued with the tribal culture of the army, in which a medal quota system applied during the Vietnam War. The Long Tan awards, for example, sparked an extraordinarily bitter forty-year struggle that warrants attention.

After the battle, Canberra sought to heal, with the balm of heroism, the national anguish over the sudden loss of eighteen soldiers. The politicians urgently needed heroes, so the battalion commander Colin Townsend rang Harry Smith on the night of 21 August 1966, the day the exhausted troops completed burying the dead. Townsend demanded recommendations for awards 'by the next afternoon'. Canberra was insistent, he said: the government needed the Queen's approval as soon as possible. Smith therefore recommended David Sabben, Geoff Kendall, Adrian Roberts and Morrie Stanley for MCs, Bob Buick, Bill Moore and Bill Akell for MMs and Gordon Sharp for a posthumous MID. Townsend, for his part, recommended Smith for a DSO.

Smith's list, however, exceeded the battalion's quota, and Townsend prevailed upon him to trim it. 'There was a ration [i.e. quota] of one decoration per 150 troops per six months,' Smith said later, arguing that after 'a decent stoush', the British set aside the quota system; they were not ruled by it.[14] Not so the Australian Army, which seemed in the thrall of a statistical fetish where awards were concerned. Smith duly pared his list to the 'absolute minimum', discarding 'maybe four MIDs'.[15] Townsend accepted the shorter list, including the four MCs.

Smith heard nothing further until 21 December 1966, when he read the actual awards in the press. All except a couple had been downgraded. Smith's DSO had become an MC; his two surviving platoon commanders had received an MID. Sharp received nothing, posthumously.[16] In the same list, an army postal worker had received an MID. Notwithstanding this man's undoubted skill with the mail, an awards system that placed Sabben's, Kendall's, Akell's and Roberts's performance at Long Tan on the same notch as a postal clerk did little to enhance its credibility. When Harry Smith tackled Townsend about the 'disgusting announcement', the latter said 'nothing could be done about it'. Higher powers had made the decision.[17]

Thirty years later, Smith read the declassified file, which showed that Brigadier Jackson, the Task Force commander, had passed Smith's recommendations up to Australian Force Vietnam in Saigon, where they sat for five weeks. In that time, Smith alleges, 'higher authorities' pressed Townsend to downgrade the awards. Lieutenant David Harris, then personal assistant to Jackson, concurs: Major General Mackay, Jackson and Townsend did a 'cosy little deal', he said.[18]

There is strong evidence for this in a hitherto unpublished letter from Townsend to Lieutenant Colonel Derek Roylance, dated May 1984. 'I believe I downgraded a few [awards] myself,' Townsend wrote, 'and scrubbed others at the time … In Harry Smith's case, for example, I recommended a DSO … but this was downgraded to an MC, and now I believe quite rightly so … If one accepts Harry Smith's MC as a fair and reasonable award, there is little other recognition the platoon commanders could have received other than an MID …'[19]

For forty years the Long Tan veterans have pressed to have their original awards reinstated — to the dismay and irritation of many in the army, who argue that others were similarly denied but have not complained. In 2005 the Howard Government responded sympathetically but refused. Such action would open a flurry of claims from other, similarly deserving soldiers and create new anomalies, it argued.[20] Then, in 2008, the Rudd Labor Government finally acknowledged the injustice, by restoring Harry Smith's original recommendation by awarding him the Australian equivalent of the DSO, and his two lieutenants (Sabben and Kendall), the equivalent of the Military Cross. And some other injustices have been addressed. In 2004 the Australian Government decided that twenty-two Long Tan veterans were entitled to wear their South Vietnamese awards granted thirty-eight years before, yet denied them, nominally because the Queen had not sent her approval. In fact, successive Veterans' Affairs ministers had tried to argue that the South Vietnamese awards were never intended — a claim roundly refuted by former South Vietnamese officials (at the time, the soldiers received dolls and cigar boxes in lieu of their medals).

The bestowal of foreign awards also proved deeply divisive: on several occasions Canberra was accused of denying the soldiers the honour of receiving high foreign decorations. This was not always justified. Consider Flight Lieutenant Garry Cooper, who received a brace of US and British Commonwealth awards. In August 1968 US commander Major General Julian Ewell personally recommended Cooper for the Congressional Medal of

Honour, America's highest award for gallantry; Canberra refused to allow the award. In reply, Ewell recommended Cooper for the Victoria Cross — similarly denied. Yet many think he deserved it: on the night of 18 August 1968, the helicopter in which Cooper was travelling took ground fire, and the pilot was shot through the head. Cooper leant over the dead airman, grabbed the controls and managed to land the hurtling aircraft in a rice paddy — amid hundreds of Viet Cong, who immediately peppered the wreckage. Although wounded in the back, Cooper dragged a more badly wounded US colonel out of the stricken Huey and into waist-deep paddy water, where they spent a terrifying night eluding Viet Cong troops who crept along the dyke. They escaped the next morning by making a dash for it into a waiting US gunship.

Often, exceptional acts of courage were denied *any* recognition. A glaring example was Mark 'Pinkie' Moloney, whose battalion commander, Eric Smith, recommended him for a VC. In the end, Moloney received no award, for procedural reasons to do with the temporary detachment of his company. And there were many moments of selfless courage that received scant recognition: Ian Ahearn, for example, recommended thirteen awards after the battle of Coral — only one was approved; witness the miraculous medevac of Vic Morrow, who, despite massive wounds, survived thanks to the efforts of six members of the 6th Battalion. Meanwhile, the government continues to deny the most basic military recognition — the service medal — to the four RAAF members left on the tarmac at Saigon in April 1975 and the RAAF pilots who flew in Detachment S, claiming that the war was over at the time of their humanitarian mission.

In summary, the Australian military awards system singularly failed to recognise many deserving soldiers. Even its own quotas were applied selectively or on the apparent nudge of higher authority, according to the evidence. Some highly placed defence personnel even claimed that the very scales used to determine awards were 'wrong'. Vice Admiral Sir Richard Peek, Chief of the Naval Staff, found, for example, that one in every seventeen RAAF, one in every thirty-eight navy and one in every sixty-one army members received an award in Vietnam. The same trend applied in Korea and World War II, Peek concluded, in a damning assessment sent to Admiral Sir Victor Smith, chairman of the Chiefs of Staff Committee, on 28 July 1972: 'As I find it impossible to accept that the RAAF is always more gallant ... than the other 2 Services; and that in Vietnam, which was essentially an infantryman's war, the Army was the least distinguished and gallant of the 3 Services, *it seems to me that the basis of the scale must be wrong.*'[21]

Of 50,000 Australian defence personnel sent to Vietnam, six were listed as missing in action (MIA) after the war. In 2007 the heroic perseverance of veteran Jim Bourke and his team in OPERATION AUSSIES HOME led to the discovery of the remains of Lance Corporal Richard Parker and Private Peter Gillson, whose bodies were left, presumed dead, after a fierce battle on the Gang Toi plateau on 8 November 1965. They were repatriated on 6 June 2007, with full military honours. Then in December 2007, the remains of Lance Corporal John Gillespie, who died in a helicopter crash on 17 April 1971, were identified and repatriated to Australia on 19 December 2007. They were similarly laid to rest with his family in attendance. Three Australians remain listed as MIA: Private David Fisher, of the SAS, who fell 30 metres from a rope attached to a helicopter winch during a hot extraction on 27 September 1969; and Flying Officer Michael Herbert and Pilot Officer Robert Carver, who disappeared on 3 November 1970 when their Canberra bomber apparently crashed mid-flight on its return home.

The Welcome Home celebrations continued throughout the weekend. On Sunday 4 October 1987 the Sydney Domain pounded to the rhythm of the 1960s. A new generation of 19-year-olds who had never heard 'We Gotta Get Outta This Place' and for whom leaving on a jet plane held little novelty value danced to the sounds of Luscombe Bowl: Lorrae Desmond, Little Pattie, Col Joye, Dinah Lee, Don Lane and Normie Rowe all performed.

The parade's greatest permanent legacy was the decision to erect a national monument in Canberra, in memory of Australia's Vietnam veterans. Designed by Ken Unsworth and Peter Tonkin, the sublime structure is in fact an empty space entombed within three massive stelae, 'wrenched in a tight helix, a spiral which sets the whole design in motion'.[22] The visitor is beckoned in, through a gap between the two foremost blocks, as though some ancient mystery, or unspeakable truth, lies hidden within. Inside, one stands under a granite halo of 500 stones — one for each of the dead — suspended by a spider's web of wires, and concealing a scroll listing the Honour Roll. Etched into the rear wall is the photo, by Sergeant Mike Coleridge, of soldiers of the 7th Battalion awaiting a helicopter airlift. The 'unique vocabulary' of the Vietnam years covers a side wall, evoking the sensations peculiar to the war: the 'thud thud thud' of the Huey; the infantryman 'who walked out front'; the rain, the jungle, the rice paddies; and the Vietnamese people.

# Chapter 49
# ... borne back ceaselessly
# into the past

My life seems little different from that of a sampan pushed
upstream towards the past. The future lied to us, there long ago in
the past. There is no new life, no new era, nor is it hope for a
beautiful future that now drives me on, but rather the opposite.
The hope is contained in the beautiful pre-war past.
*Bao Ninh, The Sorrow of War.*

I walked away from my friends to a quiet spot and cried as I had
never done before, deeply and long.
*Major Brian McFarlane.*

The tricks of destiny have yielded some heartening outcomes: the first S-
bend lavatories in Long Tan, for example. Neither the French nor
Marxist economics nor Uncle Ho's heirs achieved this basic step towards
provincial hygiene, which took a simple act of foreign charity. In 1994 Paul
Murphy, a 2nd Battalion infantryman, returned to Ba Ria–Vung Tau
province (as Phuoc Tuy is now called) to establish the Australian Veterans'
Vietnam Reconstruction Group (AVVRG). This voluntary organisation has
since channelled more than a million dollars into the province; recent
investments include 300 septic toilets for Long Tan, a dental clinic and
physiotherapy unit. Earlier, the group helped construct a local orphanage
and rebuild the primary school in Hoa Long. Elsewhere, Ba Ria–Vung Tau

is hugely prosperous: oil workers, tourists and dealers of every kind fill the bars and hotels; the Grand Hotel is full again; and new roads radiate into all corners of the province. Little of this prosperity has filtered through to the poorest rural areas and those in greatest need.

At Nui Dat, the crumbling ochre columns of the main gates and faint artillery markings on the boulders — of dates, units and kangaroos — are the only reminders of the Australian presence forty years ago. The occasional cowherd drives his oxen across the flats beneath SAS Hill. To the side of the airfield is the little one-roomed kindergarten the AVVRG built; happy children tumble onto the playground that had once been a busy tarmac, where Murphy's colleague 'Breaker' Cusack, a 6th Battalion veteran, distributes toys to delighted kids. A decorated Viet Cong major lives in a house nearby, and not far away is the headquarters of the B445 Battalion, heir to the D445, a poignant reminder of who's in charge now.

Near Long Tan, sunlight shines through the rubber canopy and falls upon a simple white cross, a memorial to the Australian fallen. It is one of two memorials to foreign soldiers in Vietnam (the other, to the French, is at Dien Bien Phu). The cross is a replica; the original is held in the museum at Dong Nai, which purchased it from the local Thinh family who had taken it from Long Tan in 1975, possibly for use on their family grave. In front of the cross, in a stone cauldron, joss sticks send up wisps of smoke in memory of the Vietnamese dead.

Long Phuoc, which the Australian troops destroyed in 1966, is now a bustling town with a large kindergarten and war memorial. The Viet Cong tunnel system that started here, and extended to Hoa Long, almost 3 kilometres away, was recently opened to tourists. 'Australians did not commit atrocities,' volunteers my tunnel guide. 'They were the most stubborn, skilled soldiers. When they crossed a dirt road, they didn't walk, they rolled, so they wouldn't leave footprints.'[1]

Further north the bustling village of Binh Gia remains predominantly Catholic — a concession by the communist government — and Binh Ba is a thriving town surrounded by extensive rubber plantations. We drove east to Xuyen Moc and the home of Nguyen Gia Ho, who served as a propaganda chief in the National Liberation Front in Phuoc Tuy during the war. As his wife served lunch, he said: 'I fought against Thais, Koreans and Americans, but mainly Australians. The Australians defeated the Vietnamese in Vietnam. They were very skilled. The people didn't hate them. The Australian Army left some good feelings here. It's true that several villages —

the Catholic ones — supported you. We tried to destroy those villages. For a while, the Australians controlled all of Phuoc Tuy. When you left the National Liberation Front took over the province.'[2] That fairly accurately summed up the Australian war.

On the summit of the Long Hais a guide led me through the caves that had once been the Viet Cong headquarters, the Minh Dam Secret Zone: the district committee cave, hospital cave, propaganda cave, army headquarters, sleeping and entertainment quarters. For years the cadres had lived and fought in this natural citadel, surviving repeated Australian infantry attacks and B52 bombs. In this sense, the US Air Force fulfilled General Curtis LeMay's threat to 'bomb 'em back to the Stone Age', then grossly underestimated the resilience of the cavemen. In a little museum nearby, beneath a glass case, sat the depressing sight of an 'Australian-manufactured mine, disassembled by our soldiers and used to wipe out the enemy's vitality'.[3]

In Hanoi, three retired North Vietnamese commanders granted me an audience; we sat back in carved wooden armchairs in a meeting room of the Hanoi Veterans Association, sipping green tea. It was November 2005. Would they explain how they defeated the greatest military power on earth? Their answers were gruff and direct.

'First, there is nothing more precious than freedom and independence,' said Lieutenant General Ngo Van Ly, commander of a tank regiment during the war. 'Second was the South's commitment to fight. Third was the support of China and Russia, and international assistance. Fourth was the civilian support in America and other countries.'[4]

'The key thing was to get the foreign soldiers out,' offered the slightly menacing Lieutenant General Mai Thuan, a former infantry commander and now the association's chairman.[5] 'The soldiers had to understand what they fought for, and why. We didn't separate national independence and communism. We didn't consider communism as something above the soldiers' minds. We brought the two together.'[6] The Politburo similarly held communism and nationalism to be mutually reinforcing — a political concept utterly lost on the American and Australian governments of 1965.

'The US strategy was wrong,' Lieutenant General Thuan concluded. 'The Americans thought they could defeat us in a short time. They were very well equipped but they lacked the spirit, the heart ... And the US troops couldn't distinguish between civilians and our troops. The Vietnamese soldier lived with the Vietnamese civilian, who became combatants.'[7]

'Our soldiers were everywhere,' concluded Ngo Van Ly.[8] We sipped our tea in silence.


The next day I joined Professor Huu Ngoc on his short walk through central Hanoi to the Sunway Hotel. There, fifteen American war veterans awaited his weekly lecture, 'Three thousand years of Vietnamese history'. It was unseasonably warm, and we walked at a steady pace amid the orderly chaos of street stalls and motorcycles. The professor moved imperturbably along: little, it seemed, and certainly not the maelstrom of modern Hanoi, could stop the advance of this 85-year-old Vietnamese historian. As we progressed, Professor Ngoc smiled in a sort of Socratic way, suggesting that he knew just how little he knew. Yet this veteran of Dien Bien Phu and the American War, historian, author and newspaper columnist, clearly knew a great deal. The history of Vietnam seemed to unwind in his mind as we advanced: it was as if each measured step plotted the progress of the past. The professor waved aside the oncoming school of motorcycles as one might dismiss a fly. 'Anarchy,' he sighed. 'But necessary anarchy.'[9] It was a fair summary of Vietnam's twenty-year transition from command economy to partial free market.

Vietnam is booming, it's true: 'the fastest growing economy in the world' prefaces every article on the nation's 'economic miracle'. All but the most stalwart Politburo members now regard Marxist ideas as slightly embarrassing anachronisms. 'Communism won the war, but capitalism won the peace' is a frequently heard refrain. At Ho Chi Minh's cottage, in the grounds of the Presidential Palace, a bust of Lenin and a photo of Marx sit on Uncle Ho's desk. 'These are here because Ho Chi Minh was really fond of Marx and Lenin,' said my student guide, as though she were telling a fairytale.

Tower cranes and the entrails of huge construction projects shape the skyline of every Vietnamese city. In 2007 the government unveiled plans for a A$33 billion rail link between Hanoi and Ho Chi Minh City. Western businesses crowd Saigon, as many locals prefer to call the 'Pearl of the Orient'. The Caravelle and Rex hotels have been rebuilt, and the bars jostle with enough energy to make Madame Nhu dance in her grave. Local entrepreneurs have cashed in on Hollywood war porn: the Apocalypse Now nightclub seethes with the full spectrum of sexual choice. The Continental trades on an earlier war, of quiet Americans along Rue Catinat (Le Loi). The American War Crimes Museum has been renamed the War Remnants Museum, in deference to tourists' sensitivities.

Hanoi, like Beijing, has discovered that you can have your communist cake and eat it too. The West simply wants to do business, not vex its nominally communist clients with an insistence on human rights. Indeed, imprisoned priests, fierce censorship laws and the continuing persecution of dissenters and the Montagnards receive little international attention. In April 2004 Hanoi brutally put down a Montagnard uprising. 'This may seem like a small issue,' said Ken Bacon, president of Refugees International, 'but this is one area where the Vietnamese are up to their old, ethnic, commie control-freak tricks.' Nor can the new Asian communist model — one party, free markets — disguise the corruption within: Transparency International routinely lists Vietnam, with Bangladesh, Myanmar and Indonesia, as the four most corrupt regimes in Asia.

I walked over the Long Bien bridge — destroyed, rebuilt, destroyed, rebuilt and twisted under Nixon's Arc Light Christmas — then wound my way back to the haunted Hoan Kiem Lake, in the centre of the ancient city. On the stone shore a deformed street urchin sold me Jon Swain's *River of Time* and Bao Ninh's *Sorrow of War*. At the Metropole Hotel I sat down to read. A 'B52' and 'Screaming Orgasm' graced the cocktail list ... choices, choices of the new market economy. As if to rid my mind of the shocking associations, I ordered a B52 and opened *The Sorrow of War*.


Should Australia have been involved in the Vietnam War? After the fall of Saigon, 66 per cent of Australians answered 'no' and 27 per cent 'yes' to this pointless question in a poll (without giving reasons). Of Liberal voters, half now disapproved of the commitment and 43 per cent approved; of Labor voters, the responses were 74 per cent against and 20 per cent in favour, respectively.[10] These replies are meaningless without specifying what one is agreeing or disagreeing with. Should we have been involved in defence of the national interest, to stop what was perceived as a real communist threat? Or in defence of a threatened minority in a distant country?

It is worth restating that from 1965 to 1968 a majority of Australians supported their government's commitment to the Vietnam War; it was seen as a morally defensible engagement in the national interest. The government felt it had little choice other than to back Washington in a war against an enemy that both the Liberal Coalition and Labor viewed as a genuine regional threat. 'The point,' said the columnist Paul Kelly, in a speech to the Australian War Memorial, 'is that the enemy was real — the Second World War generation was right, not wrong, in identifying the communist threat.'[11] Sir Arthur Tange, perhaps Australia's finest civil servant, who advised against the commitment 'when I was in a position to offer any advice', conceded years later: 'I don't think we had any choice.'[12]

No doubt, at the time the perceptions and fears of communism were real enough, but what of the actual threat to Australia? How real were those perceptions and how justified those fears? Specifically, were China and the Soviet Union seriously willing or able to launch a pan-Asian Domino Effect?

Certainly, in the 1950s the communist rhetoric blazed a trail of global revolution. Yet let us briefly separate rhetoric from reality, and examine the Soviet Union's *actual* policy in Indochina in the early 1960s. The war caught Moscow staring in the spotlight of two choices: on the one hand, the Soviets hoped to use North Vietnam 'as a channel for Soviet political penetration into this strategically important region'. The idea was 'to swing such countries as Thailand, Malaysia and the Philippines from pro-American positions to a more neutralist, if not pro-Soviet course'. In other words, very threatening. On the other hand, Moscow was not ready to sacrifice its better relations with the West in the interests of Hanoi: it feared a deep commitment to a remote conflict in alliance with the 'highly independent and nationalist-oriented Vietnamese Communists'.[13] In the end the Soviets chose a high-wire act between these extremes. They would do three things: finance Hanoi's war; preserve the détente with the West (by adjusting their Vietnam policy 'when necessary'); and press a negotiated settlement on Hanoi, as the best insurance against being drawn further into the war.[14] This was not mere rhetoric, as CIA records show: in discussions with the Americans, the Soviets did express a desire to find a peaceful settlement — until the Tonkin Gulf Incident changed their minds.[15]

And China? How serious was the Chinese threat to the region? North Vietnam was never China's puppet, and refused to kowtow to China's demands. 'We never had any fear of China taking us over,' a prominent Hanoian general told me in 2005. 'When China received Kissinger, the Chinese told us not to fight ... but we did.'[16] North Vietnam privately loathed China; the feeling, despite the propaganda, was mutual. Vietnam would not willingly, in these circumstances, serve as Mao's stepping stone into South-East Asia.

Mao's fear of nuclear war with America also curbed his global ambitions. His priority was a 'limited war' against the United States, fought through a Vietnamese proxy. His rhetoric boasted of global conquest; in practice he avoided escalation. In 1960 'Chinese leaders were not supportive of any intensification of the military struggle [in Vietnam]'.[17] In the event, Mao would confine his war with the West to Vietnam and use the Vietnamese people to bleed his arch-enemy, America. Vietnam's Prime Minister Pham Van Dong said as much to Stanley Karnow in 1981: '[Mao] was always ready to fight to the last Vietnamese.'[18]

In fact, China refused to send combat troops to Vietnam, or anywhere else in South-East Asia. In 1959 Mao rejected Hanoi's request for Chinese pilots and ground troops (China agreed, however, to send a vast arsenal of weapons and ammunition as well as 320,000 support troops to North Vietnam, between 1965 and 1973).[19] This enormous backstop freed Hanoi's best combat troops for frontline action — an incalculable gift to General Giap. 'You can regard China as your rear,' the Chinese leadership assured Ho Chi Minh.[20] Finally, China, in the 1960s, did not have a navy worthy of the name.

Moscow and Peking, in summary, did not wish to provoke America beyond the confines of 'limited' — that is, non-nuclear — war, according to new research based on original KGB and CCP documents.[21] They chose their targets carefully. China's staggering losses in the Korean War, Stalin's death in 1953 and the rupture of the Communist Bloc severely curbed their global ambitions. In 1956 Khrushchev's advocacy of 'peaceful coexistence' with the West and rejection of Lenin's theory of the inevitability of war as 'the midwife of revolution' marked the beginning of the break with Mao. The Soviets' complete split with the Chinese, in 1960, interred the nightmare vision of a Red world.

In short, the Domino Theory was a grossly simplistic, unchanging metaphor imposed on a ceaselessly changing, complex world. As Qiang Zhai concluded, in his classic account of China's role: 'Just as dominoes is a game for children, the eponymous theory was the stuff of child's play.'[22] If the Domino Theory expressed a real fear of Soviet and Chinese aggression in the 1950s, it failed to justify the strategic case for the American war in Vietnam in 1965. In 1955 the British had largely defeated the Chinese 'communist terrorists' in Malaya, a job completed by the Australians in 1960; and in 1965–66, in Indonesia, a military junta crushed the local Communist Party.[23] 'The notion that any of Thailand, Malaysia, Singapore or Indonesia would have gone communist in the 1960s because Vietnam fell strains credibility,' said Paul Kelly.[24] Indeed, even as the Australians beat the domino drum, Washington lost faith in the theory. LBJ later rejected the whole metaphor of toppling dominoes, and Dean Rusk, Secretary of State, never used the phrase; it trivialised a complex situation, he felt.

Not even Canberra's hawks backed up their rhetoric with action: if they seriously believed the Red Tide would soon be lapping our shores, then surely defence spending had increased to meet the threat? On the contrary, at the height of communist fears, between 1953–54 and 1962–63, defence spending actually fell, from 3.9 to 2.7 per cent of gross domestic product (and rose rapidly after that, to a 1960s' peak of 18 per cent of GDP, in 1966–67).[25]

A more persuasive case — in hindsight — for American (and allied) involvement in Vietnam was that it bought time for other Asian nations to develop democratic institutions and crush local communist movements. 'This gives rise to the idea, popular in many quarters, of Vietnam as a failed war with good consequences,' Kelly remarked.[26] Major General Sandy Pearson echoed this sentiment: 'It was an unwinnable but necessary war. It gave South-East Asia ten years in order to defeat communism. So the Americans achieved their objective even though they lost the war.'[27] Several historians, politicians and commanders share this view of the Vietnam War as 'necessary'; hence Lee Kuan Yew told US Admiral Zumwalt, in 1970: 'You gave us ten years against the spread of communism ... do not despair.' This may be so; but it is also an ingenious convolution of America's original goals in Vietnam, which were to contain the spread of communism. Washington did not send half a million troops and expend 58,000 lives in Vietnam so that Singapore and Indonesia might at liberty build their one-party dictatorships. Nor do these 'good consequences' justify the American war *as fought*, or imply any agreement with the political handling of the war. They serve chiefly to soothe battered US military egos and offer a justification, with dollops of hindsight, for the war.

In truth, the main reason America stayed in Vietnam was to avoid the humiliation of defeat. Three words summed up US war aims after 1968: 'America must win.' As early as January 1966 the US Assistant Secretary of Defense John McNaughton could write, 'The present US objective in Vietnam is to avoid humiliation. The reasons why we went into Vietnam ...

are largely academic.'[28] The fear of communism, falling dominoes, Red China ... in time, the interests of American national pride subsumed them all. Australia thus found itself harnessed not to an American policy or strategy but to the American ego, the preservation of which had some validity, of course: the failure of US resolve in Vietnam would have given heart to other rogue states in the Cold War.

On a more sweeping level, Western historians have recast the Vietnam War as an unfortunate setback in the Cold War, 'a mere episode in this epic'.[29] Many now see the war in this light: Australia's official historian Peter Edwards noted, 'It is easier now to think of Vietnam not as a war that was lost but as a losing battle within a bigger Cold War struggle that was won.'[30]

It may be easy; it is also a simplistic and dangerous way of viewing the Vietnam War. It packs away this human tragedy as the unfortunate ephemera in an otherwise triumphant Western victory over the Communist Bloc, and tends to absolve the grave political mistakes that led to it as minor errors in an otherwise successful political and military outcome. In consequence, the Vietnam War ceases to be a singular human catastrophe from which we might learn and becomes, in time, simply a minor battle in a sweeping allied triumph. To avoid that deadly complacency, we must always look afresh at the Vietnam War and examine it on its own terms as well as in the context of the Cold War.

Which begs the question, who won and lost the Vietnam War? The question is almost obscene. The pyrrhic victor was Hanoi's 'Democratic Republic of Vietnam', which defeated Saigon and the Americans with the same synthesised strategy it had applied against the French: the repercussive hit and run tactics of proselytising guerrillas; the pitched, belt-hugging attacks on the enemy's fortresses or 'tethered goats'; the encirclement of and invocation to the cities to rise up; and finally, the huge conventional invasion, as the People's Army fell on the wisp of resistance like a tornado around a sapling. Except that it did not happen that way: at stages during this bloody symphony the South Vietnamese resisted and tore up the communist script, most spectacularly during the great communist uprising of Tet 1968, to which the southerners refused to rally and turned to America and her allies for protection, and during Hanoi's Easter Offensive in 1972, which the South, with US air power, soundly defeated.

Of the many losers, America was the biggest and sorest. Whichever way you look at it, whatever 'terms' of victory you seek to impose, the Vietnam War was an American military and political defeat: 58,000 young Americans and countless Vietnamese had to die before Kissinger surrendered the South.[31] The revisionists refuse to accept this, and have 'redefined the meaning of winning', to paraphrase the military strategist Sir Robert Thompson.[32] True enough, America never lost a battle, in terms of bodies counted or 'real estate' captured. 'That may be so,' a North Vietnamese negotiator famously told his US counterparts, three years after the Paris peace talks, 'but it is also irrelevant.'

Shelves heave with books seeking to contest the outcome of the Vietnam War. The 'woulda-coulda-shoulda' school of military history argues that America *would* have won the war had it been allowed to attack the North; *could* have won had Congress not cut funding; *should* have won had the protesters and the press not lost the battle at home. Such excuses are hypothetical, and fail to see that Washington set the framework for the war: a limited, non-nuclear conflict restricted to South Vietnam. The US military was duty bound to defeat the insurgency *within that framework*. It failed to do so; it lost on the battlefield. It lost because the Pentagon's ill-conceived war of attrition directly served Hanoi's interests: overwhelming US force simply drove countless numbers of Vietnamese soldiers and civilians into the communist embrace. American firepower did more to turn hearts and minds to Ho Chi Minh than any amount of North Vietnamese propaganda. Beyond attrition, the USA had no clear strategic goals — unless one accepts the 'strategy' of body count, which logically led to the annihilation of most Vietnamese people and was thus doomed. This is not the wisdom of hindsight; many had sounded the alarm bells at the time, not least General Matthew Ridgway, who quizzed Hubert Humphrey in the mid-1960s, saying, 'I have never known what the mission for General Westmoreland was', to which Humphrey replied, 'That's a good question. Ask the President.'[33] Neither the President nor his staff had an answer.

Alas, the President's circle promised much and delivered little. The Vietnam War bled LBJ's budget, ended his domestic dream of a Great Society, and banished Washington's arrogant belief in America as the political and moral leader of the world. In 1965 Johnson's most evangelical apologist, his adviser Walt Rostow, had envisaged democracy and a television set in every mud hut in Asia and Africa. Such views were not only not embarrassing, they were also positively believed, at least until Robert Kennedy shed his 'role of

Hamlet' and announced his candidacy for the presidency. Yet even as the shards fell from the Tet Offensive his speech writer incorporated, to Kennedy's horror, the statement: 'At stake is not simply the leadership of our party, and even our country, it is our right to the moral leadership of the planet.'[34] The path to Khe Sanh was paved with such intentions. It was not 'necessary' to fight the Vietnam War as the Americans did, but Kennedy's gilded generation failed to heed or act on the warnings. Several diplomats and politicians — chiefly Kenneth Galbraith, George Ball and William Fulbright — warned of the folly of entering the war; several generals firmly opposed the chosen strategy.[35] The debates were sharp, thrilling, brilliant ... but to no avail. If the most eloquent shades of the ancient world had reassembled on Capitol Hill, none — not even the persuasive powers of Pericles and Cicero — could have curbed the fatal impulse that possessed this golden voyage ... until only a ghost ship sailed on, with President Johnson at the helm, his Great Society in ruins and the putrefying albatross of Vietnam slung around his neck.

The National Liberation Front also lost. These young men and women, who fought countless battles in Hanoi's interests, received not a particle of power under the new regime. They were literally sold down the Mekong River. Theirs was a tragedy of monumental dimensions. With utter contempt for its southern comrades, Hanoi reneged on the Third of its Four Points, which supposedly recognised the National Liberation Front as 'the sole genuine representative of the people of South Vietnam'. Hanoi simply ignored the NLF, whose leaders faded away and were soon forgotten.

China lost, too. 'It had shed blood and enormous amounts of material resources in Vietnam but had not secured the gratitude and goodwill of the Vietnamese,' wrote Qiang Zhai. 'Instead of having strengthened security along its southern frontier China found itself at the end of the war highly insecure, as Hanoi moved closer to the Soviet Union.'[36] The historic tension and mutual distrust between Vietnam and China resumed. In 1973–74 Hanoi refused to kowtow to Chinese demands that it stop fighting in the South; China, supposedly the great tipper of dominoes, was now actually trying to *contain* Hanoi's belligerence. Indeed, Sino–Vietnamese border clashes began as early as 1973, and confirmed the primacy of Moscow in post-war Vietnam. Beijing's paltry spoils and fury at Vietnam's invasion of Pol Pot's Cambodia boiled over: in 1979 China launched an attack on Vietnam, which failed.

★ ★ ★

And the Australians? The Australian troops won a tactical victory over a small Vietnamese province. They largely secured Phuoc Tuy, befriended and protected many villagers, and fulfilled the tactical tasks to which they were assigned. They did so bravely and, in the main, with restraint and compassion. That is not to suggest that they were better soldiers than the Americans or Vietnamese, but they certainly deployed superior tactics that were more likely to defeat the enemy. Yet the Australian tactics were in some ways forced on them, because they lacked the air and firepower of the Americans; and they made a grave error of judgement in the construction of the minefield.

Still, after Long Tan in 1966, the communist forces attempted only one further regimental attack — in September 1971 — after hearing of the Australian decision to pull out — and withdrew completely to the provincial borders in 1968–69. In the clearest sign of provincial security and growing confidence, two-thirds of the Australian forces fought outside Phuoc Tuy in May–June 1968. 'You won' the Battle of Long Tan, Brigadier Nguyen Minh Ninh told me forty years later. 'Tactically and militarily you won — but politically, we also won.' The Australians forces, he conceded, had matched or outfought the Vietnamese on the battlefield.

The SAS played a key part. By the end of 1967 the SAS psychologically dominated the province; by the war's end, SAS patrols had infiltrated every Viet Cong base, sighted a total 5,366 enemy in 1,175 patrols; clashed with the enemy 298 times; and inflicted 655 Viet Cong and North Vietnamese casualties, of which 492 were killed in action. In reply, the Viet Cong caused thirty-one SAS casualties: one killed in action, one died of wounds, one missing presumed dead and twenty-eight wounded, most of them lightly.[37]

Australian commanders could only speculate about what might have been had their tactics been more generally applied. Brigadier John Salmon believed Australia should have more strongly promoted its military philosophy to the American commanders: 'If we believed in that philosophy ... we should have been sufficiently confident to press it more — to initiate in Phuoc Tuy a model system ... and then see if we could sell it to the country overall.'[38] Major General Michael Jeffery, the future Governor-General, expressed a similar sentiment at an AATTV reunion in 2002: '... because of the superior tactics employed, we Australians had everything under control in Phuoc Tuy Province ... one wonders, if those tactics could have been employed throughout the rest of South Vietnam, whether the outcome might not have been different.'[39]

It was, in the end, a politicians' war. Politicians decided to send the troops (against sound military advice in America and Australia), set the limits on the war, and influenced the strategy and the tactics to an unusual degree — right down to decisions over bombing targets and how many troops should stay in Phuoc Tuy. Yet not a single politician has admitted his culpability, or acknowledged the simple fact that their failure to end the Vietnam War sooner was *a failure of political will*. Robert McNamara and Malcolm Fraser have recanted, and now believe the war was a mistake; but whose mistake?

On the contrary, politicians, in a slew of memoirs, have tended to portray themselves as powerless before a conflagration not of their making, a war that gathered its own momentum and spun out of their control. Not one has admitted his personal error, much less apologised for failing to intervene to stop the obscene public attack on the soldiers who were, in the end, used as scapegoats for a series of staggering political misjudgements. The Australian Parliament and people, in short, betrayed the servicemen and women — the only participants in this sorry tale who did what was asked of them — in reply to whom Serong said: 'We did not *go* to Vietnam; we were *sent*, by the people of Australia. The fact that those same people, having sent us, chose to spit upon us when we returned remains our deepest national shame ...'[40]

The human cost of the war, in terms of grief and moral degradation, is immeasurable. In our helplessness, we surrender to statistics:[41] 521 Australian soldiers killed in action, or died of wounds or accident, and about 3,000 wounded;[42] 58,193 Americans dead and about 300,000 wounded;[43] 220,357 South Vietnamese troops dead or missing in action and 1.17 million wounded;[44] 666,000 Viet Cong and North Vietnamese troops dead,[45] with the possibility that a third were civilians mistaken for enemy troops or deemed legitimate targets. Of South Vietnamese civilian casualties, about 325,000 were confirmed killed (rising to a million, depending on your source and definition of a 'civilian'), 30 per cent of whom were children younger than 13. In total, an estimated 65,000 North Vietnamese civilians died as a result of US bombing.[46] The Viet Cong assassinated 36,725 civilians between 1957 and 1972;[47] the North Vietnamese and/or Viet Cong assassinated 166,000 South Vietnamese civilians.[48] About three million Vietnamese people are believed to have suffered herbicide poisoning. In total, 3.5 million people died in Vietnam over fifteen years; in the Korean War, by contrast, 2.8 million people — mostly

Chinese — died in three years; World War I inflicted 8.5 million war deaths and 15 million total deaths; World War II killed 50 million people — military personnel and civilians — according to conservative median estimates.

The true cost of the Vietnam War, in dollar terms, is incalculable. Estimates vary. But, on the basis of the most comprehensive analysis available at the time, the total cost to Australia, to June 1972, was at least A$500 million.[49] The figure excludes future benefits, pensions to veterans and such intangibles as foregone taxes had the casualties lived. The American figure sets the Australian cost in context. Campagna's study, *The Economic Consequences of the Vietnam War*, puts the actual cost to America of the Vietnam War at US$173 billion.[50] By adding US veterans' future benefits (US$220 billion), lost earnings and conscription taxes (US$83 billion) and foreign trade costs (US$8 billion), Campagna calculated a total American loss of US$515 billion, or half a trillion dollars. 'These are staggering sums for a war that nobody won … a tragedy of epic dimensions,' he wrote.[51]

In the early 1970s the last British soldiers left Malaysia and the USA retreated into isolationism. Australia realised that it could no longer rely on its traditional allies. The 1971 Strategic Basis Paper abandoned forward defence, and over the next nine years Sir Arthur Tange strove to entrench a policy of self-reliance. Sir James Killen's 1976 Defence White Paper enshrined Tange's efforts, and self-reliance remained the basis of Australia's strategic defence policy until 2007 (when the Howard Government proposed a regional defence policy).

The anti-war protesters and draft resisters are quieter now — installed in careers, enjoying their grandchildren or pursuing new causes: climate change, Africa, AIDS. Yet some draft resisters have never recovered from their experiences. In 2006 I visited Simon Townsend, a softly spoken man with sad eyes and pale skin. 'I have two fantasies,' he told me. 'One is that a government — Labor or Liberal — will issue an apology to the country for the whole war. The second is that I will walk past a burning house and run in and save the lives of two children … because people have always called me a coward. I don't think it'll happen, because I'm now 60 and suffering the effects of a stroke. But I'm not afraid to die. I'm not afraid of bullets. But when people call you a coward, you're a coward.'[52]

★   ★   ★

The last act of war is to grieve. Undying as the snowmelt and the whisper of the wind are the memorials and services for the dead. Little reunions repeat the ritual every year, in Vietnam, America, South Korea, Thailand, the Philippines, Australia and New Zealand.

Many Vietnamese units — North and South — had few or no survivors. The entire North Vietnamese battalion of the hero of Bao Ninh's semi-autobiographical novel, *The Sorrow of War*, perished in the 'Screaming Souls Jungle'. In regretting the war's aftermath and waste, the author consigned the communist victory to a forgettable nightmare. 'My life,' Bao Ninh wrote, 'seems little different from that of a sampan pushed upstream towards the past. The future lied to us, there long ago in the past. There is no new life, no new era, nor is it hope for a beautiful future that now drives me on, but rather the opposite. The hope is contained in the beautiful pre-war past.'[53]

In South Vietnam, many elderly couples mourn their children and not, as it should be, the other way around. I encountered an old Vietnamese couple in a hamlet near Dat Do. An Australian soldier, they said, had killed their daughter when she was a teenager. They led me into the garden: against a back wall, under a shelter, stood a little shrine to the girl, with her photograph, flowers, joss sticks and various letters. The couple had tended this shrine for forty years. I felt like apologising — on behalf of whom? For what? The girl's mother smiled at my confusion. Then her eyes filled with tears, she staggered backwards, and her husband led her inside. I stayed and looked at the photo of this girl: an innocent child … a Viet Cong soldier.

In Australia, Brian McFarlane thought he had conquered his feelings; he felt the war occupied but a corner of his mind. Then one day in 2006 he took a stroll with fellow retired officers along the Memorial Walkway at Enoggera barracks. The party passed a little plaque to Private Gordon Knight, the first national serviceman in McFarlane's company to die; he was 21. McFarlane has never forgotten the sight of the young man embracing family and friends on the night of their departure for South Vietnam in 1966. The sight of Private Knight's plaque, beside the path, forty years on, summoned a rush of memories that quite overwhelmed McFarlane: 'I walked away from my friends to a quiet spot and cried as I had never done before, deeply and long. I cried for the loss of Knight and the misery it must have brought to his family, and for the whole miserable pain of this …'[54]

And the soldier wept.

# Appendix 1

## The Australian Roll of Honour for the Vietnam War 1962–1975

Dale Abbott
Dennis Eric Abraham
Richard John Abraham
Bruno Adam J.
   Adamczyk
Lex William H. Adams
Alan William Ahearn
Richard Alfred Aldersea
Norman George Allen
John Harker Andrews
Frederick John Annesley
Ross David Anton
Gary Alex Archer
Kevin John Arnold
Peter John Arnold
William John Ashton
Trevor James Attwood
Donald Raymond Aylett
Marvin Walter Ayres
Peter John Badcoe
Kenneth Wilfred Bade
Errol John Bailey
John Bain
George Terence Baines
Douglas Alfred Baker
Lindsay Ronald Bancks
David John Banfield
Stuart John Barnett
James Joseph Barrett
Glen Trevor
   Bartholomew
Karl William Baudistel
Lionel James Baxter
Brian Charles Beilken
Alec Ernest J. Bell

Ronald John Bell
Graham Rhodes
   Belleville
Ronald William Betts
Bernd George F. Binder
Martin Bink
Raymond Paul Binning
Michael James Birchell
Thomas Birnie
Robert Graham Birse
Barbara Frances Black
Trevor Ralph Black
Thomas Douglas
   Blackhurst
Wayne Allan Blanck
Alan Clarence Bloxsom
Kenneth James
   Boardman
John Albert Bond
Douglas Graham Borlace
Michael Alwyn Bourke
Donald Mackenzie
   Bourne
Robert Walter Bowtell
Dennis Hampton
   Bracewell
Gregory Vincent Brady
Peter John Bramble
David John Brennan
John Bressington
William John Brett
Kevin Frederick Brewer
David John Briggs
Dennis Lindsay Brooks
Edward Francis Brophy

Allen Roy Brown
Ian Robert Brown
Lindsay Noel Brown
Robert Buchan
John Harold Bullman
Roberts Burns
Ronald Robert Butlin
Raymond John
   Butterworth
Basil Eric Byrne
Robert Alan Byrne
John Alexander
   Campbell
Hugh Carlyle
Ronald Thomas Carroll
William Thomas Carroll
John Carruthers
Robert Charles Carver
Anthony Austin Casadio
Albert Lesley Casey
Garry Owen Cashion
Nick John Cassano
Robert John Caston
Peter Allan Chant
Rodney Stewart
   Chapman
Thomas William
   Checkley
Christopher Clark
Donald Murray Clark
Raymond Duncan Clark
Ross Tasman Clark
Peter Edward Clements
Richard William Cliff
Laurence Ian Clifford

John Raymond Cock
Kevin George Coles
Ronald Francis Connors
George Alfred Constable
Robert Tom Convery
Kevin George Conway
Geoffrey John Coombs
Alan John Cooper
Russell James Copeman
Brendan Franics Coupe
James George Cox
Raymond John Cox
Ronald Edward Coxon
Peter Craig
Noel Valintine Crouch
Bryan Thomas Cullen
Timothy Joseph Cutcliffe
Anatoly Danilenko
Gordon Henry
   D'Antoine
Barry Norton Davidson
Rex William Davies
Ronald Edward Davies
Walter Johnston Davison
Ian Kenneth Dawson
Peter Dawson
Thomas Johannes De
   Vries Van Leeuwen
Romon John P. Deed
John Walter Desnoy
Keith Ivan Dewar
Stephen Warwick
   Dickson
John Alexander Doherty
Barry Creig Donald
Denis John Donnelly
William Wayne Donnelly
David Gerard Doyle
Glenn Alfred Drabble
Roger William Driscoll
Andrew Drummond
David John Dubber

James Duff
Kenneth Allan Duffy
Milton Raymond Dufty
Alan Leslie Duncuff
Jeffrey Max Duroux
John Thomas Durrington
Philip Earle
Beresford Paul Edwards
Ronald John Engstrom
Paul Evans
Thomas Arthur Evans
Barry Edmond Fallon
Leslie Thomas Farren
Francis John Fewquandie
Ronald Eric Field
David John E. Fisher
Roger Leon Fisher
Jack Fitzgerald
Bryan Francis Fitzpatrick
Robert Fleming
Graham Leslie Foster
Alexander Henry T.
   Fotheringham
John Fraser
John William Freeman
Vivian Albert French
Ronald James Gaffney
Wallace James Galvin
Kenneth Howard Gant
Bernard Anthony
   Garland
John Edgar Garrett
John Garrigan
Barry Randolph George
Ian James Gibbs
Arthur John Gibson
George Geoffrey Gilbert
Michael William T. Gill
Robert James Gillard
John Francis Gillespie
Peter Raymond Gillson
Guy Richard Godden

Peter James Gollagher
Phillip Raymond Goody
Eric George Gould
Allan Walter Graham
Samuel Graham
Ernest Francis Grant
George Bruce Green
John Gerald Greene
Victor Roy Grice
Edward Anthony Grills
Robert Maxwell Grist
Thomas Joseph Grose
William Francis Hacking
Eric Halkyard
John Hall
Frederick George
   Hamersley
Maxwell Powell Hanley
Michael John Hannaford
Allan Robert Hansen
Bryant Victor Hansen
Peter Roy Hansen
Noel Stuart Harald
Edward William George
   Hards
Ronald Arthur Harris
Barleif Alfred Harstad
Peter Richard Hart
Gilbert John Hartney
Norman Victor G.
   Hawker
James Francis Hayes
Robert Max Hayes
Malcolm Austin
   Henderson
Terence Edward Hendle
Michael Patrick John
   Herbert
Ronald David Hewitt
Robert Bernard Hickey
Donald Cameron Hill
Reginald Hedley Hillier

Peter Aubyn Hines
Frederick William Hoare
William Joseph Hoban
Tony Holland
Anthony Edward Hollis
John Wallace Holloway
Ronald Dean Hood
Neville Wayne Horne
James Michael Houston
Kenneth Raymond
Houston
Rodney Noel Hubble
Antony Jeffrey Huelin
Robert Edward Hughes
Rodney Donald Hughes
Raymond Henry Hunt
Harold Walter Hurst
Maurice John Hutchison
Francis Arthur Hyland
Peter Joseph Jackson
Robert James Jackson
Barry James
Alan Douglas Jellie
Jack Jewry
Brian Richard Alan Jones
John Henry Kalma
Graham Robert
Kavanagh
Barry Walter Kelly
John Joseph Kennedy
Raymond John Kennedy
Raymond Charles
Kermode
James Kelly Kerr
Robert MacDonald Key
Ian William Kingston
Keith Michael Kingston-
Powles
John William Kirby
Gordon Knight
Peter Raymond Knight
Peter Francis Kowalski

Gaetano La Grasta
Everitt Murray Lance
Terrance Edward
Langlands
Paul Andrew Large
Stanley Gordon Larsson
Norman William Le
Bherz
Errol John Lee
Ronald Victor Lees
Peter Edward Lewis
Matthew Philip Linton
Anthony Lisle
Colin Thomas Lithgow
Allan Lloyd
Richard Edward Lloyd
Geoffrey Robert Locke
Barry Arthur Logan
Matthew Loughman
Noel Lowes
Robert John Lubcke
Neville Francis Luff
Trevor Lyddieth
Terance Edward Lyon
Peter James Lyons
James Alexander
MacDonald
Larry James MacLennan
Peter Anthony Malone
Joseph George Manicola
Paul Manning
Peter Robert Marks-
Chapman
William Henry Martin
Ian George Mathers
Geoffrey Francis
Mathews
Kenneth Frank
Mathieson
Reginald Nelson Maza
John Noel McCarthy
Malcolm Ross

McConachy
Albert Frederick
McCormack
Dennis James
McCormack
Leslie Charles
McDonnell
Peter Edward McDuff
Peter Shaun McGarry
William McGoldrick
Raymond Alfred
McGuire
Neil Anthony McInerney
Colin William
McLachlan
James Clyde McMillan
Ross Charles McMillan
Robert Leo McNab
Duncan Glen McNair
Lyall Hugh McPherson
Malcolm Bruce
McQualter
John Leonard McQuat
James Leslie Menz
Thomas Frederick
Meredith
David Geoffrey Milford
Robert Bruce Milligan
David Mitchell
Warren David Mitchell
Kevin Leslie Mitchinson
Barry John Moore
Raymond John Moore
Sydney Thomas Moore
John Leslie Morgan
Dayle William Morrison
Allan Brian Moss
Graeme John Moss
Brenton George
Mowbray
Michael Muc
Hans Leonhard Muller

Barry John Munday
Peter Eris Murray
Harold Robert Musicka
George Nagle
William Lynn Nalder
Paul John Navarre
Dennis William Neal
John David Needs
Dennis Edwin Nelson
Ralph James Niblett
Raymond Kevin Nichols
Kenneth Roy Nicholson
Erald Herman Nilsen
Christopher Robert
    Nisbet
Errol Wayne Noack
Michael James Noonan
Graham Leonard Norley
John William Norris
John Alfred O'Brien
John Martin O'Connor
Patrick Shane O'Connor
Stephen James O'Dal
Robert Melville
    O'Hanlon
John Laurence O'Hara
Allan Leslie O'Neill
John Barry O'Neill
Geoffrey O'Shea
Richard Harold J. Parker
Roderick Thomas Ross
    Parker
Antonio Parrello
David Paterson
Raymond Brian Patten
Allan Graham Pattison
John Gregory S. Pearce
Bernard Michael Pengilly
Desmond Hugh Penn
Peter Lawrence
    Penneyston
Robert Graham Perrin

Timo Esko A. Pesonen
Bror Ola Petersen
Victor Neils Petersen
Trevor Graham Petith
John Gordon Pettit
Leslie James Pettit
Noel Charles Pettitt
O'Brian Cedric Ignatious
    Phillips
Reginald Arthur Phillips
Thomas Dudley Phillips
Geoffrey Anthony Pike
Douglas Brian Plain
Bruce James Plane
Gary Robert Polglase
Victor Ian Pomroy
Michael Damien Poole
Robin Christian Pothof
Daryl Poulson
Robert Edward Power
Douglas Roy J. Powter
Noel Arthur Pracy
Kevin John Prior
Leslie Prowse
Anthony Thomas Purcell
Anthony Vincent
    Quigley
Stanley Edwin Radomi
Francis Lindsay Raffen
Joseph Steven Ramsay
John Milton Rands
John Robert Rapp
Paul Francis Reidy
Alexander Remeljej
Brian Rennie
Terrence James Renshaw
Maxwell Lachlan Rhodes
Adrian William Rich
Neil Thomas Richardson
Philip Mackay Richter
Wayne Maurice Riley
Kerry Patrick Rinkin

Jeffrey Clive Rivett
Arthur James Robertson
Malcolm Robert
    Robertson
John Rogers
Kerry Michael Rooney
Christopher William
    Roost
Grant Stuart Ross
Thomas Ross
James Ruddy
Arthur Ruduss
Douglas Javing Salveron
Ronald Wayne Salzmann
Richard Wayne Sandow
Christopher James
    Sawtell
Grantley James Scales
Martinus Jacobus M.
    Schuit
Ian James Scott
Ian Neil Scott
Ronald Allan Scott
Terence Ronald Scott
Ronald Seiler
Raymond Douglas Seipel
Gordon Cameron Sharp
Keith Charles Shaw
Laurence Rodney
    Sheppard
Peter James Sheriff
Noel Ervin Shipp
Anthony Peter Siggers
Thomas Simpson
Harold Leslie Slater
John Michael Slattery
Ronald George Smillie
Baron Fredrick Smith
Bernard Lyle Smith
Francis John Smith
John Smith
Noel Alan Smith

Paul Leslie Smith
Peter Charles Smith
Robert Stanley Smith
Ronald Keith Smith
Gordon Dennis
Sorrensen
Roderick James Sprigg
Donald Matthew Stahl
Henry John Stanczyk
Gregory Ian Stanford
David John Steen
John George Stevens
John Maxwell Stone
Michael Sukmanowsky
Paul Charles Sullivan
Thomas Suter
Henry Edward Suttor
Ronald James Swanton
John Robert Sweetnam
Arnold Sykes
Alan Talbot
Leonard Alexander
Taylor
Peter Tebb
Wayne Edward Teeling
David John Thomas
William Malcolm
Thomas
Barry John Thompson
Donald Leslie Thompson
Ian James Thomson
John Richard Tinkham
Vincent John Tobin
Michael Peter Tognolini

Marian Tomas
Francis Brett Topp
Michael Towler
Barry Tregear
Bevan Maxwell Trimble
Kevin John Troy
Paul Zigmund Trzecinski
Desmond John Tully
Timothy Charles Turner
Geoffrey Lawrence
Tweedie
John Warren Twomey
Paul Richard P. Van
Rijsewijk
Arie Van Valen
Patrick John Vickers
Douglas James Voyzey
Victor Neil Wagstaff
David John Waldock
Maxwell Ray Wales
Brian Geoffrey Walker
Alan John Wallis
David Anthony B. Wallis
Brian Walsh
Graham Francis A.
Warburton
Anthony Edward L.
Waring
Brian David Waters
Bryan Phillip Watson
Richard Christopher A.
Watson
David Raleigh Webster
James Clifton Webster

Garry Maxwell West
Leslie James Weston
Raymond Bruce Weston
Kevin Arthur Wheatley
John William Wheeler
Barry John Whiston
Colin Joseph Whiston
Harry Winston White
James Mungo T. White
Michael Paul White
John Hunter Whitton
Alan Charles F.
Wilkinson
Archibald Stanley
Williams
Garry Ian Willoughby
Robert Peter Wilsen
Kevin Ronald Wilson
Mervyn Arthur F. Wilson
Robert Barclay Wilson
Bogdan Kazimierz
Wojcik
Norman James Womal
Richard Mervyn
Woolford
Ivan Alfred Woolley
Jeffrey Thomas Worle
Donald Spence Wride
Alexander Henry Young
Brian Thomas Young
Robert George Young
Robert James Yule

# Appendix 2

## Australian infantry battalions and their commanders who served in Vietnam

**1RAR**

| 1st Tour | 25 May 1965 to 14 Jun. 1966 | Lt Col. Lou Brumfield |
| | | Lt Col. Alex Preece |
| 2nd Tour | 19 Jan. 1968 to 28 Feb. 1969 | Lt Col. Phillip Bennett |

**2RAR**

| 1st Tour | 1 Apr. 1967 to 7 Jul. 1968 | Lt Col. Noel 'Chic' Charlesworth |
| 2nd Tour | 28 Apr. 1970 to 4 Jun. 1971 | Lt Col. John Church |

**3RAR**

| 1st Tour | 12 Dec. 1967 to 5 Dec. 1968 | Lt Col. Jeffrey 'Jim' Shelton |
| 2nd Tour | 12 Feb. 1971 to 19 Oct. 1971 | Lt Col. Peter F. Scott |

**4RAR**

| 1st Tour | 29 Jan. 1968 to 30 May 1969 | Lt Col. Lee Greville |
| 2nd Tour | 1 May 1971 to 12 Mar. 1972 | Lt Col. Jim Hughes |

**5RAR**

| 1st Tour | 1 Apr. 1966 to 5 Jul. 1967 | Lt Col. John Warr |
| 2nd Tour | 28 Jan. 1969 to 5 Mar. 1970 | Lt Col. Colin Khan |

**6RAR**

| 1st Tour | 1 Apr. 1966 to 7 Jul. 1967 | Lt Col. Colin Townsend |
| 2nd Tour | 7 May 1969 to 28 May 1970 | Lt Col. David Butler |

**7RAR**

| 1st Tour | 2 Mar. 1967 to 26 Apr. 1968 | Lt Col. Eric Smith |
| 2nd Tour | 10 Feb. 1970 to 10 Mar. 1971 | Lt Col. Ron Grey |

**8RAR**

| Tour | 18 Nov. 1969 to 12 Nov. 1970 | Lt Col. Keith O'Neill |

**9RAR**

| Tour | 5 Nov. 1968 to 5 Dec. 1969 | Lt Col. Alby Morrison |

# Appendix 3

## Australian units involved in Vietnam

AUSTRALIAN ARMY
*Australian Force Vietnam*
Headquarters Australian Army Force Vietnam
Headquarters Army Assistance Group Vietnam
Australian Embassy Guard Platoon
Defence and Employment Platoon
Field Operations Research Section
Headquarters Australian Force Vietnam Cash Office
Australian Civil Affairs Unit
Postal Unit
AFV Provost Detachment

*1 Australian Logistic Support Group*
Australian Logistic Support Company Headquarters
1 Australian Logistic Support Group
2 Detachment Australian Force Vietnam
Detachment 1 Division Postal Unit
Detachment 1 Comm Z Postal Unit
Detachment 5 ASCO Unit
Headquarters 2 Australian Force Canteen Unit (AFCU)
Detachment 2 AFCU
1 Platoon 2 AFCU
67 Ground Liaison (GL) Section
1 Australian Rest and Convalescence Centre
AFV Amenities and Welfare Unit
1 Psychological Operations Unit
AFV Provost HQ
110 Signals Squadron

*1 Australian Task Force*
Headquarters 1 Australian Task Force
Detachment 1 Division Cash Office
Detachment Australian Force Vietnam Cash Office
Provost Section 1 Provost Company (AFV Provost)
Australian Force Vietnam Provost Unit
1 Australian Reinforcement Unit (1ARU)
Defence and Employment Platoon (Hawke Force)
104 Signals Squadron
2nd Defence and Employment Platoon (officially recognised in 2008)

*Australian Army Training Team Vietnam*

*Royal Australian Armoured Corps*
1 APC Troop
1 APC Squadron
A Squadron 3 Cavalry Regiment
B Squadron 3 Cavalry Regiment
A Squadron 1 Armoured Regiment
B Squadron 1 Armoured Regiment
C Squadron 1 Armoured Regiment
Detachment 1 Forward Delivery Troop
1 Troop A Squadron 4/19 Prince of Wales Light Horse

*Royal Australian Artillery*
105 Field Battery
1 Field Regiment
    101 Field Battery
    103 Field Battery
    105 Field Battery
4 Field Regiment
    106 Field Battery
    107 Field Battery
    108 Field Battery
12 Field Regiment
A Field Battery
102 Field Battery
104 Field Battery
Detachment 131 Divisional Locating Battery

*Royal Australian Engineers*
Detachment 198 Works Section
198 Works Section
Detachment 11 Movement Control Group
3 Field Troop
1 Field Squadron
21 Engineer Support Troop
Detachment 55 Advanced Engineer Stores Squadron
Detachment 55 Engineer Workshop & Park Squadron
55 Engineer Workshop & Park Squadron
17 Construction Squadron
Detachment 11 Movement Control Group
30 Terminal Squadron
Detachment 1 Division Postal Unit
Detachment 1 Communication Zone Postal Unit
1 Small Ship Troop (*Clive Steele*)
1 Small Ship Troop (*Harry Chauvel*)
3 Small Ship Troop (*Vernon Sturdee*)

4 Small Ship Troop (*Brudenell White*)
Detachment 32 Small Ship Squadron (*John Monash*)
Detachment 32 Small Ship Squadron (*Clive Steele*)
Detachment 32 Small Ship Squadron (*Harry Chauvel*)

*Royal Australian Survey Corps*
Detachment 1 Topographical Survey Troop A
Section 1 Topographical Survey Troop

*Royal Australian Signal Corps*
HQ 145 Signal Squadron 709 Signal Troop
527 Signal Troop, absorbed into 145 Signal Squadron
547 Signal Troop
581 Signal Troop
552 Signal Troop
506 Signal Troop
520 Signal Troop
HQ 110 Signal Squadron
HQ Signal Squadron
704 Signal Troop
557 Signal Troop
561 Signal Troop
532 Signal Troop
503 Signal Troop
103 Signal Squadron
104 Signal Squadron (TF), replaced 103 Signal Squadron
110 Signal Squadron, replaced 145 Signal Squadron
Detachment 152 Signal Squadron (SAS)
AAAGV Signal Detachment

*Royal Australian Infantry*
First Battalion Royal Australian Regiment (1RAR)
Second Battalion Royal Australian Regiment (2RAR)
Third Battalion Royal Australian Regiment (3RAR) (Old Faithful)
Fourth Battalion Royal Australian Regiment (4RAR)
Fifth Battalion Royal Australian Regiment (5RAR)
Sixth Battalion Royal Australian Regiment (6RAR)
Seventh Battalion Royal Australian Regiment (7RAR)
Eighth Battalion Royal Australian Regiment (8RAR)
Ninth Battalion Royal Australian Regiment (9RAR)
(2RAR and 4RAR [both tours] and 6RAR [second tour] served as ANZAC
    battalions; each contained two companies of New Zealand troops.)
Special Air Service Regiment (SAS)
    One Squadron Special Air Service
    Two Squadron Special Air Service
    Three Squadron Special Air Service

*Royal Australian Army Aviation Corps*
161 Reconnaissance Flight
161 (Independent) Reconnaissance Flight

*Australian Intelligence Corps*
Detachment 1 Division Intelligence Unit
1 Psychological Operations Unit

*Royal Australian Army Service Corps*
RAASC Detachment at Bien Hoa
HQ 1 Company RAASC at Vung Tau
1 Transport Platoon RAASC at Vung Tau
87 Transport Platoon RAASC at Vung Tau
Detachment 276 AD Company at Vung Tau
Detachment 1 Division Postal Unit at Vung Tau
HQ 5 Company RAASC at Vung Tau
2 Transport Platoon at Vung Tau
85 Transport Platoon (Tipper) at Vung Tau
86 Transport Platoon at Vung Tau
Saigon Detachment 1 Comm Z Postal Unit at Vung Tau
HQ 26 Company RAASC at Nui Dat
85 Transport Platoon at Nui Dat
Elm 176 AD Company at Nui Dat
Elm 1 Comm Z Postal Unit at Nui Dat
21 Supply Platoon
25 Supply Platoon
Detachment 52 Supply Platoon
Detachment 8 Petroleum Platoon

*Royal Australian Army Medical Corps*
1 Australian Field Hospital
2 Field Ambulance
8 Field Ambulance
Detachment 1 Field Medical/Dental Unit
Detachment 1 Field Medical/Dental Depot
Detachment 1 Field Hygiene Company

*Royal Australian Army Dental Corps*
33 Dental Unit

*Royal Australian Army Nursing Corps*
44 members of the RAANC served in Vietnam with:
1st Australian Field Hospital
8th Field Ambulance

*Royal Australian Army Ordnance Corps*
HQ 2 Company Ordnance Depot (Type A) (redesignated)

2 Advanced Ordnance Depot
    13 Ordnance Supply Control Platoon
    16 Ordnance Vehicle Platoon
    14 Ordnance Stores Platoon
    18 Ordnance Depot Laundry and Bath Section
    15 Ordnance Ammunition Platoon
    19 Ordnance Supply Control Platoon
    20 Ordnance Stores Platoon
Independent Armoured Sqn Workshop Stores Section (redesignated)
101 Field Workshop Stores Section
102 Field Workshop Stores Section
106 Field Workshop Stores Section
1 Independent Armoured Squadron Workshop Stores Section
1 Armoured Squadron Workshop Stores Section
1 Ordnance Field Park Detachment
6 Ordnance Field Park Detachment
1 Ordnance Field Park

*Royal Australian Electrical and Mechanical Engineers*
Detachment 131 Div Loc Bty Workshop
1 Field Squadron Workshop
106 Field Workshop (Type A)
1 TF Headquarter Light Aid Detachment
1 APC Squadron Light Aid Detachment
A Squadron 3 Cavalry Regiment Light Aid Detachment
B Squadron 3 Cavalry Regiment Light Aid Detachment
A Squadron 1 Armoured Regiment Light Aid Detachment
B Squadron 1 Armoured Light Aid Detachment
C Squadron 1 Armoured Regiment Light Aid Detachment
1 Field Regiment Light Aid Detachment
4 Field Regiment Light Aid Detachment
12 Field Regiment Light Aid Detachment
1 Independent Armoured Squadron Workshop
1 Armoured Squadron Workshop
17 Construction Squadron Workshop Detachment
1 Division ST Workshop
5 Company RAASC Workshop
101 Field Workshop (Type A)
102 Field Workshop (Type B)

*Citizens Military Forces Observers*

*Army Public Relations Service*

ROYAL AUSTRALIAN NAVY
HMAS *Sydney*
HMAS *Brisbane*

HMAS *Perth*
HMAS *Hobart*
HMAS *Vendetta*
HMAS *Jeparit* (until 1969 MV *Jeparit*)
HMAS *Boonaroo*
Clearance Diving Team 3
RAN Helicopter Flight Vietnam
    Some reassigned to US/Aus 135th Assault Helicopter Company
RAN Detachment 9 Squadron RAAF
RAN Medical officers
RAN Chaplains

## ROYAL AUSTRALIAN AIR FORCE
Headquarters Royal Australian Air Force Element
Australian Force Vietnam Headquarters
Royal Australian Air Force Contingent at Vung Tau
Royal Australian Air Force Caribou Transport Flight
Base Support Flight
Army Light Aircraft Squadron
No. 1 Operational Support Unit
No. 2 Squadron
No. 9 Squadron
Airfield Construction Squadron (Detachment B)
No. 5 Airfield Construction Unit
Royal Australian Air Force Element 161 Recce Flight
No. 35 Squadron
No. 36 Squadron
No. 37 Squadron
Detachment S
RAAF Nursing Service Medevac Flight
RAAF Chaplains

## CIVILIAN AND PHILANTHROPIC
Red Cross
Salvation Army
War correspondents
Official war artists, historians and photographers
Civilian medical teams
Australian entertainment groups
Everymans welfare organisation

Source: Vietnam Veterans Association of Australia, http://www.vvaa.org.au
'Australian Order of Battle for Vietnam 1962–1972' (Copyright © 1996 Brian Ross)

# Appendix 4

## Dust-off during a hot extraction

The helicopter medevac procedure — learned from the Americans — was a feat of astonishing coordination. A soldier could be in a clean hospital bed within 30 minutes of a radio request. The 'dust-off' Hueys often flew in under the suppressive cover of Bushranger helicopter gunships, which circled overhead, machine-gunning the jungle fringes as the wounded were stretchered or winched aboard the medical helicopter. Often the medevac came under intense ground fire, as shown in this extraordinary transcript of a radio exchange during an Australian medevac in the Hat Dich area, in July 1969 (reprinted with the kind permission of Captain David Wilkins, of the Fifth Battalion, from his account, 'A Vietnam Diary', pp. 112–22):

> 3C [*pronounced 'Three-Charlie', was the company sergeant major, Jack Lake, on the ground*]: Dust-off 2 this is Three-Charlie, do you see the smoke I threw for Bushranger? That's where I'll have the medevac, over.

> Bushranger 71 [*pronounced 'Seven-One', the helicopter gunship*]: ...We'll be suppressing just to the east of that purple smoke, over.

> Dust-off 2 [*the medevac dust-off helicopter*]: Three-Charlie this is Dust-off 2. Do you want the Stokes litter or the jungle penetrator first?

> 3C: Jungle penetrator first, over [*the jungle penetrator was a folded seat connected to a wire, dropped through thick jungle like a plumb bob; the wounded were strapped into the seat and winched up*].

> Bushranger 71: Bushranger Seven-One, rolling in from the south-west to the north-east in 20 seconds, over.

> 3C: Watch out for Dust-off, out ... Dust-off 2, this is Three-Charlie. That man is fairly bad. He has taken a hole right into the chest above the heart. WE ARE TAKING FIRE, WE'RE TAKING FIRE. PULL OUT, DUST-OFF. GET OUT, DUST-OFF.

> 30 ['*Three-Zero', the company commander Bill Titley*]: Dust-off is getting fired at. GET THAT CHOPPER OUT OF THE WAY. YOU'RE BEING FIRED AT, DUST-OFF.

Dust-off 2: ... Roger. We're taking some pretty heavy tracer from that same position also, out.

30: Bushranger Seven-One, this is Three-Zero, can you bring that fire in closer now. Dust-off has been taking enemy fire, over.

Bushranger 71: ... Roger, if Three-One can throw smoke, we'll suppress out.

31 ['Three-One', the platoon commander Ian Hosie, or his radio operator, Private Reeves]: Dust-off, be careful with those guns, we're down here too, over.

31: Three-Zero, this is Three-One, STOP DUST-OFF FROM FIRING. HE'S SHOOTING US UP.

30: ... Dust-off Two, this is Three-Zero, cease your firing. You are engaging friendly troops, over.

Dust-off 2: ... Wilco, out.

Bushranger 71: ... Rolling again in twenty seconds, over.

The dust-off took thirty enemy hits, wrote Wilkins, but the pilot remained calm, and rotated the aircraft's tail towards the fire to protect the crew. His side gunners, however, mistakenly fired on Hosie's platoon. The dust-off made a second, successful attempt and winched several wounded out. One Australian died of wounds in the operation.

# Endnotes

## Chapter 1 **Three thousand years**

1 John and Victoria Binnie, interviews, Sydney, 9 September 2005.
2 David Llewelyn, personal memoir, September 2006.
3 Paul Murphy, interview, Vung Tau, 16 November 2005.
4 Heard, *Well Done, Those Men*, p. 4.
5 Ibid., pp. 5–6.
6 Ibid., p. 7.
7 Woodard, *Asian Alternatives*, p. 27.
8 AWM89 N20; and *Hansard*, August 1954, p. 573.
9 As described by Professor Huu Ngoc, a prominent Vietnamese historian, in a lecture to American Vietnam veterans in Hanoi, November 2005.
10 Karnow, *Vietnam*, p. 100.
11 Buttinger, *The Smaller Dragon*, p. 29.
12 Ibid.
13 Huu Ngoc, *Wandering Through Vietnamese Culture*, p. 1071.
14 Ibid.
15 Buttinger, *The Smaller Dragon*, p. 45.
16 Karnow, *Vietnam*, p. 104.
17 Ibid.
18 Ibid., p. 103.
19 Ibid, p. 105.
20 Buttinger, *The Smaller Dragon*, p. 70.

## Chapter 2 **The French**

1 Buttinger, *The Smaller Dragon*, p. 86.
2 Jamieson, *Understanding Vietnam*, p. 43.
3 Karnow, *Vietnam*, p. 79.
4 Ibid., p. 82.
5 Buttinger, *The Smaller Dragon*, p. 98.
6 Karnow, *Vietnam*, p. 85.
7 Ibid., p. 87.
8 Ibid.
9 Some governors made token attempts to civilise the French *mission civilatrice*: Albert Sarrault tried and failed to outlaw the routine practice of beating the natives. That was about the extent of his duty of care: true, Sarrault built medical clinics for the villagers, but they were poorly equipped and soon useless. On the debit side, in 1917, Sarrault extended France's trade monopolies and encouraged the spread of opium houses, fast-tracking new generations of Vietnamese adolescents into addiction. Perhaps his most obscene contribution was the creation of an army of forced Vietnamese labour, 140,000 civilians, whom he shipped back to France to aid the war effort in Europe.
10 Jamieson, *Understanding Vietnam*, p. 51.
11 Ibid., p. 55.
12 Ibid., p. 56.
13 Ibid., p. 60.

14 One account of Chau's capture tells of a young Marxist called Ly Thuy (alias Nguyen Ai Quoc, alias Ho Chi Minh) proposing to his fellow communists the sacrifice of Chau to their revolutionary cause. The idea was to 'sell' Chau to the French, which would raise funds for Ho's fledgling communist movement; meanwhile Chau's imprisonment would inflame anti-French feeling and arouse world condemnation. It would also rid Ho of a dangerously popular nationalist (Chau had studied Marxism and repudiated it). As for Chau's fate, Ho anticipated that Chau's fame would save his neck, as indeed happened, according to Buttinger's account (*The Smaller Dragon*, p. 159): Ho's men abducted Chau in Shanghai, and sold him to the French for 150,000 piastres. A Criminal Commission sentenced him on 23 November 1925 to hard labour for life, commuted to house arrest.

15 Buttinger, *The Smaller Dragon*, pp. 163–4.

16 Ibid.

17 Ibid., p. 178.

18 Ibid., p. 177.

19 Ibid., p. 180.

20 Jamieson, *Understanding Vietnam*, p. 160.

21 Ibid., p. 167.

22 Buttinger, *The Smaller Dragon*, p. 179.

## Chapter 3 Ho and Giap

1 Marx and Engels, *The Communist Manifesto*, p. 39. *The Communist Manifesto* seduced millions, who accepted its exhortation to revolutionary violence in realising their socialist dreams. For them, the destruction, exile or removal of an entire social class was deemed necessary, indeed inevitable. Marx distinguished his ideas from all that went before them, asserting that 'the philosophers have only *interpreted* the world … the point is to *change* it'. Marx foretold the violent overthrow of 'the bourgeoisie' and its replacement with a dictatorship of and for the worker. No quarter would be given in this great struggle, which Marx believed was the inevitable outcome of a historic war between capital and labour. He saw the human agent as helpless before the 'iron laws' of his economic theories. Capitalists were 'mere puppets, irresistibly pulled by economic wires — by historical forces over which they have no control' (Popper, *The Open Society and Its Enemies*, Vol. 2, *Hegel and Marx*, p. 354). For Marx, greed and exploitation were consequences, not causes, of capitalist corruption. So too were the victims of unrestrained capitalism, the conditions of which Marx laid bare in *Capital*. Yet his burning sense of injustice compelled him to wreck, rather than reform, the system he so despised. Others — such as the British labour reformers and Charles Dickens — saw the inhumanity Marx saw and pleaded for social reform. The leaders of the English workers' movement in general wanted union representation, not the blood of their employers. They asked not 'Who should rule over us?' but 'How can we tame them?' (Popper, *Hegel and Marx*, p. 144). Marx and Engels must be considered as products of their time, and not across the wasteland of the greater part of their legacy. The Procrustean fury of the Manifesto reflected Marx's profound contemplation of and sympathy for the lot of ordinary workers and their families. Indeed, the case against child labour is one of the Manifesto's few persuasive pleas. Marx and Engels also recommended free education for all children in public school — a reform now universally applied throughout the capitalist West. Yet one did not have to be a communist or socialist to see, at the time, the injustice of unrestrained monopolistic capitalism and the exploitation of the poor. This hardly redeemed Marx's core prescription for a violent global revolution, the legacy of which set in train the processes that led to the Soviet Gulag, the Vietnamese re-education camp and the Khmer Rouge. In one sense it is unfair to blame Marx, because if his theory of the *inevitable overthrow of capitalism* was correct, the workers would have united anyway. In the event, they failed to do so; they pursued the course of reform. Only peasant agrarian societies in Russia and parts of Asia and Africa responded with the mass homicide Marx had predicted.

2 Marx and Engels, *The Communist Manifesto*, p. 41.

3 Marx, *The Poverty of Philosophy*.

4 Marx and Engels, *The Communist Manifesto*, p. 258.

5 Ibid., p. 96.

6 Lenin, 'The State and Revolution', in Marx, Engles and Lenin, *The Essential Left*, p. 164.

7 Ibid.

8 Karnow, *Vietnam*, p. 119.

9 Pemberton (ed.), *Vietnam Remembered*, p. 15.

10 Giap, *Unforgettable Days*, p. 10.

11 Ibid., p. 427.

12 Vu Anh, *Days with Ho Chi Minh*, p. 167.

13 Warner, *The Last Confucian*, p. 45.

14 Fall, profile of Vo Nguyen Giap; in Vo Nguyen, Giap, *People's War, People's Army*, p. xxxvii.

15 Karnow, *Vietnam*, p. 141.

16 Few regimes were less democratic. The Democratic Republic of Vietnam would not adopt its true name, the Socialist Republic of Vietnam, until after the Second Indochina War.

17 Buttinger, *The Smaller Dragon*, p. 209.

18 Ibid., p. 258.

19 Halberstam, *The Making of a Quagmire*, p. 34.

20 Karnow, *Vietnam*, p. 147.

21 Warner, *The Last Confucian*, p. 50.

22 *The Pentagon Papers*, pp. 49–50.

23 Karnow, *Vietnam*, p. 155.

24 The actual figure was probably closer to a thousand, according Vu Quoc Uy, Chairman of the Haiphong Municipal Committee, in 1981. For various descriptions of Valluy's attack, see Karnow, *Vietnam*; Jamieson, *Understanding Vietnam*; Buttinger, *The Smaller Dragon*; and Warner, *The Last Confucian*.

25 The history of the ensuing eight-year war is superbly told in Bernard Fall's classics *Street Without Joy* and *Hell in a Very Small Place*; and Martin Windrow's epic *The Last Valley*.

26 Buttinger, *The Smaller Dragon*, p. 351.

27 Fall, *Viet-Nam Witness*, p. 35.

28 Jamieson, *Understanding Vietnam*, p. 228.

29 Sexton, *War for the Asking*, p. 23. The Americans spent US$954 million backing the French in Indochina up to 1954; by comparison, the French spent US$11 billion of taxpayers' money between 1946 and 1954 on the First Indochina War, according to Bernard Fall in *Street Without Joy*. That should 'lay at rest once and for all the myth of "the American taxpayer financing the French in Indo-China"' (ibid., p. 308). Yet according to Karnow, the USA had spent US$2.5 billion on French Indochina by 1954, 'more assistance than France received in Marshall Plan aid from America …' (Karnow, *Vietnam*, p. 137).

30 Windrow, *The Last Valley*, p. 613.

31 Ibid., p. 629; and www.dienbienphu.org, the battle's official site.

Chapter 4 **The Red menace**

1 Pemberton, *All the Way*, p. 12.

2 Thompson, *No Exit from Vietnam*, p. 104.

3 Kimball, *To Reason Why*, p. 31.

4 As recorded by Clark Clifford, presidential adviser and future Secretary of Defense, during Eisenhower's briefing of JFK on foreign policy, 19 January 1961.

5 National Security Council paper 124/2 of June 1952; *Pentagon Papers*, pp. 81–8.

6 Watt, *Vietnam*, p. 58.

7 Buttinger, *The Smaller Dragon*, p. 376. The Geneva Agreements were riddled with 'semantic monstrosities', in Buttinger's apt phrase. Many clauses were open to interpretation and legal

confusion. A critical clause stated that the line dividing Vietnam was 'provisional and should not in any way be interpreted as constituting a political or territorial boundary'. The communist North had demanded this concession. But how would the two Vietnams be reconciled? By elections, of course. To the fury of the South, the communists at first insisted that these be held within months. Then, to general astonishment, the Soviet Foreign Minister, Vyacheslav Molotov, the conference's co-chairman (with Britain), proposed a two-year waiting period before elections, pending consultations between 'the competent authorities of the two zones'. Such 'competent authorities' didn't exist: the government of Saigon had ruled itself out by rejecting the proposals; the French were leaving; and if some regarded the Hanoi regime as 'competent', they certainly did not include America and Saigon. Regardless, the elections were verbally 'agreed' for July 1956. Nothing was signed (for the full text of the Geneva Agreements, see Department of External Affairs, *Select Documents on International Affairs*, No. 1 of 1964, pp. 1–15).

8 Buttinger, *The Smaller Dragon*, p. 378.
9 Qiang Zhai, *China and the Vietnam Wars 1950–1975*, p. 4.
10 For the full text of the Australian statement, see Department of External Affairs (Foreign Affairs and Trade), *Current Notes on International Affairs*, Vol. 25 (1954), p. 469.
11 Watt, *Vietnam*, p. 65.
12 Gollan, *Revolutionaries and Reformists*, p. 244.
13 *Hansard*, Vol. 201, pp. 1046–8.
14 *Hansard*, Vol. 196, p. 601.
15 Davidson, *The Communist Party of Australia*, p. xi.
16 Sexton, *War for the Asking*, p. 37.
17 Murphy, *Harvest of Fear*, pp. xvii–xviii.
18 Ibid., p. 109.
19 Albinski, *Australian Policies and Attitudes Towards China*, pp. 443–4.
20 Watt, *The Changing Margins of Australian Foreign Policy*, p. 10.
21 In an intense debate on the issue in August 1967, Opposition Leader Gough Whitlam accused the government of treason: 'If there is a profit to be made, apparently there is no treason. When treason prospers, none dare call it treason' (*Hansard*, August 1967).
22 Freudenberg, *A Certain Grandeur*, p. 189.

## Chapter 5 **The two Vietnams**

1 Fall, *The Two Viet-Nams*, p. 153.
2 Ibid., pp. 127–8; Buttinger, *The Smaller Dragon*, p. 420.
3 Fall, *The Two Viet-Nams*, p. 155.
4 Lind, *Vietnam — The Necessary War*, p. 3.
5 Chang and Halliday, *Mao*, p. 372.
6 Fall, *The Two Viet-Nams*, p. 156.
7 Taussig, cited in Fall, *The Two Viet-Nams*.
8 Giap, speech printed in *Nhan Dan*, the North Vietnamese Communist Party newspaper, 31 October 1956; also see Hoang Van Chi, *From Colonialism to Communism*, New York, 1964, pp. 209–10 (the author, a Viet Minh fighter, fled the North when he saw the true nature of the regime).
9 Fall, *The Two Viet-Nams*, p. 177.
10 Halberstam, *The Best and the Brightest*, p. 148.
11 Halberstam, *The Making of a Quagmire*, p. 47.
12 Jamieson, *Understanding Vietnam*, p. 235.
13 Warner, cited in Halberstam, *The Making of a Quagmire*, p. 41.
14 Buttinger, *The Smaller Dragon*, p. 440. Diem's four elections were held on 4 March 1956, 30 August 1959, 9 April 1961 and 27 September 1963.
15 Jamieson, *Understanding Vietnam*, p. 237.
16 Henderson, cited in Lindholm, *Vietnam*, p. 342.

17 Ibid., pp. 343–4.

18 Edwards, *Crises and Commitments*, pp. 194–5.

19 *Age, Sydney Morning Herald, Catholic Weekly* and other Australian papers, 2–9 September 1957.

20 Edwards, *Crises and Commitments*, p. 199.

Chapter 6 **Viet Cong**

1 Giap, *People's War, People's Army*, p. 46.

2 Thompson, *No Exit from Vietnam*, p. 48.

3 Giap, *People's War, People's Army*, pp. 20–1.

4 Peter Gration, 'A Comparison of Strategies in the Vietnam War' (unpublished essay), p. 1.

5 Fall, *Viet-Nam Witness*, p. 78. The South was unfairly accused of the first breach of Geneva, by refusing to hold elections (to which it had never agreed). However, Saigon swiftly copied the North, by welcoming US arms. There followed endless stories of non-compliance on both sides. When US warplanes took off from an aircraft carrier and landed in Saigon — a flagrant breach — a monitor with the International Commission explained: 'Yes — but officially we have not been informed of the presence of the aircraft carrier.' When Geneva's monitors asked why they were refused entry to the largest airfield in North Vietnam, Hanoi said: 'It belongs to a private flying club — and private property is exempted from commission control.' (Fall, *Viet-Nam Witness*, p. 79.)

6 Ang Cheng Guan, *The Vietnam War From the Other Side*, p. 19.

7 Truong Nhu Tang, *A Viet Cong Memoir*, p. 64.

8 Sheehan, *A Bright Shining Lie*, pp. 102–3.

9 Ziegler and John Paul Vann, the US colonel who first recognised the failure of America's strategy in Vietnam, tried to stop such crimes, with little success. They were not isolated incidents; Vann had heard of many similar methods of torture. Their use merely swelled the ranks of the National Liberation Front.

10 Murphy, *Harvest of Fear*, p. 88.

11 The NLF's struggle had always involved violence against civilians, as Fall shows: for example, the assassination by the Viet Cong of 1,900 village officials in 1957 and 1958, which contradicted Dr Jim Cairns's claim in his book *The Eagle and the Lotus* that the Viet Cong pursued peaceful means until 1962–3.

12 Qiang Zhai, *China and the Vietnam Wars 1950–1975*, p. 83.

13 Lewy, *America in Vietnam*, pp. 17–18.

14 Thompson, *No Exit from Vietnam*, p. 36.

15 US Department of State, *Aggression from the North: The Record of North Viet-Nam's Campaign to Conquer South Viet-Nam*, p. 57 (my emphasis).

16 AWM290 117/4/6/[2], Department of the US Army, Headquarters, 173rd Airborne Brigade, Office of the Intelligence Officer, APO US Forces [6/65], Intelligence Summaries.

17 Cited in Halberstam, *The Best and the Brightest*, p. 167.

18 Truong Nhu Tang, *A Viet Cong Memoir*, pp. 164–5.

19 Ibid.

20 AWM 3DRL/7551, Paperes of Huynh Chien Dau, Viet Cong fighter, 1961–75.

21 Truong Nhu Tang, *A Viet Cong Memoir*, pp. 164–5.

22 Gottschang Turner and Phan Thanh Hao, *Even the Women Must Fight*, p. 37.

23 Colonel Le Trong Tam, cited in ibid., p. 93.

24 In fact, the CIA overstated the Ho Chi Minh Trail's importance in supplying the enemy; most Viet Cong supplies arrived via the Cambodian port of Sihanoukville, a fact not discovered until after the war.

25 Gottschang Turner and Phan Thanh Hao, *Even the Women Must Fight*, p. 137.

26 Evans, *Caduceus in Saigon*, p. 158.

27 Pike, *Viet Cong*.

28 Ang Cheng Guan, *The Vietnam War From the Other Side*, p. 28.

29 AWM115 [68], War materiel used by the Viet Cong in South Vietnam. The Viet Cong's exotic arsenal included dogs, monkeys and bees. Large monkeys were dressed in black pyjamas with their faces painted to resemble Diem's, then let loose in Saigon and other cities bearing anti-government slogans.

30 Karnow, *Vietnam*, p. 331.

31 Sheehan, *A Bright Shining Lie*, pp. 381–2. Karnow records that the Viet Cong doubled in number in 1964 to at least 170,000 men, most of whom were recruited in the South (Karnow, *Vietnam*, p. 400).

32 Thompson, *No Exit from Vietnam*, p. 40.

33 Fall, *Viet-Nam Witness*, pp. 185–6.

34 AWM89 N[73], Viet Cong Use of Terror, March 1967 — United States Mission in Vietnam.

35 Ibid.

36 Wyllie, 'Australian surgical teams in Vietnam', letter to *Daily Telegraph*, 24 November 1966, p. 4. 'Medevac' means medical evacuation by helicopter.

37 Sheehan, *A Bright Shining Lie*, p. 115.

38 Rintoul, *Ashes of Vietnam*, p. 84. The Viet Cong terror campaign sought to deny Western aid to the villagers, as it undermined their control of the peasants. In one incident, in the early 1960s, VC troops kidnapped Wilfred Arthur, an Australian agricultural expert, sent under the Colombo Plan to help establish a dairy farm in Ben Cat. The Viet Cong released Arthur in exchange for a typewriter and cash. Meanwhile, they sniped at the dairy's employees, destroyed the new machinery and killed all the cows.

39 AWM89 N[73], Viet Cong Use of Terror, March 1967 — United States Mission in Vietnam.

40 Pike, *Viet Cong*.

41 *Pentagon Papers*, p. 130.

42 Ibid., pp. 140–1.

43 Watt, *Vietnam*, p. 111.

44 NAA CRSA4940/1, Cabinet Submission 521, SEATO Aid Programme: Aid to Vietnam, Barwick, 16 January 1963.

45 Burchett, *Vietnam — Inside Story of the Guerrilla War*, p. 37.

46 Sheehan, *A Bright Shining Lie*, p. 302.

47 *Times of Vietnam*, 28 October 1962, quoted in *Pentagon Papers*, p. 151.

48 *Pentagon Papers*, p. 153.

49 Sheehan, *A Bright Shining Lie*, p. 311.

50 'Albert' became province chief in Ben Tre, which the Viet Cong used as a rest and staging area, and was then briefly promoted to chief of military security — a post most coveted by the Viet Cong's 'Master Spy' — on the government's general staff. He literally had contacts 'everywhere', until his enemies caught up with him. He was later assassinated (Truong Nhu Tang, *A Viet Cong Memoir*, pp. 42–62).

51 AWM PR00660, Papers of Major Peter Young.

52 McCarthy, *Vietnam*, p. 66.

53 *Observer*, 21 March 1964, quoted in Fall, *Viet-Nam Witness*, p. 197.

54 Fall, *Viet-Nam Witness*, p. 281.

55 Halberstam, *The Best and the Brightest*, p. 297.

56 Thompson, *No Exit from Vietnam*, p. 27.

Chapter 7 **Enter the Americans**

1 Halberstam, *The Best and the Brightest*, p. 38.

2 Ibid.

3 Kimball, *To Reason Why*, p. 133. President Johnson initially shared Kennedy's fear of falling dominoes, and claimed that the loss of Vietnam would force America to fight on the beaches of Waikiki. LBJ, who later lost faith in the theory altogether, came to see himself as the biggest

domino: a man whose dreams were broken by 'that bitch of a war on the other side of the world' (Karnow, *Vietnam*, p. 320).

4 Kennedy 'needed a weapon', said a presidential staffer during the 1960 presidential campaign. 'Everyone else had a weapon ... Scoop Jackson had the Polaris, and Lyndon had Space, and Symington had the B-52. What could they get for a weapon for Kennedy?' A defence intellectual named Dan Ellsberg — who would later leak the Pentagon Papers to the *New York Times* — replied: 'What about the infantryman?' (Halberstam, *The Best and the Brightest*, p. 22.) In fact, the weapon most associated with JFK in Vietnam was neither the infantry nor his specially trained counter-insurgency force. It was herbicide: Kennedy personally approved OPERATION RANCH HAND, the defoliation of the South Vietnamese jungles.

5 Gration, 'A Comparison of Strategies in the Vietnam War' (unpublished essay), p. 4.

6 Quoted in Nagl, *Learning to Eat Soup with a Knife*, p. 27.

7 Karnow, *Vietnam*, p. 281. Quang Duc died aged 66; he had been a monk since the age of 15. Two younger monks had volunteered to incinerate themselves, but Duc's seniority prevailed.

8 Sheehan, *A Bright Shining Lie*, p. 335.

9 Homer Bigart, cited in Karnow, *Vietnam*.

10 Successive Saigon regimes failed to mollify the angry clerics. In 1965 Buddhist revolts and suicides spread to Hué and Da Nang, where American and Australian military advisers became targets of their attacks. In May–June 1966, over three weeks ten Buddhist monks and nuns incinerated themselves in protest at the 'American war'. The Buddhist leader Tri Quang held President Johnson personally responsible for the self-immolation of a 55-year-old nun and indicted him for having 'masterminded the repression of the Vietnamese people' (Karnow, *Vietnam*, p. 449).

11 McNeill, *The Team*, p. 122.

12 *Pentagon Papers*, pp. 738–9.

13 *Pentagon Papers*, cited in Sheehan, *A Bright Shining Lie*, p. 360.

14 Karnow, *Vietnam*, p. 307.

15 Ibid., p. 308.

16 AWM PR00660, Papers of Major Peter Young.

17 Sheehan, *A Bright Shining Lie*, pp. 262–3.

18 Ibid., p. 283.

19 Harkins soon became an 'object of ridicule' in the US Army, records Sheehan. To 'pull a Harkins' became a slang term among younger American officers for committing a stupid act. Harkins repeatedly misinformed Washington about the progress of the war, accepted fabricated casualty figures, and refused to acknowledge the manifest failure, at this stage, of the ARVN.

20 Sheehan, *A Bright Shining Lie*, p. 372.

21 Ibid., p. 374.

22 AWM89 N[73], Viet Cong Use of Terror, March 1967 — United States Mission in Vietnam.

23 Ibid.

24 Karnow, *Vietnam*, p. 370.

25 Ibid., p. 386.

26 Sexton, *War for the Asking*, p. 115; and *Hansard*.

27 McNamara, *In Retrospect*, p. 127.

28 It is often argued that the President, McNamara and Rusk deceived Congress and the American people over what happened in the Tonkin Gulf. In his book *In Retrospect*, McNamara rejected the charges as 'unfounded'. So too did Guenter Lewy: '... there is no evidence to show that the events of the second Gulf of Tonkin Incident were the result of a deliberate provocation ...' (Lewy, *America in Vietnam*, p. 36). Against this, recently released US documents suggest that the incident did involve a deliberate deception by the USA: on 30 November 2005, the US National Security Agency declassified documents on the Gulf of Tonkin Incident, including an article by NSA historian Robert Hanyok, 'Skunks, Bogies, Silent Hounds, and the Flying Fish: The Gulf of Tonkin Mystery, 2–4 August 1964' (*Cryptologic Quarterly*, Winter 2000/Spring

2001, Vol. 19, no. 4/vol. 20, no. 1). Hanyok wrote that intelligence information was presented to the White House 'in such a manner as to preclude responsible decisionmakers in the Johnson administration from having the complete and objective narrative of events'. Instead, 'only information that supported the claim that the communists had attacked the two destroyers was given to Johnson administration officials'.

29  Gaiduk, *The Soviet Union and the Vietnam War*, p. xv.
30  Ibid., p. 15.
31  Qiang, Zhai, *China and the Vietnam Wars 1950–1975*, pp. 132–3.
32  Ibid., p. 137.
33  In 1967 China agreed to send, in addition, 8,000 toothbrushes, 11,100 tubes of toothpaste, 24,700 bars of soap and 109,000 cases of cigarettes, as well as volleyballs, harmonicas and playing cards (ibid., p. 135).
34  Ibid., p. 139.
35  Kimball, *To Reason Why*, pp. 126–9.
36  Sexton, *War for the Asking*, p. 136.
37  Karnow, *Vietnam*, p. 415.
38  Lind, *Vietnam — The Necessary War*, p. 247.
39  Salisbury, *Behind the Lines — Hanoi*, p. 131.

## Chapter 8 **The quiet Australian**

1  NAA A6706/1 38.
2  In Woodard, *Asian Alternatives*, p. 67.
3  SEATO was a regional defence alliance signed in 1954. It aspired to being an Asian NATO, but had little real power. The signatories — the USA, Britain, France, Australia, New Zealand, Pakistan, the Philippines and Thailand — either ignored it or wheeled it out as a high-sounding legal prop for actions and decisions often taken for very different reasons. It called on the signatories to defend each other against attack, as well as the designated territories of South Vietnam, Laos and Cambodia, whose security was deemed to be vital. Three signatories — Britain, France and Pakistan — rarely attended meetings, ignored its provisions and declined to help defend South Vietnam.
4  Malcom Fraser, interview, Melbourne, 26 September 2006.
5  Sexton, *War for the Asking*, p. 12.
6  Text of ANZUS Treaty.
7  LBJ Library, National Security File, Country File, Asia and the Pacific, Australia, Menzies Visit to Washington, 6/24/64, Box 234 (my emphasis).
8  NAA A1838/280 3004/11/7/1.
9  NAA A1838/269 TS3014/2/1, pt 7.
10  John Rowe, interview.
11  Blair, *There to the Bitter End*, p. 21.
12  Ibid., p. 22.
13  Ibid., p. 5.
14  Ibid., p. 19.
15  McNeill, *The Team*, p. 6.
16  Training Command — Army, *The Team*, Part 1, 'A Political Gesture' (video).
17  AWM MSS1082, M. Hamilton-Smith, 'Australian Involvement in Counter-insurgency Programmes in South Vietnam' (MA thesis, University of NSW, 1984).
18  Ibid.
19  Ibid.
20  Halberstam, *The Best and the Brightest*, p. 276.
21  Blair, *There to the Bitter End*, p. 54.
22  Ibid., p. 38.
23  AWM107(1), interview with Brigadier O. D. Jackson, Army Historical Programme.

24 Blair, *The to the Bitter End*, p. 47.
25 AWM107(1), interview with Brigadier F. P. Serong, 1971, Army Historical Programme.
26 Ibid.
27 MACJO1, signed by General Paul Harkins, 18 December 1963; Davies and McKay, *The Men Who Persevered*, p. 41.
28 Woodard, *Asian Alternatives*, p. 154.
29 Letter from Ted Serong to Professor Peter Young, former member of the Australian Army Training Team, 6 July 1997, sighted by author.

## Chapter 9 **The Team**

1 AWM107(1), interview with Brigadier F. P. Serong, 1971, Army Historical Programme.
2 Petersen, *Tiger Men*, p. 6.
3 Ibid., p. 3.
4 Training Command — Army, *The Team*, Part 1, 'A Political Gesture' (video).
5 Ibid.
6 Ibid.
7 Caputo, *A Rumor of War*.
8 AWM107(1), interview with Brigadier F. P. Serong, 1971, Army Historical Programme.
9 McNeill, *The Team*, p. 11.
10 AWM PR00665 Papers of Sergeant W. F. Hacking. All extracts re Hacking drawn from this source.
11 *New Idea*, 21 January 1989.
12 Davies and McKay, *The Men Who Persevered*.
13 Ibid.
14 McNeill, *The Team*, p. 23.
15 Ibid.
16 AWM PR01214, Papers of Warrant Officer II Allan Joyce.
17 The Viet Minh and National Liberation Front had similar rules, often honoured in the breach; see Lockhart, *Nation in Arms*.
18 AWM MSS1082, M. Hamilton-Smith, 'Australian Involvement in Counter-insurgency Programmes in South Vietnam' (MA thesis, University of NSW, 1984); see also McNeill, *The Team*, p. 382.

## Chapter 10 **The Montagnard chief**

1 AWM MSS1082, M. Hamilton-Smith, 'Australian Involvement in Counter-insurgency Programmes in South Vietnam' (MA thesis, University of NSW, 1984).
2 Daly's Foreword, in Petersen, *Tiger Men*, p. vii.
3 Petersen, *Tiger Men*, p. 17.
4 AWM107(1), Interview with Brigadier F. P. Serong, 1971, Army Historical Programme.
5 Petersen, *Tiger Men*, p. 18.
6 Ibid., p. 24.
7 Ibid., p. 31.
8 Davies and McKay, *The Men Who Persevered*, p. 39.
9 AWM PR89/097, Papers of Lieutenant Colonel Barry Petersen, Annex I to Report on Attachment to US Agency: The Application of Dissemination of Propaganda and Civic Action.
10 Petersen, email, 10 April 2007.
11 O'Neill, *Vietnam Task*, p. 56.
12 AWM MSS1082, M. Hamilton-Smith, 'Australian Involvement in Counter-insurgency Programmes in South Vietnam' (MA thesis, University of NSW, 1984).
13 Cited by Fall, *Viet-Nam Witness*, pp. 192–3.
14 Burchett, *Vietnam — Inside Story of the Guerrilla War*, p. 139.
15 AWM PR89/097 Papers of Lieutenant Colonel Barry Petersen, *Vietnam* — Annex A.

16  Ibid., Annex F: Suggested preparations of Anti-communist Guerrilla Forces should a partial or complete communist takeover occur in the Republic of Vietnam.
17  Petersen, *Tiger Men*, p. 53.
18  Ibid., p. 62.
19  AWM PR89/097 Papers of Lieutenant Colonel Barry Petersen, Report on Attachment to US Agency, August 1963–October 1965, Republic of Vietnam.
20  Ibid., Annex CC.
21  Ibid., Annex H; Report on Attending a Sacrifice for Y-Bham Enuol — Night of 30/31 July 1964.
22  McNeill, *The Team*, p. 44.
23  AWM PR89/097 Papers of Lieutenant Colonel Barry Petersen, Report on Attachment to US agency, August 1963–October 1965, Republic of Vietnam.
24  Petersen, *Tiger Men*, p. 69.
25  Ibid., p. 77.
26  Ibid., p. 80.
27  AWM107(1), Interview with Brigadier O.D. Jackson, Army Historical Programme, p. 18.
28  AWM PR89/097 Papers of Lieutenant Colonel Barry Petersen, Report on Attachment to US Agency August 1963–October 1965, Republic of Vietnam, Annex CC.
29  Ibid.
30  Petersen, *Tiger Men*, p. 122.
31  Ibid., p. 146.
32  Denis Gibbons, interview, Sydney, 28 December 2005.
33  AWM107(1), Interview with Brigadier O. D. Jackson, Army Historical Programme, p. 18.
34  Petersen, *Tiger Men*, p. 159.
35  McNeill, *The Team*, p. 65.
36  AWM MSS1082, M. Hamilton-Smith, 'Australian Involvement in Counter-insurgency Programmes in South Vietnam' (MA thesis, University of NSW, 1984).

## Chapter 11  1st Battalion, Royal Australian Regiment

1  *Hansard*, 29 April 1965.
2  Edwards, *A Nation at War*, p. 55.
3  Ibid., p. 373.
4  Ibid., p. 179. The creation of the powerful Foreign Affairs and Defence Committee in 1963 completed the politicians' ascendancy over all dissenting or modifying voices. The Prime Minister and leading frontbenchers — not the Ministers for Air, Army and Navy — sat on the committee, which deliberated without reference to Parliament, lesser Cabinet ministers, back-benchers or the Australian people.
5  Clark, *In Fear of China*; see in particular the last chapter, 'Australia versus China'.
6  Some of Clark's ideas were sound; others not. He suggested that Mao was a reasonable leader and inspiration to the oppressed; in fact, Mao was responsible for the deaths of countless millions of Chinese people, and openly supported — in his rhetoric and through the supply of arms — violent communist uprisings throughout Asia (see Chang and Halliday, *Mao*). Clark also suggested that the Chinese would behave if America (and Australia) recognised Mao's regime and its claim on Taiwan (he argued, with breathtaking simplicity, that Taiwan might be 'peacefully reunited' with China, ignoring the right of 14 million Chinese nationalists *not* to live under communism). At times, Clark brings to mind a British mandarin, or 'Old China Hand', for whom the Great Leap Forward — in which millions died — can be explained away as a regrettable excess in an otherwise sound approach. Old China hands were often blinded by their fondness for their subject. In Clark's case, his frustration at government policy drove him to try to slay Australia's St George, when he might have been more usefully employed analysing the real nature of Mao's destructive dragon. Nonetheless, his book *In Fear of China* (1967) is a compelling indictment of many aspects of Australian foreign policy at the time.

7   Kelly, 'Vietnam — 30 Years On', Australian War Memorial Anniversary Oration, 11 November 2005.

8   Woodard, *Asian Alternatives*, p. 206.

9   As many books argue, chiefly Sexton, *War for the Asking*; Pemberton, *All the Way*; Freudenberg, *A Certain Grandeur*; and Woodard, *Asian Alternatives*.

10  Freudenberg, *A Certain Grandeur*.

11  Sexton, *War for the Asking*, p. 1.

12  Woodard, *Asian Alternatives*, p. 252.

13  LBJ Library, National Security File, Country File, Asia and the Pacific, Australia, Dept of State — Memorandum of Conversation, 28 April 1965, Subject: Situation in Vietnam, with Dean Rusk, Harold Holt, Sir Roland Wilson, Keith Waller, Australia Cables, Vol. 1, 11/63–12/65, Box 233 [1 of 2].

14  Sexton, *War for the Asking*, p. 1.

15  Waller also asked whether the Americans might occasionally express their appreciation for the Australian troop contribution, as this would help quell domestic opposition to the war. Waller noted that McGeorge Bundy had thanked the South Koreans but not the Australians on television a few days before. In response, the Americans agreed to find occasions to thank Australia for its war effort.

16  Sexton, *War for the Asking*, p. 149.

17  Ibid., p. 161.

18  Ibid., p. 168.

19  NAA A1838 TS 696/8/4 Part 10, Exchange of letters between the Australian Ambassador and the Prime Minister of the Republic of Vietnam, 29 April 1965 (my emphasis).

20  Woodard, *Asian Alternatives*, p. 251.

21  *Sydney Morning Herald*, 30 April 1965.

22  *Age*, 30 April 1965.

23  A selection of Australian newspapers, 30 April–6 May 1965.

24  *Bulletin*, 8 May 1965.

25  *Australian*, various reports during May 1965.

26  Saigon correspondent, *New York Times*.

27  *Hansard*, 4 March 1965.

28  After seven years of leading Labor in Opposition, Calwell resigned in 1967. Then he freely spoke his mind, a decidedly less American-friendly place: President Johnson should be impeached, he said. The bombing of North Vietnam reminded him of Goering's air raid on Coventy (*Canberra Times*, 2 February 1968).

29  Edwards, *A Nation at War*, p. 35.

30  Freudenberg, *A Certain Grandeur*, p. 53.

31  Various newspapers, 14 May 1965.

32  *Australian*, 14 May 1965.

33  Edwards, *A Nation at War*, p. 49.

34  Bill Crombie, interview, Caboolture, 8 June 2005.

35  Those aboard HMAS *Sydney*'s first voyage included: B Company, 1RAR; elements of Support and Administration Companies; 1 APC Troop (Prince of Wales Light Horse); and 1 Australian Logistics Company.

36  Breen, *First to Fight*, p. 23.

37  John Eaton, interview, Brisbane, 8 June 2005.

38  AWM MSS1160, F. J. Wilson, 'Women in the Anti-Vietnam War Anti-Conscription Movement in Sydney 1964–1972' (Honours thesis, University of NSW), p. 11.

39  AWM MSS5395, Women's International League for Peace and Freedom, Records 1960–90, Box 1(4).

40  Breen, *First to Fight*, p. 17.

41  Ibid., p. 23.

42  Don Dali, email, 25 August 2005.

43  Breen, *First to Fight*, p. 15.

44  Essex-Clark, personal papers, 'Some Rough Notes on Service with 1RAR in Vietnam, 1965–66', 20 September 2005.

Chapter 12 **The Iron Triangle**

 1  Breen, *First to Fight*, p. 21.

 2  Essex-Clark, personal papers, 'Some Rough Notes on Service with 1RAR in Vietnam, 1965–66', 20 September 2005.

 3  Breen, *First to Fight*, p. 39.

 4  AWM290 117/4/6/[2], Intelligence Summaries (Brigade), Department of the Army, Headquarters 173rd Airborne Brigade, Office of the Intelligence Officer, US Forces [6/65], Intelligence Summary, July 1965.

 5  Stone, *War Without Honour*, p. 52.

 6  *Airborne — The First Three Years — A Pictorial History of the 173rd Airborne Brigade.*

 7  Stone, *War Without Honour*, p. 66.

 8  AWM PR87/195, Papers of Corporal Ron Kelly.

 9  Nagl, *Learning to Eat Soup with a Knife*, p. 136.

10  AWM PR00659, Papers of Second Lieutenant Clive Williams.

11  AWM290 117/4/6/[2], Intelligence Summaries (Brigade), Department of the Army, Headquarters 173rd Airborne Brigade, Office of the Intelligence Officer, US Forces [6/65], Intelligence Summary, June 1965.

12  Stone, *War Without Honour*, p. 62.

13  AWM290 117/4/6/[2], Intelligence Summaries (Brigade), Department of the Army, Headquarters 173rd Airborne Brigade, Office of the Intelligence Officer, US Forces, American Field Intelligence Bulletin 4, June–July 1965.

14  AWM290 117/4/6/[2], Intelligence Summaries (Brigade), Department of the Army, Headquarters 173rd Airborne Brigade, Office of the Intelligence Officer, US Forces [6/65], Intelligence Summary, June 1965.

15  Modystack, *The Pony Soldiers*, p. 28.

16  AWM290 117/4/6/[2], Intelligence Summaries (Brigade), Department of the Army, Headquarters 173d Airborne Brigade, Office of the Intelligence Officer, US Forces [6/65], Intelligence Summary, June 1965.

17  Ibid.

18  AWM PR00659, Papers of Second Lieutenant Clive Williams.

19  AWM273 [23], 1RAR Administrative Arrangements on Arrival in Vietnam.

20  Essex-Clark, personal papers, 'Some Rough Notes on Service with 1RAR in Vietnam, 1965–66', 20 September 2005.

21  AWM PR00659, Papers of Second Lieutenant Clive Williams.

22  Ibid.

23  Stone, *War Without Honour*, p. 133.

24  Nagl, *Learning to Eat Soup with a Knife*, p. 154. Nagl would later criticise US methods in Iraq.

25  Ibid., p. 156.

26  AWM98 R1/3/6, Accidents, Deaths, Casualties, Personnel, 1RAR, 26 June 1965.

27  Breen, *First to Fight*, p. 36.

28  McNeill, *The Team*.

29  Hackworth, *About Face*, p. 495. The late David Hackworth is one of several US officers thought (wrongly) to have inspired the character of Colonel Kilgore in *Apocalypse Now*. (A more likely candidate was the Rambo-like warrior Major James 'Bo' Gritz.)

30  McNeill, *The Team*, p. 195.

31  AWM273 [31], B Coy 1RAR in South Vietnam, 1965–66.

32  Terry Burstall, interview, 4 June 2005.

33 Ibid.
34 Later, the US Special Forces replaced the Australians at Tra Bong, with tragic results. A US company decided to help defend Dong Phu, a nearby outpost, from a reported attack. It meant patrolling through the same steep-sided valley that Skardon had rejected as a perfect ambush opportunity, which in fact happened: just 900 metres short of Dong Phu, about 400 Viet Cong fell on the American-led company as it moved through a narrow defile between the river and the jungle's edge. Four Americans were killed instantly, and thirty Vietnamese irregulars were slaughtered. The Viet Cong chose not to waste a bullet on the district chief, whom they drowned.
35 Davies and McKay, *The Men Who Persevered*, p. 77.
36 Ibid., p. 78.
37 Ibid., p. 79.
38 McNeill, *The Team*, p. 321.
39 Ibid., p. 322.
40 Mangold and Penycate, *The Tunnels of Cu Chi*, p. 163.
41 Hackworth and Sherman, *About Face*, p. 559.
42 Bushby, 'Educating an Army', Canberra Papers on Stragegy and Defence, No. 126, p. 27.
43 Breen, *First to Fight*, pp. 83–4.
44 AWM273 [25]–[27], Operations General, B Coy Int Sec 1RAR, Bien Hoa 27 August 65, Lessons Learned in Past Operations.
45 John Eaton, interview, 8 June 2005.
46 Trevor Hagan, interview, 7 June 2005.
47 Ibid.
48 AWM273 [11], OPERATIONS IRON TRIANGLE and BEN CAT II, 8–14 October 1965.
49 AWM MSS5898 26 (55), Papers of Alex Carey.
50 Ibid.
51 Porter, who was wounded in action in Vietnam, died in 2006. He suffered severe post-traumatic stress disorder for most of his life, and confided in Essex-Clark, near the end, that the shooting episode had crippled him emotionally.
52 PR87/166, Papers of A.H. 'Lex' McAulay.
53 AWM273 [11], OPERATIONS IRON TRIANGLE and BEN CAT II, 8–14 October 1965.
54 Ibid.
55 AWM PR00659, Papers of Second Lieutenant Clive Williams.
56 McNeill, *To Long Tan*, pp. 100–2.

Chapter 13 **Cu Chi**

1 AWM PR00659, Papers of Second Lieutenant Clive Williams.
2 Breen, *First to Fight*, p. 104.
3 Ibid., p. 114.
4 Major John Essex-Clark planned an immediate operation to recover the bodies, but it did not proceed, under orders from superior headquarters. More than forty years later, in June 2007, Jim Bourke's OPERATION AUSSIES HOME, with the help of the Australian and Vietnamese governments, successfully located the remains of Parker and Gillson, which were returned to Australia.
5 AWM PR91/179, Papers of Second Lieutenant Clive Williams.
6 Poem by Captain Peter Rothwell, commander, D Company, 1RAR.
7 AWM PR00659, Papers of Second Lieutenant Clive Williams.
8 AWM273 [14], OPERATION NEW LIFE, Operational Analysis, 3 Field Troop RAE; Sub-Unit Operation Analysis, D Coy, Comd. Capt D. P. Rothwell.
9 Breen, *First to Fight*, p. 145.
10 AWM273 [14] OPERATION NEW LIFE, Operational Analysis, Sub-Unit Operation Analysis, C Coy, Comd. Maj J. J. Tattam.

11  In later operations, an American captain, Romie 'Les' Brownlee, a 26-year-old Texan conqueror, personified the US saturation approach. Ordered simply to 'kill Viet Cong', he led his company, nicknamed the Bulls, on noisy search-and-destroy missions. They chatted, smoked, wore colourful badges and crashed along the paths — actions that were meant to provoke ambushes from which they would blast their way out with massive firepower and napalm. The Bulls wreaked a trail of havoc, at huge cost. By December 1966 a third of Brownlee's men were dead and the rest wounded, earning 160 Purple Hearts between them. Brownlee, himself evacuated with shoulder wounds, was hailed as an American hero and awarded two Silver Stars. He later conceded that he underestimated the enemy: 'We didn't give him the credit and we paid with blood for our ignorance' (quoted in Breen, *First to Fight*, p. 227). OPERATION NEW LIFE also revealed deep flaws in US intelligence. 'You are looking at [an intelligence officer]', reported one US intelligence officer, 'who cannot tell you where one single enemy unit is located … In Vietnam intelligence is failing … Intelligence has not been adapted to the type of war that is being fought. The nature of the war is one of a war without a front. The enemy is everywhere and he is nowhere …' (quoted in McNeill, *To Long Tan*).

12  Breen, *First to Fight*, p. 160.

13  Interview with Don Lane, quoted in ibid., p. 168.

14  AWM PR87/195, Papers of Corporal Ron Kelly.

15  Mangold and Penycate, *The Tunnels of Cu Chi*, p. 45.

16  Ibid.

17  Ibid., p. 54.

18  Ibid., p. 30.

19  Ibid., p. 33.

20  Ibid.

21  Garland, *Infantry in Vietnam*.

22  Eyster, in Mangold and Penycate, *The Tunnels of Cu Chi*.

23  AWM98 R237–1–22 (i), Correspondence — General — Classified: 'Dieseline Vapour in Vietcong Tunnel Systems', background info, R. Henderson.

24  Hooper and MacGregor, 'Operation "Crimp"', in *Holdfast* magazine, p. 31.

25  Duong Huong Ly, 'The Mother — The Native Land' (Vietnamese poem).

26  Papers of Brigadier John Essex-Clark.

27  Breen, *First to Fight*, p. 190.

28  Hooper and MacGregor, 'Operation "Crimp"', in *Holdfast* magazine, p. 28.

29  Ibid., p. 27.

30  Ibid., p. 28.

31  Ibid., p. 30.

32  See Edwards, *A Nation at War*, pp. 119–21; and Horner, *The Gunners*, p. 473.

33  PR87/166, Papers of A.H. 'Lex' McAulay.

34  Breen, *First to Fight*, p. 213.

35  PR87/166, Papers of A.H. 'Lex' McAulay.

36  John Essex-Clark, email, 13 April 2007.

37  AWM PR00659, Papers of Second Lieutenant Clive Williams; letter from Nelly Clark, Padstow, NSW, 5 February 1966.

Chapter 14  **Nashos**

1  Department of Labour and National Service Call-Up Notice, sent to Eric Oswald Bensley, 15 June 1965.

2  Department of Labour and National Service Call-Up Notice, sent to John Binnie, 29 June 1966.

3  Instructions and Notes for Completing Registration Form, Commonwealth of Australia, Dept of Labour and National Service, National Service Act 1951–64.

4  Richard Hornery, emails, August 2005.

5   John Binnie, interview, Sydney, 9 September 2005.

6   Edwards, *A Nation at War*, p. 21.

7   Goot and Tiffen, 'Public Opinion', in King, *Australia's Vietnam*, p. 143.

8   Returned and Services League, 48th Annual Report, 1963.

9   LBJ Library, National Security File, Country File, Asia and the Pacific, Australia, Dept of State
    — Memorandum for McGeorge Bundy, White House, from Benjamin Read, Executive
    Secretary, 18 November 1964, Australia Memos, Vol. 1, 11/63–12/65, Box 233 [1 of 2].

10  Edwards, *Crises and Commitments*, p. 271.

11  Woodard, *Asian Alternatives*, pp. 177–8.

12  LBJ Library, National Security File, Country File, Asia and the Pacific, Australia, Dept of State
    — Memorandum from William Bundy to Secretary of State Dean Rusk, 21 November 1964
    [Subject: Visit of Hasluck], Australia Memos, Vol. 1, 11/63–12/65, Box 233 [1 of 2]. In 1964,
    the Americans were less concerned with a few token Australian conscripts than with the idea of
    chemical warfare testing in Australia. They hoped to sound out Hasluck on whether Canberra
    would allow the US 'to conduct chemical warfare tests in Australia'. Canberra declined.

13  Rintoul, *Ashes of Vietnam*, p. 14.

14  Bray, *Aboriginal Ex-Servicemen of Central Australia*, pp. 12–15.

15  Langley, *A Decade of Dissent*, p. 17.

16  Ross, 'Australian Soldiers in Vietnam: Product and Performance', in King, *Australia's Vietnam*,
    pp. 72–5.

17  Army Manning Review 1969–70; Ross, 'Australian Soldiers in Vietnam: Product and
    Performance', in King, *Australia's Vietnam*, p. 75.

18  *Hansard*, 12 November 1964.

19  Langley, *A Decade of Dissent*, p. 19.

20  Letter, Colin Khan to David Horner, 26 October 1989 (sighted by author).

21  Interviews with several national servicemen who served with the Royal Australian Regiment,
    1966–71.

22  Middleton, 'My Story' (unpublished memoir).

23  D. Wilkins, 'A Vietnam Diary' (unpublished memoir), p. 8.

24  Hall, *Combat Battalion*, p. 19.

25  McNeill, *To Long Tan*, p. 28.

26  Gregg Lindsay, email, 4 June 2006.

27  Letter, Colin Khan to David Horner, 26 October 1989.

28  Ibid.

29  Heard, *Well Done, Those Men*.

30  Ibid., pp. 11–14.

31  R. Harris, 'The New Breed' (unpublished memoir), pp. 20–1.

32  Hennessy, *The Sharp End*, p. 8.

33  R. Harris, 'The New Breed' (unpublished memoir), p. 24.

34  Ross, 'Australian Soldiers in Vietnam: Product and Performance', in King, *Australia's Vietnam*,
    p. 88.

35  Heard, *Well Done, Those Men*, p. 54.

36  *Daily Telegraph*, 25 July 1965.

37  Donnelly, *The Scheyville Experience*, p. xi.

38  Ibid.

39  Gregg Lindsay, email, 4 June 2006.

40  David Sabben, interview, 17 August 2005.

41  Transcript of interview with Larry Moon for documentary *The Scheyville Experience*, produced
    by Don Keys; also quoted in Donnelly, *The Scheyville Experience*, p. 75.

42  Gregg Lindsay, email, 4 June 2006.

43  Donnelly, *The Scheyville Experience*, p. 109.

44  Ibid.

45  Avery, *We Too Were Anzacs*, p. 43.

46  Colin Khan, interview, Canberra, 13 October 2005.

## Chapter 15 **To Nui Dat**

1  AWM107(2), interview with Major General Ken Mackay, Army Historical Programme, p. 12.

2  AWM107, interview with Lieutenant General John Wilton, Army Historical Programme, p. 25.

3  Frost, *Australia's War in Vietnam*, p. 30.

4  Nguyen Gia Ho, interview, 15 November 2005.

5  Murphy, *Harvest of Fear*, p. 18.

6  Frost, *Australia's War in Vietnam*, p. 32.

7  Murphy, *Harvest of Fear*, p. 35.

8  Ibid., p. 97.

9  Burstall, *A Soldier Returns*, pp. 39–40; different casualty figures are given in Hammond, *Reporting Vietnam*, pp. 35–6.

10  McNeill, *To Long Tan*, p. 57.

11  Burstall, *A Soldier Returns*, pp. 39–40.

12  Ang Cheng Guan, *The Vietnam War from the Other Side*, p. 101.

13  McNeill, *To Long Tan*, p. 185, and AWM PR00660, Papers of Major Peter Young. By the end of 1966, an incredible 693,000 communist troops were stationed in the South — an amalgam of Viet Cong Main Forces, Provincial and People's Forces, and North Vietnamese units (Ang Cheng Guan, *The Vietnam War from the Other Side*, p. 110). Most of these would confront America's 240,000 troops — soon to rise to half a million — in the northern provinces.

14  Nguyen Gia Ho, interview, village in Phuoc Tuy, 15 November 2005.

15  O'Neill, *Vietnam Task*, p. 17.

16  McNeill, *To Long Tan*, p. 229.

17  Frost, *Australia's War in Vietnam*, p. 38.

18  AWM107(2), Interview with Brigadier O. D. Jackson, Army Historical Programme, p. 45.

19  Ibid., p. 27.

20  Ibid.

21  McAulay, *The Battle of Long Tan*, p. 7.

22  AWM102 [46], Military Working Arrangements Between the CGS and COMUSMACV, March 1966.

23  AWM107(2), Interview with Brigadier O. D. Jackson, Army Historical Programme, p. 58.

24  AWM107(1), Interview with Major General Ken Mackay, Army Historical Programme.

25  Frost, *Australia's War in Vietnam*, p. 65.

26  AWM107(1), Interview with Major General A. L. MacDonald, Army Historical Programme, p. 6.

27  Frost, *Australia's War in Vietnam*, p. 65.

28  David Sabben, interview, Melbourne, 21 August 2005.

29  O'Neill, *Vietnam Task*, p. 26.

30  McFarlane, *We Band of Brothers*, p. 204.

31  Haran and Kearney, *Crossfire*, p. 5.

32  AWM107, Interview with Lieutenant Colonel David Rouse, Army Historical Programme, p. 7.

33  Ibid.

34  O'Neill, *Vietnam Task*, p. 27.

35  Spike Jones, interview, Bribie Island, 6 June 2005.

36  AWM107(1), Interview with Brigadier O. D. Jackson, Army Historical Programme, p. 50.

37  Colin Townsend, interview, Gympie, 19 August 2005.

38  O'Brien, *Conscripts and Regulars*, p. 23.

39  AWM107(1), Interview with Brigadier O. D. Jackson, Army Historical Programme, p. 84.

40  McNeill, *To Long Tan*, p. 200.

41  AWM 3DRL/7689, Papers of Sergeant W. L. Fogarty, 7RAR.

42  David Morgan, personal papers, autobiography.

43  Geoff Jones, interview, Brisbane, 3 June 2005.

44  Harry Smith, interview, Hervey Bay, 6 June 2005.

45  At the time, Major Holt and George Lugg were extremely concerned about, and reported on, the health aspects of working with herbicides.

46  McCulloch, *The Politics of Agent Orange*, pp. 59–61; see also: First Report, Senate Standing Committee on Science and the Environment, *Pesticides and the Health of Australian Vietnam Veterans*, November 1982.

47  As revealed years later in the Herbicide Tapes, or 'Herb Tapes', published by the USAF; see www.gmasw.com/ao_amts1.htm.

48  General William DePuy, commander of the US 1st Division, personally ordered the herbicide offensives in the Iron Triangle, on General Westmoreland's authority (under the scorched earth policy recommended, incidentally, by the ageing General Douglas MacArthur). Many insiders considered DePuy the prime architect of America's war in Vietnam: 'Wherever DePuy went he left destruction in his wake,' wrote David Hackworth (*About Face*, p. 559). As well as destroying nature, the US commanders tried to harness it as a weapon of war. 'Soil destabilising chemicals' were sprayed on infiltration and supply routes in Laos, Cambodia and South Vietnam. These were designed to promote mudslides and unbreachable bogs. The USA even attempted to control the weather. The little-known 'Weather War', under the top-secret PROJECT COMPATRIOT — approved by President Johnson — aimed to promote excessive rainfall over the roads and waterways of the supply routes, by cloud-seeding (i.e. firing into the monsoonal cloud base). In 1967 the US Joint Chiefs of Staff reported the results of the first attempt at 'weather warfare', which they described as a 'form of interdiction ... more humane than bombing'. On 23 May 1967 Donald F. Hornig, Special Assistant to the President for Science and Technology, reported to the White House on the 'possible adverse factors' of weather warfare. Hornig wrote: 'It seems likely to me that continuous flooding would provide a hazard to life, health and sanitation. In particular, the loss of the rice crop, combined with a breakdown in transportation ... is likely to cause food shortages for the very young, the aged and the infirm ... The degree of revulsion to be expected in domestic and international metereological circles at the initiation of "weather warfare" should not be underestimated ...' (LBJ Library, National Security File, Country File, Vietnam, Memorandum for Mr Rostow, 23 May 1967, Subject: Project Compatriot, Box 88, PROJECT COMPATRIOT, 5/67–7/67, Box 88.)

Chapter 16  **The village**

1  Langley, *A Decade of Dissent*, p. 49.

2  Ibid., pp. 50–1.

3  Edwards, *A Nation at War*, pp. 125–6.

4  AWM107(1), Interview with Major General Ken Mackay, Army Historical Programme, p. 31.

5  McNeill, *To Long Tan*, p. 248.

6  Such friendly fire accidents severely disturbed and sometimes broke the soldiers who pulled the trigger. A machine-gunner, for example, who accidentally shot his company second-in-command was so stricken with grief that he was psych-tested and sent home. Two years later he was found dead in his own vomit in a single-room apartment, of acute alcohol poisoning (Haran and Kearney, *Crossfire*, pp. 58–9). Fear and nerves led to a number of accidental shootings of civilians. In one case, a Vietnamese man and his daughter came running towards an Australian patrol. A witness claimed that a soldier accidentally triggered a claymore mine, which hit the man, the girl and several Australians, one of whom was cleaved in two by the blast. The child's mother then came running down the hill carrying a basket: 'Someone thought she probably had grenades in her basket ... and she was shot,' a soldier recalled. She got up, and kept coming 'with these bloody baskets'. A second shot killed her, and her baskets were found to contain vegetables (Rintoul, *Ashes of Vietnam*, pp. 64–5). Lachlan Irvine, in a separate case, claims that his platoon commander ordered that, in order to justify the unintended killing of an unarmed man and woman in an ambush, grenades be placed in their basket along with their fish and vegetables (ibid., p. 136).

7   Charlton and Moncrieff, *Many Reasons Why*, p. 103.

8   Karnow, *Vietnam*, p. 232.

9   Murphy, *Harvest of Fear*, p. 3.

10  McNeill, *To Long Tan*.

11  Corporal Robin 'Spike' Jones, 'South Vietnam, 1st Tour, May 66–67, B Coy, 6RAR' (unpublished memoir).

12  McFarlane, *We Band of Brothers*, p. 223.

13  David Sabben, interview, 21 August 2005.

14  Frost, *Australia's War in Vietnam*, p. 88.

15  AWM95, 1ATF Commander's Diary, August 1966.

16  McNeill, *To Long Tan*, p. 255.

17  Lieutenant Colonel Colin Townsend, personal papers; Oral History Recording, 18 December 1989, Official History Unit, p. 9.

18  David Sabben, interview, 21 August 2005.

19  AWM95, 1ATF Commander's Diary, September 1966.

20  McNeill, *To Long Tan*, p. 424.

21  An Australian reconnaissance unit also destroyed villages on Long Son Island, ostensibly to move the people away from 'harassment and interdiction' fire (i.e. salvoes of artillery designed to terrify and disorient the Viet Cong). Peter Haran recalls 'zippoing' a thatched hut — setting it ablaze with his Zippo lighter, which was engraved with 'Let me win your heart and mind or I'll burn your goddamned hut down' (Haran and Kearney, *Crossfire*, pp. 65–6).

22  Schell, *The Village of Ben Suc*.

23  McNeill and Ekins, *On the Offensive*, p. 22. The same week, the costliest of the US war, saw 144 Americans killed and 1,044 wounded.

24  Sheehan, *A Bright Shining Lie*, pp. 570–1.

25  Denis Gibbons, interviews, 28–29 December 2005.

26  AWM181, Survey Report at Hoa Long village, Long Le district, Phuoc Tuy Province, pp. 1–16.

27  McNeill, *To Long Tan*.

28  Haran and Kearney, *Crossfire*, p. 131.

29  AWM 3DRL/7551, Papers of Huynh Chien Dau, Viet Cong fighter, 1961–75.

30  Khien Dinh Nguyen, interview, Sydney, 6 September 2005.

31  Hennessy, *The Sharp End*, p. 46.

32  Brian McFarlane, interview, Bowral, 31 August 2005.

33  Haran and Kearney, *Crossfire*, pp. 20–1.

34  AWM103, Standard Operation Procedure, Australian Task Force Vietnam, Book 1, Parts 1–6, 10 July 1966, pp. 12–13; and AWM293 [59], 5RAR SOP for Operations in Vietnam — October 1966.

35  AWM95, 5RAR Commander's Diary, July 1966.

36  Ibid.

37  Haran and Kearney, *Crossfire*, p. 157.

38  McNeill, *To Long Tan*, p. 252.

39  Haran and Kearney, *Crossfire*, p. ix.

40  Ibid., pp. 156–7.

41  O'Neill, *Vietnam Task*, p. 56.

42  Ibid., p. 60.

43  Ibid., p. 64.

44  Ibid., p. 65.

## Chapter 17 **Long Tan — warnings**

1   Government of the Socialist Republic of Vietnam, *D445: The Heroic Battalion*.

2   AWM107(1), Interview with Brigadier O. D. Jackson, AATTV Feb 65, Army Historical Programme, p. 64.

3　McNeill, *To Long Tan*, p. 286.

4　Horner, *SAS: Phantoms of War*, pp. 191–4.

5　AWM107(1), Interview with Brigadier O. D. Jackson, Army Historical Programme.

6　Harrison, *The Most Offensive Men Alive*. In 1966, the SAS Regiment contained three squadrons, each of which comprised three troops of twenty-five men, who in turn formed five patrols of five men. The SAS were, in essence, infantrymen with a specialist bent, for example navigation, communications, tracking, cliff-climbing, demolition and so on. Many SAS troops felt uneasy about their role in Vietnam: the predatory manhunt, the shoot and scoot missions, the prowling about the scrub seemed not to fulfil their potential. The SAS in general took great care to distinguish civilians from combatants. During one patrol, two SAS soldiers stole within a few metres of a sleeping Vietnamese woman to check whether she carried a weapon (AWM103 R723/1/1/2 Part 3).

7　After the title of the book, Hayley, *Thinking Thugs*.

8　Haran and Kearney, *Crossfire*, p. 50.

9　Horner, *SAS: Phantoms of War*, p. 214.

10　McNeill, *To Long Tan*, p. 288.

11　David Harris, telephone interview, 19 December 2006.

12　Peter Young, interviews, Gold Coast, 29–30 September.

13　Cable, 'An Independent Command' (published report), p. 35.

14　Murphy, *Harvest of Fear*, p. 85.

15　McNeill, *To Long Tan*, p. 249, and O'Neill, *Vietnam Task*, p. 48.

16　AWM PR90/162, Papers of D. Horsfield.

17　McNeill, *To Long Tan*, p. 425.

18　Ibid., p. 292.

19　O'Neill, *Vietnam Task*, p. 75.

20　Ibid., p. 82.

21　Ibid., p. 82.

22　Tidey, 'The Modus Operandi and Effectiveness of Specialist Intelligence Support to 1st Australian Task Force, South Vietnam, 1966–1971' (Master of Defence Studies thesis, ADFA, 2002).

23　Blair Tidey, interview, Canberra; Steve Hart, emails, March 2006. SIGINT and electronic warfare is the most secretive branch of intelligence; and has often gone to deadly lengths to hide its sources from the enemy. The West's inner sanctum of SIGINT is the highly secretive four-power group Aus–Can–UK–US, from which New Zealand was excluded after it refused to host US nuclear warships in the 1980s.

24　After Long Tan, the circle with some access to SIGINT widened to include battalion commanders and eventually the battalion operations and intelligence officers. Later in the war, battalion subunits received signals intelligence as 'special agents' reports' (SPARs), a cover for its true provenance.

25　Tidey, 'The Modus Operandi and Effectiveness of Specialist Intelligence Support to 1st Australian Task Force, South Vietnam, 1966–1971' (Master of Defence Studies thesis, ADFA, 2002).

26　McNeill, *To Long Tan*.

27　Trevor Richards, interview, Sydney, 3 May 2006.

28　Ibid.

29　Richard 'Dick' Hannigan, personal papers, notes on the battle of Long Tan, p. 3.

30　Tidey, 'The Modus Operandi and Effectiveness of Specialist Intelligence Support to 1st Australian Task Force, South Vietnam, 1966–1971' (Master of Defence Studies thesis, ADFA, 2002), p. 35. Later in the war, SIGINT gained strong support, and proved critical in many operations. For example, it located 'Dodo', code for the radio used by a COSVN intelligence team, headquarters of the Communist Party in the southern region, to monitor allied movements (the Australian 6th Battalion captured the radio and the female radio operator, who was the subject of the alleged 'water torture' incident — see chapter 31). Signals intelligence also played a vital role in detecting 274th Regiment's movements in OPERATION PADDINGTON (1967); successfully assaulting a VC headquarters in OPERATION FEDERAL (April 1969); capturing a major logistics complex in the Nui May Taos in December 1969 (OPERATION MARSDEN); staging a hugely effective ambush near Hoa Long, in August 1970 (OPERATION HAMMERSLEY); and tracking the movements of the 3/33rd NVA Regiment in June 1971.

31  John Rowe, various interviews, Sydney 2005.

32  Ibid.

33  McNeill, *To Long Tan*, p. 309. The beaded line on the map in McNeill's book was in fact hand-drawn by the author and not generated by 547 Signal Troop, as the image suggests. When Rowe informed McNeill that 'I had not seen this beaded diagram or anything like it before', McNeill stated that he had drawn it himself. 'There was never a copy at the [Task Force],' said Rowe (note to author).

34  Ibid. An enemy regiment contained four battalions of about 350 men each.

35  John Rowe, personal papers.

36  John Rowe, various interviews, Sydney 2005.

37  John Rowe, personal papers.

38  McNeill, *To Long Tan*, p. 309.

39  John Rowe, personal papers.

40  McNeill, *To Long Tan*, p. 311.

41  Rowe, Comments on Official History.

42  Ibid.

43  Richard 'Dick' Hannigan, personal papers, notes on the battle of Long Tan, p. 2.

44  John Rowe, personal papers.

45  Mollison, *Long Tan and Beyond*, p. 127.

46  Colin Townsend, personal papers, *The Spirit of Youth and Xa Long Tan*, 'Personal Reflections on Long Tan', p. 4.

47  AWM102 [42], 6RAR After-action Report, OPERATION SMITHFIELD, 18–21 August 1966; also Colin Townsend, personal papers, List of intelligence in AA report, OPERATION SMITHFIELD, October 1966.

48  AWM181, 1ATF After-action Report, OPERATION SMITHFIELD, December 1966, p. 4.

49  David Harris, telephone interview, 19 December 2006.

50  AWM PR90/162, Papers of D. Horsfield.

51  McNeill, *To Long Tan*, p. 311.

52  AWM 3DRL/6117, Papers of Colonel C. M. Townsend.

53  AWM95, 6RAR Commander's Diary, August 1966, Command Post Log Entry 52, 17 August 1966.

54  Peter Dinham, interview, Canberra, 26 October 2005.

55  David Harris, email, 21 August 2006.

56  Spike Jones, 'With B Company at the Battle of Long Tan, 18 August 1966' (unpublished memoir).

57  David Sabben, interview, Melbourne, 21 August 2005; also McNeill, *To Long Tan*, p. 314.

## Chapter 18 Long Tan — action

1  Harry Smith, interview, Hervey Bay, 6 June 2005.

2  Grandin (ed.), *The Battle of Long Tan*, pp. 1–9.

3  Ibid.

4  AWM PR90/162, Papers of D. Horsfield; interview with Geoff Kendall, 9 November 1984.

5  Grandin (ed.), *The Battle of Long Tan*, p. 107.

6  Ibid., pp. 18–26.

7  Ibid., pp. 10–14.

8  McNeill, *To Long Tan*, p. 314.

9   AWM PR90/162, Papers of D. Horsfield; interview with Geoff Kendall, 9 November 1984.

10  Morrie Stanley, notes from discussion, 161 Battery, 2005 Reunion, Palmerston North; and Grandin (ed.), *The Battle of Long Tan*.

11  Harry Smith, interview, Hervey Bay, 6 June 2005.

12  Government of the Socialist Republic of Vietnam, *D445: The Heroic Battalion*, p. 62.

13  Nguyen Nam Hung, ex-regimental commander of 274th Regiment (1965–70), reply to questionnaire, Vung Tau, 2 October 2005.

14  Government of the Socialist Republic of Vietnam, *D445: The Heroic Battalion*.

15  Nguyen Nam Hung, commander of the 274th Regiment (now major general, retired); and Nguyen Minh Ninh, deputy commander of the D445 Battalion (now brigadier, retired), interviews, Vung Tau, 16 and 19 November 2005. In June 1988, Colonel Nguyen Thanh Hong, former operations officer of the 5th Division, and Lieutenant Colonel Nguyen Van Kiem, former commander of D445 Battalion, also confirmed the two-phase plan to destroy Nui Dat (see McNeill, *To Long Tan*, pp. 365–71).

16  The official communist versions must be treated with deep scepticism, given their many omissions, inconsistencies and plain errors (or lies). Did the Viet Cong forces intend an 'ambush'? Much ink has been spent arguing this question; partly because the very meaning of the word has been lost in translation. The Viet Cong and People's Army did not use the word 'ambush' in the narrow tactical sense applied by the Australian Army. 'Ambush' in the Vietnamese sense meant a surprise attack on an enemy company or larger on the killing field of their choice. The Viet Minh had battered the French with such battalion-sized shock offensives; the Viet Cong similarly thrashed the South Vietnamese, as the Team witnessed on many occasions. They typically chose valleys or rubber plantations for such offensives; in the latter, the regulated aisles of trees assisted the line of fire. Some argue that to deny this *intention* at Long Tan is to deny the enemy's tactical history. Yet errors and inconsistencies litter the Viet Cong narrative. According to the D445 official history of Long Tan, the plan was to mortar Nui Dat, to 'lure the tiger from the mountain', or 'bait and wait'; this happened on 17 August. There followed, however, an explicable delay of an entire day — suggesting that the mortaring had a different purpose: as a way of testing the Australians' reaction time. If the Viet Cong planned a full-scale attack on the base, they would need to know how quickly the Australians could lock on to the direction of the mortars and turn their guns. The local history, however, claims the forces of the National Liberation Front formed up in a semicircle, 3 kilometres wide, at 10.15 a.m. on 18 August 1966, in wait to entrap the Australians. In this formation, the 275th Regiment was given the critical 'middle battle' position, to spring the surprise; units of the 275th and one D445 company would fight the 'front-block battle' near Long Tan village, the 'nose' of the ambush; two more D445 companies under the command of Sau Thu would fight the 'back-block battle'; that is, the encircling action that would sweep beneath the 'tail' of the cornered enemy and destroy the Australians in a closing vice. Finally, the eighty-strong Vo Thi Sau militia company, almost all of whom were women under the command of Mrs Chin Phung, would be on hand to help drag away the wounded. Yet, as Harry Smith persuasively argues, the Australians later found little sign of the enemy lying in wait in a semicircle on the fringes of the rubber; the evidence suggests they were further away to the east, in the jungle, and became aware of Delta Company's presence in the rubber only when a North Vietnamese patrol accidentally encountered Sharp's platoon. Indeed, if the enemy were poised to entrap the Australians, why were these crack troops allowed to walk about the supposed killing field? Perhaps they were a reckless reconnaissance party. The communist narrative fails to explain other errors: such as their failure to attack Bravo Company and the absence of any clearly prepared ambush (Smith, emails to author, 2006–07). Smith rejects any talk of a prepared ambush, believing Long Tan a chance encounter of two forces in the field; David Sabben agrees, and vividly presents Long Tan as an 'encounter battle' in his novel *Through Enemy Eyes* (Allen & Unwin, Sydney, 2005). Indeed, it does appear that Delta Company's swift, in-depth assault formation caught the enemy off guard. Brigadier John Essex-Clark agrees: 'I believe that the

NVA/VC were reconnoitering and establishing an ambush where the rubber meets the jungle, when they were caught napping slightly, and casually expecting the Australians to stop often and move ponderously like the Americans and ARVN. Historically the NVA had to say they held the initiative, which they did except for our artillery fire and, finally, APC relief' (email to author, 2 May 2007). Of course, the failure of the Viet Cong 'ambush' is not an argument against the enemy's *intention*; the Australians probably upset that intention, and what followed was an encounter battle on open ground.

An equally likely scenario — and one supported by Chinese military advisers — is that the Vietnamese never intended an ambush of any type; rather, the People's Army/Viet Cong simply meant to surround and overrun Nui Dat. This possibility at least explains the mortar attack — as a way of testing the water, to check and time the Australians' reaction.

17  Brigadier John Essex-Clark described a similar phenomenon during training: 'I remember, as a tactics instructor, teaching my students how to position a defensive position or ambush to get the best fields of fire in a rubber or oil-palm plantation. One metre the wrong way and the plantation then appears to be impenetrable because the angles of tree lines confuse and interlock. The tress are planted approximately 8 metres apart and echeloned precisely, like a chess board's lines' (email to author, 2 May 2007).

18  Harry Smith, personal papers.

19  Perhaps they were an incautious and over-confident reconnaissance group. Their presence confounds the official communist version of a well-planned ambush, and suggests that the enemy was in some disorder or that his communications had lapsed.

20  Harry Smith, personal papers.

21  Government of the Socialist Republic of Vietnam, *D445: The Heroic Battalion*, p. 63: 'We watched the three Australian formations move into the rubber,' claimed a 275th regimental officer. The head observer, Nguyen Van Bung, reported to his commanders: 'Get ready! The Australians are now 650 metres from the back-block units!' They radioed the Australian position to the front-block forces. 'Keep quiet!' Ut Dang, a 275th officer, is recorded as saying, 'Wait until they come near. Fire only after receiving our order.' The Viet Cong then lost track of the Australian 'tail', the rear troops, according to the D445 account: 'The tail lasts very long!' said one mystified radio transmitter. All units were then told: 'In case of error, fire when they are at least thirty metres from the front-block forces.'

22  Former 275th commanders confirmed, in discussions with Terry Burstall, that the 'ambush' was initiated 'in the wrong place'. See Burstall, 'Long Tan: The Other Side of the Hill' in Horner, *Duty First*.

23  Mollison, *Long Tan and Beyond*, p. 133.

24  McAulay, *The Battle of Long Tan*, p. 49.

25  Grandin (ed.), *The Battle of Long Tan*, p. 157.

26  McAulay, *The Battle of Long Tan*, p. 49.

27  Grandin (ed.), *The Battle of Long Tan*, p. 126; and Stewart, 'The Ghosts of Long Tan'.

28  McNeill, *To Long Tan*, p. 318.

29  Subritzky, 'Gunfire at Long Tan: The FO's Story'.

30  Harry Smith, personal papers.

31  Stewart, 'The Ghosts of Long Tan', *Australian*, 5 August 2006.

32  Harry Smith, personal papers.

33  Ibid.

34  Ibid.

35  Colin Townsend, personal papers, 'Personal Reflections on Long Tan', p. 7.

36  Mollison, *Long Tan and Beyond*, p. 135.

37  Grandin (ed.), *The Battle of Long Tan*, p. 130.

38  McAulay, *The Battle of Long Tan*, p. 55.

39  Bill Akell, interview, Buninyong, 22 August 2005.

40  Harry Smith, personal papers.

41  David Sabben, interview, Melbourne, 21 August 2005.

42  Grandin (ed.), *The Battle of Long Tan*, p. 156.

43  McAulay, *The Battle of Long Tan*, p. 88.

44  McNeill, *To Long Tan*, p. 320.

45  Mollison, *Long Tan and Beyond*, p. 152.

46  David Sabben, interview, Melbourne, 21 August 2005.

47  Burstall, *The Soldier's Story*, p. 77.

48  To this day, members of Delta Company argue over Buick's precise words and actions. Some claim he yelled, 'Every man for himself.' Others claim he ran back, ahead of his men. Every soldier has his own perspective on a chaotic situation. The fact is that Buick's action saved what was left of his platoon. He could not get the dead out; he thought only of the living. Many seem motivated by their dislike of Buick rather than making a fair assessment of the situation. Indeed, John Beere recently wrote to film producer Martin Walsh that Buick showed no fear of enemy fire and, at one point, stood up and ran over to attend a wounded soldier. He was quite ready to die for his troops. 'Buick was among the last to return, not the first,' said Sabben. Others disagree; the truth lies with the consciences of men.

49  John Heslewood, interview, Bribie Island.

50  Mollison, *Long Tan and Beyond*, p. 152.

51  David Sabben, interview, Melbourne, 21 August 2005.

52  AWM PR90/162, Papers of D. Horsfield; interview with Geoff Kendall, 9 November 1984; interview with Paddy Todd, October 1984.

53  Adrian Roberts, email, 7 September 2006.

54  Burstall, *The Soldier's Story*, p. 133.

55  McNeill, *To Long Tan*, p. 430. The relationship between the two services was 'really very, very bad', Major Alex Piper recalled.

56  AWM Air Force Office file 566/2/215, Department of Air Organisation Directive No 9/66: Reformation and Deployment of No 9 Sqn to Vietnam, 18 April 1966, p. 2; also quoted in McNeill, *To Long Tan*, p. 322.

57  Captain Trevor Richards, Lieutenant David Harris, Colonel David Chinn and Major David Watts each confirmed the heated argument between Jackson and Raw. See McNeill, *To Long Tan*, notes, p. 549.

58  Grandin (ed.), *The Battle of Long Tan*, p. 146.

59  Bob Grandin, interview, Maroochydore, 7 June 2005.

60  Harry Smith, interview, Hervey Bay, 6 June 2005.

61  Bill Akell, interview, Buninyong, 22 August 2005.

62  *Sydney Morning Herald*, 22 August 1966, p. 1.

63  Burstall, *The Soldier's Story*, p. 102.

64  Harry Smith, email, 2 March 2006.

65  AWM PR90/162, Papers of D. Horsfield; interview with Peter Ainslie, 11 Pl D Coy, 6 Bn.

66  AWM PR90/162, Papers of D. Horsfield; interview with Brian Halls, 11 Pl D Coy, 6 Bn.

67  Stewart, 'The Ghosts of Long Tan'.

68  Government of the Socialist Republic of Vietnam, *D445: The Heroic Battalion*, p. 64.

69  Grandin (ed.), *The Battle of Long Tan*, p. 141.

70  P. Dinham, 2 Pl, A Co Involvement at Long Tan (unpublished article), 18 August 1966.

71  Adrian Roberts, emails, 7 September 2006 and 17 April 2007. Townsend refers to the rumours of the pistol incident in a letter to Derek Roylance, May 1984 (Colin Townsend, personal papers). The delays triggered a bitter dispute. Mollison, the new commander of Alpha Company, insisted that he was in overall command of the convoy and could veto Roberts's orders. Yet Roberts believed the troop commander (i.e. himself) led the carriers and their passengers while on the move and that the infantry officer resumed command only when the soldiers left the carriers. This unfortunate dispute is fully aired in McNeill, *To Long Tan*, pp. 336–8, and Modystack, *The Pony Soldiers*. The Standard Operation Procedures normally applied in other

battalions should have clarified the position, as Essex-Clark shows, in the SOPs he wrote for 1RAR (paragraph 65c): 'When troops [i.e. infantry] are travelling in APCs they are under command of the APC formation commander [in this case, Roberts]. This also applies to each carrier where the crew commander commands all in his vehicle. Command reverts to the commander of troops [i.e. Mollison] … after they have dismounted' (Essex-Clark, email, 3 May 2007). To both Roberts's and Mollison's credit, their sole purpose was to reach Harry Smith as swiftly as possible. Unfortunately, Mollison and Roberts trained their frustration on each other when the real source of the problem was the army's lack of readiness for a joint armour–infantry assault.

72  Jamieson, 'With the APCs at Long Tan'.
73  Stewart, 'The Ghosts of Long Tan'.
74  Harry Smith, Papers.
75  McNeill, *To Long Tan*, p. 340.

## Chapter 19 **Long Tan — aftermath**

1   Harry Smith, interview, Hervey Bay, 6 June 2005.
2   Spike Jones, 'With B Company at the Battle of Long Tan, 18 August 1966' (unpublished memoir).
3   Laurie Drinkwater, interview, Maroochydore, 7 June 2005.
4   AWM PR90/162, Papers of D. Horsfield; interview with Peter Ainslie, 11 Pl D Coy, 6 Bn.
5   AWM PR90/162, Papers of D. Horsfield.
6   Burstall, *The Soldier's Story*, p. 129.
7   Bob Buick, 'A Platoon Sergeant's Perspective of the Battle of Long Tan, 18 August 1966' (unpublished memoir).
8   'Hero of Long Tan's "Mercy Killing" Upsets Comrades', *A Current Affair*, ABC, 17 August 2000; see also Buick, *All Guts and No Glory*.
9   Rintoul, *Ashes of Vietnam*, p. 91.
10  Stewart, 'The Ghosts of Long Tan'; and Bob Buick, interview, Mooloolaba, 5 June 2005.
11  Bill Akell, interview, Buninyong, 22 August 2005.
12  Grandin (ed.), *The Battle of Long Tan*, p. 238.
13  Graham 'Breaker' Cusack, interview, Vung Tau, 11 November 2005.
14  AWM 3DRL/6117, Papers of Colin Townsend.
15  Dave Sabben, email, 4 August 2005; source: Denis Gibbons.
16  A selection of Australian newspapers.
17  McNeill, *To Long Tan*, p. 372.
18  AWM 3DRL/6117, Papers of Colin Townsend.
19  Harry Smith, email, 2 March 2006.
20  AWM 3DRL/6117, Papers of Colin Townsend.
21  LBJ Library, National Security File,, Head of State Correspondence, Australia, PM Holt Correspondence, 1/19/66–5/16/68, Cable LBJ to Holt re: TV report on Long Tan Aug 22 1966, *Today Show*, Vol. 1, Box 1.
22  Colin Townsend, personal papers.
23  Government of the Socialist Republic of Vietnam, *D445: The Heroic Battalion*, p. 65.
24  Burstall, 'Long Tan: The Other Side of the Hill'.
25  Nguyen Minh Ninh, commander of the D445 Battalion, and Nguyen Nam Hung, commander of the 274th Regiment, interviews, Vung Tau, 19 November 2005.
26  Government of the Socialist Republic of Vietnam, *D445: The Heroic Battalion*, p. 65.
27  Ibid.
28  Ibid. Post-battle critics condemn the Australians for failing to pursue the enemy's retreating regiments. 'The Americans were incredulous and mightly pissed off that we didn't follow up,' remarked one intelligence officer. In fairness, the Task Force did not possess a battalion-strength airlift capability or Phantom jets; only the legs of exhausted soldiers. Indeed, US troops then

engaged in OPERATION TOLEDO to the north of Phuoc Tuy tried and failed to intercept the retreating Viet Cong. Townsend changed his reasons for not pursuing the enemy: after the battle, he later claimed, the battalion wanted to pursue but was prevented from going beyond artillery range (see Colin Townsend, Oral History Recording, by David Chinn, Amamoor, Qld, 18 December 1989, Official History Unit). Later, he claimed the battalion was in no state for a sustained pursuit, 'with the enemy able to conduct battalion-sized ambushes' (AWM102/42, After-action Report, OPERATION SMITHFIELD). Jackson's failure to send a rapid relief force earlier in the battle drew the most severe criticism, yet the only troops available were Mollison's weary A Company, just back from a three-day patrol. Ford's B Company was even less prepared: on leave or somewhere in the scrub.

29 Harry Smith, interview, Hervey Bay, 6 June 2005.
30 Ibid.
31 Neville Cullen, interview, Redcliffe, 8 June 2005.
32 Bruce Fletcher, letter to author, 2006.
33 LBJ Library, National Security File, International Meetings and Travel File, Seven-Nation Conference — Potus Trip 10/16/66, White House Situation Room, Situation Report for the President, 19 October 1966, Box 4.

Chapter 20 ... **with LBJ**

1 *Hansard*, 31 March 1966, p. 865.
2 LBJ Library, National Security File, Country File, Asia and the Pacific, Australia Cables, Vol. 1, 1/66–7/67, Cable from Rusk to President, 27 June 1966, Box 233 [1 of 2].
3 LBJ Library, National Security File, Special Head of State Correspondence File, Australia–Presidential Correspondence, Letter from Holt to LBJ, 1 February 1966, Box 3.
4 *Australian*, 1 July 1966.
5 Not very far, as Paul Kelly and Peter Edwards showed. See Kelly, 'Vietnam — 30 years on', Australian War Memorial Anniversary Oration, 11 November 2005; Edwards, *A Nation at War*.
6 Murphy, *Harvest of Fear*, p. 152.
7 LBJ Library, White House Central File, CO18 7/8/66–10/15/66, Box 13.
8 NAA CRS A1209/39, Cablegram 2056, McEwen to Holt, 13 July 1966.
9 Pemberton, *All the Way*, p. 335.
10 LBJ Library, National Security File, Country File, Australia, Prime Minister Holt Visit 6/29 and 7/13/66, Memo from Rostow for President, 17 June 1966, Box 234.
11 Poll published in the Melbourne *Herald*, 6 August 1966.
12 LBJ Library, National Security File, International Meetings and Travel File, President's Trip to New Zealand, Briefing Book, 10/19–20/66, Box 11.
13 Ibid.
14 LBJ Library, National Security File, International Meetings and Travel File, Seven-Nation Conference — Potus Trip, Cable from Tom Johnson to Bill Moyers and Bob Fleming, White House, Box 3 [2 of 4].
15 LBJ Library, National Security File, International Meetings and Travel File, Seven-Nation Conference — Potus Trip, Transcript, Cronkite interview with Holyoake, 10/20/66, Box 4 [2 of 3].
16 LBJ Library, National Security File, International Meetings and Travel File, President's Itinerary, Asian Trip, Intelligence Memorandum, Security Conditions in Six Western Pacific Countries, Central Intelligence Agency, Directorate of Intelligence, 10/18/66, p. 2, Box 9 [2 of 2].
17 LBJ Library, National Security File, International Meetings and Travel File, Seven-Nation Conference — Potus Trip, Intelligence Memorandum, Security Conditions in Six Western Pacific Countries, Central Intelligence Agency Directorate of Intelligence, 10/16/66, p. 2 Box 4 [1 of 4].
18 Ibid.
19 LBJ Library, Oral History Charles Chuck Lipsen, personal statement, 13 June 1975.

20 LBJ Library, National Security File, International Meetings and Travel File, President's Itinerary, Asian Trip, Intelligence Memorandum, Security Conditions in Six Western Pacific Countries, Central Intelligence Agency, Directorate of Intelligence, 18/10/66, p. 2, Box 9 [2 of 2].

21 LBJ Library, White House Central File, Letter from LBJ to Paul Lippman, 18 January 1966, CO18 11/17/65–7/7/66, Box 13.

22 LBJ Library, Confidential File, TR100 Walt Rostow, To the President from Ambassador Clark, 25 October 1966, Box 95.

23 LBJ Library, National Security File, International Meetings and Travel File, Seven-Nation Conference — Potus Trip, White House Press Cuttings File, Box 2 [2 of 4].

24 LBJ Library, National Security File, International Meetings and Travel File, Seven-Nation Conference — Potus Trip, Press Cuttings, October 1966, and Cable, American Embassy Canberra to White House, p. 3, 10/20/66, Box 4 [2 of 3].

25 NAA CS file C4461, CRS A4940/1; also quoted in Edwards, *A Nation at War*, p. 116.

26 LBJ Library, National Security File, International Meetings and Travel File, Seven-Nation Conference — Potus Trip, Summary of Reactions to Manila Conference, Box 3 [2 of 4].

27 *Sydney Morning Herald*, 22 October 1966.

28 LBJ Library, Office Files, C. Bellinger, Australia, Remarks by the President, 'The Dynamics of Peace in the Space Age — Australia', 21–22 October 1966.

29 LBJ Library, National Security File, International Meetings and Travel File, Seven-Nation Conference — President's Asian Trip, October–November 1966, Briefing Book 10/11/66, Box 9 [1 of 2].

30 LBJ Library, Confidential File TR100, Walt Rostow, Cable from Ambassador Clark to the President, 25 October 1966, Box 95.

31 LBJ Library, National Security File, International Meetings and Travel File, Seven-Nation Conference — Potus Trip, Cable from Bromley Smith to Bill Moyers, 20 October 1966, Box 4 [1 of 3].

32 Langley, *A Decade of Dissent*, pp. 57–8. The secret servicemen included the President's personal bodyguard, Rufus Youngblood (who had hurled himself across LBJ in Dallas at the time of President Kennedy's assassination). Australian lawyers Galbally and O'Bryan later apologised on behalf of the arrested protesters, in a letter to the White House: 'Mr President … their action was not inspired by any malevolent feeling towards you or the great nation you represent … rather the effervescence of youthful gaiety and jocularity excited to a fever pitch by your presence …' (LBJ Library, Central File, CO18 10/16/66–3/20/67, Box 13).

33 LBJ Library, National Security File, Manila Conference and President's Asian Trip, 17 Oct–2 Nov 1966, Press Cuttings, October 1966, and Cable from American Embassy Canberra to Rusk, Box 46.

34 LBJ Library, Central File, CO18 10/16/66–3/20/67, Box 13.

35 LBJ Library, Confidential File ND19/CO312 Vietnam (Situation In, March 1967), Box 72 [1 of 2].

36 Vietnam Action Committee pamphlet, July 1966.

37 LBJ Library, National Security File, International Meetings and Travel File, Seven-Nation Conference — Potus Trip, Text of the Joint Communiqué issued at the Manila Conference, October 25, 1966, Box 4 [1 of 3]; see also NAA 66/7728 ATT 2 CRS A1209/80, Vietnam Manila Conference — Brief and Background Papers.

38 LBJ Library, National Security File, International Meetings and Travel File, Seven-Nation Conference — Potus Trip, Text of the Joint Communiqué issued at the Manila Conference, October 25, 1966, Box 4 [1 of 3].

39 *Age*, 25 November 1966.

40 Beazley, 'Federal Labor and the Vietnam Commitment', in King, *Australia's Vietnam*, pp. 50–1.

41 LBJ Library, Personal Papers, Papers of George W. Ball, Australia 1/24/64–7/11/66, Cable from American Embassy Canberra to Sec of State, Washington DC, 16 Jan 1967, Box 1.

42 Ibid.

43  LBJ Library, National Security File, Country File, Asia and the Pacific, Australia, Australia Memos, Vol. 2, 1/66–7/67, Impressions of Prime Minister Ky by R. Woolcott, Public Information Officer, Dept of External Affairs, Canberra, 1 February 1967, Box 233 [1 of 2].

44  Ibid.

45  Howson, *The Howson Diaries*, p. 263.

46  LBJ Library, National Security File, International Meetings and Travel File, SEATO Council Meeting, Washington, 18–20 April 1967, Background Paper, Box 36 [2 of 3].

47  Haran and Kearney, *Crossfire*, pp. 118–19.

## Chapter 21 **Draft dodgers**

1  Maddock and Stilwell, 'Boom and Recession', in Curthoys et al. (ed.), *Australians From 1939*; and Edwards, *A Nation at War*.

2  *Nation*, 15 May 1965.

3  Edwards, *A Nation at War*, pp. 67–70.

4  Ibid., p. 74.

5  Stone, *War Without Honour*, p. 49.

6  AWM ML MSS 5395 Box 1 (4), Women's International League for Peace and Freedom — NSW Branch, Records 1960–90.

7  Ron Saw, *Daily Mirror*, 18 November 1966.

8  *Australian*, 27 July 1966.

9  Macky, 'Ballad of William White', 1966, published in Scates, *Draftsmen Go Free*, p. 19, and in *Retrieval*, June–July 1975.

10  The lyrics of certain anti-war songs betrayed a gross ignorance of the Australian soldiers and helped to perpetuate the myth of the diggers as 'baby-killers'; consider, for example, Melbourne crooner Glen Tomasetti's 'The Army's Appeal to Mothers' (first published in an anti-conscription leaflet, 1966; reprinted in Scates, *Draftsmen Go Free*, p. 19; and *Retrieval*, June–July 1975):

> … Teach him killing civilians is
> Essential to our defence.
> Teach him to hate each foreign name,
> Colour, race or tongue,
> 'Cause he'll make a happier soldier
> If you brutalize him young.
>
> When it comes to twisting a bayonet,
> Or sticking in a boot,
> He'll find it so much easier,
> If you bring him up as a brute.

11  Jordens, '*Conscientious Objection and the Vietnam War*', Working Paper No. 73, p. 13.

12  Ibid., pp. 20–1.

13  Langley, *A Decade of Dissent*, pp. 37–8.

14  Examples drawn from Langley, *A Decade of Dissent*.

15  *Sydney Morning Herald*, 28 May 1968.

16  Press cuttings and *Hansard*, May 1968.

17  Simon Townsend, interview, 1 September 2006.

18  Letter to Townsend, undated. In 1976, Townsend got a job fronting the immensely popular TV show *Simon Townsend's Wonder World*, and became a much-loved Australian.

19  Gershon Gottlieb, *Hell No, We Won't Go!*, p. 62.

20  Ibid., pp. 115–16.

21  Ibid., p. 257.

22  Freudenberg, *A Certain Grandeur*, p. 94.

23  Hutchinson, *Not Going to Vietnam*, pp. 11–12.

24  Langley, *A Decade of Dissent*, p. 89.

Chapter 22 **R&R**

1   *Uc dai loi*: Australian soldiers; P: piastre, the local currency.
2   Knightley, *The First Casualty*, p. 384.
3   Greene, *The Quiet American*, p. 36.
4   Herr, *Dispatches*, p. 41.
5   McHugh, *Minefields and Miniskirts*.
6   Wilcox, 'Life at the Dat', in *Wartime* magazine; O'Brien, *Conscripts and Regulars*, p. 27.
7   Philip Ham, '25 Years On: Recollections of a National Serviceman, 1968–1970' (unpublished memoir).
8   John Rowe, various interviews, Sydney 2005.
9   Ross, 'Australian Soldiers in Vietnam: Product and Performance', in King, *Australia's Vietnam*, p. 90.
10  AWM100 2/R153/1/4, Canteens — Committees — Conferences General [2RAR].
11  The Australian entertainers were either members of 'official concert parties', organised by the government's Forces Advisory Committee on Entertainment, or private entertainers, employed by such agencies as Showgroup International. (The RSL also organised concert tours, through the Australian Forces Overseas Fund.) The official entertainers tended to be established Australian artists who performed chiefly for the Australian soldiers; for example, Lorrae Desmond, Little Pattie and Sylvia Raye. The private performers were wilder acts for whom money and excitement had a strong allure and who played mostly on US military bases, often in very dangerous circumstances. They were helicoptered to remote US bases in Plei Ku, Kon Tum and Da Nang. 'Many private acts were left to fend for themselves … getting from base to base,' recalled Don Morrisson in *My Rock 'n' Roll War*. 'Road travel was extremely hazardous.'
12  AWM290 4/R66/4/1, Amenities — Entertainment — Concert Parties.
13  Lorrae Desmond, interview, Sydney, 23 September 2005.
14  McHugh, *Minefields and Miniskirts*, p. 26.
15  AWM275 [26], Comments from Entertainers in Vietnam; and Lorrae Desmond, interview, Sydney, 23 September 2005. After the war, Desmond, the soldiers' universal mother figure, became deeply involved in veterans' affairs.
16  AWM275 [26], Comments from Entertainers in Vietnam.
17  Sylvia Raye, 'My Memories', email, 21 September 2006.
18  Morrisson, *My Rock 'n' Roll War*, pp. 191–2.
19  McHugh, *Minefields and Miniskirts*, p. 26.
20  Ibid., p. 27.
21  Ibid., p. 23.
22  Corporal Robin 'Spike' Jones, 'With B Company at the Battle of Long Tan, 18 August 1966' (unpublished memoir).
23  McHugh, *Minefields and Miniskirts*, pp. 75–6.
24  Ingrid Hart, email, 19 January 2007.
25  O'Farrell, *Behind Enemy Lines*, p. 201.
26  John Bullen, personal papers, diary, 22 May 1968.
27  Ibid.
28  Ibid.
29  O'Keefe and Smith, *Medicine at War*, pp. 204–5.
30  AWM103 R719/1/1/2, From Austforce Vietnam to 1ATF, 24 September 1966.
31  AWM103 R719/1/1/2, Chaplains' Report, HQ 1ATF, Nui Dat, 4 July 66.
32  Bob Gully, interview, Sydney, 2 June 2005.
33  O'Farrell, *Behind Enemy Lines*, pp. 141 and 192.
34  Barr, *Surgery, Sand and Saigon Tea*, pp. 97–8.
35  Corporal Robin 'Spike' Jones, 'With B Company at the Battle of Long Tan, 18 August 1966' (unpublished memoir).
36  Advertisement in the *Mighty Magenta* (newsletter, 1ALSG).

37 Corporal Robin 'Spike' Jones, With 'B' Company at the Battle of Long Tan, 18 August 1966 (unpublished memoir).

38 Lunn, *Vietnam: A Reporter's War*, pp. 164–5.

39 O'Neill, *Vietnam Task*, p. 163.

40 O'Keefe and Smith, *Medicine at War*, pp. 102–3.

41 AWM PR00202, Papers of Dr B. Dunn, 'Venereal Disease in Vietnam', Headquarters Australian Force Vietnam, 21 January 1971.

42 Anonymous, interview.

43 Rintoul, *Ashes of Vietnam*, p. 88.

44 O'Keefe and Smith, *Medicine at War*, p. 102.

45 Ibid., p. 103.

46 Ibid., pp. 178–9. Vietnamese prostitutes were not the only 'carriers' of infection. An apparently well-bred Australian entertainer infected dozens of soldiers and even her fellow musicians with the clap, it emerged. Another Australian girl slept with so many soldiers that she earned the nickname 'root rat'; by repute, she enjoyed sex with pilots while aboard their Hueys (McHugh, *Minefields and Miniskirts*.

47 AWM100 2/R153/1/4, Canteens — Committees — Conferences General, Minutes of a Meeting of the Vietnam Command Amenties Fund, 29 August 1967.

48 AWM290 4/R746/1/7, Safety — General — Aquatic — Lifesaver — Aust. Beach; and AWM95 7/1/69, Memo 20 April 1966, Beach Safety — Vung Tau.

49 Brian Sewell, interview, Vung Tau, 14 November 2005.

50 LBJ Library, National Security File, Country File, Asia and the Pacific, Australia, Memos Vol. 2, 1/66–7/67, Memo to Mr Cyrus Vance, 23 May 1967, Establishment of Australia as an R&R site, Box 233 [1 of 2]. The GIs had a habit of leaving their calling cards and other paraphernalia at the Bourbon and Beefsteak, an all-night drinking hole in Sydney's Kings Cross and an unofficial war museum until 2003, when philistine developers turned it into a backpackers' bar.

51 McHugh, *Minefields and Miniskirts*, p. 50.

52 Ibid.

53 Elkner did not report the attack; in fact, she and her assailant pursued a love affair, as she revealed years later. Elkner went on to a successful stage and television career, and became best known for the 1970s single 'Rack off Normie'; she was still performing in 2007 (Maureen Elkner, discussion, Slide nightclub, Sydney, 11 January 2007).

54 McHugh, *Minefields and Miniskirts*, pp. 57–8.

55 Ibid., pp. 60–1.

56 Ibid., p. 68.

57 AWM103 R271/1/67/1, Discipline — General — 5RAR.

58 AWM103 R271/1/71/3, Discipline — Charge Report 4RAR.

59 AWM103 R271/1/71/2, Discipline — General — 6RAR.

60 AWM103 478/1/515, Investigation Reports — General (Part 2) — 4RAR.

61 AWM103 R271/1/67/1, Discipline — General — 5RAR.

62 AWM103 478/1/515, Investigation Reports — General (Part 2) — 4RAR.

63 Ross, 'Australian Soldiers in Vietnam: Product and Performance', in King, *Australia's Vietnam*, p. 89.

64 Arnold, *Cop in a Baggy Green Skin*; and AWM103 R271/1/71/2, Discipline — General — 6RAR.

## Chapter 23 **February 1967**

1 Colin Townsend, personal papers, Oral History Recording, by David Chinn, Amamoor, Qld, 18 December 1989, Official History Unit, p. 11.

2 McNeill, *To Long Tan*, p. 427.

3 OPERATION CROWSNEST.

4 OPERATION BUNDABERG.

5  OPERATIONS CANARY and DUCK (1 and 2).

6  OPERATIONS CANBERRA and QUEANBEYAN.

7  OPERATION HAYMAN.

8  OPERATION INGHAM.

9  McFarlane, *We Band of Brothers*.

10  In 2005 I had lunch with Hung, now a brigadier general, in Vung Tau. He did not recall the loss of his diary.

11  O'Neill, *Vietnam Task*, p. 121.

12  Ibid.

13  AWM107(1), Interview with Major General Tim Vincent, Army Historical Programme, p. 32. 'Medcap' means Medical Civic Action Program; 'dentcap' means Dental Civic Action Program.

14  AWM95, 5RAR Commander's Diary, January 1967.

15  OPERATION TAMBOURINE.

16  Dr John Taske, Letter to AWM, quoted in McNeill and Ekins, *On the Offensive*, p. 82.

17  Ibid.

18  AWM103 R245/2/3, Court of Inquiry, General, Arty ACC — 6RAR. The negligence of three New Zealand gunners, from 161 Field Battery, caused the tragedy, according to a Military Court of Inquiry. The episode exposed serious failings in the battery; for example, one duty officer admitted to the court that he had had virtually no artillery training. Two others confirmed that the locking device on the gun's artillery plotter was unserviceable. This defect meant that a mere nudge could send the shells hurtling to the wrong target, as the gunner told the court: 'I must have knocked the plotter with my hand.' The battery had known about the defect for five months. Those responsible — including two officers — were not subject to Australian military law, and escaped punishment (although one returned to New Zealand for further artillery training). The tragedy was a black mark against a unit that had performed so brilliantly at Long Tan.

19  OPERATION BEAUMARIS.

20  Second Lieutenant David Harris, quoted in McNeill and Ekins, *On the Offensive*, p. 87.

21  AWM PR88/091 Records of Lieutenant M. O'Brien, 7RAR, 'The Long Hai Mountains'.

22  AWM117 [20], OPERATION RENMARK.

23  O'Neill, *Vietnam Task*, p. 221.

24  AWM107(1), Interview with Major General Tim Vincent, Army Historical Programme, p. 12.

25  White, 'Death Without Glory', *Canberra Times*, 22 February 1997.

26  Ibid.

27  AWM117 [20], Combat After-action Report, OPERATION RENMARK, 5RAR, 18 March 1967.

28  See McNeill, *The Team*, for detailed coverage of Ruff Puffs and Badcoe.

29  McNeill, *The Team*, pp. 236–7.

30  Ibid, p. 239.

31  Ekins, 'Killing ground', p. 48.

32  Mackay, letter to *Bulletin*, 23 September 2003, p. 7.

33  The official history examines the battle in detail; see McNeill and Ekins, *On the Offensive*, pp. 89–115.

34  McFarlane, *We Band of Brothers*, p. 355.

35  Brian McFarlane, interview, Bowral, 31 August 2005.

36  McNeill and Ekins, *On the Offensive*, p. 93.

37  Ibid., p. 96.

38  Ekins, 'Killing ground', p. 49.

39  Mackay, letter to *Bulletin*, 23 September 2003, p. 7.

40  Gannon, 'You'll Be Back for Breakfast', in Maddock (ed.), *Memories of Vietnam*, p. 80.

41  Ekins, 'Killing ground', p. 47; and McNeill and Ekins, *On the Offensive*, p. 102.

42  Harris, in Maddock (ed.) *Memories of Vietnam*; also quoted in McFarlane, *We Band of Brothers*, p. 359.

43  Jones, OPERATION BRIBIE, 17 February 1967.

44 McFarlane, *We Band of Brothers*, p. 359.
45 Brian McFarlane, interview, Bowral, 31 August 2005.
46 Hennessy, *The Sharp End*.
47 McFarlane, *We Band of Brothers*, pp. 364–6.
48 Brian McFarlane, emails.
49 McFarlane, *We Band of Brothers*, p. 365.
50 Hennessy, *The Sharp End*.
51 Neil Rankin, interview.
52 Jones, OPERATION BRIBIE, 17 February 1967.

## Chapter 24 **The minefield**

1 Lockhart, 'The Minefield' (essay), p. 9; see also Lockhart *The Minefield: An Australian Tragedy in Vietnam*.
2 Cable, 'An Independent Command', Canberra Papers on Strategy and Defence, No. 134, p. 34.
3 McNeill and Ekins, *On the Offensive*, p. 32.
4 Maizey, in *Vietnam Minefield*, SBS Television.
5 Nat Hardcastle, interview, Sydney, 2006.
6 Dr Greg Lockhart, a former member of the Team, is that rarity: a soldier and a scholar. A mine attack he experienced in Vietnam no doubt helped to focus him on his compelling book *The Minefield: An Australian Tragedy in Vietnam* (2007). Lockhart's post-war academic career in Vietnamese history and literature is unique among commentators on Australia's involvement in war. A passionate writer, he somehow manages to remain judicious. Since 2001 he has been Honorary Historian of the Vietnam Veterans' Federation of Australia.
7 Lockhart, 'The Minefield' (essay), p. 17.
8 Cable, 'An Independent Command', Canberra Papers on Strategy and Defence, No. 134, p. 36.
9 Lockhart, 'The Minefield' (essay), p. 22.
10 AWM107, Interview with Brigadier Stuart Graham, Army Historical Programme, p. 8.
11 LBJ Library, Westmoreland Papers, Westmoreland Diary, 29 January 1967, pp. 2–3.
12 AWM107, Interview with Brigadier Stuart Graham, Army Historical Programme, p. 9.
13 AWM107, Interview with Brigadier O. D. Jackson, Army Historical Programme, pp. 78–9.
14 McNeill and Ekins, *On the Offensive*, p. 78.
15 Ibid., p. 127.
16 Maizey, in *Vietnam Minefield*, SBS Television.
17 AWM107, Interviews with the commanders. In a letter to Dr Greg Lockhart on 11 July 2002, Major John Rowe argued that Colonel Dat, the province chief, had been the driving force behind the minefield: 'Dat asked Graham to provide him with the minefield … His major arguments were that such a barrier would make it much harder for the Main Force Viet Cong troops to raid the populated areas …' Graham, Rowe concluded, was torn between supporting the province chief and developing a supportive, long-term relationship, or pursuing an exclusively Australian agenda: 'On balance, Graham decided it was more important to support Dat's request for the minefield than to oppose it.' This account reads as a decent effort to exonerate Graham by sharing responsibility. Yet those who knew Graham knew a very stubborn man; it was simply out of character for him willingly to subordinate his authority or his tactical ideas to the province chief. No doubt they worked together, but there can be little doubt that Graham drove the barrier project.
18 Eric Smith, interview, Canberra, 6 Ocober 2006.
19 McNeill and Ekins, *On the Offensive*, pp. 134–5.
20 OPERATION LEETON.
21 See Lockhart, *The Minefield*, for a detailed analysis of its construction and impact.
22 AWM R823 1/2/1, Engineers' Mine Warfare 1970–71.
23 Walter Pearson was wounded by a mine in Vietnam; years later he co-produced the documentary *Vietnam Minefield*, SBS Television (2005).

24  Bob Coleman, interview, 2005.

25  Joe Cazey, in *Vietnam Minefield*, SBS Television.

26  Lockhart, 'The Minefield', in *Vietnam Veteran Newsletter*, p. 25.

27  Heard, *Well Done, Those Men*, p. 225.

28  McKay, *Bullets, Beans and Bandages*, p. 206.

29  Lockhart, 'The Minefield' (essay), p. 28.

30  *Holdfast* (official newsletter of the Vietnam Tunnel Rats Association), No. 4.

31  Ibid.

32  Lockhart, various discussions, 2007; see also Lockhart, *The Minefield*, for a detailed analysis.

33  Almost forty years later, Fraser could not recollect the release but said the casualties were 'an operational issue that would be better left for the army' (*Australian*, 16 August 2005).

34  AWM103, Report by Major B. G. Florence into Casualties Sustained by 1 Field Squadron RAE on Operation Leeton during May 1967, Nui Dat, 3 June 1967.

35  Thompson, in *Vietnam Minefield*, SBS Television.

36  Lockhart, 'The Minefield' (essay), p. 27.

37  Ibid.

38  Duong Son Minh (with voice-over translation), in *Vietnam Minefield*, SBS Television.

39  For a detailed account, see Phan Ngoc Danh and Tran Quang Toai, *Lich Su Dau Tranh Cach Mang Cua Huyen Long Dat* (The History of the Long Dat District Revolutionary Struggle).

40  Mac Linh Xuan (with voice-over translation), in *Vietnam Minefield*, SBS Television.

41  Burstall, *A Soldier Returns*, p. 68

42  Mac Linh Xuan (with voice-over translation), in *Vietnam Minefield*, SBS Television.

43  Kearney, 'Blunder that killed 60 troops', *Australian*, 13 August 2005.

44  Brian McFarlane, interviews, Bowral, 2005.

45  Frost, *Australia's War in Vietnam*, p. 98.

46  Ibid., p. 100.

47  Ibid., p. 101. CORDS stands for Civil Operations and Rural Development Support.

48  For example Phan Ngoc Danh and Tran Quang Toai, *Lich Su Dau Tranh Cach Mang Cua Huyen Long Dat* (The History of the Long Dat District Revolutionary Struggle); and the Dong Nai provincial history.

49  Phan Ngoc Danh and Tran Quang Toai, *Lich Su Dau Tranh Cach Mang Cua Huyen Long Dat*, (The History of the Long Dat District Revolutionary Struggle), chapter 6, p. 5; also quoted in McNeill and Ekins, *On the Offensive*, p. 155.

50  Mai Thuan, interview, Hanoi, 28 November 2005.

51  Paul Murphy, interview, Vung Tau, 16 November 2005.

52  Sandy Pearson, interview, Sydney, 4 September 2006.

53  Cable, 'An Independent Command', Canberra Papers on Strategy and Defence, No. 134, pp. 38–9.

## Chapter 25  **The hamlet without a soul**

1  Eric Smith, interview, Canberra, 6 October 2005.

2  Ibid.

3  The official historians echo Graham's view: the very title of McNeill and Ekins' official history, *On the Offensive*, as well as the chapters 'Removing the claws' and 'To the borders ...', suggest that the Task Force had determined this result and firmly controlled the destiny of the 'Australian Province'. This is a rather simplistic interpretation. The enemy, at this stage, was hardly removed or driven out of the province; he lingered, waiting to strike back, as Tet would prove.

4  The 275th Regiment even survived its disastrous assault on Lo Gom, a small fort in the path of the minefield.

5  US 1st Brigade, the US 11th Army Cavalry Regiment and the 35th Ranger (South Vietnamese) Battalion.

6   Successive Australian battalions cordoned, searched and/or destroyed Viet Cong in the same grid squares throughout the war, because the enemy made a point of trying to reoccupy areas the Australians had recently cleared. This tactic undermined the people's faith, if any, in the foreigners' ability to protect them and achieve lasting influence.

7   O'Brien, *Conscripts and Regulars*, p. 44.

8   AWM107(1), Interview with Major General Tim Vincent, 31 January 1967–30 January 1968, 20 March 1972, Army Historical Programme.

9   O'Brien, *Conscripts and Regulars*, pp. 51–2.

10  McNeill and Ekins, *On the Offensive*, p. 205.

11  Roy Savage Diaries, http://docsdiaries.tripod.com; and O'Brien, *Conscripts and Regulars*, p. 51.

12  AWM98, R569/1/57, Quarterly Operational Summary, 1 July–30 September 1967.

13  Australian Department of External Affairs, Presidential and Senate Elections in the Republic of Vietnam on 3 September 1967 — Report of the Australian Observers, Parliamentary Paper No. 145, 1967, pp. 23–5.

14  AWM98 R72/1/1, Headquarters Australian Force Vietnam (Saigon) Records, War Dogs Box 18: The Effectiveness of Tracker Dogs in SVN, 31 August 1967 (7RAR).

15  AWM290 [8/3], After-action Report, OPERATION PHOI HOP.

16  Haran, *Trackers*, p. 124.

17  AWM290 [8/3], After-action Report, OPERATION PHOI HOP.

18  AWM98 R72/1/1, Headquarters Australian Force Vietnam (Saigon) Records, War Dogs Box 18: Tracker Dogs — Operational Employment and Effectiveness — D. Vincent, Major General COMAFV, 27 October 1967.

19  Adshead, Robinson, Gillies, Jacka, Personal reflections on the battle of Suoi Chau Pha, A Company 7RAR, 6 August 1967.

20  Heard, *Well Done, Those Men*, pp. 157–62.

21  Ibid., p. 161.

22  Adshead, Robinson, Gillies, Jacka, Personal reflections on the battle of Suoi Chau Pha, A Company 7RAR, 6 August 1967.

23  Ibid.

24  AWM 3DRL/7689, Papers of Sergeant W. L. Fogarty, 7RAR.

25  AWM288 R459/1/2/1 Part 2, After-action Reports — 3RAR, 6RAR, 7RAR and 9RAR, October 1967–September 1969.

26  The Australians had protected the insertion of South Vietnam's Revolutionary Forces during OPERATION SOUTHPORT.

27  McNeill and Ekins, *On the Offensive*, p. 224.

28  AWM288 R459/1/2/1 Part 2, After-action Reports — 3RAR, 6RAR, 7RAR and 9RAR, October 1967–September 1969, OPERATION AINSLIE After-action Report.

29  Eric Smith, interview, Canberra, 6 October 2005.

30  AWM288 R459/1/2/1 Part 2, After-action Reports — 3RAR, 6RAR, 7RAR and 9RAR, October 1967–September 1969, OPERATION AINSLIE Analysis Report, 27 October 1967.

31  McNeill and Ekins, *On the Offensive*, p. 229.

32  Eric Smith, interview, Canberra, 6 October 2005. Earlier Smith had been involved in a rice denial operation that aimed to take the harvest from Viet Cong areas and redistribute it among friendly villages. 'So we surrounded a village and took the rice and gave it back to the people. But thirty angry women dressed in black approached. My interpreter explained, "Sir, you've mixed up their rice." I said, "Look, rice is rice." He said, "No, each village grows a different kind of rice. It all has a different value." So I got on the phone and told the brigadier, and he said, "Whaddya mean? Rice is rice!" I said, "No, rice *isn't* rice." They abandoned the operation.'

33  Paul Murphy, interview, Vung Tau, 16 November 2005.

34  AWM288 R459/1/2/1 Part 2, After-action Reports — 3RAR, 6RAR, 7RAR and 9RAR, October 1967–September 1969, OPERATION AINSLIE After-action Report.

35  McNeill and Ekins, *On the Offensive*, p. 229.

36  Eric Smith, interview, Canberra, 6 October 2005.

37  McNeill and Ekins, *On the Offensive*, p. 230.

38  John Bullen, personal papers, diary.

39  The land grants were valueless, as Lieutenant Colonel Kevin Latchford later discovered.

40  AWM PR87/166, Papers of A. H. 'Lex' McAulay.

41  McNeill and Ekins, *On the Offensive*, p. 236.

42  Ibid., p. 238.

43  AWM290 3/R723/1/3, Reports General — 1ATF Psy Ops, After-action Report.

44  AWM290 7/16 Part 1, OPERATION SANTA FE, After-action Report, 7RAR, 31 December 1967, p. 10.

45  McNeill and Ekins, *On the Offensive*, pp. 261–2.

46  Bob Richards, personal papers.

47  A passing consolation was the disruption of Viet Cong bases in the area. The Australians found and destroyed thirty-five enemy camps and the usual bunker networks and rice supplies. The search revealed a housing compound for 120 people, equipped with a classroom and a dispensary containing 5,000 phials of penicillin, plus a variety of domestic items, such as five sewing kits, two typewriters, one quiver, two photo albums and a violin. A few women remained inside; outside, South Vietnamese troops captured '100 chickens' (AWM290 7/16 Part 1, Intelligence Summary, OPERATION SANTA FE, 7RAR, 31 December 1967, p. 8).

Chapter 26  **To January 1968**

1  LBJ Library, National Security File, Country File, Asia and the Pacific, Australia, Visits of PM Harold Holt, 6/1–2/67 and 6/17–19/67, Box 234 [2 of 2].

2  LBJ Library, National Security File, Country File, Asia and the Pacific, Australia, Memos Vol. 2, 1/66–7/67, Memo from William Bundy to the President, 1 June 1967, Box 233 [1 of 2].

3  NAA 67/7130 Part 1, A1209/80, Press Briefing Given by the Prime Minister to Parliamentary Press Gallery, Canberra, 19 July 1967.

4  LBJ Library, National Security File, Special Head of State Correspondence File, Australia 6/1/67–8/31/67, Letter from Holt to LBJ, 4 June 1967, Box 3.

5  LBJ Library, National Security File, Australia, Text of Holt's Address to the American Australian Association, River Club, New York, 8 June 1967, Box 234.

6  Ibid.

7  LBJ Library, White House Social Files, Holt Visit to Washington, 1 June 1967.

8  LBJ Library, National Security File, Country File, Asia and the Pacific, Australia, Memos Vol. 2, 1/66–7/67, Memo from Clark to Rostow, 13 December 1967, Box 233 [1 of 2].

9  Edwards, *A Nation at War*, p. 155.

10  For a full analysis of the long-running tank debate, see McNeill and Ekins, *On the Offensive*, pp. 245–50; and Coates, 'Preparing armoured units for overseas service', in *The Australian Army and the Vietnam War 1962–72*, pp. 77–95.

11  LBJ Library, National Security File, Head of State Correspondence, Cable from American Embassy Canberra to Secretary of State, Washington DC, 1/19/66–5/16/68 Vol. 1, Box 1.

12  LBJ Library, National Security File, Head of State Correspondence File, Memo from Rostow to LBJ, 10 October 1967, Box 1.

13  *Hansard*, 17 October 1967; see also NAA 67/7130 Part 2, A1209/80, Australian Forces for South Vietnam — Policy 1967.

14  *Pravda*, 20 October 1967, quoted in cable from Australian Embassy in Moscow to Canberra, sent same day.

15  McNamara, *In Retrospect*, p. 262.

16  Dallek, *Lyndon B. Johnson*, p. 319.

17  McNamara, *In Retrospect*, p. 269.

18  Ibid., p. 270.

19  Edwards, *A Nation at War*, p. 156.

20  *Hansard*, 15 May 1968, p. 1464.

21  Scates, *Draftsmen Go Free*, p. 32.

22  *Hansard*, 14 November 1968, p. 2868.

23  Edwards, *A Nation at War*, p. 221.

24  *Age*, 2 September 2005; and Frame, *The Life and Death of Harold Holt*. A coroner's report in 2005 — delayed because the law had previously prohibited coroners' investigations of deaths where no body had been found — quashed the rumours about Holt's death.

25  LBJ Library, National Security File, International Meetings and Travel File, Australian Presidential Trip to Holt Funeral, 23 December 1967, Box 20.

26  LBJ Library, National Security File, Special Head of State Correspondence File, Australia 11/1/67–12/31/67, Cable from LBJ to Lord Casey, 18 December 1967, Box 3.

27  LBJ Library, National Security File, Country File, Asia and the Pacific, Australia, Visits of PM Harold Holt 6/1–2/67 and 6/17–19/67, Box 234 [1 of 2].

28  LBJ Library, National Security File, Special Head of State Correspondence File, Australia 11/1/67–12/31/67, Cable from Lady Bird and LBJ to Mrs Zara Holt, 17 December 1967, Box 3.

29  LBJ Library, National Security File, International Meetings and Travel File, Australian Presidential Trip to Holt Funeral, Briefing Book, 23 December 1967, Box 20.

30  LBJ Library, National Security File, Minutes of Meeting of the President with the Australian Cabinet, 21 December 1967, Canberra, Box 2.

31  Ibid.

32  LBJ Library, National Security File, International Meetings and Travel File, Australian Presidential Trip to Holt Funeral, Briefing Book, 23 December 1967, Box 20. The President's Briefing Book makes fascinating reading. It included an article by Wilfred Burchett (21 October) on the thoughts of North Vietnam's Prime Minister Dong. Rostow earlier informed the President on 9 October: '... Burchett, in fact, has quite a lot of insight into Hanoi's mind, at the present time, with respect to negotiations.' However briefly, Washington elevated the man condemned as a traitor in Australia to the status of a credible interpreter of Hanoi's thoughts on the possibility of peace talks (National Security File, Country File, Asia and the Pacific, Australia, Memo from Walt Rostow to the President, 6 October 1967, Box 233 [2 of 2]).

33  LBJ Library, National Security File, International Meetings and Travel File, Australian Presidential Trip to Holt Funeral, Briefing Book, 23 December 1967, Box 20.

34  LBJ Library, National Security File, Country File, Asia and the Pacific, Australia, Australia Cables Vol. 3, 8/67–1/69 [2 of 2], Telegram from Secretary of State, Washington to American Embassy Canberra, December 1967, Box 233 [2 of 2].

35  OPERATION FORREST incorporated OPERATIONS OODNADATTA, CANUNGRA, SHEPPARTON, DIMBOOLA, MELBOURNE, LAWLEY and LORNE.

36  O'Brien, *Conscripts and Regulars*, p. 84. Nobody knew how much rice was denied the enemy, because the Viet Cong hid its rice in secret caches away from the villages. On a larger scale, the war denied rice to everyone: in 1967, South Vietnam had to import 750,000 tons to feed itself (in 1963 it had exported a surplus 340,000 tons, a post-1945 peak); in 1968, it would be forced to import almost a million tons.

37  Bob Richards, personal papers.

38  After his wounds were stitched, Richards and other casualties spent three weeks at the Rest and Convalescence centre in Vung Tau, during which the officer commanding ordered the wounded men to 'get off their arses' and shift cases of beer. The work opened up their wounds; Richards's deep lacerations wept fluid for weeks. He lodged a report and 'the people who treated us with contempt lost their jobs and were charged and returned to Australia' (Bob Richards, personal papers).

39  McNeill and Ekins, *On the Offensive*, pp. 264–5.

40  Ibid., p. 267.

41  AWM103 R719/1/4/2, AVF Chaplains' Conference, November 1967.

42 Coates, 'Preparing Armoured Units for Overseas Service', in *The Australian Army and the Vietnam War 1962–72*.

43 Encyclical Letter of Pope Paul VI, 27 October 1966, published in Department of External Affairs, *Select Documents on International Affairs*, No. 9, Vietnam, February 1966–October 1966, Canberra, December 1966.

44 LBJ Library, White House Central File, Confidential File ND19/Co312 Vietnam, Greenville News, South Carolina, 'World Might Be Heading Toward Its Final Conflict', January 68, Box 73 [1 of 2].

45 Dallek, *Lyndon B. Johnson*, p. 325.

46 Ibid., pp. 328–9.

## Chapter 27 **The Tet Offensive**

1 Peter Young, interview, Gold Coast, 29 September 2006.

2 Warner, *Not With Guns Alone*, p. 147.

3 Peter Young, personal papers, notes on Saigon dinner, 4 October 2006.

4 Peter Young, personal papers, Input for Dr Peter Young from Colonel John M. Fitzgerald (USA Retired), 30 June 2004.

5 Peter Young, personal papers, 'The Military Situation Within South Vietnam, 9th July 1967' (intelligence report).

6 Despite Young's detractors, his intelligence proved accurate. This section draws on many sources, chiefly Young's private papers, incorporating: Young's report The Military Situation Within South Vietnam, 9th July 1967; a letter from Young to Lieutenant Colonel K. Whyte, ADMI, Directorate of Military Intelligence; a letter from Serong to Young, 18 July 1998, in which Serong states, 'Swinbourne knew nothing and was not a fast learner … Swinbourne could not handle [Young]. Personality clash. Regrettable. The AMF lost a good man …'; Input from Colonel John Fitzgerald to Dr Peter Young, 13 July 2004; and a letter from Brigadier General Phillip Davidson, Assistant Chief of Staff, MACV HQ, to the commander, Australian Force Vietnam; as well as extensive discussions with Young; AWM PR00660, Papers of Major Peter Young; email exchanges with Major Fitzgerald in America; and Warner's account in *Not With Guns Alone*, p. 152. In 1968 Young's bright career prospects paled under his new boss, the military attaché Colonel Alan Swinbourne, who distrusted him and sought to close him down. Their personalities clashed, and Swinbourne, clearly outside the intelligence loop, seemed to delight in ending Young's privileged position. Young's seven-page appeal to Lieutenant Colonel K. Whyte, Director of Military Intelligence in Canberra, in which he outlined a 'wonderful opportunity' for Australia to exploit the 'almost unlimited access' to US intelligence, went unrewarded. Young did not help his case by running down several officers and diplomats. Yet he was self-aware: 'I know that you will forgive my excesses in pushing for what I believe in (almost fanatically now).' He also knew that his military days were numbered. His 'punishment' arrived in December 1967 in the form of a transfer back to Australia, where his unflagging arrogance received a rocket from Lieutenant Colonel Nat Hardcastle, who assigned him command of a national service training company in Singleton. Firmly out in the cold, Young promptly resigned in disgust, and pursued a successful publishing and media career. The Australian Army thus severed the intelligence connections of a man who, however untamed, had in the course of six years insinuated himself into the inner circles of US Army intelligence in South Vietnam.

7 AWM293 [66].

8 Blair, *There to the Bitter End*, p. 165.

9 LBJ Library, National Security File, International Meetings and Travel File, Australian Presidential Trip to Holt Funeral, Assessment of Military Situation in Vietnam — 18 December 1967, Briefing Book, 23 December 1967, Box 20.

10 Dallek, *Lyndon B. Johnson*, p. 315.

11 LBJ Library, National Security File, International Meetings and Travel File, Australian Presidential Trip to Holt Funeral, Assessment of Military Situation in Vietnam — 18 December 1967, Briefing Book, 23 December 1967, Box 20.

12  Behr, *Anyone Here Been Raped and Speaks English?*, p. 245.
13  LBJ Library, National Security File, International Meetings and Travel File, Australian Presidential Trip to Holt Funeral, Sitrep from Rostow to LBJ — 21 December 1967, Briefing Book, 23 December 1967, Box 20.
14  Blair, *There to the Bitter End*, p. 158.
15  Ang Cheng Guan, *The Vietnam War From the Other Side*, p. 117.
16  Karnow, *Vietnam*, p. 18.
17  See Ang Cheng Guan, *The Vietnam War from the Other Side*.
18  Le Duan, *On the Socialist Revolution in Vietnam*.
19  Ang Cheng Guan, *The Vietnam War From the Other Side*, p. 121.
20  Ibid., p. 123.
21  Ibid., p. 125.
22  Sheehan, *A Bright Shining Lie*, p. 643.
23  Edwards, *A Nation at War*, p. 192.
24  AWM PR87/75, Papers of Viet Cong unit (unknown), cable from Westmoreland to Admiral Sharp, 15 January 1968.
25  Ibid.
26  Sheehan, *A Bright Shining Lie*, p. 707. Both Weyand and Wilton believed the war had reached a stalemate; Wilton had thought so as early as mid-1967.
27  O'Brien, *Conscripts and Regulars*, p. 103.
28  Herr, *Dispatches*, p. 90; and AWM107, Interview with Major General Tim Vincent, Army Historical Programme, pp. 46–7.
29  Ibid.
30  Sheehan, *A Bright Shining Lie*.
31  Herr, *Dispatches*, p. 89.
32  Ibid., p. 86.
33  AWM MSS1109, Grey, 'The Ground War in Vietnam: The Post-War Debate' (thesis).
34  AWM107(1), Interview with Major General A. L. MacDonald, 1972, Army Historical Programme.
35  Ibid.
36  Karnow, *Vietnam*, p. 527.
37  Government of the Democratic Republic of Vietnam, *South Viet Nam: A Month of Unprecedented Offensive and Uprising*, p. 15.
38  AWM290 7/18 Part 1 — 7RAR Operation Coburg, January 1968, Contact Report — D Coy Contact on 27 January with C238 VC Bn.
39  Ross Ellis, email, 25 May 2007.
40  Swaysland, notes — 8 Plt C Coy 7 Bn RAR — OPERATION COBURG.
41  M. Moloney, personal papers, notes on his tour with 7RAR — February 1968.
42  Eric Smith, interview, Canberra, 6 Ocober 2006.
43  M. Moloney, personal papers, notes on his tour with 7RAR — 1968; O'Brien, *Conscripts and Regulars*, p. 116.
44  Terry O'Brien, 'My First 24 Hours In Country', 3 February 1968 (unpublished memoir), with diary extracts by Peter McMillan.
45  Ibid.
46  Ibid.
47  Government of the Socialist Republic of Vietnam, *D445: The Heroic Battalion*, p. 76.
48  Coulthard-Clark, *The RAAF in Vietnam*, p. 112.
49  AWM117 [32], Operation in Support of Sector HQ at Baria.
50  AWM98 R698/1/5, Public Relations — General — 3RAR Record of Operation Service in SVN, 1967–68.
51  Government of the Socialist Republic of Vietnam, *D445: The Heroic Battalion*, p. 78.
52  McNeill and Ekins, *On the Offensive*, p. 308.
53  McNeill, *The Team*, p. 138.

54  Ibid.

55  Davies and McKay, *The Men Who Persevered*, pp. 114–15.

56  Sources for the Hué massacre: Sorley, *A Better War*; Lind, *Vietnam — The Necessary War*; Gee, *The Graves of Hué*. The official communist account, *South Viet Nam: A Month of Unprecedented Offensive and Uprising*, fails to mention the atrocity.

57  Gee, *The Graves of Hué*.

58  McNeill, *The Team*, p. 152.

59  Arnett, *Live from the Battlefield*, p. 256.

60  McAulay, *The Battle of Coral*, p. 16.

61  Sheehan, *A Bright Shining Lie*, p. 719.

62  LBJ Library, National Security File, Country File, Vietnam, Allies: Troop Commitments, 1967–69, Box 91.


Chapter 28  **Coral**

 1  John Bullen, personal papers, diary.

 2  Ibid.

 3  LBJ Library, National Security File, Country File, Vietnam, Memo to the President from Walt Rostow, 3 April 1968, 'Australians Unhappy About Late Notification', Box 91 [1 of 2].

 4  LBJ Library, National Security File, Country File, Vietnam, extract from transcript of news from Radio Australia, 1 April 1968, Box 91 [1 of 2].

 5  Phillip Bennett and Jim Shelton, interviews, Canberra, 17 October 2005.

 6  Ibid.

 7  'LRRPs Hit NVA Battalion Near Phu Loi, 10–12 May 1968', F/52 Inf. (LRP), www.1id.army.mil

 8  'A Closer Look at US–Australian Operations in the Vietnam War: Operation Toan Thang I and the Defense of Fire Support Base Coral, April–June 1968', www.flagsys.com/vietnam/phuloi-battle.htm

 9  Geoff Cohen, personal papers, notes on Coral and Balmoral, letter, 19 January 2006.

10  Jim Shelton, interview, Canberra, 17 October 2005.

11  Ibid.

12  McNeill and Ekins, *On the Offensive*, p. 358.

13  McAulay, *The Battle of Coral*, p. 36.

14  Ibid., p. 54.

15  Ibid., p. 39.

16  McNeill and Ekins, *On the Offensive*, p. 362.

17  McAulay, *The Battle of Coral*, p. 57.

18  The 165th and 141st regiments of the People's Army of Vietnam, respectively.

19  Gordon Alexander, personal communication.

20  Ahearn, 'Attack on 13th May 68: A Short History of 102 Battery', p. 16.

21  McAulay, *The Battle of Coral*, p. 72.

22  Ibid., p. 89.

23  Ibid., p. 93.

24  Manchester, *American Caesar*, p. 833.

25  Gordon Alexander, personal communication.

26  5 Platoon, Bravo Company, 1RAR.

27  Norden, DCM Citation, AWM Honour Roll.

28  3 Platoon, Alpha Company, 1RAR.

29  Ahearn, 'Attack on 13th May 68: A Short History of 102 Battery'.

30  Roger Wilson, interview, Witta, Qld, 19 August 2005, and diary (personal papers).

31  Wilson was later made an honourable member of the 1st Battalion — a rare compliment from the army to the RAAF.

32  Weekes, FSPB 'CORAL', email, 9 August 2006.

33 Adamson, personal papers, article on CORAL, email, 19 October 2005.

34 Phil Davies, email, 16 June 2006.

35 AWM107(2), Interview with Brigadier Phillip Bennett, 11 March 1977, Army Historical Programme.

36 Adamson, personal papers, article on CORAL, email, 19 October 2005.

37 Wally Thompson, interview, 21 June 2006.

38 McAulay, *The Battle of Coral*, p. 172.

39 Adamson, personal papers, article on CORAL, email, 19 October 2005.

40 John Dellaca, interview, 2005.

41 McKay, *Bullets, Beans and Bandages*, pp. 196–8.

42 AWM PR00076, Papers of Dr D. Beard (Colonel).

43 Ibid.

## Chapter 29 **Balmoral**

1 Jim Shelton, interview, Canberra, 17 October 2005.

2 McNeill and Ekins, *On the Offensive*, p. 382.

3 Geoff Cohen, personal papers, notes on Coral and Balmoral; letter, 19 January 2006.

4 McNeill and Ekins, *On the Offensive*, p. 384.

5 McAulay, *The Battle of Coral*, p. 243.

6 Gordon Alexander, personal communication.

7 McNeill and Ekins, *On the Offensive*, p. 387.

8 McAulay, *The Battle of Coral*, p. 249.

9 Delta Company, 3RAR.

10 McAulay, *The Battle of Coral*, p. 283. In recent years a Vietnam veteran called Brian Cleaver has been trying to locate the mass grave of North Vietnamese soldiers buried on 28 May 1968. A dig at the likely spot in May 2005 yielded nothing, and Cleaver conjectured that the families of the dead may have moved the remains to a burial ground designated for the Heroes of Vietnam.

11 John Bullen, personal papers, diary.

12 AWM107(1), Interview with Major General A. L. MacDonald, 1972, Army Historical Programme.

13 LBJ Library, White House Central File CO18 7/7/67–7/31/68, letter from Chairman of Joint Chiefs of Staff to LBJ, 29 May 1968, Box 15; see also National Security File, Country File, Vietnam, Memo for the President, 29 May 1968, Box 91 [1 of 2].

14 McAulay, *The Battle of Coral*, p. 319.

15 Phillip Bennett, email, 28 May 2007.

16 Gration, 'A Comparison of Strategies in the Vietnam War', May 1968 (essay).

17 Ibid.

18 Phillip Bennett, email, 28 May 2007.

## Chapter 30 **The air war**

1 Hans Roser, interview, Canberra, 21 October 2005.

2 Lindsay Naylor, email, 10 October 2005.

3 Hans Roser, interview, Canberra, 21 October 2005.

4 Ibid.

5 Ibid.

6 Smith, RAAF FAC History, www.fac-assoc.org; see also Coulthard-Clark, *Hit My Smoke!*; and Harrison, M., *A Lonely Kind of War*.

7 This brief history of napalm is drawn from *Encyclopaedia Britannica*, and from Lumsden, *Incendiary Weapons*.

8 Wells, *The War Within*, p. 84; *Ladies Home Journal*, Fall 1966.

9 Many other uses of napalm were proposed: the Nobel Prize-winning author John Steinbeck recommended in 1966 that the US Army equip its troops with 'napalm grenades' — packed with jellied petroleum — which he nicknamed the 'Steinbeck Super Ball'. One of America's

(arguably) greatest writers reckoned napalm grenades 'the natural weapon for the Americans' because US troops excelled at throwing baseballs. Valenti and McNamara showed interest, but did not pursue the idea. (LBJ Library, White House Central File, Confidential File, Memo from Jack Valenti to McNamara, 14 January 1966, Box 71 [1 of 2].) Incidentally, in the Australian tradition of making a joke of the most serious issue, the diggers in Vietnam nicknamed an army cook 'Napalm' because he burned everything.

10  Chong, *The Girl in the Picture*, which tells the full story of Kim Phuc.

11  Ibid., p. 364.

12  Sheehan, *A Bright Shining Lie*, p. 618.

13  Middleton, *Air War — Vietnam*.

14  Cameron, *Witness*.

15  For the detailed history of the air war, see Coulthard-Clark's *RAAF in Vietnam*; Stephens's *The Royal Australian Air Force*; and Eather's *Target Charlie*. My aim is simply to give the general reader a broad understanding of the Australian involvement in the US-led air war in Vietnam.

16  Coulthard-Clark, *The RAAF in Vietnam*, p. 50.

17  Ibid., p. 50.

18  Ibid., p. 192.

19  Ibid., p. 196.

20  Wing Commanders Rolf Aronsen, Selwyn Evans, John Whitehead, Jack Boast, Francis Downing and Thomas Thorpe.

21  Coulthard-Clark, *The RAAF in Vietnam*, p. 209.

22  Ibid., p. 211.

23  Ibid., p. 149.

24  Coulthard-Clark gives a thorough account of the dispute.

25  Coulthard-Clark, *The RAAF in Vietnam*, p. 157.

26  Bob Grandin, interview.

27  Alan Kitchen, notes; see also www.diggerhistory.info for Skippy Squadron.

28  AWM 107, Interview with Major General A. L. MacDonald, 1972, Army Historical Programme, p. 24.

29  Coulthard-Clark, *The RAAF in Vietnam*, p. 77.

30  Stephens, *The Royal Australian Air Force*, p. 264.

31  Ibid., p. 266.

32  Eric Smith, interview, Canberra, 6 October 2005.

33  Roger Wilson, interview, Witta, Qld, 19 August 2005. One No. 9 Squadron commander, Nick LeRay-Meyer, sought to undo the damage. 'I could see where the air force had gone wrong,' he said. 'I was determined to fight it: the army were hard done by. The poor buggers were out there all the time. I'd arrive in a beautifully pressed suit smelling of aftershave' (Nick LeRay-Meyer, interview, Melbourne, 21 August 2005).

34  The air commodores in Vietnam were J. Dowling, J. F. Lush, G. T. Newstead, F. S. Robey, C. H. Spurgeon and N. P. McNamara.

35  Coulthard-Clark, *The RAAF in Vietnam*, p. 83.

36  Ibid., p. 86.

37  Indeed, in 2005 Nick LeRay-Meyer, as No. 9 Squadron Association's national president, commissioned a full analysis of helo operations in Vietnam.

38  LBJ Library, CIA Intelligence Memorandum: An Appraisal of the Bombing of North Vietnam, 20 June 1966, Directorate of Intelligence, Central Intelligence Agency. In fact, LeMay's air war even failed to destroy the critical Viet Cong supply lines — and not only because communist forces used extensive tunnels and jungle cover. Nearly 80 per cent of supplies entered South Vietnam via the Cambodian port of Sihanoukville, according to intelligence gathered in Cambodia in 1970. From 1968, the Ho Chi Minh Trail was not, in fact, the key source of supplies. The Pentagon had been 'dead wrong for years about the flow patterns of supplies', wrote Frank Snepp, a former CIA agent in Saigon (Snepp, *Decent Interval*, p. 31).

39  Thompson, *No Exit From Vietnam*.
40  Sheehan, *A Bright Shining Lie*, p. 533.
41  Lind, *Vietnam — The Necessary War*, p. 252.
42  Hans Roser, interview, Canberra, 21 October 2005.
43  Komer, *Bureaucracy at War*.
44  Sheehan, *A Bright Shining Lie*, p. 619.
45  Hans Roser, interview, Canberra, 21 October 2005.
46  Karnow, *Vietnam*, p. 509.
47  Thompson, *No Exit From Vietnam*, p. 135.

## Chapter 31 **The press offensive**

1  Tiffen, 'News coverage', in Tiffen and Goot (eds), *Australia's Gulf War*, p. 177.
2  Hallin, *The Uncensored War*, p. 168.
3  AWM PR89/104, Papers of Lieutenant Colonel Peter Murray.
4  Brigadier Colin Khan DSO, address to United Services Club, Brisbane, 18 August 1992.
5  Cited by Knightley, *The First Casualty*, p. 402. Among the fifty or so reporters who redeemed the media's reputation must surely be listed the Americans David Halberstam, Charles Mohr, Neil Sheehan, Malcolm Browne, Frances FitzGerald and Stanley Karnow; the Australians Denis Warner, Murray Sayle, Pat Burgess, Neil Davis, Denis Gibbons and Richard Hughes; the Britons Jon Swain, James Cameron; the New Zealanders Kate Webb and Peter Arnett (the longest serving foreign correspondent in Vietnam); the Frenchwoman Catherine Leroy; and of course the great French-American Bernard Fall, who died in Vietnam and left the finest written legacy of the war.
6  LBJ Library, White House Central File, Confidential File, letter from Jack Valenti to LBJ, 10 December 1965, Box 71 [1 of 2].
7  Arnett, *Live from the Battlefield*, pp. 75–7.
8  AWM107(1), Interview with Major General C. A. E. Fraser, March 1974, Army Historical Programme.
9  McHugh, *Minefields and Miniskirts*, pp. 29–35.
10  Cited by Knightley, *The First Casualty*, p. 408.
11  Ibid., pp. 419–20.
12  Terry O'Brien, interview, Ballarat, 23 August 2005.
13  Denis Gibbons, interviews, 28–29 December 2005.
14  Westmoreland, *A Soldier Reports*.
15  AWM PR87/084, Papers of Lieutenant Colonel L. B. Swifte — Army Public Relations Unit, Headquarters, United States Military Assistance Command, Vietnam, MACV Directive Number 360-1, 29 March 1967.
16  Ibid.
17  Arnett, *Live from the Battlefield*, pp. 75–7.
18  Hammond, *Reporting Vietnam*, p. 68.
19  Quoted in ibid.
20  AWM PR87/084, Papers of Lieutenant Colonel L. B. Swifte — Army Public Relations Unit, News Media Representatives' Agreement before Entering Australian Areas.
21  Quoted in Burstall, *A Soldier Returns*, p. 188.
22  D. Wilkins, 'A Vietnam Diary', (unpublished memoir).
23  Ibid.
24  Cited by Knightley, *The First Casualty*, p. 396.
25  Herr, *Dispatches*, p. 173.
26  Cited by Knightley, *The First Casualty*, p. 396.
27  Ibid., p. 397.
28  Arnett was as 'hard-boiled as a Chinese thousand-year-old egg', concluded the author Marina Warner. He admitted as much: rather than try to prevent a Buddhist monk from incinerating

himself, Arnett stood by and photographed the monk catching fire, then rushed off to his office to file the story: 'As a human being, I wanted to [save the monk]; as a reporter, I couldn't' (Knightley, *The First Casualty*, p. 406).

29  Knightley, *The First Casualty*, p. 397.

30  Brian McFarlane, interview, Bowral, 31 August 2005.

31  Gee, *The Graves of Hué*, pp. 67–8.

32  McNeill, *To Long Tan*, p. 396.

33  Ibid., pp. 396–8.

34  As confirmed by Lieutenant Colonel Nguyen Van Kiem, former commanding officer of D445 Battalion, in an interview with Ian McNeill on 18 June 1988 in Vung Tau.

35  Payne, *War and Words*, p. 218; see pp. 197–240 for Payne's full account.

36  McNeill, *To Long Tan*, p. 398.

37  Payne, *War and Words*, pp. 197–240.

38  AWM PR91/114, Papers of G. Carpay, freelance photographer, 4 October 1966.

39  'Johnson Accused: Betrand Russell's Indictment of the Vietnam War Criminals', pamphlet published by the Vietnam Action Committee, Sydney.

40  Edwards, *A Nation at War*, pp. 208–11.

41  AWM PR87/084, Papers of Lieutenant Colonel L. B. Swifte — Army Public Relations Unit, 'How Aussies Behave in Vietnam', *Life*, 1 April 1968.

42  AWM MSS1009, York, 'Sources of Student Unrest in Australia with Particular Reference to La Trobe University, 1967–72' (MA thesis, University of Sydney, 1983).

43  Hallin, *The Uncensored War*, p. 3. Television found much air-time for such heroes as Hal Moore, hero of the battle of Ia Drang (on whose book Mel Gibson's film *We Were Soldiers* is based). Hal described his men at the time as 'the greatest soldiers in the world. In fact, they're the greatest men in the world … They came over here to win' (Hallin, *The Uncensored War*, p. 138).

44  Sources: Brigadier Phil Greville, 'Traitor', *Weekend Bulletin*, 3–4 December 2005; Red Harrison, 'Flesh on the Bones of Wilfred Burchett', *Weekend Australian*, 28–29 May 1988; Kane, *Exploding the Myths: The Political Memoirs of Jack Kane*; Tibor Meray, 'My Memoirs of Wilfred Burchett' (unpublished); Roland Perry, 'How the KGB Used Wilfred Burchett', *Age*, 6 March 1993; Russell Spurr, 'Wilfred Burchett: The View From the Other Side', *Times on Sunday*, 27 September 1987. Burchett's books (e.g. *Vietnam — Inside Story of the Guerrilla War* and *Vietnam Will Win!*) are prescient and well written but also riddled with communist agitprop.

45  Sorley, *A Better War*, p. 159.

46  Woodruff, *Unheralded Victory*, p. 258. Intriguingly, the harshest critics of the media's performance in Vietnam have come from academic circles. Australian reporting of the war was 'overwhelmingly timid' and 'deplorably inferior' to its US counterpart, claimed Rodney Tiffen ('News coverage', in Tiffen and Goot (eds), *Australia's Gulf War*, p. 187). Peter King reached the same conclusion; in his view, the Australian media utterly failed 'to cover the "other war" — the … struggle for the villages and the souls of the Vietnamese people' (*Australia's Vietnam*, p. 16).

## Chapter 32 **Body count**

1  AWM103 R723/1/51 Part 2, Reports — General — Monthly Statistical Report.

2  McNeill and Ekins, *On the Offensive*, pp. 411–12.

3  Kinnard, *The War Managers*, p. 69.

4  Fall, *Viet-Nam Witness*, p. 265.

5  Ang Cheng Guan, *The Vietnam War From the Other Side*, p. 112.

6  AWM103 R723/1/39/1, MACV Quarterly Summary Reports, 1969.

7  Working through an example: the Enemy Net Loss (ENL) equalled the Enemy Gross Adjusted Loss (EGAL) minus the total Enemy Replacement Rate (ERR). To find the EGAL the Americans deducted 5 per cent from the total enemy KIA in South Vietnam, 'to reflect kidnapped and recruited labourers', then added 35 per cent to the result to account for those who became 'permanently disabled or died of wounds' (DOW). To the total were added

prisoners of war and Hoi Chanh (surrendering enemy troops), thus arriving at the EGAL, which excluded those killed or wounded in artillery or air strikes, as they were impossible to estimate. The EGAL in the second quarter of 1969, for example, was 27,163 (assuming 17,423 KIA and 6,098 DOW). The total Enemy Replacement Rate (ERR) simply added reinforcements (a mere 1,125) and members of new units identified (445) to the total number of enemy infiltrators (North Vietnamese troops entering South Vietnam; i.e. 23,900 in the second quarter, 1969). The ERR for the second quarter 1969 was 25,470. Thus the Enemy Net Loss (ENL) in that period equalled 1,693 soldiers (AWM103 R723/1/39/1, MACV Quarterly Summary Reports, 1969).

8  Lewy, *America in Vietnam*, p. 79.
9  Kinnard, *The War Managers*, pp. 74–5.
10 Thompson, *No Exit from Vietnam*, p. 137.
11 Maclear, *Vietnam*, p. 165.
12 Thompson, *No Exit from Vietnam*, p. 145.
13 Charlton and Moncrieff, *Many Reasons Why*, p. 144.
14 Komer, *Bureaucracy at War*, p. 61.
15 Karnow, *Vietnam*, p. 18.
16 Kinnard, *The War Managers*, pp. 74–5.
17 With the exception of a few battalion commanders — notably Lieutenant Colonel Ron Grey — Australian officers rarely challenged the US system openly. Some, however, wrote down their feelings. In 1968 the intelligence officer John Rowe published *Count Your Dead*, a novel that indicted the senseless destruction and US obsession with body count. And others proposed different tactical methods. As early as 1966 the Australian intelligence officer Robert O'Neill showed the efficacy of measuring the progress of the war according to the number of Viet Cong 'removed per day of operational time' (i.e. detained or captured). This implied the Australian tactical methods of cordon and search of villages (and *not* their destruction), which proved remarkably successful at gaining village loyalties, flushing out enemy elements and saving lives. In five cordon and searches in 1966–67 the Australians lost one dead with none wounded, for 16 Viet Cong killed, 47 captured and 112 suspects taken (O'Neill, *Vietnam Task*, pp. 187–9). Yet the tactical priority of *protecting* over *destroying* gained little traction in the US war until 1969, when it was too late.
18 AWM107, Interview with Major General Tim Vincent, 1972, Army Historical Programme, pp. 23 and 44. In July 1967 Vincent submitted a Task Force 'kill ratio chart' to Lieutenant General Tom Daly with the rider that 'we do not measure overall success by body count kills'; securing the population was also 'important' (McNeill and Ekins, *On the Offensive*, p. 412).
19 Horner, *SAS: Phantoms of War*, p. 230.
20 In mid-1967 the SAS adjusted its methods: it sought to capture, not to kill, the Viet Cong, for the simple reason that a live enemy was a better source of intelligence than a dead one. In 1967 Australian SAS went to 'the most ludicrous' efforts to capture the enemy, as one soldier remarked: 'You never knew whether the man you had selected to capture was the Far East karate champion or the fastest draw in the North Vietnamese army' (Horner, *SAS: Phantoms of War*, p. 219). Very few were captured. 'We failed to take even one prisoner alive,' remarked Kevin Bovill of his unit. Frank Cashmore captured three enemy troops in the course of his two tours.
21 King (ed.), *Australia's Vietnam*, p. 80.
22 Cited in Horner, *SAS: Phantoms of War*, p. 235.
23 Cited in ibid.
24 AWM MSS1431, Poems, A. W. Pahl, ex-helicopter gunner, 9 Squadron RAAF.
25 When the dust-off medic, Sergeant Neville Cullen, of the 8th Field Ambulance, arrived in Vietnam in 1971, he found that few dust-off pilots were prepared to fly into combat zones. One reason that year was the loss of their colleague Corporal John Gillespie, who died trapped in a burning helicopter. Cullen promptly volunteered to fly the missions, and others soon followed. Cullen later trained with US dust-off teams, and was recommended for a Bronze Star, which

the Australian Government refused to allow because the action happened over Cambodia. Cullen is the only Australian Life Member of the American Dust-off Association.

26  McKay, *Bullets, Beans and Bandages*, p. 12.

27  Rintoul, *Ashes of Vietnam*, p. 70.

28  Barr, *Surgery, Sand and Saigon Tea*, p. 226.

29  Ibid., p. 231.

30  AWM PR00076, Papers of Dr D. Beard (Colonel).

31  Ibid.

32  Ibid.

33  Ibid. Disease exacted a far greater casualty rate than combat. During the war, Vietnam was one of the world's most infectious environments. Safe water supplies and effective sanitation systems were rare, and the list of 'exotic' illnesses included shigella dysentery, scrub typhus, Japanese B encephalitis and amoebic liver abscesses. During the war, malaria afflicted 933 Australian soldiers; gastrointestinal diseases 1,422; skin diseases 1,139; psychiatric illnesses 499; and sexually transmitted diseases an astonishing 11,384 (O'Keefe and Smith, *Medicine at War*, p. 399). Malaria did more to reduce combat strength than any other disease. In October 1968, the incidence of malaria in Nui Dat was higher 'than it has ever been', noted a report on the malaria 'epidemic' (AWM290 4/R515/1/2, Medical Diseases — General, Report on a visit by Colonel M. M. Lewis, Director of Army Health, to the Australian Forces, Vietnam, 15–22 October 1968). The parasite became resistant to Paludrine, so the Task Force used a cocktail of dapsone and Paludrine, which, along with mandatory sprays, nets, swing-fog machines and mosquito-proof jungle greens, kept the rate well below the hyperendemic levels of World War II.

34  AWM117 [82], After-action Report, OPERATION MARSDEN.

35  Interviews with civilian nurses, Sydney, 20 July 2005.

36  Barbara Ferguson, interview, Sydney, 5 September 2005.

37  Brass, *Bleeding Earth*, p. 18.

38  Ibid., p. 19.

39  AWM PR89/100, Papers of Dr Graham Wilson.

40  Ibid.

41  AWM PR00202, Papers of Dr B. L. Dunn (Major).

42  Brass, *Bleeding Earth*, pp. 65–6.

43  World Health Organisation, *The Republic of Viet-Nam — South Vietnam*, January 1968.

44  Papers of June Allen, Team Leader's Report (3/10/67–15/4/68), Long Xuyen, NSW Hospital Commission Team, p. 3.

45  Brass, *Bleeding Earth*, p. 31.

46  Interviews with civilian nurses, Sydney, 20 July 2005.

47  Brass, *Bleeding Earth*, pp. 31–2.

48  Ibid.

49  June Allen, personal papers, Team Leader's Report, 3/10/67–15/4/68, Long Xuyen, NSW Hospital Commission Team, p. 4.

50  Evans, *Caduceus in Saigon*, p. 50.

51  Brass, *Bleeding Earth*, pp. 55–7. A saving grace was a drop in the infant mortality rate, from 46.6 per cent in 1956 to a barely merciful 35–6 per cent, between 1958 and 1965; further falls occurred between 1966 and 1973.

52  Wyllie, 'Australian surgical teams in Vietnam', letter to *Daily Telegraph*, 24 November 1966.

53  Terry, *House of Love*, p. 340.

54  The story of which is recorded in Peter Eccles-Smith's book *Letters From a Viet-Nam Hospital*.

55  Brass, *Bleeding Earth*, p. 28.

56  *Say a Prayer for Me — The Chaplains of the Vietnam War* (video).

57  AWM PR00032, Papers of A. Treffry.

58  Lifton, *Home from the War*, pp. 163–4.

59  Terry Cobby, personal papers.

60  Rintoul, *Ashes of Vietnam*.

61  Michael Bindley, email, 11 May 2006.

62  Ibid.

63  AWM PR00341, Papers of T. W. Pracy, No. 9 Squadron RAAF.

64  AWM290, Accidents, Deaths and Casualties — Personnel — General.

65  AWM290 4/R237/1/15, Correspondence — General — Letters of Condolence.

66  AWM290 2/R237/1/1 Part 1, Correspondence — General — Letters of Condolence.

67  AWM290 4/R478/1/21, Investigations — General.

68  Rintoul, *Ashes of Vietnam*, pp. 105–6.

69  Ibid.

70  AWM PR89/104, Papers of Lieutenant Colonel Peter Murray.

Chapter 33  **A politicians' war**

1  Hancock, *John Gorton*, pp. 173–4.

2  Reid, *The Gorton Experiment*, p. 11.

3  LBJ Library, National Security File, Country File, Asia and the Pacific, Australia, Visit of PM Gorton, May 27–28, 1968, Box 234.

4  LBJ Library, National Security File, Country File, Asia and the Pacific, Australia, Visit of PM Gorton of Australia, May 27–28, Memo to Secretary Rusk from Winthrop Brown, 23 May 1968, Box 234.

5  LBJ Library, National Security File, Country File, Asia and the Pacific, Australia, Visit of PM Gorton of Australia, May 27–28, 1968, Scope Paper, 22 May 1968, Box 234.

6  LBJ Library, National Security File, Country File, Asia and the Pacific, Australia, Visit of PM Gorton of Australia, May 27–28, Memo to Secretary Rusk from Winthrop Brown, 23 May 1968, Box 234.

7  Ibid.

8  LBJ Library, National Security File, Country File, Asia and the Pacific, Australia, Visit of PM Gorton of Australia, May 27–28, Memo to the President from Dean Rusk, 24 May 1968, Box 234.

9  LBJ Library, National Security File, Country File, Asia and the Pacific, Australia, Visit of PM Gorton of Australia, May 27–28, Press release: Exchange of Toasts Between the President and Prime Minister John Gorton of Australia, State Dining Room, White House, Washington DC, 27 May 1968, Box 34.

10  LBJ Library, National Security File, Country File, Asia and the Pacific, Australia, Visit of PM Gorton of Australia, May 27–28, Suggestions on Approaching Australians, 22 May 1968, Box 234.

11  LBJ Library, National Security File, Country File, Asia and the Pacific, Australia, visit of PM Gorton of Australia, May 27–28, Press release: Exchange of Toasts Between the President and Prime Minister John Gorton of Australia, State Dining Room, White House, Washington DC, 27 May 1968, Box 34.

12  LBJ Library, National Security File, Country File, Asia and the Pacific, Australia, Visit of PM Gorton of Australia, May 27–28, Joint Communiqué, 27–28 May 1968, Box 234.

13  Reid, *The Gorton Experiment*, p. 57.

14  Editorial, *Daily Telegraph*, 30 May 1968.

15  Editorial, *Australian Financial Review*, 30 May 1968.

16  LBJ Library, National Security File, Country File, Asia and the Pacific, Australia, Memos Vol. 3, 8/67–1/69 [1 of 2], Memorandum of conversation, Miss Ainsley Gotto with John C. Dorrance, 19 June 1968, in cable from American Embassy, Canberra, to Department of State, 5 July 1968, Box 233 [2 of 2].

17  LBJ Library, National Security File, Country File, Asia and the Pacific, Australia, Memos Vol. 3, 8/67–1/69 [1 of 2], Memorandum of conversation, Mr Alan Reid with John C. Dorrance, 18 June 1968, in cable from American Embassy, Canberra, to Department of State, 5 July 1968, Box 233 [2 of 2].

18  LBJ Library, National Security File, Country File, Asia and the Pacific, Australia, Memos Vol. 3, 8/67–1/69 [1 of 2], Memorandum of conversation, Mr A. T. Griffith with John C. Dorrance, 18 June 1968, in cable from American Embassy, Canberra, to Department of State, 5 July 1968, Box 233 [2 of 2].

19  Edwards, *A Nation at War*, p. 198.

20  Quoted in ibid., p. 200.

21  Freudenberg, *A Certain Grandeur*, p. 139.

22  LBJ Library, National Security File, Country File, Asia and the Pacific, Australia, Memos Vol. 3, 8/67–1/69 [1 of 2], Mr Peter Lawler, with John C. Dorrance, 17 June 1968, in cable from American Embassy, Canberra, to Department of State, 5 July 1968, Box 233 [2 of 2].

23  LBJ Library, National Security File, Country File, Asia and the Pacific, Australia, Memos Vol. 3, 8/67–1/69 [1 of 2], Memo from Marshal Wright to Walt Rostow, 13 July 1968, Box 233 [2 of 2].

24  According to Freudenberg's version, LBJ *had* forewarned Gorton, who then angered Washington by absentmindedly leaking the secret, a day before the announcement; the embassy invitation was meant to soothe misunderstandings (*A Certain Grandeur*, p. 145).

25  Hancock, *John Gorton*, p. 215.

26  Ibid., pp. 215–16.

27  Ibid., pp. 219–20.

28  LBJ Library, National Security File, Country File, Asia and the Pacific, Australia, Memos Vol. 3, 8/67–1/69 [1 of 2], Memorandum of conversation, Mr Peter Lawler, Deputy Secretary, Cabinet Office, with John C. Dorrance, Political Officer, American Embassy, Canberra, 17 June 1968, in cable from American Embassy, Canberra, to Department of State, 5 July 1968, Box 233 [2 of 2].

29  LBJ Library, National Security File, Country File, Asia and the Pacific, Australia, Memos Vol. 3, 8/67–1/69 [1 of 2], Memorandum of conversation, Mr A. T. Griffith, Assistant Secretary for Defence and External Relations, Prime Minister's Department, with John C. Dorrance, Political Officer, American Embassy, Canberra, 17 June 1968, in cable from American Embassy, Canberra, to Department of State, 5 July 1968, Box 233 [2 of 2].

30  Reid, *The Gorton Experiment*, p. 87.

31  Freudenberg, *A Certain Grandeur*, p. 124.

32  AWM107(1), Interview with Major General A. L. MacDonald, 1972, Army Historical Programme.

33  AWM107(1), Interview with Major General Tim Vincent, 1972, Army Historical Programme.

34  Hall, *Combat Battalion*, p. 19.

35  Andrews, *The Department of Defence*.

36  Ibid., p. 179.

37  Stevens, *The Royal Australian Navy*, p. 209.

Chapter 34  **Australian Viet Cong**

1  The 'Swinging Sixties' list draws on many sources, chiefly: Marwick, *The Sixties*; Edwards, *A Nation at War*; Pemberton, *Vietnam Remembered*; Langley, *A Decade of Dissent*; King, *Australia's Vietnam*; the BBC and the ABC.

2  Michael Hamel-Green, telephone interview, 16 August 2006.

3  Hughes, *Things I Didn't Know*.

4  Garry MacDougall, response to questionnaire.

5  Joan Coxsedge, response to questionnaire.

6  Dr Meredith Burgmann, interview, Sydney.

7  Hutchinson, *Not Going to Vietnam*, p. 40.

8  Ibid., pp. 42–3.

9  Edwards, *A Nation at War*, p. 7; and Albinski, *Politics and Foreign Policy in Australia*, pp. 114–15. The Australian communists carefully planned this parasitic infiltration of peace organisations. At its 1948 Congress the Communist Party of Australia adopted a policy of 'working through mass

fronts as a means of popular mobilisation' (Murphy, *Harvest of Fear*, p. 56). As early as 1950 Australian Reds were trying to harness anti-nuclear feelings to the communist revolution, argued ex-communist Fred Wells in *The Peace Racket* (1964): '… an atom bomb petition', stated one member of the Central Committee of the Communist Party of Australia in July 1950, '… is the greatest weapon we have yet in bolshevizing the party … our aim must be to merge the Party with this broad mass movement, with our Party acting as its most vigorous fighting core.' The party later ejected the proposer, Jack Blake, for being too moderate (AWM MSS1068, Colebatch 'An Examination of the Sources, Ideologies and Political Importance of Peace Movements in Australia from c. 1950 to 1965', MA thesis, University of Western Australia, 1974). They succeeded: once in the system, the communists refused to allow peace groups to make any public statement that criticised the policies of the Soviet Union, China or other communist country. Note the deafening silence of the Australian Peace Council over the Soviet invasion of Hungary, which most Australian communists defended. Peace activists were thus anointed as Stalin's stooges. In March 1965 Australia's home-grown Bolsheviks sent a delegation to a 'Consultative Meeting of Representatives of Communist and Workers' Parties' in Moscow. They returned with 'instructions' from the Kremlin to 'allot the highest priority to the campaign against the United States presence and activities in Vietnam'. The meeting called for 'the international solidarity with the fraternal people of the DRV [North Vietnam] with the heroic Working People's Party of Vietnam and with the National Liberation Front of South Vietnam' (Findlay, *Protest Politics and Psychological Warfare*, pp. 12–13). Within a month of their return they activated these instructions: 'Australian communists will respond to the Moscow meeting's appeal and work for communist unity by acting yet more vigorously to defend world peace, supporting Vietnam and opposing US imperialism and Australian Government policies in South East Asia' (*Tribune*, 7 April 1965).

10  Findlay, *Protest Politics and Psychological Warfare*, p. 23.
11  Edwards, *A Nation at War*, p. 72.
12  NAA A1838 563/20 Part 3, Wednesday Commentary — 'Medi-Cong', Sydney University ALP Club, 2 March 1966, Vol. 2, No. 1; see also Breen, *First to Fight*, p. 216.
13  Albinski, *Politics and Foreign Policy in Australia*, pp. 151–2.
14  Langley, *A Decade of Dissent*, p. 89.
15  *Age*, 12 July 1969.
16  *Age*, 9 July 1969.
17  Findlay, *Protest Politics and Psychological Warfare*, p. 33.
18  Ibid., p. 51.
19  Langley, *A Decade of Dissent*, p. 116.
20  AWM MSS1009, York, 'Sources of Student Unrest in Australia with Particular Reference to La Trobe University, 1967–72' (MA thesis, University of Sydney, 1983).
21  Extracts from ASIO dossier on the ABC and dossier on Roger Milliss.
22  AWM MSS1068, Colebatch, 'An Examination of the Sources, Ideologies and Political Importance of Peace Movements in Australia from c. 1950 to 1965' (MA thesis, University of Western Australia, 1974).
23  See Noone, *Disturbing the War: Melbourne Catholics and Vietnam*.
24  Dr W. E. Murray, *Australian*, 1 May 1965.
25  Edwards, *A Nation at War*.
26  Ibid., p. 228.
27  Hamel-Green, 'The resisters: A history of the anti-conscription movement, 1964–1972'.
28  Curthoys, 'Mobilising Dissent', in Pemberton, *Vietnam Remembered*, p. 151.
29  Ibid.
30  Edwards, *A Nation at War*, p. 182.
31  Hancock, *John Gorton*, pp. 224–5.
32  Gorton's actual words were: 'Australian support would be at hand wherever the United States is resisting aggression, wherever the United States or the United Kingdom or any other country

was seeking to ensure that there will be a chance for free expression. Wherever there is a joint attempt to improve, not only the material but the spiritual standards of life of the peoples of the world, then, sir, we will go Waltzing Matilda with you' (ibid., p. 225). Waltzing with America delivered little, however, in the way of significant economic benefits to Australia. America never relaxed its tariffs on Australian goods. Asked in December 1969 whether the two countries felt economic friction, Sir Keith Waller, then Australian Ambassador to Washington, replied: 'Oh yes, very much so … You've had your high tariff on wool of course, for many, many years … It's roughly 50 cents a pound … No other industrial country in the world has a tariff of this magnitude, and so we've long made representations on that, without any great success … Most of our meat exports consist of lean meat … It's chopped up and … used in hamburgers and things … We contend that you have a shortage [the Americans admitted this]. We have a surplus, and we feel we should get better access to the American markets than we do … We don't think that's particularly fair' (LBJ Memorial Library, Sir Keith Waller, Interview, 1 December 1969.)

33  Freudenberg, *A Certain Grandeur*, pp. 167–9.
34  Greene, *The Quiet American*, p. 54.

## Chapter 35 **Accelerated pacification**

1  Sorley, *A Better War*, p. 56.
2  Record, 'How America's Own Military Performance in Vietnam Aided and Abetted the "North's" Victory', in Gilbert, *Why the North Won the Vietnam War*, p. 124.
3  Sorley, *A Better War*.
4  AWM PR83/227, Papers of Major E. M. McCormick, Unit Leader's Personal Response Handbook, Fleet Marine Force, Pacific 1968, with Foreword by Victor Krulak, Lieutenant General US Marine Corps.
5  Herr, *Dispatches*, p. 17.
6  Ibid., p. 173.
7  Many American commanders (if not their junior officers) did embrace pacification. They set up a Hamlet Evaluation System, which monitored the progress of hamlet security (by 1969, 92 per cent of South Vietnamese were said to be living in hamlets judged 'relatively secure', according to US computers); rehoused refugees, and returned a quarter of a million people to their villages. MACV pressed President Thieu to introduce land reforms — in 1970 tenancy ended, and 500,000 families received parcels of land (reversing, belatedly, Diem's disastrous land expropriation). All this paid political dividends. 'By 1972,' CIA chief William Colby wrote, 'the pacification program had … eliminated the guerrilla problems in most of the country.' Unfortunately, pacification started to succeed just as the Americans were preparing to withdraw (Sorley, *A Better War*, p. 305).
8  AWM MSS1109, Grey, 'The Ground War in Vietnam: Some aspects of the post-war debate' (BA Hons thesis, ANU, 1982), p. 19.
9  CORDS did attempt to integrate the military and political offensives. It was a 'unique experiment', said Komer, the first time the American civilian and military were bound together in a civic aid campaign. It employed 6,500 US military advisers — half the total advisers in Vietnam — at its peak. It was flexible and responsive, yet all too late to change the direction of the war.
10 Komer, *The Komer Report*, 1966, Introduction.
11 Gilbert, *Why the North Won the Vietnam War*, p. 175.
12 These conclusions are drawn chiefly from the work of Robert O'Neill, Carter Malksian and Daniel Marston, who greatly enlarge on the theme of American reluctance to apply pacification techniques.
13 Hall, *Combat Battalion*, p. 32.
14 Lewy, *America in Vietnam*, p. 82.
15 Hall, *Combat Battalion*, p. 32.

16  Ibid., pp. 35–6.

17  Ibid., p. 33.

18  Ibid., p. 36.

19  Grey, *The Australian Army*, p. 220.

20  AWM103 R719/1/1/2, 'The Role of the Australian in Vietnam' (lecture series), Annex A to HQ AFV, 23 December 1967, Suggested topics [for talks to Troops].

21  McNeill, *The Team*, p. 233. Adding to the confusion were those two terms: 'Civil Affairs' and 'Civic Action'. Civil Affairs was the departmental name as well as referring to the broad structural relationship between the military, the local authorities and the people; civic action was the actual process of distributing aid, building infrastructure and so on.

22  Frost, *Australia's War in Vietnam*, p. 172.

23  Peter Gration, interview, Canberra, 2005; and McNeill and Ekins, *On the Offensive*, p. 191.

24  McNeill and Ekins, *On the Offensive*, p. 190.

25  Ibid., p. 196.

26  For example OPERATIONS REYNELLA, NEPPABUNNA, MUNDINGBURRA.

27  AWM290 4/R4/2/7, Miscellaneous Documents about Background to Villages, Australian Military Forces 1ATF Provincial Data Handbook, Phuoc Tuy province and Long Thanh district, 10 August 1970.

28  Ibid.

29  AWM103 R723/1/12/1, Reports — General — Civic Action Report October–December 1969.

30  O'Brien, *Conscripts and Regulars*, p. 170.

31  AWM288 [106], 1 Aust Civil Affairs Unit, Nui Dat, 5RAR Civic Action Project.

32  AWM103 R723/1/12/2, Civic Action Monthly Reports, AFV Civil Affairs Monthly Report, May 1970.

33  McNeill and Ekins, *On the Offensive*, p. 195.

34  Peter Gration, interview, Canberra, 2005.

35  Elderly Vietnamese peasant, interviewed during tour of Phuoc Tuy, November 2005.

36  Coulthard-Clark, *The RAAF in Vietnam*, p. 310; for details of the RAAF's civic action program, see pp. 299–317.

37  AWM PR02075, Papers of Chaplain Pat McCormick.

38  Ibid.

39  AWM103 R723/1/12/2, Civic Action Monthly Reports, AFV Civil Affairs Monthly Report, May 1970.

40  Government of the Socialist Republic of Vietnam, *D445: The Heroic Battalion*, pp. 99–100.

41  Derrill de Heer, interview, Canberra, 18 October 2005.

42  AWM290 3/R723/1/3, Reports General — 1ATF Psy Ops (Monthly Report).

43  Schell, *The Village of Ben Suc*, pp. 15–16.

44  AWM290 3/R723/1/3, Reports General — 1ATF Psy Ops (Monthly Report).

45  Herr, *Dispatches*, p. 49.

46  AWM103 R723/1/12/2, Civic Action Monthly Reports, AFV Civil Affairs Monthly Report, May 1970.

47  AWM 290 4/R4/2/7, Miscellaneous Documents about Background to Villages, Australian Military Forces 1ATF Provincial Data Handbook, Phuoc Tuy province and Long Thanh district, 10 August 1970.

48  Bushby, 'Educating an Army', Canberra Papers on Strategy and Defence, No. 126, p. 87.

49  AWM 290 4/R4/2/7, Miscellaneous Documents about Background to Villages, Australian Military Forces 1ATF Provincial Data Handbook, Phuoc Tuy province and Long Thanh district, 10 August 1970.

50  Grey, *The Australian Army*, p. 220.

51  Carter Malkasian, email, 13 October 2005.

52  Komer, *The Komer Report*, 1966, Introduction, p. 14.

53  Brass, *Bleeding Earth*, p. 16.

54  McNeill, *The Team*, p. 245.

55  Rintoul, *Ashes of Vietnam*, p. 69.

56  AWM PR00331, Papers of Lieutenant B. L. Smith.

57  Ross, 'Australian Soldiers in Vietnam: Product and Performance', in King, *Australia's Vietnam*, p. 82.

## Chapter 36  Binh Ba

 1  Bushby, 'Educating an Army', Canberra Papers on Strategy and Defence, No 126, p. 59.

 2  AWM290 5/R841/1/40 Part 3, Joint Exercise Nulla Nulla, Shoalwater Bay.

 3  AWM290 [9/27], 9RAR Instructions, HMAS *Sydney*, Executive Officer's Temporary Memorandum, No 84/68.

 4  McAulay, *In the Ocean's Dark Embrace*.

 5  AWM PR00330, Papers of David Keating.

 6  9RAR Association, *9 Battalion, The Royal Australian Regiment*, p. 46.

 7  AWM 4/R569/1/39(A), Operations General — OPERATION GOODWOOD — After-action Report, 10 March 1969.

 8  Philip Ham '25 Years On — Recollections of a National Serviceman, 1968–1970' (personal memoir).

 9  AWM279 723/R5/56, 5RAR Combat After-action Report 3/69, Unit After-action Reports 5RAR and 9RAR — OPERATIONS SURFSIDE and GOODWOOD.

10  AWM PR00330, Papers of David Keating.

11  Herr, *Dispatches*, p. 55.

12  M. Blake, personal papers, notes on the Battle of Binh Ba, June 1969, email, 3 January 2007.

13  This account of the battle draws on the following sources: Sandy Pearson, interview; Colin Khan, interview; Murray Blake, email; Ray de Vere, interview; David Wilkins, 'A Vietnam Diary' (unpublished memoir); Brian London, 'The Battle of Binh Ba: A Platoon's View', www.5rar.asn.au; Bill O'Mara, interview; A. Burke, 'The Battle of Binh Ba', www.anzacday.org.au; *Ironsides*; and several unit after-action reports.

14  Sandy Pearson, interview, Sydney, 14 September 2006.

15  M. Blake, notes on the Battle of Binh Ba, June 1969, email, 3 January 2007.

16  London, 'The Battle of Binh Ba: A Platoon's View', www.anzacday.org.au

17  M. Blake, notes on the Battle of Binh Ba, June 1969, email, 3 January 2007.

18  D. Wilkins, 'A Vietnam Diary' (unpublished memoir), pp. 74–5.

19  M. Blake, notes on the Battle of Binh Ba, June 1969, email, 3 January 2007.

20  London, 'The Battle of Binh Ba: A Platoon's View', www.anzacday.org.au

21  Bill O'Mara, interview, Canberra, 11 January 2006.

22  D. Wilkins, 'A Vietnam Diary' (unpublished memoir), pp. 74–5.

23  Bill O'Mara, interview, Canberra, 11 January 2006.

24  D. Wilkins, 'A Vietnam Diary' (unpublished memoir), p. 77.

25  Rintoul, *Ashes of Vietnam*.

26  Bill O'Mara, interview, Canberra, 11 January 2006. Many years later, O'Mara received in the post a photograph of the North Vietnamese corpses he had helped to bury. In some distress he decided to bury the photograph next to the Vietnam War Memorial in Canberra. He later exhumed the photo, at my request.

27  *Dateline*, SBS, 29 June 2006. David Brill and veterans Bruce Burrow, Bruce Fraser, Tony Templeton and Walter Pearson returned to Binh Ba.

28  AWM117 [1], 5RAR After-action Report 6/69, OPERATION HAMMER.

29  Ibid.

30  Blake, notes on the Battle of Binh Ba, June 1969, email, 3 January 2007.

31  Ray de Vere, telephone interview, 7 September 2005.

32  London, 'The Battle of Binh Ba: A Platoon's View'.

33  Nguyen Van Tan, veteran and guide, Ba Ria–Vung Tau province, November 2005.
34  Peter Gration, interview, Canberra, 2005.
35  London, 'The Battle of Binh Ba', www.5rar.asn.au
36  AWM103 R719/1/8, Official Correspondence — Chaplains, 1ATF.

Chapter 37 **Vietnamisation**

1  John Press, notes sent to author and interviews, October 2005.
2  Wally Thompson, interview, Sydney, 21 June 2006.
3  Roy Hornsby, in Clarke et al., 'Tall Tales But True' (unpublished memoir).
4  Ibid.
5  McNeill, *The Team*, p. 277.
6  Ibid., pp. 206–14.
7  Ibid., p. 346.
8  Ray Simpson, Citation for the Victoria Cross, AWM.
9  Davies and McKay, *The Men Who Persevered*, p. 142.
10  Warrant Officer Keith Payne, VC, 'Who's Who in Australian Military History', AWM, www.awm.gov.au/people/663.asp.
11  McNeill, *The Team*, pp. 354–5.
12  Palmer, *Vietnam Veterans: Honours and Awards*, pp. 201–2.
13  Warrant Officer Keith Payne, VC, 'Who's Who in Australian Military History', AWM, www.awm.gov.au/people/663.asp
14  AWM103 R723/1/39/1, MACV Quarterly Summary Reports, 1969.
15  Pike, *Viet Cong*.
16  Valentine, *The Phoenix Program*.
17  Maclear, *Vietnam*, p. 261.
18  Sheehan, *A Bright Shining Lie*, p. 732.
19  AWM290 2/R569/1/8, Operations — General, Plan Op Phun Hoang, Phung Hoang Centre, Long Le District.
20  Blair, *There to the Bitter End*, pp. 151 and 189; and *Ted Serong*, p. 123.
21  Rintoul, *Ashes of Vietnam*, pp. 139–40.
22  Ibid.
23  AWM103 R723/1/39/1, MACV Quarterly Summary Reports, 1969.
24  Sorley, *A Better War*, p. 147.
25  Karnow, *Vietnam*, p. 617.
26  Charlton and Moncreiff, *Many Reasons Why*, pp. 194–6; Sheehan, *A Bright Shining Lie*, p. 733.
27  Maddock, 'Going Over the Limit?', in Maddock (ed.), *Memories of Vietnam*, pp. 161–3.
28  Truong Nhu Tang, *A Viet Cong Memoir*, p. 201.
29  McKay, *Bullets, Beans and Bandages*, p. 105.
30  Tidey, 'The Modus Operandi and Effectiveness of Specialist Intelligence Support to 1 Australian Task Force, South Vietnam, 1966–1971' (Master of Defence Studies thesis, ADFA, 2002), p. 14.
31  See Bryan Pannell, 'Intelligence in South Vietnam', lecture to Australian Army Staff College, Fort Queenscliffe, 1971, pp. 22–3; Tidey, 'The Modus Operandi and Effectiveness of Specialist Intelligence Support to 1 Australian Task Force, South Vietnam, 1966–1971'; Hede, 1st Australian Task Force Phung Hoang Ops, BENRPT-004, Senior Province Officer Baria Phuo Tuy, 5 October 1968 — copy held at Australian Intelligence Corps Museum, Canungra.
32  AWM103 R723/1/39/1, MACV Quarterly Summary Reports, 1969. Of the 610,412 foreign military personnel then in South Vietnam, 538,569 were American; 50,366 Korean; 11,577 Thai (double their 1968 strength); 7,734 Australian; 1,579 Filipinos; and 546 New Zealanders. Added to these were more than 500,000 South Vietnamese soldiers.
33  Ibid.
34  Chanoff and Doan Van Toai, *Vietnam at War*, p. 63.

Chapter 38 **Morale**

1 MSS1569 Papers of G. Tilley and Beverly Milner.

2 Rintoul, *Ashes of Vietnam*, p. 141.

3 AWM PR00076, Papers of Dr D. Beard (Colonel).

4 McNeill and Ekins, *On the Offensive*, p. 345.

5 Major Rex Rowe, telephone interview, 2007.

6 AWM PR01533, Papers of Frank Delaney.

7 Bill Akell, interview, Buninyong, Victoria, 22 August 2005.

8 Hall, *Combat Battalion*, p. 152.

9 Brian Honner, interview, Canberra, October 2005.

10 O'Keefe and Smith, *Medicine at War*, p. 170.

11 D. Wilkins, 'A Vietnam Diary' (unpublished memoir), p. 107.

12 AWM290 2RAR 2R569/12/1, Field Signals — OPERATION NATHAN.

13 AWM103 R478/1/31 Part 2, Investigations — General — 5RAR Mine Incident, 9 March 1969.

14 Rintoul, *Ashes of Vietnam*, pp. 93–4.

15 AWM288 569/1 Folio 2/96, OPERATION ESSO, 5RAR After-action Report.

16 Ibid.

17 O'Brien, *Conscripts and Regulars*, p. 242.

18 Hornsby, in Clarke et al., 'Tall Tales But True' (unpublished memoir).

19 AWM107, Interview with Brigadier S. P. Weir, 13 July 1972, Army Historical Programme.

20 Horner, *Australian Higher Command in the Vietnam War*.

21 AWM107, Interview with Brigadier S. P. Weir, 13 July 1972, Army Historical Programme.

22 Spragg, *When Good Men Do Nothing*, p. 92.

23 Ibid., pp. 89–99.

24 AWM107, Interview with Brigadier S. P. Weir, 13 July 1972, Army Historical Programme.

25 Hall, *Combat Battalion*, p. 53.

26 Ibid., p. 54.

27 AWM290 [8/5], After-action Report, OPERATION HAMMERSLEY.

28 AWM98 R569/1/194, Operations — General — Unusual Incident — OP HAMMERSLEY — 8RAR — Long Hais.

29 Ibid.

30 Ibid.

31 Hall, *Combat Battalion*, p. 157.

32 Ibid., p. 173.

33 Ibid., p. 172.

34 Michael Jeffery, interview, Canberra, 5 October 2005.

35 Cosgrove, *My Story*, p. 88.

36 AWM PR87/157, Papers of Lieutenant Colonel Neil C. Smith.

37 Bill Dobell, interview, Ballarat, 23 August 2005.

38 AWM98 R273/271/50, Reports Mil. Personnel — Accidental Wounding.

39 AWM290 4/R723/1/4, Australian Military Forces, Office of the Provost Marshal, 7 August 1971, Report on Major Disturbances, Vung Tau City on Evening of 3 August 1971.

40 AWM103 [634], Papers Relating to General Court Martial, Private P. D. Allen.

41 Cosgrove, *My Story*, p. 73.

42 Gilbert, *Why the North Won the Vietnam War*, p. 223.

43 Wells, *The War Within*, p. 340.

44 Karnow, *Vietnam*, p. 440.

45 Wally Thompson, interview, Sydney, 21 June 2006.

46 John Salmon, interviews, Canberra, 2006.

47 Sandy Pearson, interview, Sydney, 2006.

48 AWM290 [2/30], Captured Documents, 717 Serials 1–10, Bulletin No. 39,297, Captured Enemy Documents, 16 October 1970.

49 AWM290 2/38, Communist Document Analyst Report No. 110/69, Miscellaneous Serials, Captured Documents, CIA report, Diary of Nguyen Van Van.

50 AWM288 R569/1/69 Part 1, OPERATION FEDERAL/OVERLANDER, 5RAR.

51 AWM290 [2/31], Captured Documents, 717 Serials 11–20.

52 AWM290 [2/30], Captured Documents, 717 Serials 1–10, Bulletin No. 39, 297, Captured Enemy Documents 16 October 1970.

53 AWM PR85/254, Diary of Nguyen Vu Co, D445 Bn.

54 Ibid.

## Chapter 39 **Moratorium**

1 AWM PR86/091, Papers of Vietnam Moratorium Campaign (Organising Committee).

2 Association for International Cooperation and Disarmament; Congress for International Cooperation and Disarmament; Committee in Defiance of National Service Act; Vietnam Action Committee; Save Our Sons.

3 Edwards, *A Nation at War*, p. 249.

4 AWM MSS1009, York, 'Sources of Student Unrest in Australia with Particular Reference to La Trobe University, 1967–72' (MA thesis University of Sydney, 1983), p. 68.

5 Sheehan, *A Bright Shining Lie*, pp. 689–90.

6 Knightley, *The First Casualty*, pp. 390–1.

7 Kelman, 'The Military Establishment', *Society*, May–June 1975, pp. 18–22, cited in Kinnard, *The War Managers*, p. 52.

8 Gee, *The Graves of Hué*.

9 *Time*, 15 December 1967.

10 Edwards, *A Nation at War*, p. 246.

11 Army Museum, Hanoi, Socialist Republic of Vietnam.

12 Bob Gould, interview, Sydney, 9 February 2006.

13 AWM290 2/R499/71/1, Mail and Postal General (Including Delivery Services).

14 John Bullen, personal papers, diary.

15 Edwards, *A Nation at War*, p. 246.

16 Ibid., pp. 246–7.

17 Ibid., pp. 246–8.

18 AWM MSS1009, York, 'Sources of Student Unrest in Australia with Particular Reference to La Trobe University, 1967–72' (MA thesis, University of Sydney, 1983), p. 68.

19 Ibid.

20 Langley, *A Decade of Dissent*, p. 161.

21 Ibid., p. 108.

22 AWM PR86/091, Papers of Vietnam Moratorium Campaign (Organising Committee), Conference to End Vietnam War, Notes to speech by Arthur Calwell at Albert Hall, 2 August 1968.

23 Harry Ward, response to questionnaire.

24 Gerry Harant, email, 10 April 2006, and www.greenleft.org.au/back/1995/192/192p12.htm

25 Edwards, *A Nation at War*, pp. 256–66.

26 Ibid.

27 NAA A1209 1970/6340 Part 1, Intelligence Summary, Demonstration, Central Crime Intelligence Bureau, 29 April 1970.

28 NAA A1209 1970/6340 Part 1, Letter from C. H. Brown to the Prime Minister's Department, 13 April 1970.

29 Ibid.

30 NAA A1209 1970/6340 Part 1, Press release, Dr Cairns' Call for Demonstrations, 26 March 1970.

31 *Hansard*, Speech by the Hon T. E. F. Hughes, QC, MP, 14 April 1970.

32  Hughes cut a swashbuckling, defiant figure. When protesters nailed a list of draft resisters to his door, he appeared brandishing a cricket bat. The activists spent the rest of the day playing cricket on his street, a game he chose not to join. Hughes's chief irritants that day were Alex Robertson, editor of *Tribune*; Janice Jones, of Students for a Democratic Society; Joseph Owens, of the Builders' Labourers' Federation; and several others. (NAA A1209 1970/6340 Part 2, Commonwealth Police, Fortnightly Report, Central Crime Intelligence Bureau, 1 September 1970).

33  Liberal politicians' warning, *Age*, 23 April 1970; and *Sydney Morning Herald*, 24 April 1970.

34  Langley, *A Decade of Dissent*, p. 136.

35  Wordsworth, *The Prelude*, Book xi.

36  Langley, *A Decade of Dissent*, p. 136.

37  Bill Dobell, interview, Ballarat, 23 August 2005.

38  Gary McMahon, email to author.

39  NAA A1209 1970/6340 Part 2, Western and Wilson, 'Well, What Did the Moratorium Do?', cited in Australian Security Intelligence Organisation, Background Brief, 1970.

40  Langley, *A Decade of Dissent*, p. 169.

41  NAA A5882 CO19 Part 2, *Solace for a Free Man*, a booklet of advice to draft resisters.

42  R. Harris, 'The New Breed', p. 67.

43  Edwards, *A Nation at War*, p. 309.

44  Ibid.

45  Encyclical Letter of Pope Paul VI, 27 October 1966, published in Department of External Affairs, *Select Documents on International Affairs,* No. 9: Vietnam, February 1966–October 1966, Canberra, December 1966.

46  AWM MSS0838, MacDonald, 'Opposition Within the Church to Australia's Military Involvement in Vietnam' (B.Lett. thesis, University of New England, 1974); see also *Hansard*, 29 September 1970.

47  Langley, *A Decade of Dissent*, pp. 116–18.

48  Edwards, *A Nation at War*, p. 301.

## Chapter 40 **Platoon**

1   Cable, 'An Independent Command' Canberra Papers on Strategy and Defence, No. 134, p. 78.

2   Horner, *SAS: Phantoms of War*, p. 385.

3   Frank Cashmore, email, 2007.

4   John Church, interview, 6 January 2006.

5   AWM290 [8/13], 8RAR Combat Operation — After-action Reports — OPERATIONS DECADE and CUNG CHUNG 2 and 3.

6   AWM107(1), Interview with Major General C. A. E. Fraser, 5 March 1971, Army Historical Programme.

7   Philip McNamara, interview, Sydney, 24 January 2007; see also Church, *Second to None*.

8   Peter Cosgrove, interview, 21 February 2007.

9   Major Chinh and Brig Minh, interviews, November 2005.

10  Hall, *Combat Battalion*, p. 26.

11  AWM117 [33], OPERATION TONG, 5RAR Late Ready Reaction Coy Combat After-action Report, 7/8 June 1969 (emphasis in original).

12  Ibid., p. 513.

13  John Church, interview, 6 January 2006.

14  Krasnoff, *Krazy Hor*, pp. 106–7.

15  J. Grey, personal papers, notes on operations in Vietnam 1970–71, 7th Battalion, RAR, 17 December 1970; and AWM PR88/091, Records of Lieutenant M. P. J. O'Brien, 7RAR.

16  O'Brien, *Conscripts and Regulars*, p. 171.

17  John Church, interview, 6 January 2006.

18  Hall, *Combat Battalion*, p. 26.

19  Bob Gully, interview, Sydney, 2 June 2005.

20 O'Brien, *Conscripts and Regulars*, p. 181.

21 Ibid., p. 192.

22 Ibid., p. 198.

23 Stewart, 'Infantry Minor Tactics and the Claymore' in *Australian Infantry*.

24 *Courier-Mail*, 13 August 1970.

25 AWM290 [8/13], 8RAR Combat Operation — After-action Reports — OPERATIONS DECADE and CUNG CHUNG 2 and 3.

26 Hall, *Combat Battalion*, p. 213.

27 AWM290, Lessons Learned, After-action Report, 7RAR, OPERATION CUNG CHUNG 3.

28 AWM290 3/746/1/4, Safety General — Rules of Engagement — United States Military Assistance Command, Vietnam, Directive Number 525–13, 1 May 1971, Military Operations, Rules of Engagement (supersedes MACV 525-13 (C), 9 March 1969).

29 Ian Kortlang, interview, Sydney, 1 March 2005.

30 Church, *Second to None*, p. 177; Ian Kortlang, interview, Sydney, 1 March 2005.

31 Ian Kortlang, interview, Sydney, 1 March 2005.

32 McKay, *In Good Company*, p. 62.

33 AWM290 4/R256/1/1, Defence — General — Base Defence.

34 McKay, *In Good Company*.

35 Ibid., p. 82.

36 Carlo Mikkelsen, email, 2005.

37 Barry Middleton, 'My Story — The Way I Felt' (unpublished memoir), p. 1.

38 Bob Gully, interview.

39 Herr, *Dispatches*, pp. 54–5.

40 Ibid., p. 35.

41 Knightley, *The First Casualty*, pp. 387–8.

42 Sallah and Weiss, *Tiger Force*.

43 Hall, *Combat Battalion*, pp. 199–200.

44 Ibid., p. 209.

45 Rintoul, *Ashes of Vietnam*, p. 149.

46 Hall, *Combat Battalion*, p. 207.

47 Rintoul, *Ashes of Vietnam*, pp. 163–5.

48 Knightley, *The First Casualty*.

49 Chanoff and Doan Van Toai, *Vietnam*, p. 171.

## Chapter 41 **Last days**

1 Tom Daly, 'The Fraser Affair — February 1971' (unpublished essay; excerpts published here for the first time).

2 The details of the story, amply aired in a slew of biographies and memoirs (e.g. Reid, *The Gorton Experiment*; Ayres, *Malcom Fraser*; Hancock, *John Gorton*) need not detain us. Yet the army, tortoise-like, has hitherto failed to present its side of the story; in fact, Daly's own version of events has sat unpublished since 1988. My account draws heavily on his extraordinary narrative, as well as Brigadier Salmon's valued advice and trenchant debrief.

3 HQ AFV, Military Civic Action Plan 1971/72, 3 February 1971 (copy supplied by Malcolm Fraser, 28 September 2006).

4 John Salmon, interview, Canberra, 2006.

5 AWM107(1), Interview with Brigadier John Salmon, Army Historical Programme.

6 Tom Daly, 'The Fraser Affair — February 1971' (unpublished essay), p. 2.

7 Ibid.

8 Frost, *Australia's War in Vietnam*, p. 172.

9 Tom Daly, 'The Fraser Affair — February 1971' (unpublished essay), p. 25.

10 Ayres, *Malcom Fraser* (notes to draft manuscript).

11 *Australian*, 4 March 1971.

12 Tom Daly, 'The Fraser Affair — February 1971' (unpublished essay), p. 30.

13 Ibid., p. 41.

14 John Salmon, interview, Canberra, October 2006.

15 AWM107, Interview with Brigadier John Salmon, Army Historical Programme.

16 AWM103 [809], 1ATF Papers on Withdrawal of Personnel and Equipment from Vietnam — August 1971.

17 Ibid.

18 AWM290 3/569/71/11 Part 2, OPERATION IVANHOE.

19 David Morris, interview, Sydney, 14 August 2005.

20 McKay, In Good Company.

21 Taylor, Last Out, p. 229.

22 McKay, Bullets, Beans and Bandages, pp. 188–9.

23 AWM290 4/11 Part 3, Orders Dissolving Civilian Defence Organisation, People's Revolutionary Government, Republic of South Vietnam.

24 AWM290 4/6 Part 1, 4RAR/NZ (ANZAC) Bn — Intelligence Section, 501 Serials 4236–4513.

25 AWM290 [2/31], Captured Documents, 717 Serials 11–20.

26 AWM290 4/8 Part 1, 4RAR/NZ (ANZAC) Bn — Intelligence Section — 501 Serials 4830–5164.

27 AWM290 4/R750/1/8.

28 Arnold, Cop in a Baggy Green Skin, p. 111.

27 AWM290 4/4 Part 1, Contact Report June 1971, 4RAR/NZ (ANZAC) Bn — Intelligence Section — 501 Serials 3143–3414.

29 AWM290 4/11 Part 2, 4RAR/NZ (ANZAC) Bn — Intelligence Summaries from 29 March 1971 to 5 November 1971.

31 AWM107, Interview with Major General C. A. E. Fraser, 15 March 1974, Army Historical Programme.

32 McDonald, DSO citation, in Palmer, Vietnam Veterans: A Record of Service, p. 71.

33 AWM103 [810], Withdrawal of 1ATF from South Vietnam.

34 Initially Greville had command only of 1ALSG's local administration in Vung Tau, and not of the service operations of the logistics unit, which were answerable to Saigon. His frustration echoed the 'cries of anguish made by all my predecessors as commander 1ALSG', he said. Eventually, however, the problem was resolved by the amalgamation of 1ALSG under his command.

35 AWM290 4/R571/1/6, Orders and Instructions, 4RAR SOPs.

36 Horner, Duty First, p. 277; also Taylor, Last Out, p. 242.

37 Phillip Greville, interview, Gold Coast, 29 September 2006.

38 Walker, 'Like a Cardhouse in the Wind', p. 204.

39 Taylor, Last Out, p. 243.

40 McFarlane, We Band of Brothers, p. 400.

41 AWM103 [810], Withdrawal of 1ATF from South Vietnam.

42 AWM103 [804], 1ATF Withdrawal of Australian Forces Vietnam — August–September 1971.

43 Phillip Greville (personal papers), 'Report on OPERATION INTERFUSE — From the Point of View of 1ATF and 1ALSG', p. 5.

44 Ibid., p. 13.

45 AWM290 4/R274/5/3, Displays — Festivals and Fetes — Barbeques.

46 McNeill, The Team, p. 261.

47 The training of the Cambodian Army had started in Australia, in strictest secrecy, then continued in Phuoc Tuy, at the Van Kiep Jungle Warfare Training School (to where the ill-fated Nui Dat jungle school had relocated). The Cambodian troops seemed more disciplined than the Vietnamese, observed Lieutenant Colonel J. W. Stewart, then chief instructor of the training school. They would need all the discipline they could muster in the coming clash with Pol Pot's Khmer Rouge.

48 McNeill, The Team, p. 478.

Chapter 42 **'Baby-killers'**

1 For the full story of HMAS *Sydney* and the transport and escort ships, plus the RAN Nominal Roll, see Nott and Payne, *The Vung Tau Ferry and Escort Ships, Vietnam 1965–72*. Four hundred RAN personnel served during the Vietnam War, on HMAS *Sydney, Melbourne, Vampire, Parramatta, Duchess, Vendetta, Yarra, Derwent, Anzac, Swan* and the transport ships *Jeparit, Boonaroo* and other support craft.

2 Ian Kortlang, interview, Sydney, 1 April 2005.

3 AWM103 4/R553/1/20, Movement General — RTA — D Coy, 4RAR.

4 McKay, *Bullets, Beans and Bandages*, p. 252.

5 Coe, *Desperate Praise*, pp. 38–9.

6 Giblett, *Homecomings*, p. 23.

7 Blinco, *Down a Country Lane*, p. 458.

8 Harry Whiteside, interview, Sydney, 24 February 2005.

9 David Morgan, personal papers, autobiography.

10 Rintoul, *Ashes of Vietnam*, p. 181.

11 Claude Zavattaro, interview, Sydney, 13 September 2005.

12 Ian Kortlang, interview, Sydney, 1 April 2005.

13 Rintoul, *Ashes of Vietnam*, p. 184.

14 Ibid.

15 Not all parades were glum and subdued. In the early years, at least until 1968, large crowds turned out to cheer and shower confetti. And the soldiers' families, of course, made their sons feel proud and loved. The protesters generally stayed away.

16 AWM290 2/R270/71/1D, Discharge 1969 NS Intakes — General.

17 AWM MSS1578, Rhodes, 'Vietnam Veterans' Welcome Home Parade and Reunion' (MA thesis, Department of History, Monash University, 1990).

18 Ibid.

19 Peter Gration, interview, Canberra, 2005.

20 Wally Thompson, interview, Sydney, 21 June 2006.

21 Bill O'Mara, interview, Canberra, 11 January 2006.

22 Tim Fischer, interview, Sydney, 1 August 2005.

23 AWM MSS1578, Rhodes, 'Vietnam Veterans' Welcome Home Parade and Reunion' (MA thesis, Department of History, Monash University, 1990).

24 Terry Burstall, interview, Brisbane, 4 June 2005.

25 Peter Dinham, interview, Canberra, 26 October 2005.

26 Ibid.

27 Rintoul, *Ashes of Vietnam*, p. 187.

28 Ibid., p. 194.

29 *Say a Prayer for Me — The Chaplains of the Vietnam War* (video).

30 Kelly Lu, 'Sisters in Arms? The Postwar Relationship Between Australian Army and Civilian Nurses of the Vietnam War', (BA thesis) pp. 72–3.

31 Lorrae Desmond, interview, Sydney, 23 September 2005.

32 Ray De Vere, telephone interview, 7 September 2005.

33 Harry Whiteside, interview, Sydney, 24 February 2005.

34 Neville Cullen, interview, Redcliffe, 8 June 2005.

35 Laurie Drinkwater, interview, Maroochydore, 7 June 2005.

36 Brian Sewell, interview, Vung Tau, November 2005.

37 Hennessy, *The Sharp End*, pp. 105–6.

38 Gary McMahon, 'Why Was Vietnam Unique?' (unpublished essay).

39 David Morris, interview, Sydney, 14 August 2005.

40 Terry O'Brien, interview, Ballarat, 23 August 2005.

41 Heard, *Well Done, Those Men*, pp. 198–9.

42 Richard Hornery, email, 2005.

43  Gary McMahon, 'Why Was Vietnam Unique?' (unpublished essay).

44  Laurie Drinkwater, interview, Maroochydore, 7 June 2005.

45  Heard, *Well Done, Those Men*, pp. 198–9.

46  Philip Ham, personal papers, '25 Years On — Recollections of a National Serviceman, 1968–1970'.

47  Nick Quigley, personal papers.

48  Laurie Drinkwater, interview, Maroochydore, 7 June 2005.

49  McNeill, *The Team*, p. 107.

50  Colin Townsend, interview, Gympie, 19 August 2005.

51  AWM PR88/062, Records of Maxine Sheldrick.

52  McKay, *Bullets, Beans and Bandages*, p. 243.

53  Rintoul, *Ashes of Vietnam*, p. 198.

54  Laurie Drinkwater, interview, Maroochydore, 7 June 2005.

55  Rick Bensley, letter to author, 11 July 2007.

56  Colin Townsend, interview, Gympie, 19 August 2005.

57  Neville Cullen, interview, Redcliffe, 8 June 2005.

58  Bill O'Mara, interview, Canberra, 11 January 2006.

59  AWM MSS1578, Rhodes, 'Vietnam Veterans' Welcome Home Parade and Reunion' (MA thesis, Department of History, Monash University, 1990).

60  Bob Gould, interview, Sydney, 9 February 2006.

61  Joan Coxsedge, response to questionnaire.

62  Peter Gration, interview, Canberra, 2005.

63  Tom Daly, 'The Fraser Affair — February 1971' (unpublished essay).

64  Coe, *Desperate Praise*, pp. 111–12.

## Chapter 43 **The North invades**

1  *Sydney Morning Herald*, 14 July 1971. Gough Whitlam was undoubtedly a shrewd politician. He attacked the war — 'conceived in deceit, nurtured in deceit and … ending in deceit' — only when he decided it was politically opportune to do so; he urged conscripts to refuse to serve overseas only when he sensed a majority opposed conscription — for which Gorton accused Whitlam on television of inciting the troops to 'mutiny' (NAA A5882 CO19 Part 2, TV interview, Prime Minister John Gorton, for Channel 7 Network, 24 September 1970).

2  McKay, *In Good Company*, p. 188.

3  McNeill, *The Team*, p. 184.

4  Ibid., p. 299.

5  Ibid., p. 458.

6  Ibid., p. 456.

7  In fairness to the ARVN in Phuoc Tuy, the problem, in these latter stages, sometimes lay with members of the Team, who seemed too eager to blame their tools. If the trainees responded so poorly, what did that say about the trainers? The Team's concentration in Phuoc Tuy created a classic case of too many cooks — in 1970, eighty-four advisers in fourteen Mobile Advisory and Training Teams (called MATTs) roamed the province. Some 'over-advised' operations ended in farce. 'There were signs of utter confusion,' said Len Opie, of one action, 'largely created by advisers and others who felt it essential to interfere with or criticise almost every aspect of the operation' (McNeill, *The Team*, p. 450).

8  Ibid., p. 193.

9  Ibid., p. 469.

10  Ibid., p. 470.

11  Ibid., p. 472.

12  Sorley, *A Better War*, p. 219.

13  Morris, 'The War We Could Have Won', *New York Times*.

14  Dr Tien Nguyen, interview, Sydney, 16 March 2005.

15 A year earlier Wilfred Burchett clamoured for Kissinger's ear, claiming to be the bearer of a peace offer from Hanoi. Kissinger listened, decided Burchett had nothing new to say, and cut all further US contacts with the reporter. Thus ended Burchett's dream of acting as an intermediary between Hanoi and the West.

16 Rymer, 'Blood On Their Hands: The Victims Vietnam Peace Protesters Forgot', *Sydney Morning Herald*, 22 April 2005; also *All Points of the Compass*, ABC TV, 1 May 2005.

17 Sir Robert Menzies, personal statement to the LBJ Library, 24 November 1969, p. 10.

18 Karnow, *Vietnam*, p. 597.

19 Information pamphlet, Hanoi Army Museum.

20 Edwards, *A Nation at War*, p. 325.

21 Snepp, *Decent Interval*, p. 41.

22 Former tank commander, interview, Hanoi, November 2005 (preferred to remain anonymous).

23 Sorley, *A Better War*, p. 363.

24 *Time*, 15 April 1985.

25 US Congressional Reports; also in Sorley, *A Better War*, p. 364.

26 Blair, 'Get Me Ten Years: Australia's Ted Serong in Vietnam, 1962–1975'.

27 Serong, 'One Month in September', Papers of Ted Serong, AWM.

28 Sorley, *A Better War*, p. 370.

29 Hoang Ngoc Lung, *The General Offensives of 1968–69*.

30 Grenville, *The Saving of South Vietnam*; and David Sabben, interview, Melbourne, 21 August 2005.

31 Lockhart, *Nation in Arms*, p. 271.

32 Snepp, *Decent Interval*, p. 145.

33 Kinnard, *The War Managers*, p. 4.

34 Snepp, *Decent Interval*.

35 Ibid., p. 192.

36 Ibid., p. 199.

37 Ibid., p. 197.

Chapter 44 **The fall of Saigon**

1 One of Serong's happier roles, in the last days, was classical music critic for the English-language *Saigon News*, a role akin to that of the band that played on as the *Titanic* went down — with the rider that Serong was always a better critic than a player.

2 Blair, *There To the Bitter End*, pp. 221–2. These were noble sentiments perhaps, but they need to be set against Serong's later statements to *Quadrant* magazine: in the thick of the fall of Saigon, 'I still found myself asking, "Are these people worth saving?"' (*Quadrant*, October 1989, p. 18).

3 Blair, 'Get Me Ten Years: Australia's Ted Serong in Vietnam, 1962–1975', 1996 Vietnam Symposium paper.

4 Ibid.

5 Dr Tien Nguyen, interview, Sydney, 16 March 2005.

6 Geoff Rose, 'Vietnam — March/April 1975', emailed article, 29 September 2005.

7 Neil Davis, ABC News, 30 September 1973.

8 Rosemary Taylor, to a conference on refugees in Saigon, February 1975; Mathews, 'War Waifs Die While Australia Dithers', *Age*, 18 February 1975.

9 Geoff Rose, 'Vietnam — March/April 1975', emailed article, 29 September 2005.

10 One child died on board; others arrived sick and dehydrated. At Bangkok, the Australian Embassy staff and medical teams transferred the children to a Qantas B747 for a better flight to Australia. The RAAF's two evacuation flights that day enabled a new start for 194 children. In total, only 300 Vietnamese children were evacuated to Australia, according to very strict criteria: only those approved by Vietnam for overseas adoption, and for whom suitable Australian parents had been found, were acceptable. Canberra thus made no allowances for the tragic exception of a fifteen-year war: in 1975, Whitlam's government applied the same adoption rules to Vietnam as to any other country.

11  NAA A1838 3014/10/15/6 Part 4, Cable, Australian Embassy in Saigon to Canberra, 18 April 1975.

12  Geoff Rose, 'Vietnam — March/April 1975', emailed article, 29 September 2005.

13  Ibid. In 1993 Rose met the pilot who bombed the palace, Nguyen Thanh Trung, then chief pilot of Vietnam Airlines. Contracted from an Ansett subsidiary to Vietnam Airlines, Rose flew with and trained Trung for six months. When Rose asked him why he had bombed the palace, Trung said, 'I just wanted to do anything possible to help bring an end to the war.' Trung also led the bombing raid on Tan Son Nhut airfield on 28 April, which killed the last two US servicemen in the Vietnam War.

14  Geoff Rose, 'Vietnam — March/April 1975', emailed article, 29 September 2005.

15  Snepp, *Decent Interval*, p. 256.

16  Snepp, *Decent Interval*, pp. 70–80.

17  Le Duan, Letter, Hanoi War Museum.

18  Bouscaren, *All Quiet on the Eastern Front*, p. 164.

19  Snepp, *Decent Interval*, p. 344.

20  Ibid.

21  Mike Sheean, personal account, email, 15 November 2006.

22  Ibid.; Trevor Nye, interview, Hervey Bay, 6 June 2005.

23  Mike Sheean, personal account, email, 15 November 2006.

24  Edwards, *A Nation at War*, p. 332. The leak reached the media via Andrew Peacock, who was in Saigon at the time of the cables' dispatch. The 'cables affair' has provoked a great deal of politically charged comment, not least from Whitlam himself, who has tried to play down the episode, and from Whitlam staffers Graham Freudenberg, John Menadue, Gregory Clark and Brian Johns (see e.g. Freudenberg, *A Certain Grandeur*; and *Quadrant*, March 1997).

25  Reprinted in 'The Vietnam Experience', 10th Anniversary Lift-out, *Sydney Morning Herald*, 30 April 1985.

26  www.naa.gov.au/fSheets/fs243.html

27  Edwards, *A Nation at War*, p. 336.

28  Nye, interview, Hervey Bay, 6 June 2005.

29  Ibid.

30  Coulthard-Clark, *The RAAF in Vietnam*, p. 330.

31  Sheean, personal account, email, 15 November 2006.

32  Nye, interview, Hervey Bay, 6 June 2005.

33  Edwards, *A Nation at War*, p. 336.

34  Air Commodore J. W. Mitchell AO (retired), letter to newspapers, 2003 (exact date unknown).

35  Edwards, *A Nation at War*, p. 336.

36  Nye, interview, Hervey Bay, 6 June 2005.

37  Ibid.

38  Blair, 'Get Me Ten Years: Australia's Ted Serong in Vietnam, 1962–1975'.

39  Blair, *There to the Bitter End*, p. 232.

40  Snepp, *Decent Interval*, p. 391.

41  Ibid., p. 452.

42  Ibid., pp. 469–70.

43  Bowden, *One Crowded Hour*, p. 337.

44  Bob Gould, interview, Sydney, 9 February 2006.

45  www.gregoryclark.net/lifestory/page14/page14.html

## Chapter 45  **Cabramatta**

1  Dr Tien Nguyen, interview, 16 March 2005.

2  Ibid.

3  Snepp, *Decent Interval*, pp. 476–7.

4   Their families suffered many other humiliations; for example, North Vietnamese troops desecrated the graves of southern soldiers at the huge southern war cemetery at Bien Hoa: 'Many of the dead ARVN … had their photographs engraved on the headstones. The communists smashed these with rifle butts, even shooting out the eyes' (Swain, *River of Time*, p. 81).

5   Sorley, 'Remembering Vietnam — A Lecture to the National Archives', p. 18. A further 1.5 million were 'resettled' to 'new economic zones': impoverished areas, ravaged by hunger and disease; five million people would be thus forcibly employed by 1980.

6   Lind, *Vietnam*, p. 244.

7   Truong Nhu Tang, *A Viet Cong Memoir*, pp. 267–8.

8   Ibid., p. 270.

9   Van Tien Dung, *Our Great Spring Victory*; also Petersen, *Tiger Men*, p. 222. The Montagnard remain a persecuted minority; Hanoi's promises of more autonomy and better conditions were, of course, unfulfilled.

10  Nguyen Van Khanh, 'A Glimpse at the Situation of Land, Fields, and Agricultural Production in Viet Nam During the Years of *Doi Moi* (Renewal)', in *Vietnamese Studies*, p. 87.

11  Figes, *A People's Tragedy*, p. 723.

12  'President Ho Chi Minh's Testament', p. 52.

13  Ibid., p. 46.

14  Nguyen Van Khanh, 'A Glimpse at the Situation of Land, Fields, and Agricultural Production in Viet Nam During the Years of *Doi Moi* (Renewal)', in *Vietnamese Studies*, pp. 95–6.

15  Swain, *River of Time*, p. 197.

16  Ibid., pp. 199–200.

17  Ibid., p. 200.

18  Bob Gould, interview, Sydney, 9 February 2006.

19  Stack, 'A Controlled Intake of Vietnamese Required', 1979 Jamieson Memorial Lecture to the Neurological Society of Australia, *AMA Gazette*, 24 May 1979.

20  Ibid.

21  Khien Dinh Nguyen, interview, Sydney, 2005.

22  The Presidential Unit Citation (Army) for Extraordinary Heroism to the Studies and Observation Group, United Military Assistance Command, Vietnam, awarded 19 September 2003 at the US Naval Base, Port Hueneme, to Colonel Vo Dai Ton, RVN Special Forces.

23  Colonel Vo Dai Ton, interview, Sydney, 2005.

24  Ibid.

25  Tuan Van Phan, interview, Sydney, 2005.

## Chapter 46  Agents Orange, Purple, White, Green, Pink, Blue …

1   Hitchens, 'The Vietnam Syndrome', *Vanity Fair*, pp. 112–19.

2   McCulloch, *The Politics of Agent Orange*, p. 17.

3   Sheehan, *A Bright Shining Lie*, pp. 618–19.

4   Ellsberg, *Secrets: A Memoir of Vietnam and the Pentagon Papers*, pp. 135–6.

5   McCulloch, *The Politics of Agent Orange*, p. 66.

6   Gary McMahon, 'Why Was Vietnam Unique?' (unpublished essay).

7   O'Keefe and Smith, *Medicine at War*, p. 309. 'Between 1965 and 1971,' the New Zealand Defence Minister told his Parliament on 5 June 2003, 'a total of 487,000 US gallons (1,843,295 litres) of herbicide was sprayed on Phuoc Tuy Province from aircraft as part of Operation Ranch Hand' (submission to the NZ Health Committee Inquiry into the Health Effects of Agent Orange, 1 July 2003).

8   Senate Standing Committee, *Pesticides and the Health of Australian Vietnam Veterans*, p. 53.

9   Avery, *We Too Were Anzacs*, p. 74.

10  Rintoul, *Ashes of Vietnam*, p. 155.

11  D. Wilkins, 'A Vietnam Diary', p. 15.

12 Fred Beal, interview, Windsor, NSW, 15 April 2005.

13 McCulloch, *The Politics of Agent Orange*, p. 58.

14 Gary McMahon, 'Why Was Vietnam Unique?' (unpublished essay).

15 Crowe, *The Battle After the War*, p. 73.

16 AWM PR85/426, Agent Orange File; and *Hansard*, 23 November 1978.

17 Ibid.; and *Hansard*, 27 March 1980.

18 McCulloch, *The Politics of Agent Orange*, p. 165.

19 Crowe, *The Battle After the War*, p. 78.

20 AWM PR85/426, Agent Orange File; and *Hansard*, 1 April 1980.

21 AWM PR84/204, Submission to 'Agent Orange' Royal Commission of Vietnam Veterans Association of Australia.

22 Senate Standing Committee, *Pesticides and the Health of Australian Vietnam Veterans*, November 1982.

23 'Herb Tapes', pp. 111–33; *Agent Orange*, Vietnam Veterans' Association of Australia response to Evatt Royal Commission, 1986.

24 Senate Standing Committee, *Pesticides and the Health of Australian Vietnam Veterans*, pp. 53–69.

25 Ibid., p. 202–3 (emphasis in original).

26 The government did produce more research, for example the Case-Control Study of Congenital Anomalies and Vietnam Service (the Birth Defects Study), commissioned by the Minister for Veterans' Affairs, published in January 1983. It found no statistical evidence to suggest a link between Vietnam service and birth defects in the soldiers' children.

27 Fett, Dunn, Adena, O'Toole, Forcier, *Australian Veteran Health Studies. The Mortality Report*. Part 1, Executive Summary.

28 Evatt, P., *Royal Commission on the Use and Effects of Chemical Agents on Australian Personnel in Vietnam*.

29 *Agent Orange*, Vietnam Veterans' Association of Australia response to Evatt Royal Commission, 1986.

30 Crowe, *The Battle After the War*, pp. 121–5.

31 Ibid., pp. 118–19.

32 *Agent Orange*, Vietnam Veterans' Association of Australia response to Evatt Royal Commission, 1986.

33 The US Secretary of Veterans' Affairs commissioned the National Academy of Sciences study in 1991.

34 See US Institute of Medicine, *Veterans and Agent Orange*, a response to the NAS study.

35 Crowe, *The Battle After the War* and Department of Veterans' Affairs, *Morbidity of Vietnam Veterans*.

36 Department of Veterans' Affairs, Cancer Incidence in Australian Vietnam Veterans Study 2005; Third Australian Vietnam Veteran Mortality Study 2005; and *Australian National Service Vietnam Veterans: Mortality and Cancer Incidence 2005*, report.

37 These studies did not attempt to determine the cause of the excessive rates observed, warned Dr Justine Ward, principal medical officer, Repatriation Medical Authority. 'Many of the diseases listed were known to be caused by cigarette smoking and consumption of alcohol, and many are not known to be related to dioxin.'

38 Department of Veterans' Affairs, *Australian National Service Vietnam Veterans, Mortality and Cancer Incidence 2005*, report.

39 The RMA urges caution in making a direct link between herbicides and many veterans' conditions. 'The RMA,' said Dr Ward, 'has included factors in a number of statements of principles where there is evidence that dioxins *might* be harmful, but our standard of proof for causation is generous, as required by legislation. There is a general human tendency to attribute *all* ill health to poorly understood and strange substances (depleted uranium, chemicals generally), when the evidence for causation is actually in relation to very specific diseases, and even then is often fairly limited. On the other hand, better understood but less frightening explanations are discounted (smoking, alcohol, chance findings)' (email, 10 April 2007).

40  Interviews with DVA officials, Canberra, 2006.
41  Hitchens, 'The Vietnam Syndrome', pp. 112–19.
42  Ibid.

Chapter 47 **'Totally and permanently incapacitated'**

 1  Shakespeare, *Henry IV*, Part 1, Act 2, Scene 3, lines 44–69.
 2  D. Booth, 'Fucked in the Head' (unpublished memoir).
 3  Harry Whiteside, interview, Sydney, 24 February 2005.
 4  Rintoul, *Ashes of Vietnam*, p. 226.
 5  D. Booth, 'Fucked in the Head' (unpublished memoir).
 6  Ibid.
 7  Bernie Cox, interview, Sydney, 10 March 2005.
 8  Mick O'Halloran, email, 22 May 2006.
 9  J. Faggotter, 'Australia, Don't Forget About Us' (unpublished memoir).
10  Denis Gibbons, interviews, Sydney, 28–9 December 2005.
11  Shakespeare, *Hamlet*, Act 1, Scene 5, Line 10.
12  American Psychiatric Association, *Diagnostic and Statistical Manual of Mental Disorders*,
    pp. 428–9.
13  Muir, 'The Hidden Cost of War: The Psychological Effects of the Second World War and the
    Indonesian Confrontation on Veterans and their Families' (PhD thesis, University of
    Wollongong, 2003), pp. 186–9.
14  Mackenzie, D., 'Trauma of War Hits Troops Years Later', *New Scientist*, 25 August 2005, p. 6.
15  Senate Standing Committee, *Pesticides and the Health of Australian Vietnam Veterans*, p. 123.
16  Grossman, 'Evolution of Weaponry', www.killology.com/print/print_weaponry.htm; see also
    Grossman, *On Killing*.
17  Senior official in the Defence Department (preferred not to be named).
18  Retired brigadier (preferred not to be named).
19  Shephard, *A War of Nerves*, pp. 387, 393 and 396.
20  Atrens, 'Madness and Neuromythology', *Quadrant*, pp. 19–22.
21  Dr Graeme Killer, Principal Medical Adviser of the Commonwealth Department of Veterans'
    Affairs, quoted in J. Faggotter, 'Australia, Don't Forget About Us' (unpublished memoir).
22  Dr Justine Ward, emails, March 2007.
23  Dr Justine Ward, email, 1 March 2007.
24  Dr Karl Koller, interview, Sydney, 2006.
25  Dr Justine Ward, email, 1 March 2007.
26  Noel Payne, interview, Brisbane, 3 June 2005.
27  Rintoul, *Ashes of Vietnam*, pp. 207–8.
28  Graham Edwards, email, 11 August 2006.
29  A few remarkable examples are the Vietnam Veterans Motorcycle Clubs; the Cockscomb
    Veterans Camp, in the hills outside Rockhampton; and Pandanus Park, at Kalpowar Station, 150
    kilometres north-west of Cooktown. Pandanus, an organisation representing hundreds of old
    soldiers, including Les Hiddins, TV's 'Bush Tucker Man', has fought the Queensland
    Government to have its property, a post–World War I Soldier Settler Block, set aside as a
    veterans' retreat.
30  D. Booth, 'Fucked in the Head' (unpublished memoir).
31  Nguyen Van Mac, interview, Vung Tau, November 2006.

Chapter 48 **Welcome home**

 1  John Press, interviews, Canberra, October 2005.
 2  Peter Poulton, information relating to Welcome Home Parade.
 3  AWM MSS1578, Rhodes, 'Vietnam Veterans' Welcome Home Parade and Reunion' (MA thesis,
    Department of History, Monash University, 1990).

4 Ibid. The National Congress of the RSL, however, did not back the parade, owing to 'antipathy towards the Vietnam Veterans Association' in relation to simmering Agent Orange claims, according to veteran Keith Rossi.

5 Australian Vietnam Forces, National Reunion and Welcome Home Parade, program.

6 Khan, 'Dawn Service Address', p. 2.

7 AWM MSS1578, Rhodes, 'Vietnam Veterans' Welcome Home Parade and Reunion' (MA thesis, Department of History, Monash University, 1990).

8 Ibid.

9 McKay, *Bullets, Beans and Bandages*, p. 262.

10 Giblett, *Homecomings*, p. 63.

11 Palmer, *Vietnam Veterans: Honours and Awards, Army*.

12 Palmer, *Vietnam Veterans: A Record of Service*, p. 200.

13 Ibid., p. 127.

14 Other sources suggest the official quota was one decoration per 250 troops every six months. The Team, incidentally, functioned outside the quota system, due in part to its unusual status as an advisory unit dispatched to Vietnam under the Department of External Affairs.

15 Harry Smith, emails, August 2006.

16 Ibid.

17 Ibid.

18 David Harris, telephone interview, 2006. Harry Smith agrees: 'I am of the opinion that the citations were rewritten, redated, and re-signed by Townsend and Jackson, with an under-the-table deal for Jackson and then Townsend, both the DSO' (email).

19 Colin Townsend, personal papers, letter, Townsend to Derek Roylance, May 1984, handed to author in 2005.

20 In 1998 the Independent Review Panel of the End of War List had reached a similar conclusion (but that did not inhibit the decoration of a Bribie veteran, in 2006). Indeed, yawning anomalies have always existed in the army awards system, as David Sabben submitted to a formal government review (Sabben, 'Submission to the Review of Service Entitlement Anomalies in Respect of South-East Asian Service, 1955–1975'). For example, DSOs were almost automatically bestowed on battalion commanders, yet a DSO recipient must have shown 'conspicuous gallantry and leadership under fire or under conditions equivalent to service in actual combat with the enemy. Normally reserved for Lieutenant Colonels and Majors', states the *Honours and Awards Manual* of 1966. It added, 'For senior officers, leadership over a period under fire entailing gallantry is also necessary …' Few recipients of the DSO displayed conspicuous gallantry *under fire*, Sabben contends. Several majors did — including Smith — but not a single major received a DSO.

21 Letter, Vice Admiral Sir Richard Peek, Chief of Naval Staff, to Admiral Sir Victor Smith, KBE, CB, DSC, 28 July 1972 (my emphasis).

22 Brochure published to commemorate the Vietnam War Memorial, Canberra.

## Chapter 49 ... borne back ceaselessly into the past

1 Guide at the Long Phuoc tunnels, November 2005.

2 Nguyen Gia Ho, interview, Xuyen Moc, November 2005.

3 Museum, Long Hai Mountains, Ba Ria-Vung Tau province, South Vietnam.

4 Ngo Van Ly, interview, Hanoi, November 2005.

5 Mai Thuan, interview, Hanoi, November 2005.

6 Ibid.

7 Ibid.

8 Ngo Van Ly, interview, Hanoi, November 2005.

9 Huu Ngoc, lecture, Hanoi, 28 November 2005.

10 AWM PR00341, survey in Papers of T. W. Pracy, No. 9 Squadron, RAAF.

11 Kelly, 'Vietnam — 30 years on', Australian War Memorial Anniversary Oration, 11 November 2005.

12  Ibid.

13  Gaiduk, *The Soviet Union and the Vietnam War*, p. 18.

14  Ibid., p. 19.

15  Ibid., p. 31.

16  Three North Vietnamese commanders (now retired) — Lieutenant General Mai Thuan (infantry), Lieutenant General Ngo Van Ly (armour) and Colonel Pham Van Trung (anti-aircraft artillery) — concurred in interviews with these views, Hanoi, November 2005.

17  Ang Cheng Guan, *The Vietnam War From the Other Side*, p. 44.

18  Karnow, *Vietnam*, p. 329.

19  Gaiduk, *The Soviet Union and the Vietnam War*, p. 16.

20  Qiang Zhai, *China and the Vietnam Wars, 1950–1975*, p. 117.

21  Ibid.; Gaiduk, *The Soviet Union and the Vietnam War*; Chang and Halliday, *Mao*.

22  Qiang Zhai, *China and the Vietnam Wars, 1950–1975*, pp. 217–22.

23  One soldier better placed than many to judge the effect of the Domino Theory was Sandy Pearson (now Major General, retired). In 1964 Pearson worked in a top-secret signals intelligence unit in Singapore where he listened to radio communications throughout South-East Asia (between 1959 and Confrontation in 1964, the signals intelligence detachment in Singapore was initially known as 201, then as 121 Signal Squadron; see Blaxland, 'The Role of Signals Intelligence in Australian Military Operations', www.defence.gov.au). In the early 1960s his eavesdropping on communist radio traffic persuaded him that the Domino Theory was a myth. Asian communist parties were not organised across borders, and did not present a monolithic threat (Sandy Pearson, interview, Sydney, 4 September 2006).

24  Kelly, 'Vietnam — 30 Years On', Australian War Memorial Anniversary Oration, 11 Nov. 2005.

25  Beaumont, *Australian Defence: Sources and Statistics*, p. 32.

26  Kelly, 'Vietnam — 30 Years On', Australian War Memorial Anniversary Oration, 11 Nov. 2005.

27  Sandy Pearson, interview, Sydney, 4 September 2006.

28  Kimball, *To Reason Why*, p. 135.

29  Kelly, 'Vietnam — 30 Years On', Australian War Memorial Anniversary Oration, 11 Nov. 2005.

30  Ibid.

31  A glib argument in favour of a Free World 'victory' is that the war ended in 1973, when both sides signed the peace treaty. According to this idea, America had fought the communists to a standstill without surrendering the South; a deal was struck; and the border was agreed. Most of the Free World forces had already left. The ensuing North Vietnamese invasion was thus a new war, the 'Third Indochina War', runs this argument. This idea does not wash: only a peculiarly legalistic, or politically naive, mind would tolerate such an interpretation. True, both sides signed a piece of paper. But the Paris Peace Accords, like the Geneva Agreements, were forced upon an unwilling South, for which peace had not been secured. Even as Nixon and Kissinger hailed the deal as 'Peace with Honour', the People's Army was lining up South Vietnamese in its sights. The Free World forces had *not* finished the job: they had *not* stopped the fighting in the South. On the contrary, in agreeing to let thousands of North Vietnamese troops remain in the South, America signed a deal that assured the resumption of war and the collapse of South Vietnam. In short, Kissinger's signature was the mark of surrender. US Congress stood aside as the North overran South Vietnam. This last act compounded rather than ameliorated Washington's defeat and disgrace.

32  Thompson, *No Exit*.

33  Halberstam, *The Best and the Brightest*, p. 145.

34  Ibid., p. 41.

35  In 1961 George Ball, Under Secretary of State, famously warned against sending ground troops: within five years Vietnam would suck in 300,000 US soldiers, he said. Kennedy replied, 'George, you're crazier than hell' (Halberstam, *The Best and the Brightest*, p. 174).

36  Qiang Zhai, *China and the Vietnam Wars, 1950–1975*.

37  Horner, *SAS: Phantoms of War*, pp. 390–1.

38  AWM107(1), Interview with Brigadier John Salmon, Army Historical Programme, p. 36.
39  Governor-General Michael Jeffery, address to AATTV Reunion Dinner, Perth, 31 August 2002.
40  Clark, G., 'The Vietnam Debate Revisited', *Quadrant*, October 1989, p. 18 (Serong's emphasis).
41  The closest estimates based on the most reliable sources.
42  Australian War Memorial, 'Australian Military Statistics: The Vietnam War — Casualties and Contributions', www.awm.gov.au/atwar/statistics/vietnam.htm
43  www.archives.gov/research/vietnam-war/casualty-statistics.html and www.historynet.com/wars_conflicts/vietnam_war/3033736.html
44  Lewy, *Encyclopedia Americana*; Kutler, *Encyclopedia of the Vietnam War.*
45  Lewy, *Encyclopedia Americana*; Summers, *On Strategy.*
46  Kutler, *Encyclopedia of the Vietnam War*; Lewy, *Encyclopedia Americana*; Olson, *Dictionary of the Vietnam War*; Summers, *On Strategy.*
47  Lewy, *Encyclopaedia Americana.*
48  Rummel, *Statistics of Democide.*
49  Groenewegen, 'The Public Finance of Australia's Participation in the Vietnam War', *Australian Quarterly*, Vol. 42, No. 4, December 1970, pp. 63–73.
50  Campagna, *The Economic Consequences of the Vietnam War*, pp. 96–7.
51  Ibid., p. 108.
52  Simon Townsend, interview, Sydney, 1 September 2006.
53  Bao Ninh, *The Sorrow of War*, p. 42. His book, a literary masterpiece, is a bitter repudiation of the war; in this, it follows a Vietnamese tradition. Although Vietnam's historic experience has tended to be one of resistance to external aggression, Vietnamese literature does not glorify war or sing 'the grandeur of massacres' (Huu Ngoc, *Wandering Through Vietnamese Culture*, p. 501). Perhaps the greatest Vietnamese poem (after the classic *The Tales of Kieu*) is an implicitly anti-war poem, 'Chinh Phu Ngam' (Lament of a Wife Whose Husband Has Gone to War): 'He bade me farewell and my heart broke,' wrote the poet Doan Thi Diem (1705–48), in her adaptation of the longer original written in classical Chinese by her contemporary Dang Tran Con. The poem has been a lullaby, a guiding spirit and a source of inspiration to millions of Vietnamese families.
54  Brian McFarlane, interview, Sydney, 29 May 2006.

# Bibliography

## Interviews and discussions
In person, by post, telephone or email.

### Vietnam veterans
This section includes army, air force and navy personnel of all ranks, Australian and New Zealand, unless stated. In many cases, soldiers' wives were also interviewed.

Colin Adamson, Ian Ahearn, Bill Akell, Gordon Alexander, Phillip Anderson, Ross Anderson, Paddy Bacskai, Neil Baker, Richard Barry, Charlie Bartkus, Fred Beal, Graham Bell, Frank Benko, Phillip Bennett, Rick Bensley, Bruce Bickham, Barry Billing, Michael Bindley, John Binnie, Murray Blake, Gary Blinco, David Booth, Jim Bourke, Kevin Bovill, Bob Breen, Bob Buick, John Bullen, Terry Burstall, David Butler, Bruce Cameron, Ian Cavanough, Graeme Chapman, 'Cheyenne', Ted Chitham, Bob Church, John Church, Neville Clark, Terry Cobby, Geoff Cohen, Bob Coker, Bob Coleman, Barry Corse, Bob Cornwell, Peter Cosgrove, Bernie Cox, Rodney Cox, Ian Crangle, Richard Creagh, Bill Crombie, Neville Cullen, Graham Cusack, Don Dali (US forces), Bruce Davies, Phil Davies, Noel de Grussa, Derrill de Heer, John Dellaca, Ray De Vere, Gregg Dickson, Peter Dinham, Bill Dobell, Greg Dodds, Graeme Doolin, Laurie Drinkwater, John Eaton, Graham Edwards, Ross Ellis, Jono Elson, John Essex-Clark, Henry Fabisiak, Rory Farquasson, Mike Fernando, Tim Fischer, Jack Fitzgerald (US forces), Bruce Fletcher, Bernie Folkes, Jim Gable, Rod Gearhart, Denis Gibbons, Rick Giblett, Kev Gillett, Don Gillies, Jock Gordon, Alan Gould, Frank Grady, Bob Grandin, Peter Gration, Peter Gregory, Phil Greville, Ron Grey, John Griffin, Graham Griffiths, Bob Gully, Trevor Hagan, David Hall, Philip Ham, Richard Hannigan, Nat Hardcastle, Ron Hargrave, David Harris, Stan Harris, Steve Hart, Jack Hayes, Barry Heard, Garry Heskett, John Heslewood, Harold Heslop, John Hevey, Brian Hewitt, Brian Honner, Ross Horne, David Horner, Richard Hornery, Graham Irvine, Jim Irvine, Peter Jameson, Michael Jeffery, Geoff Jenkins, Tony Jensen, Garry Johns, Norm Johns, Chris Johnson, Geoff Jones, Spike Jones, Tony Keech, 'Ned' Kelly, Ian Kennedy, Colin Khan, Alan Kitchen, Ian Kortlang, Nick LeRay-Meyer, Theo Linden, Rick Lindmark, Gregg Lindsay, Bob Livingstone, David Llewelyn, Greg Lockhart, Charlie Lynn, Rod Lyons, Ian Mackay, Mark Moloney, Gerard Mapstone, Ern Marshall, Bernie McCartin, Gerry McCormack, Peter McDonald, Brian McFarlane, Gary McKay, Brian McKenzie, Gary McMahon, Philip McNamara, Barry Middleton, Carlo Mikkelsen, Gerry Mitten, Charles Mollison, Bob Morrow, Alan Moore, Bob Moore, David Morgan, David Morris, Paul Murphy, Lindsay Naylor, Graham Neil, John Norris, Trevor Nye, Owen O'Brien, Terry O'Brien, Paul O'Connor, Mick O'Halloran, Bill O'Mara, Bob O'Neill, Keith Payne, Noel Payne, Roger Pearce, Sandy Pearson, Norm Peatling, Barry Petersen, Garry Prendergast,

John Press, Harry Prosser, Nick Quigley, Ian Rafferty, Neil Rankin, Bruce Ravenscroft, Merv Reid, Bob Richards, Trevor Richards, Ross Riddett, James Riddle, Adrian Roberts, Bill Roche, Geoff Rose, Hans Roser, John Rowe, Normie Rowe, Rex Rowe, Barry Russ, David Sabben, John Salmon, John Salter, Tony Scott, Brian Sewell, Gavin Sharp, Mick Shave, Mick Sheean, Jim Shelton, Bryan Smith, Eric Smith, Harry Smith, Noel Sproles, John Staal, Morrie Stanley, Peter Stapleton, Iain Stewart, Ian Stiles, Ron Tait, Donald Tate, Richard Terry, Wally Thompson, Neville Tickner, Colin Townsend, Eddie Tricker, Jack van Dam, Vietnam Veterans' Motorcycle Club (various members), Roger Wainwright, Harry Wall, Stuart Wallace, Tony White (1RAR), Tony White (5RAR), William Walker, David Webster, Neil Weekes, Don Weir, Peter Westwood, Alan White, Harry Whiteside, David Wilkins, Roger Wilson, Neville Woodward, Peter Young, Claude Zavattaro.

## Australian, UK and US civilians

June Allan, Jan Bell, Victoria Binnie, Frances Byak, Meredith Burgmann, Val Campbell, Barry Cohen, Joan Coxsedge, Lorrae Desmond, Maureen Elkner, Barbara Ferguson, Malcolm Fraser, Graham Freudenberg, Bob Gould, Jeffrey Grey, John Hambly, Michael Hamel-Green, Gerry Harant, Simon Harrington, Ingrid Hart (Vass), Geoff Hodgkinson, Ian Hopley, Glynis Howarth, Mark Johnson, Karl Koller, Jean Debelle Lamensdorf, Roger Lee, Carter Malkasian, Daniel Marston, Garry McDougall, Siobhan McHugh, Wendy Moline, Don Morrisson, Kristy Muir, Rod and Rose Murray, Penny Peel, Sue Quinn, Alan Ramsey, Sylvia Raye, Stuart Rintoul, Bob Scates, Michael Sexton, Greg Sheridan, Simon Townsend, Fiona Tuckwell, Paul Vercoe, Harry Ward, Justine Ward, Andrew Williams, Peter Williams, Peter Wright.

## Vietnamese veterans and civilians, Australia

Khien Dinh Nguyen, Tien Manh Nguyen, Bich Phan, Tuan Van Phan, Vo Dai Ton, Vo Hoa Son.

## Vietnamese veterans and civilians, Vietnam

Nguyen Van Anh, Soa Binh, 'Major Chinh', Phan Chien, 'Major Dau', Hoang Xuan Hien, 'Mr Hiep', Nguyen Duc Hoan, Nguyen Nam Hung, Minh Levan, Ngo Van Ly, Hoang Minh Manh, 'Mr Mac', Huu Ngoc, Gia Ho Nguyen, Nguyen Minh Ninh, Nguyen Minh Le, Nguyen Long Quang, Pham Truong Thanh, Mai Thuan, Pham Van Trung, and many veterans and civilians in Vietnam who asked not to be named.

# Archives

## Australian War Memorial, Canberra
### Military records, Vietnam
The following files contain reports on Australian Army Training Team Vietnam, infantry, RAAF and SAS operations, intelligence reports, standing orders, messages, honours and awards, casualty figures and notifications, medical reports, letters home, charge sheets, court martial records, enemy reports, miscellaneous reports and so on

during the Australian involvement in Vietnam (1962–71) and were examined.
AWM 89, 95, 98 100, 103, 116, 117, 273, 275, 279, 284, 288, 290, 293.

In addition the following files were closely examined:

AWM95, Australian Army War Diaries — South-East Asian Conflicts.

AWM95, Long Tan After-action reports.

AWM98, Headquarters Australian Force Vietnam (Saigon) Records.

AWM101, Records of Chief of the General Staff.

AWM102, Australian Army Vietnam Records.

AWM102 [35], Records Associated with the Battle of Long Tan.

AWM102 [42], 6RAR: After-action Report, Operation Smithfield, 18–21 August 1966, Nui Dat.

AWM103, Headquarters 1st Australian Task Force (Nui Dat) records.

AWM107(1), Australian Army Historical Programme — Oral History Recordings for the Australian War Memorial. Interviews with Australian Force Vietnam and 1st Australian Task Force commanders: Major General Don Dunstan, Brigadier Phillip Greville, Major General R. A. Hay, Major General William Henderson, Major General Colin Fraser, Brigadier David Jackson, Major General A. L. MacDonald, Major General Ken Mackay, Major General Sandy Pearson, Brigadier John Salmon, Brigadier Ted Serong, Major General Tim Vincent, Brigadier Bill Weir.

AWM107(2), Australian Army Historical Programme — Oral History Recordings for the Australian War Memorial. Interviews with Battalion commanders: Lieutenant Colonels Lou Brumfield, Alex Preece, Peter Scott, Jim Hughes, Phillip Bennett.

AWM115, Headquarters 1st Australian Task Force (Nui Dat) Records of Units Under Command.

AWM117, Headquarters 1st Australian Logistic Support Group (Vung Tau) Records of Units Under Command.

AWM125, Written Records, South-East Asian Conflicts.

AWM177, Australian Army Commanders' Diaries.

AWM181, Herbicide Series, Vietnam (series of commanders' diaries and other formation records used in the preparation of the Australian Army's *Report on the Use of Herbicides, Insecticides and other Chemicals by the Australian Army in South Vietnam*. The records were made publicly available when the report was tabled in December 1982).

AWM181, Psychological Reports, Civil Affairs, Logistics and 1RAR Commander's Diary, 9RAR Commander's Diary, 161 Reconnaissance Flight.

AWM290, After-action Reports for Operations of 1RAR, 2RAR, 3RAR, 4RAR, 5RAR, 6RAR, 7RAR, 8RAR, 9RAR (all tours of duty).

AWM290, Captured Enemy Documents — many of which were declassified during my research.

AWM314, Public Presentation of US Prisoners of War.

RRC02398, Entertainment for the Troops Collection, 1912–91.

*Papers and theses*

MSS0838, MacDonald, J., 'Opposition Within the Church to Australia's Military Involvement in Vietnam', 1974.

MSS1009, York, B., 'Sources of Student Unrest in Australia with Particular Reference to La Trobe University, 1967–72', 1983.

MSS1068, Colebatch, H., 'An Examination of the Sources, Ideologies and Political Importance of Peace Movements in Australia from c. 1950 to 1965', 1974.

MSS1082, Hamilton-Smith, M. J. L., 'Australian Involvement in Counter-insurgency Programmes in South Vietnam, 1961–65', 1984.

MSS1109, Grey, J. G., 'The Ground War in Vietnam: Some Aspects of the Post-War Debate', 1982.

MSS1160, Wilson, F. J., 'Women in the anti-Vietnam War, Anti-conscription Movement in Sydney 1964–1972', 1985.

MSS1431, Pahl, A. W., Poems.

MSS1569, Tilley, G. and Milner, B., Experiences of RAAF Nursing Service — Vietnam.

MSS1578, Rhodes, C., 'Vietnam Veterans' Welcome Home Parade and Reunion', 1990.

*Personal records — Australian*

3DRL/3771(A), Papers of Brig. W. G. Henderson.

3DRL/6117, Papers of Col. C. M. Townsend.

3DRL/7689, Papers of Sgt W. L. Fogarty.

AWM265, Records of the Official Historian Peter Edwards, *A Nation at War*.

MSS 5898 26 (55), Alex Carey Papers.

PR00032, Papers of A. Treffry.

PR00076, Papers of Dr D. Beard (Col.).

PR00202, Papers of Dr B. L. Dunn (Maj.).

PR00215, Papers of Col. L. G. Clark.

PR00330, Papers of D. Keating.

PR00331, Papers of Lt B. L. Smith.

PR00341, Papers of T. W. Pracy.

PR00659, Papers of 2nd Lt C. O. G. Williams.

PR00660, Papers of Maj. P. Young.

PR00665, Papers of Sgt W. F. Hacking.

PR01214, Papers of WOII A. J. A. Joyce.

PR01533, Papers of F. Delaney.

PR01634, Papers of Able Seaman A. L. Ey.

PR01769, Papers of G. Neat (ABC correspondent).

PR02075, Papers of Chaplain P. McCormick.

PR83/227, Papers, letters of Maj. E. M. McCormick.

PR84/177, Papers and manuals of Maj. A. B. Garland.

PR84/204, Submission to 'Agent Orange' Royal Commission by Vietnam Veterans' Association of Australia.

PR85/089, Letters, photos, newspaper clippings of Maj. F. Lomas.

PR85/148, Papers of Lt D. R. Sabben.

PR85/426, J. Dux and P. J. Young, Research Notes and Material for *Agent Orange; The Bitter Harvest.*

PR86/091, Book and papers of Vietnam Moratorium Campaign (Organising Committee).

PR87/084, Papers of Lt Col. L. B. Swifte.

PR87/157, Papers of Lt Col. N. C. Smith.

PR87/163, Vietnam Veterans' Association of Australia, administration papers, 1970–87.

PR87/166, Papers of A. H. 'Lex' McAulay.

PR87/195, Papers of Cpl R. J. Kelly.

PR88/062, Records of M. Sheldrick.

PR88/091, Records of Lt M. P. J. O'Brien.

PR88/179, Miscellaneous papers of families of Vietnam soldiers 1962–72.

PR89/097, Papers of Lt Col. A. B. Petersen.

PR89/100, Papers of Dr G. Wilson.

PR89/104, Papers of Lt Col. P. T. Murray.

PR90/162, Papers of D. Horsfield.

PR91//79, Papers of 2nd Lt C. Williams.

PR91/114, Papers of G. Carpay.

*Personal records — Vietnamese*

PR85/254, Diary of Nguyen Vu Co D445 LF BN, Viet Cong, Vietnam War.

3DRL/7551, Papers of Huynh Chien Dau, Viet Cong fighter, war in Vietnam, 1961–75.

PR91/183, Papers of Tran Van Tai.

PR87/75, Papers of Viet Cong unit (unknown).

PR86/036, Page from North Vietnamese child's school book.

NATIONAL ARCHIVES OF AUSTRALIA, CANBERRA

*Department of External/Foreign Affairs files*

These files cover Australian aid to Vietnam, withdrawal of Australian forces from Vietnam, Vietnamese refugees, evacuation of Vietnamese orphans.

A1838, A1838/1, A4531/1, NAA.

*Prime Minister's Department files*

These files cover policy in Vietnam, SEATO Council meetings, Manila Conference, strategic basis of Australia's defence policy, US request for Australian defence assistance, Moratorium campaign, national service policy, Prime Minister's visits to Asian countries, control of communist propaganda in Australia, Prime Minister's correspondence, cabled reports and communiqués.

A1209/25, A1209/39, A1209/46, A1209/60, A1209/80, A1945, A5619, NAA.

*Prime Minister's Cabinet records*
A4940 NAA — Sir Robert Menzies, Harold Holt.
A5882 — John Gorton, William McMahon.
A5931 — Gough Whitlam.
A10756 — Malcom Fraser.

*Cabinet office files*
A5882/1, A5882/2, A5883, NAA.

*General files*
A4531/6 NAA — Wilfred Burchett.
A4940 NAA — Australian military aid to South Vietnam, Civil Aid Programme.

LYNDON BAINES JOHNSON LIBRARY AND MUSEUM, AUSTIN, TEXAS —
PAPERS OF LYNDON BAINES JOHNSON
*National Security files*
Agency File, Box 42.
Country File — Asia and the Pacific, Australia, Box 233.
Country File — Asia and the Pacific, Australia, Box 234.
Country File — Vietnam, Boxes 17, 88 and 91.
Files of Robert W. Komer, Box 12.
Files of Walt W. Rostow, Box 8.
Head of State Correspondence [with Menzies, Holt and Gorton], Boxes 1 and 3.
International Meetings and Travel File, Boxes 2–7, 9–11, 20 and 36.
National Security Council, Manila Conference and President's Asia Trip, 17
    October–2 November 1966, Box 46.
Special Head of State Correspondence, Boxes 3 and 4.
Subject File, 'Sequoia Trips — Diplomatic Dinners', Box 45.

*White House Aides' Office files*
Bellinger, C., Boxes 1a and 15.
Busby, H., Box 53.
Hardesty, R., Box 1 (1651).
Sparks, W., Box 11.

*White House Central files*
Asian Countries, Meeting with Leaders — 1–23 October 1966, Box 66.
Australia, CO18, Boxes 13 and 15.
Confidential File, Box 71 [2 of 2].
Confidential File, CO312, Vietnam (Situation in), Boxes 71, 72 and 73.
Confidential File, July–December 1966, Boxes 6 and 72.
Confidential File, October–December 1967, Box 73.
Confidential File, Name File, Clark, E., Box 240.
Confidential File, Name File, Gorton, J., Box 146.

Confidential File, Name File, Hasluck, P., Box 146.
Confidential File, Name File, Holt, H., Box 146.
Confidential File, Name File, Menzies, R., Box 148.
Confidential File, Name File, Waller, J., Box 152.
Confidential File, TR49, Box 95.
Confidential File TR100, Daily Reports, Box 95.
Confidential File TR136, Australia, Box 96.
White House Press Office Files, Background Briefings, February 1968,
    Box 88.
White House Social Files — Alpha, Australia, Box 48.

*Personal papers*
Ball, G., Personal Papers, Box 1.
Bellinger, C., Papers, Box 15.

*Oral histories*
Lipsen, C., Gift of Personal Statement, 13 June 1975.
Menzies, R., Gift of Personal Statement, 6 April 1972.
Waller, K., Gift of Personal Statement, 1 December 1969.

*Other files*
CBS interview with LBJ: 'Why I Chose Not to Run', Box 3.
Meeting Notes Files, Boxes 1 and 2.

## Unpublished papers, diaries, memoirs, letters

Adamson, C., Several unpublished articles covering his tour in Vietnam.
Adshead, B., Robinson, N., Gillies, D., Jacka, S., Personal reflections on the battle of
    Suoi Chau Pha, A Company 7RAR, 6 August 1967.
Ahearn, I., 'Attack on 13th May 1968: A Short History of 102 Battalion'.
Akell, W., Personal papers.
Allen, J., Personal papers.
Binnie, J., Personal papers.
Blake, M., Notes on the Battle of Binh Ba — June 1969, compiled
    January 2007.
Booth, D., 'Fucked in the Head', 1996 (a personal account of his post-war
    condition written for his doctor).
Bourke, J., General notes and maps, OPERATION AUSSIES HOME, involving the
    whereabouts of veterans listed as MIA (Parker, Gillson, Fisher and Gillespie),
    2002.
Buick, B., 'A Platoon Sergeant's Perspective of the Battle of Long Tan, 18 August
    1966' (unpublished article).
Bullen, J., Diaries, 1968.
Camm, K., Letter to author, 20 April 2005.
Chambers, L. C., Personal papers.

Clarke, 'S.', Curry, M., Grubb, W., Higgins, K., Hornsby, R., Irvine, D., Kyte, R., Morris, J., Selmes, J., Sigvart 'S.', Single, J. and Stewart, I., 'Tall Tales But True: Stories from D Company, 6RAR, 1969–70'.

Cobby, T., Letters home during his tour in Vietnam, 1968.

Cohen, J., Notes on Coral and Balmoral.

Corse, B., 'Recollections — Vietnam October 1967'.

Cubis, R., Letter on the Battle of Long Tan, 2 October 1974.

Daly, T., 'The Fraser Affair — February 1971', February–March 1971.

Desmond, L., Personal notes on her concerts in Vietnam.

Dinham, P., 2Pl, A Coy Ptl, 23 Nov 66 — Op Ingham; 2Pl, A Coy Involvement at Long Tan 18 August 1966.

8 Platoon, C Company, 7th Battalion, Royal Australian Regiment, OPERATION COBURG (no named author; an account of the operation, with photos).

Essex-Clark, J., Personal papers.

Faggotter, J. (ed.), 'Australia, Don't Forget About Us — The Vietnam War 1961–1975'.

Ferguson, B., Letters 1967–74 (covering her experiences in Vietnam as a teacher and civil aid worker).

Fernando, M., Personal papers.

Fletcher, B., Notes on his tour as official war artist.

Gration, P., 'A Comparison of Strategies in the Vietnam War', April 1968.

Greville, P., Personal papers, newspaper articles.

Grey, J., Personal papers.

Ham, P., '25 Years On — Recollections of a National Serviceman 1968–1970'.

Hannigan, R., Notes on the Battle of Long Tan.

Hargrave, R., Personal notes.

Harris, R., 'The New Breed', personal memoir.

Jones, 'Spike', 'South Vietnam — 1st Tour — May 1966–67, B Company, 6RAR'.

Kerr, W., 1ARU MAT Adviser's Diary, Parts 1 and 2, Nov.–Dec. 1968.

Khan, C., Personal papers, including speeches on the Battle of Binh Ba.

Linden, M., 'A Christmas to Remember'.

Lindmark, R., 'Another Day in Vietnam I Will Never Forget'.

Llewelyn, D., Personal papers.

Moloney, M., Notes on his tour with 7RAR.

McMahon, Gary, 'Why Was Vietnam unique?'.

Meray, Tibor, 'My Memoirs of Wilfred Burchett'.

Middleton, B., 'My Story — The Way I Felt'.

Mikkelsen, C., 'My Way to Vietnam — and My Involvement in the Vietnam War'.

Morgan, D., Autobiography (an account of his tour of Vietnam).

Nguyen Nam Hung, Ex-Regimental Commander of 274th Regiment, 1966, Statement in Response to Questionnaire About the Battle of Long Tan, Vung Tau, 2 October 2005.

O'Brien, T., 'My First 24 Hours In Country', 3 February 1968.

O'Neill, R., 'Viet Cong Structure' (notes of an intelligence officer in Phuoc Tuy province).

Peatling, N., 'My Military Career 1966/68'; notes on tour with 3RAR; after-action reports on the battle of Balmoral.

Press, J., Notes on his tour with 7RAR.

Quigley, N., Personal papers.

Richards, R., Personal papers.

Rose, G., 'Vietnam — March/April 1975'.

Rowe, J., Personal papers.

Sabben, D., Notes on his tour with 6RAR.

Salmon, J., Personal papers.

Smith, E., Personal papers.

Smith, H., Personal papers.

Townsend, C., Personal papers (numerous letters, after-action reports and articles).

Tyons, T., 'Heartbreak Hill'.

Weekes, N., 'FSPB "Coral"'.

Wilkins, D., 'A Vietnam Diary — My Story of Active Service', 2004.

Wilson, R., Diary, 1968.

Young, P., Personal papers, letters, confidential reports, articles.

## Published reports, essays, theses, articles

Atrens, D., 'Madness and Neuromythology', *Quadrant*, September 2000.

Australian Government, *The Mortality Report*, Parts 1–3, Australian Veterans Health Studies, Canberra, 1984.

Australian Military Forces, Pocketbook, South Vietnam, published by the Australian Army during the Vietnam War.

Australian Vietnam Forces, National Memorial, Commemorative Booklet, Canberra, Australian Government, October 1992.

Australian Vietnam Forces, National Reunion and Welcome Home Parade, official program, October 1987.

Blair, A., 'Get Me Ten Years: Australia's Ted Serong in Vietnam, 1962–1975', a paper to the 1996 Vietnam Symposium, After the Cold War: Reassessing Vietnam, 18–20 April 1996, Texas Tech University, Lubbock, Tex.

Blaxland, J., 'The Role of Signals Intelligence in Australian Military Operations', www.defence.gov.au/army/LWSC/Publications/journal/AAJ_Autumn05/AA J_Autumn05_blaxland

Burke, A., 'The Battle of Binh Ba', www.anzacday.org.au.

Bushby, R. N., 'Educating an Army: Australian Army Doctrinal Development and the Operational Experience in South Vietnam, 1965–72', Canberra Papers on Strategy and Defence, No. 126, Strategic and Defence Studies Centre, Research School of Pacific and Asian Studies, Australian National University, Canberra 1998.

Cable, R. W., 'An Independent Command: Command and Control of the 1st Australian Task Force in Vietnam', Canberra Papers on Strategy and Defence,

No. 134, Strategic and Defence Studies Centre, Research School of Pacific and Asian Studies, ANU, Canberra 2000.

Cairns, J., 'Vietnam: Is It Truth We Want?', Victorian Branch of the Australian Labor Party, Melbourne, 1965.

Channon, J. (compiler), *The First Three Years: A Pictorial History of the 173rd Airborne Brigade*, Brigade Information Office, Tokyo, 1968.

Clark, Gregory, 'Life Story", www.gregoryclark.net/lifestory.

Coates, J., 'Preparing Armoured Units for Overseas Service', in *The Australian Army and the Vietnam War 1962–72* (Dennis, P. and Grey, J., eds), Chief of Army's Military History Conference 2002, Army History Unit, Canberra 2002.

Crane, P. J., Burnard, D. I., Horsley, K. D. and Adena, M. A., *Mortality of Vietnam Veterans: The Veteran Cohort Study: A Report of the 1996 Retrospective Cohort Study of Australian Vietnam Veterans*, Department of Veterans' Affairs, Canberra, 1997.

Crane, P. J., Burnard, D. I., Horsley, K. D. and Adena, M. A., *Mortality of National Service Vietnam Veterans: A Report of the 1996 Retrospective Cohort Study of Australian Vietnam Veterans*, Department of Veterans' Affairs, Canberra, 1997.

*Cu Chi — The Document Album*, Vietnam Government Publishers, Ho Chi Minh City, 2004.

Dennis, P. and Grey, J. (eds), *The Australian Army and the Vietnam War 1962–72*, Chief of Army's Military History Conference 2002, Army History Unit, Canberra, 2002.

Dennis, P. and Grey, J. (eds), *Entangling Alliances: Coalition Warfare in the Twentieth Century*, Chief of Army's Military History Conference 2005, Australian History Military Publications, Canberra, 2005.

Department of External Affairs, *Presidential and Senate Elections in the Republic of Vietnam on 3 September 1967: Report of the Australian Observers*, Parliamentary Paper No. 145, Canberra 1967.

Department of External Affairs, *Select Documents on International Affairs, No. 1: Viet Nam Since the 1954 Geneva Agreements*, Canberra, December 1964.

Department of External Affairs, *Select Documents on International Affairs, No. 9: Vietnam, February 1966 to October 1966*, Canberra, December 1966.

Department of External Affairs, *Select Documents on International Affairs, No. 9: Vietnam, November 1966 to June 1967*, Canberra.

Department of External Affairs, *Select Documents on International Affairs, No. 9: Vietnam, July 1967 to December 1967*, Canberra.

Department of External Affairs, *Vietnam, Australia and Asia: Attitudes of Asian Countries to Viet-Nam and to Australia's Role There*, Canberra, 1967.

Department of Veterans' Affairs, *Australian National Service Vietnam Veterans: Mortality and Cancer Incidence 2005*, Commonwealth of Australia, Canberra, 2005.

Department of Veterans' Affairs, *Case-Control Study of Congenital Anomalies and Vietnam Service* (Birth Defects Study), Commonwealth of Australia, Canberra, 1983.

Department of Veterans' Affairs, Departmental Instructions, Fact Sheets, Statements of Principles (various conditions), Timeline, Vietnam Veterans Counselling

Service — Summary of Background Events, Commonwealth of Australia, Canberra, various dates.

Department of Veterans' Affairs, *Morbidity of Vietnam Veterans: A Study of the Health of Australia's Vietnam Veteran Community*, Vols 1 and 2, Commonwealth of Australia, Canberra, 1998.

Department of Veterans' Affairs, *The Nominal Roll of Vietnam Veterans*, Commonwealth Department of Veterans' Affairs, Canberra, 1996.

Department of Veterans' Affairs and Australian Incidence of Health and Welfare, *Cancer Incidence in Australian Vietnam Veterans Study 2005*, Commonwealth of Australia, Canberra, 2005.

Department of Veterans' Affairs and Australian Institute of Health and Welfare, *Australian Vietnam Veterans — Mortality and Cancer Incidence Studies*, Overarching Executive Summary 2006, Commonwealth of Australia, Canberra, 2006.

Department of Veterans' Affairs and Australian Institute of Health and Welfare, *The Third Australian Vietnam Veterans Mortality Study 2005*, Commonwealth of Australia, Canberra, 2005.

*Duty First*, March 1994: Vietnam special issue, with articles by Dick Hannigan, Harry Honnor, W. B. James, G. M. McCormack, Ian McNeill, Jim Shelton and Morrie Stanley.

Ekins, A., 'Killing Ground', *The Bulletin*, 16 September 2003 (and letter in reply by Ian Mackay, officer commanding B Coy 6RAR, 1966–67, *The Bulletin*, 23 September 2003).

Environmental Health Perspectives, 'A Geographic Information System for Characterizing Exposure to Agent Orange and Other Herbicides in Vietnam', www.ehponline.org/members/2003/5755/5755.html#herb

Evans, M. and Ryan, A. (eds), *From Breitenfeld to Baghdad: Perspectives on Combined Arms Warfare*, Working Paper No. 122, Land Warfare Studies Centre, Canberra, 2003.

Evatt, P., *Royal Commission on the Use and Effects of Chemical Agents on Australian Personnel in Vietnam*, Commonwealth of Australia, Canberra, 1985.

Fernando, M., 'Nasho in Nam', *Vietnam Veteran Newsletter*, 24 December 2002.

Fett, M. J., Dunn, M., Adena, M. A., O'Toole, B. I. and Forcier, L., *Australian Veteran Health Studies. The Mortality Report*, Part 1, Australian Government Publishing Service, Canberra, 1984

'Facts About the Anti-L. B. J. Demonstration', Monash University Representative Council, Melbourne, 1966.

Grey, R., *Infantry Battalion Lessons from Vietnam*, Centre for Defence Command, Leadership and Management Studies, Australian Defence College, Weston Creek, ACT, 1972.

Groenewegen, P., 'The Public Finance of Australia's Participation in the Vietnam War', *Australian Quarterly*, Vol. 42, No. 4, December 1970, pp. 63–73.

Grossman, D., 'Evolution of weaponry', www.killology.com/print/print_weaponry.htm.

Hall, R., and Ross, A., 'Lessons from Vietnam: Combined Arms Assault Against Prepared Defences', in Evans, M. and Ryan, A. (eds), *From Breitenfeld to Baghdad: Perspectives on Combined Arms Warfare*, Working Paper No. 122, Land Warfare Studies Centre, July 2003.

Hamel-Green, M., 'Vietnam: Beyond Pity', *Dissent*, Winter 1970, No. 25, pp. 30–6.

'Ho Chi Minh's Testament', Central Committee of the Communist Party of Vietnam, Hanoi, 1969.

Horner, D., *Australian Higher Command in the Vietnam War*, Canberra Papers on Strategy and Defence, No. 40, Strategic Defence Studies Centre, Research School of Pacific and Asian Studies, Australian National University, Canberra, 2000.

Hooper, J. and MacGregor, X., 'Operation "Crimp": The First Penetration of the Vietcong Tunnels', *Holdfast*, undated.

Hassett, F. (ed.), 'Counter Revolutionary Warfare', Division in Battle Pamphlet No. 11, Australian Army.

Hitchens, C., 'The Vietnam Syndrome', *Vanity Fair*, August 2006, pp. 112–19.

Hoang Ngoc Lung, *The General Offensives of 1968–69*, McLean, Va., 1981; www.vietnam.ttu.edu/virtualarchive/index.htm.

Information Booklet for National Servicemen, Military Board, Commonwealth of Australia, reprinted throughout 1960s.

Institute of Medicine, *Veterans and Agent Orange: Health Effects of Herbicides Used in Vietnam*, National Academy Press, Washington DC, 1994.

Jeffery, M., address to AATTV Reunion, Perth, 31 August 2002.

Jordens, A., *Conscientious Objection and the Vietnam War*, Working Paper No. 73, Peace Research Centre, Research School of Pacific Studies, ANU, Canberra, 1989.

Kelly, Paul, 'Vietnam — 30 Years On', Australian War Memorial Anniversary Oration, 11 November 2005.

Khan, Brigadier Colin, Dawn Service Address, reprinted in *Reveille*, Vol. 62, No. 6 (New Series), November–December 1987.

Kulka, R., Schlenger, W., Fairbank, J., Hough, R., Jordan, B. K., Marmar, C., Weiss, D. and Grady, D., *Trauma and the Vietnam War Generation: Report of Findings from the National Vietnam Veterans Readjustment Study*, Brunner/Mazel Psychosocial Stress Series No. 18, Brunner/Mazel, New York, 1990.

Lockhart, G., 'The Minefield', *Vietnam Veteran Newsletter*, September 2003.

London, B., 'The Battle of Binh Ba: A Platoon's View', www.5rar.asn.au.

Lu, K., 'Sisters in Arms? The Postwar Relationship Between Australian Army and Civilian Nurses of the Vietnam War', BA thesis.

Morris, S. J., 'The War We Could Have Won', *New York Times*, 1 May 2005.

Muir, K., 'The Hidden Cost of War: The Psychological Effects of the Second World War and the Indonesian Confrontation on Veterans and Their Families', PhD thesis, University of Wollongong, NSW, 2003.

Nelson, D. and Turse, N., 'A Tortured Past: Documents Show Troops Who Reported Abuse in Vietnam Were Discredited Even as the Military Was Finding Evidence of Worse', *Los Angeles Times*, 20 August 2006.

Nguyen Khac Vien (ed.), 'Indochina: The 1972–73 Turning Point', *Vietnamese Studies*, No. 39, Hanoi, 1979.

Nguyen Van Khanh, 'A Glimpse at the Situation of Land, Fields, and Agricultural Production in Viet Nam During the Years of *Doi Moi* (Renewal)', *Vietnamese Studies*, No. 1, Hanoi, 2004.

'Operation Hammer: The Battle at Binh Ba, South Vietnam 6–8 June 1969' (unsigned article), *Ironsides*, No. 2, 1983, Phoenix Defence Publications, Canberra, pp. 3–10.

O'Toole, B. I., Marshall, R. P., Grayson, D. A., Schureck, R. J., Dobson, M., Ffrench, M., Pulvertaft, B., Meldrum, L., Bolton, J., and Vennard J., 'The Australian Vietnam Veterans Health Study: III. Psychological health of Australian Vietnam Veterans and its Relationship to combat', *International Journal of Epidemiology*, Vol. 25, No. 2, 1996, pp. 331–40.

Pannell, B., 'Intelligence in South Vietnam', lecture to the Australian Army Staff College, Fort Queenscliffe, Vic., 1971.

Parliament of the Commonwealth of Australia, *After the March: Report of an Inquiry into Counselling and Ancillary Services for Vietnam Veterans*, Canberra, 1988.

Pegram, A., 'All the Way: Wagga Wagga's Vietnam War Experience', Bachelor of Arts dissertation, Charles Sturt University, Bathurst, NSW, 2004.

Repatriation Commission, Annual Reports 2005–06, Department of Veterans' Affairs and National Treatment Monitoring Committee, Canberra.

Ryan, A., *Australian Army Cooperation With the Land Forces of the United States — Problems of the Junior Partner*, Working Paper No. 121, Land Warfare Studies Centre, Canberra, 2003.

Ryan, A., *'Putting Your Young Men in the Mud': Change, Continuity and the Australian Infantry Battalion*, Working Paper No. 124, Land Warfare Studies Centre, Canberra 2003.

Sabben, D., Submission to the Review of Service Entitlement Anomalies in Respect of South-East Asian Service 1955–75, 7 August 1999.

Senate Standing Committee on Science and the Environment, *Pesticides and the Health of Australian Vietnam Veterans*, First Report, November 1982, Commonwealth of Australia, Canberra, 1982.

Smith, N., *Australian Army Female Service in South Vietnam 1965–1973*, Mostly Unsung Military History Research and Publications, Gardenvale, Vic., 2000.

Sorley, L., 'Remembering Vietnam', lecture delivered to the National Archives, Washington DC, 30 April 2002.

Stack, E., 'A Controlled Intake of Vietnamese Required', 1978 Jamieson Memorial Lecture to the Neuosurgical Society of Australasia, Darwin, reprinted in Australian Medical Association *Gazette*, 24 May 1979.

Stewart, I., 'Infantry Minor Tactics and the Claymore', *Australian Infantry*, Vol. 17, No. 2, May 1971.

Subritzky, M., 'The Second ANZAC Adventure — Gunfire at Long Tan: The FO's Story', www.hotkey.net.au/~marshalle/lt/fostory.htm.

Tidey, B., 'The Modus Operandi and Effectiveness of Specialist Intelligence Support to 1st Australian Task Force, South Vietnam 1966–1971', thesis, Master of Defence Studies, ADFA, Canberra, 2002.

Tracey, M., 'Australians in Vietnam: An Account of the War in Vietnam and the 30th Anniversary Commemorations of the Battle of Long Tan', *Australian Defence Force Journal*, Canberra, 1996.

University Study Group on Vietnam, *Vietnam and Australia: History, Documents, Interpretations*, USGV, Gladesville, NSW, 1966.

US Department of State Publications, *Aggression from the North — The Record of North Vietnam's Campaign to Conquer South Vietnam*, Bureau of Public Affairs, Washington DC, 1965.

Vietnam Action Committee, *Johnson Accused: Bertrand Russell's Indictment of the Vietnam War Criminals*, Comment Publishing Company, Sydney, 1972.

Vietnam Veterans' Association of Australia, Response to the Evatt Royal Commission into the Use and Effects on Australian Personnel of Chemical Agents in Vietnam, Vietnam Veterans Association of Australia, 1985.

Vo Dai Ton, former commando, Republic of Vietnam, collection of articles and poems.

Watt, A., 'The Changing Margins of Australian Foreign Policy', Roy Milne Memorial Lecture, Australian Institute of International Affairs, 1964.

Woloszuk, N., 'Professional Practice and Culture of Journalism During the Wars in Vietnam and Afghanistan', essay, University of Technology, Sydney, 2002.

Young, D. B., 'Vietnam, the Answers: A Reply to the Holt Governments "Vietnam, Questions and Answers".' Sydney, 1966.

Young, P., 'The Military Situation Within South Vietnam, Saigon, July 1967', intelligence appraisal.

World Health Organisation, 'The Republic of Vietnam — South Vietnam,' WHO study, January 1968.

## Journals, newspapers and magazines

*American Journal of Psychiatry*.

*Australian Army Journal*.

*Australian Infantry*.

*Cryptologic Quarterly*, Winter 2000, Vol. 19, No. 4; Spring 2001, Vol. 20, No. 1.

*Daily Telegraph* (key periods, 1965–75; and subsequent dates).

*Duty First*: magazine of the Royal Australian Regiment Association.

*Hansard* (Commonwealth of Australia parliamentary record, 1965–75 — key periods).

*Holdfast* (official newsletter of the Vietnam Tunnel Rats Association, Australia).

*Ironsides* (magazine of the Royal Australian Armoured Corps).

*Journal of Military History*.

*Ladies Home Journal* (USA).

*Life*.

*Los Angeles Times*.

*Mufti* (Victorian RSL official journal).

*New Scientist.*

*New York Times.*

*Pacific Stars and Stripes* (authorised publication of the US Armed Forces, Far East).

*Paulatim* (magazine of the Royal Australian Army Medical Corps).

*The Australian*, (1966–75 and subsequent dates).

*The Bulletin*, (1962–75 and subsequent dates).

*The Lancet.*

*The Sydney Morning Herald*, (1962–75; and subsequent dates).

*Time.*

*Vanity Fair.*

Vietnam Action Campaign, sundry brochures and pamphlets (e.g. *Comment, Vietnam Action, Dissent, 1966–69*).

*Vietnam Veteran Newsletter, The.*

*Vietnamese Studies* (academic journal published in Hanoi).

*Wartime* (journal of the Australian War Memorial).

## Books

Albinski, H. S., *Australian Policies and Attitudes Toward China*, Princeton University Press, Princeton, N.J., 1965.

Albinski, H. S., *Politics and Foreign Policy in Australia: The Impact of Vietnam and Conscription*, Duke University Press, Durham NC, 1970.

American Psychiatric Association, *Diagnostic and Statistical Manual of Mental Disorders*, 4th edn, Washington, 1994.

Anderson, P., *When the Scorpion Stings: The History of the 3rd Cavalry Regiment, South Vietnam, 1965–72*, Allen and Unwin, Sydney, 2002.

Andrews, E., *Australia and China: The Ambiguous Relationship*, Melbourne University Press, Melbourne, 1985.

Andrews, E., *The Department of Defence*, Vol. 5, Australian Centenary History of Defence, Oxford University Press, Melbourne, 2001.

Ang Cheng Guan, *The Vietnam War from the Other Side: The Vietnamese Communists' Perspective*, Routledge Curzon, London, 2002.

Appy, C., *Vietnam: The Definitive Oral History Told from All Sides*, Random House, New York, 2007.

Armbruster, F., Gastil, R., Kahn, H., Pfaff, W. and Stillman, E., *Can We Win in Vietnam? The American Dilemma*, Pall Mall Press, London, 1968.

Arnett, P., *Live From the Battlefield*, Simon and Schuster, London 1994.

Arnold, J., *Cop in a Baggy Green Skin: Reflections of an Australian Military Police Sergeant in Vietnam During 1971–1972*, privately published, 2002.

Arnold, J., *Tet Offensive 1968: Turning Point in Vietnam*, Osprey, Oxford, 2004.

Ashbolt, A., *Words From the Vietnam Years*, Australasian Book Society, Sydney, 1974.

Australian Broadcasting Corporation, *Vietnam: A Reporter's War*, ABC, Sydney, 1975.

Avery, B., *In the ANZAC Spirit. The Fourth Battalion, Royal Australian Regiment/NZ (ANZAC) South Vietnam 1968–1969*, Slouch Hat Publications, McCrae, Vic., 2002.

Avery, B., *We Too Were Anzacs, The 6th Battalion RAR/NZ (ANZAC), South Vietnam, 1969 to 1970*, Slouch Hat Publications, McCrae, Vic., 2004.

Ayres, P., *Malcolm Fraser: A Biography*, William Heinemann, Melbourne, 1987.

Bao Ninh, *The Sorrow of War*, Vintage, London, 1998.

Barnes, I. L., *Australian Gallant and Distinguished Service, Vietnam 1962–73*, Military Historical Society of Australia, Canberra, 1974.

Barr, M., *Surgery, Sand and Saigon Tea*, Allen and Unwin, Sydney, 2001.

Barth, R., *A Soldier's Time: Vietnam War Poems*, John Daniel, Santa Barbara, Calif., 1987.

Battle, M. R. (ed.), *The Year of the Tigers: The Second Tour of 5th Battalion, the Royal Australian Regiment in South Vietnam 1969–70*, Printcraft Press, Brookvale, NSW, 1970.

Beaumont, J. et al., *Australian Defence: Sources and Statistics*, Vol. 6, Australian Centenary History of Defence, Oxford University Press, Melbourne, 2001.

Behr, E., *Anyone Here Been Raped and Speaks English? A Foreign Correspondent's Life Behind the Lines*, Hamish Hamilton, London, 1981.

Biedermann, N., *Tears on My Pillow: Australian Nurses in Vietnam*, Random House, Sydney, 2004.

Bishop, C., *Vietnam War Diary 1964–1975*, Silverdale Books, Leicester, 2003.

Blackburn, R., *Mercenaries and Lyndon Johnson's 'More Flags' — The Hiring of Korean, Filipino and Thai Soldiers in the Vietnam War*, McFarland and Co., Jefferson, NC, 1994.

Blair, A., *Ted Serong: The Life of Australian Counter-insurgency Expert*, Oxford University Press, Melbourne, 2002.

Blair, A., *There to the Bitter End: Ted Serong in Vietnam*, Allen and Unwin, Sydney, 2001.

Blinco, G., *Down a Country Lane*, Zeus, Burleigh, Qld, 2003.

Bonds, R. (ed.), *The Vietnam War*, Salamander Books, London, 1983.

Bouscaren, A. T. (ed.), *All Quiet on the Eastern Front: The Death of South Vietnam*, Devon-Adair Company, Old Greenwich, Conn., 1977.

Bowden, T., *One Crowded Hour: Neil Davis, Combat Cameraman 1934–85*, Angus and Robertson, Sydney, 1987.

Bradford, D., *The Gunners' Doctor*, Random House Australia, Sydney, 2007.

Braestrup, P., *Big Story: How the American Press and Television Reported and Interpreted the Crisis of Tet, 1968 in Vietnam and Washington*, Westview Press, Boulder, Colo., 1977.

Brandon, H., *Anatomy of Error — The Secret History of the Vietnam War*, André Deutsch, London, 1970.

Brass, A., *Bleeding Earth: A Doctor Looks at Vietnam*, William Heinemann, London, 1968.

Bray, G., *Aboriginal Ex-Servicemen of Central Australia*, IAD Press, Alice Springs, 1995.

Breen, R., *First to Fight*, Allen and Unwin, Sydney, 1988.

Brodie, S., *Tilting at Dominoes: Australia and the Vietnam War*, Child and Associates, Brookvale, NSW, 1987.

Buick, R. with McKay, G., *All Guts and No Glory: The Story of a Long Tan Warrior*, Allen and Unwin, Sydney, 2000.

Burchett, W., *Grasshoppers and Elephants: Why Viet Nam Fell*, Urizen Books, New York, 1977.

Burchett, W., *Vietnam Will Win!*, Guardian, New York, 1968.

Burchett, W., *Vietnam — Inside Story of the Guerrilla War*, International Publishers, New York, 1965.

Burstall, T., *A Soldier Returns*, University of Queensland Press, St Lucia, 1990.

Burstall, T., *The Soldier's Story*, University of Queensland Press, St Lucia 1986.

Burstall, T., *Vietnam: The Australian Dilemma*, University of Queensland Press, St Lucia, 1993.

Buttinger, P., *The Smaller Dragon: A Political History of Vietnam*, Praeger, New York, 1958.

Buzzanco, R., *Masters of War: Military Dissent and Politics in the Vietnam Era*, Cambridge University Press, Cambridge, 1996.

Cairns, J., *Silence Kills: Events Leading up to the Moratorium on 8 May 1970*, Vietnam Moratorium Committee, Melbourne, 1970.

Cairns, J., *The Eagle and the Lotus: Western Intervention in Vietnam 1847–1968*, Lansdowne Press, Melbourne, 1969.

Cairns, J., *Vietnam: Scorched Earth Reborn*, Widescope, Camberwell, 1976.

Cameron, J., *Witness*, Victor Gollancz, London, 1966.

Camp, N., Stretch, R., and Marshall, W., *Stress, Strain, and Vietnam: An Annotated Bibliography of Two Decades of Psychiatric and Social Sciences Literature Reflecting the Effect of the War on the American Soldier*, Greenwood Press, Conn., 1988.

Campagna, A., *The Economic Consequences of the Vietnam War*, Praeger, New York, 1991.

Caputo, P., *A Rumor of War*, Arrow Books, London, 1978.

Casula Powerhouse Arts Centre, *Viet Nam Voices: Australians and the Vietnam War*, Casula, NSW, 2000.

Chang, J. and Halliday, J., *Mao: The Unknown Story*, Jonathan Cape, London, 2005.

Chanoff, D. and Doan Van Toai, *Vietnam: A Portrait of Its People at War*, IB Tauris and Co., London, 1996.

Charlton, M. and Moncrieff, A. (eds), *Many Reasons Why: The American Involvement in Vietnam*, Scolar Press, London, 1978.

Chong, D., *The Girl in the Picture: The Remarkable Story of Vietnam's Most Famous Casualty*, Simon and Schuster, London, 2000.

Church, J., *Second to None — 2RAR as the ANZAC Battalion in Vietnam, 1970–71*, Army Doctrine Centre, Sydney, 1995.

Clancy, B., *Best We Forget*, Indra Publishing, Briar Hill, Vic., 1998.

Clark, C., *Yours Faithfully: A Record of Service of the 3rd Battalion, The Royal Australian Regiment in Australia and South Vietnam, 16 February 1969–16 October 1971*, Printcraft Press, Brookvale NSW, 1972.

Clark, G., *In Fear of China*, Lansdowne Press, Melbourne, 1967.

Clunies-Ross, A. (ed.), *Grey Eight in Vietnam, The History of the Eighth Battalion, the Royal Australian Regiment, November 1969 — November 1970*, Brisbane, 1970.

Coates, J., *An Atlas of Australia's Wars*, Vol. 7, Australian Centenary History of Defence, Oxford University Press, Melbourne, 2001.

Coe, J., *Desperate Praise: The Australians in Vietnam*, Artlook Books, Perth, 1982.

Conrad, J., *Heart of Darkness*, Penguin Classics, London, 2000.

Cook, P. (ed.), *Australia and Vietnam 1965–1972*, La Trobe University Studies in History, Department of History, La Trobe University, Melbourne, 1991.

Coulthard-Clark, C., *Hit My Smoke! Targeting the Enemy in Vietnam*, Allen and Unwin, Sydney, 1997.

Coulthard-Clark, C., *The RAAF in Vietnam*, Vol. 3, *The Official History of Australia's Involvement in Southeast Asian Conflicts 1948–1975*, Allen and Unwin, Sydney, in association with the Australian War Memorial, 1995.

Crowe, A., *The Battle After the War: The Story of Australia's Vietnam Veterans*, Allen and Unwin, Sydney 1999.

Crozier, B., *South East Asia in Turmoil*, Penguin, Harmondsworth, UK, 1965.

Curthoys, A. and Merritt, J. (eds), *Australia's First Cold War: 1949–1959*, Vol. 2, *Better Dead than Red*, Allen and Unwin, Sydney, 1986.

Curthoys, A., Martin A. W. and Rowse, T. (eds), *Australians From 1939*, Fairfax, Syme and Weldon Associates, Broadway, NSW, Australia, 1987.

Dallek, R., *Lyndon B. Johnson: Portrait of a President*, Penguin, London, 2005.

Daum, A., Gardner, L., and Mausbach, W. (eds), *America, the Vietnam War, and the World*, Cambridge University Press, New York, 2003.

Davidson, A., *The Communist Party of Australia*, Hoover Institution Press, Stanford University, Stanford, Calif., 1969.

Davies, B. and McKay, G., *The Men Who Persevered*, Allen and Unwin, Sydney, 2005.

Dennis, D., *One Day at a Time: A Vietnam Diary*, University of Queensland Press, St Lucia, 1992.

Department of Veterans' Affairs, *Vietnam: Our War, Our Peace*, Commonwealth of Australia, Canberra, 2006.

Dixon, N., *On the Psychology of Military Incompetence*, Pimlico, London, 1994.

Donnelly, R., *The Scheyville Experience 1965–1973*, University of Queensland Press, St Lucia, Qld, 2001.

Dorr, R., *Vietnam: The Air War*, Osprey, London, 1991.

Eather, S., *Get the Bloody Job Done: The Royal Australian Navy Helicopter Flight — Vietnam and the 135th Assault Helicopter Company 1967–1971*, Allen and Unwin, Sydney, 1998.

Eather, S., *Target Charlie*, Aerospace Publications, Weston Creek, ACT, 1993.

Ebury, S., *Weary: The Life of Sir Edward Dunlop*, Viking, Melbourne, 1994.

Eccles-Smith, P., *Letters from a Viet-Nam Hospital*, A. H. and A. W. Reed, Wellington, New Zealand, 1969.

Edwards, P. (general editor), *The Official History of Australia's Involvement in Southeast Asian Conflicts 1948–1975*, Allen and Unwin, Sydney, in association with the Australian War Memorial (all volumes).

Edwards, P. (with Pemberton, G.), *Crises and Commitments*, Vol. 1, *The Official History of Australia's Involvement in Southeast Asian Conflicts 1948–1975*, Allen and Unwin, Sydney, in association with the Australian War Memorial, 1992.

Edwards, P., *A Nation at War*, Vol. 6, *The Official History of Australia's Involvement in Southeast Asian Conflicts 1948–1975*, Allen and Unwin, Sydney, in association with the Australian War Memorial, 1997.

Ellsberg, D., *Secrets: A Memoir of Vietnam and the Pentagon Papers*, Viking, New York, 2002.

Ellwood-Akers, V., *Women War Correspondents in the Vietnam War, 1961–1975*, Scarecrow Press, London, 1988.

Essex-Clark, J., *Maverick Soldier: An Infantryman's Story*, Melbourne University Press, Melbourne, 1991.

Evans, B., *Caduceus in Saigon: A Medical Mission to South Viet Nam*, Hutchinson, Richmond, Vic., 1968.

Faas, H. and Page, T., *Requiem, by the Photographers Who Died in Vietnam and Indochina*, Jonathan Cape, London, 1997.

Fairbairn, G., *Revolutionary Warfare and Communist Strategy: The Threat to South East Asia*, Faber and Faber, London, 1968.

Fairfax, D., *Navy in Vietnam: A Record of the Royal Australian Navy in the Vietnam War, 1965–1972*, Australian Government Publishing Service, Canberra, 1980.

Fall, B., *Hell in a Very Small Place: The Siege of Dien Bien Phu*, Da Capo Press, New York 2002.

Fall, B., *Last Reflections on a War*, Doubleday, New York, 1967.

Fall, B., *Street Without Joy*, Stackpole Books, Mechanicsburg, Pa., 1994.

Fall, B., *The Two Viet-Nams*, Pall Mall Press, London, 1963.

Fall, B., *Viet-Nam Witness 1953–66*, Frederick A. Praeger, New York, 1966.

Ferguson, B., *Rain in my Heart: Memories of Children and War in South Vietnam*, Lothian Books, Melbourne, 2006.

Figes, O., *A People's Tragedy: The Russian Revolution 1891–1924*, Random House, London, 1996.

Findlay, P., *Protest Politics and Psychological Warfare: The Communist Role in the Anti-Vietnam War and Anti-Conscription Movement in Australia*, Hawthorn Press, Melbourne 1968.

Fitzgerald, F., *Fire in the Lake: The Vietnamese and the Americans in Vietnam*, Little, Brown, Boston, 1972.

Frame, T., *The Life and Death of Harold Holt*, Allen and Unwin, Sydney, 2005.

Frazer, M., *Nasho*, Aires Imprint, West Melbourne, 1984.

Freudenberg, G., *A Certain Grandeur*, Penguin, Melbourne, 1987.

Frost, F., *Australia's War in Vietnam*, Allen and Unwin, Sydney, 1987.

Gaiduk, I., *The Soviet Union and the Vietnam War*, Ivan R. Dee, Chicago, 1966.

Garland, A. N. (ed.), *Infantry in Vietnam: Small Unit Actions in the Early Days 1965–66*, Battery Press, Nashville, Tenn., 1982.

Gee, K., *The Graves of Hué: A Short Study of the Use of Terror as a Political Weapon on the Communists of South Vietnam*, Friends of Vietnam, Sydney, 1969.

Gettleman, M. E. (ed.), *Vietnam History, Documents and Opinions on a Major World Crisis*, Fawcett Crest, New York, 1966.

Giblett, N., *Homecomings: Stories from Australian Vietnam Veterans and their Wives* (2nd edn), Australian Government Publishing Service, Canberra, 1987.

Gilbert, M. J., *Why the North Won the Vietnam War*, Palgrave, New York, 2002.

Gollan, R., *Revolutionaries and Reformists: Communism and the Australian Labour Movement 1920–1955*, ANU Press, Canberra, 1975.

Goot, M. and Tiffen, R. (eds), *Australia's Gulf War*, Melbourne University Press, Carlton, Vic., 1992.

Gottlieb, S. G., *Hell No, We Won't Go! Resisting the Draft During the Vietnam War*, Viking Penguin, New York 1991.

Gottschang Turner, K. with Phan Thanh Hao, *Even the Women Must Fight: Memories of War from North Vietnam*, John Wiley and Sons, New York, 1998.

Grandin, R. (ed.), *The Battle of Long Tan, as Told by the Commanders*, Allen and Unwin, Sydney, 2004.

Greene, G., *The Quiet American*, Penguin, Harmondsworth, UK, 1977.

Grenville, K., *The Saving of South Vietnam*, Alpha Books, Sydney, 1972.

Grey, J. and Dennis, P., *Emergency and Confrontation: Australian Military Operations in Malaya and Borneo 1950–1966*, Vol. 5, *The Official History of Australia's Involvement in Southeast Asian Conflicts 1948–1975*, Allen and Unwin, Sydney, in association with the Australian War Memorial, 1996.

Grey, J. and Doyle J. (eds), *Vietnam: War, Myth and Memory: Comparative Perspectives on Australia's War in Vietnam*, Allen and Unwin, Sydney, 1992.

Grey, J., *The Australian Army*, Vol. 1, The Australian Centenary History of Defence, Oxford University Press, Melbourne, 2001.

Grey, J., *Up Top: The Royal Australian Navy in Southeast Asian Conflicts, 1955–1972*, Vol. 7, *The Official History of Australia's Involvement in Southeast Asian Conflicts 1948–1975*, Allen and Unwin, Sydney, in association with the Australian War Memorial, 1998.

Grossman, D., *On Killing: The Psychological Cost of Learning to Kill in War and Society*, Oxford University Press, London, 1995.

Guest, R., *The Team in Pictures: A Pictorial History of the Australian Army Training Team Vietnam 1962–1972*, National Executive, AATTV Association, Canberra, 1992.

Gurney, G., *Vietnam: The War in the Air*, Crown Publishers, New York, 1985.

Hackworth, D. and Sherman, J., *About Face: The Odyssey of an American Warrior*, Macmillan, Melbourne, 1989.

Halberstam, D., *The Best and the Brightest*, Random House, New York, 1972.

Halberstam, D., *The Making of a Quagmire*, Bodley Head, London, 1965.

Hall, R., *Combat Battalion: The Eighth Battalion in Vietnam*, Allen and Unwin, Sydney, 2002.

Hallin, D., *The Uncensored War: The Media and Vietnam*, Oxford University Press, New York, 1986.

Ham, P., *Kokoda*, HarperCollins, Sydney, 2004.

Hammond, W., *Reporting Vietnam: Media and Military at War*, University Press of Kansas, Lawrence, Kans., 1998.

Hancock, I., *John Gorton: He Did It His Way*, Hodder Headline, Sydney, 2002.

Haran, P., and Kearney, R., *Crossfire: An Australian Reconnaissance Unit in Vietnam*, New Holland, Sydney, 2001.

Haran, P., *Trackers — The Untold Story of the Australian Dogs of War*, New Holland, Sydney, 2000.

Harrison, M., *A Lonely Kind of War*, Presidio Press, Novato, Calif., 1997.

Hayek, F., *The Road to Serfdom*, Routledge Classics, London, 2001.

Heard, B., *Well Done, Those Men: Memoirs of a Vietnam Veteran*, Scribe, Melbourne, 2005.

Heeson, T. I., *Historical Notes on 1 ALSC WKSP Det RAEME Bien Hoa, South Vietnam 3 May 1965–13 May 1966: A Personal View*, privately published, 1982.

Heller, J., *Catch 22: A Novel*, Simon and Schuster, New York, 1996.

Hennessy, B., *The Sharp End: The Trauma of a War in Vietnam*, Allen and Unwin, Sydney, 1997.

Hennessy, M., *Strategy in Vietnam: The Marines and Revolutionary Warfare in I Corps, 1965–1972*, Praeger, Westport, Conn., 1997.

Herr, M., *Dispatches*, Pan Books, London, 1978.

Herring, G. (ed.), *Secret Diplomacy of the Vietnam War: The Negotiating Volumes of the Pentagon Papers*, McGraw-Hill, New York, 1983.

Hill, E. F., *Communism and Australia: Reflections and Reminiscences*, Communist Party of Australia (Marxist-Leninist), Melbourne, 1989.

Hoang Van Chi, *From Colonialism to Communism*, Allied Publishers, New Delhi, 1964.

Hope, B., *Five Women I Love: Bob Hope's Vietnam Story*, Robert Hale, London, 1967.

Horner, D., *Australian Higher Command in the Vietnam War*, Strategic and Defence Studies Centre, Research School of Pacific Studies, Australian National University, Canberra, 1986.

Horner, D., *Duty First: The Royal Australian Regiment in War and Peace*, Allen and Unwin, Sydney, 1990.

Horner, D., *SAS: Phantoms of War: A History of the Australian Special Air Service*, Allen and Unwin, Sydney, 2002.

Horner, D., *The Commanders: Australian Military Leadership in the Twentieth Century*, Allen and Unwin, Sydney, 1984.

Horner, D., *The Gunners: A History of Australian Artillery*, Allen and Unwin, Sydney, 1995.

Hoskins, A., *Televising War: From Vietnam to Iraq*, Continuum, London, 2004.

Howson, P., *The Howson Diaries: The Life of Politics*, Viking, Ringwood, Vic., 1984.

Hutchinson, G., *Not Going to Vietnam: Journeys Through Two Wars*, Sceptre, Sydney, 1999.

Huu Ngoc, *Wandering Through Vietnamese Culture*, Gioi Publishers, Hanoi, 2005.

Jamieson, N., *Understanding Vietnam*, University of California Press, Berkeley, 1994.

Johnson, L. D., *The History of 6RAR/NZ (ANZAC) Battalion*, Vol. 2, 1967 to 1970, Enoggera, Brisbane, 1972.

Kahn, H., *Can We Win in Vietnam: The American Dilemma*, Pall Mall Press, London, 1968.

Kaiser, D., *American Tragedy: Kennedy, Johnson and the Origins of the Vietnam War*, Harvard University Press, Cambridge, Mass., 2000.

Kane, J., *Exploding the Myths: The Political Memoirs of Jack Kane*, Angus and Robertson, Sydney, 1989.

Karnow, S., *Vietnam*, Penguin, Harmondsworth, UK, 1983.

Keesing's Research Report, *South Vietnam: A Political History 1954–1970*, Charles Scribner's Sons, New York, 1970.

Kimball, J., *To Reason Why: The Debate About the Causes of U.S. Involvement in the Vietnam War*, Temple University Press, Philadelphia, 1990.

King, P. (ed.), *Australia's Vietnam: Australia in the Second Indo-China War*, George Allen and Unwin, Sydney, 1983.

Kinnard, D., *The War Managers: American Generals Reflect on Vietnam*, Da Capo, New York, 1991.

Kissinger, H., *The White House Years*, Little, Brown, Boston, 1979.

Kitson, F., *Low Intensity Operations: Subversion, Insurgency, Peacekeeping*, Stackpole Books, Harrisburg, Pa., 1971.

Knightley, P., *The First Casualty: From the Crimean to Vietnam: The War Correspondent as Hero, Propagandist, and Myth Maker*, Harcourt Brace Jovanovich, New York, 1975.

Kolko, G., *Vietnam: Anatomy of War 1940–1975*, Unwin Paperbacks, London, 1987.

Komer, R. W., *The Komer Report*, White House, Washington DC, 1966.

Komer, R., *Bureaucracy at War: US Performance in the Vietnam Conflict*, Westview Press, Boulder, Colo., 1986.

Krasnoff, S., *Krazy Hor: A Soldier's Story*, Allen and Unwin, Sydney, 2004.

Krasnoff, S., *Shadows on the Wall*, Allen and Unwin, Sydney, 2002.

Krepinevich, A. F., *The Army and Vietnam*, Johns Hopkins University Press, Baltimore, 1986.

Kutler, S. (ed.), *Encyclopedia of the Vietnam War*, Charles Scribner, New York, 1996.

Lamensdorf, J. D., *Write Home for Me: A Red Cross Woman in Vietnam*, Random House, Sydney, 2006.

Langley, G., *A Decade of Dissent: Vietnam and the Conflict on the Australian Home Front*, Allen and Unwin, Sydney, 1992.

Le Cao Dai, *Memoirs of War: A North Vietnamese Journal of Life on the Ho Chi Minh Trail 1965–1973*, Gioi Publishers, Hanoi, 2004.

Le Duan, *On the Socialist Revolution in Vietnam*, Vol. 2, Foreign Languages Publishing House, Hanoi, 1965.

Lennox, G., *Forged by War: Australians in Combat and Back Home*, Melbourne University Press, Melbourne, 2005.

Levin, B., *The Pendulum Years: Britain in the 60s*, Icon Books, Cambridge, 2003.

Lewis, S., *My Vietnam: Photographs of Australian Veterans of the Vietnam Conflict*, My Vietnam Trust, Adelaide, 2002.

Lewy, G., *America in Vietnam*, Oxford University Press, New York, 1978.

Lifton, R. J., *Home from the War — Vietnam Veterans: Neither Victims nor Executioners*, Wildwood House, London, 1974.

Lind, M., *Vietnam — The Necessary War: A Reinterpretation of America's Most Disastrous Military Conflict*, Touchstone, New York, 1999.

Lindholm, R. W., *Viet-Nam: The First Five Years: An International Symposium*, Michigan State University Press, East Lansing, 1959.

Lockhart, G., *Nation in Arms: The Origins of the People's Army of Vietnam*, Asian Studies Association of Australia with Allen and Unwin, Sydney, 1989.

Lockhart, G., *The Minefield: An Australian Tragedy in Vietnam*, Allen and Unwin, Sydney, 2007.

Lumsden, M., *Incendiary Weapons*, MIT Press, Cambridge, Mass. and Almqvist and Wiksell, Stockholm, 1975.

Lunn, H., *Vietnam: A Reporter's War*, Hodder Headline, Sydney, 2002.

Lyles, K., *Vietnam Anzacs: Australian and New Zealand Troops in Vietnam 1962–72*, Osprey Publishing, Oxford, 2004.

Lynn, J., *Battle: A History of Combat and Culture*, Westview Press, Boulder, Colo., 2003.

MacGregor, S., *No Need for Heroes: The Aussies Who Discovered the Viet Cong's Secret Tunnels*, Calm, Sydney, 1993.

Maclear, M., *Vietnam: The Ten Thousand Day War*, Thames Methuen, London, 1980.

Maddock, K. (ed.), *Memories of Vietnam*, Random House, Sydney, 1991.

Maddock, K. and Wright, B. (eds), *War: Australia and Vietnam*, Harper and Row Publishers, Sydney, 1987.

Manchester, W., *American Caesar, Douglas MacArthur, 1880–1964*, Little, Brown, Boston, c1978.

Mangold, T. and Penycate, J., *The Tunnels of Cu Chi*, Presidio Press, Random House, New York, 2005.

Mansford, G., *The Mad Galahs*, George Mansford, Gordonvale, NSW, 1999.

Marr, D., *Barwick*, Allen and Unwin, Sydney, 1980.

Martin, A. W., *Robert Menzies: A Life*, Vols 1 and 2, Melbourne University Press, Melbourne, 1993 and 1999.

Marwick, A., *The Sixties: Cultural Revolution in Britain, France, Italy, and the United States c.1958–c.1974*, Oxford University Press, Oxford, 1998.

Marx, K., *Capital*, Vols 1 and 2, Progress Publishers, Moscow, 1978.

Marx, K., *The Poverty of Philosophy: Answer to the Philosophy of Poverty by M. Proudhon*, Foreign Languages Press, Peking, 1978.

Marx, K. and Engels, F., *The Communist Manifesto*, Penguin Classics, London, 2002.

Marx, K., Engels, F., Lenin, V., *The Essential Left: Four Classic Texts on the Principles of Socialism*, Unwin Books, London, 1974.

Matthews, L. J. and Brown, D. E., *Assessing the Vietnam War: A Collection from the Journal of the US Army War College*, Pergamon-Brassey's International Defense Publishers, Washington, DC, 1987.

McAulay, L. (aka Alexander, D.), *When the Buffalo Fight*, Hutchinson, Melbourne, 1980.

McAulay, L., *Blue Lanyard, Red Banner: The Capture of a Vietcong Headquarters by 1st Battalion, the Royal Australian Regiment — Operation CRIMP 8 — 14 January 1966*, Banner Books, Maryborough, Qld, 2005.

McAulay, L., *Contact: Australians in Vietnam*, Hutchinson, Sydney, 1989.

McAulay, L., *In the Ocean's Dark Embrace — Royal Australian Navy Clearance Diving Team 3, Vietnam 1967–71*, Banner Books, Maryborough, Qld, 1997.

McAulay, L., *The Battle of Coral: Vietnam Fire Support Bases Coral and Balmoral, May 1968*, Century Hutchinson, Melbourne, 1988.

McAulay, L., *The Battle of Long Tan: The Legend of Anzac Upheld*, Hutchinson, Melbourne, 1986.

McAulay, L., *The Fighting First: Combat Operations in Vietnam, 1968–69, the First Battalion, the Royal Australian Regiment*, Allen and Unwin, Sydney, 1991.

McCarthy, M., *Vietnam*, Weidenfeld and Nicolson, London, 1968.

McClelland, J., *Names of all Australian Armed Forces People Killed in Action 1939 to 1947, Korea 1950 to 1953, Vietnam 1963 to 1973*, James McClelland Research, Silverdale, NSW, 1990.

McCulloch, J., *The Politics of Agent Orange: The Australian Experience*, Heinemann, Richmond, Vic. 1984.

McFarlane, B., *We Band of Brothers*, Brian W. McFarlane, Bowral, NSW, 2000.

McHugh, S., *Minefields and Miniskirts: Australian Women and the Vietnam War*, Doubleday, Sydney, 1993.

McKay, G. and Stewart, E., *Vietnam Shots: A Photographic Account of Australians at War*, Allen and Unwin, Sydney, 2002.

McKay, G., *Bullets, Beans and Bandages: Australians at War in Viet Nam*, Allen and Unwin, Sydney, 1999.

McKay, G., *Delta Four: Australian Riflemen in Vietnam*, Allen and Unwin, Sydney, 1996.

McKay, G., *In Good Company: One Man's War in Vietnam*, Allen and Unwin, Sydney, 1987.

McNamara, R. with VanDeMark, B., *In Retrospect*, Times Books, New York, 1995.

McNeill, I. and Ekins, A., *On the Offensive: The Australian Army in the Vietnam War 1967–1968*, Vol. 8, *The Official History of Australia's Involvement in Southeast Asian Conflicts 1948–1975*, Allen and Unwin, Sydney, in association with the Australian War Memorial, 2003.

McNeill, I., *The Team: Australian Army Advisers in Vietnam, 1962–1972*, Allen and Unwin and Australian War Memorial, Canberra, 1984.

McNeill, I., *To Long Tan: The Australian Army and the Vietnam War, 1950–1966*, Vol. 2, *The Official History of Australia's Involvement in Southeast Asian Conflicts 1948–1975*, Allen and Unwin, Sydney, in association with the Australian War Memorial, 1993.

McPhedran, I., *The Amazing SAS*, HarperCollins Publishers, Sydney, 2005.

Mendes, P., *The New Left, the Jews and the Vietnam War 1965–1972*, Lazare Press, Sydney, 1993.

Middleton, D. (ed.), *Air War: Vietnam*, Arms and Armour Press, London, 1978.

Modystack, N., *The Pony Soldiers: With the Australian Light Horse in Vietnam, 1965–1966*, Australian Military History Publications, Loftus, NSW, 2003.

Mollison, C., *Long Tan and Beyond: Alpha Company 6 RAR in Vietnam 1966–67*, Cobb's Crossing Publications, Woombye, Qld, 2005.

Morrisson, D., *My Rock 'n' Roll War*, Dog-Tag Books, Bracken Ridge, Qld, 1977.

Murphy, J., *Harvest of Fear: A History of Australia's Vietnam War*, Allen and Unwin, Sydney, 1993.

Nagl, J., *Learning to Eat Soup with a Knife: Counter-insurgency Lessons from Malaya and Vietnam*, Praeger, Westport, Conn., 2002.

*Nam: The Vietnam Experience 1965–75* (various contributors), Hamlyn, London, 1990.

Nelson, R., Margan, F., Breen, P., Reid, S. and Evans, D., *A Pictorial History of Australians at War*, Hamlyn, Sydney, 1970.

Newman, K., *The ANZAC Battalion: A Record of the Tour of 2nd Battalion, The Royal Australian Regiment, 1st Battalion, the Royal New Zealand Infantry Regiment (The Anzac Battalion) in South Vietnam, 1967–68*, Printcraft Press, Brookvale, NSW 1968; rev. edn, John Burridge Military Antiques, Swanbourne, WA, 1995.

Nguyen Tuen Hung and Schecter, J., *The Palace File: The Remarkable Story of the Secret Letters from Nixon and Ford to the President of South Vietnam and the American Promises that Were Never Kept*, Harper and Row, New York, 1986.

Nicosia, G., *Home to War: A History of the Vietnam Veterans' Movement*, Crown Publishers, New York, 2001.

9RAR Association, *9th Battalion, The Royal Australian Regiment: Vietnam Tour of Duty, 1968–1969: On Active Service*, Enoggera Barracks, Brisbane, 1992.

Nixon, R., *No More Vietnams*, Arbor House, New York, 1985.

Noone, V., *Disturbing the War: Melbourne Catholics and Vietnam*, Spectrum, Melbourne, 1993.

Norden, E., *The Hidden War: South Vietnam*, Peace Action, Sydney, 1964.

Nott, R. and Payne, N., *The Vung Tau Ferry and Escort Ships, Vietnam 1965–1972*, Noel and Margaret Payne, Nerang, Qld, 1998.

O'Brien, M., *Conscripts and Regulars — With the Seventh Battalion in Vietnam*, Allen and Unwin in association with Seventh Battalion, Royal Australian Regiment Association, Sydney, 1995.

O'Farrell, T., *Behind Enemy Lines: An Australian SAS Soldier in Vietnam*, Allen and Unwin, Sydney, 2001.

O'Keefe, B. and Smith, F., *Medicine at War: Medical Aspects of Australia's Involvement in Southeast Asia 1950–1972*, Allen and Unwin in association with the Australian War Memorial, Sydney, 1994.

O'Neill, R., *General Giap: Politician and Strategist*, Cassell Australia, Melbourne, 1969.

O'Neill, R., *Vietnam Task: The 5th Battalion, the Royal Australian Regiment 1966–1967*, Cassell Australia, Melbourne, 1968.

Odgers, G., *Pictorial History of the Royal Australian Air Force*, Child and Henry, Brookvale, NSW, 1984.

Olson, J. (ed.), *Dictionary of the Vietnam War*, Greenwood Press, Westport, Conn., 1988.

Page, T., *Derailed in Uncle Ho's Victory Garden*, Touchstone, London, 1995.

Palmer, A., *Vietnam Veterans: A Record of Service*, Military Minded, Mosman Park, WA, 1995.

Palmer, A., *Vietnam Veterans: Honours and Awards*, Military Minded, Mosman Park, WA, 1995.

Parry, W., *Just a Nasho*, Winston Parry, Alderley, Qld, 2003.

Payne, P., *War and Words: The Australian Press and the Vietnam War*, Melbourne University Press, Melbourne, 2007.

Pemberton, G., *All the Way: Australia's Road to Vietnam*, Allen and Unwin, Sydney, 1987.

Pemberton, G., *Vietnam Remembered*, Weldon, Sydney 1993.

Pennington, V., *The Team in Vietnam: The Lighter Side*, Wakefield Press, Kent Town, SA, 1992.

*Pentagon Papers: The Defense Department History of United States Decision-making in Vietnam*, Senator Gravel Edition, Vols I and II, Beacon Press, Boston, 1971.

Petersen, B. with Cribbin, J., *Tiger Men: An Australian Soldier's Secret War in Vietnam*, Macmillan, Melbourne, 1988.

Phan Ngoc Danh and Tran Quang Toai, *Lich Su Dau Tranh Cach Mang Cua Huyen Long Dat* (A History of the Revolutionary Struggle of the Long Dat District), NXB, Dong Nai, 1986.

Pierce, P., Grey, J. and Doyle, J., *Vietnam Days: Australia and the Impact of Vietnam*, Penguin, Ringwood, Vic., 1991.

Pike, D., *History of Vietnamese Communism, 1925–1976*, Hoover Institution, Stanford, Calif., 1978.

Pike, D., *PAVN: People's Army of Vietnam*, Presidio Press, Novato, Calif., 1986.

Pike, D., *Viet Cong: The Organization and Techniques of the National Liberation Front of South Vietnam*, MIT Press, Cambridge, Mass., 1966.

Pilger, J. (ed.), *Tell Me No Lies: Investigative Journalism and its Triumphs*, Jonathan Cape, London, 2004.

Pimlott, J. (ed.), *Vietnam: The History and the Tactics*, Macdonald and Co., London, 1988.

Pimlott, J., *Vietnam: The Decisive Battles*, Michael Joseph, London, 1990.

Popper, K., *The Open Society and Its Enemies*, Routledge and Kegan Paul, London, 1966.

Qiang Zhai, *China and the Vietnam Wars 1950–1975*, University of North Carolina Press, Chapel Hill, NC, 2000.

Reid, A., *The Gorton Experiment*, Shakespeare Head Press, Sydney, 1971.

Renouf, A., *The Frightened Country*, Macmillan, Melbourne, 1979.

Rickards, G., *Twelve in Focus: 12th Field Regiment in South Vietnam 1971: A Memento for All Ranks of the Tour in South Vietnam*, 12th Field Regt RAA, Ingleburn, NSW, 1971.

Rintoul, S., *Ashes of Vietnam*, Australian Broadcasting Corporation, Sydney, 1988.

Robinson, A. (ed.), *Weapons of the Vietnam War*, Bison Books, Greenwich, Conn., 1983.

Roser, Iris Mary, *Ba Rose: My Years in Vietnam 1968–1971*, Pan Books, Sydney, 1991.

Rowe, J., *Australians at War: Vietnam*, Time-Life Books, Sydney, 1987.

Rowe, J., *Count Your Dead*, Angus and Robertson, Sydney, 1968.

Royal Australian Regiment, *Soldier's Field Handbook* (various battalions, 1965–71).

Rummel, R. J., *Statistics of Democide: Genocide and Mass Murder Since 1900*, Transaction Publishers, Charlottesville, Va., 1997.

Ryan, M., *Vietnam Conscript*, Independent Book Publishers, UK, 1993.

Sabben, D., *Through Enemy Eyes*, Allen and Unwin, Sydney, 2005.

Salisbury, H., *Behind the Lines: Hanoi*, Secker and Warburg, London, 1967.

Sallah, M. and Weiss, M., *Tiger Force: A True Story of Men and War*, Little, Brown, New York, 2006.

Sayce, R. and O'Neill, M., *The Fighting Fourth: A Pictorial Record of the Second Tour in South Vietnam*, 4RAR, Brookvale, NSW, 1972.

Scates, R., *Draftsmen Go Free: A History of the Anti-conscription Movement in Australia*, R. Scates, Richmond, Vic., 1988.

Schell, J., *The Village of Ben Suc*, Knopf, New York, 1967.

Scott, P., *Command in Vietnam: Reflections of a Commanding Officer*, Slouch Hat Publications, McCrae, Vic., 2007.

7th Battalion, Royal Australian Regiment, *Notes on Operations, Vietnam 1970–71*, 7RAR Association, c. 1971.

7th Battalion, Royal Australian Regiment, *Seven in Seventy: A Pictorial Record of Seventh Battalion, the Royal Australian Regiment, 1970–71*, 7th Bn RAR, 1971.

Sexton, M., *War for the Asking: Australia's Vietnam Secrets*, Penguin, Ringwood, Vic., 1990.

Shakespeare, W., *The Complete Works*, Wells, S. and Taylor, G. (eds), Oxford University Press, Oxford, 1986,

Sheehan, N., *A Bright Shining Lie: John Paul Vann and America in Vietnam*, Vintage, New York, 1988.

Sheehan, N., Smith, H., Kenworthy, E. and Butterfield, F., *The Pentagon Papers*, Bantam and New York Times, New York, 1971.

Shephard, B., *A War of Nerves: A History of Military Psychiatry*, Jonathan Cape, London, 2000.

Smith, H. and Broome, S., *A Bibliography of Armed Forces and Society in Australia*, 3rd edn, Department of Government, Faculty of Military Studies, University of NSW at the Australian Defence Force Academy, Canberra, 1987.

Smith, H., *Conscientious Objection to Particular Wars: The Australian Approach*, Strategic and Defence Studies Centre, Australian National University, Canberra, 1986.

Snepp, F., *Decent Interval: The American Debacle in Vietnam and the Fall of Saigon*, Penguin, Harmondsworth, UK, 1980.

Sorley, L., *A Better War: The Unexamined Victories and Final Tragedy of America's Last Years in Vietnam*, Harcourt Brace and Co., New York, 1999.

Spector, R., *After Tet: The Bloodiest Year in Vietnam*, Vintage, New York, 1993.

Spragg, G., *When Good Men Do Nothing*, Australian Military History Publications, Loftus, NSW, 2003.

Stephens, A., *The Royal Australian Air Force*, Vol. 2, Australian Centenary History of Defence, Oxford University Press, Melbourne, 2001.

Stevens, D., *The Royal Australian Navy*, Vol. 3, The Australian Centenary History of Defence, Oxford University Press, Melbourne 2001.

Stone, G. L., *War Without Honour*, Jacaranda, Brisbane, 1966.

Stuart, R., *3 RAR in South Vietnam, 1967–1968: A Record of the Operational Service of the Third Battalion, the Royal Australian Regiment in South Vietnam, 12th December 1967–20th November 1968*, Printcraft Press, Brookvale, NSW, 1968.

Summers, H., *On Strategy: A Critical Analysis of the Vietnam War*, Presidio Press, Novato, Calif., 1982.

Swain, J., *River of Time*, Minerva, London, 1996.

Taylor, J., *Last Out: 4RAR/NZ (ANZAC) Battalion's Second Tour in Vietnam*, Allen and Unwin, Sydney, 2001.

Terry, S., *House of Love: Life in a Vietnamese Hospital*, Lansdowne Press, Melbourne, 1967.

Terzani, T., *Giai Phong! The Fall and Liberation of Saigon*, Angus and Robertson Publishers, UK, 1976.

Thanh, H. et al., *Days with Ho Chi Minh*, Foreign Languages Publishing House, Hanoi, 1962.

Thayer, C., *War By Other Means: National Liberation and Revolution in Vietnam 1954–60*, Allen and Unwin, Sydney, 1989.

Thompson, R., *No Exit From Vietnam*, Chatto and Windus, London, 1969.

Thurgar, J. and Crothers, R. (comp.), *Australian Vietnam Forces National Memorial: A Photographic History of the Dedication Weekend*, R. W. Crothers and Associates, Canberra, 1992.

Thurgar, J. and Wright, C. (comp.), *Welcome Home Photographs of the Welcome Home Parade, 3rd October 1987*, Austwide Communications, Canberra, 1988.

Truong Nhu Tang (with Chanoff, D. and Doan Van Toai), *A Viet Cong Memoir: An Inside Account of the Vietnam War and Its Aftermath*, Vintage, New York, 1986.

US Department of State, Office of Media Services, *Aggression From the North: The Record of North Viet-Nam's Campaign to Conquer South Viet-Nam*, Department of State, Washington DC, 1965.

Valentine, D., *The Phoenix Program*, William Morrow, New York, 1990.

Van Tien Dung, *Our Great Spring Victory: An Account of the Liberation of South Vietnam*, Monthly Review Press, New York, 1977.

Vo Nguyen Giap, *People's War, People's Army: The Viet Cong Insurrection Manual for Underdeveloped Countries*, Frederick A. Praeger, New York, 1967.

Vo Nguyen Giap, *Unforgettable Days*, Foreign Languages Publishing House, Hanoi, 1975.

Walters, I., *Dasher Wheatley and Australia in Vietnam*, Northern Territory University Press, Darwin, 1998.

Warner, D., *Not With Guns Alone: How Hanoi Won the War*, Hutchinson, Melbourne, 1977.

Warner, D., *Reporting South East Asia*, Angus and Robertson, Sydney, 1966.

Warner, D., *The Last Confucian*, Angus and Robertson, Sydney, 1964.

Watt, A., *Vietnam: An Australian Analysis*, F. W. Cheshire, Melbourne, 1968.

Webb, J. and Drake, L., *Mission in Vietnam*, 4RAR, Townsville, Qld, 1969.

Weiss, P., *Notes on the Cultural Life of the Democratic Republic of Vietnam*, Calder and Boyars, London, 1971.

Welch, N., *A History of the Sixth Battalion, the Royal Australian Regiment, 1965–1985*, 6th Battalion RAR, Enoggera, Qld, 1986.

Wells, F., *The Peace Racket*, F. Wells, Sydney, 1964.

Wells, R. and Boulton, E., *Uc Dai Loi: No 1: Words and Images of the Vietnam War*, Access Press, Perth, 2000.

Wells, T., *The War Within: America's Battle Over Vietnam*, University of California Press, Berkeley, 1994.

Welsh, D., *The History of the Vietnam War*, Bison Books, London, 1981.

West, B., *The Village*, Simon and Schuster International, New York, 2003.

Westmoreland, W. C., *A Soldier Reports*, Doubleday, Garden City, N.Y., 1976.

Wheen, F., *Karl Marx*, Fourth Estate, London, 1999.

Williams, I., Wickens, B. and Sabben, D., *Vietnam: A Pictorial History of the Sixth Battalion, the Royal Australian Regiment*, Printcraft Press, Brookvale, NSW, 1967.

Williams, J., *Cry in the Wilderness: Guinea Pigs of Vietnam*, Homecoming Press, Nambour, Qld, 1998.

Williams, J., *Harvest of Tears*, Homecoming Press, Nambour, Qld, 1995.

Williams, J., *The Devil's Rainbow: Conscripts, Chemicals, Catastrophe*, Homecoming Press, Nambour, Qld, 1996.

Windrow, M., *The Last Valley: Dien Bien Phu and the French Defeat in Vietnam*, Weidenfeld and Nicolson, London, 2004.

Woodard, G., *Asian Alternatives: Australia's Vietnam Decision and Lessons on Going to War*, Melbourne University Press, Carlton, Vic, 2006.

Woodruff, M., *Unheralded Victory: Who Won the Vietnam War?*, HarperCollins Publishers, London, 1999.

Woolf, C. and Bagguley, J. (eds), *Authors Take Sides on Vietnam*, Peter Owen, London, 1967.

Wordsworth, W., *The Complete Poetical Works*, Bartleby, New York, 1999.

## Documentaries, television, films

IPCCC, *Vietnam: 30 Years After the War*, Vietnamese documentary, 2005.

Keyes, D., *In Search of the Tiger: Operation Coburg During the Tet Offensive*, directed by A. Williams for Army Headquarters Training Command, 1996.

Keyes, D., *Say a Prayer For Me: The Chaplains of the Vietnam War*, directed by A. Williams, Heritage Series, 1995.

Milliarium Zero and Winterfilm, *Winter Soldier*, 1971.

*Operation Coburg*, 13-part series, Army Headquarters Training Command, 1996.

Pearson, W., *Vietnam Minefield*, SBS Television, 2006.

Red Dune Films, *The Battle of Long Tan*, directed by Martin Walsh, 2006.

Reinbott, R., McLaren, L. and Williams, A., *Fragments of War — Vietnam*, narrated by Jack Thompson, Heritage Series.

Rymer, J., *All Points of the Compass*, ABC TV.

Snomoat, *Aussie Trackers — Vietnam*, two-part, privately produced documentary on war dogs.

'The Scheyville Experience', Heritage Series.

Training Command — Army, *The Team*, five-part documentary on the Australian Army Training Team Vietnam, Heritage Series, 2001.

War File, *Vietnam: The Chopper War*.

White, T., *The Doc's Movie: 5RAR Vietnam, 1966–67*, personal documentary.

'Withdrawal from Saigon', *This Day Tonight*, ABC current affairs, 1975.

## Museums, libraries, field sources

Army Museum, Hanoi.

Australian War Memorial, Canberra.

Cu Chi Tunnels.

Dong Nai Museum, Dong Nai.

LBJ Memorial Library, Austin, Texas.

National Archives of Australia, Canberra.

Reunification Palace, Ho Chi Minh City.

Vietnam War Remnants Museum, Ho Chi Minh City.

## Reunions attended

1RAR and 173rd Airborne Brigade, Penrith, NSW, 30 June–1 July 2005.

6RAR Reunion and Gala Dinner Dance, Brisbane, 3–5 June 2005.

7RAR Reunion, Fremantle, WA, 26–27 April 2006.

161 Battery, Royal New Zealand Artillery, Palmerston North, NZ, 15–16 July 2005.

## Websites

For the websites of all Australian units in Vietnam, key in the unit's name into a search engine, such as Google.

Agent Orange information pack, www.vvnw.org/Educational_Material/agent_orange.htm.

Australian Army Aviation Association, www.fourays.org

Australian Army Trackers and War Dogs Association, http://aussietrackers.tripod.com/main-index.html

Australian casualties, www.thecasualtylist.com

Australian Centre for Post-traumatic Mental Health, www.acpmh.unimelb.edu.au

Australian Diggers, www.diggerz.org

'Australian Involvement in Vietnam, The', www.hotkey.net.au/~marshalle

Australian Vietnam veterans health study III, www.ncbi.nlm.nih.gov/entrez/query

Australian Vietnam veterans' organisations, http://grunt.space.swri.edu/ozorgs.htm

Australian War Memorial, www.awm.gov.au

Centre for Military and Veterans Health, research protocol for health study of children of Vietnam veterans, www.uq.edu.au/cmvh/index.html

Coxcomb Veterans Camp, http://veteranretreat.tripod.com

Department of Veterans' Affairs, www.dva.gov.au

Department of Veterans' Affairs, 'Australians at War Film Archive', www.australiansatwarfilmarchive.gov.au

Dien Bien Phu, www.dienbienphu.org

Digger History, www.diggerhistory.info

Hackworth, David, www.hackworth.com

Herbicide spray map: http://cybersarges.tripod.com/aomap2.html

'Herb Tapes', www.gmasw.com/ao_amts1.htm

History Net, www.historynet.com/wars_conflicts/vietnam_war

National Archives of Australia, www.naa.gov.au

National Archives of Australia, 'The Fall of Saigon, 1975', Fact Sheet 243, www.naa.gov.au/fSheets/fs243.html

National Archives of Australia, 'Statistical information about casualties of the Vietnam Conflict', www.archives.gov/research/vietnam-war/casualty-statistics.html

Operation Aussies Home, www.austmia.com

Pandanus Veterans' Sanctuary, http://veteransanctuary.tripod.com

RAAF FAC History, www.fac-assoc.org

Veterans Support and Advocacy Service Australia, www.ausvets.powerup.com.au

Vietnam Center and Archive, Texas Tech University, www.ttu.edu/vietnam

Vietnam Veterans Association of Australia, www.vvaa.org.au

Vietnam War, www.vietnamwar.com

# Index

Clunies-Ross, Captain Adrian 101–2
Cobby, Private Terry 429
Cobham, Lord 258
Coburg (Operation) 351
Cochinchina 18, 20, 25, 37, 180
Cocker, Joe 450
Coe, John 572
Cohen, Major Geoff 365, 366, 379
Col Joye and the Joy Boys 218, 280
Colby, William 93, 493, 496
Cold War 6, 75, 90, 303, 595, 659
Cold War Warrior 75, 90, 303
Cole, Major Kevin 534
Coleman, Sapper Bob 308
Coleridge, Sergeant Mike 650
Collett, Edgar 270
Collins, Provost Corporal Bill 203
Collinson, Warrant Officer Reg 140
Colmer, Corporal Les 156
colonialism in Asia
    British withdrawal 85
    Dutch Antilles 85
    French in Indochina 7, 12, 15, 16–28, 85, 106,
        180–18, 187, 262 see also Cochinchina
Columbus (Christopher) 85
Combined Studies Division (CIA) see Covert
    Action Branch (CIA)
Commander of the Order of the British Empire
    (CBE) 646
Committee in Defiance of the National Service
    Act (CDNSA) 458, 517, 521
Common Agricultural Policy (EEC) 86
Commonwealth Club (Canberra) 389
communism 17, 26, 41, 54, 91, 114, 262, 303, 337,
    387, 653, 658
    Australia, perceived threat to 47–49, 85, 118, 119,
        120, 123–25, 126, 253, 254, 329, 445, 656, 658
    China, in see People's Republic of China
    see also Domino Theory
Communist Bloc 6, 53–54, 55, 73, 81, 255, 347,
    388, 657, 658
Communist Party Dissolution Act 46
Communist Party of Australia (CPA) 45–47, 129,
    259, 275, 449, 452, 453, 456, 521, 568
    see also Independent Communist Party (Australia)
Communist Party of Indochina 33, 36, 181
Communist Party of North Vietnam 60, 346, 514,
    608
Communist Party (Soviet Union) 33, 63
Communist Revolutionary Warfare (book) 130
Companion of the Order of the Bath (CB) 645
Conein, Lucien 74
Confucianism 8, 9, 12, 23
Congress for International Cooperation and
    Disarmament (CICD) 517, 523
Congress (US) 660
    aid support 279
    military support, repeal of 586, 595, 660
    Tonkin Gulf Resolution 80, 81
    repeal of 586

Congressional Medal of Honour (US) 320, 648
Connolly, Graham 128
conscientious objection
    Australia, in 268–73, 274, 335–36, 338
    US, in 274
conscription 127, 165–77, 257, 263, 328, 335, 443
    abolition of 558
    national ballot 169–70, 171
    referenda on 166
    resistence against 267–73, 457–59, 527–28 see
        also anti-war movement; conscientious
        objection; draft resistance
Conspicuous Gallantry Medal 397
Continental Hotel (Saigon) 106, 279, 404, 654
Convery, Second Lieutenant Robert 512
Conway, Sergeant Kevin 102–3
Cooper, Dale 521
Cooper, Flight Lieutenant Garry 391, 648–49
Cop in a Baggy Green Skin (book) 288, 512
Coral see Fire Support Patrol Base Coral
CORDS program see Civil Operations and
    Revolutionary (later Rural ) Development
    Support program (CORDS)
Cosgrove, Lieutenant Peter 509–10, 512–13, 531
COSVN see Central Office of South Vietnam
    (COSVN)
Cottrell, Flying Officer Mac 391
Coughlan, Corporal John (Snow) 397
Count Your Dead (book) 213
Counter-insurgency Manual (UK) 73–74
Country Party 5, 45, 48, 263, 440
    see also Liberal-Country Coalition
Courier-Mail 88
    Nixon, Gorton's meeting with 460
Covert Action Branch (CIA) 91, 103, 106–7
    Montagnard operation 106–17
Covich, Danilo 270
Coward, Noel 443
Cox, Bernie 632
Coxsedge, Joan 452, 528, 571
CPA see Communist Party of Australia (CPA)
Crean, Frank 275
Credlin, Sergeant Austin 377
Creedence Clearwater Revival (band) 450
Crimes Act 520, 528
Crimp (Operation) 152–58
Cripps, Sir Stafford 33
Crombie, Private Bill 128
Cronkite, Walter 258, 403
Crook, William 441
Crosby, 'Bing' (formerly Colonel) 552
Cross of Gallantry with Palm (Republic of
    Vietnam) 396
Cross of Gallantry with Silver Star (Republic of
    Vietnam) 391
Cu Chi district 143, 152–55, 195, 596
    tunnel complex 143, 152–55, 390
Cu Huu Can (poet) 28
Cuban missile crisis (1963) 6
Cubis, Lieutenant Colonel Richard (Dick) 231

Cudmore, Padre Gerry 130
Cullen, Bryan 338
Cullen, Neville 249, 565, 567, 571
Cultural Revolution (China) 347
Cung Chung (Operation) 535–37
Currie, Michael 495
Curthoys, Ann 435, 449, 459
Curtin Government 168
Curtin, Prime Minister John 166, 260
Cusack, Graham (Breaker) 236, 245, 652
Cutler, Sir Roden 374, 527
Cyclone Tracy (Darwin) 592
Czechoslovakia 269, 456
   Soviet invasion of 434–35, 518, 577

D445 Battalion (Viet Cong) 182, 209, 290, 354, 355, 468, 469–70, 515, 531, 581, 652
   Battle of Long Tan 238, 239, 240, 246–47
   Operation Cung Chung 535
   Operation Hammersley 507–9
Da Costa, Major Joe 101
Da Lat training school 494
Da Nang 18, 82, 88, 99, 287, 343, 347, 351, 423, 557–58, 580, 581
   fall of 589–90, 592, 596, 615
dadaism 450
Dai Viet (Nationalist Party) 121, 355, 357–58
   see also Vietnamese Nationalist Party (VNQDD)
Daily Mirror 128
Daily Telegraph (London) 406
Daily Telegraph (Sydney)
   Daly/Fraser stoush 548
   Gorton's White House visit 438
   Tet Offensive 403
Dainer, Ian 597–601
Dak Seang fort 492
Dak Son (hamlet) 519–20
Dali, Private Don 130
Dalton, Tony 449, 516, 527
Daly, Private Jim 157, 159
Daly, Lieutenant General Tom (later Sir) 106, 306, 344, 506, 508, 551, 572
   Fraser, media stoush with 546–50
Dam San see Petersen, Captain Barry
Damita, Lili 405
Dao see Tran Hung Dao, General
d'Argenlieu, Admiral Thierry 37
Darlac province 107, 110, 112
Darwin Quarantine Station 612
Dat Do district 182, 305, 469, 487, 503, 552, 580, 581
Dat Do (village) 180, 190, 195, 291, 306, 467, 508, 515, 665
Dat, Lieutenant Colonel 182, 210, 306
Davies, B. 100
Davies, Captain Phil 360, 375
Davis, (Doc) 231
Davis, Neil 593, 603, 614
Davison, General Michael 350, 536
Day, Brian 622
De Tham 22

De Vere, Captain Ray 480, 484, 566–67
Deak, Lieutenant Mick 290
deaths and casualties, statistics of 416–19, 663
   Americans 103, 133, 136, 137, 146, 148, 158, 159, 160, 195, 250, 270, 345, 349, 363
   ARVN 77, 133, 181, 250, 345, 586, 606
   Australians 100, 102, 103, 137, 142, 145, 146, 158, 217, 245, 250, 376, 502
   civilians 152, 196–97, 357–58, 400, 415, 418, 425–26, 484, 492, 495, 518–19, 586, 606
   kill rates 418–19, 464, 495
   New Zealanders 145
   Viet Cong/NVA 77, 135–36, 137, 146, 148, 150, 158, 159, 195, 197, 245, 250, 270, 317, 327, 345–46, 349, 357, 358, 373, 484–85, 495, 496, 579, 662
Debelle, Jean 245
DeBomford, Corporal Barry 534
Declaration of Independence of the Democratic Republic of Vietnam 35
Deed, Sapper Ray 309
Deep Throat (film) 450
Defence and Employment Platoon (1ATF) 540
Defence and Employment Platoon (2ATF) 531–32
Defence, Department of 49, 89, 119, 120, 123, 444, 624, 635
   Daly/Fraser media stoush 547–49
   Joint Intelligence Organisation 548
   soldiers' remains, reversal of policy 142
Defence Force Protection Act (1967) 276, 453
Defence White Paper (1976) 664
Defense, Department of (US) 417
defoliation see chemical war
Delafosse, Jules 20
Delaney, Sapper Frank 503
Dellaca, Bombardier John 377
Dellwo, Sergeant Gerard 492
Delta Company (1RAR) 150, 160, 367, 370, 373, 381
Delta Company (2RAR) 5, 312, 323
Delta Company (3RAR) 367
Delta Company (4RAR) 555
Delta Company (5RAR) 480
Delta Company (6RAR) 190, 218, 219, 220, 248–49, 291, 565
   Battle of Long Tan 218–41, 242–50, 646
   Presidential Unit Citation (US) 248, 646
Delta Company (7RAR) 323, 351–52
Demilitarised Zone (DMZ)
   Korea 303
   Vietnam 43, 53, 88, 95, 179, 347, 348, 390
Democrat Party (US) 78
Democratic Labor Party (DLP) 46, 47–48, 57, 89, 263, 276, 440, 453, 457, 460, 524, 526
Democratic Republic of Vietnam see North Vietnam
Democritus League 259
Deng Xiaoping 62
Denistone East Primary School (NSW) 269
Dental Civil Action Project (dentcap) 465, 466

Highway 15 182, 289
Hill 937 (Hamburger Hill) 350
Hill, Brian 76, 213
Hill, Captain Bob 143
Hilsman, Roger 93
Hines, Sir Colin 642
Hitchens, Christopher 617, 628
Hitler, (Adolf) 265, 269, 524, 583
HMAS *Boonaroo* 275, 644
HMAS *Brisbane* 644
HMAS *Hobart* 644
HMAS *Perth* 644
HMAS *Jeparit* 189, 275, 280, 520, 556, 644
HMAS *Sydney* 3, 4, 128, 129–30, 171, 186, 187,
     476, 555, 556, 557, 560, 644
HMAS *Vendetta* 644
HMS *Terrible see* HMAS *Sydney*
Ho Bo Woods 143, 155, 156
Ho Chi Minh 7, 10, 17, 64, 71, 78, 223, 346, 347,
     414, 449, 451, 525, 587, 595, 603, 608, 609,
     654, 660
  August Revolution 32, 35–37
  death of 514, 515
  early travels 31–33
  Geneva Agreements *see* Geneva Agreements
     (1954)
  Mao Tse-tung, meetings with 80–81
  writings and quotations 29, 32, 35, 37, 52
Ho Chi Minh City 12, 153, 180, 604, 654
  *see also* Saigon
Ho Chi Minh Trail 65, 94, 108, 148, 191, 390, 490,
     514, 585, 586
Hoa Hao (gangster sect) 55
Hoa Long (village) 182, 188, 189, 195, 196, 197,
     198, 203, 289, 290–91, 303, 318, 411, 467,
     504, 536, 554, 581, 651, 652
Hoang Phuong, General 189
Hobart (Operation) 199
Hogarth, Major 556
Hoi An 351
'Hoi Chan' program 151
Hollingsworth, Brigadier General Jim 158
Hollingworth, Clare 406
Hollingworth, General James F. 542
Holmberg, Sergeant 490–91
Holsworthy Barracks (Sydney) 128, 186
Holsworthy military prison (Sydney) 272
Holsworthy (Operation) 210–11
Holt Government 275
  medals, Battle of Long Tan 248
Holt, Harold (as Prime Minister) 183, 246, 334,
     396, 398, 436, 445
  1966 election 263
  additional Australian troops, US request for
     331–33
  death and funeral 336–37, 435
  Johnson, relationship with 253, 255–57,
     260, 330
  Manila Conference (1966) 262–63
  SE Asia, British withdrawal from 329

support for war 253–55, 265, 328
  White House, visits to 255–56, 330–31
Holt, Harold (as Treasurer) 121, 122, 127–28
Holt, Major E.S. (Tim) 190, 502
Holt, Zara 336
Holyoake, Prime Minister Keith 257, 258
Hon Me Island, raid on 79
Honeywell 527
Hong Kong 33, 286, 385
Hong Kong Bar (Vung Tau) 511
Honner, Major Brian (Bronx) 283, 503–4
Honnor, Major Harry 217, 222
Honolulu Conference (1964) 120
Hope, Bob 152
Hopkins, Frank 86
Hoppner, Private (Hoppy) 320
Horne, Donald 266
Hornery, Richard 166, 568
Hornsby, Private Roy 487–88, 505–6
Hornung, Brian 228
Horseshoe (hill at Nui Dat) 190, 288, 302,
     306, 559
Hotel Darlac (Darlac) 107
'House of the Five Hundred Girls' (brothel) 279
Howard Government 648, 664
Howard, Major Horrie 354
Howard, Prime Minister John 572
Howson, Peter 265, 398
Hudson, Captain Peter 325
Hudson, D. 516
Hué 14, 15, 18, 20, 31, 75, 99, 294, 295, 347, 395,
     443, 577, 580
  fall of 588, 596
  Tet Offensive 347, 351, 355–58, 394
  VC massacre of civilians 357–58, 403, 410, 615,
     616
Hughes, Billy 166
Hughes, Brigadier Jim 326
Hughes, Brigadier Ron 337–38, 349, 377, 378, 385,
     477
Hughes, Lieutenant Colonel Jim 538–39
Hughes, Robert 451
Hughes, Tom 267, 520, 524
Huguette (Fort) 38
Hump (Operation) 148–50
Humphrey, Hubert 331, 459, 660
Hung Kings (Hong Bang dynasty) 7
Hung Manh 310
Hunter, Mayo 128
Hutchens, Major James 149
Hutchinson, Garrie 449, 453
Huu Ngoc (Professor) 654
Huy (Foreign Minister) 594
Huynh Chien Dau 64, 198–99
Hyde, Michael 276, 449, 453, 454, 529
Hyland, Private Frankie 338

Ibbetson, James 643
illnesses related to chemical exposure 617–28
  Evatt Royal Commission 622–26